CRITICAL SURVEY

OF

POETRY

CRITICAL SURVEY

OF

POETRY

Second Revised Edition

Volume 2

Giosuè Carducci - William Empson

Editor, Second Revised Edition
Philip K. Jason
United States Naval Academy

Editor, First Edition, English and Foreign Language Series
Frank N. Magill

SALEM PRESS, INC.
Pasadena, California   Hackensack, New Jersey

Editor in Chief: Dawn P. Dawson
Managing Editor: Christina J. Moose
Developmental Editor: Tracy Irons-Georges
Research Supervisor: Jeffry Jensen
Acquisitions Editor: Mark Rehn
Photograph Editor: Philip Bader
Manuscript Editors: Sarah Hilbert, Leslie Ellen Jones,
Melanie Watkins, Rowena Wildin
Assistant Editor: Andrea E. Miller
Research Assistant: Jeff Stephens
Production Editor: Cynthia Beres
Layout: Eddie Murillo

∞ The paper used in these volumes conforms to the American National Standard for Permanence of Paper for Printed Library Materials, Z39.48-1992(R1997).

Library of Congress Cataloging-in-Publication Data

Critical survey of poetry / Philip K. Jason, editor.—2nd rev. ed.
    p.   cm.
Combined ed. of: Critical survey of poetry: foreign language series, originally published 1984, Critical survey of poetry: supplement, originally published 1987, and Critical survey of poetry: English language series, rev. ed. published 1992. With new material. Includes bibliographical references and index.
    ISBN 1-58765-071-1 (set : alk. paper) — ISBN 1-58765-073-8 (v. 2 : alk. paper) —
    1. Poetry—History and criticism—Dictionaries. 2. Poetry—Bio-bibliography. 3. Poets—Biography—Dictionaries. I. Jason, Philip K., 1941 -   .

PN1021 .C7 2002
809.1′003—dc21   2002008536

First Printing

PRINTED IN THE UNITED STATES OF AMERICA

CONTENTS

COMPLETE LIST OF CONTENTS

VOLUME 1

VOLUME 2

VOLUME 3

VOLUME 4

VOLUME 6

VOLUME 7

VOLUME 8

POETRY AROUND THE WORLD

RESEARCH TOOLS

INDEXES

CRITICAL SURVEY
OF
POETRY

GIOSUÈ CARDUCCI

Born: Val di Castello, Italy; July 27, 1835
Died: Bologna, Italy; February 16, 1907

PRINCIPAL POETRY

Rime, 1857
Juvenilia, 1863
Giambi, 1867 (also as *Giambi ed epodi*, 1882)
Levia gravia, 1868
Decennalia, 1871
Poesie, 1871
Nuove poesie, 1872
Odi barbare, 1877 (*Barbarian Odes*, 1939)
Nuove odi barbare, 1882 (*New Barbarian Odes*, 1939)
Ca ira, 1883
Rime nouve, 1887 (*Rime nouve of Carducci*, 1916; *The New Lyrics*, 1942)
Terze odi barbare, 1889 (*Third Barbarian Odes*, 1939)
Rime e ritmi, 1899 (*The Lyrics and Rhythms*, 1942)
A Selection of His Poems, 1913
A Selection from the Poems, 1921
The Barbarian Odes of Giosuè Carducci, 1939, 1950 (includes *Barbarian Odes*, *New Barbarian Odes*, and *Third Barbarian Odes*)

OTHER LITERARY FORMS

Giosuè Carducci had a long career as a scholarly critic as well as a poet and combined the two activities well. He wrote many volumes of literary history and criticism and edited several editions of Italian authors, including Petrarch and Politian. His two volumes on Giuseppe Parini have been called "the most impressive monument of his indefatigable industry." His best-known essays include "Di alcune condizioni della presente letteratura," "Dello svolgimento della letteratura nazionale," "Del rinnovamento letterario in Italia," and "Confessioni e battaglie." The major fault in his prose, as in his poetry, is a tendency toward bombast, though at his best he was the finest essayist of his time. Often asked to speak on public occasions, he displayed disciplined classical eloquence, speaking on Vergil,

Dante, Petrarch, Giovanni Boccaccio, Alessandro Manzoni, and Giacomo Leopardi. His greatest speech, delivered in Bologna on June 4, 1882, was his extemporaneous eulogy for Giuseppe Garibaldi, who had died two days previously: "Per la morte di Giuseppe Garibaldi" (on the death of Giuseppe Garibaldi). All his nonfiction, as well as his poetry, is collected in his complete works, *Opere complete* (1940).

ACHIEVEMENTS

The first Italian to win the Nobel Prize for Literature, which he received in 1906, Giosuè Carducci synthesized two great literary traditions to create a distinctive, original body of work. Although he came to maturity in the Romantic era, Carducci adhered to and helped maintain the values of the classical tradition; indeed, he became the outstanding exponent of the classicism which lay beneath the surface of Romanticism throughout the 1800's. Unlike his contemporaries, who looked nostalgically back to the Middle Ages, Carducci turned his attention toward ancient Rome and Greece. His fusion of a classical aesthetic with essentially Romantic sentiments exerted a powerful influence, particularly in the last decades of the century. Poets such as Enrico Panzacchi, Lorenzo Stecchetti, Giovanni Marradi, and Severino Ferrari were all part of Carducci's circle. Both for his influence and for his work, Carducci is recognized as the major Italian poet of the late 1800's.

BIOGRAPHY

Giosuè Carducci was born to Dr. Michele Carducci and Ildegonda Celli in Val di Castello, a small town near Viareggio, in Tuscany. Carducci's father was greatly affected by the patriotism which would lead to the Risorgimento. An active Carbonaro (a member of a secret society seeking the unification of Italy), he was confined for a year in Volterra because of his participation in the Revolution of 1831. When Carducci was three, his family moved to Bolgheri, in the wild and desolate Maremma region south of Pisa. Maremma, with its Etruscan tombs, became the emotional landscape of Carducci's later poetry, appearing in such poems as "Idillio maremmano" ("Maremma Idyll") and "Traversando la Maremma Toscano" ("Crossing the Tuscan Maremma"). Carducci's mother reared him on the tragedies of Vittorio

Alfieri, a writer in the French neoclassical style who had sought to revive the national spirit of Italy. For his part, Carducci's father attempted to impart to his son his own fervent enthusiasm for the writings of Manzoni, but Carducci, always an independent thinker, never acquired a taste for Manzoni. The boy was also taught Latin by his father and delighted in the works of Vergil and other ancient authors. He avidly read Roman history and anything dealing with the French Revolution. His first verse, satirical in nature, was written in 1846.

In 1848, the Carduccis were obliged to move when the attempt at independence failed. The threat of violence became too great for Carducci's father, and the family relocated first to Laiatico, then to Florence. Carducci went to religious schools until 1852, and was influenced by his rhetoric teacher, Father Geremia Barsottini, who had translated into prose all the odes of Horace. The boy became further impassioned in the cause of Italian reunification and discovered the works of Ugo Foscolo and Giuseppe Mazzini. After completing his education, Carducci followed his wandering father to Celle on Mount Amiata but soon after won a scholarship to the Normal School of Pisa. In 1855, he published his first book, *L'arpa del populo*, an anthology, and a year later he received his doctoral degree and a certification for teaching. He took a position as a rhetoric teacher in a secondary school at the *ginnasio* in San Miniato al Tedesco.

With several friends, among them Giuseppe Chiarini, Carducci founded a literary society, Amici Pedanti, a group that was essentially anti-Romantic and anti-Catholic. They believed that Italy's only hope for the future was in the revival of the classical, pagan spirit of the ancient world, which was emphasized as still existing in the Italian land and blood. Such opinions naturally provoked violent objections, both from Romantics and from those who favored the status quo. Carducci freely and ferociously responded in prose to the attacks many times. His first collection of poetry, *Rime*, appeared in July, 1857.

Although Carducci won a competition for the chair of Greek in a secondary school in Arezzo, the granducal government did not approve his appointment, so, in 1857, he returned to Florence and eked out a living by giving private lessons. In November, his depression became worse when his brother Dante killed himself for unknown reasons. A year later, Carducci's father died, and Carducci became the head of his impoverished family. In 1858, he moved his mother and brother Walfredo into a very poor house in Florence, continuing his private lessons and editing the texts of the Bibliotechina Diamante of publisher Gaspare Barbèra. Together with Barbèra, he founded a short-lived periodical, *Il poliziano*. Despite his financial situation, Carducci married Elvira Menicucci in March, 1859.

With the union of Tuscany and Italy, Carducci's fortunes turned for the better. First, he was offered the chair of Greek in the secondary school of Pistoia, where he remained for nearly a year; then, the minister of education, Terenzio Mamiani, appointed him to the chair of Italian Eloquence at the University of Bologna. Carducci was somewhat ambivalent toward his professorial role and its traditional philological orientation and fretted about its effect on his poetry, but the position allowed him to deepen his acquaintance with the classics and with the literature of other nations. His political views also changed. Under Victor Emmanuel II, Carducci had been an idealistic monarchist in support of the union of Italy, but after Garibaldi was wounded and captured

Giosuè Carducci (Library of Congress)

by government troops at Aspromonte in 1862, Carducci allied himself with the democratic republicans and became more pronouncedly Jacobin and anti-Catholic, venting his intense feelings in aggressive poetry.

Carducci published his *Giambi* (iambics; later *Giambi ed epodi*), a collection of polemical poems, under the pseudonym "Enotrio Romano"; the poems reveal Carducci's affinities with Victor Hugo and Heinrich Heine. "Inno a Satana" ("Hymn to Satan") was in a similar vein and became one of his most famous poems, though his work suffered in quality as he became more vituperative. By 1872, however, he had begun to control his polemical instincts, and some of his finest poems, later collected in *The New Lyrics*, were written in the 1870's. *Barbarian Odes*, begun in 1873, became his most influential work.

Indeed, following the publication of the collection *Barbarian Odes*, Carducci became an object of adulation for younger poets throughout Italy. Periodicals such as *Fanfulla della Domenica*, *Cronaca bizantina*, and *Domenica letteraria* helped spread his fame. *New Barbarian Odes* solidified his reputation, and he assumed the role of national poet.

In part, Carducci's position as a leader of young Italian poets was the result of the efforts of Angelo Sommaruga, who had founded *Cronaca bizantina* to encourage native Italian writing and gathered newcomers such as Marradi, Matilde Serao, Edoardo Scarfoglio, Guido Magnoni, and Gabriele D'Annunzio for its pages. Sommaruga sought out Carducci to give credibility to the group, and Sommaruga's encouragement spurred Carducci to intense activity in verse and prose. During this period, Carducci's political and philosophical views shifted; he resigned himself to the monarchy and acquired a more religious attitude, with some appreciation of the Church's mission, though he remained fundamentally anticlerical.

The last two decades of Carducci's life were filled with misery. In 1885, he became ill. Five years later he was made a senator, but in 1899, a stroke paralyzed his hand and nearly deprived him of speech. He continued working, despite the setbacks, publishing his last volume of poetry in 1899 and collecting his works from 1850 to 1900. In 1904, he resigned from teaching. He received the Nobel Prize for Literature the year before he died.

ANALYSIS

When granting Giosuè Carducci the 1906 Nobel Prize, the Swedish Academy stated that the award was given "not only in consideration of his deep learning and critical research, but above all as a tribute to the creative energy, freshness of style, and lyrical force which characterize his poetic masterpieces." Carducci's works are exceptional in their synthesis of literary qualities often seen as opposites. Though his life coincided with the height of Romanticism in Italy, he took the classical mode as his paradigm of artistic creation. This might have made him a curious anachronism, but his passion and his agility with classical form kept his works free of the servility that mars much neoclassical poetry. Carducci had too great a heart to let formal considerations neuter him and too much poetic skill not to exploit the opportunities of form.

Indeed, Carducci's great learning gave him the ability to scrutinize his own work, to evaluate and revise it with a living sense of literary history. Full of the passions of the Risorgimento and the nationalism of the new Italian state, he nevertheless viewed his work as part of a long historical tradition; whatever the Romans had been in essence was still in the Italian landscape, soil, and blood. Though Italy had drifted from the unity and glory of its past, it was always possible to restore those qualities, which were not dead but merely submerged. Classicism thus became a way of restoring to the Italian nation and people their rightful identity and heritage. Carducci himself wrote:

> Great poetry aspires ceaselessly to the past and proceeds from the past. The dead are infinitely more numerous than the living, and the spaces of time under the Triumph of Death are incomparably more immense and more tranquil than the brief moment agitated by the phenomenon of life.

JUVENILIA

Carducci collected his earliest poetry (that written between 1850 and 1860, including that published in *Rime*) in *Juvenilia*. In these early poems, the young Carducci was searching for his voice, but he had already adopted many of the values which inform his mature work. *Juvenilia* reveals a familiarity with Greek and Latin models as well as with Italian poetry; the values that antedate Romanticism are stressed, along with a natural humanism free of the sentimentality and egotistic aberrations of Romanticism. *Juvenilia* is highly patriotic in tone and often violently anti-Catholic because of the Church's opposition to the reunification of Italy. Carducci revives the memory of ancient poetry and pagan strength by saluting the ancient gods; he praises ancient Greece, "Mother Rome," and "free human genius." He reminds Italy of the greatness of Rome and the heroic example of the French Revolution. He salutes the heroes of Italian unity, such as Garibaldi, Mazzini, and Victor Emmanuel II, the latter in a joyous celebration of the imminent war with Austria in 1859. Many of the poems are violently emotional: Carducci attacks those whom he perceives as the enemies of Italy and plunges into depression over the contemporary state of the country and its people.

One of Carducci's most famous and controversial poems was "Hymn to Satan." Later in his life, the poet would disavow the poem and call it "vulgar sing-song," but he stood defiantly behind it when it was published, astounding the public and causing great outrage at the University of Bologna and elsewhere. The critic Querico Filopanti, for example, asserted that it was not a poem at all but an intellectual orgy. In it, Carducci gives full vent to his anticlerical feelings, seeking to shock Italians out of their spiritual apathy. Satan becomes the symbol of nature and reason: He is Lucifer, carrier of light, enemy of asceticism and of a Church which denies the natural rights of man. Free thought, progress, and physical vitality are Satan's promises. Curiously, the poem praises Girolamo Savonarola for his defiance, ignoring the religious reformer's own asceticism. Carducci's Satan has been likened to Charles Baudelaire's in *Les Fleurs du mal* (1857, 1861, 1868; *Flowers of Evil*, 1909), but a more fruitful comparison can be drawn with the English Romantics' interpretation of John Milton's Satan in *Paradise Lost* (1667) as a Romantic hero. Carducci's Satan is clearly more Promethean than Satanic.

LEVIA GRAVIA AND GIAMBI ED EPODI

Levia gravia (light and heavy) has a tone of somberness and bitter disappointment, reflecting the events of the 1860's. During this time, the conquest of Rome was delayed, the disaster at Aspromonte occurred, and Carducci himself was drifting from his belief in the

monarchy. The largely political inspiration and the tendentiousness which characterize *Levia gravia* also mar *Giambi ed epodi*, in which Carducci's combative nature overcomes his sense of poetry. "Canto dell'amore" ("Song of Love"), the last poem in *Giambi ed epodi*, provides a departure from this combativeness and reveals a depth greater than that of many of his earlier works. Most of this collection simply attacks and satirizes Pope Pius IX and the problems of the newly formed Italian government. "Song of Love," however, expresses a simple, robust view of life. Looking from Perugia, where the fortress of Paolina (a symbol of tyranny razed by the people in 1860) once stood, the poet is filled with the beauty of spring and lifted above the level of ordinary human struggle. The song of love fills him. The ancient Etruscans and Romans and foreign invaders of the Umbrian plain are evoked as symbolic of the ongoing cycles of nature. The poet even invites his enemy the pope to drink a glass of wine to liberty with him. He hears a chant rising from the hills, the voice of people of the past saying, "Too much we hated, suffering. So love!/Holy and fair the world shall be always."

NUOVE POESIE

Some critics, such as Eugenio Donadoni, remark on the gracefulness of images and rhythms in *Levia gravia* and date Carducci's beginnings as a major poet from this volume. Others, however, would delay his "arrival" as a major poet to the more mature *Nuove poesie*, four years later. One notable poem from the latter is "I poeti di parte bianca" ("Poets of the White Faction"), which makes reference to the factions in Dante's Florence and evokes that moment in history as well as the poetry of the fourteenth century. "Francesco Petrarca" celebrates the great sonneteer and speaks of raising an altar to him in the deep, green woods, combining Carducci's sense of landscape with his love for the tradition of Italian poetry.

BARBARIAN ODES, NEW BARBARIAN ODES, AND THIRD BARBARIAN ODES

At the center of Carducci's oeuvre is the highly influential and original sequence comprising *Barbarian Odes*, *New Barbarian Odes*, and *Third Barbarian Odes*. "I hate the outworn meters," Carducci proclaimed, and he began to adapt such classical forms as the Alcaic, the Asclepiad, and the Sapphic, all commonly used by Horace.

Carducci's adaptations of classical meters are extraordinarily successful; the demanding requirements of the ancient forms are satisfied gracefully and unobtrusively. When, late in life, he returned to modern forms, the musicality and facility of his verse were markedly enhanced.

Among the most successful poems of the *Barbarian Odes* is the pensive love poem "Alla stazione in una mattinata d'autunno" ("To the Station on an Autumn Morning"), in which Carducci evokes the melancholy feeling of the autumn season. "Miramar," the title of which is derived from the name of the castle near Trieste from which Maximilian began his voyage to Mexico, also conveys a tragic, pensive mood, using vivid natural imagery of the Adriatic Sea in the context of the story of the ill-fated Emperor Maximilian of Mexico. "Alla fonti del Clitunno" ("At the Sources of the Clitumnus"), a protest against Christianity, lacks the sharp edge of Carducci's earlier poems on the same topic. The poet celebrates the peasants who live along the quiet river, condemns the fanatic humility of medieval life, and hails the fecund vitality of Italy, mother of crops, laws, arts, and industry. "Presso l'urna di P. B. Shelley" ("Near the Urn of P. B. Shelley") is one of Carducci's many poems making reference to great persons, living or dead. Written in elegiac distichs (a dactylic hexameter followed by a pentameter), the poem portrays a faraway island where mythical and literary figures meet. Siegfried and Achilles walk along the sea; Roland and Hector sit together under a tree; Lear tells his story to Oedipus. Ophelia and Iphigenia, Cordelia and Antigone, Durendala and Andromache, Helen and Iseult, Lady Macbeth and Clytemnestra are paired. Shelley, the only modern poet present, has been brought to the island by Sophocles. The narrator speaks: "The present hour is in vain; it but strikes and flees;/ only in the past is beauty, only in death is truth." Like many classicists, Carducci believed that it is possible to cheat death only by the immortality of art.

THE LYRICS AND RHYTHMS

In *The Lyrics and Rhythms*, his final book of poetry, Carducci abandoned the classical meters of *Barbarian Odes* and returned to modern forms. Many of the poems in this volume were composed in the Alps and have a clear, wide-ranging vision, as if written in imitation of the clear, broad expanses visible from the mountains. Standing on the "mount of centuries," the poet looks deeply into the past in order to see the future. The landscape is rich with associations from his memory, from history, from ancient myth and legend. The tone of the collection is generally solemn, as if Carducci, who had been obsessed with death since his brother's suicide and the death of his infant son, were contemplating his own end. In the gravity of its tone and the sweep of its vision, this last book of poems offers a fitting valediction.

OTHER MAJOR WORKS

EDITED TEXT: *L'arpa del populo*, 1855.

MISCELLANEOUS: *Opere*, 1889-1909 (includes prose and poetry); *Opere complete*, 1940 (30 vols.; includes all his prose and poetry).

BIBLIOGRAPHY

Bailey, John Cann. *Carducci*. Oxford, England: Clarendon Press, 1926. A brief biographical and critical study of Carducci.

Brand, Peter, and Lino Pertile, eds. *The Cambridge History of Italian Literature*. Rev. ed. New York: Cambridge University Press, 1999. Includes bibliographical references and index.

Donadoni, Eugenio. *A History of Italian Literature*. Translated by Richard Monges. New York: New York University Press, 1969. A two-volume history of Italian literature.

Scalia, Eugene. *Carducci: His Critics and Translators in England and America, 1881-1932*. New York: S. F. Vanni, 1937. A history of the critical reception of Carducci's work in England and America. Includes bibliographic references.

Williams, Orlo. *Giosuè Carducci*. New York: Houghton Mifflin, 1914. A short biography of Carducci. Includes bibliographic references.

J. Madison Davis;
bibliography updated by the editors

THOMAS CAREW

Born: Kent, England; 1594 or 1595
Died: London, England; 1640

PRINCIPAL POETRY

Poems, 1640, 1642
Poems, with a Maske, by Thomas Carew Esquire, 1651
Poems, Songs, and Sonnets, Together with a Masque, 1671
The Poems of Thomas Carew with His Masque, 1949 (Rhodes Dunlap, editor)

OTHER LITERARY FORMS

Thomas Carew wrote a number of songs for plays that were presented at the court of Charles I. The only other major work he produced, however, was his masque *Coelum Britannicum* (1634).

ACHIEVEMENTS

To discuss the achievements of Thomas Carew is a difficult, if not an impossible, task because the first printed edition of his work did not appear until after his death. As a result, his poems were not widely known—which is no reflection, of course, on their merit. Whatever impact he had on the literary climate of the Caroline period was limited to a small audience at court who knew his poems from the manuscript copies that were circulated. With this qualification in mind, Carew's accomplishments can be counted as significant. Alexander Witherspoon and Frank Warnke assess Carew's achievements as follows: "Unquestionably a minor poet, he has the distinction of being one of the best in an age when minor poetry often touched greatness" (*Seventeenth Century Prose and Poetry*, 1963). Certainly Carew achieved this greatness in "An Elegie upon the Death of the Deane of Pauls, Dr. John Donne," his unquestioned masterpiece. He more often produced verse that was trite or contrived. Somewhere between these two levels of achievement, however, lies a body of genuinely agreeable poetry that is valuable to the student of literature not so much because of its own innate merit but because it so effectively captures the spirit of Cavalier po-etry. Indeed, one can gain a satisfactory knowledge of the themes and techniques of the Cavaliers through reading Carew alone, for he is in a sense the perfect example of the court poet during the reign of Charles I.

BIOGRAPHY

Despite the recurring popularity of his verse and his reputation as a significant Cavalier poet, little is known about the life of Thomas Carew (generally agreed to be properly pronounced "Cary," as spelled by English author and biographer Izaak Walton) other than that which one might infer from his poems or speculate about the life of a courtier at the court of Charles I. Carew was born in Kent in either 1594 or 1595. His father Matthew was a master in Chancery, and his mother, Alice Rymers, was descended from a noble family. Although nothing is known of Carew's boyhood, there is a record of his having begun study at Merton College, Oxford, in 1608. In 1610 he entered Cambridge and apparently took his degree in 1612. Again, one can only speculate about Carew's academic career, but he no doubt studied the basic curriculum in rhetoric, mathematics, and philosophy.

After graduating from Cambridge, Carew studied law, although his father's letters about his son's preparation for the bench suggest that Carew's inclinations were not toward a legal career. Rhodes Dunlap in *The Poems of Thomas Carew* (1949) speculates that Carew may have been distracted by the notoriously frivolous life of an Inns of Court student. Matthew Carew shared this and other concerns with his friend Sir Dudley Carleton, English ambassador to Italy, who, at the request of his friend, employed the youthful Carew in 1613. Although records do exist about Carleton's Italian activities, no mention is made of Carew. No doubt the intelligent and lively Carew availed himself of the opportunities for learning and licentiousness that Italy offered until he was released from Carleton's employ in 1616, apparently the result of Carew's making a rather foolish suggestion in writing about Lady Carleton's lack of fidelity to her husband.

Carew returned to England, where he apparently fell ill with syphilis. Perhaps it was this bout with the illness that led to one of the better anecdotes concerning Carew. Apparently thinking himself to be dying, he sent for

John Hale, a former school fellow from Merton College who had gone into the ministry. On his death bed, or so he thought, Carew asked for absolution and repented his wayward life. Carew recovered and continued his ways. When he again lay ill and sent for Hale, he was refused by his former friend.

Matthew Carew tried to heal the wounds between his son and Carleton, but to no avail. No doubt the elder Carew was still completely frustrated with his son when he died in 1618.

A year later Carew attended Sir Edward Herbert on his embassy to Paris. In 1624 Carew was recalled to England, and soon after his poetry began to circulate in manuscript form (only a few of his poems were published during his lifetime). In 1630, Carew was appointed to a court position, where he remained until his death.

Little is known about Carew's life at court. In 1634 his masque *Coelum Britannicum* was presented there; the designer was the famous Inigo Jones, who had worked closely with Ben Jonson. Carew was highly regarded by contemporary literary figures, counting among his friends such men as John Donne, Ben Jonson, Sir William Davenant, James Shirley, and Richard Lovelace, with whom he apparently had a close relationship. Like so many of the "Tribe of Ben," Carew was a staunch Royalist.

Another interesting anecdote told about Carew is that he saved the queen from being caught in a compromising position with Jermyn, Lord St. Albans. He had obviously learned something from the affair with Lady Carleton. For saving her secret, the queen apparently rewarded Carew with her highest devotion.

Carew died in 1640, probably after joining the king in his Scottish campaign. He was buried next to his father at St. Anne's Chapel. No trace of either grave is discernible today.

ANALYSIS

A man with many masters—John Donne, Ben Jonson, Giambattista Marino—Thomas Carew was slave to none, although as a Cavalier poet he has been generally regarded as one of Jonson's followers. Like Jonson, Carew commanded many lyric forms and his lines often read as beautifully as do those of Jonson. In fact, many

of Carew's verses have been effectively set to music. Proficiency with meter, however, was only part of Carew's art. He used the conceit effectively, although at times his images strain to such an extent as to warrant Samuel Johnson's attacks on the Metaphysical poets. Carew more effectively associated himself with the Metaphysical school with his use of paradox and argument, adding an intellectual quality to his poems that he so highly valued in Donne.

Jonson and Donne account for the main influences on Carew. He was equally capable of borrowing from Petrarch, Edmund Spenser, or Marino, however, for both theme and technique. In fact, because most of Carew's poems deal with the theme of love, the forsaken lover in particular, writers such as Petrarch and Spenser were often models better suited to his purpose.

"UPON SOME ALTERATIONS IN MY MISTRESS, AFTER MY DEPARTURE INTO FRANCE"

There has been a fair amount of speculation about whether Carew's love poems, particularly those addressed to Celia (probably a pseudonym) or to the unidentified mistress, have an autobiographical basis. Such speculation aside, the poems are interesting for both their lyric excellence and their range of themes. The peak of Carew's lyric accomplishment occurs in "Upon some Alterations in my Mistress, after my Departure into France," where the central image of the lover lost on the troubled ocean of his lady's altered affections is enhanced by the equally varying meters, thus well fusing theme and structure. Thematically, one sees in Carew a movement from Petrarchan despair to bitter vindication against his inconstant mistress. The very range of Carew's work thus demands admiration.

What this brief analysis suggests is that in Carew's work one can see many of the themes and techniques that had dominated Elizabethan and Jacobean poetry and that were equally important to the Caroline poets. Carew also polished his use of the rhyming couplet in anticipation of the Augustan Age. Despite his limitations, Carew paints an accurate picture of poetic achievement and direction in the late Renaissance.

"Upon some Alterations in my Mistress, after my Departure into France" warrants comment, first, because it demonstrates an attitude in love poetry that Carew would reject for the bitter vindictiveness of later poems, such as "Disdaine returned," and second, because Carew's technique in the poem, even when not effective, is interesting. The poem is more likely autobiographical than are many of his other love poems. The poem appears to be Carew's response to his mistress's change of feeling after he had gone to France with Sir Edward Herbert. Unlike later works showing Carew bitter about his lady's rejection, this short lyric poem presents the poet as a forlorn Petrarchan lover. Appropriately, its theme is developed in the extended image of a poet lost on the troubled ocean of inconstant love and his lady's waning affections.

Carew's use of the extended image is interesting not only because it is so typical of Petrarchan poetry, but also because this technique varies from his general approach, which, like Donne's, usually fuses diverse elements. In this poem, the first stanza quickly presents the image that will be elaborated:

> Oh gentle Love, doe not forsake the guide
> Of my fraile Barke, on which the swelling tide
> Of ruthless pride
> Doth beat, and threaten wrack from every side.

It was a well-worn figure by the time Carew came to employ it, and Carew in no way used it with originality. The varied line lengths and metrical feet, however, suggesting the tempestuous seas, show Carew effectively combining idea and form.

Carew's reference to the "mystie cloud of anger" in the second stanza identifies the alterations to which the title refers. Still, Carew follows this line by calling his lady his "faire starre," seeming to say that despite her alterations she remains for him a guiding passion. The last line of the poem, however—"In the deep flood she drown'd her beamie face"—suggests the more defiant train of thought of his later poems as he turns his back on his lady and tells her that her own treatment of him will be her destruction.

"SONG, TO MY INCONSTANT MISTRESS"

In Carew's "Song, To my inconstant Mistress," as in "Disdaine returned," he pictures himself as the scorned Petrarchan lover, though, rather than suffering in frustration, he methodically points out why his mistress will at some point regret her attitude. This intellectual response to an emotional situation is characteristic of the school

of Donne, while the lyric excellence of the poem, in five-line tetrameter stanzas rhyming ababb, follows the influence that governed the "Tribe of Ben." Carew thus illustrates his ability to absorb diverse influences.

Underlying the entire thematic structure of "Song, To my inconstant Mistress" is the poet's paralleling of love and religion. The opening stanza portrays him as a man with a "strong faith," while his mistress is a "poor excommunicate." These early parallels suggest a point that the poet will later develop: that true faithfulness in love will, as in religion, be rewarded by salvation. The focus of this poem, however, is on the damning of the unfaithful mistress.

The second stanza develops one of Carew's typical themes, that love demands an equal commitment by both parties. The poet says that his inconstant mistress will be replaced by a "faire hand" and that this new love and the poet will be "both with equall glory crown'd." At this point, Lynn Sadler suggests, the tone of the poet has something of the "swagger of bravado." The point is well taken; moreover, the swagger is to become more bitter in the final stanza.

In the third stanza the implications of the first are at last fulfilled. The poet has already established the bliss he will enjoy because of his constancy to the ideal of love. His main point, however, is to show the despair that awaits the one who has violated the spirit of love. Her reward, moreover, will be equal to her sin, for she will suffer to the degree that she caused suffering. Finally, again in religious terms, she will be "Damn'd for (her) false Apostasie."

"Song, To my inconstant Mistress" is one of Carew's best lyric love poems. His fusion of religious and erotic imagery enhances the latter without mocking or trivializing the former, an achievement which distinguishes the poem from the common run of Cavalier lyrics.

"DISDAINE RETURNED"

One of Carew's best-known poems, "Disdaine returned" demonstrates two significant aspects of his art: the lyric beauty that he inherited from Jonson and his smooth integration of several typical Elizabethan and Jacobean themes. The basic structure of the poem is simple. It has three six-line stanzas in tetrameter, rhyming *ababcc*. In the last stanza, however, the closing couplet varies slightly in its meter and thus draws the poem to a decisive close, suggesting that the poet has cured himself of his lovesickness. Unlike many of the other Celia poems in which Carew expounds the poet's frustrations in love with a typical Petrarchan lament, "Disdaine returned" shows the spirit and style that were characteristic of Donne in such poems as "The Broken Heart." The poem opens with a *carpe diem* statement, "As old Time makes these decay/ So his flames must waste away." Rather than using these lines to make the basic live-for-the-moment argument, however, Carew suggests a feeling of depressed reconciliation; his lady has lost the opportunity for a genuine love that would not fade with the passing of time or the loss of beauty. The second stanza justifies the claim as Carew defines in basically Platonic terms his ideas about love which his mistress has not been able to accept: "Hearts with equal love combined kindle never-dying fires."

In the third stanza, the frustrated poet, whose love is genuine, is forced to return his lady's rejection. As the second stanza suggests, there must be equal commitment for the relationship to prosper. The poet says, however, that he has not found his love returned: "I have searched thy soul within/ And find naught but pride and scorn." He decides to return these feelings of disdain, ending his pointless suffering.

"AN ELEGIE UPON THE DEATH OF THE DEANE OF PAULS, DR. JOHN DONNE"

Generally accepted as Carew's best poem, "An Elegie upon the Death of the Deane of Pauls, Dr. John Donne" is one of the few poems by Carew to be published during his own lifetime. It was published in 1633, although it was probably written much nearer the time of Donne's death in 1631.

The poem opens with an indictment of an age that finds only "unkneaded dowe-bak't prose" to praise the loss of its greatest poet. Carew's frustration with this situation is intensified throughout the poem as he reviews the many changes in the use of language that Donne had wrought. He freed the poet from "senile imitation" of the ancients and then "fresh invention planted." Carew devotes a large part of the poem, in fact, to making this point, using a concept which Donne would have appreciated: Donne paid the "debts of our penurious bankrupt age," which had so long struggled in borrowed images and forms. So great was Donne's power, Carew says,

that "our stubborne language bends, made only fit/ With her tough-thick-rib'd hoopes to gird about/ Thy Giant phansie."

Because Donne is gone, Carew declares, the advances that he initiated are vanishing as well, since they are "Too hard for Libertines in Poetrie." To further build on this theme, the poet uses the image of the wheel that will cease to turn after losing its "moving head." Still, Carew's final image is that of the phoenix, a popular image in Donne's poetry, to suggest that perhaps from the ashes the spirit of Donne will rise in another era.

Finally, Carew apologizes for his poor effort by saying that Donne is "Theme enough to tyre all Art." He then presents the closing epitaph:

> Here lies a King, that rul'd as hee thought fit
> The universall Monarchy of wit;
> Here lie two Flamens, and both those, the best,
> Apollo's first, at last, the true God's Priest.

This best of Carew's poems is a rather accurate projection of what would be the course of poetic achievement after the death of Donne. Not until Alexander Pope, about one hundred years later (excluding John Milton), did England see a genius to compare with Donne, yet between these two giants, such poems as this one by Carew kept alive the spirit of poetic achievement that distinguished the Renaissance.

OTHER MAJOR WORK

PLAY: *Coelum Britannicum*, pr. 1634 (masque).

BIBLIOGRAPHY

Benet, Diana. "Carew's Monarchy of Wit." In *"The Muses' Common-Weale": Poetry and Politics in the Seventeenth Century*, edited by Claude J. Summers and Ted-Larry Pebworth. Columbia: University of Missouri Press, 1988. Focuses on three poems: "To my much honoured friend Henry Lord Cary of Lepington upon his translation of Malvezzi," "Upon Occasion of his Ode of defiance annext to his Play of the new Inne" (to Ben Jonson), and "To my worthy Friend, M. D'Avenant, Upon his Excellent Play, *The Just Italian*." Argues that Carew, using the absolutist rhetoric of James and Charles, consciously constructs a realm of wit in which the writer reigns supreme. Shows the problems faced by writers in the Stuarts' attempts to limit free speech.

Corns, Thomas N., ed. *The Cambridge Companion to English Poetry: Donne to Marvell*. Cambridge, England: Cambridge University Press, 1993. Presents a brief but balanced biography of Thomas Carew and an analysis of his work.

Parker, Michael P. "'To my friend G. N. from Wrest': Carew's Secular Masque." In *Classic and Cavalier: Essays on Jonson and the Sons of Ben*, edited by Claude J. Summers and Ted-Larry Pebworth. Pittsburgh: University of Pittsburgh Press, 1982. Surveys the seventeenth century genre of the country-house poem and places Carew's piece as the turning point between Jonson's "To Penshurst" and Marvell's "Upon Appleton House." Supplies information about Wrest and its owners, which was for many years obscured through historical error. Shows how the structure of the poem owes much to the masque tradition.

Sadler, Lynn. *Thomas Carew*. Boston: Twayne, 1979. This critical biography, part of Twayne's English Authors series, presents a straightforward introduction to Carew's life, times, and works. Sadler does not rate the poet as highly as some later critics have done, and though she covers his entire output, her emphasis is on the better-known lyrics at the expense of the country-house poems and Carew's masque. Perhaps the most accessible single work on Carew for the general reader. Includes a well-selected bibliography with annotations.

Selig, Edward I. *The Flourishing Wreath*. New Haven, Conn.: Yale University Press, 1958. Reprint. Hamden, Conn.: Archon Books, 1970. The first full-length serious study of Carew's verse, this work began as an undergraduate thesis. Remains the most thorough attempt to justify Carew's fame in his own time. Selig's chapter ("The Well-Tempered Lyre") on the poet's song lyrics is still valuable; he points out that a third of Carew's poems were written for singing, and sixty settings survive. The book's examination of patterns of imagery in Carew is also useful.

Semler, L. E. *The English Mannerist Poets and the Visual Arts*. Madison, N.J.: Fairleigh Dickinson University Press, 1998. Includes an introduction to mannerism as it applies to visual as well as poetic work. Each of the five poets covered, including Carew, is shown to have one or more of the characteristics of the mannerist style.

Sharpe, Kevin. "Cavalier Critic? The Ethics and Politics of Thomas Carew's Poetry." In *Politics of Discourse: The Literature and History of Seventeenth-Century England*, edited by Kevin Sharpe and Steven Zwicker. Berkeley: University of California Press, 1987. Distances Carew from the usual image of the Cavalier and argues that he was a serious writer with an orderly and hierarchical vision of a kingdom of nature and love. Emphasizes Carew's often misunderstood, positive view of marriage and connects this idea to his political vision.

Walton, Geoffrey. "The Cavalier Poets." In *From Donne to Marvell*. Vol. 3 in *New Pelican Guide to English Literature*, edited by Boris Ford. New York: Penguin Books, 1982. The rise in Carew's modern reputation is clearly demonstrated by the fact that, of the five poets covered in this chapter, Carew now receives the most attention. Stresses Carew's complexity and range, and singles out for praise the sense of social responsibility shown in Carew's two country-house poems, "To Saxham" and "To my friend G. N., from Wrest."

Gerald W. Morton;
bibliography updated by the editors

LEWIS CARROLL

Charles Lutwidge Dodgson

Born: Daresbury, Cheshire, England; January 27, 1832

Died: Guildford, Surrey, England; January 14, 1898

PRINCIPAL POETRY

Phantasmagoria and Other Poems, 1869

The Hunting of the Snark: An Agony in Eight Fits, 1876

Rhyme? and Reason? 1883

Three Sunsets and Other Poems, 1898
The Collected Verse of Lewis Carroll, 1932, 1960
   (as *The Humorous Verse of Lewis Carroll*)
For "The Train": Five Poems and a Tale, 1932

OTHER LITERARY FORMS

Lewis Carroll is remembered for his long fiction, the children's classics *Alice's Adventures in Wonderland* (1865) and *Through the Looking-Glass and What Alice Found There* (1871). Immediate popular and critical successes, they are now among the world's most quoted and translated books, enjoyed by children and adults alike, and their characters are part of the world's folklore. His sentimental and tendentious *Sylvie and Bruno* (1889) and *Sylvie and Bruno Concluded* (1893) were far less successful.

Carroll's prose fiction is best classified as anatomy, which, unlike the novel, is about ideas rather than people and engages the mind rather than represents life realistically. The characters of *Alice's Adventures in Wonderland* and *Through the Looking-Glass and What Alice Found There* are personifications of philosophical or linguistic problems and function, much as counters in a game whose rules change according to Carroll's fancy.

Lewis Carroll (Library of Congress)

The books have rudimentary characteristics of the *Bildungsroman*—Alice's changes in size or status suggesting puberty and development—but Alice herself is static. Like Gulliver or Candide, she is the "straight man" in the comedy, less important as a character than as a stabilizing perspective—that of the "normal" child in a mad world. The anatomy's distinguishing formal characteristic is, paradoxically, its refusal to take any one form—its protean, adaptive quality. In *Alice's Adventures in Wonderland* and *Through the Looking-Glass and What Alice Found There*, the dream-narrative dissolves into a structure of dialectic or symposium which is almost infinitely transformable—into poetry, parody, literary criticism, riddles, or verbal games for the sake of the play.

The tendency of Carroll's work to turn into wordplay is not confined to his fiction and poetry. He published more than three hundred separate works, consisting of formal mathematical and logical treatises, essays on cranky subjects, satires on Oxford's academic politics, numerous acrostics, puzzles, and trivia. In addition, he wrote faithfully in his diaries, now published, and composed delightful letters, also published. His work in formal mathematics is sober, systematic, and unoriginal. His contribution in logic was made indirectly and intuitively by way of his "nonsense," which dramatized in paradoxes and wordplay concepts later taken up by linguistic philosophers such as Bertrand Russell and Ludwig Wittgenstein. In general, Carroll wrote best when least serious and when working in a hybrid form somewhere between linguistic analysis and literature. In his best art, in works such as *A Tangled Tale* (1885), a cross between narrative and mathematics, or the philosophical dialogue "What the Tortoise Said to Achilles," the logician and poet combine forces.

ACHIEVEMENTS

Lewis Carroll created a new kind of children's literature that was sheer fun in the most serious sense; its combination of fantasy, humor, and wordplay stimulated the mind and the imagination. In rejecting the rational, moralistic approach of the children's literature of the eighteenth and nineteenth centuries, Carroll turned the trend toward lesson-free imaginative literature in the twentieth.

Now that Alice is known to children largely through the popular media, Carroll's books have become the territory of adults—adults from a considerable range of intellectual disciplines. Physicists, psychologists, philosophers, linguists, and computer scientists, as well as mathematicians and literary critics, have written about or in response to his work. In the twentieth century, his view of the world as a fascinating if unsolvable puzzle continued to grow on readers, presenting a difficulty in classifying his literary influence. Theoretically, "nonsense" is humor's equivalent of Symbolist poetry or abstract painting in its concern with the play of verbal surfaces and textures rather than function or content. As nonsense's purest and best practitioner, Carroll is a forerunner of Surrealism, Dadaism, and similar schools. Certainly, Carroll has made connections, directly or indirectly, with the most important of the modernists and postmodernists. T. S. Eliot, James Joyce, Franz Kafka, Wallace Stevens, Jorge Luis Borges, and Vladimir Nabokov all owe something to the nonsense perspective: alinear structure, the play of intellectual wit, the view of literature as a game of language, and the concept of autonomous art.

Carroll contributed the Mad Hatter, the Cheshire Cat, and the Jabberwock to the world's folklore; provided an abundance of popular quotations; and added several new words to the English language. While other, more ambitious works of the era have become dated, *Alice's Adventures in Wonderland*, *Through the Looking-Glass and What Alice Found There*, and *The Hunting of the Snark* survive and seem inexhaustible. This is because Carroll's gift was a language which opened minds to the infinity of worlds within words.

BIOGRAPHY

Charles Lutwidge Dodgson's literary achievement under the pseudonym of Lewis Carroll is often separated from his career as a Victorian mathematician and don. As Dodgson the reserved bachelor, he lived an extremely regular life, most of it at Christ Church College, Oxford, where he matriculated in 1850, taught mathematics from 1855 until 1881, and thereafter served as curator of the Senior Common Room. Despite the academic conventionality of these externals, Dodgson had diverse interests: photography, at which he excelled in his special in-

terest areas (children and celebrities); visits with his child-friends; theatergoing; occasional preaching; and writing. As Lewis Carroll, he wrote what he, to some extent, considered children's humor, indeed calling it "nonsense," and this side of his work is often viewed as a form of sublimation. Carroll thus becomes the rebel who escaped from the tedium of being Dodgson. Certainly, Dodgson had his part in confining Carroll to the nursery: He allowed only little girls to use his pseudonym and refused in later life to acknowledge letters addressed to Lewis Carroll at his quarters. The Dodgson/Carroll split is too simple in one respect, however; at his best and most distinctive, he merges the perspectives of the logician and the poet. His intellectual agility is behind the playfulness that inspires the word magic.

Dodgson was the third child and eldest son of the eleven children of the Reverend Charles Dodgson and Frances Jane Lutwidge. His authoritarian father may have contributed to the reserved character of his later public image. His affection for his mother was unusually strong and may have hindered his ability to develop attachments to grown women. A lifelong stammer contributed to his introversion but also may have had something to do with his fascination with portmanteau words, funny sounds, puns, and nonsense in general.

As a child educated at home until he was twelve, Dodgson was happy and precocious. To entertain his siblings, he invented games with whimsically elaborate systems of rules, wrote and staged marionette plays for home theatricals, and edited and illustrated several family magazines which contain the early expressions of the logician and poet in puzzles, nonsense, and parodies. He continued producing and contributing to these family periodicals until he was twenty-three.

Although he went on to Richmond Grammar School and Rugby, where he suffered the usual fate of the introverted egghead, the precocious child of Dodgson's idyllic years in a sense never grew up. He turned into Lewis Carroll, the persona who talked only to "child-friends," as he called the little girls whose friendship he cultivated until they reached puberty. These friendships began with Alice Liddell, daughter of the dean of Christ Church, who became Alice of Wonderland. Collectively, the girls became the inspiration, ideal readers, and mediating perspective for most of Carroll's works. This absolutely sure sense of his audience—beginning with his siblings and continuing with his child-friends—has much to do with what makes Carrollian nonsense work. It provided a creative rapport that directed him in transforming what might have been unlikely material— mathematics, logic, and linguistics, as well as wild fantasies—into poetry.

ANALYSIS

The name of Lewis Carroll is now almost synonymous with "nonsense." Carroll did not invent nonsense verse, for it is as old as children's games and nursery rhymes. With Carroll, however, it grows up and becomes something more than nonsense as that term is usually defined. The term refers to humorous verse that does not make sense, which in turn suggests a kind of non-poetry, verse with all the surface characteristics of poetry—rhyme, meter, and figures of speech—but without meaning. As the title of Carroll's *Rhyme? and Reason?* implies, it is sound gone berserk and completely overtaking sense. Superficially, this definition fits his "Jabberwocky," which seems to have the authentic ring of a brilliant poem in a foreign language which does not exist. As such "nonsense," "Jabberwocky" is a piece of ingenuity but little more. The reader's appreciation of Carroll's poetry is far more complex than the term will admit, however, as the enduring popularity of "Jabberwocky" suggests.

The fact that Carroll, a mathematician and logician, felt most alive when playing or inventing games, puzzles, stories, and rhymes with children, leads to the uncommon meaning of his nonsense. As his life seems to show (and in an analogy suggested by Kathleen Blake and Carroll critic Richard Kelly), he viewed the world as a vast puzzle that could never be solved but which must be worked to the end, for the sake of the game itself. Through wordplay of all sorts, from conundrums and acrostics to parodies and paradoxes, Carroll's poetry engages the reader in that game. His "nonsensical" poetry is like that unsolvable puzzle of the world in inviting and resisting interpretation simultaneously. To solve it or extract a meaning would be to end the game and destroy the poem.

ALICE'S ADVENTURES IN WONDERLAND

As quirky as Carroll might seem, his development as a poet follows a common pattern: He began writing what is predominantly parody, in his juvenilia and *Alice's Adventures in Wonderland*, and moved on to poems that are complete in themselves, "Jabberwocky" and *The Hunting of the Snark*. Most of the poems of *Alice's Adventures in Wonderland* are parodies of popular verses and songs that Victorian children were taught and often called upon to recite. In Wonderland, where the world is out of joint, these are consistently misquoted, either by the Wonderland characters, who are all mad, or Alice, whose verbal memory is understandably deranged.

Soon after falling down a rabbit hole and experiencing sudden and strange changes in size, Alice attempts to remember who she is, trying out the names of various friends. As a final effort to regain her identity, she tries to recite Isaac Watts's "Against Idleness and Mischief," which begins "How doth the little busy bee," the bee providing nature's model of virtuous industry. The resulting parody is "How doth the little crocodile," which turns Watts's pathetic fallacy into a sadistic one. The crocodile's work, in contrast to the bee's, consists of floating passively with "gently smiling jaws" open to welcome "little fishes in." In place of Watts's cozy wholesomeness, Alice seems to have constructed a Darwinian world of "Nature red in tooth and claw" or a Freudian one of oral aggression.

To extract "Eat or be eaten" as Carroll's moral would be missing the point, however, even though this theme arises in almost every parody and episode in the book. In Wonderland, as in slapstick comedy, violence is the rule, but it remains, with emotions, on a purely verbal level, as in the case of the Queen of Hearts's universal panacea, "Off with your head!" Although Carroll juxtaposes the law of the jungle against the tea-and-bread-and-butter decorum of the Victorian nursery, the point is to disrupt the normal or preconceived order. Even the trauma of Alice's loss of identity is short-lived. After misquoting the poem, she cries a pool of tears that becomes an ingenious obstacle course for the next episode.

The parodied poems are easy targets, insipid and platitudinous doggerel, and the parodies themselves are part of a larger satire on Victorian children's literature and spoon-fed education, as suggested elsewhere in the Mock Turtle's curriculum of "Reeling and Writhing" and "Ambition, Distraction, Uglification, and Derision." Carroll's parody tends to get broader, as satire on specific children's literature diffuses into satire on education and moral instruction in general, and then into wordplay which does violence on language itself and all its rules. In the parodies as a whole, the target is didacticism, but the main reason for reading is to engage in a game of transformation that surprises and stimulates.

The dramatic situation, in which Alice is called upon to recite and invariably delivers a parody, itself becomes a game, especially for Victorian readers, who immediately recognized the parodied poems and appreciated the play of the parody against the original. The episode in which Alice is told to recite "Father William" by the hookah-smoking caterpillar must have further delighted children who could share her cool upward glance at the adult world, with its arbitrary orders and rules. Her recitation, "wrong from beginning to end," as the Caterpillar comments condescendingly afterward, begins as Robert Southey's "The Old Man's Comforts," a strenuously righteous portrait of old age: "In the days of my youth I remember'd my God/ And He hath not forgotten my age." Carroll's Father William is a slapstick character; eccentrically and wonderfully athletic, he maintains his strength by standing on his head or balancing eels on his nose. He is also voracious, eating a goose with "the bones and the beak," and short tempered: The poem ends as he shouts at his son, "'Be off, or I'll kick you down stairs.'"

In this and the next parody, also on the subject of that Victorian shibboleth, the home and family, Carroll's antididacticism is at its wildest. The Duchess's lullaby is a parody of G. W. Langford's morbidly sentimental "Speak gently to the little child!/ . . . . It may not long remain." Carroll inverts this advice (rule by love rather than by fear) into the loudly comic violence of "Speak roughly to your little boy,/ And beat him when he sneezes." The onomatopoeic chorus of "Wow! Wow! Wow!" is a cacophonous child-pleaser. One feels no sympathy for the Duchess's baby, to whom this advice is applied, because his feelings, like the parodied poem, are turned into a sound effect. As soon as Alice takes pity on him, he turns into a pig.

By the mad tea party episode, at which point in the narrative most of the foundations of Alice's normal, above-ground order have been destroyed, the parodies get broader and more irrelevantly playful. The Mad Hatter's song is a misquotation of Jane Taylor's "Twinkle, twinkle, little star," but it surprises and entertains as a piece of sheer incongruity. Arbitrarily, it seems, the Hatter substitutes "bat" for "star" and "tea-tray" for "diamond," producing "Twinkle, twinkle, little bat!/ How I wonder what you're at!/ Up above the world you fly,/ Like a tea-tray in the sky." The images surprise by failing to relate, either to reality or to one another. Not only do bats fail to "twinkle," but also they have nothing in common with tea-trays. Much as the Duchess's baby is turned into a thing—a sound effect and then a pig—the potential simile is neutralized, its images turning back into discrete, therefore unpoetic and senseless, objects.

Surprise and laughter are nonsense's equivalent of poetic emotion. Its "sense" is more difficult to explain. The Mad Hatter's song, however, makes Wonderland sense in several ways. As a mad inversion of a sentimental song, it corresponds with the mad tea party as the counterpart of Victorian high tea. It is also the perfect expression of the Mad Hatter, who challenges Alice's sense of time, logic, and decorum. The tea tray in the sky is the appropriate marker in the Hatter's world of eternal teatime, and the indecorous but twinkling little bat fits in with his tea-drinking companions, the March Hare and, especially, the Dormouse, who tells a story of little girls who live at the bottom of a treacle well ("well in") and draw things beginning with "M." The meaning of the Hatter's song is like that of his riddle with no answer, "Why is a raven like a writing-desk?" Through arbitrary or nonsense correspondences, the words take the reader on an exhilarating trip to nowhere and everywhere at the same time.

The Mock Turtle's two songs, which come just before the book's conclusion in the trial scene, are more playfully nonsensical, musical, and complete than the previous poems, and so prevent one's reading any moral into Wonderland. The songs also prepare for Alice's awakening, precipitated by her "Stuff and nonsense!" response to the increasingly irrational court, which, as she suddenly realizes, is "nothing but a pack of cards."

The first song upsets the previously established pattern by turning a sadistic poem into harmless play. It parodies the meter and obvious dramatic situation of

Mary Howitt's "The Spider and the Fly," in which the spider invites the fly into her "prettiest little parlour." Carroll adapts Howitt's inappropriately rollicking rhythm to a fittingly gay song and dance, the "Lobster Quadrille." "Will you walk a little faster?" says a whiting to a snail, who is then exhorted to join in a "delightful" experience. Lest the snail, like the fly, fear danger—indeed, the dance involves being thrown out to sea—he is told to be adventurous and reminded that "The further off from England the nearer is to France—." The song ends jollily enough as the invitation extends to Alice and the reader: "Will you, won't you, will you, won't you, won't you join the dance?"

Similarly, "Turtle Soup" teases the reader with hints of danger and opportunities for morals, only to cancel them out. The situation reeks with dramatic irony: The Mock Turtle sings about his destiny as food and sobs all the while. Yet the verbal connection between Mock Turtle and turtle soup which makes the irony possible has a fallacy embedded in it. A mock turtle cannot be made into turtle soup—or any soup, for that matter. Realizing that the implied relationship is pure wordplay, the reader is reminded that, as his name suggests, the character and indeed the whole book is a fiction. "Mock" also suggests fakery and underscores the character's sentimentality, another level of unreality. "Mock" additionally suggests ridicule, and this turtle's song is a parody of James Sayles's treacley "Star of the Evening," with lowly and also rather sloppy soup substituted for the star. Finally, riddled with too many ironies and puns of which to make sense, "Turtle Soup" turns, like the previous song, into an invitation—to eat, slurp, and sing: "Beau—ootiful Soo—oop!/Soo—oop of the e—e—evening,/ Beautiful, beauti—FUL SOUP!"

THROUGH THE LOOKING-GLASS AND WHAT ALICE FOUND THERE

Carroll's parody becomes a sustained and sophisticated art, and perhaps something more than parody, in *Through the Looking-Glass and What Alice Found There*, but only once, in the White Knight's ballad, which adapts the rhyme and meter of Thomas Moore's "My Heart and Lute" to the content of William Wordsworth's "Resolution and Independence." In its comment on Wordsworth's profoundly serious treatment of an experience that can strike one as less than edifying, the

story shows Carroll's keen sense of the absurd. Wordsworth's narrator meets an old man on the moor, comments on the fine day, and asks him his occupation. As the old man feebly and wanderingly answers, his words, compared to a stream, flow into one another, and his interrogator gets lost in elevated meditation. When, after further interrogation, the message finally comes through, it is merely that he wanders and gathers leeches and makes do. The leech-gatherer then becomes a symbol of independence and sanity to comfort the narrator in anxious times.

So summarized, the poem sounds like a non sequitur, an effect that Carroll intensifies through sustained nonsensical dialogue and slapstick. When Carroll's "aged, aged man," sitting precariously on a gate, mumbles so incoherently that his words trickle away "like water through a sieve," his interrogator repeatedly shouts "How is it that you live?" and thumps him on the head. Wordsworth's symbol of sanity turns into Carroll's decidedly eccentric inventor of such things as mutton pies made of butterflies and waistcoat buttons out of haddocks' eyes. Like Wordsworth's, Carroll's speaker is moved to emotional recollection of the aged man, but in moments of clumsiness rather than tranquillity—when he drops something on his toe or shoves "a right-hand foot" into a "left-hand shoe." In the *buffo* finale, Carroll maintains one rhyme for twelve lines to create an unforgettable impression of that old man he "used to know," whose "look was mild, whose speech was slow," who "muttered mumblingly and low/ As if his mouth were full of dough."

In the early and more hostile 1856 version entitled "Upon the Lonely Moor," the parody's targets were sentimentality and Wordsworth. In *Through the Looking-Glass and What Alice Found There*, the parody becomes a joke on the White Knight and then, through a hierarchy of analogies, on Carroll himself. The poem is about an eccentric inventor whom the speaker cannot forget. The White Knight is a similar eccentric inventor whom Alice cannot forget; and the quixotic White Knight is often seen as a caricature of Carroll (in life as well as in art, an eccentric inventor) who hopes Alice Liddell will not forget him. Carroll was fond of reversals and regressions such as this series, which works like a mirror reflecting the mirror reflection of an object ad infinitum.

This reversal turns a hilarious but rather mean parody into a self-referential joke. Finally, it turns that joke into a poem, as the leech-gatherer, Wordsworth, the "aged, aged man," the White Knight, and Carroll become an unfolding series of mild and mumbling quixotic inventors who hope to stumble onto the key to the treasure of the universe. The poem comments on itself as poetry, for each of these figures is a poet in some questionable sense, beginning with the leech-gatherer whose feeble words transcend themselves and on through the White Knight and Carroll (both of whom, as Alice detects, got the "tune" from somebody else). By reflecting backward and forward, the parody inverts itself into a poetically suggestive surface.

As a rule, the poems of *Through the Looking-Glass and What Alice Found There* are not parodies or, like the White Knight's ballad, become something else through the reflective magic of the mirror—its main structural principle as well as the device behind the "logic" of its poetry. The book begins by reversing Wonderland's premises. Instead of a spring day's dream about falling down a rabbit hole, the sequel is a logically constructed game of "Let's pretend" that takes place indoors on a November afternoon. Though Wonderland is chaos, the universe behind the Looking Glass is determined, artificial, and abstract. The mirror principle means that everything goes backward, and reversal extends to the relationship between words and reality.

The mirror world corresponds roughly with philosophical idealism; thus, Alice becomes a figment of a dream of the Red King, who plays George Berkeley's God. Similarly, language and art shape life, and poems can make things happen. Nature imitates art in comical ways when imported nursery-rhyme characters must act out their lines. Egghead Humpty-Dumpty persists in sitting on his wall; Tweedledum and Tweedledee periodically take up arms over a rattle. Looking-Glass insects are like concrete poems, as the Bread-and-Butterfly and the Rocking-horse Fly are materialized words. Trees bark by saying "Bough-wough." Poetry is part of the logician's demonstration of how language can create self-contained worlds.

"JABBERWOCKY"

Shortly after Alice steps through the mirror, she discovers a book that appears to be in a foreign language, but she soon realizes that it is a Looking-Glass book. Holding it to the mirror, she reads the poem "Jabberwocky." Carroll originally planned to print the entire poem in reverse, which would have made reading it a visual joke, an infinite regression of text within text. Even when read in normal order, "Jabberwocky" works according to the rule of the world behind the mirror. The meanings one derives from it refer one back to its surface, obliterating the usual distinctions between form and content. As the title suggests, "Jabberwocky" is gibberish about the Jabberwock, which is identified with the same gibberish. As a poetry of surfaces, this nonsense works much like abstract painting or music; the play of patterns, textures, and sounds is the point.

The first quatrain, like all of Carroll's poetry, has a deceptive simplicity; it is a common ballad stanza in clear English syntax. Therefore "Twas brillig, and the slithy toves/ Did gyre and gimble in the wabe" seems to say something but does not—quite. Later on in the book, Carroll has Humpty-Dumpty provide an elaborate interpretation—made suspect from the beginning by his assertion that he can explain all poems, even those that "haven't been invented." Defining some of the coinages as "portmanteau" words—two words combined to make a new one—he seems to clear up "mimsy" (miserable and flimsy) and "slithy" (slimy and lithe), but the principle fails with "toves" as a fusion of badger, lizard, and corkscrew, and "brillig" as the time "when you begin broiling things for dinner." If one takes Humpty Dumpty's analysis in all seriousness, one ends up with another Mad Hatter's song composed of disparate objects such as bats and tea trays. Its main purpose is to combine insights with false leads and so lure the reader into the game.

The puzzling first quatrain made its first appearance in 1855 in *Mischmasch*, the last of the family periodicals, in a quaint, archaic-looking script, under the heading "Stanza of Anglo-Saxon Poetry." Evidently, from the beginning Carroll wanted a mock-medieval effect. To turn it into "Jabberwocky," he added five middle stanzas—with a motif deriving, perhaps, from the eighth century *Beowulf* and from St. George—and framed them with the repeated first stanza, thus turned into a refrain. To genre and structure, Carroll *has* applied the portmanteau principle, creating a clever mishmash of epic and ballad—a mock-epic ballad.

Thus identified, the poem does mean something—or, at least, it provides at strategic points just enough to lead the reader on. As Alice says, it gives its readers ideas, even though they "don't know exactly what they are!" The story line, starting with the second stanza, is easy to follow, having a beginning, middle, and end, as Alice perceives when she says that *somebody* killed *something.* A young man is warned by his father of the Jabberwock, goes off and kills it, and returns to the praises of his father. The elements of the epic are also present, abstracted and compressed into a balladlike miniature, a toy. Carroll uses the mock-heroic for the "pure" purpose of reducing content to patterns or game structures with which to play.

The poem includes the ominous warning of the seer; the chimerical beast and its familiars, the Jubjub and the Bandersnatch; the quest, with its dark night of the soul by the Tumtum tree; the confrontation, battle, and victory; and the glorification of the hero. In good nonsense fashion, Carroll understates motivation—for example, the hero's object in killing the creature—reducing it to the simplest of elements: He is a subject, and it is the direct object. Carroll also foreshortens significant episodes with humorous effect. The interminable quest is dismissed in a mechanically efficient line, "Long time the manxome foe he sought—" and the Jabberwock's appearance and slaying are anticlimactic. Its "eyes of flame" are stereotypical dragon paraphernalia, and it comes "whiffling" and "burbling" asthmatically rather than horrifically. The battle takes all of two lines, and it is as easy as "One, two! One, two! And through and/ through"—so easy that the only sound comes from the final, decapitating blow: "snicker-snack!"

As a "silly" epic in miniature, these five stanzas make perfect sense. The nonsense words, most of them adjectives, nouns, or onomatopoeic verbs, are coined and arranged to produce a single impression. It is difficult not to see the "beamish" hero who has "uffish" thoughts and "gallumphs" as a high-spirited boy, because the "new" words are close enough to real ones suggestive of emotional states (gruff, beaming, and gallop). He is left as merely an impression, moreover,

as one means of conveying the playful spirit in which the poem is intended to be read. Similarly, the Jabberwock is reduced from a monster to a sound machine producing wonderful gibberish: whiffles, burbles, and ultimately, of course, jabberwocky. "Snicker-snack" is thus the appropriate blow for finishing it off. Not only is it a toylike sound; it is no more than a sound. The monster is thus reduced to a noise destroyed by a sound that "snickers" in gleeful triumph. Similarly, the story line ends in the father's joyous "chortle" (chuckle and snort).

As in the parodies, Carroll neutralizes potentially disturbing events and forces the reader's attention on the patterns and words. In doing so, he opens worlds of experience shut off from Victorian readers accustomed to a literary climate of "high seriousness" and utilitarian purpose. "Jabberwocky" thus had the effect of renewing poetry and language. It continues to do so each time it is read. Even through mock Anglo-Saxon, it brings back the feel of the incantatory power of oral alliterative verse and the liberation of a primal lyrical utterance. Indeed, the mockery, the fact that it contains words that remain "foreign," makes it more magical, for what "gibberish" there is in the poem offers the child in every reader the experience of creating his own inner language. In reading the coined words, and regardless of whether they translate as portmanteaus, one makes old sounds and meanings into new ones, recreating language in one's own image. So the reader is allowed to return momentarily to that purest creative experience, the act of uttering, naming, and making worlds out of words.

The notion that "Jabberwocky" is a meaningless poem is thus both false and true. Its "nonsense" is perhaps best thought of as pure or uncommon sense. Carroll, moreover, structured his ballad to insure that no moral or theme could be derived from it other than an experiencing of the primacy of the word. At precisely the point in the poem at which one expects the emergence of a theme, when the Jabberwock is conquered and the father rejoices, one is back where one started—with "'Twas brillig" leading further back through the "borogroves" to the pure nowhere of "the mome raths outgrabe." For those who continue to play the game, content keeps leading back to the verbal surface, the Jabberwock to Jabberwocky, ad infinitum. As in a Möbius Strip, neither side is up. Because it behaves so much like the Looking-Glass cake that must be handed around before it can be cut, whereupon it is no longer there, "Jabberwocky" might seem to make frustrating reading. By so resisting interpretation, paradoxically, the poem does teach a lesson—that a poem should not *mean* but *be*. Carroll's nonsense at its best shows how poetry should be read as a linguistic artifact—a premise taken seriously by the modernist poets and the New Critics.

In the poetry of nonsensical double-talk, Carroll was preceded by Edward Lear and followed by the Dadaists, Surrealists, Italian Futurists, Gertrude Stein, and E. E. Cummings, among others. No one, including Carroll himself, has since achieved the artless perfection of "Jabberwocky." One reason is that his followers were not playing; hyperconscious of having a serious theme to impart, they used nonsense in its various forms as a metaphor for meaninglessness in a fundamental philosophical sense. Carroll reduces, dehumanizes, and demystifies the content of his poem to make a toy or game out of it. Modernists such as T. S. Eliot used similar techniques, in the "Sweeney" poems or the game of chess in *The Waste Land* (1922) for example, to comment on the deracination of modern urban man and the failure of communication in a world bereft of external standards of value. *The Hunting of the Snark*, Carroll's longest and most elusive poem, is more problematic, however, and has perhaps justifiably invited comparison with modern literature of the absurd.

THE HUNTING OF THE SNARK

In the preface to *The Hunting of the Snark*, Carroll hints playfully that his new poem is "to some extent" connected with "the lay of the Jabberwock" and thus is sheer nonsense. He also directs attention to Humpty-Dumpty's portmanteau principle, suggesting that *The Hunting of the Snark* will be a sequel, a culmination of that delightful form of wordplay. Readers are likely to feel misled. The only new words are its principle terms, "Snark" (snail and shark, snarl and bark) and "Boojum" (boo, joke, and hokum?); the rest of the coined words are stale borrowings from "Jabberwocky." In other important ways, the similarities that Carroll leads his readers to expect only set off the differences.

"Jabberwocky" is quintessentially innocent wordplay; *The Hunting of the Snark*, appropriately subtitled *An Agony in Eight Fits*, is embedded with elaborately juxtaposed systems of rules, involving syllogistic logic, numerical and alphabetical sequences, equations, diagrams, paradoxes, acrostics, and puns, none of which are consistent with common sense, one another, or their own terms. All this is the stuff of Wonderland, but Alice's mediating perspective is missing here. In Snarkland, the reader plays Alice's role, which consists of searching for the rules of a game that defies logic. Reading the poem is like being at a Mad Hatter's tea party culminating in a riddle with no answer, or worse—a joke at the reader's expense.

In *The Hunting of the Snark*, Carroll has reversed the terms of "Jabberwocky." It is a mad sea adventure and another mock-heroic quest in ballad form for an elusive monster which associates with the Bandersnatch and the Jubjub bird. Yet, while the Jabberwock is dispensed with promptly, the Snark is never even seen, unless by the nearest thing to a protagonist, the Baker, who vanishes before he can reveal what he has perhaps found. The search and the monomania inspiring it are the whole story until the very end, where the poem more or less self-destructs. In short, the Snark or, as it turns out to be, Boojum wins, and in a most disconcerting way.

The narrative begins *in medias res* as the Bellman lands his crew on an island which he swears three times is "just the place for a Snark," reasoning backward that "what I tell you three times is true." The reader learns that this sort of reasoning is typical, and not only of the Bellman: The chart he has provided for his approving crew, who scorn conventional signs, is an absolute blank, and his only "notion for crossing the ocean" is to tinkle his bell. Circular reasoning also seems to be behind the plot, which veers off into digressions and returns to confirm a course that it has arbitrarily taken. The reader finds that the Baker's uncle has warned his nephew that some Snarks are Boojums, which if met with, make one "softly and suddenly vanish away." The Baker sees a Snark, whereupon he "softly and suddenly vanishe[s] away" along with the Snark, who "*was* a Boojum, you see," as the narrator smugly informs the reader. The tale is uniquely anticlimactic. The reader is not disappointed, satisfied, or surprised; one laughs partly in bewilderment. It is not only that the Snark—or Boojum—wins, but one is never quite sure what it is other than the visible darkness that swallows the Baker, much less *why* it is. Carroll's answer seems to be a mocking "why not?"

It is no wonder that some of its early critics found this agony in eight fits less than funny. Carroll, besieged with questions as to whether it contained a hidden moral, answered inconsistently, saying alternately that it was nonsense, that he did not know, and, in two letters of 1896, that it concerned the search for happiness. As his response suggests, the poem almost demands allegorization but resists it just as strongly. The problem is shown in the wide divergence and crankiness of the various attempts to explain the poem. One explanation of the poem is that it is an antivivisectionist tract, another idea is that it is a tragedy about a business slump; other suggestions have been that the poem is a satire on Hegelian philosophy, an Oedipal quest, or an existentialist piece.

If the poem is regarding a search for happiness, as Carroll suggested, then the existentialist reading (offered by Carroll scholar Martin Gardner) seems inevitable, for the threat of annihilation is an undercurrent in all Carroll's major works. Accordingly, the search becomes life, the Snark an illusory goal, and the Boojum the absurd reward—the vanishing signifies nothingness, the void. If the poem has symbols, they certainly point in an absurd direction. The Bellman's blank map suggests the human condition of knowing nothing, neither where humanity is nor where it is going. Because the bowsprit gets mixed with the rudder, the ship goes backward, and considering the entire absence of dimension or direction, it goes nowhere other than the route that is the Bellman's arbitrary choice. The Baker, Everyman, dreams each night of a "delirious fight" with the Snark and thus exists in a state of eternal anxiety, dreading his inevitable extinction. He is so anxious, in fact, that he stammers, "It is this, it is this" three times before he can state precisely the "notion" that he "cannot endure."

Logic and language

Carroll would not have been able to endure such an allegory, however, for he had a slightly different notion of the absurd: the agonizing but strangely pleasing illogicality of language. Moreover, he consistently evaded or sublimated his existential concerns in the game of logic and language. Carroll was less Sartrean than Wittgensteinian, concerned less with the philosophical absurd, the fundamentals of being and nothingness, than with the epistemological absurd, the problem of how humankind knows and does not know, and knowledge's fallacy-prone medium, language. His direction is indicated in what absorbs the reader's attention, the poem's labyrinth of nonsense structures. The title refers to the reader's hunting of the Snark, and the Snark is the problem of the poem, its "hidden meaning" which "vanishes" or was a Boojum, nothing, all along.

The peculiar way the poem was composed—backward—suggests how it should be read, as a puzzle or riddle. The last line flashed into Carroll's mind when he was out strolling. He wrote a stanza to fit the nonsense line and made up the poem to fit the stanza. In other words, he derived the poem's premises (If the Snark is a Boojum, you will vanish away) from its conclusion: "For the Snark *was* a Boojum, you see." The poem works much like the absurd syllogisms found in his *Symbolic Logic: Part I, Elementary* (1896). Its premises are fallacious, its conclusion a joke, and its terms absurd; a parody of systematic reasoning, it exists to be puzzled out.

Language is frequently the culprit, for it can generate systems that relate to nothing but themselves. The prefatory poem to Gertrude Chataway is a key to showing how language works in *The Hunting of the Snark*. The preface at first appears to be a nostalgic meditation on childhood, but on second reading it turns up an acrostic spelling Gertrude's name, and on third reading a double acrostic: The first word of each quatrain spells out "Girt Rude Chat Away." The surface poem has been generated from an arbitrary system, in a sense another language, imposed on it, and it exists primarily for the sake of the game, the search for correspondences. It means little more than the playful joke that it is.

Similarly, in *The Hunting of the Snark*, one tries to follow the arbitrary systems embedded in it to learn the rules of the game. Not only are the rules arbitrarily made, however; they are inconsistently applied, continuously bringing one back to the primary fact of the poem. The rule underlying the plot follows the Bellman's example of going nowhere; the quest veers off into tales within the tale as the various crew members pursue their monomanias. The Butcher and Beaver cross paths and become diverted from the Snark hunt at first by what they take to be the "voice of the Jubjub," then by the Butcher's threefold mock-syllogistic proof that it is the voice of the Jubjub, then by his elaborately circular equation for proving his proof is threefold, and finally in a natural history lesson on the attributes of the Jubjub. The pair's memory of the Jubjub's song, the reader learns later, has cemented their friendship, but whether they heard it or whether it ever existed is impossible to know. "The Barrister's Dream" turns the Snark hunt into another level of unreality and logical absurdity. It is about a Kafkaesque trial in which the Snark, the defending lawyer, takes over the functions of prosecution, jury, and judge, and pronounces the defendant, a pig who is already dead, guilty. In this sequence, as in the poem as a whole, the Snark symbol takes on so many potent meanings that it becomes meaningless.

As a dream and a tale within the tale, the mad trial is less bewildering than the "rule of three" motif with which the poem begins. Three is a teasing potential symbol, suggestive of the Trinity, but Carroll sets up the Bellman's absurd rule of "What I tell you three times is true" as a parody of the syllogism, reducing it to a kind of ultimate question-begging. Not only does it fail logically, but also no one applies it the same way, so that no conclusions whatsoever can be drawn. The Baker is on the verge of confessing and thus effecting his ultimate fear of extinction when he stammers three times "It is this, it is this," but never says what "It" is. The incident becomes a mock omen of sorts, but one that finally mocks the reader's utter inability to establish a causal relation. Similarly, the Butcher applies the rule to prove that he hears the "voice of the Jubjub" but alters his terms to "note" and "song," leaving the Jubjub somewhere between reality and fiction. The final absurdity is that the rule apparently works, if at all, only for the Bellman, who has said, "What *I* tell you three times is true" (italics added).

In Snarkland, classification is subordinate to the arbitrary principle of alphabetical priority. The normal impulse is to view the motley crew as a microcosm, the world satirized as a "ship of fools," especially when the crew members are designated by their occupations: the Bellman, Baker, Barrister, Billiard-marker, Banker, Bonnet-maker, Broker, Boots, Butcher—and absurdly, the Beaver, who is a lacemaker designated by species. The Beaver's inclusion signals that the whole crew "means" no more than the rule of "B." Even the "rule of B" fails, however, when one applies it to characters in general—perhaps to conclude that the Snark was a Boojum by alphabetical priority. The Jubjub bird is the one exception. One is reminded of that other sea tale of the nursery, "Rub a dub dub,/ Three men in a tub,/ The Butcher, the Baker, the Candlestick-maker," in which the characters exist for the sake of rhyme rather than reason.

The Baker, however, throws out classification altogether, for he is of the null class, Nobody. He can bake only bride-cake, for which there are no ingredients; therefore he is a nonbaker. He is distinguished for the number (forty-two) of items he has left behind upon boarding ship: his umbrella, watch, jewels, clothes—and, worst of all, his name. He is therefore called anything from "Thing-um-a-jig" to "Toasted-cheese."

The Snark is the Baker in reverse in this respect; a hodgepodge of identities and attributes, it has five "unmistakable" marks: its hollow but crisp taste, its habit of rising late, its slowness in taking a jest, its fondness for bathing machines, and its ambition. The methods of hunting a snark are equally disparate and unrelated to its marks. One may seek it with thimbles, care, forks, hope, a railway-share, smiles, and soap. The final absurdity is that all of this information fails to connect with the main problem, the Boojum—with one notable exception.

For those searching for a solution to the puzzle, Carroll ended the poem with a multileveled joke which refers back to the poem itself as a joke. The third characteristic of a snark is its "slowness in taking a jest." Should "you happen to venture on one,/ It will sigh like a thing that is deeply distressed," and it is particularly antagonized by a pun, at which it "looks grave." The poem ends in a grand mock apocalypse except for the intrusion, between the sighting of the Snark and the vanishing, of a pun, the worst of all bad jokes, which appears to have been the fatal provocation. As the Baker ecstatically wags his head, accompanied by the cheers and laughter of the crew, the Butcher puns, "He was always a desperate wag." The Baker then vanishes in the middle of the awful word, squeaking out "It's a Boo—" before "jum" is absorbed into a sound that "some fancied" a vast "weary and wandering sigh."

Carroll turns his mock-epic ballad into something like a conundrum, a riddle with an answer buried in an absurd pun. In so ending the hunt, he makes the poem dissolve like the Cheshire cat, leaving the reader with no more than the mocking terms of the last line: "For the Snark *was* a Boojum, you see." The pun refers back through the poem, reverberating mockery. "Wag" reminds the reader that the Baker is a joker, a joke, and thus nobody, really. His annihilation therefore means nothing; he never *was* to begin with, except as a figment in the dream of Carroll, the "wag" desperate to end a "bad" joke. A conundrum that puns on its being a bad joke, *The Hunting of the Snark* is the most dazzling of Carroll's infinite regressions. It regresses back into "Boojum," a metaphor for nothing, specifically the nothing that the poem means other than what it sounds like: "Boo!" enunciated jokingly and with a little hokum tossed in.

Because the poem was, as the Bellman suggests in the second fit, "so to speak, 'snarked'" from the beginning, it also teaches a lesson in the illogic of language. If one "solves" the riddle in the planted conundrum, one commits a post hoc, moreover resting the burden of proof on the arbitrary connotations of language—puns on the "grave" look of the Snark and the purely speculative meanings of the "weary and wandering sigh" that "some fancied" they heard. The poem shows how language can *seem* to tell how and why IT, the Boojum, happened but also tells nothing. This elaborate riddle is a metaphor for the impossibility of knowing final causes, and the Snark's vanishing into Boojum is the palpable unknown.

The Hunting of the Snark illustrates Carroll's nonsense technique at its most complex, correlating fundamental philosophical paradoxes with semantic play. Here as elsewhere, he turns a "joke" into a poem by turning the joke on itself, thus making it embody the elusive thing that it is about. This antididactic "nonsense" has sometimes been seen as an evasion of the poem's responsibility to mean—and an evasion of the issue of meaninglessness that it raises, as well.

Paradoxically, it is precisely because it *is* that evasion that the poem speaks so well to the twentieth century. By sublimating his anxiety in a logician's "agony," Carroll's formal and semantic absurdities embody the urgent epistemological issues of the modern world. In another sense, then, Carroll's humor is not an evasion but rather a metaphor for what everyone must do if he does not drop out: play the game. As such, Carroll's point corresponds with that of James Joyce and the postmodern fabulators, who explore the absurd facility through which language creates reality and meaning.

OTHER MAJOR WORKS

LONG FICTION: *Alice's Adventures in Wonderland*, 1865; *Through the Looking-Glass and What Alice Found There*, 1871; *The Wasp in a Wig: The "Suppressed" Episode of "Through the Looking-Glass and What Alice Found There,"* 1977.

NONFICTION: *The Fifth Book of Euclid Treated Algebraically*, 1858, revised 1868; *A Syllabus of Plane Algebraical Geometry*, 1860; *The Formulae of Plane Trigonometry*, 1861; *A Guide to the Mathematical Student in Reading, Reviewing, and Writing Examples*, 1864; *An Elementary Treatise on Determinants*, 1867; *Euclid, Book V, Proved Algebraically*, 1874; *Euclid and His Modern Rivals*, 1879; *The Principles of Parliamentary Representation*, 1884; *The Game of Logic*, 1887; *Curiosa Mathematica, Part 1: A New Theory of Parallels*, 1888; *Curiosa Mathematica, Part 2: Pillow Problems Thought During Wakeful Hours*, 1893; *Symbolic Logic: Part I, Elementary*, 1896; *Feeding the Mind*, 1907; *The Diaries of Lewis Carroll*, 1954; *The Unknown Lewis Carroll*, 1961; *The Magic of Lewis Carroll*, 1973; *Lewis Carroll's "Symbolic Logic: Part I, Elementary," 1896, Fifth Edition, "Part II, Avanced," Never Previously Published: Together with Letters from Lewis Carroll to Eminent Nineteenth-Century Logicians and to His "Logical Sister" and Eight Versions of the "Barber-Shop Paradox,"* 1977; *The Letters of Lewis Carroll*, 1979; *The Oxford Pamphlets, Leaflets, and Circulars of Charles Lutwidge Dodgson, Vol. 1*, 1993; *The Mathematical Pamphlets of Charles Lutwidge Dodgson and Related Pieces*, 1994.

CHILDREN'S LITERATURE: *A Tangled Tale*, 1885; *Sylvie and Bruno*, 1889; *Sylvie and Bruno Concluded*, 1893; *"The Rectory Umbrella" and "Mischmasch,"* 1932; *The Pig-Tale*, 1975.

BIBLIOGRAPHY

Blake, Kathleen. *Play, Games, and Sport: The Literary Works of Lewis Carroll*. Ithaca, N.Y.: Cornell University Press, 1974. A very insightful study of Carroll's work, with emphasis on the Alice books, *Sylvie and Bruno*, and *The Hunting of the Snark*. Emphasis is placed on systems of logic and language constructions. Supplemented by an index.

Clark, Anne. *Lewis Carroll: A Biography*. London: J. M. Dent & Sons, 1979. A critical biography that includes more than thirty plates. Includes detailed analysis of the Alice books and *Sylvie and Bruno*, as well as other works, and a wealth of biographical material. One of the most comprehensive works on Carroll. Supplemented by extensive references, a select bibliography, and an index.

Collingwood, Stuart Dodgson. *The Life and Letters of Lewis Carroll*. London: T. F. Unwin, 1898. The authorized biography of Lewis Carroll. Contains numerous illustrations and much anecdotal information about Lewis Carroll and his associates. Includes a discussion of several of Carroll's works, an index, and a chronology.

Cohen, Morton N. *Lewis Carroll: A Biography*. New York: Random House, 1995. Cohen has devoted more than three decades to Carroll scholarship. Using Carroll's letters and diaries, he has provided what many regard as a definitive biography. Illustrated with more than one hundred of Carroll's photographs and drawings.

De la Mare, Walter. *Lewis Carroll*. London: Faber & Faber, 1932. This well-written book places Lewis Carroll in a historical context and analyzes the different genres he utilizes. Contains a detailed discussion of the two Alice books and a brief treatment of other works. Supplemented by an index and a bibliography.

Guiliano, Edward. *Lewis Carroll: An Annotated International Bibliography, 1960-1977*. Charlottesville: University Press of Virginia, 1980. This excellent re-search source contains more than fifteen hundred entries and is divided into four sections: "Primary Works," "Reference and Bibliographic Works," "Biography and Criticism," and "Miscellaneous." Supplemented by an index.

Jones, Jo Elwyn, and J. Francis Gladstone. *The Alice Companion: A Guide to Lewis Carroll's Alice Books*. New York: New York University Press, 1998. Full of information, a commentary on the people and places that make up Carroll's and Alice Liddell's world in mid-nineteenth century Oxford and a sourcebook to the extensive existing literature on this period in Carroll's life.

_____. *The Red King's Dream: Or, Lewis Carroll in Wonderland*. London: Jonathan Cape, 1995. By the authors of *The Alice Companion*, a look at Carroll in his life and times, including his literary milieu, friends, and influences. Bibliographical references, index.

Leach, Karoline. *In the Shadow of the Dreamchild: A New Understanding of Lewis Carroll*. Chester Springs, Pa.: Peter Owen, 1999. Leach uses new research to argue that the long-standing image of Lewis Carroll, his exclusively child-centered and unworldly life, his legendary obsession with Alice Liddell, and his supposedly unnatural sexuality, are in fact nothing more than myths.

Pudney, John. *Lewis Carroll and His World*. London: Thames and Hudson, 1976. A historical study of Carroll and his culture, with more than one hundred illustrations. It is both insightful and broad in scope. Supplemented by a chronology, a select bibliography, and an index.

Thomas, Donald. *Lewis Carroll: A Portrait with Background*. London: John Murray, 1996. Thomas revels in the less savory interests of his subject, from prostitution to lunatic asylums, yet renders Carroll a curiously appealing figure.

Williams, Sidney H., and Falconer Madan. *The Lewis Carroll Handbook*. London: Oxford University Press, 1962. An extensive, definitive bibliographic study of Lewis Carroll's works. Supplemented by illustrations, a chronology, an appendix, and an index.

Linda C. Badley;
bibliography updated by the editors

HAYDEN CARRUTH

Born: Waterbury, Connecticut; August 3, 1921

PRINCIPAL POETRY

The Crow and the Heart, 1959
Journey to a Known Place, 1961
The Norfolk Poems, 1962
Nothing for Tigers, 1965
For You, 1970
The Clay Hill Anthology, 1970
From Snow and Rock, from Chaos, 1973
Dark World, 1974
The Bloomingdale Papers, 1975
Brothers, I Loved You All, 1978
The Sleeping Beauty, 1982, rev. ed. 1990
If You Call This Cry a Song, 1983
Asphalt Georgics, 1985
The Oldest Killed Lake in North America, 1985
The Selected Poetry of Hayden Carruth, 1985
*Tell Me Again How the White Heron Rises and Flies
    Across the Nacreous River at Twilight Toward
    the Distant Islands*, 1989
Collected Shorter Poems, 1946-1991, 1992
Collected Longer Poems, 1993
Scrambled Eggs and Whiskey: Poems, 1991-1995,
    1996
A Summer with Tu Fu: A Sequence of Poems, 1996
Jazz Doctor, 2001

OTHER LITERARY FORMS

Hayden Carruth edited *The Voice That Is Great Within
Us* (1970), a highly regarded and widely taught anthology
of modern American poetry, and *The Bird-Poem Book*
(1970). *Working Papers: Selected Essays and Reviews*
(1982) and *Effluences from the Sacred Caves: More Selected Essays and Reviews* (1983) collect essays and reviews, mainly of modern and contemporary poetry. *Sitting In: Selected Writings on Jazz, Blues, and Related
Topics* (1986) collects Carruth's music criticism.

ACHIEVEMENTS

Versatile, independent, and prolific, Hayden Carruth
has had a long and distinguished career as poet, editor,

critic, and teacher. He has been poetry editor of *Poetry*
(1949-1950) and *Harper's* (1977-1982) and has received numerous awards, including the Shelley Memorial Award (1978), the Lenore Marshall Prize (1979),
Guggenheim Fellowships (1965, 1979), a Senior Fellowship from the National Endowment for the Arts
(1988), and the Ruth Lilly Poetry Prize (1990). He received honorary degrees from New England College
(1987) and Syracuse University (1993), and the National
Book Critics Circle Award in Poetry (1993). *Scrambled
Eggs and Whiskey: Poems, 1991-1996* earned him two
distinguished honors: the National Book Award in poetry and the Pulitzer Prize.

BIOGRAPHY

Born in Waterbury, Connecticut, in 1921, Hayden
Carruth has spent most of his life in New England. He
was graduated from the University of North Carolina,
and he earned his master's degree from the University of
Chicago in 1948.

Carruth's military experience during World War II is
important to his work. Perhaps even more important, by
his own account, have been his struggles with mental illness. The long and painful recovery from his institutionalization in 1953 led to his living in relative isolation and
considerable poverty in northern Vermont for much of
his working life. He earned his living as a freelance reviewer and editor before taking a teaching position at
Syracuse University in 1979. Married four times (the
fourth time to Joe-Anne McLaughlin in 1989), Carruth
has two children, Martha, who died of cancer in her forties, and David Barrow II, the latter present in many poems as "Bo." He accepted a one-year professorship at
Bucknell University from 1985 to 1986, and returned to
Syracuse University until 1991, when he was made a
professor emeritus. He then turned his energy to owning
and operating Crow's Mark Press in Johnson, Vermont.

ANALYSIS

The work of this lifelong New Englander reflects a
sustained engagement with his region and its literary traditions, but his interests and sources range widely
through space and time. Sometimes regarded as a poetic
conservative because of his interest in fixed forms,
Carruth is better seen as an experimental traditionalist

Hayden Carruth (© Pat Orviss)

whose exhaustive knowledge and mastery of formal verse allow him to use a wide variety of poetic resources. His poems range from brief lyrics to Frostian blank-verse monologues and character studies to extended sonnet sequences, notably *The Sleeping Beauty*, a book-length exploration of the spirit of romance in the late twentieth century. Carruth's reviews and essays demonstrate his tough-mindedness and fairness, his insistence on careful judgment and sharp distinctions. A self-described "New England anarchist," independent and widely read, he has been a significant voice for intelligence, humanity, and craft in American letters.

Hayden Carruth's great themes are old ones: madness and music, isolation and community, despair at the human capacity for destruction and hope in the beauty and terror of love and of art, "the joy and agony of improvisation," as he puts it in *Brothers, I Loved You All*. Carruth has lived a life at once set apart—he began the teaching career typical of his fellow poets only in his late fifties—and finely attuned to his place and his age. Few poets are more deeply knowledgeable about literary traditions and about the range of work being done in their own time, as

Carruth's work as poet, anthologist, and critic reveals. His achievement has been to fuse his learning, his keen eye and ear, his remarkable poetic craft, and his thoroughgoing integrity and self-awareness into a body of writing distinguished in both form and substance.

Virtually every one of Carruth's poems shows his interest in the formal qualities of verse; unlike many of his contemporaries, he did not leap from formal to free verse in midcareer but has continued to experiment with a variety of stanzaic and rhythmical patterns. Although his writing has always drawn deeply from the natural world, his best early poems deal with the sober human experiences of war and madness, and their austere formal patterns create a sense of barely achieved emotional control. "On a Certain Engagement South of Seoul," from *The Crow and the Heart*, recalls the alienation and disorientation of Carruth's combat experience in crisp *terza rima*:

> We were unreal,
> Strange bodies and alien minds; we could not cry
>
> For even our eyes seemed to be made of steel;
> Nor could we look at one another, for each
> Was a sign of fear.

The poem ends with the speaker still turning over the experience, struggling for some kind of clarity or understanding: Does it "make us brothers" or merely "bring our hatred back?" The horror and sorrow of the war create a kinship among those who suffered them, but it is a strange bond that does not bring joy.

"ADOLF EICHMANN"

"Adolf Eichmann" uses *terza rima* to very different effect, in a grim meditation that modulates into a horrifying curse on the Nazi executioner: "I say let the dung/ Be heaped on that man until it chokes his voice." The curse continues, wishing a plague of leprosy on Eichmann in a manner reminiscent of the imprecatory psalms. The curse's culmination, however, is a sentence of emotional rather than physical punishment:

> But let his ears never, never be shut,
> And let young voices read to him, name by name,
> From the rolls of all those people whom he has shut
>
> Into the horrible beds.

Few poems so direct, aimed at such easy targets, avoid lapsing into sentimentality or cliché. Throughout his career, however, Carruth has taken the risk of addressing the most pressing and difficult topics. (He has repeatedly criticized his fellow poets for avoiding the subject of nuclear holocaust.) Here the heavy, exact rhymes on "dung" and "shut" give the poem the awful resonance of a huge bell.

MENTAL ILLNESS

Carruth's struggles with mental illness are a recurrent theme in all of his work. During his hospital stay in 1953 and 1954 he wrote the long sequence *The Bloomingdale Papers*, which was lost for some twenty years and was published in full only in 1975 (although parts appear in *The Crow and the Heart*, and the sequence "The Asylum," in fifteen-line near-sonnets, was printed in *For You*). The sequence incorporates many forms, including passages of prose, sonnets, lists, and psalms. The asylum poems confront psychological terror and trace the search for stability and coherence with remarkable acuity, honesty, and courage, refusing the temptations of easy self-dramatization or confessionalism: "Prison grows warm and *is* the real asylum." Carruth pictures himself and the other asylum inmates sitting in a deep winter stillness to face "all the terrors of our inward journeys,/ The grave indecencies, the loathsome birds." This terrifying inward journey requires a "strange bravery" of one who calls himself "unbrave." Without romanticizing his suffering, the poems humanize it.

Among the poems written against the fear of madness and the correlative fear of a meaningless universe, "Contra Mortem" from *For You* is Carruth's personal favorite. Written in the fifteen-line stanzas he has used repeatedly, it is a moving meditation on the endurance of being in the face of nothingness. In its hard-won refusal to allow despair the last word, it strikes a characteristic note: "Some are moralists and some have faith/ but some who live in the free exchange of hearts/ as the gift of being are lovers against death."

FROM SNOW AND ROCK, FROM CHAOS

With *From Snow and Rock, from Chaos*, Carruth found a confidence and a characteristic voice that remains through all the widely various work he has published since. Overtones of the poets he has chosen for masters—William Butler Yeats, Ezra Pound, and Robert Frost, among many others—can still be heard, along with the voices of his New England neighbors, which he often captures with uncanny accuracy. Yet through and above them all, Carruth's gruff, blustery presence remains constant, acute without being merely "sensitive," open to his own faults and failings without overdramatizing them, refusing easy consolations and hero worship as well:

> this was the world foreknown
> though I had thought somehow
> probably in the delusion
> of that idiot thoreau
> that necessity could be saved
> by the facts we actually have

"FREEDOM AND DISCIPLINE"

Carruth's long-standing interest in music, particularly jazz, informs his poetics in essential ways. (His instrument is the clarinet.) "Freedom and Discipline," from the early *Nothing for Tigers*, describes concerts by Sergei Rachmaninoff and Coleman Hawkins, ponders "Why I went to verse-making . . . this grubbing art," and concludes, "Freedom and discipline concur/ only in ecstasy." He has written sympathetic and insightful jazz criticism, paying special attention to the capacity of music to capture the streams of human feeling.

BROTHERS, I LOVED YOU ALL

Music is also central to *Brothers, I Loved You All*, arguably Carruth's best single volume, and the most fully represented in *The Selected Poetry of Hayden Carruth*. There are many fine lyrics, and several long, Frostian dramatic monologues, but the centerpiece is the long poem "Paragraphs," another sequence in fifteen-line near-sonnets. "Paragraphs" draws on Carruth's deep investment in New England culture and expresses grief at the decline of that culture under industrial urbanization, the "superadded trailers, this prefab, damned fashion/ out of Monterey or Bronxville, God knows where." The poem incorporates reports of war atrocities, memories of jazz musicians (the "brothers" of the title), celebrations of natural energy, a marvelous Puerto Rican folktale of a transparent bird that flies until it dies, quotations from the anarchist Mikhail Bakunin, and much more. Amid the ravages and human destructiveness the poem traces, Carruth isolates a few sustaining factors: his own old poems, "their inside truth that was/ (is, is!) crucial," the human effort "to wrench lucidity out of nowhere," and especially the treasured presence of the old jazzmen he regards as his superiors, and the joy and beauty of their improvising together:

>   not singular, not the rarity
> we think, but real and a glory
> our human shining, shekinah . . .   Ah,
>   holy spirit, ninefold
> I druther've bin a-settin there, supernumerary
> cockroach i'th' corner, a listenin, a-listenin,,,,,,,
>   than be the Prazedint ov the Wuurld.

Carruth's master, Pound, used to blend high intellection and dialectical misspellings like this, and the influence is plain here, though Carruth's subject matter is very much his own. Two key parts of the modernist project were to bring past and present together so that history and modernity might coexist in the poem and to create a poetic language that would include both sophisticated abstractions and the most common, rude speech. A good case can be made for Carruth as one of the most successful inheritors of that project. Considered as a whole, in fact, his work bears up well against that of the modernist masters. He is certainly more accessible than Pound, less squeamish than T. S. Eliot, more in touch with American life than Wallace Stevens; moreover, his language is more capacious and capable of dealing in abstractions than William Carlos Williams's. Carruth would not make such presumptuous claims for himself, but his work has consistently been of a magnitude befitting such comparisons.

THE SLEEPING BEAUTY

The Sleeping Beauty is Carruth's book-length tribute to his third wife, Rose Marie Dorn. A reworking of the Briar Rose myth, it is also an ambitious exploration of the spirit of romance, of the multiple dangers and attractions of the romantic tradition. The poem blends a series of the sleeping princess's dreams—in which she is visited by Homer, Hesiod, Henry Hudson, the fictional character Heathcliff, and Adolf Hitler, among others—with the poet's memories and reflections, conversations with a gruff Vermont ghost named Amos, and hauntingly repeated glimpses of a sculpture of a woman's face

buried in a stream. The face is an emblem of the mysterious, sleeping, ideal beloved, the one whom "the prince who is human, driven, and filled with love" must pursue, and of whom he must prove himself worthy. Consistently reviewed as one of the most successful long poems of the 1980's, it deserves to be better known.

IF YOU CALL THIS CRY A SONG

If You Call This Cry a Song gathers poems written between about 1964 and 1979. As the time span would suggest, it is a varied collection, with poems in many styles and modes. Difficult to summarize briefly either thematically or formally because of its diversity, the book is filled with unpredictable treasures, including an exuberant dialect version of the myth of Hermes, "A Little Old Funky Homeric Blues for Herm."

ASPHALT GEORGICS

As early as *The Norfolk Poems* Carruth showed his fascination with popular culture and the language of ordinary people. His most memorable and sustained treatment of that subject matter comes with *Asphalt Georgics*, thirteen poems in rhyming quatrains in the common speech of upstate New York and filled with the Kmarts and semiurban clutter of their lives.

> What a mishmash—the suburbs! You
>   know it. So I pray for
> Crawford, the street, the smokebush, the
>   works. I pray for no more
>
> Reagan. Well, you got to keep your
>   wig on, you can't give in
> to the dead. So what if it don't
>   mean much. It means something.

The poems are wry and stoic at once, whimsical and grim, elegiac and defiant, an engaging blend of grumpy accommodation and high spirits. They balance common speech against the rigid stanza form with a deftness reminiscent of Frost. Yet these poems do not imitate or resemble Frost's; they are far less idealized and selective in their presentation of New England, much closer to the slang and materiality of the true American colloquial.

TELL ME AGAIN HOW THE WHITE HERON RISES . . .

The title of Carruth's 1989 collection, *Tell Me Again How the White Heron Rises and Flies Across the Nacre-*

ous River at Twilight Toward the Distant Islands, suggests its main formal experiment. The lengthy titles—others include "Sometimes When Lovers Lie Quietly Together, Unexpectedly One of Them Will Feel the Other's Pulse," "The Necessary Impresario, Mr. Septic Tanck," and "Ovid, Old Buddy, I Would Discourse with You a While"—are at once elevated and farcical, ambitious and self-deprecating, whimsical and somber. Like the poems themselves, they are emblematic of a man who has won through to a deep and difficult sanity, to a knowledge of self, craft, and world that is occasionally cranky, often idiosyncratic, but always marked by a hard-edged lucidity and a rich and integral compassion. Filled with sharply realized details, carefully worked patterns of sound, and honed and balanced abstractions, the poems integrate Carruth's lifelong concerns for the music of music and of poetry, for the mysteries of love and language, for the ways human beings find to destroy and to sustain one another.

The volume closes with "Mother," an agonized and agonizing elegy, and with a vision of his mother on her deathbed, "Penitent for the crime committed against you, victim of your own innocence./ (Existence is the crime against the existing),/ Drifting, drifting in the uncaused universe that has no right to be." To recognize that neither humankind nor the universe has any "right" to be and yet to persist, to make such painful eloquence from that recognition: This is the achievement of Hayden Carruth.

SCRAMBLED EGGS AND WHISKEY

Carruth earned several major honors for his collection of poetry titled *Scrambled Eggs and Whiskey: Poems, 1991-1995*, including the National Book Award for poetry and the Pulitzer Prize. Centered on meditations of such themes as politics, history, aging, nostalgia, guilt, and love, the volume carries a voice of dejection while also expressing a kind of gratitude for the people and things which have made his later life remarkably satisfying. In "Flying to St. Louis," he uses the phrase "alone and desperate" twice, and goes on to say "I've blamed my mother and father" for the "pain, the desperation" for sixty-five years. He mentions that "he drinks wine and swallows more pills" in "Wife Poem" and that he will "finish the wine, take/ the sleeping pills" in "Five-thirty A.M." While a tone of defeat and melancholy finds a significant place in this collection, this

mood makes the moments of deep satisfaction that much more vivid. The book is dedicated to Joe-Anne, his wife, and in "Wife Poem," he writes that she

> dropped
> down from the moon, not like some
> sylphy Cynthia at Delphi, after all she's
> not seventeen, but with the sexual grace
> and personal implacability
> of a goddess of our time.

The central focus of the book thus seems to be Carruth's recognition that he has been blessed with a gift, an offering from the cosmos.

His experience in a mental hospital in the 1950's always informs his works to some degree and here, for example in "Franconia," he notes that despite the experience, he had the good fortune to find a person whose presence and support have made him "as happy, as gratified, as I've ever been,/ old friend, in all these seventy-two years." He continues in amazement in "Resorts" to say "My dear, we are in love. It's a fact, certifiable." While he admits that as an old man, he's "too old to write love songs now" ("Birthday Cake"), that impulse is at the core of the collection.

JAZZ DOCTOR

In *Jazz Doctor*—published following Carruth's numerous books of poetry and as he entered his eighth decade—Carruth lauds the unexpected power of "petty endurance." The collection celebrates his devotion to jazz, as the title references: In one piece, he lovingly describes the trumpeter Dizzy Gillespie's cheeks in midblow—"monstrous fruit about to burst,/ Blood and flesh all over the bandstand." Other sections, like "Afterlife," "Basho," and "Faxes," have Carruth conversing with a range of personas, in lines of varying lengths. "While Reading Basho," with its combination of classic haiku form with contemporary idiom, displays some of Carruth's jauntiness: "Basho, you made/ a living writing haiku?/ Wow! Way to go, man." The emotional center is a fifteen-page-long poem in memory of the poet's daughter Martha, who died of cancer in her forties. It is a pungent and furious work that details her hospital stays, ranging from the day of her birth to a final period when she looked like "a young crone."

OTHER MAJOR WORKS

LONG FICTION: *Appendix A*, 1963.

NONFICTION: *Working Papers: Selected Essays and Reviews*, 1982; *Effluences from the Sacred Caves: More Selected Essays and Reviews*, 1983; *Sitting In: Selected Writings on Jazz, Blues, and Related Topics*, 1986; *Suicides and Jazzers*, 1992; *Reluctantly: Autobiographical Essays*, 1998; *Beside the Shadblow Tree: A Memoir of James Laughlin/Hayden Carruth*, 1999.

EDITED TEXTS: *The Voice That Is Great Within Us*, 1970; *American Poetry of the Twentieth Century*, 1970; *The Bird-Poem Book*, 1970.

BIBLIOGRAPHY

Booth, Philip. "On *Brothers, I Loved You All*." *American Poetry Review* 8 (May/June, 1979): 13-16. Fellow poet Booth praises Carruth's immediacy and vitality, the "tensile strength" of his use of abstractions, and his willingness to risk direct statement. Not compelled by the Frostian poems in *Brothers, I Loved You All*, Booth is cogently appreciative of the rest of the book.

Feder, Lillian. "Poetry from the Asylum: Hayden Carruth's *The Bloomingdale Papers*." *Literature and Medicine* 4 (1985): 112-127. Feder gives a brief account of the writing and publication history of *The Bloomingdale Papers* and a rather stiff but useful analysis of its depiction of the poet's struggle to remake his self. She also notes connections with later works, including *Brothers, I Loved You All* and *The Sleeping Beauty*, and calls particular attention to the ongoing search for self-realization through love.

Flint, R. W. "The Odyssey of Hayden Carruth." *Parnassus* 11, no. 1 (1983): 17-32. Flint praises *The Sleeping Beauty* as one of the most important poems of the 1980's. He commends Carruth's tough-minded sanity, comparing *The Sleeping Beauty* to Robert Lowell's long poems and John Berryman's *The Dream Songs* (1969), he finds that Carruth's poem has a much better plot, if less mere excitement. Flint also briefly discusses *Working Papers*.

Howard, Richard. "To a Known Place." *Poetry* 107 (1966): 253-258. Howard surveys Carruth's poetry through *Nothing for Tigers*, finding in the early books debts to Wallace Stevens, John Crowe Ransom, W. B. Yeats, and Allen Tate, but celebrating and briefly analyzing the psychological and visionary impulses of *Journey to a Known Place* and *Nothing for Tigers*.

Robbins, Anthony. "Hayden Carruth: An Interview." *The American Poetry Review* 22, no. 5 (September/October, 1993): 47-49. Robbins gives a brief biography of Carruth and summarizes an interview covering many subjects including Marxist ideology, E. L. Doctorow's influence on *The Sleeping Beauty*, and the development of poetic philosophy.

Weiss, David, ed. *In the Act: Essays on the Poetry of Hayden Carruth. Seneca Review* 20 (1990). This special issue of *Seneca Review* features twelve essays on Carruth's work by Wendell Berry, David Rivard, Maxine Kumin, Sam Hamill, David Budbill, and others; an interview with Carruth; and new poems. The essays range from personal reminiscences to formal literary criticism, and discuss Carruth's work from his earliest poems to *Tell Me Again How the White Heron Rises and Flies Across the Nacreous River at Twilight Toward the Distant Islands*. An extensive and valuable resource.

Jeff Gundy,
updated by Sarah Hilbert

RAYMOND CARVER

Born: Clatskanie, Oregon; May 25, 1938
Died: Port Angeles, Washington; August 2, 1988

PRINCIPAL POETRY

Near Klamath, 1968
Winter Insomnia, 1970
At Night the Salmon Move, 1976
Two Poems, 1982
If It Please You, 1984
This Water, 1985
Where Water Comes Together with Other Water, 1985
Ultramarine, 1986
A New Path to the Waterfall, 1989
All of Us: The Collected Poems, 1996

Raymond Carver (© Marion Ettlinger, courtesy of Atlantic Monthly Press)

OTHER LITERARY FORMS

Raymond Carver is perhaps best known as a writer of short fiction. In addition, he wrote a screenplay and edited a collection of short stories.

ACHIEVEMENTS

Raymond Carver has been credited with rescuing both poetry and the short story from the elitists and obscurantists and giving them back to the people. His honors include the National Endowment for the Arts Discovery Award for Poetry in 1970, the Joseph Henry Jackson Award for fiction in 1971, a Wallace Stegner Creative Writing Fellowship, Stanford University, in 1972-1973, a National Book Award nomination in fiction in 1977, a Guggenheim Fellowship in 1977-1978, a National Endowment for the Arts Award in fiction in 1979, the Carlos Fuentes Fiction Award in 1983, the Mildred and Harold Strauss Living Award in 1983, a National Book Critics Circle Award nomination in fic-

tion in 1984, a Pulitzer Prize nomination in fiction in 1984, and *Poetry* magazine's Levinson Prize in 1985. Carver was elected to the American Academy of Arts and Letters in 1988 and in that same year was awarded a Doctorate of Letters from the University of Hartford.

BIOGRAPHY

Raymond Carver was born in Clatskanie, Oregon, and grew up in Yakima, Washington, where his father worked as a saw filer in a lumber mill. Like most young men growing up in that heavily forested, sparsely populated region, Carver enjoyed hunting and fishing; possibly from some remote ancestor, however, he seems to have inherited unusual intelligence, sensitivity, and ambition. His life is a story of his struggle to achieve self-actualization in spite of an impoverished background. His parents were poor and uneducated, and he himself was extremely ignorant about literature. In his teens he enrolled in a correspondence course in creative writing, but he never finished it. His early reading was typically the Westerns of Zane Grey, the fantasies of Edgar Rice Burroughs, and magazines celebrating rugged outdoor adventure.

At the age of nineteen he married his teenage sweetheart, who gave birth to their first child less than six months later. Another child was born the following year, and from then on Carver was torn between the desire to become a writer and the need to support his family. "Nothing—and, brother, I mean nothing—that ever happened to me on this earth," he said, "could come anywhere close, could possibly be as important to me, could make as much difference, as the fact that I had two children."

In 1958, Carver and his family moved to Paradise, California, where he enrolled at Chico State College. One of the major turning points in his life was a course in creative writing taught by the inspiring writer and teacher John Gardner. Carver began publishing poems and short stories in college literary magazines. He continued to do so when he transferred to Humboldt State College in Arcata, California, and finally his work began to be accepted by respected literary quarterlies.

He was tortured by the fact that he had to support himself and his family by working at a series of mindless and often physically exhausting dead-end jobs.

Among other things, he worked as a mill hand, a farm laborer, a delivery boy, a service station attendant, a stock clerk, and a janitor. His poems and stories are haunted by guilt. He felt guilty because he was not providing his family with a decent standard of living, and he felt guilty because he did not want to be burdened with a family at all. He drank because he felt guilty, and then he felt guilty for drinking. Many American writers have been heavy drinkers, including Ernest Hemingway, William Faulkner, and Sinclair Lewis, but none has admitted it so frankly or used it so freely as subject matter for his work.

In 1967, he obtained his first white-collar job, as an editor of textbooks for Science Research Associates in Palo Alto, California. By this time he had become a heavy drinker, and only a few years later he was fired. Still, he had continued to write stories and poetry, and in 1970 he received a National Endowment for the Arts Discovery Award for Poetry. Other monetary awards helped him to devote more time to writing. In 1971, his poems and stories began to appear in magazines such as *Esquire*, *Harper's Bazaar*, and *Playgirl*.

Part-time teaching assignments helped Carver survive to produce more stories and poetry. In 1971 he began teaching creative writing at the University of California at Santa Cruz; in 1972 he began teaching at both UC Santa Cruz and Stanford University. In 1975 he had to drop out of an assignment at the University of California at Santa Barbara because of his alcoholism; in the late 1970's, however, Carver was back teaching writing again, even though he said he felt uncomfortable doing it.

Carver taught at Goddard College in the late 1970's and then at the University of Texas in El Paso and at the University of Vermont. He was appointed professor of English at Syracuse University in 1980. In 1983 he was at last able to give up teaching and devote his full time and attention to writing, after receiving a Strauss Living Award, which guaranteed him an annual stipend for five years.

Carver was separated from his wife in the late 1970's and began living with Tess Gallagher, a poet and college teacher like himself who had also been born in the Pacific Northwest. Gallagher helped him to cope with his drinking problem and provided him with understanding and emotional support. She was with Carver until the time of his death from lung cancer in 1988; they had been married in Reno, Nevada, less than two months before he died. Years of worry, chronic insecurity, and hard living had cut short the career of one of America's most promising writers at the age of only fifty.

ANALYSIS

Raymond Carver certainly had his faults, but he also had many strengths that were responsible for making him better loved than most other writers of his generation and ultimately more famous. He was humble, modest, honest, sincere, and dedicated. He was not ashamed to acknowledge his lower-class background or the fact that he had done a considerable amount of work that required him to get his hands dirty. He did not pretend to know all the answers or even to know any of the answers. The reader senses that Carver was someone like himself or herself, struggling to make sense out of a life that actually did not make much sense at all.

Carver's writing was always personal and autobiographical. He did not seem to know how to write any other way. This quality made him seem primitive and a mere literary curiosity to certain sophisticated critics but also endeared him to ordinary readers, many of whom felt betrayed by the trickery and emotional emptiness of much modern literature. Carver said, "My poems are of course not literally true" but acknowledged that, as in most of his short stories, "there is an autobiographical element."

Carver never got on a pulpit or a soapbox. He never blamed anyone but himself for his troubles. His writings are remarkably devoid of allusions to religion and politics, the Scylla and Charybdis of most modern writers. This was probably another thing that annoyed his critics: They wanted him to take a position—preferably one aligned with their own. A writer can toil in obscurity forever without a glance from such people, but if he begins receiving recognition, then they immediately want to bring him into their camp. Thus critics have complained that in Carver's poems there are no resolutions, no epiphanies—as if resolutions and epiphanies were something that came in boxes of twelve at the supermarket. One of Carver's writing mottos was "No cheap tricks." He steered by this motto all his life, and it always guided him in the direction of unadorned self-revelation. The photographs that appear on the backs of many of his published volumes show a big, awkward, shy-looking man with questioning eyes that are hard to look at and hard to look away from. He was the sort of plain-spoken American that Americans have always admired, not unlike Abraham Lincoln, Mark Twain, Will Rogers, and Jimmy Stewart. In an age when every television personality seems to have all the answers to life's biggest questions, it is refreshing to come upon a writer such as Carver who has no easy answers to offer. Carver will be remembered not for his depth of thought but for his depth of feeling. He saw life as a mystery, but a wonderful and fascinating mystery.

FIRES: ESSAYS, POEMS, STORIES

When Raymond Carver published *Fires: Essays, Poems, Stories* in 1983, he said that he had collected in the book everything he had previously written that he considered worth keeping. In addition to two very illuminating essays about his life and his writing values, the book contains fifty of his poems dating back to 1968. Most of the themes that would appear in his later poems are evident in these early works. "Near Klamath," for example, is one of many expressions of his love for nature and particularly for fishing. Many of Carver's poems about nature remind the reader of Ernest Hemingway's passionate love for physical action in the outdoors. Hemingway was one of Carver's early literary models; they have a similar simple, straightforward style of writing and have a similar reticence to express sentimental feelings.

With Carver, one senses that his love of nature was connected with a yearning for escape from the responsibilities that plagued him—the menial jobs, the laundromats, the crying children, the endless bills, the junk cars, the squatter's life in cheap apartments and borrowed dwellings—and kept him from his writing, the only thing that gave his life meaning. In one of his better-known poems, "Winter Insomnia," he writes:

> The mind would like to get out of here
> onto the snow. It would like to run
> with a pack of shaggy animals, all teeth.

"Drinking While Driving" is one of the many pieces Carver wrote about drinking during his lifetime. "Bank-

ruptcy" tells with wry humor how he became bankrupt for the first time at the age of twenty-eight. A similar story is told in a later poem titled "Miracle," published in *A New Path to the Waterfall*; the wry humor is still there (as it remained for the rest of his life), but his wife's reaction to this second bankruptcy was far more violent. "Deschutes River" is an interesting poem because it brings together his love for the out-of-doors and his personal guilt and anxiety: The poem ends with the lines "Far away—/ another man is raising my children,/ bedding my wife bedding my wife."

Some of the poems collected in *Fires* show the bad habits a naïve beginner can pick up from other writers who substitute stylistic legerdemain, erudition, wit, and exoticism for genuine feeling. "Rhodes," "The Mosque in Jaffa," and "Spring, 480 B.C." are among the poems in which Carver deals with foreign sights and sounds, evidently trying to evoke refined sentiments. Poems with this foreign flavor continue to appear in his subsequent volumes and are among the least appealing of his works. Many of them have a certain artificial or chapbook quality, as if written by a professor on sabbatical. It was inevitable that Carver's growing fame as well as his exposure to academia would tempt him to seem more cultivated than he actually was; he was most likable and most effective, however, as a simple lad from the Pacific Northwest who had barely managed to obtain a bachelor's degree.

ULTRAMARINE

The poems collected in *Ultramarine*, published in 1986, represent Carver at his best. These poems are longer, more confident. The words march across the pages almost with the brave assurance of John Milton's iambic pentameter in *Paradise Lost* (1667). Carver, however, always shunned rhyme and meter. Stylistically he belongs to that vast modern school of poets who have abandoned all poetic conventions and try to write like someone talking to a close friend. Though his poems have rhythm, rhyme and meter would seem as grossly out of place in a poem by Carver as he himself would look in an Elizabethan costume with lace ruffles.

The question arises, why then did he continue to arrange his words in lines to look like poems? Why did he not abandon this last vestige of conventional poetry and write his thoughts as plain prose? There are several possible answers. Probably the most important one is that the appearance of a poem gives the author more freedom. Prose poems such as those written by Charles Baudelaire have never gained wide popularity. A reader faced with a prose paragraph expects a reasoned utterance, a logical progression of ideas from the first to the last sentence. The poetic format allows Carver and other workers in this dominant movement the freedom to use exclamations, interjections, incomplete sentences, neologisms, allusions, abrupt changes of subject, or whatever else they wish. Here are the first four lines of "In the Lobby of the Hotel del Mayo," from *Ultramarine:*

> The girl in the lobby reading a leather-bound book.
> The man in the lobby using a broom.
> The boy in the lobby watering plants.
> The desk clerk looking at his nails.

These fragments would seem surrealistic in a straight prose paragraph; such prose might remind one of the experimental writing of Gertrude Stein. An arrangement in lines like those of a traditional poem, however, prepares the reader to approach the words in a different way.

One of the most interesting poems in *Ultramarine* consists entirely of short fragments describing an old car that Carver once owned—or that once owned Carver.

> The car with a cracked windshield.
> The car that threw a rod.
> The car without brakes.
> The car with a faulty U-joint.
> The car with a hole in its radiator.
> The car I picked peaches for.

The poem continues in this vein for forty-four more lines and ends with the words "My car." By the time the reader finishes the poem, he or she has formed a remarkably complete picture not only of the car, but also of Carver's life and state of mind over the long period during which he was chained to this horrible automobile. It is characteristic of Carver to take his imagery from the external world rather than search for it in his own memory. There seems to be a Japanese influence here, perhaps by way of his favorite poet, William Carlos Williams. Like many of the poems in *Ultramarine*, "The Car" deals with themes of alcoholism, debt, meaningless work, domestic unhappiness, and the longing for escape. As always, there is also a note of unconquerable humor even in this Job-like litany of despair.

There is, however, a slightly different note, a slightly different perspective. In most of these poems, Carver is now talking about the past. Life has improved for him. He has achieved recognition. He is earning some money and not having to do it with a mop or a broom. He has quit drinking. Perhaps most significantly, *Ultramarine* is dedicated to Tess Gallagher, a fellow writer and evidently a real soul mate, someone who would be with him for the rest of his life.

"NyQuil" is one of the poems in which he remembers his nightmare with alcohol. NyQuil is a well-known cold medicine, but Carver was doggedly drinking it down as a substitute for liquor. An acquaintance, he says, was similarly trying to break his addiction to Scotch whiskey by drinking Listerine by the case. This externalization or projection of feelings is a common characteristic of Carver's writing—both in his poems and in his short stories. The image of a man drinking NyQuil by the tumblerful gives the reader a vivid conception of the depth of Carver's addiction to alcohol.

"Jean's TV" is another poem in which an external object serves as an extended metaphor. A former girlfriend and drinking companion named Jean calls to ask when he plans to return the black-and-white television set she had left with him when she moved out. He hems and haws until the reader finally understands: He must have sold it a long time ago to buy liquor. Carver has confessed in interviews that he was capable of doing almost anything in his drinking days; he was also apparently unusually susceptible to feelings of remorse.

In "The Possible" he talks about another former drinking companion, this one a fellow college teacher, and makes the following interesting statement about his many years of teaching: "I was a stranger,/ and an impostor, even to myself." "Where They'd Lived" is among the poems that deal with his unhappy marriage. Like most of the poems collected in this volume, these two pieces seem to be looking back at a receding past.

One new theme appears quite prominently among the poems collected in *Ultramarine*, the book that established Carver's reputation as a poet. It is the theme of unexpected death. "Egress" tells of a man who "fell dead/ one night after dinner, after talking over some business deal." "Powder-Monkey" is the story of a coworker who is killed in a head-on collision with a logging truck. In "An Account," a friend dies of a heart attack while watching *Hill Street Blues* on television. In each of these poems, Carver seems stunned. "What does this mean?" he seems to be asking the reader. "How can this happen?"

Somehow the black shadow of death makes Carver's message to the world suddenly stand out bright and clear. Life itself is beautiful in any aspect. The human tragedy and the human comedy are two sides of the same coin. Drinking, toiling, fighting, and lying to the landlords and the bill collectors are all a part of life, and consequently they all contain their own weird beauty. Clearly, Carver was experiencing strong premonitions of his own approaching death.

A NEW PATH TO THE WATERFALL

Carver finished *A New Path to the Waterfall* shortly before he died of lung cancer. The title of the book is taken from one of the poems in the volume, "Looking for Work." The speaker dreams that he is out fishing: "Suddenly, I find a new path/ to the waterfall." His wife wakes him up, however, and tells him that he must go out and find a job. The themes of unhappy marriage, responsibilities, shortage of cash, and a desire to escape to nature are still here, even though Carver's troubles were at this point only ghosts of the past. One of the most harrowing poems in the book is "Miracle," in which he matter-of-factly and in excruciating detail describes the aftermath of his second bankruptcy proceeding. On the way home on the airplane, his wife turns in her seat and begins hitting him in the face with clenched fists.

> All the while his head is pummeled,
> buffeted back and forth, her fists falling
> against his ear, his lips, his jaw, he protects
> his whiskey.

Yet the shadow of death is the subject that dominates this last collection of Carver's poetry. What he sensed intuitively in *Ultramarine* has become an unblinking reality. Early in his career, he had chosen to write short stories and short poems because his struggle to support a family left him no time to contemplate larger projects; ironically, now that he had leisure and a certain amount of financial security, death was pressing him even harder

than the bosses and bill collectors of old. In September, 1987, Carver, a heavy cigarette smoker for many years, was diagnosed with lung cancer. Two-thirds of his left lung was removed, but this hideous disease recurred as a brain tumor in March of the following year. He underwent seven weeks of full-brain radiation; however, by early June the doctors found tumors in his lungs again. He knew he had only a short time left to live.

Some of Carver's last poems are not only his most moving but also his most successful in terms of realizing his artistic aims. "Poems" reveals how he understood his creative process. His poems "came to him," and he wrote them down as if he had heard them whispered in his ear. Frequently they came to him in the form of dreams, as was the case with "Looking for Work." He was never satisfied with the original versions of his poems, however, and he polished them painstakingly for a long time before letting them out of his hands. At their best, these poems seem to have no need for rhyme or meter or any of the other paraphernalia of conventional poetry. His method might be described as functionalism: The thought finds its own form, so that thought and form seem molded to each other. "Through the Boughs" comes close to perfection in this style of poetic composition.

> Down below the window, on the deck, some ragged-
>   looking
> birds gather at the feeder. . . .
> The sky stays dark all day, the wind is from the west and
> won't stop blowing. . . . Give me your hand for a time.
>   Hold on
> to mine. That's right, yes. Squeeze hard. Time was we
> thought we had time on our side. *Time was, time was,*
> those ragged birds cry.

These last poems by Carver are almost the royal road to understanding what many modern poets have been trying to do. They have abandoned rhyme and meter. They have abandoned what used to be called poetic diction. They write in a conversational style. They attempt to allow the poetic message to dictate the poem's own unique form. No one has expressed the essential notion behind modern poetry better than the great American thinker Ralph Waldo Emerson, who said in his essay "The Poet": "For it is not metres, but a metre-making argument that makes a poem—a thought so passionate and alive that like the spirit of a plant or an animal it has an architecture of its own, and adorns nature with a new thing."

Ironically, the circumstances that originally kept Carver from writing became the principal material of much of his poetry and fiction. His recognition of this fact may partially explain the wry humor found in many of his most doleful poems. Drinking bouts, hangovers, guilt, divorce, and debt were recurring themes of his stories and poems. He recognized that even his own terminal illness was a powerful subject for his poetry. With characteristic naïveté and improvidence, Carver had chosen precisely the two literary forms that are hardest to sell and pay the least money when they do sell—poetry and short stories. These choices automatically condemned him to long years of poverty, with all the problems that accompanied it. (John Gardner had not warned Carver and his classmates of this reality when he advised them to forget about the "slicks" and concentrate on the "little" magazines, "where the best fiction in the country was being published, and all of the poetry.") Even had he lived longer, Carver would have had a hard time making a living as a writer: He was dependent upon the various disguised forms of charity that are the creative writer's lot in the age of television.

"Proposal," "Cherish," "Gravy," "No Need," and "After-Glow" all confront the imminence of death. "What the Doctor Said," in which Carver relates how a doctor informed him that he had at least thirty-two malignant nodules on one lung and was doomed, still is tinged with that ineradicable Carver humor, his most endearing quality. Though he has no resolutions or epiphanies to offer the reader, his invincible spirit, his truthfulness and dedication, and his admirable humanity are resolution and epiphany in themselves.

He had started as a country yokel in a rocky region whose literary roots did not run deep; he had made the painful climb from ignorance to enlightenment, from inarticulate frustration to masterful eloquence, from anonymity to fame. Many of his poems and stories are confessions of his sins, but readers have forgiven him because they recognize in him their own faults as well as some of their virtues. He had more than mere talent with words: He had the extra quality of soul that only great writers possess. He saw literature not as a stylish game but as the most important job a person can do. When he died on the morning of August 2, 1988, his works were being read in twenty different languages, and he has a better chance of being remembered for the next few centuries than most of his contemporaries. His career was a striking illustration of what Ralph Waldo Emerson meant when he said in "The Poet," "Thou must pass for a fool and a churl for a long season. This is the screen and sheath in which Pan has protected his well-beloved flower. . . . and though thou shouldst walk the world over, thou shalt not be able to find a condition inopportune or ignoble."

OTHER MAJOR WORKS

SHORT FICTION: *Put Yourself in My Shoes*, 1974; *Will You Please Be Quiet, Please?*, 1976; *What We Talk About When We Talk About Love*, 1981; *Cathedral*, 1983; *Where I'm Calling From*, 1988; *Elephant and Other Stories*, 1988; *Short Cuts: Selected Stories*, 1993.

SCREENPLAY: *Dostoevsky*, 1985.

EDITED TEXT: *American Short Story Masterpieces*, 1987 (with Tom Jenks).

MISCELLANEOUS: *Fires: Essays, Poems, Stories*, 1983; *No Heroics, Please: Uncollected Writings*, 1991; *Call If You Need Me: The Uncollected Fiction and Other Prose*, 2001.

BIBLIOGRAPHY

Carver, Raymond. *Conversations with Raymond Carver*. Edited by Marshall Bruce Gentry and William L. Stull. Jackson: University Press of Mississippi, 1990. A collection of twenty-five previously published interviews with Carver, conducted between 1977 and 1988, the period when he was at the peak of his career. Full of information about his life, his values, his opinions of other authors, and his literary aspirations.

Gallagher, Tess. Introduction to *A New Path to the Waterfall*, by Raymond Carver. New York: Atlantic Monthly Press, 1989. The collection in which this essay appears, a collection of Carver's last poems, includes some moving reflections on his life and values as he faced the fact that he was dying of cancer. The writer of the informative and moving introduction is the person who knew him best, the poet Tess Gallagher, who lived with him for many years and was with him at the time of his death.

Halpert, Sam. *Raymond Carver: An Oral Biography.* Iowa City: University of Iowa Press, 1995. An expanded edition of a collection of conversations originally published in 1991 as *When We Talk About Raymond Carver.* Includes contributions from Carver's first wife, his daughter, an early writing instructor, and some of his lifetime friends.

Kuzma, Greg. "*Ultramarine:* Poems That Almost Stop the Heart." *Michigan Quarterly Review* 27 (Spring, 1988): 355-363. In her introduction to *A New Path to the Waterfall*, Tess Gallagher calls Kuzma's review of *Ultramarine* "the most astute essay on [Carver's] poetry."

Nesset, Kirk. *The Stories of Raymond Carver: A Critical Study.* Athens: Ohio University Press, 1995. The first book-length study of Carver's work, Nesset calls the book, "a preliminary exploration." Includes an extensive bibliography.

Saltzman, Arthur M. *Understanding Raymond Carver.* Columbia: University of South Carolina Press, 1988. An excellent short overview of Carver's life and work; emphasizes Carver's short stories, but one chapter is devoted to his poetry. Contains a valuable bibliography of works by and about Carver.

Stull, William L., and Maureen P. Carroll, eds. *Remembering Ray: A Composite Biography of Raymond Carver.* Santa Barbara, Calif.: Capra Press, 1993. Though not a formal biography, this collection of essays covers Carver's working-class origins, his troubled first marriage, his battle with alcoholism, his teaching style, and his ultimate happiness until his death from cancer.

Wolff, Tobias. "Raymond Carver Had His Cake and Ate It Too." *Esquire* 112 (September, 1989): 240-248. A personal friend and fellow author and teacher relates a series of anecdotes about Carver in his wild drinking days. The essay highlights Carver's zest for life, his interest in people, his kindly personality, and his unconcealed delight in the critical recognition he began receiving toward the end of his life.

Bill Delaney;
bibliography updated by the editors

TURNER CASSITY

Born: Jackson, Mississippi; January 12, 1929

PRINCIPAL POETRY

Watchboy, What of the Night?, 1966
"The Airship Boys in Africa," 1970
Steeplejacks in Babel, 1973
Silver Out of Shanghai: A Scenario for Josef von Sternberg, Featuring Wicked Nobles, a Depraved Religious, Wayfoong, Princess Ida, the China Clipper, and Resurrection Lily, with a Supporting Cast of Old Hands, Merchant Seamen, Sikhs, Imperial Marines, and Persons in Blue, 1973
Yellow for Peril, Black for Beautiful: Poems and a Play, 1975
The Defense of the Sugar Islands: A Recruiting Poster, 1979
Keys to Mayerling, 1983
Hurricane Lamp, 1986
Between the Chains, 1991
The Destructive Element: New and Selected Poems, 1998

OTHER LITERARY FORMS

While primarily a poet, Turner Cassity has also written several uncollected short stories, a poetic drama (*Men of the Great Man*, contained in *Yellow for Peril, Black for Beautiful*), and an essay on the cataloging of periodicals, "Gutenberg as Card Shark," published in *The Academic Library: Essays in Honor of Guy R. Lyle* (1974).

ACHIEVEMENTS

Perhaps because of its traditional form, Turner Cassity's poetry has received less attention than it deserves. Cassity won the Blumenthal-Leviton-Blonder Prize for poetry in 1966 and has gained an increasingly large group of supporters, but he seems to have had little influence on the course of contemporary writing, except perhaps as a precursor of the new formalist school. Detractors, and occasionally even champions, argue that while technically polished, the poems are often unrewardingly distant or difficult, and that although the poet's formal talent is considerable, his range is somewhat limited. A closer reading of Cassity's work as a whole, however, reveals the complexity to be a necessary outgrowth of the poet's vision—not merely cleverness for its own sake—and the limited scope to be a false modesty. The wealth of allusion never makes the writing pedantic or pretentious; instead it reflects the poet's refusal to adopt a single, narrow perspective as his guide. Conscious of his heritage, the poet is able to distance himself ironically from that past and to discover his present. Further attention to Cassity's work should continue to reveal both the significance of his refusal to write a less traditional, more accessible type of poetry, and the importance of his unique and challenging view, a view that rewards even as it frustrates the reader's expectations of what contemporary poetry should be.

BIOGRAPHY

Allen Turner Cassity was born in Jackson, Mississippi, on January 12, 1929. His father, who died when Cassity was four, was in the sawmill business; his mother was a violinist and his grandmother a pianist in silent film theaters. The family moved to Forrest, Mississippi, in 1933 and later back to Jackson, where Cassity attended Bailey Junior High School and was graduated from Central High School. Cassity was graduated from Millsaps College with a B.A. in 1951 and from Stanford University with an M.A. in English in 1952; at Stanford he studied poetry with Yvor Winters in a program that he likens to "the strict technical training a musician would get at a good conservatory."

He was drafted in 1952 during the Korean War and spent the two years of his duty in Puerto Rico, an experience that provides the basis for his sequence *The Defense of the Sugar Islands*. He received an M.S. in library science from Columbia University in 1956 and served as an assistant librarian at the Jackson Municipal Library for 1957-1958 and for part of 1961. From 1959 to 1961, Cassity was an assistant librarian for the Transvaal Provincial Library in Pretoria, South Africa. Observations from his stay in Pretoria and Johannesburg frequently appear in his poems. In 1962, Cassity accepted a job at the Emory University Library in Atlanta, where he remained until his retirement in 1991.

Cassity's travels have taken him to the desert and the tropics, and he has spent much time in California. He has referred to his poems as "tropical pastorals," but this description conceals the sense of amusement and horror with which many of his speakers perceive the past. Cassity has also described himself as "a burgher" in temperament and conviction, and this label is also somewhat misleading, for his poems seldom reveal a complacent attitude; his scrutiny of colonialism, while not obviously polemical, often reveals more the flaws inherent in the underlying psychology of the colonist than do more tendentious poems.

ANALYSIS

Ever since his first volume of poetry, *Watchboy, What of the Night?*, Turner Cassity has continued to write terse, elliptical poems in unfashionably strict metrical form. For Cassity, the discipline of writing in meter and rhyme is prerequisite to his creative process: "without it, nothing comes into my head." Yet, while traditional, his verse avoids monotony and is typically supple and lively. His poems often include exotic settings or historical figures, juxtaposing them to the tawdriness of the familiar modern world. The combination of this irony with the restrained meter and diction yields a body of poetry that is formal and wittily aloof; the polish and urbanity, however, do not conceal the poet's ongoing search for a deliverance from decay and loss. Ultimately, the poet returns to his medium, language, and to his craftsmanship to find this deliverance, and in this sense Cassity is truly modern—in contrast to many contemporary poets, who, though severing ties with traditional form, fail to understand the relationship of past to present and their role in defining that relationship.

Clearly, Cassity is to some extent an heir of earlier modern poets writing in traditional modes, especially of Yvor Winters, with whom Cassity studied; many have also noted similarities between Cassity's work and that of W. H. Auden, Wallace Stevens, and Robert Frost. Equally evident, though, is the deft, colloquial irony of French post-Symbolists such as Jules Laforgue; and the formal control, epigrammatic wit, and social concern of eighteenth century poetry, particularly that of Alexander Pope, are, for some readers, evident in many of Cassity's poems. Still, the density of Cassity's allusions and the complexity of his contrasts—past and present, great and trivial, historical and personal—distinguish his writing from that of the traditional poet.

The growing acceptance of Cassity's terse, restrained style has led to a greater appreciation of his poetry; still, the work of Turner Cassity has yet to receive a full, comprehensive critical account. Perhaps only when the historicity of what is now called contemporary poetry becomes clear will it be possible to understand the unique merit of Cassity's contribution. In the meantime, his poetry may gradually become for the general reader less of a curiosity and more of a hallmark of a complex and significant response to the modern age.

"SEVEN DESTINATIONS OF MAYERLING"

The fact that Cassity frequently juxtaposes the noteworthy with the mundane may in part account for his being labeled a satirist. Such a strategy, however, is a means more of evaluating the past than of ridiculing the present, a means of understanding change and loss. The poem "Seven Destinations of Mayerling," for example, imaginarily relocates the castle of a German baron's suicide/murder to seven sites: Arizona (across from the London Bridge, which was actually relocated there), Orlando (another Disney World), Dallas (the Budapest Hymnbook Depository), Nashville (an attraction at the Grand Ol' Opry), Milwaukee (a beer hall), Tokyo (a brothel), and Montana (a hunting lodge). Cassity's purpose here, in spite of his witty and acerbic parodies, is not to lament the banality of modern culture, for the castle, like Europe itself, is no holy relic to be venerated. Rather, by juxtaposing the contrasting and even conflicting worlds, the poet simultaneously depicts the difficulty of living outside time and change, and the capacity of the imagination, wit, poetic language, and form to create an amusement, which itself becomes the sought-after haven, the refuge.

"GUTENBERG AS CARD SHARK"

A key to Cassity's attitude toward the past may be found in his essay "Gutenberg as Card Shark," an essay primarily about the cataloging of periodicals. Cassity criticizes the tendency of librarians to efface the traces of a periodical's original state (such as deleting the advertisements from magazines); he finds these indexes of the ephemeral nature of the publication often more revealing of the time than the verbal text itself, and points out that an emphasis on the more academic nature of the publication simplifies and hence falsifies the text's reality. Behind this priority lies the preference for the genuine though ephemeral artifact (which may in fact be genuine because it is ephemeral) over the self-consciously didactic and hence derivative and unreal artwork. The article concludes: "The Gutenberg Bible was no doubt a towering achievement, but if we could retrieve entire the cultural environment of those printed playing cards which preceded it, who would not trade Scripture away?"

WATCHBOY, WHAT OF THE NIGHT?

Cassity's first collection, *Watchboy, What of the Night?*, like most of his works, is divided into several sections. The first section, "Rudiments of Tropics," consists primarily of scenes and recollections from such places as Indochina and Haiti. These poems reflect on change and chance and loss, as in "La Petite Tonkinoise," a monologue by a Vietnamese prostitute who is an object of exploitation but also the force that controls the colonizer: "Yet I and wheel, meek where your glance is hurled,/ Combined, were Fortune, Empress of the World." The second section, "Oom-Pah for Oom Paul," extends the analysis of imperialism to South Africa. In "Johannesburg Requiem," the blacks lament a social, linguistic, and economic structure that is not theirs but which they must serve.

The section "In the Laagers of Burgherdom" celebrates with deft irony the comforts of kitsch: Café musicians complain of having to play the same tunes repeatedly (though they do have steady employment), heaven is depicted as a Hollywood production number, lovers are compared to the Katzenjammer Kids, and elderly ladies find "Grace at the Atlanta Fox" (an art deco film theater in the style of a Turkish mosque).

"THE AIRSHIP BOYS IN AFRICA"

The forty-page poem "The Airship Boys in Africa: A Serial in Twelve Chapters," published in *Poetry* in 1970, is dedicated "To the Crabbes: George and Buster" (a reference to the eccentric early nineteenth century poet who described simple village life in eighteenth century couplets and to the swimmer/actor hero of Tarzan films). Here again Cassity relies on an urbane mixture of kitsch and culture, in this instance to convey the failure that results when one culture attempts to impose itself on another for mere gain; the story depicts the doomed flight of a German Zeppelin in World War I to secure territory in Africa. Interweaving past with present, reality with mirage, the poet presents a wry but frightening vision. The heroism of the German crew, like their airship, is finally deflated, their mission pointless. The first chapter describes a Namibian who, talking and thinking in clicks, watches the airship crash; the poem then, in the *in medias res* fashion of epics, reverts to the beginning of the story and follows the crew on their mission. The final chapter describes the survivors searching for the last remaining German stronghold, one of them falling back and clicking his tongue against his teeth. This unexpected union of conqueror with conquered is repeated in the epitaph, a conclusion with nightmarish overtones of the Flying Dutchman legend:

> Full throttle low above the high savannah;
> Game running into, out of pointed shadow.
> Herr, between drummed earth and silent heaven,
> We pursue a shade which is ourselves.

Cassity's preoccupation with kitsch, as represented here and in other works, signifies neither an amused cynicism nor a predilection for form over content but an awareness of the liberating power of coming to terms with one's own culture. While admiring its technical virtuosity, Donald Davie has criticized "The Airship Boys in Africa" for what he calls a tendency toward campiness, in which the poet seeks "to always astonish, outsmart, upstage any conceivable reader." Though characterized by cleverness and wit, Cassity's poems do not lack a seriousness or a sincerity, nor are they marred by what Davie calls a lack of shapeliness; rather, they assume a shape that, while unexpected or startling, is in fact the only shape that can convey the poet's meaning. The reference to Buster Crabbe, for example, reminds the reader of the naïve and ethnocentric assumptions of the Hollywood film about civilization and savagery, progress and technology. Yet whereas the naïveté of the Hollywood production obscures one's awareness of reality, so can culture—the failed Parsifal myth, the Germanic heroic code—stifle with its insistence on the reenactment of the past.

In a later poem in *Hurricane Lamp*, "Advice to King Lear," the poet describes a San Antonio theater with seats on one side of a river and a stage on the other side. During a production of *King Lear*, as the weather on-stage grows more and more threatening (thanks to the arbitrary aid of wind machines) and as Lear's situation becomes increasingly tragic, a boat passes between the stage and the audience, and the speaker admonishes the protagonist, "Get on the boat, Old Man, and go to summer." The very tackiness of the theatrical setup allows the audience to free itself from its dependence on illusion and from its slavery to the single prescribed ending. In "The Airship Boys in Africa," the poet's exposing of the tawdriness of the Teutonic myth undermines the repressive nature not only of fascism but also of the unquestioning allegiance to myth and culture.

SILVER OUT OF SHANGHAI

Even more than "The Airship Boys in Africa," Cassity's narrative poem *Silver Out of Shanghai: A Scenario for Josef von Sternberg, Featuring Wicked Nobles, a Depraved Religious, Wayfoong, Princess Ida, the China Clipper, and Resurrection Lily, with a Supporting Cast of Old Hands, Merchant Seamen, Sikhs, Imperial Marines, and Persons in Blue*, as its full title indicates, builds a poetic world out of the soundstage exoticism of such films as *Shanghai Express* (1932). Ostensibly the story describes the attempt of a wealthy British merchant, Sir V. M. Grayburn, to smuggle silver out of Shanghai without causing a drop in silver prices; he hires a South African engineer to suggest that the ship carries gold instead, but his rivals have the ship sunk, and a last-minute salvage effort by the engineer saves the day, or at least the silver. While overtly mocking the heroics of the adventure genre, with its exaggerated characterizations, its moral chiaroscuro, and its contrived resolution, *Silver Out of Shanghai* also attacks the attempt of the colonialist to create, through manipulation, a world without change. As a character remarks to Grayburn,

> "Oh, V., you've missed the point. It's *temporary*.
> Daddy thought the Boxer Wars would end it;
> Then the Straits.
>
> . . . .
>
>   The rest of us
> Know better, Take that Afrikaaner boy
> He knows a country has to be reconquered
> Day by day.

Yet while the narrative of *Silver Out of Shanghai*, if not its purpose, is clear, the form of *Steeplejacks in Ba-*

bel is much more perplexing, primarily because of the elliptical nature of the diction and the allusions. Here, as elsewhere, the poet dissects the fascist and colonialist mentalities, but in several poems, he treats more sympathetically the colonialist as displaced person, particularly in "Two Hymns" ("The Afrikaaner in the Argentine" and "Confederates in Brazil"). Technically, the poems of *Steeplejacks in Babel* are among Cassity's tersest and densest; as Richard Johnson has observed, the poet has removed "all but the essentials." The strictures of brevity, along with the formal discipline exacted by the rhymed couplets of iambic pentameter, create a poetry whose knowledge comes from its form and not the reverse. The first and last poems, "What the Sirens Sang" and "Cartography Is an Inexact Science," underscore this characteristic truth.

THE DEFENSE OF THE SUGAR ISLANDS

The Defense of the Sugar Islands marks a significant change in Cassity's writing; these poems, based on his experience as a soldier in Puerto Rico during the Korean War, are first-person accounts of events and memories (though in a sense these poems are no more or less autobiographical than is any other of his poems, and one need not know the poet's life to understand the poems). From musing on his past, the speaker comes to realize and rejoice in his own fragility: "Those airs, without their scouring sand, seem more,/ Not less, sand's vessel set to measure time." In "A Walk with a Zombie" (another reference to a kitschy Hollywood film), the speaker contrasts himself as rememberer with a mummified Pharaoh: "If in my eyes the light is less,/ Yours, Pharaoh, have not looked on loss/ As mine have looked"; through memory and imagination, he can "sustain/ One blood unmummied: living wound/ Of armless mills that mock the wind,/ Of crystal words I cannot say,/ Of bladed cane I cannot see."

HURRICANE LAMP

Hurricane Lamp returns to the less obviously reflective style of the earlier works, but it, too, is a progression forward, although a subtle one. The disciplined meters and richly textured allusions again contrast with the wit and ironic distance of the speaker. Here, however, the speaker begins to adopt a more colloquial diction and a less reserved stance, particularly in such poems as "Berolina Demodee" and "A Dialogue with the Bride of Godzilla."

"MAINSTREAMING" AND "SOLDIERS OF ORANGE"

In the mid-1980's, Cassity began to move away from the terse formality of his short lyrics in a series of medium-length poems (about one hundred lines long), conversational poems which are more relaxed in meter and tone than longer narratives but equally rich in juxtaposition of past and present. "Mainstreaming" and "Soldiers of Orange" are, with *The Defense of the Sugar Islands*, among Cassity's few directly autobiographical poems: "Mainstreaming" recounts the experience of soldiers assigned to work with a unit of mentally defective draftees; "Soldiers of Orange" blends memories of a meeting with a former girlfriend and her daughter, including an encounter with Dutch colonial soldiers, with present-day observations of a drive through a Louisiana which has been colonized by Vietnamese refugees.

THE DESTRUCTIVE ELEMENT

In *The Destructive Element*, there is little in the way of a new mode or vein of work for Cassity, and in fact, his style remains constant and therefore recognizable and distinctive: He has found something that works and continues to do it. The poems run the gamut from clear, witty, and brief epigrams to complex, allusion-laden meditative poems. The poet's distinctive mix of philosophical speculation, irony, nose-thumbing at current pieties, and complex wordplay is a constant throughout this book. Yet while he remains firmly placed in the new formalist movement, several of his poems here are also frankly humorous and deliberately ornamental, displaying a cultivated idiosyncrasy.

Cassity is, at heart, a satirist, and while his work displays hard-bitten formalism and moral seriousness, the best satirists care deeply about their subjects, and humor is their weapon of choice for assailing human shortcoming. His passion comes clear with his use of emphatic tone and acute wit, evident in "Sitting Behind Ben-Hur."

> I've a tan. I look at backs a lot. I deeply understand
> teamwork.
> I live in filth. Was I fastidious
> When I was free? Here sharks will have us;
> It's not as though elsewhere there are not jackals.
> Bear up. Hand and heart grow calloused.

While the persona's rationalizations of the situation are amusing, it captures his awful resignation to fate, and, by extension, our immense capacity for endurance, even as it begs the question, At what cost?

Cassity's poetry here is also frequently fun, using liguistic delight—witness "Vegetarian Mary and the Venus Flytrap" and "Never Use a Stock Ticker Without a Geiger Counter"—and playful scenarios.

> My young grandfather, for the me of four,
> Blew smoke rings. I, these long years more,
> Without much gift, can, nonetheless
> Redeem my breath from utter shapelessness.

His life of travels acts as a springboard for many of the poems. His years in Africa, military service in the Caribbean, and frequent jaunts across the globe form what he calls his "colonial pastorals." He analyzes how history and place intersect, and in turn produces poems that serve as a moralistic consideration on the conflict between beauty and practicality, and the many ironies that result from this conflict. He examines a place in its natural state in order to uncover the ironic contrast after it has been changed by technology and use—that is, once it has been colonized.

BIBLIOGRAPHY

Ash, John. "A Brash Yankee and a Southern Dandy." Review of *Hurricane Lamp. The New York Times Book Review*, April 20, 1986, 19. Appreciates this work's juxtaposition of the ordinary and the exotic. Remarks that Cassity's insistence on formality does make for rigid and monotonous reading. It is, however, never self-indulgent or maudlin. Comments that Cassity combines at his best "elegance with an attractive pungency."

Barth, R. L., Susan Barth, and Charles Gullans. *A Bibliography of the Published Works of Turner Cassity, 1952-1987*. Florence, Ky.: Author, 1988. Useful compendium of Cassity's titles.

Flint, R. W. "Exiles from Olympus." *Parnassus: Poetry in Review* 5 (Spring/Summer, 1977): 97-107. Reviews Cassity's works, in particular *Yellow for Peril, Black for Beautiful*, and *Steeplejacks in Babel*. Sympathetic to Cassity inasmuch as Flint values his taciturnity and declares him a poet to watch. Quotes from *Watchboy, What of the Night?* and compares his work to Nadine Gordimer's uncompromising style.

Gioia, Dana. "Poetry and the Fine Presses." *The Hudson Review* 35 (Autumn, 1982): 438-498. Gives extravagant praise to Cassity by calling him the "most brilliantly eccentric poet in America." Clearly, Gioia enjoys Cassity's poetry but regrets how "few of his poems really show all he is capable of." Notes that *The Defense of the Sugar Islands: A Recruiting Poster* makes a real breakthrough for Cassity. According to Gioia, these poems have as much emotional and intellectual force as technical virtuosity, and Cassity's full range of talents come into being.

Steele, Timothy. "Curving to Foreign Harbors: Turner Cassity's 'Defense of the Sugar Islands.'" Review of *The Defense of the Sugar Islands: A Recruiting Poster. The Southern Review* 17 (Winter, 1981): 205-213. Outlines the structure of the retrospective poem. Argues for its success on balance but acknowledges some reservation, notably the "frequent density of Cassity's syntax" and the fact that important details are withheld.

Tillinghast, Richard. "Poems That Get Their Hands Dirty." *New York Times Book Review*, December 18, 1991, 7. Compares Cassity's *Between the Chains* to Adrienne Rich's *An Atlas of the Difficult World* and Philip Levine's *What Work Is*.

Steven L. Hale,
updated by Philip K. Jason and Sarah Hilbert

ROSALÍA DE CASTRO

Born: Santiago de Compostela, Spain; February 24, 1837
Died: Padrón, Spain; July 15, 1885

PRINCIPAL POETRY
La flor, 1857
A mi madre, 1863
Cantares gallegos, 1863
Follas novas, 1880

En las orillas del Sar, 1884 (*Beside the River Sar*, 1937)

Obras completas, 1909-1911 (4 volumes)

Poems, 1964

OTHER LITERARY FORMS

Rosalía de Castro was a novelist as well as a poet. Her five novels—*La hija del mar* (1859; *Daughter of the Sea*, 1995), *Flavio* (1861), *Ruinas* (1866; ruins), *El caballero de las botas azules* (1867; the knight with the blue boots), and *El primer loco* (1881; the first madman)—span the transition from Romanticism to realism. Although Castro herself put considerable stock in her novels, she is remembered only for her poetry.

ACHIEVEMENTS

Rosalía de Castro has been called Spain's foremost woman poet; Gerald Brenan has gone further, asserting that if she had written more in Spanish than in her native Galician dialect, she would be recognized as the greatest woman poet of modern times. Her unabashedly heart-throbbing lyrics are saved from mawkishness by her disciplined style. Castro's poetry, along with that of Gustavo Adolfo Bécquer, is the most representative of Spanish poetry at the time of its transition from Romanticism to the modern lyric. Some critics believe that she interacted with Bécquer—that in fact she lent him in 1857 a copy of Gérard de Nerval's translation of Heinrich Heine's *Tragödien, nebst einem lyrischen Intermezzo* (1823), a book said to have influenced Bécquer. It was not until the second decade of the twentieth century, when Azorín (José Martínez Ruiz) and Miguel de Unamuno y Jugo recommended her to the public, that her reputation as a poet became assured. Later, even poet Luis Cernuda, who found her work uneven and sentimental, recognized the rare timelessness of her observations. Antonio Machado borrowed images from her poetry, Juan Ramón Jiménez referred to her as "our Rosalía," and Gerardo Diego used her name as a metaphor in his own poetry. Her Galician poetry inspired Federico García Lorca to write his own "poemas gallegos," including a "Canzón de cuna pra Rosalía Castro, morta" ("Lullaby for the Late Rosalía de Castro").

With her contemporaries Manuel Curros Enríquez (who wrote an elegy for her) and Eduardo Pondal, Castro made up a triad of Galician poets who effected a renaissance of their provincial literature. Using the folk songs of Galicia as her models, she bonded modern Spanish poetry to oral forms that would have otherwise been lost. She led the way for subsequent poets to utilize folk tradition, and her work tolled the death knell for urban Romanticism. Modernist poets availed themselves of the revolutionary meters used by Castro (her enneasyllabic verse in *La flor*—the flower—predates the so-called innovations of Rubén Darío), and her use of free verse heralded the boldness of contemporary poetry.

To a remarkable extent, Castro's Galician and Spanish poetry has been accepted into English-language anthologies of world verse, especially in those of women's poetry (such as *The Penguin Book of Women Poets*, 1979, and *A Book of Women Poets: From Antiquity to Now*, 1981).

BIOGRAPHY

Rosalía de Castro was born in Santiago de Compostela in 1837, the child of María Teresa de la Cruz de Castro y Abadía. Her mother, who came from a once-wealthy family, was thirty-three when Rosalía was born; her father, Jose Martínez Viojo, was thirty-nine and a priest. Although her father could not acknowledge Rosalía as his daughter, he may have taken some interest in her welfare. Rosalía was brought up by Francisca Martínez, who, despite her surname, does not appear to have been the priest's sister. By 1853, Rosalía was living with her real mother, and there developed between them a deep bond. In Rosalía's eyes, her mother sanctified whatever sin she may have committed by reaffirming her obligation to her daughter in defiance of a hypocritical society.

A precocious child, Castro was writing verses by the age of eleven, and by sixteen she could play the guitar and the piano, had developed a fine contralto voice, and could draw well and read French. She read the foreign classics in translation and was fond of George Gordon, Lord Byron; Heinrich Heine; Edgar Allan Poe; and E. T. A. Hoffmann. Judging from the spelling errors in hand-written manuscripts of her poetry, however, her formal education may not have been extensive.

As a teenager, Castro was taken from Padrón to Santiago, where she attended school and where she participated in the city's cultural life. At a young people's cultural society, she met Aurelio Aguirre, one of the most representative figures of the Romantic movement in Galicia, a man who was later to be the model of Flavio in her novel of the same name, and who dedicated to her a work called "Improvisation"—apparently an attempt to console her for the discrepancy between her enchanting poetry and her less than enchanting physical appearance. Perhaps it is too facile to attribute the characteristic wistfulness of her poetry to a failed love affair, but it has been suggested that the lost love recalled in her poems and her fiction was Aurelio Aguirre. Among the poems not included in her own collections but included in *Obras completas* is an elegy for Aguirre.

In 1856, Castro went to Madrid, where she stayed at the home of a relative. It is generally said that she went "on family business," but it is possible she left home with the idea of becoming an actress in Madrid. Exposed to the cultural life of the Spanish capital, she devoted herself to writing and was able to meet other contemporary writers. In 1857, her first book of poetry *La flor* appeared and was favorably reviewed by Manuel Murguía in *La Iberia*. According to Murguía, he was not acquainted with the young author, but this is rather unlikely, not only because some of his comments presuppose a direct knowledge of Castro's personality, but also because he, too, had recently come from Galicia and, in fact, was Aguirre's best friend. Castro and Murguía were married in Madrid on October 10, 1858. Murguía, like Aguirre a Galician of Basque descent, was a journalist and historian destined to be honored in Galicia for his role in promoting regionalist literature. The couple had seven children. Their first child, a daughter, was born in 1859; their second child, also a daughter, was not born until ten years later. One of the twins Castro bore in 1871, Ovidio, was an accomplished painter of Galician landscapes but died young. Her youngest son died in his second year as the result of a fall, and her youngest daughter was stillborn in 1877.

In 1862, Castro's beloved mother died, and Castro honored her with a privately printed collection of poems, *A mi madre* (to my mother) of limited literary value but elegiac and emotional.

It remains unclear what kind of a marriage Castro had with Murguía. Gerald Brenan believes that Murguía,

envious of his wife's talents, mistreated her; it is certain that Murguía destroyed his wife's correspondence after her death. Castro scholar Marina Mayoral, on the other hand, prefers to see in Murguía—who survived his wife by thirty-eight years and wrote lovingly and abundantly about her—one of the few mainstays of Castro's sad life. Despite the fulfillment of children and the security of family life, she was frequently bored, and in both her poetry and her fiction, she mourned lost happiness.

It is important, however, not to exaggerate the pathetic nature of Castro's life. She loved the arts and took great pleasure from her endeavors in the fields of music, drawing, and acting. She was a great success when she acted in Antonio Gil y Zárate's play *Rosamunda* (1839), and for the greater part of her life she enjoyed exchanging ideas with her friends. Her daughter Gala, who lived until 1964, was especially concerned that her mother not be remembered as morose. As Victoriano García Martí points out, people who are authentically sorrowful often develop a profound love of humankind and achieve a different kind of contentment. This was especially true of Castro, and after her death a legend grew concerning her generosity to others, endowing her with a kind of saintliness.

Between 1859 and 1870, the couple lived in Madrid and Simancas, where Murguía had a position as a government historian, and they traveled extensively throughout Spain. To Castro, any terrain that was not green, damp, and lush like her native Galicia was disappointing; thus, she disliked most of the rest of Spain. She became so consumed with nostalgia for her native land that she began her *Cantares gallegos* (Galician songs), written in Galician but given a Spanish title. In the 1870's, Murguía held positions in Galicia, and Castro spent much of her time at Padron, which she considered home. Having suffered from vague ill-health all of her life, she withdrew completely from society in her last decade; she died of uterine cancer in 1885. In the moments before her death, she received the Sacraments, recited her favorite prayers, and begged her children to destroy her unpublished manuscripts. With her last breath, she asked that the window be opened, for she wished to see the ocean—which in fact was not visible from her home.

Castro was buried near her mother in the peaceful cemetery of Adina in Padron, a place whose enchantment she had evoked in *Follas novas* (new leaves). On the very day of her death, accolades began to arrive, and as a result of the homage paid her in death, her remains were moved in 1891 to a marble tomb in the Convent of Santo Domingo de Bonaval in Santiago. In 1917, her compatriots, together with an organization of Galician emigrants in America, organized a campaign to raise a statue to their poet in the Paseo de la Herradura in Santiago, looking toward Padron. According to biographer Kathleen Kulp-Hill, this statue is faithful to portraits and descriptions of Castro. The figure is seated in a calm, pensive attitude, projecting an aura of strength and warmth.

ANALYSIS

As Frédéric Mistral is to Provence and Joan Maragall to Catalonia, Rosalía de Castro is to Galicia, the northwest corner of the Iberian peninsula, linked politically with Spain but tied ethnically, linguistically, and temperamentally with Portugal. When Castro was nine years old, there was an unsuccessful insurrection in Galicia against the Spanish government. The unpleasant memory of the savage reprisals undertaken by the government may help explain her strong hostility toward Castile and Castilians, as in the lines, "May God grant, Castilians,/ Castilians whom I abhor,/ that rather the Galicians should die,/ than to go to you for bread."

Santiago de Compostela, Castro's birthplace, possesses the bones of Saint James the Apostle, for which reason Galicia became in the Middle Ages the third most holy shrine in Christendom (after Jerusalem and Rome). The steady stream of pilgrims traveling to Galicia from all parts of Europe made Santiago a medieval cultural center, and in the thirteenth century, Galician became the language of lyrical poetry throughout the Iberian peninsula. The Galician *jograles* (minstrels) sang characteristically of melancholy (designated in Spanish by its Galician and Portuguese name, *saudades*), as in, for example, their *cantigas de amigo*, the songs of women whose lovers were absent, either away at sea or fighting the Moors in Portugal. After the thirteenth century, however, there was an eclipse of Galician poetry, and it was not until the nineteenth century that an interest in the poetic potential of the Galician language was reawakened.

The poetry of Rosalía de Castro flows from line to line in a musical sequence and does not, as Gerald Brenan observes, condense well into a single epithet or phrase. She was not fond of metaphors but rather relied heavily on repetition—in such lines as ("Breezes breezes, little breezes/ breezes of the land I come from")—and contrast—as in "To them those frosts/ are the promise of early flowers;/ To me they are silent workers/ weaving my winding sheet." In her earlier poems, she sometimes used the *leixa-pren*, a special feature of the medieval *cantigas de amigo*, whereby each new stanza begins with an echo from the last line of the previous stanza. Her diction is almost colloquial, her syntax uninverted (except in her earliest poetry and in some of her later poetry), and her adjectives are always the least ornamental possible. There abound words for the lushness of Galicia, names of animals and birds, and especially of trees (such as the oaks sacred to the ancient Celts of Galicia; giant chestnuts; and the cedars of "our own" Lebanon). In her somber moods, she draws repeatedly on Spanish adjectives such as *torvo* (grim), *amargo* (bitter), and *triste* (sad), and uses verbs such as *anonadar* (to destroy), *agostar* (to wither up as in August), *hostigar* (to scourge), while she uses words such as *guarida* (lair), *nido* (nest), and *egida* (aegis) to express the security and coziness of home in Galicia. Galician, more than Spanish, is a nasal language (for example, Galician *min*, "my," as opposed to Spanish *mí*), and Castro uses its humming nasals as a tool to craft more sharply the gloom she suffers on Earth, as in the line "Pra min i-en min mesma moras" (for me and in myself you live), from "Cando penso que to fuche" (when I think that you have gone), in *Follas novas*.

"I USED TO HAVE A NAIL"

One remarkable poem that reveals Castro's attitude toward sorrow is "Una-ha vez tiven un cravo" ("I Used to Have a Nail") in *Follas novas*. This painful nail, whether made of gold, iron, or love, leads the poet, weeping like Mary Magdalen, to entreat God to effect a miracle for its removal. When at last she gathers the courage to pluck it out, the void it leaves is something like a longing for the old pain. Some critics have speculated that without an abundant supply of sorrow for her to sublimate into poetry, Castro felt lost. This contradictory hunger for suffering cannot be reduced to the level of a personal neurosis, for it reflects the ideals of traditional Christianity. Castro believed that thistles, though harsh to the flesh, mark the road to heaven, and in "Yo en mi lecho de abrojos" ("I on My Bed of Thistles," from *Beside the River Sar*), avowedly preferred her destiny to a "bed of roses and feathers," which have been known to "envenom and corrupt."

RELIGION AND SUPERSTITION

Castro was conventionally religious; she needed God and sought him everywhere, and she fought herself for her faith, as Unamuno did. There are biblical references in her poetry, as well as her marginally Christian *sombras* (shades), the souls of persons no longer living whom Castro "invokes" from time to time and who respond by intervening in the lives of the living. She also draws on Galician lore concerning the supernatural world. Witches (*meigas, lurpias*), warlocks (*meigos*), and elves (*trasgos*) inhabit her forests, and the safety of the unwary nocturnal traveler may be jeopardized by the Host of Souls in Torment. In "Dios bendiga todo, nena" ("God Blesses Everything, Child," from *Cantares gallegos*), an old woman warns a young girl of the dangers of the world, whereupon the girl declares her intention never to leave her village without scapularies, holy medals, and amulets to protect her from witches. The fine line between religion and superstition is typified in "Soberba" ("Foolish Pride") in *Follas novas*, where a family frightened by a storm tries to placate God with candles, olive leaves, and prayers, and by scouring from their personal slates offenses that might have incurred his wrath. Nor is the imagery of the supernatural always to be taken literally. In an aubade, Castro has the heroine address her lover affectionately as "warlock" while he prepares to leave her bed, and elsewhere employs the same word to create a metaphor for sorrow: "N' hay peor meiga que un-ha gran pena" (there is no worse demon than a great sorrow).

CANTARES GALLEGOS

Castro's first important book of poems was *Cantares gallegos*. In the prologue to this volume, she acknowledges the inspiration of *El libro de los cantares* by Antonio de Trueba, published the previous year, and apologizes for her shortcomings as a poet, claiming that her only schooling was that of "our poor country folk." The poems are dedicated to Fernan Caballero (Cecilia Böhl de Faber), the pioneer of the realistic novel in Spain, who won Castro's appreciation with her unprejudiced portrayal of Galicians. Working without a grammar, Castro apologizes for her Galician; indeed, it is not a pure dialect unaffected by Castilian influence, and lexical and orthographic inconsistencies abound. She attempted to imitate modern Portuguese in her use of diacritical marks, contractions, and elisions, and included a short glossary of Galician words for the sake of her Castilian readers.

Castro's usual procedure was to begin her poems with a popular couplet and then to elaborate it into a ballad. Her masterpiece is perhaps "Airiños, airiños, aires" ("Breezes, Breezes, Little Breezes") in which she portrays the nostalgia of a Galician emigrant, playing upon the dual meaning of *airiños* as "little breezes" and "little songs." Everywhere this unfortunate emigrant turns in the strange country of her destination, people peer curiously at her, and she longs for the sweet breezes of home, those "quitadoiriños de penas" (takers-away of sorrow) that enchant the woods and caress the land. Similarly as Galician poetry inspired the Castilian lyric of the fifteenth and sixteenth centuries, this poem influenced the revival of Spanish poetry that began thirty years after Castro's death. The *Romancero gitano* (1928; *Gypsy Ballads*, 1951, 1953) of Federico García Lorca, for example, with its themes and repetitions derived from folk tradition, owes much to this poem.

In "Pasa rio, pasa rio" ("Pass by, River, Pass By"), a disconsolate lover weeps tears into the ocean in hope that they may reach her beloved in Brazil, where he has had to emigrate. The plight of the Galician emigrant forced to leave his homeland because of economic necessity troubled Castro deeply. There are many poems of praise for Galicia, such as "Cómo chove mihudiño" ("How the Rain Is Falling Lightly"), in which she describes Padrón, lulled by the river where the trees are shady, and reminisces about the great house owned by her humanitarian grandfather. She dares to ask the Sun of Italy if it has seen "more green, more roses,/ bluer sky or softer colors/ where foam stripes your gulfs with whiteness"; and is reminded by a wandering cloud of the sad shade of her mother wandering lonely in the spheres before she goes to glory.

FOLLAS NOVAS

The poems of *Follas novas* are meant to be read and reflected upon, as opposed to the folk poems of *Cantares gallegos* with their marked oral quality. The 139 poems of *Follas novas* are more subjective and personal and bleaker than those of the earlier book, which radiate innocence and hope; they are also more innovative in form: Castro employed varying line lengths with metrical combinations then regarded as inappropriate for Spanish verse, such as combinations of eight with ten or eleven syllables or eight with fourteen. Dedicated to the Society for the Welfare of Galicians in Havana, the book was published simultaneously in Havana and Madrid in 1880. In her prologue, Castro expresses her concern for the suffering of Galicians in distant lands, and she also asserts her artistic independence as a woman. Certainly the successive deaths of her two youngest children within three months of each other in 1876-1877 did much to intensify her tragic sense of life, but many of the poems in this collection were written as long as ten years before the publication date.

Here, Castro's poetry is no longer concerned with aubades but rather with the departures of lovers and their separation. Love is no longer hopeful but rather furtive and anxious. In "¿Que lle digo?" ("What Should I Tell Her?") the emigrant may be plagued by *saudades* for his homeland, but may wax cynical about love as well: "Antona is there, but I have Rosa here." The landscape of Galicia is always in the background, but is no longer decorative and is now interwoven with more complex emotions. Death is seen as a cure for the disease of life, and the poet asks God why suicide must be deemed a crime.

Although she occasionally dedicated her poems to worthy persons (such as her husband and Ventura Ruíz de Aguilera), Castro did not often exalt either historical figures or living persons in her poetry. One notable exception, written in classical form, is her elegy on the tomb of Sir John Moore, the affable British general who led a retreat to Corunna that ended in the British victory over the Napoleonic forces there in 1809, but which cost Moore his life. *Follas novas* also includes a translation into Galician of the poem "Armonias d'a tarde" (harmonies of the afternoon), by Ventura Ruíz de Aguilera, a contemporary poet who drew on the folk motifs of the Salamanca area.

BESIDE THE RIVER SAR

As a result of complaints made by her Galician readers that some of her material was scandalous, Castro vowed never again to write in Galician, and it is to this decision and the Spanish poems of her last collection, *Beside the River Sar,* that she owes her prominence in Spanish literature. Not all the critics, however, proclaim the superiority of these poems. Gerald Brenan, who prefers the softer, more tender tone of her Galician verse, finds the aloofness of her Castilian poems chilling. Many of the poems collected in *Beside the River Sar* were written between 1878 and 1884 and were published in periodicals, some as distant as *La nación española* of Buenos Aires. These late poems reflect a greater concern with ideas; they are characterized by unusual combinations of lines and broken rhythms, with lines of as many as sixteen or eighteen syllables, and by a syntactical complexity not previously seen in Castro's work.

In *Beside the River Sar,* Galicia is no longer a focal point, assuming instead the role of a backdrop, and the folk element is even less in evidence. Castro continues to excel in nature poetry, displaying in "Los robles" ("The Oaks") a distinctly modern concern for ecology when she protests the wasteful destruction of trees in Galicia with an almost druidic reverence for arboreal vitality. The river Sar of the title, the beloved river of her homeland, is a symbol for the flowing of life toward its unknown and unknowable destination.

In what is possibly her most frequently anthologized poem, "Dicen que no hablan las plantas" ("They Say That Plants Do Not Speak"), Castro asserts the importance that natural phenomena such as plants, brooks, and birds have for her. Although it seems that these natural phenomena view her as a "madwoman" because of her outlandish dreams, she exhorts them not to poke fun at her, because without those dreams, she would lack the wherewithal to admire the beauty that they themselves so generously display.

In her valorization of dreams (*sueños* or *ensueños*) and her refusal to accept the pathetic constraints by which man is necessarily bound, Castro prefigures the concerns of the *generación del 98*, of poets such as Unamuno, Antonio Machado, and Azorín. Nevertheless, she must acknowledge that dreams can lead to folly, as they do in the poignant "La canción que oyó en sueños el viejo" ("The Song Which the Old Man Heard in His Dreams"), in which an old man, designated crazy in the poem, feels his blood pump and surge as his youthful passions return when in truth he should be reckoning with "infallible death" and "implacable old age."

In *Beside the River Sar*, the winter, symbolic of despair and the end of life in Castro's earlier work, is friendly, a herald, in fact, of spring, and is "a thousand times welcome." Even the desert of Castile, anathema in her earlier poetry and so drastically opposed to the lushness of Galicia, assumes a positive guise, coming to represent the realm beyond carnal suffering, lit by "another light more vivid than that of the golden sun."

One of the most interesting poems in the collection is the questioning and subsequently epiphanic "Santa Escolástica" ("Saint Scholastica"). In Santiago on a drizzly April day, the poet allows herself to absorb the dismal atmosphere. "Cemetery of the living," she exclaims, as she contrasts the gloom she sees around her with the city's medieval glory. This leads to her own rephrasing of that tortured question, "Why, since there is God, does Hell prevail?" She enters the Convent of San Martín Pinario in search of comfort. Her female soul begins to feel the sacred majesty of the temple as vividly as it has felt the satisfactions of motherhood. Suddenly, the sun strikes the statue of Saint Scholastica and brings into sharper focus the saint's ecstasy, which in turn produces an ecstasy in Castro, who exclaims exultantly, "There is art! There is poetry! . . . There must be a heaven,/ for there is God."

Kathleen Kulp-Hill contrasts this joyous poem from *Beside the River Sar* with a poem from *Follas novas* having the same setting, "N'a catedral" ("In the Cathedral"). In the latter, although the sun shines briefly into the dimly illuminated room, the shadows return, and the poet withdraws without consolation. As the contrast between the two poems suggests, Castro's last volume was a testament to hope.

In an age when poets declaimed, Rosalía de Castro had the courage to write honestly and realistically about issues that troubled her. She was unashamed to examine and interpret the feelings of the Galician peasantry, creating from their own forms and phrases a new poetry of rare beauty. As she explored her own hope and hopelessness and pondered the human condition in general, she translated her findings into poetry that speaks to all men.

OTHER MAJOR WORKS

LONG FICTION: *La hija del mar*, 1859 (*Daughter of the Sea*, 1995); *Flavio*, 1861; *Ruinas*, 1866; *El caballero de las botas azules*, 1867; *El primer loco*, 1881.

BIBLIOGRAPHY

Courteau, Joanna. *The Poetics of Rosalía de Castro's "Negra sombra."* New York: Edwin Mellen Press, 1995. A close critical examination of one of Castro's poems. Includes bibliographical references and index.

Dever, Aileen. *The Radical Insufficiency of Human Life: The Poetry of R. de Castro and J. A. Silva.* Jefferson, N.C.: McFarland, 2000. A comparison of Castro's and Silva's poetry. Their works have meaningful differences but share remarkable likenesses in theme, tone, and style, though it is unlikely that they knew of each other's work. Of interest to feminist critics is an interpretation of Castro's literary vocation within a patriarchal society.

Kulp-Hill, Kathleen. *Manner and Mood in Rosalía de Castro: A Study of Themes and Style.* Madrid: Ediciones José Porrua Turanzas, 1968. A thorough critical study of Castro's writing and a bibliography of her works.

_____. *Rosalía de Castro.* Boston: Twayne Publishers, 1977. Introductory biography and critical analysis of selected works. Includes an index and bibliography of Castro's writing.

Jack Shreve;
bibliography updated by the editors

CATULLUS

Gaius Valerius Catullus

Born: Verona, Italy; c. 85 B.C.E.
Died: Probably in Rome, Italy; c. 54 B.C.E.

PRINCIPAL POETRY

Catullus was well known to Augustan Rome, but he fell into obscurity as the Roman Empire declined. In the fourteenth century, a manuscript of his works was discovered containing 116 of his poems, varying from a short couplet to a long poem of more than four hundred lines. Catullus wrote in Latin. His Latin texts, edited by Elmer Truesdell Merrill with extensive notes and information about his life and works, are available in *Catullus* (1893). A good modern translation of his poems is that of Frank O. Copley, *Gaius Valerius Catullus: The Complete Poetry, a New Translation with an Introduction* (1957).

OTHER LITERARY FORMS

Catullus is remembered only for his poetry.

ACHIEVEMENTS

Catullus is one of the greatest lyric poets of all time. He lived in Rome when that city was the center of the world and when it was rocked to its foundations by political and social revolution. Catullus was in his early twenties when, in 62 B.C.E. under the consulship of Cicero, the Catiline Conspiracy occurred. The poet lived to see the coalition of Julius Caesar, Pompey, and Crassus form in 60 B.C.E. and Caesar's subsequent rise to power. Catullus had been dead only about five years when civil war broke out between Caesar and Pompey. Pompey's death at the battle of Pharsalus occurred in 48 B.C.E., and Caesar was assassinated in 44 B.C.E. References to Julius Caesar, Pompey, and Cicero appear in various poems of Catullus. He wrote during the stormy period when the Roman Empire was established, immediately prior to the reign of Augustus (27 B.C.E.-C.E. 14). Catullus bitterly attacked Caesar and his favorites in early poems but eventually came to support the Caesarian party. His poetry precedes the somewhat later literary wave of Vergil (Publius Vergilius Maro, 70-19 B.C.E.) and the Augustan poets.

Catullus was the leading representative of a revolution in poetry created by the *neoteroi* or "new men" in Rome. Rather than writing about battles, heroes, and the pagan gods, Catullus draws his subjects from everyday, intensely personal life. He writes about lovers' quarrels, arguments, indecent behavior, and his love for his brother and for his Italian countryside. Whatever he writes is marked by a high level of passion, rather than by the Augustan ideal of calm detachment. His poetry is personal, intense, and excited. His language is that of the street: slang, profanity, dialect. His poems are frequently dramatic monologues in which an aggrieved suitor addresses his mistress or an injured party pours malediction on his enemy. The reader must envision many of Catullus's poems as little one-act plays, with a persona speaking the lines, a dramatic audience listening to the

Catullus (Library of Congress)

speech, and a particular situation in which these words might be spoken appropriately.

Although the content, topics, and language of Catullus's poems were drawn from the seamy streets of Rome, his poetic forms were not. Catullus studied and imitated the meters of late Greek literature of the Alexandrian school; probably for this reason, he was called in ancient times the "learned" Catullus. The late Greek poets developed complicated metrical patterns which Catullus translated into the Latin language. (This subject is discussed extensively in Merrill's edition of Catullus.)

Catullus was a precursor of the Augustan age, a conveyor of the Alexandrian formal tradition into Latin poetry, with a genius for intense, passionate, personal poetry. Even in translation, he is funny and obscene, furious and touching.

BIOGRAPHY

Very little biographical information about Gaius Valerius Catullus is known with certainty. From references in his poetry and from legend, a series of traditional hypotheses about his life have evolved. Ancient sources indicate that he was born in what is now Verona. His family must have been wealthy and powerful, although he never mentions any family member except his brother. Catullus was probably a younger son who went at an early age to Rome to make his way. He owned a villa at Sirmio in the lake district of northern Italy and another in the Sabine Hills. It appears that he lived a life of ease and culture. The only documented fact about his career is that he traveled to the province of Bythinia on the staff of the Governor Gaius Memmius in about 57 to 56 B.C.E. The likely motive for such a trip would be to earn a fortune, but later unfavorable references in Catullus's poems suggest that the undertaking was not completely successful.

The poems of Catullus are often dramatic, like the sonnets of William Shakespeare: A lover sings the praises of his beloved or heaps scorn on a rival. While it is not accurate to consider such poems as directly autobiographical, it has become customary to assume that they reflect to some degree real happenings in the life of the poet. If the reader considers the poems to be mainly nonfiction, an emotional tale emerges about love and

hate in Rome long ago. The poet falls in love with Lesbia, a married woman. She toys with his affection and keeps him in torment. She is unfaithful to him with many men. The poet attacks his rivals viciously in words, but he is nevertheless enslaved by Lesbia's charms, until he flees from Rome on his venture to Bythinia to escape her treacheries.

Modern scholars suggest that Lesbia is a pseudonym for a real woman, Clodia, the sister of Publius Clodius Pulcher and the wife of Q. Caecillius Metellus Celer, who was consul in the year 60 B.C.E. This hypothesis seems to be supported by several references in the poems and suggests that Catullus really was involved in an affair that followed the outlines suggested in his poems. Sophisticated readers of poetry, however, will hesitate to accept such easy equations of art and reality. It is equally possible that Lesbia and her lover are both merely fictional inventions of a clever writer.

Whether Catullus left Rome to forget his cruel beloved or to get rich, he apparently was unhappy with his experience as a follower of the Governor Memmius, who became an object of attack in several of Catullus's later poems. While in Bythinia, he wrote a tribute to his dead brother's grave, and he celebrated in poetry his own return to Italy. In Rome once again, the poet celebrated a new beloved, the boy Juventius, who also proved unfaithful. Catullus viciously attacked a character whom he called "Mentula" (the word literally means "penis" in Latin) thought to be based on Caesar's associate, Mamurra. Although critical of Caesar, Catullus eventually was reconciled with the Caesarian political group. He died in his thirtieth year.

It was probably an admirer who collected Catullus's poems in a book after his death and divided it into three parts according to the verse forms of the poems. The first group includes sixty poems on various themes, all in iambic or logaoedic rhythm. The middle group includes longer poems and begins with three epithalamia. The third group consists of shorter poems in elegiac meter. Gradually, the poems of Catullus fell out of favor, and he became an unknown figure until the fourteenth century when Benvenuto Campesino rediscovered the texts, probably in Verona. From that original, many copies were made, so that the works of Catullus were well-known to the great writers of the Italian Renaissance.

ANALYSIS

Gaius Valerius Catullus was a master of erotic poetry. Modern attitudes toward sexual love derive from conventions of courtship which can be traced back to Catullus. Some of his sexual poems seem wholesome and agreeable to the modern "liberated" reader; others may seem "unnatural" or obscene. In either case, Catullus was one of the first writers to codify a set of conventions for courtship: the blazon or praise of the beloved, the lover's lament at his unfaithful love, the abasement of the lover captivated by his unworthy beloved, the vilification of the rival for the beloved's affection, the antiblazon or enumeration of the beloved's defects, the comparison of married to adulterous love. These topics or themes have become commonplace in Western literature, but Catullus was one of the first to invent and systematically explore them. The 116 poems of Catullus can be grouped into several categories: those celebrating sexual love, those that taunt and insult, travel and locodescriptive verse, and mythological material such as the stories of Theseus and Ariadne, Peleus and Thetis, and Attis. Although these themes overlap, almost all of his verse fits into one or more of these categories.

IN PRAISE OF PHYSICAL LOVE

Examples of his praise for sexual love include poems 5, 7, 8, 51, 70, 86, 87, 109, and others. Poem 5 is rightly famous as the prototype of the address of the lover to his beloved, "gather ye rosebuds while ye may." It is a poem of seduction in which the lover reminds the beloved that life is short, and time is fleeting, and she had better not delay too long in consenting to their union. The lover reminds the beloved that soon they will die and sleep one long eternal night; he asks for a thousand or a hundred thousand kisses. Carried away by the passion of these lines, the reader may fail to notice how contrary this erotic sentiment is to conventional morality. Rather than directing his attention to loftier matters, the lover elevates sexual union to a position of supreme importance. Such an exaltation of love is basic to the courtly tradition which developed later in the Renaissance.

Poem 70 introduces the notion that the beloved is not to be trusted, for lovers' promises are as fleeting as words written in dust or running water. Poem 109 expresses the lover's fervent wish that his beloved speak the truth when she promises to love him. Poem 86 presents a comparison or combat between the beloved Lesbia and another woman called Quintia. The poem is in the form of a blazon and begins by enumerating all of Quintia's outstanding physical features: her complexion, size, and shape. The lover grants that Quintia is physically well made but argues that she lacks personality. Only Lesbia has the inner spark, the charm that can truly be called beautiful. A cruder but nevertheless amusing version of this kind of love poem, sometimes called antiblazon, is poem 43. The lover's rival is called Mentula; Mentula has a girl whom some might call pretty, but the lover systematically examines her nose, feet, eyes, fingers, lips, and tongue, concluding that only a country bumpkin would call such a girl pretty. In every way, Lesbia far surpasses his rival's girl.

To elevate the significance of physical love to that of a religion and to make the beloved a goddess of love turns the lover into a helpless suppliant at the mercy of an unpredictable deity. Poem 8 is the lover's lament. He knows that Lesbia is merely toying with him, and he resolves not to run after her, not to be a foolish slave to desire. The lover rages at his unfaithful mistress—for example, in poems 37 and 58 where he accuses her of becoming a common whore; in poem 38, however, he is begging her to take him back again. Strangely, the worse the beloved treats him, the more the lover desires her. Poem 72 explains that Lesbia's behavior breaks the lover's heart but inflames his lust for her. Catullus encapsulates the lover's lament in a couplet, justly called the best two lines of psychological analysis ever written, poem 85. The lover says that he hates and he loves her. If you ask him why, he cannot explain. He simply feels that he is crucified. The final word, *excrucior*, literally "to be crucified," is particularly well-chosen because the crossed feelings of love and hate catch the lover when they intersect and nail him, as it were, to a cross.

In addition to his passion for the woman Lesbia, Catullus also celebrates a homosexual love for the boy Juventius. The poet's addresses to the boy follow conventions of romantic love similar to those which govern his speeches to Lesbia. Poem 48 celebrates the boy's kisses much as poem 5 does the woman's. Poem 99 tells how the once-sweet kisses of the boy turn bitter because he is unfaithful. Poem 81 mocks the boy for having a new boyfriend, a country hick unworthy of him. Poem 40 threatens a rival who has stolen the affection of the lover's boy. In general, Catullus endorses wine, women (or boys), and song. Poem 27, for example, is a famous drinking song; but, there is always pain close beneath the revelry. Not only does he both love and hate Lesbia, but he is also crucified by conflicting feelings about Rome, about all of his acquaintances, about life in general. He sees the ugliness barely hidden beneath the fashionable woman's makeup, the betrayal lurking behind the hearty greeting of the politicians and lawyers of the capitol, and death everywhere—the death of a pet sparrow, death pursuing golden boys and girls, the death of his beloved brother.

POETIC TAUNTS AND INSULTS

Catullus is also the master of poetic taunts and insults. Seldom has a writer humiliated so many public figures so effectively, so obscenely, so inventively. There are too many poems of this sort to analyze them in detail. Mentula, the supposed rival for Lesbia's favors, heads the list of those in the poet's disfavor. Mentula's virility, wit, poetry, courage, and personal hygiene all come into question. Usually, Catullus uses some common Roman name, the equivalent of English names such as Jimmy or Wayne, as a pseudonym for a historical personage. Modern scholars have spent much effort trying to discover who the characters attacked in the poems really are. No doubt this provided sport for the Roman audience as well, as readers whispered about the true identity of the characters ridiculed or, perhaps, libeled in Catullus's lines.

Sometimes, however, he does not hesitate to name names. Poem 93, for example, is a couplet addressed to Caesar by name, and it says that the poet does not care what the great man thinks. Poem 29 names Mamurra, who was Caesar's prefect in Gaul. The poem accuses Mamurra of looting Gaul for his own profit and refers repeatedly and mockingly to Mamurra as the degenerate descendant of the founding fathers of Rome. After maligning Mamurra's sexual habits and his wasteful financial practices, the poem concludes that men like Mamurra have brought Rome to ruin. It is not necessary to know the exact identity of the unfortunate people who suffered the scathing attacks of Catullus. They are better understood as comic types, like caricatures. As such,

they show the poet's ability to sketch a portrait of human deviance in a few biting lines. Thallus in poem 25 is the softest, most cunning, most delicate homosexual—and he steals personal belongings from the clothing of people at the public baths. Flavius in poem 6 has a new girl who is too spirited for him. Suffenus in poem 22 is the prolific poet who writes and writes, but who never rises above mediocrity. Furius in poem 23 is the poor man who toadies to the rich and powerful, not realizing that he is better off in poverty than he would be as a client. Egnatius in poem 39 is the ingratiating man who always smiles. In a court of law or a business deal, he remains smiling. Catullus speculates obscenely about how Egnatius polishes his shining teeth. Scatology and references to personal uncleanliness abound in these verses—for example, the attack on Rufus in poem 69. Unfaithfulness and lack of decency in small personal dealings also infuriate Catullus, as in poem 77. Sexual behavior is commonly ridiculed—for example, the poems numbered 88 and 91, which accuse Gellius of incest and other unusual practices. Usually these attacks are framed in the most offensive language imaginable, as the attack on Aemillius in poem 97.

TRAVEL AND RURAL LIFE

A number of the poems are about travel and celebrate the Italian rural life. Poem 10 humorously explains that Catullus did not get rich on his trip to Bythinia. Poem 31 celebrates his return from the barbarian province to his beautiful villa in Sirmio. Even in modern times, this lake-dotted area in northern Italy is a delightful place to visit, but the poem by Catullus is not merely a reflection of the real peace of such a landscape. It is an example of the pastoral convention, a celebration of the virtues of the simple life. Not only is the barbarian province of Bythinia contrasted to the homely peace of Sirmio, but the poem also implies that the country life has a simplicity and virtue lacking in the nasty city. Catullus seems to have a contradictory set of attitudes in this regard. In some poems, his worst insult is to accuse someone in Rome of being a hick or a country bumpkin. At other times, the sexual rivalry and power struggles among greedy Romans seem to turn sour, and he longs for the simplicity and honesty of the farm. Poem 44 is an example of this longing for the rural life. Thus, Catullus turns at times to recall the few moments in his life where decency and faithfulness have appeared—for example, the touching references to his brother's death in poems 65 and 68, and especially the lovely elegy, poem 101.

POEM 64

The most important single poem by Catullus is poem 64, a wedding song or epithalamium for Peleus and Thetis, sometimes called his "little epic." It celebrates the marriage of two sets of mythical characters, Peleus/Thetis and Theseus/Ariadne. The poem actually consists of two legendary stories, one embedded within the other. The outer story concerns the wedding of the man Peleus with the goddess Thetis. According to the myth, from this union was born the great Greek hero Achilles. The inner story concerns Theseus and Ariadne. According to the myth, the island of Crete had exacted a tribute of youths and maidens from Athens who were to be sacrificed to a monster, the Minotaur. Prince Theseus of Athens goes to Crete and, with the help of the Cretan princess Ariadne, slays the Minotaur. He takes Ariadne with him back to Athens but stops along the way at the island of Naxos. There he abandons her and sails to Athens alone.

Ariadne's grief on Naxos is the topic of the embedded story in poem 64. The inner and outer stories are linked together by a clever device. The wedding bed of Peleus and Thetis is decked with an embroidered cloth which depicts the earlier legend of Theseus and Ariadne. As the poet describes the scene of the consummation of the marriage of Peleus and Thetis, he digresses to describe the embroidery, thus juxtaposing and contrasting the two pairs of lovers. Although the language and situation of this poem is much more elegant than the rough "street talk" of the poems concerning Lesbia and of the taunts and insults, there is a certain similarity in subject. The epithalamium celebrates sexual union in extremely frank terms. Both the legend of Peleus and Thetis and that of Ariadne on Naxos involve the mating of a human being with a divinity. Both, therefore, imply that love can elevate man to superhuman states of being.

Both poems also recognize that the joy of eros is all the more keen because it is fleeting and subject to change. The opening lines of poem 64 tell how Thetis, the daughter of Jupiter and princess of the sea, became enamored of Peleus, the mortal prince of Thessaly. Jupi-

ter himself approves of the match. The wedding takes place in Thessaly, and the poet describes the gathering of the guests and the decoration of the house. Among the decorations of the wedding chamber there is a wonderfully designed cloth depicting the abandonment of Ariadne on Naxos by her careless lover, Theseus. About half of the poem, from line 50 to line 266, describes the embroidered scene, contrasting the unhappy love of Ariadne to the happy expectations of Peleus and Thetis on their wedding day. The story begins with a lush description of the aggrieved Ariadne wading in the wake of her departing lover's ship. The poet then digresses to tell how Ariadne came to this sorry situation, how Theseus set out from Athens to slay the Minotaur on Crete and free his people from the annual tribute, how Ariadne helped Theseus slay the Minotaur in its labyrinth and so left Crete with him. Although Ariadne had abandoned her family and friends to follow Theseus, he forgets her and sails away from Naxos. In a long speech, Catullus rehearses a theme common to his Lesbia poems: faithless love. Ariadne cries out her complaint to the faithless Theseus in a brilliant and heart-wrenching dramatic scene, but she realizes that Theseus is so far away that he cannot even hear her.

Ariadne is finally avenged, however. Her complaint echoes to heaven, and Jupiter ordains a terrible revenge. Theseus had promised his father that, if he succeeded in slaying the Minotaur and returned alive from Crete, he would carry new white sails on his return voyage so that his father could see from afar his success; but, if he died in the attempt, the sails of his ship would be black. The gods see to it that Theseus's forgetfulness is total; he not only forgets Ariadne, but he also fails to hoist the new white sails, so that his father, watching from the headland for the return, imagines his son to be dead and commits suicide in despair. Thus, Theseus has cause to grieve for his forgetfulness exactly as Ariadne did. Moreover, the weeping of Ariadne inflames Bacchus, the god of revelry, with love for her. With luxuriant pomp and procession he comes to Naxos and takes Ariadne for his own. This apotheosis of Ariadne through love is depicted on the veil which decks the wedding bed of Peleus and Thetis. In addition to this wonderful fabric, other gifts come to the lovers. The centaur Chiron comes down from the mountains with woodland gifts.

The Naiads, spirits of streams and springs, bring their greenery. Prometheus, too, who gave man fire, is a guest. At the wedding party, the three Fates sing, foretelling that a son will be born to the couple, a son who will be the great Achilles. The poem thus implies that the wedding will benefit all of Greece.

Catullus concludes by observing that the gods were once friends and guests at human events, such as this wedding, long ago. Since those ancient times, however, man has fallen on evil ways—greed, fratricide, incest, lechery of all sorts—and the gods no longer consort familiarly with humankind. This poem of 408 lines is not as massive an accomplishment as the *Aeneid* (c. 29-19 B.C.E.) of Vergil, which is the epitome of epic poetry in Latin. On the other hand, jewel-like perfection and economy characterize the little epic of Catullus, making it a glory of the Latin language.

LEGACY

Catullus is a major poet because he transmitted important features of the literary tradition which he received from earlier classical writers and, also, because he modified tradition and literally invented new styles, themes, and modes of thinking which are still used in modern poetry. The "traditional" Catullus learned from Greek models a number of lyric meters and stanzaic forms. He translated these into Latin, and from his experiments, the later vernacular poets of Europe were able to develop a formal richness in the short poem. He also reworked traditional stories from classical mythology and passed them on, enriched and embroidered more elegantly than they were before passing through his hands. The story of Theseus and Ariadne is ancient and common in classical times, but the modern reader remembers it in the words of Catullus's depiction of Ariadne on Naxos wading after her false lover's departing ship and crying out her grief. If Catullus had done nothing but purvey the poetic forms and stories of Greek culture to modern readers by way of Latin, he would still deserve a major place in literary history. Catullus was more than a merely traditional writer, however. He exhibited a major, original, inventive power in several aspects of his work.

Catullus brought to his poetry an unusual sense of immediate, personal involvement. It is no accident that readers tend to look at his poems as if they were autobiographical. They are written so that it seems certain that they express some lived, deeply felt, personal experience: betrayed love, petty insult, grief at the loss of a brother. Such intense involvement in the poems is created in part by the use of a highly dramatized form of speaking, like the dramatic monologues of Robert Browning. When one reads Catullus, one is compelled to imagine the speaker of the lines as a character in a play. One is forced to construct a persona speaking, and one must imagine the dramatic circumstances under which these words might be uttered. The heightened immediacy of the lines supports Catullus's use of highly colloquial vocabulary and sentence structure. Many students of Latin, approaching Catullus for the first time, are baffled by his language—his use of profanity, slang, neologisms, and sentence fragments. Yet, to base poetry in language as it is really spoken by ordinary men rather than in some artificial "poetic" dialect was a remarkable achievement, well understood by modern writers.

Catullus invented, too, the introverted concentration of his lyric poetry. His poems almost all turn inward on the speaker's own feeling and attitudes. The speaker may be talking about X, but the poem's real focus is on how the speaker feels about X and not on the ostensible subject of the work. When Catullus writes about the Caesarian party, the reader is interested in how Catullus feels, not about what the Caesarians were or what they did. History tells readers the facts; Catullus understood that poetry tells readers how human beings respond to history.

Because Catullus turned inward and attempted to analyze human emotions, he naturally found himself talking mainly about love and hate. His poems externalize feelings, especially erotic feelings. He used traditional forms of poetry to express attitudes seldom defined before. His poetry, for the first time in Western literature, systematically developed the ideas and conventions of courtly love. When his poems were rediscovered in the Renaissance, writers such as Petrarch saw there a prototype for the conventions of courtly love. Contemporary attitudes toward the sexual relationship are so pervasive and powerful that one seldom stops to consider their origins. Turn on the popular radio stations, however, listen to a few songs and ask where these ideas come from: Why is erotic love elevated to such a high place in the contemporary system of values? Why is faithless love lamented so extravagantly? Why is erotic rivalry the source of so much hostility and anxiety? Why is the woman given a dominant position in the relationship, like a goddess giving her favors or denying them? Such modern attitudes toward erotic love were, in many cases, first stated in Catullus, transmitted through the courtly love-poets of Europe to emerge scarcely changed in lyrics today.

Catullus's greatest accomplishment was to express intensely personal feelings in traditional poetic forms. Like all the greatest artists, he united a command of tradition with an individual talent which caused him to change and expand the possibilities he inherited.

BIBLIOGRAPHY

Adler, Eve. *Catullan Self-Revelation.* New York: Arno Press, 1981. Considers the poetry as having two major ends—delight and instruction—and analyzes the formal and rhetorical devices by which Catullus pursues these two goals.

Arkins, Brian. *An Interpretation of the Poems of Catullus.* Lewiston: Edwin Mellen Press, 1999. Surveys Catullus's life and literary influences and offers a reading of his poetry that emphasizes its modernity and accessibility to modern readers.

Dettmer, Helena. *Love by the Numbers: Form and Meaning in the Poetry of Catullus.* New York: Peter Lang, 1997. Offers a reading of Catullus's entire corpus of poetry as a unified body of work organized along thematic, structural, and metrical groupings.

Fitzgerald, William. *Catullan Provocations: Lyric Poetry and the Drama of Position.* Berkeley: University of California Press, 1995. Fitzgerald interprets Catullus's lyrics and emphasizes his manipulation of the reader's point of view. Does not require knowledge of Latin. Includes bibliographic references.

Havelock, Eric Alfred. *The Lyric Genius of Catullus.* New York: Russell & Russell, 1929. A formal and stylistic study of Catullus's poetry and personality, emphasizing the paradoxical blend of emotional sincerity and scholarly sophistication in his work.

Wheeler, Arthur Leslie. *Catullus and the Traditions of Ancient Poetry.* Berkeley: University of California Press, 1934. Approaches Catullus's poetry as a problem in literary history, defining his artistic achievement by locating it within the wider context of ancient Greek and Roman poetry.

Wiseman, T. P. *Catullus and His World: A Reappraisal.* Cambridge University Press, 1985. Includes general chapters introducing the reader to the political and social life of Rome in the first century B.C., which are followed by a contextual reading of Catullus's poetry.

Todd K. Bender;
bibliography updated by William Nelles

CONSTANTINE P. CAVAFY

Konstantionos Petrou Kabaphes
Born: Alexandria, Egypt; April 17, 1863
Died: Alexandria, Egypt; April 29, 1933

PRINCIPAL POETRY

Poiemata, 1935 (Alexander Singopoulos, editor)
The Poems of C. P. Cavafy, 1951
The Complete Poems of Cavafy, 1961
Poiemata, 1963 (George Savidis, editor)
K. P. Kabaphe: Anekdota poiemata, 1968 (Savidis, editor)
Passions and Ancient Days, 1971
Collected Poems, 1975 (Savidis, editor)
Before Time Could Change Them: The Complete Poems of Constantine P. Cavafy, 2001

OTHER LITERARY FORMS

Except for a few essays on literary topics and short notes on language and metrics to be found in his papers, Constantine P. Cavafy did not work in any literary form other than poetry. Greek poet George Seferis, in *On the Greek Style* (1966), quotes Cavafy as having said, near the end of his life, "I am a historical poet. I could never write a novel or a play; but I hear inside me a hundred and twenty-five voices telling me I could write history."

ACHIEVEMENTS

Constantine P. Cavafy did not achieve public acclaim during his lifetime. The fortunes of war, however, marooned two English novelists—E. M. Forster and Lawrence Durrell—in Alexandria during World War I and World War II, respectively. Forster had one of Cavafy's best poems, "The God Abandons Antony," translated and printed in his *Alexandria: A History and Guide* (1922) and spread his name among such literary figures as T. S. Eliot, T. E. Lawrence, and Arnold Toynbee, so that after Forster's stay in Alexandria, Cavafy received many European visitors. Lawrence Durrell modeled aspects of Cavafy in the figures of the brooding old poet of the city and the homosexual physician, Balthazar, important characters in his masterwork *The Alexandria Quartet* (includes *Justine*, 1957; *Balthazar*, 1958; *Mountolive*, 1958; *Clea*, 1960). Thus, the Alexandria which tantalizes the imagination of the modern Western reader is to no small degree the city as imagined by Cavafy.

Cavafy remained almost unknown in Greece until after his death. In 1963, the centenary of his birth was marked by the publication of a collected edition of his works, including both his poetry and volumes of previously unpublished prose and other prose. The 1968 publication of seventy-five previously unpublished poems was the major literary event of the year in Athens.

Adding weight to Cavafy's reputation was W. H. Auden's statement in 1961 (in his introduction to *The Complete Poems of Cavafy*, translated by Rae Dalven) that Cavafy had influenced his writing for more than thirty years. Auden singled out for praise "the most original aspect of [Cavafy's] style, the mixture, both in his vocabulary and his syntax, of demotic and purist Greek," and paid tribute also to Cavafy's rich evocation of Alexandria and of Hellenic culture.

In the early 1880's, when Cavafy began to write, the official language of Greece—the language employed by the government and taught in the schools—was *Katharevousa* or purist Greek, "a language," in the words of Linos Politis in *A History of Modern Greek Literature* (1973), "based on popular speech, but 'corrected' and 'embellished' on the model of the ancient." At the same time, there were in Greece passionate advocates of the demotic or spoken tongue, who believed that it alone should be the language of Greek literature and the Greek state. Although this linguistic controversy persists in Greece even today, modern Greek writers have over-

whelmingly adopted the demotic. The tension between a demotic base and borrowings from purist, classical, and the other evolutionary forms of the language accounts in part for the remarkable vitality of modern Greek poetry—a development in which Cavafy played a significant role. Cavafy himself said, "I have tried to blend the spoken with the written language . . . trembling over every word." The remarkable result was a poetic diction that not only draws on the traditions of Greek from its entire history but also, on occasion, is able to combine phrases and whole lines of ancient Greek with the modern, demotic language and yet remain entirely clear and understandable to any educated Greek reader.

Cavafy's distinctive language can be appreciated only in the original Greek, but even a reader who knows Cavafy's poems in translation can appreciate one of his principal achievements: the creation, in Auden's words, of a unique "tone of voice, a personal speech . . . immediately recognizable." Cavafy's poetic voice represents a "style of deliberately prosaic quality, simple, concentrated, almost dry, economical, unadorned, divested of every element which would cause it to deviate from the strictest austerity—at its best inevitable," as Petroula Ruehlen puts it in *Nine Essays in Modern Literature* (1965). It is above all Cavafy's *voice* that, in translation, has exercised a powerful influence on contemporary American poetry.

BIOGRAPHY

Constantine Peter Cavafy was born Konstantionos Petrou Kabaphes, the youngest and most beloved son of a wealthy Alexandrian merchant; both Cavafy's father and his mother came from prosperous families in Constantinople. By the time of Cavafy's birth, his father's business in cotton, grain, and buffalo hides had benefited from the Crimean War and the family had settled in a luxurious house in the fashionable rue Cherif in Alexandria. The poet's first seven years were spent in a household accustomed to elaborate balls and parties and the company of wealthy business people and professionals of various nationalities. A generous man of European outlook who had lived for some time in England, Cavafy's father saw to it that the children were tended by an English nurse, a French tutor, and Greek servants. Unfortunately, he died in 1870 without leaving the family well provided for; though the family was always "respectable," and though the Cavafy brothers retained the cachet of a wealthy, upper-class milieu, the family fortune was severely reduced.

In 1872, Cavafy's mother, Haricleia, took the family to Liverpool. Because of the economic crisis of 1876 and the three eldest sons' inexperience and ill-advised speculation, the family farm had to be liquidated in 1879, whereupon the Cavafys returned to Alexandria actually impoverished. Cavafy had thus spent seven formative years, from the age of nine to the age of sixteen, in England, where he acquired an excellent facility with the English language and a lifelong love for the works of William Shakespeare, Robert Browning, and Oscar Wilde. For the rest of his life, Cavafy spoke Greek with a slight English accent and often spoke or corresponded in English with his brothers; in the position he held for thirty years immediately under British superiors in the Irrigation Department of the Ministry of Public Works in Alexandria, he was valued for his ability to teach Egyptian employees the English language.

Upon his return to Alexandria in 1879, Cavafy enrolled for three years in a business school, the Hermes Lyceum. In 1882, political and military disturbances by Egyptian nationalists seeking to end foreign rule and expel foreigners led to the bombardment of the city by British warships anchored in the harbor. Along with many other Europeans, the Cavafy family left, this time for Constantinople and the home of Haricleia Cavafy's father, George Photiades, a wealthy diamond merchant. While living in Constantinople from 1882 to 1885, Cavafy wrote his first poetry and had his first homosexual experiences. These two activities were to become the chief concerns of his life. He wrote both prose and poetry in French and English as well as in Greek. It was also during this period in Constantinople that Cavafy first became familiar with demotic Greek.

In 1885, Haricleia Cavafy moved the family back to Alexandria for the last time; Cavafy really never left the city again. He took several trips at odd intervals, once visiting France and England and a number of times journeying across the Mediterranean to Athens, but his attachment to Alexandria was profound. When asked late in his life to move to Athens, Robert Liddell reports Cavafy replied: "Mohammed Aly Square is my aunt. Rue Cherif Pacha is my first cousin and the Rue de Ramleh my second. How can I leave them?" He lived with his mother until her death in 1899, when he was thirty-six, then with his brother Paul, taking in 1907 an apartment on the third floor of 10 Rue Lepsius. This apartment was to remain Cavafy's residence until his death twenty-six years later.

In 1891, the death of Cavafy's second eldest brother led him to seek a permanent position in the Irrigation Department, where he had been working part-time for three years. At the same time, he began a chronological listing of all of his poems to date—a list that shows how many he wrote but did not publish. From 1892, Cavafy's life assumed the routine in which his poetry, work, and personality took their characteristic form. His hours as a bureaucrat were not long, from 8:30 in the morning until 1:30 in the afternoon, but the work was tedious and paid minimally; more often than not, Cavafy came to work as much as an hour late. He was reasonably dutiful, if often too scrupulous about his responsibility for all European correspondence; a "trifle overdeliberate" is the phrase cited in his record for 1913, and his subordinates complained that he was overly strict in requiring fastidiously correct records and translations. Cavafy recognized the cost to his art; Liddell quotes him from 1905: "How often during my work a fine idea comes to me, a rare image, and sudden ready-formed lines, and I'm obliged to leave them, because work can't be put off. Then when I go home and recover a bit, I try to remember them, but they're gone." He never forgot that he was the son of a rich man. Nevertheless, records show that regular increases in pay and annual leave (finally reaching twelve weeks) marked his path to the position of subdirector of his section. He also supplemented his income by speculation on the Egyptian Stock Exchange, occasionally with great success.

Away from his job, Cavafy's life centered on his apartment at 10 rue Lepsius, where friends and literary figures visited, and on his nocturnal activities in the cafés and shady quarters of Alexandria. While still living with his mother, Cavafy had bribed the servants or persuaded his brothers to ruffle up his bed so that it looked as if he had spent the night at home. Then he had to cross from the respectable section of the city where he lived with his mother to the area of taverns, bars, and brothels. Living alone after 1910, he enjoyed greater freedom; the old Greek quarter called Massalia, to which he had moved, gradually deteriorated, so that at some point a brothel occupied the ground floor in his building. Cavafy did not have a single long-standing relationship during his entire life; his closest friends, Pericles Anastassiades (as of 1895) and Alexander Singopoulos (whom he met in 1915), were both considerably younger. He did not dislike or avoid women, however, counting several among his closest friends.

Cavafy never published his most explicitly erotic poetry during his life. It is clear that he suffered some guilt concerning his homosexuality, perhaps in part because of his genteel background and his desire to maintain a certain social standing. A secretive man, an engaging poseur, Cavafy was extremely vain, about both his looks (cultivating his boyish demeanor past middle age) and his literary reputation, which he often urged others to spread, but he was also a lively and informed conversationalist. His method of distributing his poetry, with its calculated air of mystery, suggests the mixture of arrogance and reticence which characterized both his life and his work. Cavafy died on his seventieth birthday from cancer of the larynx and was buried in the family plot in the Greek cemetery in Alexandria.

Analysis

To enter the world of Constantine P. Cavafy's poetry is to embrace simultaneously the significance of historical, artistic, and erotic experience, to enter a world with an "atmosphere of refinement and passion . . . just perceptible pathos . . . reserve . . . mystery" in Marguerite Yourcenar's memorable phrasing. This is possible because, as C. M. Bowra points out,

Cavafy risks no stunning effects. His is a great poetry strictly truthful and circumstantial and realistic, concerned above all to present human nature as it is and to make its presentation entirely convincing not merely to the imagination but to the intelligence. This quiet air, which looks so easy to maintain and must have in fact demanded the greatest self-control and critical judgment, is Cavafy's special triumph.

George Seferis, an important younger contemporary of Cavafy, explains how Cavafy's poetic language makes this possible: "Cavafy stands at the boundary where poetry strips herself in order to become prose." Because he is an "unpoetic" poet, his poetry is both easy and difficult to translate—that is, he rarely employs such devices as internal rhyme, alliteration, simile, or metaphor. Instead, he employs unadorned, factual description. His preference after 1900 for free verse reinforced the deliberately prosaic quality of his poetry.

Cavafy himself classified his poetry thematically into three categories: the historical, the artistic or philosophical, and the erotic, though it is essential to remember that these three kinds of experience often appear in the same poem. Many other divisions are also possible: sequences of poems sharing similar themes, drawn from the same historical period or incident, using the same real or similar imaginary characters. The sum of Cavafy's experience, however, as well as his own statement, make the poet's own classification illuminating.

Cavafy identified both one of the historical periods most important for his work and his own method of using history when he said that the Byzantine historians "cultivated a kind of history that has never been written before or since. They wrote history dramatically." These historians created a sense of the living presence of figures and events, transcending time and assuming eternal significance, just as the Byzantine mosaic artist represented life in timeless, two-dimensional forms. To read about the Alexandrians in 100 B.C.E. today, for example, is to compress the two thousand years between the two epochs and to share the experience of both periods simultaneously. Cavafy's method of dramatizing history is marvelously economical; he need not draw explicit comparisons between the past and present, for he makes the past present by depicting people and events of universal human significance.

"Waiting for the Barbarians"

In "Waiting for the Barbarians," for example, one of Cavafy's best-known poems, two imaginary citizens in an unspecified Roman city discuss events in the local senate on a day when the barbarians are coming to take power. No speeches are being given, no laws are being passed. All the political leaders have adorned themselves in their finest attire; bedecked with jewels, they have prepared a scroll to give to the barbarians. The poem is in the form of a dialogue between the first speaker, who asks naïve questions, and the second, apparently as worldly-wise as the first is unknowing, who answers in a dry, flat tone, matter-of-fact to the point of testiness, as if speaking to a child. Lacking any description of events in the third person, the poem creates a sense of live observation with its dialogic form. The naïve questioner is as awed by the splendid throne, garments, and jewelry he asks about as the seemingly more knowing speaker is unimpressed, but the poem's penetrating irony is that both are blind to the truth of their corruption—the first in refusing to see it, as his repeated "why" shows, the second in accepting it so readily with a self-conscious air of world-weary sophistication. Cavafy thus implies that the final truth of a historical situation can never be known, creating a double irony for the reader: The truth is that the truth cannot be known. Nevertheless, on the surface, the poem merely records a simple conversation.

"EXILES"

The dialogue is not as common a form in Cavafy's poetry as the dramatic monologue, which offers him, in Yourcenar's words, "the possibilities of *acting* in every sense of the word . . . to have his own emotions confirmed by another mouth." Two such dramatic monologues are "Exiles," in which the speaker accepts the surface of political or historical events with the culpable naïveté of the questioner in "Waiting for the Barbarians," and "Phihellene," in which the speaker is another self-deluded sophisticate.

Exiled to Alexandria by political events in Constantinople in the ninth century, the speaker of "Exiles" is overly certain that he and his fellow exiles will be able to overthrow the Macedonian usurper Basil, who, in reality, ruled for twenty-two years after killing his co-emperor, Michael III. The activities of the exiles are a kind of game: Their use of fictitious names and their superficial enthusiasm in studying literature both suggest their immaturity. Their confidence that they will overthrow Basil is clearly unfounded, and much of the irony of the poem derives from the speaker's complacency, from his tone of voice.

"PHIHELLENE"

Quite different is the cutting, ironic realism of the speaker of "Phihellene," who thinks he knows all the world's tricks. The speaker is the insignificant monarch of an unspecified territory on the eastern fringe of the Roman Empire; the poem consists of his instructions to a subordinate concerning a coin that is to be minted in his honor. The inscription which will accompany his image on the coin, he specifies, should not be "excessive or pompous—/ we don't want the proconsul to take it the wrong way;/ he's always smelling things out and reporting back to Rome—/ but of course giving me due honor." For the obverse of the coin, he suggests a depiction of a "good-looking" discus-thrower, but above all ("for God's sake," he urges, "don't let them forget"), he is concerned that the inscription testify to his appreciation of Hellenic culture—"that after 'King' and 'Savior,'/ they add 'Phihellene' in elegant characters." The central irony of the poem is the consuming desire of this petty monarch to be celebrated as a man of culture, a desire that has its counterpart in the cultural pretensions of many twentieth century dictators.

HISTORICAL AND POLITICAL PERSPECTIVES

In several poems on Mark Anthony, Cavafy further manipulates dramatic situation and point of view to present the unusual perspectives on historical figures for which his poetry is noted. The speaker of "In a Township of Asia Minor" has just dictated a lavishly flattering proclamation in honor of Anthony's anticipated victory at Actium. Learning that Octavius has defeated Anthony, the speaker merely instructs his amanuensis to substitute Octavius's name for Anthony's, adding "It all fits brilliantly." In "Alexandrian Kings" and "In Alexandria, 31 B.C.E.," Cavafy also shows the superficiality and triviality of politics, here in the third person. The Alexandrians, faced with the parade of Cleopatra's children, who all receive important titles, "knew of course what all this was worth,/ what empty words they really were, these kingships." Just as calmly, they allow a peddler from a nearby village to sell his perfumes for the celebration of Anthony's triumph because "someone tosses him the huge palace lie:/ that Antony is winning in Greece" ("In Alexandria, 31 B.C.E.").

In "The God Abandons Antony," Cavafy uses the second person to give Anthony advice. Whether the speaker lives in Anthony's or Cavafy's time does not matter; he tells Anthony right to his face to accept courageously his loss of Alexandria. Anthony should not mourn his luck or "say/ it was a dream"; rather, he should "go firmly to the window/ and listen with deep emotion" to the city's "exquisite music," confirming the city's delights and his pleasure in them. Here, Cavafy speaks in the poetic voice of an Alexandrian who has dignity, confidence, and self-knowledge.

ARTISTIC PROCESS AS THEME

In the second major category of his poems, Cavafy shows artists at work and presents some of his ideas on the artistic process. Although Cavafy cannot automatically be identified with the speakers of these poems, it is clear that many of them do, in fact, express his attitude toward his art. The need for craftsmanship and the relationship between art and reality are recurring themes in this group of poems.

Two poems concerning the relationship between art and life are "I've Brought to Art" and "Melancholy of Jason Kleander, Poet in Kommagini, C.E. 595." In the first poem, the poet says he has brought life to art, "desires and sensations . . ./ indistinct memories/ of unfulfilled love affairs," and art has known how "to shape forms of Beauty,/ almost imperceptibly completing life,/ blending impressions, blending day with day." In the second, in the voice of the poet Jason Kleander, he says that art has "a kind of knowledge about drugs:/ certain sedatives, in Language and Imagination," which relieve the pain of the "wound from a merciless knife" that age inflicts.

In many of the poems in this group, Cavafy reveals the sense of secrecy and isolation underlying his art. The first-person speaker in "Hidden Things" says he will be understood only "From my most unnoticed actions,/ my most veiled writing," but that "Later, in a more perfect society,/ someone else made just like me/ is certain to appear and act freely." "Walls," written as early as 1896 and printed as the first poem by Keeley and Sherrard in the authoritative *C. P. Cavafy: Collected Poems*, indicates just how isolated Cavafy may have felt. His oppressors, identified only as "they," have built walls around him: "But I never heard the builders, not a sound./ Imperceptibly they've closed me off from the outside world." In "The First Step," however, another early poem, he speaks of the necessary difficulty of art: Theocritos rebukes a young poet who says that he has "been writing for two years/ and . . . [has] composed

only one idyll"; even the artist who has completed only one work is "above the ordinary world/ . . . a member of the city of ideas." Here, the artist's isolation from the "ordinary world" becomes a badge of pride.

THE EROTIC POEMS

The private world of Cavafy's art is nowhere seen more clearly than in the third division of his work, the erotic poems, the most explicit of which he never published himself. Cavafy perhaps believed that he could publish "Pictured" and "When They Come Alive" within three years of their composition because both justify imaginary erotic experience by the art which it helps to create and nurture. In "Pictured," a writer, discouraged by the slow progress of his work, gazes at a picture of "a handsome boy/ . . . lying down close to a spring." The picture revives the poet's inspiration: "I sit and gaze like this for a long time,/ recovering through art from the effort of creating it." Though it could be argued that there is little art in the picture, the image of the youth has nevertheless inspired the very poem which describes it. "When They Come Alive" is addressed to an unidentified poet (perhaps Cavafy, addressing himself?); the poem begins: "Try to keep them, poet,/ those erotic visions of yours,/ . . . Put them, half-hidden, in your lines." The poem concludes by urging the conscious cultivation of such erotic fantasies.

It is interesting to compare these two poems with another erotic poem "At the Theatre," written before them but never published in Cavafy's lifetime. Here, erotic reverie is not justified as a stimulus to artistic creation but is rather celebrated for its own sake. Addressed to a young man whose "strange beauty" and "decadent youthfulness" have aroused the speaker's "mind and body," the poem concludes: "in my imagination I kept picturing you/ the way they'd talked about you that afternoon." In "Half an Hour," another poem never published by Cavafy, the speaker recounts a "totally erotic" half hour at a bar in which the sight of "your lips . . . your body near me" were all his imagination needed. As the poet says, "we who serve Art,/ sometimes with the mind's intensity/ can create pleasure that seems almost physical"—as strong a statement of the power of imagination as could be asked for.

Another poem unpublished during Cavafy's lifetime, "And I Lounged and Lay on Their Beds," again justifies debauchery for the sake of art. The poet says that "When I went to that house of pleasure/ I didn't stay in the front rooms where they celebrate,/ with some decorum, the accepted modes of love"; instead, in "the secret rooms," he "lounged and lay on their beds"—a line more suggestive than any fuller description of the experience would be. It was a consummate artistic touch to begin the title with "And," here deliberately ambiguous: It may suggest that much more took place than is explicitly described in the title. In Cavafy's poetry, all experience takes on the sacred value of ancient and mysterious temple rites.

A final poem, "Craftsmen of Wine Bowls," serves to show how Cavafy combined erotic, artistic, and philosophical themes in a single poem. In a dramatic monologue, a silversmith describes how his memory, which he begged to help him, enabled him to see "the young face I loved appear the way it was"—a difficult achievement, because "some fifteen years have gone by since the day/ he died as a soldier in the defeat at Magnesia." Magnesia was the battle that established Rome's supremacy in the Hellenized East; thus, the trouble the silversmith takes to commemorate his fallen love seems justified by the nobility of the soldier's cause. Carved on what is only a small bowl, the figure is of a "beautiful young man,/ naked, erotic, one leg still dangling/ in the water," an appropriate image for Cavafy's delicate, refined, and passionate art.

BIBLIOGRAPHY

Anton, John P. *The Poetry and Poetics of Constantine P. Cavafy: Aesthetic Visions of Sensual Reality*. Newark, N.J.: Gordon & Breach Science, 1995. Discusses Cavafy's early development and the creation of his own original poetic voice. Includes autobiographical elements and background of ancient Alexandria as a way to further the understanding of the poetry.

Jusdanis, Gregory. *The Poetics of Cavafy: Textuality, Eroticism, History*. Princeton, N.J.: Princeton University Press, 1987. Discusses Cavafy's conception of the poet; his conception of his audience; his formalistic concerns, especially within the context of the redemptive powers of art; and his language and textuality. Explores Cavafy's affiliations with modernism and Romanticism, and his poetics and poetic concerns, especially the role of the poet and the value of art.

Keeley, Edmund. *Cavafy's Alexandria*. Princeton, N.J.: Princeton University Press, 1996. Important study of Cavafy's deployment of the city of Alexandria in his poetry, which demonstrates that from 1911 to 1921, Cavafy developed his own imaginative version of his home city Alexandria. Suggests Cavafy's image of Alexandria is a various one, including visions of Alexandria as a contemporary homoerotic Sensual City, a Metaphoric City, and a Mythical, Hellenistic City.

Liddell, Robert. *Cavafy: A Biography*. 1974. Reprint. London: Gerald Duckworth & Co., 2001. Gracefully written and appreciative biography of Cavafy and an important resource for all Cavafy scholars. Discusses Cavafy's family background, his early years, his relationship with his mother, his life in Alexandria, his homosexuality, his poetry, and his last years. Numerous illustrations and a bibliography.

John M. Lee;
bibliography updated by Margaret Boe Birns

GUIDO CAVALCANTI

Born: Florence, Italy; c. 1259
Died: Florence, Italy; August 27 or 28, 1300

PRINCIPAL POETRY
Le rime, 1527
The Sonnets and Ballate of Guido Cavalcanti, 1912
   (Ezra Pound, translator)
The Complete Poems, 1992

OTHER LITERARY FORMS
   Guido Cavalcanti is remembered only for his poetry.

ACHIEVEMENTS
   The extant poems of Guido Cavalcanti number fewer than threescore; when taken together, however, they are compelling evidence that he was one of the finest Italian

poets of his age. Ezra Pound, Cavalcanti's translator into English, even exalted him above Dante, noting in 1929 that "Dante is less in advance of his time than Guido Cavalcanti." While Pound's enthusiasm for Cavalcanti was perhaps excessive, there is little doubt that, except for Dante, Cavalcanti was the most outstanding member of the famous "school" of *il dolce stil nuovo* (the sweet new style). Although some critics question the existence of such a school in late thirteenth century Italy, it is generally conceded that a number of poets of the period constituted an informal group defined by common linguistic and thematic concerns. In addition to Dante and Cavalcanti, this group included Guido Guinizzelli, the founder of the school, and several writers of love lyrics: Lapo Gianni, Gianni degli Alfani, Dino Frescobaldi, and Cino da Pistoia.

The major themes of *il dolce stil nuovo* are outlined in Guinizzelli's seminal canzone "Al cor gentil ripara sempre amore" ("To the Noble Heart Love Always Returns"). Foremost is a new concept of nobility, which is no longer tied to birth or social rank but rather to spiritual perfection or moral worth. Second is the identification of love with the noble heart, meaning that love is reserved for the heart of a truly noble soul (as defined above) and that the noble heart is likewise reserved for love. Last is the theme of the spiritualization of woman. Since women inspire love, and love in turn is the cause and product of a noble heart, women may prove to be instruments of moral perfection. Every lady is a potential *angelicata crïatura* (angelic creature), to use Cavalcanti's phrase and to employ terminology characteristic of the *stilnovisti*.

The phrase "the sweet new style" derives from *Purgatorio* (*Purgatory*) in Dante's *La divina commedia* (c. 1320; *The Divine Comedy*). It is Bonagiunta Orbicciani da Lucca's term for the poetics espoused by Dante, Cavalcanti, and several of their contemporaries. The "sweetness" of the new style refers primarily to the gentleness of the subject matter (love), the purity of the language (vernacular Italian), and the graciousness of the chosen poetic rhythms (implying an avoidance, for example, of harsh rhymes). The "newness" derives from the originality of the poets' inspiration—that is, an inner, emotional need to write verse as opposed to a purely intellectual decision to compose—and from

the abundance of new expressions, rather than stereotypical phrases, designed to communicate the psychological state of the poet. Cavalcanti's careful depiction of the various states of his emotions, such as self-pity and bewilderment, is noteworthy for its innovative departure from timeworn clichés. An even more important achievement, however, was the remarkable influence Cavalcanti exerted on his onetime friend Dante, who early in his career referred to Cavalcanti as his *primo amico*, or "first friend," and to whom he dedicated *La vita nuova* (c. 1292). It was Cavalcanti who encouraged Dante to write his poetry in the vernacular instead of in Latin; Dante's decision to follow his friend's advice changed forever the course of Italian poetry.

BIOGRAPHY

Guido Cavalcanti was born in Florence, Italy, a few years prior to Dante's birth. The exact year of Cavalcanti's birth has never been established. While some have placed it as early as 1240, Natalino Sapegno and many others believe that the poet was born just before 1260. His father was Cavalcante de' Cavalcanti, a descendant of Guelph merchants and the same figure who appears next to the Ghibelline Farinata degli Uberti in one of the burning tombs of the heretics in the *Inferno*. Dante's treatment of Cavalcanti's father and father-in-law in this famous episode has led to much speculation about Cavalcanti's own philosophical and religious beliefs and was in part responsible for the depiction of Cavalcanti as a heretic in various stories by Giovanni Boccaccio and others. What is known of Cavalcanti's life comes in large part from the contemporary chronicles of Filippo Villani and Dino Compagni. At an early age, Cavalcanti was betrothed by his father to Beatrice (Bice) degli Uberti, daughter of Farinata. This was essentially a political marriage, one designed, like so many of the time, to put an end to the internecine wars between the Guelphs and the Ghibellines, who supported the papacy and the emperor respectively. Cavalcanti was among the Guelph representatives at the peace negotiations held by Cardinal Latino in 1280; he took part in the general council of the commune in 1284, together with Compagni and Brunetto Latini, and his friendship with Dante dates from this period. He was a fierce adversary of Corso Donati, leader of the Black Guelphs. Because of his hatred for Donati, he joined the opposing White Guelph faction. His allegiance to that faction led to his exile in Sarzana, Italy, on June 24, 1300. It was on that date that the priors of Florence, of which Dante was one, attempted to resolve the city's political strife by banishing the leaders of both factions. While banished, Cavalcanti contracted malaria. Although he was recalled to Florence soon thereafter, he never recovered, and he died in his native city on August 27 or 28 of the same year. His death was recorded on August 29, 1300, in the register of the dead in the Cathedral of Santa Reparata.

These meager facts about Cavalcanti's life and death shed little light on the poet's personality, which is largely shrouded in legend. Perhaps because Dante attributes *disdegno* (disdain) to him in a verse of the previously cited episode in the *Inferno*, other authors have also characterized Cavalcanti as haughty, aristocratic, and solitary. Dante's portrayal of his supposedly best friend as disdainful has led many to conclude that their friendship sharply diminished at some point during their later years. Some speculate that this happened because of conflicts over literary values, with Dante preeminently interested in ethical understanding and Cavalcanti in aristocratic expression. Others argue that the differences in their perception of love formed the basis for the breakdown of their friendship. A disagreement over political matters is yet another possible explanation, although both Dante and Cavalcanti were White Guelphs, and Dante's permanent exile followed Cavalcanti's temporary exile by only a year or so. Whatever the case, Compagni describes Cavalcanti as a "noble knight" and as "courteous and bold" but also as "disdainful and solitary and devoted to study." Villani writes that the poet was a "philosopher of antiquity, not a little esteemed and honored for his dignity." It is Villani also who outlines the rancor and bitterness that Cavalcanti felt toward Donati, who evidently attempted to assassinate Cavalcanti as he made a pilgrimage to Santiago de Compostela. Boccaccio, in his commentary on the *Inferno*, speaks of Cavalcanti as a "most well-bred man and wealthy and of a lofty intellect." Regardless of who paints the portrait, Cavalcanti always appears as intelligent but a man apart, a solitary person destined to exile by his temperament if not by his politics.

ANALYSIS

Guido Cavalcanti's poetry, like that of other *stilnovisti*, may be viewed, in part, as a reaction to the poetry of Guittone d'Arezzo and his followers. Guittone's mid-thirteenth century poetry was largely imitative of the Provençal tradition: Hermetic in nature, it also emphasized rhetorical, metrical, and verbal complexities. Poets of "the sweet new style," on the other hand, deemphasized technical elements so that aspects such as meter and rhyme were generally subservient to meaning. Also, whereas Guittonian poetry covered a wide range of subjects, Guinizzelli and his disciples focused almost entirely on love and its effects. Cavalcanti, however, should not be seen as a mere conformist to Guinizzelli's dicta, for Cavalcanti in turn distinguished himself from many of his own school. In his concentration on love's psychology, he was philosophically more sophisticated than all other *stilnovisti* except Dante. He introduced, for example, the concept of *spiriti* (spirits) into his poetry in order to dramatize the conflicting emotions and behaviors that love elicits. The term "spirit" is a technical term of Scholasticism; it refers, according to Albertus Magnus, to the "instrument of the soul" or the "vehicle of life." Spirits represent the essence of life. They shine in the eyes of the beloved and console the heart of the lover. They are forced to flee, however, when love invades. Their flight results in man's metaphorical death. It is not surprising, then, that closely related to the theme of spirits in Cavalcanti's poems is the theme of death.

LYRICAL WORKS

If one facet of Cavalcanti's poetry may be characterized as highly philosophical, the other can be described only as profoundly lyrical. The preoccupation with love and death, for example, results in a melancholy portrayal of the poet's mercurial emotions: Happiness is poignantly juxtaposed to sadness. Tears and sighs become appropriate symbols of the persona's ever-changing state of being because they can stand either for joy or sorrow, pleasure or pain. Love is always the culprit that renders the lover defenseless, a helpless observer. Love causes both agony and ecstasy; eventually, it generates a deep-seated desire for release via death. The poet's sense of helplessness before such an all-powerful conqueror is reflected in the presentation of the lover as spectator.

This distancing technique leads to a highly dramatic tension and a beautiful lyric expression. It allows the poet to observe and record the effects of love but does not permit him to intervene.

SONNETS

Cavalcanti's known works include thirty-six sonnets, eleven ballads, two canzones, two isolated stanzas, and one motet. In addition, two ballads of questionable authenticity are occasionally attributed to him. The sonnets, because of their large number, seem to represent the poet's preferred form. The major theme of most of the sonnets relates, not unexpectedly, to the pain and weakness that love inflicts on the lover. Love, however, is not the only argument in the compositions. The sonnets of correspondence, for example, are the most important in the collection from a historical perspective, and they show the range of topics covered. These sonnets were dedicated or written to other men, including the poets Dante, Alfani, Guittone d'Arezzo, Guido Orlandi, and a certain Bernardo da Bologna (about whom very little is known).

The five sonnets addressed to Dante are either responses to rhymes on love by Dante or words of friendly encouragement. "Vedeste, al mio parere, onne valore" ("You Saw, in My Opinion, Every Valor") is a reply to Dante's famous call to love's faithful, "A ciascun' alma presa e gentil core" ("To Every Captured Soul and Noble Heart"). On the other hand, one sonnet to Orlandi, "Di vil matera mi conven parlare" ("Of a Vile Matter I Must Speak"), constitutes a rather caustic personal attack. Another sonnet, addressed to Guittone and entitled "Da più a uno face un sollegismo" ("From Many to One Makes a Syllogism"), falls in the tradition of the harsh literary criticism of Guittone also found in Dante's writings. A sonnet to Nerone Cavalcanti, "Novelle ti so dire, odi, Nerone" ("News I Know to Tell You, So Hear, Nerone"), testifies to the fierce fight between the Cavalcanti and Buondelmonti families.

BALLADS

In the ballads, one finds themes such as that of exile in "Perch'io non spero di tornar giammai" ("Because I Hope Not Ever to Return") and of country delights in "In un boschetto trova' pasturella" ("In a Woods I Found a Shepherdess"). As noted earlier, the theme of death often accompanies or weaves through the prevailing theme of love. This is seen in the ballad "Quando di morte mi conven trar vita" ("When I Must Take Life from Death"). On the poet's pilgrimage to Santiago de Compostela, he stops in Toulouse. There, in the Church of the Daurade, he imagines an encounter with Mandetta, a beautiful woman recalled in the ballad "Era in penser d'amor quand'io trovai" ("I Was Thinking of Love When I Found"). The beauty of Mandetta is also described in the sonnet "Una giovane donna di Tolosa" ("A Young Woman of Toulouse"). The young woman reminds him of his faraway lady, whom Cavalcanti never mentions by name in his poetry. Dante, however, refers to her as Vanna, short for Giovanna, and states in *La vita nuova* that she was also known, because of her beauty, as Primavera, or Springtime.

"MY LADY ASKS ME"

The poet's most famous poem, which is also his most difficult, is neither a sonnet nor a ballad. Perhaps the most-discussed canzone in all of Italian literature, "Donna me prega" ("My Lady Asks Me"), a poem of seventy-five lines, has been described by John Colaneri as "an intellectual, philosophical, and somewhat obscure exposition of the essence of love." Most scholars would agree with this description, especially the reference to the poem's obscurity. Interpretations of the work differ widely, drawing variously on Arab mysticism, Averroist thought, Arab-Christian Platonism, Thomist philosophy, and neo-Aristotelianism.

From a technical viewpoint, "My Lady Asks Me" is a virtuoso performance, offering unequivocal proof of the poet's exceptional rhyming ability. The poem is meant to be a treatise on the philosophy of love as well as a highly lyrical composition, however, and in the canzone's opening stanza, Cavalcanti raises the following questions: Where does love exist? Who creates it? What is its virtue, its power, and its essence? The answers to these queries are contained in the remainder of the poem but in a rather complicated philosophical knot.

In most of his poetry, Cavalcanti has a great desire to render visible that within man which is invisible, such as the movements of the human soul. The poet transforms these actions into images of real beings. Thus, "spirits" (as the term was used in Scholastic philosophy, to designate the vital faculties of man) were introduced into love poetry. All of the *stilnovisti* made use of them for the purpose of artistic representation, but it was principally with Cavalcanti that the systematization of the spirits took place. Indeed, it was primarily because of Cavalcanti that spirits became an integral part of the literary expression of the amorous theme and that they remained there for centuries.

BIBLIOGRAPHY

Dronke, Peter. *Medieval Latin and the Rise of European Love Lyric.* 2d ed. New York: Oxford University Press, 1968. In the chapter on Cavalcanti, Dronke depicts the poet as a master of *stilnovisti* poets. He briefly examines *Canzone* in light of contemporary lyric poetry and Scholastic philosophy.

Nelson, Lowry. "Cavalcanti's Centrality in Early Vernacular Poetry." In *Poetic Configurations.* University Park: Pennsylvania State University Press, 1992. This short overview places Cavalcanti's work in his own cultural and intellectual contexts and discusses his influence on poets from Dante to Ezra Pound.

Pound, Ezra. *Literary Essays of Ezra Pound.* London: Faber and Faber, 1954. Pound's classic essay "Cavalcanti" offers his view of the poet who influenced him deeply early in his career. He has a scholar's eye as well, for his analysis of "Donna mi prega" is thorough in both senses.

Shaw, J. E. *Guido Cavalcanti's Theory of Love: The "Canzone d'Amore" and Other Related Problems.* Toronto: University of Toronto Press, 1949. Shaw's close commentary precedes his own translation of the work. His appendix is a discussion of critical commentaries from 1327 to 1940.

Wilhelm, James J. *Dante and Pound: The Epic of Judgment.* Orono: University of Maine Press, 1974. On Cavalcanti, who influenced both great poets, see chapters 4 and 5. Chapter 4 details Cavalcanti's influence on Dante and Dante's reaction to Cavalacanti, especially as registered in *Inferno.* Chapter 5 explores Pound's critical attitude toward Cavalcanti and how this differed from his poetic use of him.

Madison U. Sowell;
bibliography updated by Joseph P. Byrne

PAUL CELAN

Paul Antschel

Born: Czernowitz, Romania; November 23, 1920
Died: Paris, France; April, 1970

PRINCIPAL POETRY

Der Sand aus den Urnen, 1948
Mohn und Gedächtnis, 1952
Von Schwelle zu Schwelle, 1955
Gedichte: Eine Auswahl, 1959
Sprachgitter, 1959 (*Speech-Grille*, 1971)
Die Niemandsrose, 1963
Gedichte, 1966
Atemwende, 1967 (*Breathturn*, 1995)
Ausgewählte Gedichte: Zwei Reden, 1968
Fadensonnen, 1968 (*Threadsuns*, 2000)
Lichtzwang, 1970
Schneepart, 1971
Speech-Grille and Selected Poems, 1971
Nineteen Poems, 1972
Selected Poems, 1972
Gedichte: In zwei Bänden, 1975 (2 volumes)
Zeitgehöft: Späte Gedichte aus dem Nachlass, 1976
Paul Celan: Poems, 1980 (rev. as *Poems of Paul Celan*, 1988)
Gedichte: 1938-1944, 1985
Sixty-five Poems, 1985
Last Poems, 1986
Das Frühwerk, 1989
Gesammelte Werke in sieben Bänden, 2000 (7 volumes)
Glottal Stop: 101 Poems, 2000

OTHER LITERARY FORMS

Paul Celan's literary reputation rests exclusively on his poetry. His only piece of prose fiction, if indeed it can be so described, is "Gespräch im Gebirg" (1959), a very short autobiographical story with a religious theme. Celan also wrote an introductory essay for a book containing works by the painter Edgar Jené; this essay, entitled *Edgar Jené und der Traum vom Traume*, (1948; *Edgar Jené and the Dream About the Dream*, 1986), is an important early statement of Celan's aesthetic theory. Another, more oblique, statement of Celan's poetic theory is contained in his famous speech, "Der Meridian" (1960), given on his acceptance of the prestigious Georg Büchner Prize. (An English translation of this speech, "The Meridian," is available in the Winter, 1978, issue of *Chicago Review*.)

ACHIEVEMENTS

Paul Celan is considered an "inaccessible" poet by many critics and readers. This judgment, prompted by the difficulties Celan's poetry poses for would-be interpreters seeking traditional exegesis, is reinforced by the fact that Celan occupies an isolated position in modern German poetry. Sometimes aligned with Nelly Sachs, Ernst Meister, and the German Surrealists, Celan's work nevertheless stands apart from that of his contemporaries. A Jew whose outlook was shaped by his early experiences in Nazi-occupied Romania, Celan grew up virtually trilingual. The horror of his realization that he was, in spite of his childhood experiences and his later residence in France, a German poet was surely responsible in part for his almost obsessive concern with the possibilities and the limits of his poetic language. Celan's literary ancestors are Friedrich Hölderlin, Arthur Rimbaud, Stéphane Mallarmé, Rainer Maria Rilke, and the German Expressionists, but even in his early poems his position as an outsider is manifest. Celan's poems, called hermetic by some critics because of their resistance to traditional interpretation, can be viewed sometimes as intense and cryptic accounts of personal experience, sometimes as religious-philosophical discussions of Judaism, its tradition and its relation to Christianity. Many of his poems concern themselves with linguistic and poetic theory to the point where they cease to be poems in the traditional sense, losing all contact with the world of physical phenomena and turning into pure language, existing only for themselves. Such "pure" poems, increasingly frequent in Celan's later works, are largely responsible for the charge of inaccessibility which has been laid against him. Here the reader is faced with having to leave the dimension of conventional language use, where the poet uses language to communicate with his audience about subjects such as death or nature, and is forced to enter the dimension of metalanguage, as Harald Weinrich calls it, where language is used to discuss only language—that is, the *word* "death," and not death itself.

Paul Celan (© A. van Mangoldt)

Such poems are accessible only to readers who share with the poet the basic premises of an essentially linguistic poetic theory.

In spite of all this, much of Celan's poetry can be made accessible to the reader through focus on the personal elements in some poems, the Judaic themes in others, and by pointing out the biblical and literary references in yet another group.

BIOGRAPHY

Paul Celan was born Paul Ancel, or Antschel, the only child of Jewish parents, in Czernowitz, Romania (later Chernovtsy, U.S.S.R.), in Bukovina, situated in the foothills of the Carpathian Mountains in what is today northern Romania. This region had been under Austrian rule and thus contained a sizable German-speaking minority along with a mix of other nationalities and ethnic groups. In 1918, just two years before Celan's birth, following the collapse of the Austro-Hungarian Empire, Bukovina became part of Romania. Thus, Celan was reared in a region of great cultural and linguistic diversity, the tensions of which energized his poetry.

Little is known of Celan's early childhood, but he appears to have had a very close relationship with his mother and a less satisfying relationship with his father. Positive references to his mother abound in his poems, whereas his father is hardly mentioned. After receiving his high school diploma, the young Celan went to study medicine in France in 1938, but the war forced his return in the following year to Czernowitz, where he turned to the study of Romance languages and literature at the local university. In 1940, his hometown was annexed by the Soviet Union but was soon occupied by the Germans and their allies, who began to persecute and deport the Jewish population. Celan's parents were taken to a concentration camp, where they both died, while the young man remained hidden for some time and finally ended up in a forced-labor camp. These events left a permanent scar on Celan's memory, and it appears that he had strong feelings of guilt for having survived when his parents and so many of his friends and relatives were murdered. After Soviet troops reoccupied his hometown, he returned there for a short time and then moved to Bucharest, where he found work as an editor and a translator. In 1947, his first poems were published in a Romanian journal under the anagrammatic pen name Paul Celan. In the same year, he moved to Vienna, where he remained until 1948, when his first collection of poetry, *Der Sand aus den Urnen*, was published.

After moving to Paris in the same year, Celan began to frequent avant-garde circles and was received particularly well by the poet Yvan Goll and his wife. Unfortunately, this friendship soured after Goll's death in 1950, when Goll's wife, Claire, apparently jealous of Celan's growing reputation as a poet, accused him of having plagiarized from her husband. A bitter feud resulted, with many of the leading poets and critics in France and Germany taking sides. During this period, Celan also began his work as a literary translator, which was to be a major source of both income and poetic inspiration for the rest of his life. He translated from the French—notably the writings of Rimbaud, Paul Valéry, and Guillaume Apollinaire—as well as the poetry of William Shakespeare, Emily Dickinson, and Marianne Moore from the English and the works of Aleksandr Blok, Sergei Esenin, and Osip Mandelstam from the Russian.

In the following years, Celan married a French graphic artist, Gisèle Lestrange, and published his second volume of poetry, *Mohn und Gedächtnis* (poppy and memory), containing many poems from his first collection, *Der Sand aus den Urnen*, which he had withdrawn from circulation because of the large number of printing mistakes and editorial inaccuracies it contained. *Mohn und Gedächtnis* established his reputation as a poet, and most of his subsequent collections were awarded prestigious literary prizes.

Celan remained in Paris for the rest of his life, infrequently traveling to Germany. During his later years, he appears to have undergone many crises both in his personal and in his creative life (his feud with Claire Goll is only one such incident), and his friends agree that he became quarrelsome and felt persecuted by neo-Nazis, hostile publishers, and critics. His death in April of 1970, apparently by suicide—he drowned in the Seine—was the consequence of his having arrived, in his own judgment, at a personal and artistic dead end, although many critics have seen in his collections *Lichtzwang*, *Schneepart*, and *Zeitgehöft*, published posthumously, the potential beginning of a new creative period.

ANALYSIS

Paul Celan's poetry can be viewed as an expressive attempt to cope with the past—his personal past as well as that of the Jewish people. Close friends of the poet state that Celan was unable to forget anything and that trivial incidents and cataclysmic events of the past for him had the same order of importance. Many of his poems contain references to the death camps, to his dead parents (particularly his mother), to his changing attitude toward the Jewish religion and toward God. In his early collections, these themes are shaped into traditional poetic form—long, often rhymed lines, genitive metaphors, sensuous images—and the individual poems are accessible to conventional methods of interpretation. In his later collections, Celan employs increasingly sparse poetic means, such as one-word lines, neologisms, and images that resist traditional interpretive sense; their significance can often be intuited only by considering Celan's complete poetic opus, a fact which has persuaded many critics and readers that Celan's poems are nonsense, pure games with language rather than codified expressions of thoughts and feelings which can be deciphered by applying the appropriate key.

MOHN UND GEDÄCHTNIS

Mohn und Gedächtnis, Celan's first collection of poetry (discounting the withdrawn *Der Sand aus den Urnen*), was in many ways an attempt to break with the past. The title of the collection is an indication of the dominant theme of these poems, which stress the dichotomy of forgetting—one of the symbolic connotations of the poppy flower—and remembering, by which Celan expresses his wish to forget the past, both his own personal past and that of the Jewish race, and his painful inability to erase these experiences from his memory. Living in Paris, Celan believed that only by forgetting could he begin a new life—in a new country, with a non-Jewish French wife, and by a rejection of his past poetic efforts, as indicated by the withdrawal of his first collection.

Mohn und Gedächtnis is divided into four parts and contains a total of fifty-six poems. In the first part, "Der Sand aus den Urnen" ("Sand from the Urns"), Celan establishes the central theme of the collection: The poet "fills the urns of the past in the moldy-green house of oblivion" and is reminded by the white foliage of an aspen tree that his mother's hair was not allowed to turn white. Mixed with these reflections on personal losses are memories of sorrows and defeats inflicted upon the Jewish people; references to the conquest of Judea by the Romans are meant to remind the reader of more recent atrocities committed by foreign conquerors.

The second part of *Mohn und Gedächtnis* is a single poem, "Todesfuge" ("Death Fugue"), Celan's most widely anthologized poem, responsible in no small part for establishing his reputation as one of the leading contemporary German poets. "Death Fugue" is a monologue by the victims of a concentration camp, evoking in vivid images the various atrocities associated with these camps. From the opening line, "Black milk of daybreak we drink it at sundown . . ."—one of the lines that Claire Goll suggested Celan had plagiarized from her husband—the poem passes on to descriptions of the cruel camp commander who plays with serpent-like whips, makes the inmates shovel their own graves, and sets his pack of dogs on them. From the resignation of the first lines, the poem builds to an emotional climax in the last stanza in which the horror of the cremation chambers is indicated by im-

ages such as "he grants us a grave in the air" and "death is a master from Germany." While most critics have praised the poem, some have condemned Celan for what they interpret as an attempt at reconciliation between Germans and Jews in the last two lines of the poem. Others, however, notably Theodor Adorno, have attacked "Death Fugue" on the basis that it is "barbaric" to write beautiful poetry after, and particularly about, Auschwitz. A close reading of this long poem refutes the notion that Celan was inclined toward reconciliation with the Germans—his later work bears this out—and it is hard to imagine that any reader should feel anything but horror and pity for the anonymous speakers of the poem. The beautifully phrased images serve to increase the intensity of this horror rather than attempting to gloss it over. "Death Fugue" is both a great poem and one of the most impressive and lasting documents of the plight of the Jews.

"Auf Reisen" ("Travel"), the first poem of the third part of the collection, again indicates Celan's wish to leave the past behind and to start all over again in his "house in Paris." In other poems he makes reference to his wife, asking to be forgiven for having broken with his heritage and married a Gentile. As the title of the collection suggests, the poppy of oblivion is not strong enough to erase the memory of his dead mother, of his personal past, and of his racial heritage. In poems such as "Der Reisekamerad" ("The Traveling Companion") and "Zähle die Mandeln" ("Count the Almonds"), the optimistic view of "Travel" is retracted; in the former, the dead mother is evoked as the poet's constant travel companion, while in the latter, he acknowledges that he must always be counted among the "almonds." The almonds *(Mandeln)* represent the Jewish people and are an indirect reference also to the Russian Jewish poet Osip Mandelstam, whose work Celan had translated. The irreconcilable tension between the wish to forget and the inability to do so completely is further shown in "Corona," a poem referring to Rainer Maria Rilke's "Herbsttag" ("Autumn Day"). Whereas the speaker of Rilke's poem resigns himself to the approaching hardships of winter, Celan converts Rilke's "Lord: it is time" into the rebellious "it is time that the stone condescended to bloom."

The poems in *Mohn und Gedächtnis* are not, for the most part, innovative in form or imagery, although the long dactylic lines and the flowery images of the first half begin to give way to greater economy of scope and metaphor in the later poems. There is a constant dialogue with a fictional "you" and repeated references to "night," "dream," "sleep," "wine," and "time," in keeping with the central theme of these poems. Celan's next collections show his continued attempts to break with the past, to move his life and his poetry to new levels.

VON SCHWELLE ZU SCHWELLE

In *Von Schwelle zu Schwelle* (threshold to threshold), Celan abandoned his frequent references to the past; it is as if the poet—as the title, taken from a poem in *Mohn und Gedächtnis*, suggests—intended to cross over a threshold into a new realm. Images referring to his mother, to the persecution of the Jews, to his personal attitude toward God, and to his Jewish heritage are less frequent in this volume. Many German critics, reluctant to concentrate on Celan's treatment of the Holocaust, have remarked with some relief his turning away from this subject toward the problem of creativity, the possibilities of communication, and the limits of language. Indeed, if one follows most German critics, *Von Schwelle zu Schwelle* was the first step in the poet's development toward "metapoetry"—that is, poetry which no longer deals with traditional *materia poetica* but only with poetry itself. This new direction is demonstrated by the preponderance of terms such as "word" and "stone" (a symbol of speechlessness), replacing "dream," "autumn," and "time." For Celan, *Von Schwelle zu Schwelle* constituted a more radical attempt to start anew by no longer writing about—therefore no longer having to think about—experiences and memories which he had been unable to come to grips with in his earlier poems.

SPEECH-GRILLE

Speech-Grille is, as the title suggests, predominantly concerned with language. The thirty-three poems in this volume are among Celan's finest, as the enthusiastic critical reception confirmed. They are characterized by a remarkable discipline of expression, leading in many cases to a reduction of poetry to the bare essentials. Indeed, it is possible to see these poems as leading in the direction of complete silence. "Engführung" ("Stretto"), perhaps the finest poem in the collection and one of Celan's best, exemplifies this tendency even by its title, which is taken from musical theory and refers to the fi-

nal section of a fugue. A long poem which alludes to "Death Fugue," it is stripped of the descriptive metaphors which characterized that masterpiece, such as the "grave in the air" and "the black milk of daybreak"; instead, experience is reduced to lines such as "Came, came./ Came a word, came/ came through the night,/ wanted to shine, wanted to shine/ Ash./ Ash, ash./ Night."

DIE NIEMANDSROSE

Celan's attempt to leave the past behind in *Speech-Grille* was not completely successful; on the contrary, several poems in this collection express sorrow at the poet's detachment from his Jewish past and from his religion. It is therefore not surprising that Celan's next collection, *Die Niemandsrose* (the no-one's rose), was dedicated to Osip Mandelstam, a victim of Joseph Stalin's persecutions in the 1930's. One of the first poems in this collection makes mention of the victims of the concentration camps: "There was earth inside them, and/they dug." Rather than concentrating on the horrors of camp existence, the poem discusses the possibility of believing in an omnipotent, benevolent God in the face of these atrocities; this theme is picked up again in "Zürich, zum Storchen" ("Zurich, the Stork Inn"), in which Celan reports on his meeting with the Jewish poet Nelly Sachs: "the talk was of your God, I spoke/ against him." Other poems contain references to his earlier work; the "house in Paris" is mentioned again, and autumn imagery, suggesting the memory of his mother, is used more frequently. Several other poems express Celan's renewed and final acceptance of his Jewish heritage but indicate his rejection of God, culminating in the blasphemous "Psalm," with its bitter tribute: "Praised be your name, no one."

LATER YEARS

Celan's poetry after *Die Niemandsrose* became almost inaccessible to the average reader. As the title *Breathturn* indicates, Celan wanted to go in entirely new directions. Most of the poems in Celan's last collections are very short; references to language and writing become more frequent, and striking, often grotesque, portmanteau words and other neologisms mix with images from his earlier poems. There are still references to Judaism, to an absent or cruel God, and—in a cryptic form—to personal experiences. In the posthumously published *Schneepart*, the reader can even detect allusions to the turbulent political events of 1968. The dominant feature of these last poems, however, is the almost obsessive attempt to make the language of poetry perform new, hitherto unimagined feats, to coerce words to yield truth which traditional poetic diction could not previously force through its "speech-grille." It appears that Celan finally despaired of ever being able to reach this new poetic dimension. The tone of his last poems was increasingly pessimistic, and his hopes, expressed in earlier poems, of finding "that ounce of truth deep inside delusion," gave way to silence in the face of the "obstructive tomorrow." It is the evidence of these last poems, more than any police reports, which make it a certainty that his drowning in the Seine in 1970 was not simply the result of an accident.

Celan's poetry can be understood only by grasping his existential dilemma after World War II as a Jewish poet who had to create his poetry in the German language. Desperate to leave behind everything which would remind him of his own and his people's plight, he nevertheless discovered that the very use of the German language inevitably led him back to his past and made a new beginning impossible. Finally, the only escape he saw still open to him was to attempt to abandon completely the conventions of German lyric poetry and its language, to try to make his poetry express his innermost feelings and convictions without having to resort to traditional poetic diction and form. Weinrich suggests that Celan, like Mallarmé before him, was searching for the "absolute poem," a poem which the poet creates only as a rough sketch and which the reader then completes, using private experiences and ideas, possibly remembered pieces of other poems. If this is true, Celan must have ultimately considered his efforts a failure, both in terms of his poetic intentions and in his desire to come to terms with his personal and his Jewish past.

OTHER MAJOR WORKS

SHORT FICTION: "Gespräch im Gebirg," 1959.

NONFICTION: *Edgar Jené und der Traum vom Traume*, 1948 (*Edgar Jené and the Dream About the Dream*, 1986); "Der Meridian," 1960 ("The Meridian," 1978); *Collected Prose*, 1986.

TRANSLATIONS: *Der goldene Vorhang*, 1949 (of Jean Cocteau); *Bateau ivre/Das trunkene Schiff*, 1958 (of Arthur Rimbaud); *Gedichte*, 1959 (of Osip Man-

delstam); *Die junge Parzel/La jeune Parque*, 1964 (of Paul Valéry); *Einundzwanzig Sonette*, 1967 (of William Shakespeare).

BIBLIOGRAPHY

Baer, Ulrich. *Remnants of Song: Trauma and the Experience of Modernity in Charles Baudelaire and Paul Celan*. Stanford, Calif.: Stanford University Press, 2000. Baer sees a basis for comparison of the nineteenth and the twentieth century poet. Bibliographical references, index.

Bernstein, Michael André. *Five Portraits: Modernity and the Imagination in Twentieth-Century German Writing*. Evanston, Ill.: Northwestern University Press, 2000. Compared with Celan are four other German poets and philosophers: Rainer Maria Rilke, Robert Musil, Martin Heidegger, and Walter Benjamin. Bibliographical references, index.

Block, Haskell M. *The Poetry of Paul Celan*. New York: P. Lang, 1991. A collection of papers from a conference at the State University of New York at Binghamton in 1988.

Chalfen, Israel. *Paul Celan*. New York: Persea Books, 1991. A biography of Celan's youth and early career. Includes bibliographic references.

Del Caro, Adrian. *The Early Poetry of Paul Celan: In the Beginning Was the Word*. Baton Rouge: Louisiana State University Press, 1997. A detailed treatment of the early volumes *Mohn und Gedächtnis* (1952) and *Von Schwelle zu Schwelle* (1955).

Felstiner, John. *Paul Celan: Poet, Survivor, Jew*. 1995. Reprint. New Haven, Conn.: Yale University Press, 2001. Illuminates the rich biographical meaning behind much of Celan's spare, enigmatic verse. Bibliographic references, illustrations, map, index.

Fioretos, Aris. *Word Traces: Readings of Paul Celan*. Baltimore: Johns Hopkins University Press, 1994. Close readings. Bibliographical references, index.

Glenn, Jerry. *Paul Celan*. New York: Twayne Publishers, 1973. Biography and criticism of Celan's work. Includes a bibliography of Celan's work.

Rosenthal, Bianca. *Pathways to Paul Celan*. New York: P. Lang, 1995. An overview of the varied and often contradictory critical responses to the poet. Illustrated, bibliographical references, index.

Wolosky, Shira. *Language and Mysticism: The Negative Way of Language in Eliot, Beckett, and Celan.* Stanford, Calif.: Stanford University Press, 1995. A useful comparative study that helps to place Celan in context. Bibliographical refernences, index.

Franz G. Blaha;
bibliography updated by the editors

LUIS CERNUDA

Born: Seville, Spain; September 21, 1902
Died: Mexico City, Mexico; November 5, 1963

PRINCIPAL POETRY
Perfil del aire, 1927
Egloga, elegía, oda, 1927
Un río, un amor, 1929
Los placeres prohibidos, 1931
Donde habite el olvido, 1934
Invocaciones, 1935
La realidad y el deseo, 1936, 1940, 1958, 1964
Las nubes, 1940
Como quien espera el alba, 1947
Poemas para un cuerpo, 1957
Desolación de la quimera, 1962
The Poetry of Luis Cernuda, 1971
Poesía completa, 1973
Selected Poems of Luis Cernuda, 1977
34 Poemas, 1998

OTHER LITERARY FORMS

Although Luis Cernuda is best known for his poetry, he was also a prolific essayist and critic. He published several works in prose, three of which, devoted to criticism, appeared during his lifetime. In his *Estudios sobre poesía española contemporánea* (1957; studies on contemporary Spanish poetry), Cernuda analyzes the most important trends in Spanish poetry since the nineteenth century. He bestows upon Gustavo Adolfo Bécquer the distinction of having reawakened poetry after more than one hundred years of lethargy, and he lauds Miguel de Unamuno y Jugo as the most important Spanish poet of

Luis Cernuda

the twentieth century. Cernuda's *Pensamiento poético en la lírica inglesa (siglo XIX)* (1958; poetic thought in English lyricism), a study of the theory of poetry as practiced by nineteenth century British poets, reveals Cernuda's deep appreciation of and attachment to English verse of the Romantic and Victorian periods. Many of Cernuda's essays and magazine and newspaper articles—which appeared originally in such publications as *Caracola, Litoral, Octubre, Cruz y raya, Heraldo de Madrid,* and *Insula*—have been collected in the two-volume *Poesía y literatura* (1960, 1964; poetry and literature) and in *Crítica, ensayos, y evocaciones* (1970; criticism, essays, and evocations). *Variaciones sobre tema mexicano* (1952; variations on a Mexican theme), often referred to as poetic prose, is an affectionate reflection by the poet on the people of Mexico, their music, their art, their churches, and their poverty and misery. Mexico was the poet's adopted homeland, after some years in what he perceived to be alien environments, and he felt warmed by the Mexicans, their culture, and their climate, so reminiscent of his native Andalusia. *Ocnos*

(1942, 1949, 1964) is a meditation upon time, a prose poem that becomes the lyrical confession of a poet writing about himself and his art. Because it contains Cernuda's analysis of his work, this volume is a useful companion to his poetry. Cernuda also undertook the translation into Spanish of the poetry of Friedrich Hölderlin, Paul Éluard, William Wordsworth, and William Blake, as well as plays by William Shakespeare. He did not devote much effort to fiction, leaving behind only three short pieces: "El indolente" ("The Indolent One"), "El viento en la colina" ("The Wind on the Hill"), and "El sarao" (the dancing party), all published in the collection *Tres narraciones* (1948; three narratives).

ACHIEVEMENTS

While Luis Cernuda is recognized as an important member of the *generación del 27* (considered by some a second Spanish Golden Age), he did not receive during his lifetime the acclaim and recognition extended to some of his contemporaries, such as Federico García Lorca, Jorge Guillén, Rafael Alberti, and Vicente Aleixandre. Furthermore, Cernuda never enjoyed financial or professional security. His position as a self-exile—he never returned to Spain, even for brief periods, after 1938—might explain his lack of popularity during the 1930's and 1940's; his political sympathies (staunchly Republican), his open homosexuality, his reticence, and even the seemingly simple structure and language of his poetry were all factors that may have distanced him from an entire generation of readers. More recently, Cernuda's audience has been growing: A number of important critical studies have appeared in the last fifteen years, a complete edition of his poetry has been published, and a collection of many of his extant essays was issued in 1970—clear indications that Cernuda is being reappraised by a new generation of Spanish poets and critics.

Even now, however, as Carlos-Peregrín Otero has observed, it might be premature to evaluate Cernuda's impact and his role as an innovator in Spanish letters. Cernuda displayed, first and foremost, a commitment to poetry and to the creative act. His work allowed him to express himself and served to sustain him. It was through his poetry that he came to understand himself and the world, and this understanding helped him to endure the solitude and melancholy of his alienated and withdrawn existence. Through his writing, he was able to objectify his desire, his passion, and his love and to liberate himself in ways that his social persona never could. He also used his poetry to battle against his obsession with time and its relentless passage. These were the principal themes of Cernuda's works. He expressed them with increasing clarity and simplicity of language, yet, toward the end of his life, his work began to acquire the quiet, meditative tone of a man who is confident in the knowledge that his art, if nothing else, will escape decay.

BIOGRAPHY

Born to a comfortable middle-class family of Seville, Luis Cernuda y Bidón was the youngest of the three children of Bernardo Cernuda Bousa, a colonel of a regiment of engineers, and Amparo Bidón y Cuellar. In Cernuda's poem "La familia" ("The Family"), which appeared in *Como quien espera el alba* (like someone awaiting the dawn), the domestic environment of his youth is portrayed as grave, dark, and rigid like glass, "which everyone can break but no one bends." The poet does not reveal any warmth or affection for his parents or his two sisters. His parents, he adds, fed and clothed him, and even provided him with God and morality. They gave him all: life, which he had not asked for, and death, its inextricable companion. From an early age, Cernuda displayed a timidity and reticence which were to characterize his social interaction throughout his life.

Cernuda first began to appreciate poetry at the age of nine, when he came across some poems by Gustavo Adolfo Bécquer (1836-1870), the Romantic poet whose remains were transferred from Madrid to Seville for permanent interment in 1911, causing excitement among the residents of the city and renewed interest in the poet's work. After completing secondary school in a religious institution, Cernuda enrolled at the University of Seville to study law in 1919. He received his law degree in 1925 but never practiced. His most important experience during his university years was his contact with Pedro Salinas, the eminent poet whose first year as a professor at the university coincided with Cernuda's first year as a student. Their association—at first formal, impersonal, and restricted to the classroom—developed in the course of the next few years, as Salinas encouraged Cernuda and other students to pursue their poetic inclinations. Salinas recommended that Cernuda begin to read French authors, among them Charles Baudelaire, Stéphane Mallarmé, and André Gide. Gide's works helped Cernuda to confront and to reconcile himself to his homosexuality. Through the influence of Salinas, Cernuda was able to publish nine poems in the prestigious magazine *Revista de occidente* when he was only twenty-three. Two years later, in 1927, Cernuda published his first collection, *Perfil del aire* (air's profile). In spite of the coolness with which it was received, with one or two notable exceptions, Cernuda had determined to devote his life to writing, putting an end to any professional indecision he had felt earlier.

Upon the death of his mother in 1928—his father had died in 1920—Cernuda left Seville for good, traveling first to Málaga and then to Madrid, and meeting a number of the writers and poets who would be known as the *generación del 27*, among them Manuel Altolaguirre and Emilio Prados (the editors of *Litoral*), Vicente Aleixandre, and Bernabé Fernández-Canivell (future director of the literary magazine *Caracola*, an outlet for Cernuda's poetry). He had met García Lorca in Seville in 1927. In the fall of 1928, through Pedro Salinas, Cernuda was offered an appointment as Spanish lecturer at the École Normale de Toulouse, a position that afforded the young poet the opportunity to spend some time in Paris. During his year in France, he immersed himself in the Surrealist movement and adopted a style and point of view to which he would adhere for the next four years.

The decade of the 1930's was one of steady productivity for Cernuda, marked by increasing recognition of his gifts among other writers of his generation. At the same time, it was a period of political instability that forced writers to take sides. Cernuda was a staunch supporter of the Spanish Republic, and for a brief period, around 1933, a member of the Communist Party, contributing several political articles to *Octubre*, a magazine edited by Rafael Alberti. In 1934, for a short time, he worked for Misiones Pedagógicas (pedagogic missions), an educational program sponsored by the Republican government to bring culture to remote areas of the country. Cernuda's job was to explain the great masterpieces of Spanish painting, presented to the audience in reproduction. Cernuda spent the first summer of the Spanish Civil War, in 1936, in Paris as a secretary to the Spanish ambassador to France, Alvaro de Albornoz, whose daughter Concha was a friend of Cernuda. Upon his return to Spain, Cernuda joined the Republican popular militia and fought in the Guadarrama. In the winter of 1938, he traveled to England to deliver a series of lectures arranged for him by the English writer Stanley Richardson. A few months later, while returning to Spain through France, Cernuda decided to go into exile permanently, first to Great Britain, where he taught in Surrey, Glasgow, Cambridge, and London, and then to the United States, where he arrived in the fall of 1947. His appointment as professor of Spanish literature at Mount Holyoke College, negotiated for Cernuda by Concha Albornoz, initiated the most stable and financially untroubled period of the poet's life. The New England climate and the isolation of the school, however, made Cernuda restless and caused him to explore the possibility of a teaching post at a university in Puerto Rico. In 1953, after several summers spent in the more hospitable Mexico, he resigned his tenure at Mount Holyoke and settled in Mexico, where he would remain—with only brief returns to the United States to teach at San Francisco State College and the University of California at Los Angeles—until his death from a heart attack in 1963. While in Mexico, he supported himself by his writing and by teaching several courses at the Universidad Autónoma in Mexico City.

ANALYSIS

In the case of Luis Cernuda, it is impossible to separate the poet from the man—his personality from his literary production. As much as Cernuda himself protested that he loathed the intrusion of the person in the poem, he, much more than most of his contemporaries, can be said to have revealed himself through his writing. He offered readers a glimpse of his poetic world from one window only, as Jenaro Talens states, and that window is open to the main character, who is frequently—if not always—Cernuda himself. As a consequence, his poetic production reflects his development as a man and his awareness of himself. This, in turn, tends to focus most analyses of his work along closely chronological lines, as his poetry evolves from the vague and dreamy musings of youth to the bitter acceptance of the relentlessness of time and the inevitability of death. Beginning with the first book of poems, *Perfil del aire*—published as a supplement to the magazine *Litoral* and edited by Manuel Altolaguirre and Emilio Prados in 1927—Cernuda embarked upon a journey of self-discovery. In this first collection, the youthful poet presents an indifferent, indolent attitude toward the world; he is there, but he dreams and is surrounded by emptiness. Dreams and walls protect him, provide him with a haven for his loneliness; there, he can savor his secret pleasures and his unfulfilled yearnings. This first major effort, retitled "Primeras poesías" and revised before reappearing in the first edition of *La realidad y el deseo* (reality and desire), was not well received. Cernuda was criticized sharply for imitating Jorge Guillén, and his production was judged unoriginal. More recent criticism, while acknowledging Cernuda's debt to Guillén, dismisses these charges as exaggerated, praising this early work for its fine sensibility and for the musical quality of its language.

EGLOGA, ELEGÍA, ODA

The negative reception of his first book encouraged Cernuda to withdraw, at least personally, from what he considered the literary mainstream and, by his own admission, "to wish to cultivate that which is criticized by others." He began work on a second collection, *Egloga, elegía, oda* (eclogue, elegy, ode), a series of four poems patterned after classical and neoclassical models, particularly the works of Garcilaso de la Vega, whose meter and rhyme Cernuda imitated deliberately. Some years later, reflecting on his development as a writer, Cernuda said that, while this second work had permitted him to experiment with classical themes and strophes, its style did not satisfy him, for he was unable to find what he loved in what he wrote. Nevertheless, in *Egloga, elegía, oda*, the poet was able to express more forcefully some of the feelings first introduced in *Perfil del aire*. Vague yearnings have become a compelling attraction to beauty in all its forms; the poet's need to satisfy his desires is confronted by the opposition of desire to such satisfaction. In this set of poems, he begins to remove his cloak of ennui, revealing a strong, sensuous nature. The

pursuit of pleasure replaces indifference as the antidote for solitude and sadness. Desiring to express himself in a more daring fashion and to rebel against the constraints of bourgeois society, which misunderstood him and his sexuality, Cernuda gravitated toward the Surrealists. He read the works of Louis Aragon, André Breton, and Paul Éluard, whose poetry he translated into Spanish.

UN RÍO, UN AMOR AND LOS PLACERES PROHIBIDOS

Cernuda's Surrealist stage began, not coincidentally, with his year in France (1928-1929) and resulted in two important works, *Un río, un amor* (a river, a love) and *Los placeres prohibidos* (forbidden pleasures). The most notable technical characteristic of *Un río, un amor* is Cernuda's use of free verse, which was also being adopted during this period by other Spanish poets, such as Aleixandre, García Lorca, and Alberti. Freed of external constraints, Cernuda's verse nevertheless retained a strong sense of meter, and the rhythm of his lines was preserved through accentuation and cadence. He also made use of reiteration, anaphora, and anastrophe. From this period onward, Cernuda began to experiment with longer lines, although they seldom exceeded eleven syllables. In *Los placeres prohibidos*, Cernuda continued to discard technical conventions, alternating between verse and prose poems. Thematically, Surrealism provided Cernuda with the opportunity to liberate himself from social restrictions. Asserting his linguistic and stylistic freedom, he wrote of "night petrified by fists," "towers of fear," "iron flowers resounding like the chest of man," "tongue of darkness," and "empty eyes."

Toward the end of *Un río, un amor*, Cernuda intimates what is expressed openly in *Los placeres prohibidos*; he accepts his homosexuality and admits to being possessed by love. This love takes the form of passionate physical desire, rendered no less glorious and pure because of its carnality; only the outside world tarnishes this love with its opprobrium. In *Un río, un amor*, love produces an emptiness and a vacuum. Man is like a phantom, without direction; he is indifferent to the world, as if he were dead. In *Los placeres prohibidos*, however, love ceases to be the object of dreams; it becomes something real, the primary goal of man's desire, the motive behind all he does and feels: To give in to this love, without reservation, is man's purpose. Its attainment is nevertheless elusive—except for some fleeting moments—and contains an element of pain; herein lies the source of the solitude and the impotence of man.

DONDE HABITE EL OLVIDO

A third work published during this period, *Donde habite el olvido* (where oblivion dwells), closes out Cernuda's Surrealist phase. It was written after a failed love affair, one that the author naïvely had believed would last forever. This accounts for the bitterness of its tone, the poet's desire for death, and the harsh indictment of love, which, once it disappears, leaves nothing behind but the "remembrance of an oblivion." In the fourth poem of this collection, Cernuda retraces his personal history, as if it were a life already lived, replete with regrets and unfulfilled expectations. The first part of the poem exudes optimism, expansiveness, and anticipation, conveyed by the spring moon, the golden sea, and adolescent desire. The light, however, turns into shadows; the poet falls into darkness and is ultimately a living corpse.

LAS NUBES

With his next major publication, *Las nubes* (the clouds), Cernuda introduced two important new themes into his poetry: historical time, with its specific focus on Spain as the abandoned and beleaguered homeland, and man's spirituality and religiosity. Love, the recurring topic of much of Cernuda's work, plays virtually no role in this collection. In "Un español habla de su tierra" ("A Spaniard Speaks of His Homeland"), the poet writes nostalgically of the happy days of the past, before his land succumbed to the conquering Cains. The bitter days of the present find sustenance in the fond memories of years gone by, an idealized past that might someday be re-created yet to which the poet cannot return. When that day comes, and his homeland is free, it will come looking for him—only to discover that death has come to call first. Ironically, as one critic has pointed out, this poem was prescient in its chronology. In "Impresión de destierre" ("Impression of Exile"), the dislocated narrator—then in London—overhears a fatigued voice announce the death of Spain; "'Spain?' he said. 'A name./ Spain has died. . . .'"

Las nubes also contains the clearest expression of Cernuda's views on traditional religion. While his poetic use of belief in the supernatural has been described as a type of pantheistic hedonism based on Mediterranean mythology, his spiritual quest included attempts to find answers in more traditional Christian imagery by positing the existence of a God through whom man can achieve love. Cernuda devoted four poems in this collection to the broad question of the existence of God: "La visita de Dios" ("God's Visit"), "Atardecer en la catedral" ("Dusk in the Cathedral"), "Lázaro" ("Lazarus"), and "La adoración de los magos" ("The Adoration of the Magi"). In the long poem "God's Visit," the protagonist, in a voice filled with anguish, confronts God with the terrible wreckage of what is now the speaker's country, the poet's paradise of years gone by, perhaps destroyed by the casual wave of his hand. As the last hope for renewal, the protagonist begs God to restore to the world beauty, truth, and justice; without these, he warns, God could be forgotten.

"THE ADORATION OF THE MAGI"

More firmly rooted in Christianity is the five-part poem "The Adoration of the Magi," in which Cernuda's debt to T. S. Eliot is clear. The poem opens with a meditation by Melchior on the existence of God, reaching the conclusion that if he himself is alive, God, too, might well exist. This knowledge does not fully satisfy Melchior. To reason the existence of God is not enough; some more evocative proof is needed. The second part of the poem, "Los reyes" ("The Kings"), presents the Magi, each with a distinctive voice which expresses the conflicting visions of a single character: Melchior the idealist, Gaspar the hedonist, and Balthasar the skeptic. Through their intertwined monologues, the pilgrim searches for proof of the existence of God. The next section, "Palinodia de la esperanza divina" ("Palinode of Divine Hope"), is perhaps the most inventive; in it, the author expresses the disenchantment and disappointment felt by the Magi upon arriving in Bethlehem after a long journey and finding nothing but a poor child, a life "just like our human one," after expecting "a god, a presence/ radiant and imperious, whose sight is grace." In the fourth part, "Sobre el tiempo pasado" ("On Time Past"), the protagonist is the old shepherd (Father Time?) who remembers a period in his youth, long past, when three wise men came to look at a newborn child. The old man, however, has no recollection of a god; how can a humble shepherd, whose knowledge of man is so lacking, have seen the gods? The poem closes with a short fifth part "Epitafio" ("Epitaph"), wherein man, as searcher, is told that he once found the truth but did not recognize it; now he can console himself by living his life in this world, as a body, even though he cannot be free from misery.

PASSAGE OF TIME AS THEME

The publication of *Las nubes* marked a new beginning for Cernuda, the man and the poet. He had departed from Spain; he was approaching the age of forty—an age which, for a man who associated beauty with youth and joy with youthfulness, must have created much anxiety. His prospects for recognition in Spain had been shattered by political events. Cernuda responded to this situation by creating a protagonist with a distinct identity; he created *the poet*, whose role it was to substitute as the main character for the author and who would, when called upon, assume all responsibility for failure. Thus, Cernuda created what Phillip Silver calls his "personal myth" and entered into the mature stage of his poetic production. Poetry became a means to understand and preserve the past. The need to fulfill a grand passion was discarded; man must resign himself to a world that belongs to the gods, a world in which he cannot partake of paradise. If man can be made into a myth, however, his life will be eternal and his beauty everlasting. In poems such as "Noche del hombre y su demonio" ("A Man's Night and His Demon") and "Río vespertino" ("Evening River") from *Como quien espera el alba*, Cernuda expresses an attitude of acceptance, as if recounting a life already lived. He anticipates, without fear, the inevitability of death. There is but one small consolation: There is no ash without flame, no death without life. In the long poem "Apología pro vita sua" from the same collection, the poet gathers up all the suffering of his existence: his obsessions as a poet, the war, his agnosticism, and his need and hope for a personal, intimate God. From his bedside, the protagonist summons first his lovers—some of whom he loved—to help illuminate his world growing dim, for "Is passion not the measure of human greatness . . . ?" He then calls in his friends to help him renounce the light. As in a confessional, he admits to regrets, but only for those sins which he has not had the opportunity or the strength to commit. He asserts that he has lived without God because he has

not manifested himself to him and has not satisfied his incredulity. The protagonist maintains that to die, man does not need God; rather, God needs man in order to live. In an apparent contradiction, a few lines later, he asks God to fill his soul with the light that comes with eternity.

The past, that which has been, and the inevitable passage of time become the dominating theme of the remainder of Cernuda's poetic output. In his mature verses, he recounts his life and his loves with the pessimistic tone of one who knows that they will never come again. Splendor, beauty, passion, and joy are juxtaposed to solitude, old age, and death.

OTHER MAJOR WORKS

SHORT FICTION: *Tres narraciones*, 1948.

NONFICTION: *Ocnos*, 1942, 1949, 1964; *Variaciones sobre tema mexicano*, 1952; *Estudios sobre poesía española contemporánea*, 1957; *Pensamiento poético en la lírica inglesa (siglo XIX)*, 1958; *Poesía y literatura*, 1960, 1964 (2 volumes); *Crítica, ensayos, y evocaciones*, 1970.

ANTHOLOGY: *Prosa completa*, 1975

BIBLIOGRAPHY

Harris, Derek. *Luis Cernuda: A Study of His Poetry*. London: Tamesis, 1973. A critical study of Cernuda's poetry. Includes bibliographic references.

_____. *Metal Butterflies and Poisonous Lights: The Language of Surrealism in Lorca, Alberti, Cernuda and Aleixandre*. Anstruther, Fife, Scotland: La Sirena, 1998. An analysis of the use of surrealism in the poetry of Cernuda and other poets. Includes bibliographical references.

Jiménez-Fajardo, Salvador. *Luis Cernuda*. Boston: Twayne, 1978. An introductory biographical and critical analysis of selected works by Cernuda. Includes bibliographic references.

Jiménez-Fajardo, Salvador, ed. *The Word and the Mirror: Critical Essays on the Poetry of Luis Cernuda*. Rutherford, N.J.: Fairleigh Dickinson University Press, 1989. A collection of critical essays dealing with Cernuda's works.

McKinlay, Neil C. *The Poetry of Luis Cernuda: Order in a World of Chaos*. Rochester, N.Y.: Tamesis,

1999. A brief biographical and critical study. Includes bibliographical references and index.

Martin-Clark, Philip. *Art, Gender, and Sexuality: New Readings of Cernuda's Later Poetry*. Leeds, England: Maney, 2000. A critical interpretation of selected works by Cernuda. Includes bibliographical references and index.

Clara Estow;
bibliography updated by the editors

LORNA DEE CERVANTES

Born: San Francisco, California; August 6, 1954

PRINCIPAL POETRY

Emplumada, 1981

From the Cables of Genocide: Poems on Love and Hunger, 1991

OTHER LITERARY FORMS

Nearly all Lorna Dee Cervantes' literary work is poetry. She was the founder and editor of Mango Publications, which published the literary review *Mango*, and she also founded and has edited the literary magazine *Red Dirt*.

ACHIEVEMENTS

Lorna Dee Cervantes' first collection of poems, *Emplumada*, won the American Book Award (from the Before Columbus Foundation) in 1982. Her second collection, *From the Cables of Genocide: Poems on Love and Hunger*, won the Paterson Prize for Poetry and the Latino Literature Award and was nominated for a National Book Award in 1992. Cervantes has also been named Outstanding Chicana Scholar by the National Association of Chicano Scholars.

BIOGRAPHY

Lorna Dee Cervantes was born in 1954 in San Francisco and moved to San Jose (the setting for several of her best-known poems) after her parents' divorce in 1959. Her ethnic identification is not only Mexican American but also Native American, and she draws on

this dual heritage in her poetry. She began writing poetry at an early age and first came to notice reading "Refuge Ship" at a drama festival in Mexico City in 1974. Her poems began to appear in Chicano journals such as *Revista Chicano-Riquena* and *The Latin American Literary Review*, and in 1981 the University of Pittsburgh Press published her first volume of poetry, *Emplumada*, to widespread praise.

Cervantes gained her B.A. from San Jose State University in 1984, received her doctorate from the University of California at Santa Cruz in 1990, and has taught creative writing at the University of Colorado at Boulder. In addition to her academic position, Cervantes has done a good deal of editorial work, encouraging other Chicano writers, and has read her poetry at national and international literary festivals.

ANALYSIS

Lorna Dee Cervantes is one of the major Latina poetic voices writing in English, and at least half a dozen of her poems have been reprinted widely. While she has written on a variety of topics, including a number of love poems, she is best known for those poems that define the situation for Mexican Americans at the end of the twentieth century, poems that are feminist and political. More than any other poet, Cervantes describes what it is like to live in two cultural worlds—or between them—and the tensions and difficulties such a limbo creates for a woman.

EMPLUMADA

Many of Cervantes' best-known poems were printed in her first collection, published in 1981. *Emplumada* immediately established Cervantes as a major voice in contemporary American poetry, and its best poems raised the themes and issues with which many women were struggling. While her language is simple and direct, Cervantes uses a number of Spanish words and phrases (and includes a two-page "glossary" at the end of the book which translates them into English). What is most striking in the collection is its colorful imagery; the poems are filled with visuals of birds and flowers. The collection's title, for example, *Emplumada*, comes from the combination of two Spanish words: *emplumado*, meaning "feathered or in plumage, as in after molting," and *plumada*, a "pen flourish." The title thus implies both change and growth and the flourish of a pen. The two emerge in this collection in a woman defining her new self through her poetry. As she writes at the end of "Visions of Mexico While at a Writing Symposium in Port Townsend, Washington,"

> as pain sends seabirds south from the cold
> I come north
> to gather my feathers
> for quills.

Poet Lynette Seator has written that *Emplumada* contains "poetry that affirms Mexican-American identity as well as the identity of the poet as woman coming-of-age." While there are love poems in this collection as well ("Café Solo," "The Body Braille"), the best poems ("Lots: I" and "Lots: II," "Poema para los Californios Muertos") have larger feminist, ethnic, and historical subjects.

"REFUGEE SHIP"

"Refugee Ship" is the poem that first gained notice for Cervantes. It is a remarkable work for such a young poet, for its brief fourteen lines capture the feelings of many earlier immigrants caught between two cultures. The first stanza establishes her Latina identity and her link to her *abuelita* (grandmother). In the five lines of the second stanza, she describes her estrangement from her native culture in language and in name:

> Mama raised me without language.
> I'm orphaned from my Spanish name.
> The words are foreign, stumbling
> on my tongue. . . .

Even her physical appearance, she concludes in this stanza, looks alien: "I see in the mirror/ my reflection: bronzed skin, black/ hair." The four lines of the third and final stanza give the image of the title that so perfectly describes her situation and dilemma:

> I feel I am a captive
> aboard the refugee ship.
> The ship that will never dock.
> *El barco que nunca atraca.*

The repeated final line, in English and then Spanish, emphasizes her estrangement, the sense not only of dislocation but also of being caught between two places, two lives, and never able to land or reside in either. "Refugee Ship" captures that feeling of estrangement for genera-tions of immigrants to America, from the nineteenth century on, who were torn between two cultures, and at home in neither.

"OAXACA, 1974"

Closely linked to "Refugee Ship" in *Emplumada* is "Oaxaca, 1974," which originally appeared under the ti-tle "Heritage," in which form it has several times been anthologized. In the poem, the narrator looks for her Mexican heritage "all day in the streets of Oaxaca," but the children laugh at her, calling to her "in words of an-other language." Although she has a "brown body," she searches "for the dye that will color my thoughts," or make "this bland pochaseed" ("an assimilated Mexican American," as Cervantes translates the phrase in the glossary) more Latino in her thinking. She did not ask to be brought up "tonta" (stupid), she concludes, but "Es la culpa de los antepasados" (It is her ancestors' fault):

> Blame it on the old ones.
> They give me a name
> that fights me.

If the name is Lorna, it is obviously English in derivation and says nothing of her Mexican American heritage. It is significant that "Heritage" was the first title of the poem, and that in collecting it as "Oaxaca, 1974" Cervantes took out the poem's original first word, "Heritage," but the idea still runs beneath the poem's lines and images. The poem, like "Refugee Ship," is an evocative description of the immigrant living uncomfortably between two cultures.

"FREEWAY 280" AND "BENEATH THE SHADOW OF THE FREEWAY"

Two other poems in this first collection complement each other and have been reprinted in several antholo-gies. Deborah L. Madsen wrote, "Cervantes' poetry re-veals an acute sense of the importance of geographical and cultural place," and that is nowhere more true than in these two related poems. "Freeway 280" has the theme of human versus nature: In spite of the "raised scar" of the freeway, the narrator tells readers, life thrives. Once, she wanted to leave on the same freeway, but now she has returned.

> Maybe it's here
> en los campos extraños de esta ciudad ["in the strange
> fields of this city"]
> where I'll find it, that part of me

mown under
like a corpse
or a loose seed.

The opposition between humans and nature has become the means of the narrator's finding her own identity in a hometown destroyed by urban development, but where "wild mustard remembers, old gardens/ come back stronger than they were."

"Beneath the Shadow of the Freeway" is a longer and more complex poem (and probably Cervantes' best-known single poem) and starts in the same San Jose setting. In spite of its title and all its natural imagery, however, "Beneath the Shadow of the Freeway" is really a celebration of the power of women. In language that lifts her thoughts to a mythic level, Cervantes creates a powerful statement of Latina strength, and a reminder about those—particularly men—who so often take it away.

The poem is broken into six numbered parts; all except the first contain verse stanzas themselves. In the first section, the narrator describes the house she lives in with her mother and her grandmother, who "watered geraniums/ [as] the shadow of the freeway lengthened." "We were a woman family," the narrator declares in the next stanza, and introduces her main theme. Her mother warns her about men, but the narrator models herself more on her grandmother, who "believes in myths and birds" and "trusts only what she builds/ with her own hands." A drunken intruder (perhaps the mother's ex-husband) tries to break into the house in section 5 but is scared away. In the final stanza the mother warns the narrator, "'Baby, don't count on nobody,'" but the narrator confesses to the reader that "Every night I sleep with a gentle man/ to the hymn of the mockingbirds," plants geraniums, ties her hair up like her grandmother, "and trust[s] only what I have built with my own hands." The poem is thus a celebration of three generations of women and contains the promise that women can be independent and still find love.

"POEM FOR THE YOUNG WHITE MAN WHO ASKED ME HOW I, AN INTELLIGENT, WELL-READ PERSON COULD BELIEVE IN THE WAR BETWEEN RACES"

This may be Cervantes' most blatantly political poem in *Emplumada*, but it mirrors ideas and images found throughout the collection. "I believe in revolution," she tells the Anglo man who has questioned her, "because everywhere the crosses are burning" and "there are snipers in the schools." They are not aimed at her interrogator, she says, but "I'm marked by the color of my skin."

Racism is not intellectual.
I can not reason these scars away.

Outside my door
there is a real enemy
who hates me.

"I am a poet," the persona declares, "who yearns to dance on rooftops." Her "tower of words," however, cannot silence "the sounds of blasting and muffled outrage." This contradiction is continued in the poem's last lines:

Every day I am deluged with reminders
that this is not
my land
and this is my land.

I do not believe in the war between races

but in this country
there is war.

As in "Refugee Ship" and "Oaxaca 1974," the narrator is torn between two lands—but here within her own country.

FROM THE CABLES OF GENOCIDE

Cervantes' second collection of poems a decade later failed to match the quality and power of *Emplumada*. In four sections—"From the Cables of Genocide," "On Love and Hunger," "The Captive Verses," and "On the Fear of Going Down"—the poems in *From the Cables of Genocide* tend to be longer, and the style more complex. At least four of the poems are written "after Neruda," several others "after García Lorca," and there are more classical allusions here than in *Emplumada*. While the distinctively sharp Cervantes language and intense imagery grace the poems in the collection, fewer of them have been reprinted. There is also less use of Spanish in the second collection.

Many of the poems in *From the Cables of Genocide* record the pain and loss suffered at the ending of love, and "My Dinner with Your Memory" may be representative of this recurrent subject and situation. The imagery of a feast (bread, butter, cheese, plum brandy) works counter to the sense of pain here: "when the moon slivers my heart/ into poverty's portions." The concluding lines are ambiguous at best but certainly convey the poem's sense of loss:

> Who would hunger at the brink of this
> feast? Who would go, uninvited,
> but you and your ghost of a dog?

Other poems in the collection—"On Love and Hunger," "Macho"—continue this theme. There are fewer poems here that deal with ethnic or multicultural issues ("Flatirons" and "Pleiades from the Cables of Genocide" are two strong exceptions), and more that deal with the personal plight of a woman ("On Finding the Slide of John in the Garden"). Some of the best poems in the second collection—like "Shooting the Wren"—are reminiscent of poems in the first, such as "Uncle's First Rabbit."

BIBLIOGRAPHY

Candelaria, Cordelia. *Chicano Poetry: A Critical Introduction.* Westport, Conn.: Greenwood Press, 1986. In an early evaluation of Cervantes' poetry, Candelaria writes that *Emplumada* "discloses a talent that is fresh, forceful, and multifaceted" and places her work in the "*Flor y Canto*," third and final phase of Chicano poetry (after "Movement" or protest poetry and the development of a "Chicano Poetics").

Crawford, John F. "Notes Toward a New Multicultural Criticism: Three Works by Women of Color." In *A Gift of Tongues: Critical Challenges in Contemporary American Poetry*, edited by Marie Harris and Kathleen Aguero. Athens: University of Georgia Press, 1987. One of the first analyses of *Emplumada* (along with Joy Harjo's *She Had Some Horses*, 1983, and Janice Mirikitani's *Awake in the River*, 1978) sees the volume as "a fabulous narrative of development," in which Cervantes is finding her own voice.

McKenna, Teresa. "'An Utterance More Pure than Word': Gender and the Corrido Tradition in Two Contemporary Chicano Poems." In *Feminist Measures: Soundings in Poetry and Theory*, edited by Lynn Keller and Cristanne Miller. Ann Arbor: University of Michigan Press, 1994. Detailed analyses of Juan Gomez-Quinoñes's "The Ballad of Billy Rivera" and Cervantes' "Visions of Mexico While at a Writing Symposium in Port Townsend, Washington," which also touches on several other key poems in *Emplumada*.

Madsen, Deborah L. *Understanding Contemporary Chicana Poetry.* Columbia: University of South Carolina Press, 2000. Excellent overview of Cervantes' poetry in final chapter of this study finds that her work "is characterized by her angry use of language, her passionate expression of emotions, and a complex interweaving of imagery to represent a feminist view of Chicana life in contemporary America."

Savin, Ada. "Bilingualism and Dialogism: Another Reading of Lorna Dee Cervantes' Poetry." In *An Other Tongue: Nation and Ethnicity in the Linguistic Borderlands*, edited by Alfred Arteaga. Durham, N.C.: Duke University Press, 1994. Using the linguistic theory of Mikhail Bakhtin, Savin finds that Cervantes' "poetic discourse is fragmented, divided, lying somewhere in the interspace between two cultures," but *Emplumada* is "an eloquent literary expression of the Chicanos' paradigmatic quest for self-definition."

Seator, Lynette. "*Emplumada*: Chicana Rites-of-Passage." *MELUS* 11 (Summer, 1984): 23-38. Reads Cervantes' first collection not only as "poetry that affirms Mexican-American identity" but also as "presentation of a woman in the *process* of coming of age" as well. Contains detailed analyses of many of the best poems in the collection, including "Lots: I" and "Lots: II," "Caribou Girl," "For Edward Long," and "For Virginia Chavez."

Wallace, Patricia. "Divided Loyalties: Literal and Literary in the Poetry of Lorna Dee Cervantes, Cathy Song, and Rita Dove." *MELUS* 18 (Fall, 1993): 3-19. In all three of these ethnic poets, Wallace shows, "the poet's creative use of language seeks to overcome what appears to be fixed or closed. . . . Cervantes' poems are often acts of assertion against restrictive social and linguistic structures."

David Peck

AIMÉ CÉSAIRE

Born: Basse-Pointe, Martinique; June 26, 1913

PRINCIPAL POETRY

Cahier d'un retour au pays natal, 1939, 1947, 1956
(*Memorandum on My Martinique*, 1947; better
known as *Return to My Native Land*, 1968)
Les Armes miraculeuses, 1946 (*Miraculous Weapons*, 1983)
Soleil cou coupé, 1948 (*Beheaded Sun*, 1983)
Corps perdu, 1950 (*Disembodied*, 1983)
Ferrements, 1960 (*Shackles*, 1983)
Cadastre, 1961 (*Cadastre: Poems*, 1973)
State of the Union, 1966 (includes abridged translations of *Les Armes miraculeuses* and *Ferrements*)
Moi, Laminaire, 1982
Aimé Césaire: The Collected Poetry, 1983
Non-vicious Circle: Twenty Poems, 1985
Lyric and Dramatic Poetry, 1946-1982, 1990
La Poésie, 1994

OTHER LITERARY FORMS

Poet, dramatist, and essayist Aimé Césaire is recognized not only for his poetry but also for his political and dramatic works. The first major poem he wrote, *Return to My Native Land*, set the tone and thematic precedence for his subsequent writings. *Tropiques*, a cultural magazine of which the poet was one of the principal founders, featured Césaire's own poems, which were reprinted in the Gallimard edition of *Miraculous Weapons* in 1946. As well as a vehicle for literary content, the magazine was used to arouse the cultural and political consciousness that would continue to mark Césaire's personality throughout his life.

While Césaire's poetry attests his exceptional talent as an artist, his polemical and historical works, *Discours sur le colonialisme* (1950; *Discourse on Colonialism*, 1972), born of the poet's disillusionment with the inferior role Martinique continued to play in its relations with France, and *Toussaint Louverture* (1960), named after the black hero Toussaint-Louverture, who led the 1802-1803 revolution in Haiti, demonstrate the poet's effort to assail racism, colonialism, and the cultural alienation of blacks from all sides. He continued to explore the problems of the existence of blacks in the world and African culture, especially the issue of decolonization, in his drama—which is more accessible than his poetry.

His plays include *La Tragédie du Roi Christophe* (1963; *The Tragedy of King Christophe*, 1964), *Une Saison au Congo* (1966; *A Season in the Congo*, 1968), and a reworking of William Shakespeare's play *The Tempest* (1611) entitled *Une Tempête d'après "La Tempête" de Shakespeare: Adaptation pour un théatre nègre* (1969; *The Tempest*, 1974).

ACHIEVEMENTS

Aimé Césaire's contribution to literature goes beyond his exceptional use of Surrealist techniques, his extraordinary mastery of the French language, and his attempt to articulate the inhumane effects of racism and colonialism. In 1982, he received the French Grand Prix National de la Poésie. By his example, Césaire helped to give impetus to the first great outpouring of written literature in Africa and the West Indies.

BIOGRAPHY

One of several children, Aimé Césaire was born on June 26, 1913, in Basse-Pointe, Martinique; his father, Ferdnand, was a comptroller with the revenue service. Most of his childhood was spent in the midst of poverty, and as Césaire grew older, he became acutely aware of the oppressive conditions of the majority of the Martinicans. At the Lycée Schoelcher in Fort de France, he excelled in his studies, winning a scholarship to the Lycée Louis-le-Grand in Paris. Ironically, this sojourn in Paris paved the way for Césaire's political maturation.

His friendship with Léopold Senghor, whom he met at Louis-le-Grand, was instrumental in changing Césaire's view of Africa, which would serve time and again as a source of inspiration for him. Once he completed his studies, he returned to Martinique with his wife, Suzanne, whom he had married while he was a student at the École Normale Supérieure. They would have six children.

Césaire's return to Martinique, a journey he had envisioned in his first poem, was as significant as his departure. He (as well as his wife) enjoyed a brief teaching career (1940-1945) at his former *lycée* in Fort-de-France. As usual, Césaire left his mark, inspiring his students with his love of poetry and instilling in them an enthusiasm for learning. Like many of his black contemporaries, Césaire took on the dual role of artist and political leader. Elected mayor of Fort-de-France (1945) and deputy to the National Assembly in France (1946), Césaire worked diligently to improve the plight of the Martinicans. During his fourteen years in office in the National Assembly, he was a member of the French Communist Party. He left the party when he perceived its indifference to the particular interests of Martinique.

In 1957, Césaire founded the Martinican Progressive Party (Parti Progressiste Martiniquais), and, despite his disillusionment, he never ceased to play an active role in shaping the political life of his homeland. He assumed the presidency of the local "regional council," but he retired from electoral politics entirely in 1993. Although he has not published any new poetry since 1982, the collection of his work published in Paris in 1994 by the prestigious Seuil firm was a major event. Césaire remains the best-known writer of the West Indies.

Aimé Césaire

ANALYSIS

Aimé Césaire arrived in France in 1931, at a time when Surrealism had already begun to dominate the literary scene. Instead of an ideology, this movement provided Césaire with the poetic vision and creative license to set his own creative Muse into action. Fleeing the oppressive poverty of his native Martinique, Césaire was ripe for the ideals put forth by the Surrealists. He was attracted, in particular, to the notion of *écriture automatique* (automatic writing) and the Freudian concept of the self, hidden in the recesses of the subconscious, waiting only for a propitious moment to reveal itself. Armed with these two concepts, Césaire destroyed the poems he had written previously and began writing his epic poem *Return to My Native Land*, which would eventually gain for him great fame. More significant, he adopted the methods of the Surrealists in the service of a truly revolutionary cause.

Thus, Césaire's sojourn in France, originally envisioned as an escape from the hopeless conditions in Martinique, resulted instead in his own cultural and political awakening. While pursuing his studies in Paris at the Lycée Louis-le-Grand, he met Léopold Senghor (who later became the first president of Senegal and one of Africa's greatest francophone writers). Thanks to their friendship, Césaire acquired a greater knowledge and appreciation of Africa. Together, they joined forces with Léon Damas, another young poet, to establish the journal *L'Étudiant noir*, which replaced a previous journal, *Légitime défense*, that had been silenced after its first publication. Thus, Césaire's cultural and political consciousness gradually began to take on a more concrete form. Before, racism and colonial exploitation were, in his perception, limited mainly to the geographical confines of the West Indies and, especially, to Martinique. Once in Paris, however, he began to realize that the suffering of blacks extended well beyond the boundaries of his homeland. For Césaire, Senghor, and Damas, the creation of *L'Étudiant noir* was an acknowledgment that blacks in the West Indies, Africa, and elsewhere underwent a common experience.

Although Césaire worked zealously to produce a poem that would express the range, depth, and complexity of his poetic vision, his efforts were not initially received with enthusiasm. The first publisher to whom he submitted *Return to My Native Land* refused to publish the poem. Césaire succeeded in having only excerpts from the poem published in the magazine *Volonté* in 1939. Consequently, both the poet and his work went unnoticed for the most part, but this did little to dampen his creative spirit. When Césaire finally returned to Martinique, where he founded the journal *Tropiques* with the aid of his wife, Suzanne Césaire; René Menil; and Aristide Maugée, he continued to bring to life his poetic inspirations. It was not, however, until Césaire met André Breton (who became aware of Césaire's poetic genius after having read, in *Tropiques*, the poems that make up *Miraculous Weapons*) that Césaire was reintroduced to France's reading public. Subsequent admiration of Césaire's work was not limited to writers or political figures. The 1950 deluxe edition of *Disembodied* contained thirty-two engravings by Pablo Picasso that richly illustrated the ten poems in the collection. The poetic genius which caught the attention of Breton continues to be recognized by Césaire's critics.

RETURN TO MY NATIVE LAND

In his preface to the first complete edition of Aimé Césaire's *Return to My Native Land*, André Breton remarked that this poem represented the "greatest lyrical monument of the times." Indeed, Césaire's first major poem has left an indelible mark upon literature. Of all his works, *Return to My Native Land* is, by far, the most criticized, analyzed, and quoted.

If poetry allows the human spirit to liberate itself from the bonds of reason, as the Surrealists suggest, then it becomes quite clear why Césaire's first major work has such a strong autobiographical tone. The ever-present "I" calls attention to the poet's desire to become rooted once again in his history and culture. Thus, *Return to My Native Land*, a poem of revolt, self-awakening, and "engagement," represents, first and foremost, the poet's personal testimony. From the start, it recalls the town where Césaire grew up, an image which seems both to attract and to repel him. He vividly evokes the stagnant existence of black peasants in Martinique, trapped in poverty and despair, resigned and silent. The emphasis placed on the geographical isolation of the island reinforces, as well, the idea of cultural alienation from the African sources of the black people.

Césaire presents a distressing picture of the poverty in which he and his six brothers and sisters lived. His father's health was being destroyed by an unknown illness, and his mother spent her days and nights operating a Singer sewing machine to help provide the family's daily sustenance. Yet poverty and illness were not the most tragic effects of colonialism and racism, for Césaire saw an entire race reduced to a state of intellectual and emotional apathy, convinced of their inability to build, to create, to take control of their own destiny. It was in response to this sense of apathy and self-contempt that Césaire developed the concept of *négritude*, emphasizing a very proud self-awareness of "blackness" and the distinctive qualities of black culture.

Césaire's recognition and acceptance of Martinique's history, which also represents his own as well, makes it possible for him to purge himself of his feelings of cultural inferiority and to begin his ascent toward a new sense of racial consciousness. From the abyss of despair there arises a magnificent cry of protest. In *Return to My Native Land*, Césaire undertakes what he envisions as a messianic mission: He becomes the voice of the downtrodden, the victims, the exploited, the oppressed—those who are unable to verbalize and articulate their own cry of protest. Critics often compare the poet to Christ, citing as examples the lines in which Césaire takes on himself the prejudices held against blacks. At one point, his account of the inhumanities suffered by blacks is reminiscent of the scourging of Christ. Césaire's acceptance of his Christ-like role strongly underscores the message of "engagement," the poet's role as a socially and politically committed artist.

SHACKLES

The themes and motifs found in Césaire's first major poem recur throughout his oeuvre. *Shackles*, published in 1960, explores the vicissitudes of the black experience in Martinique and the evolution of African culture. The title, which denotes the forging of iron, suggests the era of slavery. Césaire recaptures this brutal moment in black history in the title poem, which is replete with nautical expressions used to evoke the voyage of the slave ship. He uses this image to draw a comparison between the agony suffered by the slaves and the misery which plagues the lives of the Martinicans, "arrimés de cœurs lourds" (stowing heavy hearts). It is with this new generation of slaves, who are not necessarily physically bound by chains, that Césaire is primarily concerned.

The poet recognizes the need to reconcile the present with the past, heretofore rejected and denied, before there can be any real and permanent cultural revolution. Therein lies the salvation of Martinique, cut off physically and emotionally from its African roots. The past represents, in Césaire's words, an old "wound" which has never healed, an "unforgettable insult." Thus, Césaire, with other *négritude* writers, has finally been able to set the record straight, to place colonialism and slavery in their proper perspective. Like all the other sons and daughters of humanity, black people were not destined to be slaves for all time.

African independence has signaled the beginning of a new phase in the history of blacks. Suddenly, it became apparent that the masters of colonialism were not entirely invincible. This is a positive sign for Césaire, who sees in these events a confirmation of the latent force among blacks—a force needed to overcome years of inferiority and submission. His poem "Pour saluer le Tiers Monde" ("Salute to the Third World") is above all one of praise and exaltation. The poet feels an immense sense of pride in the advent of a new African. Césaire punctuates the text, several times, with the emphatic words "I see," calling attention to the fact that he is a witness to these changing times. The image Césaire presents of Africa, unexpectedly standing upright, contrasts, significantly, with his image of Martinique, made powerless by its somnolence. Césaire laments the lack of racial and cultural consciousness among the Martinicans and celebrates Africa, the maternal source of his people. Indeed, to some degree, Césaire places the burden of leadership for the West Indies on Africa. The poet depicts a symbolic ritual in which he covers his body with the soil of Africa in such a way as to infuse himself with her strength. It is important to note that Césaire's treatment of Africa in *Shackles* recalls his original theme of the "return to his native land," which signifies not only a physical journey but also a return to his African heritage.

While he grapples with the larger problems of Martinique's fate, Césaire continues to confront his personal dilemma as a committed artist. His situation is not a unique one; it is one he shares with the educated elite of all Third World nations. With this privileged status comes the awesome responsibility to represent the voice of the masses. In his public life, Césaire does this through his active involvement in the political affairs of Martinique. In the same way, his poetry reaffirms continually his message of racial consciousness and commitment. There is no "art for art's sake" in Césaire's work; style and content are so closely intertwined that it is virtually impossible to talk about one without the other.

In *Return to My Native Land*, Césaire refers to the creative power of words, a power which enables the individual to alter reality. Poetry has allowed the poet the freedom to manipulate and violate the French language in ways that would not have been possible in prose. Thus, the very texture of his language is political; his style is a declaration of independence, shattering conventions associated with the oppressors of his people.

Despite the thematic consistency that characterizes Césaire's oeuvre, a certain movement can be traced from *Return to My Native Land* to *Shackles*. The former deals with the necessity to affirm and reclaim the dignity of blacks. It was the product of a period of intense soul-searching for the poet, who had to overcome his own sense of cultural and racial inferiority. In *Shackles*, on the other hand, Césaire seeks to reconcile the ideals of *négritude* with the existing realities in the West Indies. The masses do not appear to be ready to take their destiny into their own hands, and Césaire has come to realize that the effects of years of silent resignation will be reversed only gradually. In all his works, however, Césaire has remained committed to his people, serving them as visionary, storyteller, historian, and poet.

OTHER MAJOR WORKS

PLAYS: *Et les chiens se taisaient*, pb. 1956; *La Tragédie du Roi Christophe*, pb. 1963 (*The Tragedy of King Christophe*, 1964); *Une Saison au Congo*, pb. 1966 (*A Season in the Congo*, 1968); *Une Tempête, d'après "La Tempête" de Shakespeare: Adaptation pour un théâtre nègre*, pr., pb. 1969 (*The Tempest*, 1974).

NONFICTION: *Discours sur le colonialisme*, 1950 (*Discourse on Colonialism*, 1972); *Toussaint Louverture*, 1960.

MISCELLANEOUS: *Œuvres complètes*, 1976.

BIBLIOGRAPHY

Arnold, A. James. *Modernism and Negritude: The Poetry and Poetics of Aimé Césaire*. Cambridge, Mass.: Harvard University Press, 1981. Crítcal interpretation of Césaire's work presented in its political and cultural context. Aimé Césaire's surrealism is seen as subverting, in the name of black experience, the very European high moderism he assimilated and employed. Includes bibliography and index.

Bailey, Marianne Wichmann. *The Ritual Theater of Aimé Césaire*. Tübingen, Germany: G. Narr, 1992. Analysis of the use of myth and ritual in Aimé Césaire's writing. Includes bibliography.

Confiant, Raphaël. *Aimé Césaire: Une Traversée paradoxale du siècle*. Paris: Stock, 1993. Fellow West Indian writer and professor of literature Confiant examines Césaire in literary, cultural, and political context. In French.

Davis, Gregson. *Aimé Césaire*. New York: Cambridge University Press, 1997. Examines Aimé Césaire's dual career as writer and elected politician. Gregson Davis's account of Aimé Césaire's intellectual growth is grounded in a careful reading of the poetry, prose, and drama that illustrates the full range and depth of his literary achievement.

Eshelman, Clayton, and Annette Smith. Introduction to *Aimé Césaire: The Collected Poetry*. Berkeley: University of California Press, 1983. In this illustrated collection of more than four hundred pages, Eshelman and Smith offer commentary on Césaire to accompany their translations of a selection of his poems for the English-language audience and students. Bibliographical references.

Kesteloot, Lilyan. *Aimé Césaire*. 5th ed. Paris: P. Seghers, 1979. An in-depth critical analysis of Aimé Césaire's work. Includes bibliography. In French.

Martin, Gerald, ed. *Men of Maize*. Pittsburgh: University of Pittsburgh Press, 1993. A collection of essays by various authors relevant to Césaire, poetry as a genre, and Caribbean culture.

Pallister, Janis L. *Aimé Césaire*. New York: Twayne, 1991. Short biography and a critical analysis of Aimé Césaire's work and career. Includes bibliography and index.

Scharfman, Ronnie Leah. *Engagement and the Language of the Subject in the Poetry of Aimé Césaire*. Gainesville: University Presses of Florida, 1987. This monograph addresses issues of race awareness and politics as well as literature. Bibliography, index.

Cherie R. Maiden,
updated by Gordon Walters

GEORGE CHAPMAN

Born: Near Hitchin, England; c. 1559
Died: London, England; May 12, 1634

PRINCIPAL POETRY

The Shadow of Night, 1594
Ovid's Banquet of Sense, 1595
Hero and Leander, 1598 (a completion of Christopher Marlowe's poem)
Euthymiae Raptus: Or, The Tears of Peace, 1609
An Epicede or Funerall Song on the Death of Henry Prince of Wales, 1612
Eugenia, 1614
Andromeda Liberata: Or, The Nuptials of Perseus and Andromeda, 1614
Pro Vere Autumni Lachrymae, 1622

OTHER LITERARY FORMS

In his own time, George Chapman was equally well-known for his poetry and plays. As a leading playwright for the children's companies that performed at the Blackfriars theater, he achieved distinction in both tragedy and comedy. His greatest success in tragedy was *Bussy d'Ambois* (pr. 1604), followed by a sequel, *The Revenge of Bussy d'Ambois* (pr. c. 1610). His other tragedies include the two-part *The Conspiracy and Tragedy of Charles, Duke of Byron* (pr., pb. 1608), as well as *The Tragedy of Chabot, Admiral of France* (pr. c. 1635; with James Shirley) and *Caesar and Pompey* (pr. c. 1613). Chapman also composed the first comedy of humors, *An Humorous Day's Mirth* (pr. 1597), followed by romantic and satiric comedies, including *The Blind Beggar of Alexandria* (pr. 1596), *The Gentleman Usher* (pr. c. 1602), *All Fools* (wr. 1599, pr. c. 1604), *Monsieur d'Olive* (pr. 1604), *The Widow's Tears* (pr. c. 1605), and *May Day* (pr. c. 1609).

A<small>CHIEVEMENTS</small>

George Chapman regarded his English translations of Homer's *Odyssey* and *Iliad* (both c. 800 B.C.E.) as "the work that I was born to do." An arduous, demanding task which occupied him for thirty years, his translation was commissioned by the youthful son of James I, Prince Henry, whose untimely death at the age of eighteen left the poet without a patron. Although he continued to work in spite of the lack of patronage, he turned to the stage and to original verse to make his living. That John Keats found looking into Chapman's Homer a thrilling discovery, which he subsequently immortalized in a sonnet, is a tribute to the quality of this work, which has not been generally admired. Chapman's translation has receded into obscurity as an archaic and quaint achievement.

Chapman's original poetry, which is characterized by a remarkable range of theme and style, is often considered difficult or even obscure for the modern reader. A largely philosophical poet, Chapman incorporates challenging intellectual concepts and images in his verse. Some of his more explicitly philosophical poems, such as *The Shadow of Night*, are rich in Neoplatonic thought, an abstruse subject. Others, such as his continuation of Christopher Marlowe's unfinished *Hero and Leander* (1598), convey ideas through emblematic and iconographic techniques. In the poem *Ovid's Banquet of Sense*, he writes partly in the manner of the erotic epyllion and partly in the more Metaphysical vein of sharply intellectual conceits, while in *Euthymiae Raptus* he writes more in the style of satiric allegory, with pointed, polished heroic couplets. Some of his poems are occasional, such as the *Andromeda Liberata*, which celebrates the notorious marriage of the king's favorite, Robert Carr, to Lady Frances Howard, later implicated in the murder of Thomas Overbury. Chapman's choice of the Andromeda myth to represent Frances's unconsummated marriage with the young Earl of Essex was extremely tactless, and the poet had to publish a justification and explication of what was interpreted as an insulting poem. Some of his poems are mystical, as is the

first section of *Euthymiae Raptus*, where he relates his encounter with the flaming vision of Homer's spirit, which inspired him to his translation, and as is the "Hymn to Our Savior," included in the collection called *Petrarch's Seven Penitential Psalms* (1612), and concerned with the theme of transcending fleshly experience. Finally, Chapman also wrote two fine elegies, *Eugenia*, written on the death of Lord Russell, and *An Epicede or Funerall Song on the Death of Henry Prince of Wales*, on the death of the much loved and genuinely lamented Prince Henry.

B<small>IOGRAPHY</small>

Although George Chapman was born into a fairly wealthy and well-connected family, it was his fate to suffer poverty because he was the younger son. Not much is known about his early years. He spent some time at Oxford but did not take a degree there. After a brief period of service in the household of a nobleman, he saw military action on the Continent, participating in the Low Country campaigns of 1591-1592. His first literary accomplishment was the publication of *The Shadow of Night*, an esoteric poem reflecting his association with a group of erudite young scholars, including Sir Walter Ralegh, all of whom reputedly dabbled in the occult. His publication of a continuation of Marlowe's *Hero and Leander* clearly established his relationship with the ill-fated younger playwright.

His own early career as a playwright barely supported him, and Chapman was imprisoned for debt in 1600. After his release, he attempted to supplement his income from the stage by seeking patronage for his nondramatic poetry. The youthful Prince Henry, a genuine patron of the arts, offered to support Chapman's proposed translation of the complete works of Homer. Unfortunately, the death of the young prince put an end to such hopes, and Chapman was never to be completely free from the specter of poverty. When he collaborated with Ben Jonson and John Marston on the city comedy *Eastward Ho!* (pr., pb. 1605), Chapman found himself in prison again, this time for the play's supposed slander against Scots. Largely through his own epistolary efforts directed toward both the king and other dignitaries, Chapman and fellow prisoner Jonson were released without having their noses slit, the usual punishment for the given offense.

After his release from prison, Chapman continued to write both plays and poetry and to continue the laborious work of translation even without the aid of patronage. He eventually became an acknowledged literary success in all these endeavors, honored in *The English Parnassus* (1657), lauded by the critic Francis Meres as one of the best in both comedy and tragedy, and believed by some modern critics to have been the "rival poet" of William Shakespeare. Although little is known about his later years, historian Anthony à Wood's description of the elderly poet as "reverend, religious, and sober" suggests his continuing dedication to the serious art of poetry and to the subtle art of life.

When Chapman died at the age of seventy-four, his monument was fashioned by Inigo Jones, the noted theatrical designer with whom Chapman had collaborated on court masques. His Latin inscription was "Georgis Chapmanus, poeta Homericus, Philosophers verus (etsi Christianus poeta)."

ANALYSIS

George Chapman's poetry is unusually diversified. It does not reveal a consistent individual style, technique, or attitude, so that an initial reading does not immediately divulge a single creative mind at work. A skilled experimenter, Chapman tried the Metaphysical style of John Donne, the satirical heroic couplet in a manner anticipating John Dryden, and in his translations reverted to the archaic medieval fourteener. His poetry is also unusually difficult. His allusions are often esoteric, his syntax strained or convoluted, and his underlying ideas verging on the occult. His is not primarily a lyrical voice, and his verses are almost never musical. For Chapman the content of poetry is supreme, and the poet's moral calling is profound. His work, in consequence, is essentially didactic.

Chapman's poetics, as expressed in scattered epistles and dedications attached to his verses, help clarify his intentions and to reveal the purpose behind what may strike the reader as willful obscurity. Philosophically, Chapman was a Platonist, and he was well read in Neoplatonic writings. His poetic theories are a metaphorical counterpart to Platonic dualism. The fact that precious minerals are buried in the ground rather than easily available on the surface suggests to Chapman that the spirit of poetry must lie beneath the obvious surface meaning of the words. The body of poetry may delight the ear with its smooth, melodious lines, but the soul speaks only to the inward workings of the mind. Thus, Chapman rejects the Muse that will sing of love's sensual fulfillment in favor of his mistress Philosophy, who inspires the majesty and riches of the mind. The reader must not be misled by the outer bark or rind of the poems, to use another of his analogies, but should rather seek the fruit of meaning deep within. Scorning the profane multitude, Chapman consecrates his verses to those readers with minds willing to search.

ALLEGORY AND EMBLEM

Two of the techniques that Chapman employs most often to achieve his somewhat arcane didactic purposes are allegory and emblem. His poems are frequently allegorical, both in the sense that he introduces personified abstractions as spokesmen for his ideas and in the sense that a given event or personage stands for another. He reveals his allegorical cast of mind in dealing with such objects as love, war, or learning by envisioning them as personified abstractions, clothing them in appropriate iconographical garments, and situating them in emblematic tableaux. His use of emblems thus grows out of his allegorical mode of thought. Drawing on the popular emblem books of the Renaissance, he depicts scenes or images from nature or mythology as iconographic equivalents of ideas. A torn scarf, for example, becomes a confused mind, and an uprooted tree a fallen hero. The technique is symbolic and highly visual, but static rather than dramatic.

Since Chapman regarded his Homeric translations as his major poetic mission in life, he did not consider his own poetry as a great achievement. He regarded the calling of the poet with great seriousness, however, and his poems as a result have much of importance to say. In spite of their difficulty and partly because of it, his unusual poems speak to the sensitive reader willing to dig below the often formidable surface.

THE SHADOW OF NIGHT

Chapman's first published poem, *The Shadow of Night*, consists of two complementary poems, "Hymnus in Noctem" and "Hymnus in Cynthiam." The first is a lament, the second a hymn of praise. The first is concerned with contemplation, the second with action. Both celebrate the intellect and assert the superiority of darkness over daylight. Sophisticated in structure, esoteric in allusion, and steeped in the philosophy of Neoplatonism, the work is a challenge to the general reader.

The object of lament in "Hymnus in Noctem" is the fallen state of the world. Chapman contrasts the debased world of the present day, rife with injustice, to the primal chaos that existed when night was ruler. In that time before creation, there was harmony, for chaos had soul without body; but now bodies thrive without soul. Men are now blind, experiencing a "shadow" night of intellect which is a reversal of genuine night. The poet then calls upon the spirit of night to send Furies into the world to punish the rampant wickedness of men. He will aid the Furies by castigating sinful humankind in his verses and by writing tragedies aimed at moral reformation.

As night is praised for its creative darkness, the source of inner wisdom, daylight is regarded negatively, associated with whoredom, rape, and unbridled lust. Chapman warns the great virgin queen, here equated with the moon goddess, that an unwise marriage would eclipse her virtue, removing her from the wise mysteries of the night and exposing her to brash daylight. The poem ends with an emblematic scene, as Cynthia appears in an ivory chariot, accompanied by comets, meteors, and lightning.

"Hymnus in Cynthiam" proclaims praise for Cynthia as pattern of all virtue, wisdom, and beauty, at once moon goddess, divine soul of the world, and Queen Elizabeth I. Cynthia is portrayed here in her daytime role, and the active life of daylight is contrasted to night as the time for contemplation. During the day Cynthia descends from the moon to earth, where she fashions a nymph named Euthymia, or Joy, out of meteoric stuff. Out of the same vapors, she creates a hunter and his hounds. Chapman's narrative of a shadowy hunting scene is probably based on the myth of Acteon and his hounds. The poet's allegorical version of the myth depicts the hunt as appropriate to the daylight, a time of sensual and otherwise sinful behavior. The object of the hunt is debased joy, which attracts the base affections (the hunting hounds) and the rational souls, submitting to passion (the hunters on their horses), follow after. This pageant of desire is essentially unreal, however, as daytime itself is unreal, and Cynthia promptly disposes of the hounds when night arrives. The mystical darkness offers an opportunity for true joy found only in the spiritual and intellectual fulfillment made possible by contemplative, nocturnal solitude.

The major themes of this two-part poem are thus the Platonic vision of inward contentment, the true joy afforded by contemplation, and the superiority of darkness over daylight. Writing partly in the ancient tradition of the Orphic hymns, Chapman veils his meaning in a mysterious religious atmosphere. The allegorical hunt and the emblematic scenes are, however, vividly described and poetically clear. The poem ends with a tribute to the immutability of Cynthia. Although the original harmony of primal darkness is gone, Cynthia will try to restore virtue to the degenerate world.

OVID'S BANQUET OF SENSE

Prefacing the volume of poems featuring Chapman's next major poem, *Ovid's Banquet of Sense*, is a brief statement of the poet's convictions about his craft. Here he admits that he hates the profane multitude, asserts that he addresses his intentionally difficult poetry to a select audience, and appeals to those few readers who have a "light-bearing intellect" to appreciate his arcane verses. At first reading, the 117 stanzas of this poem do not seem very esoteric at all. Ostensibly, *Ovid's Banquet of Sense* follows the currently popular mode of the erotic epyllion, as exemplified in William Shakespeare's *Venus and Adonis* (1593). If one follows Chapman's warning, however, one feels committed to search beneath the surface for deeper meaning.

The narrative structure of the poem follows the experience of Ovid in the garden of his mistress Corinna. In the garden he is able to feast his senses on her while he remains hidden from her view. The first of his senses to be gratified is hearing, or *auditus*, as Corinna plays on her lute, fingering the strings and sweetly singing delightful lyrics. Then, as Ovid draws somewhat nearer to where she is seated at her bath, he is greeted by the overpowering fragrance of the spices she uses in bathing her body. His sense of smell, or *olfactus*, is now enchanted. Moving closer to the arbor in order to see her more clearly, Ovid is next able to feast his eyes on her inviting nakedness. The longest section of the poem is devoted to this languorous satisfaction of sight, or *visus*. The poet indulges in lavish sensual imagery to describe the experience. Ovid's intense pleasure in the sight of his unclothed mistress ends abruptly, however, when she looks into her glass and suddenly sees him staring at her. Quickly wrapping herself in a cloud, she reproaches him for his immodest spying on her private bath. Ovid defends himself very convincingly, arguing that since his senses of hearing, smell, and sight have already been satisfied, he has a right to ask for a kiss to satisfy his sense of taste, or *gustus*. She grants him the kiss, which is also described in richly provocative language, but the ingenious would-be lover then argues for gratification of the ultimate sense, touch, or *tactus*.

Corinna is responsive to Ovid's seductive plea, and when he lightly touches her side, she starts as if electrified. Like Ovid, the reader is aroused by the prolonged erotic buildup, but both are doomed to a letdown. At this climactic moment the scene is interrupted by the sudden appearance of several other women, Corinna's friends, who have come to paint in the garden. Having led both his hero and his reader to expect more, the poet now drops the narrative with a somewhat smug remark that much more is intended but must be omitted.

In the final stanza Chapman refers to the "curious frame" of his poem, suggesting that it resembles a painting, wherein not everything can be seen, some things having to be inferred. The meaning beneath the surface, about which Chapman warned the reader, emerges from this awareness. The reader, like Ovid, has been put in the position of voyeur. Chapman has tricked the reader into false expectations and into assuming a morally ambiguous role. Indeed, the frustration seems worse for the suspenseful reader than for the abandoned lover, for Ovid is not disappointed by the anticlimax but instead is inspired to write his *Ars amatoria* (c. 2 B.C.E.; *Art of Love*). It is the reader who is trapped forever inside the curious frame. In spite of this trickery, *Ovid's Banquet of Sense* is likely to be one of Chapman's most appealing poems for the general reader. The primarily pictorial imagery, the undercurrent of irony, the escalating narrative movement through the five sensory experiences, and the vivid sensuality of Ovid's responsiveness to his mistress combine to make it at once a dramatic and lyrical reading, unlike Chapman's usual heavy didacticism.

"A CORONET FOR HIS MISTRESS PHILOSOPHY"

The didactic point of view is supplied by the series of interlinked sonnets which follow, "A Coronet for His Mistress Philosophy." Offering a moral perspective on the ambiguity of *Ovid's Banquet of Sense*, this series is circular, as its title implies, with the last line of each sonnet becoming the first line of the next, coming full circle at the end by repeating the opening line. Here Chapman renounces the Muses that sing of love's "sensual emperie" and rejects the violent torments of sexual desire in favor of devotion to the benevolent mistress, Philosophy. The poet's active and industrious pen will henceforth devote itself to the unchanging beauty of this intellectual mistress, whose virtues will in turn inspire him to ever greater art.

HERO AND LEANDER

Chapman's continuation of Christopher Marlowe's *Hero and Leander* is also a narrative love poem. Marlowe's premature death in 1594 left unfinished his poetic version of this tragic love story from the classical world. What survives of Marlowe's work is two sestiads, which leave the narrative incomplete. Chapman undertook to finish the poem, publishing his own four sestiads in 1598. Chapman claims that he drank with Marlowe from the fountain of the Muses, but acknowledged that his own draft inspired verse more "grave" and "high." Whereas Marlowe had been concerned with the physical beauty of the lovers and exalted their passion, Chapman takes a moral approach to their relationship, condemning their failure to sacramentalize physical love through marriage.

In the third sestiad the goddess Ceremony descends from heaven to reproach Leander. Her body is as transparent as glass, and she wears a rich pentacle filled with mysterious signs and symbols. In one hand she carries a mathematical crystal, a burning-glass capable of destroying Confusion, and in the other, a laurel rod with which to bend back barbarism. Her awesome reproof of Leander likens love without marriage to meat without seasoning, desire without delight, unsigned bills, and unripened corn. Leander immediately vows to celebrate the requisite nuptial rites. Meanwhile, Hero lies on her bed, torn between guilt and passion. Her conflict gradually gives way to resolution as thoughts of her lover's beauty prevail over her sense of shame. In the end, love triumphs over fear.

In the fourth sestiad, Hero offers a sacrifice to the goddess Venus, who accuses her devotee of dissembling loyalty to her. Venus darts fire from her eyes to burn the sacrificial offering, and Hero tries to shield herself from the rage of the deity with a picture of Leander. The divinely repudiated offering is clearly a bad omen.

The fifth sestiad is introduced with Hero's expression of impatience for night to bring her lover. The marriage theme is also reinforced in the form of an allegorical digression about a wedding staged and observed by Hero in order to make the time seem to pass more quickly and pleasantly. The wedding scene also introduces a wild nymph, Teras, a name given to comets portending evil. Teras sings a tale to the wedding party, following it with a delicately lyrical epithalamium. As she finishes the song, however, she suddenly assumes her comet nature, and with her hair standing on end, she glides out of the company. Her back appears black, striking terror into the hearts of all, especially Hero, who anxiously awaits her lover.

Night finally arrives in the sixth sestiad, bringing with it the tragic climax of the poem. Determined to swim the Hellespont in order to see Hero, Leander takes his fatal plunge into the stormy sea. Vainly he calls upon first Venus, then Neptune, for help against the violent waves tormenting his body, but the swimmer is doomed. Angry Neptune hurls his marble mace against the fates to forestall the fatal moment, but to no avail. The god then brings the drowned body of Leander on shore, where Hero sees him and, grief-stricken, dies calling his name. Moved by pity, the kindly god of the sea transforms the lovers into birds called Acanthides, or Thistle-Warps, which always fly together in couples.

Although Chapman's continuation lacks the classical grace and sensuous imagery of Marlowe's first two sestiads, it is poetically successful. His poem has a variety of styles, ranging from classical simplicity to Renaissance ornateness. The inevitable tragic plot is deepened by Chapman through the theme of moral responsibility and the role of form and ritual in civilization. He uses personified abstractions effectively, as in the case of the imposing goddess Ceremony, and he demonstrates his mythmaking skills in the person of the comet-nymph

Teras. His emblematic verse intensifies the visual effects of the poem, often making it painterly in the manner of *Ovid's Banquet of Sense*. In his poem, his didacticism is happily integrated with story and character rather than being imposed from without. Of all Chapman's poems, *Hero and Leander* is the most accessible to the contemporary reader.

EUTHYMIAE RAPTUS

Euthymiae Raptus is a substantial (1,232-line) allegorical poem. The immediate occasion which called it forth was the truce in the war with The Netherlands, which had been brought about through the mediation of King James, and the poem is dedicated to the young Prince Henry. It is, however, much more than an occasional poem. Partly autobiographical and partly philosophical, as well as partly topical, it is a major achievement.

The opening *inductio* has primary autobiographical value. Here Chapman relates his personal, mystical encounter with the spirit of Homer. The poet had been meditating when he suddenly perceived a figure clothed in light with a bosom full of fire and breathing flames. It is at once obvious that the apparition is blind, though gifted with inward sight. The spirit then identifies itself as Homer, come to praise Chapman for his translations and to reveal the reason why the world has not achieved a state of peace. Invisible until this moment, Homer has been inspiring Chapman's poetry for a long time. At the end of this section, Homer shows Chapman a vision of the lady Peace mourning over a coffin, despairing the death of Love. A brief *invocatio* follows, spoken by the poet, while Peace, pouring out tears of grief, prepares to speak.

The third and major section of the poem is structured as a dialogue between Peace and the poet as Interlocutor. This section is essentially a thoughtful and impassioned antiwar poem. Typical of Chapman's philosophical cast of mind, the poem probes the cause of war throughout human history. Peace's lament for Love clearly relates the fact of war to the death of Love, but why has Love died? Peace attributes the demise of Love to lack of learning among people in general. Genuine learning, according to Peace, implies a capability for original thought, without which men can never arrive at a true knowledge of God. It is this deprived state of mind and soul that has made war possible. The failure of learning keeps men from knowing God, thereby bringing about the end of Love, and Love is necessary to sustain Peace.

The concept of learning elucidated in this poem is not so much intellectual as ethical. Learning is viewed as the art of good life. Chapman cites three classes of men in particular who are dangerous enemies of this ideal: first, the active men, who aim only at worldly success and reject learning in favor of ruthlessly pursuing ambition; second, the passive men, who simply neglect learning while they waste time in mere pleasures; and, finally, the intellective men, who debase learning because they pursue their studies only for the sake of social and financial reward. Genuine learning, to be attained for its own sake, empowers the soul with control over the body's distracting passions and perturbations. Those who are called scholars in this world are all too often mere "walking dictionaries" or mere "articulate clocks" who cannot "turn blood to soul" and who will therefore never come to know God. These three categories of nonlearners and perverters of learning willingly enter the destructive toils of war.

LEGACY

These four long poems, along with the elegies *Eugenia* and *An Epicede or Funerall Song on the Death of Henry Prince of Wales* and the occasional pieces, *Andromeda Liberata* and *Pro Vere Autumni Lachrymae*, represent most of Chapman's original verse. There are also a few short pieces called *Petrarch's Seven Penitential Psalms*, consisting largely of translations. The body of Chapman's original poetry is thus limited in scope but impressive in quality. Although *The Shadow of Night* is occasionally obscure in poetic diction, and although *Euthymiae Raptus* at times proves slow going in its didacticism, both of these poems are nevertheless rich in thought and are distinguished by several passages of high poetic caliber. *Ovid's Banquet of Sense* and *Hero and Leander* are actually two of the finest narrative poems of the English Renaissance.

The modern reader has much to gain from Chapman. His subtlety and irony appeal to the intellect, and his emblematic and metaphorical language pleases the aesthetic imagination. His is a distinctive Renaissance voice not circumscribed by the formulaic patterns of that highly conventional age. He is above all a serious writer, committed to the lofty calling of poetry as a vehicle of ideas through the medium of figurative language.

OTHER MAJOR WORKS

PLAYS: *The Blind Beggar of Alexandria*, pr. 1596 (fragment); *An Humorous Day's Mirth*, pr. 1597; *All Fools*, wr. 1599, pr. 1604 (also known as *The World Runs on Wheels*); *The Gentleman Usher*, pr. c. 1602; *Monsieur d'Olive*, pr. 1604; *Bussy d'Ambois*, pr. 1604; *Eastward Ho!*, pr., pb. 1605 (with Ben Jonson and John Marston); *The Widow's Tears*, pr. c. 1605; *The Conspiracy and Tragedy of Charles, Duke of Byron*, pr., pb. 1608; *May Day*, pr. c. 1609; *The Revenge of Bussy d'Ambois*, pr. c. 1610; *The Masque of the Middle Temple and Lincoln's Inn*, pr. 1613 (masque); *Caesar and Pompey*, pr. c. 1613; *The Ball*, pr. 1632 (with James Shirley); *The Tragedy of Chabot, Admiral of France*, pr. 1635 (with Shirley).

TRANSLATIONS: *Iliad*, 1598, 1609, 1611 (of Homer); *Petrarch's Seven Penitential Psalms*, 1612; *Odyssey*, 1614 (of Homer); *Georgics*, 1618 (of Hesiod); *The Crown of All Homer's Works*, 1624 (of Homer's lesser-known works).

BIBLIOGRAPHY

Braunmuller, A. R. *Natural Fictions: George Chapman's Major Tragedies*. Newark: University of Delaware Press, 1992. Braunmuller presents Chapman's plays in their relation to the poet's theory of art and its connections to the world of history and experience that censored two of his plays and punished him because these dramas offended the French court.

Donno, Elizabeth Story. "The Epyllion." In *English Poetry and Prose, 1540-1674*, edited by Christopher Ricks. New York: Peter Bedrick Books, 1986. Donno's essay provides an excellent introduction to Elizabethan narrative poetry, especially the mythological variety. Her account of Chapman's narrative verse is sound; another chapter covers his dramatic poetry. The index offers good cross-referencing. Includes a select bibliography.

Hulse, Clark. *Metamorphic Verse: The Elizabethan Minor Epic*. Princeton, N.J.: Princeton University

Press, 1981. Hulse has accomplished the most complete redefinition of Elizabethan narrative poetry of modern times. His account of Chapman and his contribution is thorough and complete. The bibliographical apparatus is professional.

Huntington, John. *Ambition, Rank, and Poetry in 1590's England*. Urbana: University of Illinois Press, 2001. Huntington uncovers a form of subtle social protest encoded in the writings of aspiring Elizabethan poets, and argues that these writers invested their poetry with a new social vision that challenged a nobility of blood and proposed a nobility of learning instead. Huntington focuses on the early work of George Chapman and on the writings of others who shared his social agenda and his nonprivileged status.

Kermode, Frank. "The Banquet of Sense." In *Shakespeare, Spenser, Donne*. London: Routledge & Kegan Paul, 1971. Presents a revelatory commentary on Chapman's narratives; the insights are simply unparalleled. Includes substantial notes, a bibliography, and an index.

MacLure, Millar. *George Chapman: A Critical Study*. Toronto: University of Toronto Press, 1966. This full-scale critical analysis of all Chapman's writing includes extensive coverage of his narrative poetry and integrates it well with the rest of his life's work. MacLure pays particular attention to his diction and his use of poetic devices. Contains an index, notes, and a bibliography.

Snare, Gerald. *The Mystification of George Chapman*. Durham, N.C.: Duke University Press, 1989. The title is slightly misleading. This first-rate critical analysis actually attempts to demystify Chapman and his work, which had suffered from a prevailing view that it was unnecessarily obscure and contorted. Snare's discussions are lucid. Includes good notes, an index, and a bibliography.

Spivack, Charlotte. *George Chapman*. New York: Twayne, 1967. This brief volume offers a good overview of Chapman's life and provides instructive surveys of his works; the account is coherent and clear. Includes a chronology, notes and references, a select bibliography, and an index.

Waddington, Raymond B. *The Mind's Empire: Myth and Form in George Chapman's Narrative Poems*.

Baltimore: The Johns Hopkins University Press, 1974. Focuses exclusively on Chapman's poems; analyzes them exhaustively and relates them to their cultural and historical backgrounds. Emphasis is on structural analysis. Contains an extensive bibliography, an index, and complete notes.

Charlotte Spivack;
bibliography updated by the editors

RENÉ CHAR

Born: L'Île-en-Sorgue, France; June 14, 1907
Died: Paris, France; February 19, 1988

PRINCIPAL POETRY

Les Cloches sur le cœur, 1928
Arsenal, 1929
Ralentir travaux, 1930 (with Paul Éluard and André Breton)
Le Marteau sans maître, 1934
Moulin premier, 1937
Placard pour un chemin des écoliers, 1937
Dehors la nuit est gouvernée, 1938
Le Visage nuptial, 1938 (*The Nuptial Countenance*, 1976)
Seuls demeurant, 1945
Feuillets d'Hypnos, 1946 (*Leaves of Hypnos*, 1973)
Le Poème pulvérisé, 1947
Fureur et mystère, 1948
Les Matinaux, 1950
Lettera amorosa, 1953
Hypnos Waking, 1956
Poèmes et prose choisis, 1957
Cinq Poésies en hommage à Georges Braque, 1958
La Parole en archipel, 1962
Commune présence, 1964
Le Nu perdu, 1971
La Nuit talismanique, 1972
Aromates chasseurs, 1976
Poems of René Char, 1976
Selected Poems of René Char, 1992

OTHER LITERARY FORMS

Like many French poets, René Char has written a great number of prose poems and is considered one of the finest practitioners in this genre since Charles Baudelaire and Arthur Rimbaud, by whom he was heavily influenced. These works are scattered throughout Char's poetry collections, suggesting that he does not distinguish the prose poem as a separate form. Char has published several volumes of essays, including *Recherche de la base et du sommet* (1955; inquiry into the base and the summit) and *Sur la poésie* (1958; on poetry). He has also contributed a number of prefaces, introductions, and catalogs for art shows, such as the 1973 Picasso exhibit in Avignon. Char's lifelong interest in painting is reflected in essays on Georges Braque, Joan Miró, and other contemporary artists; he has also been active in other arts, writing the scenario for the ballet *L'Abominable Homme des neiges* (1956; the abominable snowman), for example, and the play *Le Soleil des eaux* (1949). Char's work has been set to music by composer Pierre Boulez.

René Char (© Irisson)

ACHIEVEMENTS

Early in his poetic career, René Char was deeply involved in Surrealism, coauthoring several works with Paul Éluard and André Breton and gaining some recognition for his work. Under that influence, he was encouraged in his taste for the fragment—the incomplete line and "broken" metaphor, which he called *le poème pulvérisé*. These Surrealist techniques led to his being identified with the movement but did not lead to serious individual recognition.

After World War II, Char dedicated his *Leaves of Hypnos* to Albert Camus, a fellow Resistance fighter, who called Char France's greatest living poet, praising his shift from the self-absorption of Surrealism to a more universal view. Char thereby became associated with the rising tide of existentialism and achieved recognition as a major poet. Char also is credited with achieving a new validation for the prose poem, which, though it had a long tradition in France, was still regarded as a stepchild of "real" poetry.

BIOGRAPHY

René-Émile Char was born on June 14, 1907, the son of Émile Char, a manufacturer, and Marie-Thérèse-Armand Rouget of Cavaillon. Char's father, who served as the mayor of L'Île-en-Sorgue, was the son of a ward of the state who had been given the name "Charlemagne," later shortened to "Char-Magne" and, eventually, to "Char." Char spent his childhood in L'Île-en-Sorgue in the Vaucluse region in the south of France. The Vaucluse has a lush landscape ringed with mountains, the beauty of which would later fill his poetry. It is also an area of diverse industries, and the young Char became familiar with men of many occupations, especially craftsmen, peasants, and Sorgue River fishermen. Their rugged independence helped to instill in him a lifelong love of freedom. The boy had begun his education in the public schools when his father died in 1918. He then continued to the *lycée* in Avignon (the closest large city) for his *baccalauréat*. In 1924, he spent some time in Tunisia, where he developed a distaste for colonialism. He returned to study briefly at the École-de-Commerce in Marseilles, leaving from 1927 to 1928 for artillery service in Nîmes. In 1928, he published his first book of poems, *Les Cloches sur le cœur*.

Char sent a copy of his second collection, *Arsenal*, to Paul Éluard, the chief poet of Surrealism, in Paris. Éluard was impressed with Char's work and went to L'Île-en-Sorgue to meet him. They became lifelong friends, and Char moved to Paris, where Éluard introduced him to the leading figures of Surrealism, including André Breton. Char cowrote the poem *Ralentir travaux* (works slowed down) with Éluard and Breton and helped found the periodical *La Surréalisme au service de la révolution*. In 1933, Char married Georgette Goldstein (they were divorced in 1949) and a year later published *Le Marteau sans maître* (the hammer without a master). During the early 1930's, he resided sometimes in Paris, sometimes in L'Île-en-Sorgue, and made several trips to Spain.

By the mid-1930's, the political climate in Europe was changing, and Char broke with the Surrealists in 1934, as Éluard soon would, sensing a need for the kind of action hinted at in *Le Marteau sans maître*: the defense of the oppressed and the fight for justice. In 1935, Char accepted a job as manager of the chalk pits in Vaucluse, but he soon resigned. In 1936, he was seriously ill as a result of blood poisoning, and he spent a year—the same year the Spanish Civil War began—convalescing in Cannes. He published *Placard pour un chemin des écoliers* (sign for a bypath) and *Dehors la nuit est gouvernée* (somewhere night is ruled) in the late 1930's, both titles indicating his growing sense of commitment. As 1939 ended, Char found himself mobilized into the artillery in Alsace, where he fought until the French surrender.

Returning to L'Île-en-Sorgue, Char was suspected by the Vichy police of being a communist because of his association with Surrealism. He fled with Georgette to the Alps and there began his activities as a *maquisard* in the Armée Secrète. Using the name Captain Alexandre from 1943 to 1945, Char became the departmental commander of the Parachute Landing Division of the Second Region of the *Forces françaises combattantes*, and deputy to the regional commander of the Free French operations network. He was wounded in combat against the Germans in June, 1944, and, after being cared for by Resistance doctors, he continued to Algeria in July, 1944, in response to a summons from the North Africa Allied Council. Subsequently, he was parachuted into

France and participated in the battles to liberate Provence. Demobilized in 1945, he received several decorations for his service, including the Croix de Guerre and the Médaille de la Résistance.

From 1939 to the liberation of France, Char had not published any poetry. When *Seuls demeurant* (the only ones left) and *Leaves of Hypnos* appeared, he became famous. Georges Mounin's critique *Avez-vous lu Char?* (1947; Have you read Char?) praised Char's work and contributed to his success. Char again began to live part of each year in Paris and part in the Vaucluse; he did not, however, participate in the "official" literary life. He has generally declined the honors offered to him, although he was made a Chevalier de la Légion d'Honneur and received the Prix des Critiques in 1966, and he argues that poetry should not be considered a means of making a living. He also stood apart from the partisan political involvements which entangled many French writers of the time—especially those who shared Char's leftist sympathies.

One of Char's closest friends was the novelist Albert Camus, who, like Char, linked literature with the struggle toward freedom and human dignity. Char also exchanged letters with the Russian poet and novelist Boris Pasternak and, beginning in 1955, kept in close contact with the German philosopher Martin Heidegger.

Throughout the 1950's and 1960's, the audience for Char's poetry grew, and he was translated into numerous foreign languages. Beginning with his association with Georges Braque in 1947, Char has often published his poetry in beautiful editions, illustrated by celebrated contemporary artists such as Picasso, Nicolas de Staël, Louis Broder, and Louis Fernandez. Char also illustrated his poetry himself. His interest in philosophy has dominated his later poetry, and since the 1950's, Char saw his role as poet as that of a commentator on society, a revolutionary in the service of humankind. He died in Paris on February 19, 1988.

ANALYSIS

Albert Camus once wrote that René Char's poetry was both ancient and new, subtle and simple, carrying both daytime and night: "In the brilliant landscape where Char was born, the sun . . . is something dark." Camus thus identified one of the predominant characteristics of Char's poetic method: the juxtaposition of opposites. According to critic Robert W. Greene, Char has rejected one of the fundamental concepts of Western thought: the Aristotelian principle that a thing cannot be anything other than what it is at one moment in time. Any poem working within different principles seems as obscure and vaporous as Eastern religions which deny the reality of the world. Char, however, deeply admires the fragments of Heraclitus—who believed in the unity of opposites—and sets up oppositions throughout his poetry. Similar concepts can be found in earlier poetry influenced by Eastern thought, such as Ralph Waldo Emerson's "Brahma," in which the slayer is simultaneously the one who is slain. Char's rejection of the identity principle, however, has different implications in its twentieth century context. It reflects the linguistic, subjective philosophies developing in the late nineteenth and early twentieth centuries, and though Char has a tendency toward the fragmentary aphorism (possibly influenced by the fragments of Heraclitus), he grapples with modern problems in a specific way. Thus, as Camus rightly observed, Char's poetry is both "ancient and new."

"COMMUNE PRÉSENCE"

The concluding lines of Char's important early poem "Commune présence" are characteristic in their conjunction of opposites: "You have been created for extraordinary moments . . . Adjust yourself and disperse without regret." Here, a near-heroic proclamation of identity is immediately followed by a line advising assimilation. The following line, "According to a soft hardness," embodies yet another contradiction and illustrates Char's technique of opposing semantic units. It furthermore conveys Char's fundamental view of a world of unsynthesized opposites. Life is simultaneously total resistance and total acceptance. One is reminded of the existentialist assertions that whatever a person does is completely absurd, yet that it is necessary to act as if each moment had meaning. The final two lines of the poem contain a command: "Swarm the dust/ No one will decelerate your union." The penultimate line is a contradiction because a swarm of bees is similar to a cloud of dust only in appearance. Dust moves at random, each mote in its own direction; bees move in rough unison. Dust dissipates into nothingness; bees have a vi-

tal purpose. The final line promises that nothing can oppose the eventual union, however—the union that comes from an initial scattering. In political terms, one sees the allusion to humankind as a collection of individual, meaningless units (like dust), which can gain new meaning by union (like a swarm). All those meaningless units (bees, motes, people), added together, become meaning. Metaphorically, darkness becomes the sun.

SURREALIST PERIOD

Char's early association with Surrealism might be regarded as an influence in that direction, or it may be seen as a reflection of what Char already was reaching for in his work. As Camus wrote, "No doubt he did take part in Surrealism, but rather as an ally than as an adherent, and just long enough to discover that he could walk alone with more conviction." This is the general critical appraisal. Anna Balakian, however, asserts that Char carries on the tradition of Surrealism better than anyone else. As Char describes in *Le Poème pulvérisé*, he faces—like Breton and the others—"this rebellious and solitary world of contradictions" and cannot live without the image of the unknown before him. In this vast unknown, this world finally impossible to understand (hence the Surrealist's despair), one can only be an explorer, and poetry is the medium of exploration: words and meaning in conflict. Irrationality is crucial in setting aside the world of illusion and seeing beyond, to the more legitimate world of dreams. *The Nuptial Countenance* has been cited as exhibiting this trait in its mixing of objects that defy classification; it has many resemblances to the works of Breton and Éluard.

Critic Mechthild Cranston argues that Char took two important insights with him when he broke with Surrealism: He saw that the existing world order was in need of reexamination, along with the canons of art, and that violence and destruction would not solve the problems of his generation. The first idea has remained with him throughout his career, in his commitment to the Resistance and in his generally leftist politics. The second, however, has undergone modification. In Char's Surrealist period, he speaks of the need for violence, catastrophes, and crimes to help create a new concept of art. "Les Soleils chanteurs" mentions specific kinds of violence which will revitalize poetry. Char's poetry of this period is filled with images of chemicals, metals, and machinery, like the works of the Futurists, and has a similar purpose: to destroy the florid, false language of late Romanticism. Char's experience of the real—not metaphorical—violence of World War II changed his orientation. In his poetry published since the war, he has abandoned the rhetoric of the Surrealists, achieving a new humility and seeking the simplicity of a child's vision.

LATER POETRY

Char's later poetry is also distinguished by its moral intensity, particularly its commitment to freedom. In Char's view, anything that inhibits human freedom is immoral. The poet's duty is to do battle continually against anything that would restrict humankind's ability to seek meaning. This includes any preconceived ideas, even the idea of liberty itself. One might see in this stance a combination of the didactic nature of Surrealism and the call to action and freedom in existentialism. Like the existentialists, Char attempts to recreate ethics for modern man, yet in doing so he invokes the mystery so important to Surrealist art. Thus, for Char, poetry is an existential stance, a *becoming*, an invitation to return to natural insights and to reject mechanical materialism.

OTHER MAJOR WORKS

PLAY: *Claire: Théâtre de Verdure*, 1949; *Le Soleil des eaux*, 1949; *L'Abominable Homme des neiges*, pb. 1956 (ballet scenario); *Trois coups sous les arbres: Théâtre Saisonnier*, 1967.

NONFICTION: *Recherche de la base et du sommet*, 1955; *Sur la poésie*, 1958.

MISCELLANEOUS: *En trente-trois morceaux*, 1956 (aphorisms).

BIBLIOGRAPHY

Caws, Mary Ann. *The Presence of René Char*. Princeton, N.J.: Princeton University Press, 1976. Critical interpretation of selected works by Char. Includes bibliographical references and index.

_____. *René Char*. Boston: Twayne, 1977. An introductory biography and critical interpretation of selected works by Char. Includes an index and bibliography.

Eichbauer, Mary E. *Poetry's Self-Portrait: The Visual Arts as Mirror and Muse in René Char and John Ashbery*. New York: P. Lang, 1992. An analysis of the relationship to visual art of the poetry of Char and Ashbery. Includes bibliographical references and index.

Lawler, James R. *René Char: The Myth and the Poem*. Princeton, N.J.: Princeton University Press, 1978. A critical analysis of Char's poetry. Includes bibliographic references.

Minahen, Charles D., ed. *Figuring Things: Char, Ponge, and Poetry in the Twentieth Century*. Lexington, Ky.: French Forum, 1994. A critical study and comparison of the works of René Char and Francis Ponge. Includes bibliographic references.

Piore, Nancy Kline. *Lightning: The Poetry of René Char*. Boston: Northeastern University Press, 1981. A short critical study of selected poems. Includes an index and bibliography.

J. Madison Davis;
bibliography updated by the editors

CHARLES D'ORLÉANS

Born: Paris, France; May 26, 1391
Died: Amboise, France; January 4, 1465

PRINCIPAL POETRY

Livre contre tout péché, 1404
Retenue d'amours, 1414
Ballades, c. 1415-1460
Chansons, c. 1415-1460
Songe en complainte, 1437
Rondeaux, c. 1443-1460
The English Poems of Charles of Orleans, 1941-1946 (2 volumes)
The French Chansons, 1986

OTHER LITERARY FORMS

In addition to his poetry, Charles d'Orléans left a long and partly autobiographical speech which he had presented in defense of the Duke of Alençon at the latter's trial. The speech, which dates from 1458, contains reminiscences of Charles's captivity and of his early life.

ACHIEVEMENTS

Charles d'Orléans is by any measure one of the preeminent poets of the latter Middle Ages; most critics would in fact rank him second in France only to François Villon. They would, however, doubtless consider him a rather distant second and that would represent both an accurate assessment and something of an injustice. He is by no means the literary equal of Villon, one of the world's great poets. Yet Charles is often underestimated, not only because he is inferior to Villon, but also because, quite simply, he is *not* Villon.

To many readers, Charles's poetry may seem somewhat dated, in contrast to the timeless texts of his contemporary. Indeed, Charles uses images, formulas, and conventions associated with the literature of courtly love, which enjoyed its greatest vogue during the twelfth and thirteenth centuries. His allegories and personifications have been dismissed as delicate and cultivated playthings, valuable witnesses to an age but of quite limited appeal to modern readers.

It is important, however, to meet Charles on his own terrain and on his own terms; there he is found to be an extraordinary poet. Charles was a wealthy and refined prince; for him and for many of his contemporaries, poetry was both a pastime and an art to be cultivated. A poem might be a witty rejoinder in a literary debate with friends, or it might be an artistic creation of the highest order, an artifact to be sculpted carefully and consciously. In such a system, Charles's use of traditional materials—his allegories and personifications and courtly images—was fully justified. An attentive reading, moreover, reveals that he was by no means a slave to tradition. What he borrowed he was able to renew, and his best poems derive much of their appeal from his subtle re-creation of traditional materials.

Re-creation occurs within the bounds of individual poems as well; there are, for example, few poets more adroit than Charles at leading gracefully into a refrain so as to alter its meaning slightly with each stanza. He is a master of style, of wit, of verbal color, yet he is sometimes considerably more than that. No sooner is the reader lulled by an extended series of abstractions and personifications than Charles suddenly shifts to an unadorned declaration of the pain he felt at his captivity, deprived as he was not simply of love but of his homeland and his freedom.

Charles engaged frequently in poetic contests and games, and poetry was for him avocation as well as art. Under the circumstances, repetition and unevenness are inevitable. More often than not, however, he proves himself to be an extraordinary practitioner of his art—that of the refined and delicate poem which deserves admiration for what it is rather than criticism for what it lacks.

BIOGRAPHY

Charles d'Orléans was born in Paris on May 26, 1391; his father was Louis, Duke of Orléans, whose brother was King Charles VI. In 1406, a marriage was arranged between Charles and his cousin Isabelle of France. The following year (in November, 1407), his father was assassinated by Jean-sans-Peur, Duke of Burgundy, and Charles himself became Duke of Orléans. Isabelle died in 1409, and the next year, following an alliance with the Count of Armagnac, he married eleven-year-old Bonne d'Armagnac. He spent several years trying to avenge his father's death, doing battle with the Burgundians, concluding more than one unsuccessful treaty, and occasionally seeking the aid of the English.

France's troubles were not limited to the regional struggles which occupied much of Charles's early life; he had, in fact, been born at the midpoint of the Hundred Years' War, and before his twenty-fifth birthday he was taken prisoner by the English in the Battle of Agincourt (October 25, 1415). He spent the next twenty-five years as a prisoner in England. It was a curious kind of imprisonment; although he was frequently moved from place to place, he was never held behind bars. He was allowed to receive visitors, money, and servants from France, and he had access to various amenities and pleasures, which (according to some reports) may have included female companionship. It was hardly a difficult existence, but Charles was nevertheless separated from his homeland and family, and many of his poems from the period bitterly lament his plight.

Changes in the political and military situation (along with the payment of a substantial ransom and a promise never again to take up arms against the English) secured Charles's release in November, 1440, and, his second wife having died five years earlier, he soon married Marie de Clèves, niece of the Duke of Burgundy. For the remainder of his life, he dabbled occasionally in military and political affairs but was largely content to devote his time to poetic pursuits, especially at his castles in Blois and Tours.

During the night of January 4, 1465, he died at Amboise, at the age of seventy-three.

ANALYSIS

The subjects of Charles d'Orléans's poetry are love, his imprisonment in England, and the pain he suffers from both. These are not necessarily discrete subjects; they frequently overlap and merge. For example, in the courtly idiom adopted by Charles, love always entails the lover's loss of freedom. Accordingly, the poet often appears to have transformed his captivity into an amorous metaphor (without, however, diluting its literal force); he was the prisoner of the English in much the same way that his persona was the prisoner of love. His themes are also related in a more direct way, for his imprisonment deprived him not only of freedom but also of love and pleasure. Thus, even in one of his more clearly patriotic poems, "En regardant vers le pays de France," ("While Looking Towards the Country of France"), where the source of his suffering is his separation from his homeland, his pain is caused in part by the loss of "the sweet pleasure that I used to experience in that country," one of his specific pleasures obviously being that of love.

During his years in England, Charles often lamented the separation from "his lady." Critical efforts to identify that lady (with Isabelle, with Bonne d'Armagnac, or with an English acquaintance) have not met with success; this failure is both inevitable and appropriate. The fact is that courtly convention would be likely to preserve the anonymity of the lady, and also, more to the point, her identity is simply irrelevant. She may thus have been *any* woman or an amalgam of several women—or she may not even have existed except as an abstraction. Indeed, in some poems she appears to represent not a particular lady but France itself, for Charles uses the same general terms to describe his absence from his lady and his separation from his country. Again, Charles's emotion is his principal focus, and a shifting, ambiguous relation exists between the major causes of it. For a poet like Charles, given to persistent metaphorical associations, his lady and his country easily become almost interchangeable or doubled poetic referents throughout the period of his captivity.

POEMS ABOUT CAPTIVITY

There are many places where Charles makes explicit reference to his experiences in England. Even though his captors treated him comparatively well, his poems could hardly have conveyed more anguish and melancholy. His best-known work of the period is doubtless the poem "While Looking Towards the Country of France," in which Charles, from Dover, laments his fate and declares: "Peace is a treasure that cannot be praised too highly. I detest war, for it has long prevented me from seeing my beloved France." Later, he was to remark in another context that he would prefer to have died in battle rather than endure his English captivity. Other works express his sorrow at France's lot and his later exultation at the English defeat ("Rejoice, Noble Kingdom of France"). Such passages offer a good deal of interest for reasons both historical and biographical, and even though their artistic value is uneven, some of them are likely to appeal to modern readers more than do Charles's love poems.

LOVE POETRY

On first reading, the love poems may appear dated— and, indeed, some of them are. Charles is generally thought of as a poet of courtly love, and that is the way he began his literary career. At that time, he cultivated (not always with much originality) all of the conventions of courtly love inherited from Guillaume de Lorris (in *Le Roman de la rose*, thirteenth century; *The Romance of the Rose*, 1900) and from others who wrote two centuries or more before Charles. Not only his ideas but also his modes of expression are traditional. Thus, in Ballade 29 he writes: "I do not fear Danger or his followers,/ For I have reinforced the fortress/ In which my heart has stored its goods/ . . . And I have made Loyalty mistress of it." Such passages are often ingenious, but the premises underlying them offer nothing new.

With time, however, his ideas evolved, and later he either turned against courtly love or (according to John Fox) simply found it largely irrelevant. Thus, while he had earlier noted without much apparent conviction that "Sadness has held me in its power for so long that I have entirely forgotten Joy," his protestations begin to assume a more personal and intense tone. He points out that "the poor souls of lovers are tormented in an abyss of sorrow" (Rondeau 140); he wonders if it is Fortune's desire that he suffer so much (Rondeau 217); he orders Beauty out of his presence, because "you tempt me too often" (Rondeau 236). In some cases, to be sure, the later poems are superficially indistinguishable from the traditional laments of the courtly lover, but one can generally discern a subtle shift of tone, and some texts go further and constitute a clear rejection of courtly premises. For example, replacing the traditional notion that suffering tempered by hope is adequate recompense for the lover is Charles's insistence (in Rondeau 65) that he can love only if his love is reciprocated, and in Rondeau 160 he states cynically that a medicine can surely be found to help those who are in love.

RETENUE D'AMOURS AND SONGE EN COMPLAINTE

A revealing example of the evolution in Charles's thought is provided by the contrast between his two long poems, *Retenue d'amours* (love's retinue) and *Songe en complainte* (dream in the form of a complaint). The former, written prior to Agincourt, offers a traditional allegorical presentation of a young man's initiation into love: He leaves *Enfance* (childhood) and entrusts his life to Lady Youth. He is afraid, because Youth has long served the God of Love, and Charles has heard many men tell of "the pains that Love makes them endure." Considering himself unable to bear the torment, he is reluctant to expose himself to Love's power. Youth assures him that those who complain are not true lovers who know what joy is and that honor and great good come to those who love. After meeting other members of Love's retinue, he awakens to love in a traditional way: Beauty shoots an arrow into his heart through his eyes. Becoming Love's vassal, he swears to accept the ten commandments of Love (to remain honorable, loyal, discreet, and so on).

More than twenty years later, Charles composed *Songe en complainte*, which serves in one sense as a continuation of the earlier poem, but which also proves to be its converse, its mirror image. Here, noting that his heart requires repose, his purpose is to *disengage* himself from love, to reclaim his heart, long held captive by the God of Love. Whereas he had earlier emphasized the joy of love and had accepted its pain as a natural, even desirable phenomenon, the older Charles now finds pain too high a price to pay for love and desires release from his vows. His attitude toward love is now melancholy, heavily tinged with skepticism.

The two long poems are important as a dramatic illustration of Charles's evolution, but artistically they are not particularly impressive creations. They are straightforward and (especially in the former case) derivative, and emphasis remains primarily on the elaboration of theme to the virtual exclusion of expressive subtlety and poetic effect. In fact, it could be said, with little injustice to Charles, that his poetic temperament is reductive not expansive. He is generally more successful in his shorter forms. Thus the ballades are usually better than the long poems, and the rondeaux are better still. His most successful pieces approach the status of Imagist poems, presenting a single, self-contained, vivid image, generally in the opening lines. The body of the poem is largely an elaboration of this image, often involving the subsidiary images derived from and supporting the principal one. Ironically, the elaboration may at times dilute the power of the image instead of intensifying it. Charles himself must have realized as much; he gradually began to abandon the ballade in favor of the shorter rondeau (a fixed-form poem containing three brief stanzas, usually of four or five lines each, with the beginning of the first stanza serving as the refrain of the other two). The dimensions of this form were ideally suited to Charles's talent and temperament, and his rondeaux present what John Fox describes as "an art form at its peak." Many of the themes, images, and personifications used in the long poems find their way into the shorter ones as well, although in the latter Charles molds them to his purposes with greater originality and flexibility.

POETIC TECHNIQUE

Despite the fact that Charles is often considered to have made extensive use of allegory, it is essential to define his technique with more precision. Ann Tukey Harrison correctly suggests that Charles reduces allegories and personifications to metaphors tailored to his purposes. Often the narrative element in his poems is radically diminished or entirely eliminated, leaving him with *Esperance* (hope), *Beauté* (beauty), *Bon Acceuil* (welcome), or some other quality which appears to be a dramatized personification but in fact simply represents an aspect of his own experience. Thus, one of his famous poems, "La Forêt de longue actente" (the forest of long awaiting), provides not the locus of a sustained series of events (as it might have for Guillaume de Lorris, for example) but rather a simple indication of a psychological or emotional state.

Moreover, while Charles may appear to maintain a static set of personifications adopted from earlier tradition, his system is in reality remarkably flexible, each figure being freely fashioned to the need created by a particular poem and by a particular dramatic situation. Thus, Comfort (for example) may be specific or abstract, ally or foe, as the context dictates. Each figure exists within a rather wide range of possible functions, and, as a result, Charles's poetic cosmos is constantly shifting and developing with each text and with each artistic choice.

"LA FORÊT DE LONGUE ACTENTE"

The stylistic pattern employed in "La Forêt de longue actente" (that is, the conjoining of a natural or architectural object with an abstraction) occurs in many of Charles's poems and pulls them in opposing directions, creating a tension between the concrete and the abstract: the Cloud of Sadness, the Ship of Good News, the Doorway of Thought, the Window of the Eyes. Such formulas are simple stylistic inversions that present a metaphor (thought is a doorway) as an apparent allegory. Charles is clearly fashioning a very personal version of allegory—or, rather, using the appearance of allegory to amplify and deepen the meaning of his images.

Several of Charles's images (castles, forests, ships) suggest confinement or containment, and the temptation to propose a biographical reading is not easily resisted. Obviously, such images reflect the poet's own imprisonment. Such a reading may seem plausible, but it ultimately does an injustice to Charles as a poet, because it reduces the text to an item of biographical evidence. Critical focus must remain on the poem itself, and instead of seeing the text as an index to his life, the critic should regard Charles's experience as material and inspiration for an autonomous series of texts. Some of his poems do indeed speak directly and explicitly of his captivity in England, yet loss of freedom is a familiar metaphor in the tradition of courtly love, to say nothing of love poetry of other ages.

As Charles had first been the willing poetic prisoner of love, and as he had later been imprisoned by the English, he gradually came to see himself as the captive of old age. He began to consider love an inimical force, and for him it was explicitly linked to the aging process. The culmination of this development is found in *Songe en complainte*. He notes that it ill befits an old man to make a fool of himself with regard to love, and he announces that "Love and Old Age are incompatible." Here the melancholy that characterizes many of his poems takes on a new tone; instead of a gentle melancholy presumably felt by all lovers (and accepted by Charles's persona during his earlier years), this poem offers a note of genuine sadness and almost forlorn resignation. Such an evolution is in one sense typical of his work. There are few themes or images that he either adopts or discards during the course of his career; rather, it is the use of them that changes, the tone of them that evolves. His originality thus lies not in the fashioning of new themes, but in the particular ways his persona comes to react to conventions borrowed from earlier poets.

Charles d'Orléans thus represents the continuation and culmination of a style and a tradition two centuries old or older, but he also represents their renewal. He puts a personal stamp on the allegorical method, and at the same time he manages to raise his poetry—which participates in venerable tradition—above the level of the personal. His poems do not present a broad and elaborate canvas; they are far closer to the refined art of the miniature: diminutive, delicate, intimate. In the rondeau, Charles found his ideal form and cultivated it extensively, leaving a body of work that not only presents unusual historical interest but also preserves a number of small and often exquisite masterpieces.

BIBLIOGRAPHY

Arn, Mary-Jo, ed. *Charles d'Orléans in England, 1415-1440*. Rochester, N.Y.: D. S. Brewer, 2000. A biography of Charles's life while imprisoned in England. Includes bibliographical references and index.

Coldiron, A. E. B. *Canon, Period, and the Poetry of Charles of Orleans: Found in Translation*. Ann Arbor: University of Michigan Press, 2000. An analysis of the history and critical reception of Charles's poetry in English translation. Includes bibliographical references and index.

Fein, David A. *Charles d'Orléans*. Boston: Twayne, 1983. An introductory biography and critical study of selected works by Charles. Includes an index and a bibliography.

Fox, John. *The Lyric Poetry of Charles d'Orléans*. Oxford, England: Clarendon Press, 1969. A critical analysis of Charles's poetry. Includes bibliographic references.

Goodrich, Norma Lorre. *Charles of Orléans*. Geneva, Switzerland: Droz, 1967. Goodrich analyzes the themes in Charles's poetry in French and in English. Includes a bibliography.

McLeod, Enid. *Charles of Orleans: Prince and Poet*. New York: Viking Press, 1970. A thorough biography of Charles offering invaluable insights into his life and works.

Norris J. Lacy;
bibliography updated by the editors

ALAIN CHARTIER

Born: Bayeux, France; c. 1385
Died: Avignon, France; c. 1430

PRINCIPAL POETRY

The Poetical Works of Alain Chartier, 1974 (J. C. Laidlaw, editor)

OTHER LITERARY FORMS

Traditional literary history has judged Alain Chartier's poetry to be less important than his prose works. This evaluation is based on the fact that many of the poems are conventional, courtly creations, whereas the prose works deal with substantial moral and political issues. Modern scholars, however, have adopted a new perspective on Chartier's poetry, seeing in it a symbolic extension of the content found in the prose works. This new approach reveals a continuity and balance in Chartier's works.

Chartier wrote in both Latin and French. His major prose works in French are *Le Quadrilogue invectif* (1489; *The Invective Quadrilogue*, late fifteenth century), written in 1422, and *Le Traité de l'espérance: Ou, Consolation des trois vertus* (1489; *The Treatise on Hope: Or, The Comfort of the Three Virtues*; late fifteenth century) written about 1428. *The Invective Quadrilogue*, composed after the Battle of Agincourt, is a patriotic allegory in which France exhorts the orders of society— chivalry, the clergy, and the common people—to seek peace together. Chartier takes a firm stand in this work, which many critics consider his most important, for national unity, for the poor, and for the Dauphin Charles. The author's longest work and among his last, *The Treatise on Hope*, was inspired by Boethius. Allegorical and historical figures paint a vivid tableau of a country distressed by continual conflict and then offer a religious solution to national problems. The treatise is a combination of verse and prose, with prose predominating.

Chartier's Latin works include official diplomatic speeches and letters, personal letters to his family and friends and *De vita curiali* (1489; *The Curial*, 1888), the shortest of the prose works and of uncertain date. *The Curial*, written first in Latin, then translated into French, as *Le Curial*, is a vehement attack on the practices of court life. Because of the problems presented by the manuscript tradition, several theories on date of composition and authorship have been advanced. Scholars are not certain whether Chartier composed one or both parts.

Above all, Chartier's prose writings are distinguished by their eloquence. Both his contemporaries and successors appreciated and imitated his conciseness and oratorical style. Modern scholars have appreciated the extent to which he consecrated his literary skill to addressing the problems of his times. One critic, Edward J. Hoffman, in his 1942 study, *Alain Chartier: His Work and Reputation*, sees in Chartier's literary contribution "a crusading spirit . . . an eloquence born of sincerity and genuine sympathy, all put to the service of a high moral purpose: the regeneration of a stricken, prostrate nation."

ACHIEVEMENTS

Alain Chartier has been called the "Father of French Eloquence" and one of the first of France's great patriots.

Literary history has admired him most for his patriotism, his humanism, and his erudition. During his lifetime and in the century that followed, Chartier was held in high esteem for his oratorical and poetic ability. Then, for many years, he fell out of critical favor and was rarely mentioned with judgment other than disdain for the excessively traditional aspects of his work. Modern critics have benefitted from the studies of Arthur Piaget, Pierre Champion, and Gaston Paris, as well as by the clarification of the confusing and extensive manuscript tradition. In addition to Hoffman, scholars such as J. C. Laidlaw, William W. Kibler, and C. J. H. Walravens have based their evaluations on more reliable texts and have viewed Chartier in his historical as well as his literary context.

BIOGRAPHY

Constructing an accurate biography of Alain Chartier has proved an arduous task for scholars. Biographers have had to deal with many problems—scarce information, variable spellings of the author's surname, and frequently contradictory references—in order to propose an approximate chronology. Account books, political and diplomatic documents, and the author's own works have been fruitful sources of information.

Chartier was born toward the end of the fourteenth century, probably 1385, into a property-holding family in Bayeux, Normandy, in France. His father was Jean Chartier. Alain was older than his two brothers, Guillaume and Thomas, and preceded them to high office. Thomas was to become a royal secretary and notary; Guillaume, bishop of Paris and royal adviser. Although little information concerning Alain's youth and years as a student is available, it is known that he left his native province to study at the University of Paris. It may be assumed from his scholarly knowledge and ability to write well in Latin and in Middle French that Chartier was an able student and that he received an excellent classical education. In addition to his mastery of language, his works bear witness to a broad knowledge of ancient history, philosophy, and literature.

The artistically nourishing atmosphere of the Anjou court was pivotal in the development of the young Chartier's literary talent, and his courtly love poems must have found an appreciative audience in royal circles. Chartier entered royal duty about 1418 and continued in the services of the Dauphin after the latter was declared King Charles VII. No mention is made of Chartier in royal records after 1429. As royal secretary, it was Chartier's duty to act as spokesman, deliver speeches, and present credentials during diplomatic missions. His work involved him in negotiations in Hungary, Venice, and Scotland, where he distinguished himself as an orator. Chartier's embassy to Scotland in 1428 is remembered through a famous anecdote. According to the legend, the Dauphiness Margaret of Scotland, daughter of James I and future wife of the Dauphin Louis (later Louis XI), approached Chartier, who was asleep in a chair, and kissed him on the mouth, saying that she did not kiss the man but rather the mouth that had spoken so many virtuous and beautiful words.

Although it is not known if Chartier was a member of the clergy, it is known that he held several ecclesiastical titles, such as canon, curate, and archdeacon, which the French king could have bestowed on a public servant. The emphasis on religion in his works would substantiate his close affiliation with the Church. Furthermore, that he neither married nor had children supports the hypothesis that he became a priest.

Chartier's disappearance in 1429 has been a subject for scholarly research. It is possible that, because of the harshly critical nature of his writings about politics, he fell out of royal favor and was even exiled. It must be remembered that Chartier lived in disillusionment and despair over the moral and political corruption that he had witnessed at first hand. Sensitive to the plight of his beloved country and of his compatriots, Chartier reacted constantly to his times. At the height of his literary career, France was torn by conflict without and within: the Hundred Years' War (1337-1453), the Burgundian-Armagnac civil wars, and the troubled reign of Charles VI. Clearly, Chartier dedicated his life to calling his fellow human to return to the virtuous ways of the past. Scholars find no evidence to prove that he lived after 1430 and believe that he is buried at the Church of Saint-Antoine in Avignon, France.

ANALYSIS

Chartier was an erudite author, trained in a traditional medieval background that profoundly influenced the formation of his poetic canon. His frequent use of allegory, personification, and courtly themes characterizes his poetry. Yet beyond mastery of conventional form and the expression of traditional themes, the poet devoted his scholarship and literary skill to communicating moral ideas to his readers. This aspect of his work issued from his observations of his contemporaries and his participation in the political events of his lifetime. Because he was deeply affected by conflict and suffering, Chartier moved from a purely aesthetic to a more realistic thematic conception.

The 1974 Laidlaw edition of Alain Chartier's poetry is comprehensive in its discussion of the background and manuscript tradition of each poem and also in its review of previous critical editions and bibliography. Students of Chartier will benefit from this work. All the poems discussed in this section are found in the Laidlaw edition.

"THE LAY ON PLEASURE"

Chartier's poetry, though begun in the courtly tradition, illustrates a maturing process and a consequent passage from less serious thematic concerns to moral and political issues. His earliest love poems are traditional in form and at times somewhat awkward. "Le Lai de plaisance" ("The Lay on Pleasure"), dating from about 1414, provides an example of the young poet's early tendency to concentrate on metrical complexity and accurate rhyme scheme rather than on subject matter. Although it is not difficult to identify the poem's theme—thoughts on pleasure on New Year's Day—nor to detect its sad tone, it is nevertheless somewhat perplexing to follow the thematic development through the forty-eight stanzas. The poet presents the subject in a courtly manner in the form of advice on how to be an honorable lover, yet the message is obscured at times by the poet's intention to fulfill all the technical requirements of the lay's fixed form. Chartier engaged in technical exercises with other fixed forms as well. His poetry shows him respecting and occasionally mastering the stanzaic, metric, and rhythmic uniformity of the ballad, the rondeau, and the chanson. Although Chartier was not innovative in the fixed-form genres, his poems possess graceful movement and harmony.

"THE BOOK OF FOUR LADIES"

Chartier's longest poetic work, "Le Livre des quatre dames" ("The Book of Four Ladies"), written after the Battle of Agincourt, about 1416, represents a transition between his idealized poetry and realistic prose. This work holds special interest because, though it was written shortly after the very traditional "The Lay on Pleasure," it contains political ideas that Chartier develops later in his prose. In addition, "The Book of Four Ladies" describes the poet's personal sentiments at some length in a prologue of twelve stanzas. While on a solitary spring walk to forget his sadness over a love affair, the narrator meets four women who in turn reveal their grief at having lost their lovers in battle; one has been killed, one has been captured, another is missing, and the last has fled. It is possible, according to Laidlaw, to speculate on the identities of the women, placing them in the historic context of the conflicts of the Burgundian-Orléanist. Through the lamentations of these women, Chartier expresses far more than grief. He criticizes energetically and eloquently those in power who allowed France to fall into ruin and those who refused to defend their country. Although structurally traditional in its description of an idealized landscape and its plan of debate, the poem is an impassioned patriotic work heralding Chartier's important prose works.

"THE PATRIOTIC DEBATE"

Another poem that gives evidence of Chartier's transition to serious subjects is "Le Débat patriotique" ("The Patriotic Debate"), written sometime between 1416 and 1420. The poetic form is a debate between two noblemen during the course of which the author expresses his scorn for the behavior of the nobility, particularly toward peasants. Thematically, the poem is in the same current as *The Invective Quadrilogue* and *The Curial* because of its attack on the noble class, which, according to Chartier, has lost its nobility of spirit. The poet exhorts members of the privileged classes to return to honor and to earn the respect of those who follow their directions and their examples—it is through valor, not wealth and position, that men acquire distinction. The structural plan of the work, too, reinforces its important message. Hoffman points out that for modern readers, the dramatic, playlike format of this poem is especially realistic and convincing. In addition, he notes, Chartier's vivid vocabulary and energetic movement produce an atmosphere that is radically different from the allegories and didactic debates that characterize many of Chartier's poetic works. Because of the effective manner in which form supports meaning, several critics have ranked "The Patriotic Debate" as one of Chartier's best poems.

Also in the category of moral poetry is "Le Bréviaire des nobles" ("The Breviary for Nobles"), written about 1424. In this work, Chartier is again concerned with honor and virtue, which the poet invites his noble readers to emulate. Although the structure of the poem is completely traditional, it conveys the high moral message that lies at the heart of Chartier's serious writings.

"THE BEAUTIFUL, PITILESS LADY" AND "THE EXCUSE"

It is interesting that Chartier's oeuvre is not chronologically consistent in its development toward greater moral and political expression. One of his most famous and popular poems, "La Belle Dame sans merci" ("The Beautiful, Pitiless Lady"), written in 1424, shows the poet moving in a different direction. Although many of his love poems became increasingly more realistic and influenced by events in French history, in this poem the poet looks inward and seems touched by worldly happenings only in the desire to take refuge from them. Here, Chartier seems to reject contemporary reality in favor of creating a more satisfactory, even courtly universe. Yet, strangely enough, the poetic world that he envisions is not a happy one. The hero is a sorrowful and scorned lover; the heroine is skeptical and independent. The two of them never succeed in communicating with each other. The portrayal of the cruel heroine angered Chartier's courtly readers to the extent that they demanded, through a noble, protofeminist institution called the Court of Love, that the poet explain his intentions in belittling both his heroine and love. Chartier answered their accusation in a second poem, "L'Excusation" ("The Excuse"), in which he claimed that Cupid had forgiven him and that he would always serve and respect women. Allusions by other French poets of the period suggest that Chartier was expelled from the poetic Court of Love. This suggestion has not been proved; taken symbolically, however, it can be interpreted as a reflection of Chartier's rupture with the traditional aesthetic system of his day.

OTHER MAJOR WORKS

NONFICTION: *Le Quadrilogue invectif*, wr. 1422, pb. 1489 (*The Invective Quadrilogue*, late fifteenth century); *Le Traité de l'espérance: Ou, Consolation des trois vertus*, wr. c. 1428, pb. 1489 (*The Treatise on Hope: Or, The Comfort of the Three Virtues*, late fifteenth century); *De vita curiali*, 1489 (*The Curial*, 1888).

BIBLIOGRAPHY

Brown, Cynthia J. "Allegorical Design and Image-Making in Fifteenth-Century France: Alain Chartier's Joan of Arc." *French Studies* 53, no. 4 (October, 1999): 385-404. Brown argues that it was the late medieval tendency to allegorize moments of crisis in order to understand and overcome them that set the stage for the construction of Joan's image.

Giannasi, Robert. "Chartier's Deceptive Narrator: 'La Belle Dame sans mercy' as Delusion." *Romania* 114 (1996): 362-384. Analyzes the narrator's persona as distinct from that of the author, reading the poem as the rejected lover's revenge fantasy.

Hoffman, Edward J. *Alain Chartier: His Work and Reputation*. Geneva, Switzerland: Slatkine Reprints, 1975. A comprehensive introduction to Chartier's life, works, and critical reputation. As is typical of earlier criticism, Hoffman dismisses much of Chartier's poetry as frivolous and conventional, indifferent to external events.

Hult, David F. "The Allegoresis of Everyday Life." *Yale French Studies* 95 (1999): 212-233. Argues that the major innovation of Chartier's work lies in its interpretive ambivalence, its power to encode or accommodate both realistic and allegorical readings.

Kibler, William W. "The Narrator as Key to Alain Chartier's 'La Belle Dame sans mercy.'" *French Review* 52 (1979): 714-723. Defends Chartier's poem from charges of escapism and conventionality. Reads it rather as an indictment of the breakdown of the traditional feudal virtues of honesty and honor in French society.

Laidlaw, J. C., ed. *The Poetical Works of Alain Chartier*. Cambridge, England: Cambridge University Press, 1974. The poems themselves are presented in French, but the extensive introduction surveys Chartier's life and works and analyzes the manuscript tradition in detail. The editor refers to previous critical studies and editions by André du Chesne, G. du Fresne de

Beaucourt, Arthur Piaget, and Pierre Champion. The Laidlaw edition has filled gaps and corrected errors of former editions.

Shapely, C. S. *Studies in French Poetry of the Fifteenth Century*. The Hague, Netherlands: Nijhoff, 1970. Unlike most earlier critics, Shapely argues in his chapter on Chartier that "La Belle Dame sans merci," read closely and with attention to the full context of Chartier's literary production, offers a moral critique of contemporary cultural mores.

Ann R. Hill;
bibliography updated by William Nelles

THOMAS CHATTERTON

Born: Bristol, England; November 20, 1752
Died: London, England; August 24, 1770

PRINCIPAL POETRY

Poems Supposed to Have Been Written at Bristol, by Thomas Rowley, and Others in the Fifteenth Century, 1777 (Thomas Tyrwhitt, editor)
Poetical Works, 1871 (Walter Skeat, editor)

OTHER LITERARY FORMS

Thomas Chatterton, obsessed with the creation of antique literature, did not limit his artistic output to the poetry he pretended was written by the fictional fifteenth century cleric Thomas Rowley, even though any claim for his literary recognition is based on the Rowley collection. Although Chatterton's prose writings are generally imitative and unoriginal, at a time of rampant literary forgeries, he created a pastiche of spurious historical manuscripts, maps, drawings, genealogies, and pedigrees for credulous, if historically ignorant dilettantes seeking to restore the lost treasures of Great Britain. Such exotic esoterica served two purposes: substantiation of his insistent claim of authenticity for his fraudulent poetry, and a means to ingratiate himself with the circle of those who passed as the literate antiquarians in Bristol. In 1768, at the dedication of the new Bristol Bridge across the Severn River, he fabricated and

had published a minutely detailed account of the three-hundred-year-old ceremonies on the occasion of the opening of the old bridge; the manuscript, he attested, was found in St. Mary Redcliff Church and appeared to be written in authentic Old English.

In exploring various modes for presenting the life and character of his medieval hero William Canynges (Chatterton dropped the final "s"), a famous mayor of Bristol under Henry VI in the fifteenth century, Chatterton created illuminating letters from both him and his wholly fictional priest-confessor, the poetic monk Thomas Rowley. Such epistolary prose develops both the historical fabric of the era, the War of the Roses, and the vivid characters of the correspondents. Another nonpoetic aspect of Chatterton's work was his political essays and letters, similar to those of the infamous and anonymous eighteenth century satirist "Junius." The influence of Alexander Pope is certainly obvious in these epistles. Two other curious prose works of Chatterton deserve special notice. One is "The Ryse of Peyncteynge yn Englande wroten bie T. Rowleie, 1469, for Mastre Canynge," a work the unknown adolescent sent to the famed antiquarian Horace Walpole, hoping he would include it in his *Anecdotes of Painting in England* (1762-1771). The other is *The Last Will and Testament of Me, Thomas Chatterton, of the City of Bristol* (1770), enabling him to break his indenture to a lawyer by accompanying it with the threat of suicide.

During his final brief episode in 1770 as a Grub Street hack writer in London, Chatterton wrote whatever the journalistic market would bear; short stories and musical works attest his creative versatility. The prose selections fall roughly into two classes, the sentimental and the comic. Examples of the former were often moralistic: "Maria Friendless," a plagiarism from Samuel Johnson; "The False Step"; and "The Unfortunate Fathers," each filled with pathos and appeals to conventional emotional response. Comic works were generally picaresque tales in the manner of Tobias Smollett, reflecting Chatterton's own necessity to live by his wit(s). Had these short stories been refined, rather than turned out hastily in a desperate bid for recognition and remuneration, Chatterton might have developed into a skilled and entertaining writer of fiction.

Thomas Chatterton (Library of Congress)

At this time of frenetic literary activity in London, Chatterton completed one satiric birletta and several other fragments. This dramatic form, a popular eighteenth century version of the pantomime, was generally a drama in contemporary English rhyme, and Chatterton's contribution to this genre was *The Revenge* (1770), a low burlesque opera with mythological characters as well as miscellaneous songs. He also wrote several scenes of another set in the London social scene entitled *The Woman of Spirit* (1770).

ACHIEVEMENTS

Riding the crest of popular Gothic taste, Thomas Chatterton freed himself of the excessive mannerisms of that eighteenth century genre—those narratives stressing only terror—and instead created tales portraying a benevolent and simple medieval world of minstrelsy where courtesy, beauty, and honor were the hallmarks. There can be little question, however, that far more significant than the value of any of his literary works is his

sensational, intriguing, and complex life viewed from the standpoint of his influence as a precursor of those poets and other artists who venerated him as a heroic martyr in the cause of aesthetic creativity. Born in the age of neoclassicism, Chatterton, because of his incredible dedication to the medieval world, tapped that vein of primitive wonder, escape, and sensibility both to nature and humanity that would become Romanticism.

From Chatterton, the major Romantic writers took the inspiration to defy not only what many increasingly saw as rampant philistinism but also many of their themes, modes, and structural forms. Samuel Taylor Coleridge's "Kubla Khan," John Keats's "To Autumn," and William Wordsworth's "Resolution and Independence" are only several of the major Romantic works in which Chatterton's influence echoes. It was not from his poetry, however, that the Romantics took greatest inspiration. The notion of isolated genius, neglected and scorned by unfeeling worldly hypocrites, coalesced around the mythic circumstances of the life and death of

Chatterton; sympathetic artists championed as their epitome the poet who died so young. Wordsworth's reference to him as "the marvellous Boy" represents the esteem in which he was held, and Keats especially appears inspired both personally and poetically by the youth, for his "Endymion" was "inscribed to the memory of Thomas Chatterton."

The influential Victorian Robert Browning sought to vindicate Chatterton, citing his abandonment of the fraudulent Rowleyan world and his determined attempt to begin a new, creative life in London as evidence of a different direction from that as a literary forger. To the romantic Pre-Raphaelites, at the height of England's industrialization, Chatterton persisted as a symbol of escape from an increasingly hostile society, and it is the pathos-filled painting of Chatterton's death scene by one of its members, Henry Wallis, that has forever fixed the young poet's fate in the conscience of the world. Late nineteenth century devotion to Chatterton might be viewed as a projection of unresolved contemporary dilemmas, but for whatever reason, the eighteenth century poet's myth began to fade with the rising popularity of realism. Perhaps it is only now, when people strive to assert their identity in the face of technological anonymity, and when the cult of the youthful dead apotheosizes its casualties, that the image of Thomas Chatterton will again rise, not as the desperate literary impostor, not even as a poet, but as one who sacrificed everything on the altar of creative individualism.

BIOGRAPHY

No consideration of Thomas Chatterton can proceed without first relating the poet to Bristol, the city of all but the final four months of his brief life, particularly the environs of the St. Mary Redcliffe Church. Born in its shadow, Chatterton was the posthumous son of another Thomas, a sometime schoolmaster, choir singer, and sexton of the imposing edifice. His mother, a colorless woman of whom little is known, struggled after her husband's death to maintain the household, which also included her mother and a daughter. Poverty haunted the family, and young Thomas was forced to be educated in charity schools.

Judged dull and unteachable at the age of five at the schoolhouse in which he had been born, the child retreated into a private world of his own, haunting the church and yard of St. Mary Redcliffe, to whose legends and corners he was introduced by his uncle, a sexton. He taught himself to read from a huge black-letter Bible and soon became an omnivorous reader. The solitary child early discovered Edmund Spenser's *The Faerie Queene* (1590-1596) and scraps of history books, and they, along with the church building and his family, were his life.

When he was eight, Chatterton was admitted to a charity school at Colston Hospital, a seemingly benevolent yet oppressive situation, especially to one of Chatterton's sensitivity. Little more than a training prison, at the school success in the mercantile world was the only goal of the exhausting regime, and after seven difficult years, young Chatterton's nature took logical form as a result: the dreamy, romantic escapist coexisting with the cynical, expedient realist. In the eighteenth century, Bristol physically resembled a medieval city with its walls, gates, winding narrow streets, and primitive facilities. The spirit of the city, however, was far from that of the Middle Ages, for it bustled with industry and the overpowering necessities of mercantilism. The getting and spending of money was the basis of both civic and personal status, and in such a competitive environment, young Chatterton soon realized that he must find a way to secure both fame and wealth as a means of escaping unimaginative, prosaic contemporary Bristol.

At age fourteen, he was indentured for a term of seven years to a local attorney, John Lambert, as a scrivener apprentice. Although the work was not arduous, the youth chafed in his position, his excessive pride suffering as he saw himself a slave. With little to do in the office, Chatterton had plenty of time to pore over what volumes of ancient lore he could find, as well as to write voluminously. It was from Lambert's office that he sent forth his fabricated history of the old Bristol Bridge as well as the myriad other "antique" manuscripts and other documents that filled both his time and imagination. It was also in Lambert's office that the mythical fifteenth century priest-poet Thomas Rowley first appeared; Chatterton calculated that fame for a fifteenth century monk was far easier to attain than for an obscure eighteenth century youth.

Also, while serving as Lambert's clerk, Chatterton found an eager market for his fraudulent historical documents among the tradespeople of Bristol who entertained a taste for antiquity; he palmed off bogus pedigrees as well as manufactured manuscripts that found their way into a history of Bristol then being written. It is important to recognize that eighteenth century Bristol was a provincial, middle-class citadel with few intellectual resources. Even elsewhere in England knowledge of that country's history was sketchy and legend-riddled, especially of that period before Elizabeth's reign. Only because true scholarship was practically nonexistent could such amateurish and naïve forgeries of Chatterton go undetected.

Every free moment that Chatterton could escape from the watchfulness of his master he spent roaming around Bristol, especially in the precincts of St. Mary Redcliffe, with its hidden manuscript-filled chests. It was here in the so-called muniment room over the North Porch that he claimed he found the Rowley manuscripts that he wanted to share with the world.

Chatterton's life as a drudging scrivener increasingly oppressed him. He felt he must escape and be free to pursue his creative work, and one means seemed to be recognition by the literary world with its consequent rewards. In an attempt to effect this goal, the young apprentice offered "ancient poems" to James Dodsley, the London publisher of Thomas Percy's *Reliques of Ancient English Poetry* (1765), a relatively successful collection of authentic old ballads as well as some spurious additions. Receiving no reply, Chatterton then audaciously, but anonymously, wrote to Horace Walpole, a titled and wealthy literary figure, seeking to secure him as a patron, much in the same relationship as William Canynge's to Rowley.

Initially intrigued, Walpole responded to Chatterton's letter enthusiastically, but then the youth ill-advisedly revealed his identity and position in life, enclosing several Rowleyan manuscripts. The patrician Walpole recoiled from the brash youth, sensing a hoax, especially in the light of the current literary furor swirling around the Ossianic poems claimed by James Macpherson to be translated from third century bardic writings. Walpole himself had also exploited the rage for the antique, for the first edition of his popular *The Castle of Otranto* (1765) masked the author's true identity with the claim that the medieval terror story was "translated by William

Marshal, Gent, from the original Italian of Onuphrio Muralto" and supposedly first printed "at Naples in the black letter, in the year, 1529."

Because Walpole was famous, influential, and wealthy, because he had a private printing press at his "Gothick" estate, Strawberry Hill, and because he too had perpetrated literary imposture, Chatterton had sensed that he would be enthusiastic about the Rowley poems. In point of fact, the ingenious Bristol youth could not have been more mistaken. After consulting other literary figures to confirm his suspicions, Walpole self-righteously and vindictively condemned Chatterton's work as fraudulent and wrote the youth an insulting letter advising him to stick to his trade as a scrivener. Walpole, however, kept Chatterton's manuscripts for several months, despite three importuning letters requesting their return; Walpole eventually complied with no word of explanation for the delay.

His hopes for publication and patronage shattered, Chatterton became more determined to escape Bristol by any means he could, assuming that if he could work in London, he would find an appreciative audience. Yet, service to Lambert bound him, so he devised a plot to threaten suicide, including execution of a last will and testament. The lawyer now had suffered enough from his difficult and insolent apprentice, so the indenture was broken, and Chatterton departed immediately for London. He was seventeen years old.

Demonstrating herculean efforts to secure literary recognition and a means to survive there, the youth undertook a spartan existence, accepting any and all menial writing jobs he could locate. Still proud and unyielding, however, and writing falsely optimistic letters home, he refused help from those who recognized his increasingly desperate situation, and four months after he arrived in London, starving, alone, and ill, he drank arsenic and died at the age of seventeen.

ANALYSIS

At the outset, the troubling problem of Thomas Chatterton's identity as a literary forger must be faced. Traditionally, critics either piously indict him as an outcast and impostor in the history of belles lettres or else strain to rationalize the situation and dismiss his fabrications as only a boyish prank. Resolution of these biased positions is both impossible and unnecessary, for moral judgments are outside the task of criticism, the works themselves providing its proper basis. Thomas Rowley, like any of Chatterton's other characters, stands beside Hamlet or Huckleberry Finn as a literary creation; the fraudulent means by which he was introduced to the world are irrelevant.

Chatterton's poetry falls into three loose classes: the Rowley cycle, the non-Rowleyan miscellany, and that of the final stage in both Bristol and London. In all, there is evidence of Chatterton's remarkable but uneven efforts to vary his modes and to perfect his poetic skills in order to secure patronage and an audience. In the Rowley poems, he seeks to glorify his idealized patron figure, the fifteenth century William Canynge, and to represent both the reality and spirit of the imaginary Bristol as an enlightened cultural center in those times under his leadership. It is here that Chatterton's greatest artistic gifts lie: in his ability both to realize fresh and imaginative worlds of experience within realistic temporal and geographic frames, and to offer brief but beautiful glimpses into the pleasures of living in such a Camelot-like society.

Certainly much poetry that Chatterton wrote is lost, for he was not careful to preserve his work. Also, when depressed, he frequently tore his poems to bits. It is not surprising that a boy as precocious as Chatterton would be this erratic or that he would begin composing at a very early age, even though such juvenilia, whether religious hymns, didactic fables, or satiric verses, is highly derivative. The most noteworthy of these early works is "Eleanoure and Juga." Although the controversy over the date of its composition is as yet unresolved, most critics place it in 1764, making it the first of Chatterton's poems of antiquity. Also, it was the only Rowley poem published during the lifetime of the poet, appearing in *Town and Country Magazine* in 1769. A simple pastoral ballad in form, with a vivid setting but little characterization or plot, the two speakers, young maidens left alone by the deaths of their lovers in the Wars of the Roses, relate their sorrows to each other, futilely seeking comfort in their mutual loss.

THE "BLANK YEARS"

All his early work was completed by 1764, and then for a four-year period—what has been called his "blank years"—no Chatterton literary production remains. The boy poet apparently was totally occupied in creating in his imagination the idealized Bristol of the fifteenth century, the incredibly detailed setting for Thomas Rowley's poems, as well as perfecting the special antique language in which he could express himself through Rowley. The minor poems that began to appear in 1768 are mostly nonlyrical and include several satires, both anti-Tory diatribes and attacks on specific individuals. Chatterton also wrote a number of insipid love lyrics for another youth to use in his courtships, but critics suggest that they too are in fact satiric, with only the poet recognizing them for what literary mockery is there. Quite moving is a 1769 elegy on the death of the poet's good friend Thomas Phillips: "Now rest, my muse, but only rest to sleep." Yet another side of his genius is found in his lines addressed to Horace Walpole after the connoisseur's denial of help, even though the youth was persuaded not to send them to his would-be patron. He scorns Walpole's mean heart and accuses him of perpetrating the same scheme—literary deceit—for which he now scorns Chatterton. Finally, the poet asserts that he and Rowley will stand united forever, even after Walpole has gone to hell.

NON-ROWLEYAN POEMS

Significant among the later non-Rowleyan poems of 1770 were the three "African Eclogues," the first written in Bristol and the final two in London. These poems indicate Chatterton's sensitivity to the plight of blacks and perhaps his identification with them as victims of unwarranted cruelty. Also part of the final Bristol period were the long, trenchant, satiric poem "Resignation," assailing contemporary governmental crises and the philippic "Kew Gardens" (originally conceived as "The Whore of Babylon"), a malicious attack on the unpopular Dowager Princess of Wales. "The Exhibition: A Personal Satyr" was the initial Chatterton London poem, an extended prurient and vulgar treatment of the trial of a Bristol cleric on moral charges. Shortly thereafter, Chatterton returned to his concern with African suffering in the sensuous and primitive "Narva and Mored" and "The Death of Nicou."

"AN EXCELENTE BALADE OF CHARITIE . . ."

The last Rowley poem, "An Excelente Balade of Charitie, as wroten by the gode Prieste Thomas Rowley, 1464," was in fact written in July, 1770, little more than a month before the poet's suicide. As in much of Chatterton's work, the style and dramatic imagery is more Elizabethan than medieval. The stanzaic form is rime royal, with occasional modifications of the iambic pentameter lines with a Spenserian Alexandrine. A fifteenth century version of the biblical Good Samaritan story, it is more personal than anything Chatterton had previously written. He alludes poignantly to his own helplessness and need in that of the "moaning pilgrim" with no home, friends, or money. Most critics now view it as one of his finer achievements, even though it was rejected when Chatterton offered it for publication.

ROWLEYAN YEARS

Other than the early "Eleanoure and Juga" and the late "An Excelente Balade of Charitie," the main body of the poems Chatterton wrote and attributed to the Bristol monk Rowley are of the year beginning in the summer of 1768, and on this Middle Ages romance cycle rests any claim to genius that might be sought for the precocious youth. Chatterton even fabricated a prose biography to authenticate his ancient poet, having him born in Somersetshire at Norton Malreward, a loyal servant of the Yorkist monarch Edward IV and a dutiful parish priest. In the prose narrative "The Storie of Wyllyam Canynge," the priest describes in the first person his lifelong friendship and patronage with the Bristol mayor, making continual reference to Canynge's enthusiastic reception of certain of his dramatic poems. In Rowley's words, here Chatterton seems to be describing Canynge as the character of the father-patron figure of his own dreams. Chatterton's main concern in the Rowleyan works was with heroism, both traditional and particular, especially that exemplified by the secular mayor Canynge. Several of the poems glorify heroes of old, pointing to obvious correspondences with the bourgeois Canynge, while villains demonstrate negatively those characteristics absent in this fifteenth century paragon.

If the juvenile effort "Eleanoure and Juga" is considered as outside the Rowley canon by nature of its probable composition by a twelve-year-old poet, then the highly dramatic "Bristowe Tragedie: Or, The Death of Syr Charles Bawdin" is the first extant Rowley poem. A vivid and dramatic character portrayal, the story is told in slow-moving ballad stanzas of the authentic political execution of the brave Sir Charles and his fellow conspirators for high treason against the obdurate King Edward IV, despite the moving intercession for clemency by William Canynge. Bawdin's defiance and courage as he stood fast by his principles under duress form the bulk of the narrative, but Canynge too demonstrates bravery and loyalty to his friends at considerable personal risk. Chatterton here employs all the stock ballad features as they were utilized by poets seeking to revive the medieval form, and to a certain degree, he succeeds in dramatizing a historical event of epic dimensions.

The next four Rowleyan works are all fragmentary: "Ynn Auntient Dayes," "The Tournament" (also known as "The Unknown Knyght"), and the "Battle of Hastyngs," I and II. Metrically in all these epics except "The Tournament," Chatterton utilizes a pentameter line, while the stanza forms vary. Subject matter still concerns itself with heroic fifteenth century Bristol happenings and characters, and the familiar St. Mary Redcliffe Church looms dominantly in the settings, especially in "Ynn Auntient Dayes." Heraldic trappings and pageantry obviously form the background for "The Tournament," but even several rewritings failed to give life to this linear narrative of medieval competition. In dealing initially with the Battle of Hastings, Chatterton tackled a familiar and difficult topic, much inspired by Alexander Pope's handling of the Trojan siege in his 1715 to 1718 translation of the *Iliad*, but the vast material was more than he could handle, particularly the repetitious and overly realistic butchery of the combatants. Despite the scale of the battle, however, little heroic fervor was generated in his first effort, so bloodthirsty in tone. Sensing increasing powers, he again took up the subject, but the second digressive version, in truth, is little better than the first, except for a few isolated instances of well-handled poetic passages, especially the descriptions of Stonehenge and the Salisbury Plain.

At the same time that Chatterton was undertaking then abandoning these four ambitious works, he also wrote four celebrations of traditional heroes in the lyric mode, thereby exalting the role of the hero into which he intended Canynge to take his place. These poems are significant for reasons both biographic and aesthetic: Two based on fictional saints associated with the glorification of St. Mary Redcliffe were designed to accompany Chatterton's spurious prose "Bridge Narrative" and enhance his reputation as an antiquarian to secure local patronage; another, the Pindaric ode "Songe toe Ella" introduces the Bristol Castle lord, the Saxon hero of the tragic poem "Aella: A Tragycal Enterlude," Chatterton's most ambitious and successful Rowleyan work; the fourth was probably bait for Horace Walpole; and all reveal a new spirit of experimentation, a higher degree of complexity in Chatterton's formulation of the Rowleyan language, and the growth of confidence in the poet.

Chatterton produced five Rowleyan verse dramas: the comic "The Merrie Tricks of Laymyngetowne," the Bristol local-color-filled "The Parlyamente of Sprytes" which celebrated Canynge's heroic deeds, "Aella," "The Tournament: An Interlude," and the fragmentary "Goddwyn: A Tragedie." Other than in occasional successful passages—for example, in the ringing martial chorus with its startling personifications praising Saxon freedom and the heroic Harold in "Goddwyn"—in none of these works, with the exception of "Aella," does Chatterton handle his material maturely and produce memorable poetry. "Aella," his masterpiece, stands alone as his most ambitious and successful verse drama and demonstrates his ability to sustain complex dramatic interest. For these reasons some attention should be given to its plot.

"AELLA"

The brave Aella, Warden of Bristol Castle, marries the lovely Saxon Birtha, who is secretly loved by his friend, the dishonorable Celmonde. After the newly-weds are serenaded by minstrels at their wedding banquet, a messenger announces a new Danish invasion threatening the West Country, and Aella, although torn by love for his bride, responds to the call to arms. At Watchet, scene of the ensuing battle, the Danish leaders argue but are soon routed by the heroic forces led by Aella, who is wounded in the fray. Meanwhile, Birtha's attendants attempt to cheer the lonely bride with more minstrelsy, but she cannot respond.

Celmonde bursts into the room to tell her in private of her husband's wounds, which he deceitfully says are mortal, and begs her to leave with him to rush to Aella's side before it is too late. She complies impetuously, telling no one the reason for her flight. Once in the dark woods, the base traitor professes his love and attempts to

ravish Birtha, but her screams attract the scattered Danish forces under their defeated leader Hurra, and in the scuffle, Celmonde is killed. Birtha identifies herself to the Danish leader who chivalrously promises her safe conduct back to Bristol.

Aella, however, was able to return to the castle, and finding Birtha missing, he succumbs to jealousy and what he conceives as wounded honor by Birtha's departure with another man, and he stabs himself. Birtha returns and, finding her husband dying, explains her actions, and they are reconciled. As the hero dies, his bride faints over his dead body, and the play ends.

The minstrel's songs interspersed in the narrative are some of Chatterton's best-known and finest lyrics, particularly the skillfully rendered lyric with the refrain "Mie love ys dedde,/ Gon to hys death-bedde,/ Al under the wyllowe tree." Perhaps Chatterton's musical inheritance here is manifest in these poetic lines.

No reader of "Aella" could miss its primarily Shakespearean derivation. Aella is Othello, foiled by the treacherous Celmonde-Iago, and Birtha is Desdemona. Other Shakespearean plays echo in "Aella" also: *Henry V* (1598-1599), *Hamlet* (1600-1601), and *The Tempest* (1611) have been traced in Chatterton's lines. Ultimately, however, it is not in its sources but in its original execution that the merit of "Aella" lies. Chatterton's shaping of the material demonstrates particularly well his lyrical imagery, especially in the minstrel songs, and has rarely been excelled in English poetry.

The few remaining works of the Rowley cycle are notable in that Chatterton continues the overriding theme of exalting Canynge's greatness. Probably the most effective of these shorter Rowley poems is another celebration in verse, "The Storie of Wyllyam Canynge," presented by means of a lovely visionary dream related by the elderly Rowley, who traces the life of his paragon and recalls valorous deeds not only of Canynge but also of other heroes of Bristol. In all, these final, relatively brief but successful lyrics, which also include "The Accounte of W. Canynges Feast," "Englysh Metamorphosis," "The Worlde," and several eclogues ("Robert and Raufe," "Nygelle," and "Manne, Womanne, Syr Rogerre") support the overall image and spirit of ancient Bristol and of Canynge that Chatterton meant to portray and glorify. Taken as a whole with the rest of the Rowleyan works, the cycle forms the youthful Chatterton's finest, most astonishing accomplishment.

OTHER MAJOR WORKS

PLAYS: *The Revenge*, pr. 1770 (opera); *The Woman of Spirit*, pb. 1770 (burletta).

NONFICTION: *The Last Will and Testament of Me, Thomas Chatterton, of the City of Bristol*, 1770.

MISCELLANEOUS: *The Complete Works of Thomas Chatterton: A Bicentary Edition*, 1971 (2 volumes; Donald S. Taylor and Benjamin Hoover, editors).

BIBLIOGRAPHY

Bronson, Bertrand H. "Thomas Chatterton." In *The Age of Johnson: Essays presented to Chauncey Brewster Tinker*, edited by Wilmarth S. Lewis. New Haven, Conn.: Yale University Press, 1949. This relatively short study is filled with useful information about the larger context in which Chatterton's work appeared. Examines not only biographical curiosities but also critical issues brought up by the poems themselves.

Fairchild, Hoxie Neale. "Aesthetic Sentimentalists." In *Religious Trends in English Poetry: Religious Sentimentalism in the Age of Johnson, 1740-1780*. Vol. 2. New York: Columbia University Press, 1939. Takes a special approach to Chatterton by concentrating on the religious elements in his poetry. The popular religious influences of the age, combined with the interest in medieval and gothic cultures, provide color and arresting images which make Chatterton's poems richly textured, even if they are not theologically deep.

Folkenflik, Robert. "Macpherson, Chatterton, Blake, and the Great Age of Literary Forgery." *The Centennial Review* 18 (1974): 378-391. This brief survey of the pre-Romantic period places Chatterton's work in context with that of another minor poet, James Macpherson, and with the great poet William Blake. All three of these poets worked with assumed identities and created personas with whom they identified in varying degrees.

Groom, Nick, ed. *Thomas Chatterton and Romantic Culture*. New York: St. Martin's Press, 1999. A collection of diverse essays by scholars, critics, and writers such as Peter Ackroyd and Richard Holmes. They show the mercurial Chatterton in exciting new contexts and restore him as a seminal figure in English literature. Includes bibliographical references and index.

Kelly, Linda. *The Marvellous Boy: The Life and Myth of Thomas Chatterton*. London: Weidenfeld & Nicolson, 1971. Building upon earlier studies, this comprehensive biography draws its title from a line in William Wordsworth's "Resolution and Independence." Kelly seeks to show that Chatterton was more than a literary oddity and to examine his place in the development of English Romantic poetry.

Meyerstein, E. H. W. *A Life of Thomas Chatterton*. London: Igpen and Grant, 1930. Although this study is old, it is not out of date and is considered essential to the study of Chatterton. It is objective and comprehensive, as opposed to the sentimentalized biographies of former eras.

Maryhelen Cleverly Harmon;
bibliography updated by the editors

GEOFFREY CHAUCER

Born: London(?), England; c. 1343
Died: London, England; October 25(?), 1400

PRINCIPAL POETRY

Book of the Duchess, c. 1370

Romaunt of the Rose, c. 1370 (translation, possibly not by Chaucer)

Hous of Fame, 1372-1380

The Legend of St. Cecilia, 1372-1380 (later used as "The Second Nun's Tale")

Tragedies of Fortune, 1372-1380 (later used as "The Monk's Tale")

Anelida and Arcite, c. 1380

Parlement of Foules, 1380

Palamon and Ersyte, 1380-1386 (later used as "The Knight's Tale")

The Legend of Good Women, 1380-1386

Troilus and Criseyde, 1382

The Canterbury Tales, 1387-1400

OTHER LITERARY FORMS

In addition to the early allegorical dream visions, the "tragedy" of *Troilus and Criseyde*, and the "comedy" *The Canterbury Tales*, Geoffrey Chaucer composed various lyrical poems, wrote a scientific treatise in prose, and translated two immensely influential works from Latin and Old French into Middle English. The shorter works have received little attention from critics. "An ABC," Chaucer's earliest poem adapted from the French of Guillaume Deguilleville, and the various ballades, roundels, and envoys are in the French courtly tradition. They also reflect the influence of the Roman philosopher Boethius and often include moral advice and standard *sententiae*. Somewhat longer are the *Anelida and Arcite* and the complaints to Pity and of Venus and Mars, which develop the conventions of the languishing lover of romance.

The prose works include the interesting astrological study, *A Treatise on the Astrolabe* (1387-1392), written for "little Lewis my son," and the *Boece* (c. 1380) a translation of Boethius's *De consolatione philosophiae* (523; *The Consolation of Philosophy*) which particularly influenced Chaucer's *Troilus and Criseyde* and "The Knight's Tale." The prologue to *The Legend of Good Women* notes that Chaucer also translated *Romaunt of the Rose* (c. 1370). Certainly the great Old French dream vision, particularly the first part by Guillaume de Lorris, influenced Chaucer's early dream allegories as well as his portrayal of certain characters and scenes in *The Canterbury Tales*—the Wife of Bath, for example, and the enclosed garden of "The Merchant's Tale." Scholars, however, are uncertain whether the extant Middle English version of *Romaunt of the Rose* included in standard editions of Chaucer is by the poet.

ACHIEVEMENTS

Seldom has a poet been as consistently popular and admired by fellow poets, critics, and the public as has Geoffrey Chaucer. From the comments of his French contemporary Eustache Deschamps (c. 1340-1410) and the praise by imitation of the fifteenth century Chaucerians to the remarks of notable critics from John Dryden and Alexander Pope to Matthew Arnold and C. S. Lewis, Chaucer has been warmly applauded if not always understood. His poetic talent, "genial nature," wit,

charm, and sympathetic yet critical understanding of human diversity are particularly attractive. To D. S. Brewer, Chaucer "is our Goethe, a great artist who put his whole mind into his art."

Yet sometimes this praise has been misinformed, portraying Chaucer rather grandly as "the father of English literature" and the prime shaper of the English language. In fact, English literature had a long and illustrious tradition before Chaucer, and the development of Modern English from the London East Midland dialect of Chaucer has little to do with the poet. Chaucer has also been credited with a series of firsts. G. L. Kittredge identified *Troilus and Criseyde* as "the first novel, in the modern sense, that ever was written in the world." Its characters, to John Speirs, are also poetic firsts: Pandarus "the first rounded comic creation of substantial magnitude in English literature," and Criseyde "the first complete character of a woman in English literature." Others see Chaucer's poetry as "Renaissance" in outlook, a harbinger of the humanism of the modern world. Such views reveal an element of surprise on the critics' part that from the midst of Middle English such a poetic genius should emerge. In fact, typical discussions of Chaucer's

Geoffrey Chaucer (Library of Congress)

career, dividing it into three stages as it develops from French influence (seen in the dream allegories) to Italian tendencies (in *Troilus and Criseyde*, for example) and finally to English realism (in *The Canterbury Tales*), imply an evolutionary view not only of Chaucer's poetry but also of English literary history. These stages supposedly reflect the gradual rejection of medieval conventionalism and the movement toward modern realism.

Whatever Chaucer's varied achievements are, the rejection of conventions, rhetoric, types, symbols, and authorities is not among them. Charles Muscatine has shown, moreover, that Chaucer's "realism" is as French and conventional as are his early allegories. Chaucer's poetry should be judged within the conventions of his time. He did experiment with verse forms, establishing a decasyllabic line which, to become the iambic pentameter of the sonnet, blank verse, and heroic couplet, is English poetry's most enduring line. His talent, however, lies in manipulating the authorities, the rhetoric, and conventional "topics" and in his mastery of the "art poetical." As A. C. Spearing notes, "Once we become aware of Chaucer's 'art poetical,' we gain a deeper insight into his work by seeing how what appears natural in it is in fact achieved not carelessly but by the play of genius upon convention and contrivance."

Such an approach to Chaucer will recognize his achievement as the greatest poet of medieval England, not as a forerunner of modernism. It will note his remaking of French, Latin, and Italian sources and treatment of secular and religious allegory as being, in their own way, as original as his creation of such characters as the Wife of Bath and the Pardoner. Chaucer's achievement is in his ability to juxtapose various medieval outlooks to portray complex ideas in human terms, with wit and humor, to include both "heigh sentence" and "solaas and myrthe," and to merge the naturalistic detail with the symbolic pattern. In this attempt to synthesize the everyday with the supernatural and the homely with the philosophical and in his insistence on inclusiveness—on presenting both the angels and the gargoyles—Chaucer is the supreme example of the Gothic artist.

BIOGRAPHY

For a medieval poet, much is known about Geoffrey Chaucer's life, his association with the English court, his diplomatic activity on the Continent, and his public appointments. He was born in the early 1340's, the son of John Chaucer, a London wine merchant. He spent time in the military, serving with the English forces in France in 1359 where he was captured; he was ransomed in 1360. Around 1366 he married Philippa Roet and probably fathered two sons. He served the crown most of his life. Originally (c. 1357) he was connected to the household of Princess Elizabeth, who was married to Prince Lionel, the son of King Edward III. He also served another son of the king, John of Gaunt, the Duke of Lancaster, who later married Chaucer's sister-in-law, Katherine Swynford. Chaucer's public service survived the death of Edward III and the tumultuous reign and deposition of Richard II. It included numerous diplomatic missions to the Continent, his appointment as controller of customs and subsidy for the port of London (1374-1386), his service as a justice of the peace and member of parliament for Kent (1386), his demanding duties as clerk of the King's Works (1389-1391), and, finally, his appointment as deputy forester of North Petherton royal forest in Somerset (after 1391). Chaucer lived in London, Greenwich, and Calais, the French port then controlled by the English. In 1399, he leased a house in the garden of Westminster Abbey. He probably died on October 25, 1400, and was buried in the nearby abbey, the first of a long line of English authors to rest in the Poets' Corner.

These biographical details provide little evidence of Chaucer's position as a poet, although in a general way they do cast light on his poetry. Chaucer's association with courtly circles must have provided both the inspiration for and the occasion of his early poetry. It is certain that he wrote the *Book of the Duchess* to commemorate the death of Blanche, the wife of John of Gaunt. He probably also composed *The Legend of Good Women* for a courtly patron (the queen, according to John Lydgate), and read *Troilus and Criseyde* to a courtly audience, as he is portrayed doing in a manuscript illustration. In more general terms, his early poetry reflects the French literary taste of the English court.

Chaucer's public career, furthermore, reveals that he was far from being the withdrawn versifier of artificial courtly tastes. His duties at the port of London and as chief supervisor of royal building projects suggest that he was a practical man of the world. Certainly these responsibilities brought him into contact with a wide variety of individuals whose manners and outlooks must have contrasted sharply with those of members of the court. In the past, such scholars as J. M. Manly searched historical records to identify specific individuals with whom Chaucer dealt in an attempt to locate models for the portraits of the pilgrims in *The Canterbury Tales*. Like any artist, Chaucer was no doubt influenced by those with whom he worked, but such research gives a false impression of Chaucer's characters. Even his most "realistic" creations are often composites of traditional portraits. Nevertheless, the studies of J. A. W. Bennett (*Chaucer at Oxford and at Cambridge*, 1974) show that careful attention to the records of fourteenth century England can enlighten modern understanding of the social, intellectual, and cultural trends of Chaucer's time and thus provide a setting for his life and work.

One aspect of Chaucer's public career must certainly have influenced his poetry. Repeatedly from 1360 to 1387 Chaucer undertook royal missions on the Continent. During these journeys he visited Flanders, Paris, perhaps even Spain. More important, in 1373 and again in 1378 he visited Italy. These trips to what in the fourteenth century was the center of European art brought him into contact with a sophisticated culture. They may have also introduced him to the work of the great Florentine poets, for Chaucer's poetry after these visits to Italy reflects the influence of Dante, Petrarch, and particularly Boccaccio. Finally, the diplomatic missions suggest certain features of Chaucer's personality that lie behind his poetry, although these features seem deliberately masked by his self-portraits in the poetry. Of middle class origin, expert in languages and trusted at court, Chaucer as a diplomat sent on at least seven missions to the Continent must have been not only convivial and personable—the usual view of the poet—but also self-assured, intelligent, and a keen judge of character.

ANALYSIS

When reading Geoffrey Chaucer's works one is struck by a sense of great variety. His poetry reflects numerous sources—Latin, French, and Italian—ranging from ancient authorities to contemporary poets and including folk tales, sermons, rhetorical textbooks, philosophical meditations, and ribald jokes. Equally varied are Chaucer's poetic forms and genres: short conventional lyrics, long romances, exempla, fabliaux, allegorical dream visions, confessions, saints' legends, and beast fables. The characters he creates, from personified abstractions, regal birds, and ancient goddesses to the odd collection of the Canterbury pilgrims and the naïve persona who narrates the poems are similarly varied. Finally, the poems present a wide variety of outlooks on an unusual number of topics. Like the Gothic cathedrals, Chaucer's poetry seems all-inclusive. Not surprisingly, also like the Gothic cathedrals, his poems were often left unfinished.

"Experience, though no authority," the Wife of Bath states in the prologue to her tale, "is good enough for me." Unlike her fifth husband, Jankin the clerk, the Wife is not interested in what "olde Romayn gestes" teach, what Saint Jerome, Tertullian, Solomon, and Ovid say about women and marriage. She knows "of the woe that is in marriage" by her own experience. This implied contrast between, on one hand, authority—the established positions concerning just about any topic set forth in the past by Scripture, ancient authors, and the Church fathers and passed on to the present by books—and, on the other hand, the individual's experience of everyday life is central to medieval intellectual thought. It is a major theme of Chaucer's poetry. Often Chaucer appears to establish an authority and then to contrast it with the experience of real life, testing the expected by the actual. This contrast may be tragic or comic; it may cast doubt on the authority or further support it. Often it is expressed by paired characters, Troilus and Pandarus, for example, or by paired tales, the Knight's and the Miller's. The characters' long recital of authorities may be ludicrous and pompous, Chaucer's parody of the pedant, but the pedant may be right. After Chanticleer's concern with what all the past has said about the significance of dreams, readers probably sympathize with Pertelote's comment that he should take a laxative. Nevertheless, once the rooster is in the fox's mouth, the authorities are proven correct. Similarly, the sum total of the Wife of Bath's personal experience is merely the proving, in an exaggerated form, of the antifeminist authorities. As Chaucer states in the prologue to the

Parlement of Foules, out of old fields comes new corn, and out of old books new knowledge.

Related to the contrast between authority and experience are a series of other contrasts investigated by Chaucer: theological faith versus human reason, the ideal versus the pragmatic, the ritual of courtly love versus the business of making love, the dream world versus everyday life, the expectations of the rule versus the actions of the individual, the Christian teaching of free will versus man's sense of being fated. Again, these contrasts may be treated seriously or comically, may be represented by particular characters and may be brought into temporary balance. Seldom, however, does Chaucer provide solutions. The oppositions are implicit in human nature, in the wish for the absolute and the recognition of the relative. As novelist and critic Arthur Koestler comments on a modern political version of this dilemma (as represented by the extremes of the Yogi and the Commissar), "Apparently the two elements do not mix, and this may be one of the reasons why we have made such a mess of our History." Chaucer's poetic and highly varied treatment of these nonmixers may help to explain why his poetry continues to speak to readers today.

Chaucer's concern with these topics—a fascination not unusual in the dualistic Gothic world—imbues his poetry with a sense of irony. Since the 1930's, readers have certainly emphasized Chaucer's ironic treatment of characters and topics, a critical vogue that may be due as much to the fashions of New Criticism as to the poetry itself. Yet Chaucer's characteristic means of telling his stories clearly encourages such readings. One can never be sure of his attitude because the poet stands behind a narrator whose often naïve attitudes simply cannot be identified with his creator's. Perhaps the creation of such a middleman between the poet and his audience was necessary for a middle-class poet reading to an aristocratic audience, or perhaps it is the natural practice of a diplomatic mind, which does not speak for itself but for another. Whatever the reasons, Chaucer's narrators are poetically effective. They provide a unifying strand throughout his varied work. Scholar A. C. Spearing notes that "the idiot-dreamer of *The Book of the Duchess* develops into the idiot-historian of *Troilus and Criseyde* and the idiot-pilgrim of *The Canterbury Tales*." Later, he comments that when Chaucer assigns the doggerel

poem, "Sir Thopas," to Chaucer the pilgrim as a joke, he "takes the role of idiot-poet to its culmination."

One result of the use of such narrators is that, in contrast with the contemporary dream vision, *The Vision of William, Concerning Piers the Plowman* (c. 1362)— with its acid attacks on English society, the failures of government, and the hypocrisy of the church—Chaucer's poetry seems aware of human foibles yet accepting of human nature. He implies rather than shouts the need for change, recognizing that in this world at least major reform is unlikely. His essentially Christian position, hidden behind the naïve narrator and his concern with surface details, naturalistic dialogue, and sharp description, is implied by the poem's larger structures. They often provide symbolic patterning. The contrast in the *Parlement of Foules* between the steamy atmosphere of the temple of Venus and the clear air of Nature's dominion or in *Troilus and Criseyde* between the narrator's introductory devotion to the god of love and his concluding epilogue based on Troilus's new heavenly point of view imply Chaucer's position concerning his favorite topic, human love. Similarly, the traditional Christian metaphor identifying life as a pilgrimage and the Parson's identification of Canterbury with the New Jerusalem suggest that the pilgrimage from a pub in Southwark to a shrine in Canterbury is a secular version of an important traditional religious theme. The reader of Chaucer, while paying careful attention to his realism which has been found so attractive should also be aware of the larger implications of his poetry.

Behind the medieval interest in dreams and the genre of dream visions lies a long tradition, both religious and secular, originating in biblical and classical stories and passed on in the Middle Ages in the works of Macrobiuss and Boethius. As a literary type, the dream vision, given impetus by the *Romaunt of the Rose*, was particularly popular in fourteenth century England. The obtuse dreamers led by authoritative guides found in such works as *Piers Plowman* and *The Pearl* (c. 1375-1400) are typical of dream visions and may have suggested to Chaucer the creation of his characteristic naïve narrator. Certainly Chaucer's four dream visions, as different as they are from one another, already develop this narrative voice as well as other typical Chaucerian characteristics.

BOOK OF THE DUCHESS

The earliest of Chaucer's very long poems, *Book of the Duchess* (1,334 lines), is a dream elegy in memory of the duchess of Lancaster. The poem begins with the narrator reading in bed about dreams, specifically the Ovidian story of the tragic love of Ceyx and Alcyone. After her husband's death, Alcyone is visited in a dream by Ceyx, leading to Alcyone's eventual brokenhearted death. This introductory section, which as usual refers to numerous authorities on dreams, combines Chaucer's concern with both dreams and love. These authorities provide background for the narrator's experience in a dream. After praying to Morpheus, the narrator falls asleep to dream of another couple divided by death, a man in black (John of Gaunt) and his lost lover, "faire White" (Blanche). The dreamer's foolish and tactless questions allow the grieving knight to express his love and sense of loss, sometimes by direct statement, on other occasions by such elaborate devices as describing a game of chess in which fortune takes his queen. The traditionally obtuse dreamer is here used in a remarkably original way. The poet is able to place the praise of the dead and the feelings of anguish in the mouth of the bereaved. Thus, this highly conventional poem, with its conscious borrowing from Ovid, *Romaunt of the Rose*, Jean Froissart, and Guillaume de Machaut, is an effective elegy in the restrained courtly tradition.

HOUS OF FAME

The *Hous of Fame*, Chaucer's second dream vision, breaks off suddenly after 2,158 lines. It creates a series of allegorical structures and figures in an analysis of the relationship between love, fame, rumor, fortune, and poetry. The dreamer is here provided with a guide, Jupiter's eagle, that probably derives from Dante's *Purgatorio IX*. In Book I he relates the romance of Aeneas and Dido, two lovers of some poetic fame whose story is portrayed in panels on a temple of glass dedicated to Venus. This temple is contrasted with the house of Fame which the dreamer sees in Book III when the eagle rather unceremoniously whisks him into the heavens. In this second allegorical structure, the dreamer views the goddess Fame surrounded by the great poets of antiquity on pedestals. They represent the authorities who, like Vergil, record the stories of such lovers as Aeneas and Dido. The dreamer realizes, however, that Fame (and thus presumably the poets of Fame) deals out good and bad at random, suggesting that there is little relationship between actuality and reputation. He next sees the house of Rumor. Full of noise and whispering people, it is perhaps an allegorical representation of the character of everyday life. In any case, this chaotic structure is no more attractive than the house of Fame. Still searching for "tydinges of Loves folk," the dreamer sees "a man of greet auctoritee," but the poem breaks off before the man can speak. The reader, like the dreamer, is left in the air; the poem is left without an ending. As Muscatine comments, "It is hard to conceive of any ending at all that could consistently follow from what we have." In fact, the poem lacks a sense of unity. Its multiple topics and elaborate descriptions are best studied as set pieces. Of particular interest is the often comic dialogue between the dreamer and the eagle in Book II.

PARLEMENT OF FOULES

The *Parlement of Foules* (699 lines) is a more satisfactory poem, although it shares much in common with *Hous of Fame*, including a series of allegorical portraits and locales, a guide who tends to shove the dreamer around, and birds as characters. A poem describing the mating of birds on Saint Valentine's day, the *Parlement of Foules* begins, like the *Book of the Duchess*, with the narrator reading a book about a dream. The book is Cicero's *Dream of Scipio*, the standard textbook on dreams, found in the last part of *De republica* (52-51 B.C.E.). Its guide, Scipio Africanus the elder, becomes the dreamer's guide in the *Parlement of Foules*. He dreams of the typical enclosed garden of romance, guarded by a gate. The gate's contrasting inscriptions alluding to the gates of Dante's *Inferno*, suggest the dual nature of love: bliss, fertility, and "good aventure" on the one hand, and sorrow, barrenness, and danger on the other. Within the garden the dreamer again sees two versions of love, although, as naïve as ever, he seems bewildered and unsure of what he witnesses.

Like the Renaissance masterpiece painting of "Sacred and Profane Love by Titian," the poem contrasts two traditional ideals of love. One is symbolized by Venus, whose entourage includes Flattery, Desire, and Lust as well as Cupid, Courtesy, and Gentleness. Her religion of love is the subject of the poets and ancient authorities whom the narrator so often reads. Her palace is dark and mannered, painted with the tragic stories of doomed lovers. In contrast, the dreamer next sees in the bright sunlight "this noble goddess Nature," who presides over the beauty of natural love and mating of the birds. These ceremonies include description of all levels of the hierarchy of the birds, from the pragmatic arrangements of the goose and the love devotion of the turtledove to the courtly wooing of the former by the eagles. The language of the birds, often comic, similarly ranges from the sudden "kek, kek!" and "kukkow" to elaborate Latinate diction. Although lighthearted and sometimes chaotic, the openness and social awareness of Nature's realm is clearly to be preferred to the artificiality and self-absorption of the temple of Venus. The poem ends under Nature's skillful guidance as the birds sing a song of spring, which awakens the dreamer. In the prologue, the narrator states that he wishes to learn of love. This dream has provided much to learn, yet he seems in the end unchanged by his experience and once again returns to his authorities.

THE LEGEND OF GOOD WOMEN

Of great interest as a forerunner of *The Canterbury Tales*, *The Legend of Good Women* is Chaucer's first experiment with decasyllabic couplets and with the idea of a framed collection of stories. Like the much grander later collection, it begins with a prologue and then relates an unfinished series of stories. Although the prologue plans nineteen stories, the poem breaks off near the conclusion of the ninth, after 2,723 lines. Unlike "The General Prologue" to *The Canterbury Tales*, with its detailed portraits of the pilgrims set in the Tabard Inn, the prologue to *The Legend of Good Women* is set as yet another dream. It presents the god of love and his daisy queen in conversation with the Chaucerian narrator. Once again, the narrator is a reader of books anxious to learn from life about love. More interesting, he is here also a writer of books and is harassed by the god of love for not presenting lovers in a good light in his poetry. Specific reference is made to his translation of the *Romaunt of the Rose* and to *Troilus and Criseyde*. As penance for his grievous sins against the religion of love, the narrator promises to write about the faithful lovers of ancient legend.

Comparisons with *The Canterbury Tales* are perhaps unfair, but the poem, lacking the dynamic characters and varied tales of the later collection, seems grievously repetitious. Its recital of love tragedies is borrowed from Ovid and other authorities. Nevertheless, the legends do encompass a wider range of classical stories than might at first be expected, including the stories of Cleopatra and Medea, who to the modern reader, at least, hardly qualify as "good women." The luscious yet natural scenery of the prologue is superb. Furthermore, the work is fulfillment of Chaucer's poetic development in the courtly tradition. Whatever the poem's weaknesses, it is unlikely that Chaucer would have agreed with Robert Burlin's judgment that the poem was "a colossal blunder."

TROILUS AND CRISEYDE

In his elaborate panegyric, the French poet Émile Deschamps refers to Chaucer as a "Socrates, full of philosophy, Seneca for morality . . . a great Ovid in your poetry." The poem that most fully deserves such praise is *Troilus and Criseyde*, Chaucer's longest complete poem (8,259 lines) and, to many readers, his most moving work. Here for the first time in a long poem, Chaucer turns from the dream-vision form and the participating narrator but not from his concern with authorities and the nature of love. He now adds, however, a Boethian philosophical touch. Although it is a poem about love, Fortuna rather than Venus is the controlling goddess of Chaucer's "little tragedy." Although the career of Troilus is based on Boccaccio's *Filostrato* (c. 1335-1340), it would seem that *The Consolation of Philosophy* exerted the greatest influence on the poem.

The five books of *Troilus and Criseyde* rather than being, as modern critics like to assert, the first novel or a drama in five acts, represent the various stages of Troilus's tragic love affair. Describing the "double sorrow" of Troilus, the son of King Priam of Troy, the poem begins with his initial love-longing, then traces his increasingly successful courtship of Criseyde culminating in their fulfilled love, the intervention of the Trojan War in the midst of their happiness, their forced separation, Criseyde's eventual acceptance of the Greek Diomede, and finally Troilus's gallant death at the hand of Achilles. While telling this story, Chaucer paints a series of scenes, both comic and serious, sometimes absurd, often movingly romantic, examining various outlooks on human love. Troilus's excessive idealism seems to parody the courtly lovers of French romances, whereas the pragmatic, often cynical attitudes of Pandarus, the uncle of Criseyde and confidant of Troilus, remind one of the waterfowl in the *Parlement of Foules* and the later fabliaux of *The Canterbury Tales*. Criseyde's views of love shift between these two extremes, varying according to her feelings and the exigencies of circumstance.

Calling *Troilus and Criseyde* Chaucer's "great failure," Ian Robinson (*Chaucer and the English Tradition*, 1972) believes that the poem includes "many great parts but they don't cohere into a great whole." Yet the poem does have a unifying structure, based on the rising and falling stages of the Wheel of Fortune. The notion of Fortune turning a wheel which sometimes takes man to the height of success and sometimes drags him down to failure is standard in medieval thought and very popular in both literature and art. The stages of the wheel, along with the poem's narrative units, are set forth in the invocations which introduce the books of *Troilus and Criseyde*. In the first, when Troilus is at the bottom of the wheel, the narrator invokes Tesiphone, "thou cruel fury." As Morton Bloomfield comments ("Distance and Predestination in *Troilus and Criseyde*"), Tesiphone was characterized as the "sorrowful fury" who laments her torments and pities those whom she torments. The choice is thus appropriate for the description in Book I of the hero's initial love torments and for the events of the entire poem. The Chaucerian narrator presents himself as "the sorrowful instrument" of love, required to tell the "sorrowful tale."

The invocation in Book II, to Clio the Muse of history, suggests that the second stage represents a rather neutral and objectively historical description of the rise of Troilus on the wheel, whereas the invocation to Venus in Book III is appropriate for the stage when the lovers are at the top of the wheel and consummate their love. As all readers of Boethius know, however, if one chooses to ride to the top of the wheel, one in all fairness cannot be surprised when the wheel continues to turn downward. Thus, Book IV begins with an invocation to Fortune and her wheel, which throws down the hero and sets Diomede in his place. There is also an appropriate reference to Mars, suggesting the growing influence of the war on the romance. Book V follows without an in-

vocation, probably because it is a continuation of the fourth book and implying that the downward movement of the wheel is one continuous stage. Certainly the poem's last book does not introduce any new elements. Its major concerns are Troilus's fatalism and the details of the Trojan War.

This pattern clearly interweaves two problems which dominate the poem: the perplexities of human love and man's sense of being fated. Troilus is the character overwhelmed by both problems. Although many critics are fascinated by the inscrutable Criseyde and attracted by the worldly-wise Pandarus, Troilus is the poem's central figure. Readers may become frustrated by his passive love-longing and swooning and his long-winded and confused discussion of predestination and free will; however, he is treated sympathetically and his situation must be taken seriously. One can argue, using Boethius as support, that the solution to the human predicament is simply never to accept the favors of Fortune—to stay away from her wheel—but what man would not do as Troilus did for the love of Criseyde? Similarly, one can agree with the moralizing narrator at the poem's conclusion that the solution is to avoid worldly vanity and the love associated with Venus and to look instead to heavenly love.

Certainly Troilus recognizes this view as his soul ascends to the seventh sphere. Yet the poem as a whole hardly condemns the love of the two Trojans. On the contrary, it describes their long-awaited rendezvous in bed with great sensitivity and poetic beauty, with warmth and sensuous natural imagery. As Spearing states, "There is probably no finer poetry of fulfilled love in English than this scene." In this great tragic romance, Chaucer seems to juxtapose human and divine love and to intermingle the sense of predestination and the Christian teaching of free will; not until the end does he speak as the moralist and condemn worldly vanity. Perhaps the tragedy of Troilus and of the human situation in general is that the distinctions are not sufficiently clear until it is too late to choose.

THE CANTERBURY TALES

Near the end of *Troilus and Criseyde*, Chaucer associates his "little tragedy" with a long line of classical poets and then asks for help to write "some comedie." Donald Howard and others have seen this as a reference to the poet's plans for *The Canterbury Tales.* Whether Chaucer had this collection planned by the time he had completed *Troilus and Criseyde, The Canterbury Tales* can certainly be understood as his comedy. If, as the Monk notes at the beginning of his long summary of tragic tales, a tragedy deals with those who once "stood in high degree, and fell so that there was no remedy," in the medieval view comedy deals with less significant characters and with events that move toward happy endings. *The Canterbury Tales* is thus a comedy, not because of its comic characters and humorous stories—several tales are actually tragic in tone and structure—but because its overall structure is comic.

Like Dante's *The Divine Comedy* (c. 1320) which traces the poet's eschatological journey from Hell through Purgatory to Heaven, shifting from a pagan guide to the representatives of divine love and inspiration, and concluding with the beatific vision, Chaucer's comedy symbolically moves from the infernal to the heavenly. From the worldly concerns of the Tabard Inn in Southwark and the guidance of the worldly-wise Host, through a variety of points of view set forth by differing characters on the pilgrimage road, the poem moves to the religious goal of the saint's shrine in Canterbury Cathedral and the Parson's direction of the pilgrims to "Jerusalem celestial."

Although with differing effects, since the Christian perspective of *Troilus and Criseyde* lies beyond the narrative itself, Chaucer's tragedy and comedy thus share a similar moral structure. Like the tragedy, *The Canterbury Tales* moves from an ancient story of pagan heroes to a Christian perspective. In *Troilus and Criseyde* the narrator develops from being the servant of the god of love to being a moralist who condemns pagan "cursed old rites" and advises the young to love him who "for love upon a cross our souls did buy." The collection of tales similarly moves from the Knight's "old stories" set in ancient Thebes and Athens and relating the fates of pagan lovers to the Parson's sermon beginning "Our swete lord god of hevene." In contrast with the earlier poem, *The Canterbury Tales* is a comedy because its divine perspective is achieved within the overall narrative. Yet as in the earlier poem, this divine perspective at the end does not necessarily cancel out the earlier outlooks

proposed. The entire poem with its multiplicity of characters and viewpoints remains.

Such an approach to *The Canterbury Tales* assumes that, although unfinished, the poem is complete as it stands and should be judged as a whole. Like the Corpus Christi cycles of the later Middle Ages, which include numerous individual plays yet can (and should) be read as one large play tracing salvation history from creation to doomsday, *The Canterbury Tales* is more than the sum of its parts. "The General Prologue," that masterpiece of human description with its fascinating portraits of the pilgrims, establishes not only the supposed circumstances for the pilgrimage and the competition to tell the best story but also the strands that link the tales to the characters and to one another. Although only twenty-four tales were finished, their relationship to one another within fragments and their sense of unity within variety suggest that Chaucer had an overall plan for *The Canterbury Tales.*

The famous opening lines of "The General Prologue," with the beautiful evocation of spring fever, set forth both the religious and the secular motivations of the pilgrims. These motivations are further developed in their description by the pilgrim Chaucer. He again is the naïve narrator whose wide-eyed simplicity seems to accept all, leaving the discriminating reader to see beyond the surface details. Finally, in his faithful retelling of the stories he hears on the way to Canterbury—for once his experience has become an authority to which, he explains, he must not be false—the narrator again unwittingly implies much about these various human types. Several of the prologues and tales that follow then continue to explore the motivations of the individual pilgrims. The confessional prologue of "The Pardoner's Tale" and its sermon filled with moral exempla, for instance, ironically reflects the earlier description of the confidence man, Pardoner, as one "with feigned flattery and tricks, made the parson and the people his apes."

It would be a mistake, however, to interpret the various tales simply as dramatic embodiments of the pilgrims. Certainly Chaucer often fits story to storyteller. The sentimental, self-absorbed, and prissy Prioress tells, for example, a simplistic, anti-Semitic tale of a devout little Christian boy murdered by Jews. The implications of her tale make one question the nature of her spirituality. The tales given the Knight, Miller, and Reeve also reflect their characters. The Knight tells at great length a chivalric romance, a celebration of his worldview, whereas the Miller and Reeve tell bawdy stories concerning tradesmen, clerks, and wayward wives.

Yet these tales also develop the larger concerns of *The Canterbury Tales* implied by Chaucer's arrangement of the tales into thematic groups. "The Knight's Tale," with its ritualized action and idealized characters, draws from Boethian philosophy in its symmetrically patterned examination of courtly love, fate, and cosmic justice. The Miller then interrupts to "quite" or answer the Knight with a bawdy fabliau. Developing naturalistic dialogue and earthy characters, it rejects the artificial and the philosophical for the mundane and the practical. In place of the Knight's code of honor and courtly love, elaborate description of the tournament, and Stoic speech on the Great Chain of Being, the drunken Miller sets the stage for sexual conquest, a complex practical joke, and a "cherles tales" involving bodily functions and fleshly punishment. In "The Miller's Tale," justice is created not by planetary gods but by human action, each character getting what he deserves. The Reeve, offended by both the Miller and his tale, then follows with another fabliau. His motivations are much more personal than those of the Miller: The Reeve feels that the Miller has deliberately insulted him, and he insists on returning the favor. Yet even in this tale Chaucer provides another dimension to the issues originally set forth by the Knight.

The clearest example of Chaucer's thematic grouping of tales is the so-called Marriage Cycle. First noted by G. L. Kittredge and discussed since by various critics, the idea of the cycle is that Chaucer carefully arranged particular tales, told by suitable pilgrims, so that they referred to one another and developed a common theme, as in a scholarly debate. The Marriage Cycle examines various viewpoints on love and marriage, particularly tackling the issue of who should have sovereignty in marriage, the husband or the wife. The cycle is introduced by the Wife of Bath's rambling commentary on the woes of marriage and her wishful tale of a young bachelor who rightly puts himself in his wife's "wyse governance." After the Friar and Summoner "quite" each other in their own personal feud, the cycle continues with an extreme example of wifely obedience, "The

Clerk's Tale" of patient Griselda. Such an otherworldly portrait of womanly perfection spurs the Merchant, a man who is obviously unhappy in marriage, to propound his cynical view of the unfaithful wife. The saint's legend of the scholarly Clerk is thus followed by the fabliau of the satirical Merchant, and the debate is no nearer conclusion. Finally, the Franklin appears to "knit up the whole matter" by suggesting that in marriage the man should be both dominant as husband and subservient as lover. Yet the Franklin's view is hardly followed by the characters of his tale. Interestingly, the two solutions to the issue of sovereignty proposed—those of the Wife of Bath and of the Franklin—are developed in Breton lays, short and highly unrealistic romances relying heavily on magical elements. Is it the case that only magic can solve this typically human problem? Chaucer, at least, does not press for a definitive answer.

The great sense of variety, the comic treatment of serious issues, the concern with oppositions and unsuccessful solutions, and the lively and imaginative verse that so typifies *The Canterbury Tales* are best exemplified by "The Nun's Priest's Tale." A beast fable mocking courtly language and rhetorical overabundance, the tale at once includes Chaucer's fascination with authorities, dreams, fate, and love, and marriage, and suggests his ambivalent attitudes toward the major philosophical and social concerns of his day. The elevated speeches of Chanticleer are punctuated by barnyard cries, and the pompous world of the rooster and hen are set within the humble yard of a poor widow.

Here the reader is provided with a comic version of the detached perspective that concludes *Troilus and Criseyde*. After deciding that dreams are to be taken seriously and refusing to take a laxative, Chanticleer disregards his dream and its warning and makes love to his favorite wife in a scene that absurdly portrays chickens as courtly lovers. Interestingly, Chanticleer now cites a standard sentiment of medieval antifeminism: *In principio/ Mulier est hominis confusio* ("In the beginning woman is man's ruin"), which alludes to the apostle John's famous description of the creation (John 1:1). The learned rooster, moreover, immediately mistranslates the Latin as "Womman is mannes ioye and al his blys," perhaps the Priest's subtle comment on the Nun he serves or the rooster's joke on Pertelote. Yet the joke ultimately is on Chanticleer when "a colfox ful of sley iniquitee" sneaks into this romance "garden." Noting that the counsel of woman brought woe to the world "And made Adam from paradys to go," the Nun's Priest then relates the temptation and fall of Chanticleer and the subsequent chasing of the fox and rooster out of the barnyard. The adventure is full of great fun, a hilarious scene, yet strangely reminiscent of the biblical story of the fall of man. It is not clear what one is to make of such a story.

Although Chaucer was not the first author to create a framed collection of stories, *The Canterbury Tales* is assuredly the most imaginative collection. Earlier the poet had experimented with a framed collection in *Legend of Good Women*. His Italian contemporary, Boccaccio, also created a collection of stories in *The Decameron* (1348-1353), although scholars cannot agree whether Chaucer knew this work. Earlier collections of exempla and legends were probably known by the poet, and he certainly knew the great collection of Ovid, *The Metamorphoses* (c. 8 A.D.). Like Ovid's collection, *The Canterbury Tales* is organized by thematic and structural elements which provide a sense of unity within diversity. Chaucer's choice of the pilgrimage as the setting for the tales is particularly effective, since it allows the juxtaposition of characters, literary types, and themes gathered from a wide range of sources and reflecting a wide range of human attitudes.

Here, perhaps, is the key to Chaucer's greatness. Like the medieval view of the macrocosm, in which constant change and movement take place within a relatively unchanging framework, Chaucer's view of the microcosm balances the dynamic and the static, the wide range of individual feeling and belief within unchanging human nature. *The Canterbury Tales* is his greatest achievement in this area, although earlier poems, such as the *Parlement of Foules*, with its portrayal of the hierarchy of birds within Nature's order, already show Chaucer's basic view. Ranging over human nature, selecting from ancient story and supposed personal experience, with a place for both the comic and the tragic, Chaucer's poetry mixes mirth and morality, accomplishing very successfully the two great purposes of literature, what the Host calls 'sentence and solas,' teaching and entertainment.

OTHER MAJOR WORKS

NONFICTION: *Boece*, c. 1380 (translation of Boethius's *The Consolation of Philosophy*); *A Treatise on the Astrolabe*, 1387-1392.

MISCELLANEOUS: *Works*, 1957 (second edition, F. N. Robinson, editor).

BIBLIOGRAPHY

Brewer, Derek. *Chaucer and His World*. New York: Dodd, Mead, 1978. A social history of the late fourteenth century in England as well as a biographical study, this work presents Chaucer as a man at the center of his culture exploring his early life and civic career, as well as his art and artistry. Many excellent illustrations give a lively sense of the period.

_____. *A New Introduction to Chaucer*. New York: Longman, 1998. Brewer, an expert in the field, provides ample biographical and historical material for anyone who is unfamiliar with Chaucer's life and work. Includes a thorough bibliography and index.

_____, ed. *Chaucer: The Critical Heritage*. 2 vols. Boston: Routledge & Kegan Paul, 1978. A two-volume selection of essays on Chaucer. Volume 1 (1385-1837) contains contributions ranging from Émile Deschamps to Samuel Taylor Coleridge; Volume 2 (1837-1933) includes criticism by Virginia Woolf, among others. In the vast resources on Chaucer, this volume edited by an eminent Chaucerian stands as an excellent source for reviewing Chaucer's scholarship and criticism.

Howard, Donald R. *Chaucer and the Medieval World*. London: Weidenfeld & Nicolson, 1987. This literary biography portrays Chaucer in a public and private context using the previously published facts of his life found in *Chaucer Life-Records* (Martin M. Crow and Clair C. Olson, eds., 1966). Howard is indebted to previous biographies, especially John Champlin Gardner's *The Life and Times of Chaucer* (1977) and Derek Brewer's volume cited above. A spirit of inquiry and an empathy akin to Chaucer's own pervade this study.

_____. *The Idea of "The Canterbury Tales."* Berkeley: University of California Press, 1976. This study endeavors to understand the idea of the poem in a historical perspective. It looks at language, customs, institutions, values, and myths, as well as the use of visual models like rose windows and pavement labyrinths to understand the sprawling form. Special attention is paid to the darker side of Chaucer, the concept of pilgrimage and medieval aesthetics. Howard elucidates the implied meanings behind the juxtapositions of some of the tales. Excellent bibliographical references appear in the footnotes.

Kittredge, G. L. *Chaucer and His Poetry.* Cambridge, Mass.: Harvard University Press, 1915. This classic of Chaucerian scholarship includes a critical appraisal of the chief works based on lectures given by the author in 1914. The first chapter is a short discussion of the man and his times, but the meat of the criticism develops around the poems with two chapters devoted to *The Canterbury Tales.* A reading knowledge of the poems is recommended.

Muscatine, Charles. *Chaucer and the French Tradition.* Berkeley: University of California Press, 1957. A history of literary style in the medieval period, this study proposes that Chaucer adapted his personal style from the courtly and bourgeois styles of French literature. It presents Chaucer as fusing the traditions of the idealized court romances and the "fabliaux," beast epics, and fables.

Pearsall, Derek Albert. *The Life of Geoffrey Chaucer: A Critical Biography.* Cambridge, Mass.: Blackwell, 1994. Derek Pearsall shows that Chaucer's immersion in his troubled times was more intimately expressed in his work than is admitted by traditional accounts. Includes bibliography and index.

Percival, Florence. *Chaucer's Legendary Good Women.* New York: Cambridge University Press, 1998. Suitable for introductory students yet containing challenging insights for scholars. Percival attempts to provide a comprehensive interpretation of the puzzling *Legend of Good Women* without ignoring any of the contradictory views that it contains about women.

Robertson, D. W., Jr. *Preface to Chaucer: Studies in Medieval Perspectives.* Princeton, N.J.: Princeton University Press, 1962. This is the classic of Chaucerian new historicism developed by Robertson partly in reaction to G. L. Kittredge and the New Criticism which downplay the religious and cultural influences on Chaucer. Robertson clearly presents the principles of medieval aesthetics through which Chaucer can be processed and given richer meaning. He focuses on the prevalent ideas of Chaucer's time, the importance of allegory in medieval theories of literature and religion in medieval life. Amplified with more than one hundred illustrations.

West, Richard. *Chaucer 1340-1400: The Life and Times of the First English Poet.* New York: Carroll & Graf, 2000. A discussion of the history surrounding Chaucer's achievements and the events of his life. Chapters take up such matters as the Black Death's impact on the anti-Semitism evident in "The Prioress's Tale" and the impact of the great English Peasants' Revolt of 1381 on Chaucer's worldview.

Richard Kenneth Emmerson;
bibliography updated by the editors

MARILYN CHIN

Born: Hong Kong; January 14, 1955

PRINCIPAL POETRY
Dwarf Bamboo, 1987
The Phoenix Gone, the Terrace Empty, 1994

OTHER LITERARY FORMS

Besides writing poetry, Marilyn Chin has translated poetry, written short fiction, and published literary interviews. She translated Gozo Yoshimasu's *Devil's Wind: A Thousand Steps or More* in 1980, and, with Pen Wenlan and Eugene Eoyang, *Selected Poems of Ai Qing* (1982). Her short story "Moon" was anthologized in *Charlie Chan Is Dead* (1993), and an interview of Maxine Hong Kingston was published in *MELUS* in 1989.

ACHIEVEMENTS

Marilyn Chin, a Chinese American poet, has garnered numerous awards, including the Wallace Stegner Award from Stanford University, more than one National Endowment for the Arts Writing Fellowship, the

Mary Robert Rinehart Award, a MacDowell Colony Fellowship, a Josephine Miles Award, and several Pushcart Prizes, among others.

Chin is passionately devoted to her craft, alert to the sociopolitical events of her times, and always sensitive—even indignant—about the situation of women in their relationships, their families, and their societies. Coming into print in the 1980's, Chin's poetic work belongs with the second decade of a contemporary renaissance of Asian American poetry. During the 1970's, and in the wake of the Black Arts movement, poets such as Lawson Fusao Inada, Jessica Hagedorn, and Nellie Wong had broken a generation-long silence during which Asian American poetry had waned to a whisper. Like her immediate predecessors, Chin is engaged and caustic about the shortcomings and inequities of American life, society, and policy. However, she possesses a more highly attuned awareness of Asian events, and her study of classic Chinese texts has endowed her with a width of allusiveness and a profundity of feeling for things Chinese that are rarely equaled in her contemporaries.

BIOGRAPHY

Marilyn Mei-Ling Chin was born in Hong Kong but grew up in Portland, Oregon, and San Francisco, the daughter of George and Rose (Yuet Kuen Wong) Chin. Her father was a Chinese restaurateur who abandoned his family for a blond woman. Attending the University of Massachusetts, Amherst, Chin earned a B.A. in Chinese literature in 1977. She became a translator for the international writing program at the University of Iowa, working with the Chinese poet Ai Qing, and received an M.F.A. in poetry from Iowa in 1981. She joined the M.F.A. faculty at San Diego State University in 1988 and lived more than a decade in San Diego in what she has described as a state of exile, for she considers San Francisco her spiritual home.

Chin's issues of familial discord—the abandonment of her father, her mother's grief, and her own need to connect with her ancestry—have had a profound impact upon her poetry. In an interview with Bill Moyers, Chin recalled her family's dissolution as "the fragmentation that I write about over and over again, hoping to resolve this pain; . . . I was raised by a matriarchy."

ANALYSIS

Marilyn Chin has said that, in addition to issues of family and feminism, her thematic interests include those of "bicultural identity, . . . assimilation, . . . political and global questions." Chin has been quick to add that the poet's "most formidable challenge is that presented by the art itself. . . . A poet may spend days contemplating on the next sentence, or the next image." Characteristically, Chin's imagery is brilliant, and her turns of thought and feeling are complexly personal and sociopolitical, often taking an ironic or dialectical twist. Her allusiveness is immensely adroit and plays richly with classic Chinese poets such as Li Bo, Tao Qian, or Bo Juyi, as well as Western moderns such as Robert Frost, William Carlos Williams, Charles Baudelaire, and Constantine P. Cavafy.

Her books of poetry show Marilyn Chin to be a magisterial weaver of words and crafter of images. Witty, earthy, and wise, she expertly and sensitively works with Asian and Western traditions of expression, personalizing intensely complex issues of immigration and assimilation as they affect family relations, female identity, and political consciousness.

DWARF BAMBOO

Chin's preoccupation with the poetic craft is abundantly evident in *Dwarf Bamboo*, which is much more than a capable first book. The whole is the product of a subtle, gifted intelligence, a redoubtable maker of images; it forms an intensely persuasive portrayal of a woman's sensibility grappling with the perplexity and the experience of being American, and Asian, and female.

One of the most striking qualities of Chin's poetry is her use of imagery—tinglingly sensuous, precise, yet often expansively allusive within both Western and Asian cultural contexts. One poem, for instance, begins: "Red peonies in a slender vase/ blood of a hundred strangers/ Wateroat, cut wateroat/ tubes in my nose and throat." The first line is precisely visual, suggestive of a painting, be it a French Impressionist still life or a scroll painting of the Ming or Qing Dynasty. The clipped second line is allusively resonant of Chinese poetry, beginning with its lack of article and continuing with the "hundred" strangers, a typical Chinese locution (whereas, perhaps, the Western equivalent might be "dozens" of strangers). The literal object, the reader realizes with a pleasurable aftershock of recognition, is a blood transfusion being given to a hospital patient. Phrasings such as this point out the qualities of Chin's image-making at its best—subtle, original, sharp, and producing resonances both Asian and Western in an American context.

Chin's images are often borne on a sweeping cadence that lends grandeur to a familiar subject. Writing of the Chinese poet Ai Qing, a victim of the Cultural Revolution, Chin says: "wherever you are, don't forget me, please—/ on heaven's station[e]ry, with earth's chalk/ write, do write." The two-part cadence of the second line reinforces its images that defamiliarize and elevate a personal letter to cosmic proportions and prepare for the briefer but even more insistent two-part cadence of the last line, which must physically take the reader's breath away.

The structuring theme of Chin's book itself is Asian and American, organic and cross-cultural. The book's title posits the organic plant image and metaphor which derives from the Tang Dynasty populist poet Po Chü-i. Elaborating the metaphor, the book's first part is titled "The Parent Node" and consists of poems set in the Asian motherlands of China and Japan. These poems also evoke ancestors, familial ones such as grandfather and uncle and literary ones such as Basho, and there are poems that provide poignant, emotionally charged snapshots of life during several phases of modern Chinese history.

The second section, titled "American Soil," shifts its scenes to the North American continent; there is a road trip from Boston to Long Beach, California, a glimpse of the Chinese American ghost town of Locke in the Sacramento Valley, a vignette from the bigoted and eccentric Louisiana countryside. "We are Americans Now, We Live in the Tundra" announces one poem's title, and it provides an ironic critique of America as the promised land of immigrant dreams, which is turning out to be an antispiritual and hugely industrial wasteland, a "tundra/ Of the logical, a sea of cities, a wood of cars." (The poem does not spare the immigrants' blighted country of origin either: "China, a giant begonia—// Pink, fragrant, bitten/ By verdigris and insects"). Another poem pictures the dilapidation of "Where We Live Now" in

America: "A white house, a wheelless car/ In the backyard rusted// Mother drags a pail of diapers to the line." In many of these poems, one senses a young person's point of view.

"Late Spring," the book's third section, presents a more mature persona as its speaker. The poems crisscross national boundaries, resting momentarily in Hong Kong, Nagasaki, Oregon, and Oakland; they explore love, sensuality, relationships, and art; they ponder feminine identity, Asian American identity: "*This wetsuit protects me/ Wherever I go.*"

"American Rain" is the ironic title of the fourth and final section of the book, which concludes with a mood of skepticism, if not pessimism. The long poem "American Rain" is a surrealistic and nightmarish indictment of the Vietnam War, a vortex of imagery whirling between beautiful blooms and the marl of the dead, between Ben Hai in Vietnam and Seaside in Oregon, between life-giving rain and death-dealing bombs. Ultimately, the book closes on a pessimistic phrase ("another thwarted Spring") in a poem dominated by inkwash-like bleakness ("a black tree on a white canvas/ and a black, black crow"), for though the speaker may strive "towards the Golden Crane Pavilion," she is also aware of "the shape of Mara," the Buddhist symbol of death and destruction.

Dwarf Bamboo, then, is an organically unified volume of poems that starts with the metaphor of Chinese bamboo nodes, progresses to a transplantation on American soil, continues to maturity in spring, and undergoes an ambiguous season, whether of battering or of nurturing under American rain.

THE PHOENIX GONE, THE TERRACE EMPTY

The title of this book derives from a poem by the Tang Dynasty poet Li Bo titled "Climbing Phoenix Terrace at Chin-ling." Li Bo's eight-line lyric remarkably touches on the themes of loss ("the terrace empty"), fleeting time ("the river flows on"), death ("ancient mounds"), separation ("the two-forked stream"), and exile ("I do not see Ch'ang-an"). These are the themes that dominate Chin's second book.

The book is organized into six sections. Not surprisingly, the first section is titled "Exile's Letter," and it contains grouped poems lamenting the loss of Chinese culture. For instance, "The Barbarians Are Coming" presents a woman defending a portion of the Great Wall from its invaders' penetration—in imagery both militaristic and suggestively sexual. "Barbarian Suite" laments how Western modes of life, thought, and speech have supplanted Chinese modes in the speaker. "How I Got That Name" is a bitter narrative raising issues of stereotyping and identity. It tells how the author's father ("a tomcat in Hong Kong trash") became so enchanted by Marilyn Monroe, the stereotypical Western blond, that he changed his daughter's Chinese name to Marilyn "after some tragic white woman/ swollen with gin and Nembutal." It also rails against the stereotype of the "'Model Minority'" pinned on Asian Americans by the majority to use against other minorities.

The book's second section, "The Tao and the Art of Leavetaking," is full of a sense of someone or something missing, eventually of death. The poem "Sad Guitar," for instance, projects images of incompleteness—an immigrant (missing a homeland) is blindly (missing a sense) strumming a guitar with only three fingers (missing two), and touching through his music fire, wood, and water (three of the five Chinese elements). This section's title poem is a complex and elegiac meditation on absence that stems from the experience of deep personal loss, perhaps that of a mother or a lover. It attempts to come to terms with antitheses such as utilitarianism and aestheticism, being and nothingness, plenitude and emptiness. Several positive thoughts are suggested, for example, "all fruits lead to God"—whether a peach be a utilitarian fruit to be eaten or an aesthetic object of a still life, its roots are in creation/creativity—and again "Emptiness is but one mind./ One mind is of no mind," suggesting that one must empty the mind of the distractions of "speakable" and "nameable" material things and rational thought before the nonrationalist and nonmaterialistic Tao can enter in, the Tao which is even "above" Plato's "form." Yet the poem ends despairingly in images of blocked or crippled creativity ("last night the verses halted") and of thwarted desire, aridity, and perhaps impotence ("the rice paper lay idle./ The black ink dry in the receptacle."

The next section, "The Phoenix Gone, the Terrace Empty," is replete with a sense of loss. The lengthy title poem is permeated with images of exile, death, and melancholy. Its speaker narrates a journey, which begins in an arduous Chinese landscape and ends in the West in regret and isolation. The speaker also travels into time to the Asian past of her immigrant parents and working-class grandparents, and to the afterlife of her ancestors, before returning to her American present. Throughout, images of nostalgia, conflict, and death dominate. Finally, taking stock of herself, the speaker's American assimilation incurs only the disappointment of her ancestors, "child, child/ they cried,/ 'Ten thousand years of history and you have come to this.'" Yet the traditions of Asia fit ill in America: "Shall I walk/ into the new world/ in last year's pinafore?" This inability causes "deep regret," even hints of violence: a moon "shaped . . ./ like a woman's severed ear" appears when her mother meets her Caucasian boyfriend. To her, the image of Uroborus, the snake biting its own tail, does not represent renewal but self destructiveness: a snake "eating herself into extinction." To seek sustenance from the past is to court a "dead prince" whose love only inflicts pain: "you kiss me tenderly/ where arch meets toe meets ankle,/ where dried blood warbles" in an image of footbinding. At the end of the poem, the phoenix, a symbol of renewal (and of woman), has flown, and the speaker finds herself in the present, gazing into a pond, seeing "not lotus, not lily"—neither tranquillity nor purity—but the "yellow crowfoot" creeping over her aging face.

In tune with the book's theme of loss, its fourth section, "Homage to Diana Toy," gathers into several poignant lyrics Chin's thoughts about a patient dying of anorexia in a psychiatric hospital, while its fifth section, "Love Poesy," contains several visceral poems centering on disappointment and betrayal in love relationships: For instance, one poem ends on this wry allusion to the Tang Dynasty poet Du Fu: "My roommate's in the bathroom [expletive] my boyfriend,/ and all I have is Tu Fu."

The final section of Chin's book is "Beijing Spring," poems occasioned by the brutal crushing of the pro-Democracy movement in Tiananmen Square in 1989. They demonstrate the depth and breadth of Chin's political conscience. Anger and sorrow fill these pages, together with a mood of disillusion delicately captured in the poem "New China," whose tone and imagery hauntingly echos the "Poems on Returning to Dwell in the Country" by the fourth century poet Tao Qian.

OTHER MAJOR WORKS

SHORT FICTION: "Moon," 1993.

TRANSLATIONS: *Devil's Wind: A Thousand Steps or More*, 1980 (of Gozo Yoshimasu); *Selected Poems of Ai Qing*, 1982 (with Pen Wenlan and Eugene Eoyang).

EDITED TEXTS: *Writing from the World*, 1985; *Dissident Song: A Contemporary Asian American Anthology*, 1991.

BIBLIOGRAPHY

Browne, Michael Dennis. "Cousin to a Million." *Hungry Mind Review*, Summer, 1994, 40. Browne posits exile as the central theme of *The Phoenix Gone, the Terrace Empty* and argues Chin documents identity formation in Asian American women.

Chin, Marilyn. "Marilyn Chin." In *The Language of Life: A Festival of Poets*. Interview by Bill Moyers. New York: Doubleday, 1995. This interview records Chin's views on her poetry and its personal, social, and political motivations and provides insight into several poems. She sees herself as a conduit for "historical voices, ancient voices, contemporary feminist voices."

Slowick, Mary. "Beyond Lot's Wife: The Immigration Poems of Marilyn Chin, Garrett Hongo, Li-Young Lee, and David Mura." *MELUS* 25, no. 3 (Fall/Winter, 2000): 221-242. Slowick argues that the central aim of these four poets, as Asian Americans and children of immigrants, is to break the silence surrounding immigrant and challenge the typical American "first person, meditative poetry of self-examination."

Svoboda, Terese. "Try Bondage." *The Kenyon Review* 17, no. 2 (Spring, 1995): 186-191. Svoboda claims that Chin is searching for a complex type of freedom, in which oppressed and oppressor coexist. Tiananmen Square is a symbol for such a freedom. She also discusses the inevitable pain of assimilation in Chin's poetry.

Uba, George. "Versions of Identity in Post-Activist Asian American Poetry." In *Reading the Literatures of Asian America*, edited by Shirley Lim and Amy Ling. Philadelphia: Temple University Press, 1992. Uba compares Chin with David Mura and John Yau, pointing out the importance of identity and ideology for her.

Zheng, Da. Review of *The Phoenix Gone, the Terrace Empty*, by Marilyn Chin. *Amerasia Journal* 24, no. 2 (Summer, 1998): 186-191. The reviewer notes the variety of themes in Chin's poetry and argues that her poetry is a "special form of protest" reacting to all types of social injustice. He also indicates some of the Chinese literary allusions in her poem.

C. L. Chua and Teresa Ishigaki

CHRISTINE DE PIZAN

Born: Venice, Italy; c. 1365
Died: Probably at the Convent of Poissy, near Versailles, France; c. 1430

PRINCIPAL POETRY

L'Epistre au dieu d'amours, 1399 (*The Letter of Cupid*, 1721)
Le Livre du dit de Poissy, 1400
Le Livre de la mutacion de fourtune, 1400-1403
Le Livre du chemin de long estude, 1402-1403
Le Dit de la rose, 1402
Le Livre du duc des vrais amans, 1405 (*The Book of the Duke of True Lovers*, 1908)
Cent Ballades d'amant et de dame, c. 1410
Le Ditié de Jeanne d'Arc, 1429 (*The Tale of Joan of Arc*, 1977)

OTHER LITERARY FORMS

Christine de Pizan's oeuvre was not limited to poetry but included an impressive number of prose works as well. Composed primarily between 1400 and 1418, these works cover a broad thematic range and bear witness to a powerful and erudite ability; they include letters, short narratives, memoirs, manuals, autobiography, treatises, allegorical psalms, and meditations. Many represent an expansion and development of ideas expressed initially in her poetry; her early poetic commitment to scholarship, political ethics, religious devotion, and women's rights was amplified in the prose works of her maturity.

ACHIEVEMENTS

Christine de Pizan is rightly recognized as France's first woman of letters, professional writer, and feminist. Although scholars of the past acknowledged and respected her ability, modern scholarship has elevated Christine (as she is known by scholars) to a deserved place in world literature. If this recognition has been somewhat tardy, the delay has been the result of the general inaccessibility of her work, spread among dispersed manuscripts. A number of modernized versions from the original Middle French, translations, editions, and critical studies have dramatically heightened interest in her work. Especially remarkable are her learned vocabulary, her knowledgeable use of mythological allusions, and her feminism.

Christine excelled thematically and structurally in both traditional and innovative forms. As an accomplished lyrical poet, she received acclaim from her contemporaries for her conventional courtly poetry. In this category, for example, she demonstrated mastery of the ballad, rondeau, lay, pastoral, and lover's lament. These poems were designed to please the aristocracy at court through an idealized concept of love. Her skill in writing traditional poetry earned the admiration and support of many important members of the nobility, such as the Dukes of Orléans, Burgundy, and Berry as well as King Charles V. Although she was composing in the conventional style, Christine often interjected her own personality by describing events in her life, by referring to a noble benefactor, or by expressing her opinions on the important issues of her day. In this regard, the works possess a documentary value.

Although Christine's poetry exhibits a high degree of technical mastery, she was never content with virtuosity for its own sake. Central themes of the necessity for justice and responsibility in government, concern for all women, and religious devotion imbue her writings. As a whole, Christine's works bear witness both to a vast knowledge of history and to a profound moral commitment to the age in which she lived.

BIOGRAPHY

Although Christine de Pizan ranks as France's first woman of letters, she was not of French but of Italian birth. Born about 1365 in Venice, she spent only her first years in Italy, leaving her birthplace when her father received the position of astrologer at the court of Charles V of France. Tommaso di Benvenuto da Pizzano, known as Thomas de Pizan after his arrival in France, brought his family to Paris around 1368, and it was there that Christine had an experience that was to shape the course of her lifework. With her father's encouragement, she received the kind of education usually reserved for boys in the Middle Ages. A precocious child, Christine was eager to learn, and this unique educational opportunity proved to be the single most important factor in her life, for it provided the young artist with the scholarly tools and knowledge upon which she was to draw during her entire career. On these early foundations in classical languages, literature, mythology, history, and biblical studies, Christine would build a rich and varied literary edifice. In addition, her educational background influenced her perspective by prompting her to view her subjects in a historical, comprehensive, and ethical light.

Because of her creative talent and her ability to please the court with her poetry, Christine became a favorite and never lacked noble patronage. Yet at age fif-

Engraving of Christine de Pisan. (© Gianni Dagli Orti/Corbis)

teen, in 1380, she married not a nobleman but a court notary from Picardy, Étienne de Castel. According to *Lavision-Christine* (wr. 1405, pb. 1969), an autobiographical work, it was a happy marriage, and the couple had three children.

Two extremely unhappy events sharply influenced Christine's life and career before she was twenty-five years old. The first of these was the death of Charles V in 1380 and the subsequent government during the minority of Charles VI. During the regency period of the Dukes of Bourbon and Burgundy, Christine's father lost his court position. This demotion meant a loss of prestige as well as severe financial losses from which the scholar and former court astrologer never recovered. A few years later, in 1385, Thomas de Pizan died. Then, in 1389 or 1390, a second, even more devastating, event occurred when Christine's husband died in an epidemic. Thus, her ten-year marriage came to an abrupt end, leaving her with the heavy responsibility of rearing three children alone.

Instead of lamenting the loss of those who had supported and encouraged her literary talents, Christine turned to her art as a source of income as well as a refuge from grief. She was successful in her literary pursuits and regained noble patronage, moving gradually yet not exclusively into prose and producing a wide range of works. Although it is difficult to reconstruct her biography for these years, it is thought that she entered the Dominican convent at Poissy around 1418, the time of the Burgundian massacres. Scholars base this hypothesis on the description of a visit to her daughter at Poissy in "Le Dit de Poissy" (the proverb of Poissy). She did not break the silence of her retreat until 1429, when she composed the poem "Le Dittié de Jeanne d'Arc" (Joan of Arc). Thus, Christine concluded her literary career appropriately, honoring a woman who, like herself, had risen above adversity to pursue her goals. The exact date of her death is not known.

ANALYSIS

The most striking characteristics of Christine de Pizan's work are her breadth of knowledge and her active engagement of the social and political issues of her day. While these attributes would be considered typical rather than extraordinary in a modern writer, they are indeed in-

triguing in a woman living at the turn of the fifteenth century. Clearly, credit for the wealth of knowledge seen in her works must be given to the exceptional education which she received. Nevertheless, an analysis of the artist must include recognition of the artistic sensitivity and the reverence for life which she brought to her career. Because of the broadness of her vision, she transcended the traditional courtly style of poetry in which she was trained and began to include significant personal, political, and moral issues in her poems. Her works weave innovation into traditional background by passing from idealized medieval expression to realistic humanist concerns that are closer in spirit to the Renaissance.

CENT BALLADES

Christine's first published works in verse reveal her conformity to the literary standards of the era. The aesthetic canon governing late medieval poetry did not accept expressions of individual joy or sorrow but instead required these emotions to be placed in a universal framework. Christine's early works demonstrate not only her respect for the existing literary system but also her mastery of it. In her ballads, lays, and rondeaux, there is a harmonious relationship between form and meaning. An example of the traditional mold can be seen in *Cent Ballades* (one hundred ballads). In ballad 59, following the social code of the era, the poet advises young lovers to be noble, peaceful, and gracious. Written in decasyllabic lines, the ballad follows the prescribed form in stanzaic composition, regular rhyme, and refrain. The tone is appropriately elevated by the use of virtuous, abstract vocabulary, and verbs in the imperative and subjunctive moods. This ballad is typical of Christine's courtly love poems, which in their grace and elegance meet and even surpass the criteria of the times.

At the beginning of her career, Christine was dependent upon the approval of her patrons, and it was important to please them by adhering to acceptable forms and also to amuse them with clever versatility and occasional flattery. She accomplished this by writing a group of rondeaux, very brief poems in lines of two to four syllables in equally short stanzas. These poems on the chagrin of love are typical of the clever, though sometimes exaggerated, metric exercises with which late medieval poets experimented. Christine also excelled at occasional verse; several of her poems in this category go beyond flattery by conveying a secondary message which in the course of the poem emerges as the main theme. For example, in a series of poems honoring Charles d'Albret, a patriotic high constable, Christine salutes his royal lineage, then hastens to one of her favorite and most important themes, the defense of the honor of women, particularly those in need. Although Christine continues to observe the fixed form of the ballad, she transmits her intense interest in her subject through a passionate tone, a concrete vocabulary, and a rhythmic pattern that dramatically emphasizes key words. The contemporary theme is anchored to ancient history as the poet compares the champion of her sex to the virtuous Roman Brutus.

Many of Christine's poems are centrally concerned with women's rights. It would appear that the genesis of this theme in her work was twofold. First, as a woman who herself had to work for a living, Christine could identify with women who had suffered misfortune, most of whom did not have her advantages. Many times in her works, she pleads for widows and orphan girls. While Christine's feminism thus had its roots in her own experience, it was also given force by her rejection of widely accepted literary stereotypes of women. She abhorred, for example, the image of her sex in *Le Roman de la rose* (thirteenth century; *The Romance of the Rose*), where women are portrayed as greedy, inconstant, and egocentric.

THE TALE OF JOAN OF ARC

Christine's final literary work provides an appropriate conclusion to a survey of her poetic career. In terms of both theme and structure, *The Tale of Joan of Arc* represents a culminating point because in it, the poet restates and unites both forcefully and creatively the concerns that inspired her whole literary career. Of the inspirations, the most prominent is religious devotion. The poem, which extols Joan of Arc's mission to save France, is a pious work, praising God's grace and power. Joan is uniquely qualified to champion France because she is God's handmaiden: "Blessed is He who created you!/ Maiden sent from God," exclaims the poet in the twenty-second stanza. Two secondary themes, patriotism and political concern, are welded to the religious motif; they also give the poem documentary value.

The poem reflects the attitude of a nation already weary from what was to be known as the Hundred Years' War (1337-1453) yet exhilarated by the victory of Orléans and the coronation of Charles VII at Rheims in 1403. Christine's sense of reality does not allow her to be swept away by optimism. Instead, realizing that there are further civil dangers to be faced, she encourages mutual cooperation between citizens and their King.

The final theme of the poem, yet certainly not the least in importance, is explicitly feminist: The heroine, supported and uplifted by the author's belief that women are able to do all things, confers unity and balance to this hymn of praise. In her enthusiastic expression of admiration for Joan as a woman, Christine employs a range of technical devices which convincingly reinforce her message. Written in sixty-one stanzas of eight octosyllabic lines each, the poem adheres to a traditional stanzaic structure, yet within the stanzas, all formality disappears; marked by exclamations, direct address, rhetorical questions, concrete and picturesque vocabulary, and conversational movement, the style is highly innovative. In this final work, Christine left an eloquent testimony to her accomplishments as a woman and as a poet.

OTHER MAJOR WORKS

NONFICTION: *L'Epistre d'Othéa à Hector*, 1400 (*The Epistle of Othea to Hector: Or, The Boke of Knyghthode*, c. 1440); *Les Epistres sur "Le Roman de la rose,"* 1402; *Le Livre des fais et bonnes meurs du sage roi Charles V*, 1404; *Le Livre de la cité des dames*, 1405 (*The Book of the City of Ladies*, 1521); *L'Avision-Christíne*, 1405 (*Christine's Vision*, 1993); *Le Livre des trois vertus*, 1405 (*The Book of the Three Virtues*, 1985); *Le Livre du corps de policie*, 1406-1407 (*The Body of Polycye*, 1521); *Les Sept Psaumes allégorisés*, 1409-1410; *La Lamentation sur les maux de la guerre civile*, 1410 (*Lament on the Evils of Civil War*, 1984); *Le Livre des fais d'armes et de chevalerie*, 1410 (*The Book of Fayttes of Arms and of Chivalry*, 1489); *Le Livre de la paix*, 1412-1413; *L'Epistre de la prison de la vie humaine*, 1416-1418.

BIBLIOGRAPHY

Blumenfeld-Kosinski, Renate, ed. *The Selected Writings of Christine de Pizan*. Translated by Blumenfeld-Kosinski and Kevin Brownlee. New York:

Norton, 1997. Includes selections from a wide range of de Pizan's writing as well as seven critical essays on her work and a selective bibliography.

Brabant, Margaret, ed. *Politics, Gender, and Genre: The Political Thought of Christine de Pizan.* Boulder, Colo.: Westview, 1992. Fourteen critical essays examining de Pizan's political writings and assessing her contribution to Western political thought.

Brown-Grant, Rosalind. *Christine de Pizan and the Moral Defence of Women: Reading Beyond Gender.* Cambridge, England: Cambridge University Press, 1999. Examines the cultural contexts that define de Pizan's choice of literary and rhetorical strategies to counter misogyny.

Quilligan, Maureen. *The Allegory of Female Authority: Christine de Pizan's "Cité des dames."* Ithaca: Cornell University Press, 1991. A page-by-page commentary on the *Livre de la cité des dames,* explicating it as an antimisogynistic allegory.

Richards, Earl Jeffrey, ed. *Christine de Pizan and Medieval French Lyric.* Gainesville: University Press of Florida, 1998. Nine critical essays on the lyrical works, all but one written expressly for this volume and first published here.

_____. *Reinterpreting Christine de Pizan.* Athens: University of Georgia Press, 1992. Sixteen critical essays, organized thematically under the headings of feminism, medieval literature, and Christian humanism. Includes a selective bibliography covering scholarship from 1980 to 1987.

Willard, Charity Cannon. *Christine de Pizan: Her Life and Works.* New York: Persea, 1984. A full-length biography that includes extensive discussion of her literary works and of the social and historical contexts within which she wrote them.

Ann R. Hill;
bibliography updated by William Nelles

JOHN CIARDI

Born: Boston, Massachusetts; June 24, 1916
Died: Edison, New Jersey; March 30, 1986

PRINCIPAL POETRY

Homeward to America, 1940
Other Skies, 1947
Live Another Day, 1949
From Time to Time, 1951
As If: Poems New and Selected, 1955
I Marry You: A Sheaf of Love Poems, 1958
Thirty-nine Poems, 1959
In the Stoneworks, 1961
In Fact, 1962
Person to Person, 1964
This Strangest Everything, 1966
Lives of X, 1971
The Little That Is All, 1974
Limericks: Too Gross, 1978 (with Isaac Asimov)
A Grossery of Limericks, 1981 (with Asimov)
Selected Poems, 1984
The Birds of Pompeii, 1985
Echoes: Poems Left Behind, 1989
The Collected Poems of John Ciardi, 1997 (Edward Cifelli, editor)

OTHER LITERARY FORMS

John Ciardi's career as a poet both generated and nourished his other remarkably varied and prolific literary activities, particularly his influential work as a teacher, critic, and author of two popular textbooks, *How Does a Poem Mean?* (1959) and *Poetry: A Closer Look* (1963). Ciardi served as an often controversial poetry editor of the *Saturday Review* (originally the *Saturday Review of Literature*) from 1956 to 1977. There he was responsible for selecting the verse that would be published in the magazine, as well as writing highly subjective columns covering a broad range of aesthetic subjects. Several volumes of his selected essays appeared, including *Dialogue with an Audience* (1963), *Manner of Speaking* (1972), and *Ciardi Himself: Fifteen Essays in the Reading, Writing, and Teaching of Poetry* (1989). The titles themselves suggest Ciardi's awareness of the vital role of the reader (or "audience") with whom the artist must communicate and his delight in the power and versatility of words. *The Selected Letters of John Ciardi* was published in 1991.

Ciardi's work as a translator of Dante's *The Divine Comedy* (c. 1320) was closely related to his recognition as a poet, for he chose to present all three sections of the classic work in his characteristically forceful, idiomatic American verse, professing to offer not another scholarly translation but one that based its appeal on its ability to be understood by the average reader. Ciardi worked more than twenty years on Dante's poem. The first section, *The Inferno*, appeared in 1954, *The Purgatorio* in 1961, and *The Paradiso* in 1970. A one-volume edition, with a new introduction by Ciardi, was published in 1977. Although critical opinion of his translation has varied, Ciardi himself evaluated his effort as one that "has not been a scholar's but a poet's work."

On innumerable other occasions, Ciardi commented on his own poetry (he was an especially good self-analyst) and on art in general. Essays of this sort appeared not only in his *Saturday Review* columns but also in various periodicals and prefaces to his poetry collections.

Other facets of Ciardi's talent and personality are revealed in his numerous volumes of poetry for children, mostly nonsense verse in the grand tradition of Edward Lear and Lewis Carroll. The first of these collections, *The Reason for the Pelican*, appeared in 1959, and another volume, *Fast and Slow: Poems for Advanced Children and Beginning Parents*, was published in 1975. Ciardi also published *Limericks, Too Gross* (1978) with Isaac Asimov and *A Browser's Dictionary, and Native's Guide to the Unknown American Language* (1980).

Not content with the printed word, Ciardi recorded many of his poems for children, as well as his more serious work (including the Dante translations) and several discussions of poetry in general and how it can be understood. In the early 1980's, he presented a series of programs on National Public Radio entitled *A Word in Your Ear*, in which he both instructed and entertained his listeners with nontechnical etymological lore.

ACHIEVEMENTS

Ideally, John Ciardi's poems should be read as a whole, not as individual works, for their total effect is much greater than the sum of their various parts. Ciardi's engaging "personality" constitutes an integral informing intelligence, a presence that becomes more complex and developed as the experience of his poetry grows. His work is comparatively accessible—indeed

his "first law" for all poetry is that it be easily understood by the general reader.

Whether Ciardi ranks among the finest of contemporary poets remains to be seen; he himself defined a "modern poet" as one who has yet to stand the test of continued critical acclaim. Because he has never been identified with a "movement" and was never the spokesman for a conspicuous cause, his popular reputation has been solely based on his poetry, essays, and personal efforts to effect a mutually meaningful dialogue with a middlebrow audience.

BIOGRAPHY

Born in 1916 in the Italian neighborhood of South Boston, John Ciardi was the fourth child and only son of Italian immigrants Concetta DeBenedictis and Carminantonio Ciardi. When he was only three years old, his father died in an automobile accident. In 1921 his mother moved the family to the Boston suburb of Medford, where Ciardi attended public school. After finishing high school in 1933, he worked a year to earn money before entering the pre-law program at Bates College in Maine, where his academic career was not very successful. In 1935 he transferred to Tufts College in Boston, where he abandoned his pre-law studies for literature and took his B.A. degree magna cum laude in 1938. In that same year he entered University of Michigan graduate school on a tuition scholarship.

Ciardi's main interest in the Michigan program was its Avery Hopwood Awards in poetry, and he was determined to compete for both the money and the prestige. He won first prize, a stipend of $1,200, and saw his first book of poetry, *Homeward to America*, published in 1940; his career as a poet was launched. His master of arts degree was granted in 1939, and in 1940 he began his teaching career, a vocation he pursued, with only the interruption of service in World War II, until 1961. His first position was in Missouri as instructor in English at the University of Kansas City.

In 1942 Ciardi enlisted in the United States Army Air Force and was discharged in 1945 as a technical sergeant after duty as an aerial gunner on a B-29 bomber in the air offensive against Japan. In both 1943 and 1944, while still in the service, he received prestigious prizes for his verse from *Poetry* magazine. After discharge

John Ciardi (© Bettmann/Corbis)

from the Air Force, he returned briefly to his teaching post in Kansas City in 1946, that year marrying Myra Judith Hostetter, an instructor in journalism. He also received another prize from *Poetry* and in the fall joined the faculty of Harvard University as an instructor.

In 1947, Ciardi's second volume of poetry was published, and he joined the staff of the Bread Loaf Writers' Conference, an affiliation he continued until 1972. In 1948 he became an assistant professor at Harvard, a position he held with distinction until 1953, once being voted "the most popular professor at Harvard." The depth and strength of his vocational commitment is evident in his 1949 statement that "I make my living by writing and by teaching others to write." During this period he was an editor at Twayne Publishers, and another collection of his poetry, *Live Another Day*, appeared. In 1950 he edited his anthology *Mid-Century American Poets*, and in 1951 lectured in Salzburg, Austria. In 1952 he was elected a fellow of the American Academy of Arts and Sciences.

That same year the first of his three children, a daughter, was born; in 1953 and 1954 two sons were born. In 1953, Ciardi left Harvard for Rutgers University, where he remained until his resignation as a tenured professor in 1961, no longer determined to pursue the academic life of

"planned poverty." In 1956 he spend much of the year in Rome on a fellowship in literature at the American Academy of Arts and Letters, also beginning in that year his long association (lasting until 1977) as poetry editor of the *Saturday Review*. In 1958 he served as president of the College English Association and the following year published his initial juvenile poetry book. In 1960, Ciardi received the first of many honorary degrees, and in 1961 he began appearing on educational television.

Working on his Dante translations, on his almost annual publications of verse collections, and at the *Saturday Review* (he reported reading approximately one thousand poems a week in his position as poetry editor), Ciardi produced an enormous literary output. From 1973 to 1974 he was a visiting professor at the University of Florida, and for a number of years was a literary "circuit rider," filling year-round lecture engagements throughout America. Ciardi remained active in various literary activities into the 1980's; he died in Edison, New Jersey, in 1986.

ANALYSIS

In an important prefatory essay to the 1949 volume *Live Another Day*, John Ciardi set down thirteen prescriptive principles of his poetic creed. These fundamental rules served him as a guideline for his own poetry and as a standard for the evaluation and judgment of the works of others. An understanding of these critical precepts is important to the analysis of Ciardi's poetry.

Ciardi's first and most important rule is that the reader should be able to understand a given poem. Ciardi had little use for certain poets (T. S. Eliot and Ezra Pound among them) whom he called "baroque," inbred mannerists writing to other writers rather than generating their work from the raw material of nature "outward to the lives of men." Moreover, Ciardi believed that a poem should be affirmative and specific "about the lives of people." He recalled the origins of the genre by reminding readers that poetry should be read aloud, that its effect is to the ear not the eye. Ciardi asserted that poetry can be about any subject, and may utilize any diction (no word is "not fit"), thus echoing William Wordsworth's democratic principles set forth in his preface to *Lyrical Ballads* (1800). Ciardi also believed that "personality" must emerge from the work, otherwise it "is dead." Pursuing more technical prosodic elements, his premises include the opinion that to succeed, a poem "must create its own form," and that ambiguities must be recognized and understood in each of their separate possibilities.

One can recognize that much of Ciardi's poetic credo is derivative, especially from the modern New Critical approach. In reference to his translations of Dante, Ciardi confessed unabashedly that he was "a thief of other men's scholarship" but argued logically and persuasively that such work has "no better purpose" than to serve other men's needs. In his own poetic principles, however, he went beyond any limited doctrinaire critical tenets and stressed the totality of a specific work, each line being "a conceived unit" of the whole. His final points were technical: He saw rhyme in the poem as "part of the total voice-punctuation" and metrics as being more successful when the conventional iambic pentameter line is less strictly observed.

Critics have declared that no two of Ciardi's poems are alike. While that observation may be something of an overstatement, certainly both his subjects and his forms, his diction and his tone, all demonstrate both poetic inventiveness and a remarkably broad range of personal interests. Indeed, in their subjectivity lies the primary theme of this most autobiographical poet: himself and his search for orientation and stability in a protean and often hostile and uncertain world. Readers, however, soon notice certain recurring themes: the pervasive influence of his first-generation Italian background, the shattering personal loss of his father, and the anxieties and contradictions, as well as the joys, of everyday contemporary urban life. The universal problem of discovering "a self" amid its distractions lies at the heart of Ciardi's work.

In his preference for the short, usually lyric poem, Ciardi consistently used closed forms and tightly structured traditional stanzas, whether or not he employed rhyme; more often than not the reader is aware of a beginning, middle, and end. Following his own dictum advocating "common speech," Ciardi's lively vernacular diction is honestly direct, sometimes irreverent, and even crude, often employing colloquialisms. Often faulted for being repetitious and belaboring the obvious as well as for lacking a direct emotional charge in his choice of diction, Ciardi nevertheless refused to assume a philosophical stance alien to his nature, nor did he depart from his own particular "sense of the form." Perhaps his anecdotal subjects were often not equal to his masterful technical skills, but when one considers the number of poets of whom the reverse is true, Ciardi's remarkable poetic achievement comes into focus.

HOMEWARD TO AMERICA

In Ciardi's first book, *Homeward to America*, the volume that launched his career by winning the Hopwood Prize at the University of Michigan, he exhibited many of the characteristics that mark all his work—the search for and development of a self presented with wit and irony. Drawing obvious analogies between his parents' migration to America—their search for a "home"—and his own experience, he concludes (in "Letter to Mother") that despite their courageous and dramatic precedent, he must find his way alone. While the weaker poems in the collection are little more than externalizations of emotions dimly felt by the young poet, in his maturity this same protesting voice rings true.

OTHER SKIES

A tone of protest is a distinctive characteristic of Ciardi's verse, especially in his early work, yet the iconoclast is no nihilist. Affirmation of life underlies even his most violent social criticism. Beginning in 1947, Ciardi began publishing strongly worded, often cynical poems. The volume *Other Skies* reflects Ciardi's war years; the forty-two poems reveal the intellectual growth forged by his military experience. Indicative of his new personal confidence and his mastery of the ironic tone is the tightly rhymed "Elegy Just in Case" that begins "Here lie Ciardi's pearly bones," in which he speculates about what would become of his decaying corpse rotting in the jungle. The bantering observations belie the grisly truth of war and its victims, yet the poem is no less effective for its flippant tone. More somberly intense is his "Poem for My Twenty-ninth Birthday," in which he identifies himself with "the soaring madness of our time," a crewman of a bomber whose mission is "to save or kill us all" by destroying the lives of unseen and unknown enemy victims. Also in this important collection is "On a Photo of Sgt. Ciardi a Year Later," one of his most widely read poems. Here he considers himself in an earlier snapshot. He appears as an illusory costumed figure, and he concludes that the reality of a subject invariably eludes the camera's eye: "The shadow under the shadow is never caught."

LIVE ANOTHER DAY

In succeeding collections the flippancy diminishes; perhaps the newly married poet underwent a humanizing transformation, an affirmation of his growing responsibilities. In *Live Another Day, From Time to Time*, and *As If*, he continues to recall and chronicle earlier experiences, the raw material of his emerging consciousness of self. In *Live Another Day* he includes both his prefatory credo as a poet and a profile of his hypothetical reader. In these transitional volumes the poet begins his attempt to reconcile his own introspective incursions with the interests of the public with whom he feels increasingly compelled to create a "dialogue."

AS IF AND I MARRY YOU

In *As If*, Ciardi includes several poems inspired by his wife Judith, later reprinted in *I Marry You*. At the time of this collection, Ciardi was deeply involved in his translations of Dante, an involvement which forced him to reexamine his Italian roots. Much of this personal exploration is evident in powerful poems about his father. In a sharply drawn poem typical of another less elegiac strain ("Thoughts on Looking into a Thicket") the poet offers one of his most succinct statements of his thematic stance: "I believe the world to praise it."

I Marry You, despite its popularity, is a private collection, a tribute by the poet to his happy and inspirational marriage and family life. Some critics see it as self-conscious sentimentality, but perhaps this opinion is a judgment on modern attitudes toward such intimate revelations rather than on the emotions themselves or the quality of their presentation. Not all of the poems in this collection, however, are conjugal, for what some consider to be Ciardi's finest poem, "Snowy Heron," is included. Here the poet follows his earlier admonition to praise and extends the idea of espousal to include the

world of nature; "I praise without a name," he proclaims, the power of the heron's flight. He feels that by whatever name one calls this spirit, the crucial act is to express glorification, adding emphasis by both beginning and ending the second six-line stanza with the imperative "but praise."

THIRTY-NINE POEMS

With the publication of *I Marry You*, Ciardi approached the height of his poetic powers. In his next collection, *Thirty-nine Poems*, which appeared in 1959, he strives to illustrate his belief that intensely personal truths about one man might well illumine the life of another. "Bridal Photo, 1906" was inspired by a picture of his parents in a frozen moment; it ends with a prayer and a benediction by their son. In his explanatory notes for this poem, Ciardi says that from this communion of a man with a piece of paper, he found himself "knowing more and more truly about myself, and about all of us."

THE 1960'S

Four collections by Ciardi appeared during the 1960's: *In the Stoneworks*, *In Fact*, *Person to Person*, and *This Strangest Everything*. The first two works are generally seen as competent, but merely covering Ciardi's familiar and recognized poetic territory. His third volume of the decade is more successful. The title poem of *Person to Person* reaffirms his ceaseless efforts to make connections with his readers despite the difficulty of any genuine personal communication ("I can reach no one"). Another commendable poem in this group is "Autobiography of a Comedian," in which "Lucky John" Ciardi honestly profiles himself; being a comic, he confesses, is the only alternative to death. Materialistic rewards, however, do not satisfy the humanist instincts and yearnings of the soul: The comedian admits, "I'm still winning what I have no real use for." Protesting the absurdity that "even scholars take me seriously," he asks plaintively and in desperation (apparently extending himself to be a spokesman for Everyman), "How do we make sense of ourselves?"

"TENZONE"

A well-known poem from *Person to Person* is "Tenzone," an ironic debate between the poet's soul and his body. In the guise of "soul," the effaced poet (again obviously Ciardi) describes himself complacently and realistically as "the well-known poet, critic, editor, and middle-high aesthete of the circuit" for whom "some weep" because he wastes his talents, while others find the very thought of his abilities laughable. "Soul" denounces him as a "greedy pig," dead to art, a confidence man concerned only with money and whiskey. In response, "body" accuses "soul" of having a father-fixation, of being a failed poet who knows it after discovering that a "poem is belly and bone." In "Nothing Is Really Hard but to Be Real" the poet taunts his readers by declaring that the aphoristic title is "fraudulent," only hollow "gnomic garbage." What is important is to find the truth of "our own sound" that reveals "what a man is." This argument, as well as his rhetorical gambit, is familiar Ciardi material, the theme and style not only of much of his poetry but also of his essays and lectures.

THIS STRANGEST EVERYTHING

Less successful than *Person to Person*, his best and most significant volume of this decade, is *This Strangest Everything*. Here there are no excellent poems, nor, for that matter, any embarrassments; Ciardi seems content to cover old ground, to write not for critical acclaim but to fulfill the expectations of his growing audience of devoted readers.

THE 1970'S

In *Lives of X*, the first of Ciardi's two collections of the 1970's, the poet offers fifteen longer narratives in blank verse, one critic seeing it as "the closest thing to a formal autobiography [Ciardi] has yet attempted." Here he traces his rich and varied life from birth onward, recalling and expanding on events described in earlier poems and offering new details from memory, especially on his desperate search for a name and an identity, as well as his struggle with the Catholic Church. The other collection of this decade, *The Little That Is All*, has been called "vintage Ciardi" and is a random yet ultimately affirmative collection that expresses his concerns with objects and events in the life of a typical twentieth century man. Ranging from power mowers and blue movies to hiring a lawyer to fix his son's fourth "pot bust," the volume reflects both Ciardi's wit and his hard-won wisdom and above all his ultimately triumphant coming to terms with life. His terse yet perceptive self-assessment of the chaos of suburban existence (in "Memo: Preliminary Draft of a Prayer to God the Father") is: "I do not complain: I describe."

OTHER MAJOR WORKS

NONFICTION: *How Does a Poem Mean?*, 1959, rev. 1975; *Poetry: A Closer Look*, 1963; *Dialogue with an Audience*, 1963; *Manner of Speaking*, 1972; *For Instance*, 1979; *A Browser's Dictionary, and Native's Guide to the Unknown American Language*, 1980, 1983, 1988 (3 volumes); *Good Words to You*, 1987; *Ciardi Himself: Fifteen Essays on the Reading, Writing, and Teaching of Poetry*, 1989; *The Selected Letters of John Ciardi*, 1991 (Edward Cifelli, editor).

TRANSLATIONS: *The Divine Comedy*, 1977 (*The Inferno*, 1954, *The Purgatorio*, 1961, and *The Paradiso*, 1970; of Dante's *La divina commedia*)

CHILDREN'S LITERATURE: *The Reason for the Pelican*, 1959; *Scrappy the Pup*, 1960; *I Met a Man*, 1961; *The Man Who Sang the Sillies*, 1961; *You Read to Me, I'll Read to You*, 1962; *The Wish-Tree*, 1962; *John J. Plenty and Fidler Den*, 1963; *You Know Who*, 1964; *The King Who Saved Himself from Being Saved*, 1965; *An Alphabestiary*, 1966; *Someone Could Win a Polar Bear*, 1970; *Fast and Slow: Poems for Advanced Children and Beginning Parents*, 1975; *Doodle Soup*, 1985.

EDITED TEXT: *Mid-Century American Poets*, 1950.

BIBLIOGRAPHY

Ciardi, John. *The Selected Letters of John Ciardi*. Edited by Edward M. Cifelli. Fayetteville: University of Arkansas Press, 1991. Collection of correspondence with various literati including Isaac Asimov, Theodore Roethke, Muriel Rukeyser, and John Frederick Nims. Includes an index.

Cifelli, Edward M. *John Ciardi: A Biography*. Fayetteville: University of Arkansas Press, 1997. Cifelli, an expert on Ciardi's work, chronicles the rise and fall of the poet's fortune from his high profile in the 1940's and 1950's to his relative obscurity when the Beats and the confessional poets arrived.

Clemente, Vince, ed. *John Ciardi: Measure of the Man*. Fayetteville: University of Arkansas Press, 1987. This collection of essays is essential for any student of Ciardi. Authors as varied as Isaac Asimov and Maxine Kumin comment on Ciardi's multifaceted life and writing career. Covers Ciardi's work as a poet, a science-fiction writer, and an author for children.

Krickel, Edward Francis. *John Ciardi*. Boston: Twayne, 1980. This volume is a valuable introduction to the work of Ciardi. It contains a brief biography and an analytic overview of the body of his work. Supplemented by a thorough primary and secondary bibliography and an index.

Nims, John Frederick. "John Ciardi: The Many Lives of Poetry." In *John Ciardi: The Measure of the Man*, edited by Vince Clemente. Fayetteville: University of Arkansas Press, 1987. Nims addresses Ciardi as a poet and reveals his poetic bias when he praises Ciardi as a man of the world who gave up his career to write. Ciardi's experience informed his poetry, which was rich and varied.

White, William. *John Ciardi: A Bibliography*. Detroit: Wayne State University Press, 1959. Contains a statement by Ciardi. The bibliography is not complete but it is useful, as it lists the first publication dates of many of Ciardi's works that do not appear in book collections or periodical guides. It dramatizes Ciardi's amazing versatility by showing that he wrote in many different literary genres.

Williams, Miller. "John Ciardi: 'Nothing Is Really Hard but to Be Real.'" In *The Achievement of John Ciardi*, edited by Miller Williams. Glenview, Ill.: Scott, Foresman, 1969. Williams edited a selection of Ciardi's poems published from the mid-1940's to the mid-1960's. Williams's essay on Ciardi is one of the best available. Suitable for all students.

Maryhelen Cleverly Harmon;
bibliography updated by the editors

AMY CLAMPITT

Born: New Providence, Iowa; June 15, 1920
Died: Lenox, Massachusetts; September 10, 1994

PRINCIPAL POETRY

Multitudes, Multitudes, 1974
The Isthmus, 1981
The Summer Solstice, 1982
The Kingfisher, 1983
A Homage to John Keats, 1984
What the Light Was Like, 1985
Archaic Figure, 1987
Westward: Poems, 1990
Manhattan: An Elegy and Other Poems, 1990
A Silence Opens, 1994
The Collected Poems of Amy Clampitt, 1997

OTHER LITERARY FORMS

Although Amy Clampitt is known primarily for her several collections of poems, her first serious literary efforts took the form of fiction. Clampitt wrote two full-length novels in the 1950's, although they remain unpublished. She did however produce some noteworthy critical work late in her career. Clampitt provided the introduction and selected the poems for Ecco Press's *The Essential Donne*, published in 1988. *Predecessors, Et Cetera: Essays*, published by the University of Michigan Press in 1991, includes several of her essays on the aesthetics of writing and on seminal literary figures she found influential on her own work. Clampitt begins the book by posing the most fundamental of questions, "What do you need to know to be a writer?" She then uses this question as a springboard for a candid and remarkably lucid discussion of the ideas of literary figures as diverse as nineteenth century novelist Henry James and twentieth century eschatologist Hal Lindsey. In this way the essays of *Predecessors, Et Cetera* reflect the intellectual eclecticism that informs her most memorable poems.

ACHIEVEMENTS

Amy Clampitt graduated with honors from Grinnell College in Iowa in 1941, where she was also elected to Phi Beta Kappa. Her poetry began to gain significant attention relatively late in her life, but during roughly the last decade of her life she received a number of important awards. In 1982 she received a John Simon Guggenheim Fellowship and in 1984 an American Academy and Institute of Arts and Letters Award. In 1985, Clampitt won an Academy of American Poets Fellowship and and in 1991 a three-year Lila Acheson Wallace Reader's Digest Fellowship. She was also writer in residence at

The College of William and Mary in 1984-1985, at Amherst College in 1986-1987, and at Smith College in 1992-1993.

She was named visiting Hurst Professor at Washington University in 1988. Clampitt's first major collection, *The Kingfisher*, was nominated for the National Book Critics Circle Award in 1983 and widely received by a number of major critics as one of the most important volumes of American poetry to appear in the 1980's.

BIOGRAPHY

In a rare interview with Judson Brown for *Daily Hampshire Gazette* in 1987, then sixty-seven-year-old poet Amy Clampitt remarked, "I'm very much put off by this whole thing of making human interest stories about someone who published late." Clampitt was addressing one of the most remarkable facts about her life as a poet: that her work remained relatively unnoticed until she was in her sixties. However, although she published "late," her work is generally viewed as some of the most accomplished lyric poetry to come out of the United States in the late twentieth century.

Helen Vendler remarked of Clampitt's landmark 1983 collection *The Kingfisher*,

A century from now, . . . it will still offer beautiful objects of delectation, but it will have taken on as well the documentary value of what, in the twentieth century, made up the stuff of culture.

Although she was held in similar esteem as a "culture maker" by a host of other reviewers, who championed *The Kingfisher* and its highly anticipated 1985 follow up *What the Light Was Like* as monumental achievements, Clampitt shunned the limelight that her late-found fame afforded her. Thus, the facts of her life, especially of those sixty years before she burst upon the literary scene, remain scant and sporadic. It is generally known, however, that Clampitt was born in 1920 in the farming town of New Providence, Iowa.

Even though poems like "Imago" document that she was raised very much a pragmatic, hardworking daughter of the Iowa prairie ("the shirker propped/ above her book in a farmhouse parlor"), her parents did strongly encourage her to pursue her gift for language, which she

Amy Clampitt (© Thomas Victor)

demonstrated even as a girl, writing poems as early as age nine. Clampitt was schooled at Grinnell College, where she earned election to Phi Beta Kappa and received a bachelor of arts degree with a concentration in English, graduating with honors in 1941. Upon graduation, she was awarded a fellowship for graduate study at Columbia University, but she left before completing her first year when she found graduate study largely unfulfilling.

Clampitt found greater satisfaction in the world of work, taking a job at Oxford University Press as promotional director for college textbooks, a position she kept until 1951, when a trip to Europe beckoned. In 1952 Clampitt returned to New York to take a position as reference librarian for the National Audubon Society. She remained there, first as a researcher and later in an editorial capacity, until 1977. Turning her efforts more toward her poetry during this period, Clampitt was eventually able to publish enough in distinguished magazines and reviews in the 1970's to secure a job in 1977 as a poetry editor with E. P. Dutton. She remained there until 1982, when she left to pursue her own writing full-time.

Throughout the 1980's and until her death from ovarian cancer in 1994, Clampitt supported herself entirely from the proceeds from her books, fellowships, and personal appearances. *The Kingfisher* alone sold in excess of ten thousand copies, an almost unprecedented feat in poetry.

ANALYSIS

Often compared to the work of decidedly "metaphysical" poets like John Donne, Wallace Stevens, and Marianne Moore, Clampitt's poetry is, in comparison to that of most of her contemporaries, metaphorically dense, richly allusive, and structurally complex. Although she shares with many late twentieth century poets a penchant for the short lyric, her predispositions differ markedly from those of poets like Adrienne Rich, Robert Lowell, and Sylvia Plath. Whereas these writers use poetry primarily as a vehicle for intimate self-examination, Clampitt's work celebrates the textures and intricacies of the external rather than the internal. Her poetry, time and again, looks to the natural world as the wellspring of imagination and uniformly basks in its glory. The sometimes terse, sometimes playful, always challenging idiom in which she works reflects the complexity of a world of which she is both observer and taxonomist, subject and object.

MULTITUDES, MULTITUDES AND THE ISTHMUS

Some have dismissed Clampitt's early collections *Multitudes, Multitudes* and *The Isthmus* as "a mere foreshadowing" of her later work, but writing the entry on Clampitt for *Dictionary of Literary Biography*, Robert Hosmer observed that both books contain a number of exciting poems worthy of consideration, particularly for their mythological resonance and visionary force. Poems like "A Christmas Cactus" and "The Eve of All Souls" take on what Hosmer calls a "liturgical" assertiveness as they seek to fuse both Christian and personal mythologies into a unifying logos. Although at a mere fifteen poems *The Isthmus* is a much briefer project, it signals an important turning point in Clampitt's work. *The Isthmus* largely turns its attention from myth and allusion to natural imagery and the delights of the physical world, particularly of the place where land meets sea. Poems such as "The Lighthouse" achieve a balance between immediacy and abstraction that anticipates Clampitt's later, better-known efforts:

A dripping sleeve of incandescence
sweeps the cove, unrolls the corridor . . .
like a sleepwalking familiar—
lightening mollified, a newly
calibrated force of nature.

"THE KINGFISHER"

Critic Paul Olson observed of Clampitt's first major volume *The Kingfisher*, that it is "a book of tough stuff, full of dirt and doctrine." Indeed his description aptly characterizes the collection's title poem, which struggles to find the meeting point between the "doctrine" of abstraction and the "dirt" of physical immediacy. Echoing Wallace Stevens's classic "Sunday Morning" in both theme and structure, "The Kingfisher" seeks to reconcile the paradox inherent in the fact that careful observation of the physical world yields both experience and distance from that experience. In effect, closeness in itself creates its own brand of chasm between subject and object.

Clampitt chooses the Bronx Zoo's aviary as primary locus for the poem. For urbanites its lavish variety of birds promises a refuge from the "dazzled pub crawl" of their artificial workaday environs, from a world from which "the poetry is gone." As naturally beautiful and free as the aviary's stunning variety of kingfishers, thrushes, and bellbirds are, however, the fact remains that each bird is nonetheless caged and just as confined by its environs as its observers are. This fact leads the speaker to conclude that even the birds are therefore abstractions, their sight and songs eroding, through the prism of human perception, into "a burnished, breathing wreck that didn't hurt at all."

Curiously, the poet does not see this relegation of natural beauty, this "kingfisher's burnished plunge" into abstraction, as an entirely negative thing. Instead, echoing Stevens, Clampitt asserts that the transformative nature of the imagination, that process through which it makes experience tacit to the perceiver, is precisely what makes nature real. She confidently characterizes the imagination as "an arrow/ through landscapes of untended memory: ardor/ illuminating with its terrifying currency" the process of perception.

"IMAGO"

One of the few poems that refers directly to the poet's girlhood on the Iowa prairie, "Imago" is unique among her works in its copious use of autobiographical elements. Where most of her contemporaries would no doubt choose the first person for so obviously autobiographical a poem, even here Clampitt opts for the third person "she." Nonetheless, the reader clearly sees this poem's attempts to infuse childhood memory with mythmaking fancy. Of her Iowa childhood Clampitt writes:

> Sometimes, she remembers, a chipped flint
> would turn up in a furrow,
> . . . .
> a nomad's artifact fished from the broth,
> half sea half land—hard evidence
> of an unfathomed state of mind.

Resonant with the land/sea imagery so prominent in her early poem "The Isthmus," "Imago" suggests likewise that the place where earth and water intersect is a flashpoint for understanding the connection between external truth and internal myth.

Clampitt conjures from sparse instants of childhood recollection the stuff of a resoundingly textured poem, one that the possible detractors she addresses may argue "has no form," but one that in her own aesthetic "trundle[s] . . . dismantled sensibility everywhere."

In a sense, it is "dismantled sensibility" that epitomizes Clampitt's poetry, particularly poems like "Imago." Weary of narrative, they seek a more sublime architecture—one that borrows heavily from both archetypal symbolism and Christian iconography. Here one sees in the same eclectic, wildly associative stanzas Jungian archetypal imagery ("the predatory stare out of the burrow") and an almost liturgical celebration of what is simultaneously both Christian and pagan ("a luna moth, the emblem/ of the born-again, . . . a totem-garden of lascivious pheromones").

"A HERMIT THRUSH"

One of the quintessential themes in Clampitt's poetry is her reminder, as friend and reviewer Mary Jo Salter puts it, that "even our memories have their physical home, and could lose it." In "A Hermit Thrush," one of the more vibrant poems from 1987's *Archaic Figure*, Clampitt meditates on both the tentativeness and

tangibility with which memory informs imagination. Choosing as her setting a picnic that is for the speaker both a getaway from and a sojourn into her private myth of the world, Clampitt uses this scenario from which to announce some of her most memorable metaphysical messages. The poem formidably opens "Nothing's certain," proceeds to assert, of our relationship with our memories, that "to/ hold on in any case means taking less and less for granted," and ends, as she does in so many of her poems, in a veiled but nonetheless omnipresent sense of triumph over the indirect but tacit with which our world makes itself known to us:

> . . . —there's
>
> hardly a vocabulary left to wonder, uncertain
> as we are of so much in this existence, this
> botched, cumbersome, much-mended,
> not unsatisfactory thing.

OTHER MAJOR WORKS

PLAY: *Mad with Joy*, pr. 1993 (staged reading).

NONFICTION: *Predecessors, Et Cetera: Essays*, 1991.

EDITED TEXT: *The Essential Donne*, 1988.

BIBLIOGRAPHY

Fairchild, Laura. "Amy Clampitt: An Interview." *American Poetry Review*, 16 (July/August, 1987): 17-20. In one of her few widely circulated interviews, Clampitt candidly discusses her poetry's emphasis on sound, as well as the impact classic poets Gerard Manley Hopkins and Emily Dickinson have had on her work. Although she observes that "I don't have a lot of the teacher in me," she muses amicably about her tenure as writer in residence at The College of William and Mary as well.

Morrisroe, Patricia. "The Prime of Amy Clampitt." *New York* 17 (October 15, 1984): 44-48. Part interview and part critical analysis, Morissroe's article emphasizes the differences between Clampitt's poetry and that of her most widely read contemporaries, "confessional" poets, such as Sylvia Plath. Whereas such poets are routinely celebrate for their ability to "bleed all over the page," Morrisroe observes that poetry such as Clampitt's, which markedly deemphasizes the personal in favor of drawing attention to the natural world, has merits of its own. As Morrisroe deftly points out, "the intensity of [Clampitt's] response to nature can turn the mundane into the magical without turning the magical into a prettified cliché."

Salter, Mary Jo. Introduction to *The Collected Poems of Amy Clampitt*. New York: Knopf, 1997. One of the most illuminating and personal sketches of Clampitt available, Salter's introduction to her posthumously published collected poems bristles with surprising and heretofore undocumented information and anecdotes about the poet. It is Salter who makes public the fact that Clampitt wrote two unpublished novels in the 1950's and only claimed publicly to be a poet in 1971. Salter also provides a moving account of the poet's final days before she died of ovarian cancer in 1994.

Stein, Jean C., and Daniel G. Maroski, eds. *Contemporary Literary Criticism* 32. Detroit: Gale Research, 1985. Focuses on the critical reception for Clampitt's seminal collection *The Kingfisher*. Points out that several critics—including Helen Vendler, Paul Olson, Peter Stitt, and Richard Howard—viewed Clampitt as "the most important new poet on the American scene" in the last quarter of the twentieth century.

Vendler, Helen. "On the Thread of Language." *New York Review of Books* 30 (March 3, 1983): 19-22. Probably the most celebrated (and quoted) review of Clampitt's work to appear in her lifetime, Vendler's ebullient review of *The Kingfisher* notes that its progression over her previous work is "dumbfounding" and that the collection as a whole serves as a remarkable "triumph over the resistance of language, the reason why poetry lasts."

White, Edmund. "Poetry as Alchemy." *Nation* 236 (April 16, 1983): 485-486. White concentrates on what he views as a profound and poignant contradiction in Clampitt's work: that her poems simultaneously both suggest and shy away from narrative. As he observes of Clampitt's work, "one senses [in it] not awkwardness but rather a strange fusion of an ambition to narrate and a talent for suppressing the tale."

Gregory D. Horn

JOHN CLARE

Born: Helpston, England; July 13, 1793
Died: Northampton, England; May 20, 1864

PRINCIPAL POETRY

Poems Descriptive of Rural Life and Scenery, 1820
The Village Minstrel and Other Poems, 1821
The Shepherd's Calendar, 1827
The Rural Muse, 1835
The Later Poems of John Clare, 1964 (Eric Robinson and Geoffrey Summerfield, editors)
The Shepherd's Calendar, 1964 (Robinson and Summerfield, editors)
Selected Poems and Prose of John Clare, 1967 (Robinson and Summerfield, editors)
The Midsummer Cushion, 1979
The Later Poems of John Clare, 1837-1864, 1984
The Early Poems of John Clare, 1804-1822, 1988-1989

OTHER LITERARY FORMS

John Clare attempted little systematically except poetry. He left manuscript drafts of several unfinished essays, and part of what was intended as a natural history of Helpston. He wrote two lengthy autobiographical essays, one of which was published in 1931: *Sketches in the Life of John Clare, Written by Himself*. The other appeared in a collection of his prose in 1951. He also left one year of a journal in which he recorded his reading and his speculations on religion, politics, and literature. His best-known essay is probably his "Journey Out of Essex," an account of his escape from an asylum and his harrowing journey home on foot with no food or shelter; it has been published several times.

ACHIEVEMENTS

John Clare overcame obstacles that would have defeated most other people and became an important poet of the Romantic period in England. His family was illiterate and desperately poor though ambitious for their son to rise in the world. His formal schooling was minimal, and he lived all his life isolated from the literary currents of his day. His editors censored his work heavily, misled him about royalties, and were generally insensitive to what he was trying to do in his verse. He suffered for years from malnutrition and then from incurable mental illness. Despite everything, he was not only enormously prolific as a poet—more than three thousand poems in a fifty-five-year career that began at the age of sixteen—but also wrote a number of poems that may deservedly be called masterpieces. In particular, his descriptive poems have come to be recognized for their originality and anticipation of certain trends in twentieth century nature poetry. His dedication to poetry was intense, surviving, in addition to all other trials, the almost complete financial failure of three of the four books he published during his lifetime. His *The Shepherd's Calendar* is one of the truest and most delightful evocations of English rural life ever written. The "animal" poems of his middle years (the most famous of which is probably "Badger") are stark and powerful expressions of his increasing alienation and despair. He carried his dedication to poetry undiminished into confinement in an asylum, where he wrote poems which show his "sane" grasp of his own insanity. These later poems rise to a universality which has made them widely admired ever since some of them were published in 1873.

Clare was almost completely ignored by the critics until the commentary of Arthur Symons in 1908, and the first textually reliable selection of his poems did not appear until 1920. Even at that, the student of Clare must still exercise extreme caution when using certain editions. In particular, the largest existing selection of his poems, the most complete editions of his prose, and the only one of his letters (all edited by J. W. and Anne Tibble), as well as one of the two existing selections of his asylum poems (edited by Geoffrey Grigson), contain serious misprintings of the manuscripts on almost every page. Much better selections have appeared, published by the Oxford University Press. His reputation began to rise after the work of Symons and especially after the edition by Edmund Blunden in 1920. Much criticism and analysis has appeared since the centennial of Clare's death in 1864, and his reputation has risen rapidly since then.

BIOGRAPHY

John Clare's childhood was spent laboring in the fields near his native village and in the "dame schools" which provided a rudimentary education for those of the rural poor who understood their value. Clare's father was a ballad singer of some local note, and this early exposure to village folk culture, together with his bent for reading, provided a solid base for his later accomplishments. His interest in writing seems to have awakened at the age of sixteen when he acquired a copy of James Thomson's narrative-descriptive poem, *The Seasons* (1746). Finding time and opportunity to write at all, however, proved difficult. Unable to afford much paper, he recorded his earliest efforts on scraps kept in his hat; thus they were easily lost or damaged. The extremely long hours of an agricultural laborer and the distrust of learning among his fellow villagers restricted him further. Nevertheless, by his early twenties he had assembled a fairly substantial body of work which he showed to a nearby storekeeper with literary connections in London. His first book, *Poems Descriptive of Rural Life and Scenery*, was brought out in 1820 by John Taylor, publisher of Charles Lamb and John Keats. It was an immediate success, going through four editions within a year. Taylor then published a second volume, *The Village Minstrel and Other Poems*, in 1821, but its sale was disappointing. Clare's first book had caught the very end of a craze for "peasant poets," Over the next several years he made a few trips to London, meeting and socializing

John Clare (© Bettmann/Corbis)

with Lamb, William Hazlitt, Thomas De Quincey, and others. Nevertheless, problems quickly developed. He began to have disagreements with his publishers over the editing of his poems, the size of his family increased rapidly (he had married a local woman in 1820), and so did his debts. He could not seem to get an accurate or satisfactory explanation of how much of his royalties were needed to pay publishing expenses.

From then until 1837, Clare lived in Helpston almost without interruption, writing increasingly good poetry with almost no public recognition at all. A third volume, *The Shepherd's Calendar*, was finished in 1823 but not published until four years later when it, too, sold poorly. He suffered from malnutrition and his mental health began to deteriorate. Regular employment was scarce in his region, and a move to a neighboring village in 1832 (to a cottage given him by a patron) did not substantially alter his prospects. His sense of place was so strong that he found it difficult to adjust to the move, and he grew increasingly deluded. In 1835 he managed to have a fourth volume published, *The Rural Muse*. The book was well received by the critics but did not sell well.

Finally, in late 1837, he was taken to Matthew Allen's experimental asylum at High Beech, in the Epping Forest near London. There he was well-treated and recovered some of his physical health, but he wrote little for several years. In the spring of 1841, he began writing poetry again, and in July he escaped. He made his way home by walking for several days, surviving by eating grass along the roadside. Although he was not violent, he was clearly not sane, and in late 1841, he was again committed, this time nearer home at the asylum in Northampton. There he remained until his death in 1864 at the age of seventy. His asylum poetry was written almost entirely in the last few months at High Beech and during the brief stay at home and the first several years at Northampton. When a sympathetic asylum supervisor who had preserved his work departed in 1850, his deteriorating condition and lack of encouragement from the staff seemingly closed off his inspiration.

ANALYSIS

The poetry of John Clare shows throughout its development the influence of three forces: the culture of his village and social class, nature, and the topographical

and pastoral poetry of the eighteenth century. Clare's view of human life as lived in close relationship with nature is presented in his poetry as a series of contrasts between the freer, socially more equal, open-field village of his childhood and the enclosed, agriculturally "improved," and socially stratified village of his manhood; between the Eden of a wild nature untouched by human beings and the fallen nature of fences, uprooted landmarks, and vanished grazing rights; between the aesthetic response to nature which loves it for what it is and the scientific response which loves it for profit and social status. Further, as a self-educated poet in a land of illiterate laborers, Clare had difficulty resolving the tension between his temptation to idealize village life and his equally strong temptation to expose its squalid ignorance. One evidence of this is the fact that he wrote *The Shepherd's Calendar*, a celebration of the beauty and activity of a village, in the same year that he wrote "The Parish," a brutally frank attack on its ignorance and cultural isolation. In his best poetry, Clare is able to see each reality as only a part of the truth.

"GYPSIES"

A typical Clare poem of his pre-asylum years will seek, above all, concreteness in its imagery and a structure designed to make the images reveal the maximum amount of meaning. Clare is a master at creating multiple levels of significance through what at first seems like an almost random collection of sights and sounds. A poem that well illustrates this technique is his unrhymed sonnet "Gypsies." It is a poem which deftly combines Clare's love of rural life with his awareness of its darker side. He begins the poem, as he does so many others, with a sense of the mystery of nature: "The snow falls deep; the forest lies alone," but he immediately introduces the theme of human suffering amid the beauty: "the boy goes hasty for his load of brakes/ Then thinks upon the fire and hurries back." The cold is beautiful but potentially deadly. Then he transports the reader to the gypsy camp where there are only bushes to break the wind, where "tainted mutton wastes upon the coals," and the scrawny dog squats nearby "and vainly waits the morsel thrown away." Clare's use of internal rhyme is very successful, as "tainted" and "vainly" resonate against each other in interesting ways. In a sense, the gypsies are "tainted" in the settled village society and thus hope in vain for acceptance. Clare has provided hints of an attitude, then, while allowing the details to carry the implications. He seems to reject both the villagers' ethnic bigotry and the hopelessness of gypsy life: "'Tis thus they live—a picture to the place/ A quiet, pilfering, unprotected race." The seeming offhandedness of "'Tis thus they live" is acceptance and rejection, simultaneously, as the remaining line and one half so neatly demonstrate by balancing "quiet" against "pilfering" against "unprotected." The sudden rise from specific images to broad generalization at the end does not surprise the reader because the details have been so carefully chosen throughout. Clare refuses to idealize gypsy life just as he refuses to excuse the villagers for their prejudice. The sonnet as he uses it here retains most of the traditional Shakespearean form except for the lack of rhyme. It is all the more impressive because Clare encloses his argument in a description which values the gypsies for the beauty they add to life. This determination to see life for what it is and an equal determination not to allow its bitterness to defeat him or prevent him from seeing its beauty is one of Clare's most admirable qualities as a poet and as a man.

The themes of Clare's poetry grow directly out of the ways of seeing human life and nature illustrated in "Gypsies." Perhaps the most important of his themes is the contrast between the village and landscape of the past and of the present. In making this contrast in his poetry, Clare is not simply engaging in private history-making which would leave modern readers uninterested because they occupy a space and a time far removed from Clare's. Rather, he is comparing two fundamentally different approaches to the relationship between human beings and the natural world. The choice between these two approaches is as crucially important today as it was then, and for this reason alone Clare's poetry has lost none of its cogency for the modern world.

"THE MORES"

In Clare's time, enclosure of the land for purposes of agricultural improvement was the issue that divided people in rural areas. No Clare poem speaks more eloquently to what enclosure did, psychologically as well as physically, to village life and to him as a poet than "The Mores" (that is, moors). It is written in a familiar eighteenth century form and style: the locodescriptive poem in heroic couplets. Nevertheless, Clare handles it in original ways. The heroic couplet in the eighteenth century embodies the polished wit and rational completeness which characterized the view of life held by the Age of Reason. Clare's couplet has a slow, solemn movement which is equally as impressive, though far different in effect. At the beginning of the poem, for example, the same sense of mystery in primeval nature seen in "Gypsies" is present here, although that mystery is more obviously a part of the argument to be made: "Far spread the moorey ground a level scene/ Bespread with rush and one eternal green/ That never felt the rage of blundering plough." Here again, balance: the quietness of the pre-enclosure view versus a barely suppressed anger; nature's innocence and eternity against the "blundering" greed of human beings.

Clare's description is always visually precise and yet capable of entertaining several levels of meaning: "uncheckt shadows of green green brown and grey," where "uncheckt" means both "without limits" and "not in checkered patterns as enclosed fields are." A few lines later, "one mighty flat undwarfed by bush or tree/ Spread its faint shadow of immensity." Here, "flat" functions both as a noun and as a kind of suspended adjective: The reader pauses in suspense at this unusual caesura, so that the line reinforces the idea that the reader cannot see the limits of this "faint shadow of immensity/ In the blue mist the (h)orisons edge surrounds." Human pride erupts into the poem, for "inclosure came and trampled on the grave/ Of labours rights." From here to the end of the poem there is continual tension between longing for the old freedom and the reality of the new concern for boundaries, profits, and class distinctions. When these two value systems begin to clash more directly in the poem, the descriptive style becomes harsher, befitting the new dispensation: "And sky bound mores in mangled garbs are left/ Like mighty giants of their limbs bereft." Everywhere there is a pettiness, a separation rather than a communion: "Fence now meets fence in owners little bounds . . ./ In little parcels little minds to please/ With men and flocks imprisoned ill at ease."

As the poem proceeds it becomes clearer that Clare is really talking about a failure of vision: "Each little tyrant with his little sign/ Shows where man claims earth glows no more divine." The problem with the human desire to dominate nature is finally that it destroys that which makes us most human. In Clare's view, then, beauty, freedom, open fields, and social harmony have been succeeded by ugliness, fences, and social antagonism. Under these circumstances, poetic creativity becomes as difficult as any other activity requiring vision. The moors "are vanished now with commons wild and gay/ As poets visions of lifes early day." The cumulative force of the couplets, the measured movement of the lines, the masterful control over the reader's "eye" as it moves over the landscape, all create an emotional impact which makes "The Mores" typical of Clare at his best in the descriptive-narrative poem.

Clare's poetry grew increasingly lyric and less narrative-descriptive as the years passed. As with John Keats, Clare was particularly interested in taking the sonnet in new directions. They both believed that the sonnet might function as a stanza form for longer poems. In Keats's case, the result was the great odes of 1819; in Clare's, the very different but impressive poems on animals of the mid-1830's. Clare's poems had always been filled with a variety of animal life, but these poems move to a new attitude toward nature, emphasizing its otherness from human beings. By a seeming paradox, they move also toward an increased empathy *with* nature. The paradox is resolved by seeing that it is precisely the alienation of wild nature from human society (especially of certain hunted animals) with which Clare could identify because he, too, felt thus cut off from human understanding. The actions of animals in and around nests, caves, and hollow trees fascinated him. These were places where relatively helpless creatures might hope to escape.

"SAND MARTIN"

In the poem "Sand Martin," for example, the bird inhabits the "desolate face" of a wasted landscape far away from man where it flits about "an unfrequented sky." Clare seems to admire most the sand martin's ability to "accept" the desolation of its habitat because of the protection it affords. The speaker of the poem feels "a hermit joy/ To see thee circle round nor go beyond/ That lone heath and its melancholy pond." Clare knew that a person's roots and his resulting sense of place might make him part of a scene that could enervate his spirit; yet, he might be unable to function in any other place.

Clare is a pioneer in using the sonnet to center on a single, unified experience by ignoring the traditional octave-sestet break and using instead accumulation of detail to create meaning. Thus, his early reading in the topographical poetry of the eighteenth century, with its emphasis on a collection of images moving toward a visual as well as an emotional climax, served him well when he wished to make his poetry express through details his anguish and sense of isolation. Meaning emerges in a Clare description almost in slow motion, and it is sometimes late in the poem before the reader realizes what power the accumulated detail has acquired.

LYRIC POEMS

Clare is one of the great lyric poets of the English language. His roots were in a culture which valued the ballad and the oral tale as art forms as well as sources of tradition. Clare himself was a lifelong collector of ballads and folk songs (noting down music as well as words), and he played the violin well. Many of his finest lyrics come from the 1830's and the asylum years, when the bulk of his output became lyric rather than narrative of descriptive. The good lyric can sometimes succeed in reaching the widest audience when it is most personal and "private." From the mid-1830's come four of Clare's best: "Remembrances," "Song's Eternity," "With Garments Flowing," and "Decay." A brief comparison of these four will serve to illustrate the command that Clare exercised over a variety of forms, moods, and themes in the lyric.

In "Remembrances," Clare uses a device so simple and well known—the stages of human life compared to the seasons of the year—that in the hands of a lesser poet it would become trite and shopworn. This ballad-like poem has octameter lines and a typical rhyme scheme of *aaabcccddd*; it is marvelously adapted to the leisurely memories of childhood which the poem treats. From the first line, "Summers pleasures they are gone like to visions every one," Clare manages to imbue the commonest scenes from the past with a haunting quality which the incantatory rhythm of the verse reinforces perfectly.

"Song's Eternity" is a very different kind of lyric. Instead of unusually long lines, it has unusually short ones: alternating lines of four beats and two. Rather than the expansiveness of the quasi-narrative ballad, Clare offers the crisp conciseness of

What is song's eternity?
Come and see.
Melodies of earth and sky.
Here they be.
Songs once sung to Adam's ears.
Can it be? . . .
Songs awakened with the spheres
Alive.

It is Clare's frequently heard theme of the eternity of nature which will provide the necessary stay against the confusion of modern life.

The third lyric, "With Garments Flowing," represents still another form and another purpose. It is a love lyric written in a meter often found in Clare's poetry: stanzas with alternating nine and eight syllables, all tetrameter, rhyming *ababcdcd*. It is more regular than the forms used in "Remembrances" and "Song's Eternity" and was probably chosen because he wanted the ballad-like stanza without its looseness and conversational tone together with the conciseness and rhythm of "Song's Eternity" without the absolute regularity of that poem. The success of "With Garments Flowing" lies also in the metonymy of the garments of the lover's dress standing for the lover herself. To the speaker in the poem she is the type of all that is beautiful. Yet in describing her Clare retains homely details of village life while avoiding the sentimentality that can threaten such an attempt.

Finally, "Decay" is another quite different kind of lyric, and equally successful. Clare wrote it apparently as a means of understanding what was happening to his poetic voice as a result of the move in 1832 to another village, as a way of regaining his poetic voice or at least of explaining its loss. He skillfully controls the reader's response through subtle variations in the rhyme scheme in the ten-line stanzas, as well as through modulations in the simple theme: "O poesy is on the wane/ I hardly know her face again," which acts as a kind of refrain throughout. Personification is also important in this poem: The sun is a "homeless ranger" that "pursues a naked weary way/ Unnoticed like a very stranger." The blend of the local and the universal, as is so often true in Clare's poetry, is here perfectly calculated to communicate disorientation in a coherent manner: "I often think that west is gone/ Oh cruel time to undeceive us." Time has taken away the visionary gleam: "The stream it is a naked stream/ . . .

The sky hangs o'er a broken dream/ The bramble's dwindled to a bramble." The tone becomes more bitter, and the speaker more puzzled even while attaining a new understanding: "And why should passing shadows grieve us/ . . . And hope is but a fancy play/ And joy the art of true believing." Here the sarcasm and the grief somehow perfectly complement each other.

ASYLUM POEMS

Clare's creativity followed a different pattern in the asylum years. Long periods of virtual poetic silence were followed by relatively brief times of sustained production. The dominant theme of his asylum poems is the assertion of his identity as a free man and as a poet. Indeed, Clare had always believed that freedom of the eye and of the mind were necessary preconditions of artistic creativity. His determination to be remembered as a poet, decades after his work had been largely forgotten, is probably responsible both for the quality of his asylum work and for the fact that madness did not completely engulf his mind any sooner than it did. Clare's first sustained asylum production was a continuation of George Gordon, Lord Byron's *Childe Harold's Pilgrimage* (1812-1818, 1819), written in 1841 under the delusion that he was Byron. While it was left unfinished, the work demonstrates that his descriptive and lyric talents were not only unimpaired but also still developing. It was, however, in the first few years of his confinement at Northampton Asylum (from 1842 to about 1848) that some of Clare's finest poems were written. Three of these may be examined briefly for the light they cast on the theme of self-identity and on his level of achievement in these years.

In one, "Peasant Poet," Clare seems to sum up what his poetic life had been about, emphasizing, of course, simplicity and love of nature. His gift for juxtaposing images of ordinary things in order to achieve fresh meaning is undiminished: "the daisy-covered ground" immediately next to "the cloud-bedappled sky"; the sound of the brook leading the eye to the swallow "swimming by." This peasant poet of whom he speaks (clearly himself) was not a great achiever "in life's affairs." He was just two things: "A peasant in his daily cares/ The poet in his joy." It is a descriptive lyric containing the essence of his poetic credo: poetry as joy, transforming the face of daily life.

The second poem, "An Invite to Eternity," is Clare's most sustained attempt to define the perception of the insane mind; not to define it as a dictionary would but to re-create for the reader its vision of the world—making the reader participate in it and so identify with it. Like so many of Clare's poems, whenever written, this one begins with an invitation—in this case to a "sweet maid" who is to travel with him through the landscape of madness. In the same sort of personification seen in "Decay," both the sun and the path have forgotten where they are to go. In this "strange death of life to be," what the reader sees is inverted, made into its opposite: "Where stones will turn to flooding streams/ Where plains will rise like ocean waves." The swaying rhythm of the tetrameter lines creates an almost hypnotic effect. It is an existence without identity: being and nonbeing at the same time. In this twilight existence, they will not know each other's face, and time itself will cease to exist: "The present mixed with reasons gone/ And past and present all as one." Knowing all this, he asks the maid, can her life be led "to join the living with the dead?" If so (and he seems to await her answer with the serenity of absolute knowledge), "Then trace thy footsteps on with me/ We're wed to one eternity." Logic, time, identity, and ordinary perception of the "real" have all been suspended, to be replaced by their opposites. The perfectly ordered form of the poem, its calm account of the horrors of irrationality, provide remarkable evidence of Clare's ability at times in the asylum to view his own insanity from outside, as it were. Perhaps more important, the poem demonstrates how much he was still a poet in control of his art.

The third poem is entitled simply, "I Am." If "Peasant Poet" sums up Clare's view of himself as poet, and "An Invite to Eternity" his view of himself as insane, "I Am" may be said to provide the essence of Clare as child of God. In the poem he creates a persona supremely tragic: the good man bereft of that which gave his life purpose and left to experience the moment of self-understanding completely alone. The poem turns on the idea of existence without essence, and the first stanza reiterates the "I Am" four times in its six lines: Since no one knows anything of him except that he exists, he becomes "the self-consumer of [his] woes." They have no outlet, they meet with no understanding. The tremen-dous psychological pressure that this would ordinarily create is somehow controlled and made to yield calm resignation rather than anger, as the speaker surveys "the vast shipwreck of my lifes esteems." Instead, in the third and final stanza he returns to a familiar Clare theme: the Eden of nature. There, where there is neither man nor woman, only God, peace is at last possible: "Untroubling and untroubled where I lie/ The grass below, above, the vaulted sky." In Clare's fen country, the two essential facts had always been the moors and the sky—both flat, immense, bare, unchanging, losing themselves at the edge in mist and shadow.

OTHER MAJOR WORKS

NONFICTION: *Sketches in the Life of John Clare, Written by Himself*, 1931; *John Clare's Birds*, 1982; *John Clare's Autobiographical Writings*, 1983; *The Natural History Prose Writings of John Clare*, 1983; *The Letters of John Clare*, 1985; *Selected Letters*, 1988 (Mark Storey, editor).

BIBLIOGRAPHY

Blythe, Ronald. *Talking About John Clare*. Nottingham, England: Trent, 1999. A commentary on the relationship between the English rural writer and the places that inform his work. Includes passages on many writers who are thematically associated with John Clare.

Chilcott, Tim. *"A Real World and Doubting Mind": A Critical Study of the Poetry of John Clare*. Hull, England: Hull University Press, 1985. The title of this volume is taken from Clare's *The Shepherd's Calendar*. Chilcott argues that the real world and doubting mind are two distinct aspects of Clare's poetry. Discusses both his preasylum and asylum periods. A challenging critical study recommended for readers familiar with Clare.

Clay, Arnold. *Itching After Rhyme: A Life of John Clare*. Tunbridge Wells, England: Parapress, 2000. An in-depth biography with bibliographical references and index.

Howard, William. *John Clare*. Boston: Twayne, 1981. A useful introduction to Clare's poetry. Includes Clare's own statements about his method of composing poetry and emphasizes more his form than content or philosophy. Devotes a chapter each to the sonnets and one to *Childe Harold's Pilgrimage.*

Storey, Edward. *A Right to Song: The Life of John Clare.* London: Methuen, 1982. A full-length biography sympathetic to Clare that looks at the complexity of his poetic landscapes. The thoroughly researched biography stays close to his works and is recommended for Clare scholars.

Storey, Mark. *The Poetry of John Clare: A Critical Introduction.* London: Macmillan, 1974. Explicitly an introduction, this volume traces the development of Clare's poetry from his humble beginnings to his maturation. Chooses *The Shepherd's Calendar* as the focal point for an examination of Clare's mature descriptive technique. An appreciative study of Clare that highlights both the appeal and the variety of his work.

Tibble, J. W., and Anne Tibble. *John Clare: A Life.* 1932. Reprint. London: Michael Joseph, 1972. Considered the standard biography for many years but now superseded by Edward Storey's biography. Still useful, although some of the details of Clare's early life are sketchy and inaccurate.

Mark Minor;
bibliography updated by the editors

AUSTIN CLARKE

Born: Dublin, Ireland; May 9, 1896
Died: Dublin, Ireland; March 19, 1974

PRINCIPAL POETRY

The Vengeance of Fionn, 1917 (based on the Irish Saga "Pursuit of Diarmid and Grainne")
The Fires of Baal, 1921
The Sword of the West, 1921
The Cattledrive in Connaught and Other Poems, 1925 (based on the prologue to *Tain bo Cuailnge*)
Pilgrimage and Other Poems, 1929
The Collected Poems of Austin Clarke, 1936
Night and Morning, 1938

Ancient Lights, 1955
Too Great a Vine: Poems and Satires, 1957
The Horse-Eaters: Poems and Satires, 1960
Collected Later Poems, 1961
Forget-Me-Not, 1962
Flight to Africa and Other Poems, 1963
Mnemosyne Lay in Dust, 1966
Old-Fashioned Pilgrimage and Other Poems, 1967
The Echo at Coole and Other Poems, 1968
Orphide and Other Poems, 1970
Tiresias: A Poem, 1971
The Wooing of Becfolay, 1973
Collected Poems, 1974
The Selected Poetry of Austin Clarke, 1976

OTHER LITERARY FORMS

Besides his epic, narrative, and lyric poetry, Austin Clarke published three novels, two volumes of autobiography, some twenty verse plays, and a large volume of journalistic essays and literary reviews for newspaper and radio. He also delivered a number of radio lectures on literary topics and gave interviews on his own life and work on Irish radio and television.

ACHIEVEMENTS

In a poetic career that spanned more than fifty years, Austin Clarke was a leading figure in the "second generation" of the Irish Literary Revival. Most of his career can be understood as a response to the aims of that movement: to celebrate the heroic legends of ancient Ireland, to bring the compositional technique of the bardic poets into modern English verse, and to bring poetry and humor together in a socially liberating way on the modern stage.

Clarke's earliest efforts to write epic poems on pre-Christian Ireland were not generally successful, although his first poems do have passages of startling color and lyric beauty which presage his later work. When, in the 1930's, he turned to early medieval ("Celtic Romanesque") Ireland, he found his métier, both in poetry and in fiction. To the celebration of the myth of a vigorous indigenous culture in which Christian ascetic and pagan hedonist coexisted, he bent his own disciplined efforts. Unlike William Butler Yeats and most of the leading writers of the Revival, Clarke had direct access to the language of the ancient literature and worked to reproduce its rich assonantal effects in modern English. In this effort he was uniquely successful among modern Irish poets.

In his later years, Clarke turned to satirizing the domestic scene, living to see cultural changes remedy many of his complaints about Irish life. Although writing in obscurity through most of his career, in his later life Clarke was belatedly recognized by several institutions: He was awarded an honorary D.Litt. in 1966 from Trinity College, received the Gregory Medal in 1968 from the Irish Academy of Letters, and was the "Writer in Profile" on Radio Telifís Éireann in 1968.

BIOGRAPHY

Austin Clarke was born into a large, middle-class, Catholic, Dublin family on May 9, 1896. He was educated by the Jesuits at Belvedere College and took a B.A. and an M.A. in English literature from University College, Dublin, in 1916 and 1917, and he was appointed assistant lecturer there in 1917. In his formative years, he was heavily impressed by the Irish Literary Revival, especially Douglas Hyde's Gaelic League and Yeats's Abbey Theatre, and his political imagination was fired by the Easter Rising of 1916. In 1920, following a brief civil marriage to Geraldine Cummins, he was dismissed from his university post; shortly thereafter, he emigrated to London and began to write his epic poems on heroic subjects drawn from the ancient literature of Ireland.

In 1930, Clarke married Nora Walker, with whom he had three sons, and between 1929 and 1938 he wrote a number of verse plays and two novels—both banned in Ireland—before returning permanently to Ireland in 1937. Since in his creative career and national literary allegiance he was from the beginning a disciple of Yeats, he was sorely disappointed to be omitted from *The Oxford Book of Modern Verse* which Yeats edited in 1936. Nevertheless, with the publication of *Night and Morning*, Clarke began a new and public phase in his creative career: The following year, he began his regular broadcasts on poetry on Radio Éireann and started to write book reviews for *The Irish Times*. Between 1939 and 1942, he was president of Irish PEN and cofounder (with Robert Farren) of the Dublin Verse-Speaking So-

ciety and the Lyric Theatre Company. Subsequently, his verse plays were produced at the Abbey and on Radio Eireann.

Clarke's prolonged creative silence in the early 1950's seems, in retrospect, oddly appropriate to the depressed state of Ireland, where heavy emigration and strict censorship seemed to conspire in lowering public morale. Yet, as if he were anticipating the economic revival, he published *Ancient Lights* in 1955. Here began a new phase in his poetic career, that of a waspish commentator on contemporary events, composing dozens of occasional poems, some of which can lay claim to a reader's attention beyond their particular origins. Between 1955 and his death, a collection of these pieces appeared every two or three years, as well as two volumes of autobiography. His public profile was maintained through his radio broadcasts, his regular reviews in *The Irish Times*, his attendance at many PEN conferences, and his visits to the United States and the Soviet Union. In 1972, he was nominated for the Nobel Prize in Literature. He died on March 19, 1974, shortly after the publication of his *Collected Poems*.

ANALYSIS

The first phase of Austin Clarke's poetic career, 1917 to 1925, produced four epic poems which are little more than apprentice work. Drawing on Celtic and biblical texts, they betray too easily the influences of Yeats, Sir Samuel Ferguson, and other pioneers of the Revival. Considerably overwritten and psychologically unsure, only in patches do they reveal Clarke's real talent: his close understanding of the original text and a penchant for erotic humor and evocative lyrical descriptions of nature. The major preoccupations of his permanent work did not appear until he assimilated these earliest influences.

Clarke's difficulties with religious faith, rejection of Catholic doctrine, and an unfulfilled need for spiritual consolation provide the theme and tension in the poems from *Pilgrimage and Other Poems* and *Night and Morning*. These poems arise from the conflicts between the mores of modern Irish Catholicism and Clarke's desire for emotional and sexual fulfillment. These poems, therefore, mark a departure from his earlier work in that they are personal and contemporary in theme. Yet they are also designedly Irish, in setting and technique.

In searching for a vehicle to express his personal religious conflicts while keeping faith in his commitment to the Irish Literary Revival, Clarke found an alternative to Yeats's heroic, pre-Christian age: the "Celtic Romanesque," the medieval period in Irish history when the Christian Church founded by Saint Patrick was renowned for its asceticism, its indigenous monastic tradition, its scholastic discipline, its missionary zeal, and the brilliance of its art (metalwork, illuminated manuscripts, sculpture, and devotional and nature poetry). Although this civilization contained within it many of the same tensions which bedeviled Clarke's world—those between the Christian ideal and the claims of the flesh, between Christian faith and pagan hedonism—it appealed to his imagination because of his perception of its independence from Roman authority, the separation of ecclesiastical and secular spheres, and its respect for artistic excellence. This view of the period is selective and romanticized but is sufficient in that it serves his artistic purposes.

Clarke's poetry is Irish also in a particular, technical sense: in its emulation of the complex sound patterns of Gaelic verse, called *rime riche*. In this endeavor, he was following the example set by Douglas Hyde in his translations of folk songs and by the poems of Thomas MacDonagh. This technique employs a variety of rhyming and assonantal devices so that a pattern of rhymes echoes through the middles and ends of lines, playing off unaccented as well as accented syllables. Relatively easy to manage in Gaelic poetry because of the sound structure of the language, *rime riche* requires considerable dexterity in English. Yet Clarke diligently embraced this challenge, sometimes producing results which were little more than technical exercises or impenetrably obscure, but often producing works of unusual virtuosity and limpid beauty. Clarke summed up his approach in his answer to Robert Frost's inquiry about the kind of verse he wrote: "I load myself with chains and I try to get out of them." To which came the shocked reply: "Good Lord! You can't have many readers."

Indeed, Clarke is neither a popular nor an easy poet. Despite his considerable output (his *Collected Poems* runs to some 550 pages), his reputation stands firmly on a select number of these. Of his early narrative poems, adaptations of Celtic epic tales, only a few passages transcend the prevailing verbal clutter.

PILGRIMAGE AND OTHER POEMS

With the publication of *Pilgrimage and Other Poems*, however, the focus narrowed, and the subjects are realized with startling clarity. Perhaps the most representative and accomplished poem in this volume is the lyric "Celibacy." This treatment of a hermit's struggle with lust combines Clarke's personal conflicts with the Catholic Church's sexual teachings and his sympathy with the hermit's spiritual calling in a finely controlled, ironic commentary on the contemporary Irish suspicion of sex. Clarke achieves this irony through a series of images which juxtapose the monk's self-conscious heroism to his unconscious self-indulgence. The rhyming and assonantal patterns in this poem are an early example of the successful use of the sound patterns borrowed from Gaelic models that became one of the distinctive characteristics of his work.

NIGHT AND MORNING

With the publication of *Night and Morning*, there is a considerable consolidation of power. In this collection of sterling consistency, Clarke succeeds in harnessing the historical elements to his personal voice and vision. In the exposition of the central theme of the drama of racial conscience, he shows himself to be basically a religious poet. The central problems faced here are the burden to the contemporary generation of a body of truth received from the centuries of suffering and refinement, the limitations of religious faith in an age of sexual and spiritual freedom, and the conflicts arising from a sympathy with and a criticism of the ordinary citizen. Clarke's own position is always ambivalent. While he seems to throw down the gauntlet to the dogmatic Church, his challenge is never wholehearted: He is too unsure of his position outside the institution he ostensibly abjures. This ambivalence is borne out in the fine title poem in this volume, in the implications of the Christian imagery of the Passion, the candle, the celebration of the Mass, the Incarnation, and the double lightning of faith and reason. A confessional poem, "Night and Morning" protests the difficulties in maintaining an adult faith in the Christian message in a skeptical age. While it criticizes the lack of an intellectual stiffening in modern Irish Catholicism and ostensibly years for the medieval age when faith and reason were reconciled, the poem's passion implies an allegiance to the Church that is more emotional than intellectual. These ambiguities are deftly conveyed by the title, design, tone, and imagery of the poem.

Almost every poem in this volume shows Clarke at his best, especially "Martha Blake," "The Straying Student," and "The Jewels." In "Martha Blake," a portrait of a devout daily communicant, Clarke manages multiple points of view with lucidity and ease. From one perspective, Martha's blind faith is depicted as heroic and personally valid; from another, Martha is not very aware of the beauty of the natural world around her, although she experiences it vicariously through the ardor of her religious feelings; from a third, as in the superb final stanza, the poet shares with his readers a simultaneous double perspective which balances outer and inner visions, natural and supernatural grace. The ambiguity and irony which permeate this last stanza are handled with a sensitivity that, considering the anguish and anger of so much of his religious verse, reveals a startling degree of sympathy for ordinary, sincere Christians. He sees that a passionate nature may be concealed, and may be fulfilling itself, beneath the appearances of a simple devotion.

ANCIENT LIGHTS

When, after a long silence, *Ancient Lights* appeared in 1955, Clarke had turned from his earlier historical and personal mode to a public and satirical posture. These poems comment wittily on current issues controversial in the Ireland of the early 1950's: the mediocrity and piety of public life, "scandalous" women's fashions, the domination of Irish public opinion by the Catholic Church, the "rhythm" method of birth control, and the incipient public health program. Many of these poems may appear quaint and require annotations even for a post-Vatican II Irish audience. The lead poem, "Celebrations," for example, in criticizing the smug piety of post-revolutionary Ireland, focuses on the Eucharistic Congress held in Dublin in 1932. The poem is studded with references to the Easter Rising of 1916, its heroic antecedents and its promise for the new nation. These are set in ironic contrast with the jobbing latter-day politicians who have made too easy an accommodation with the Church and have thus replaced the British with a native oppression. Clarke vehemently excoriates the manner in which the public purse is made to subscribe to Church-mandated institutions. Despite its highly compressed

content, this poem succeeds in making a direct statement on an important public issue. Unfortunately, the same is not true of many of Clarke's subsequent satires, which degenerate into bickering over inconsequential subjects, turn on cheap puns, or lapse into doubtful taste.

This cannot be said, however, of the title poem of this volume, one of Clarke's best achievements. Autobiographical and literally confessional, it can be profitably read in conjunction with his memoir, *Twice 'Round the Black Church: Early Memories of Ireland and England* (1962), especially pages 138-139. It begins with the familiar Clarke landscape of Catholic Dublin and the conflict between adolescent sex and conscience. Having made a less than full confession, the persona guiltily skulks outside, pursued by a superstitious fear of retribution.

Emerging into the light like an uncaged bird, in a moment reminiscent of that experienced by James Joyce's Stephen Daedalus on the beach, the protagonist experiences an epiphany of natural grace which sweeps his sexual guilt away. The Church-induced phobias accumulated over the centuries drop away in a moment of creative self-assertion. This experience is confirmed in nature's own manner: driven by a heavy shower into the doorway of the Protestant black church (for the full significance of the breaking of this sectarian taboo, see again his memoir), he experiences a spiritual catharsis as he observes the furious downpour channeled, contained, and disposed by roof, pipe, and sewer. With the sun's reappearance, he is born again in a moment of triumphant, articulate joy.

The narrative direction, tonal variety, and especially the virtuosity of the final stanza establish this poem as one of Clarke's finest creations. It weaves nostalgia, humor, horror, vision, and euphoria into a series of epiphanies which prepare the reader for the powerful conclusion. This last stanza combines the images of penance with baptism in a flood of images which are precisely observed and fraught with the spiritual significance for which the reader has been prepared. It should be noted, however, that even here Clarke's resolution is consciously qualified: The cowlings and downpipes are ecclesiastical, and the flood's roar announces the removal of but "half our heavens." Nevertheless, in the control and energy of its images and sound patterns, the poem realizes many of Clarke's objectives in undertaking to write poetry that dramatizes the proverbial tensions between art, religion, and nature in the national conscience.

SATIRE AND IRONY

In the nineteen years following the publication of *Ancient Lights*, Clarke produced a continuous stream of satires upon occasional issues, few of which rise above their origins. They are often hasty in judgment, turgid almost beyond retrieval, or purely formal exercises. These later volumes express a feeling of alienation from modern Ireland, in its particular mix of piety and materialism. Always mindful of the myths lying behind Irish life, his critique begins to lose its currency and sound quixotically conservative. Then in the early 1960's, with the arrival of industrialization in Ireland, relative prosperity, and the Church reforms following Vatican II, many of Clarke's criticisms of Irish life become inapplicable and his latter-day eroticism sounds excessively self-conscious and often in poor taste. Nevertheless, some of his later lyrics, such as "Japanese Print," and translations from the Irish are quite successful: lightly ironic, relaxed, matching the spirit of their originals.

MNEMOSYNE LAY IN DUST

The most impressive personal poem of this last phase in his career is the confessional *Mnemosyne Lay in Dust*. Based on his experiences during a lengthy stay at a mental institution some forty years before, it recrosses the battleground between his inherited Jansenism and his personal brand of secular humanism. In harrowing, cacophonic verse, the poem describes the tortured hallucinations, the electric shock treatment, the amnesia, the pain of rejection by "Margaret" (his first wife), the contemplated suicide, and the eventual rejection of religious taboos for a life directed to the development of reason and human feeling. For all its extraordinary energy, however, this poem lacks the consistency and finish of his shorter treatments of the same dilemma.

FINAL PHASE

The last phase of Clarke's poetic career produced a group of poems on erotic subjects which affirm, once again, his belief in the full right to indulge in life's pleasures. The best of these—such as "Anacreontic" and "The Healing of Mis"—are remarkably forthright and witty and are not marred by the residual guilt of his earlier forays into this subject.

Austin Clarke's oeuvre is by turns brilliant and gauche. Learned and cranky, tortured and tender, his work moves with extraordinary commitment within a narrow range of concerns. His quarrels with Irish Catholicism and the new Irish state, his preoccupation with problems of sexuality, with Irish myth and history, and his technical emulation of Irish-language models set him firmly at the center of Irish poetry after Yeats. These considerations place him outside the modernist movement. In Ireland, he has been more highly rated by literary historians than by the younger generation of poets. Recognition abroad is coming late: In about twenty poems, he has escaped from his largely self-imposed chains to gain the attention of the world at large.

OTHER MAJOR WORKS

LONG FICTION: *The Bright Temptation*, 1932, 1973; *The Singing Men at Cashel*, 1936; *The Sun Dances at Easter*, 1952.

PLAYS: *The Son of Learning*, pr., pb. 1927 (as *The Hunger Demon*, pr. 1930); *The Flame*, pb. 1930, pr. 1932; *Sister Eucharia*, pr., pb. 1939; *Black Fast*, pb. 1941, pr. 1942; *As the Crow Flies*, pr. 1942 (radio play), pb. 1943, pr. 1948 (staged); *The Kiss*, pr. 1942, pb. 1944; *The Plot Is Ready*, pr. 1943, pb. 1944; *The Viscount of Blarney*, pr., pb. 1944; *The Second Kiss*, pr., pb. 1946; *The Plot Succeeds*, pr., pb. 1950; *The Moment Next to Nothing*, pr., pb. 1953; *Collected Plays*, pb. 1963; *The Student from Salamanca*, pr. 1966, pb. 1968; *Two Interludes Adapted from Cervantes: "The Student from Salamanca" and "The Silent Lover,"* pb. 1968; *The Impuritans: A Play in One Act Freely Adapted from the Short Story "Young Goodman Brown" by Nathaniel Hawthorne*, pb. 1972; *The Visitation*, pb. 1974; *The Third Kiss*, pb. 1976; *Liberty Lane*, pb. 1978.

NONFICTION: *Poetry in Modern Ireland*, 1951; *Twice 'Round the Black Church: Early Memories of Ireland and England*, 1962; *A Penny in the Clouds: More Memories of Ireland and England*, 1968; *The Celtic Twilight and the Nineties*, 1969; *Growing Up Stupid Under the Union Jack: A Memoir*, 1980.

BIBLIOGRAPHY

Algoo-Baksh, Stella. *Austin C. Clarke: A Biography.* Toronto: ECW Press, 1994. Combines a narrative of

Austin Clarke's life with thoughtful interpretations of some of his major works. Gives a portrait of Clarke's puplic persona but few details of his personal life. Includes bibliographical references and index.

Garratt, Robert F. *Modern Irish Poetry: Tradition Continuity from Yeats to Heaney.* Berkeley: University of California Press, 1986. This important book devotes a chapter to Clarke, the main figure of transition for twentieth century Irish poetry. Clarke's early poetry followed William Butler Yeats in retelling Irish myths, his middle work focused on medievalism, and his later poems echoed James Joyce in their critical analysis of religion. Contains an index and select bibliography that includes material on Clarke.

Halpern, Susan. *Austin Clarke: His Life and Works.* Dublin: Dolmen Press, 1974. Introducing Clarke as the most significant Irish poet since William Butler Yeats, Halpern studies his memoirs before analyzing his work. First, she examines his poetry as early, later, and latest. Then, she presents his criticism, and finally, she studies his drama and prose romances. Complemented by an appendix, a bibliography, notes, and an index.

Harmon, Maurice. *Austin Clarke, 1896-1974: A Critical Introduction.* Dublin: Wolfhound Press, 1989. The introduction covers the life of Clarke, the contexts for his writing, his Catholicism, and his participation in nationalist movements. Two phases are then examined: first, his prose, drama, and poetry from 1916 to 1938; second, his sustained work in poetry, short and long, from 1955 to 1974. Supplemented by a portrait, notes, a bibliography, and an index.

Loftus, Richard J. "Austin Clarke: Ireland of the Black Church." In *Nationalism in Modern Anglo-Irish Poetry.* Madison: University of Wisconsin Press, 1964. Focuses on Clarke's contributions to Irish verse: use of Gaelic prosody, creation of beauty from harsh peasantry, and experimental verse drama. Most of the chapter reviews Clarke's satirical anger at the Irish Catholic church. Includes notes, a bibliography, and an index.

Murphy, Daniel. "Disarmed, a Malcontent." In *Imagination and Religion in Anglo-Irish Literature, 1930-*

1980. Blackrock, Ireland: Irish Academic Press, 1987. Analyzes Clarke's lyrics and satires. Also examines religious tensions in *Mnemosyne Lay in Dust,* reviews Clarke's use of history, examines Clarke's satirical style, and finally sketches Clarke's use of nature. The chapter is supplemented by notes and a bibliography. The book contains an index.

Ricigliano, Lorraine. *Austin Clarke: A Reference Guide.* New York: Maxwell Macmillan International, 1993. A chronology of the major works by Clarke; an alphabetical list of all the individual poems and plays in the volumes cited; and a secondary bibliography, also arranged chronologically from 1918 to 1992, with descriptive annotations.

Tapping, G. Craig. *Austin Clarke: A Study of His Writings.* Dublin: Academy Press, 1981. After calling Clarke's tradition "modern classicism," Craig sketches a background of Romanticism to "Celto-Romanesque." Five chapters study the poetic drama, the novels, the poetry from 1938 to 1961, the poetry of the 1960's, and the new poems as treatments of old myths. Augmented by bibliographies, notes, an appendix, and an index.

Cóilín Owens;
bibliography updated by the editors

PAUL CLAUDEL

Born: Villeneuve-sur-Fère, France; August 6, 1868
Died: Paris, France; February 23, 1955

PRINCIPAL POETRY

Connaissance de l'est, 1900, 1952 (*The East I Know*, 1914)

Art poétique, 1907 (*Poetic Art*, 1948)

Cinq Grandes Odes, 1910 (*Five Great Odes*, 1967)

Vers d'exil, 1912

Corona Benignitatis Anni Dei, 1915 (*Coronal*, 1943)

La Messe là-bas, 1921

Poèmes de guerre, 1922 (partial translation, *Three Poems of the War*, 1919)

Feuilles de saints, 1925

Cent Phrases pour éventails, 1927 (*A Hundred Movements for a Fan*, 1992)

La Cantate à trois voix, 1931

Dodoitzu, 1945

Poèmes et paroles durant la guerre de trente ans, 1945

Visages radieux, 1947

Premiers Vers, 1950

Poésies diverses, 1957

Autres Poèmes d'après le chinois, 1957

Petits Poèmes d'après le chinois, 1957

Traductions de poèmes, 1957

Œuvre poétique, 1957

Poèmes retrouvés, 1967

OTHER LITERARY FORMS

Although Paul Claudel's poetry occupies a prominent place in his writings, it was his theater that brought him a worldwide reputation. Gallimard published Claudel's *Œuvres complètes* (1950-1967) in twenty-seven volumes. Claudel stated repeatedly that human drama is not complete unless a supernatural element enriches it and brings to it a vertical sense. From the day of his conversion to Roman Catholicism on December 25, 1886, the Bible became his daily companion. In his poetry, the influence of the Bible manifests itself in an exuberant lyric vein, while in his plays it is evident in his conception of the conflict between good and evil—not so much a question of metaphysics as a struggle that takes place within the soul, among Satan, man, and God. Claudel's study of the Bible also resulted in a series of exegetical works that constitute a third important part of his creative artistry. Finally, the numerous volumes of Claudel's correspondence and the two volumes of his journal are indispensable guides to his inner life.

ACHIEVEMENTS

The literary fate of Paul Claudel can be compared to that of Stendhal (Marie-Henri Beyle), who, despite the initial indifference and lack of enthusiasm with which people of his generation received his writings, predicted that his works would be understood and successful by the end of the nineteenth century. Stendhal even dedi-

cated his novel, *La Chartreuse de Parme* (1839; *The Charterhouse of Parma*, 1895), not without irony, "to the happy few" who were able to understand his art and thought. Time has proved that Stendhal judged with perspicacity both his own work and the evolution of the literary taste of his country. In the same way, when Symbolism was giving clear signs of its vitality, Ferdinand Brunetière, very skeptical of the success of the new movement, in an article published by *La Revue des deux mondes* on November 1, 1888, dared challenge all the members of it by saying: "Give us a masterpiece and we will take you seriously." Literary scholar Henri Guillemin is surprised that Brunetière did not recognize the signs that were pointing to the man who was to come: "He was there, the man of masterpiece," he says, and in less than two years Claudel would publish his play *Tête d'or* (1890; English translation, 1919). Yet, despite this and many other masterpieces, Claudel remained unknown to the general public until after World War II.

Claudel was too religious for the secular Third Republic of France; his poetry ignored the Alexandrine meter and largely did without rhyme, while his plays dramatized a soul-searching and soul-saving adventure in which the eternal destiny of man took priority over psychology. Above all, Claudel did not use the literary language most of the French cherished, and he was accused of writing French poetry in German.

Nevertheless, Claudel persisted on his solitary course, largely undistracted by the literary fashions of the twentieth century. By the end of his life, he was numbered among the preeminent poets and playwrights of modern France.

BIOGRAPHY

Paul-Louis-Charles-Marie Claudel was born in Villeneuve-sur-Fère (Tardenois), France, on August 6, 1868. He was the youngest of three children, with two sisters, Camille and Louise. Their father, Louis-Prosper Claudel, was a civil servant who came to Villeneuve-sur-Fère from La Bresse, a small town in the Vosges region. By nature, he was an unsociable and taciturn person. His profession as civil servant left him little time for his children. Claudel's mother, born Louise Cerveaux, came from a family that had its origins in Villeneuve-sur-Fère. Like her husband, she was an unaffectionate parent; according to Claudel, she never kissed her children. The difficult character of the oldest child, Camille, may have been responsible for the mother's attitude and, indeed, adversely affected all the relationships in the family. In 1882, after many years of following her husband from place to place—Louis-Prosper Claudel had held posts in Villeneuve-sur-Fère, Bar-le-Duc, Nogent-sur-Seine, Wassy, Rambouillet, and Compiègne—Louise Claudel yielded to the pressure of Camille and agreed to settle with her children in Paris. Camille was eighteen years of age, Louise sixteen, and Paul fourteen.

Contrary to what one might expect, Paris did not fascinate the young Claudel: The crushing feelings of loneliness and boredom from which he suffered became even more frightening in the big city. Nor did Paris offer a respite from the endless family quarrels. In the restless atmosphere of the country's capital and under the pressure of his anarchist instincts, Claudel at one time contemplated suicide. Fortunately, as he grew into adulthood, he saw the positive side of Parisian life. He discovered the "mystical" beauty of Richard Wagner's music; at the age of nineteen, he was admitted to Stéphane Mallarmé's circle; and while still in the *lycée*, he enjoyed the company of classmates who were to become leading figures in French cultural and political life in the first half of the twentieth century. In 1886, purely by accident, Claudel discovered Arthur Rimbaud, in the June issue of *La Vogue* magazine, when he read Rimbaud's *Les Illuminations* (1886; *Illuminations*, 1932) and *Une Saison en enfer* (1873; *A Season in Hell*, 1932).

On December 25, 1886, Claudel went to Notre-Dame of Paris, and there, during the early afternoon Office of Vespers, his "heart was touched" and he "believed." The nightmares that had haunted his youth were banished; his life and his obvious talent acquired a purpose. A creative enthusiasm inspired him to "evangelize" all the layers of his being. The process of this evangelization was to be reflected in his writings, both poetry and drama; he was to remain forever a poet committed to God and men.

After passing the examination for the Ministry of Foreign Affairs, Claudel entered into a diplomatic career that lasted until 1935. His first consular assignment took him to New York City and Boston in 1893. By that time, he had published *Tête d'or* and *La Ville* (1893; *The City*,

1920). His visit to the United States inspired him to write *L'Échange* (1954; the exchange), a masterpiece that presents a realistic image of American life and civilization. His diplomatic life took him next to China; between 1895 and 1900, Claudel held posts in Foochow, Shanghai, and Hankow. It was at this time that he turned to poetry. Upon his return to France, in 1900, Claudel thought of abandoning poetry and becoming a monk, but he was not accepted in either Solesmes or Ligugé. He decided then to pursue his diplomatic career, which took him back to China.

It was in 1900, on shipboard en route to China, that he met a married Polish woman, "Ysé" (Rose Vetch). They shared an adulterous affair which lasted four years. In 1906, while on vacation in France, Claudel married Reine Sainte-Marie Perrin, daughter of the architect of the Basilica of Fourvière in Lyons. Three days after his marriage, Claudel returned to China, accompanied by his wife. From that year on, Claudel's professional life never knew an eclipse; from China, he went on to Prague, Frankfurt, Rome, and Brazil. Finally, as ambassador, he served in Japan, the United States, and Belgium.

The last years of Claudel's life were filled with honors and recognition. Even the Académie Française reversed its 1936 rejection of him, and in 1946 Claudel was elected one of the Immortals of France. Perhaps the most striking symbol of Claudel's success is the fact that, on the night of his death in February, 1955, the Comédie-Française was rehearsing *L'Annonce faite à Marie* (1912; *The Tidings Brought to Mary*, 1916).

ANALYSIS

One of the outstanding characteristics of Paul Claudel's work is its cosmic dimension. His poetry does not form an exception to this general rule, for Claudel chose as its subject the visible world, enriching it with the invisible things of his faith. He was tempted neither to sacrifice the visible for the sake of the spiritual nor to do the opposite.

When he refers to his poetry in "La Maison fermée" ("Within the House") of *Five Great Odes*, Claudel uses this analogy: "The Word of God is the way that God gives himself to humankind. The created word is that way by which all created things are given to man." The universe of Claudel, one might say, is a man-centered world but certainly not to the exclusion of God. In an analogous sense, the poet is called upon to redeem visible things from the corruption of time and to elevate them, by his created word, to the heights of eternity. "To name a thing," Claudel says in his *Poetic Art*, "means to produce it inextinguishable, for it is to produce it in relationship to its principle, which does not include cessation." In a sense, therefore, the peculiar vocation of the poet is to be a prophet in the etymological sense of the word: He speaks for the visible universe.

However ironic it may sound, one has the impression that Claudel, after his conversion, wanted to "convert his conversion" to his own powerful nature, to the splendor of visible things, and to invite God himself to join him in his celebration of this world. By embracing nature and by calling things by their names, however, the poet determines their place in the intention of their Creator. There is nothing that horrified Claudel more than the idea of a material infinite; he considered it a "scandal of the reason." Speaking of Dante's poetic endeavor, Claudel reminds himself that a true poet does not need "greater stars" or "more beautiful roses" than those nature furnishes. His task is to use words, those "resonant phantoms," to produce an enjoyable and intelligent picture of the universe.

If it is true that Claudel attained in *Five Great Odes* the summit of his poetic creation, it is because his genius had reached a level of synthesis where painful experiences and poetic inspiration were molded into a harmonious unity. Yet this synthesis was achieved only after a lengthy poetic development, beginning with Claudel's assimilation of Arthur Rimbaud and Stéphane Mallarmé.

When, in June, 1886, Claudel discovered in *La Vogue* Rimbaud's *Illuminations* and *A Season in Hell*, he recognized in these poems the sign of his own deliverance. Rimbaud's poetic language fascinated Claudel; the simplest term Claudel could find to describe the fascination was "bewitchment." In an age marked by secularism and aggressive materialism, a young poet dared to speak of the nostalgia of the soul for freedom and of the reality of invisible things. Claudel was not naïve; he could hear blasphemy and cursing in the desperate cries of Rimbaud, but he was happy to inhale that "living and

almost physical impression of the supernatural" that the poems of Rimbaud communicated to his soul. Claudel learned much from Rimbaud, not least the daring juxtaposition of images with no clear link among them. Above all, however, Rimbaud made Claudel aware that the material world, when it comes into contact with the spirit, becomes very fragile. Upon reading Rimbaud, Claudel said, he had the impression of hearing the voice of the most authentic genius of his time.

Like most poets of his generation, Claudel was also influenced by Mallarmé. As early as 1887, Claudel was among those who went to listen to the master of the Symbolist movement. It was a great privilege to be admitted to Mallarmé's salon; in the quasi-religious ambience of the Symbolists, to be recognized by Mallarmé was to be consecrated. Little is known of the extent of their personal relationship, but, while on his first diplomatic mission in China, Claudel was eager to continue his correspondence with the "master"; he even dared to express his reservations concerning Mallarmé's aesthetic principles. In his "La Catastrophe de l'Igitur," published in *Positions et propositions I* in 1928, Claudel recognizes that Mallarmé was the first poet to place himself in front of an object and ask the question, "What does that mean?" Claudel acknowledges that Mallarmé's way of trying to infuse the lifeless object with life was worthy of admiration, but he also underscores Mallarmé's failure to give the necessary answer to, or explanation of, his own question.

According to Claudel, if things and objects mean something, the poet has the obligation to speak for them. Mallarmé, on the contrary, hoped to condense in his verse the whole reality of things, by transferring them from the realm of "sensibility" to that of "intelligibility." The difference, then, between Claudel and Mallarmé is that, whereas Mallarmé believed that poetry is the ultimate forum of intelligibility and that there is nothing else to be understood beyond it, Claudel said that *through* the poetic word the visible reality becomes a key to another reality, that which is *meant* by the first one. In other words, and to paraphrase a thought of Claudel, the world is indeed a text that speaks "humbly and joyfully" of its own "absence" and of the presence of its Creator. Claudel rightly calls the adventure of Mallarmé a "catastrophe." One has but to remember the experience of Rimbaud, who, having tried to reach the ultimate and absolute power of the creative word, was forced to abandon poetry altogether, for absolute power pertains only to the absolute Word.

THE EAST I KNOW

The prose poems of *The East I Know*, the composition of which was spread out over a period of ten years, were written under the influence of Mallarmé. Claudel at first called them "impressions," later "poems in prose." In some cases, they are less impressions than precise descriptions of the emotional significance that various elements of the Chinese universe held for him. Some aspects of the descriptiveness that one finds in *The East I Know* do not, it is true, have their origin in Mallarmé; they derive, rather, from one of Claudel's contemporaries, Jules Renard. In 1896, Renard sent a copy of his recently published book, *Histoires naturelles* (1896; *Natural Histories*, 1966), to his friend Claudel in China. It was in this book that Claudel found what he considered the ideal manner of describing nature. He states delightedly that the book is "full of nature"; he also found that Renard's sentences were better balanced than those of Mallarmé. Yet Mallarmé's distinctive sentences, composed entirely of subordinate clauses (main clauses were indicated by their absence), continued to excite Claudel with their suggestive juxtapositions. Ultimately, *The East I Know* led Claudel to a fusion of the two trends; that is, he had to learn how to harmonize the sentence with the message it contained and the exterior world with the spiritual world of which it offered signs. In achieving this synthesis, Claudel found his voice as a poet.

Claudel's achievement in *The East I Know* is exemplified in "L'Heure jaune" ("The Golden Hour"). The title signifies both the ripeness of the wheat field and the sunset hour. As the poet walks through the wheat field, a path opens in it. Suddenly, the wheat field turns into a table (a bread table) at which the poet can rest. He is invited by God to this universal banquet table, which is illuminated by the sun. Before the sun sets, the poet, raising himself above the table, takes a last look over the universe, which has reached the last phase of its maturity. Indeed, the whole universe has become like the sun, and the only wish the poet can utter is that he not perish before he reaches the "golden hour": "I wander through the lanes of the harvest, up to the neck in gold. . . . All is ripe. . . . Suddenly, to my eyes, the earth is like a sun. Let me not die before the golden hour!"

FIVE GREAT ODES

With *The East I Know*, Claudel completed his poetic apprenticeship. Having done so, he undertook a new genre, the ode. In 1900, he made two important literary discoveries: Thanks to his friend André Suarès, he read Pindar, whose odes he savored for their rhythmic invention and absolute freedom of form. In the same year, while he was seeking admittance to monastic life in Solesmes, his attention was called to the English poet Coventry Patmore, a convert to Catholicism who enjoyed an extraordinary vogue late in the nineteenth century but whose works are scarcely read today. Claudel liked Patmore so much that he translated some of his poems into French. Patmore furthered Claudel's knowledge of the art of the ode; he also taught Claudel how to use the theme of love in poetry—as both a profane subject and a mystical reality expressing the only possible relationship between man and God. A third element that greatly contributed to the making of *Five Great Odes* was Claudel's visit to the Louvre in 1900, during which he noticed for the first time a Roman sarcophagus with the nine Muses.

These three sources furnished him with sufficient material for the new work. Suddenly, as if a new revelation had filled his being, he realized with exuberant joy that he had something to say, that he possessed the words he needed to speak in the name of the silent universe. It is not surprising that he began to write the first of the odes, "Les Muses" ("The Muses"), in the monastery of Solesmes. He felt at the same time that he was "all alone," "detached, refused, abandoned, without a task, without vocation, an outcast in the middle of the world," yet called to something that he could not fathom. As if in answer to the question that Mallarmé addressed to things, Claudel affirms in the odes that he has found the secret; he knows now how to speak and how to tell what each thing *means*. It is not a slight change that has occurred: He has regained his voice, has recovered his poetic health, and, having been told that he has no religious vocation, is now free to return to his poetic one. He walked out of the monastery in Liguié, "The Muses" yet to be finished; soon, he boarded a ship to China to resume his diplomatic post. On the ship, he met Ysé, the great love of his life, and he completed "The Muses." The joy that the muse inspired had turned into a question that he would make explicit in his play *Partage de midi* (pr. 1906; *Break of Noon*, 1960): "Why suddenly this woman on the ship?" Claudel could not answer the question; instead, for six years he kept silent. It was not until 1906 that he started to work on the second ode. He wrote about his illicit adventure in *Break of Noon* and ended his relationship with Ysé. The crisis of conscience that had paralyzed him for six years had finally come to a happy resolution. The illicit love had a purpose: Having discovered the "other" embodied in Ysé, Claudel was able to see the world anew, a "world now total" because it was seen with the eyes of the "other" as well as with his own. It was therefore fitting that Claudel should have transformed his love into an imperishable rose.

From the time of his meeting with Ysé, the rose is used in his poetry both allegorically and as a proper name, for Rose was the true name of Ysé. In a sense, his is a "roman de la rose," with the difference that Claudel possessed not so much the rose as the "interdiction." Because of this restraint, the rose brought him neither happiness nor fulfillment; knowing it was like knowing the "source of thirst." The rose, then, in *Five Great Odes*—it is presented throughout the poem—is a mystical rose with all the symbolism associated with it in the Western literary tradition. Claudel exploits this traditional symbolism and adds to it his own interpretation of the rose's perfume as the very essence of the flower. When inhaled (*respiré*), this perfume gives in an instant a sense of the fullness of eternity. The message of the rose is that, time having been abolished, one lives in eternity.

"THE MUSE WHO IS GRACE" AND "WITHIN THE HOUSE"

In "La Muse qui est la grâce" ("The Muse Who Is Grace"), Claudel continues the theme of the rose, although not without a certain irony. Having spent so many years meditating on the meaning of love, the poet realizes that it would be easier to live without women, but then he must also realize that the Muse herself is a woman—a woman with the face of Wisdom. It is therefore perfectly orthodox to say that in the fifth ode, "Within the House," Claudel substitutes Wisdom for the mystical rose. In doing so, he closed one of the major circles of his poetic and spiritual evolution. The night of

his conversion on December 25, 1886, when he went home and opened his sister Camille's Bible, his eye fell on the passage in Proverbs that speaks of Wisdom. Finally, he was led back to this Wisdom through the power of the mystical rose, which is Love.

Wisdom also taught Claudel that Creation is finite. "We have conquered the world," he says in "Within the House," "and we have found that Your Creation is finite." It appears contradictory that, while on one hand Claudel never ceases looking for signs of phenomena to prove that eternity is available to human understanding and is anxious to replace the signifying with the signified, on the other hand he berates the idea of indefinite and infinite within the realm of Creation. According to Claudel, if there is a contradiction, it is certainly not going to surface in the right relationship between the world and God; on the contrary, it is always found in the deification of the finite universe. He believes that God so planned the world that everything should return to him. Claudel thus conceives of the universe not as an automatic machine blindly traveling toward an undetermined goal, but as an entity within a perfect circle in which the vocation of the poet is to remind rational as well as irrational beings of the primordial unity their universe must achieve. That is why, in the midst of his joyous celebration in "Magnificat," he raises his voice against Voltaire, Joseph Ernest Renan, Jules Michelet, Victor Hugo, and all those who continue to have nightmares or dreams of a self-sufficient, man-created world. In his essay "Introduction à un poème sur Dante" (*Positions et propositions I*), Claudel takes issue with Hugo's cosmology, as expressed in the poem "Plein Ciel" ("Up in the Sky"), in which the Romantic poet imagines "Un Fini sans bornes" ("A Finite Without Limits"). Claudel does not hesitate to call this idea "a scandal for the reason, a disaster for the imagination." In contrast to these figures, he offers the portrait of Christopher Columbus, who, when he sailed to the West in order to reach India, was not led by any thought of discovery; he was, rather, led by the desire to prove that the Earth was a "circle," having its existence within the orbit of God. Thus, Columbus resembles the poet, who by vocation is the "sower of the measure of God," and the symbolism of the last ode's title becomes intelligible: "Within the House" is a perfect "circle," the movement of which is determined by the creative act of God and the redemptive charity of his Son.

LA MESSE LÀ-BAS

The very form of Claudel's verse was biblical in inspiration. He employed from the beginning of his poetic career a form that has come to be known as the *verset claudélien*. Among the influences that shaped this distinctive form, the most significant was the Bible, as Claudel was quick to acknowledge—in particular, the Psalms and the books of the prophets. In the long swell of the Claudelian verset, the cadence and the length of the lines are determined by units of breath, which in turn are conditioned by the nature of the thought that is being expressed. The lyric breath demands a more regular form, and it may even take rhyme and assonance, whereas drama, which is charged with interior struggles and tensions, demands a less regular form.

In 1917, Claudel was charged with a new diplomatic mission, this time to Brazil. The journey there was more painful than previous ones: Claudel had to leave his wife, his children, and his country behind in the midst of a raging war and all its uncertainties. The poem *La Messe là-bas*, written during this period, reflects his sense of exile. There is, however, another equally important theme in the poem—perhaps new at this point in Claudel's life—in the images of bread and wine as they become symbols in a liturgical and sacramental sense.

It should be remarked that the whole poem in its exterior form corresponds to the structure of the Catholic Mass and, as such, is a celebration of Communion. The question, then, can be raised in the following fashion: Communion with whom—and under what species? The first part of the question does not present any major problem; the poet has been separated from his family, and it is fitting that he should attempt to stay in communion with them in some way. On a deeper level, communion is reestablished between the two lovers, Claudel and Ysé. After all, they met on a ship that took both of them into exile, where they were to experience for years the desert of their love. On yet another level, Claudel savors communion with Rimbaud, whose poetry reminded him of the voice of the prophet in the desert announcing the breaking of the dawn. Finally, on the deepest level of his thought, Claudel celebrates that Communion with God which Rimbaud was unable to

reach, for neither the method of Mallarmé nor the desire of Rimbaud proved capable of containing the absolute, in the poet's word. Faith, on the contrary, assures Claudel that, since God made himself available to the understanding of the human soul in his own Word, the Catholic Mass is the only worthy celebration of this Communion: God instituted the Mass to commemorate his Communion with humankind. That is the reason Claudel selected the frame of the Mass to signify both poetry and communion.

It would be quite absurd to state that in Claudel's symbolism a tree, say, refers to man, or that bread represents an invisible celestial food. An object never refers to another object, only to itself. Claudel does not deny that there is something to be signified. In his system, whether aesthetic or spiritual, the physical and the spiritual realms coexist. What Claudel wants to say is that the bread and wine convey something in addition to the reality constituted by their molecular structure; their reality consists also in man's hunger and thirst for them. In the same way, one could say that light is provided because of man's need to see. Now, human hunger and thirst, if they are authentic, constitute a desire for something absolute—indeed, nothing but the absolute can satisfy them. In the Eucharistic celebration, the bread and wine lend, first of all, their physical appearance, but they are more than that: The word of the poet raises them into that region where the "object" can convey what the human desire is seeking. The poet can tell Ysé that they cannot satisfy their mutual desire and love unless they give priority to the Absolute Who is All in all. Rimbaud is recalled (as Mallarmé might have been) because he, too, was tempted to use the sacramental and liturgical symbolism of the Word without accepting the need for perfect communion.

LOVE BEGETS WISDOM

Claudel believed that every poet enters this world with one purpose. "The thing of beauty" which is ultimately the message of all poets, while gaining shape and identity, traces its own history. In the case of Claudel, this poetic message evolved and developed like a seed—the word is found even on his tombstone—which goes through death and resurrection before producing new life. At the beginning of his poetic career, he gave way to his sentiments of exile: He found himself far from home and from Heaven; at the other end of his career, in a peaceful recognition, he humbly bowed before the solidity of the universe of God. Between these two points, Claudel seems to have run a double itinerary: While he poured into his drama all his joys and sorrows, he reserved for his poetry the history of a rose, as if his life had been a "roman de la rose." In his poetry, however, this rose is transformed into a person, "Rose," who, in turn, having given the poet the joy of loving, is transfigured into a "mystical rose." In Claudel's poetry, love is a blessing when it arrives, but it is also meant to signify the absence of what it promises. Love therefore leads to Wisdom, which alone holds the keys to the mystery of the universe and the destiny of man; totality is found neither in woman's love nor in the fascination of the created universe, but in the eternal love of God.

OTHER MAJOR WORKS

PLAYS: *L'Endormie*, wr. 1886-1888, pb. 1925; *Tête d'or*, pb. 1890, second version wr. 1895, pb. 1901 (English translation, 1919); *Fragment d'un drame*, pb. 1892; *La Jeune Fille Violaine*, wr. 1892, pb. 1926, second version pb. 1901; *La Ville*, pb. 1893, second version pb. 1901 (*The City*, 1920); *L'Échange*, wr. 1893-1894, pb. 1901, second version pr. 1951; *Le Repos du septième jour*, wr. 1896, pb. 1901; *Partage de midi*, pb. 1906, second version pr., pb. 1948 (*Break of Noon*, 1960); *L'Otage*, pb. 1911 (*The Hostage*, 1917); *L'Annonce faite à Marie*, pr., pb. 1912, second version pr. 1948 (*The Tidings Brought to Mary*, 1916); *Le Pain dur*, wr. 1913-1914, pb. 1918 (*The Crusts*, 1945); *Protée*, pb. 1914, second version pb. 1927 (*Proteus*, 1921); *La Nuit de Noël*, pb. 1915; *Le Père humilié*, wr. 1915-1916, pb. 1920 (*The Humiliation of the Father*, 1945); *L'Ours et la lune*, pb. 1919; *Le Soulier de satin*, wr. 1919-1924, pb. 1928-1929 (*The Satin Slipper: Or, The Worst Is Not the Surest*, 1931); *L'Homme et son désir*, pr., pb. 1921; *La Femme et son ombre*, pr. in Japanese 1923, pb. 1927; *Le Peuple des hommes cassés*, wr. 1927, pb. 1952; *Sous le rempart d'Athènes*, pr., pb. 1927; *Le Livre de Christophe Colomb*, pb. 1929 (libretto; music by Darius Milhaud; *The Book of Christopher Columbus*, 1930); *Le Festin de la sagesse*, wr. 1934, pb. 1939; *Le Jet de Pierre*, wr. 1937, pb. 1949;

Jeanne d'Arc au bûcher, pr. in German 1938, pb. 1938 (English translation, 1939); *L'Histoire de Tobie et de Sara*, pb. 1942 (music by Milhaud); *Le Ravissement de Scapin*, wr. 1949, pb. 1958.

NONFICTION: *Jacques Rivière et Paul Claudel*, 1926 (*Letters to a Doubter: Correspondence of Jacque Rivière and Paul Claudel*, 1929); *Positions et propositions I*, 1928; *L'Oiseau noir dans le soleil levant*, 1929; *Écoute, ma fille*, 1934; *Positions et propositions II*, 1934 (*Ways and Crossways*, 1933); *Conversations dans le Loir-et-Cher*, 1935; *Un Poète regarde la Croix*, 1935 (*A Poet Before the Cross*, 1958); *Figures et paraboles*, 1936; *Toi, qui es-tu?*, 1936; *Les Aventures de Sophie*, 1937; *L'Épée et le miroir*, 1939; *Contacts et circonstances*, 1940; *Présence et prophétie*, 1942; *Seigneur, apprenez-nous à prier*, 1942 (*Lord, Teach Us to Pray*, 1948); *Le Livre de Job*, 1946; *L'Oeil écoute*, 1946 (*The Eye Listens*, 1950); *Discours et remerciements*, 1947; *Du côté de chez Ramuz*, 1947; *La Rose et le rosaire*, 1947; *Paul Claudel interroge le Cantique des Cantiques*, 1948; *Sous le signe du dragon*, 1948; *Accompagnements*, 1949; *André Gide et Paul Claudel, 1899-1926*, 1949 (*The Correspondence, 1899-1926, Between Paul Claudel and André Gide*, 1952); *Emmaüs*, 1949; *Une voix sur Israël*, 1950; *André Suarès et Paul Claudel*, 1951; *L'Évangile d'Isaïe*, 1951; *Francis Jammes-Gabriel Frizeau et Paul Claudel*, 1952; *Introduction au Livre de Ruth*, 1952; *Paul Claudel interroge l'Apocalypse*, 1952; *Le Symbolism de la Salette*, 1952; *J'aime la Bible*, 1955 (*The Essence of the Bible*, 1957); *Conversation sur Jean Racine*, 1956; *Qui ne souffre pas? Reflexions sur le problème social*, 1958; *Darius Milhaud et Paul Claudel*, 1961; *Aurélien Lugné-Poe et Paul Claudel*, 1964; *Au milieu des vitraux de l'Apocalypse*, 1966; *Jacques Copeau-Charles Dullin-Louis Jouvet et Paul Claudel*, 1966; *Journal I*, 1968; *Journal II*, 1969; *Mémoires improvisés*, 1969.

MISCELLANEOUS: *Œuvres complètes*, 1950-1967 (27 volumes).

BIBLIOGRAPHY
Caranfa, Angelo. *Claudel: Beauty and Grace*. Lewisburg, Pa.: Bucknell University Press, 1989. Clearly

explains the complex relationship between Claudel's aesthetics and his belief in Catholicism, as expressed both in his plays and in his poetry. The clearest introduction to Claudel's religious beliefs.

Chiari, Joseph. *The Poetic Drama of Paul Claudel*. New York: Gordian Press, 1969. Critical apraisal of Claudel's plays. Includes bibliography.

Griffiths, Richard. *Claudel: A Reappraisal*. Chester Springs, Pa.: Dufour Editions, 1970. Criticism of Claudel's major works with bibliography.

Humes, Joy. *Two Against Time: A Study of the Very Present Worlds of Paul Claudel and Charles Péguy*. Chapel Hill: University of North Carolina Press, 1978. Contains an excellent analysis of the two major French Catholic poets of the twentieth century. The paradox in the title of this book refers to the fact that both Péguy and Claudel were more concerned with the representation of the divine in this life and in the next than with meditations on social and political events.

Knapp, Bettina L. *Paul Claudel*. New York: Ungar, 1982. Critical analysis of Claudel's plays.

Longstaffe, Moya. *Metamorphoses of Passion and the Heroic in French Literature*. Lewiston, N.Y.: Edwin Mellen, 1999. A historical and critical interpretation of the works of Pierre Corneille, Stendhal, and Paul Claudel.

Moses, Nagy. "When the Heart Speaks of Its Reasons: *Cinq Grandes Odes*." *Claudel Studies* 21 (1994): 45-57. This American scholarly journal appears annually and includes excellent essays on Claudel's works. This article contains a thoughtful analysis of his poetic masterpiece.

Paliyenko, Adrianna. *Mis-reading the Creative Impulse: The Poetic Subject in Rimbaud and Claudel*. Carbondale: Southern Illinois University Press, 1997. Claudel found inspiration in the visionary poetry of the late nineteenth century French poet Arthur Rimbaud, but he transformed the agnostic Rimbaud into an orthodox Catholic believer. Palijenko explains that Claudel's clear misreading of Rimbaud's poetry had a profound influence on his own attempt to reconcile modernity and Catholicism in his own poetry.

Waters, Harold. *Paul Claudel*. New York: Twayne,

1970. Remains the best general introduction in English to Claudel's long career as a diplomat and to his plays and poetry. Contains an excellent annotated bibliography of studies on Claudel.

Watson, Harold. *Claudel's Immortal Heroes: A Choice of Deaths*. New Brunswick, N.J.: Rutgers University Press, 1971. An analysis of the characters in Claudel's work. Includes bibliographic references.

Moses M. Nagy;
bibliography updated by Edmund J. Campion

LUCILLE CLIFTON

Thelma Lucille Sayles
Born: Depew, New York; June 27, 1936

PRINCIPAL POETRY
Good Times, 1969
Good News About the Earth, 1972
An Ordinary Woman, 1974
Two-Headed Woman, 1980
Good Woman: Poems and a Memoir, 1969-1980, 1987
Next: New Poems, 1987
Quilting: Poems, 1987-1990, 1991
The Book of Light, 1993
The Terrible Stories, 1996
Blessing the Boats: New and Selected Poems, 1988-2000, 2000

OTHER LITERARY FORMS

In addition to her poetry, Lucille Clifton has written prose, often for children but also for adults. *Generations: A Memoir* (1976), is included as a part of *Good Woman: Poems and a Memoir, 1969-1980*. She began publishing for children in 1970 with *Some of the Days of Everett Anderson*, short poems in a picture-book format that spawned a series about the life of a young black boy. *The Times They Used to Be* (1974) is written as a narrative poem. She has written other picture books in prose: *The Boy Who Didn't Believe in Spring* (1973), *All Us*

Come Cross the Water (1973), *My Brother Fine with Me* (1975), *Three Wishes* (1976), and *Amifika* (1977), as well as a short novel, *The Lucky Stone* (1979). In response to questions her own six children had, Clifton wrote *The Black BC's* (1970), an alphabet book which blends poetry with prose. A departure from her usual perspective, *Sonora Beautiful* (1981) features a white girl as the protagonist.

ACHIEVEMENTS

In 1988, Lucille Clifton became the only poet ever to have two books chosen as finalists for the Pulitzer Prize in the same year: *Next: New Poems* and *Good Woman: Poems and a Memoir, 1969-1980*. Lucille Clifton won the National Book Award for *Blessing the Boats, New and Selected Poems, 1988-2000*; previously, she was a National Book Award finalist for *The Terrible Stories*. She also won the Coretta Scott King Award for *Everett Anderson's Goodbye* in 1984. Other honors include an Emmy Award from the American Academy of Television Arts and Sciences, the Shelley Memorial Award, the Charity Randall Citation, the Shestack Prize from the American Poetry Review, the Lannan Literary Award, and two creative writing fellowships from the National Endowment for the Arts. She holds honorary degrees from the University of Maryland and Towson State University. Clifton was elected to the American Academy of Arts and Sciences and appointed chancellor of the Academy of American Poets in 1999. In 1991, Clifton became a distinguished professor of humanities at St. Mary's College in Columbia, Maryland.

BIOGRAPHY

Thelma Lucille Sayles Clifton, daughter of Samuel L. and Thelma Moore Sayles, was born in New York, near Buffalo, and grew up with two half sisters and a brother. Her father worked for the New York steel mills. Her mother was a launderer, homemaker, and aspiring poet but once had to burn all her poems because her husband told her, "Ain't no wife of mine going to be no poetry writer."

Ironically, by both parents, Clifton was encouraged to be anything she wanted to be. She was named for her great-grandmother, who, according to her father, was the first black woman to be legally hanged in the state of Virginia. The first in her family to finish high school or consider attending college, at sixteen, Clifton entered college at Howard University, having earned a full scholarship. After majoring in drama and attending for two years, Clifton lost her scholarship. She told her father,

> I don't need that stuff. I'm going to write poems. I can do what I want to do! I'm from Dahomey women!

After transferring to Fredonia State Teachers College in 1955, Clifton worked as an actor and began her writing career. While at Fredonia, she met novelist Ishmael Reed at a writers' group, and he showed some of her poems to Langston Hughes, who was the first to publish Clifton's writing.

In 1958 she married Fred James Clifton. They had six children, four daughters, Sidney, Fredrica, Gillian, and Alexia, and two sons, Channing and Graham. In 1969, poet Robert Hayden entered her poems into competition for the Young Men's-Young Women's Hebrew Association Poetry Center Discovery Award. Clifton won the award and with it the publication of her first volume of poems, *Good Times*, which was chosen as one of the ten best books of the year by *The New York Times*. Prior to 1971, when she became poet in residence at the historically black Coppin State College in Baltimore, Maryland, Lucille Clifton worked in state and federal government positions. She remained at Coppin until 1974. From 1979 through 1982, she was poet laureate of the state of Maryland. From 1982 to 1983, she was a visiting writer at Columbia University School of the Arts and at George Washington University. Subsequently, she taught literature and creative writing at the University of California at Santa Cruz, and later at St. Mary's College. Besides appearing in more than one hundred anthologies of poetry, her poems have come to popular attention through her numerous television appearances.

ANALYSIS

Distinguished by her minimalist style, Clifton is sometimes compared with poets Gwendolyn Brooks and Emily Dickinson. Clifton is usually considered one of the prominent Black Aesthetic poets, along with Sonia Sanchez and Amiri Baraka, who were con-

Lucille Clifton (AP/Wide World Photos)

sciously breaking with Eurocentric conventions in their work. The characteristics of Clifton's craft—her concise, often untitled free verse, use of vernacular speech, repetition, puns and allusions, lowercase letters, sparse punctuation, and focused use of common words—have become her trademark style, which is clearly unfettered by others' expectations. Without worrying about convention, about boundaries—created either physically or emotionally—Clifton shares her perceptions of life by writing about the feelings humans share. Her rationale for writing poetry is to assert the importance of being human. In an interview with Michael Glaser, Clifton stated that

> writing is a way of continuing to hope. When things sometimes feel as if they're not going to get any better, writing offers a way of trying to connect with something beyond that obvious feeling . . . a way of remembering I am not alone."

She states further that she sees writing as a way to bear witness, to hold back the darkness by acknowledging the pain of the past and then choosing a more joyful future.

GOOD TIMES

Clifton's early work was frequently inspired by her family, especially her children, and was often a celebration of African American ancestry, heritage, and culture. In the title poem of this collection, Clifton reminds all children, "oh children think about the/ good times." She juxtaposes society's perceptions and her own in the opening poem of the collection—"in the inner city/ or/ like we call it/ home"—in order to honor the place she lives. Believing in the humanity of all people, she calls on each person, regardless of ancestry, to take control of his or her life. Of Robert, in the poem by the same name, she states he "married a master/ who whipped his mind/ until he died," suggesting through the image that the union was one of mutual consent. Her impatience with humans of all kinds who do not strive to improve their lot is a theme begun with this collection and continued throughout her more than three decades of publishing. Another theme that arises here is optimism, as in "Flowers": "Oh / here we are/ flourishing for the field/ and the name of the place/ is Love."

GOOD WOMAN: POEMS AND A MEMOIR

One theme of the poems in this collection involves Clifton's ethnic pride, as is reflected in "After Kent State": "white ways are/ the way of death/ come into the/ black/ and live." This volume also contains a section called "Heroes," which directly extends this first theme, and ends the book with a section called "Some Jesus."

> I have learned
> some few things
> like when a man
> walk manly
> he don't stumble
> even in the lion's den.

While the gender is male, Clifton would not limit the message to men. Overall, her early work heralds African Americans for their resistance to oppression and their survival of racism.

AN ORDINARY WOMAN

An Ordinary Woman includes poems divided into two sections, beginning with "Sisters," a celebration of family and relationships. "The Lesson of the Falling Leaves" includes the following line:

> the leaves believe
> such letting go is love
> such love is faith
> such faith is grace
> such grace is god
> i agree with the leaves.

It is a testimony to hope, a theme that runs throughout her work. Consistently juxtaposing past with present, Clifton provides wisdom to guide the future, as in the example of "Jackie Robinson":

> ran against walls
> without breaking.
> in night games
> was not foul
> but, brave as a hit
> over whitestone fences,
> entered the conquering dark.

TWO-HEADED WOMAN

Two-Headed Woman, which invokes the African American folk belief in a "Two-Headed Woman," with its overtones of a voodoo conjurer, begins with a section entitled "Homage to Mine," moves onto "Two-Headed Woman," and concludes with "The Light That Came to Lucille Clifton." While Clifton's works often have allusions to Christianity, as in the "Some Jesus" series in *Good News About the Earth*, she refers to other faiths as well, including the Hindu goddess Kali, from "An Ordinary Woman," providing evidence of her openness to multiple ways of knowing. As a "Two-Headed Woman," in the opening poem of that section, Clifton says she has "one face turned outward/ one face/ swiveling slowly in." Spirituality and mysticism pervade this collection, as the final poem attests, with its reference to the "shimmering voices" of her ancestors, whom the poet has heard singing in the "populated air."

QUILTING

In five parts, each of the first four named for traditional quilt patterns, "Log Cabin," "Catalpa Flower," "Eight-Pointed Star," and "Tree of Life," *Quilting* seems pieced together, as a quilt. It ends with a single poem, "Blessing the Boats," in "prayer," as if the spiritual life serves as the connecting threads. Clifton honors those whose roles in history have brought about change, like "February 11, 1990" dedicated to "Nelson Mandela and Winnie," and "Memo" which is dedicated "to Fannie Lou Hamer." The poem's "questions and answers" ends with "the surest failure/ is the unattempted walk."

THE TERRIBLE STORIES

In *The Terrible Stories*, Clifton chronicles the terrible stories of her own life, which include her struggle with breast cancer, and the terrible stories of her people, which include slavery and the prejudice that has survived time. The book ends with a section called "From the Book of David," which ends with a question from the poem "What Manner of Man." Referring to the biblical David, the poet asks how this David will be remembered "if he stands in the tents of history/ bloody skull in one hand, harp in the other?" Clifton's ability to look at history—ancient, contemporary, or personal—and find redemption in it gives humanity a way to face and survive its failures; this perspective shows her consistent faith in grace.

BLESSING THE BOATS

This anthology includes new poems as well as selected poems from *Next*, sometimes called a collection of sorrow songs, as loss is the overriding theme. Once more, "New Poems," the opening section of the anthology, records and comments on contemporary events of the twentieth century, such as school shootings, referred to in "The Times," and the bombing of black churches, referred to in "Alabama 9/15/63." It also addresses private occurrences, such as the traumas that gave rise to such poems as "Dialysis" and "Donor."

OTHER MAJOR WORKS

CHILDREN'S LITERATURE: *The Black BC's*, 1970; *Some of the Days of Everett Anderson*, 1970; *Everett Anderson's Christmas Coming*, 1971; *All Us Come Cross the Water*, 1973; *The Boy Who Didn't Believe in Spring*, 1973; *Everett Anderson's Year*, 1974; *The Times They Used to Be*, 1974; *My Brother Fine with Me*, 1975; *Everett Anderson's Friend*, 1976; *Three Wishes*, 1976; *Everett Anderson's 1-2-3*, 1977; *Amifika*, 1977; *Everett Anderson's Nine Month Long*, 1978; *The Lucky Stone*, 1979; *Sonora Beautiful*, 1981; *Everett Andersons' Goodbye*, 1983.

NONFICTION: *Generations: A Memoir*, 1976.

BIBLIOGRAPHY

Anaporte-Easton, Jean. "Healing Our Wounds: The Direction of Difference in the Poetry of Lucille Clifton and Judith Johnson." *Mid-American Review* 14, no. 2 (1994). This essay suggests that Clifton's voice is distinctive because of her use of physical imagery, particularly of the body, in order to write a work that seeks to unite it with both mind and spirit.

Bennett, Bruce. "Preservation Poets." *The New York Times Book Review*, March 1, 1992, pp. 22-23. Poet and critic Bennett discusses Clifton's *Quilting*, noting that the first four sections are named after traditional quilting designs, yet the final section, "prayer," consists of a single poem. He believes readers familiar with Clifton's work will witness recurrent themes section by section: importance of history on the present and future, celebration of women, and life as a personal journey of spiritual growth and discovery.

Cahill, Susan, ed. *Writing Women's Lives: An Anthology of Autobiographical Narratives by Twentieth Century American Women Writers.* New York: HarperPerennial, 1994. This collection of narratives, more than five hundred pages in length, provides extensive points of comparison as the careers of nearly fifty female writers are featured. The women included cut across cultures and span the century, but all are contemporaries of Clifton.

Clifton, Lucille. "I'd Like Not to Be a Stranger in the World: A Conversation/Interview with Lucille Clifton." Interview by Michael Glaser. *The Antioch Review* 58, no. 3 (2000): 310-328. In an extensive interview, Clifton discusses why she writes and explores the genesis of the topics about which she writes. She emphasizes the importance of family in her writing, particularly her heritage and the storytelling tradition, epitomized in her husband's last words to her: "Tell my story."

Jordan, Shirley, ed. *Broken Silences: Interviews with Black and White Women Writers.* New Brunswick, N.J.: Rutgers University Press. 1993. In an interview format, Jordan and Clifton explore the differences in perception between black and white women and how that impacts how each approaches their writing. Focuses on *Sonora Beautiful*, one of the few works by a female African American writer told from the perspective of a white protagonist.

Alexa L. Sandmann

ARTHUR HUGH CLOUGH

Born: Liverpool, England; January 1, 1819
Died: Florence, Italy; November 13, 1861

PRINCIPAL POETRY

The Bothie of Tober-na-Vuolich, 1848 (first published as *Toper-na-Fuosich*)
Ambarvalia, 1849 (with Thomas Burbridge)
Amours de Voyage, 1858 (serial)
Poems, 1862
Mari Magno, 1862 (written in 1861)
Dipsychus, 1865 (written in 1850)
The Poems of A. H. Clough, 1951 (H. F. Lowry, editor)

OTHER LITERARY FORMS

Arthur Hugh Clough, although primarily a poet, was also a distinguished essayist. Clough's essays tend to cluster around two topics—literary criticism, and social, especially religious, issues. His prose works appeared primarily in newspapers and periodicals. They have been collected in *The Poems and Prose Remains of Arthur Hugh Clough* (1869) and *Selected Prose Works* (1964).

ACHIEVEMENTS

Most assessments of Arthur Hugh Clough's achievements raise the question, "Why did he not achieve more?" This question originated with his contemporaries and reflects the social attitudes and professional expectations of Victorian times. A young man who was well begun, that is, one who was graduated from Oxford or Cambridge, and who enjoyed the respect of his colleagues, and who was expected to rise to eminence in his profession. Clough began with these high expectations. Subsequently, however, he surrendered a fellowship at Oxford, took an administrative post at the University of London, became an examiner in the Education Office, and, finally, an aide to the famous nurse Florence Nightingale. Contemporaries saw this path as a continual falling off. Furthermore, his real accomplishments in poetry occur in just a single decade of his life. Perhaps a more generous way of assessing Clough's achievement is to concentrate on his creative work itself.

In his writing one finds a ferocious intellectual honesty which, by its clarity of vision, allows subsequent generations to see more clearly what were the inner tensions of the reflective person in an age of religious, scientific, and political ferment. Clough is an articulate observer of the age which witnessed the rapid spread of evangelicalism, the sharp reaction against it by the Oxford Movement, the open attacks on historic Christianity, and the fervent reply of a beleaguered orthodoxy. Moreover, he is not only an observer; he is also a sympathetic participant drawn in painfully divergent directions by the conflicts of his times.

BIOGRAPHY

When Arthur Hugh Clough was three years old, his family moved from Liverpool to Charleston, South Carolina. During the six years he spent in America, he lived under the constant influence of his mother's evangelical piety. In spite of a subsequent religious disillusionment, the concerns and temperament of the evangelical disposition marked Clough's poetry for the rest of his life.

In 1828 Clough was sent back to England for his education. In the following year, he entered Rugby and so fell under another of the dominant influences upon his life and work—namely, the family of the headmaster, Thomas Arnold. Arnold and his two sons Tom and Matthew (later the poet) fostered in Clough the ideals of a commitment to reason, rigorous self-discipline in pursuit of high goals, and a deep moral sobriety in contemplating public affairs. At Rugby, Clough was editor of the *Rugby Magazine* and head of the School House.

Clough won a prestigious scholarship to Balliol College, Oxford, which he entered in 1827. In 1841, he took a second-class degree, to the considerable surprise of friends who had expected more, and he was denied a fellowship in his own college after his graduation. Nevertheless, he was elected to a fellowship in Oriel College and so remained at Oxford, where he became one of the most popular tutors.

Throughout Clough's years at Oxford, he had watched the progress of the Oxford Movement. The polemical context of religious discussions on the Oxford campus at the time may have contributed to a growing skepticism, which culminated in Clough's resigning the Oriel fellowship in 1848 as an act of conscience. He could not endorse the Thirty-nine Articles (the Creed of the Anglican Church), as Oxford dons were expected to do. The soul-searching struggle of his departure from Oxford may be intimated in his poem *The Bothie of Tober-na-Vuolich*, written shortly thereafter.

Clough was not "ruined" in English education, however, and in 1849, after a trip to Italy during which he witnessed the French suppression of Giuseppe Mazzini's Roman Republic, he became the principal of University Hall, University College, London. From the Italian trip came his *Amours de Voyage*. He returned to Italy the following year and, while there, began his long and perhaps best-known poem, *Dipsychus* (first published in *Letters and Remains*, 1865).

In 1852 Clough resigned his duties at University Hall in a dispute over the manner in which religious instruction should be administered and over his refusal to recruit actively students in this prototype of a modern university. He set sail for America, where he enjoyed some reputation for his *The Bothie of Tober-na-Vuolich*, and the favor of such American literary figures as Ralph Waldo Emerson, James Russell Lowell, Henry Wadsworth Longfellow, and Charles Eliot Norton. Nevertheless, he could not find a position which would allow him an income sufficient to marry the girl he had left in England—Blanche Smith. Thus, he returned to England when Thomas Carlyle secured for him a position with the Education Office.

Clough and Blanche Smith were married in June, 1854, and for the remaining seven years of his life he continued his rather routine work as a bureaucrat. This employment, compounded by the increasing duties he performed for Florence Nightingale, Blanche's cousin, crowded out his efforts at poetry. This busy employment helps to account for the fact that Clough's most prolific period of creativity was confined to a single decade of his life.

During 1859, Clough was stricken ill with scarlatina. Traveling about the Continent in an effort to recover his health gave him opportunity to think of poetry once again. He had written a good deal of the unfinished *Mari Magno* (first published in *Poems*, 1862) when he died in Florence in 1861. He was buried in the Protestant cemetery there, just four months after Elizabeth Barrett Browning had been interred in the same place.

ANALYSIS

Arthur Hugh Clough's poetry is the effort of a man reared in deep religious faith to discover whether, following his apostasy, an honest skepticism could produce high-minded contentments equal to those of the idealism he had repudiated.

THE BOTHIE OF TOBER-NA-VUOLICH

Although he wrote occasional poems throughout his life and published a number in the school magazine at Rugby, Clough's career as a serious poet extends only from 1848 to 1858, with a resurgence of activity in the last year of his life, 1861. *The Bothie of Tober-na-Vuolich*, his first major work, appeared at the end of a long year of soul-searching. Early in 1848 he had resigned as tutor, and in October he resigned his fellowship at Oriel. In November the poem appeared. It is a long account of a group of Oxford scholars who retire to the Scottish highlands to read for examinations. The most distinctive member of the party, Philip Hewson, is a freethinking radical who falls in love three different times during the extended stay—the last time with the girl who lives in the bothie (cottage) at Tober-na-Vuolich. Philip's various personal experiences have a softening effect on his political views. Early in the poem he makes a high-strung and doctrinaire attack on the privileged classes, but the women he meets have to be dealt with as actual and complex beings. When he finally falls in love with the peasant girl Elspie, he comes to realize that his economic account of the peasantry is far too simple to explain the living person. In the belief that Oxford scholasticism is too far removed from the life of experience, Philip declines to return—for reasons similar to those of the poet himself. Even Philip's skepticism now seems to him too doctrinaire to account for the stress of his inner life, and the poem ends with Philip and Elspie emigrating to New Zealand where he "hewed and dug; subdued the earth and his spirit." Clough suggests that his late skepticism might be as doctrinaire as

his early faith, and he looks to the leavening of actual experience to moderate his own abstract scholasticism.

The Bothie of Tober-na-Vuolich is written in hexameters. This fact has produced a long-running controversy over the metrical effects of the poem. Wendell Harris has given a comprehensive account of the arguments (*Arthur Hugh Clough*, 1970). Clough's defenders—such as Matthew Arnold—believe that his use of hexameters gives his poem the primitive, homespun forcefulness which is also to be found in the poetry of classical antiquity—in the *Iliad* (c. 800 B.C.) for example: "So in the golden morning they parted and went to the westward." Critics of the poem believe that for a sustained work the meter, tending to "break down into anapests" (Harris), flows against the natural iambs of English narrative discourse. It falls somewhere between prose and poetry: "So in the cottage with Adam the pupils live together/ Duly remained, and read, and looked no more for Philip." If there is to be found a justification for the meter, it is in Clough's expectation that the rough-hewn meter would reinforce his theme: the rejection of doctrinaire scholasticism (and the modern poetic conventions) in favor of an experientially authenticated sense of love and social justice.

AMBARVALIA

Ambarvalia appeared in January, 1849—only three months after *The Bothie of Tober-na-Vuolich. Ambarvalia* is a collection of poems on several topics. The title refers to an ancient Roman festival in which animals were sacrificed to ensure the fertility of the fields. By this title Clough may have intended to remove himself from a sectarian Christian ideal of the world and to evoke the image of a mythology at once more primitive and closer to nature. The leading poem of the collection implies this sort of skepticism; it is called "The Questioning Spirit." In it one human spirit confronts all the others with troubling questions, and they reply that they neither know nor need to know the solution to such rarefied philosophical problems. The poem is an attack on a mindless sort of orthodoxy: "Only with questionings pass I to and fro,/ Perplexing these that sleep, and in their folly/ inbreeding doubt and sceptic melancholy." That melancholy questioning, coupled with a persistent but vague hope which always attends his agnosticism, could be the theme of Clough's entire poetry. The poem

"Why Should I Say I See the Things I See Not" is a well-nigh militant refusal to say that reality rests on things not manifest, "Unfit, unseen, unimagined, all unknown." The last of the twenty-nine poems in *Ambarvalia* asks the ancient question whether there actually are gods who treat human beings in the apparently shabby ways that fate seems to dictate. He answers his own question in this problematical way:

> If it is so let it be so
> And we will all agree so;
> But the plot has counterplot,
> It may be, and yet be not.

DIPSYCHUS

In 1850, Clough began his long poem *Dipsychus*. Although it did not appear until 1865 (indeed it was never truly finished), this poem has since become Clough's best-known work. It consists of fourteen scenes, an epilogue, and four more scenes of a continuation. The poem is set in Venice. Its protagonist is Dipsychus, the divided soul, who is engaged in a lengthy dialogue with Spirit (who, as the reader later learns, is Mephistopheles). Some readers have believed that the Spirit is the projected voice of the skeptical "half" of Dipsychus's mind. A better reading seems to be that Dipsychus represents the mind torn between faith and doubt, and Spirit represents the distractions which would alleviate his inward tensions through the pleasures of everyday life: sex, wealth, the struggle for power, and the like. Dipsychus, however, does not want to be merely mollified; he wants to know the honest truth of the world.

Dipsychus is not only reminiscent of Johann Wolfgang von Goethe's *Faust* (1790-1832) but also challenges comparison. Goethe's poem has more action and pageantry, a grander scale and more subtle inquiry, but Clough's poem presents the issues with a bold forthrightness which marks the possibility of a clearly skeptical voice in Victorian society even before the publication of *On the Origin of Species* (1859). The clause "Christ is not risen" becomes a recurring refrain in the opening scenes. Spirit (Mephistopheles) replies that if such is the case, all Dipsychus's metaphysics would be futile and he might as well console himself with the pleasures of the flesh:

> This lovely creature's glowing charms
> Are gross illusion, I don't doubt that;
> But when I pressed her in my arms
> I somehow didn't think about that.

Finally, Dipsychus, having succumbed to Spirit's temptation to "Enjoy the minute," despairs of a metaphysic which will give authenticity to his actions and resigns himself to live the common life. In the continuation, however, when he has lived long and become a successful lord chief justice, he must face the woman he debauched thirty years earlier. He must face the fact that even if his actions seem not to be subject to the guidance of metaphysics, they nevertheless have consequences: "Once Pleasure and now Guilt." The poem ends with the inference that because actions have results, experience may after all generate meanings and values even when doctrinaire ideologies fail.

AMOURS DE VOYAGE

Amours de Voyage was written in 1849, although it did not appear publicly until 1858. In this poem Clough is still trying to make hexameters carry a rather plain narrative. Structurally, the poem is a series of letters, one group from Claude to Eustace describing his travels in Italy and his infatuation for an English girl he has encountered. The interspersed letters are from Georgiana Trevellyn to Louisa. Georgiana's letters are filled with girlish gossip and observations on political affairs, but such comments give way to an increasing preoccupation with the Trevellyns' new acquaintance—Claude. In postscripts to Georgiana's letters and then in a correspondence of her own, Mary Trevellyn describes first her contempt, then her aloofness, then her interest, then her obsession with Claude. Their first acquaintance, which left them at cross-purposes, gives way to real love for each other. Claude and Mary miss connections at various Continental watering places until Mary reports that she is returning to England, and the reader concludes that the protagonists have missed their chance for love, because Claude is going to Egypt.

The letters, however, are not only about an ironic love affair which never occurred, but they are also about the events which undermine other features of Claude's high-minded idealism. In this regard, *Amours de Voyage* is much like Friedrich Schiller's philosophical letters.

Claude decides to leave Europe not merely because he cannot locate Mary but also because "Rome will not suit me; the priests and soldiers possess it." The authoritarian spirit of European orthodoxy and the militant spirit of European politics offer no consolation to a young free-thinker who sees that Europe is going to miss its chance for peace as he has missed his chance for love.

MARI MAGNO

Clough worked little at poetry after 1858 until it became evident that his failing health was not yielding to treatment. At the time of his death he was hard at work on *Mari Magno*. The poem is a Chaucerian collection of tales told by travelers aboard a transatlantic ship bound for America, across the "great sea." The tales are told on six different nights of the voyage. The clergyman tells two, the lawyer two, an American one, the narrator one in his own voice, and the mate one.

At this late hour of his life, Clough's stories tell of love missed or nearly missed. The failure of idealized love and the necessity of going on with practical life are forced on the protagonists by impersonal chance, by odd coincidences, a too-late arrival at a rendezvous, a ship which leaves too soon. There is little searching here for the great idea, no return to the struggle for a secular metaphysic which will justify actions and values. Rather, there is merely a plaintive lament for a lost idealism that has no home in this pragmatic world, and a sad sense that even true hearts and high-minded spirits must come to grips with a world of unkept promises and missed appointments. A poignant longing for this hopeless idealism is balanced against the tranquillity which comes from a resignation to life as it is.

LEGACY

Clough's poetry, taken altogether, considers the common themes of love, faith, and learning; makes them vulnerable to the disillusionments of modern skepticism; and then asks certain questions. First, does intellectual honesty necessarily erode the authority of these traditional ideals? Second, is there some new, coherent perception of the world (in *Dipsychus* he calls it a "Second Reverence") which will satisfy the demands of both a rigorous honesty and the spiritual needs which our ideals have traditionally satisfied? These questions make Clough a representative figure among the young intellectuals of mid-nineteenth century Europe. His friend

Matthew Arnold described his dilemma as a struggle "between two worlds, one dead the other powerless to be born." Clough does seem to have acquired some tranquillity in the years following his marriage, and critics disagree whether he found it because he quit struggling or because he discovered what he was looking for—a high-minded skepticism which was humane and satisfying. Perhaps the safest way to interpret his life and work is to affirm that their outward expressions suggest an inward acceptance complex enough to tantalize biographers, effectual enough to redeem Clough's sense of well-being.

OTHER MAJOR WORKS

NONFICTION: *Letters and Remains*, 1865 (Mrs. Clough, editor); *Prose Remains*, 1888; *Selected Prose Works*, 1964 (B. B. Trawick, editor).

MISCELLANEOUS: *The Poems and Prose Remains of Arthur Hugh Clough*, 1869 (2 volumes).

BIBLIOGRAPHY

Biswas, Robindra Kumar. *Arthur Hugh Clough: Towards a Reconsideration*. Oxford, England: Clarendon Press, 1972. This somewhat laborious biographical-critical study of Clough makes a case for his success around the period 1847-1852, particularly in *Amours de Voyage*, in which Clough "confidently fulfills his potential as a poet." His is a "minor key," or "a footnote" illuminating a "major argument" in the text of Victorian poetry. Good bibliography.

Chorley, Katharine. *Arthur Hugh Clough: The Uncommitted Mind*. Oxford, England: Clarendon Press, 1962. This biography assumes that "Clough wrings his criticism of life out of his own experience." His poetry is a fight to "save himself" from his own intellectual honesty by fixing on some faith, but he "dared not commit himself to any answer," because of an Oedipal conflict with the authority of his mother.

Christiansen, Rupert. *The Voice of Victorian Sex: Arthur H. Clough, 1819-1861*. London: Short Books, 2001. A short biography focused on the interior, psychological aspects of Clough and his work. He is placed in context in Victorian England and Cristiansen details Clough's struggle with natural physical urges and the shame they caused him all his life.

Greenberger, Evelyn Barish. *Arthur Hugh Clough: The Growth of a Poet's Mind*. Cambridge, Mass.: Harvard University Press, 1970. Studies Clough's prose writings on political and religious matters and shows him in a new light, as an energetic reformer and committed thinker. Traces his growth from naïve abstractions through active polemics and some disappointment to a greater wisdom concerning individual virtue within the social structure.

Harris, Wendell V. *Arthur Hugh Clough*. New York: Twayne, 1970. A brief, sound, introductory study of the poet's career. Most revaluations of Clough see him as a poet of Victorian doubt who quit poetry when he found no resolution. Harris argues that when Clough had "beaten out a form of belief he could accept, the anvil ceased to ring." Contains a chronology and a bibliography with helpful annotations.

Houghton, Walter E. *The Poetry of Clough: An Essay in Revaluation*. New Haven, Conn.: Yale University Press, 1963. Houghton's book is still the best discussion of Clough's poetry and poetics, with a focus on technique. A master of the "intellectual lyric," Clough streamlined his language and rhetoric in his search for certainty, his idiomatic and straightforward style qualifying him as "one of the best of Victorian poets" and "perhaps the most modern."

Moore, Richard. "Arthur Hugh Clough." *Notes and Queries* 46, no. 1 (March, 1999): 53-55. A discussion of two previously unpublished letters by Clough sent to Lady Harriet Ashburton which clarify some details in his biography.

Thorpe, Michael, ed. *Clough: The Critical Heritage*. New York: Barnes & Noble Books, 1972. This volume in the Critical Heritage series contains contemporary letters, views, and reviews of Clough from 1847 to 1869, as well as posthumous reactions up to 1920. Contributors include Matthew Arnold, Ralph Waldo Emerson, Algernon Charles Swinburne, and E. M. Forster.

Timko, Michael. *Innocent Victorian: The Satiric Poetry of Arthur Hugh Clough*. Athens: Ohio University Press, 1966. Concentrates on Clough's satire and emphasizes the importance of placing the poet within the context of the "vital influence" of the so-ciety that is his satire's target. The poetry is driven by a "moral aesthetic" of "positive naturalism," which not only recognizes but also embraces human contradictions and limitations.

L. Robert Stevens;
bibliography updated by the editors

JEAN COCTEAU

Born: Maisons-Laffitte, France; July 5, 1889
Died: Milly-la-Forêt, France; October 11, 1963

PRINCIPAL POETRY

La Lampe d'Aladin, 1909
Le Prince frivole, 1910
La Danse de Sophocle, 1912
Le Cap de Bonne-Espérance, 1919
L'Ode à Picasso, 1919
Poésies, 1917-1920, 1920
Escales, 1920
Discours du grand sommeil, 1922
Vocabulaire, 1922
Plain-Chant, 1923
Poésie, 1916-1923, 1924
Cri écrit, 1925
Prière mutilée, 1925
L'Ange Heurtebise, 1925
Opéra, 1927
Morceaux choisis, 1932
Mythologie, 1934
Allégories, 1941
Léone, 1945
Poèmes, 1945
La Crucifixion, 1946
Anthologie poétique, 1951
Le Chiffre sept, 1952
Appogiatures, 1953
Clair-obscur, 1954
Poèmes, 1916-1955, 1956
Gondole des morts, 1959
Cérémonial espagnol du phénix, 1961
Le Requiem, 1962

OTHER LITERARY FORMS

Jean Cocteau was a formidable artist in many genres and awesomely prolific. Among his seven novels, little read today, the most important is *Les Enfants terribles* (1929; *Enfants Terribles*, 1930, also known as *Children of the Game*, 1955). Among his many plays, some of the most notable are *Orphée* (pr. 1926; *Orpheus*, 1933), *La Voix humaine* (pr., pb. 1930; *The Human Voice*, 1951), *La Machine infernale* (pr., pb. 1934; *The Infernal Machine*, 1936), *Les Parents terribles* (pr., pb. 1938; *Intimate Relations*, 1952), and *La Machine à écrire* (pr., pb. 1941; *The Typewriter*, 1948). In the opinion of many critics, Cocteau's greatest achievements were in the cinema. His masterpieces—which he both wrote and directed—include *Le Sang d'un poète* (1932; *The Blood of a Poet*, 1949), *La Belle et la bête* (1946; *Beauty and the Beast*, 1947), *Les Parents terribles* (1948; *Intimate Relations*, 1952), *Les Enfants terribles* (1950), *Orphée* (1950; *Orpheus*, 1950), and *La Testament d'Orphée* (1959; *The Testament of Orpheus*, 1968). Cocteau also wrote scenarios for ballets by various composers, notably for Erik Satie's *Parade* (1917), for Darius Milhaud's *Le Boeuf sur le toit* (1920), and for *Les Mariés de la tour Eiffel* (1921) which had music by "Les Six." Cocteau also collaborated on two opera-oratorios, *Oedipus-Rex* (1927) with Igor Stravinsky, and *Antigone* (1922; English translation, 1961) with Arthur Honegger. Cocteau's nonfiction includes a variety of idiosyncratic autobiographical and critical works.

ACHIEVEMENTS

Jean Cocteau was one of the most remarkable figures in twentieth century art. Extremely versatile, he unified his diverse interests by seeing them as merely different aspects of *poésie: poésie de roman* (poetry of the novel), *poésie de théâtre* (poetry of the drama), *poésie cinématographique* (poetry of the film), and even *poésie graphique* (poetry of draw-

ing). Curiously, with poetry as the metaphorical center of Cocteau's artistic achievement, critics are still uncomfortable with his accomplishment as a poet. Some consider him a central figure through whom the major currents of art in the early 1900's passed, while others regard him as a dilettante, interested only in stylishness and facile demonstrations of his considerable talents, lacking substance under the sparkling facade. Many of his contemporaries were uncertain of his importance because he remained always on the periphery of "serious" art. Looking back, however, it is clear that, at the very least, Cocteau's poetry is another brilliant aspect of one of the most versatile artistic minds of the century and that it has been underrated largely because of the difficulty in grasping Cocteau in all his variety.

BIOGRAPHY

Jean Cocteau was born in a prosperous suburb of Paris to Georges and Eugénie Lecomte Cocteau, a cultivated bourgeois couple who exposed Jean, his brother

Jean Cocteau (National Archives)

Paul, and their sister Marthe to the fine arts. When at their suburban home, the children played on the grounds of a nearby castle designed by François Mansart. When in Paris—Cocteau would always consider himself a Parisian above all—his family lived with his grandparents, whose house contained classical busts, vases, a painting by Eugène Delacroix, and drawings by Jean-Auguste-Dominique Ingres. Cocteau's grandfather was a cellist and would often be visited by the renowned violinist Pablo de Sarasate. Some of Cocteau's fondest memories of his early life were of trips to the circus, the ice palace, and the theater, especially the Comédie-Française. Years later, in his own drama, he would attempt to duplicate the lighting or brilliancy of theatrical events in his memory and would discover from lighting technicians that it had been technically impossible to do such things when he was a child. Time had increased the splendor of his memories, including those of the castle and of his grandparents' house. He thus began to perceive his own life as having mythological dimensions, as even his personal experiences had become exaggerated and distorted over time.

In 1899, Cocteau's father committed suicide as a result of financial problems. Cocteau became an indifferent student at the Petit Lycée Condorcet and, later, at the Grand Condorcet. Like many creative personalities, he found the institutional atmosphere oppressive. Besides having a weak constitution, which often led to legitimate absences, he was frequently truant. During his illnesses, he often had his German governess stitching doll clothes for his model theater. One of his closest childhood friends was Réné Rocher, later to become a director, who spent much time with Cocteau and his miniature theaters. After a trip with his mother to Venice, Cocteau began study for his baccalaureate, had his first love affair (with Madeleine Carlier, ten years his senior), and became more involved with the theater—meeting Edouard de Max, who acted opposite Sarah Bernhardt. Quite naturally, with all this to entertain him, Cocteau failed the examination.

On April 4, 1908, de Max sponsored a reading of Cocteau's poetry, by de Max, Rocher, and other prominent actors and actresses, at the Théâtre Fémina. Because the event was attended by many of the elite of Paris, including several leading literary critics, Cocteau

became instantly well known. Subsequently, he became acquainted with such literary notables as Edmond Rostand, Marcel Proust, Charles Péguy, Catulle Mendès, and Jules Lemaître. He became quite enamored of Comtesse Anna de Noailles and tried to write poetry like hers, with a refined sensibility and enhanced sensuality. He was one of three founders of a literary magazine, *Schéhérazade*, which was dedicated to poetry and music, and rented a room at the Hôtel Biron, where Auguste Rodin and his secretary, Rainer Maria Rilke, were also staying.

When Cocteau was introduced to the great impresario Sergei Diaghilev of the Ballets Russes, he begged Diaghilev to permit him to write ballets. Diaghilev eventually said "Étonne-moi!" ("Astonish me!"), and Cocteau took this injunction as an order to give shape to the rest of his life's work. His first ballet, *Le Dieu bleu* (1912), was not successful, though Diaghilev produced it for the coronation of George V. Convinced the music was at fault, Cocteau began to associate with Igor Stravinsky, living with him for a while. During this period, Cocteau was also trying to defend himself against the accusation of Henri Ghéon in the *Nouvelle Revue française*, who charged that he was an entirely derivative poet. Around 1914, Cocteau underwent what he called a "molting," breaking free of the influence of Rostand and the Comtesse de Noailles and moving toward his eventual association with Max Jacob and Guillaume Apollinaire.

As World War I broke out, Cocteau attempted to enlist but was rejected for health reasons. Illegally, he became an ambulance driver on the Belgian front, but after being discovered, he was sent back to Paris. These experiences would later form a large part of his novel *Thomas l'imposteur* (1923; *Thomas the Impostor*, 1925). Back in Paris, he met Amedeo Modigliani and Pablo Picasso and introduced the latter to Diaghilev, thereby creating the association which would produce Erik Satie's 1917 ballet *Parade*, with scenario by Cocteau, costumes and set by Picasso, and choreography by Léonide Massine. *Parade* created a scandal with its atonal music and extraordinary set and costumes. Only the presence of Apollinaire, in uniform and wearing a bandage over his head wound, kept the outraged spectators from attacking the creators of the ballet. Cocteau responded vigorously, attacking the musical influences of Claude Debussy, Richard Wagner, and Stravinsky and linking himself with the composers known as "Les Six" (Georges Auric, Louis Durey, Arthur Honegger, Darius Milhaud, Francis Poulenc, and Germaine Tailleferre).

In 1919, Cocteau met and fell in love with Raymond Radiguet, who was fifteen, handsome, and a poetic genius—or so Cocteau believed. Radiguet caused Cocteau to reevaluate his aesthetics and move toward a simpler, classic style; thus inspired, he found new energy and created a number of new works, including *Le Grand écart* (1923; *The Grand Écart*, 1925) and the volume of poems *Plain-Chant*. Radiguet, however, died of typhoid in December, 1923, and Cocteau was devastated. Diaghilev tried to shake Cocteau from his despair by taking him on a trip to Monte Carlo. The trip itself did little good, however, and the discovery of opium there proved to be Cocteau's only solace. His addiction eventually provoked his friends and family to persuade him to enter a sanatorium in 1925. There, he came under the influence of Jacques Maritain, the Catholic philosopher, who briefly restored Cocteau's faith in religion. He was able to pick up the pieces of this life and create such works as *L'Ange Heurtebise, Orpheus*, and *Children of the Game*. He even patched up his friendship with Stravinsky and wrote the words for Stravinsky's oratorio *Oedipus-Rex*.

In the 1930's, Cocteau seemed inexhaustible, even though he suffered a bout with typhoid in 1931. Plays, poems, songs, ballets, art criticism, and even a column for *Ce soir* poured forth from his pen. He took a trip around the world in imitation of Jules Verne's *Le Tour du monde en quatre-vingt jours* (1873; *Around the World in Eighty Days*, 1873). He became the manager of the bantamweight boxer Alphonse Theo Brown. Perhaps the most important of his activities during this period was his first attempt at *poésie cinématographique*, when he wrote and directed *The Blood of a Poet*.

Cocteau, always controversial, found himself squeezed between his artistic enemies and new political ones during the Nazi occupation of France. He was viciously attacked in the press. His play *The Typewriter* was banned. He never backed off, however, even when beaten by a group of French Fascists for failing to salute the flag.

After the war, Cocteau found himself a "grand old man" of the artistic world, but he refused to rest on his laurels and continued arousing controversy. He traveled and wrote plays, journals, and films. He made recordings and designed frescoes for the city hall at Menton, the Chapel of St. Pierre at Villefranche-sur-Mer, the Chapel of Notre Dame in London, the Church of Saint Blaise-des-Simples in Milly-la-Forêt, and the Chapel of Notre-Dame-de-Jerusalem at Fréjus. He also designed fabrics, plates, and posters. He was made a member of the Royal Belgian Academy and the Académie Française in 1955 and received an honorary doctorate of letters from Oxford University in 1956. He died on October 11, 1963, shortly after hearing of the death of his friend Edith Piaf.

ANALYSIS

Jean Cocteau's first three books of poetry enjoyed the kind of success which works that essentially flatter the prevailing literary establishment are prone to have. He was instantly praised and compared to various great poets, present and past, yet never aroused the outrage or bewilderment provoked by significant breakthroughs. Very much a salon poet and dandy, Cocteau had yet to discover his own voice. *La Lampe d'Aladin* contained poems dedicated to the various actors and actresses who had read them at Cocteau's "debut" in the Théâtre Fémina. Like much of the poetry of the early 1900's, the poems of this first volume seem self-serving, overly and insincerely emotional, and very immature, though occasionally some charming cleverness may emerge.

LE PRINCE FRIVOLE

Cocteau's second collection, *Le Prince frivole* (the frivolous prince), is little better than the first. Its title came to be applied to its author, and Cocteau would later refer to the book as elevating him to the "Prince du Ridicule." The creation of poetry here is still an amusing game. Cocteau rather dutifully insists on melancholy in many of the works, but it comes off as posing, even though it may be indicative of an indefinable feeling that all the praise he was receiving was undeserved.

LA DANSE DE SOPHOCLE

After the publication of *La Danse de Sophocle*, the inadequacy of Cocteau's artistic commitment was brought home to him in a review by Henri Ghéon in

Nouvelle Revue française (André Gide may have had a hand in its authorship). Ghéon pointed out the derivative qualities of Cocteau's three books and implied that the poet was immature, frivolous, and greatly overestimated. Ghéon said that Cocteau was undeniably gifted but that he had not devoted himself to his gift. The review was more important in Cocteau's life than the book itself, though one can see in *La Danse de Sophocle* the beginning of Cocteau's lifelong interest in the eternal truths found in ancient Greek mythology and literature. The review provoked Cocteau to understand "that art and poetry aren't a game, but a descent into a mine, down toward the firedamp and danger. . . ."

LE CAP DE BONNE-ESPÉRANCE

Cocteau did not publish another collection of poetry until seven years later, after working for the Ballets Russes, associating with a more radical set of artists, and after his experiences in World War I. Later, when republishing his works, he ignored the earlier three books and dated his beginnings as a poet from *Le Cap de Bonne-Espérance* (the Cape of Good Hope), which was inspired by his association with the aviator Roland Garros. Garros would take Cocteau on daily flights from Villacoublay. He performed numerous acrobatics with Cocteau in the plane, and the poet was inspired by the sensation of flying and the view of Paris from the air. In 1918, after a remarkable escape from a German prison, Garros was shot down and killed. A proof copy of Cocteau's long poem dedicated to Garros was found in his cockpit. In the book, the airplane symbolizes the modern era: It frees humankind from earthly considerations, putting the pilot or passenger into a realm of new visions and solitude, where he can find his soul. At the same time, he faces death.

The poems in *Le Cap de Bonne-Espérance* are extremely sensual, despite the abstract element, and attempt to re-create the physical sensations of flying with fragmented lines and onomatopoeic vowels. These techniques were not original to Cocteau; the typographical effects had been used by Stéphane Mallarmé, Apollinaire, and Pierre Reverdy, and the *lettriste* effects by Pierre Albert-Birot. Yet, as Adrienne Monnier points out, it was daring of Cocteau to employ these still-radical devices. André Breton, among others, considered the collection not radical enough and had a sour

expression the whole time Cocteau was reading it in Valentine Gross's apartment. Cocteau is said to have called his work old-fashioned, in an effort to charm Breton, but many see the reading as the beginning of Cocteau's long battle with the Surrealists. The book also provoked a letter from Proust, who gently asked whether it did not display a certain indiscriminate use of images.

DISCOURS DU GRAND SOMMEIL

Discours du grand sommeil (discourse of the great sleep) consists of eleven poems written between 1916 and 1918 and was inspired by Cocteau's experiences with the Fusiliers Marins, among whom he lived, illegally wearing the Marine uniform until discovered by an officer. A day after Cocteau was ejected from the front, most of the Fusiliers Marins were killed. Cocteau attempted in these poems to end once and for all his role as the "prince of frivolity." Though flippancy was always part of Cocteau's demeanor, he once asserted that it was the bourgeois way of dealing with catastrophe—that what appeared to be frivolity to others was actually Cocteau's way of dealing with his profound sadness. *Discours du grand sommeil*, writes Wallace Fowlie, is "a plunge downward," "a contact with the grim presence of death." The poems are quite effective in conveying the horror of war, of the exhausting marches, the screams of the dying, and the endless suffering. There is also an awakening sense of the soldier as symbolic of the tragedy of human existence and a movement toward a more classical style and attitude. The volume clearly points toward Cocteau's later aesthetic.

VOCABULAIRE

Vocabulaire also reveals a cleaner, purer style than that of Cocteau's youthful works yet still betrays the inordinate influence of the artistic movements of the war years, such as Dadaism, Futurism, Imagism, and cubism. Cocteau's fixation upon certain images (such as snow turning to marble) is notable throughout his career. In this collection, the rose appears often, with obvious allusions to Pierre de Ronsard, in clear homage to French classicism. One finds Cocteau in search of himself, struggling as he had since the Ghéon review to achieve originality. The poems consist largely of philosophical speculations on the nature of change and the poet's role in metamorphosis. The endless flow of change is represented by the changes in clouds, aging, swans, the dissolution of salt statues, death, and snow. Cocteau's private mythology is fully developed here; several poems, such as "Tombeaux" (tombs) and "Oiseaux sont en neige" (birds are in snow), connect homosexuality to the themes of change and death. In these poems, Cocteau seems to be taking stock of his life, trying to find a direction and meaning to it.

POÉSIES, 1917-1920

Under Radiguet's influence, Cocteau was moving toward the tradition of French literature that employs the brief, clear, precise sentence. Cocteau renewed himself with this classicism and rediscovered the themes of classical antiquity. In *Poésies, 1917-1920*, Cocteau introduced a new set of topics, themes, and motifs, such as the clown, circus, angel, sailor, and athlete. Perhaps the most significant poem in the collection is "L'Ode à Picasso" (ode to Picasso), an attempt to grasp the complexity of the painter and artist whom Cocteau often watched at work for hours on end. The poem reveals Picasso as a man possessed by an inner fire, an embodiment of the concept, expressed by Socrates in Plato's Ion, of the madness of the poet. Painting, sculpture, film, and any other expression of art are therefore merely facets of the same thing: *poésie*. Cocteau sees in Picasso a man in constant contact with the Muses, free of mundane considerations. The poem expresses much of what Cocteau would attempt to be, would have the courage to be, after being inspired by Radiguet. The final poem of *Poésies, 1917-1920*, "Mouchoir" (handkerchief), bids farewell to influences of the past and sets the poet out on a voyage into the unknown. To be a poet is thus to move ahead relentlessly, to be uncertain of the results, to follow no one.

PLAIN-CHANT

Plain-Chant reveals in its title a further move toward simplification and, in Fowlie's view, is central to the work of Cocteau. It is classically metered and uses the imagery of Angel, Muse, and Death, symbolism which recurs in much of the rest of Cocteau's oeuvre. The Angel in this lyric poem is clearly Radiguet, and the poem expresses Cocteau's great love for him and also his fear of the death which will inevitably separate them. The Angel is his guide through the mysteries of poetic art and also his protector when the Muse leaves him or

Death presses in on him. As Bettina Knapp has observed, however, Death becomes a restorative power, a bridge to another world: "He burrowed within and reached new depths of cognition, with beauty of form and classical restraint." The poem was also strangely prescient, as Radiguet died in 1923, emotionally shattering Cocteau.

OPÉRA

Cocteau's discovery of his identity as a poet under the guidance of Radiguet was not lost in his plummet into despair brought about by the young man's death. The collection *Opéra* mixes Cocteau's visions induced by opium with lucid language and precise control. Even in his agony, he rigorously adheres to a classical detachment, a coolness that enhances the feelings and mythological dimensions of the works. A blending of Christian and pagan mythology points toward Cocteau's extensive revising and adapting of works of classical mythology for the stage and film. "L'Ange heurtebise" in *Opéra* is usually thought to be one of Cocteau's most significant poems. It explores the question of angels, which he had discussed in an essay, *Le Secret professionnel* (1922). The poet is stuck on an earthly plane, struggling to understand a larger reality, while the Angel stands above. The Angel reappears in work after work of Cocteau, inspiring poets and urging them to look upon the human predicament with detachment.

LATER YEARS

Cocteau did not cease writing poetry until his death, but most critics seem indifferent to the large number of his works after *Opéra*. Perhaps his work in film and prose detracted from his development in poetry, though Cocteau himself saw all his artistic works as facets of the same creative impulse: It was all poetry to him. His influence on the literary scene waned, perhaps because he had finally found his own unique path, and artists and critics found it difficult to categorize and thus assess the measure of Cocteau's achievement. His variety contributes to the difficulty of an overall assessment: He began each mature collection of poems as if he had only recently become a poet.

At the very least, Cocteau's poetry exhibits many of the primary traits of twentieth century poetry in its clean, precise form, its development of personal mythology, and its exploitation through adaptation of traditional mythological and literary themes. These traits are significant elements of the mainstream of modern poetry, and Cocteau is clearly in the middle of it.

OTHER MAJOR WORKS

LONG FICTION: *Le Potomak*, 1919; *Le Grand Écart*, 1923 (*The Grand Écart*, 1925); *Thomas l'imposteur*, 1923 (*Thomas the Impostor*, 1925); *Le Livre blanc*, 1928 (*The White Paper*, 1957); *Les Enfants terribles*, 1929 (*Enfants Terribles*, 1930; also known as *Children of the Game*); *Le Fantôme de Marseille*, 1933; *La Fin du Potomak*, 1939.

PLAYS: *Antigone*, pr. 1922 (libretto; English translation, 1961); *Orphée*, pr. 1926 (*Orpheus*, 1933); *Oedipus-Rex*, pr. 1927 (libretto; English translation, 1961); *La Voix humaine*, pr., pb. 1930 (*The Human Voice*, 1951); *La Machine infernale*, pr., pb. 1934 (*The Infernal Machine*, 1936); *L'École des veuves*, pr., pb. 1936; *Les Chevaliers de la table ronde*, pr., pb. 1937 (*The Knights of the Round Table*, 1955); *Les Parents terribles*, pr., pb. 1938 (*Intimate Relations*, 1952); *Les Monstres sacrés*, pr., pb. 1940 (*The Holy Terrors*, 1953); *La Machine à écrire*, pr., pb. 1941 (*The Typewriter*, 1948); *Renaud et Armide*, pr., pb. 1943; *L'Aigle à deux têtes*, pr., pb. 1946 (*The Eagle Has Two Heads*, 1946); *Bacchus*, pr. 1951 (English translation, 1955); *Théâtre complet*, pb. 1957 (2 volumes); *Five Plays*, pb. 1961; *L'Impromptu du Palais-Royal*, pr., pb. 1962; *The Infernal Machine and Other Plays*, pb. 1964.

SCREENPLAYS: *Le Sang d'un poète*, 1932 (*The Blood of a Poet*, 1949); *Le Baron fantôme*, 1943; *L'Éternel retour*, 1943 (*The Eternal Return*, 1948); *La Belle et la bête*, 1946 (*Beauty and the Beast*, 1947); *L'Aigle à deux têtes*, 1946; *Ruy Blas*, 1947; *Les Parents terribles*, 1948 (*Intimate Relations*, 1952); *Les Enfants terribles*, 1950; *Orphée*, 1950 (*Orpheus*, 1950); *Le Testament d'Orphée*, 1959 (*The Testament of Orpheus*, 1968); *Thomas l'Imposteur*, 1965.

NONFICTION: *Le Coq et l'Arlequin*, 1918 (*Cock and Harlequin*, 1921); *Le Secret professionnel*, 1922; *Lettre à Jacques Maritain*, 1926 (*Art and Faith*, 1948); *Le Rappel à l'ordre*, 1926 (*A Call to Order*,

1926); *Opium: Journal d'une désintoxication*, 1930 (*Opium: Diary of a Cure*, 1932); *Essai de la critique indirecte*, 1932 (*The Lais Mystery: An Essay of Indirect Criticism*, 1936); *Portraits-souvenir, 1900-1914*, 1935 (*Paris Album*, 1956); *La Belle et la bête: Journal d'un film*, 1946 (*Beauty and the Beast: Journal of a Film*, 1950); *La Difficulté d'être*, 1947 (*The Difficulty of Being*, 1966); *The Journals of Jean Cocteau*, 1956; *Poésie critique*, 1960.

BALLET SCENARIOS: *Le Dieu bleu*, 1912 (with Frédéric de Madrazo); *Parade*, 1917 (music by Erik Satie, scenery by Pablo Picasso); *Le Boeuf sur le toit*, 1920 (music by Darius Milhaud, scenery by Raoul Dufy); *Le Gendarme incompris*, 1921 (with Raymond Radiguet; music by Francis Poulenc); *Les Mariés de la tour Eiffel*, 1921 (music by Les Six; *The Wedding on the Eiffel Tower*, 1937); *Les Biches*, 1924 (music by Poulenc); *Les Fâcheux*, 1924 (music by George Auric); *Le Jeune Homme et la mort*, 1946 (music by Johann Sebastian Bach); *Phèdre*, 1950 (music by Auric).

TRANSLATION: *Roméo et Juliette*, 1926 (of William Shakespeare's play).

BIBLIOGRAPHY

Brown, Frederick. *An Impersonation of Angels: A Biography of Jean Cocteau*, 1968. Study of the life and work of Cocteau, with emphasis on his artistic milieu and his collaborators and sources of inspiration, such as poet Guillaume Apollinaire, artist Pablo Picasso, novelist André Gide, and filmmaker Jean Marais. Illustrations, bibliography.

Crosland, Margaret. *Jean Cocteau: A Biography*. New York: Knopf, 1956. A charming biography written with the help and encouragement of Cocteau himself. The goal is to relate Cocteau's work to his life and to relate the different aspects of his work to one another. Lively comments by fellow artists, as well as discussion and interpretation of individual works by Cocteau. With excerpts from letters of Cocteau and numerous illustrations.

Fowlie, Wallace. *Jean Cocteau: History of a Poet's Age*. Bloomington: Indiana University Press, 1966. A biography relating the events of Cocteau's life to contemporary events.

Knapp, Bettina L. *Jean Cocteau*. Boston: Twayne, 1989. Discusses Cocteau's writings from a literary and psychological point of view in an effort to determine his influences. Sees Cocteau as a many-sided individual often in need of a collaborative creator or as inspired by other creative people around him. Suggests Cocteau's poetic imagination was most vital and original in the domain of film, theater, and the novel. Research includes material based on interviews with Cocteau himself. Chronology and bibliography.

Lowe, Romana N. *The Fictional Female: Sacrificial Rituals and Spectacles of Writing in Baudelaire, Zola, and Cocteau*. New York: P. Lang, 1997. Highlights a the sacrificial victim common in nineteenth and twentieth century French texts: women. Lowe traces structures and images of female sacrifice in the genres of poetry, novel, and theater with close readings of Baudelaire, Zola, and Cocteau.

Mauriès, Patrick. *Jean Cocteau*. London: Thames and Hudson, 1998. A brief biography illustrated with many photographs.

Peters, Arthur King, ed. *Joan Cocteau and the French Scene*. New York: Abbeville Press, 1984. Eight essays, plus a preface and impressively detailed chronology. Discusses such topics as Cocteau's biography, his intellectual milieu, his literary and artistic influences, and his place in the arts of his period and as the first true multimedia artist. Numerous photographs of Cocteau, his colleagues, and his own artwork.

Sprigge, Elizabeth, and Jean-Jacques Kihm. *Jean Cocteau: The Man and His Mirror*. New York: Coward-McCann, 1968. Biography with bibliographic references.

Steegmuller, Francis. *Cocteau*. Boston: D. R. Godine, 1986. A major biography of Cocteau. Discusses his childhood, the influence of his mother, and fellow poets. Defines him as a "quick-change" artist with a propensity for constant self-invention, discarding old views and activities and assuming new roles or guises with remarkable facility. Twelve appendices plus numerous illustrations. Bibliography, index.

J. Madison Davis;
bibliography updated by Margaret Boe Birns

SAMUEL TAYLOR COLERIDGE

Born: Ottery St. Mary, England; October 21, 1772
Died: Highgate, London, England; July 25, 1834

PRINCIPAL POETRY

Poems on Various Subjects, 1796, 1797 (with Charles Lamb and Charles Lloyd)
A Sheet of Sonnets, 1796 (with W. L. Bowles, Robert Southey, and others)
Lyrical Ballads, 1798 (with William Wordsworth)
The Rime of the Ancient Mariner, 1798
Christabel, 1816
Sibylline Leaves, 1817
The Complete Poetical Works of Samuel Taylor Coleridge, 1912 (2 volumes; Ernest Hartley Coleridge, editor)

OTHER LITERARY FORMS

Samuel Taylor Coleridge's original verse dramas—*The Fall of Robespierre* (1794, with Robert Southey), *Remorse* (1813, originally *Osorio*), and *Zapolya* (1817)—are of particular interest to readers of his poetry, as is *Wallenstein* (1800), his translation of two dramas by Friedrich Schiller. His major prose includes the contents of two periodicals, *The Watchman* (1796) and *The Friend* (1809-1810, 1818), two lay Sermons, "The Statesman's Manual" (1816) and "A Lay Sermon" (1817), the *Biographia Literaria* (1817), "Treatise on Method," originally published in *The Encyclopaedia Metropolitana* (1818), and a series of metaphysical aphorisms, *Aids to Reflection* (1825). His lectures on politics, religion, literature, and philosophy have been collected in various editions, as have other short essays, unpublished manuscripts, letters, records of conversations, notebooks, and marginalia. These prose works share common interests with his poetry and suggest the philosophical context in which it should be read. Coleridge's literary criticism is particularly relevant to his poetry.

ACHIEVEMENTS

It is ironic that Samuel Taylor Coleridge has come to be known to the general reader primarily as a poet, for poetry was not his own primary interest and the poems with which his name is most strongly linked—*The Rime of the Ancient Mariner*, "Kubla Khan," and *Christabel*—were products of a few months in a long literary career. He did not suffer a decline in poetic creativity; he simply turned his attention to political, metaphysical, and theological issues that were best treated in prose. That Coleridge is counted among the major poets of British Romanticism is, for this reason, all the more remarkable. For most poets, the handful of commonly anthologized poems is a scant representation of their output; for Coleridge, it is, in many instances, the sum of his accomplishment. His minor verse is often conventional and uninspired. His major poems, in contrast, speak with singular emotional and intellectual intensity in a surprising range of forms—from the symbolic fantasy of *The Rime of the Ancient Mariner* (which first appeared in *Lyrical Ballads*) to the autobiographical sincerity of the conversation poems—exerting an influence on subsequent poets far beyond what Coleridge himself anticipated.

BIOGRAPHY

Samuel Taylor Coleridge was born October 21, 1772, in the Devonshire town of Ottery St. Mary, the youngest of ten children. His father, a clergyman and teacher, died in October, 1781, and the next year Coleridge was sent to school at Christ's Hospital, London. His friends at school included Charles Lamb, two years his junior, whose essay "Christ's Hospital Five-and-Thirty Years Ago" (1820) describes the two sides of Coleridge—the "poor friendless boy," far from his home, "alone among six hundred playmates"; the precocious scholar, "Logician, Metaphysician, Bard!," holding his auditors "entranced with imagination." Both characteristics—a deep sense of isolation and the effort to use learning and eloquence to overcome it—remained with Coleridge throughout his life.

He entered Cambridge in 1791, but never completed work for his university degree. Depressed by debts, he fled the university in December, 1793, and enlisted in the Light Dragoons under the name Silas Tompkyn Comberbache. Rescued by his brothers, he returned to Cambridge in April and resumed his studies. Two months later he met Robert Southey, with whom he

soon made plans to establish a utopian community ("Pantisocracy") in America. Southey was engaged to marry Edith Fricker, and so it seemed appropriate for Coleridge to engage himself to her sister Sara. The project failed, but Coleridge, through his own sense of duty and Southey's insistence, married a woman he had never loved and with whom his relationship was soon to become strained.

As a married man, Coleridge had to leave the university and make a living for his wife and, in time, children—Hartley (1796-1849), Berkeley (1798-1799), Derwent (b. 1800), and Sara (1802-1852). Economic survival was, it turned out, possible only with the support of friends such as Thomas Poole and the publisher Joseph Cottle and, in 1798, a life annuity from Josiah and Tom Wedgwood. The early years of Coleridge's married life, in which he lived with his family at Nether Stowey, were the period of his closest relationship with the poet William Wordsworth. Inspired by Wordsworth, whom he in turn inspired, Coleridge wrote most of his major poetry. Together, the two men published *Lyrical Ballads* in 1798, the proceeds of which enabled them,

Samuel Taylor Coleridge (Library of Congress)

along with Wordsworth's sister Dorothy, to spend the winter in Germany, where Coleridge studied metaphysics at the University of Göttingen.

Returning to England the following year, Coleridge met and fell deeply in love with Sara Hutchinson, a friend of Dorothy who later became Wordsworth's sister-in-law. This passion, which remained strong for many years, furthered Coleridge's estrangement from his wife, with whom he moved to Keswick in the Lake District of England, in July, 1800, to be near the Wordsworths at Grasmere. Coleridge's health had always been poor, and he had become addicted to opium, which, according to current medical practice, he had originally taken to relieve pain. Seeking a change of climate, he traveled to Malta and then Italy in 1804 to 1806. On his return, he and his wife "*determined* to part absolutely and finally," leaving Coleridge in custody of his sons Hartley and Derwent (Berkeley had died in 1799).

In 1808, Coleridge gave his first public lectures and in the next two years published the twenty-seven issues of *The Friend*. By now, he was a figure of national standing, but his private life remained in disarray. Sara Hutchinson, who had assisted him in preparing copy for *The Friend*, separated herself from him, and in 1810 he quarreled decisively with Wordsworth. (They were later reconciled, but the period of close friendship was over.) Six years later, after various unsuccessful attempts to cure himself of opium addiction and set his affairs in order, he put himself in the care of James Gillman, a physician living at Highgate, a northern suburb of London. Under Gillman's roof, Coleridge was once again able to work. He wrote the two lay Sermons, "The Statesman's Manual" and "A Lay Sermon"; completed the *Biographia Literaria*, originally planned as an autobiographical introduction to *Sibylline Leaves* but ultimately two volumes in its own right; and revised the essays he had written for *The Friend*, including among them a version of the "Treatise on Method" which he had composed for the first volume of *The Encyclopaedia Metropolitana*. He also resumed his public lectures on philosophy and literature and in time became a London celebrity, enthralling visitors with his conversation and gradually attracting a circle of disciples. Meanwhile, he worked at the magnum opus that was to synthesize his metaphysi-

cal and theological thought in a single intellectual system. This project, however, remained incomplete when Coleridge died at Highgate, July 25, 1834.

ANALYSIS

Samuel Taylor Coleridge's major poems turn on problems of self-esteem and identity. Exploring states of isolation and ineffectuality, they test strategies to overcome weakness without asserting its antithesis—a powerful self, secure in its own thoughts and utterances, the potency and independence of which Coleridge feared would only exacerbate his loneliness. His reluctance to assert his own abilities is evident in his habitual deprecation of his own poetry and hyperbolic praise of William Wordsworth's. It is evident as well in his best verse, which either is written in an unpretentious "conversational" tone or, when it is not, is carefully dissociated from his own voice and identity. Yet by means of these strategies, he is often able to assert indirectly or vicariously the strong self he otherwise repressed.

"THE EOLIAN HARP"

Writing to John Thelwall in 1796, Coleridge called the first of the conversation poems, "The Eolian Harp" (written in 1795), the "favorite of *my* poems." He originally published it, in 1796, with the indication "Composed August 20th, 1795, At Clevedon, Somersetshire," which dates at least some version of the text six weeks before his marriage to Sara Fricker. Since Sara plays a role in the poem, the exact date is crucial. "The Eolian Harp" is not, as it has been called, a "honeymoon" poem; rather, it anticipates a future in which Coleridge and Sara will sit together by their "Cot o'ergrown/ With white-flower'd Jasmin." Significantly, Sara remains silent throughout the poem; her only contribution is the "mild reproof" that "darts" from her "more serious eye," quelling the poet's intellectual daring. Yet this reproof is as imaginary as Sara's presence itself. At the climax of the poem, meditative thought gives way to the need for human response; tellingly, the response he imagines and therefore, one must assume, desires, is reproof.

"The Eolian Harp" establishes a structural pattern for the conversation poems as a group. Coleridge is, in effect, alone, "and the world *so* hush'd!/ The stilly murmur of the distant Sea/ Tells us of silence." The eolian harp in the window sounds in the breeze and reminds him of "the one Life within us and abroad,/ Which meets all motion and becomes its soul." This observation leads to the central question of the poem:

> And what if all of animated nature
> Be but organic Harps diversely fram'd,
> That tremble into thought, as o'er them sweeps
> Plastic and vast, one intellectual breeze,
> At once the Soul of each, and God of all?

Sara's glance dispells "These shapings of the unregenerate mind," but, of course, it is too late, since they have already been expressed in the poem. (Indeed, the letter to Thelwall makes it clear that it was this expression of pantheism, not its retraction, that made the poem dear to Coleridge.) For this reason, the conflict between two sides of Coleridge's thought—metaphysical speculation and orthodox Christianity—remains unresolved. If the poem is in any way disquieting, it is not because it exemplifies a failure of nerve, but because of the identifications it suggests between metaphysical speculation and the isolated self, religious orthodoxy and the conventions—down to the vines covering the cottage—of married life. Coleridge, in other words, does not imagine a wife who will love him all the more for his intellectual daring. Instead, he imagines one who will chastise him for the very qualities that make him an original thinker. To "possess/ Peace, and this Cot, and thee,/ heart-honour'd Maid!," Coleridge must acknowledge himself "A sinful and most miserable man,/ Wilder'd and dark." Happiness, as well as poetic closure, depends upon this acceptance of diminished self-esteem. Even so, by embedding an expression of intellectual strength within the context of domestic conventionality, Coleridge is able to achieve a degree of poetic authority otherwise absent in the final lines of the poem. The ability to renounce a powerful self is itself a gesture of power: The acceptance of loss becomes—as in other Romantic poems—a form of strength.

The structure of "The Eolian Harp" can be summarized as follows: A state of isolation (the more isolated for the presence of an unresponsive companion) gives way to meditation, which leads to the possibility of a self powerful through its association with an all-powerful force. This state of mind gives place to the acknowledgment of a human relationship dependent on the poet's recognition of his own inadequacy, the reward for which is a poetic voice with the authority to close the poem.

"THIS LIME-TREE BOWER MY PRISON"

This pattern recurs in "This Lime-Tree Bower My Prison" (1797). The poem is addressed to Charles Lamb, but the "gentle-hearted Charles" of the text is really a surrogate for the figure of Wordsworth, whose loss Coleridge is unwilling to face head-on. Incapacitated by a burn—appropriately, his wife's fault—Coleridge is left alone seated in a clump of lime trees while his friends—Lamb and William and Dorothy Wordsworth—set off on a long walk through the countryside. They are, like Sara in "The Eolian Harp," there and yet not there: Their presence in the poem intensifies Coleridge's sense of isolation. He follows them in his imagination, and the gesture itself becomes a means of connecting himself with them. Natural images of weakness, enclosure, and solitude give way to those of strength, expansion, and connection, and the tone of the poem shifts from speculation to assertion. In a climactic moment, he imagines his friends "gazing round/ On the wide landscape" until it achieves the transcendence of "such hues/ As veil the Almighty Spirit, when yet he makes/ Spirits perceive his presence."

As in "The Eolian Harp," the perception of an omnipotent force pervading the universe returns Coleridge to his present state, but with a new sense of his own being and his relationship with the friends to whom he addresses the poem. His own isolation is now seen as an end in itself. "Sometimes/ 'Tis well to be bereft of promised good," Coleridge argues, "That we may lift the soul, and contemplate/ With lively joy the joys we cannot share."

"FROST AT MIDNIGHT"

"Frost at Midnight," the finest of the conversation poems, replaces silent wife or absent friends with a sleeping child (Hartley—although he is not named in the text). Summer is replaced by winter; isolation is now a function of seasonal change itself. In this zero-world, "The Frost performs its secret ministry,/ Unhelped by any wind." The force that moved the eolian harp into sound is gone. The natural surroundings of the poem drift into nonexistence: "Sea, and hill, and wood,/ With all the numberless goings-on of life,/ Inaudible as dreams!" This is the nadir of self from which the poet reconstructs his being—first by perception of "dim sympathies" with the "low-burnt fire" before him; then by a process of recollection and predication. The "film" on the grate reminds Coleridge of his childhood at Christ's Hospital, where a similar image conveyed hopes of seeing someone from home and therefore a renewal of the conditions of his earlier life in Ottery St. Mary. Yet even in recollection, the bells of his "sweet birth-place" are most expressive not as a voice of the present moment, but as "articulate sounds of things to come!" The spell of the past was, in fact, a spell of the imagined future. The visitor he longed for turns out to be a version of the self of the poet, his "sister more beloved/ My play-mate when we both were clothed alike." The condition of loss that opens the poem cannot be filled by the presence of another human being; it is a fundamental emptiness in the self, which, Coleridge suggests, can never be filled, but only recognized as a necessary condition of adulthood. Yet this recognition of incompleteness is the poet's means of experiencing a sense of identity missing in the opening lines of the poem.

"Frost at Midnight" locates this sense of identity in Coleridge's own life. It is not a matter of metaphysical or religious belief, as it is in "The Eolian Harp" or "This Lime-Tree Bower My Prison," but a function of the self that recognizes its own coherence in time. This recognition enables him to speak to the "Dear Babe" who had been there all along, but had remained a piece of the setting and not a living human being. Like the friends of "This Lime-Tree Bower My Prison," who are projected exploring a landscape, the boy Hartley is imagined wandering "like a breeze/ By lakes and sandy shores." The static existence of the poet in the present moment is contrasted with the movement of a surrogate. This movement, however, is itself subordinated to the voice of the poet who can promise his son a happiness he himself has not known.

In all three poems, Coleridge achieves a voice that entails the recognition of his own loss—in acknowledging Sara's reproof or losing himself in the empathic construction of the experience of friend or son. The act entails a defeat of the self, but also a vicarious participation in powerful forces that reveal themselves in the working of the universe, and through this participation a partial triumph of the self over its own sense of inadequacy. In "Frost at Midnight," the surrogate figure of his son not only embodies a locomotor power denied the static speaker, but he is also, in his capacity to read the "language" uttered by God in the form of landscape, associated with absolute power itself.

THE RIME OF THE ANCIENT MARINER

Although written in a very different mode, *The Rime of the Ancient Mariner* centers on a similar experience of participation in supernatural power. At the core of the poem is, of course, the story of the Mariner who shoots the albatross and endures complete and devastating isolation from his fellow man. The poem, however, is not a direct narrative of these events; rather, it is a narrative of the Mariner's narrating them. The result of the extraordinary experience he has undergone is to make him an itinerant storyteller. It has given him a voice, but a voice grounded on his own incompleteness of self. He has returned to land but remains homeless and without permanent human relationships. In this respect, *The Rime of the Ancient Mariner* is Coleridge's nightmare alternative to the conversation poem. As "conversations," they suggest the possibility of a relationship with his audience that can in part compensate for the inadequate human relationships described in the poem. The Mariner's story is a kind of conversation. He tells it to the Wedding-Guest he has singled out for that purpose, but the relationship between speaker and audience can scarcely be said to compensate for the Mariner's lack of human relationships. The Wedding-Guest is compelled to listen by the hypnotic power of the Mariner's "glittering eye." He "beats his breast" at the thought of the wedding from which he is being detained and repeatedly expresses his fear of the Mariner. In the end, he registers no compassion for the man whose story he has just heard. He is too "stunned" for that—and the Mariner has left the stage without asking for applause. His audience is changed by the story—"A sadder and a wiser man,/ He rose the morrow morn"—but of this the Mariner can know nothing. Thus, the power of the Mariner's story to captivate and transform its audience simply furthers his alienation from his fellow human beings.

Structurally, the poem follows the three-stage pattern of the conversation poems. A state of isolation and immobility is succeeded by one in which the Mariner becomes the object of (and is thus associated with) powerful supernatural agencies, and this leads to the moralizing voice of the conclusion. Unlike the conversation poems, *The Rime of the Ancient Mariner* prefaces individual isolation with social isolation. The Mariner and his shipmates, in what has become one of the most familiar narratives in English literature, sail from Europe toward Cape Horn, where they are surrounded by a polar ice jam. An albatross appears and accepts food from the sailors; a fair wind springs up, and they are able to resume their journey northward into the Pacific Ocean; the albatross follows them, "And every day, for food or play,/ Came to the mariner's hollo!"—until the Mariner, seemingly without reason, shoots the bird with his crossbow. Coleridge warned readers against allegorizing the poem, and it is fruitless to search for a specific identification for the albatross. What is important is the bird's gratuitous arrival and the Mariner's equally gratuitous crossbow shot. The polar ice that threatens the ship is nature at its most alien. Seen against that backdrop, the albatross seems relatively human; the mariners, accordingly, "hailed it in God's name"; "As if it had been a Christian soul." Like the "film" in "Frost at Midnight"—a poem in which crucial events are also set against a wintry backdrop—the bird offers them a means of bridging the gap between man and nature, self and nonself, through projecting human characteristics on a creature of the natural world. By shooting the albatross, the Mariner blocks this projection and thus traps both himself and his shipmates in a state of isolation.

The Mariner's act has no explicit motive because it is a function of human nature itself, but it is not merely a sign of original sin or congenital perversity. His narrative has until now been characterized by a remarkable passivity. Events simply happen. Even the ship's progress is characterized not by its own movement but by the changing position of the sun in the sky. The ice that surrounds the ship is only one element of a natural world that dominates the fate of the ship and its crew, and it is against this overwhelming dominance that the Mariner takes his crossbow shot. The gesture is an assertion of the human spirit against an essentially inhuman universe, aimed at the harmless albatross because aimed at the act of self-deceptive projection by which his shipmates attempt to mitigate their sense of isolation.

He is punished for this self-assertion—first, by the crewmen who blame him for the calm that follows and tie the albatross around his neck as a sign of guilt. It is only after this occurs that the Mariner, thirsty and guilt-ridden, perceives events that are explicitly supernatural and the second stage of his punishment begins. Yet the Mariner's isolation, even after his shipmates have died and left him alone on the becalmed ship, remains a consequence of his assertion of self against the natural world, and the turning point of the poem is equally his own doing. In the midst of the calm, the water had seemed abhorrently ugly: "slimy things did crawl with legs/ Upon the slimy sea," while "the water, like a witch's oils,/ Burnt green, and blue and white." Now, "bemocked" by moonlight, the same creatures are beautiful: "Blue, glossy green, and velvet black,/ They coiled and swam; and every track/ Was a flash of golden fire." In this perception of beauty, the Mariner explains, "A spring of love gushed from my heart,/ And I blessed them unaware." At the same moment, he is once again able to pray, and the albatross falls from his neck into the sea. Prayer—the ability to voice his mind and feelings and, in so doing, relate them to a higher order of being—is a function of love, and love is a function of the apprehension of beauty. In blessing the water snakes, it should be noted, the Mariner has not returned to the viewpoint of his shipmates when they attributed human characteristics to the albatross. When he conceives of the snakes as "happy living things," he acknowledges a bond between all forms of organic life, but their beauty is not dependent on human projection.

Yet achieving this chastened vision does not end the Mariner's suffering. Not only must he endure an extension of his shipboard isolation, but also when, eventually, he returns to his native land, he is not granted reintegration into its society. The Hermit from whom he asks absolution demands quick answer to his own question, "What manner of man art thou?" In response, the Mariner experiences a spasm of physical agony that forces him to tell the story of his adventures. The tale told, he is left free of pain—until such time as "That agony returns" and he is compelled to repeat the narrative: "That moment that his face I see,/ I know the man that must hear me:/ To him my tale I teach." The Mariner has become a poet—like Coleridge, a poet gifted with "strange power of speech" and plagued with somatic pain, with power to fix his auditors' attention and transform them into "sadder and wiser" men. Yet the price of this power is enormous. It entails not only the shipboard suffering of the Mariner but also perpetual alienation from his fellow human beings. Telling his story is the only relationship allowed him, and he does not even fully understand the meaning of his narration. In the concluding lines of the poem, he attempts to draw a moral—

> He prayeth best, who loveth best
> All things both great and small;
> For the dear God who loveth us,
> He made and loveth all.

These words are not without bearing on the poem, but they overlook the extraordinary disproportion between the Mariner's crime and its punishment. Readers of the poem—as well as, one supposes, the Wedding-Guest—are more likely to question the benevolence of the "dear God who loveth us" than to perceive the Mariner's story as an illustration of God's love. Thus, the voice of moral authority that gave the conversation poems a means of closure is itself called into question. The soul that acknowledges its essential isolation in the universe can never hope for reintegration into society. The poet whose song is the tale of his own suffering can "stun" his reader but can never achieve a lasting human relationship. His experience can be given the aesthetic coherence of narrative, but he can never connect the expressive significance of that narrative with his life as a whole.

It is in part the medium of the poem that allows Coleridge to face these bleak possibilities. Its ballad stanza and archaic diction, along with the marginal glosses added in 1815 to 1816, dissociate the text from its modern poet. Freed from an explicit identification with the Mariner, Coleridge is able both to explore implications of the poet's role that would have been difficult to face directly and to write about experiences for which there was no precedent in conventional meditative verse.

"KUBLA KHAN"

A similar strategy is associated with "Kubla Khan," which can be read as an alternative to *The Rime of the Ancient Mariner*. The poem, which was not published until 1816, nearly two decades after it was written, is Coleridge's most daring account of poetic inspiration and the special nature of the poet. In the poem, the poet's isolation is perceived not as weakness but strength. Even in 1816, the gesture of self-assertion was difficult for Coleridge, and he prefaced the poem with an account designed to diminish its significance. "Kubla Khan" was, he explained, "a psychological curiosity," the fragment of a longer poem he had composed in an opium-induced sleep, "if that indeed can be called composition in which all the images rose up before him as *things*, with a parallel production of the correspondent expressions, without any sensation or consciousness of effort." Waking, he began to write out the verses he had in this manner "composed" but was interrupted by a visitor, after whose departure he found he could no longer remember more than "the general purport of the vision" and a few "scattered lines and images."

The problem with this explanation is that "Kubla Khan" does not strike readers as a fragment. It is, as it stands, an entirely satisfactory whole. Moreover, the facts of Coleridge's preface have themselves been called into question.

Just what was Coleridge trying to hide? The poem turns on an analogy between the act of an emperor and the act of a poet. Kubla Khan's "pleasure-dome" in Xanadu is more than a monarch's self-indulgence; symbolically, it attempts to arrest the process of life itself. His walls encircle "twice five miles of fertile ground," in the midst of which flows "Alph," the sacred river of life, but they control neither the source of the river nor its conclusion in the "lifeless ocean" to which it runs. The source is a "deep romantic chasm" that Coleridge associates with the violence of natural process, with human sexuality, and with the libidinal origins of poetry in the song of a "woman wailing for her demon lover." Kubla's pleasure-dome is "a miracle of rare device," but it can exert no lasting influence. The achievement of the most powerful Oriental despot is limited by the conditions of life, and even his attempt to order a limited space evokes "Ancestral voices prophesying war!"

In contrast, the achievement of the poet is not bounded by space and time and partakes of the dangerous potency of natural creativity itself. Yet the nature of inspiration is tricky. The speaker of the poem recollects a visionary "Abyssinian maid" playing a dulcimer, and it is the possibility of reviving "within me/ Her symphony and song" that holds out the hope of a corresponding creativity: "To such a deep delight 'twould win me,/ . . . I would build that dome in air, . . ." The poet's act is always secondary, never primary creativity. Even so, to re-create in poetry Kubla's achievement—without its liabilities—is to become a dangerous being. Like the Mariner, the inspired poet has "flashing eyes" that can cast a spell over his audience. His special nature may be the sign of an incomplete self—for inspiration depends on the possibility of recovering a lost recollection; nevertheless, it is a special nature that threatens to re-create the world in its own image.

CHRISTABEL

Nowhere else is Coleridge so confident about his powers as a poet or writer. *Christabel*, written in the same period as *The Rime of the Ancient Mariner* and "Kubla Khan," remains a fascinating fragment. Like "Kubla Khan," it was not published until 1816. By then, the verse romances of Sir Walter Scott and George Gordon, Lord Byron, had caught the public's attention, and among Coleridge's motives in publishing his poem was to lay claim to a poetic form he believed he had originated. More important, though, his decision to publish two parts of an incomplete narrative almost two decades after he had begun the poem was also a means of acknowledging that *Christabel* was and would remain unfinished.

To attribute its incompletion to Coleridge's procrastination evades the real question: Why did the poem itself preclude development? Various answers have been offered; the most convincing argue a conflict between the metaphysical or religious significance of Christabel—whose name conflates Christ and Abel—with the exigencies of the narrative structure in which she is placed. As Walter Jackson Bate explains it, the "problem of finding motives and actions for Christabel . . . had imposed an insupportable psychological burden on Coleridge." The problem that Coleridge fails to solve is the problem of depicting credible innocence. Christabel, the virgin who finds the mysterious Lady Geraldine in the forest and brings her home to the castle of her father, Sir Leoline, only to fall victim to Geraldine's sinister spell,

is either hopelessly passive and merely a victim, or, if active, something less than entirely innocent. At the same time, Geraldine, who approaches her prey with "a stricken look," is potentially the more interesting character. Christabel is too much like the albatross in *The Rime of the Ancient Mariner*; Geraldine, too much like the Mariner himself, whose guilt changes him from a simple seaman to an archetype of human isolation and suffering. Christabel's name suggests that Coleridge had intended for her to play a sacrificial role, but by promising to reunite Sir Leoline with his childhood friend, Roland de Vaux of Tryermaine, whom she claims as her father, Geraldine, too, has a potentially positive function in the narrative. Whether or not her claim is true, it nevertheless initiates action that may lead to a reconciliation, not only between two long-separated friends but also between Sir Leoline's death-obsessed maturity and the time in his youth when he was able to experience friendship. There is, therefore, a suggestion that Geraldine is able to effect the link between childhood and maturity, innocence and experience, of particular concern to Coleridge—and to other Romantic poets as well. If Christabel and Geraldine represent the passive and active sides of Coleridge, then his failure to complete the narrative is yet another example of his inability to synthesize his personality—or to allow one side to win out at the expense of the other.

A few other poems from 1797 to 1798 deserve mention. "The Nightingale" (1798), although less interesting than the other titles in the group, conforms to the general structure of the conversation poems and so confirms its importance. "Fears in Solitude" (1798) is at once a conversation poem and something more. Like the others, it begins in a state of isolation and ends with social reintegration; its median state of self-assertion, however, takes the form of a public political statement. The voice of the statement is often strident, but this quality is understandable in a poem written at a time when invasion by France was daily rumored. "Fears in Solitude" attacks British militarism, British materialism, and British patriotism. Yet it is itself deeply patriotic. "There lives nor form nor feeling in my soul," Coleridge acknowledges, "Unborrowed from my country," and for this reason the poem is not a series of topical criticism but an expression of the dilemma of a poet divided between moral judgment of and personal identification with his native land.

"DEJECTION"

When Coleridge returned from Germany in the summer of 1799, his period of intense poetic creativity was over. The poems that he wrote in the remaining years of his life were written by a man who no longer thought of himself as a poet and who therefore treated poetry as a mode of expression rather than a calling. "Dejection: An Ode," which Coleridge dated April 4, 1802, offers a rationale for this change and seems to have been written as a formal farewell to the possibility of a career as a poet. The poem's epigraph from the *Ballad of Sir Patrick Spence* and its concern with perception link it with *The Rime of the Ancient Mariner*; its use of the image of the eolian harp links it with the poem by that name and, by extension, with the free-associational style of the conversation poems as a group. Its tone and manner are also close to those of the conversation poems, but its designation as an ode suggests an effort to elevate it to the level of formal statement. At the same time, its recurrent addresses to an unnamed "Lady" (Sara Hutchinson) suggest that the poem was primarily intended for a specific rather than a general audience, for a reader with a special interest in the poet who will not expect the poem to describe a universal human experience. Thus, the poem is at once closely related to Coleridge's earlier verse and significantly different from it.

In keeping with the conversation-poem structure, "Dejection" begins in a mood of solitary contemplation. The poet ponders the moon and "the dull sobbing draft that moans and rakes/ Upon the strings of this Aeolian lute." Together, they portend a storm in the offing, and Coleridge hopes that the violence of the "slant night shower" may startle him from his depression. His state, he explains, is not merely grief; it is "A stifled, drowsy, unimpassioned grief,/ Which finds no natural outlet, no relief,/ In word, or sign, or tear." All modes of emotional expression are blocked: He is able to "see" the beauty of the natural world, but he cannot "feel" it, and thereby use it as a symbol for his own inner state. He has lost the ability to invest the "outward forms" of nature with passion and life because, by his account, his inner source of passion and life has dried up. This ability he calls "Joy"—"the spirit and the power,/ Which wedding Na-

ture to us gives in dower/ A new Earth and new Heaven." The language of apocalypse identifies "Joy" with religious faith; the notion of language suggests a more general identification with the expressive mode of his earlier poetry and its ability to transform an ordinary situation into an especially meaningful event. To have no "outlet. . ./ In word" is to have lost the voice of that poetry; to make the observation within a poetic text is to suggest one more difference between "Dejection" and Coleridge's earlier poetry.

"Dejection" may seem like a restatement of the notion of a possible harmony—now lost—between nature and the human that was expressed in the earlier poetry. In fact, "Dejection" denies the grounds of the harmony advanced in the earlier poems. In "Frost at Midnight," for example, the "shapes and sounds" of the natural world are perceived as an "eternal language, which thy/ God utters." In "The Eolian Harp," man is conceptualized (tentatively) as only one of the media through which the eternal force expresses itself. "Dejection," in contrast, identifies the source of "Joy" in man himself. In feeling the beauty of nature, "we in ourselves rejoice." While the earlier poems toyed with pantheism, this focus on the state of mind of the individual soul is squarely orthodox, but the religious conservatism of "Dejection" does not in itself explain the termination of Coleridge's poetic career.

Coleridge himself attributes this termination to his own self-consciousness. As he explains in "Dejection," he had sought "by abstruse research to seal/ From my own nature all the natural man." This scientific analysis of the self got the better of him, however, and now his conscious mind is compelled to subject the whole of experience to its analytic scrutiny. Nothing now escapes the dominance of reason, and insofar as the power of Coleridge's greatest poetry lay in its capacity to dramatize or at least imagine a universe imbued with supernatural meaning, the power is lost. Theologically, this capacity can be associated with pantheism or the vaguely heterodox natural theology of the conversation poems; psychologically, its potency, derived from primal narcissism, is related to the animism given explicit form in the spirits who supervise the action in *The Rime of the Ancient Mariner*. The power of this poetry, it can be argued, lies in its ability to recapture a primitive human experience of the world.

The psychological awareness that Coleridge gained by his own self-analysis made this primitive naïveté impossible. "Dejection" is thus potentially a poem celebrating the maturity of the intellect—its recognition that its earlier powerful experience of nature, even when attributed to a Christian deity, was a matter of projection and therefore a function of his need to associate himself with an objective expression of his own potency. If the poem is not celebratory, it is because the consequences of this recognition amount to an admission of the importance of his individual self at odds with Coleridge's need for social acceptance. At the same time, it deprives him of that powerful confirmation of self derived from the illusionary sense of harmony with the animistic forces of the natural world. "Dejection" should have been a poem about Coleridge's internalization of these forces and triumphant recognition of his own strength of mind. Instead, he acknowledges the illusion of animism without being able to internalize the psychic energy invested in the animistic vision.

In disavowing belief in a transcendental power inherent in nature, Coleridge disavows the power of his own earlier poetry. "Dejection" lacks the ease and confidence of the conversation poems, and its structure is noticeably mechanical. The storm that ends "Dejection" replaces the voice of authority that defined their closure, but, despite being anticipated by the opening stanzas, it is a *deus ex machina* without organic connection with the poet. For reasons that the poem itself makes clear, it can effect no fundamental transformation of his being. Hence, it is simply unimportant, and to expect it to have greater effect is, in the words of "The Picture" (1802), to be a "Gentle Lunatic."

LATER POETRY

Having forgone "Gentle Lunacy," the best of Coleridge's later poetry speaks with an intense but entirely naturalistic sincerity. In poems such as "The Blossoming of the Solitary Date-Tree" (1805), "The Pains of Sleep" (1815), and "Work Without Hope" (1826), Coleridge makes no attempt to transform his poetic self into the vehicle for universal truth. He simply presents his feelings and thoughts to the reader. He complains about his condition, but there is no sense that the act of complaint, beyond getting something off his chest for the time being, can effect any significant alteration of the

self. Other poems lack even this concern for the limited audience whom he might have expected to be concerned with his personal problems. Poems such as "Limbo" (1817) and "Ne Plus Ultra" (1826?) are notebook exercises in conceiving the inconceivable—in this case, the states of minimal being, in which even the Kantian categories of space and time are reduced to uncertain conceptions, and absolute negation, "The one permitted opposite of God!" With other poems written for a similar private purpose, they are remarkable for the expressive power of their condensed imagery and their capacity to actualize philosophical thought. Coleridge's mastery of language never deserted him.

The greatness of the half dozen or so poems on which his reputation is based derives, however, from more than mastery of language. It derives from a confidence in the power of language that Coleridge, for legitimate reasons, came to doubt. Those half dozen or so poems assume that Coleridge is not a great poet, but that the grounding medium of poetry, like the "eternal language" of nature, is itself great. The very fact of his achievement in 1797 to 1798 presented to him the possibility that it was Coleridge and not poetry in which greatness lay; and, given that possibility, Coleridge could no longer conceive of himself as a poet. He would continue to write, but in media in which it was the thought behind the prose, and not the thinker, that gave meaning to language.

OTHER MAJOR WORKS

PLAYS: *The Fall of Robespierre*, pb. 1794 (with Robert Southey); *Remorse*, pr., pb. 1813 (originally *Osorio*); *Zapolya*, pb. 1817.

NONFICTION: *The Watchman*, 1796; *The Friend*, 1809-1810, 1818; "The Statesman's Manual," 1816; "A Lay Sermon," 1817; *Biographia Literaria*, 1817; "Treatise on Method," 1818; *Aids to Reflection*, 1825; *On the Constitution of the Church and State, According to the Idea of Each: With Aids Toward a Right Judgment on the Late Catholic Bill*, 1830; *Specimens of the Table Talk of the Late Samuel Taylor Coleridge*, 1835; *Letters, Conversations, and Recollections of S. T. Coleridge*, 1836; *Letters of Samuel Taylor Coleridge*, 1855 (2 volumes; E. H. Coleridge, editor); *Coleridge's Shakespearean Criticism*, 1930;

Coleridge's Miscellaneous Criticism, 1936; *Notebooks*, 1957-1986 (4 volumes).

TRANSLATION: *Wallenstein*, 1800 (of Friedrich Schiller's plays *Die Piccolomini* and *Wallensteins Tod*).

MISCELLANEOUS: *The Collected Works of Samuel Taylor Coleridge*, 1969-2001 (Kathleen Coburn et al., editors).

BIBLIOGRAPHY

Alexander, Caroline. *The Way to Xanadu*. New York: Knopf, 1994. The author relates her travels to the places that inspired Coleridge's "Kubla Khan" and describes the texts that inspired Coleridge.

Ashton, Rosemary. *The Life of Samuel Taylor Coleridge: A Critical Biography*. Cambridge, Mass.: Blackwell, 1996. Examines Coleridge's complex personality, from poet, critic, and thinker to feckless husband and guilt-ridden opium addict. Coleridge's life is placed within the context of both British and German Romanticism.

Barfield, Owen. *What Coleridge Thought*. Middletown, Conn.: Wesleyan University Press, 1971. One of the most lucid expositions of Coleridge's philosophical thought, which is explained in its own terms rather than in its connections with other systems of thought. Emphasizes Coleridge's concept of "Polar Logic" and fully discusses such Coleridgean topics as fancy and imagination, understanding and reason. Assumes that Coleridge's later philosophy was implicit in the earlier, an assumption that has been questioned by other Coleridge scholars.

Bate, Walter Jackson. *Samuel Taylor Coleridge*. New York: Macmillan, 1968. An excellent, concise critical biography. Examines all aspects of Coleridge's life and career with fairness and insight. Provides influential readings of the major poems, especially *The Rime of the Ancient Mariner*, "Christabel," and "Kubla Khan." Discusses Coleridge's projected magnum opus, his literary theories and criticism, and his religious thought.

Beer, J. B. *Coleridge the Visionary*. London: Chatto & Windus, 1959. Delves into Coleridge's reading in such diverse sources as George Berkeley, Jacob Boehme, Neoplatonism, Egyptian and Indian my-

thology, and contemporary science, in order to illuminate the ideas which inform the poetry, particularly *The Rime of the Ancient Mariner*, "Christabel," and "Kubla Khan." Provides fine insight into the range and depth of Coleridge as he attempted to understand the links between human society and the spiritual and physical laws of the universe.

Coburn, Kathleen, ed. *Coleridge: A Collection of Critical Essays*. Englewood Cliffs, N.J.: Prentice-Hall, 1967. Fourteen essays on all aspects of Coleridge's work. The overview of Coleridge's life and work by I. A. Richards is a good place for the beginner to start. Also important are Edward E. Bostetter's seminal essay "The Nightmare World of the Ancient Mariner" and A. Gérard's "The Systolic Rhythm: The Structure of Coleridge's Conversation Poems," both of which make excellent starting points for further study.

Holmes, Richard. *Coleridge: Early Visions*. New York: Viking Press, 1990. The first volume of a two-volume biography. Covers Coleridge's life up to his departure for Malta in 1804. This splendid book is virtually everything a biography should be: well researched, lively, full of insight, and sympathetic to its subject without ignoring other points of view. Fully captures Coleridge's brilliant, flawed, fascinating personality.

Prickett, Stephen. *Coleridge and Wordsworth: The Poetry of Growth*. New York: Cambridge University Press, 1970. The poetry of Coleridge and Wordsworth will always be linked together, and this is one of many books that discuss the relationship between the two poets. Unlike a number of scholars who have emphasized the ultimately destructive nature of the relationship, Prickett focuses on the benefits both men derived from the lively interplay of sometimes conflicting ideas. Prickett discusses in particular the poets' ideas of perception and creativity, and how these ideas combined to form a "model of growth."

Yarlott, Geoffrey. *Coleridge and the Abyssinian Maid*. London: Methuen, 1967. Analyzes the reasons for Coleridge's failure as a poet after 1802 and argues that Coleridge changed his views on poetry as a result of his failure. Some of this is on the psychology of the man, particularly his emotional insecurity, but Yarlott avoids the excesses of some psychoanalytic critics and does not allow his thesis to distort his critical judgment. Excellent readings of all the major poems.

Frederick Kirchhoff;
bibliography updated by the editors

MICHAEL COLLIER

Born: Phoenix, Arizona; May 25, 1953

PRINCIPAL POETRY

The Clasp and Other Poems, 1986
The Folded Heart, 1989
The Neighbor, 1995
The Ledge, 2000

OTHER LITERARY FORMS

Michael Collier has edited a number of anthologies, including *The Wesleyan Tradition: Four Decades of American Poetry* (1993), *The New Bread Loaf Anthology of Contemporary American Poetry* (1999; coedited with Stanley Plumly), and *The New American Poets: A Bread Loaf Anthology* (2000).

ACHIEVEMENTS

Michael Collier was awarded two National Endowment for the Arts Fellowships (1984 and 1994) as well as a Guggenheim Fellowship. On the strength of his first volume of poetry, Collier received the Alice Day Di Castagnola Award from the Poetry Society of America. His landmark collection, 2000's *The Ledge*, was nominated for the National Book Critics Circle Award. In 2001, he was named poet laureate of the state of Maryland.

BIOGRAPHY

Michael Collier grew up during the boom years of post-World War II prosperity in a comfortable upper-middle-class Catholic family, the son of a homemaker and a military pilot who became a salesman. Collier at-tended a parochial school in Arizona and a Jesuit high school. After graduating from Connecticut College in 1976, where he had studied under the poet William Meredith, Collier received his master's degree from the University of Arizona in 1979.

During his education, Collier held a number of odd jobs, including house painting and plumbing, that contributed both to his compassion for ordinary people and to his fascination with technology, specifically the intricate systems of everyday machines. For two years following graduation, he lived in London and traveled to exotic lands. He experienced strikingly different cultures, visiting Africa, Japan, even Siberia.

After returning to the United States, Collier moved to the East Coast in the early 1980's to serve as the director of poetry programs for the Folger Shakespeare Library in Washington, D.C., before joining the English department of the University of Maryland, College Park, in 1984. He became that institution's director of creative writing. He began publishing poetry in the mid-1980's and met with immediate critical praise for a distinctive verse style recognized for its maturity, exquisite music, and graceful subtleties. While at Maryland, he accepted a number of visiting professorships at universities, including The Johns Hopkins and Yale Universities. He has also served since 1992 on the faculty of the creative writing program at Warren Wilson College in North Carolina.

In 1992 Collier began his association with the prestigious Bread Loaf Writers' Conference and was named its sixth director in 1995, a post previously held by, among others, Robert Frost and John Ciardi. As editor of three critically lauded anthologies of contemporary American poetry, Collier has established himself as an important critical voice. He married Kathleen Branch, a librarian, in 1981, and together they had two sons.

ANALYSIS

To read Michael Collier is to confront a series of contradictions. Although he was part of the generation that came of age during a decade of intense social and political activism, a generation caught up in the agenda of civil rights, women's rights, and the peace movement, Collier's poetry speaks of a fascination with the domestic landscape of his own childhood. His vision recalls

Edwin Arlington Robinson's compassionate portraits of the misfits and eccentrics of Tilbury Town.

Although he has worked as an activist on issues ranging from local education reform to environmentalism, Collier writes verse that seldom touches such hot-button contemporary questions but is rather focused on the unsuspected dramas that occur next door and down the street. More interesting, despite his academic background, Collier writes verse that is accessible, gently musical, and inviting. Reassuringly immediate, such verse exploits the natural inflections and collisions of sound that occur in colloquial English. Collier finds such unadorned language sufficiently musical to sustain the rich tones of verse. More notable, his verse forsakes the expected academic posturings of ironic distancing and cynicism; Collier's vision is at once compassionate and humane, exhibiting a depth of emotion for his characters, who exist along the margins of the ordinary.

Collier is clearly fascinated by things, by gizmos and machines, by the sheer mechanical complex of the contemporary world: "I'm a consumer," he has said. "I like things. I'm fascinated by the mechanical world." Collier is ultimately, however, tuned to the subtler interior worlds of those who come in contact with such machines—their vulnerabilities and eccentricities amid the overwhelmingly technical culture of the modern world.

THE CLASP AND OTHER POEMS

The opening poem of this collection, "Ancestors," sets Collier's agenda: He admits that he descends from village dentists, and the poem captures those long-ago, often difficult surgical excavations into the "fleshy rose/ pulsing in the root like the heart's/ faintest hint." By comparing the rotted tooth to the heart, Collier offers the image of the clumsy dentist's painful surgeries as fitting metaphor for the work of the poet, necessarily rooting out the painful experiences of the heart, explorations that may seem barbaric but are essentially therapeutic. Despite being barely in his thirties at the time of this collection's writing, Collier clearly felt the gravitational pull of time, the uneasy responsibility of memory, and the heavy intrusion of recollection.

These poems exist simultaneously in two tenses, crossed by the shadows and dreams where the forgotten and the neglected persist: "I don't believe that what we lose/ is lost forever." Collier draws on those occasions when the difficult past unexpectedly resurfaces: rummaging among old photographs, conducting otherwise innocuous conversations, being suspended delicately between sleep and wakefulness, ministering to an ailing loved one.

In the poignant poem "Eyepiece," Collier struggles to glimpse the moon through a neighbor's telescope, only to find his view unexpectedly blocked when the scope snaps shut. Such denial of a fuller view unexpectedly compels him to remember his college roommate's suicide and to concede how, eventually, everyone will similarly, suddenly, inexplicably disappear. Despite the heavy pressure of the past, the persistence of memory is revealed without sentimentality or melodramatic anxiety. Musically, the poems are executed with languid sounds, with rich, long vowels and rolling consonants in a meticulous orchestration of stresses and syllables that effect a quiet, hushed reading appropriate to verse that exists on the border between past and present.

THE FOLDED HEART

Collier's second collection reinforces the premise of his first: There is no larger perspective than that of the personal past. As the title suggests, here is the gift of Collier's heart, investigations into his past that are neatly, precisely fashioned (folded) within the lines of polished verse. Gathered here are recollections drawn from Collier's childhood and adolescence, narratives of his family and his Arizona neighbors, episodes that are cast in verse not to indulge nostalgia or inflate ego but rather to explore the dimensions of each experience.

Few poems are written in the present tense, although, "Tonight" is a beautiful exception, in which the poet considers the view outside his office window. The mood of the rest of this collection is consistently retrospective and somber. Careful detailing makes vivid a past that Collier, distanced in time from the events, finds nevertheless pressing and immediate. The sound of the poems is appropriately gentle, a weave of soft and rolling sounds that quietly create rhythms through the light beat of syllables, one stanza frequently flowing uninterrupted into the next without the harsh intrusion of punctuation.

As though following William Carlos Williams's dictum "no ideas but in things," Collier is able to fashion a symbolic landscape without heavy-handedness. For instance, in "Lagoon" he recounts a boyhood episode when he stole onto a closed golf course to steal lost balls and was chased by a guard dog, whose pursuit was ultimately curtailed by the course fence. What does the dog symbolize? Under Collier's manipulation, the dog becomes a multilayered symbol that suggests more than it means: It may represent lost youth, the thwarted hand of authority, the uselessness of rules for a boy, the shattering intrusion of the dangers of the adult world, or, perhaps, the sheer thrill of disobedience. Thus Collier ranges over his adolescence—recollections of performing in a third-grade theater production, purchasing a pigeon from a crafty neighbor, playing air guitar, skimming a dead bat out of a neighbor's pool, waiting anxiously at the age of five for an operation to remove his appendix, eagerly anticipating his father's return from sales trips—and reclaims them, revealing how pedestrian experience, under the appropriately sensitive observation, can be coaxed into the symbolic.

In the closing poem, "The Cave," Collier audaciously refashions the living room, where his family would watch home movies of his sister's competitive diving performance, into Plato's allegorical cave. The suburban tableau thus becomes a potent symbol suggesting the timeless struggle to wish into existence the unreachable perfect.

THE NEIGHBOR

As the title suggests, Collier moves outward in his third collection, out of the confines of his own experience to re-create empathetically the shattered interior lives of those who live about him. With compassion, Collier selects those whose quiet lives belie their emotional pain: a neighbor determined to hoist, unaided, his boat onto its hitch, a door-to-door tree trimmer saddled with a hanging goiter, an Indian neighbor versed in spirituality but unable to manipulate his power mower, a boyhood friend so unsettled by the prospects of spending the night that his mother must rescue him, a neighborhood priest in a dunking booth at a parish festival, a classroom of children ducking under desks during a safety drill, the schoolyard terrorism casually visited on a helpless fat boy.

These are characters trapped in their own lives, haunted by a higher sense, an awareness of some sort of spirituality, sensitive innocents mired in the brutal realities of a world that will not affirm a higher plane. They are victims of forces they cannot even identify. Without heavy authorial intrusion to manipulate the reader's response to these characters, Collier relies on telling details to reveal the characters' interior devastations.

In "The Magician," for instance, Collier creates the portrait of suburban ennui by focusing on a neighbor who, when he walks his dogs, does simple (if mesmerizing) magic tricks for a swarm of enthralled neighborhood children until, the walk finished, he returns to his decidedly unmagical suburban home, unchains his dogs, and quietly empties his pockets of "the tiny vehicles of magic."

Other poems are far darker. In "The Rancher" a father, a sheep rancher, meets for the first time a boy who comes to his house to pick up his daughter for a date. The father's curious fascination with the sex life of his daughter (after her dates, he "lifts her dress or puts/ his hand in her Levis") reveals a disquieting, even perverted psychology. Before the two depart, the father shows the young man his collection of frozen castrated sheep testes and intones darkly, "She'll do to you/ what I did to sheep to get these." Then, as he shuts the freezer door, the father whispers to the stunned young man that he would be glad to listen to details about what sex with his daughter is like. His, the reader understands with shattering immediacy, is a heart without love that has long ago reduced people to meat.

In "2212 West Flower Street" Collier writes of how, after a neighbor had killed his wife and committed suicide, the shocked neighborhood struggled to restore the dead man's humanity. This is precisely Collier's achievement: the humane gesture of making even his most aberrant characters accessible and human. The poet never intrudes on the revelation of these characters; quietly, carefully, he acts as a witness to their suffering. Collier's compassionate interest in such characters emerges in lines that are elegant and subtly rhythmic, giving music and dignity to such haunted souls.

THE LEDGE

If *The Neighbor* explores the residents of a physical geography, a matrix of homes and streets, backyards and bedrooms, *The Ledge* signals that in his mid-forties, Collier is prepared to explore that most daunting of artistic terrain, the interior of the heart. In this effort, Collier is drawn to reassuring extremes (lost and found, youth and maturity, known and unknown, sacred and profane, familiar and exotic, clear and shadowy) and to those epiphanic moments when such absolutes are revealed to be inoperative, those moments when the familiar becomes suddenly strange, the near-at-hand becomes irretrievably lost, and the everyday becomes mysterious, even unknowable.

Here, surfaces deceive and conceal. In "Safe" a man squirrels away mementos from his emotional savagings in a quarried-out book. Bosco, a neighborhood dog in "A Real-Life Drama," stands in the street with a mangled rabbit bleeding beneath his paws, a pet "taken over by the dark corner of his nature." In another, Halloween guests wearing masks reveal interior psychologies as they stand mesmerized by a raccoon casually terrorizing their outdoor picnic spread. A boy at swimming lessons, who has only to pass alone through a locker room, is overwhelmed by the experience and sends up a terrified scream, "frightened/ of the ordinary world." Bored in a hotel, Collier struggles to watch the "erotic chaos" of the scrambled signal of an adult pay-per-view channel, the familiar sexual routine becoming suddenly mesmerizing, tantalizing. The calm of a country club is shattered, literally, when a man accidentally walks through a closed sliding-glass door.

In "My Crucifixion" Collier recalls, when in the charge of a baby-sitter, reenacting the crucifixion with his sisters and finding himself oddly aroused as they gleefully "hammer" his hands and feet. A man swimming in a pool appears to be some sort of grotesque, finned, aquatic monstrosity. Again and again, the familiar becomes disquietingly strange—a moment of bleacher camaraderie, the familiar stadium wave, reveals uncertain anxieties over the hopelessness of such forced cheering. In the haunting "The Dolphin," Collier compares tracking the fin lines of a coursing dolphin to understanding the intricate turns of a ten-year marriage.

Familiarity cannot sustain understanding. It is the sort of world revealed by the deep dive in "Fathom and League," in which the poet is stunned by the intricate, roiling underworld of volcanoes beneath the placid calm of the ocean surface. Amid such uncertainties, Collier offers as strategy the position of a "brave sparrow" perched on the thinnest of ledges, poised, ever vigilant, amid the inexplicable terrors of the apparently ordinary: neighborhood cats, starlings, owls, blue jays. As

Collier ironically reveals the mysterious in the familiar, his style is appropriately unadorned and direct. He delivers his epiphanic moments in a colloquial narrative voice, without emotional exclamations, allowing the disconcerting revelations themselves to unsettle the reader.

In the closing poem, "Pax Geologica," Collier dreams of the ocean's bottom scattered with the detritus of his own home, a mingling of the exotic and the familiar which is a fitting emblem for his poetic achievement.

OTHER MAJOR WORKS

EDITED TEXTS: *The Wesleyan Tradition: Four Decades of American Poetry*, 1993; *The New Bread Loaf Anthology of Contemporary American Poetry*, 1999 (coedited with Stanley Plumly); *The New American Poets: A Bread Loaf Anthology*, 2000.

BIBLIOGRAPHY

Henry, Brian. Review of *The Ledge*. *The New York Times Book Review*, April 20, 2000, p. 21. Sensitive, if brief, overview of Collier's emerging poetic legacy and themes.

Longenbach, James. "Poetry in Review." *Yale Review* 83 (October, 1995): 144-147. Places Collier within a school of contemporary academic poets.

Reel, Monte. "Everyday Life, Uncommon Passion: Poet Laureate Offers New View." *The Washington Post*, March 25, 2001, p. C5. Discusses Collier's intention to become an ambassador for poetry throughout the state of Maryland.

Joseph Dewey

BILLY COLLINS

Born: New York, New York; March 22, 1941

PRINCIPAL POETRY
Pokerface, 1977
The Apple That Astonished Paris, 1988
Questions About Angels, 1991
The Art of Drowning, 1995
Picnic, Lightning, 1998

Taking off Emily Dickinson's Clothes, 2000
Sailing Alone Around the Room: New and Selected Poems, 2001

OTHER LITERARY FORMS

Billy Collins has confined his work in print mostly to poetry; however, he has been quick to embrace other means of communicating his work. *Video Poems* (1980) is a video of Collins reading some print-published works. *The Best Cigarette* (1993) is a compact disc reading. Collins has also published online in *The Cortland Review*, an electronic literary magazine that has published a number of well-known American writers. In 2001 he published the nonfiction work *The Eye of the Poet: Six Views of the Art and Craft of Poetry*.

ACHIEVEMENTS

Billy Collins has been called arguably "the most popular poet in America," not only for his accessible and often humorous work in print but also for his appearances on National Public Radio (on both *Prairie Home Companion* and *Fresh Air* in 1997), during which he read and talked about his work with engaging charm. Collins has received poetry fellowships from the New York Foundation for the Arts, the National Endowment for the Arts, and the Guggenheim Foundation. He has received the Bess Hokin Award, the Oscar Blumenthal Award, the Frederick Bock Prize, and the Levinson Prize from *Poetry* magazine; he has been named Literary Lion by the New York Public Library, and *Questions About Angels* won the National Poetry Series competition for 1991. In 2001, Collins was named U.S. poet laureate.

BIOGRAPHY

Billy Collins was born on March 22, 1941, in New York, New York, the son of William and Katherine Collins, an electrician and a nurse, respectively. He attended parochial schools and received a B.A. degree from College of the Holy Cross in 1963 and a Ph.D. from the University of California, Riverside, in 1971. His primary study was the Romantic poets. His career has been mainly academic; he began teaching at Lehman College of the City University of New York in 1971 as a professor of English. He married and settled in Westchester County with his wife, Diane.

Billy Collins (Courtesy of Random House)

Despite the domestic setting of much of his poetry, Collins's writing reveals little of his private life except perhaps his love of jazz. In 1999, however, his career received considerable publicity because of a publishers' conflict which delayed the publication of his new and selected poems. The volume had been scheduled for publication by Random House but was blocked when Collins's previous publisher, the University of Pittsburgh Press, refused to allow Random House to reprint some of Collins's earlier poems, ostensibly because the university press still found them profitable. The conflict was covered in *The New York Times* and the on-line magazine *Salon*, leading Collins to say that he would like to forget about the mechanics of publishing and "get back to writing poems." As writing, originally a sidelight to his academic career, has become increasingly important to Collins, he has developed a lively schedule of readings and workshops, several of the latter in Ireland.

ANALYSIS

Poet Stephen Dunn, in a review of *Picnic, Lightning*, wrote, "We seem always to know where we are in a Billy Collins poem, but not necessarily where he is going." Collins himself has expressed his distaste for poetry in general, which sometimes seems to have been written in code, accessible only to the cognoscenti. Such poems, he implies in the poem "Introduction to Poetry," create readers who believe that the only way to approach a poem is to "tie the poem to a chair with rope/ and torture a confession out of it," while the writer longs for readers who can "waterski/ across the surface of a poem/ waving at the author's name on the shore." That suggests why his subjects tend to be drawn from the ordinary, the events of everyone's life—driving, shoveling snow, eating dinner or breakfast. It also suggests why he so often uses humor to lead the reader into the place, often a serious and surprising place, of the poem's conclusion. Collins's humor and accessibility go a long way in accounting for his enormous popularity as a contemporary poet.

A reviewer for *Questions About Angels* said that Collins's technique produces poems that evoke no emotional response from the reader, but many readers would disagree. John Taylor, reviewing *Picnic, Lightning* for *Poetry* magazine, argued that melancholy lies just below the surface in Collins's work; indeed, his humor often seems simply a means, an invitation to serious reflection. These qualities of accessibility, humor, and regard for the everyday are present in all Collins's work from the earliest to the latest, but certainly *The Art of Drowning* and *Picnic, Lightning* seem to mark a movement into poems of greater reflection, a reduction in the number of poems of pure playfulness that marked earlier volumes.

THE APPLE THAT ASTONISHED PARIS

In *The Apple That Astonished Paris*, the poems establish a list of typical Collins subjects and his approaches to them: History is represented here, along with travel, writing, books, and some examples of playful imagination. In "Flames," for example, Collins imagines Smokey the Bear, discouraged and angry at the perennial failure of his campaign against forest fires: "He is sick of dispensing/ warnings to the careless,/ the half-wit camper,/ the dumbbell hiker." Looking oddly threatening, Smokey sets out with gasoline and matches. The poem concludes, "He is going to show them/ how a professional does it."

Collins often uses an abstract title which he subsequently explores in a variety of concrete images. In "Books," for example, the abstract title leads, in the first stanza, to a picture of an academic library at night, empty of patrons but humming with the voices of its authors resting on their dark shelves. The second stanza pictures a man in the act of reading; he is "a man in two worlds"—the physical world he lives in as well as the book's world of imagination. The third stanza recalls the narrator's mother, reading to him in a voice that offered him the same duality. The mother's voice was both her own and at the same time the vehicle of the frightening events of the story. The narrator finally imagines "all of us reading ourselves away from ourselves." The words become like "a trail of crumbs," the trail which the reader follows into the forest of the book.

"Death" is constructed similarly. From its abstract title, Collins moves swiftly to imagining how the news of a death in the family traveled in the past and then describes the telephone as the modern means of delivering bad news. Telephones are everywhere; the reader can almost hear one ringing—"ready to summon you, ready to fall from your hand."

Many of the poems in the volume are shorter than in Collins's later work, but they foreshadow many of his later themes and subjects—visits to Tuscany and Ireland; the imaginative creation of a town called "Schoolsville," peopled by all the students the speaker has ever taught; a miniature world history, an organization that Collins uses often, in "Personal History," where the speaker courts his love from the Middle Ages through the Industrial Revolution only to end up in this postmodern age, driving with her to the movies in a Volkswagen.

QUESTIONS ABOUT ANGELS

Questions About Angels seems to move to a level beyond that of *The Apple That Astonished Paris* while still using themes and subjects familiar to Collins's readers. The writer's voice, too, continues in its range of irony, meditation, and amusement. In this volume, however, the humor often leads to a more sharply serious conclusion. "Forgetfulness," for example, seems at first to be a humorous consideration of what happens to one's memory in middle age:

The name of the author is the first to go
followed obediently by the title, the plot,

the heartbreaking conclusion, the entire novel
which suddenly becomes one you have never read, never
    even heard of. . . .

Collins goes on to catalog other things one might forget—the names of the Muses, the order of the planets,
the address of a relative. They are so completely lost that
it is as if they have retired to a remote fishing village
"where there are no phones." The list and its attendant
images are funny, but the poem concludes on a suddenly
melancholy note: "No wonder the moon in the window
seems to have drifted/ out of a love poem that you used
to know by heart."

"First Reader" offers a similar experience, beginning
comically with a picture of Dick and Jane, characters
from the popular series of elementary school readers in
the 1940's and 1950's. Collins calls them "the boy and
girl who begin fiction," for that is how they functioned
for children learning to read. Collins quotes a line of frequent dialogue from those school texts. "Look!" Dick
and Jane constantly command each other, "pointing at
the dog, the bicycle, or at their father." At the end, Collins puns on the word "look"; even as children, with our
growing literacy "we were forgetting how to look, learning how to read."

The title poem of this volume exemplifies a quality
Collins admires in poems—the ending that leads the
reader in a direction that was not forecast by the opening.
Collins has said that too often writers overplan their poems, leaving no room for imagination to begin work during
the process of composition. "Questions About Angels"
opens with the old question from medieval theology:
"How many angels can dance on the head of a pin?"
Collins labels that the only question which is ever asked
about angels and offers other possibilities, questions
about how angels spend their time, what their clothes are
made of, particulars about their flight. Then the poem
returns to the pinhead and suggests that the answer is
that only one angel can dance there, an angel which Collins pictures as a jazz singer in a nightclub, one of Collins's favorite subjects, where she is dancing forever.

The Art of Drowning

The Art of Drowning introduces a slight shift in Collins's style—a movement to longer poems and a narrow-
ing of subject matter. Several poems here rise from Col-

lins's interest in jazz, notably "Sunday Morning with the
Sensational Nightingales" and "Exploring the Coast of
Birdland." In "Nightclub" Collins playfully works
changes on the common musical idea that "you are so
beautiful and I am a fool/ to be in love with you." No
one, he says, ever sings "you are a fool to be in love with
me." The poem concludes with the narrator performing
a fantasy bebop solo which asserts "We are all so fool-
ish/ . . ./ so damn foolish/ we have become beautiful
without even knowing it."

This volume also establishes firmly Collins's sense
of the beauty of the mundane, his nearly sacramental
reverence for the ordinary delights of a good meal
("Osso Buco") or the sight of a student writing an exam
("Monday Morning," with its allusions to Wallace
Stevens's poem "Sunday Morning"). These events make
him "feel like the secretary to the morning," in "Tues-
day, June 4, 1991," whose task is to chronicle the
weather, his coffee, the arrival of the house painters, and
the antics of the new kitten, and in doing so he seems to
drench them in an almost holy light.

Picnic, Lightning

Picnic, Lightning continues with tones and subjects
of *The Art of Drowning*. Again, Collins writes about the
beauties of the day ("Shoveling Snow with Buddha,"
"Morning," "In the Room of a Thousand Miles") and
jazz ("I Chop Some Parsley While Listening to Art
Blakey's Version of 'Three Blind Mice'"). What seems
new in this volume is the number of poems that make
specific reference to other literary works. As a literature
teacher, Collins naturally refers to others' writings in all
his collections, but in *Picnic, Lightning* the reader finds
Samuel Taylor Coleridge's "The Nightingale" in Collins's "Moon," W. H. Auden's "Musée des Beaux Arts"
in "Musée des Beaux Arts Revisited," and a whole array
of writers in "Marginalia," to name a few examples.
"Paradelle for Susan" makes another literary reference
as Collins creates a new verse form, a loopy combination of villanelle, pantoum, and sestina, to form a gentle
spoof of a type of poem often produced in workshops (a
subject he satirized more directly in the previous volume). "Paradelle" is accompanied by a mock-serious
footnote outlining the form's complex requirements.
Overall, *Picnic, Lightning* feels very much like a second
part of the *Art of Drowning*.

OTHER MAJOR WORKS

NONFICTION: *The Eye of the Poet: Six Views of the Art and Craft of Poetry*, 2001.

BIBLIOGRAPHY

Allen, Dick. Review of *The Apple That Astonished Paris*, by Billy Collins. *Hudson Review* 42, no. 2 (Summer, 1989): 321. Allen praises Collins for his accessibility, noting his "friendly lines" and calling the volume an "irrepressible delight."

Laird, Nick. "Not So Mean Streets." *Times Literary Supplement* 8 (September, 2000): 29. Laird's review of *Taking Off Emily Dickinson's Clothes* notes that it is Collins's first publication outside the United States. It is composed of selections from four earlier volumes. Laird praises Collins's writing in a "Whitmanesque tradition of celebrating America and its language."

Lehman, David. "A Poetry-Free Presidency." *Salon* 19 (January, 2001). http://www.salon.com/books/feature/2001/01/19/lehman. David Lehman, the founder of the *Best American Poetry* series, considers the significance of presidents choosing poets to read at their inaugurations. Collins wonders whether it is appropriate for poets to speak for the political establishment.

Taylor, John. Review of *Picnic, Lightning*. *Poetry* 175, no. 4 (February, 2000): 273. In this review article of *Picnic, Lightning*, Taylor gives a serious discussion of this book and of *The Art of Drowning*. He describes the qualities that create Collins's "soft metaphysical touch" and the consolations his poems offer.

Weber, Bruce. "On Literary Bridge, Poet Hits a Roadblock." *The New York Times* 19 (December, 1999): 1. Weber gives an account of the contest between Random House and University of Pittsburgh Press over the reprint rights to Collins's poems. The article also contains some biographical information and an account of Collins's readings. The article was answered by Dennis Loy Johnson in "Billy and the Bullies" in the June 2, 2000, issue of the on-line magazine *Salon* (http://www.salon.com/books/feature/2000/06/02/bullies), in which Johnson focuses on the economics of publishing poetry.

Ann D. Garbett

WILLIAM COLLINS

Born: Chichester, England; December 25, 1721
Died: Chichester, England; June 12, 1759

PRINCIPAL POETRY

Persian Eclogues, 1742

An Epistle: Verses Humbly Address'd to Sir Thomas Hanmer on His Edition of Shakespeare's Works, 1744

Odes on Several Descriptive and Allegoric Subjects, 1746 (dated 1747)

An Ode on the Popular Superstitions of the Highlands of Scotland, Considered as the Subject of Poetry, 1788 (written in 1749)

OTHER LITERARY FORMS

The form of William Collins's literary accomplishments was limited to poetry.

ACHIEVEMENTS

William Collins's achievements in poetry do not embody the results of careful observation of life, his best poems being descriptive and allegorical. His feelings were intense when he contemplated abstractions such as simplicity, an aesthetic ideal to which his ode gives subtle definition by means of description. His ability to think about abstractions and intellectual concepts in pictorial terms was Collins's most remarkable gift. A second gift was his ability to link every part of his poem to the next, so that the poem flows along in an unbroken stream.

His best work was done in the ode. Of the twelve such pieces published under the title *Odes on Several Descriptive and Allegoric Subjects* in 1746, three stand out for special effects. The "Ode on the Poetical Character" roughly approximates the true Pindaric ode, and, unlike Augustan forms, shows the poet to be an inspired creator and projects imagination as the prime essential of a true poet. "The Passions, an Ode for Music" is a pseudo-Pindaric ode in the tradition of John Dryden's "Alexander's Feast." Its richness of image and appropriate variety of movement have made it the poet's most popular piece. *An Ode on the Popular Superstitions of the Highlands of Scotland, Considered as the Subject of Poetry* is Collins's longest poem, containing his invention of the seventeen-line stanza of iambic pentameter ending with an Alexandrine. It was also the first significant attempt in English literature to concentrate on the Romantic elements of Scottish legend and landscape.

Collins's themes are significant because they anticipate the interests of the early nineteenth century Romantic poets and thus the broad concerns found in modern poetry. Five themes are noteworthy. First, Collins is concerned with the role of imagination in poetry. He believes that imagination rather than reason, an Augustan concern, is the essential trait of the poet. Second, he is a critic of literature, one whose commentary is conditioned by his concern for the imagination. Third, Collins shows a strong interest in folklore and its relation to literature, anticipating Samuel Taylor Coleridge and William Wordsworth. Fourth, he often emphasizes patriotic and political themes, themes which promote ideas of freedom, liberty and justice, all special concerns of the early Romantic writers. Finally, Collins continually expresses concern for psychological issues in his poetry. All these themes are tied directly to the problem of imagination.

BIOGRAPHY

William Collins was born at Chichester in Sussex in December, 1721. His early years seem to have been those of a favored child. Whether Collins attended a school or learned his first letters at home or under the tutelage of a local curate, he was well enough prepared by the time he was eleven to be admitted as a scholar to Winchester College. His years at Winchester were important. It was there that he made friendships with Joseph Warton, William Whitehead, and James Hampton, and studied mythology and legend in Homer and Vergil. He both wrote and published his first poems while at Winchester.

Some scholars believe that it was Warton's friendship and influence that led Collins to become interested in literature. The Warton family was thoroughly literary, and it is possible that Joseph's example first persuaded the youth from his Chichester home and encouraged him to begin cultivating his literary interests. In any case, Collins's literary powers developed while he was at Winchester. One of the poems which he wrote during these years, "Sonnet," was published in the *Gentlemen's Magazine* in October, 1739.

After completing his studies at Winchester, Collins was admitted to Queen's College, Oxford, on March 21, 1740. On July 29, 1741, he was appointed demy of Magdalen College, allowing him some stipend, and in 1743 he took the bachelor's degree and left Oxford. Before leaving college, he had published his *Persian Eclogues* and, although the work was published anonymously, the publication was Collins's first serious claim to public notice and ironically remained his chief popular accomplishment during his lifetime. While at Oxford, Collins also published *An Epistle*, which, like *Persian Eclogues*, was well received. The book went into a second edition in 1744, which in itself might have been the inspiration that caused Collins to leave for London to try his hand at the literary life. He moved to the city for a brief period, but eventually settled in Richmond where he worked for a time and established new friendships, in particular one with James Thomson.

When Bonnie Prince Charles landed in Scotland in 1745 and sounds of war spread, Collins turned to writing patriotic verse. During the early part of 1746, Collins was working on his odes. Perhaps they had been in progress for some time; in any event, scholars are quite sure that by the summer of 1746 they were nearing the form in which they now exist. It may have been at this time that Collins traveled to the Guildford races, where he met Joseph Warton. In time they mutually decided to publish their poems. The publication of his *Odes on Several Descriptive and Allegorial Subjects* in 1746 was the high-water mark of Collins's life, even though he probably did not realize it at the time, primarily because the public took very little note of them. Scholars do not know what his reaction to this relative failure may have been, but they do know that he was engaged in various literary projects in 1747 and that he remained active in literary circles. The depressing malady to which Thomas Warton refers in one of his letters did not begin to afflict Collins until 1750 at the earliest.

Collins began disposing of his share of the family property in Chichester in 1749 and when he made his last trip there in October for final legalities he met John Home, beginning another fertile creative period in his life. By 1750 there were announcements that a new translation by Mr. William Collins of Torquato Tasso's *Jerusalem Delivered* (1575) would appear. Although no copy seems to exist, there is every reason to believe that Collins did translate the poem. After meeting Home, Collins also went on to write the famous ode on the superstitions of Scotland.

It must have been about the end of 1750 or in 1751 that Collins's illness began. Eventually he was committed to an insane asylum. Warton mentions that at Easter, 1751, Collins was "given over and supposed to be dying." Samuel Johnson's account is probably substantially accurate—except that he has him dying in 1756 rather than in 1759. No one since the eighteenth century has added to the knowledge of the last period of Collins's life.

ANALYSIS

Although the heroic couplet had achieved its dominance by the time of William Collins, lyric poetry was still alive, albeit somewhat in reserve as a popular mode of expression. The lyric poet of the second quarter of the eighteenth century had available a number of traditional forms: the Pindaric ode for exalted subjects, the Horatian ode for a variety of urban and meditative themes, the elegy, and the song. A new type appeared, another type of "ode" which centered around a personified abstraction treated in a descriptive way. Borrowing from John Milton's style in "L'Allegro" and "Il Penseroso," the Wartons and Collins played a major role in developing this form.

Collins did not achieve fame with his odes during his lifetime, and perhaps this lack of recognition contributed to his early mental instability and eventual death at thirty-seven. His odes never attain warmth and personal intimacy, but they do achieve particular effects which are unsurpassed in eighteenth century poetry: pensive melody, emotionally charged landscape, vigorous allegory, and rich romanticism.

Collins, like his friends the Wartons, advocated concepts of poetry that would eventually dominate poetic thought by the turn of the nineteenth century. His belief that poetry should be freely imagined and passionately felt, that it should be blessed with *furor poesis*, puts him basically into the Wordsworthian camp. His formalism and abstraction, ties to his Augustan background, obviously hamper his style. Collins is much like Edwin Arlington Robinson's Miniver Cheevy, born out of time. He has one poetic foot in the past, but the other, much larger one, extends far into the future, since it would be some forty years after his death before the publication of William Wordsworth and Samuel Taylor Coleridge's *Lyrical Ballads* (1798), the recognized *locus classicus* of Romanticism. Collins has been compared with the early nineteenth century poet Percy Bysshe Shelley in his use of abstraction; in the work of both poets, personifications become real figures which help to express a delicate mood without recourse to great detail: "Spring with dewey fingers cold" and "Freedom a weeping hermit" illustrate the method well. This personification of natural phenomena in eighteenth century verse for the most part symbolizes affective states, where the allegorical figure sums up the meaning which the phenomenon has for the poet.

Collins does seem at times to strive for scholarly classicism. His mixture of classical and medieval sources illustrates his "two voices" long before Alfred, Lord Tennyson's metaphor and poems come into overt expression. He was the most free of all the early precursors of Romanticism, and his predominant concern was the spirit of beauty. Most critics compare Collins favorably with his contemporaries, especially with Thomas Gray, generally agreeing with William Hazlitt's assessment. Hazlitt argued that Collins possessed genuine inspiration, and that even though his work is marred by affectation and certain obscurities, "he also catches rich glimpses of the bowers of paradise."

"ODE ON THE POETICAL CHARACTER"

Perhaps the best guide to Collins's attitude toward inspiration and imagination is his "Ode on the Poetical Character." Early in the ode, Collins asserts that the true poetical character is godlike, for the bard is one "prepared and bathed in heaven." Following this apotheosis, Collins pursues the idea by describing God's creation of the world as analogous to the poet's act of creation. A bit of sixteenth century pagan/Christian syncretism is reflected in his analogy: God was the original type of all poets and the contemporary poet imitates his divine power. Collins, however, adds allegorical layers to this analogy. He suggests that Fancy is a separate female entity and not merely an attribute of God, and he adds the rather confusing metaphor of a girdle of poetic imagination.

Collins turns to the examples of John Milton and Edmund Spenser, suggesting that the true poet will find his voice in a kind of wedding of their diverse styles. One finds such a poet, according to stanza three, "high on some cliff . . . of prospect wild," accompanied by holy genie and surrounded by an Eden-like environment. In this ode there is a sense of a new aesthetic attitude that later comes to be described as "Romantic"; John Langhorne says that the ode is so wild it seems to have been written under the Romantic tyranny of the imagination.

PERSIAN ECLOGUES

The wedding of the styles of Spenser and Milton which results in this strong emotional verse can be related to Collins's earlier work entitled *Persian Eclogues*. He prefaces his eclogues with the statement that "The style of my countrymen is as naturally strong and nervous as that of an Arabian or Persian is rich and figurative." Spenser is a writer whom Collins associates with Persian genius because of his luxuriously expansive style. Following the contemporary attitude toward Hebraic poetry as being energetic but brief rather than copious, Collins thinks of Milton as an example. The fusion of these two styles results in rich, emotional verse.

Persian Eclogues was published in 1742 while Collins was at Oxford, but the individual eclogues had been written sometime between his birthday in 1738 and the winter of 1740. According to Joseph Warton, Collins wrote them at a time when he was studying Persian history. In Collins's time, exotic Eastern interests were becoming popular, and features of Oriental poetry had become fascinating to the post-Augustan generation. Thomas Rymer comments that fancy dominated Oriental verse, "wild, vast and unbridled." Obviously, such a style met with Collins's approval; the pretense that he was actually translating Persian poetry allowed him to attempt a rich elegance and wildness of thought, traits which became characteristic of his mature Romanticism.

Most critics agree that the eclogues contain little genuine Orientalism. In diction and structure they closely follow conventions of the eighteenth century pastoral, especially those of Alexander Pope. There are several significant differences, however, between Pope and Collins, the first of which is simply that Collins's setting is exotic, not English. Also, there is a difference in theme; although both writers follow the conventional emphasis on the power of time, Collins's tone is secular rather than Christian, as in Shelley's pastoral elegy "Adonais." Collins does not see the essence of pastoral as the recognition of man's fall and of modern man's desire to repudiate Adam and inherited sin. By using the seasons, Pope, for example, is able to trace man's decline from a golden age to an age of error, with a final eclogue showing the transforming power of Christ, who can bring the golden age back for all humankind. Collins does not use the seasons for his structure and he does not use the sacred closing eclogue. Rather, he suggests that the usable values of the past should be put into practice in contemporary society.

There is little borrowing in *Persian Eclogues* from other sources. The third eclogue may be a variation of a story of a king of Persia who, after witnessing the simple life of his peasant subjects, gives up his kingship for a time in order to live with shepherds. The king eventually returns to court with a favorite shepherd, who in turn longs continually for his rural home. This story appeared in Ambrose Phillips's periodical *The Free-Thinker* in 1719 and 1739, thus making it possible for Collins to have seen it.

"ODE TO LIBERTY"

Another poem reflecting Collins's orientation toward Romanticism is the 1746 "Ode to Liberty." The background for the ode is the War of the Austrian Succession. The war with France saw the city of Genoa fall prey to allied invasion because of Austrian occupation: Genoa is another example of the democratic fight for liberty, paralleling Austria's own William Tell who refused to bow to the dictatorial governor's demands. The "Ode to Liberty" suggests a desire for peace, implying throughout a great sympathy for those who suffer innocently. Collins's question in Strophe 1, perhaps alluding to the exhortations of Tyrtaus to the Spartans in the Second Messenian War to fight with courage, stresses the disgrace of cowardice and the glory of patriotism. He also alludes to William Tell in Epode 1, and his closing remarks suggest that England will welcome to its shores for peaceful play the dedicated youth who fought so bravely.

AN ODE ON THE POPULAR SUPERSTITIONS OF THE HIGHLANDS OF SCOTLAND

It is generally observed that the ode which expresses Collins's Romantic temperament at its best is one of his last works, originally entitled *Ode to a Friend on His Return* but published posthumously in 1788 as *An Ode on the Popular Superstitions of the Highlands of Scotland*. The ode was addressed to a friend and fellow writer, John Home, who was leaving London after his failure to place one of his plays on the London stage.

The Romantic nature of the piece is seen in the opening lines as Collins asks his friend to rediscover a region inhabited by "Fairy People" and ruled by "Fancy." The ancient bards seem to rise in masque-like manner around Home, whose mind is "possest" by strange powers. The "matted hair with bough fantastic crown'd" enhances the supernatural mood that Collins establishes. Collins admonishes Home to make use of such forces in writing his plays. By employing supernatural tales such as are found in the folklore of Scotland, Collins says, the modern poet can partake of the visionary power found therein and share in its creative force. Probably the most alluring section of the ode is the story of the hapless swain caught up in the force of the kelpie's wrath. The swain is led astray by glimmering mazes that cheer his sight. These lights are actually the will-o'-the-wisps, a vision deluding and drawing him to the water monster, whose malignant design becomes obvious to the reader at this point. The poor swain becomes a passive, helpless wretch in the clutches of the evil kelpie. His death leads to his transformation into a supernatural being, unable to bridge the gap between his former and his present life.

In the closing lines, Collins invokes a natural environment that is sustained by supernatural traditions. The ode is undoubtedly a celebration of the new visionary source which would further liberate poetry in the Romantic period.

BIBLIOGRAPHY

Doughty, Oswald. *William Collins*. London: Longmans, Green, 1964. A brief, handy book recommended for its accessibility. A brief view of Collins's life is followed by succinct readings of his major poems. Includes useful bibliography.

Sherwin, Paul S. *Precious Bane: Collins and the Miltonic Legacy*. Austin: University of Texas Press, 1977. Sherwin's "anxiety of influence" approach, though perhaps inapplicable to all poets, is certainly applicable to Collins and the poets of the "Age of Sensibility," who consciously looked back to the towering figures of Edmund Spenser, William Shakespeare, and John Milton. The reading of Collins's "Ode on the Poetical Character" is particularly recommended.

Sigworth, Oliver F. *William Collins*. New York: Twayne, 1965. This is a very good introduction to the life and work of Collins. Lodged between a biographical account of Collins and a long treatment of the poetry is a particularly useful consideration of "the poetry and the age." Supplementing the text are a chronology, notes, and a bibliography.

Sitter, John. *Literary Loneliness in Mid-Eighteenth-Century England*. Ithaca, N.Y.: Cornell University Press, 1982. Sitter is a major authority on the so-called Age of Sensibility in England during the 1740's and 1750's—the period that Collins has come to exemplify. Contains excellent discussions of other writers important to the period, as well as an extended treatment of Collins and his poetry.

Weiskel, Thomas. *The Romantic Sublime: Studies in the Structure and Psychology of Transcendence*. Baltimore: The Johns Hopkins University Press, 1976. An impressive book, demanding and difficult but containing an important reading of Collins and his poetry, especially the crucial "Ode on the Poetical Character."

Wendorf, Richard. *William Collins and Eighteenth-Century English Poetry*. Minneapolis: University of Minnesota Press, 1981. Perhaps the single best study of Collins. Also an editor of Collins, Wendorf begins with an informed, sensible treatment of Collins's "madness"—for years a critical and biographical stumbling block—then moves on to consider Collins's career and poetry. The treatment of Collins's "musical odes" is highly interesting. A useful "note" on modern criticism of Collins is included.

White, Deborah Elise. *Romantic Returns: Superstition, Imagination, History*. Stanford, Calif.: Stanford University Press, 2000. Intended for readers with a background in literary theory, the book covers the theorization and operation of "imagination" in pre-Romantic and Romantic writing. The ways in which the aesthetics of Romanticism inform its political and economic speculations are explored in an analysis of the poetry and prose of William Collins, William Hazlitt, and Percy Bysshe Shelley.

Woodhouse, A. S. P. "Collins and the Creative Imagination: A Study in the Critical Background of His Odes (1746)." In *Studies in English by Members of University College, Toronto*, edited by M. W. Wallace. Toronto: University of Toronto Press, 1931. A classic early study of Collins, still vital for Woodhouse's discussion of the ode in the mid-eighteenth century and his treatment of Collins's most important poem, the "Ode on the Poetical Character."

John W. Crawford;
bibliography updated by the editors

PADRAIC COLUM

Born: County Longford, Ireland; December 8, 1881
Died: Enfield, Connecticut; January 11, 1972

PRINCIPAL POETRY
Wild Earth: A Book of Verse, 1907
Dramatic Legends and Other Poems, 1922
Creatures, 1927
Way of the Cross, 1927
Old Pastures, 1930
Poems, 1932
The Story of Lowry Main, 1937
Flower Pieces: New Poems, 1938
The Collected Poems of Padraic Colum, 1953
The Vegetable Kingdom, 1954
Ten Poems, 1957
Irish Elegies, 1958
The Poet's Circuit: Collected Poems of Ireland, 1960
Images of Departure, 1969
Selected Poems of Padraic Colum, 1989 (Sanford Sternlicht, editor)

OTHER LITERARY FORMS

Padraic Colum was a prolific writer who expressed himself in many different genres during the first seven decades of the twentieth century. He helped found the Abbey Theatre in Dublin with William Butler Yeats, and he wrote three major plays: *The Land* (1905), *The Fiddler's House* (1907), and *Thomas Muskerry* (1910). All three plays deal with the dignity of Irish farmers. He wrote numerous short stories; two major novels, *Castle Conquer* (1923) and *The Flying Swans* (1957); and numerous essays on Irish history and politics. After his immigration to the United States in 1914 with his wife, Mary Colum, he became especially famous for his elegant retelling of folk tales for children. Some of his most admired books for children are *The King of Ireland's Son* (1916), *The Golden Fleece and the Heroes Who Lived Before Achilles* (1921), and *Legends of Hawaii* (1937).

Padraic Colum (Library of Congress)

ACHIEVEMENTS

Unlike other great writers of the literary movement called the Irish Renaissance, such as William Butler Yeats, Lady Augusta Gregory, and James Joyce, who were his friends, Padraic Colum was from a peasant background. He understood profoundly the beliefs and moral values of Irish farmers. Although he moved to the United States in 1914, his thoughts never really left the Irish countryside of his youth. In his poetry and prose, he wrote in a deceptively simple style. His poetry captured the simple dignity of Irish peasants, whose emotions and struggles he presented as representations of the rich diversity of human experience. Some of his poems, including "An Old Woman of the Roads" and "A Cradle Song," have been learned by heart by generations of Irish and Irish-American students. His poetry is immediately accessible to young readers, but more mature readers also appreciate the simple eloquence and evocative power of his poems. He captured the essence of Irish folklore and popular culture and transmitted to readers its profound universality. In 1952, Padraic Colum won an Academy of American Poets Fellowship. He received the Gregory Medal of the Irish Academy of Letters in 1953 and the Regina Medal in 1961.

BIOGRAPHY

Padraic Colum was born in a workhouse in Ireland's County Longford on December 8, 1881. His original name was Patrick Columb, but in his early twenties he changed his name to Padraic Colum to make it sound more Irish and less English. He was the first of eight children born to Susan and Patrick Columb. During his youth, he learned about Irish folklore and traditions by listening to the oral tales told by those who lived in County Longford. He never wavered in his commitment both to the Catholic faith of his ancestors and to the values of Irish peasant culture. His formal education ended when he was sixteen, and he was in many ways a self-educated man.

His family moved to Dublin in 1891, and after his studies ended, Colum became a clerk for the Irish railroads. He soon developed a deep interest in Gaelic culture and discovered his abilities as a writer. With the encouragement of William Butler Yeats and Lady Augusta Gregory, he wrote plays for the newly founded Abbey Theatre in Dublin as well as lyric poetry. A monetary

grant in 1908 from American businessman Thomas Kelly enabled Colum to resign from his job with the railroads and to concentrate solely on his writing. From then on, Colum earned his living as a writer. He married Mary Maguire in 1912, and they moved to the United States two years later.

While in the United States, the Colums often wrote together. They were popular lecturers and visiting professors at various American universities, especially at Columbia University, where they taught literature for many years. They spent most of their time in New York City, but they traveled frequently. Although they had no children, Colum earned his living largely by retelling folk tales for children. These books were enormously popular. In 1924 the provincial legislature in Hawaii decided to preserve traditional Hawaiian folk tales, and it decided that Padraic Colum was the most qualified person to undertake this project. The Colums spent two years in Hawaii, where Padraic learned Hawaiian and became so erudite in Hawaiian culture that he gave numerous lectures on Hawaiian history and culture in Honolulu's Bishop Museum.

During his nearly six decades in the United States, Colum remained a prolific writer. He was a humble man who preferred speaking about his wife and their numerous fellow writers, especially their close friend James Joyce, to talking about himself. One year after Mary's death in 1957, Colum completed a biography the two of them had been writing of Joyce, which he titled *Our Friend James Joyce*. At that time Colum began receiving care from his nephew Emmet Greene, who assisted him in his many trips around the New York area. Although Colum never wrote an autobiography, American scholar Zack Bowen recorded a series of interviews with him in the 1960's. In the interviews, Colum spoke extensively of his literary career. Bowen relied on these interviews for his 1970 biography of Colum, and he donated these tapes to the library of the State University of New York, Binghamton, which houses Colum's papers. Colum died in a nursing home in Connecticut on January 11, 1972. His body was flown to Ireland, where he was buried next to his beloved Mary.

ANALYSIS

In nineteenth century British and American plays, a common character type was the "stage Irishman." This artificial Irish character was not very bright or sensitive. He tended to be a buffoon whose major interest in life was drinking. These plays revealed no understanding of the harsh reality of colonial rule and economic exploitation in rural Ireland. Until the very end of the nineteenth century, Catholics could not own land in Ireland, and farmers were forced to pay rent to absentee landlords. A desire for stability and a profound love of the land were deeply felt by Irish peasants. Padraic Colum expressed their feelings in a poetic voice that was authentic.

"AN OLD WOMAN OF THE ROADS"

Colum's 1907 book *Wild Earth* includes some of his most admired poems. The very title suggests that generations of Irish peasants had resisted British efforts to suppress their culture and their Catholic faith. One of Colum's most famous early poems is "An Old Woman of the Roads." Its title refers to so-called tinkers, itinerant peddlers who traveled the roads of Ireland in their wagons and sold their goods. Because of their trade, tinkers did not develop roots in a specific village. In this twenty-four-line poem, which is composed of six four-line stanzas, the old woman speaks in the first person. She is a humble but proud woman with simple desires. She dreams of having a house with a hearth, heated by sod, in which she could have a bed and a dresser. She imagines that this house would also be her store, in which she could display her goods to eager customers. She is tired of endless traveling in her wagon, and she dreams of stability, which she associates with peace. Like almost all Irish peasants, she is deeply committed to the Catholic faith that gives her the strength to endure suffering with quiet dignity. In the final stanza, the old woman realizes that she may never have a house in this life, but she still dreams of paradise where she will be "out of the wind's and the rain's way." As she travels the roads of Ireland, she prays to God "night and day."

As for other Irish peasants, God's presence in their daily lives and the resurrection are realities that she does not question. She is tired of the constant struggle to survive in abject poverty, but she never forgets that God loves her, and she believes that she will eventually return to her true "house" in heaven. With many different uses of the word *house*, Colum enables his readers to appreciate the quiet dignity and profound spirituality of ordinary Irish people. It is not at all surprising that "An Old Woman of the Roads" remains a poem beloved by generations of Irish readers and readers of Irish descent.

"A CRADLE SONG"

Another 1907 poem that has remained popular is the sixteen-line poem "A Cradle Song." As in "An Old Woman of the Roads," each stanza contains four lines of free verse. The scene evoked in this poem is universal. Parents around the world sing to their babies in order to calm them and to help them sleep. Just as in "An Old Woman of the Roads," Colum includes a clear religious reference because the mother of whom he speaks in "A Cradle Song" is the Virgin Mary.

He transfers the infancy of Christ to an Irish country setting, and he refers to Mary by the Irish term of endearment "Mavourneen," which means "darling." The Gospel according to St. Matthew tells how three wise men, or magi, came to adore the infant Jesus just after Mary had given birth. In "A Cradle Song," Colum transforms these wise men into "men from the fields" whom a new mother has invited to come see her infant son, whom she has protected with "her mantle of blue." The great respect due Christ and all babies and mothers requires that the "men from the fields" enter the house "gently" and "softly," lest they disturb the mother or child. Colum evokes the poverty of these surroundings by pointing out that the floor in this house is cold, and farm animals are "peering" at the mother and baby "across the half door." Despite the lack of material comfort, the mother is incredibly happy because she is experiencing the miracle of a new life. In this poem, Colum expresses very eloquently to his readers the incredible joy which new life brings.

"ROGER CASEMENT"

Colum wrote several elegies in praise of distinguished Irish people who had died. His most famous elegy was for the Irish patriot Roger David Casement (1864-1916), whom the British hanged on a charge of treason. Colum and others who favored Irish independence from Great Britain never believed the accusations against Casement, whom they considered to be a martyr. This elegy contains two eight-line stanzas. Four of the sixteen lines contain the Gaelic words for mourning, "ochone, och, ochone, ochone!" One could translate the word *ochone* as "alas," but these are words people say at an Irish country burial. Casement was hanged in a British jail, but Colum imagines that Irish peasants have reserved for him the honors owed to a worthy person who has left this earth to spend eternity in heaven. Colum states that those who respect Roger Casement's memory are not respectable English people named Smith, Murray, or Cecil, who approved of the execution of an Irish hero, but rather "outcast peoples . . . who laboured fearfully." These social outcasts, whom the British disdain and with whom Colum identifies, will "lift" Roger Casement "for the eyes of God to see."

Although Casement was executed for the alleged crime of treason, Colum reminds his readers that although a colonial power can reduce individuals to silence by killing them, it can never destroy in the minds of ordinary people the martyr's dignity. Casement's heroism in the face of death only serves to remind Irish people of his "noble stature . . . courtesy and kindliness" that Colum evokes in this very powerful elegy.

"AFTER SPEAKING OF ONE WHO DIED A LONG TIME BEFORE"

Although Colum wrote poems of very high quality for seventy years, just three years before his death he completed an extraordinary collection of twenty poems, titled *Images of Departure*. These exquisite poems express the joy of life felt by an eighty-eight-year-old poet who had survived his wife and almost all his friends. Perhaps the finest poem in this collection is the twenty-four-line poem "After Speaking of One Who Died a Long Time Before." This short poem is composed of an eleven-line stanza and a thirteen-line stanza. He links his personal loss of his beloved wife and best friend, Mary, with the "tenderness and grief" simultaneously felt by people when they think of dead loved ones who profoundly touched their lives. Near the very end of his long life, Colum still demonstrated his masterful ability to use ordinary words and images in order to help his readers appreciate the rich complexity of human emotions.

OTHER MAJOR WORKS

LONG FICTION: *Castle Conquer*, 1923; *The Flying Swans*, 1957.

SHORT FICTION: *Selected Short Stories of Padraic Colum*, 1985 (Sanford Sternlicht, editor).

PLAYS: *The Children of Lir*, pb. 1901 (one act);

Broken Soil, pr. 1903; *The Land*, pr., pb. 1905; *The Fiddler's House*, pr., pb. 1907 (revision of *Broken Soil*); *The Miracle of the Corn*, pr. 1908; *The Destruction of the Hostel*, pr. 1910; *Thomas Muskerry*, pr., pb. 1910; *The Desert*, pb. 1912; *The Betrayal*, pr. 1914; *Three Plays*, pb. 1916, revised 1925, revised 1963 (includes *The Land*, *The Fiddler's House*, and *Thomas Muskerry*); *Mogu the Wanderer: Or, The Desert*, pb. 1917, pr. 1932 (revision of *The Desert*); *The Grasshopper*, pr. 1917 (adaptation of Eduard Keyserling's play *Ein Frühlingsofer*); *Balloon*, pb. 1929; *Moytura: A Play for Dancers*, pr., pb. 1963; *The Challengers*, pr. 1966 (3 one-act plays: *Monasterboice*, *Glendalough*, and *Cloughoughter*); *Carricknabauna*, pr. 1967 (also as *The Road Round Ireland*); *Selected Plays of Padraic Colum*, pb. 1986 (includes *The Land*, *The Betrayal*, *Glendalough*, and *Monasterboice*; Sanford Sternlicht, editor).

SCREENPLAY: *Hansel and Gretel*, 1954 (adaptation of Engelbert Humperdinck's opera).

NONFICTION: *My Irish Year*, 1912; *The Road Round Ireland*, 1926; *Cross Roads in Ireland*, 1930; *A Half-Day's Ride: Or, Estates in Corsica*, 1932; *Our Friend James Joyce*, 1958 (with Mary Colum); *Ourselves Alone: The Story of Arthur Griffith and the Origin of the Irish Free State*, 1959.

CHILDREN'S LITERATURE: *A Boy in Eirinn*, 1913; *The King of Ireland's Son*, 1916; *The Adventures of Odysseus*, 1918; *The Boy Who Knew What the Birds Said*, 1918; *The Girl Who Sat by the Ashes*, 1919; *The Boy Apprenticed to an Enchanter*, 1920; *The Golden Fleece and the Heroes Who Lived Before Achilles*, 1921; *The Big Tree of Bunlahy: Stories of My Own Countryside*, 1933; *Legends of Hawaii*, 1937; *A Treasury of Irish Folklore*, 1954; *Story Telling, New and Old*, 1961; *The Stone of Victory, and Other Tales of Padraic Colum*, 1966.

BIBLIOGRAPHY

Bowen, Zack. *Padraic Colum: A Biographical-Critical Introduction*. Carbondale: Southern Illinois University Press, 1970. This excellent introduction to Padraic Colum's works was based on a careful study of his writings but also on extensive interviews between Padraic Colum and Zack Bowen in the 1960's.

Journal of Irish Literature 2, no. 1 (1973). This special issue deals solely with Padraic Colum. Includes many excellent essays on his works.

Murphy, Ann. "Appreciation: Padraic Colum (1881-1972), National Poet." *Eire-Ireland: A Journal of Irish Studies* 17, no. 4 (Winter, 1982): 128-147. A thoughtful essay that describes well the important place of Padraic Colum in twentieth century Irish poetry.

Murray, Christopher. "Padraic Colum's *The Land* and Cultural Nationalism." *Hungarian Journal of English and American Studies* 2, no. 2 (1996): 5-15. A short but accurate description of Colum's support for Irish independence from Great Britain.

Sternlicht, Sanford. *Padraic Colum*. Boston: Twayne, 1985. This solid introduction to Padraic Colum's life and works contains an excellent annotated bibliography. It describes clearly why Padraic Colum was the most important Irish American writer of the twentieth century.

_____. "Padraic Colum: Poet of the 1960's." *Colby Literary Quarterly* 25, no. 4 (1989): 253-257. A short but insightful analysis of *Images of Departure* elegies written by Padraic Colum in the 1960's.

Edmund J. Campion

WILLIAM CONGREVE

Born: Bardsey, Yorkshire, England; January 24, 1670

Died: London, England; January 19, 1729

PRINCIPAL POETRY

Poems upon Several Occasions, 1710

OTHER LITERARY FORMS

William Congreve's major works are his plays: four comedies, *The Old Batchelour* (1693), *The Double-Dealer* (1693), *Love for Love* (1695), and *The Way of the World* (1700), and one tragedy, *The Mourning Bride* (1697). Congreve also wrote criticism, *Amendments of Mr. Collier's False and Imperfect Citations* (1698); a no-vella, *Incognita: Or, Love and duty Reconcil'd* (1692); a masque, *The Judgement of Paris* (1701); and an opera, *Semele* (1710). Some of his letters were published in a collection edited by John Dennis (1696). His other miscellaneous writings include contributions to *The Gentleman's Journal* (1692-1694), an essay for *The Tatler* (February 13, 1711), and the "Dedication to John Dryden's *Dramatick Works*" (1717).

ACHIEVEMENTS

In his own day William Congreve had a considerable reputation as a poet. John Dryden, in his poem "To My Dear Friend Mr Congreve," crowned him as his successor, and, as a political poet supporting William III, Congreve performed much the same function as Dryden did for Charles II and James II. Contemporary writers such as Jonathan Swift and the lesser known Charles Hopkins and William Dove praised Congreve's verse extravagantly. Almost all this praise, however, stemmed from Congreve's reputation as a dramatist and from his pleasing personality. By the middle of the eighteenth century critics began looking at Congreve's poetry in isolation and harshly condemned it. In the nineteenth century Thomas Macaulay pronounced Congreve's poetry to be of little value and long forgotten, and Edmund Gosse concentrated on Congreve the man, giving no very favorable judgment. After such a great fall in Congreve's reputation, critical judgment of his poetry has settled: He is considered an elegant minor poet, whose real fame rests on his plays. His best poems are his light love songs and his witty prologues; his greatest contribution to poetry was his condemnation of the irregular Cowleyan Pindaric, a form which had led to much laxness and mediocrity in poetry.

BIOGRAPHY

William Congreve was born in Yorkshire but grew up in Ireland, where his father served as an army lieutenant. Unlike many poets of his day, he belonged to the gentry: His grandfather was squire of Stretton Hall in Staffordshire. Congreve attended Kilkenny College, where he is reported to have written his first poem on the death of his headmaster's magpie. Swift was an older classmate of Congreve at Kilkenny and later at Trinity College, Dublin. After college, Congreve moved to London to study law but soon became entranced by the literary life. He frequented Will's coffeehouse, published a novel, and began writing odes and songs. His translations of Homer won Dryden's praise and friendship, and Dryden edited and then sponsored Congreve's first play, *The Old Batchelour*. During the play's run Congreve fell in love with the young actress Anne Bracegirdle, for whom he wrote many poems and the part of Millamant in *The Way of the World*. For his promise as a propagandist for William III, Congreve was given his first of a long series of political posts, commissioner for hackney coaches; in gratitude, he produced the standard celebratory odes. *The Mourning Bride*, Congreve's only tragedy, was his greatest popular success, although he is most acclaimed now for *The Way of the World*, a relative failure in its own day.

After the less-than-rapturous reception of *The Way of the World*, suffering from increasing blindness and painful gout, Congreve declined to expend the enormous amount of energy and concentration needed to write plays. He continued to write verses on occasion and became a gentleman about town, friend of prominent writers, and gallant of Henrietta, Duchess of Marlborough. Although he stopped writing for the theater, his love for it never waned; in 1705 he became the director of the new Haymarket Theater. His government posts continued; in 1714 he was made searcher of customs and then secretary to the island of Jamaica, an office which gave him an adequate income for the rest of his life. He died in 1729 and was buried in Westminster Abbey, where the duchess was buried beside him a few years later.

ANALYSIS

William Congreve's best poetry, like his plays, brings Restoration society to life: the intricacies of the courtship dance and the war in the theaters between playwrights and critics. When Congreve strays from his own milieu into political propaganda, however, or makes attempts at the sublime, his poetry rarely rises above the mediocre.

COURTSHIP

Congreve's poems, particularly his songs, reveal the feelings of both partners in the courtship dance. His men are not confident and promiscuous Horners who accumulate conquest after conquest but insecure young men

William Congreve (Library of Congress)

who often have been hurt or discarded by women. One song, in anapests, mimics the headstrong impetuosity and lumbering clumsiness of a young man in love: "I Look'd, and I sigh'd, and I wish'd I cou'd speak." Another song, "The Reconciliation," reminds one of John Donne's "Go and Catch a Falling Star": A cynical young man insists that women prove ungrateful whenever men are true and claims that the joys women give are "few, short, and insincere." "Song," one of Congreve's best-known and most-liked poems, purportedly composed for Anne Bracegirdle, is written in the calm yet bittersweet manner of Sir Thomas Wyatt. A lover, remembering the past joys of his inconstant mistress, determines not to seek revenge but to be grateful for what has been. Many of Congreve's songs sound this same theme of a young man bemoaning his lost love.

Congreve's women fall into two categories: honorable women torn between their desire to love and be loved and their need to maintain their virtue and inconstant women who leave heartbroken, hapless men in their wake. Congreve shows great sensitivity to the plight of women in the love-honor struggle of Restoration society. In "Song in Dialogue, for Two Women" the two women speakers decide whether or not to yield to their lovers' enticements. The first speaker claims she will but changes her mind after listening to the second. Both sing a chorus which acknowledges how quickly men can lose interest: "And granting Desire,/ We feed not the Fire,/ But make it more quickly expire." In another song Selinda is caught between her religious desire for purity and her secular desire to keep her lover: She runs to the church if he asks her favor yet cries when she thinks he will leave her. Selinda's lover wittily reveals the pressure put on a Restoration woman: "Wou'd she cou'd make of me a Saint,/ Or I of her a Sinner."

Like Alexander Pope, Congreve has his essay on women: three short poems on Amoret, Lesbia, and Doris. "Doris," which was much praised by Sir Richard Steele, presents a fully rounded picture of a promiscuous "Nymph of riper Age" who shines on various lovers in the night and quickly forgets them the next day. "Lesbia" describes a young man's discovery of the empty head of the idol he worships: the "trickling Nonsense" from her coral lips like balm heals his heart wounded by love. "Amoret" presents a contradictory young woman, who affects "to seem unaffected" and laughs at others for what she prizes in herself. A blind hypocrite, she does not see that "She is the Thing that she despises."

Congreve claimed to be a moralist, exposing the vice and folly of his society. He is indeed harsh in his condemnation of unfaithful, hypocritical wives. In his epilogue to Thomas Southerne's *Oroonoko* (1695) he satirizes town ladies who profess to be Christian and virtuous yet despise their spouses and take their marriage vows lightly. Promiscuous single women may leave angry, unhappy men, but they do not undermine the foundations of society—marriage and family.

PROLOGUES AND EPILOGUES

Congreve's prologues and epilogues, though less vigorous and daring than Dryden's, comment on the state of the theater and society through the use of witty imagery. His prologues are fitting appetizers for the feasts which follow. The prologue to *The Old Batchelour* begins seriously, with an image that Congreve was to use on other occasions: the play as a battleground between critics and writers. The prologue is the drum signaling the opening of the skirmishes. This prologue, however, ends in a burlesque, with the pretty spokeswoman (Anne Bracegirdle) forgetting her lines, pleading with the audience to like the play, and running offstage in confusion.

Critics habitually drew the fire of Restoration playwrights, and Congreve regularly traded insults with them. The epilogue to *The Old Batchelour* sandwiches a witty comparison of young women and playwrights in between the standard pleading to be approved and the standard insulting of the critics ("If he's an ass, he will be tried by's peers"). Once the end is gained, both women and playwrights are damned (discarded).

The prologue to *The Double-Dealer* is more sophisticated, with fewer drops in tone. It compares the play to a Moorish infant, thrown by its father (the playwright) into the sea (the pit) to prove its legitimacy. The image serves Congreve well; he can describe the pit as tempestuous and call the critics sharks. The epilogue to *The Double-Dealer* classifies the audience of the Restoration theater, critics all: the men of learning, the pit, the ladies, the beaux, and the witlings, each of whom has different exacting requirements for a successful play. The same theme recurs in Congreve's epilogue to *Oroonoko*. The poet divides his time among the different tastes; his one foot wears the sock, the other the buskin, and in striving to please he is forced to hop in a single boot.

In addition to condemning the critics and the problems they create for authors, Congreve condemns the amateur playwrights who at the time were drowning the stage. He laments that the theater has become a church whose main activity is funerals, not christenings. In another witty metaphor, he tells the wits that Pegasus—that is, the art of writing—has tricks which take more to master than merely getting up and riding. He ridicules the lady playwrights in lines as good as Pope's in *The Dunciad* (1728-1743): "With the same Ease, and Negligence of Thought,/ The charming Play is writ, and Fringe is wrought." One important theme of Congreve is the hard task serious writers have, not in writing itself but in presenting their works, when they are assailed by ignorant critics and torpedoed by amateurish mishmash.

Jeremy Collier attacked Congreve's licentiousness in his "Short View of the Immorality and Profaneness of the

English Stage," but Congreve blamed the audience for the type of plays which were popular. Reciting his "Epilogue at the Opening of the Queen's Theatre," Bracegirdle told the audience that the beaux may find it hard to spend one night without smutty jests, but she promises them soon "to your selves shew your dear selves again" and display "in bold Strokes the vicious Town." Congreve whirls in defensive fury against the pseudoreformers. In "Prologue, to the Court, on the Queen's Birthday," he claims that playwrights seek to war against vice and folly but reformers force the Muse to assume the very forms she has been fighting. Reformers break the mirror (the plays) which reflect their own ignorance and malice. Congreve renounces the stage, saying his Muse will now pursue the nobler tasks of painting the "Beauties of the Mind" and, by showing the court the virtues of one such as the queen, "shame to Manners an incorrigible Town." He says he will remain a moralist although his means have changed. Unfortunately, when he praises the virtuous queen, his lines lack the strength of the earlier diatribe: The only line in this prologue that matches the eloquence of his fury is one in which the Muse "secretly Applauds, and silently Admires" the queen.

IMAGERY

When Congreve leaves writing for the stage or writing about the stage, his poetic powers by and large desert him and his claim of remaining a moralist is specious; it is hard to find any morality in "poet laureate" praises. The only thing which redeems Congreve's laudatory verses to William and to Mary is his imagery, which leaps out from the sycophantic meanderings. In "To the King, on the Taking of Namure" Congreve admits that his proper sphere is singing simple love songs, but he underestimates his own abilities. His description of the battle of Namure rises above the commonplace, with its discordant consonants imitating the clash and clang of battle (before Pope's strictures on sound and sense) and his images of the earth in labor giving birth to the "dead Irruptions" and the air tormented by the cannon fire and smoke. Warlord man is shown to victimize nature.

On the other hand, nature befriends human beings when they are gentle. In "The Mourning Muse of Alexis, Lamenting the Death of Queen Mary," Congreve describes the beauty and peace of nature mourning Queen Mary: Sable clouds adorn the chalk cliffs, bees deposit their honey on Mary's tomb, and glowworms light the dirges of fairies. The imagery is beautiful, but if one comes to the poem with the expectation that it will give solace, it is disappointingly silly.

Although the classical set pieces in Congreve's poems to King William are disastrous, the set piece in the irregular ode "On Mrs. Arabella Hunt, Singing" works well. Much like Pope's portrayal of dullness in *The Dunciad*, Congreve's mighty god Silence is wrapped in a melancholy thought, wreathed by mists and darkness, lulled by poppy vapors, and sitting on an "ancient" sigh. Silence is vanquished by the beauty of Hunt's singing, and her listeners are left in a state reminiscent of the lovers on John Keats's Grecian urn, "For ever to be dying so, yet never die."

Congreve's "A Hymn to Harmony, in Honour of St. Cecilia's Day, 1701" and Pope's "Ode for Musick, on St. Cecilia's Day," when compared, illustrate the difference between a great poet and a minor one. In both poems the authors describe the ability of music to soothe troubled minds. Congreve says that the Muses with balmy sound assuage a wrathful and revengeful mind, while Pope turns the idea into a concrete image, personifying melancholy, sloth, and envy and showing rather than explaining the effect of music on them. Pope may have mined Congreve's ore for ideas, but he cut, polished, and presented the more beautiful gems.

Congreve's technical abilities never equal the power of his imagery. He squirms and struggles under the burden of rhyming. In order to achieve his rhymes, he often destroys his syntax or creates a jingle of sound rather than a flow. Even when he does find a rhyme, it frequently is only an eye-rhyme or a jarring approximation of a rhyme. Perhaps one reason that Congreve was able to create exquisite poetry in *The Mourning Bride*, lines which Samuel Johnson called "the most poetical paragraph" in the "whole mass of English poetry," is that he was not forced into rhyme and could write blank verse.

Like other writers who experiment in genres other than their major ones, Congreve does not repeat the brilliance of his plays in his poetry. Lacking technical virtuosity, flawed by absurd and frozen set pieces, and distinguished by no more than ordinary political praise, his poems nevertheless can sparkle with striking imagery and wit. Above all, Congreve's poems, with their views of the theater and of love and honor in Restoration society, add to the reader's understanding of his plays.

OTHER MAJOR WORKS

LONG FICTION: *Incognita: Or, Love and Duty Reconcil'd*, 1692 (novella).

PLAYS: *The Old Bachelor*, pr., pb. 1693; *The Double-Dealer*, pr. 1693; *Love for Love*, pr., pb. 1695; *The Mourning Bride*, pr., pb. 1697; *The Way of the World*, pr., pb. 1700; *The Judgement of Paris*, pr., pb. 1701 (masque); *Squire Trelooby*, pr., pb. 1704 (with Sir John Vanbrugh and William Walsh; adaptation of Molière's *Monsieur de Pourceaugnac*); *Semele*, pb. 1710 (libretto), pr. 1744 (modified version); *The Complete Plays of William Congreve*, pb. 1967 (Herbert Davis, editor).

NONFICTION: *Amendments of Mr. Collier's False and Imperfect Citations*, 1698; *William Congreve: Letters and Documents*, 1964 (John C. Hodges, editor).

TRANSLATIONS: *Ovid's Art of Love, Book III*, 1709; *Ovid's Metamorphoses*, 1717 (with John Dryden and Joseph Addison).

MISCELLANEOUS: *Examen Poeticum*, 1693; *The Works of Mr. William Congreve*, 1710; *The Complete Works of William Congreve*, 1923, repr. 1964 (4 volumes; Montague Summers, editors).

BIBLIOGRAPHY

Hoffman, Arthur W. *Congreve's Comedies*. Victoria, B.C.: University of Victoria, 1993. Analysis and interpretation of Congreve's comic plays. Includes bibliography.

Lindsay, Alexander, and Howard Erskine-Hill, eds. *William Congreve*. New York: Routledge, 1989. A valuable collection of essays on Congreve's life and work. Provides a history of the scholarly approaches by major critics of Congreve. Contains a useful introduction, notes, and an index.

Morris, Brian, ed. *William Congreve*. London: Ernest Benn, 1970. A collection of nine important essays devoted to placing Congreve's plays in a historical and cultural context. The introduction by Morris is first rate. Supplemented by an index and a list of abbreviations.

Novak, Maximillian E. *William Congreve*. New York: Twayne, 1971. After a detailed introduction to Congreve's life, Novak discusses each of Congreve's five plays in depth and devotes a concluding chapter to Congreve's poetry and other writings. Supplemented by an excellent select bibliography (including secondary sources), notes, an index, and a chronology.

Thomas, David. *William Congreve*. New York: St. Martin's Press, 1992. Critical analysis of Congreve's plays with bibliographic references and an index.

Van Voris, W. H. *The Cultivated Stance*. Dublin: Dolemen, 1965. A detailed and comprehensive analysis of Congreve's plays in terms of dramatic structuring, including dialogue, plot, unity, characterization, and major themes. Complemented by a chronology and an index.

Williams, Aubrey L. *An Approach to Congreve*. New Haven, Conn.: Yale University Press, 1979. This insightful study provides a discussion of the historical context from which Congreve's work emerged, as well as discussions of Congreve's five plays and one novella. Supplemented by notes and an index.

Ann Willardson Engar;
bibliography updated by the editors

HENRY CONSTABLE

Born: Flamborough(?), England; 1562
Died: Liège, France; 1613

PRINCIPAL POETRY

Diana, 1592, 1594
Spiritual Sonnets, 1815
The Poems of Henry Constable, 1960 (Joan Grundy, editor)

OTHER LITERARY FORMS

Henry Constable's other writings were political and religious prose works. While still a Protestant, he wrote a pamphlet called *A Short View of a Large Examination of Cardinall Allen His Trayterous Justification of Sir W.*

Stanley and Yorck (c. 1588). This was an answer to a work of 1587 in which the Roman Catholic cardinal had justified the surrender of Daventer to the Spaniards by Stanley, one of Leicester's chief officers. Constable answered specific arguments of Allen's work with arguments based on justice and Protestant theology. He mocked the cardinal, implying that he was a "purple whore." He also wrote the *Examen pacifique de la doctrine des Huguenots* (1589, *The Catholike Moderator: Or, A Moderate Examination of the Doctrine of the Protestants*, 1623), published anonymously in Paris. The work was pro-Huguenot, but in it, the author pretended to be a Catholic. It was translated into English in 1623. The work was an enlargement of a response that he wrote to another tract. Again, Constable was concerned with politics, theology, and justice, but he also indicated that he desired the union of the Protestant and Roman Catholic Churches. Constable was soon to become a Catholic. He wrote an unpublished theological work (c. 1596) that has been lost, and another work on English affairs (c. 1597). He is presumed to be the author or co-author of an anonymous book in defense of King James's title in 1600, which was an answer to another work supporting Spain that was erroneously attributed to him. He also collaborated with Dr. W. Percy on a work against the Spanish and Jesuits in 1601. It is clear that Constable was deeply involved in the political and religious matters of his day. His religious interests were to affect greatly his life and his poetry, and he wrote an important group of religious sonnets after his conversion to Catholicism. As the prose works mentioned above showed this commitment to the Protestant cause, his religious sonnets showed his strong feelings for the Catholic faith.

ACHIEVEMENTS

In his best-known work, *Diana*, Henry Constable wrote highly polished courtly sonnets. Some modern critics consider his undated *Spiritual Sonnets*, which appeared only in manuscript, to be superior to the *Diana* in their originality and strong sense of feeling. Both his secular and his religious poems, however, were sonnets of praise. His love of argument is evident in the logical patterns of his sonnets, particularly in his use of symmetrical antitheses, often with accompanying alliteration. The openings of many of his sonnets are striking, and he made use of clever conceits, including some of the extended Metaphysical variety that are memorable. His diction was simple and unaffected, though his style was marked by considerable repetition.

Although today he is considered to be a minor poet, he was regarded as a major talent by his contemporaries. He was one of the earliest of Elizabethan sonnet writers and helped to create the fashion. Many of his sonnets had been written before 1591, when Sir Philip Sidney's *Astrophel and Stella* was published. The *Diana* of 1592 was one of the earliest collections of sonnets. Samuel Daniel, the author of *Delia* (1592), may have been influenced by Constable rather than the other way around. William Shakespeare seems to have borrowed specific details from Constable, and Michael Drayton also showed Constable's influence. Francis Meres in *Palladis Tamia* (1598) praised him highly. Ben Jonson's "An Ode" (c. 1600) listed Constable with Homer, Ovid, Petrarch, Pierre de Ronsard, and Sidney, and his name is mentioned in the company of excellent poets by Drayton and Gabriel Harvey. In the anonymous play *Returne from Parnassus* (c. 1600), he is spoken of as "Sweate Constable." Edmund Bolton in the *Hypercritica* (1618) termed Constable "a great master in the English Tongue, nor had any Gentleman of our Nation a more pure, quick, or higher Delivery of Conceit. . . ." The contemporary poet Alexander Montgomerie wrote a Scottish version of one of his poems, and a Latin translation of another is included in the *Poemata* (1607) of Dousa (Filius). After his own time, he was largely known until the nineteenth century, when his poetry was edited by W. C. Hazlitt and was included in anthologies of Elizabethan sonnets.

BIOGRAPHY

Henry Constable came from a line of distinguished ancestors on both his father's and his mother's side. The surname originated from the office of Constable in Chester, which had been held by members of his father's family since the time of William the Conqueror, although his father's branch of the family had settled in Yorkshire. The poet must have been born in 1562, since he was thirteen years old in 1575, and was presumably born at Flamborough. There is no information about his childhood. He attended St. John's College, Cambridge, his rank being recognized there by special distinctions. After receiving his bachelor's degree in 1579 or 1580 by a special grace, the reason not made clear, he was admitted to Lincoln's Inn on February 21, 1583. Later in the same year, a letter he wrote to his father indicates that he was with the English ambassador, Sir Francis Walsingham, in Scotland. Walsingham recommended the young Constable to the English ambassador in Paris, who was distantly related to Constable, and he became an emissary. He seems to have been a proponent of the Protestant cause at Paris, remaining there until 1585. He wrote indignantly about the actions of English Catholics in Paris, and he was recommended to Walsingham by Stafford as a good choice to help the Protestant Henry of Navarre stand firm in the face of Catholic arguments. After Constable left Paris, he traveled to Heidelberg, to Poland, to Italy, perhaps to Hamburg, and probably to the Low Countries. His pamphlet in answer to a work by Cardinal Allen was probably written in 1588.

It seems likely that Constable spent the years 1588 and 1589 at court, and he was said to have been a favorite of the queen. He wrote sonnets, including ones to Penelope Rich, and was much in the company of Arabella Stuart. He was friendly with many Protestants of the Continent, including followers of Henry of Navarre. One of these, Claude d'Isle, Seigneur de Marivaux, sent several letters by James VI of Scotland to their destination by way of Constable. Another follower of Henry of Navarre and friend of Constable was Jean Hotman, who wished to see the Protestant and Roman Catholic Churches united. Constable was involved with him and others, including Penelope Rich, in an intrigue to obtain the favor of James VI for the earl of Essex. Constable met with the king and assured him of his loyalty despite the fact that Arabella Stuart was the chief rival of James in his claims to the throne of England. The scheme was, however, not successful. Constable was at the Scottish court some weeks before October 21, 1589, when he returned to London. While at the Scottish court, he of course met the members of James's literary circle. In 1589, he also wrote the work defending the Huguenots in which he pretended to be a Catholic.

By 1590, Constable had decided to become a Roman Catholic. By the end of that year, all his secular sonnets had probably been written and collected. In 1591 he went to France with Essex on an expedition to assist Henry IV militarily. Not long afterward, however, he apparently joined the other side and publicly became a Catholic. His father was said to have died as a result. Constable wrote a letter to the Countess of Shrewsbury, protesting that if his safety in England were not assured, he would stay in France. After a trip to Rome, he remained in France, living in Paris, occasionally traveling to Rouen, Scotland, Rome, Antwerp, and Brussels. He was often in need of money, although he had an irregular pension from Henry IV. Although he was a Catholic exile, he did not support the claim of Spain to the throne of England. He supported instead the claim of James VI of Scotland, from whom Catholics at least hoped for tolerance. For several years Constable schemed to assure the safety of English Catholics, the return of England to the Roman Catholic Church, and the union of Catholics and Protestants. He tried to use the influence of Henry IV to secure some toleration for Catholics in England; he was part of a plot to convert the Queen of Scots to Catholicism; and he tried to convert James IV as well. He wrote some theological and political pieces, and in 1600 he went to Rome to persuade the pope to support him in another excursion to Scotland. The attempt failed.

Constable returned to England after James I became king in 1603 and was permitted to possess his family's lands. He hoped, with the help of others, to convert James I, but in 1604 he was committed to the Tower of London after some letters revealing the scheme had been seized in France and sent back to England, probably by the king of France. Released in a few months, Constable was confined to his house. Once more deprived of his inheritance, he became dependent on kinsmen. For the next few years he was in and out of prison, until in 1610 he was either banished or simply permitted to leave the country.

After Henry IV's death, Constable returned to France. He died at Liège in 1613 after going there to help convert a Protestant minister. He lay meditating on the crucifix for several days before he died, demonstrating the truth of the words he had written while imprisoned in the Tower of London: "whether I remayn in prison, or go out, I have learned to live alone with God."

ANALYSIS

In his courtly sonnets, collected in the *Diana*, Henry Constable used the traditional conventions of the Petrarchan sonnet. He was also influenced by the French and Italian sonnets of his contemporaries, particularly Philippe Desportes. The title *Diana* is borrowed from Desportes's chief sonnet sequence, and the Italian headlines in the work (sonnetto primo and so on) reveal the Italian influence.

Joan Grundy, one of his editors, considers the Todd manuscript of this work to be the closest thing to an authoritative text, having been assembled before Constable's departure from England from poems that had been written over a period of time. There is an elaborate framework divided into three parts; these parts are then further divided into groups of seven sonnets. Constable provided explanatory titles, some notes on numerical symbolism, and the disclaimer that the sonnets are "vayne poems." In all his sonnets, Constable used the Petrarchan sonnet form *abba abba cde cde*, with variations.

DIANA

Many of the sonnets in the *Diana* are love poems. In the sonnet "To his Mistrisse," which begins, "Grace full of grace," he declares that although these verses include love complaints to others, he now loves only her. The last three lines play on the word "grace" again, vowing that he flies to God for grace that he may live in delight or never love again. Grace was a theological concept with varying interpretations, as well as being part of a noble address and a woman's name. Louise Imogen Guiney in *Recusant Poets* (1939) speculated that the "Grace" might be Grace Talbot, youngest daughter of George Talbot, sixth earl of Shrewsbury. The last sonnet in the manuscript is "To the diuine protection of the Ladie Arbella the author commendeth both his Graces honoure and his Muses aeternitye." Arabella Stuart was the granddaughter of the Countess of Shrewsbury. Constable's sonnet "To the Countesse of Shrewsburye vpon occasion of his dear Mistrisse whoe liu'd vnder her gouer[n]ment" (Part III, group 3, sonnet 2), indicates that he loved someone in her company. It is not even certain, however, whether the sonnet was written to the countess or to the dowager countess. The countess has also been suggested as a candidate for Constable's Di-

ana, and even Mary, Queen of Scots, has been mentioned because she was in the custody of the dowager countess at one time. Another possibility is Penelope Rich. The Harrington manuscript consists of twenty-one sonnets appearing under the title "Mr. Henry Constable's sonetes to the Lady Ritche, 1589." Penelope Rich had requested Constable in a letter to Hotman "qu'il ne soit plus amoureux." This lady was Philip Sidney's Stella, and she was involved in political intrigue with Constable.

In Part I, sonnet 3 of group 1, which deals with the "variable affections" of love, Constable uses repetition to great effect, combining it with antithesis. The first, fifth, and ninth lines begin, "Thyne eye," and the second, sixth, and tenth lines begin, "Myne eye." Her eye, he declares, is the mirror where he sees his heart, and his eye is a window through which her eye may see his heart; there, he says, she may see herself painted in bloody colors. Her eye is the "pyle" or pointed tip of a dart, and his eye is the aiming-point she uses to hit his heart. "Myne eye thus helpes thyne eye to work my smarte." Her eye is a fire and his eye a river of tears, but the water cannot extinguish the flames, nor can the fire dry up the streams from his eye. Constable's technique in this poem is to proceed by a series of parallel and antithetical metaphors. Some of them are traditional, but "thine eye the pyle" is presumably original, at least in English, since the *Oxford English Dictionary* cites this poem as the earliest example of the word's usage. Shakespeare is thought to have imitated lines 1-4 of this poem in his Sonnet XXIV. Constable's contemporary, Alexander Montgomerie, wrote a Scots version of the sonnet.

In the first sonnet of the second group, "An Exhortation to the reader to come and see his Mistrisse beautie," Constable combines repetition with hyperbole. He repeats the word "come" twice in both line 1 and line 6, while in the sestet, "millions" becomes the dominant note, being repeated in lines 9, 10, and 12. Here he uses hyperbole ingeniously to praise the subject of the poem, who is a wonder of nature. He exhorts the reader to come and see her in order to write about her so that the next generation will lament being born too late to see her. Everyone should come and write about her, he protests, for the time may be too short and men too few to write the history of her least part, even though they should write constantly and about nothing else. In the sestet, he declares that the millions who write about her are too few to praise one of her features and can only write about one aspect of her eye, her lip, or her hand, such as "the light or blacke the tast or red the soft or white." This poem was inspired by Petrarch's Sonnet CCXLVIII.

While the first part of *Diana* is about the "variable affections of loue," Constable points out in his "The order of the booke" that the first seven poems are about the beginning of love, the second seven are in praise of his mistress, and the third seven concern specific events in his love experience. In the second sonnet of this third set, "Of his Mistrisse vpon occasion of her walking in a garden," he personifies some of the flowers, making the roses red because they blush for shame when they see her lips and the lilies white because they become pale with envy of her. He indicates his own love by stating that the violets take their color from the blood his heart has shed for her. In the sestet, she becomes a kind of nature goddess. All flowers take their "vertue" from her and their smells from her breath; the heat from her eyes warms the earth, and she manages to water it as well by making him cry. Shakespeare imitated the opening of this sonnet in *The Rape of Lucrece* (1594), lines 477-479.

In the second sonnet of that same set, "To his Ladies hand vpon occasion of her gloue which in her absence he kissed," Constable uses a traditional theme, for there were many French and Italian poems addressed to the lady's hand, and the theme going back to Petrarch's Sonnet CXCIX. The idea of the hand shooting out arrows was also traditional, but Constable goes on to compare his five wounds caused by her five ivory arrows (her fingers) with the Stigmata of St. Francis. This poem, then, uses remarkably specific religious imagery. The stigmata were the impressions of the five wounds of Christ that St. Francis received on his flesh. Constable uses contrasts cleverly here, declaring that St. Francis did not feel the wounds, while he (Constable) lives in torment, and that the wounds of St. Francis were in his hands and feet, while his own wounds are in his heart. The metaphor becomes an elaborate conceit, for if he is therefore a saint like St. Francis, the bow which shot the shafts is a relic, and thus her hand should be kissed. Her glove is a divine thing because it is the quiver of her arrows (the covering of her hand) and the shrine of a relic (her hand).

SPIRITUAL SONNETS

Constable's *Spiritual Sonnets* praise God and his saints rather than an earthly love. The sequence begins with three sonnets to God the Father, the Son, and the Holy Ghost. The one praising God the Father begins by declaring that his essence and his existence are the same, the terminology being derived from scholastic philosophy. The essence of a being was the nature of the being, and existence was the actuality of the being. God's nature was to exist, for he was contingent on no other cause. The next lines reflect the idea that the mind of God reflects God, and thus that the Son of God is the image of God the Father. The doctrine is based on St. Paul's description in Hebrews of the Son as "being the brightness of his glory, and the express image of his person." Constable makes use of this material in the poem, saying that there is mutual love between Father and Son, as the sighs of lovers become one breath, while both breathe one spirit of equal deity, the Holy Ghost. That the Holy Ghost proceeds from both the Father and the Son was orthodox Catholic doctrine. Constable ends the poem by asking God the Father, who wishes to have the title of Father, to engrave his mind with heavenly knowledge so that it may becomes his Son's image (continuing the image figure but applying it to himself), and by praying that his heart may become the temple of the spirit, thus neatly linking the abstract theological discussion of the early part of the sonnet with the individual experience of God.

"To God the Sonne," the middle sonnet, is less abstract. The poet addresses Christ as "Great Prynce of heaven," begotten of the King and of the Virgin Queen, descendant of King David. After this royal beginning, he contrasts the angels singing at his birth with the shepherds playing their pipes; likewise, kings become as humble shepherds for Christ's sake. Heaven and earth, high and low estate, all have a claim to Christ's birth, for he was begotten in heaven, was of kingly race on his mother's side, and was poor. In "To God the Holy Ghost," Constable becomes more abstract and theological again by way of allegorical personification, likening the Holy Ghost in heaven to the love with which the Son and the Father kiss. He describes how the Holy Ghost took the shape of a dove and of fiery tongues and asks the Holy Ghost to bestow upon his love of God his wings and His fire, so that he may appear a seraphim in his sight. The burning quality of the seraphim in theological writings, such as Pseudo-Dionysius the Areopagite's *De caelesti hierarchia* (c. 500; *The Celestial Hierarchy*, 1894), is here in keeping with the fiery nature of the Holy Ghost, for Constable asks the Holy Ghost for his wings and fire, two qualities of the seraphim that he wants to possess. This trinity of poems has sources in such writers as St. Augustine and Thomas Aquinas, but each poem is a personal prayer addressed to an aspect of God.

In "To the Blessed Sacrament," Constable relates the red wine and white Eucharist of the communion service to the red blood and white body of Christ, the body pale because of the shedding of blood. Christ's body is now veiled in white to be received by Constable in the Eucharist, as though in his burial sheet, making Constable into a burial vault or monument for the corpse. He prays that the Christ whom he has received into his body in the Eucharist will appear to his soul, which is imprisoned in earth the way his forefathers were suspended in Limbo when Christ gave them light. He asks Christ to clear his thoughts and free him in a similar way from the flames of evil desire. The poem is a unified sequence of Metaphysical conceits.

In "To the Blessed Lady" (the first of his poems with that title), Constable speaks of the Virgin Mary as a Queen of Queens, born without original sin. God the Father provided his Spirit for her spouse, and she conceived his only Son, and so she was linked with the whole Trinity. Queens of this earth should no longer glory in their role, for much greater honor is due the queen "who had your God, for father, spowse, & sonne." Constable here delights in the realization of Mary's multiple relationships with God, an intellectual concept that holds the element of surprise.

At the beginning of the first of Constable's four poems on Mary Magdalen, he alludes to the saint's legendary retiring to a penitential life in Provence, saying that "for few nyghtes solace in delitious bedd," she did penance "nak'd on nak'd rocke in desert cell" for thirty years. He speaks directly to her in the poem, saying that for each tear she shed, she has a sea of pleasure now. The poem develops through a series of contrasts. In one of his other poems to the same saint, he begins by saying that she can better declare to him the pleasures of heavenly love than someone who has never experienced any other loves or than someone who is not a woman, for his soul will be like a woman once moved by lust but then betrothed to God's Son. His body is "the garment of my spryght" in the daytime of his life, and death will bring "the nyght of my delyght." His soul will be "vncloth'd," and resting from labor, "clasped in the armes of God," will "inioye/ by sweete coniunction, everlastying ioye." The poem proceeds by a complicated sequence of analogies and contrasts: Mary Magdalen knew earthly love, knew heavenly love; his soul is like her, having experienced lust and spiritual love; in the day, his soul is covered with the garment of his body, but in the night of mystical union with God it will be naked.

In his sonnets Constable praises his subjects, both secular and religious, by comparisons (some traditional and some highly original and Metaphysical), and often by ironic contrasts expressed with grammatical parallelism. His wording is simple, and there is much deliberate repetition. Through his carefully reasoned and highly-polished sonnets he communicates very well both his love of Diana and his love of God.

OTHER MAJOR WORKS

NONFICTION: *A Short View of a Large Examination of Cardinall Allen His Trayterous Justification of Sir W. Stanley and Yorck*, c. 1588; *Examen pacifique de la doctrine des Huguenots*, 1589 (*The Catholike Moderator: Or, A Moderate Examination of the Doctrine of the Protestants*, 1623).

BIBLIOGRAPHY

Fleissner, Robert F. *Resolved to Love: The 1592 Edition Of Henry Constable's "Diana."* Salzburg: Institut für Anglistik und Amerikanistik, Universität Salzburg, 1980. Part of the Salzburg Studies in English Literature series, this monograph is one the few book-length studies of Constable.

Grundy, Joan. *Henry Constable.* Liverpool, England: Liverpool University Press, 1960. The most comprehensive work written on the poet. Includes a biographical essay, complete facsimiles of his poems, discussions about his life, poems, and texts, and evaluations of his influence and reputation. Further increasing the value of this book are its exhaustive footnotes and bibliographic entries.

Lee, Sidney. "Henry Constable, Poet and Courtier." *Biographical Studies* 2, no. 4 (1954): 272-300. An excellent and detailed work that examines both the poet's political and theological life and his secular and spiritual work. Featured events include his conversion to Catholicism and its effect upon his poetry, his time spent in the court of James VI in the late 1500's, and his involvement with luminaries of the age such as the earl of Essex and the archbishop of Glasgow.

Mazzaro, Jerome. "Recusant Sincerity: Henry Constable and Spiritual Sonnets." *Essays in Literature* 17, no. 2 (Fall, 1991): 147. An analysis of Constable's *Spiritual Sonnets* and their focus on divine and human love.

Pritchard, R. E. "Milton and Constable." *Notes and Queries* 41, no. 2 (June, 1994): 166. A discussion of the similarities between Constable's "Spiritual Sonnets" and John Milton's poem "Methought I Saw."

CID CORMAN

Born: Boston, Massachusetts; June 29, 1924

PRINCIPAL POETRY

Subluna, 1945
A Thanksgiving Ecologue from Theocritus, 1954
The Precisions, 1955
The Responses, 1956
Stances and Distances, 1957
The Marches, 1957
A Table in Provenance, 1958
The Descent from Daimonji, 1959
For Sure, 1959
Sun Rock Man, 1962
In Good Time, 1964
In No Time, 1964

Nonce, 1965
For You, 1966
For Granted, 1966
Words for Each Other, 1967
And Without End, 1968
No More, 1969
Plight, 1969
Livingdying, 1970
Out and Out, 1972
O/I, 1974
Once and for All: Poems for William Bronk, 1975
Aegis: Selected Poems, 1970-1980, 1983
And the Word, 1987
Of, 1990
How/Now: Poems, 1995
Nothing Doing, 1999

OTHER LITERARY FORMS

Cid Corman's oeuvre is immense. In addition to his many volumes of poetry, he has published a large number of translations from the French, German, Italian, and Japanese. These not only have appeared as separate volumes, including the work of such diverse writers as Matsuo Bashō, Shimpei Kusano, René Char, Francis Ponge, and Philippe Jaccottet, but also lie scattered throughout his books and magazine publications. These latter include a virtual pantheon of major writers, among them Eugenio Montale, Mario Luzi, René Daumal, and Paul Celan, as well as many little-known European and Asian writers.

Corman has been equally prolific as an essayist and commentator on contemporary letters. Some of his essays have been collected in *Word for Word: Essays on the Art of Language* (1977-1978) and *Where Were We Now: Essays and Postscriptum* (1991). Corman has also maintained an enormous literary and cultural correspondence with other writers and intellectuals.

ACHIEVEMENTS

Among poets of his generation, no figure stands more at the center of both poetic activity and influence than Cid Corman. As poet, translator, and one of contemporary letters' most important editors, Corman has been generator, clearing house, arbitrator, and gadfly, presiding over one of the most fertile and creative periods of American poetry. Through his own poetry and through his editorship of *Origin* magazine, Corman has been a central reference point in the poetic battleground of the postwar years. *Origin*, which published William Carlos Williams, Louis Zukofsky, Charles Olson, Robert Creeley, Denise Levertov, and Robert Duncan, performed for its time what T. S. Eliot's *Criterion*, *The Dial*, and *The Literary Review* performed for theirs as major forums for modern writing.

Both Corman's poetry and his translations, still in need of major critical attention, have been of great importance to younger writers. The essential lines of Corman's poetic style were established in his earliest books, and its simplicity of structure and depth of realization marked a maturity of stance that younger poets, in the ongoing literary ferment, have turned to as a kind of spiritual and intellectual benchmark. This early maturity, based on Corman's desire for a poetry that would not engage in the more self-indulgent (hence more popular) styles of writing of its time, claimed for poetry a philosophical sense of anonymity, a nonaggressive quality that seemed, given Corman's unique position, to be an eye in the center of the literary storm. This quality, evident in all Corman's work, gives his voice a peculiarly important place among his contemporaries, for its tact and quiet come not out of diffidence but out of a difficult assuredness not often found in American literary life. In 1975, Corman won the Lenore Marshall Poetry Prize for *O/I*.

BIOGRAPHY

The two major poles of Cid Corman's life have been the United States and Japan, specifically Boston and Kyoto. Close study of his work shows how it embodies both the tensions of urban American life, social and literary, and the qualities of philosophical serenity and complex identification with nature associated with the Orient. Corman was born in Boston and attended the Boston Latin School and then Tufts University, where he was graduated (Phi Beta Kappa) in 1945. He did graduate work at the University of Michigan, where he won a Hopwood Award in Poetry. Back in Boston, Corman ran what was to be the first of his "editorial" contributions to modern poetry, a weekly radio program on WMEX which presented the best of contemporary poets in the Boston area. In 1951, he began *Origin* magazine. A

Fulbright to Paris and a year as an English instructor in Matera, Italy (the source for much of the material of Corman's early volumes of poetry), were the initial phases of Corman's voyaging away from America in order to discover and resolve the contradictions of literary self-exile. Such exile was, and is, Corman's major theme. After returning to the United States, Corman made the first of his trips to Kyoto, spent two years in San Francisco, and then returned to Kyoto.

In Kyoto, Corman's work and influence flourished. There he not only wrote an enormous amount of poetry but also published in a simple and elegant format *Origin* magazine, sending it back to the United States for argument, discussion, and protest, as well as distribution. For Corman, the activity in Kyoto, along with the influence of the city's famous Zen teachers, made the Japanese city one of the necessary places of pilgrimage of American poetry. To contemporary poets who visited or lived in Kyoto, such as Gary Snyder, Philip Whalen, and Clayton Eshleman, Corman's activities and, indeed, his physical presence in the coffee shop that he and his Japanese wife, Shizumi, ran, meant serious engagement and encounter with some of the strongest literary currents of the 1960's and 1970's.

Since that time Corman has continued to be active as a poet, translator, editor, essayist, and maker of fine books. His most recent projects, including several large volumes of poetry, influenced by Asian masters, are outlined in an interview with Gregory Dunne.

ANALYSIS

In one of his earliest books, *Sun Rock Man*, Cid Corman writes: "Already I feel breathless/ as if I have come too far,/ to find peace, to have found it." The thread linking more than thirty years of Corman's poetry, translation, and editorship is the quest back toward some deep original peace, some attempt to find a permanent home in exile. Corman's work is one long and moving dialectic, informed by his sense of having "come too far" and yet of being unable to return. The shifts, both technical and in terms of subject matter, that one discovers in his poems are like signposts pointing both forward and backward at once; they remind the reader that every act of creation has been one of destruction as well, that self-exile for Corman means also new territory.

In Corman's career, this new territory has meant, geographically, first Europe, then Japan. One sees, in particular, the Japanese influence in the details of Corman's verse: his affinity for natural objects and the short, almost Asian, tightness of his forms. Yet, far more important has been the psychological and literary territory Corman has traversed. Psychically, this terrain embraces the open spaces of poetic activity, of "making it new" as chartered by such forebears as William Carlos Williams, Ezra Pound, and Louis Zukofsky. Like the poetry of these predecessors, Corman's work is a departure from the traditional verse conventions of its time; it is marked, as well, by a willingness to bear the immediate deflections of incident, encounter, or thought much as Williams's poetry submitted to the "local" or Zukofsky's to the dictates of the musical phrase. Corman's work can be said to seek its timelessness in its very moment. Thus his poems are spontaneous registers of isolation, of immersion in somewhat alien landscapes where both the native or local language and its cultural iconography are essentially mute; yet it is also immersion in that deeper awareness of world and people caught in the inarticulateness of their situations. In Corman much is characterized as silent, as unknowable. Rather than raiding the inarticulate, Corman's work attempts to come to terms with it, to construct a language that seems to represent a shared act of man and world.

SUN ROCK MAN AND EARLY POEMS

Corman's earliest published poems, such as those in *Sun Rock Man*, attempt to render precisely these occasions of inarticulateness. In them, Corman employs an imagist or objectivist technique, which rigorously favors the recording eye over the conceptualizing mind. The poet is an agency or a recording instrument, and the abject poverty and hopelessness of Matera, an impoverished Italian hill town, is witnessed "objectively." Authorial control is maintained, as it were, only by the details to be selected. Poems such as "the dignities" or "Luna Park" operate under the force of Williams's "no ideas but in things," realized with an eye and ear for detail and tone that are compelling and satisfying; they seem to present an almost pure externality which speaks so eloquently and powerfully that comment is superfluous.

In the end, however, one feels that such poems may rely too heavily on their being a form of *exotica*, particularly when their occasion is almost solely the function of the poet's arrival on the scene. Indeed, the less formally accomplished poems of *Sun Rock Man* suggest a troubled and yet more fruitful ambivalence, for they sound the note which in Corman's career has its most significant distinction: a deepening capacity to express simultaneously the subjective and the objective terms of situations. As he says of his stay in Matera, "Nothing displaces us/ like our own intelligence."

MATURE POEMS

This displacement, suggesting a leave-taking that is both poetic and physical, is the major theme of all Corman's mature work. The exile is not simply one of banishment to strange lands but to a kind of Rilkean soul-work of facing out on the "speechlessness" of the world. Thus, in nearly all the poems after *Sun Rock Man*, the visual imagistic technique, while not abandoned, is forsworn in favor of rendering the physicality of voicing itself, in an attempt to say without inflation or rhetoric the meaning for the poet of such speechlessness.

Corman's poems often begin within an action, as though the poet finds himself surprised by circumstance into utterance. The prepositions or relational conjunctions, the statements containing continuous verb forms ("finding," "remembering," and so on) found at the head of many of Corman's poems are devices for signaling the organic connection between the active and changing content of the poet's situation and the arising of the poem. Rather than the "picture-making" or mimesis of the earlier poems (or of the more imagistically inclined poet), these poems are specifically linguistic occasions, not meant to hold the mirror up to nature but to sound it.

Thus, in one poem about a bell in *And Without End*, it is, as he puts it, "as if the/ air needed clearing,/ as if the sweet sound/ were a vanishing." The poem may be said to seek, like the sound of the bell, to have both its distinctness and its completeness, completeness in the sense that though sound is invisible and adds nothing visual to the picture, it permeates and thus colors everything within hearing. Such soundings have a tactful and nonjudgmental quality about them; there is, as in many other of Corman's poems, a Buddhistic or Zen-like sense of aesthetic appreciation that is, as the poem continues "so clear/ it hardly matters to say more than 'See if you can hear it'/ and 'it' is a bell."

Corman's poems have a way of establishing an equa-nimity or resting place for memory. They involve an un-covering effect, moving from an unspecified dramatic statement to a highly qualified core of meaning. This meaning often resides less in a particular line or state-ment than in the cumulative effect of passage through the poem. In a poem entitled "Back" (from *O/I*), for ex-ample, a device similar to the "bell" sound of the poem discussed above utilizes repetition and variants of tone or phrase to advance and specify meaning. Generalized "man" becomes "me" "given to go on"; a "call/ sum-moning/ all plays on" until the "event" is so "taken to/ heart" that "heart at/ height flings out." The intelligence of the poem resolves itself not only ideationally but vir-tually at the level of the syllable (something Corman has learned well from Zukofsky and Olson), where each moment of development is anticipated musically. In Corman, the minims of speech are deployed much like the quavers of traditional song, as both accents and resistances to the plain meanings of words.

Such fine-tuning informs all Corman's work. The poems seem to draw attention to little more than their own process of realization, as though the form of thought that the poet engenders—though given as language—takes on the characteristics of a visual construct, some-thing cleanly and sparingly drawn. Critics have referred to the "haiku-like" qualities of Corman's verse, but it is perhaps more accurate to note its peculiar transforma-tion of imagistic technique into the realm of thought, as though the processes of the mind could be delineated as carefully as the leaf on a plum branch.

This confrontation with silence—since silence can-not respond, only evoke—becomes in Corman a form of self-realization, an embodying of poetic utterance which has its root in both estrangement and participation. The poet is at all costs trying to make a home in this home-lessness, and the tension of his poetry is the attempt to give this silence its due:

> Don't make me laugh
> or I'll cry: that's the cry,
> Here me, my silence,
> in silence.

The key to such poetry is that both its solipsistic and playful qualities are embedded in the ironies of ambigu-ity and tone. There is something deeply comic and even lighthearted in Corman's address to a language-less world—comic in the very basic sense that seriousness and any heavy-handed desire to mean are always opera-tive under the meaning-canceling sign of death. As Corman notes in one poem:

> in time go
> words also, however true
> Man's life is a conjuring
> finally nothing once more.

This air of "finally nothing" pervades much of Corman's later work, giving the sense of exile both ease and humor, transfiguring the past and its pains into a newer richness and balance. Here the self fully recog-nizes itself as a transparency, an agency that works on and gives voice to its interferences. Poetic tension comes out of the drama and new knowledge is gained in recon-ciliation with the modalities of the past. Thus, Corman writes:

> To bear back the lost
> is at all events
> much like entering
> the enemy's lines
> to plead for one's dead
> for burial.

Corman's poems seek out what the phenomenolo-gists would call the "preobjective world"; that is the world existing before overlaps of human concept and understanding. At the same time, they suggest that the self, about which it is easy to be glib, is no more easily grasped than that exterior world. The strength of the po-etry derives from Corman's urge to pare down to that world, to reduce, to silence language to all but its essen-tial qualities, to make it, as he says in "Morion," a poem about a gem which resembles a Hans Arp sculpture: "Nothing extra,/ all edge./ solid heart. What one/ offers another."

Such poetry has the feel of a natural object; its spare-ness resists the desire to appropriate it, calling instead for tact and subtlety in response. Unlike much contem-porary poetry, Corman's poems refuse to trade on pres-ent anxieties, refuse to be converted into a form of moral coinage—there is barely a word in these poems about the "big issues." Nevertheless, they insinuate themselves into one's moral consciousness by going to ground, by addressing the self at its most affective point, the economy of its own organization:

> Doorways
> reveal my
> shadow and
> make me ask
> myself once
> more if this
> mask I wear
> of words keeps
> my body
> clear of breath.

This grounding acts like an Archimedean lever on ordinary notions of identity and thus gives an astonishing capaciousness to the small forms that Corman so skillfully uses. One would almost want to claim for this poetry a ripple effect, or claim—and here its comparison to haiku is warranted—that it introduces an irruption into the quotidian while at the same time preserving the flavor of the quotidian intact. Such poetry does not easily lend itself to paraphrase or exegesis, nor are its larger incursions into consciousness as immediate as certain more fashionable confessional modes of writing.

This delayed effect and the fact that Corman's work is both large in bulk (he is one of the most prolific poets writing today) and scattered throughout many volumes and little-known magazines, accounts for the lack of a larger critical effort directed at his work. Another reason may be that his work, seen only fitfully, is regarded as only another part of the vast output of American lyricism.

Yet Corman, rightly perceived, is not a lyric poet at all, but, like Ezra Pound, a poet of the epic. It can be said of modern poetry that the lyric has overshadowed the epic, that given the alienated or fragmented sense of self which constitutes contemporary life, the narrative drive required for the epic form can no longer be sustained. One can also read much contemporary poetry as a counter-epic, celebrating, instead of a hero's overcoming obstacles, the hero's sense of loss, discovering, like Eliot, the fragments to shore against the ruins. By contrast, Corman's poetry would intimate a third way,

where the epic has merely gone interior, where the story's arc travels across and engages the adventures of consciousness. Surely Corman's poems might be letters home from such a voyage, reminders in their cumulative reconciliations of sight and sound, of place and identity, that self and world are indeed home for each other.

OTHER MAJOR WORKS

NONFICTION: *William Bronk: An Essay*, 1976; *Word for Word: Essays on the Art of Language*, 1977-1978 (2 volumes); *Where Were We Now: Essays and Postscriptum*, 1991.

POETRY TRANSLATIONS: *Back Roads to Far Towns*, 1967 (Matsuo Bashō); *Things*, 1971 (Francis Ponge); *Leaves of Hypos*, 1973 (René Char); *Breathings*, 1974 (Philippe Jaccottet); *One Man's Moon*, 1984.

BIBLIOGRAPHY

Dunne, Gregory. "Interview with Cid Corman." *American Poetry Review* 29, no. 4 (July/August, 2000): 23-28. Dunne provides useful insights into Corman's long career, affinities with other poets, his use of the syllabic line, and his many years living in Japan.

Evans, George. "A Selection from the Correspondence: Charles Olson and Cid Corman, 1950." *Origin* 5, no. 1 (1983): 78-106. Evans presents the first 14 of 175 letters between Corman and Charles Olson. In 1950, Corman was attempting to launch a new poetry magazine. He wrote to Olson to persuade him to take on the position of contributing editor. Interesting to all students of the Objectivist movement.

Heller, Michael. *Conviction's Net of Branches: Essays on the Objectivist Poets and Poetry*. Carbondale: Southern Illinois University Press, 1985. Corman was a major figure in the Objectivist poetry movement. These essays shed light on the nature and convictions of the Objectivists. This study is suitable for advanced undergraduate and graduate poetry students.

Hinten, Marvin D. "Corman's 'The Tortoise.'" *The Explicator* 54 (Fall, 1995): 43-44. One of the few academic readings of any of Corman's poems, this one elucidates without overkill, paying attention to the functional use of syllabic lines and enjambment.

Olson, Charles. *Letters for "Origin," 1950-1956*. Edited by Albert Glover. New York: Paragon House, 1989. Cid Corman founded *Origin* magazine as a forum for Objectivist poets, and he hired Charles Olson to be its contributing editor. Their letters discuss the struggles of the periodical and of the Objectivist poetic movement. Suitable for serious Corman students.

Olson, Charles, and Cid Corman. *Charles Olson and Cid Corman: Complete Correspondence, 1950-1964*. Edited by George Evans. 2 vols. Orono: National Poetry Foundation, University of Maine, 1987. Evans presents the 175 extant letters between the founder of *Origin* magazine and its contributing editor. They reveal that Olson was initially skeptical of Corman's aims, fearing that Corman was starting a magazine with too broad a scope to serve the needs of the Objectivist poets.

Pater Faranda, Lisa. "'Between Your House and Mine': The Letters of Lorine Niedecker to Cid Corman, 1960-1970." *Dissertation Abstracts International* 44 (February, 1984): 2474A. Pater Faranda annotates the correspondence between Lorine Niedecker and fellow poet Corman, who was Niedecker's editor in the last years of her life. Their correspondence has a dramatic shape to it because it begins before her marriage and ends just before her death.

Michael Heller,
updated by Philip K. Jason

GREGORY CORSO

Born: New York, New York; March 26, 1930
Died: Robbinsdale, Minnesota; January 17, 2001

PRINCIPAL POETRY

The Vestal Lady on Brattle and Other Poems, 1955
Gasoline, 1958
The Happy Birthday of Death, 1960
Minutes to Go, with Others, 1960
Long Live Man, 1962
Selected Poems, 1962
The Mutation of the Spirit, 1964
There Is Yet Time to Run Back Through Life and Expiate All That's Been Sadly Done, 1965
Ten Times a Poem, 1967
Elegiac Feelings American, 1970
Earth Egg, 1974
Herald of the Autochthonic Spirit, 1981
Mindfield: New and Selected Poems, 1989

OTHER LITERARY FORMS

Although Gregory Corso published mainly poetry, he also wrote a short play, *In This Hung-up Age*, produced at Harvard University in 1955; a novel, *The American Express* (1961); and two film scripts: *Happy Death*, with Jay Socin, produced in New York in 1965, and *That Little Black Door on the Left*, included in a group of screenplays entitled *Pardon Me, Sir, But Is My Eye Hurting Your Elbow?* (1968). He also wrote, with Anselm Hollo and Tom Raworth, a series of parodies, *The Minicab War*, published in London by the Matrix Press in 1961.

ACHIEVEMENTS

Perhaps Gregory Corso's greatest contribution to the Beat movement specifically and American poetry generally lies in his role as a literary paradigm for the "New Bohemianism" that appeared in America after World War II and through the 1950's. Despite the fact that Corso never went beyond elementary school, he gained a reputation as one of the most talented of the Beat poets, a "poet's poet," a sort of *enfant terrible* of the Beats. He received teaching appointments on the basis of his reputation as a major figure in the Beat movement, and in this context he was awarded the Longview Foundation Award in 1959 for his poem "Marriage," the Poetry Foundation Award, and the Jean Stein Award for Poetry from the American Academy and Institute of Arts and Letters in 1986.

BIOGRAPHY

More than any of his contemporaries, Gregory Corso lived the true Beat life. Brought up in the slums of New York City, with practically no formal education, Corso was, in the words of the poet-critic Kenneth Rexroth, "a genuine *naif*. A real wildman, with all the charm of a hoodlum . . . a wholesome Antonin Artaud."

He was born in New York City to poor Italian immigrant parents, Fortunato Samuel and Michelina (Colloni) Corso. His mother died when he was a child, and about this loss Corso wrote: "I do not know how to accept love when love is given me. I needed that love when I was motherless young and never had it." His unhappy childhood was marked by his being sent to an orphanage at eleven and to the Children's Observation Ward at Bellevue Hospital when he was thirteen. At that time, Corso later wrote, "I was alone in the world—no mother and my father was at war . . . to exist I stole minor things and to sleep I slept on the rooftops and in the subway." In summarizing his thirteenth year, however, Corso insists that although he went "through a strange hell that year" of 1943, it is "such hells that give birth to the poet."

After three years on the streets of New York, having lived with five different foster parents, Corso was arrested with two friends while attempting to rob a store. Instead of being sent to a boys' reformatory, Corso was sentenced to three years at Clinton Prison, where he began to write poetry. According to Corso, prison "proved to be one of the greatest things that ever happened to me." He even dedicated his second book of poems, *Gasoline*, to "the angels of Clinton Prison" who forced him to give up the often "silly consciousness of youth" to confront the world of men.

After his release from prison in 1950, Corso took on a number of short-term jobs, including manual labor from 1950 to 1951, reporting for the *Los Angeles Examiner* from 1951 to 1952, and sailing on Norwegian vessels as a merchant seaman from 1952 to 1953. He also spent some time in Mexico and in Cambridge, Massachusetts, where he was encouraged in his writing of poetry by an editor of the *Cambridge Review* and where, with the support of several Harvard students, he published his first book of poetry, *The Vestal Lady on Brattle and Other Poems*, in 1955.

Between that time and his departure for Europe in 1959, Corso attracted widespread attention with a series of poetry readings he gave in the East and Midwest. Following the 1955 publication of *The Vestal Lady on Brattle and Other Poems* and his meeting with Jack Kerouac, Allen Ginsberg, and Gary Snyder a year later, his poetry began to appear often in such publications as *Esquire*, *Partisan Review*, *Contact*, and the *Evergreen Review*. In

1958, Lawrence Ferlinghetti first published Corso's famous poem "Bomb" as a broadside at his City Lights Bookshop in San Francisco, as well as the book *Gasoline* in the same year. After an extended tour of England, France, Germany, Italy, and Greece, Corso returned to the United States in 1961. During the following three years he was hired to teach poetry for a term at New York State University at Buffalo. In November, 1963, he married Sally November.

For Corso, the decade of the 1960's was marked by a divorce and more travel in Europe. After the publication of *The Happy Birthday of Death* in 1960, which included such celebrated poems as "Bomb," "Power," "Army," and the award-winning "Marriage," the work that he did in the following decade was very uneven, frequently bordering on flippancy and sentimentality, such as some of the poems comprising *Long Live Man* and *The Mutation of the Spirit*. *Elegiac Feelings American* and *Herald of the Autochthonic Spirit* were published a decade apart, appearing in 1970 and 1981, respectively. The increased intervals between offerings indicate a shift in Corso's attitude toward the relationship between the poet and his poems. During the salad days of the Beat movement, Corso had taken his cue from his contemporaries (notably Kerouac) by rejecting any mode of writing except pure spontaneity, but his later poems are much more carefully revised and tightly crafted works. This can be seen in the newer poems that appear in *Mindfield*.

Corso traveled widely over the course his lifetime, in Mexico and Eastern Europe as well as Western Europe, and in addition to teaching at the State University of New York at Buffalo, he taught in Boulder, Colorado. He was married three times and had five children. In his later years, he became somewhat reclusive, taking part in the occasional tribute or event. He made an appearance at the funeral of Ginsberg in 1996 to say good-bye to his old friend. Ill health forced Corso to move from New York City to Minneapolis, where he lived with a daughter. He died in Robbinsdale, Minnesota, on January 17, 2001, at the age of seventy.

ANALYSIS

Two strains pervade the poetry of Gregory Corso: the Dionysian force of emotion and spontaneity, and a preoccupation with death. From Corso's early poems to his later work, one finds the recurring persona of the clown as an embodiment of the Dionysian force, as opposed to the Apollonian powers of order, clarity, and moderation. The clown's comedy, which has its root in the very fact of being "a poet in such a world as the world is today," ranges from the mischievous laughter of the child to the darker, often somber irony of the poet-in-the-world. This exuberance is bound up with the rebelliousness and political activism of the 1960's, as is evident in one of Corso's early and most widely anthologized poems, "Bomb." In this poem—typographically shaped like a bomb in its original 1958 publication by City Lights—Corso confronted the unalterable reality of the nuclear age and his inability "to hate what is necessary to love."

A large part of Corso's Dionysian spirit is romantic—and Corso is certainly in the tradition of Romantic poets John Keats and Percy Bysshe Shelley. He sees the child as a pure, spontaneous Dionysian being: always naturally perceptive, always instinctively aware of sham, pretense, and deception. Such perception runs throughout American literature, from the character of Pearl in Nathaniel Hawthorne's *The Scarlet Letter* (1850) to the child who "went forth" in Walt Whitman to Huckleberry Finn in Mark Twain's novel of 1884 to Holden Caulfield in J. D. Salinger's *The Catcher in the Rye* (1951). Similarly, in Corso's poetry the child (particularly the self of the poet's recollection) stands for pure Dionysian perception without the intervening deceptions of rules and conventions.

The other strain in Corso's poetry is a passionate concern with the mystery of death, a theme that is more pervasive in his work than any other, with the exception of the pure experience of childhood. Indeed, the intermingling of these two motifs essentially characterizes the Dionysian spirit of Corso—as well as the art of the Beat generation in general. In a poem dedicated to one of his heroes, entitled "I Met This Guy Who Died" (from *Mindfield*), Corso writes about a drunken outing with his friend Jack Kerouac. Taken home to see Corso's newborn child, Kerouac moans: "Oh Gregory, You brought up something to die." "How I love to probe life," Corso once wrote in an autobiographical essay. "That's what poetry is to me, a wondrous prober. . . . It's not the metre or measure of a line, a breath not 'law' music, but the assembly of great eye sounds placed into an inspired measured idea."

GASOLINE

In an early collection, *Gasoline*, Corso solidifies his poetic identity in a directly autobiographical poem, "In the Fleeting Hand of Time." Here the poet casts his lot not with the Apollonian academics, who "lay forth sheepskin plans," but with life in the "all too real mafia streets." In another poem from this early collection, entitled "Birthplace Revisited," the poet captures what Allen Ginsberg referred to as "the inside sound of language alone" by virtually overturning the expected or commonplace. This brief poem opens with a mysterious figure wandering the lonely, dark street, seeking out the place where he was born. The figure resembles a character from a detective story—"with raincoat, cigarette in mouth, hat over eye, hand on gat"—but when he reaches the top of the first flight of stairs, "Dirty Ears aims a knife at me . . . I pump him full of lost watches." This is not exactly the kind of image one would expect to find in the language of the standard-bearers of Corso's time, such as Allen Tate or John Crowe Ransom. In fact, in an act of Dionysian rebellion, Corso, in a poem entitled "I Am 25," bluntly proclaims "I HATE OLD POET-MEN!"—especially those "who speak their youth in whispers." The poet-clown, in true Dionysian fashion, would like to gain the confidence of the "Old Poetman," insinuating himself into the sanctity of his home, and then "rip out their apology tongues/ and steal their poems."

THE HAPPY BIRTHDAY OF DEATH

The Happy Birthday of Death presents the best example of Corso as Dionysian clown. In the lengthy ten-part poem entitled simply "Clown," Corso presents this persona more explicitly than he does in any other place when he asserts, "I myself am my own happy fool." The fool or the clown is the personification of the "pure poetry" of Arthur Rimbaud or Walt Whitman, rejecting the academic Apollonian style of the formalists. "I am an always clown," writes Corso, "and need not make grammatic Death's diameter."

Several of the poems of *The Happy Birthday of Death*, notably the award-winning "Marriage," offer critiques of respected institutions of bourgeois society.

This poem, perhaps Corso's most popular, is structured around the central questions: "Should I get married? Should I be good?" In a surrealistic feast of language-play, Corso contrasts the social ritual of marriage ("absurd rice and clanky cans and shoes," Niagara Falls honeymoons, cornball relatives) with the irrational and spontaneous phrases he inserts throughout the poem, such as "Flash Gordon soap," "Pie Glue," "Radio Belly! Cat Shovel!" and "Christmas Teeth." In opposition to the conformist regimentation of suburban life, the speaker contrives unconventional schemes, such as sneaking onto a neighbor's property late at night and "hanging pictures of Rimbaud on the lawnmower" or covering "his golf clubs with 1920 Norwegian books."

LONG LIVE MAN

In his later work, *Long Live Man*, Corso continued his Dionysian assault on established literary conventions. The poem "After Reading 'In the Clearing,'" for example, finds the speaker admitting that he likes the "Old Poetman" Robert Frost better now that he knows he is "no Saturday Evening Post philosopher." Nevertheless, Frost is "old, old" like Rome, and, says the poet, "You undoubtedly think unwell of us/ but we are your natural children." What Corso intends is not to suggest that youth should respect age, but rather, as William Wordsworth wrote in "Ode: Intimations of Immortality," that "the child is father to the man." As Corso points out in his urban poem, "A City Child's Day," the "Grownups do not go where children go/ At break of day their worlds split apart."

Two short poems in the earlier *Long Live Man*, viewed together, seem to foreshadow the approach Corso later used to criticize the institution of marriage and, still later, in *Elegiac Feelings American* and *Herald of the Autochthonic Spirit*, Corso maintains his Dionysian critique of Apollonian standards. The first poem is entitled "Suburban Mad Song"; the second, "The Love of Two Seasons." The first asks how the wife will look at the husband after "the horns are still," when the celebration is ended "and marriage drops its quiet shoe." In other words, when the Dionysian passions of the first experiences become the frozen form, the institution of marriage, the once-happy couple "freeze right in their chairs/ troubled by the table." The only solution for such stasis, Corso seems to be saying in the other short poem,

"The Love of Two Seasons," is "the aerial laughter [of] mischief."

ELEGIAC FEELINGS AMERICAN

In "The American Way," a long poem from *Elegiac Feelings American*, Corso worries that the prophetic force of Christ is becoming frozen by American civil religion. "They are frankensteining Christ," the poet says despairingly; "they are putting the fear of Christ in America" and "bringing their Christ to the stadiums." Christ, for Corso, is the pure force of reality, while religious institutions are merely perversions even as love between two people is a pure and sacred force, while marriage is profane. "If America falls," writes Corso, "it will be the blame of its educators preachers communicators alike."

HERALD OF THE AUTOCHTHONIC SPIRIT

Herald of the Autochthonic Spirit suggests not only that the poet has not withered with age but also that he has mastered an ironic voice while maintaining his comic, childlike energy. In a simple poem, "When a Boy," he remarks, first of all, how he "monitored the stairs/ alter'd the mass" in church, as opposed to the pleasure of summer camp, when he "kissed the moon in a barrel of rain." Similarly, in the poem "Youthful Religious Experience" he tells how he found a dead cat when he was six years old and compassionately prayed for it, placing a cross on the animal. When he told this to the Sunday school teacher, she pulled his ears and told him to remove the cross. The old, Corso maintains, can never comprehend the eternally young.

In another poem from this collection, "What the Child Sees," Corso depicts the child as "innocently contemptuous of the sight" of old age's foolishness. "There's rust on the old truths," Corso contends in "For Homer," and "New lies don't smell as nice as new shoes." What the poet, like the child, perceives as pleasurable is the immediate, sensual experience, such as the smell of new shoes, not the abstractions of dried-up old lies. The sadness at the root of this pleasure, however, is a sadness that appears in much of Corso's poetry, evoked by the perennial reality of death.

MINDFIELD

In the 1989 collection *Mindfield* is a compilation of Corso's favorite poems throughout his career, along with new poems. Here, one can trace the maturation of the poet across three decades. Particularly revealing are the seven poems written after the appearance of *Herald of the Autochthonic Spirit* in 1981 but previously published. These poems illustrate the growth of Corso as a poet who, at the half-century point in his life, had broadened the range and scope of his poetry while maintaining some of the themes that have dominated his work from the early 1950's.

In the poem "Window," written in 1982, Corso confronts the painful reality of his own mortality. The horror of death, however, becomes merely an evil invention of the older generation which, asserts the man-child Corso, is notoriously "unreliable." Writes Corso:

> . . . your parents your priest your guru are people
> and it is they who tell you that you must die
> to believe them is to die . . .

As a romantic, Corso draws his lessons from nature. Proclaiming his "contempt for death" and asserting that "the spirit knows better than the body," Corso offers the reader lines of poetry as moving as many of Wordsworth's in his assertion of immortality:

> As the fish is animalized water
> so are we humanized spirit
> fish come and go   humans also
> the death of the fish
> is not the death of the water
> likewise the death of yr body
> is not the death of life
> So when I say I shall never know my death, I mean it . . .

To Corso, death is merely another limit or restraint that he challenges throughout his poetry. When he writes, at one point, "Death I unsalute you," Corso illustrates his resistance to all limits that restrict what he sees as the limitless strength of the human spirit.

In the longest of the previously unpublished poems, "Field Report," Corso confronts the inevitable approach of old age with words that are gentle and not fearful. That poem, like most of his other later works, seems to give support to the words of Corso's contemporary and friend, Allen Ginsberg, who writes in his introduction to *Mindfield* ("On Corso's Virtues") words that, while written about a single poem ("The Whole Mess . . . Almost" from *Herald of the Autochthonic Spirit*), could be said about most of Corso's later poetry: The poem is "a masterpiece of Experience, the grand poetic abstractions Truth, Love, God, Faith Hope Charity, Beauty, money, Death, & Humor are animated in a single poem with brilliant & intimate familiarity."

In others of his previously unpublished poems from the 1980's, particularly "Hi" and "Fire Report—No Alarm," Corso grapples with such large metaphysical issues as God, mortality, immortality, and the identity of Jesus. Without God, Corso concludes ironically, the Reverend Jerry Falwell (leader of the conservative Moral Majority and today's Christian Right) might well be putting onions on hamburgers. Such pithy, concrete insights are what give humor and vividness to Corso's later poetry.

OTHER MAJOR WORKS

LONG FICTION: *The American Express*, 1961; *The Minicab War*, 1961 (with Anselm Hollo and Tom Raworth).

PLAYS: *In This Hung-up Age*, pr. 1955; *Standing on a Streetcorner*, pb. 1962; *That Little Black Door on the Left*, pb. 1967.

SCREENPLAYS: *Happy Death*, 1965 (with Jay Socin); *That Little Black Door on the Left*, 1968.

MISCELLANEOUS: *Writing from Unmuzzled Ox Magazine*, 1981.

BIBLIOGRAPHY

Cook, Bruce. "An Urchin Shelley." In *The Beat Generation*. New York: Charles Scribner's Sons, 1971. Cook discusses the lives and works of key figures of the Beat generation. Corso, in a 1974 interview, charged Cook with lying about him in an interview that he conducted. About *The Beat Generation*, Corso said, "I thought it sucked because he lied."

Gifford, Barry, and Lawrence Lee. *Jack's Book: An Oral Biography of Jack Kerouac*. New York: St. Martin's Press, 1978. An extensive biography of Kerouac and his relationships with other persons of the Beat generation, including Gregory Corso. Under the influence of Kerouac, Corso put words together in an extremely abstract, apparently accidental manner. According to Corso, Kerouac, who was offered a football scholarship from Columbia University, was a "strong, beautiful man; he didn't have to show his strength. He took a Columbia University offer and then decided he wanted to write."

Knight, Arthur, and Kit Knight, eds. *The Beat Vision: A Primary Sourcebook*. New York: Paragon House, 1987. This fascinating collection includes an interview with Corso as well as a letter from Corso to Gary Snyder. The book includes vintage photographs and critical discussion of the Beat poets' place in American literature and the impact of their controversial ideas in shaping and defining American society.

Masheck, Joseph, ed. *Beat Art*. New York: Columbia University Press, 1977. Some of Corso's drawings were included in an exhibition of work by writers associated with the Beats, and although the catalog is not illustrated, the comments on the drawings are interesting and instructive. Corso's drawings, which are also featured in *Mindfield*, are significant but often overlooked artifacts of the Beat generation.

Miles, Barry. *The Beat Hotel: Ginsberg, Burroughs, and Corso in Paris, 1958-1963*. New York: Grove Press, 2000. A narrative account of Beat poets in Paris, where some of their most important work was done. Based on firsthand accounts from diaries, letters, and interviews.

Selerie, Gavin. *Gregory Corso*. New York: Binnacle Press, 1982. The interview by Selerie is particularly provocative because of Corso's comments on his books—such as *Gasoline, The Happy Birthday of Death*, and *Elegiac Feelings American*—as well as friends such as Jack Kerouac, Allen Ginsberg, and William S. Burroughs. Corso also provides information on his youthful crimes and time spent in prison.

Skau, Michael. *A Clown in a Grave: Complexities and Tensions in the Works of Gregory Corso*. Carbondale: Southern Illinois University Press, 1999. An examination that covers the complete works of Gregory Corso and his complex imagination, his humor, and his poetic techniques in dealing with America, the Beat generation, and death. Includes a bibliography of Corso's work.

Donald E. Winters, Jr.;
bibliography updated by the editors

CHARLES COTTON

Born: Beresford Hall, Staffordshire, England; April 28, 1630
Died: London, England; February 16, 1687

PRINCIPAL POETRY

"An Elegie upon the Lord Hastings," 1649
A Panegyrick to the King's Most Excellent Majesty, 1660
"The Answer," 1661
Scarronides: Or, Virgile Travestie, 1664
A Voyage to Ireland in Burlesque, 1670
Horace, 1671 (translation of Pierre Corneille's play, with original lyric poetry)
Burlesque upon Burlesque, 1675
"To My Dear and Most Worthy Friend, Mr. Izaak Walton," 1675
"The Retirement," 1676
The Wonders of the Peake, 1681
Poems on Several Occasions, 1689
Genuine Works, 1715

OTHER LITERARY FORMS

Apart from his original poetry, Charles Cotton also published translations and burlesques (now of minor interest), books on planting and gaming, and a treatise on fly fishing that became part 2 of Izaak Walton's *The Compleat Angler* (1676). He is not known to have written fiction, essays, or pamphlets. As with most seventeenth century figures, there is no diary and not much correspondence. Consequently, information on Cotton's day-to-day life is sparse, and many of his poems (which circulated in manuscript) cannot be precisely dated.

ACHIEVEMENTS

During his lifetime and throughout the eighteenth century, Charles Cotton was known almost exclusively as a writer of burlesques and translations. His rendering of Michel de Montaigne into idiomatic English prose was particularly admired. Today, however, Cotton is esteemed as a congenial minor poet of the Restoration period who anticipated aspects of Romanticism in his verse and who collaborated belatedly with Walton to produce one of the most popular books in English literature. Yet, Cotton is a significant landscape poet, a perceptive observer of rural life, an often graceful lyricist, and a distinguished regionalist.

Not until the Romantic period was Cotton taken seriously as an original versifier. Charles Lamb, a lover of old books, rediscovered Cotton's *Poems on Several Occasions* more than a century after their publication and quoted several of them delightedly in a letter of March 5, 1803. He selected four examples of Cotton's work to be included in Robert Southey's *Specimens of the Later English Poets (1807)*: "Song. Montross," "The Litany," "The Retirement," and the "Morning" quatrain. William Wordsworth discussed, praised, and quoted Cotton's "Winter" quatrains in his famous preface to the *Poems of 1815*. Samuel Taylor Coleridge extolled Cotton's *Poems on Several Occasions* in *Biographia Literaria* (1817), Chapter 19. Lamb, again, called special attention to Cotton's poem "The New Year" in his essay "New Year's Eve" (*Essays of Elia*, 1823), and with this, Cotton's poetic reputation was at its peak. Cotton lost favor during the Victorian years and proved less interesting to the earlier twentieth century than more complicated Metaphysical poets such as John Donne. Though holding a place in the literary history of seventeenth century England, Cotton has never been regarded as a major writer.

BIOGRAPHY

Charles Cotton was born at Beresford Hall, Staffordshire, on April 28, 1630. The only child of Charles and Olive Stanhope Cotton, he was, like his father, a country squire with literary interests—and a Royalist. The English Civil War, which began when he was twelve, inspired Cotton with a vision of worldwide chaos that he soon expressed in verse through descriptions of the adjacent Peak District scenery in Derbyshire. From about 1648 to 1655, young Charles was tutored by Ralph Rawson, who is mentioned in several of Cotton's early poems and who in turn addressed a poem to him. Cotton's first published poem was "An Elegie upon the Lord Hastings" (1649); Hastings had died the same year at the age of nineteen. Other poems lamenting Hasting's death were written by John Dryden, Robert Herrick, Andrew Marvell, John Denham, Sir Aston Cokayne, Alexander Brome, and John Bancroft. It cannot be said that Cotton's was the best. In 1651, he wrote another elegy, on Lord Derby, a Royalist who was captured after the Battle of Worcester and beheaded on October 15, 1651. His strong political feelings were made further apparent in "The Litany" and in "To Poet E—— W——," the latter castigating Edmund Waller for his servile obsequiousness in the face of the Cromwellian regime. Cotton wrote all these potentially seditious poems as a young bachelor in his twenties. Like almost all his shorter verse, they remained unpublished during his lifetime.

Throughout the winter of 1655-1656 Cotton was in France. From there, he addressed several poems of amorous longing to Isabella Hutchinson ("Chloris"), whom he married on June 30, 1656, and who bore him nine children before her death in 1669. She may also have been the inspiration for "On Christmas-Day, 1659," which is the only one of Cotton's major poems to be concerned with orthodox religion. Its happy mood anticipated the impending restoration of the monarchy, which took place on May 29, 1660; Cotton then wrote *A Panegyrick to the King's Most Excellent Majesty*, cele-

Charles Cotton (© Michael Nicholson/Corbis)

brating a day that must have been as exhilarating to him as that of his own wedding.

For the next twenty-five years Cotton published the literary works (not all of them precisely datable) upon which his immediate reputation would rest. Thus, in 1661, "The Answer" (to Alexander Brome) celebrated that "dusty corner of the World" which Cotton called his own and the return of his humble Muse, which for the next few years manifested itself primarily in translations. A prose translation of *The Morall Philosophy of the Stoicks* (1664), from the French of Guillaume Du Vair, preceded Cotton's famous *Scarronides*, a daringly bawdy verse burlesque of Vergil. Named for a previous French work (Paul Scarron's *Virgile travesti*, 1648), it became Cotton's most popular poem, which Samuel Pepys, among others, thought "extraordinary good" (*Diary*, March 2, 1664). To a modern critic such as James Sutherland, on the other hand, it seems nothing more than a "crude, sniggering, schoolboy denigration" of an immortal poet whom force-fed students of the classics were all too willing to disparage. Whatever its worth as literature, *Scarronides* remained central to Cotton's reputation until the nineteenth century. In 1666, however, he wrote the "Winter" quatrains, which were later to be praised by Wordsworth.

When his wife died in 1669, Cotton (who married again five years later) left Beresford Hall long enough to head a military expedition to Ireland, with his agreeable poetic narrative *A Voyage to Ireland in Burlesque* the only significant result. Consisting of three cantos of rhymed hexameters, *A Voyage to Ireland in Burlesque* is a good-hearted diary of travel vexations, candid and earthy. Cotton's translation of Pierre Corneille's drama *Horace* (1671), appearing the next year, included ten songs and choruses of his own, the largest body of Cotton's lyric poetry to be published in his lifetime. He was now at the height of his literary productivity. In 1674, Cotton published more translations from the French, including one of Blaize de Montluc, and an original work in prose, *The Compleat Gamester*, which was reprinted at frequent intervals for the next fifty years. *The Planters Manual* (1675), also an original prose, was less successful, being only a guide to successful horticulture. His next major success was a burlesque in verse of the Roman poet Lucian. Called *Burlesque upon Burlesque*, it

was written in Hudibrastic tetrameter (imitating Samuel Butler). Having created a taste for such literary travesties with his earlier demolitions of Vergil, Cotton now replied to his own imitators by providing them with a further model from which to steal.

These were also the years of his close friendship with Izaak Walton, whose *The Compleat Angler* (1653, with innumerable later editions) had already influenced Cotton's *The Compleat Gamester* of 1674. That same year, Cotton built the famous fishing house in which his initials and Walton's were intertwined over the front door. He published one of his best poems, "To My Dear and Most Worthy Friend, Mr. Izaak Walton," in the 1675 edition of Walton's *Lives* (of Donne, Richard Hooker, and George Herbert) after having written it three years earlier. When Walton's *The Compleat Angler* was next published (1676, fifth edition), it included a second part by Cotton, the treatise on fly-fishing that is surely his best-known and most-read work today. Cotton's idyllic poem "The Retirement," published in the same volume, ends with Cotton's hope of living "sixty full years." He actually died just short of fifty-seven.

In 1678, the philosopher Thomas Hobbes published *De Mirabilibus Pecci*, a Latin poem extolling the already well-known wonders of the Peak District in Derbyshire, including caverns, springs, and a great house. Alongside the Latin in this edition there was an English translation "by a person of Quality" who may have been Cotton but probably was not. In any case, Hobbes's versified horseback journey through this anomalous landscape led Cotton to compose his longest poem, *The Wonders of the Peake*, published in 1681. The year of its appearance was also one of almost unbearable financial stress for Cotton, who had inherited a deeply entailed estate from his father (died 1658) and could no longer cope with the accumulated debts. He was therefore obliged to sell Beresford Hall at auction. Fortunately, it was immediately purchased by his cousin John Beresford, who allowed Cotton to remain until his death six years later. It was thus an ebullient Cotton who cheerfully defied the severe winter of 1682-1683 in a "Burlesque upon the Great Frost," addressed of John Bradshaw. Much of his confinement was probably devoted to his translation of Montaigne (1685), which eighteenth century readers generally considered to be the most notable of all his works. Two memorable late poems were "To Astraea" (1686), addressed to Aphra Behn, the first professional woman author in England, and the "Angler's Ballad," which, with its reference to King James II (reigned 1685-1688), is usually regarded as Cotton's last. These and others were collected as *Poems on Several Occasions* in 1689, two years after Cotton's death, and the *Genuine Works* followed in 1715. Alexander Chalmers published "The Poems of Charles Cotton"—including almost all his poetry—in *The Works of the English Poets* (1810), and Thomas Campbell included selections in *Specimens of the British Poets* (1819). There were no further substantial editions of Charles Cotton's poetry until the twentieth century.

ANALYSIS

When Charles Cotton was twelve years old, Puritan insurgents overthrew the monarchy of Charles I and established a Presbyterian commonwealth in its place. During the last years of his life, James II sought to restore Roman Catholicism, and Cotton just missed seeing the Bloodless Revolution of 1688, which banished James to the Continent and returned the monarchy to Protestantism. Of these momentous events, Cotton had surprisingly little to say. While "The Litany," for example, is outspokenly anti-Cromwellian, it regards the Protector only as a vile nuisance, on a level with "ill wine" and "a domineering Spouse." Similarly, Cotton was even more predisposed to ignore the religious controversies of his time. Only "On Christmas-Day, 1659" is, of all his works, significantly Christian; even in his several elegies, there is no specifically Christian consolation. Of the great subjects available to him, Cotton did little with politics (after 1651), very little with religion, and nothing with discovery or science.

Cotton's subjects are the traditionally Horatian ones of leisure, relaxation, friendship, love, and drinking, with some special attention in his case to the river Dove, fishing, his fellow poets, and the scenery of the Peak. He is also especially observant of rural life, so that many of his poems are designedly pastoral, including eclogues in which Cotton himself appears as a lovesick shepherd. When sadness intrudes upon these idyllic scenes, it is generally economic in origin: Poverty is another of Cotton's themes, especially as it affects the literary life.

For all his love of retirement and solitude, Cotton was not a literary elitist. There are few barriers to the enjoyment of his poems, which are straightforwardly written in plain, colloquial English, as was thought appropriate to pastoral and the burlesque. Though influenced by his Metaphysical predecessors, John Donne especially, Cotton is more akin to Robert Herrick. Both Cotton and Herrick, for example, are observant regionalists particularly ready to celebrate the rewarding, if seemingly inconsequential, joys of rural life and of the milder emotions. Thus, Cotton generally prefers well-observed pastoral details and witty asides to complex imagery or erudite mythology. His contempt for classical learning was probably quite real. There is throughout Cotton's work a serene complacency regarding the adequacy of his own lighthearted perceptions and the healthiness of his instincts. While Romantic critics such as Charles Lamb appreciated the accuracy and vigor of Cotton's outlook, Victorians (such as the American James Russell Lowell) were frequently dismayed by his unapologetic "vulgarity" regarding bodily parts and functions.

A more serious objection to Cotton's verse is its apparent lack of substance. Without quite achieving the epigrammatic quotability of, for example, Richard Lovelace or Andrew Marvell, Cotton resembles both in his largely traditional thematic concerns. He writes most obviously to amuse himself, and sometimes to amuse, compliment, or insult others, but rarely to inspire deep feeling or thought. In several instances, his poems are overlong and drift into lower reaches of the imagination. In others, potentially fine lyrics are marred by inadequacies that a more serious poet would have been at pains to remove. Because poetry for Cotton was private and usually recreational, his work often lacks finality and polish. From a generic point of view, Cotton was most original in bringing to public notice the burlesque and the travel narrative as poetic forms. The other forms that he uses are generally conventional and had been used by his immediate predecessors. His lyrics, for example, are in form, technique, and substance, largely unoriginal, except insofar as they are infused by a unique and engaging personality.

Ultimately, this personableness is his greatest strength. Within his best poems (and his prose addition to Walton), Cotton is superbly himself, and nowhere more so than in "The Answer," a verse epistle to Alexander Brome, whose minor verse helped to reawaken Cotton's neglected Muse, which thrived on solitude. "No friends, no visitors, no company" were desired, "So that my solace [wrote Cotton] lies amongst my grounds,/ and my best companie's my horse and hounds." In a second epistle to Brome, also in heroic couplets, Cotton laments the neglected poet who "knows his lot is to be Poor." A related panegyric, "On the Excellent Poems of My Most Worthy Friend, Mr. Thomas Flatman" (another minor poet of the time), is Cotton's fullest statement of his own concept of poetry, which involves the balancing of old and new, judgment and wit, knowledge and feeling, naturalness and style, propriety and vigor. In many of his literary poems, however, Cotton denigrates his own poetic abilities and himself. If his burlesques are often mock-heroic, he is sometimes even antiheroic in his lyrics. Thus, in his "Epistle to John Bradshaw Esq.," Cotton describes his return to Beresford Hall after a four-month business trip to London. He remains

> The same dull Northern clod I was before,
> Gravely enquiring how Ewes are a Score,
> How the Hay-Harvest, and the Corn was got,
> And if or no there's like to be a Rot;
> Just the same Sot I was e'er I remov'd,
> Nor by my travel, nor the Court improv'd.

Cotton is at his best when most incorrigible.

THE WONDERS OF THE PEAKE

The Wonders of the Peake, probably written two years earlier, is Cotton's longest original poem, being almost fifteen hundred lines of his favorite heroic couplets. In organization and substance it is straightforward, as the reader is led to visit each of the seven "wonders" (traditional before Cotton) in turn: Poole's Hole, a cave; St. Anne's Well, a spring; Tydes-well, another spring; Elden-Hole, a second cave; Mam-Tor, a disintegrating mountain; Peak Cavern ("Peake's-Arse"), the third and most important cave; and Chatsworth, seat of the Duke of Devonshire, a splendid mansion inexplicably situated in this wilderness of geological oddities. Although undistinguished as verse, the poem is of major historical significance as a journey poem, when examples in that genre were unusual, and as a then rare attempt to describe an uncultivated landscape in English verse.

Prior to the seventeenth century, landscape was generally neglected in British literature and art (consider William Shakespeare's plays). Only following the Restoration in 1660 did scenery in literature become increasingly common. Among the reasons for its popularity were the influence of Dutch landscape painting (with an Italian influence following somewhat later), the popularity of Vergil, the rise of Baconian science, and a new naturalism (as in the thought of Thomas Hobbes, whose Latin poem on the Peak preceded Cotton's English one). As Marjorie Hope Nicolson has shown (in her book *Mountain Gloom and Mountain Glory*, 1959), with some understandable oversimplification, Cotton is of special interest in the history of British landscape aesthetics because *The Wonders of the Peake* articulates so powerfully the genuine disgust, and yet interest, which irregular terrain such as that of Derbyshire evoked. For Cotton, the limestone caverns of the Peak are both sexual and theological. They are also theaters of the imagination, wherein the mind is invited to transform ambiguously shaped dripstone formations into what it will. Cotton, in other words, substantially discovered the cavern imagery that many later poets, William Blake especially, would use in discussing the subconscious mind. Thus, Cotton was a precursor of eighteenth century landscape aesthetics and of Romantic landscape imagery.

SHORTER POEMS

Cotton's shorter poems, almost all of them published posthumously in 1689 from an uncertain text, are easily categorized (since they cannot be dated) into form and subject areas: poems of nature and the rural life, love poems, odes, elegies and epitaphs, epistles, epigrams, narratives, and burlesques and satires. The nature poems include "The Retirement"; sets of quatrains to morning, noon, evening, and night; various eclogues; and "Winter," which consists of fifty-three quatrains of tetrameter couplets full of the rural imagery and controlled understatement that Wordsworth admired; it is probably Cotton's best poem.

The love poems include songs, odes, madrigals, sonnets, and a rondeau. Those addressed to "Chloris," his future wife, and others inspired by her (such as "The Separation") are among Cotton's finest works, reaching a depth of feeling that he seldom again achieved. Yet other poems by him addressed to or concerning women are crudely sensual and even misogynistic, if maliciously funny. Thus, "Resolution in Four Sonnets, of a Poetical Question put to me by a Friend, concerning four Rural Sisters" estimates the relative ability of each to be seduced, while "To Aelia" (which begins "Poor antiquated slut, forbear") admonishes an overaged debauchee.

Though Cotton wrote odes on many subjects, particularly love, he also composed a series of Pindaric ones on hope, melancholy, woman, beauty, contentment, poverty, and death. Those to hope, melancholy, and death are serious poetry reminiscent of Donne and Herbert. Some of his earliest poems were elegies; those still capable of moving modern readers were written in honor of his first wife ("Gods! are you just?") and of his fellow poet Richard Lovelace.

Several of the epitaphs, like that on Robert Port, are long enough to compete with the elegies; that on M. H., a whore, is a macabre evocation of necrophilia and grief. The shorter epitaphs and Cotton's epigrams are generally ineffective. His narrative poems, such as those on Ireland and the Peak, grade into his epistles, as in "A Journey into the Peak. To Sir Aston Cockain." Finally, several of the odes and epistles are really drinking songs, as Cotton in his later years cheerfully faced the prospects of poverty and old age.

POEMS ON SEVERAL OCCASIONS

Despite its variety and excellence, Cotton's *Poems on Several Occasions* was little noticed in its own time, even though, as James Sutherland has suggested, it contained "more and better poetry . . . than is to be found in any other minor poet of the Restoration." By the time it appeared, naturalness and honesty were out of fashion, and Cavalier morality had been circumscribed. Though Cotton's burlesques continued to be read, his accomplishments in more important genres were almost totally forgotten until appreciative Romantic readers established a new assessment of Cotton that has since become the basis for his modern reputation.

OTHER MAJOR WORKS

PLAY: *Horace*, pb. 1671 (translation of Pierre Corneille's play, with original lyric poetry).

NONFICTION: *The Compleat Gamester*, 1674; *The Planters Manual*, 1675; *The Compleat Angler, Part II*, 1676.

TRANSLATIONS: *The Morall Philosophy of the Stoicks*, 1664 (of Guillaume Du Vair); *The History of the Life of the Duke of Espernon*, 1670; *The Fair One of Tunis*, 1674; *The Commentaries of Messire Blaize de Montluc, Mareschal of France*, 1674; *Essays of Michael Seigneur de Montaigne*, 1685; *Memoirs of the Sieur De Pontis*, 1694.

BIBLIOGRAPHY

Beresford, John, ed. *The Poems of Charles Cotton, 1630-1687*. New York: Boni and Liveright, 1923. The introduction to this selection contains a lengthy biography, with primary source material, and draws on the poems themselves as biographical sources. Includes an overview of the poet's general qualities and the range of his subjects. Examines the publication history and the credibility of the original 1689 edition of the poems.

Buxton, John, ed. *The Poems of Charles Cotton*. Cambridge, Mass.: Harvard University Press, 1958. The introduction updates and expands on John Beresford's earlier biographical notes. Explains the editor's selections, which include important material from a previously lost manuscript. A section of critical commentary on Cotton contains notes, verse tributes, and references by other writers. The introductory material accompanies a good selection of the poet's work.

Hartle, P. N. "Mr. Cotton, of Merry Memory." *Neophilologus* 74 (October, 1989); 605-619. This excellent essay examines the range of styles and the high quality found in Cotton's poetry. Points out Cotton's particular skill as a writer of burlesques and his sometimes obscene sense of humor. Contains quotations from *Scarronides* and *Burlesque upon Burlesque*. This lively piece captures the spirit of the writer in a most engaging way. Highly recommended.

Nicolson, Marjorie Hope. *Mountain Gloom and Mountain Glory*. Ithaca, N.Y.: Cornell University Press, 1959. The author explores the reasons behind the differing perceptions of mountains in seventeenth, eighteenth, and nineteenth century thought. The short reference to Cotton concerns only one poem, *The Wonders of the Peake*, and examines his attitude toward nature.

Robinson, Ken, ed. *Charles Cotton: Selected Poems.* Manchester: Fyfield Books, 1983. This representative selection of poems includes a handy chronological table and an introduction with explanatory textual notes. Places Cotton in a historical, social, and intellectual context, characterizing him as a classical skeptic. The author also looks at the simplicity in both his style and his worldview.

Dennis R. Dean;
bibliography updated by the editors

HENRI COULETTE

Born: Los Angeles, California; November 11, 1927
Died: South Pasadena, California; March 26, 1988

PRINCIPAL POETRY

The War of the Secret Agents and Other Poems, 1966
The Family Goldschmitt, 1971
The Collected Poems of Henri Coulette, 1990
And Come to Closure, 1990 (included in *The Collected Poems of Henri Coulette*)

OTHER LITERARY FORMS

Henri Coulette edited or coedited several volumes, including *Midland: Twenty-five Years of Fiction and Poetry from Writing Workshops of the State University of Iowa* (1961; with P. Engle), *The Unstrung Lyre: Interviews with Fourteen Poets* (1965), and *Character and Crisis: A Contemporary Reader* (1966; with Philip Levine).

ACHIEVEMENTS

Henri Coulette's collections of poetry have received considerable critical if not popular recognition. Throughout his career, he wrote in traditional meters and beautifully crafted lyrics; in addition, he had a deft touch with the satiric epigram. The lyrics are very unusual since they are not mere description but investigations of the imagination which stretch the boundaries of reality. For Coulette, the imagination is supreme; it creates and refines the world of appearance.

BIOGRAPHY

Born in Los Angeles, Henri Anthony Coulette attended local schools, including the institution with which he continued to be associated for most of his life, California State University at Los Angeles. He taught high school English for a while. At the University of Iowa, he attended the Writers Workshop and obtained an M.F.A. and a Ph.D. His first collection of poetry, *The War of the Secret Agents and Other Poems* was published in 1966. It received the Lamont Poetry Award, given by the Academy of American Poets, and was well received by critics. He continued to teach at California State University at Los Angeles and produced his next collection, *The Family Goldschmitt*, in 1971. A number of his subsequent poems appeared in journals such as *The Iowa Review* and *The New Yorker.*

Coulette died in 1988, but a manuscript he left was turned into a collection, *And Come to Closure*, which was published in 1990 as part of *The Collected Poems of Henri Coulette.*

ANALYSIS

Coulette also had a way of transforming contemporary events into poetry. *The Family Goldschmitt* touches on the assassinations of the Kennedys and Martin Luther King, Jr., as well as linking the mythical family in that volume to the concentration camps.

Coulette created an alternative to the long poem by turning his sequence in *The War of the Secret Agents and Other Poems* into a unified whole. The tale of the secret agents is taken from Jean Overton Fuller's *Double Webs* (1958). Coulette is less interested in the individual poem than in the relationship of poem to poem. His last collection, *And Come to Closure*, is perhaps his finest work, with a broad range of beautifully crafted poems.

THE WAR OF THE SECRET AGENTS AND OTHER POEMS

Henri Coulette's first book, *The War of the Secret Agents and Other Poems*, is not a random assortment of poems but a whole in which each poem connects with the others. It is divided into five sections. The first section, "The Junk Shop," portrays a world of objects that take on life when observed by the designing mind. In the first poem, "Intaglio," a picture comes alive as the speaker assigns "roles" to the persons in the picture: the bitch, the actress, and the acrobat. The figures in the picture are his "family." The speaker knows them "as an author knows a book"; it is a literary and not a personal relationship. The poem ends as the speaker is momentarily startled by the playing and calling of children outside, and he turns to "dust the frame and set the picture straight." The real world had faded as the created world of the picture became his true reality.

In "The Junk Shop," an array of objects created by wrights, milliners, and smiths lie in disorder and disarray, but their "pride" still "abides." The end of the poem extends the role and nature of objects; they "contain us" and are "the subjects of our thought." This poem is central to the section, since it defines objects as things with power to provoke the imagination. They can tease the contemplater out of thought and lead people to important insights about the world and themselves.

"Life with Mother," another poem on the imagination, is quite different. Mother says, "everything's left to the imagination," and that enables her to become Queen Elizabeth and Alexander Hamilton. She is certain that she is being watched "by agents of the Kremlin" and is an agent herself. Actually, however, she is a "poor Irish daughter of the man/ who invented the Nabisco fig newton." The boy, presumably her son, is not charmed but appalled by her wild imagination; however, he cannot speak. The poem ends with his imagined reply to his mother's delusions: "There are ashes on all your sidewalks, Mother/ Where are ashes in my mouth." The image of ashes succeeds in puncturing her imagined world, but his negative and disloyal revelation harms him.

The last poem in this section is "The Wandering Scholar." The scholar is having a difficult time; he is pushed into the rain and on the road by his own restlessness. He proceeds to curse himself as "the libertine of verse/ Whose meters lurch where they should tread." He prays to "St Golias," a guide who can take him through the rain "into the grove no change can mar," and begs to be brought "where the Muses are." The poem is a rather conventional lyric evoking a historical situation and connecting the poet to an earlier counterpart.

The second section of the book is a group of translations of Latin poems. The first of these, three brief poems by Heredia, tell the story of Mark Antony and Cleopatra. Initially seen as heroic and imaged as "Hawk" and "Eagle," they are quickly reduced to "two parakeets upon a single perch." In the second poem Cleopatra is defeated by Antony, and their defeat is anticipated and suggested in the third.

Coulette's translation of Gaius Valerius Catullus's famous poem on love is very fine; it is racy and contemporary without violating the spirit of the Latin original. The last poem in the sequence is an amusing translation of a poem by Philippe Jaccottet; Coulette's witty style is very fitting here.

The third section, "Hermit," consists of two poems. The first of these, "Evening in the Park," is reminiscent of the poems in the first section. Sitting in his room, the speaker looks out upon an empty park. He counts "tin cans and comic books" and awaits the night. The poetic description of night is immediately brought closer to earth and described by the factual "rush of stars." It then becomes more active as a "rush of thought," bringing images that take the speaker by surprise. The images bring back the day, which was filled with anger and danger. He sits thinking about the hermit of the park: "Does he name the trees?" "Does he conjure numbers?" In the last stanza, the speaker returns to observation of the park; the cans are now "jewelled with the stars," and the comic book whispers. Yet "to keep my mind/ Familiar and American," he must leave, rejecting the call of the imagination, which can transform the familiar into something rich and strange, and settling for ordinary life.

"The War of the Secret Agents" has seventeen sections that tell the story of an amateurish yet heroic group of agents in World War II. In "Proem," they are described as being "out of a teen-age novel"; they came "ready to die for England" and quickly revealed their situation. The Nazi Gestapo leader in Paris, Keiffer, learns of them through the betrayal of Gilbert, one of the members of the group. Keiffer describes those he will soon arrest as his flock of sheep. He makes a deal with the leader of the secret agents, Prosper: "No harm will come to his men,/ none at all, if he cooperates." The exigencies of war, however, make his promise meaningless; in the end fifteen hundred are sent to death, although a few survive. Keiffer is, perhaps, the most interesting character in the poem. He has an aesthetic sense and a personal style.

What happens after the death of the agents is the most intriguing aspect of the story. In the second poem of the sequence, Jane Alabaster (perhaps Jean Overton Fuller, author of *Double Webs*, 1958) writes a letter to T. S. Eliot, her editor at Faber and Faber, about her discovery that Gilbert is the traitor who sacrificed the others. Gilbert and the few who survived will give their version of the events. In the seventh poem, Cinema speaks about how he saw Prosper on the train that brought them to Germany. He speaks of how he traveled the Metro each day as a different person and how his own identity has been lost in his code name. He cannot explain the dead; they are gone and cannot speak. Phono was with Prosper when he was marched out to death. He recalls his bravado: "*Show these bastards how to die. . .*" Somewhat uncharacteristically, Prosper replied, "You show them." Phono waited for death, but it never came.

A letter from Prosper to his wife is found in poem 15; lamenting his difficulties with his agents, "Lumbering Phono, mad Cinema," Prosper says, "I must play the greybeard for these children." The poem shows Prosper to be quite human, not at all the foolish idealist of the earlier poem.

Poem 16 is the climax of the series. Jane Alabaster confronts Gilbert and his betrayal; Gilbert at first tries to deny it but finally is forced to admit that he is the one. Yet his action was not treason; he was under orders from London. There was "an underground beneath the underground," and the agents were sacrificed to protect it.

The last section in the book, "Moby Jane," is satiric. It contains a poem to a computer that writes poetry, a very amusing piece called "The Academic Poet," and the title poem. In the latter, Moby Jane speaks of Herman Melville as "a terrible man" who indulged in "useless scribblings" on an unknown whale. The real "beast" was the manuscript. Moby and Jane reject "signing the necessary papers," since that would be playing Melville's game. In Coulette, even the whales have a voice and a place.

THE FAMILY GOLDSCHMITT

A less important collection than *The War of the Secret Agents and Other Poems*, *The Family Goldschmitt* begins with Coulette's imaginative identification with that family when his German landlady insists that his name is Goldschmitt. He then expands the identification by noting, "There is gas escaping somewhere." Is he on a train to Deutschland? In response, he writes a letter "to

the world, no! to the people/ I love, no! to my family, yes!/ The Family Goldschmitt." Members of this mythical family are portrayed near the end of the book, and their comments mark section divisions. Coulette has a wonderful ability to transform the ordinary world into something exotic and threatening.

The section "1968" is filled with social poems on that troubled year. "On the Balcony" is on the death of Martin Luther King, Jr. The speaker is King himself, contemplating "the face in that window," presumably his killer. His friends "look up at me, lingering"; the evening is "hushed and ready." Everything seems primed for some momentous event. "It will come to me, and does,/ And I am made public." This very effective poem conveys the anticipation and completion of King's assassination without melodrama. Death is seen as a transformation from the state of a private man to another plane; King now has only a "public" existence.

The short poems on the Kennedys are, perhaps, less successful. Coulette portrays the events as sensations: "Bang!Bang!Bang!/ And always in the head." The public's response is to watch television and "drive with our lights on." These poems are effective reframings of the memorable events, but not much more.

There are other political poems in this section, a satiric poem on Richard M. Nixon and one on Ernesto (Che) Guevara. Guevara's death is caused not by the Central Intelligence Agency but by the "damned Indians." His end is described as a mistake, "like being lost/ On a family picnic." Coulette then renders the facts of the death: "a body in a sink, uniforms heavy/ With braid, a group portrait." The poem ends with an image of coldness and distance: "The earth,/ it is said, is a blue star." This image suggests inappropriate feelings about the death of one so significant.

The most interesting poem in the third section, "Walking Backwards," is the title poem. As the poem opens, the speaker is walking backward beyond people and tall buildings. Failing to make a connection with the people he passes, he makes "small talk" and shows the boredom in his face. He leaves them and "the squares/ Of which I am an angle." The last stanza comments on his departure from society: He has left behind the "great truths," the voices of orthodoxy, "at the end of their chains, barking." It is a marvelous metaphor of Coulette's opposition to and spurning of conventionality and conformity.

A short section called "Simples, Nostrums" contains a comical poem on Coulette's "first novel" and three poems on family memories. "The Invisible Father" is the best of the three. Coulette addresses his father as a "wound,/ Or at best an absence." The father is described as the sun "behind us" and as "fathering our shadows toward" the mother. Finally, he "has become the music" that he practiced, and his location is "elsewhere in that strange house." The poem ends with his coming to life as the speaker hears a passage the father had practiced "suddenly in context." In this affectionate and moving poem, the father's absence is evoked and his presence restored with a new understanding.

AND COME TO CLOSURE

Coulette's last volume, *And Come to Closure*, was published two years after his death in *The Collected Poems of Henri Coulette*; it is by far his finest collection. It begins with a brilliant translation of Horace's *Odes*, "IV" (23 B.C.E., *The Odes of Horace*, 1963) and quickly moves on to a section called "Coming to Terms"; the title poem takes the speaker back to childhood, when all is possible and "everything is in our grasp." When childhood passes, however, one is an adult, "which is to say *metaphysical*, which is to say *bored*." He asks whether the "explosion" in the desert exists, and how. Is it "invisible even to itself," or does it remain in the "desert of the mind?" Should one welcome it, "as wisemen an oasis, as children mirage?" The only refuge from aging and the inevitable boredom it brings is coming to terms with the limitations of the world and the necessity for imagination, Coulette's persistent theme.

The last poem in the section is the amusing "At the Writers Conference," in which the speaker is asked, "*Why do you write?*" He answers with a few words: "love," "feeling," and "thought." The answer is greedily accepted, but the questioners are really after something else; "they want to publish, for they perish soon." The speaker wonders what it is like to live "bereft of a title page,/ Vanity without signature and spine." The question cannot be answered, for the secret to publication cannot be given. He exits "to their sweet applause"—actually a mockery, since he cannot satisfy their vanity or provide the key to fame.

In a short section called "The Blue Hammer," there is one fine poem, the third section of "The Desire and Pursuit of the Part." The poem begins by announcing separation: "The whole is not/ Implicit in the part." The speaker is filled with fear at the "crab/ in my gut," the "spider/ In my head." When he gets up in the cold, however, he sees before him his cats, Jerome and Miss Coots. The last stanza celebrates this simple joy: "It is enough,/ Or all I have just now." Such quiet experiences may be only a "part," but they are sufficient. This settling for ordinary pleasures is a welcome development in Coulette's work.

The fifth section contains epigrams, one of which goes beyond the narrowness of the form. The sixteenth portrays a perfect moment: "A one-eyed cat Hathaway on my lap,/ A fire in the fireplace, and Schubert's 5th" on the radio. Listening, the speaker concludes, "This is, I think,/ As close as I may come to happiness." This is a gem of a poem in which the details create a compelling world; the poet is no longer reaching beyond material things but accepting them and their joy.

The sixth section, "An Unofficial Joy," contains a number of wonderful poems. Coulette's elegy, "Night Thoughts," on his friend David Kubal, is beautiful. It is not at all somber but celebrates Kubal's life with vignettes; Kubal roams the street with his dog, "pillar to post, and terribly alive." A favorite Coulette word, "elsewhere," perfectly catches Kubal's desire for escape to "some secret inner place." Having died, he is now "elsewhere," and his dead body is compared to "a windblown rose" that is "ushered to repose." The poem ends with an imaginative identification of the poet with a brother. The poem is both a joyful reminiscence and the mourning of what is gone.

"Postscript" is a brilliant villanelle in which the speaker contemplates a failed relationship. Nearly every stanza speaks of decay or undoing. The thorn outsmarts "the cunning of the rose"; there are allusions to the serpent in the garden, the "interiors none may map or chart." The last stanza sums up: "We had too little craft and too much art./ We thought two noes would make a perfect yeas." Coulette handles the complicated scheme of the villanelle with great skill and ease; the repeated line, "Who was it said, Come let us kiss and part?" communicates the speaker's regret and lack of consolation in the shattering of the relationship.

"Petition" is a perfect short poem in which the speaker prays for his cat: "Lord of the Tenth Life,/ Welcome my Jerome." The second and last stanza speaks of what Jerome loves, "bird and mouse," a "man's lap," "and in winter light,/ Paws tucked in, a nap." The invention of a cat god and the portrayal of this "fierce, gold tabby" are memorable, apt exemplars of Coulette's brilliant imagination and warm affection for what is.

OTHER MAJOR WORKS

EDITED TEXTS: *Midland: Twenty-five Years of Fiction and Poetry from Writing Workshops of the State University of Iowa*, 1961 (with P. Engle); *The Unstrung Lyre: Interviews with Fourteen Poets*, 1965; *Character and Crisis: A Contemporary Reader*, 1966 (with Philip Levine).

BIBLIOGRAPHY

Anthony, Mary. "Some Translations by Henri Coulette." *Western Humanities Review* 21 (Winter, 1967): 67-71. Anthony Coulette's translations of Catullus, Heredia, and Jaccottet very highly. She states that Coulette is not a literalist but a creative translator who preserves the poetry. Coulette's "rightness" in the poems, she says, is remarkable.

Clements, Robert J. "The Muses Are Heard." *Saturday Review* 49 (May 21, 1966): 30-31. In this brief review of *The War of the Secret Agents and Other Poems*, Clements dismisses Coulette as a "Californian" poet. He does acknowledge that the poems are "contemporary" but sees little value in the book.

Coulette, Henri. Interview by Michael S. Harper. *The Iowa Review* 13 (Spring, 1982): 62-84. In this intriguing interview Coulette reveals some of his influences and sources. Some of his poems are shown to be directly based on Coulette's life. *The Family Goldschmitt*, for example, came out of Coulette's trip to Europe in 1967. The father in the poems is Coulette's own musician father.

Donoghue, Denis. "The Long Poem." *The New York Review of Books* 6 (April 14, 1966): 18-21. A brief and neutral review of Coulette's long poem "The War of the Secret Agents." Explaining that he does not know the book Coulette used as a source for the poem, Donoghue admits to some puzzlement.

Fitts, Dudley. "Quartet in Varying Keys." *The New York Times Book Review* 71 (April 17, 1966): 46-47. A very positive review of *The War of the Secret Agents and Other Poems*. Fitts praises Coulette's "technical adroitness" in many of the short poems in the collection. He calls Coulette "a poet to watch."

Santos, Terry. "Remembering Henri Coulette." *The Kenyon Review* 14, no. 1 (Winter, 1992): 137. A brief biographical profile of the poet.

James Sullivan;
bibliography updated by the editors

ABRAHAM COWLEY

Born: London, England; 1618
Died: Chertsey, England; July 28, 1667

PRINCIPAL POETRY

Poeticall Blossomes, 1633
The Mistress: Or, Several Copies of Love Verses, 1647
Poems, 1656 (also published as *Miscellanies*)
Verses Lately Written upon Several Occasions, 1663
Poemata Latina, 1668

OTHER LITERARY FORMS

From time to time, Abraham Cowley interrupted his poetic activity with bits of drama and prose. The former were light, immature attempts: a pastoral drama, *Loves Riddle* (1638); a Latin comedy entitled *Naufragium Joculare* (1638); another comedy, *The Guardian* (1641), hastily put together when Prince Charles passed through Cambridge, but rewritten as *Cutter of Coleman-Street* (1663). His serious prose is direct and concise, although the pieces tend to repeat the traditional Renaissance theme of solitude. His most notable prose work was a pamphlet, *A Proposition for the Advancement of Experimental Philosophy* (1661), which may have hastened the founding of the Royal Society.

ACHIEVEMENTS

In the 1930's, the respected critic and literary historian Douglas Bush suggested that Abraham Cowley needed to be seen and understood as a man of his own age, rather than as an artist whose appeal is timeless. That statement may well be the key to assessing Cowley's achievement. During his own day, he secured a considerable reputation as a poet that endured well into the eighteenth century. Then, in 1779, Samuel Johnson issued, as the initial piece to what became *Lives of the Poets* (1779-1781), his *Life of Cowley*. With his usual rhetorical balance, Johnson described Cowley as a poet who had been "at one time too much praised and too much neglected at another." The London sage, through laborious comparison, classified his subject among the Metaphysical poets of the first half of the seventeenth century—a group that he could not always discuss in positive terms. Johnson, however, did single out Cowley as the best among the Metaphysicals and also the last of them. In general, Johnson praised the "Ode of Wit" (1668), turned a neutral ear toward the *Pindarique Odes* (1656), and evaluated the prose as possessing smooth and placid "equability." Cowley was all but forgotten during the nineteenth century, and not until after World War I, when critics such as Sir Herbert J. C. Grierson and T. S. Eliot began to rediscover Metaphysical verse, did his achievement begin to be understood.

Perhaps Cowley's greatest achievement as a poet was that, even in retirement, he stood willing to consider the intellectual challenges of a new world, a world at the edge of scientific and political revolution. He seemed extremely sensitive to the need for the poem as a means for expressing the intellectual essence of that new world, yet he never forsook the Renaissance tradition in which he had been taught. Cowley gave to English poetry a sensible mixture of seriousness, learning, imagination, intelligence, and perception. Although he often wrestled with himself, caught between authority and reason, between the rational and the imaginative, between the rejected past and the uncertain future, he managed to control his art, to triumph over the uncertainty and confusion of his time. Through poetry, Cowley searched for order; through poetry he achieved order—classical, scientific, and religious order—in a world that had itself become worn from passion. The achievement of Cowley is that he showed his successors—especially the Augustans of the early eighteenth century—that a poet

should seek and find new material and new methods without having to sever the strong cord of the past.

BIOGRAPHY

Abraham Cowley was born in the parish of St. Michael le Quern, Cheapside, in London, sometime after July, 1618, the seventh child and fifth son (born posthumously) of Thomas Cowley, a stationer and grocer, who left £1000 to be divided among his seven children. His mother was Thomasine Berrye, to whom Thomas Cowley had pledged his faith sometime in 1581. The widow did the best she could to educate her children through her own devices and then managed to send the boys off to more formal institutions. Thus, she obtained young Abraham's admission as a king's scholar at Westminster School, to which he proceeded armed with some acquaintance with Edmund Spenser. By the age of fifteen, he was already a published poet; his first collection of five pieces, entitled *Poeticall Blossomes*, was followed by a second edition three years later. One of the poems, "Pyramus and Thisbe," some 226 lines long, had been written when he was ten; another, "Constantia and Philetus," was written during the poet's twelfth year.

Cowley's scholarly skills unfortunately did not keep pace with the development of his poetic muse. Apparently the boy balked at the drudgeries of learning grammar and languages; furthermore, his masters contended that his natural quickness made such study unnecessary. In the end, he failed to gain election to Cambridge University in 1636 and had to wait until mid-June of the following year, at which time he became a scholar of Trinity College. Cambridge proved no deterrent to young Cowley's poetic bent; in 1638, he published a pastoral drama, *Loves Riddle*, written at least four years previously. Then, on February 2, 1638, members of Trinity College performed his Latin comedy, *Naufragium Joculare*, which he published shortly thereafter. After taking his B.A. in 1639, Cowley remained at Cambridge through 1642, by which time he had earned the M.A. The year before, when Prince Charles had passed through Cambridge, the young poet had hastily prepared for the occasion a comedy entitled *The Guardian*; the piece was acted a number of times prior to its publication in 1650 and it continued to be performed, privately, of course, during the Commonwealth and the suppression of the theaters.

Leaving Cambridge in 1643, Cowley continued to write poetry, principally at St. John's College, Oxford, where he had "retired" and become intimate with Royalist leaders. Joining the family of Jermyn (later St. Albans), he followed the queen to France in 1646, where he found a fellow poet, Richard Crashaw. The exiled court employed Cowley for a number of diplomatic services, particularly on missions to Jersey and Holland; other activities included transmitting a correspondence in cipher between Charles I and his queen. During this period, several of Cowley's works appeared in London: a collection of poems entitled *The Mistress* and a satire ascribed to him, *The Foure Ages of England: Or, The Iron Age* (1648). His poetic output was restricted, however, because his diplomatic work occupied all his days and most of his evenings. In 1656, his employers sent him to England on what can only be termed an espionage mission under the guise of seeking retirement. He was arrested, but only because the authorities mistook him for someone else; released on bail, he remained under strict probation until Charles II reclaimed the throne of England in 1660.

For Cowley, however, the big event of 1656 was the publication of his most important collection, *Poems*—including the juvenile pieces, the elegies to William Hervey and Crashaw, *The Mistress*, the *Pindarique Odes*, and *Davideis*. The last item, an epic of four books (out of twelve that he had originally planned), actually belonged to the poet's Cambridge period, and Cowley finally admitted that he had abandoned plans to complete it. After the publication of the *Poems*, Cowley, still in the employ of the exiled Royalists in France, suddenly took up the study of medicine—as a means of obscuring his espionage activities. Seemingly without difficulty, he earned his medical doctor's degree at Oxford in December, 1657, and then retired to Kent, where he studied and produced a Latin poem, "Plantarum Libri duo" (published in 1662). After the Restoration, Cowley's best poetry and prose appeared: "Ode upon the Blessed Restoration" (1660), *A Vision, Concerning His Late Pretended Highnesse, Cromwell the Wicked* (1661), *A Proposition for the Advancement of Experimental Philosophy* (1661), "Ode to the Royal Society" (1661), and *Verses Lately Written upon Several Occasions*.

Cowley's early employer, Jermyn, by then the earl of St. Albans, helped to obtain for him some royal land at Chertsey, where he could spend the remainder of his days in easy retirement. There he settled in April, 1665. His health began to decline, however, and the fact that his tenants balked at paying their rents did little to improve his physical and emotional condition. In late July, 1667, after being outdoors longer than necessary, he caught a severe cold; he died on the twenty-eighth of that month. Cowley was buried with considerable ceremony in Westminster Abbey, near Geoffrey Chaucer and Edmund Spenser, and for the rest of the seventeenth century, poets and critics continued to view him as the model of cultivated poetry.

ANALYSIS

Abraham Cowley is a transitional figure, a poet who tended to relinquish the emotional values of John Donne and George Herbert and grasp the edges of reason and wit. He was more versatile than the early Metaphysicals: He embraced the influence of Donne and Ben Jonson, relied upon the Pindaric form that would take hold in the eighteenth century, conceived of an experimental biblical epic in English (*Davideis*) well in advance of John Milton's major project, and demonstrated an open-mindedness that allowed him to write in support of Francis Bacon, Thomas Hobbes, and the Royal Society. Cowley's elegies on the deaths of William Hervey and Richard Crashaw are extremely frank poems of natural pain and loss, while at the same time the poet recognized the need for the human intellect to be aware of "Things Divine"—the dullness of the earthly as opposed to the reality of the heavenly.

Indeed, Cowley's versatile imagination ranged far and wide, and he easily adapted diverse subjects to fit his own purposes. Unlike the poets of the Restoration and the early eighteenth century who followed him, he ignored various current fashions and concentrated upon economy, unity, form, and imagination; he did not have to force the grotesque upon his readers, nor did he have to inundate them with a pretense of art. Cowley was a master at what Bishop Thomas Sprat termed, in 1668, "harmonious artistry." He turned his back upon wild and affected extravagance and embraced propriety and measure; he applied wit to matter, combined philosophy with charity and religion. Even when writing amorous verse, he took inspiration both from the courtier and from the scholar—the passion of the one and the wisdom of the other.

POETICALL BLOSSOMES

Abraham Cowley launched his career as a serious poet at the age of fifteen, while still a student at Westminster School, with the publication of *Poeticall Blossomes*. In fact, there is evidence that the volume had been prepared in some form at least two years earlier. At any rate, what appeared was a rather high level of poetic juvenilia, five pieces in which both sound and sense reflected an ability far beyond the poet's youth. The first, "Pyramus and Thisbe," 226 lines, does not differ too markedly from Ovid's tale, although Cowley's Venus seems overly malevolent and the (then) ten-year-old poet carried to extremes the desired but untasted joys of love. Otherwise, the piece evidences a sense of discipline and knowledge often reserved for the mature imagination, as young Cowley attempted to control his phrasing and his verse form. The second poem in the collection, "Constantia and Philetus," may serve as a companion to "Pyramus and Thisbe," although it is certainly no mere imitation. Cowley, now about twelve, again chose as his subject a tragic love story, keeping hold upon Venus, Cupid, and other deities. However, he shifted his setting from ancient Rome to the suburban surroundings of an Italian villa, there to unfold a rather conventional poetic narrative: two lovers, a rival favored by the parents, a sympathetic brother, and a dead heroine. He adorned the entire scene with amorous conceits and characters yearning for the beauties of the country and the consolations of nature.

In addition to the larger pieces, *Poeticall Blossomes* contained an interesting trio of shorter efforts. In "A Dream of Elysium," Cowley, seemingly engaged in an exercise in poetic self-education, parades before a sleeping poet a host of classical favorites: Hyacinth, Narcissus, Apollo, Ovid, Homer, Cato, Leander, Hero, Portia, Brutus, Pyramus, Thisbe. The final two poems of the volume constitute the young writer's first attempts at what would become, for him, an important form—the occasional poem. Both pieces are elegies: One mourns the death of a public official, Dudley, Lord Carleton and Viscount Dorchester, who attended Westminster School,

served as secretary of state, and died in February, 1632; the other was occasioned by the death of Cowley's cousin, Richard Clerke, a student at Lincoln's Inn. Naturally, the two poems contain extravagant praises and lofty figures, no doubt reflecting what the boy had read in his favorite, Spenser, and had been taught by his masters. There are those who speculate that had Cowley died in adolescence, as Thomas Chatterton did in the next century, the verses of *Poeticall Blossomes* would have sustained at least a very small poetic reputation in a very obscure niche of literary history. Cowley, however, despite a number of purely political distractions during his adult life, managed to extend his poetic talents beyond childhood exercises, and it is to the products of his maturity that one must turn for the comprehension and appreciation of his art.

POEMS

Perhaps Cowley's most important contribution to poetry came in 1656 with the publication of his extensive collection, *Poems*, several additions to which he made during his lifetime. Of more than passing interest is the preface to this volume, wherein Cowley attempts, by reference to his own personal situation, to explain the relationship between the poet and his environment. In 1656, he had little desire to write poetry, mainly because of the political instability of the moment, his own health, and his mental state. He admitted that a warlike, unstable, and even tragic age may be the best for the poet to write about, but it may also be the worst time in which to write. Living as he did, a stranger under surveillance in his own homeland, he felt restricted in his artistic endeavors. "The soul," he complained in the preface, "must be filled with bright and delightful ideas when it undertakes to communicate delight to others, which is the main end of poesy." Thus, he had given serious thought to abandoning Puritan England for the obscurity of some plantation in the Americas, and the 1656 *Poems* was to be his legacy to a world for whose conflicts and confrontations he no longer had any concern.

The *Poems* contain four divisions: the *Miscellanies*, including the *Anacreontiques*; *The Mistress*, a collection of love poems; *Pindarique Odes*; and the *Davideis*, a heroic epic focusing upon the problems of the Old Testament king. In subsequent editions, Cowley and his editors added "Verses on Various Occasions" and "Several

Discourses by Way of Essays in Prose and Verse." Cowley himself informed his readers that the *Miscellanies* constituted poems preserved from earlier folios (some even from his school days); unfortunately, he made no distinction between the poor efforts and those of quality. Thus, an immature ode, "Here's to thee, Dick," stands near the serious and moving elegy "On the Death of Mr. William Hervey," in which he conveys both universal meaning and personal tragedy and loss. Cowley, however, rarely allowed himself to travel the route of the strictly personal; for him, poetry required support from learning, from scholastic comparisons that did not always rise to poetical levels. The fine valedictory "To the Lord Falkland," which celebrates the friendship between two interesting but divergent personalities, is sprinkled with lofty scientific comparisons to display the order that reigns in the crowded mind of his hero. Indeed, there are moments in Cowley's elegies when the reader wonders if the poet was more interested in praising the virtues of science and learning than in mourning the loss of friends. Such high distractions, however, do not weaken the intensity of Cowley's sincerity.

THE MISTRESS

The Mistress, originally published as a separate volume in 1647, comprises one hundred love poems, or, in Cowley's own terms, feigned addresses to some fair creature of the fancy. Almost apologetically, the poet explains in the prefatory remarks that all writers of verse must at one time or another pay some service to Love, in order to prove themselves true to Love. Unfortunately, Cowley evidences difficulty in warming to the occasion, perhaps held back by the prevalent mood of Puritan strictness that then dominated the art. Thus, many of his physical and psychological images of Love come from traditions rather than from the heart: Love is an interchange of hearts, a flame, a worship, a river frozen by disdain. On the other hand, Cowley's original, nontraditional images and similes are often wildly incongruous, even unintentionally comical, and lacking in true feeling.

Tears are made by smoke but not by flame; the lover's heart bursts upon its object "Like a grenado shot into a magazine"; a love story cut into bark burns and withers the tree; a young lady's beauty changes from civil government to tyranny. Certainly, *The Mistress* re-

veals that Cowley could employ an obvious degree of playfulness in verse; he could counterfeit, with ease and ingenuity, a series of love adventures; he could sustain some semblance of unity in a seeming hodgepodge of romantic episodes; he could amuse his readers. For those of his age who took their love poetry seriously, however—for those who expected grace, warmth, tenderness, even truth—*The Mistress* must have been rather disappointing.

PINDARIQUE ODES

There is some confusion concerning the form of the *Pindarique Odes*. Cowley may have wanted readers to believe that he was writing the true Pindaric ode: strophe, antistrophe (alike in form), and epode (different in form from the first two divisions), with varying meter and verse lengths within a strophe, but nevertheless regular metrical schemes established for corresponding divisions. Actually, he created a new form, an irregular ode: He discarded the usual stanza patterns, varied the length of lines and the number of lines within the strophes, and varied the meter with shifts in emotional intensity. He obviously knew what he was doing and probably chose the title for the section to disguise a questionable innovation. In fact, he doubted (in the preface) whether the form would be understood by most of his readers, even those acquainted with the principles of poetry. Nevertheless, he employed sudden and lengthy digressions, "unusual and bold" figures, and various and irregular numbers. Cowley's purpose throughout was to achieve a sense of harmony between what he viewed as the *liberty* of the ode and the moral *liberty* of life, the latter combining responsibility and freedom. Through moral liberty he hoped to find simplicity, retirement, and charm; the liberty of the ode, he thought, might allow for a greater participation in intellectual exercise.

In practice, the ode allowed Cowley the opportunity to subject his readers to a host of what he had termed "bold figures," images that would have occurred to no one other than he. Thus, on one occasion he asks his Muse to "rein her Pindaric Pegasus closely in," since the beast is "an unruly and a hardmouthed horse." At another time, the Muse appears in her chariot, with Eloquence, Wit, Memory, and Invention running by her side. Suddenly, Cowley stops the action to compare the

Muse with the Creator and with the two worlds that they have created. Such comparisons, with their accompanying "bold" images, allowed the poet to display his learning, to set down explanatory notes of definition, explication, and interpretation—whether his readers needed them or not. As long as he could serve as his own explicator, there seemed no limit to his invention. Generally, though, Cowley's odes fall short of their intentions as *complete* pieces of poetry. The digressions—the instruments of the poet's new-found intellectual freedom—may strike and impress the reader momentarily, but they also distract and divert the attention from the main idea of the poem.

Not all of Cowley's odes fall short of the mark. He succeeded when his subject interested him enough to say something substantive about it. In both "To Mr. Hobbes" and "Brutus" he followed the serious thinkers of his time. The first poem finds him looking beyond the transitory troubles of the moment to a new day. The second allows him to observe Oliver Cromwell, the Caesar of his time and, like the conscientious Royalist of the period, seek contemplation rather than action. He looks to history and philosophy to explain the evils of tyranny and to find parallels with other evils that eventually gave way to good. In the ode to Hobbes, Cowley finds solace in the fact that all ideas and concepts of permanent value must remain young and fresh forever. In the ode to Brutus, the poet discovers that odd events, evil men, and wretched actions are not themselves sufficient to destroy or even obscure virtue. Again, the particular circumstances of the moment and his deep personal disappointment gave Cowley the conviction to express what he actually felt.

DAVIDEIS

It is tempting to dismiss *Davideis* as another example of Cowley's juvenilia. Of the twelve books planned, only four were finished, and those were written while Cowley was still at Cambridge. By 1656, and perhaps even before, Cowley had lost his taste for the epic and determined not to finish it. If anything can be salvaged from *Davideis* it may be found in the preface, where the poet makes an eloquent plea for sacred poetry. Cowley complains that for too long wit and eloquence have been wasted on the beggarly flattery of important persons, idolizing of foolish women, and senseless fables. The

time has come, he announces, to recover poetry from the devil and restore it to the kingdom of God, to rescue it from the impure waters of Damascus and baptize it in the Jordan.

Unfortunately, the epic that follows never rises to the elegance or merit of the prefatory prose. The poem simply sinks from its own weight. Cowley's Hell, for example, is a labyrinth of cosmic elements: caverns that breed rare metals; nests of infant, weeping winds; a complex court of mother waters. The journey there is indeed long and laborious, and the relationship between all those cosmic details (gold, winds, voices, tides, and tidelessness) and Hell is never made clear. Cowley himself acknowledged the immaturity and weakness of the epic, but he also saw it as an adumbration of the poetic potential of biblical history. Eleven years after the publication of *Davideis* in the collected *Poems*, John Milton published *Paradise Lost* (1667).

"HYMN TO LIGHT"

Cowley added to the collected editions of his poems as they were issued between 1656 and his death in 1667. As with the contents of the first edition, the pieces vary in quality. In "Hymn to Light," the poet manages to achieve a proper balance between his learning and his imagination. The reader senses that Cowley has actually observed the "winged arrows" shooting from the "golden quiver of the sky," the result of a long succession of fresh and bright dawns rising in the English countryside. Those very dawns seem to have frightened "sleep, the lazy owl of night," turning the face of "cloudy care" into a "gentle, beamy smile." During those blessed years of retirement, away from the unnatural complications and intrigues of the political world, Cowley turned more and more toward the beauty of nature as a source of pleasure. Although in "Hymn to Light" he labels light an offspring of chaos, its very beams embrace and enhance the charms and beauty of the world, while at the same time tempting the selfish and inconsiderate by shining upon valuable elements. Toward the end of the poem, he conceives of light as a "clear river" that pours forth its radiance from the vast ocean of the sky; it collects in pools and lakes when its course is opposed by some firm body—the earth, for example. Such a conceit may appear overly abstract and abstruse, but it is perhaps the most extreme figure of the poem, demonstrating the degree to which the mature Cowley had advanced beyond his juvenile epic endeavors.

"ODE TO THE ROYAL SOCIETY"

There are critics who assert that with the "Ode to the Royal Society" (1667), Cowley rose to his highest level. That is debatable, but it is certainly his last important poem. The poem was written at the request of Cowley's friend, the diarist John Evelyn, who asked for a tribute to the Royal Society to complement the official history being undertaken by Thomas Sprat, Bishop of Rochester. The poem, published the same year as Sprat's *History of the Royal Society*, focused not so much upon the institution in question or even on science in general but upon the evolution of philosophy, which Cowley placed into two chronological periods: before and after Francis Bacon. The poet dwells briefly on the constrictions of the early philosophies, which merely wandered among the labyrinths of endless discourse, with little or no positive effect upon humankind. Then follows an impassioned attack upon pure authority, which arrived at erroneous scientific and intellectual conclusions and stubbornly clung to them.

Cowley compares Francis Bacon, who, with his *Advancement of Learning* (1605), *Novum Organum* (1620), and *De Augmentis Scientiarum* (1623), had initiated a new age of philosophy, with Moses; men of intellect were led out of the barren wasteland of the past to the very borders of exalted wit. Only Bacon, maintains Cowley, was willing to act and capable of routing the ghostlike body of authority that had for so long misled people with its dead thoughts. The philosophers of the past were but mechanics, copiers of others' work; Bacon summoned the mind away from words, the mere pictures of thoughts, and redirected it toward objects, the proper focus of the mind. Thus, the poet paid tribute to the philosopher as the proper predecessor of the Royal Society; his investigations paved the way for the significant accomplishments of that institution. The immediate success of the poem may have been due in part to Cowley's personal ties with the Royal Society—particularly as a friend of both Sprat and Evelyn and as the author of *A Proposition for the Advancement of Experimental Philosophy*. Those critics who have praised the piece for its pure poetic merit, however, have rightly identified it as the culmination of Cowley's contributions to the English ode.

LEGACY

Beginning with Joseph Addison's negative criticism (*The Spectator* 62, May, 1711) and extending through the critique in Samuel Johnson's *Lives of the Poets*, Cowley's reputation has endured the accusations of mixed wit and strained metaphysical conceits. Obviously, Addison and Johnson, even though they represent opposite chronological poles of the eighteenth century, were still too close to their subject to assess him objectively and to recognize him as a transitional figure. Cowley lived during the end of one intellectual age and the beginning of another. He belonged alongside John Donne, Richard Crashaw, George Herbert, Henry Vaughan, Thomas Traherne, and Andrew Marvell; he owed equal allegiance to the writers of the early Restoration, to such classicists as John Denham and Edmund Waller. Thus, his poetry reflects the traditions of one period and the freshness of another, the extravagances of youth and the freedom to combine ingenuity with reason and learning. Cowley also had the distinct advantage of a point of view resulting from the mastery of several positive sciences and of practically all the literature of Europe. Knowledge, reflection, control, clear judgment: These he carried with him from the Puritan Revolution into the Restoration and then to his own retirement. He belonged to an age principally of learning and of prose; he wrote poetry with the sustained rhetorical and emotional force that often results in greatness. Unfortunately, his meteor merely approached greatness, flaring only for a brief moment on the literary horizon.

OTHER MAJOR WORKS

PLAYS: *Loves Riddle*, pb. 1638; *Naufragium Joculare*, pr., pb. 1638; *The Guardian*, pr. 1641 (revised as *Cutter of Coleman-Street*, 1663).

NONFICTION: *A Proposition for the Advancement of Experimental Philosophy*, 1661; *A Vision, Concerning His Late Pretended Highnesse, Cromwell the Wicked*, 1661; *Several Discourses by Way of Essays in Prose and Verse*, 1668.

MISCELLANEOUS: *The Works of Mr. Abraham Cowley*, 1668, 1681, 1689.

BIBLIOGRAPHY

Dykstal, Timothy. "The Epic Reticence of Abraham Cowley." *Studies in English Literature* 31, no. 1

(Winter, 1991): 95. An analysis of Cowley's *Davedeis* and Milton's *Paradise Lost*.

Hinman, Robert B. *Abraham Cowley's World of Order.* Cambridge, Mass.: Harvard University Press, 1960. Hinman summarizes Cowley's scholarship, outlines Cowley's notions about art, examines the influence of Bacon and Hobbes, reads the poems in terms of "order," and evaluates Cowley's position as a poet. Contains an extensive bibliography.

Nethercot, Arthur H. *Abraham Cowley: The Muse's Hannibal.* 1931. Reprint. New York: Russell & Russell, 1967. The definitive biography, Nethercot's book also discusses Cowley's literary work, citing his composition of the first religious epic in English, his development of the Pindaric ode, and his literary criticism. Includes an extensive bibliography, several illustrations, and some documents, one of which is Cowley's will.

Pebworth, Ted-Larry. "Cowley's *Davideis* and the Exaltation of Friendship." In *The David Myth in Western Literature*, edited by Raymond-Jean Frontain and Jan Wojcik. West Lafayette, Ind.: Purdue University Press, 1980. Pebworth's essay concerns the friendship of David and Jonathan, which is compared to the classical friendships of Damon and Pythias, Cicero and Atticus, and Orestes and Pylades and the topical friendship of Cowley and William Hervey. Examines the friendship in *Davideis* in terms of the three-step Neoplatonic progression of love.

Revard, Stella P. "Cowley's *Pindarique Odes* and the Politics of the Inter-Regnum." *Criticism* 35, no. 3 (Summer, 1993): 391. An examination of Royalist celebration and resistance in Cowley's *Pindarique Odes*. It is assumed that these texts and the political agenda they encode were produced under censorship.

Taaffe, James G. *Abraham Cowley.* New York: Twayne, 1972. An excellent overview of Cowley's literary work. Contains readings of many of Cowley's works, with extensive commentary on *Davideis*. Of the shorter works, "The Muse," the poems on the deaths of Richard Crashaw and William Hervey, and the Cromwell poem are treated in some detail. Includes a chronology and an annotated select bibliography.

Trotter, David. *The Poetry of Abraham Cowley.* Totowa, N.J.: Rowman & Littlefield, 1979. Tends to downplay political and social contexts and to stress the role of form in Cowley's work. The lyric poems (especially *The Mistress*), the sacred poems, the Pindaric odes, and Cowley's relationship to Richard Crashaw are treated in separate chapters. Contains a helpful bibliography.

Walton, Geoffrey. "Abraham Cowley." In *From Donne to Marvell.* Vol. 3 in *A Guide to English Literature*, edited by Boris Ford. London: Cassell, 1956. Walton regards Cowley as the bridge between Metaphysical wit and neoclassical poetry and relates Cowley's poetry back to Jonson and Donne and ahead to Dryden and Pope, but Walton's focus is on Cowley's neoclassical verse, especially in the shaping of the Pindaric ode and the creation of the first neoclassical epic in English, *Davideis*.

Williamson, George. *Six Metaphysical Poets: A Reader's Guide.* New York: Farrar, Straus & Giroux, 1967. Williamson's chapter on Cowley provides a good overview of the metaphysical elements in Cowley's poetry. Contains several one-page discussions of individual poems and concludes with an informative comparison between Cowley and Donne. For Williamson, Cowley's love poetry is located between Donne's metaphysical poetry and Waller's verse.

Samuel J. Rogal;
bibliography updated by the editors

MALCOLM COWLEY

Born: Belsano, Pennsylvania; August 24, 1898
Died: New Milford, Connecticut; March 27, 1989

PRINCIPAL POETRY
Blue Juniata, 1929
The Dry Season, 1941
Blue Juniata: Collected Poems, 1968
Blue Juniata, a Life: Collected and New Poems, 1985

Malcolm Cowley (Library of Congress)

OTHER LITERARY FORMS

Although Malcolm Cowley began his literary career as a poet and remained a practicing poet, critic of poetry, and adviser to scores of American poets for most of his more than sixty-year career, his literary reputation derives chiefly from his prose works, which include literary criticism and literary and cultural history as well as numerous essays and book reviews written for newspapers, magazines, and literary journals. Many of Cowley's critical essays are considered to be seminal studies of major American poets and novelists, such as Hart Crane, Ernest Hemingway, and William Faulkner. In addition, Cowley's major works of literary and cultural history, including *Exile's Return* (1934, 1951); *The Literary Situation* (1954); *A Second Flowering: Works and Days of the Lost Generation* (1973); *And I Worked at the Writer's Trade* (1978); and *The Dream of the Golden Mountains: Remembering the 1930's* (1980), have served as primary sources of information about the intellectual, social, political, and historical events and issues that shaped the aesthetic practices and the social and political beliefs of modern American writers. Cowley's published books range from pioneering translations of important novels and essays by French writers of the 1920's and 1930's, such as Maurice Barrès, Paul Valéry, Louis Aragon, and André Gide, to editions of the works of several of America's classic nineteenth century writers, such as Walt Whitman and Nathaniel Hawthorne. His publications also include a volume analyzing the intellectual history of modern Western civilization, *Books That Changed Our Minds* (1939), and a historical study of the African slave trade, *Black Cargoes: A History of the Atlantic Slave Trade, 1518-1865* (1962), written in collaboration with Daniel P. Mannix.

Cowley edited anthologies of several of his contemporaries, editions that significantly contributed to expanding their audience and to establishing their literary reputations. The most notable of these are *The Portable Hemingway* (1944), *The Portable Faulkner* (1946), *The Stories of F. Scott Fitzgerald* (1951), and *Three Novels of F. Scott Fitzgerald: The Great Gatsby . . . Tender Is the Night . . . The Last Tycoon* (1953).

Cowley's literary journalism has been partially collected in two volumes, *Think Back on Us: A Contemporary Chronicle of the 1930's* (1967), and *A Many-Windowed House: Collected Essays on American Writers and American Writing* (1970). The only portion of Cowley's literary correspondence (most of which is housed in Chicago's Newberry Library) that has been published is a volume of letters, with explanatory narration, between Cowley and William Faulkner regarding their eighteen-year friendship, *The Faulkner-Cowley File: Letters and Memories, 1944-1962* (1966).

ACHIEVEMENTS

Malcolm Cowley was formally honored by the American cultural and educational community relatively late in his career. His fellow writers honored him early and continuously, however, by both public recognition and private expression. Since a significant portion of his work is concerned with the writer in the modern world, in a way that James Atlas has described as almost unique in the history of American letters, Cowley was an acknowledged leader and spokesman for the American literary community for fifty years. Consequently, many of Cowley's honors were bestowed for his service to the profession of letters as much as for his individual achievements as a poet and writer.

In 1921 Cowley was granted an American Field Service Fellowship permitting him to spend two years in France studying at the University of Montpellier, an experience that was crucial in exposing him to the revolutionary ideas and practices of modern artists in France. In 1927 he received the Levinson Prize for poetry. In 1939 *Poetry* magazine awarded him the Harriet Monroe Memorial Prize. In 1946 he received a grant from the National Institute of Arts and Letters, and in 1967 the newly created National Endowment for the Arts gave Cowley a ten-thousand-dollar award in recognition of his service to American letters. The Modern Language Association of America awarded Cowley its Hubbel Medal in 1978 for services to American literature. In 1980 the American Book Publishers Council voted Cowley its American Book Award in the autobiography category, paperback division, for *And I Worked at the Writer's Trade*.

Cowley was elected to the National Institute of Arts and Letters in the early 1950's, and the institute membership shortly thereafter honored him by twice electing him president, from 1956 to 1959 and from 1962 to 1965. Cowley was also elected to the senior body of the National Institute, the American Academy of Arts and Letters, and he served as chancellor of that body from 1967 to 1977. These tenures were periods in which Cowley helped to supervise the creation and granting of a number of prizes and monetary awards to scores of writers both for individual works of literature and for contributions to literature over entire careers. For more than forty years Cowley also served as an adviser, director, and vice-president of Yaddo, the private foundation that provides subsidized residence for writers and artists in Saratoga Springs, New York.

Cowley served as a distinguished visiting professor at the University of Washington in Seattle in 1950; at Stanford University in 1956, 1959, 1960-1961, and 1965; at the University of Michigan in 1957; as Regents Professor at the University of California, Berkeley, in 1962; at Cornell University, 1964; at the University of Minnesota in 1971; and at the University of Warwick in England in 1973. He was awarded honorary doctorates of literature by Franklin and Marshall College, 1961;

Colby College, 1962; the University of Warwick, England, 1975; the University of New Haven, 1976; and Monmouth College, 1978.

Though Cowley began publishing in the 1920's, his work remained uncollected until relatively late in his career. Yet his influence on other critics, academic scholars, poets, and novelists has been substantial. His essays written while serving as literary editor of *The New Republic* from 1929 until 1944 made Cowley one of the most widely read voices of literary and cultural analysis during the years of the Great Depression and World War II. In the postwar period academic scholars considered his writing to be a critical guide to American literature and American literary history in the entire first half of the twentieth century. When Robert Spiller, Willard Thorp, and Henry Seidel Canby began work on the now standard reference work *The Literary History of the United States* (1948-1953), they asked Cowley to write the sections concerning the social history of modern American authors and the influence of American literature on foreign nations.

As adviser to one of America's foremost publishing companies, the Viking Press, for more than thirty years, Cowley played a role in developing Viking's literary publications, including such ventures as the Viking Portable Library, the paperback Compass editions, the Viking Critical Editions, and the first significant publication in America of many new writers, among them authors such as Jack Kerouac, Ken Kesey, and Tillie Olson, and a number of poets, such as Donald Hall, Philip Booth, and A. D. Hope. In the late 1940's Cowley served on the committees that inaugurated the National Book Awards and the Bollingen Prize for Poetry, and in the early 1950's he helped to advise the Rockefeller Foundation on the funding of literary magazines.

Cowley's critical acumen concerning his own generation of writers was matched by his ability to recognize and sponsor other talented writers. He first published John Cheever and discussed his fiction with him for more than forty years. He promoted Nelson Algren from his first reading of his work in 1942 until Algren's death in 1981. In addition, a number of academic critics, such as John W. Aldridge, Michael Millgate, Larzer Ziff, and Philip Young, have attested to the influence Cowley had on their careers.

One of only a handful of American poets who have become successful literary journalists, historians, and critics, and whose prose work belongs to the canon of American literature, Cowley gained a reputation as one of the most perceptive of modern literary analysts. He has been described as one of the most lucid English prose stylists of the twentieth century. Because of his belief in the cultural value and importance of poetry (indeed of all literature), he saw the use of language, particularly by artists and journalists, as an expression of the moral character of society, and his analysis of modern writers and their history became the distinctive achievement of his career.

Biography

Malcolm Cowley was born on August 24, 1898, in the small farming village of Belsano in the Allegheny hills east of Pittsburgh. His father, William Cowley, was a homeopathic physician who maintained his office in a building in an older section of Pittsburgh. The family rented an apartment in the same building, so Cowley grew up in an urban business neighborhood with few children for companionship. The Cowley summer house in Belsano had been left to William Cowley by the poet's grandmother, and it was there that Cowley's mother, Josephine (Hutmacher) Cowley, took her only child to spend the summers while her husband worked in Pittsburgh. The farm community of Belsano and Cowley's experiences there during the long summers had a profound impact on his life and poetry. He was never comfortable in urban environments. Cowley's childhood was, like that of many writers, one of periodic solitude and long hours spent alone reading and imagining. Though he received most of his early schooling in Pittsburgh, Cowley was most comfortable in the farming community of Belsano.

He entered Harvard College in 1915 on a scholarship from the Harvard Club of Pittsburgh. There he made several important literary friendships, some of them with older poets such as S. Foster Damon, Conrad Aiken, and E. E. Cummings. These friends, themselves innovators in the modern poetry movement, introduced Cowley to the work of the nineteenth century French Symbolists and to older New England poets such as Edwin Arlington Robinson and Amy Lowell, who was then a proponent of Imagism.

In the spring of 1917, Cowley volunteered for the American Field Service in France, and he served, like other Harvard writers such as Cummings, John Dos Passos, and Robert Hillyer, as part of the earliest group of Americans to see the battlefronts of World War I. Cowley drove a munitions truck for the French Army for six months, then returned to New York, where he lived for several months in Greenwich Village waiting to return to college. While living a life of poverty, and writing some poetry and book reviews to survive, he met and later married an older artist, Marguerite Frances Baird (Peggy), who was a confirmed bohemian painter divorced from her first husband, the New York poet Orrick Johns. Peggy Baird introduced Cowley to many older Greenwich Village artists, and to Clarence Britten, then literary editor of *The Dial*, who gave Cowley books for review and indirectly initiated his career in literary journalism.

Cowley returned to Harvard in September, 1919, and was graduated in the winter of 1920 after another absence spent in Army ROTC training. He had been elected president of *The Harvard Advocate* in the spring of 1918 and spent his last two college terms working to keep alive what little literary life there was at Harvard during the war years.

After college, Cowley returned to Greenwich Village, where he and Peggy lived a bohemian life again in a cheap tenement while Cowley worked as a copywriter for *Sweet's Architectural Catalogue*. He continued to do some freelance book reviewing and wrote poems and essays for magazines.

In July, 1921, Cowley went to France for two years. There he studied at the University of Montpellier and lived for short periods in Claude Monet's village of Giverney outside Paris. In Paris, his New York friend Matthew Josephson introduced him to the French Dadaist and Surrealist writers and painters, and Cowley met most of the American expatriate writers who had gone to Europe after World War I to escape the conservative, sometimes reactionary political, aesthetic, and social ideas dominating American culture in the postwar years. In France, Cowley also worked as an editor and writer for two of the most famous "little magazines" of the expatriates in those years, *Broom* and *Secession*. While most of the American expatriates absorbed a good deal of the social, political, and aesthetic ideas of the modern European avant-garde art movement, Cowley rebelled against such ideas and began to defend the traditional aesthetic values of Western artistic realism and mimesis. His experiences in France resulted in his understanding of the aesthetic brilliance of the modern artistic revolution, but he became sharply critical of many of the modernist doctrines and practices.

When Cowley returned to New York in August, 1923, he embarked on a career that he hoped would emulate the ideal of a professional man of letters. In the latter half of the 1920's Cowley wrote poems, essays, and book reviews for a number of the most prominent literary journals and newspapers of the time, and translated books of French literature, some of which became bestsellers. Cowley was also the friend of a number of writers living near New York in the 1920's, such as Hart Crane, Allen Tate, Robert Penn Warren, and Katherine Anne Porter.

When Edmund Wilson retired as literary editor of *The New Republic* in the summer of 1929, he chose Cowley to succeed him. For sixteen years thereafter Cowley served in a job he loved and exhausted himself in attempting to connect the world of literature and books with the world of politics, public affairs, and social history. His own poetry and prose of the time provide cultural historians with one of the best records of the tumultuous intellectual and political fervor of the Depression and World War II years.

After being forced to resign by Congressman Martin Dies in the spring of 1942 from his position as aide to Archibald MacLeish at the Roosevelt Administration's Office of Facts and Figures, for allegedly being a "communist threat" to America because of his left-wing political sympathies during the Depression, Cowley retired from any active political involvement and moved to Sherman, Connecticut, where he had already remodeled an old barn. Thereafter he worked as a freelance writer, editor, part-time college teacher, and adviser to the Viking Press, writing and editing the books that consolidated his reputation as one of the finest American literary critics and historians of the twentieth century.

In 1932 Cowley had divorced his first wife and married Muriel Maurer, with whom he lived for more than fifty years. His son, Robert, became a magazine and book editor in New York. Malcolm Cowley died in New Milford, Connecticut, in March of 1989, by that time revered as an American literary institution.

ANALYSIS

To appreciate Malcolm Cowley's poetry, it is necessary to see it in relation to the major cultural movement of his time, usually described by historians as artistic or cultural modernism, or simply modernism. Modernism represented a radical break with the centuries-long traditions of Western humanistic, realistic art. The humanistic tradition was characterized by a belief that art has a moral and social function in the larger process of human civilization.

The theories and practice of modern artists developed in reaction to both the humanistic tradition of Western civilization and the profound changes in Western society that resulted from the rising prestige of science and technology, the industrial revolution, and the organized use of scientific knowledge and technology by modern financial capitalism. Characteristic ideas of modern art included a repudiation of any criteria except the aesthetic as a basis for judging art, and the contention that the artistic imagination is an essentially irrational, as opposed to rational, process that governs scientific investigation and ordinary human communication.

The complex and revolutionary impulse of modern art, its antinaturalist aesthetic, its repudiation of the traditions of Western art, the social alienation and rebellion of modern artists, and their profound hostility to modern society constituted an epochal change in art history. The sometimes confused and alienated psychology that they represented together with the explosion of experimental forms that it produced were manifested while Malcolm Cowley was beginning his literary career. His critical study of that historical epoch and its influence on modern American writers was the subject of his most famous book, *Exile's Return*. It was also the subject of his first published book of poetry, *Blue Juniata*.

BLUE JUNIATA

When Cowley published *Blue Juniata* in 1929, the book was described by Allen Tate as an important historical record of the entire literary generation of the 1920's. *Blue Juniata* was published at the urging of Hart Crane, who wanted it organized to reflect the "emotional record" of its author in accord with the values of modern poetics. Instead, Cowley structured the book historically in five sections, each containing poems describing periods and places that Cowley experienced with his contemporaries. The sections include poems about his years of adolescence and World War I, the years of expatriate artists in France and Europe after the war, the migration to New York and the frenzied life of the Jazz Age, and a section of miscellaneous poems reflecting the poet's sense of upheaval in the decade of the 1920's. The book mirrors Cowley's private reaction to his time and the time itself.

If the aesthetic of modern art was antinatural, the title section of *Blue Juniata* is filled with poems celebrating nature. The title is taken from a river in west-central Pennsylvania, the rural environment that Cowley loved but to which, like the childhood homes of Thomas Wolfe, Hemingway, Fitzgerald, and others of his generation, he could not "go home again."

Cowley's poems reflect the modern poetry movement in other ways. In the second section of the book, called "Adolescence," he reprints poems written during his bohemian days after the war. Poems such as "Kelly's Barroom" imitate the style of the French Symbolist poet Jules Laforgue and his theme of youthful disillusionment. Laforgue had been recommended to younger American poets such as Cowley by Ezra Pound and T. S. Eliot, whose "The Love Song of J. Alfred Prufrock" was also derivative of Laforgue.

The third section of *Blue Juniata* consists of poems written in Europe, where many of Cowley's American friends had been influenced by the French Dadaist artists and by the international avant-garde centered in Paris and led by James Joyce, Marcel Proust, Pablo Picasso, and other European artists. Cowley's poems of those years include English versions of some of the great modern poems, such as Guillaume Apollinaire's "Marizibill," and an ironic poem undercutting a classical theme which he entitled "Mediterranean Beach." Such poems as "Valuta" satirize the exploitation by artists of postwar Europe's economic situation, while "Sunrise over the Heiterwand" hints at the political confusion of Pound, Eliot, and other symbolists. Another poem of Cowley's Paris years, "Château de Soupir: 1917," is a satire on Marcel Proust's monumental novel, *À la recherche du temps perdu* (1913-1927; *Remembrance of Things Past*, 1922-1931). A poem entitled "Two Swans" is a commentary on the outlaw sensibility of Charles Baudelaire and later Symbolists, who maintained that poetic beauty was to be found in the bizarre and criminal underworld.

Many of the poems of the fourth section of *Blue Juniata* ("The City of Anger, Poems: 1924-1928") are portraits of literary friends. In "The Narrow House," Cowley describes Kenneth Burke as a pastoral recluse of vast ambition and hopes who has husbanded his land in rebellion against the industrial age. Another remarkable poem, "The Flower in the Sea," portrays Hart Crane's obsession with the Symbolist idea of the "Poète Maudit" and his fascination with the sea. It is a portrait whose prophecy Crane fulfilled several years later, when he committed suicide by jumping overboard in the Gulf of Mexico. One poem, "Buy 300 Steel," satirizes Cowley's friend Matthew Josephson, who was forced to work at a job he hated as a stockbroker in the Roaring Twenties. Harold Loeb, an heir to a small portion of the Guggenheim copper fortune and the man who financed the avant-garde art magazine *Broom*, is described in Cowley's poem "Tumbling Mustard" as representing the frenzied energy of the artists of the 1920's. Allen Tate, with his taste for classical poetry and poetic styles, is addressed by Cowley in his sonnet "Towers of Song."

SOCIAL AND POLITICAL THEMES

Even in his poems about New York, Cowley reveals a social consciousness that distinguished him from his peers. Two poems of the late 1920's, "The Lady from Harlem: In Memory of Florence Mills" and "For St. Bartholomew's Eve (August 23, 1927)," are overtly political, reacting to the injustices felt by liberal artists at famous trials in New York, as well as in Boston in 1927 where the anarchist immigrants Nicola Sacco and Bartolomeo Vanzetti were tried and executed. Many of Cowley's pastoral poems in *Blue Juniata* also imply a social theme. In several short narrative and descriptive poems, such as "Laurel Mountain," "Seven O'Clock," "Hickory Cove," "The Farm Died," and "Empty Barn, Dead Farm," Cowley's tone is elegiac, lamenting the declining farm communities of nineteenth century America displaced by the growing urban industrialization of the twentieth century. Two other poems, "The Hill

Above the Mine" and "Mine No. 6," are stark descriptions of the ruin brought to Cowley's boyhood Pennsylvania by the greed of the mining industry. All those poems reflect Cowley's deep emotional attachment to the American landscape.

Though Cowley gave a more complete and analytical history of his literary generation in *Exile's Return*, *Blue Juniata* contains many of the themes and ideas that he later developed in that book. Indeed, the final poems of his collection, "The Urn," is a concise statement, in formal stanzas, of the central experience of the entire "lost generation," their experience of exile, uprootedness, and aching memory for a country of childhood which could never be regained in the modern world.

As a critical analyst of the Depression-era literature of social commitment and a historian of modern American literature, Cowley's major prose works are descriptive, analytical, and narrative. His deepest response to the literary and political culture of the Great Depression is revealed, however, in a slim volume of poems, his second collection, published in 1941.

THE DRY SEASON

The Dry Season contains seventeen poems, most of them written between 1935 and 1941. A few poems in the collection go back to the late 1920's but had been omitted from *Blue Juniata*. These poems, such as "Tar Babies," which was originally published in the avant-garde magazine *transition* in 1928, satirize the decadent, often sexually aberrant behavior of the artistic culture of the 1920's. "The Eater of Darkness," a poem dedicated to Cowley's friend and early Dadaist enthusiast Robert Coates, describes the bizarre literary world of New York by presenting the Jazz Age in terms of *Alice's Adventures in Wonderland* (1865). The chaotic, sometimes destructive, rebel society of modern American art had been the theme of Coates's novel *Yesterday's Burden's* (1933), which Cowley cited in *Exile's Return* as evidence of the turn by American artists in the early 1930's from modernist art and social rebellion to social involvement.

The poetry of *The Dry Season* reveals the emotional history of Cowley's own social involvement. For example, two poems, "The Mother" and "The Firstborn," are autobiographical, written after the death of his mother. Both poems reveal a sense of guilt on the part of a son

who felt unable to help his parents while they suffered, like millions of Americans, from deprivation. On a visit to Pittsburgh shortly before his mother's death, Cowley had been stunned to find that his father, a doctor unable to collect payment from most of his patients, had become a partial invalid and that his mother sometimes did not have enough to eat. The plight of his family reinforced his conviction that radical measures were needed to change the American economic structure. He also felt that writers and artists could find hope, a renewed sense of relevance, and a large audience if their art mirrored the human issues of their age.

His poems "The Last International" and "Tomorrow Morning" reflect the hopes and humanist faith that comprised Cowley's passionate response to the turmoil of the time. The imagery of "The Last International" alludes to Homer, Vergil, and Dante and their visions of Hell. In Cowley's poem, however, the dead rise up to revolutionize contemporary life.

An important aspect of "Tomorrow Morning" is its intuitive recognition that radical politics and solidarity with the politically and economically disadvantaged required affiliation with political fringe groups that would taint artistic integrity and would probably tragically fail to change historical conditions anyway. Given the evils of fascism, and the economic chaos against which Cowley believed a coalition was necessary, the poem implies that artists have no choice but to work with all factions opposed to the reactionary forces and ideas of the time.

What Cowley was unprepared for was the enormity of human evil that fascism revealed and that Soviet Communism initially masked from the often naïve writers of the 1930's. He was also surprised and hurt by the sometimes savage bitterness engendered among artists by the failed political hopes of the age. After observing the bitter factionalism of intellectuals in the late 1930's and suffering with his friends from vicious attacks by apologists for both fascism and Communism, Cowley became disillusioned by his entire political experience. Poems such as "The End of the World," "Seven," "The Lost People," and "The Dry Season" metaphorically imply that the poet's heart, mind, and spirit are despondent, like stream beds in a drought, and he yearns for some answers in an age when all myths, all beliefs, and all values seem destroyed by man's terrible capacity for evil.

Like W. H. Auden in his poem "New Year Letter" (1940), Cowley felt the political confusion of the late 1930's as a deep void, the collapse of humanistic hopes and ideals.

The Dry Season also contains a few poems written in the late 1930's that reveal Cowley's renewed love for the American landscape, pointing the way toward solace for his political disillusionment. "This Morning Robins," "Eight Melons," and "The Long Voyage" are pastoral lyrics celebrating spring and the late summer harvest when the abundance of nature provides men with sustenance to last through the "dry winter" of nature and the human heart: "Now the dark waters at the bow/ fold back, like earth against the plow;/ foam brightens like the dogwood now/ at home, in my own country." Cowley returned to the country in the 1940's, the country of American farmers and craftsmen, of small-town friendliness and the world of nature. He spent the remainder of his active literary career there defending the values in which he deeply believed.

When Cowley's collected poems were published in 1968, Kenneth Rexroth wrote in a review of the year's poetry that Cowley was an important American poet, somewhat overlooked because of his more famous peers and the brilliance of his prose.

BLUE JUNIATA: COLLECTED POEMS

The 1968 collection *Blue Juniata: Collected Poems* stands as a summary of Cowley's entire literary career. The book contains most of the poems from his two previous collections, with several changes of titles, some rearrangement of order, and minor revisions of content. Several previously uncollected poems are also included, while new poems from the 1950's and 1960's are collected in two final sections called "The Unsaved World" and "Another Country."

The book's structure is both thematic and historical, and it reveals the remarkable consistency of its author. The new work in the volume again reveals a writer with a strong satiric style and an acute sense of history. Poems such as "Ode in a Time of Crisis" and "The Enemy Within" are witty, ironic commentaries on the political paranoia and undemocratic practices of the McCarthy era in the early 1950's. With allusive irony, Cowley compares McCarthy's political tactics to another great scandal of American history, the Salem witchcraft trials.

Several of Cowley's finest poems of his late years are further meditations on his favorite theme, the relationship between man and nature. Poems such as "Natural History," a sequence in five parts, "The Living Water," a poem with echoes of the nature poetry of Henry David Thoreau and Ralph Waldo Emerson, and "Here with the Long Grass Rippling," perhaps Cowley's finest long poem (with clear allusions to Walt Whitman's "Song of Myself"), indicate again his almost religious feeling for the American landscape. "Here with the Long Grass Rippling" in particular embodies a recurring theme of the American poetic tradition, a nondoctrinaire, noncreedal, yet mystical faith in the spiritual made manifest in the world of nature.

LEGACY

While modern artists often sought frantically, sometimes tragically, to revive a sense of myth, ritual, and religious emotion in the secular, materialistic culture of modernity, seeking impossible modes of escape from nature by means of art, Cowley's vision of the sacred value of the smallest insect or flower, and the interconnectedness of the natural environment with the culture of the world, reiterated his lifelong literary theme. Literature at its best is a mirror of human history and a moral criticism of contemporary society. The profound meditation of "Here with the Long Grass Rippling" also helps to explain Cowley's great analyses of the illustrious members of his own literary generation and his sensitive response to writers such as Faulkner, Hemingway, and Thomas Wolfe, and their affinities with nineteenth century America. Having himself been shaped by the revolutionary culture of modern art, Cowley journeyed backward to find his own beliefs best expressed by the radically democratic values of America's classic writers.

His collected poetry and prose thus describes the literary odyssey of modern American writers, many of whom were his closest friends. Those writers created a new aesthetic and a new ethic that was fundamentally shaped by their experience of modern art and politics. They also modified that art by their own "long voyages" back to rediscover their moral heritage in the art of Hawthorne, Whitman, and Thoreau. Cowley's "lost generation" began as Symbolists in technique and temperament, but in the end they remained faithful to the great humanistic tradition of their nineteenth century forebears, who were, after all, as Cowley was one of the earliest to notice, America's first truly modern writers.

OTHER MAJOR WORKS

NONFICTION: *Exile's Return*, 1934, 1951 (as *Exile's Return: A Literary Odyssey of the 1920's*); *The Literary Situation*, 1954; *Writers at Work: The "Paris Review" Interviews*, 1958; *Black Cargoes: A History of the Atlantic Slave Trade, 1518-1865*, 1962 (with Daniel Pratt Mannix); *The Faulkner-Cowley File: Letters and Memories, 1944-1962*, 1966; *Think Back on Us: A Contemporary Chronicle of the 1930's*, 1967; *A Many-Windowed House: Collected Essays on American Writers and American Writing*, 1970; *A Second Flowering: Works and Days of the Lost Generation*, 1973; *And I Worked at the Writer's Trade*, 1978; *The Dream of the Golden Mountains: Remembering the 1930's*, 1980 (memoir); *The View from Eighty*, 1980 (memoir); *The Flower and the Leaf: A Contemporary Record of American Writing Since 1941*, 1985; *The Selected Correspondence of Kenneth Burke and Malcolm Cowley, 1915-1981*, 1988.

TRANSLATIONS: *On Board the Morning Star*, 1925 (of Pierre Macorlan's novel *À Bord de L'Étoile Matutine*); *Joan of Arc*, 1926 (of Joseph Delteil's biography *La Passion de Jeanne d'Arc*); *Variety*, 1927 (of volume 1 of Paul Valéry's essay collection *Variété*); *Catherine-Paris*, 1928 (of Marthe Bibesco's novel); *The Green Parrot*, 1929 (of Bibesco's novel *Le Perroquet vert*); *The Count's Ball*, 1929 (of Raymond Radiguet's novel *Le Bal du comte d'Orgel*); *Imaginary Interviews*, 1944 (of André Gide's essay collection *Interviews imaginaires*); *Leonardo, Poe, Mallarmé*, 1972 (with James R. Lawler; volume 8 of *The Collected Works of Paul Valéry*).

EDITED TEXTS: *After the Genteel Tradition: American Writers Since 1910*, 1936, rev. 1946; *Books That Changed Our Minds*, 1939 (with Bernard Smith); *The Portable Hemingway*, 1944; *The Portable Faulkner*, 1946; *The Portable Hawthorne*, 1948; *The Complete Poetry and Prose of Walt Whitman*, 1948; *The Stories of F. Scott Fitzgerald*, 1951; *Tender Is the Night*, 1951 (by F. Scott Fitzgerald); *Three Novels of F. Scott Fitzgerald: The Great Gatsby . . . Tender Is the Night . . . The Last Tycoon*, 1953; *Great Tales of the Deep South*, 1955; *Leaves of Grass, the First (1855) Edition*, 1959 (by Walt Whitman); *Fitzgerald and the Jazz Age*, 1966 (with Robert Crowley); *The Lessons of the Masters: An Anthology of the Novel from Cervantes to Hemingway*, 1971 (with Howard E. Hugo).

MISCELLANEOUS: *The Portable Malcolm Cowley*, 1990.

BIBLIOGRAPHY

Aldridge, John W. *In Search of Heresy: American Literature in an Age of Conformity.* New York: McGraw-Hill, 1956. These ten essays derive chiefly from the Christian Gauss lectures delivered by Aldridge at Princeton University in 1954. They lament boldly the tendency toward orthodoxy, and consequently mediocrity, in the literary sphere. One chapter, "The Question of Malcolm Cowley," appraises the role of Cowley in the shaping of the literature. The criticism is perceptive and stimulating.

Bak, Hans. *Malcolm Cowley: The Formative Years.* Athens: University of Georgia Press, 1993. Bak focuses on Cowley's formative years and draws on personal interviews conducted shortly before Cowley's death as well as published and unpublished writings to trace the unfolding of his thinking and influence.

Cowley, Malcolm. *Exile's Return: A Literary Odyssey of the Nineteen Twenties.* New York: Viking Press, 1951. This autobiography presents Cowley's own account of his role in the expatriate movement of the 1920's. Defines and explains the "lost generation" and is an energetic, witty, sometimes touching account of the ideas that dominated the period. Provides engaging portraits of Cowley's fellow writers: John Dos Passos, Ernest Hemingway, T. S. Eliot, F. Scott Fitzgerald, and others.

Dolan, Marc. *Modern Lives: A Cultural Re-reading of "The Lost Generation."* West Lafayette, Ind.: Purdue University Press, 1996. A study of the "lost generation" that locates autobiographical works by Ernest Hemingway, Malcolm Cowley, and F. Scott Fitzgerald in the context of their contemporaries and within an understanding of modernism.

Eisenberg, Diane U. "A Conversation with Malcolm Cowley." *Southern Review* 15 (Spring, 1979): 288-299. This essay is a verbatim recording of an interview of Cowley in dialogue form by the compiler of *Malcolm Cowley: A Checklist of His Writings, 1916-1973*. What emerges are Cowley's impressions of the craft of writing and his recollections of his literary associates.

Gambaccini, Peter. "Last of the 'Lost Generation.'" *Yankee*, March 3, 1983, 92-93, 123-130. Cowley is interviewed at his home in Sherman, Connecticut. The chatty dialogue provides a sketchy biography, especially the growth of Cowley's reputation as a critic, and provides vivid reminiscences of Hart Crane, Robert Frost, William Faulkner, and Ernest Hemingway.

Hoffman, Frederick. *The Twenties: American Writing in the Postwar Decade*. New York: Viking Press, 1955. This is a work of solid literary scholarship, a penetrating analysis of the literary flowering that occurred during the 1920's. Provides, in addition to helpful literary criticism, a stimulating account of the cultural and social history. The essay on Cowley shows his role in the arena of Ezra Pound, Ernest Hemingway, H. L. Mencken, F. Scott Fitzgerald, E. E. Cummings, William Faulkner, and Hart Crane.

Jay, Paul, ed. *The Selected Correspondence of Kenneth Burke and Malcolm Cowley, 1915-1981*. New York: Viking Press, 1988. This collection is a must for those who want to understand the development of Cowley's thought and critical opinions. Provides a lively narrative and a historical dialogue between two lifelong friends. The editing is masterful. The literary theories and social criticism of both Cowley and Burke are vividly accounted for. The early letters are particularly interesting.

Kempf, James Michael. *The Early Career of Malcolm Cowley: A Humanist Among the Moderns*. Baton Rouge: Louisiana State University Press, 1985. This study in six chapters, limited to Cowley's formative years at Harvard, in Greenwich Village, and in Paris, is an effort to correct earlier misrepresentation of the critic's influence and opinions. Provides a substantial basis for an evaluation of Cowley's whole career. The best chapters detail Cowley's postwar years in France. Bibliography.

Simpson, Lewis P. "Malcolm Cowley and the American Writer." *Sewanee Review* 84 (Spring, 1976): 220-247. Reprinted in Simpson, *The Brazen Face of History*. Baton Rouge: Louisiana State University Press, 1980. One of the very best essays on Cowley, this article is a very readable substantial examination of Cowley's writings, particularly *Exile's Return* and *A Second Flowering*. Provides a perceptive and searching commentary on the "poetics of exile" and on the "pragmatics of the writer's life," noting that Cowley's most graphic images are those of loneliness and showing how the basic motive of alienation runs through all his work.

James M. Kempf;
bibliography updated by the editors

WILLIAM COWPER

Born: Great Berkhampstead, England; November 26, 1731

Died: East Dereham, England; April 25, 1800

PRINCIPAL POETRY

Olney Hymns, 1779 (with John Newton)
Poems, 1782
The Task, 1785
Complete Poetical Works, 1907 (standard edition)

OTHER LITERARY FORMS

The *Olney Hymns* are now commonly studied as poems. Of the sixty-four hymns contributed to the volume by William Cowper, only a very few still appear in church hymnals. The hymn, however, while certainly kin to the poem, presents unique demands on the author and cannot be judged fairly by the same critical standards. The hymn must try to reflect universal Christian feelings on a level immediately recognizable to all the human souls and intellects that make up a congregation. It must be orthodox and express only the expected. It must be simple, and above all it must not reveal what is individual about the author. To the extent that Cowper's unique genius could not always be restrained by conven-

William Cowper (Hulton Archive)

tion, he is not consistently as good a hymnist as Isaac Watts or Charles Wesley.

In the eighteenth century, the familiar letter became so artistically refined that modern literary scholars now regard it as a minor literary form. Cowper's collected correspondence fills four volumes (Wright edition, 1904) and treats an incredible range of subjects and themes with great insight, humor, and style. Literary historians regard him as one of the finest letter writers in English.

ACHIEVEMENTS

Modern literary historians commonly assign William Cowper to the ranks of the so-called pre-Romantics, and to be sure, his subjective voice, preference for the rural to the urban, and social concern are qualities more easily discernible in the poetry of the early nineteenth century than of the late eighteenth century. Cowper, however, was not attempting to create a literary movement. The poetry characteristic of his later years is clearly a perfection of themes and forms that occupied his attention from the first, and those early efforts are not radical

departures from what is considered mainstream neoclassicism. Satire, mock-heroic, general nature description, all are present, but Cowper grew in his art and was not concerned that his growth made him into something a bit different.

Cowper's satires, for example, are notable for a measure of charity toward their subjects, charity which he saw was lacking in the satires of Alexander Pope and his contemporaries. Moreover, Cowper was greatly interested in poetic structure but also felt that the poetry of his age put too much emphasis on structure at the expense of real human personality. The canon of Cowper's work is of a very uneven quality, but his finest efforts, such as *The Task*, display an unobtrusive structure and identifiable human presence uncommon in the neoclassical age, and they are fine by the standards of any age. Perhaps his outstanding structural achievement is the conversational blank verse used in *The Task*. There is no more interesting development in that form between John Milton and William Wordsworth. Yet, while Cowper's critical reputation is quite good, he is not regarded as one of the major figures in English letters. The conventions of neoclassical poetry had been manipulated with greater skill by Pope, and the new directions suggested by Cowper would be shortly perfected by Wordsworth. Thus, the achievement of Cowper, by no means insignificant, is somewhat obscured by the giants who surround him.

BIOGRAPHY

William Cowper was born on November 26, 1731, in Great Berkhampstead, Hertfordshire, England. He was the fourth child of the Reverend Dr. John Cowper, rector of Great Berkhampstead, and Ann Donne. Both parents represented distinguished families. The Cowpers had distinguished themselves by loyalty to the Crown, and John Cowper's uncle, Sir William, had been created baron in 1706 and earl in 1718. The Donnes were of even nobler lineage and traced descent from Henry III. The famous seventeenth century poet, John Donne, was of the same illustrious family. John and Ann had seven children, but only William and their last child, also named John, survived infancy. Very shortly after the birth of John, Ann died; William was only six at the time.

Cowper's father appears to have been neither a cruel nor especially loving parent. Shortly after Ann's death, young William was sent away to school. This early separation from his parent—not unusual in upper-class households—seems to have affected the poet greatly, for, several years later, Cowper attacked the practice and the school system in general in a poem, *Tirocinium* (1785). While a student at Westminster, Cowper met his first love, his cousin Theodora. The affair was terminated in 1756, but it is commemorated in nineteen sentimental love poems addressed to Delia. Cowper suffered his first severe attack of depression in 1752. He was studying law at the time and was called to the bar in 1754. Although he had no great fondness for the profession, his family had thought it best that he have some livelihood.

In 1759, Cowper was appointed commissioner of bankrupts, a minor governmental post that paid very little. Out of the need for financial security, he applied for an appointment to the post of clerk of the journals of the House of Lords. When the incumbent clerk died, Cowper's appointment was put forward only to be challenged by supporters of another candidate. In 1763, Cowper learned that he would have to face an examination to determine the best applicant. This prospect greatly aggravated his already depressed state, and he experienced a severe mental breakdown during which he unsuccessfully attempted suicide. Clearly, he could not occupy a government post. The sense of rejection as a consequence of this realization joined with the recollection of his mother's death, and the broken affair with Theodora led Cowper to imagine that his exile from normal human relationships was God's sign to him that he was also excluded from the company of the blessed for all eternity.

Following an eighteen month residence in an asylum, Cowper moved to the country where he soon made the acquaintance of the Unwin family. He resided with that cheerful and cordial family in Huntingdon and then accompanied Mrs. Unwin in her move to the town of Olney following the sudden death of her husband. Here, Cowper met the revivalist minister John Newton, and, for a time, he enjoyed a useful and productive existence. He became interested in the problems of the poor and various charitable activities and joined with Newton in writing a collection of hymns which was later published as the *Olney Hymns*. In January, 1773, however, shortly before his planned marriage to the widowed Mrs. Unwin, Cowper again suffered a period of instability. Convinced by a terrifying dream that it was God's will, he once again attempted suicide. His failure only added to his distress, for now, sure that he had failed to obey God's command, he became utterly convinced of his damnation. Although he recovered from the 1773 breakdown, despair never left him.

Largely as a distraction, Cowper turned his attention to writing poetry, and in February, 1782, he published his first significant collection. The early 1780's were made happier for Cowper by his friendship with Lady Austin, who had taken up residence near Olney. It was at the suggestion of this good-humored lady that in July, 1783, he began his masterpiece, *The Task*. That poem provided the title for his next collection which appeared in 1785. Yet, whatever joy Cowper may have derived from the favorable public response to his new volume was soon erased by the death of Mrs. Unwin's son, William. This shock, plus the anxiety caused by moving from his beloved Olney to Weston, was more than Cowper could endure, and in 1787 he again lost his grip on reality.

Following his recovery, Cowper again turned to writing. He began a translation of Homer and addressed himself to social issues, especially the fight against slavery. For a few years at least he was able to reproduce the routine and uneventful living he had enjoyed at Olney. In December, 1791, however, Mrs. Unwin suffered a stroke; in May, 1792, she suffered another which rendered her immobile and speechless. She recovered somewhat, but the guilt Cowper felt at recalling how her life had been spent in his care, plunged him again into deep melancholy. His feelings are well expressed in "To Mary," written in the fall of 1793. Not even the satisfaction of his great poetic fame and an annual pension of three hundred pounds from George III could lift him from despair or silence the voices of eternal doom which came to him at night. On December 17, 1796, Mrs. Unwin died. "The Castaway," composed in 1799, is one of the bleakest poems in English and itself sufficient comment on the last three years of Cowper's life. On April 25, 1800, after a one-month struggle with edema, he died. A witness described his last facial expression as one of "holy surprise."

ANALYSIS

William Cowper's poetic achievement is marked by a tension between subjectivity and objectivity, a tension which, at its best, produces a unique poetry defying easy classification as either neoclassical or Romantic. Cowper wrote poetry to preserve his sanity. It was a way to distract himself from the terrible brooding on the inevitability of his damnation, and even when his gloom made it impossible to focus on subjects other than his own condition, at least the very act of writing, the mechanical business of finding rhymes or maintaining meter, defused the self-destructive potential of the messages of despair that crowded his dreams and came to him in the whisperings of mysterious voices. Because the poetry was not only by Cowper but also *for* Cowper, it displays a subjectivity uncommon in the neoclassical tradition. Although Cowper had his own opinions about poetry and disliked the formal, elegant couplet structure that dominated the verse of his day, he was not completely a rebel. Objectivity, Horatian humor, sentimentality, respect for the classics, the very qualities that define neoclassicism are all present in Cowper's verse. Unlike William Wordsworth, he never issued a manifesto to revolutionize poetry. Indeed, the levelheaded detachment of the Horatian persona, so popular with Cowper's contemporaries, was a stance that he often tried to capture for the sake of his own mental stability. When Cowper manages a balance between the subjectivity that injects his own gentle humanity into a poem and the objectivity that allows universal significance, he is at his best.

"ON THE RECEIPT OF MY MOTHER'S PICTURE OUT OF NORFOLK"

One of Cowper's most famous poems illustrates the poet at less than his best when he manages almost fully to withhold his own personality and allows convention to structure his message. "On the Receipt of My Mother's Picture Out of Norfolk" was written in 1790, fifty-three years after his mother's death and only ten years before his own. The poem avoids the theme of death and rather focuses on the mother with the only tool available to it: convention. The poem begins with a reference to the power of art to immortalize, a theme which might have supported some interesting content. The poet then introduces yet another worthy theme: "And while that face renews my filial grief,/ Fancy shall weave a charm for my relief"; while the art of the picture kindles an old grief, the art of the poem will provide the balm. Neither theme, however, survives beyond the first few lines of the poem. Instead, Cowper turns to the popular conventions of eighteenth century verse to produce a proper comment on a dead mother.

The verse form is the heroic couplet, the dominant form of the age. The diction is formal because the neoclassical notion of decorum—words appropriately matched to the subject matter—demanded formality in the respectful approach of a child to a parent. Ann Cowper, the poet's mother, is unrecognizable in the poem; she has no individuality, no visual reality for the reader. Consistent with the neoclassical emphasis on the general and ideal rather than the particular and commonplace, Cowper creates a cloud of expected motherly virtues through which the face of Ann can be seen but dimly. Here it should be remembered, however, that the poet is reacting to a picture, an eighteenth century portrait, not to a tangible human being, and that portrait itself would have been an idealized representation reflective of the aesthetic principle voiced by Sir Joshua Reynolds: "The general idea constitutes real excellence. . . . Even in portraits, the grace, and, we may add, the likeness, consists more in taking the general air than in observing the exact similitude of feature."

The poem, then, does accurately treat its subject if that subject is indeed the portrait. Still, the treatment is for the most part a catalog of hackneyed images—"sweet smiles" and "dear eyes"—mixed with a few images that need more than originality to save them, such as the extended simile which likens the mother to "a gallant bark from Albion's coast" that "shoots into port at some well-havered isle," a rather unflattering analogy if the reader attempts to use it to help visualize the mother. The overall sentimentality of the poem is also no departure from neoclassical convention. Sentimentalism in all literary genres had emerged as a popular reaction to the great emphasis placed on reason by so many eighteenth century thinkers. The universe, it was held, is logical and ordered, and all nature, including human nature, is ultimately understandable by the human ability to reason. Sentimentalism answered this by calling attention to emotions and feelings. Humanity is not merely rational; there are finer qualities beyond the power of logic to comprehend. At its best, sentiment could add an element of emotion to reason and make a work more reflective of the real human psyche. At its worst, sentiment drowned reality in maudlin fictions and saccharine absurdities. Cowper's poem does not completely sink in the quagmire of sentimental syrup. It hangs on by the thread of an idea about the immortalizing power of art, a thread which is visible at the beginning and then again at the end but which for the greater part of the poem is lost in the swamp.

All this is not to say that "On the Receipt of My Mother's Picture Out of Norfolk" is a bad poem. Indeed, it remains one of Cowper's most frequently anthologized works. If it is conventional, it is still worth studying as a good example of several aspects of the neoclassical tradition unknown to readers who name the age after Alexander Pope or Samuel Johnson. Cowper, however, was capable of doing better. The problem with the mother poem was that rather than writing about his mother he pretended to write about his own feelings and memories. The memories after so many years were probably dim, and he seems to have chosen to avoid an expression of his dark fears and utter isolation in favor of a conventional grieving son persona.

"THE CASTAWAY"

Cowper succeeds more fully when his reaction to a situation or event includes, but also goes beyond, the feelings most readers would experience when he injects enough of his purely subjective response to allow the reader to see a somewhat different but still believable dimension to what it is to be human. The loss of a mother is certainly an appropriate correlative to the emotions expressed in the poem. Moreover, the emotional response is certainly believable; it is not, however, unique. The loss of a seaman overboard during a storm is also an appropriate correlative to the emotions of the speaker in "The Castaway," but here Cowper does more than simply respond to a situation.

The episode of the seaman swept overboard in a storm, an account of which Cowper had read in George Anson's *Voyage* (1748) some years before writing the poem, is actually an extended metaphor for the poet's own condition. Interestingly, the analogy between poet and sailor is only briefly pointed out at the very beginning and again at the end of the poem. The metaphor, the story of the sailor, is for the most part presented with curious objectivity. The facts of the tragedy are all there: the storm, the struggles of the seaman, the futile attempts at rescue. There is also a respectable measure of grief in the subdued tone of the speaker; the reader, however, could not be misled by this seeming objectivity. It is at once apparent that the poem is really about the tragic fate of the poet, but it is precisely in this tension between the objective and subjective that the poem says so much. The effect of the long metaphor in keeping the poet's ego in the background is to illustrate that indeed the poet is an insignificant thing—a tiny, isolated being beyond the help of his fellows and the concern of his God. That curious objectivity is in fact the attitude of the universe toward Cowper. It does not seem to care, and it is not hostile. It has simply excluded Cowper from the scheme of things, a scheme which allows for the possibility of salvation for all humans.

The God in "The Castaway" seems strangely Deistic. He is unwilling to interfere with the predetermined operation of his universe, but unlike many of his contemporaries who viewed the universe with optimism, believing that if God was remote at least the system that he set in motion was good, Cowper sees no goodness in his own portion. In "The Castaway," Cowper can neither bless nor curse his fate, for any action would detract from the utter futility he wishes to convey. "The Castaway," then, is highly subjective. The poet is in no way suggesting that the fate of the metaphorical sailor describes the universal human condition. Indeed, humanity is on board the ship, which survives the storm. Cowper is talking about himself, but the air of objectivity in the presentation stresses the futility and isolation he wishes to convey. In other words, the structure of the poem contributes greatly to its message. What is Cowper in the eyes of God? He is no more than the minimal first-person intrusion in the sixty-six lines that constitute "The Castaway."

"THE POPLAR FIELD"

Cowper was a fine craftsman in the structuring of poems. His collected works clearly show a fondness for experimentation, and as is to be expected, some of those experiments were more successful than others. An interesting example is "The Poplar Field," a frequently anthologized lyric that deals with the fleeting glories of this world. Here, Cowper deliberately violates decorum and adopts a sprightly, heavily accented meter. The mere four feet to a line gallops the reader through musings on various reminders of mortality. The meter seems to mock the expected seriousness of the theme to produce a parody of melancholy landscape verse. The content of the poem consists, for the most part, of uninspired platitudes and clichés, but this is the necessary fodder for parody. A less generous reading might assert that parody is not an issue. The poem is rather a straightforward presentation of the joys of melancholy, the pleasures of the contemplative life. The meter is the vehicle for communicating the pleasure idea to the audience, and Cowper's "The Poplar Field" is really a direct descendant of John Milton's "Allegro." If this is the case, the trite content cannot be justified as fuel for a satiric fire and must be held to be just that: trite content. Perhaps, then, "The Poplar Field" is of the same family as "On the Receipt of My Mother's Picture Out of Norfolk": Both poems suffer from the substitution of conventions for the presence of the real Cowper.

"THE DIVERTING HISTORY OF JOHN GILPIN"

An experiment of unchallenged success is "The Diverting History of John Gilpin." Structure is everything in this delightful ballad about the misadventures of a linen draper on his twenty-year delayed honeymoon. The lively meter and rhyming quatrains are ideally suited to the rollicking humor of the piece. Gilpin, a rather bombastic but totally good-natured hero, has his adventure told by a narrator who is himself satirized by the deceptively careless method of his composition. It soon becomes clear that the poem is everything and that the narrator will not be stopped or the rhythm broken by such concerns as taking time to find an appropriate figure rather than a silly one or even by running out of content to fill the quatrain: "So like an arrow swift he flew,/ Shot by an archer strong;/ So did he fly—which brings me to/ The middle of my song." For Cowper, the poem lived up to its title; it seems to have diverted him indeed, for the reader familiar with Cowper's voice will look in vain for a trace of the brooding author of "The Cast-

away." Yet, beneath the funny story, the brilliant metrics, and the silly narrator, there is still the gentle poet who prefers to laugh with his characters rather than reduce them to the grotesque fools that populate so much of eighteenth century satire.

Despite the success of "The Diverting History of John Gilpin," Cowper has never been considered a leading satirist of the age. Satire, especially in the popular Horatian mode, must have had its attractions for him. The detached, witty observer who by choice leaves the herd to remark upon the foibles of humanity presented an ideal persona, but it was a stance that Cowper could seldom sustain. The satirist must appear objective; the folly must appear to be a genuine part of the target and not merely in the satirist's perception of the target. Cowper could maintain that kind of objectivity only when there was really nothing at stake. Poking fun at the world of John Gilpin is harmless, for there is no suggestion that the world is real beyond the confines of the poem. When the subject is real, however, Cowper cannot stand aside. He lacks wit, in the neoclassical sense of the word. Wit consisted of the genius needed to conceive the raw material of art and the acquired good taste to know how to arrange bits of that material into a unified whole. Wit did not allow for the subjective intrusion of the author's personal problems. Cowper's genius was so intertwined with his special mental condition that he could not remain detached, and when he tried, his acquired skill could only arrange conventions, substitutes for his unique raw material. Moreover, Cowper lacked the satirist's willingness to ridicule. He had nothing against humanity. The shipmates are guiltless in the tragedy of the castaway. Humanity, to be sure, has its delusions and vanities, but Cowper preferred the deflected blow to the sharp thrust.

THE TASK

The Task is Cowper's major achievement, and it is the satiric Cowper who introduces the work. His friend, Lady Austin, had suggested a sofa as an appropriate topic for a poem in blank verse. Of course, such a subject could only be addressed satirically, and Cowper elected the conventional form of mock-heroic. Specifically, he alluded to *The Aeneid* with "I sing the sofa" and thereby suggested that a modern Vergil would be hard pressed to find in eighteenth century society a topic deserving heroic treatment. Yet, the sofa is more than simply a mean subject, it is a quite appropriate symbol for sloth and luxury, the very qualities responsible for society's falling away from the truly heroic. Having called attention to the problem, there is little more for the sofa to do, except that it led Cowper to something worth saying, and he needed a structure less restrictive of his own involvement than the mock-heroic. So with a comment on how he prefers walks in the country to life on the sofa, Cowper shifts to an appreciation of nature theme and the *I* who had been the Vergilian persona of the satire suddenly becomes Cowper himself.

The Task is far too long a work for detailed analysis here. Its five thousand lines are divided into six parts: "The Sofa," "The Time-Piece," "The Garden," "The Winter Evening," "The Winter Morning Walk," and "The Winter Walk at Noon." The question of the overall unity of the work has probably attracted the greatest amount of critical attention. Cowper's own comments about the poem indicate that he was not aiming at tight thematic development; rather, the ideas were naturally suggested by immediately preceding ideas with the whole moving along with the ease of an intelligent but unplanned conversation.

Cowper's style, once the mock-heroic has been dropped, certainly suggests conversation. The diction is elegant but natural, quite different from the language of the other popular eighteenth century nature poet James Thomson, whose baroque language in *The Seasons* (1730) imitated the grand style of John Milton. Moreover, Cowper's blank verse avoids the end-stopped lines used by Thomson, which detracted from the conversational effect by their epigrammatic regularity. The deceptively artless ease of the poem with its several scenes, frequent digressions, and inclusion of highly personal material might easily lead the reader to conclude that the poet is recording a stream of consciousness with no central purpose or theme in mind. In fact, *The Task* is concerned with the need and search for balance in nature and human life. The sofa itself suggests the theme, for if it represents the scale tipping toward excessive luxury, there must somewhere in the range of experience be an ideal condition against which such excesses can be recognized and measured.

The ultimate excess to which the sofa points is the city, London, which on a physical plane reveals squalor, corruption, and insanity; its spiritual reality is sin. The opposite side of the scale also has a spiritual and physical existence. Spiritually, this extreme is the untempered wrath of God, pure divine power; on the physical level, such power is reflected in disturbances in nature and the brutalism that is the alternative to civilization. The early books explore the extremes and present the rural countryside as perhaps the best balance. This balance is insecure, however, for intrusions of both natural and human turmoil bring constant disturbance. The latter parts of the poem demonstrate the futility of finding a secure position in the physical environment. For those who enjoy God's grace, conversion can clarify the balance and bring freedom and order. The final book reveals God as the ultimate source of harmony. In his infinite kindness and infinite sternness, the Father judges all, and that judgment is perfection.

Among the landscape descriptions, character sketches, social criticism, and personal confessions, a unifying theme is perceptible if not obvious in *The Task*, and interestingly, it is the theme that best describes Cowper's life and art, the quest for a place of stability, a point of balance. In his art, he experimented to find his own voice, and he found it between the extremes of objectivity, toward which most art of his age tended, and the subjectivity that would characterize the art of the next generation. In the task of his life, he sought the balance of sanity, a quiet place of his own between the stress of urban society and the horror of being utterly alone, a castaway in a sea of despair. Tragically, he could not occupy that stable middle ground for very long; but in his best poetry, he created a remarkable sanity and said still-important things in a way that cannot easily be pigeonholed as neoclassical or Romantic but is uniquely Cowper.

OTHER MAJOR WORKS

NONFICTION: *Correspondence, Arranged in Chronological Order*, 1904 (4 volumes); *The Centenary Letters*, 2000 (Simon Malpas, editor).

BIBLIOGRAPHY

Cowper, William. *The Centenary Letters*. Edited by Simon Malpas. Manchester, England: Fyfield, 2000. A collection of Cowper's correspondence with a biographical introduction by Malpas.

Ella, George Melvyn. *William Cowper: Poet of Paradise.* Durham, England: Evangelical Press, 1993. Criticism and interpretation of Cowper's work with an extensive bibliography.

Free, William Norris. *William Cowper.* New York: Twayne, 1970. This 215-page work takes a biographical approach to interpretations of *The Task, Olney Hymns*, and Cowper's short poems. Norris suggests that Cowper's experiences had influence on poetic elements such as theme, structure, tone, and metaphor. Includes a lengthy bibliography, notes, and an index.

Hartley, Lodwick. *William Cowper, Humanitarian.* Chapel Hill: University of North Carolina Press, 1938. Examines how Cowper's poetry reflects humanitarian interests of the century such as slavery and treatment of animals. Hartley demonstrates that Cowper was not the total recluse many critics have made him out to be. The 277 pages offer not only Cowper's opinions of contemporary social problems but also a good overview of the humanitarian movement in England. Includes an index.

King, James. *William Cowper: A Biography.* Durham, N.C.: Duke University Press, 1986. The standard biography that corrected many of the oversights and inaccuracies of early biographies. The poetical works are discussed as markers in the chronology of Cowper's life. The 340-page work includes an extensive index and notes.

Newey, Vincent. *Cowper's Poetry: A Critical Study and Reassessment.* Totowa, N.J.: Barnes & Noble Books, 1982. Newey's intelligent approach closely examines Cowper's work psychodramatically and sees the poet as a genius craftsman of complex, contemporary, relevant poetry. The 358-page volume looks at *The Task*, moral satires, hymns, and comic verse. Includes a chronology and index of persons and works.

Nicholson, Norman. *William Cowper.* London: John Lehman, 1951. A comprehensive critical work that primarily discusses the influence of the evangelical revival on Cowper. Nicholson sees Evangelicalism as a vigorous and emotional movement that paralleled Romanticism. Although Cowper's poetic sensibility first developed under Evangelicalism, his early poetry reflects contemporary religious and social thought and later becomes partially independent of the movement to share aspects with Romanticism.

Ryskamp, Charles. *William Cowper of the Inner Temple, Esq.* Cambridge, England: Cambridge University Press, 1959. This 270-page book studies Cowper's life and works before 1786, focusing on his life and literary activities as a Templar and gentleman. Appendices include previously uncollected letters, essays, poems, and contributions to magazines. Supplemented by illustrations, notes on Cowper's friends and relatives, and an index.

William J. Heim;
bibliography updated by the editors

GEORGE CRABBE

Born: Aldeburgh, England; December 24, 1754
Died: Trowbridge, England; February 3, 1832

PRINCIPAL POETRY

Inebriety, 1775
The Candidate, 1780
The Library, 1781
The Village, 1783
The News-Paper, 1785
Poems, 1807
The Borough, 1810
Tales in Verse, 1812
Tales of the Hall, 1819
Poetical Works, 1834 (8 volumes)

OTHER LITERARY FORMS

Of George Crabbe's writings in forms other than verse, little has survived. Extant are critical prose prefaces to various of his published verse collections, a treatise on "The Natural History of the Vale of Belvoir" which appeared in 1795, an autobiographical sketch published anonymously in *The New Monthly Magazine* in 1816, a selection of his sermons published posthumously in 1850, and certain of his letters, journals, and notebook entries which have been published in varying formats throughout the years since his death. With the exception of several of the critical prefaces, particularly that which accompanies *Tales in Verse*, and portions of the letters and journal entries, these do not shed significant light on Crabbe's poetic accomplishments. In the period 1801-1802, Crabbe is known to have written and subsequently burned three novels and an extensive prose treatise on botany.

ACHIEVEMENTS

The problem of assessing George Crabbe's achievements as a poet has proved a difficult one from the start. It vexed Crabbe's contemporaries and continues in some measure to vex scholars today. To a large extent this may be caused by the difficulties in classification. His works bridge the gap between neoclassicism and Romanticism and on separate occasions—or even simultaneously—display characteristics of both movements. As the bewildering variety of labels which have been applied to Crabbe indicate, the multifaceted nature of his canon defies easy categorization. He has been termed a realist, a

George Crabbe (Hulton Archive)

naturalist, an Augustan, a Romantic, a sociological novelist in verse, a psychological dramatist, a social critic, a poetic practitioner of the scientific method, a didactic moralist, a social historian, a "Dutch painter," and a human camera. Such labels, often supportable when applied to selected portions of Crabbe's work, do not appear useful in describing his total achievement. Nevertheless, it is upon such restricted interpretations that estimations of Crabbe have frequently been built. While attesting to his artistic versatility and providing a focal point for isolated instances of detailed analysis and appreciation, the result has been in large part detrimental to the establishment of a sound critical tradition with respect to Crabbe, for readers of all types—and especially the critics—are most often reluctant to give serious consideration to an artist who cannot be conveniently classified.

Crabbe's earliest literary productions were clearly derivative, most often fashionable satires and other forms in the Augustan mode, but after the appearance of *The Village* one begins to find such terms as "original," "unique," and "inventive" being consistently applied to him. Dr. Samuel Johnson, who read *The Village* in manuscript, praised it as "original, vigorous, and elegant." The sensation surrounding the publication of *The Village* proved to be a mixed blessing, for while it won Crabbe many admirers it also served to fix him in the popular imagination as an antipastoralist and as the "poet of the poor," tags which are misleading and inaccurate when applied to a large part of his work. Crabbe's art showed consistent development throughout his long writing career, particularly in the progressively sophisticated manner in which he articulated his main form, narrative verse. He experimented frequently with narrative techniques and with innovative framing concepts for his collections of verse tales and is often credited with having influenced such writers of prose fiction as Jane Austen and Thomas Hardy. On the other hand, he remained doggedly faithful to that stalwart of eighteenth century prosody, the heroic couplet, departing from it only rarely in his more than sixty-five thousand lines of published verse. Following the appearance of *The Village*, Crabbe's reputation continued to grow, despite a twenty-two-year hiatus in his publishing career, finally declining in his later years largely as a result of the predominant influence of Romantic literary tastes. In his time, he was praised highly by Dr. Johnson; Sir Walter Scott; George Gordon, Lord Byron, and even William Wordsworth, with whom he had little in common in either taste or technique; his most consistent and eloquent champion, however, was Francis Jeffrey, the formidable critic of *The Edinburgh Review*. His harshest critics, on the other hand, were Samuel Taylor Coleridge and William Hazlitt, both of whom found him significantly deficient in "imagination" (as the Romantics were prone to define that term) owing to his meticulous attention to realistic detail. The high estimation of Crabbe's achievements drifted slowly downward throughout the course of the nineteenth century but began to revive in the twentieth century with largely favorable critical reassessments by such figures as E. M. Forster, F. L. Lucas, and F. R. Leavis. His work has been the subject of several extended critical studies, and, while it is doubtful that he will ever be awarded a place among the highest ranking English poets, it appears certain that he is again being accorded some of the critical and popular esteem in which he once was held.

BIOGRAPHY

George Crabbe was born on Christmas Eve, December 24, 1754, in Aldeburgh (or, as it was then known, Aldborough), Suffolk, the eldest son of the local collector of salt duties, who early recognized the intellectual potential of his son and endeavored to provide educational opportunities for him beyond those normally accessible to one in his station. Once a busy and prosperous seaport, Aldeburgh had dwindled in size and importance by the middle of the eighteenth century and contained a populace whose general poverty, ignorance, and ill-nature was matched by the isolated, inhospitable conditions of a seacoast plagued by tempestuous weather and surrounded by a dreary countryside consisting largely of salt marshes, heaths, and tidal flats. Crabbe's early experiences in this setting left a lasting impression: Throughout his life Aldeburgh retained a strong hold on his imagination. This strange mixture of fascination and repugnance formed the basis for a large number of the characters and settings which are possibly the most striking features of his poetry.

Between the ages of eight and thirteen, Crabbe's father arranged for him to attend grammar schools in Bungay and Stowmarket, both in Norfolk, where he received the foundations of a classical education and is known to have made his first attempts at composing doggerel verse. Unable to continue financing his son's education and having determined that the field of medicine would be the most suitable to his son's talents and inclinations, the elder Crabbe in 1768 engaged for George to be bound as an apprentice to an apothecary and surgeon at Wickhambrook, near Bury St. Edmund's, in Suffolk. Used more as a farm hand than as a surgical apprentice, young Crabbe was exceedingly unhappy there and, in 1771, was removed by his father to a more favorable situation in Woodbridge, Suffolk. These were to prove relatively happy years, for, though he seems to have shown no great interest in his medical studies, life in Woodbridge was an agreeable contrast to what he had known in Aldeburgh and Wickhambrook. It was also during this period that he met and courted his future wife, Sarah Elmy, and saw his first poem of any consequence, *Inebriety* (1775), appear in print.

In the summer of 1775, his apprenticeship over, Crabbe returned to Aldeburgh, and, after a period of uncertainty during which he worked as a common laborer on the docks (much to the dismay of his father), he finally began to practice his profession late in the year. The next four years were particularly frustrating and unhappy ones for the young doctor: It is clear that he never had any real confidence in his abilities as a physician and that he felt himself to be surrounded by people who did not appreciate him and to whom he felt in every way superior. His practice was unsuccessful and his continuing poverty made it appear doubtful whether he would ever find himself in a position financially stable enough to marry his beloved Sarah. Thus, in early 1780, he abandoned his practice, borrowed five pounds from a local philanthropist, and journeyed to London to take his chances as a poet. Although he would never again return to the profession of medicine, the years spent in training and practice were not entirely wasted ones, for they are undoubtedly responsible for such often-noted features of his poetry as his minute attention to detail and his fascination with aberrant psychological states.

London did not treat Crabbe kindly. Although he did manage to publish *The Candidate*, a dull, unreadable poem, his attempts to secure patronage were singularly unsuccessful, and his increasingly desperate financial state brought him to the point where, by early 1781, he was threatened with debtors' prison. At this propitious moment he found the patron he had been seeking, the influential statesman Edmund Burke, who eased his financial straits, helped him find publishers for his poetry, and introduced him to such eminent figures of the day as Sir Joshua Reynolds, Charles James Fox, and Dr. Johnson. It was Burke also who convinced Crabbe to take holy orders in the Anglican Church and who used his influence to get the young poet ordained, which occurred in 1782. Burke then secured for him a position which allowed him to pursue his duties as a clergyman while at the same time leaving sufficient leisure to write poetry.

His financial worries finally over, his career set, Crabbe entered a largely productive and happy phase in his life. He and Sarah were married in 1783, and over the years Crabbe was assigned to various livings in Suffolk and Leicestershire. In the early 1790's, the deaths of several of their children affected Sarah's mental state in a way that would become progressively more desperate until her death in 1813. At about the same time Crabbe began to suffer from vertigo and digestive ailments. Opium was prescribed, and he continued to use the drug for the remainder of his life. For these and perhaps other reasons, he published no poetry for a period of twenty-two years, though he is known to have continued writing poems and other literary works, the majority of which he ultimately destroyed. Crabbe's literary reemergence in 1807 marked the beginning of his most significant period of poetic production, culminating in the 1819 publication of *Tales of the Hall*. Following Sarah's death, he assumed the livings at Trowbridge, in Wiltshire, where he passed the remaining years of his life as a celebrated member of his community, taking occasional trips to London and Suffolk to visit old friends. Though he never remarried, he maintained a lively correspondence with admiring female readers in several parts of the British Isles. Crabbe died in the rectory at Trowbridge on February 3, 1832.

ANALYSIS

No critical assessment of George Crabbe's work has ever isolated his essence more precisely than do the words he himself provided in the concluding lines of Letter I of *The Borough*:

Of sea or river, of a quay or street,
The best description must be incomplete;
But when a happier theme succeeds, and when
Men are our subjects and the deeds of men;
Then may we find the Muse in happier style,
And we may sometimes sigh and sometimes smile.

Any reader who has generously sampled Crabbe's work would likely agree with the point suggested here: It is indeed people and their actions that form the central focus in the majority of his poems. Crabbe was, above all else, a narrative poet, and in the estimation of some critics second only to Geoffrey Chaucer. Paradoxically, however, his reputation in his own day (and to some extent even in the present) was not primarily based on that fact. Rather, he was seen as a painter in words—a master of highly particularized visual imagery who conjured up vivid landscapes and interior settings, most often for the purpose of emphasizing the sordid and brutal elements of existence. Though people might be present in these scenes, they were generally seen as little more than corollary features to the inanimate components dominating the whole (such as the famous description of the aged shepherd in the poorhouse found in book 1 of *The Village*). Hence, Sir Walter Scott's well-known epithet, "nature's sternest poet" ("nature" in the nineteenth century sense of the term), has come to epitomize the predominant attitude toward Crabbe as a poet. That view is indeed unfortunate, for the narrowness of its emphasis ignores the very features of Crabbe's work upon which his surest claim to significance might be built. Missing in this approach, for example, is any notion of the richness and diversity of Crabbe's humor, surely one of his most delightful features. Furthermore, such a limited view fails to note the increasingly optimistic tone of Crabbe's work, in its progress from *The Village* to *Tales of the Hall*. Most important, however, the opinion reverses what surely must be the proper emphasis when considering Crabbe's poetry as a whole: People, rather than merely serving to enhance Crabbe's realistic descriptions, are in fact the subject and center of his concern. Nature and external detail, while present to a significant degree in his poetry, exist primarily to illuminate his fascination with character.

If any one reason might be cited for the disproportionate emphasis given to Crabbe's descriptive and pessimistic qualities, it would most likely be the influence of *The Village*. This poem, a sensation in its own day and still the most consistently anthologized of Crabbe's works, paints an unrelentingly bleak picture of human existence in a manner which is essentially descriptive and which makes extensive use of external detail. These same concerns and techniques may also be seen to operate in large portions of Crabbe's next two major works, *The Parish Register* (1807) and *The Borough*. In all these, the influence of Crabbe's early life, and especially his perceptions of his native town of Aldeburgh, form the controlling focus. At the same time, however, as early as *The Village* itself and certainly in the works which follow it, the perceptive reader can note Crabbe's increasing interest in character and narration. By the time *Tales in Verse* was published the mode had become completely narrative and continued to be so throughout the poet's writing career.

Moreover, a concomitant softening of the hard lines presented in Crabbe's early poetry becomes increasingly evident as he moved more and more in the direction of a psychological and sociological examination of the factors necessary for successful human interaction. True, social criticism, human suffering, and the stultifying effects of an inhospitable environment are factors which never disappear entirely from Crabbe's writings. As time goes on, however, they retreat significantly from their earlier position of predominance and assume no more than their proportionate role in what Jeffrey referred to as "the pattern of Crabbe's arabesque."

With a canon as large as Crabbe's, it is perhaps to be expected that a remarkably large and diverse array of themes and motifs may be cataloged when examining his work as a whole. Nevertheless, certain patterns recur frequently enough in dynamic variation so as to be considered dominant. Proceeding, as they invariably do, from an intense interest in character and in human interaction, they are all rich in psychological and sociological insights. Chief among them are the problems of moral isolation, of the influence of relatives upon young minds, of success and failure in matters of love, courtship and marriage, and of the search for reconciliation as an antidote to bitterness and estrangement. To watch these thematic concerns grow in texture and complexity as Crabbe explores them in a succession of tales is one

of the pleasures of reading a generous and representative selection of his works. Of no less interest is the process of experimentation and refinement by which Crabbe first discovers and then seeks to perfect the stylistic and structural mechanisms best suited to his characteristic narrative voice.

THE VILLAGE

From the moment of its first appearance in 1783 to the present, the most immediate response of critics and general readers alike has been to see *The Village* as a poem written in response to Oliver Goldsmith's *The Deserted Village* (1770), published thirteen years earlier. This is certainly understandable. The respective titles invite such comparison, and Crabbe himself explicitly alludes to Goldsmith's poem on several occasions. Furthermore, it is apparent to even the most casual reader that Crabbe's Aldeburgh (for most assuredly it is Aldeburgh that forms the model for *The Village*) is in every conceivable way the very antithesis of Goldsmith's Auburn. While all this is true, the notion of Crabbe's poem as a simple rebuttal of Goldsmith is far too limiting; rather, it should be seen as a poem which constitutes in large part a reaction against the entire eighteenth century literary convention which governs Goldsmith's poem. The term antipastoral is a convenient label to use here, but only if one keeps in mind the fact that Crabbe's bias against the pastoral mode is somewhat specialized. It is not classical pastoralism which Crabbe objects to or even its manifestations in earlier English poetry but rather the manner in which, in the eighteenth century, poets and public alike had irrationally come to accept the conventions of pastoral description as constituting accurate and useful representations of rural life. If it is somewhat difficult to understand the tone of outrage which underlies the cutting edge of Crabbe's realism in this poem, it is perhaps because most modern readers, unlike Crabbe, have been spared the effusions of countless minor poets, most of them deservedly now forgotten, whose celebrations of the joys of pastoral rusticity filled the "poet's corner" of many a fashionable eighteenth century magazine. It is to them that he speaks when he says: "Yes, thus the Muses sing of happy swains,/ Because the Muses never knew their pains." Crabbe knew their pains; he had felt many of them himself, perhaps too many to assure his own objectivity. For, whatever the merits of seeing *The Village* as a realistic rejoinder to an artificial and decadent literary tradition, one must always remember that Crabbe's brand of realism may at times in itself be somewhat suspect by virtue of the conscious and unconscious prejudices he bears toward his subject matter.

The Village consists of two parts—Books 1 and 2—but it is Book 1 which has always commanded the greatest interest. This portion of the poem is dominated by a number of descriptive set pieces, perhaps the most frequently quoted passages in all Crabbe's works. The first of these, and the one which perhaps best epitomizes the poem's uncompromisingly harsh view of rural life, concerns the countryside which surrounds the village—the coastline and adjoining heaths. It is a bleak, barren, forbidding prospect which Crabbe presents, a landscape inhospitable to man and barely capable of sustaining life of any sort. Images of decay and sickness, of despair, of almost anthropomorphic hostility pervade the descriptions, chiefly of vegetation, of this isolated sector of the East Anglian seacoast. Almost imperceptibly, Crabbe moves from this dominant sense of place to his initial, tentative descriptions of the inhabitants, the first of many instances in his poetry where people and physical setting are juxtaposed in meaningful counterpoint.

The next of the famous set pieces in the poem is a description of the village poorhouse, the vividness and intensity of which so struck Crabbe's contemporaries that the language they frequently used to discuss it is of a sort most generally reserved for discussions of painting. Several modern commentators have argued that in this section of the poem Crabbe is functioning primarily as a social critic, calling into question, among other things, the prevailing Poor Laws and their administration in local parishes. This may be so; nevertheless, it is again the pure descriptive vividness of this scene which remains its most memorable feature. The details relating to the exterior and interior of the building form a backdrop to the cataloging of its miserable inhabitants. Again, the predominant images are of decay, oppressiveness, and despair. Amid these scenes of not-so-quiet desperation, Crabbe gives particular attention to one inhabitant of the poorhouse, an old shepherd, worn out, useless, lodged there to pine away his days in loneliness and frustration. Perhaps nowhere else in the poem does Crabbe so bru-

tally and cynically mock the pastoral ideal. Book 1 ends with vicious satirical portraits of the doctor and priest who, paid by the parish to attend to the needs of the inhabitants of the poorhouse, openly and contemptuously neglect their duties.

Book 2 is considerably less successful in its execution, primarily owing to a lack of consistency in tone and format. Crabbe begins by intimating that he wishes to soften his harsh picture of village life by showing some of its gentler moments; soon, however, this degenerates into a description and condemnation of the drunkenness of the villagers, a subject that he had previously explored in the youthful *Inebriety*. Even more disturbing, however, is the poem's conclusion, which takes the form of an unrelated and lengthy eulogy on Lord Robert Manners, late younger brother of the Duke of Rutland, the man whom Crabbe was currently serving as private chaplain.

Although it is probably his best-known work and contains some of his finest descriptive writing, *The Village* is hardly Crabbe's most representative poem. In his treatment of the aged shepherd, in the satiric portraits of the doctor and priest, one may sense the embryonic forms of the distinctive narrative voice which would ultimately come to dominate his poetry; before this manifested itself, however, a number of years had intervened.

POEMS

With the exception of *The News-Paper*, a lukewarm satire on the periodical press very much in the Augustan mode, Crabbe published no poetry in the period between the appearance of *The Village* in 1783 and the release of the collection, *Poems*, in 1807. That he was not artistically inactive during this period, however, is evidenced by the vigor and diversity of the poems found in the 1807 volume, and there is ample reason to lament the many efforts in manuscript he is known to have destroyed at this time. In addition to his previously published works, the 1807 *Poems* contained a number of commendable new efforts, including "The Birth of Flattery," "The Hall of Justice," and the provocative "Sir Eustace Grey." All these works show Crabbe experimenting with various narrative techniques. The star attraction of the new collection, however, was a much longer poem entitled *The Parish Register*.

THE PARISH REGISTER

Readers who enjoyed the angry, debunking tone of Crabbe's antipastoralism in *The Village* were probably delighted by the first several hundred lines of *The Parish Register*, which seem to signal a continuation of the same interests. "Since vice the world subdued and waters drown'd,/ Auburn and Eden can no more be found," Crabbe notes wryly and then proceeds to unveil a number of highly particularized descriptions, the most memorable of which outlines in vivid and often disgusting detail the vice and squalor of a poor village street. If anything, Crabbe appears to be well on his way to outdoing his previous efforts in this vein. At this point, however, the poem suddenly takes a new tack and begins to present a series of narratives which in the aggregate constitute its dominant feature.

The plan of *The Parish Register* is, in essence, simple and ingenious. A narrative voice is created by Crabbe; it is that of the parish priest of a small village who, at year's end, reviews the records in his church register and comments in varying fashion on the real-life stories which lie behind the cold names and dates. The poem has three divisions—"Baptisms," "Marriages," and "Burials"—and in each the loquacious speaker presents a number of narratives ranging in length and complexity from simple vignettes of a few lines to more ambitious efforts resembling full-blown tales. Generally, the best narratives are found in "Baptisms" and "Burials," particularly in the latter. Two stories of chief interest in the "Baptisms" section are that of Lucy, the daughter of a proud and wealthy miller, who conceives a child out of wedlock, is ostracized by her father and the community, and slowly goes mad, and that of Richard Monday, a foundling brought up and abused in the village poorhouse, who leaves the village to become an enormous success in the world and on his deathbed leaves only a pittance to his native town. "Burials" contains a number of memorable portraits, including those of the prudent, matriarchal Widow Goe and of old Sexton Dibble, who managed to outlive the five parsons he successively served. The most interesting, however, are the stories of Robin Dingley and Roger Cuff. In the first of these, Robin, a poor but contented man, becomes the victim of a clever attorney who leads him to place all his hopes on the possibility of a rich inheritance; when these are dashed, the loss drives him crazy and makes him a wanderer for life. The acuteness of Crabbe's psychological perceptions are noteworthy in this story, one of the first of a number of tales in which he explores the bases of aberrant behavior. Borrowing certain motifs from older folk tales, the story of Roger Cuff tells of a young man who has a falling out with his kin, goes off to sea, and years later, having made his fortune, returns disguised as a beggar to test the moral fiber of the surviving members of his family. Refused by the closest of them, he shares his wealth with an unpretentious distant relative who lives as a reclusive hermit in the forest. Years later, in "The Family of Love," one of the stories from his posthumous collection of tales, Crabbe returned to this theme but with significant alterations.

In *The Parish Register* one can observe Crabbe in the process of discovering his considerable talents as a writer of narrative verse. His experimentations with frame, point of view, dialogue and character interaction, and a host of other practical and thematic considerations, point the way toward more sophisticated efforts yet to come. Even as he was finishing this poem, he was hard at work on a far more ambitious undertaking, *The Borough*.

THE BOROUGH

One of Crabbe's longest poems—approximately eight thousand lines—*The Borough* is also one of his most perplexing and in many ways his least successful efforts when considered as a whole. Within its vast scope, however, there are isolated instances of writing which rank among the poet's best. As in *The Village* and *The Parish Register*, the subject of Crabbe's third major poem is once again a thinly disguised Aldeburgh. This time, however, the scale is much more ambitious, for, as he makes clear in his lengthy prose preface and in the opening section of the poem, the aim of *The Borough* is nothing less than complete description: All aspects of the town, its buildings, trades and professions, public institutions, social activities, and inhabitants are to be revealed. Naturally, the scheme is so grandiose as to preclude its complete achievement, but the efforts which Crabbe makes in pursuing it are in themselves somewhat remarkable. The result, unfortunately, sometimes seems more akin to social history than to poetry. In structure, the poem is epistolary, consisting of a series of twenty-four verse letters written by a resident of the borough to a friend in a far distant part of the country who has requested a description of the place. Among them are some of the dullest pieces of writing in Crabbe's entire canon, including the letters on "Elections," "The Hospital and Governors," and "Schools." Paradoxically, however, this same ponderous framework yields some of Crabbe's finest narrative pieces.

Letters XIX to XXII, collectively entitled "The Poor of the Borough," provide the most fully developed narratives found in Crabbe's work to this point. They are, in essence, short stories in verse, each one focusing on a different character type and probing the psychological dimensions of motivation and consequence. "Ellen Orford" (Letter XX), a story in which Crabbe broadens his narrative technique by having Ellen tell a large part of her own history, is an account of cumulative personal tragedy, borne stoically by a woman whose essential goodness and faith in God enable her to rise above what Hamlet termed "the slings and arrows of outrageous fortune." No such inspirational note is provided in "Abel Keene" (Letter XXI), in which a pious man is seduced into abandoning his faith, the process ending in despair and suicide. A fascinating study of self-deception and its disastrous results is presented in "The Parish Clerk" (Letter XIX), which tells the story of Jachin, the spiritually proud clerk of the parish who feels he is above sin and alienates everyone with his smug sanctimony. Tempted by his poverty and secure in the rationalizations he has constructed for his conduct as well as in the foolproof method he has devised for its implementation, Jachin begins to steal from the collection plate during services. Eventually caught and publicly disgraced, he goes the way of many of Crabbe's moral outcasts, retreating from the society of men to blend into the bleakness of the surrounding countryside, where his mental and physical energies are gradually dissipated and death comes as a welcome relief.

By most accounts the finest story in *The Borough*, perhaps the best in all Crabbe's canon, is "Peter Grimes" (Letter XXII), upon which Benjamin Britten based his well-known opera. The tale has so many remarkable features—its implicit attack on the abuses of the apprentice system, its subtle articulation of the notion that the ultimate responsibility for deviant behavior may rest within the society which fosters it, its powerful juxtapositions of external description and interior states of mind, and its surprisingly modern probing of the psychological bases of child abuse—that it is difficult to isolate any one of them as the key factor in assessing the impact it has had upon most readers. A misanthropic fisherman who lives on the fringes of his community, Peter Grimes emerged from a childhood in which he irrationally hated the father who loved him. As an adult, he acquires and successively destroys three young orphans from London who are bound to him as apprentices. The townspeople, aware of what is occurring, turn their backs on what they view as none of their business ("Grimes is at his exercise," they say when the cries of his victims are heard in the town's streets), until the death of the third boy proves to be more than they can ignore. Although they cannot legally punish him—nothing can be proved conclusively—Grimes is forbidden to take any more apprentices and is ostracized by the community. He withdraws into the desolation of the tidal flats and salt marshes surrounding his village and there, brooding alone under the hot sun, he becomes possessed by wild and persistent visions of his father and the murdered apprentices, who dance on the waters and beckon him to join them in their element. His mind shattered, he sinks to death in an agony of terror and desperation. "Peter Grimes" is a story of considerable power, owing in large part to Crabbe's masterful conception of the title character, who, like William Shakespeare's Iago and Herman Melville's Claggart, taxes the limits of critical understanding.

Despite the ponderous framing device employed by Crabbe in *The Borough*, it is possible in the narrative portions of that poem to see him working toward the use of a narrator who is to a certain degree effaced, as well as toward an occasional reliance on multiple points of view. In *Tales in Verse*, which appeared in 1812, he continued those trends and abandoned, temporarily, the use of any sort of framing device. Here, in his first collection of poetry devoted entirely to narrative themes, Crabbe presents a series of twenty-one discrete verse tales in which, as he notes in his preface

the attempt at union therefore has been relinquished, and these relations are submitted to the public, connected by no other circumstance than their being the productions of the same author, and devoted to the same purpose, the entertainment of his readers.

Ironically, what Crabbe himself half-apologetically presented as a loose compendium of disparate elements may, in fact, be his most thoroughly integrated work, for there is one factor that the vast majority of the individual tales share in common: They are, in large part, variations from every conceivable point of view on the themes of love, courtship, and marriage.

TALES IN VERSE

In the collection, *Tales in Verse*, Crabbe presents a number of his most memorable stories. One useful method of approaching the collection is to distinguish between those tales in which two persons have successfully found the basis for compatibility, avoiding the numerous pitfalls which at any point in the love-courtship-marriage continuum can destroy the entire process, and those in which the reverse has occurred. Thus, in the latter category may be grouped such tales as "Procrastination" (IV), "The Patron" (V), "The Mother" (VIII), "Squire Thomas: Or, The Precipitate Choice" (XII), and "Resentment" (XVII), while the former is represented by "The Parting Hour" (II), "The Frank Courtship" (VI), "The Widow's Tale" (VII), "Arabella" (IX), "The Lover's Journey" (X), "Jesse and Colin" (XIII), "The Confidant" (XVI), and "The Wager" (XVIII). Myriad influences may affect the delicate balance of the relationships explored in these tales, ensuring their ultimate success or failure, but two situations recur in a variety of forms. In the first of them, Crabbe explores the power, for better or for worse, that a third person may exert on a couple's life. The influence may range from a healthy one, as in the case of the emancipated aunt in "The Frank Courtship," to that which is destructive, as in "The Mother." In other situations, the influence may present an obstacle which must be overcome and resolved in order that the relationship may achieve its true potential, as is demonstrated in "The Confidant." The other recurring situation, one which came to be a dominant motif in Crabbe's remaining work, is the need to seek out and establish the compassionate basis of understanding which must ultimately be the cornerstone of any successful, lasting human relationship. Frequently this is seen in the context of a major disrupting incident in a couple's life which tests the ability of one of them to display the qualities of forgiveness and understanding necessary to keep the relationship alive. The opposite effects of this type of situation are presented, respectively, in "Resentment" and "The Confidant," as well as in certain other of the tales.

Beyond its thematic articulations, which are at once perceptive and sophisticated, "The Frank Courtship" is a tale which commands attention by virtue of its tone and stylistic qualities. Perhaps nowhere else in Crabbe is dialogue used to such delightful effect as in the courting scene between Sybil and her young suitor, Josiah; it is a piece of dramatic interchange which in the sharpness and vivacity of language reminds one of the best of Shakespeare's romantic comedies. Further, the optimistic, at times almost playful, tone of this composition may be cited as one of several memorable instances in Crabbe which serve to balance the elements of somberness and pessimism most frequently ascribed to him.

TALES OF THE HALL

In *Tales in Verse*, while not abandoning his interests in individual psychological observation, Crabbe moved strongly in the direction of exploring the dynamics of social interaction between people. This interest carried over strongly into his next major production, *Tales of the Hall*. One of the features most immediately apparent in *Tales of the Hall* is the author's return to the use of a comprehensive framing device for the presentation of a number of separate tales. Crabbe has integrated within the controlling frame of his new collection the same sort of thematic cohesiveness which serves to connect the individual narratives of *Tales in Verse*. Again, the great majority of the various tales (here called "books") represent diverse angles of vision from which to observe the many features inherent in the love-courtship-marriage syndrome. As if to emphasize his desire to pursue these studies from as many angles as possible, Crabbe further complicates his design by experimenting freely with multiple points of view and with other structural complexities in certain of the tales.

The frame itself is of considerable interest and, in its complex pattern of development, has led more than one critic to the conclusion that *Tales of the Hall* may justifiably be termed a novel in verse. As outlined in

"The Hall" (I) and the several books which immediately succeed it, the collection is bound by the story of two half brothers, George and Richard, who after a long separation have come together on a somewhat experimental basis to see what, if anything, they might have in common. Here, on the elder brother George's recently purchased estate (the Hall), they spend some weeks together, gradually wearing away the reserve and potential misunderstandings which at various points threaten to disturb the growing bond between their vastly differing personalities. In the course of this process, they tell tales of various sorts, some concerning themselves, others about people they have known in the past or have recently met in the surrounding area, and are frequently joined by a third companion and narrator, the local vicar. As the various tales unfold, the story of George and Richard itself develops in texture and complexity, resolving itself amicably, if somewhat flatly, in the final book. If the overall form of *Tales of the Hall* may be compared to that of the novel, however, it also bears certain affinities in substance to the type of long autobiographical poem which was proving increasingly popular among poets during this period (as, for example, those of Wordsworth and Byron). A convincing case might be made for seeing George and Richard—and to a certain extent even Jacques, the vicar—as varying projections of Crabbe's own conceptualized self-image.

The quality of the individual stories of *Tales of the Hall* is perhaps more uneven than that of *Tales in Verse*. The best of the stories, however, are definitely of a very high order. One is "Smugglers and Poachers" (XXI), an intricately plotted tale which, in addition to evidencing Crabbe's ongoing concern with social injustices, provides in its depiction of the enmity between the brothers James and Robert a bitter and dramatic counterpoint to the happier circumstances of the brothers found in the frame tale. Estrangement and failure in matters of love continue to find expression, as in the powerfully tragic "Ruth" (V) or the more philosophical "Lady Barbara: Or, The Ghost" (XVI); but on the whole, the tone of this collection is more consistently optimistic than in any of Crabbe's previous efforts and the note of forgiveness and reconciliation which dominates a number of the tales continues a trend first noticed in *Tales in Verse*. Two tales which illustrate this rather well are "William

Bailey" (XIX) and the structurally complex "Sir Owen Dale" (XII), both of which feature central characters who ultimately come to realize that the errors of the past cannot be allowed to poison the present forever. If there is a moral lesson to be drawn from the essentially nondidactic poetry of the later Crabbe, it is surely this point.

Two years after Crabbe's death there appeared the most complete edition of his poetry available up to that time. Edited by his son and including as its final volume the highly readable biographical account of his father's life, the *Poetical Works* of 1834 featured a number of poems never published by Crabbe during his lifetime, many of which were obviously still in a state of manuscript revision at the time of his death. Of chief interest among them is the group known collectively as *Posthumous Tales*.

POSTHUMOUS TALES

Actually, the twenty-two tales which constitute this final collection of narrative verse fall into two groups. Tales VI through XXII represent what may be described as draft versions of a new collection of poems which Crabbe had tentatively entitled *The Farewell and Return*. Crabbe's organizing principle in the collection posits a situation in which a young man leaves his native town and returns many years later to find it immensely changed. Each tale is divided into two basic parts, the first of which provides a description of a person or thing at the time of the narrator's departure, while the second involves an updating on the part of a friend whom the narrator encounters upon his return. The concept, while ingenious in nature and serving to demonstrate Crabbe's continuing preoccupation with the problem of narrative frames, is far from successful; the individual tales often resolve themselves into a depressingly predictable series of variations on the theme of destructive mutability. These evident shortcomings should not be judged too harshly, however, since it is reasonable to assume that, given the chance for suitable revision, Crabbe would ultimately have rendered the collection consistent with the quality of his previous work. One tale from *The Farewell and Return* group, "The Boat Race" (XVIII), is deserving of special mention, if only by virtue of its splendidly effective description of a sudden storm on the river and its disastrous effects.

In some respects the best narratives in the *Posthumous Tales* are found in the five unrelated tales which begin the collection, including the delightful "Silford Hall: Or, The Happy Day" (I), a highly autobiographical account of an impressionable young lad's sense of wonder and delight on receiving a guided tour of an aristocrat's palatial estate. Also of significant interest is "The Family of Love" (II), a tale in many ways reminiscent of the account of Roger Cuff found in *The Parish Register*, but with the significant difference that the central character of this later narrative finds it within himself to forgive his erring kin, reestablishing the bond of human understanding he could so easily and irrevocably destroy. In this contrasting treatment of an earlier theme, one can again gauge the distance which Crabbe has traveled in his attitude toward the potential for social fulfillment.

In the last analysis, one cannot escape the conclusion that there is a certain amount of unevenness in Crabbe's work, perhaps enough to justify his exclusion from the first rank of English poets. His occasional difficulty in blending new characters into a narrative, his sometimes annoying penchant for wordy digressiveness, his periodic lapses in tone and in the handling of dialogue, even those infrequent examples of "bad lines" which his nineteenth century detractors so loved to quote—all these and perhaps others as well might be charged to him as observable defects in technique. To dwell too long and too hard on these factors, however, is to miss the true essence of Crabbe, and to a large degree his power. In his relentless scrutiny of psychological and sociological themes, from the dark, brooding malevolence of "Peter Grimes" to the delicate social harmonies of "The Frank Courtship" and the frame of *Tales of the Hall*, one can clearly see the elements which link him securely to such widely divergent masters of English storytelling as Emily Brontë and Jane Austen. A later commentator on Crabbe, Oliver Sigworth, strikes the proper balance when he notes that "we may wish for various perfections which Crabbe did not attain, but, unique as he is, some may be happy in those which he possessed."

OTHER MAJOR WORKS

NONFICTION: "The Natural History of the Vale of Belvoir," 1795.

BIBLIOGRAPHY

Bareham, Tony. *George Crabbe*. New York: Barnes & Noble Books, 1977. Examines how Crabbe's poetry reflects contemporary ideas on religion, politics, psychology, and aesthetics. Bareham emphasizes that Crabbe was a "proper spokesman" for mainstream English thought. The 245-page text includes an index and a chronology of major events in Crabbe's career.

Crabbe, George. *The Life of George Crabbe by His Son*. 1834. Reprint. London: Cresset, 1947. This standard biography, written from the unique perspective of the poet's son, offers a benign yet candid glimpse into the poet's personality. An introduction by Edmund Charles Blunden provides further criticism of Crabbe's poetry, including an interesting discussion on the influence Crabbe's training as a physician and clergyman had on his writing.

Edwards, Gavin. *George Crabbe's Poetry on Border Land*. Studies in British Literature 7. Lewiston, N.Y.: Mellen, 1990. This 222-page critical work, organized by subject, takes a social historical approach to Crabbe's poems, dealing with Crabbe's ability to reflect his time accurately. It thoroughly discusses the concept of Crabbe as a realist, suggesting his poetry has a more complex relationship to history than just simple realism.

Hatch, Ronald B. *Crabbe's Arabesque: Social Drama in the Poetry of George Crabbe*. Montreal: McGill-Queen's University Press, 1976. This 284-page book attempts to show how Crabbe grew beyond being simply a social critic by focusing on his handling of social issues in his poetry. Hatch suggests that Crabbe's development can be seen in the way his poems' dramatic structures handle conflicting questions which either clash or are reconciled. Includes a chronology of Crabbe's life, a selected bibliography, and index.

Pollard, Arthur, ed. *Crabbe: The Critical Heritage*. The Critical Heritage series. London: Routledge & Kegan Paul, 1972. This work is an interesting compilation of criticism of Crabbe's writings by his contemporaries, including William Hazlitt, William Wordsworth, and Samuel Taylor Coleridge, along with later commentary. Arranged by individual works, the 495-page book also contains an informative introduction on Crabbe and his writing, and indexes to names, works, characteristics, and periodicals.

Sigworth, Oliver F. *Nature's Sternest Painter: Five Essays on the Poetry of George Crabbe*. Tucson: University of Arizona Press, 1965. The titles of the five essays—"Crabbe and the Eighteenth Century," "Crabbe in the 'Romantic Movement,'" "Crabbe as a Nature Poet," "Crabbe as a Narrative Poet," and "Criticism and Critique"—show the range of topics this critical work covers. Included in the 191-page book are an index and a lengthy bibliography of books and articles.

Whitehead, Frank S. *George Crabbe: A Reappraisal.* Cranbury, N.J.: Associated University Presses, 1995. A critical assessment of Crabbe's work with bibliographical references and an index.

Richard E. Meyer;
bibliography updated by the editors

HART CRANE

Born: Garrettsville, Ohio; July 21, 1899
Died: Gulf of Mexico; April 27, 1932

PRINCIPAL POETRY

White Buildings, 1926
The Bridge, 1930
The Collected Poems of Hart Crane, 1933 (Waldo Frank, editor)

OTHER LITERARY FORMS

Hart Crane's principal literary production was poetry. Other writings include reviews, several essays on literature, and two essays on poetry: "General Aims and Theories" and "Modern Poetry." His letters have been published, including those between Crane and the critic Yvor Winters and Crane's letters to his family and friends.

ACHIEVEMENTS

Hart Crane is acknowledged to be a fine lyric poet whose language is daring, opulent, and sometimes magnificent. Although complaints about the difficulty and obscurity of his poetry persist, the poems are not pure glittering surface. When Harriet Monroe, editor of *Poetry*, challenged metaphors of his such as the "calyx of death's bounty" in "At Melville's Tomb," Crane demonstrated the sense within the figure.

Crane is significant, moreover, in being a particularly modern poet. He wrote that poets had to be able to deal with the machine as naturally and casually as earlier poets had treated sheep and trees and cathedrals. His aim was to portray the effects of modern life on people's sensibilities. In his poetry Crane caught the frenzied rhythms and idioms of the jazz age.

Crane's stature also rests on his having created a sustained long poem, *The Bridge*. Early critics looking for a classical epic deplored the poem's seeming lack of narrative structure. Some critics also objected to Crane's joining the party of Walt Whitman at a time when Whitman and optimism were in disfavor. Later critics, however, have seen *The Bridge* as one of the great poems in modern American literature. They find in it a more Romantic structure, the structure of the poet's consciousness or the structure of human consciousness.

BIOGRAPHY

Harold Hart Crane's parents were Grace Hart, a Chicago beauty, and C. A. (Clarence Authur) Crane, a self-made businessman who became a successful candy manufacturer. An only child, Crane felt that he was made the battleground of his parents' conflicts. When Crane was fifteen years old, a family trip to his grandmother's Caribbean plantation, the Isle of Pines, erupted in quarreling. Crane subsequently made two suicide attempts.

When he was seventeen, Crane went to New York to become a poet, not to prepare to enter college as his father thought. In the next several years Crane alternated between living in Cleveland and New York, working at low-paying jobs, primarily in advertising, jobs that drained his energy for writing poetry. Crane received little financial support from his father, who wanted Crane to commit himself to a business career. In 1917, siding with his mother in a family argument, Harold Crane began using the name Hart Crane.

In this period Crane's poems were being published in "little" magazines. To stimulate his creativity, Crane often relied on drink and music, a habit that led him to later problems with alcohol. (His poem "The Wine Menagerie" pays tribute to the connection he found between intoxication and poetic vision.) Crane's homosexual lifestyle, which involved him in brawls and run-ins with the police, also provided him the experience of love.

"For the Marriage of Faustus and Helen" was published in 1923, a breakthrough for Crane, who previously had written only short lyrics. Poor and often unemployed, he applied in 1925 for a grant from Otto Kahn, a financier and patron of the arts. Crane received money to help support him while he worked on *The Bridge*, a poem which was to be a synthesis of the American identity. The next summer Crane wrote a major part of his masterwork at his grandmother's plantation on the Isle of Pines, Cuba. In 1926 a collection of his poetry, *White Buildings*, was published.

Crane's stormy family life continued. In 1928, in California, after helping to nurse his sick grandmother, Crane had a final quarrel with his mother, Grace, and

they never saw each other again. Shortly thereafter Crane received a legacy from his grandmother Hart's estate and he traveled to London and Paris. There he met Harry and Caresse Crosby, who offered to publish *The Bridge* in a special edition. In 1930 in Paris and then in New York *The Bridge* was published.

That winter Crane was reconciled with his father. A few months later in 1931 Crane received a fellowship from the Guggenheim Foundation. He spent a year in Mexico preparing to write a poetic drama on the conquest of Mexico. The year was marked by drinking sprees and trouble with the police for brawling and homosexuality. After traveling back briefly to Ohio for his father's funeral, Crane returned to Mexico.

At the end of his stay in Mexico, Crane had a close relationship with Peggy Cowley, who was being divorced from Malcolm Cowley. The two had plans to be married, but Crane had fits of despondency, fears about his difficulty with writing, and anxieties about the quality of his latest poem, "The Broken Tower." After a suicide attempt that Crane feared would attract police attention, he and Peggy Cowley set sail for New York on the *Orizaba*. A stop at Havana in which Crane and Cowley lost track of each other was followed by a night on board ship during which Crane went on a violent drinking spree and was robbed and beaten. The next day at noon Crane jumped overboard from the deck of the *Orizaba* and was never found.

ANALYSIS

Hart Crane's characteristic mode of poetry is visionary transformation. His language is that of transformation aimed at a reality beyond the surface of consciousness. Crane called the technique that subtly converts one image into another the "logic of metaphor." Like that of the French Symbolist poets—Charles Baudelaire, Arthur Rimbaud, Jules Laforgue, and Paul Verlaine—Crane's language is often vivid and obscure, a "jeweled" style that juxtaposes apparently alien entities. It is a poetry of indirection, not naming but suggesting objects or using them for an evocation of mood, for their magic suggestiveness. Sometimes choosing words for their music or texture, Crane employs the technique of synaesthesia, the correspondence between different sense modalities. Symbolists such as Crane, intuiting a correspondence

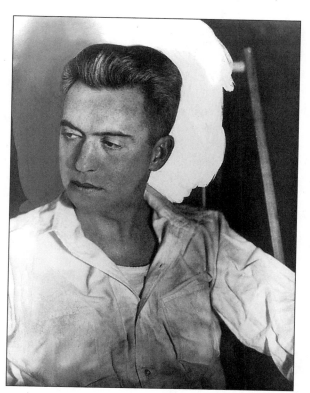

Hart Crane (Library of Congress)

between the material world and spiritual realities, aim to elicit a response beyond the level of ordinary consciousness.

Influenced by T. S. Eliot (but wanting to counteract the pessimism of the early Eliot), Crane used ironic mythological, religious, and literary echoes interspersed with snatches of banal conversation and lines from popular songs and slang. His method of achieving various perspectives almost simultaneously by the juxtaposition of such unlikely elements has been called "cubist." The tension between his cubist and Symbolist methods and his Whitmanian sentiments accounts for the unique quality of Crane's style.

Crane's poetry uses visionary transformations in an attempt to encompass the modern experience. In *The Bridge*, historical figures such as Christopher Columbus, legendary characters such as Rip Van Winkle, and mythic figures such as Maquokeeta (the consort of Pocahontas) are made part of the poet's consciousness, associated with personal memories of his childhood and with scenes of modern urban soullessness. The modern scene is transmuted by the elements, which provide a standard of value and a range of alternatives. In "For the Marriage of Faustus and Helen" the classic figure of Helen of Troy is brought together with the Renaissance figure of Dr. Faustus, and the two figures with their complex contexts bring a new perspective to the streetcar, the nightclub, and the aerial battle they visit in Crane's poem. Crane learned from the Symbolists that an image can become symbolic within a private context, calling up a dense network of meanings, emotions, and associations. Such images, unlike traditional symbols, draw on the cumulative force of the poet's personal associations—his personal "language"—rather than on the common cultural heritage. Crane's poetry fuses such personal symbols with traditional symbols from the sweep of Western culture.

"FOR THE MARRIAGE OF FAUSTUS AND HELEN"

"For the Marriage of Faustus and Helen," a poem of almost 140 lines, is Crane's first long poem. It is a marriage song for Faustus, the poet in search of spiritual fulfillment, and Helen, a figure of ideal beauty. The poem begins, however, in the tawdry modern world with the mind fettered by artificial distinctions and smothered

with the trivial: stock quotations, baseball scores, and office memos. "Smutty wings" in the first stanza becomes "sparrow wings" in the second as evening brings freedom from the strictures of the office.

The poet enters his experience by getting lost, forgetting his streetcar fare and forgetting to get a transfer. Between green and pink advertisements he sees Helen's eyes across the aisle from him, half laughing. The poet wants to touch her hands as a sign of love. Helen offers him words, inspiring his poetry. The poet's promise of love makes Helen ecstatic, and, like a Romantic poet, the modern poet dedicates his vision to her praise.

The setting of the next section is a rooftop nightclub with dancers cavorting to jazz played by black musicians. The scene of wild revelry is Dionysian. The abandon of the dancers is contrasted with the passivity of relatives, sitting home in rocking chairs. The poet invites the reader to experience a fortunate fall "downstairs" into sensual abandon. ("National Winter Garden" in *The Bridge* presents a much more somber and sordid version of the Fall.) Here the scene is a fallen world where people titter at death. The flapper who is the incarnation of Helen in the fallen realm should not be frowned on, however; even though it is "guilty song," sensual love, that she inspires, she is young and still retains some of the innocence of the ideal Helen.

The scene changes again in the third section, with the poet addressing a fighter pilot as an emissary of death (a problem that Crane would explore again in *The Bridge*). Crane treats war and the desecration of the heavens as the ultimate problem for the poet who would love the world and see beauty in it. It is not only eternity and abstract beauty that the poet praises but also the years, and beauty in and out of time, to which the bleeding hands of the poet pray. More advanced than business or religion, the imagination of the poet reaches beyond despair.

THE BRIDGE

The Bridge, a poem of more than twelve hundred lines, is Crane's masterwork, comparable to T. S. Eliot's *The Waste Land* (1922) and William Carlos Williams's *Paterson* (1946-1958). Although it is not a classical epic because it is not a narrative, the poem's seriousness and magnitude are reflected in its theme: The poet tries to find in himself and in America the possibility of the redemption of love and vision. Crane wanted the poem to be not an expression of narrow nationalism but a synthesis of the spiritual reality of America.

The central symbol of the poem is the Brooklyn Bridge, a product of contemporary technology that seemed in its beauty to embody man's aspirations for transcendence. In the poem the bridge is seen as a musical instrument, a harp; as the whitest flower, the anemone; as a ship, a woman, a world. In a letter to Otto Kahn, his patron, Crane said that the bridge symbolizes "consciousness spanning time and space." It is a figure of power in repose, a quality that Crane ascribes in the poem to God. The bridge also symbolizes all that joins and unifies, as the bridge unites the material and the spiritual in its existence.

"To Brooklyn Bridge"

"To Brooklyn Bridge," the proem, is an invocation to the bridge, in which the central opposition of the poem is sketched out—the life-giving spirituality of the bridge versus the deadening influence of the materialistic, commercial city. The freedom of the soaring seagull in the sky is contrasted with the destructive compulsion of the "bedlamite" who jumps from the bridge, amid the jeering onlookers. The poet asks the bridge to "lend a myth to God," to be the means of belief and transcendence in the city that seems to have no ideals and nothing in which to believe.

"Ave Maria"

In the next section, "Ave Maria," Crane goes back to the beginnings of America and to an age of faith, to Columbus after his discovery. Journeying back to Spain, Columbus meditates that he will tell the queen and her court that he is bringing back "Cathay." He will announce his discovery of a new reality, something that the poet accomplishes in his journey into history and myth. (In this section the sea acts as a bridge between the two continents.) Columbus's dedication has its counterweight, however, in Fernando, Isabella's husband, who anticipates a "delirium of jewels." Even in the discovery of America the motive for its exploitation was present.

"Powhatan's Daughter"

The next section of the poem, "Powhatan's Daughter," includes five sections. The first part, "The Harbor Dawn," is set in the present, with the sounds of fog horns, trucks passing, and stevedores yelling—back by the Brooklyn Bridge but enshrouded in fog. The blurring of sights and sounds by fog and water is in preparation for a blurring of time and space for a visionary journey with the poet. In the sanctuary of his room by the bridge or in his dream, the poet has an experience of love, in which his beloved is portrayed in mythic terms. Her eyes drink the dawn, and there is a forest in her hair. The mythic past lives in the present or at least in the love of the poet.

"Van Winkle"

The next section, "Van Winkle," shifts abruptly with the mention of macadam roads that leap across the country and seem to take the poet back to his childhood as well as to figures in American history that he learned about in school: Francisco Pizarro, Hernán Cortés, Priscilla Alden, Captain John Smith, and Rip Van Winkle. Van Winkle, who was legendary rather than historical, was a man out of time, displaced, because he refused to grow up. Here Van Winkle forgets the office hours and the pay and so ends up sweeping a tenement. He can get only menial work in a commercial society that demands a dedication to materialistic values. Van Winkle has a different, uncommercial vision. He looks at Broadway and sees a springtime daisy chain. Instead of the lifeless city, he sees a beautiful natural world.

Lines about Van Winkle are interspersed with memories of the poet's own childhood. The memories pick up equivalents for recurring symbols of the poem—the eagle for space and the snake for time. The poet remembers stoning garter snakes that "flashed back" at him. Instead of eagles, his space figures were paper airplanes, launched into the air.

Mythic journeys often involve the search for the father or the mother as a part of the search for identity. Crane introduces a possible need for that search in recounting two memories of disjunction from his parents: a glimpse of his father whipping him with a lilac switch and a more subtle denial by his mother, who once "almost" brought him a smile from church and then withheld it. Together with the smile, the mother seems to be withholding her approval and love. The final image of the section is of Van Winkle, ready for a streetcar ride, warned that it is getting late. It is time for the journey to continue.

"The River"

"The River" begins with a jumble of sounds, fragments of conversations—perhaps on the streetcar—

mention of commercial products such as Tintex and Japalac, and slogans from advertising, with fragments slapped against one another, making no sense. A misplaced faith links "SCIENCE—COMMERCE and the HOLY GHOST." Unlike the sermons in stones that William Shakespeare's world could find, the slogans and jingles are meaningless.

From the streetcar the scene switches to a magnificent train, the Twentieth Century Limited, roaring cross-country. The poem focuses on the hoboes who ride the rails and who, like Van Winkle, refuse to grow up. The men who did grow up, however, killed the last bear in the Dakotas and strung telegraph wires across the mountain streams. Those who want progress and a world of "whistles, wire, and steam" have a different time-sense from that of the wanderers. Although people like the poet's father would call the hoboes useless clods, the wanderers sense some truth and know the body of the land as alive and beautiful. In that knowledge they are like the poet who knows the land "bare"—intimately—and loves her. The eagle of space and the serpent of time appear, adorning the body of the beloved land, but the old gods need to be propitiated because the iron of modern civilization (and especially of the railroad) has split and broken the land and the mythic faith.

The train seems now to follow the river or to become the river. Everyone becomes part of the river, that is timeless because eternal; lost in the river, each one becomes his father's father. The poet and the poem are not only traveling across the country but are journeying back into time as well. Affirming again the possibility of love, the river whose one will is to flow is united with the gulf in passion.

"THE DANCE"

In "The Dance," the poet returns to the time of Native American greatness, the time of Pocahontas. The poet imagines himself a Native American, initiated into the worldview of the brave, at home in nature, speeding over streams in his canoe. He salutes Maquokeeta, the medicine man and priest. He commands Maquokeeta to dance man back to the tribal morning, to a time of harmony between man and nature when he had power even over rainbows, sky bridges. Maquokeeta is named the snake that lives before and beyond, the serpent Time itself. The time that he creates in his dance is the time of

mythic wholeness. Pocahontas, the earth, is his eternal bride, and in the dance he possesses her; time and space are made one. The poet has become one with Maquokeeta by calling him up and participating imaginatively in the dance.

"INDIANA"

The next section, "Indiana," a transitional one, is a letdown of poetic energy and drama. The verse is more prosaic and the rhymes seem strained. The explicit function of the piece is to have the national spirit passed from the Native American to the white settlers in a continuation of American history. It also chronicles the parting of a mother from a son, who is now to be independent (an important struggle in Crane's own life). The mother's pleas and clinging continue to the end of the section and almost beyond, binding the son by his pledge. Unwilling to let go, she begs for remembrance, naming the young man "stranger," "son," and finally "my friend." The relationship of friend, however, seems more request than fact, and nothing is related from the son's point of view.

"CUTTY SARK"

Once the poet has succeeded in getting away, in the "Cutty Sark" section, his verse returns to the energy and style of "The River" and earlier sections. The narrator is again the poet, introducing a tall, eerie sailor he has met in a South Street bar. Like the hoboes and perhaps like the poet, the sailor is an outcast. (In various ways he resembles Herman Melville's Captain Ahab and Samuel Taylor Coleridge's Ancient Mariner.) Like the hoboes in "The River," this sailor has a different sense of time from that of the commercial city. Instead of being tuned to the cycles of nature, the sailor's time-sense has been disturbed by the expanse of Arctic white, eternity itself. The sailor, who says he cannot live on land any more, is almost run down by a truck as he tries to cross the street, a sign of the break between the inarticulate, prophetic sailor and the cynical city.

The poet starts walking across the Brooklyn Bridge to get home, and his thoughts are still filled with memories of the clipper ships, related to the bridge in shape by being called "parabolas." Just as Ferdinand's greed was part of Columbus's discovery of America, part of the motive for the sailing ships was "sweet opium" and the tea the imperial British sought. The poet's experience and the American experience are still a mixture of the ideal and the sordid.

"CAPE HATTERAS"

"Cape Hatteras" is a substantial section of almost 250 lines. It begins with a primitive setting, with a dinosaur sinking into the ground and coastal mountains rising out of the land. In contrast to the impersonal geological processes, the poet, who has been wandering through time and space, tells the reader that he has returned home to eat an apple and to read Walt Whitman. From Marseille and Bombay, he is going home to America, to the body of Pocahontas and the sweetness of the land under the "derricks, chimneys," and "tunnels." He is returning to try to get a perspective on the exotic experiences he has had.

Next, the poet contemplates the infinity of space that is not subjugated by time and the actions of man, even though modern man can know space by "an engine in a cloud." The poet invokes Whitman and asks if infinity was the same when Whitman walked on the beach in communion with the sea. The poet's answer is that Whitman's vision lives even in the stock-market society of the present and in the free paths into the future. Opposed to Whitman's vision, however, is the fallen world of the machine, a demoniac world of unleashed power. The din and the violence of slapping belts and frogs's eyes that suddenly appear, vulnerable in the midst of such uncontrolled machinery, make the world a nightmare, an apocalyptic vision. The dance of the machines is a devilish parody of the heavenly, creative dance of the poet as the Native American priest, and America as Pocahontas.

The poet presents the scene of Wilbur and Orville Wright at Kitty Hawk with their silver biplane, praising their daring but deploring the use of the invention for war. A demoniac image that is parallel to the later image of the bridge as an anemone is the grenade as a flower with "screaming petals." Such terrible power is rationalized with theories as destructive as hail to the fertile earth. Imaginative vision cannot control the machines that have splintered space, even as the iron railroad split the land. The poet reminds the pilot that at the great speed of the airplane, the pilot has no time to consider what doom he is causing: He is intoxicated with space. The pilot's real mission is to join the edges of infinity, to bring them together in a loving union, to conjugate them. The poet follows his warning with a scene of the fighter pilot's destruction. Hit by a shell, the plane spirals down in a dance of death, and all that bravery becomes "mashed and shapeless debris."

If the fighter pilot represents a false relationship with space and infinity, Whitman is a figure with the right relationship, one whose vision of the earth and its renewal makes possible a new brotherhood. Whitman makes himself a living bridge between the sky and man through song. Whitman is also chief mourner of the men lost in wars, from the Civil War to Crane's time.

The next part of "Cape Hatteras" reads like a Romantic poet's declaration of his awakening to the beauty and inspiration of nature in its rhapsodic description of flowers and of heights that the poet has climbed. The declaration is followed by an apostrophe to Whitman as the awakener of the poet. Whitman is named his poetic master, the bread of angels in a eucharistic sense, and the one who began work on the bridge, the myth or imaginative construction that the poet is here creating. In Whitman the poet seems to have claimed his poetic father: He says that Whitman's vision has passed into his hands.

"THREE SONGS"

In the next section, "Three Songs," the poet tries to work through his relationship with the feminine. In the first song, "Southern Cross," he says that he yearns for a relationship that would be heavenly, ideal, and also real. (He pictures night and the constellation of the Southern Cross.) What he has found, however, is not woman, nameless and ideal, but Eve and Magdalene, fallen women, and a Venus who is subhuman and apelike. All the women lead to one grave, to death. The poet seems to feel disgust at the physical being of woman. He next pictures woman as a ship. Like the Ancient Mariner in Coleridge's poem, he is revolted by the generative (physical-sexual) nature of the sea. In Crane's poem, however, it is the feminine ship that is pictured as promiscuous, defiled by the masculine sea. The feminine also has qualities of a sea monster that can sting man. The Southern Cross, the poet's idealization of the feminine, drops below the horizon at dawn and what is left is woman's innumerable spawn, evidence of her indiscriminate sexuality.

The next song, "National Winter Garden," may seem to be a continuation of the poet's disgust with women, but it is different in being given an actual, rather than an archetypal, setting. The scene is a striptease in a burlesque show. The stripper's dance is a vulgar parody of sexuality and another parody of the creative, ecstatic dance of the Indian Priest-poet and Pocahontas. The burlesque queen awakens sexual appetite, but she is only pretending to have youth and beauty. Her pearls and snake ring are also fake, and the poet, who is waiting for someone else, runs away from the final "spasm." Here, however, the poet can make a reconciliation with Magdalene, with feminine sexuality, admitting its finality. Both men and women are physical and sexual; their natures are inescapable. If a woman is an agent of death, she is also an agent of birth. If each man dies alone in sexual union with her, he is also somehow born back into life, into his own sexual nature.

A third song for woman is "Virginia." The woman, Mary, is young, childlike, and possibly innocent. The poet seems to be using echoes of a popular song. Mary is working on Saturday at an office tower. She is described in chivalric terms; the poet is serenading her, and she is at least temporarily inaccessible. Flowers are blooming and bells are ringing, even if they are "popcorn bells." Like Rapunzel in the fairy tale, Mary is asked to let down her golden hair. All seems light and graceful (even though in the fairy tale the prince pays for his courtship with Rapunzel with a period of wandering in the forest, blinded). At the end of the song the poet calls the girl "Cathedral Mary," sanctifying her, perhaps ironically.

"QUAKER HILL"

In "Quaker Hill" the tone changes from the light, playful tone of the previous song. The section begins with a diatribe against weekenders descending on the countryside. Self-absorbed, they are out of tune with nature. They also have a distorted relation with time, being eager to buy as an expensive antique a cheap old deal table whose finish is being eaten by woodlice. The poet says that time will make strange neighbors.

Meditating on time as a destroyer, the poet asks where his kinsmen, his spiritual fathers are. To find his heritage, he has to look past the "scalped Yankees" to the mythic world of the Native Americans and accept his "sundered parentage." The poet says that men must come down from the hawk's to the worm's viewpoint and take on their tongues not the eucharist but the dust of mortality.

This humiliation is associated with the artist's abject position in modern society. Emily Dickinson and Isadora Duncan are introduced as examples of artists scorned in their day, and the only consolation the poet offers is that pain teaches patience. He asserts that patience will keep the artist from despair, implying that time will vindicate him. The section closes with a motif that is parallel to the fall of the fighter pilot to shapeless debris. Like the plane spiraling down, a leaf breaks off from a tree and descends in a whirling motion, but the leaf is part of a natural cycle, and the poet has put his faith in time and nature.

"THE TUNNEL"

The scene shifts back to the city in the next section, "The Tunnel." The natural world is left behind, and the poet is in the center of the gawdy theater district. References to hell, death, and "tabloid crime-sheets" make the area a wasteland. The subway, the fastest way home, is a descent into hell. The traveler cannot look himself in the eye without being startled and afraid. The sound of the subway is a monotone, but fragments of conversation are lewdly suggestive. The subway riders are the walking dead, living on like hair and fingernails on a corpse, yet "swinging" goes on persistently "somehow anyhow." The sounds of the subway make a phonograph of hell that plays within the poet's brain. This labyrinth of sound even rewinds itself; from this hell there is no exit. Love is a "burnt match." In "For the Marriage of Faustus and Helen," the flapper, the modern embodiment of beauty, was like a skater in the skies. Here the discarded match is skating in the pool of a urinal.

Suddenly the poet sees a disembodied head swinging from a subway strap. The apparition, figure of the artist scorned and destroyed by his society, is Edgar Allan Poe. Poe's eyes are seen below the dandruff and the toothpaste ads. In this banal setting death reaches out through Poe to the poet. At this point the subway comes to a dead stop. A sight of escape is momentary, and then the train descends for the final dive under the river.

As the train lurches forward again, the poet sees a "wop washerwoman." In the midst of the inferno there is a positive figure of a woman. Although she is not a discoverer like Columbus, her work has dignity: She cleans the city at night. A maternal figure, she brings home to her children her eyes and hands, Crane's symbols of vision and love. A victim like Poe and the poet, the cleaning woman is bandaged. Other birth imagery here is demoniac: A day being born is immediately slaughtered. The poet's greatest agony is that in this nightmare he failed to preserve a song.

In his great agony the poet feels the train start to ascend. Both the poet and the train are, like Lazarus, resurrected. They are returning to the natural world above ground. His vocation renewed, the poet can affirm the everlasting word. Once above ground again the poet is at the river bank, ready to turn to the bridge.

"ATLANTIS"

With the poet resurrected, "Atlantis"—the final section of the poem—is a song of deliverance. It is an ecstatic paean to the bridge, seen as music, light, love, joy, and inspiration. More dynamic than the music of the spheres, the music of the bridge creates a divinity. It is a myth that kills death: It gives death its utter wound, just by its light, its lack of shadow. By the myth of the bridge the cities are endowed with ripe fields. They have become natural, organic, and fruitful. The bridge is the city's "glittering pledge" forever. It is the answerer of all questions. In the poet's vision and in the poem it is unutterably beautiful.

"Atlantis" acts as a synthesis, subsuming earlier motifs such as stars, seagulls, cities, the river, the flower, grass, history and myth, circles and spirals. The question "Is it Cathay?" links the end of *The Bridge* with Columbus's discovery of America in the beginning, not in a mood of anxiety but in wonder at an America transfigured. The final two lines bring together time and space—the serpent and the eagle—with the music and radiance and energy of the bridge transcendent.

OTHER MAJOR WORKS

NONFICTION: *The Letters of Hart Crane*, 1952 (Brom Weber, editor).

MISCELLANEOUS: *The Complete Poems and Selected Letters and Prose of Hart Crane*, 1966 (Brom Weber, editor); *O My Land, My Friends: The Selected Letters of Hart Crane*, 1997 (Langdon Hammer, editor).

BIBLIOGRAPHY

Berthoff, Warner. *Hart Crane: A Re-introduction.* Minneapolis: University of Minnesota Press, 1989. Offers the first fresh approach in a generation to the work of one of the major poets of the first half of the twentieth century. Even though Crane died before the century was far advanced, there is room for reassessment. The passing of time allows Berthoff perspective for setting Crane in his cultural context and evaluating his work. This is a valuable first reference, opening up the most difficult of Crane's passages. Contains full notes, an excellent bibliography, and an index.

Crane, Hart. *O My Land, My Friends: The Selected Letters of Hart Crane.* Edited by Langdon Hammer and Brom Weber. New York: Four Walls Eight Windows, 1997. Crane left few literary essays or book reviews. As a result, these letters stand as a significant expression of his ideas about art, poetry, and culture. More significantly, they show his struggle to develop as a poet. Includes an introduction and commentary by Langdon Hammer.

Hammer, Langdon. *Hart Crane and Allen Tate: Janus-Faced Modernism.* Princeton, N.J.: Princeton University Press, 1993. Called a "brilliant study" by the reviewer for the *Times Literary Supplement*, this book focuses on the friendship between Crane and Tate, analyzing modern American poetry's progress toward professionalism and institutionalization. Includes an index.

Hazo, Samuel. *Hart Crane: An Introduction and Interpretation.* New York: Barnes & Noble Books, 1963. Hazo's small volume served as commentary of choice for several years and remains readable, informative, and enlightening. Begins with a biographical survey, then stakes out several avenues of approach to the poems. Although it includes a small number of illustrations, it has no notes. A chronology, a select, dated bibliography, and an index compensate somewhat.

Leibowitz, Herbert A. *Hart Crane: An Introduction to the Poetry.* New York: Columbia University Press, 1968. Begins with a biographical chapter which is followed by extended critical discussions of individual books. These commentaries are extraordinarily accessible to novice readers and reveal much about the poetry. Includes helpful notes, a bibliography good for its period, and an index.

Mariani, Paul L. *The Broken Tower: A Life of Hart Crane*. New York: W. W. Norton, 1999. In his fourth biography of major American poets, Mariani examines the life of Hart Crane, who held a pivotal role in the development of American literature's avant-garde. Quotes from Crane's letters and poems are included throughout the narrative.

Quinn, Vincent. *Hart Crane*. New York: Twayne, 1963. A good small volume in what was a good series of introductions. The commentary is more analytic than biographical; a chronology compensates. Contains full notes, a select bibliography, and a good index.

Unterecker, John. *Voyager: A Life of Hart Crane*. New York: Farrar, Straus & Giroux, 1969. A complete scholarly critical biography—a detailed, removed, objective account that is both thoroughly researched and readable. The illustrations alone, a minor part of the book, make the book worthwhile. Although it has a substantial index, it has no notes or bibliography.

Kate Begnal;
bibliography updated by the editors

STEPHEN CRANE

Born: Newark, New Jersey; November 1, 1871
Died: Badenweiler, Germany; June 5, 1900

PRINCIPAL POETRY

The Black Riders and Other Lines, 1895
A Souvenir and a Medley, 1896
War Is Kind, 1899
The University Press of Virginia Edition of the Works of Stephen Crane, 1970 (volume 10)

OTHER LITERARY FORMS

Stephen Crane is best known as a novelist and short-story writer, and deservedly so. His first novel, *Maggie: A Girl of the Streets* (1893) was an early and almost pure example of naturalistic fiction. About the time of his twenty-fourth birthday, *The Red Badge of Courage* (1895) made him famous. Of his other novels—*George's Mother* (1896), *The Third Violet* (1897), *Active Service* (1899), and *The O'Ruddy: A Romance* (1903, with Robert Barr)—only *The Monster* (1899), a novella, may lay claim to greatness. Of the scores of tales, sketches, and journalistic pieces that verge on fiction, the best are "The Reluctant Voyagers" (1893), "The Open Boat," "The Bride Comes to Yellow Sky," "Death and the Child," and "The Blue Hotel" (all in 1898). Of Crane's dramatic efforts, there is *The Ghost* (1899, with Henry James) performed in a room at Crane's home in England. According to one contemporary review, the play was a mixture of "farce, comedy, opera, and burlesque." His only other play is a slight closet drama called *The Blood of the Martyr* (wr. 1898?, pb. 1940).

ACHIEVEMENTS

As one of the first impressionistic writers—Joseph Conrad called him "The Impressionist"—Stephen Crane was among the first to express in writing a new way of looking at the world. Impressionism grew out of scientific discoveries that showed how human physiology, particularly that of the eyes, determines the way everything in the universe, everything outside the individual body and mind, is seen. People do not see the world as it is, yet the mind and eye collaborate to interpret what is for Crane, at least, a chaotic universe as fundamentally unified, coherent, and explainable. The delusion is compounded when human beings get together, for then they tend to create even grander fabrications, such as religion and history. Although Crane is also seen as one of the first American naturalistic writers, a Symbolist, an Imagist, and even a nihilist, the achievements which justify these labels all derive from his impressionistic view of the world.

Crane's major achievement, both as a fiction writer and a poet, is that he so unflinchingly fought his way through established assumptions about the way life is. He is the logical end of a long line of American Puritans and transcendentalists who believed in the individual pursuit of truth. The great and perhaps fitting irony of such logic is that Crane repudiated the truths in which his predecessors believed. In his fiction, he uses the old genres, but his impressionistic style denies their validity; in his poetry he attacks tradition directly, in part through what he says and in part by how he says it. Rejecting everything conventional about poetry in his day—rhyme, rhythm, conventional images, "safe" metaphors that never shocked Victorian sensibilities—Crane ends by denying things much more important: nationalism, patriotism, the greatness of individual and collective man, the existence of supernatural powers which care and protect and guide. In his best fiction and occasionally in his poetry, Crane faces squarely the horror of a meaningless universe, although he was unable to build a new and positive vision on the rubble of the old.

BIOGRAPHY

Born in a Methodist parsonage in Newark, New Jersey, Stephen Crane was the fourteenth and last child of a minister whose family had been in America for more than two centuries. On his mother's side, almost every male was a minister; one became a bishop. By the time his father died in 1880, Crane had lived in several places in New York and New Jersey and had been thoroughly indoctrinated in the faith he was soon to reject. Also around that time, he wrote his first poem, "I'd Rather Have—." His first short story, "Uncle Jake and the Bell Handle," was written in 1885, and the same year he enrolled in Pennington Seminary, where he stayed until 1887. Between 1888 and 1891, he intermittently attended Claverack College, the Hudson River Institute, Lafayette College, and Syracuse University. He was never graduated from any of these schools, preferring baseball to study. In 1892, the New York *Tribune* published many of his New York City sketches and more than a dozen Sullivan County tales. Having apparently forgotten Miss Helen Trent, his first love, he fell in love with one Mrs. Lily Brandon Munroe. That year, too, the mechanics union took exception to his article on their annual fete, which resulted in Crane's brother, Townley, being fired from the *Tribune*.

In 1893, Crane published at his own expense an early version of *Maggie*. William Dean Howells introduced him to Emily Dickinson's poetry, and in the next year he met Hamlin Garland. Also in 1894, the Philadelphia *Press* published an abridged version of *The Red Badge of Courage*.

Stephen Crane (Library of Congress)

The year 1895 is notable for three things: During the first half of the year he traveled in the West, where he met Willa Cather, and in Mexico for the Bachellor Syndicate; *The Black Riders and Other Lines* was published in May, and *The Red Badge of Courage* appeared in October. By December, he was famous, having just turned twenty-four. In 1896, he published *The Little Regiment and Other Episodes of the American Civil War* and fell in love with Cora Stewart (Howorth), whom he never married but with whom he lived for the rest of his life.

In January, 1897, on the way to report the insurgency in Cuba, he was shipwrecked off the Florida coast. Four months later he was in Greece reporting on the Greco-Turkish War. Moving back to England, he became friendly with Joseph Conrad, Henry James, Harold Frederic, H. G. Wells, and others. During that year, he wrote most of his great short stories: "The Open Boat," "The Bride Comes to Yellow Sky," and "The Blue Hotel."

Never very healthy, Crane began to weaken in 1898 as a result of malaria, which he had contracted in Cuba while reporting on the Spanish-American War. By 1899, Crane was back in England and living well above his means. Although he published *War Is Kind*, *Active Service*, and *The Monster and Other Stories*, he continued to fall more deeply in debt. By 1900, he was hopelessly debt-ridden and fatally ill. Exhausted from overwork, intestinal tuberculosis, malaria, and a will to experience life almost unmatched in literary history, Crane died, not yet twenty-nine years old. He left behind works that fill ten sizable volumes.

ANALYSIS

Stephen Crane's poetry, like his life and fiction, consists almost entirely of "enormous repudiations." Filled with vivid animism, startling metaphors, strident naturalism, and bitter nihilism, the poetry repudiates the God of Crane's father, the natural order seen as benevolent by the Romantics and transcendentalists, the brotherhood of man in any areas except sin and blind conformity, the rightness and glory of war, the possibility of justice, the grandeur of love, even man's ability to perceive a modicum of truth clearly. Repudiation is fundamental to his poetry. He rejects rhyme, among other things, and in doing so he anticipates Ezra Pound, Carl Sandburg, and Wallace Stevens, whose poetry came to fruition only in the twentieth century. Crane often went further than these poets by eschewing the rhythms that had defined lyric and narrative verse for more than two thousand years.

Crane never referred to his work as "poetry"; he almost invariably referred to his "lines." Once, however, he alluded to the didactic, nearly therapeutic, nature of his poems by calling them "pills." Unlike the fiction, which is often hauntingly and ironically lyrical, the poetry consciously strives for what Crane called a "tongue of wood." This tongue produced a sound which jarred against the ears of his contemporaries, and for the most part, as Crane himself observed, "in truth it was lamentable." Although Crane managed to avoid writing in the rhymed and metered style that filled the poetry libraries of his day, the cost to the quality of his lines was great. For example, few poets with Crane's credentials could write the following without knowing just how lamenta-

ble it was: "Now let me crunch you/ With the full weight of affrighted love."

While he was seldom this guilty of what Pound later called "emotional slither," Crane nevertheless failed, most of the time, to re-create and liberate in his poetry the intensity of his thought and emotion. Love, for example, is sometimes a biological trap and sometimes a vehicle for defying the Protestant ethic that damned those caught in love's sensuality. As a trap, love can even descend to a pathological fetishism, producing some of Crane's most "lamentable" lines: "I weep and gnash/ And I love the little shoe/ The little, little shoe." On the other hand, as a way of throwing down a gauntlet before accepted Protestant belief, it can produce some of Crane's most beautiful lines. "Should the wide world roll away," depicts a love so enthralling and encompassing that the speaker denies any need for the other props that support humankind. The poem flies in the face of convention by adding sex to Huck Finn's decision to "go to Hell" rather than betray Jim: "Neither God nor man nor place to stand/ Would be to me essential/ If thou and thy white arms were there/ And the fall to doom a long way."

GOD AND THE CHURCH

Not always so summarily dismissed, God appears in a score or more of the poems as himself, nature, or some other metaphor. It could even be said that God manifests three different faces: as God the Father, he is malevolent and capricious; as God the Son, he is kindly and pitying; as the Holy Ghost, he is indifferent. "A man said to the universe," Crane's most anthologized poem, depicts a God who responds to man's insistent cry for recognition ("Sir, I exist!") by both acknowledging the "fact" and refusing to be bound by any "sense of obligation" as a result of it. God is similarly indifferent in "God fashioned the ship of the world carefully." Only here the indifference is more clearly deistic: Once the world was made, God went bowling.

A kindly God appears in the second stanza of "The livid lightnings flashed in the clouds" as "whispers in the heart" and as "melodies,/ Distant, sighing, like faintest breath." A pitying God appears obliquely as Christ in a Spanish-American War poem called "The Battle Hymn." He is a sacrifice not only of God (the "Father of the Never-Ending Circles") but also to God from the jingoistic war spirit of American patriots during that "splendid little war." In "There was One I met upon the road," where man is presented to God as a mass of sin, God's response is to look "With kinder eyes" and say, "poor soul." Conversely, if the poem is read ironically—that is, if God is taken as the creator of sin—then the God of this poem is not pitying, but rather, cruel and malevolent.

Most often, God is malevolent and unyielding, hateful and unworthy of worship. In many poems, man looks at him with "grim hatred," as a capricious dealer of death, a denier of man's suffering, a bully, and a firm upholder of the Darwinian belief in the survival of the fittest. In "To the Maiden" and "The Ocean said to me once," God is nature, but still basically malevolent, instructing the seeker in the latter poem to tell a nearby woman that her lover has been "laid/ In a cool hall" with a "wealth of golden sand." In the next stanza, she is also to be told that her lover's hand will be heaped with corpses "Until he stands like a child/ With surplus of toys."

Since Crane also heaps bitter abuse upon the Church, it sometimes remains unclear as to whether the God that Crane depicts as malevolent is Crane's God or whether it is God as seen by the Church. In a number of poems, the Church is viewed as the betrayer of the New Testament God of compassion. Everywhere, "figures robed in black" are revealed as hypocritical and evil: "You say you are holy," "With eye and with gesture," "There was a great cathedral," "Walking in the sky," "Two or three angels," "A row of thick pillars," "If you would seek a friend among men," and a host of others bitterly accuse the Church of irrelevance. As Crane sees it, the Church not only fails to help man live on this planet, this "space-lost bulb," as he calls it in "The Blue Hotel," but also actively makes life more difficult.

THE MYTH OF BROTHERHOOD

Another of man's beliefs pilloried by Crane is brotherhood. The "subtle battle brotherhood" which fails to keep Henry Fleming from running away in *The Red Badge of Courage* becomes a banal and damnable conformity in the poetry. "'Think as I think,' said a man" is a short piece in which the speaker chooses instead to "be a toad." Patriotism is a collective "falsity," a "godly vice" that "makes us slaves." The rather good poem, "When a

people reach the top of a hill" is one long irony against "the blue battalions" of collective action. Responding to a question about mob courage, Crane once wrote in a letter: "The mob? The mob has no courage. That is the chatter of clubs and writers." In his poetry, as elsewhere, Crane shared the nineteenth century's fear of the mob. The only brotherhood that exists in Crane's poetry is a brotherhood of sin, as shown in "I stood upon a high place."

Although the most obviously insane use of the mob occurs in war, and although Crane made his reputation on war fiction, war as a theme does not loom very large in his poetry. "I suppose I ought to be thankful to 'The Red Badge,'" Crane wrote, "But I am much fonder of my little book of poems, 'The Black Riders.'" *The Black Riders and Other Lines*, Crane thought, was "about life in general," while *The Red Badge of Courage* is a "mere episode in life." Aside from a few poems which allude to the Spanish-American War, war is more generalized, as in the poem beginning "There exists the eternal face of conflict."

INJUSTICE

The theme of injustice ranges among the poems from the yellow journalism of American newspapers in Crane's day to the cosmic injustice of God to man. In all cases, Crane is bitterly insistent that justice simply does not exist. One particular injustice, however, overshadows all others: the injustice of wealth. Wealth as wealth is not questioned but rather what it seems to do to people who have it and to those who do not. Charity, for example, is "a lie." It is given by "bigoted men of a moment" as food that "turns into a yoke." The recipients are expected "to vanish/ Grateful because of full mouths." Yet, the poem warns the charitable that their turn will come: "—Wait—/ Await your turn." Only once in the ten volumes of his collected works does Crane complain about his poverty, and even then he does so in self-mockery, choosing a Chaucerian "complaint to his purse." The wealthy are "fat asses," "too well-dressed to protest against infamy." Successful people are "complacent, smiling," and "stand heavily on the dead."

The major theme of Crane's poetry, as Milne Holton's *Cylinder of Vision* (1972) has shown about the fiction, is man's utter inability to perceive the truth and his amazing willingness to believe that he does indeed see it. For Crane, the world is chaotic, and all man's beliefs about God and nations, about religions and history, are almost entirely delusory. He never resolves, for example, the conflict between the malevolent and the pitying God, choosing instead to let it stand in several two-stanza poems in which one stanza describes God the beast and the other the God of compassion. "When a people reach the top of a hill" is read by Daniel Hoffman as praise of the American nation and the triumph of man over fate, but it may also be read ironically as an exposure of utter delusion. Everywhere in the poetry, there are "gardens lying at impossible distances." In one poem, "A man saw a ball of gold in the sky," Crane uses his characteristic cosmic point of view to allow the man to climb into the sky only to find the gold ball made of clay. When he returns, the man finds the ball again made of gold: "By the heavens, it was a ball of gold." Misperception can involve delusion, as in "I saw a man pursuing the horizon," and monumental egotism, as in "I looked here," which takes William Shakespeare's "My mistress' eyes are nothing like the sun" another step by saying that her real beauty is irrelevant since he perceives her as beautiful. In another poem, Crane says it more directly. In the thirteen lines of "If you would seek a friend among men," the speaker notes seven times that all one needs to know about people is that they are "crying their wares." As with most of Crane's poetry, this theme can be traced to the Bible: All is vanity.

Ultimately, Crane's poetry is a protest against the conditions of life and against the lies man tells himself to make life tolerable. That protest sustained his brief poetic career, although in time, he did become less angry with God for not existing or at least for not paying attention. Crane is modern in the sense that, like most modern poets, he rejected both the theism and the humanism of the nineteenth century, but he lived too soon to benefit from the experiments of others who were also soon to reject them.

OTHER MAJOR WORKS

LONG FICTION: *Maggie: A Girl of the Streets*, 1893; *The Red Badge of Courage: An Episode of the American Civil War*, 1895; *George's Mother*, 1896; *The Third Violet*, 1897; *Active Service*, 1899; *The Monster*, 1898 (serial), 1899 (novella; pb. in *The Monster and Other Stories*); *The O'Ruddy: A Romance*, 1903 (with Robert Barr).

SHORT FICTION: *The Little Regiment and Other Episodes of the American Civil War*, 1896; *The Open Boat and Other Tales of Adventure*, 1898; *The Monster and Other Stories*, 1899; *Whilomville Stories*, 1900; *Wounds in the Rain: War Stories*, 1900; *Last Words*, 1902.

PLAYS: *The Ghost*, pr. 1899 (with Henry James); *The Blood of the Martyr*, pb. 1940 (wr. 1898?).

NONFICTION: *The Great Battles of the World*, 1901; *The War Dispatches of Stephen Crane*, 1964.

BIBLIOGRAPHY

Bassan, Maurice, ed. *Stephen Crane: A Collection of Critical Essays*. Englewood Cliffs, N.J.: Prentice-Hall, 1967. Divided into three sections—portraits, general discussions, and discussions of individual works—this comprehensive collection with an especially fine introduction by the editor surveys the development of Crane's career and the most significant studies of his work. Includes a detailed chronology of important dates and an incisive bibliographical essay.

Benfey, Christopher E. G. *The Double Life of Stephen Crane*. New York: Knopf, 1992. A narrative of Crane's life and literary work that argues that the writer attempted to live the life his works portrayed. Includes bibliography and index.

Berryman, John. *Stephen Crane: A Critical Biography*. 1950. Rev. ed. New York: Farrar, Straus & Giroux, 1977. Originally published in 1950, this biography by a distinguished American poet remains the single most authoritative study of Crane's life and work. Berryman makes especially good use of modern psychology in interpreting Crane's personality and the evolution of his writing. Berryman includes a separate chapter on Crane's art and an extensive bibliographical note.

Cady, Edwin H. *Stephen Crane*. Rev. ed. Boston: Twayne, 1980. An excellent, introductory, chronological account of Crane's career, with chapters on his biography, his early writing, *The Red Badge of Courage: An Episode of the American Civil War*, notes, a chronology, an updated bibliographical essay, and an index. Cady has revised some of his judgments, especially of *Maggie: A Girl of the Streets*, and identified some "elusive" evidence in Crane's studies.

Davis, Linda H. *Badge of Courage: The Life of Stephen Crane*. Boston: Houghton Mifflin, 1998. Davis's biography emphasizes the revolutionary nature of Crane's writing in a narrative of the author's struggle to re-create the early success he achieved with *The Red Badge of Courage*.

Gullason, Thomas A., ed. *Stephen Crane's Career: Perspectives and Evaluations*. New York: New York University Press, 1972. A useful source book on Crane's life and career, including documents on his family history and various biographical sketches, estimates and reminiscences, studies of the sources and influences on his work, studies of individual works, and Crane's literary and philosophical attitudes. The bibliography has a separate section on studies of Crane's poetry collections and individual poems.

Knapp, Bettina L. *Stephen Crane*. New York: Frederick Ungar, 1987. A succinct, up-to-date introduction to Crane's life and career, with a separate chapter on his biography, several chapters on his fiction, and an extensive discussion of two poetry collections, *The Black Riders and Other Lines*, and *War Is Kind*. Includes a detailed chronology, a bibliography of primary and secondary sources, and an index.

Robertson, Michael. *Stephen Crane, Journalism, and the Making of Modern American Literature*. New York: Columbia University Press, 1997. Although this work focuses on Crane's nonfiction, specifically how journalism and fiction feed into each other both in Crane's and in other early twentieth century writers' work, the insights into American literature and culture in general inform Crane's life and work.

Stallman, R. W. *Stephen Crane: A Biography*. New York: George Braziller, 1968. Stallman takes issue with John Berryman's biography, particularly with his use of evidence and his psychological interpretations. Stallman provides a wealth of new material, an impressive scholarly command of sources, several important photographs and illustrations, extensive notes, and a comprehensive checklist of Crane's writings.

Weatherford, Richard M., ed. *Stephen Crane: The Critical Heritage*. Boston: Routledge & Kegan Paul, 1973. Divided into sections which provide contemporary British and American reviews of Crane's work as it was published. Similarly, the introduction charts Crane's career in terms of each published text, noting the critical reception of his work and the details of his publishing career. Includes a brief annotated bibliography and an index.

Chester L. Wolford;
bibliography updated by the editors

RICHARD CRASHAW

Born: London, England; c. 1612
Died: Loreto, Italy; August 21, 1649

PRINCIPAL POETRY

Epigrammatum Sacrorum Liber, 1634
Steps to the Temple, 1646, 1648
Carmen Deo Nostro, 1652
Poems: English, Latin, and Greek, 1927, 1957
Complete Poetry of Richard Crashaw, 1970

OTHER LITERARY FORMS

Richard Crashaw wrote primarily religious poetry reflecting the life of Christ and the symbols of Christianity.

ACHIEVEMENTS

Richard Crashaw occupies his niche in literary history as a sort of maverick Metaphysical whose poetry, although displaying many of the techniques and characteristics of John Donne and George Herbert, is unique in its baroque flamboyance and its strong Roman Catholic sensibilities.

A poet of fluctuating popularity, Crashaw has had his work treated as decadent Metaphysical poetry, as an outstanding example of ornate wit, as conventional Catholic devotion, and as intensely personal expression. His poems are longer and more elaborate than those of his model George Herbert, although his themes are narrower in focus. Crashaw is sometimes ranked with Donne and Herbert as a "major" Metaphysical poet; alternately, he is linked with such significant but "minor" writers as Abraham Cowley and Henry Vaughan.

In his intense rendering of Counter-Reformation Roman Catholic spirituality, as well as in his use of powerful visual experiences, Crashaw is distinctive. His poetry, widely popular in his own day, continued to attract readers and critical appreciation through the end of the seventeenth century and early in the eighteenth; it waned with the pre-Romantics and their successors and received relatively little notice until early in the twentieth century, when a host of major critics rediscovered religious poetry.

BIOGRAPHY

The only child of William Crashaw, Richard Crashaw was born in London in either 1612 or 1613. His mother died when he was an infant; William Crashaw's second wife, Elizabeth, died when Richard was seven.

William Crashaw, Anglican divine, seems an unlikely parent for one of England's most famous converts to Roman Catholicism. Staunchly Low Church (some say Puritan) in his theology and in his lifestyle, the elder Crashaw devoted his life to preaching and writing, partly against the Laudian or High Church excesses in the Church of England but principally against what he perceived as the far greater dangers of the Church of Rome itself. In his efforts to know the full strength of the enemy, William Crashaw amassed an impressive collection of "Romish" writings; the critic can only speculate what effect these works, as well as his father's convictions, may have had on the spiritual development of Richard Crashaw.

After two years at London's famed Charterhouse School with its austere regime and classical curriculum, Crashaw was admitted, in 1631, to Pembroke College at Cambridge University. He would receive his A.B. in 1634 and his A.M. in 1638. He came to Pembroke with something of a reputation as a poet, a reputation which grew steadily as he produced Latin and Greek epigrams as well as English models, translations of the Psalms, and various occasional verses. These works form the basis of his 1634 publication, *Epigrammatum Sacrorum Liber*, the only work Crashaw himself would see through the printing process.

In 1635, Crashaw was appointed to a fellowship at Peterhouse College and sometime shortly thereafter was ordained to the Anglican priesthood. At Peterhouse he was in direct contact with a circle of Laudian churchmen whose devotion, emphasis on liturgical ceremony and propriety, and reverence marked another step in Crashaw's eventual spiritual journey to Rome. During this period between 1635 and 1643 Crashaw also learned Spanish and Italian, moving with ease into the reading of the Spanish mystics, among them Teresa of Avila and John of the Cross, as well as the rich tradition of Italian devotional literature. This material would strongly influence his later poetry, to the extent that his work is sometimes described as Continental rather than English.

Another significant event of the Peterhouse years was Crashaw's acquaintance with the community at Little Gidding, the religious retreat founded by George Herbert's friend Nicholas Ferrar. At Little Gidding, daily communal prayers and other religious observances were prescribed and orderly; the ancient church building was restored by the community to a Laudian elegance; the sanctuary fittings were rich and reverent. Although Ferrar and his followers steadfastly maintained their allegiance to Canterbury, the community was sometimes criticized as Papist.

These same criticisms were being levied at Peterhouse, where John Cosin, Master of Peterhouse and a friend of Crashaw, was restoring and adorning the college chapel with equal devotion. Reports of the candles, incense, and crucifixes at Peterhouse continued to arouse Puritan suspicions; in the early 1640's Cosin, along with Crashaw, was censured for "popish doctrine." In 1643 Parliament, goaded by the growing Puritan forces, forbade all altar ornaments as well as all pictures of saints. In these early years of the Civil Wars, Cosin, Crashaw, and four others were formally expelled from their fellowships and forced to depart.

The last six years of Crashaw's life, the key years of his conversion and the flowering of his poetry, are difficult to trace with any certainty. In 1644, he wrote from Leyden, speaking of his poverty and his loneliness. He may have revisited England, probably only for a short period. At some point he made the acquaintance of Queen Henrietta Maria, who, as a devout Catholic, took up his cause in a letter to Pope Innocent. Somewhere in his physical and spiritual travels, Crashaw decided—or discerned a call—to commit himself to Roman Catholicism; this central experience cannot be dated. He continued to write, completing the poems his editor would entitle *Steps to the Temple* (a humble compliment to George Herbert's *The Temple*, 1633), revising many of his earlier poems, and working on the pieces which would form his last volume, *Carmen Deo Nostro*.

Crashaw spent time in Rome and in Paris, absorbing the rich art of these cities as well as their expressions of Catholicism. In Paris, he was befriended by the poet Abraham Cowley who, appalled at his friend's physical condition, obtained care and financial assistance for him. Back in Rome, Crashaw was appointed to the service of a cardinal and subsequently was sent to Loreto, the house where, according to Catholic tradition, the Virgin Mary received word of the Annunciation. Crashaw had barely reached this Marian shrine when he fell ill; he died August 21, 1649.

ANALYSIS

Richard Crashaw's poetry may be divided into three groups of unequal significance for the scholar: the early epigrams, the secular poetry, and the religious poetry. The early epigrams and translations are studied, meticulous, and often occasional. The 178 Latin epigrams in *Epigrammatum Sacrorum Liber* show the influence of Martial and other classical writers. Crashaw also uses biblical motifs, particularly for his several English epigrams, displaying in his treatment of these themes an example of the close reading which will underlie his later work.

As a book of poetry, these early pieces are significant for the discipline they reveal and for their fascination with wordplay—puns, quips, repetitions, conceits—which Crashaw will later elevate to such exuberance. They are finger exercises, and if they lack the genius of John Milton's college ventures, they nevertheless suggest later greatness.

DELIGHTS OF THE MUSES

Crashaw's second body of verse, the secular or nonsacred poetry, comprises much of the work found in *Delights of the Muses*, the volume appended to and published with *Steps to the Temple*. In that volume, Crashaw

displays the Donnean Metaphysical, writing poems with titles such as "Wishes. To His (Supposed) Mistress," "A Picture Sent to a Friend," "Venus Putting on Mars His Armor," and "Loves Horoscope." Witty, polished, urbane, these poems show an accomplished and sophisticated writer delighting in the possibilities of English poetry. Intensely visual, these poems often select a single image and elaborate it in a manner reminiscent of the earlier emblem tradition. The classical tradition is still strong but the metrics are clearly English.

Although the poems in *Delights of the Muses* are often Donne-like in their wit, there is a certain reticence to them. The robust speaker of Donne's songs and sonnets is absent in Crashaw; there is relatively little use of the personal pronoun and none of the speechlike abruptness which makes so many of Donne's poems memorable. The meter is usually highly regular, most often iambic tetrameter or pentameter, and the cadences are smooth. There is an unsubstantiated tradition that Crashaw was a trained musician; these poems would support that claim.

From time to time there is a baffling half-revelation, for example in the two-line "On Marriage," when the speaker declares that he would "be married, but I'd have no wife,/ I would be married to the single life." Whether this is witty posturing, cynical disclaimer, or an honest account of his own state (Crashaw never married), the reader cannot tell. Crashaw's work would appear in anthologies even if he had written only the secular poetry, but his name would definitely be in smaller type. The poet himself spent far less effort in revising these secular poems, suggesting that he too considered them of secondary importance.

STEPS TO THE TEMPLE AND CARMEN DEO NOSTRO

Turning to Crashaw's major works, those rich poems which he wrote and revised for the collections that would become *Steps to the Temple* and *Carmen Deo Nostro*, one is confronted with a lavish, even bewildering, highly sensuous, celebration of the Christianity which so fired the poet. If Donne argues with God in his holy sonnets and Herbert prays through *The Temple*, then Crashaw contemplates and exclaims. Apparently gifted with mystical experiences even in the midst of his English tradition, Crashaw's mode of prayer is much more akin to that of Teresa of Avila than to the Book of

Common Prayer. Like Teresa, who said that she could meditate for hours on the opening two words of the Lord's Prayer, Crashaw, confronted by the mysteries of Christ's life, death, and resurrection, meditates, celebrates, sorrows, refines, ponders, *sees*. Faced with mystery, he expresses it in paradox and strains to reconcile the opposites. Christianity does, after all, continually join flesh and spirit, God and man, justice and mercy, life and death. Crashaw's poetry does the same: It reveals rather than persuades. Unlike Henry Vaughan and especially Thomas Traherne, whose religious poetry is almost unflaggingly optimistic, Crashaw focuses on both the joys and sufferings of Christianity and more on the sufferings of Christ and the Virgin Mary, although he involves himself in the joyous mysteries of Christianity as well.

"IN THE HOLY NATIVITY OF OUR LORD"

"In the Holy Nativity of Our Lord," one of his best-known, most tightly written poems, makes a most appropriate introduction to the poet. Starting with the paradox of the revelation of Christ's birth to humble shepherds, Crashaw structures his hymn in a series of dualities and paradoxes: "Loves noone" meets "Natures night," frost is replaced by flowers, a tiny manger provides a bed for "this huge birth" of God who becomes man. The dualities in the poem are underscored by the shepherds themselves, classically named Tityrus and Thursis, who alternate verses and sing the chorus together.

The contrasts lead to the central question of the hymn, where to find a "fit" bed for the infant Jesus. When the "whitest sheets of snow" prove pure but too cold and the "rosie fleece" of angels' wings is warm but cannot "passe for pure," the shepherds return to the nativity scene to discover that the Christ child has vividly and dramatically reached his own solution:

> See see, how soone his new-bloom'd cheeke
> Twixt's mother's brests is gone to bed.
> Sweet choice (said I!) no way but so
> Not to lye cold, yet sleep in snow.

The paradox is resolved in the person of the Virgin Mother, Mary; the "I" of the shepherds becomes the "we" of all the faithful; the celebration of "Eternitie shut in a span/ Summer in winter, day in night,/ Heaven in Earth and god in man" ends in a full chorus, followed by an anthem of liturgical joy.

Several traits elevate this poem well above the countless conventional, albeit sincere, Nativity poems of this period. The central image is vivid and personal; the Christ child is presented not as king but as nursing infant. Crashaw brilliantly takes the biblical motif of the Son of man, who has no place to lay his head, and transforms it into image. The poem moves gracefully from opening question to resolution, celebrating that resolution and concluding with the offering: "at last . . . our selves become our owne best sacrifice." It is a poem of liturgical color: The images of white and gold which weave through the stanzas are reminiscent of the vestments worn for the Christmas liturgy as well as the sunrise of Christmas Day.

One of Crashaw's simpler poems because of its traditional subject matter, "In the Holy Nativity of Our Lord" exemplifies the gifts of the poet. Crashaw is a worker with color: gold and silver, red and crimson and scarlet, and blinding white fill the poems along with modifiers such as "bright," "rosy," "radiant," and a score of others. The poet is highly conscious of textures and surfaces, forever describing his images as "soft," "rough," "slippery." Predominantly Anglo-Saxon in his diction (his most repeated nouns are monosyllables— "die," "birth," "sun," "flame," "heart," "eyes"), Crashaw betrays his early fondness for Latin in some of his favorite adjectives: "immortal," "triumphant," "illustrious," and "supernatural." He alliterates constantly, playing with vowel and consonant sounds to achieve unity of tone as well as musical qualities.

"SAINTE MARY MAGDALEN: OR, THE WEEPER"

Ironically, Crashaw's most characteristic gifts as a poet, particularly his enthusiasm for the refined and elaborate image, are responsible for some of his most-criticized efforts. Of these, the most famous is "Sainte Mary Magdalen: Or, The Weeper," a long poem commemorating the legend of Mary Magdalene, the sinner forgiven by Jesus, who, according to tradition, wept tears of repentance for many years. The motif is a beloved one in the seventeenth century; poems celebrating (and recommending) tears abound, often with Mary Magdalene, Saint Peter, or another grieving Christian as the focal point. Crashaw's poem is really not about Mary Magdalene at all; rather it is about the tears themselves which, after falling from Mary Magdalene's eyes, follow a circuitous, thirty-seven stanza route, develop a speech of their own, and finally go up to Heaven to meet "a worthy object, Our Lords Feet." In between his opening salutation of Magdalene's eyes ("Ever bubling things! Thawing crystall! Snowy hills!) and the final image of Jesus, Crashaw scatters images and conceits with such abandon as to bewilder the unwary. Some of these conceits are richly apt: Magdalene is "pretious prodigall! Faire spendthrift of thy self!" Others (and there are many more of these) are extravagant, incredible, even ludicrous:

> And now where e're he strayes
>
> . . . .
>
> He's follow'd by two faithfull fountaines,
> Two walking Bathes; two weeping motions;
> Portable and compendious Oceans.

"The Weeper" has been cited as the prime example of all that is bad, even bathetic, in Crashaw, and surely today's reader, accustomed to a leaner poetic style and certainly to a less visible religious expression, confronts major problems. These can be partially alleviated, however, with at least some consideration of the traditions out of which Crashaw is writing. He is, in a sense, doing in "The Weeper" what Teresa of Avila is doing with the Lord's Prayer: He is taking a single image and pondering it at length, refining and embroidering and elaborating the object of his meditation until it reaches a conclusion.

Crashaw is also influenced by the Christian tradition of litanies. A litany is a long series of short prayers, each one a single phrase or epithet, often recited by a priest with responses ("pray for us" or "have mercy on us") from the congregation. A litany does what the poem does: It presents aspect after aspect of the holy person or mystery so that the faithful may, in some sense, *see*. The petitions of a litany are not related to one another but to the person or mystery they are celebrating: The Virgin Mary, for example, is called Ark of the Covenant, Morning Star, Mystical Rose, Tower of Ivory, not because these phrases have any relationship to one another, but because they are figures or conceits of her. De-

pending on one's scriptural background or perhaps spiritual disposition, some phrases suggest more devotion than others.

Much has been said of Crashaw's affinities with the movement in art called baroque—that richly decorative aesthetic which suggests tension, opposites pulling at each other, extravagant gestures and ornate detail, which somehow connotes a sense of unworldliness or otherness. "The Weeper," in its maze of images and conceits, suggests that within it lies a significant truth which the reader cannot follow but at which he can only guess. The poem is perhaps less baroque than some of Crashaw's other works but it has that same energy, tension, and movement.

Finally, one might consider the fact that the poem celebrates Mary Magdalene, who wept repeatedly, even for years. The poem, too, celebrates repeatedly, with a focus on image after image, indeed perhaps doing the very thing it celebrates. Like Mary Magdalene, the poem reverences the Lord again and again. Read in this sense, "The Weeper" may well be a hieroglyph, the term used by Joseph Summers to describe George Herbert's poetry (*George Herbert: His Religion and Art*, 1954).

All the above is not intended as a defense of "The Weeper" so much as an attempt to view Crashaw in his contexts. Like many of the mystics, he has little need for discursive structure, preferring instead the intuitive, associative mode for communicating his experiences. If some images are banal, they are still a part of his contemplation and they stay in the poem. It is an unfamiliar aesthetic but not one without some validity. It is worth noting that nearly all Crashaw's numerous revisions of his poetry are toward length; he rarely discarded and never shortened.

SAINT TERESA POEMS

As a Roman Catholic, Crashaw was more free than his Church of England contemporaries to consider the lives of the saints. Although the biblical Mary Magdalene and the Virgin Mary were appropriate for the devotions of at least High Church Anglicans, saints such as Teresa of Avila were less so, even though Teresa's works had appeared in English as early as 1611 and would surely have been familiar to devout readers. It is not known whether William Crashaw possessed a copy of Teresa's classic *The Interior Castle* (1583); if he did, and if he preached against it, there is an intriguing poetic justice in his son's selection of Teresa for his richest poems. The two Saint Teresa poems rank among Crashaw's finest.

The poems contrast as well as match; "A Hymn to the Name and Honor of the Admirable Saint Teresa" is a legend or story made into a lesson, whereas "The Flaming Heart" is a meditation upon an image, possibly, as Louis Martz (in *The Wit of Love*, 1969) suggests, the painting by the Antwerp artist Gerhard Seghers, or perhaps the more famous Gian Lorenzo Bernini statue in the Coronaro Chapel, Saint Maria della Vittoria, Rome. Crashaw could have seen either representation, and he may well have seen both.

"A Hymn to the Name and Honor of the Admirable Saint Teresa" begins with the story of the child Teresa who, wanting martyrdom and heaven for her faith, persuades her little brother to go off with her in search of the Moors who will, she hopes, put them to death. The poet, meditating on the greatness of heart in the six-year-old Teresa, is both witty and moving when he breaks in, "Sweet, not so fast!" A richer, more demanding martyrdom awaits the adult Teresa; she will be called to the contemplative life, reform the Carmelite order, write magnificent works, and give herself totally to the love of God. Dying to self in the most ancient tradition, she will indeed be a spiritual martyr. The poem combines, in the richest Metaphysical tradition, intellect and emotion, tough demands and profoundly intuitive responses. Teresa is not free to choose her martyrdom any more than were the first Christians; she can only respond to the choice that God makes for her.

In the poem, Crashaw is working in the best tradition of Anglican preaching as well as with Roman Catholic sensitivity. He begins with a story, an exemplum, good clear narrative, aphorisms ("Tis Love, not years nor limbs, that can/ Make the Martyr, or the man"), vivid drama, and a totally believable picture of the child Teresa and her ardent love of God. The regular tetrameter lines with their *aabb* rhymes move the story gracefully, even inevitably, along. Then, with "not so fast," the poet moves into a new vein altogether, summoning back Teresa—and the reader—to contemplate what giving oneself to God really means. The poetry moves from narrative to lyrical, intuitive expression and is filled with images, exclamations, and apostrophes. Instead of martyrdom as a child, Teresa will face numerous mystical deaths, which will prepare her for the final death which brings total union with the Lord; these mystical deaths "Shall all at last dye into one,/ And melt thy soules sweet mansion." The diction becomes more and more simple as the concepts underneath the poetry become increasingly mystical. The poem concludes in a dazzling combination of Anglican neatness ("decorum") and Roman Catholic transcendence: The one who wishes to see Jesus "must learne in life to dye like Thee." The poem is simultaneously a meditation upon a holy life and a lyrical celebration of one who was chosen by God to live totally for him. The women in Crashaw's poetry, whether the Virgin Mary, Magdalene, Teresa, or even that "not impossible she" of the poem "Wishes. To His (Supposed) Mistress," are all great souled, larger than life, intensely vivid, and visual. Later, Crashaw would write "An Apologie" for the hymn as "having been writt when the author was yet among the protestantes"; one wonders whether its discursive, even preachy, tone is a manifestation of this state of mind. Surely, the poem needs no "apologie."

In the second Teresa poem, "The Flaming Heart," Crashaw keeps his tetrameter rhymed couplets but adopts a totally different stance, moving from story-with-lesson to contemplation. The thirteenth century theologian Thomas Aquinas defines contemplation as simultaneously knowing and loving one of the divine mysteries, and the poem illustrates that definition. The speaker is gazing at a picture or statue of Teresa in which she is visited by a seraphim, a celestial being, who, holding a burning dart, prepares to transfix the saint. The scene is taken from Teresa's own journal account of her divine revelations and translates the momentary interior apprehension into external narration. Teresa's language is explicitly sexual; the cherub with the dart, the piercing, the pain followed by ecstatic joy, all these are a part of that long tradition which uses the language of physical love for God's encounters with his people. It is the language of Donne's holy sonnets. Catholic artists, directed by the Council of Trent to make the mysteries of faith more vivid for believers, are drawn to this incident; it is not surprising that the newly converted

Crashaw, already enamored of image and mystery, would be drawn to the story of Teresa, another "not impossible she."

"The Flaming Heart" welcomes "you that come as friends" almost as though the readers are pilgrims to the church where the image is displayed. The faithful viewers are, however, immediately corrected by the wit of the speaker; although "they say" that one figure is the seraphim and the other is Teresa, the speaker assumes the role of correcting guide, asking, "be ruled by me." The figures must be reversed; the saint is the seraphim.

With that flashing insight, "Read HIM for her and her for him," the poet moves into the entire burden of the long poem, constantly juxtaposing Teresa and the seraph, celebrating her angelic virtues and total love of God, casting the seraph in the role of a "rivalled lover" who needs to veil his face, singing praise of the "flaming heart" of Teresa which is so afire with love. The couplets race in their eagerness to show this instant, moving from abstract to concrete, from Teresa to the seraph. The colors are rich here, crimson, golden, and fiery; the sense of pain becoming joy is almost tangible; the transcendence of the moment breaks out of the visual representation as the speaker also moves out of time and space and into the world of mystical prayer. The closing lines, perhaps Crashaw's most intense and most often cited, are litany, prayer, celebration, vision.

BIBLIOGRAPHY

Bertonasco, Marc F. *Crashaw and the Baroque.* Tuscaloosa: University of Alabama Press, 1971. Traces Crashaw's key images to seventeenth century emblem books and finds Saint Francis de Sales's meditative method the major influence on Crashaw's spiritual development. Provides a detailed analysis of "The Weeper" which demonstrates these influences. The appendix contains a review of Crashaw's scholarship and a bibliography.

Cousins, Anthony D. *The Catholic Religious Poets from Southwell to Crashaw: A Critical History.* London: Sheed & Ward, 1991. History of the criticism and interpretation of these English poets from a Christian perspective. Bibliographical references, index.

Healy, Thomas F. *Richard Crashaw.* Leiden, the Netherlands: E. J. Brill, 1986. Explains that Crashaw's poetry owes much to his Cambridge years at Pembroke and Peterhouse, when the religious, intellectual, and poetic environment shaped his ideas and his work. Includes extended criticism of "Musick's Duell" and, particularly, "To the Name of Jesus."

LeVay, John. "Crashaw's 'Wishes to His (Supposed) Mistresse.'" *Explicator* 50, no. 4 (Summer, 1992): 205. A critique of Crashaw's "Delight of the Muses," which includes a wishful reverie of the poet's ideal woman.

Mintz, Susannah B. "The Crashavian Mother." *Studies in English Literature* 39, no. 1 (Winter, 1999): 111-129. A study of the history of critical thought regarding Crashaw's relationship to women.

Parrish, Paul A. *Richard Crashaw.* Boston: Twayne, 1980. Surveys Crashaw's life and work and contains several relatively long explications of individual Crashaw poems. Provides a biography, followed by chapters on Crashaw's early work, the secular poems, *Steps to the Temple,* the major hymns, and the Teresa poems. Includes a selected, annotated bibliography.

Sabine, Maureen. *Feminine Engendered Faith: The Poetry of John Donne and Richard Crashaw.* London: Macmillan Academic and Professional, 1992. Examines these two poets' religious imagery and content with particular emphasis on the impact of the Virgin Mary. Bibliographical references, index.

Wallerstein, Ruth C. *Richard Crashaw: A Study of Style and Poetic Development.* 1935. Reprint. Madison: University of Wisconsin Press, 1959. One of the best early studies of Crashaw. Contains invaluable commentary on the translations Crashaw wrote in his formative years. Provides detailed information about the emblem tradition and lists many early primary sources in the bibliography.

Warren, Austin. *Richard Crashaw: A Study in Baroque Sensibility.* Ann Arbor: University of Michigan Press, 1939. An early influential overview of Crashaw's achievement. Examines the Counter-Reformation and chronicles Crashaw's life. Contains a detailed study of Baroque art, comments on Crashaw's secular and sacred verse, and summarizes the critical response to his subject. The bibliography is valuable for its listing of primary sources.

Williams, George Walton. *Image and Symbol in the Sacred Poetry of Richard Crashaw*. Columbia: University of South Carolina Press, 1963. Provides a well-written catalog of Crashaw's symbols, which he groups in three clusters: quantity (God's magnificence and man's insignificance), color (red and white), and "liquidity" (tears, blood, wine, and water). Also provides an extensive bibliography and indexes to symbols and poems.

Young, R. V. *Doctrine and Devotion in Seventeenth-Century Poetry*. Rochester, N.Y.: D. S. Brewer, 2000. History and criticism of Christian poetry in seventeenth-century England. The works of Richard Crashaw, George Herbert, Henry Vaughan, and John Donne are analyzed. Includes bibliographic references.

_____. *Richard Crashaw and the Spanish Golden Age*. New Haven, Conn.: Yale University Press, 1982. Places Crashaw within a metaphysical context and argues that Crashaw's poetry is impersonal and public, that he was familiar with contemporary Spanish literature, and that his poems about saints and feast days ("The Flaming Heart," "Hymn to the Name of Jesus," and "A Hymn to the Name and Honor of the Admirable Saint Teresa") deserve the extended criticism he devotes to them.

Katherine Hanley;
bibliography updated by the editors

ROBERT CREELEY

Born: Arlington, Massachusetts; May 21, 1926

PRINCIPAL POETRY

For Love: Poems, 1950-1960, 1962
Words, 1967
Pieces, 1969
A Day Book, 1972
Robert Creeley: An Inventory, 1945-1970, 1973
Hello, 1976 (expanded edition published as *Hello: A Journal, February 29-May 3, 1976*, 1978)
Selected Poems, 1976

Later, 1979
The Collected Poems of Robert Creeley, 1945-1975, 1982
Mirrors, 1983
Memory Gardens, 1986
Window: Paintings, 1988
Selected Poems, 1991
Life and Death, 1993 (expanded edition in 1998)
So There: Poems, 1976-1983, 1998
For Friends, 2000
Drawn and Quartered, 2001 (with Archie Rand, artist)
Just in Time: Poems, 1984-1994, 2001

OTHER LITERARY FORMS

Robert Creeley has worked in a number of literary genres, including the short story (a collection, *The Gold Diggers*, was published in 1954 and revised in 1965) and the novel (*The Island*, 1963). *A Day Book* includes both prose and poetry. Creeley's nonfiction includes *A Quick Graph* (1970), *Presences* (1976), *Collected Es-*

Robert Creeley (© Bruce Jackson, courtesy of New Directions)

says (1983), and *The Collected Prose* (1984). His ten-volume correspondence with Charles Olson began to be published in 1980 as *Charles Olson and Robert Creeley: The Complete Correspondence*. His *Day Book of a Virtual Poet* appeared in 1998.

ACHIEVEMENTS

Robert Creeley has become one of the most celebrated among American postwar poets. Early identified as a member of the Black Mountain, or Projectivist, school, he has established his individuality with a series of striking works and has transcended early factionalism to find a place in most anthologies of the period for a poetry that has no peer. He brought the modernist vision and achievements of William Carlos Williams and Ezra Pound through the changes that profoundly altered the world after 1945 to give them fresh life in his distinctive wry diction and approach to poetic conventions. *For Love*, his first collection to receive wide distribution, had by 1978 sold more than forty-seven thousand copies; it was nominated for a National Book Award in 1962, the year of its publication.

He has won a range of additional awards during his long career: the Levinson Prize in 1960 and a Leviton-Blumenthal Prize in 1964 for groups of poetry published in *Poetry*, a Guggenheim Fellowship in poetry from 1964 to 1965 and in 1971, a Rockefeller Foundation grant in 1966, and a Union League Civic and Arts Foundation Prize in 1967. He won many honors in the 1980's, including the Shelley Memorial Award, a Frost Medal, a National Endowment for the Arts grant, Leone d'Oro Premio Speziale in Venice, a Fulbright Award, and a Walt Whitman citation of merit. He was named poet laureate of New York State (1989-1991) and won the America Award for Poetry in 1995, the 1996 Lila Wallace/*Reader's Digest* Writers Award, the Bollingen Prize and a Chancellor Norton Medal in 1999, and in 2001, the Lannan Lifetime Achievement Award from the Lannan Literary Foundation.

BIOGRAPHY

Robert Creeley was born in Arlington, Massachusetts, in 1926 (a year that was to prove an *annus mirabilis* for American poetry, for others born that year include Allen Ginsberg, Frank O'Hara, Paul Blackburn,

and Lew Welch). Creeley lost his father, Oscar, a doctor, at the age of four, and thereafter lived with his mother and sister in the nearby town of West Acton. At fourteen, he won a scholarship to the Holderness School in Plymouth, New Hampshire. He entered Harvard University in 1943. When he turned eighteen, being unfit for military service because of a childhood accident that had cost him an eye, he joined the U.S. Ambulance Corps and was sent to Burma. After World War II ended, he returned to Harvard, but he eventually left without taking a degree.

In 1946, Creeley was married to his first wife, Ann McKinnon. About this time he also struck up the close friendship with Cid Corman that was to lead to the launching of Corman's groundbreaking journal *Origin*. This journal published much of Creeley's early work and also the work of Charles Olson, an older poet with whom Creeley corresponded daily for two years. At that time Olson was rector of Black Mountain College in North Carolina, and Creeley became editor (*in absentia*) of the *Black Mountain Review*, another key vehicle of what came to be called projective verse (after Olson's essay of that name), Black Mountain poetry, or, more generally, the New American Poetry. Creeley had been living in the south of France and then in Mallorca, Spain, but upon the dissolution of his marriage in 1955, he came to teach at Black Mountain College. That same year he was awarded his bachelor's degree at Black Mountain.

In 1956, however, Black Mountain College dissolved, and Creeley made his way to San Francisco, where he met the Beat writers Jack Kerouac, Allen Ginsberg, Kenneth Rexroth, and Gary Snyder. He then moved to Albuquerque, New Mexico. In 1960 he earned an M.A. from the University of New Mexico, where he was then teaching. During this period he met Bobbie Louise Hawkins, who became his wife.

During the 1950's Creeley had published seven volumes of verse, as well as a book of short stories, *The Gold Diggers*. A substantial selection of his poems was included in Donald Allen's 1960 Grove Press anthology, *The New American Poetry, 1945-1960*, a landmark collection that helped make the reputation of Creeley and of a number of his peers and associates. In 1962 Scribner's issued *For Love*, essentially a collection of the poems that had appeared in the seven earlier books; the following year his novel *The Island* was published, also by Scribner's.

After teaching at the University of British Columbia in 1962-1963, Creeley returned to New Mexico. In 1966 he took a job teaching at the State University of New York at Buffalo, and in 1978 he was appointed to an endowed chair there, so that he became the Gray professor of poetry and letters. Although he has taught for short stints at other universities, Buffalo remains his residence, and he continues his affiliation with SUNY. In 1991, he served as the director of the poetics program at San Francisco State College for one year, and throughout the 1990's and into the twenty first century, he has participated in numerous poetry readings and writers' conferences.

In 1976, his second marriage ended; shortly thereafter, he was married once more, to Penelope Highton. Creeley and Highton would have two children; Creeley also has several children from his previous marriages.

ANALYSIS

Robert Creeley focuses on the difficult turning points of relationships, on the role language has to play in such moments, given that expectations are governed by one's vocabulary—one thinks as one's language allows. Although his work is far from therapeutic, it has found an audience that to some extent had been readied by the increasing experience of psychotherapy among Americans of the late twentieth century and a growing awareness of the individual as instance of a system. Yet this is to view the work's appeal from the base of the pyramid, as it were; its great strength is its vertical appeal, that it has something in it for readers who know little of modern poetry but also yields much when subjected to critical scrutiny. In his writing Creeley takes up where Samuel Beckett left off: Creeley addresses his readers from a world in which the worst has already happened, yet one in which there is still life and the need to act.

Creeley's greatest strength has been to write a poetry of immediacy while "saving the appearances" by preserving traditional forms. Although he departed from these formal conventions for a period, he was to return to them. In any case, it was his ability to combine the radical content and approach of his early work with the use of conventional form that won for him fame and a wide readership. Colleagues such as Charles Olson, Robert Duncan, and Edward Dorn did more, arguably, to align their vision with its mode of expression; yet it may be that Creeley, in giving voice to his vision within the more recognizable confines of traditional verse, rendered a clearer picture of the gulf that separated the second half of the twentieth century from the first. He appears to be saying, "This is how the quatrain or the couplet must be used, given our new content." In this way, Creeley becomes one of the new sensibility's foremost translators into forms apprehensible to those still imbued with the old. No doubt part of his success derives from the fact that both sensibilities exist—and sometimes battle each other—within him; in several passages he alludes to the nineteenth century expectations with which he was reared.

What was the essence of this other, radically new sensibility? It was an awareness of the atomic bomb, the Nazi death camps, a Europe that had been left "like a broken anthill" (as Ezra Pound said) with twenty million dead, gigantic catastrophe brought about by long-range human design, unimaginable chaos created by careful planning. This was a world in which lamp shades were made out of human skin, in which human beings were persuaded to surrender in the service of abstract causes. Readers today have heard of these horrors so often and for so long that perhaps only a poem or an anecdote can break through the scar tissue that shields their feelings and revive something of the shock and despair so widely, and so deeply, felt when Creeley began his writing career. Creeley teaches by the anecdote, and perhaps the two that follow will give some sense of that time, and of the approach this poet and others took toward the grim events of the 1940's: to face them down and survive, to attempt to lead their generation out of the shadows toward some possible faith in life upon which action might be based.

Asked about his empty socket, and whether he had ever thought of wearing a glass eye, Creeley said that at one time he had used one. One evening in barracks in India, however, he had taken out the glass eye for the night and set it on the bedside table. As he reclined on his bed, he watched an Indian janitor sweeping the floor, coming closer and closer to the bedside table, and then bumping against it, so that the glass eye fell to the floor, where it broke. Because of wartime conditions, it would, he knew, take at least four months to get a replacement shipped to India. By that time he might have been moved on to the theater of war, and in any case his socket would have shrunk so that the new eye would not fit. Therefore he took to wearing an eyepatch over the empty socket. In the early 1950's, when Creeley was living in a village in France, there were around him so many who had been maimed in the war—who were minus an arm or a leg, fingers or toes—that he saw no point in covering up his own loss. Protecting others from the shock of his empty socket and pretending to himself that the facts were otherwise struck him as equally futile in a world so substantially damaged.

The second illustrative incident took place during Creeley's time in Burma. His ambulance team had been assured by the local military unit that a certain village had been taken by the U.S. Army and that the enemy had been driven out. Yet when Creeley and his crew arrived at the village, the first thing they spotted was a Japanese tank driving down the main street. Fortunately, they were able to back into the forest without being spotted. As the poet himself remarked of this incident, however, if they had taken the official word for it, and not trusted the evidence of their senses, they would have been dead.

While Creeley's poetry and prose of the 1950's contains little in the way of content that refers explicitly to wartime conditions or to the great horrors alluded to above, they are nevertheless permeated with the kind of wry awareness these two anecdotes suggest. For Creeley, as for other of the American poets of his generation, linear logic is less to the point than immediate perception, a plan is probably inferior to a hunch, and now always packs the possibility of transcending history. Still, any such attitude toward experience must allow for self-contradiction and ambivalence: What was a sensible line of conduct a moment ago can suddenly become not so.

"THE IMMORAL PROPOSITION"

Creeley developed a very sure way of presenting such knowledge in his poetry—for example, in "The Immoral Proposition":

If you never do anything for anyone else
you are spared the tragedy of human relation-

ships. If quietly and like another time
there is the passage of an unexpected thing:

to look at it is more
than it was. God knows

nothing is competent nothing is
all there is. The unsure

egoist is not
good for himself.

To turn this poem into a prose precis—"If you never do anything for anyone else, you are spared the tragedy of human relationships. If quietly and like another time there is the passage of an unexpected thing: to look at it is more than it was. God knows nothing is competent nothing is all there is. The unsure egoist is not good for himself"—is no doubt to obtain part of the information being transmitted. What is lost in this alteration, however, reveals the essence of Creeley's poetry. In the first place, much happens around the line breaks. A Creeley line, being a breath line—speech-based, that is, with the line being the cluster of speech between two pauses—is always end-stopped: to hear the poet read aloud from his own work, a thing he has made a frequent practice of doing, is to be assured of this fact. That brief but telling pause makes all the difference in the world between the last two lines. One reading thus yielded is "The unsure egoist is not"— period; another is "The unsure egoist is not [all there is]" or "is not [competent]." To add these to the first probable reading, "is not good for himself," enriches the mix. When one realizes that one has the alternative of hearing the final line as a kind of postscript, "[and therefore] good for himself," either ironic or not, one begins to appreciate the full complexity of both the poem and the general type of situation the poem addresses. Creeley made himself master of the pivotal word or phrase that, set at the end of a line, could be read both ahead and back—as with "egoist is not"—to embody more fully the kind of charged situation to which the poet found himself drawn. "To look at it is more/ than it was. God knows" is another cluster that stands on its own, as well as leading on to become part of a further statement. Remarkable also is the line break between lines 2 and 3, isolating the fourth syllable of "relationships" so that it takes on a peculiar autonomy and tangibility, as if to become those well-known "ships that pass in the night."

"The Immoral Proposition" is free verse, but it does not look much like the kind of poem that rubric brings to mind; it is too even, too balanced, too symmetrical. In fact, lines 1 and 2 consist of thirteen syllables each, while there is only a syllable's difference between lines 3 and 4, lines 5 and 6, and lines 9 and 10. Although they lack end rhyme, then, these have close similarity in length and thus have the feel of true couplets. Creeley showed great adroitness with his management of line length, as he did with his line breaks; the poem "The Warning" is a shining example of this:

> For love—I would
> split, open your head and put
> a candle in
> behind the eyes.
>
> Love is dead in us
> if we forget
> the virtues of an amulet
> and quick surprise.

Lines 1, 3, and 4 of the first stanza are four syllables long; line 2—the line that speaks of splitting something open in order to insert something extra—has seven syllables, or three extra. In this poem one finds end rhyme also, though in no regular pattern, and to some extent dependent upon the reader's ear for half rhyme.

"BALLAD OF THE DESPAIRING HUSBAND"

Perhaps Creeley's most hilarious use of rhyme is in a poem called "Ballad of the Despairing Husband," where the measure used, that of the old song "Little Brown Jug," is played with and against to good effect:

> My wife and I lived all alone,
> contention was our only bone.
> I fought with her, she fought with me,
> and things went on right merrily.

As this and the following two quatrains disclose, Creeley is an accomplished humorist, with a sure grasp of the use of exaggeration for comic effect. Humor is not often as open in Creeley's work as it is here, but it occurs

frequently enough that the practiced reader has learned to listen for the comic twist in any Creeley piece.

AESTHETIC VS. ACTUAL

In Creeley's work one finds a wide range of tones, with the sentimental occurring about as often as the comic. Sentimentality breaks in toward the end of "Ballad of the Despairing Husband," when the poet abandons the quatrains in iambic tetrameter in favor of longer, looser lines. Despite some playful phrases—"Oh lovely lady, eating with or without a spoon" (rhymes with "afternoon"); "Oh most loveliest of ladies"—the speaker has in effect stepped outside the frame of the poem to implore a woman who is no longer an amusing caricature but a real person.

This tension between the aesthetic and the otherwise actual sometimes is a strength in Creeley's work, but there are occasions, as here, where the reader might well judge Creeley's decision to step outside the poem to have been mistaken. The poem had been a deliberately two-dimensional rendering of important affairs of the heart, telling its portion of the truth most winningly. It ought not to have been interrupted with this other implied truth—that poems are limited, while the heart overflows. Yet this is a risk run by the poet who draws extensively on personal experience for his material—especially personal experience of love.

At times Creeley appears to judge it honest and human to break the aesthetic frame and speak in his own person. He is right in one sense; as Marianne Moore wrote of poetry, "There are things important beyond all this fiddle." Still, "this fiddle" is precisely what poetry is, and it is one thing to replace one set of conventions with another, but an entirely different enterprise to assume—perhaps unwittingly—that conventions can ever be dropped. Creeley's least satisfactory prose work, *A Day Book*, suffers greatly because this distinction is overlooked. In all fairness, it must be acknowledged that there are readers who prize such works and passages above Creeley's others and are thrilled to find the poet reduced to such vulnerability. Yet these readers would probably not think very much of such raw confession emanating, word for word, from a less notable personage. They confuse gossip with art.

WORDS

By the mid-1960's, Creeley's reputation was secure. Two hugely popular poetry conferences, one at the University of British Columbia, the other at the University of California at Berkeley, had brought Creeley and his colleagues together with an audience of younger poets, professors, and counterculture enthusiasts, guaranteeing dissemination of their works and words. Creeley was being invited to read and speak in many distinguished venues in North America, Europe, and Asia; he had won Guggenheim and Rockefeller grants; his books were selling far beyond the usual for poetry. In 1967, *Words*, his first collection since *For Love*, appeared, earning for him further critical acclaim. Here the focus is less on domestic crises—at least explicitly—and more on the crisis in language. For a lyric poet who is attempting to close the gap between self and the person who utters the poem, to reduce authorial irony, and to abolish the fiction of the dramatic monologue, the contemporary disturbance in language, the growing unease concerning the gap between the word and the thing, must be a constant concern. In his poem "The Pattern," in *Words*, Creeley writes:

> As soon as
> I speak, I
> speaks. It
> wants to
> be free but
> impassive lies
> in the direction
> of its
> words.

Such is the difficulty that these stanzas verge on nonsense verse, not least because the line breaks enforce many alternate readings beyond what syntax states. One thing is clear, though: The poet (and perhaps the poem itself) speaks of being trapped in an identity for which the habits of a vocabulary and the rules of a language, with their host of associations, are not flexible enough to allow entry or exit. This quandary becomes increasingly the burden of Creeley's writing in the late 1960's and the 1970's.

PIECES AND A DAY BOOK

In the late 1960's the twin courses of Creeley's poetry and prose began to be combined, first in *Pieces* and next in *A Day Book*. The latter consists of entries for thirty days during the course of a year, together with poems written more or less during the same period.

Pieces consists of much briefer notebook jottings, many too short to be classified unequivocally as either poetry or prose. Among these are both prose passages and distinct poems, including "The Finger," one of the clearest embodiments of Creeley's thought. This poem speaks of the act of attention as paramount, certainly taking precedence over any plan, and it exemplifies its conclusions throughout, shifting from instance to instance as the poet recalls these.

Elsewhere in *Pieces* are many short registrations of event and thought, "quick takes," mental snapshots, the germs from which more conventional poems might have been built, had Creeley seen the point of such superstructure. At this time, however, he decided to avoid such conventions. The process of these pieces is as important as the product.

RANGE OF PROSE WORK

Creeley's innovative drive produced, in 1976, the work *Presences*, a series of prose texts written according to his preconceived system—permutations of 1, 2, 3, in a variety of sequences, a page to a number (for example, 2 = 2 pages). Within these restrictions, and rather obliquely addressing himself to the work of the sculptor Marisol, Creeley wrote an astonishing range of prose styles, from fairly conventional narrative to "cut-ups"—or pieces that read like cut-up material. The overall effect is to foreground the language—the means and the material of the writer's craft—even while delivering many of the familiar aspects of fiction and autobiography. Later, in 1984, when Calder & Boyars published Creeley's *The Collected Prose*, which included *The Island*, *The Gold Diggers*, and *Presences*, he included a newly written work, *Mabel*. Here too he writes according to permutations of 1, 2, 3. The range of style and tone is less than in *Presences*, and for much of the book the narrative means are quite straightforward; yet the conception is innovative—to write an autobiography by focusing on the women in his life, a life not so much fictionalized in this work as at times exaggerated and seen in the light of gender.

SO THERE: POEMS, 1976-1983

As his prose creations have continued to be innovative, Creeley's poetry in later years has tended to settle for the same verse conventions as at the outset, but without the torque whereby the statement plays against the line breaks. The lines in the later work tend to be more pedestrian, and the poems more a recording of something noted than a drama of assertion and denial. The medium, poetry, is more taken for granted, without the challenging and questioning of *Words* and *Pieces*. Creeley's world, too, has changed profoundly during the course of his career.

In bringing together the works of three volumes of poetry from the late 1970's and early 1980's (*Hello: A Journal, February 29-May 3, 1976*; *Later*; *Mirrors*), *So There: Poems, 1976-1983* calls attention to important changes in the poet's life: the end of one marriage, the beginning of another, the birth of a son, and the transition from middle age to life as, in Creeley's words, "a young old man." Readers can also discern changes in his poetry: a movement away from proto-language-writing and a movement toward the preoccupations that have come to characterize his later work, themes centered on the past, bleak reflections on the future and death, and affirmations of the present, despite losses past and still to come: "But now—/ but now the wonder of life is/ that it is at all."

Creeley calls forth the American language as he hears it in its varied forms, from the cheerful repetitions of pop music ("Hello"), to the poignance of familiar phrases— be happy, be good—when sounded as a final good-bye to his friend, Max Fienstein ("Oh Max"). "Later" returns to locations from the poet's boyhood while "Hello" captures the reader's interest for its unusual groupings of poems: the poems are organized by date and place yet offer few details of place. Instead, they tend to focus on the self in new and unfamiliar places—alone, apart, and occasionally confused. His experiences in travel bring to his mind a number of his present circumstances: decrepit houses in Singapore prompt him to muse on his own body's impermanence; the whir of a hotel air conditioner reminds him of the American Southwest. As he notes, "Same clock ticks/ in these different places."

LIFE AND DEATH

Creeley's poetry in the late 1990's showed a growing difference when compared to his earlier work. In *Life and Death*, for example, short, abstract poems find a place in the volume, as in collections past, but here they are balanced by longer sequences: "Histoire de Florida," "The Dogs of Auckland," "There," "Inside My Head," and the title poem itself. Critics have noted that here his poems, dealing with old age and the closure of life itself,

take up the problems of poetic closure and resistance to closure—a theme so central to Creeley's poetics—in ways that appear more flexible and wise than the attitude of his earlier work. He seems no longer absolutely committed to a poetics of indeterminacy but attempts to reconcile the open-ended process of writing with the recognition that consciousness eventually comes to an end. While death "will separate/ finally/ dancer from dance" and ends what was a continuing process, it also is a form of absolute openness: It means the dissolution of boundaries and embodiment altogether.

It is apt, then, that the themes of this book center on this binary of life and death, and the chasms and similarities between them: old age, the death of friends, the persistence of love and memory even when the known object disappears from the world. The long poem that opens the volume, "Histoire of Florida," uses a colorful palette in describing a Floridian landscape to render an image of old age as a sunny promontory from which to look back:

> Waking, think of sun through
> compacted tree branches,
> the dense
> persistent light.
>
> Think of heaven,
> home,
> a heart of gold,
> old song of friend's
>
> dear love and all
> the faint world it
> reaches to,
> it wants.

OTHER MAJOR WORKS

LONG FICTION: *The Island*, 1963.

SHORT FICTION: *The Gold Diggers*, 1954, 1965.

NONFICTION: *A Quick Graph*, 1970; *Presences*, 1976; *Charles Olson and Robert Creeley: The Complete Correspondence*, 1980-1996 (10 volumes); *Collected Essays*, 1983; *The Collected Prose*, 1984; *Day Book of a Virtual Poet*, 1998.

EDITED TEXTS: *The Mayan Letters*, 1953 (with Charles Olsen); *Selected Poems*, 1993 (by Olsen).

BIBLIOGRAPHY

Altieri, Charles. "Robert Creeley's Poetics of Conjecture: The Pains and Pleasures of Staging a Self at War with Its Own Lyric Desires." In *Self and Sensibility in Contemporary American Poetry*. Cambridge, England: Cambridge University Press, 1984. Brilliant discussion of a key element in Creeley's work: the struggle between representation and the *activity* of representing. The imperatives of this struggle, says Altieri, connect Creeley's poetry to the romantic attempt to create a language, a rhetoric, that can express "the opposition between thinking and thought."

_____. "The Struggle with Absence: Robert Creeley and W. S. Merwin." In *Enlarging the Temple*. Lewisburg, Pa.: Bucknell University Press, 1979. Altieri provides a useful discussion of Creeley's aesthetics of presence, an epistemological inquiry into the dialectics of presence and absence in his writings. "Creeley . . . is trying to resolve the dualisms of man and nature, subject and object, and embody their harmonious inter-relationships. . . . But [his] solution tends to be solipsistic."

Bernstein, Charles. "Hearing 'Here': Robert Creeley's Poetics of Duration." In *Content's Dream: Essays, 1975-1984*. Los Angeles: Sun & Moon Press, 1986. This essay features an approach, incorporating, without specific attribution, many phrases and sentences from Creeley's writing into Bernstein's arguments. Focuses on how language intervenes in any investigation—even or especially the investigation of the self conducted by Creeley. Qualifies Creeley's "heroic stance" in interesting ways.

Clark, Tom. *Robert Creeley and the Genius of the American Common Place: Together with the Poet's Own Autobiography*. New York: New Directions, 1993. A biography from the author's conversations with Creeley. Includes Creeley's "Autobiography," a talk he gave at New College of California in 1991, and photographs of Creeley and family and friends.

Ford, Arthur. *Robert Creeley*. Boston: Twayne, 1978. A journeyman account of the work up to 1976, with biographical linkages that give this book much of its utility. Strong on the notion of development from *For Love* through *Words* to *Pieces*. Attention is also given to the prose works. In poetry and prose alike, says Ford, Creeley is most concerned to give shape to "the moment."

Fredman, Stephen. "'A Life Tracking Itself': Robert Creeley's *Presences: A Text for Marisol*." In *Poet's Prose: The Crisis in American Verse*. Cambridge, England: Cambridge University Press, 1983. An excellent study of *Presences* in the larger context of the new form of prose poetry. Fredman remarks that Creeley views autobiography as a form of conjecture—in the poet's own words, "in and out of the system . . . of valuation, habit, complex organic data, the weather, and so on." Fredman thoroughly investigates the application of this idea in *Presences*, rendering both idea and text more accessible.

Rifkin, Libbie. *Career Moves: Olson, Creeley, Zukofsky, Berrigan, and the American Avant-Garde*. Madison: University of Wisconsin Press, 2000. A collective group portrait covering a significant amount of twentieth century literary and intellectual history. Rifkin investigates the career choices of writers and the development of the literary canon.

Von Hallberg, Robert. "Robert Creeley and John Ashbery: Systems." In *American Poetry and Culture, 1945-1980*. Cambridge, Mass.: Harvard University Press, 1985. Von Hallberg's piece is exceptionally interesting, illuminating Creeley's oeuvre from a striking perspective: that of the systemization of American thought and culture. In the period he examines significance has come to derive from the mediating systems, not from direct contact of the individual with the ultimate objects of reference. Von Hallberg notes that Creeley seeks out "the edges of convention, where a system is ill known . . . or under strain."

David Bromige,
updated by Sarah Hilbert

SOR JUANA INÉS DE LA CRUZ

Juana Inés de Asbaje y Ramírez de Santillana
Born: San Miguel Nepantla, Mexico; November, 1648 (baptized December 2, 1648)
Died: Mexico City, Mexico; April 17, 1695

PRINCIPAL POETRY

Inundación castálida, 1689

Segundo volumen de las obras, 1692 (the long poem "Primero sueño" translated as *First Dream*, 1983)

Fama y obras póstumas, 1700

The Sonnets of Sor Juana Ines de la Cruz in English Verse, 2001

OTHER LITERARY FORMS

Sor Juana Inés de la Cruz's most readable prose work, the *Respuesta de la poetisa a la muy ilustre Sor Filotea de la Cruz* (1700; reply of the poetess to the illustrious Sister Filotea de la Cruz), is an appealing autobiographical defense of her precocious interest in learning, an emotional plea for acceptance as a woman and a scholar, and an obsessive declaration of faith. Sor Juana tries to convince her superiors that, despite her lifelong curiosity about the material world, theological concerns are still the most important to her.

El divino Narciso, pr. c. 1680 (*The Divine Narcissus*, 1945), a religious one-act play, is a tasteful and imaginative treatment of divine love in which Narcissus, as a figure of Christ, falls in love with human nature as a reflection of himself. With this short play, the fantasy of desire which takes so many forms throughout Sor Juana's work finds its ultimate synthesis of eros and agape.

ACHIEVEMENTS

Sor Juana Inés de la Cruz was a Mexican literary virtuoso who was called the "tenth muse" during her lifetime and who is generally considered the most important writer of colonial Spanish America. Although she wrote more than four hundred poems, twenty-three short plays, two full-length *comedias*, and various prose works, Sor Juana's reputation rests on a handful of poems (about two dozen in all), *El divino Narciso*, and *Respuesta de la poetisa a la muy ilustre Sor Filotea de la Cruz*. Although a reassessment of her works begun in the 1950's promises a more extensive list of her most important writings, it is likely that, with the exception of her extremely complex "Primero sueño" (*First Dream*, 1983), the few pieces which earned her the admiration of Marcelino Menendez y Pelayo one hundred years ago will continue to be the ones that will assure her a place of prominence in Spanish letters.

Sor Juana Inés de la Cruz (Library of Congress)

At her best, Sor Juana was able to manipulate the often unwieldy and intricate language of the Spanish Baroque, with its rich heritage from the Golden Age, into expressions of delicate, feminine vision and sensibility. Her aesthetic documentation of the search for knowledge, love, and God is the most complete personal and artistic record of any figure from the colonial period. Sor Juana's love poetry appears to reflect frustrating and painful experiences prior to her entry into the convent at about the age of seventeen. Few of the poems are concerned with fulfillment or the intimate communication of personal feelings; most are, instead, variations on the themes of ambivalence and disillusionment in love. Sor Juana's philosophical poems are linked to her amatory verse by a sense of disenchantment. An exception to her general pessimism is *First Dream*, in which the poet takes delight in depicting the joys and dangers of her intellectual explorations. More of Sor Juana's writings bear witness to her theological concerns. Although some of her religious lyrics express the same kind of anguish about God's love that she expressed about human love, she clearly attempted in her *villancicos* to use her poetic talent in the service of the Church.

BIOGRAPHY

Juana Inés de Asbaje y Ramírez de Santillana was born in November, 1648, in San Miguel Nepantla, some sixty kilometers southeast of Mexico City. She was the illegitimate child of a Spanish captain and a Creole mother. In the charming *Respuesta de la poetisa a la muy ilustre Sor Filotea de la Cruz*, she tells how she learned to read at the age of three, and tagged along with one of her sisters to La Amiga, an elementary school, where she took her first formal lessons. She says that, at the age of eight, she begged her mother to let her cut her hair and dress like a boy so she could attend the university. That being denied her, she continued her self-education by reading the classics she found in her grandmother's house. Around 1659, she was allowed to go to Mexico City and live with the family of one of her aunts. Although not enrolled in the university, Juana privately continued her studies, which included twenty lessons in Latin. Twenty was apparently sufficient, for subsequently she was able to write Latin poetry as well as anyone in the viceroyalty.

By 1664, Sor Juana was a member of the viceregal court and was the darling of the vicereine. She so impressed the viceroy, the Marques de Mancera, with her knowledge, that he arranged for forty professors from the university to give her tests. Sor Juana passed them all, amazing the local elite. Her several years of court life must have been intense, emotional years. She was a beautiful woman and was doubtless wooed by gentlemen of some wealth and position. Nevertheless, by 1669, she had entered the convent and had taken religious vows, as much from aversion to marriage as from attraction to the celibate life. It was her desire to be free to learn, she states in the *Respuesta de la poetisa a la muy ilustre Sor Filotea de la Cruz*, that was the primary motivation for her vocation.

For the next twenty-three years, Sor Juana was the major literary figure in colonial Spanish America, composing everything from love sonnets to a treatise on music, almost all her writing being done on request from high-ranking officials of the Church or the state. She wrote elaborate pieces for performance at liturgical functions, occasional verse for political events, and scenarios and scripts for afternoons of royal entertainment. Not long after the brilliant defense of her studies in *Respuesta de la poetisa a la muy ilustre Sor Filotea de la Cruz*, and at the height of her career, when her collected works were beginning to be published and acclaimed in Spain, pressures by her religious superiors induced her to give away her library of more than four thousand volumes and all her scientific and musical instruments, and to abandon her writing altogether. Several years later, on April 17, 1695, she died in an epidemic that swept Mexico City.

ANALYSIS

Although most of the compositions have merit, the lyric poems, in the order of their treatment here, are usually considered to be the best, and they may be used as a point of departure for delineating a canon of Sor Juana Inés de la Cruz's most significant writings.

Sor Juana Inés de la Cruz was a deeply passionate and intelligent woman who dedicated her life to knowledge and spiritual perfection. On the one hand, she seems to have renounced love for intellectual freedom, and from her amatory and philosophical writings, it appears that her renunciation of the world, along with her commitment to learning, paradoxically caused an obsession with intimacy and a profound disillusionment with any reality except that of spiritual intimacy. On the other hand, judging from her other prose and verse, Sor Juana was also a writer engaged with her society, closely involved with its institutions and its native culture. An anthology of Sor Juana's most popular compositions may slight this more social side of her personality, but it is important to remember as one reviews her major poems of love and disillusionment that the poetess wrote more concerning religion than about any real or imaginary love and that she was as adept at elaborate versification about current events and visitors to the viceroyalty as at revealing her most private feelings. It is not difficult to dwell on the more romantic side of the "tenth muse," to use certain of her poems to enhance the image of a jilted, precocious, disenchanted teenage intellectual sequestering herself in a convent and spending her life in extremely elaborate sublimation. Her most famous pieces contribute to such an image, but as the reader is exposed to a wider spectrum of her talents, a more balanced picture emerges; a trajectory of maturation becomes visible in which Catholicism and the Baroque are means to the self-fulfillment and self-expression originally thwarted in her youth by her lack of social position and her fascination with scholarship.

"ESTA TARDE, MI BIEN"

If one reads Sor Juana's writings to observe a progression from human to divine love, it is appropriate to begin with the sonnet "Esta tarde, mi bien" (this afternoon, my love). The poem is one of the few in which she relates a moving encounter with another person, and it contrasts the impotency of words with the efficacy of tears in the communication of love. Here, there is none of the love-hate dialectic which colors most of her amatory poems; instead, one finds the description of a delicately feminine, sensitive, and formidably talented personality in a moment of unguarded abandon. It is only a slight exaggeration to say that after "Esta tarde, mi bien," one sees in Sor Juana's verse the psychological effects of an unhappy affair rather than the experience of love itself. Even the tender *lira* "Amado dueño mio" (my beloved master), while documenting in a poetic sense the dimensions of intimacy, is a conventional lament of the lover separated from the beloved. The lover, like a Renaissance shepherdess, tells her misfortunes to the wind, which carries her complaints, her passion, and her sadness to the distant partner. Alfonso Méndez Plancarte states that the poem contains some of Sor Juana's finest lines and that it may surpass the eclogues of Garcilaso de la Vega. The comparison with Garcilaso is appropriate, and poetry in his likeness is fitting to express the absence of consummation rather than its presence; significantly, the *lira* keynotes a thematic transformation from completion to emptiness.

EXPLORATION OF PASSION

The sonnet "Detente, sombra de mi bien esquivo" (stay, shadow of my scornful love) can be considered an introduction to a series of poems which admit both the positive and negative effects of passion as well as the inconclusive status of unconsummated love. In "Detente, sombra de mi bien esquivo," the beloved himself eludes the poet, but his image cannot escape the prison of her fantasy. Important in this and the poems under discussion below is the counterpoint of conceits and emotions about the love "por quien alegre muero" (for whom I would happily die) but also "por quien penosa vivo" (for whom I live in agony), which develops to

an extreme in the sonnet "Al que Ingrato me deja, busco amante" (I seek the one who spurns me) and "Que no me quiera Fabio, al verse amado" (that Fabio does not love me as I love him), and the *redondilla* "Este amoroso tormento" (this torment of love). In the latter piece, as in the other poems of this group, the poet never finds fulfillment, "porque, entre alivio y dolar, hallo culpa en el amor y disculpa en el olvido" (because between relief and pain, I find blame in love and exoneration in forgetfulness).

Beyond frustration and the love-hate duality which the poet attributes to romantic feeling lie disillusionment and bitterness. The sonnets "Silvio, yo te aborezco" (I hate you, Silvio), "Amor empieza por desasosiego" (love begins uneasily), and "Con el dolor de la mortal herida" (with the pain of a mortal wound) are among Sor Juana's strongest denunciations of the men she once might have loved, as well as of herself for having given in to loving them: "no solo a tí, corrida, te aborrezco,/ pero a mí por el tiempo que te quise" (not only do I abhor you/ but myself for the time that I loved you). Here the bittersweet of "Este amoroso tormento" turns to anger. The image of the lover purposely retained in "Detente, sombra de mi bien esquivo" is repeatedly banished, and it is a logical movement from such rejection to the *sátira filosófica*, "Hombres necios" (foolish men), one of Sor Juana's more popular denunciations of men as the source of all women's problems. In these feminist *redondillas*, the poet exposes the ways in which men "acusan lo que causan" (blame us for the things they cause). Why, she asks, do men want women to be good if they tempt them to be bad? Who, she questions, is the greater sinner, "la que peca por la paga o el que paga por pecar" (she who sins for pay or he who pays for sin)?

Since Sor Juana's poems are not usually dated, there is no way of knowing whether the progression from the delicate, loving "Esta tarde, mi bien" to the sarcastic "Hombres necios" reflects the sequential effects of an increasingly unhappy situation. In any case, these poems of erotic experience do fit a pattern which begins with brief reciprocal affection and degenerates into ambivalence, then finally into contempt. There are, at the same time, a great number of poems written to women which do not fit this generalization. Sor Juana apparently had very meaningful relationships with the wives of two of the Mexican viceroys, and her many verses to Lysi show a far more consistent emotional response than that depicted in poems of male-female interaction. Certainly the Lysi poems, perhaps especially the ornate "Lámina sirva el cielo al retrato" (the sky is lamina of your portrait), are a moving contrast to her more widely read poems' heterosexual canon.

PHILOSOPHIC POEMS

Sor Juana's philosophic poems complement her negative attitude toward worldly love. "Verde embeleso de la vida humana" (green charm of human life) rejects illusions and hope as deceptive: "solamente lo que toco veo" (I only see what I can touch). It represents the repression of vain dreams, the acceptance of life without romance or even platonic fantasy. "Diuturna enfermedad de la Esperanza" (lasting infirmity of hope) reiterates this concept, and "Este que ves, engaño colorido" (this painted lie you see), a sonnet on her portrait, is an intense affirmation of the Catholic view that the flesh is "polvo, es sombra, es nada" (is dust, is a shadow, is nothing). Her "Rosa divina" (divine rose) is a variation on the universal theme of the brevity of beauty and life. Perhaps her most powerful renunciation is "Finjamos que soy feliz" (pretend that I am happy), in which she denies the validity of knowledge and maintains that because man can know nothing for certain, ignorance is preferable to imperfect knowing: "aprendamos a ignorar" (let us learn to not know). This poem is a moment of despair within the context of Sor Juana's self-confessed lifelong passion, the pursuit of knowledge. Her monumental *First Dream*, the only work which she admitted to writing for her own pleasure and not to please someone else, is far more balanced in presenting her attitude toward learning.

"PRIMERO SUEÑO"

The "Primero sueño," which is among the best philosophic poems in Spanish, is the height of Sor Juana's exploration of the Baroque. The poem begins with a description of nightfall, in which the entire physical world eventually succumbs to sleep. The human spirit, freed from the constraint of the body, soars upward to find a perspective from which it can comprehend the immensity of the universe. Once it glimpses the overpowering dimensions of creation, the soul retreats to the shadows.

Finding a mental shore on the sea of knowledge, it decides to approach the challenge of learning by dividing things into categories and mastering each division separately. In spite of doubts that the mind can really know anything, echoes of the dark vision of "Finjamos que soy feliz," the soul continues its search for truth. Dawn arrives, however, and the dream ends inconclusively. Universal knowledge has eluded the soul, but the dreamer has not despaired.

Once considered to be on the fringe of literature because of its purposeful Gongorism, "Primero sueño" is enjoying the positive reconsideration accorded the entire Spanish Baroque, in the course of which Luis de Góngora y Argote himself has been reinstated into the canon of major Spanish poets. Accepting the style of this poem as not only valid but also essential to its meaning, one can better appreciate Sor Juana's most mature and complex statement about the human condition. It is the culmination of a lifetime of study and reflection.

SACRED BALLADS

Sor Juana's religious writings include several "sacred ballads," among which "Amante dulce del alma" (sweet love of my soul), "Mientras la Gracia me exita" (while Grace moves me), and "Traigo conmigo un cuidado" (I have a deep concern) are generally held in high regard. All three attempt to express the effects of divine love. "Amante dulce del alma" asks why Christ might have willed to visit the poet in Holy Communion: Has he decided to be present from love or from jealousy? She decides for the former, reflecting that since God knows all things, he can see into her heart and has no reason to be jealous. "Mientras la Gracia me exita" tries to clarify some of the feelings involved in the inner struggle between "la virtud y la costumbre" (virtue and habit). Like "Amante dulce del alma," this is a poem of scruples rather than a meditation of universal religious significance. "Traigo conmigo un cuidado" carries the analysis of spiritual love further and contrasts it with the poet's experience of human love. "La misma muerte que vivo, es la vida con que muero" (the same death that I live is the life in which I die), she writes at the end of the poem, attempting to sum up her contradictory mental state. Even though it is divine love which causes her to feel the way she does, there are parallels between the contrarias penas (contradictory anxieties) of "Este amoroso tormento" and those expressed in "Traigo conmigo un cuidado."

It is more fruitful to look for a developed sense of religious experience in Sor Juana's *villancicos* and her play *El divino Narciso* than in her personal religious lyrics. Although these works have generally been neglected, scholar Alfonso Méndez Plancarte and others have made convincing defenses of their genres as well as of the verse itself. *El divino Narciso* contains some of Sor Juana's best writing, and, with the *loa* (or one-act play) which precedes it, shows how she introduced local themes into her work. The most significant element of the play, however, is the successful depiction of divine love, sufficiently anthropomorphized to give it comprehensible human beauty. Here is also the full evolution of a spiritual maturity which finally quiets the older, worldly concerns.

OTHER MAJOR WORKS

PLAY: *Amor es más laberinto*, wr. 1668, pr. 1689 (with Juan de Guevara); *El divino Narciso*, pr. c. 1680 (*The Divine Narcissus*, 1945); *Los empeños de una casa*, pr. c. 1680 (based on Lope de Vega Carpio's play *La discreta enamorada*; *A Household Plagued by Love*, 1942); *El mártir del Sacramento, San Hermenegildo*, pr. c. 1692; *El cetro de José*, pb. 1692; *The Three Secular Plays of Sor Juana Inés de la Cruz*, 2000.

NONFICTION: *Respuesta de la poetisa a la muy ilustre Sor Filotea de la Cruz*, 1700.

MISCELLANEOUS: *Obras completas de Sor Juana Inés de la Cruz*, 1951-1957 (4 volumes: I, *Lírica personal*, poetry; II, *Villancicos y letras sacras*, poetry; III, *Autos y loas*, drama; IV, *Comedias sainetes y prosa*, drama and prose; Méndez Plancarte, ed.); *A Sor Juana Anthology*, 1988.

BIBLIOGRAPHY

Flynn, Gerard. *Sor Juana Ines de la Cruz*. New York: Twayne, 1971. A concise work of criticism that serves to introduce the reader to Sor Juana. One chapter emphasizes her biography, the other chapters her poetry and theater. Presents Sor Juana as a woman of strong philosophical bent who wrote some of the best lyrical and dramatic poetry of colonial Latin America.

McKenna, Susan M. "Rational Thought and Female Poetics in Sor Juana's 'Primero sueno.'" *Hispanic Review* 68, no. 1 (Winter, 2000): 37-42. Clear and informative scholarly article includes detailed analysis of the imagery in "Primero sueno," Sor Juana's major work. Explains the rational and scientific influences of René Descartes on Sor Juana's thought, and how she veiled these influences in metaphor to elude, for a time, the censure of conservative church authorities.

Merrim, Stephanie. *Early Modern Women's Writing and Sor Juana Inés de la Cruz*. Nashville, Tenn.: Vanderbilt University Press, 1999. Situates the work of Sor Juana within the field of seventeenth century women's writing in Spanish, English, and French. The protofeminist writings of Sor Juana are used as a benchmark for the examination of the literary production of her female contemporaries. Includes bibliographical references and index.

_____, ed. *Feminist Perspectives on Sor Juana Ines de la Cruz*. Detroit: Wayne State University Press, 1991. A collection of essays by important literary critics and translators of Sor Juana. Discusses her life, time, and work in the context of feminist criticism.

Paz, Octavio. *Sor Juana: Or, The Traps of Faith*. Cambridge, Mass.: The Belknap Press of Harvard University Press, 1988. A definitive work on Sor Juana. Dense and scholarly study of the age in which she lived and consideration of her life and works. A blend of history, biography, and literary criticism.

Pedén, Margaret Sayers, trans. *A Woman of Genius: The Intellectual Autobiography of Sor Juana Inés de la Cruz*. Salisbury, Conn.: Lime Rock Press, 1982. One of the premier translators from Spanish renders Sor Juana's memoirs in English.

William L. Felker;
bibliography updated by Susan Butterworth

VICTOR HERNÁNDEZ CRUZ

Born: Aguas Buenas, Puerto Rico; February 6, 1949

PRINCIPAL POETRY

Papo Got His Gun! and Other Poems, 1966
Snaps, 1969
Mainland, 1973
Tropicalization, 1976
By Lingual Wholes, 1982
Rhythm, Content, and Flavor, 1988
Red Beans: Poems, 1991
Panoramas, 1997
Maraca: New and Selected Poems, 1965-2000, 2001

OTHER LITERARY FORMS

Victor Hernández Cruz wrote about poetry in an early pamphlet, *Doing Poetry* (1970). In *Stuff: A Collection of Poems, Visions and Imaginative Happenings from Young Writers in Schools--Opened and Closed* (1970), coedited with Herbert Kohl, he offers a gathering of young writers' poems which outline his fundamental commitment to poetry and poetic expression, as well as his dedication to teaching. With Leroy Quintana and Virgil Suarez, Cruz edited *Paper Dance: Fifty-five Latino Poets* (1995). This was the first anthology of Latino poets from diverse origins: Cuba, Colombia, Dominican Republic, Ecuador, Guatemala, Puerto Rico, and Mexico.

In addition to short fiction, Cruz has written the unpublished novels "Rhythm Section/Part One" and "Time Zones," both of which explore the migration and musical themes of his poetry. Excerpts from the former appear in Maria Theresa Babin's *Borinquen: An Anthology of Puerto Rican Literature* (1974). In four of his major poetry collections, Cruz has included prose works that offer insights into his life and aesthetics. He has also published articles in various journals, including *The New York Review of Books*, *Ramparts*, *Evergreen Review*, and *The Village Voice*.

ACHIEVEMENTS

In New York, Victor Hernández Cruz edited *Umbra* magazine from 1967 to 1969 and was cofounder of the East Harlem Gut Theater. In 1970, he was invited to be a guest lecturer at the University of California at Berkeley and then served in the ethnic studies department of San Francisco State College from 1971 to 1972. He worked with the San Francisco Art Commission (1976) and the Mission Neighborhood Center (1981). With novelist Ishmael Reed, he formed the Before Columbus Foundation.

He served as a visiting professor at the University of California at San Diego (1993), and at the University of Michigan, Ann Arbor (1994). In 1974, he was given the Creative Arts Public Service Award, and in April, 1981, *Life* magazine featured Cruz in its celebration of twelve North American poets. He also earned a National Endowment for the Arts creative writing award (1989) and a John Simon Guggenheim Memorial Foundation Fellowship (1991). Cultural critic Bill Moyers interviewed Cruz for an eight-part Public Broadcasting Service series, *The Language of Life*, which aired June 23 to July 28, 1995. This program was subsequently released in book and audiocassette formats.

His legendary ability to give dynamic poetry readings has twice made him World Heavyweight Poetry Champion in Taos, New Mexico. He has also participated in discussions and readings sponsored by La Fundación Federico García Lorca and at the Universidad de Alcalá.

BIOGRAPHY

Victor Hernández Cruz was born in Aguas Buenas, Puerto Rico, a small town about twenty miles from San Juan. The streets were unpaved, but he absorbed the native song and poetry as well as the poetic declamations of his grandfather and uncle. His family migrated to New York in 1954 and settled in the tenements of the Lower East Side of Manhattan. He attended Benjamin Franklin High School and began to write verse. At sixteen, he composed his first collection of poetry, *Papo Got His Gun! and Other Poems*. Cruz and his friends duplicated and distributed five hundred copies to local bookstores.

In 1967, the *Evergreen Review* helped launch his career when it featured several of these poems. Thus, while still in high school, he became a published poet. In 1969, he released his second collection of poems, *Snaps*, and gained national attention. In the 1960's, his neighborhood had become a center of intellectual and social ferment as part of the Civil Rights movement. Beat poetry, protest poetry, feminist poetry mixed with political activism and music to form the social milieu. Ishmael Reed, Allen Ginsberg, and LeRoi Jones (Amiri Baraka) were major influences, and Cruz was intrigued by the developing Nuyorican (New York/Puerto Rican) poetry movement, which often claims him.

In 1969, he moved to Berkeley, California, to become poet in residence at the University of California. In 1973, he published a third collection of poems, *Mainland*, which chronicles his migrations from New York to California and back again. In *Tropicalization*, Cruz expands his Caribbean and Spanish sensibility. His next work, *By Lingual Wholes*, includes some poems printed in both Spanish and English, for in San Francisco he found many Latino artists who helped him develop from North American poet into a poet for both English- and Spanish-speaking people.

After the publication of *Rhythm, Content, and Flavor*, Cruz moved back to Aguas Buenas, where he was born. He came into close contact with the local oral traditions and was deeply affected by them. In 1991, he recorded these sensations in *Red Beans*, and next he began working on a book of poems in Spanish. *Panoramas* provides a sensuous blend of Puerto Rico's Taino, Spanish, and African legacies in fantastic imagery which illuminates the Caribbean culture for the world. In 2001, Cruz published *Maraca*, a collection of new and selected poems spanning the years 1965 to 2000. Although he continues to travel, performing his poems from Madrid to San Francisco, he is the only well-known Puerto Rican poet writing in English who chose to return to live on the island of his birth.

ANALYSIS

Victor Hernández Cruz was the first of the Puerto Rican poets writing in the English language to reach a broad American audience. However, rather than labeling him an English-language poet, it is more accurate to view him as a bilingual or a multilingual writer. Cruz enjoys his native language, with its Arabian and African words and its unique rhythms and patterns. His poetry incorporates many strains: his family's vital oral tradition, traditional Spanish, New York-Puerto Rican slang, and black English. He discovered various "Englishes," and was intrigued by fellow writers, such as Polish author Joseph Conrad, who wrote in English as a second language.

SNAPS

After the early success of *Papo Got His Gun! and Other Poems*, a chapbook which had gained notice in *Evergreen Review*, Random House published *Snaps*. This collection's hip, barrio voice, its jazzy rhythms, and its snapshot technique of realistically portraying street life bought Cruz immediate recognition. Random House honored his irreverence for grammar and formalities of style and thus helped launch the young poet's ongoing fascination with the relationship of sound and sense, of language and life.

The poems capture the true essence of urban ghetto life. Clacking subways, dance clubs, smoking, girl-watching, and knife fights form the gritty realities of street life. The rapid staccato of half-learned English enriches the poems. Cruz's language here is the sub-language used to present Spanish Harlem's subculture. His speaker in these primarily narrative poems uses street slang as well as surrealistic humor to create a vivid picture of the danger and energy of the culturally diverse Lower East Side. There is constant movement: on subways, uptown, downtown, inside, outside, walking, driving. In "Megalopolis," the speaker presents snapshots from the window of a car moving through the urban sprawl of the East Coast:

> let those lights & trees & rocks
> talk/ going by / go by   just sit
> back/ we / we go into towns/   sailing the
> east coast / westside drive   far-off
> buildings look like castles / the kind
> dracula flies out of / new england of houses

The poem goes on to end with quick vignettes of a poet inciting riot, urban bombs, "laurence welk-reader's digest ladies" with bouffant hairdos secured with hair spray, billboards "singing lies," and "the night of the buildings/ . . . singing magic words/ of our ancestors." This ending points to another aspect of Cruz's poetry: traveling through time as well as space.

MAINLAND

Mainland records Cruz's poetic migration across the United States. The motion/mobility theme of *Snaps* here moves from intracity travel to interstate and, finally, to international migrations. The collection begins in New York, traverses the Midwest to California and the Southwest, and ends with a visit to Puerto Rico, followed by the return to New York.

These poems show the power of the memory of the Caribbean—its music and dance, its food, language, people, and culture—all working to recenter the poet once he returns to the realities of New York urban life. "The Man Who Came to the Last Floor," which ends the collection, employs surrealistic humor. A Puerto Rican immigrant with a bag of tropical seeds arrives in New York and rents a sixth floor apartment. Singing and dancing in his apartment, he accidentally flings the seeds of tropical fruits from his window.

> A policeman was walking down the avenue
> and all of a sudden took off his hat
> A mango seed landed nicely into his
> curly hair

The policeman does not notice the seed, which then grows into a flourishing five-foot tree which bears a mango. With this surreal image, Cruz presents the subtle, almost subversive, "tropicalization" accomplished by immigrants as they plant seeds to revitalize the northern urban landscape.

TROPICALIZATION

In an increasingly lyrical vein, Cruz collects in *Tropicalization* the images and rhythms of the Caribbean in poetry and prose poems. This collection presents a renewed vision of the United States, tropicalized, surrealistically transformed by the beat of its Hispanic population. Here Cruz uses more experimental structures to capture the spiritual side of barrio life, and he also enlarges upon the blending of Spanish and English ("Spanglish," or code-switching), always a characteristic of his work. He handles English as an amalgam capable of easily incorporating new words and innovative syntaxes.

In "Side 24," he cheerfully juxtaposes English and Spanish, cement and tropical oranges (*chinas*):

> Walk el cement
> Where las chinas roll
> Illuminating my path
> Through old streets

As part of the "ethnic" avant-garde, Cruz does not regard his Puerto Rican home with anger or despair, as Abraham Rodriguez does, nor does he look back with sadness, as does Judith Ortiz Cofer. He cheerfully delights in his ethnic identity, which he sees as tropicalizing the North, as bringing oranges and salsa to the cement and the chill of the United States.

BY LINGUAL WHOLES

Continuing his themes of contrasting and merging the sounds of two cultures and languages, Cruz again includes both poetry and prose in his 1982 *By Lingual Wholes*. This collection is slower paced and more pensive than the earlier works; again, music, dance, and Spanglish coalesce in a dynamic and positive expression of multiculturalism. Cruz removes barriers of culture and language, illustrating the wholeness possible in living in and creating from two cultures and languages.

The title suggests the wordplay that will follow as Cruz proves himself a master of pun, whimsy, paradox, and concrete poetry. In addition, these poems explore a deeper heritage of Puerto Rican folklore and myth, as well as a whole range of historical events and characters. Never didactic, Cruz invites the reader to participate in genial handshakes across cultures.

In the sixth poem of the collection, "Listening to the Music of Arsenio Rodriguez Is Moving Closer to Knowledge," Cruz plays tribute to the blind African-Cuban musician and composer. In New York, the Caribbean community enjoyed this music under the label "salsa." The speaker raves about salsa's power and gaily ridicules researchers who attempt to study it and "understand" it. They totally miss the dance music's intrinsic warmth and tropical passion, which is to be experienced and absorbed, not analyzed and understood.

RHYTHM, CONTENT, AND FLAVOR

In his collection, *Rhythm, Content, and Flavor*, Cruz selects poems from his earlier works and adds a new work, "Islandis: The Age of Seashells." Here he continues to interweave images of the urban and natural worlds. Also the poet reaffirms his Puerto Rican culture as the source of music and knowledge. Like lost Atlantis, with its tropical breezes and its kinship with the ocean, Puerto Rico creates a music reminiscent of the medieval "music of the spheres." As he also notes elsewhere, poetry for Cruz is "la salsa de Dios"; God is the origin of all poetry and music, and poetry is the music of God.

RED BEANS

Red Beans contains poems, prose essays, and a manifesto on poetry. The "red" of the title is the color of beans, shirts, earth, the Red Sea, "Red pepper/ In a stew," all representing the vitality and urgency Cruz finds in the "red beings," his Puerto Rican ancestors. He also draws on his earliest memories of hearing English in "Snaps of Immigration": "At first English was nothing/ but sound/ Like trumpets doing yakity yak." Later, the sound of poetic language is celebrated in "An Essay on Williams Carlos Williams":

> I love the quality of the
> spoken thought
> As it happens immediately
> uttered into the air
> Not held inside and rolled
> around for some properly
> schemed moment

Cruz continues to emphasize the naturalness, the oral spontaneity of true poetry. "Corsica" adds a focus on the joyful interplay of cultures and languages which had always been a theme in Cruz's poetry. He announces that Puerto Rico and Corsica are "holding hands" underneath the "geologic plates," that both islands see the same moon. Never narrowly ethnic, Cruz celebrates the creative merger of culture and language. He ends this volume showing his receptivity to other cultures:

> I wait with a gourd full
> of inspiration
> For a chip to fall from
> The festival fireworks
> To favor me
> And set me on fire.

PANORAMAS

The poems and essays of *Panoramas* present a civilized and gracious tone as they transport the reader to the magic world of the Caribbean, which celebrates its blend of Taino, African, and Spanish legacies. They also illuminate Latin American/Caribbean culture in the United States and beyond. Rather than conflict, Cruz suggests a harmonious merger and a creative synthesis of disparate ideas and people.

OTHER MAJOR WORKS

NONFICTION: *Doing Poetry*, 1970.

EDITED TEXTS: *Stuff: A Collection of Poems, Visions and Imaginative Happenings from Young Writers in Schools—Opened and Closed*, 1970 (with Herbert Kohl); *Paper Dance: Fifty-five Latino Poets*, 1995 (with Virgil Suarez and Leroy V. Quintana).

BIBLIOGRAPHY

Aparicio, Frances R. "'Salsa,' 'Maracas,' and 'Baile': Latin Popular Music in the Poetry of Victor Hernández Cruz." MELUS 16 (Spring, 1989-1990): 43-58. Explores and delineates the sound, beat, and rhythm of popular Latin American music in Cruz's poetry; also shows how this music tropicalizes American culture and gives a sense of cohesion and identity to immigrants.

Cruz, Victor Hernández. "Victor Hernández Cruz." Interview by Bill Moyers. In *The Language of Life: A Festival of Poets*. New York: Doubleday, 1995. In an interview with the poet, Moyers examines the blend of cultures that have influenced Cruz's poetry; also outlines the poet's rural roots and his absorption of bolero and salsa musical rhythms.

Kanellos, Nicolás. *Victor Hernández Cruz and La Salsa de Dios*. Milwaukee: University of Wisconsin, 1979. Focuses on the essentially Puerto Rican side of Cruz's poetry with special emphasis on the African-Caribbean strains of salsa, whose origins Cruz locates in Africa and the pre-Columbian West Indies.

Torrens, James. "U.S. Latino Writers: The Searchers." *America* 167 (July 18-25, 1992). Takes a sociological and psychological approach, noting that Cruz writes of numbing poverty and of the immigrant's struggle for dignity; he also explores the immigrant writer's need to belong to a group.

Waisman, Sergio Gabriel. "The Body as Migration." *Bilingual Review* 19 (May 1, 1944): 188-192. Explores Cruz's understanding of the three influences in Puerto

Rican culture: indigenous (Taino), Spanish (including that of Arabs, Gypsies, and Jews), and African (especially that of the Yorubas). Also examines his use of wordplay, metaphor, and synaesthesia. The primary focus here is on *Red Beans*.

Marie J. K. Brenner

COUNTÉE CULLEN

Born: New York, New York; May 30, 1903
Died: New York, New York; January 9, 1946

PRINCIPAL POETRY
Color, 1925
Copper Sun, 1927
The Ballad of the Brown Girl: An Old Ballad Retold, 1927
The Black Christ and Other Poems, 1929
The Medea, and Some Poems, 1935
On These I Stand: An Anthology of the Best Poems of Countée Cullen, 1947

OTHER LITERARY FORMS

Countée Cullen wrote nearly as much prose as he did poetry. While serving from 1926 through most of 1928 as literary editor of *Opportunity*, a magazine vehicle for the National Urban League, Cullen wrote several articles, including book reviews, and a series of topical essays for a column called "The Dark Tower" about figures and events involved in the Harlem Renaissance. He also wrote many stories for children, most of which are collected in *My Lives and How I Lost Them* (1942), the "autobiography" of Cullen's own pet, Christopher Cat, who had allegedly reached his ninth life. Earlier, in 1932, the poet had tried his hand at a novel, publishing it as *One Way to Heaven* (1932). In addition to articles, reviews, stories, and a novel, the poet translated or collaborated in the writing of three plays, one of them being a musical. In 1935, Cullen translated Euripides' *Medea* for the volume by the same name; in 1942, Virgil Thomson set to music the seven verse choruses from Cullen's translation. With Owen Dodson, Cullen wrote

the one-act play *The Third Fourth of July*, which appeared posthumously in 1946. The musical was produced at the Martin Beck Theater on Broadway, where it ran for 113 performances; this production also introduced Pearl Bailey as the character Butterfly.

ACHIEVEMENTS

Countée Cullen's literary accomplishments were many. While he was a student at DeWitt Clinton High School, New York City, he published his first poems and made numerous and regular contributions to the high school literary magazine. From DeWitt, whose other distinguished graduates include Lionel Trilling and James Baldwin, Cullen went to New York University. There he distinguished himself by becoming a member of Phi Beta Kappa and in the same year, 1925, by publishing *Color*, his first collection of poems. In June, 1926, the poet took his second degree, an M.A. in English literature from Harvard University. In December,

Countée Cullen in Central Park, New York. (Library of Congress)

1926, *Color* was awarded the first Harmon Gold Award for literature, which carried with it a cash award of five hundred dollars. Just before publication in 1927 of his second book, *Copper Sun*, Cullen received a Guggenheim Fellowship for a year's study and writing in France. While in France, he worked on improving his French conversation by engaging a private tutor and his knowledge of French literature by enrolling in courses at the Sorbonne. Out of this experience came *The Black Christ and Other Poems*. In 1944, the poet was offered the chair of creative literature at Nashville's Fisk University, but he refused in order to continue his teaching at the Frederick Douglass Junior High in New York City.

BIOGRAPHY

Despite his several trips abroad, Countée Porter Cullen lived most of his life in New York City, spending his childhood years with his grandmother. When he reached adolescence, he was adopted by the Reverend and Mrs. Frederick A. Cullen; Reverend Cullen was minister of the Salem Methodist Episcopal Church of Harlem. The years spent with the Cullens in the Methodist parsonage made a lasting impression on the young poet; although he experienced periods of intense self-questioning, Cullen appears never to have discarded his belief in Christianity.

During his undergraduate years at New York University, the young poet became heavily involved with figures of the Harlem Renaissance; among these Harlem literati were Zora Neale Hurston, Langston Hughes, Carl Van Vechten (a white writer who treated black themes), and Wallace Thurman. After the appearance of *Color* in 1925 and the receipt of his Harvard M.A. in June, 1926, Cullen assumed the position of literary editor of *Opportunity*. At the end of October, 1926, he wrote one of the most important of his "Dark Tower" essays about the appearance of that great treasure of the Harlem Renaissance, the short-lived but first black literary and art quarterly *Fire* (issued only once). He contributed one of his best poems, "From the Dark Tower," to *Fire*. About the solitary issue, Cullen wrote that it held great significance for black American culture, because it represented "a brave and beautiful attempt to meet our need for an all-literary and artistic medium of expression."

On April 10, 1928, Cullen married Nina Yolande Du Bois, daughter of one of the most powerful figures of twentieth century black American culture, W. E. B. Du Bois; the two were married at Salem Methodist Episcopal Church. This star-crossed union proved to be of short duration, however; while Cullen was in Paris on his Guggenheim Fellowship, Yolande was granted a decree of divorce. The marriage had not lasted two years. Much of Cullen's poetry deals with disappointment in love, and one senses that the poet was himself often disappointed in such matters.

In 1940, however, after Cullen had taught for several years at the Frederick Douglass Junior High School of New York, he married a second time; on this occasion he chose Ida Mae Roberson, whom he had known for ten years. Ida Mae represented to the poet the ideal woman; she was intelligent, loyal, and empathetic, if not as beautiful and well-connected as his former wife.

When Cullen died of uremic poisoning on January 9, 1946, only forty-two years old, the New York newspapers devoted several columns to detailing his career and praising him for his distinguished literary accomplishments. Yet in later years, Houston A. Baker deplored (in *A Many-Colored Coat of Dreams: The Poetry of Countée Cullen*, 1974) the fact that to date no collection of Cullen's poetry had been published since the posthumous *On These I Stand*, nor had any of his previously published volumes been reprinted. Indeed, many volumes of this important Harlem Renaissance poet can be read today only in rare-book rooms of university libraries.

ANALYSIS

In his scholarly book of 1937, *Negro Poetry and Drama*, Sterling A. Brown, whose poems and essays continue to exert formidable influence on black American culture, remarked that Countée Cullen's poetry is "the most polished lyricism of modern Negro poetry." About his own poetry and poetry in general, Cullen himself observed: "good poetry is a lofty thought beautifully expressed. Poetry should not be too intellectual. It should deal more, I think, with the emotions." In this definition of "good poetry," Cullen reflects his declared, constant aspiration to transcend his color and to strike a universal chord. Yet the perceptive poet, novelist, essayist and critic James Weldon Johnson asserted that the best of Cullen's poetry "is motivated by race. He is always seeking to free himself and his art from these bonds."

The tension prevalent in Cullen's poems, then, is between the objective of transcendence—to reach the universal, to enter the "mainstream"—and his ineluctable return to the predicament his race faces in a white world. This tension causes him, on one hand, to demonstrate a paramount example of T. S. Eliot's "tradition and the individual talent" and, on the other, to embody the black aesthetic (as articulated during the Harlem Renaissance); in his best poems, he achieves both. Transcending the bonds of race and country, he produces poetry which looks to the literature and ideas of the past while it identifies its creator as an original artist; yet, at the same time, he celebrates his African heritage, dramatizes black heroism, and reveals the reality of being black in a hostile world.

"YET DO I MARVEL"

"Yet Do I Marvel," perhaps Cullen's most famous single poem, displays the poet during one of his most intensely lyrical, personal moments; yet this poem also illustrates his reverence for tradition. The sonnet, essentially Shakespearean in rhyme scheme, is actually Petrarchan in its internal form. The Petrarchan form is even suggested in the rhyme scheme; the first two quatrains rhyme *abab, cdcd* in perfect accord with the Shakespearean scheme. The next six lines, however, break the expected pattern of yet another quatrain in the same scheme; instead of *efef* followed by a couplet *gg*, the poem adopts the scheme *ee ff gg*. While retaining the concluding couplet (*gg*), the other two (*eeff*) combine with the final couplet, suggesting the Petrarchan structure of the sestet. The poem is essentially divided, then, into the octave, wherein the problem is stated, and the sestet, in which some sort of resolution is attempted.

Analysis of the poem's content shows that Cullen chooses the internal form of the Petrarchan sonnet but retains a measure of the Shakespearean form for dramatic effect. The first eight lines of the poem express by means of antiphrastic statements or ironic declaratives that the poem's speaker doubts God's goodness and benevolent intent, especially in his creation of certain limited beings. The poem begins with the assertion that "I doubt not God is good, well-meaning, kind" and then

proceeds to reveal that the speaker actually believes just the opposite to be true; that is, he actually says, "I do doubt God is good." For God has created the "little buried mole" to continue blind and "flesh that mirrors Him" to "some day die." Then the persona cites two illustrations of cruel, irremediable predicaments from classical mythology, those of Tantalus and Sisyphus. These mythological figures are traditional examples: Tantalus, the man who suffers eternal denial of that which he seeks, and Sisyphus, the man who suffers the eternal drudgery of being forced to toil endlessly again and again only to lose his objective each time he thinks he has won it.

The illustration of the mole and the man who must die rehearses the existential pathos of moden human beings estranged from God and thrust into a hostile universe. What appeared to be naïve affirmations of God's goodness become penetrating questions which reveal Cullen himself in a moment of intense doubt. This attitude of contention with God closely resembles that expressed by Gerard Manley Hopkins in his sonnet "Thou Art Indeed Just, Lord." The probing questions, combined with the apparent resolve to believe, are indeed close; one might suggest that Cullen has adapted Hopkins's struggle for certainty to the black predicament, the real subject of Cullen's poem. The predicaments of Tantalus and Sisyphus (anticipating Albert Camus's later essay) comment on a personal problem, one close to home for Cullen himself. The notion of men struggling eternally toward a goal, thinking they have achieved it but having it torn from them, articulates the plight of black artists in America. In keeping with the form of the Petrarchan sonnet, the ninth line constitutes the *volta* or turn toward some sort of resolution. From ironic questioning, the persona moves to direct statement, even to a degree of affirmation. "Inscrutable His ways are," the speaker declares, to a mere human being who is too preoccupied with the vicissitudes of his mundane existence to grasp "What awful brain compels His awful hand," this last line echoing William Blake's "The Tyger." The apparent resolution becomes clouded by the poem's striking final couplet: "Yet do I marvel at this curious thing:/ To make a poet black, and bid him sing!"

The doubt remains; nothing is finally resolved. The plight of the black poet becomes identical with that of

Tantalus and Sisyphus. Like these figures from classical mythology, the black poet is, in the contemporary, non-mythological world, forced to struggle endlessly toward a goal he will never, as the poem suggests, be allowed to reach. Cullen has effectively combined the Petrarchan and the Shakespearean sonnet forms; the sestet's first four lines function as an apparent resolution of the problem advanced by the octave. The concluding couplet, however, recalling the Shakespearean device of concentrating the entire poem's comment within the final two lines, restates the problem of the octave by maintaining that, in the case of a black poet, God has created the supreme irony. In "Yet Do I Marvel," Cullen has succeeded in making an intensely personal statement; as James Johnson suggested, this poem "is motivated by race." Nevertheless, not only race is at work here. Rather than selecting a more modern form, perhaps free verse, the poet employs the sonnet tradition in a surprising and effective way, and he also shows his regard for tradition by citing mythological figures and by summoning up Blake.

REGARD FOR TRADITION

Cullen displays his regard for tradition in many other poems. "The Medusa," for example, by its very title celebrates once again the classical tradition; in this piece, another sonnet, the poet suggests that the face of a woman who rejected him has the malign power of the Medusa. In an epitaph, a favorite form of Cullen, he celebrates the poetry of John Keats, whose "singing lips that cold death kissed/ Have seared his own with flame." Keats was Cullen's avowed favorite poet, and Cullen celebrates him in yet a second poem, "To John Keats, Poet at Spring Time." As suggested by Cullen's definition of poetry, it was Keats's concern for beauty which attracted him: "in spite of all men say/ Of Beauty, you have felt her most."

"HERITAGE"

Beauty and classical mythology were not the only elements of tradition which Cullen revered. Indeed, he forcefully celebrated his own African heritage, exemplifying the first of the tenets of the Black Aesthetic. "Heritage" represents his most concentrated effort to reclaim his African roots. This 128-line lyric opens as the persona longs for the song of "wild barbaric birds/ Goading massive jungle herds" from which through no fault of

his own he has been removed for three centuries. He then articulates Johnson's observation that this poet is ever "seeking to free himself and his art" from the bonds of this heritage. The poem's speaker remarks that, although he crams his thumbs against his ears and keeps them there, "great drums" always throb "through the air." This duplicity of mind and action force upon him a sense of "distress, and joy allied." Despite this distress, he continues to conjure up in his mind's eye "cats/ Crouching in the river reeds," "silver snakes," and "the savage measures of/ Jungle boys and girls in love." The rain has a particularly dramatic effect on him; "While its primal measures drip," a distant, resonant voice beckons him to "'strip!/ Off this new exuberance./ Come and dance the Lover's Dance!'" Out of this experience of recollection and reclaiming his past comes the urge to "fashion dark gods" and, finally, even to dare "to give You [the one God]/ Dark despairing features."

THE BLACK CHRIST

The intense need expressed here, to see God as literally black, predicts the long narrative poem of 1929, *The Black Christ*. This poem, perhaps more than any other of Cullen's poems, represents his attempt to portray black heroism, the second tenet of the Black Aesthetic. Briefly the poem tells the tale of Jim, a young black man who comes to believe it is inevitable that he will suffer death at the hands of an angry lynch mob. Miraculously, after the inevitable lynching has indeed occurred, the young man appears to his younger brother and mother, much as Jesus of Nazareth, according to the Gospels, appeared before his disciples. Christ has essentially transformed himself into black Jim. Although the poem contains such faults as a main character who speaks in dialect at one point and waxes eloquent at another and one speech by Jim who, pursued by the mob, speaks so long that he cannot possibly escape (one may argue that he was doomed from the start), it has moments of artistic brilliance.

Jim "was handsome in a way/ Night is after a long, hot day." He could never bend his spirit to the white man's demands: "my blood's too hot to knuckle." Like Richard Wright's Bigger Thomas, Jim was a man of action whose deeds "let loose/ The pent-up torrent of abuse," which clamored in his younger brother "for release." Toward the middle of the poem, Jim's brother, the narrator, describes Jim, after the older brother has become tipsy with drink, as "Spring's gayest cavalier"; this occurs "in the dim/ Half-light" of the evening. At the end, "Spring's gayest cavalier" has become the black Christ, Spring's radiant sacrifice, suggesting that "Half-light" reveals only selective truths, those one may be inclined to believe are true because of one's human limitations, whereas God's total light reveals absolute truth unfettered. Following this suggestion, the image "Spring's gayest cavalier" becomes even more fecund. The word cavalier calls up another poem by Hopkins, "The Windhover," which is dedicated to Christ. In this poem, the speaker addresses Christ with the exclamation, "O my chevalier!" Both cavalier and chevalier have their origins in the same Latin word, *caballarius*. Since Cullen knew both French and Latin and since Hopkins's poems had been published in 1918, it is reasonable to suggest a more than coincidental connection. At any rate, "Spring's gayest cavalier" embodies an example of effective foreshadowing.

Just before the mob seizes Jim, the narrator maintains that "The air about him shaped a crown/ Of light, or so it seemed to me," similar to the nimbus so often appearing in medieval paintings of Christ, the holy family, the disciples, and the saints. The narrator describes the seizure itself in an epic simile of nine lines. When Jim has been lynched, the younger brother exclaims, "My Lycidas was dead. There swung/ In all his glory, lusty, young,/ My Jonathan, my Patrocles." Here Cullen brings together the works of John Milton, the Bible, and Homer into one image which appears to syncretize them all. Clearly, the poet is attempting to construct in Jim a hero of cosmic proportions while at the same time managing to unify, if only for a moment, four grand traditions: the English, the biblical, the classical, and of course, the African American.

INTERPRETATING "THE BLACK EXPERIENCE"

While *The Black Christ* dramatizes black heroism, it also suggests what it means to be black in a hostile, white world. Not all the black experience, however, is tainted with such unspeakable horror. In "Harlem Wine," Cullen reveals how blacks overcome their pain and rebellious inclinations through the medium of music. The blues, a totally black cultural phenomenon, "hurtle flesh and bone past fear/ Down alleyways of

dreams." Indeed the wine of Harlem can its "joy compute/ with blithe, ecstatic hips." The ballad stanza of this poem's three quatrains rocks with rhythm, repeating Cullen's immensely successful performance in another long narrative poem, *The Ballad of the Brown Girl*.

Although not as notable a rhythmic performance as "Harlem Wine" or *The Ballad of the Brown Girl*, "From the Dark Tower" is, nevertheless, a remarkable poem. It contains a profound expression of the black experience. Important to a reading of the poem is the fact that the Dark Tower was an actual place located on New York's 136th Street in the heart of Harlem; poets and artists of the Harlem Renaissance often gathered there to discuss their writings and their art. Perhaps this poem grew out of one of those gatherings. The poem is more identifiably a Petrarchan or Italian sonnet than "Yet Do I Marvel"; as prescribed by the form, the octave is arranged into two quatrains, each rhyming *abbaabba*, while the sestet rhymes *ccddee*. The rhyme scheme of the sestet closely resembles that in "Yet Do I Marvel."

"FROM THE DARK TOWER"

The octave of "From the Dark Tower" states the poem's problem in an unconventional, perhaps surprising manner by means of a series of threats. The first threat introduces the conceit of planting, to which the poem returns in its last pair of couplets. The poet begins, "We shall not always plant while others reap/ The golden increment of bursting fruit." The planting conceit suggests almost immediately the image of slaves working the fields of a Southern plantation. Conjuring up this memory of the antebellum South but then asserting by use of the future tense ("We *shall* not") that nothing has changed—that is, that the white world has relegated today's African Americans to their former status as slaves, not even as good as second class citizens—Cullen strikes a minor chord of deep, poignant bitterness felt by many contemporary blacks. Yet, what these blacks produce with their planting is richly fertile, a "bursting fruit"; the problem is that "others reap" this "golden increment." The poet's threat promises that this tide of gross, unjust rapine will soon turn against its perpetrators.

The next few lines compound this initial threat with others. These same oppressed people will not forever bow "abject and mute" to such treatment by a people who have shown by their oppression that they are the inferiors of their victims. "Not everlastingly" will these victims "beguile" this evil race "with mellow flute"; the reader can readily picture scenes of supposedly contented, dancing "darkies" and ostensibly happy minstrel men. "We were not made eternally to weep" declares the poet in the last line of the octave. This line constitutes the *volta* or turning point in the poem. All the bitterness and resentment implied in the preceding lines is exposed here. An oppressed people simply will not shed tears forever; sorrow and self-pity inevitably turn to anger and rebellion.

The first four lines of the sestet state cases in defense of the octave's propositions that these oppressed people, now identified by the comparisons made in these lines as the black race, are "no less lovely being dark." The poet returns subtly to his planting conceit by citing the case of flowers which "cannot bloom at all/ In light, but crumple, piteous, and fall." From the infinite heavens to finite flowers of earth Cullen takes his reader, grasping universal and particular significance for his people and thereby restoring and bolstering their pride and sense of worth.

Then follow the piercing, deep-felt last lines: "So, in the dark we hide the heart that bleeds,/ And wait, and tend our agonizing seeds." As with "Yet Do I Marvel," Cullen has effectively combined the structures of the Petrarchan and Shakespearean sonnets by concluding his poem with this trenchant, succinct couplet. The planting conceit, however, has altered dramatically. What has been "golden increment" for white oppressors will yet surely prove the "bursting fruit" of "agonizing seeds." The poem represents, then, a sort of revolutionary predeclaration of independence. This "document" first states the offenses sustained by the downtrodden, next asserts their worth and significance as human beings, and finally argues that the black people will "wait" until an appropriate time to reveal their agony through rebellion. Cullen has here predicted the anger of James Baldwin's *The Fire Next Time* (1963) and the rhetoric of the Black Armageddon, a later literary movement led by such poets as Amiri Baraka, Sonia Sanchez, and Nikki Giovanni.

Whereas these figures of the Black Armageddon movement almost invariably selected unconventional forms in which to express their rebellion, Cullen demonstrated his respect for tradition in voicing his parallel feelings. Although Cullen's work ably displays his knowledge of the traditions of the Western world, from Homer to Keats (and even Edna St. Vincent Millay), it equally enunciates his empathy with black Americans in its celebration of the Black Aesthetic. At the same time that his poetry incorporates classicism and English Romanticism, it affirms his black heritage and the black American experience.

OTHER MAJOR WORKS

LONG FICTION: *One Way to Heaven*, 1932.

PLAYS: *Medea*, pr., pb. 1935 (translation of Euripides); *One Way to Heaven*, pb. 1936 (adaptation of his novel); *St. Louis Woman*, pr. 1946 (adaptation of Arna Bontemps's novel *God Sends Sunday*); *The Third Fourth of July*, pr., pb. 1946 (musical).

CHILDREN'S LITERATURE: *The Lost Zoo (a Rhyme for the Young, but Not Too Young)*, 1940; *My Lives and How I Lost Them*, 1942.

EDITED TEXT: *Caroling Dusk*, 1927.

BIBLIOGRAPHY

Baker, Houston A., Jr. *A Many-Colored Coat of Dreams: The Poetry of Countée Cullen*. Detroit: Broadside Press, 1974. This brief and somewhat difficult volume examines Cullen's poetry in the context of a black American literature that is published and criticized largely by a white literary establishment. Presents a new view of Cullen's poetry by holding it up to the light of black literary standards.

Bronz, Stephen H. "Countée Cullen." In *Roots of Negro Racial Consciousness: The 1920's, Three Harlem Renaissance Writers*. New York: Libra Publishers, 1964. After a brief summary of Cullen's early life, Bronz examines Cullen's writings in chronological order. He is most interested in the poetry and in whether Cullen succeeds in creating characters who are interesting individuals rather than vague representatives of their race. His conclusion is that Cullen fails.

Ferguson, Blanche E. *Countée Cullen and the Negro Renaissance*. New York: Dodd, Mead, 1966. The only book-length study of Countée Cullen for many years, this volume is a highly fictionalized biography. In a pleasant and simple style, Ferguson walks readers through major events in Cullen's life. Includes eight photographs, a brief bibliography, and an index.

Onyeberechi, Sydney. *Critical Essays: Achebe, Baldwin, Cullen, Ngugi, and Tutuola.* Hyattsville, Md.: Rising Star, 1999. A collection of Onyeberechi's criticism and interpretation of the work of several African American authors. Includes bibliographic references.

Perry, Margaret. *A Bio-bibliography of Countée Cullen.* Westport, Conn.: Greenwood Press, 1971. After a brief biographical sketch, Perry offers a valuable bibliography of Cullen's works and a sensitive reading of the poetry.

Tuttleton, James W. "Countée Cullen at 'The Heights.'" In *The Harlem Renaissance: Revaluations,* edited by Amritjit Singh, William S. Shiver, and Stanley Brodwin. New York: Garland, 1989. Examines Cullen's years at New York University and analyzes his senior honors thesis on Edna St. Vincent Millay. Tuttleton argues that this period was very important to Cullen's emergence as a poet.

John C. Shields;
bibliography updated by the editors

E. E. CUMMINGS

Born: Cambridge, Massachusetts; October 14, 1894
Died: North Conway, New Hampshire; September 3, 1962

PRINCIPAL POETRY

Tulips and Chimneys, 1923
&, 1925
XLI Poems, 1925
Is 5, 1926
W: Seventy New Poems, 1931
No Thanks, 1935
1/20 Poems, 1936
Collected Poems, 1938
Fifty Poems, 1940
1 × 1, 1944

Xiape, 1950
Poems, 1923-1954, 1954
Ninety-five Poems, 1958
One Hundred Selected Poems, 1959
Selected Poems, 1960
Seventy-three Poems, 1963
E. E. Cummings: A Selection of Poems, 1965
Complete Poems, 1913-1962, 1968
Etcetera:The Unpublished Poems, 1983, revised and expanded 2000

OTHER LITERARY FORMS

In addition to poetry, E. E. Cummings also published two long prose narratives, *The Enormous Room* (1922) and *Eimi* (1933); a translation from the French of *The Red Front,* by Louis Aragon (1933); a long play, *Him* (1927); two short plays, *Anthropos: The Future of Art* (1944) and *Santa Claus: A Morality* (1946); *Tom: A Ballet* (1935); a collection of his own drawings in charcoal, ink, oil, pastels, and watercolor, *CIOPW* (1931); his autobiographical Harvard lectures, *i: six nonlectures* (1953); and a collection of his wife's photographs with captions by Cummings, *Adventures in Value* (1962).

Of these, *The Enormous Room* and *Eimi* are of particular interest because of their contributions to Cummings's critical reputation and to his development as an artist. The former is the poet's account of his three-month confinement in a French concentration camp in 1917. It was hailed upon its appearance as a significant firsthand account of the war and has become one of the classic records of World War I. It is also significant in that it is Cummings's first book, and, although prose, it reflects the same kinds of linguistic experimentation and innovation apparent in his poetry. Also reflecting his stylistic innovations is *Eimi,* Cummings's account of a trip to Russia, which has a topical vitality similar to the war experiences. The major themes of the critical response to Cummings's poetry, which developed in the 1920's, were implicit in the responses to *The Enormous Room.* Those themes, explicit by 1933, also helped to shape the criticism of *Eimi.*

Similar to the two prose narratives, *Him,* a long, expressionistic drama, is also representative of Cummings's development and of his critical reputation. Experimental and distinctive, the drama was produced in

E. E. Cummings (Library of Congress)

1928 by the Provincetown Players. In the program notes, Cummings cautioned the audience against trying to understand the play. Instead, he advised the audience to "let it try to understand you." As with the poetry and the prose, there were outraged cries claiming that the play was unintelligible, although there was also an affirmation of the lyrical originality and intensity of the play. The recognition of Cummings's lyrical talents was gradually to replace the often angry rejections of his work because of its eccentricity.

Stylistically distinctive and important in any full assessment of his achievement is the collection of Cummings's presentations as the annual Charles Eliot Norton Lecturer in Poetry at Harvard, *i: six nonlectures*. Of immediate interest, however, is the autobiographical content of the lectures. Lecture One is titled "my parents" and contains poetic and affectionate sketches of his mother and father; Lecture Two is titled "their son." The final four, less pointedly autobiographical in the usual sense of the word, are an exploration of the relationship between the poet's values and his sense of personal identity, between what he believes and what he is.

ACHIEVEMENTS

E. E. Cummings is not usually included in the first rank of modernist poets, which always begins with T. S. Eliot, William Butler Yeats, and Ezra Pound and is, more often than not, rounded out with Wallace Stevens and William Carlos Williams. Two aspects of his career, however, give his achievement a great deal of significance. First, he was on the cutting edge of the modernist, experimental movement in verse. Pound, at the center of that movement, was dedicated to restoring value and integrity to the word by breaking the mold of the past, and in that cause, he evangelically admonished the poets of his generation to "make it new." Although a disciple of no one, Cummings led the assault on conventional verse, pushing experimentation to extremes and beyond with his peculiarly distinctive typography and his unconventional syntax, grammar, and punctuation. Although he paid the price of such experimentation, which brought charges of superficiality and unintelligibility, he served the modernist movement well by helping to educate an audience for the innovations in verse and prose of the second and third decades of the twentieth century.

Second, Cummings was not only a leading experimenter in an age of experimentation but also an intense lyric poet and an effective satirist. As a lyricist, he celebrated those experiences, values, and attitudes which lyric poets of all times have celebrated; and high on his list was love—sexual, romantic, and ideal or transcendental. His love poetry often reminds readers of Renaissance poets because of its subject matter, diction, and imagery. He is often bawdy, often sentimental, sometimes concrete, sometimes abstract, but almost always intense. Many of his lyrics express a childlike joy before nature and the natural state; he also celebrated personal relationships, particularly in his well-known tributes to his father and mother.

As a satirist, Cummings's principal target is man en masse. This thrust is the opposite of the celebration of individuality, a principal subject of his lyricism. In poems with a military setting, he satirically attacks not the military but the submergence of the individual into the mass which the military often brings about. He attacks the same submergence in poems that seem to be attacking modern advertising or salesmen. Neither, however, is the real object of his scorn; it is not modern advertising but the mass mind of the mass market which it engenders that he lashes out at in several of his most effective satiric pieces.

Cummings celebrates love, spontaneity, individuality, and a childlike wonder before nature. He attacks conformity, the mass mind, progress, and hypocrisy. His greatest achievement is that in an age of experimentation in verse, and in an age defensive and self-conscious about feeling, he fashioned a personal, highly idiosyncratic style which at its best provided him with effective vehicles for some of the finest lyric and satiric poetry of the modernist period.

Among the honors and awards he received were the Dial Award in 1925 for "distinguished service to American letters"; two Guggenheim Fellowships, in 1933 and 1951; the Shelley Memorial Award in 1944 and the Academy of American Poets Fellowship in 1950; and a special citation by National Book Awards in 1955 for *Poems, 1923-1954*. In 1957, he received the Bollingen Prize in Poetry and the Boston Arts Festival Award.

BIOGRAPHY

Edward Estlin Cummings was born in Cambridge, Massachusetts, on October 14, 1894, the first of two children born to Edward Cummings and Rebecca Haswell Clarke. His father was a Harvard graduate and lecturer, an ordained Unitarian minister, and pastor of the South Congregational Church from 1909 to 1925. Cummings received his degree magna cum laude from Harvard in 1915 and a Harvard M.A. the following year. A landmark in his career came in 1952 when he returned to Harvard to deliver the Charles Eliot Norton Lectures. Subsequently published as *i: six nonlectures*, all of which are highly personal and autobiographical, the first is of particular interest because of its affectionate, idealized portraits of his parents.

Cummings went to France in 1917 to join Norton Harje's Ambulance Corps. A combination of unfortunate and nearly ludicrous events led to his incarceration by the French authorities on suspicion of disloyalty. He and a friend were confined in a concentration camp at La Ferté Macé from late September through December, 1917. That experience is the subject matter of Cummings's first book, *The Enormous Room*, which has come to be regarded as a classic account of personal ex-

perience in World War I. Although prose, it launched the poet's career and, because of its style, set the tone and, implicitly, some of the basic themes that were to characterize the responses to his poetry for the next two decades. Before 1922, Cummings had published poems in the *Harvard Monthly*, in *The Dial*, and six poems in *Eight Harvard Poets*, but it was *The Enormous Room* that began his critical reputation. His first book of poems, *Tulips and Chimneys*, was published in 1923.

In 1923, Cummings moved to Patchin Place in New York City and lived there, spending the summers at his family's place in New Hampshire, until his death in 1962. Cummings traveled to Russia in 1931 and converted that experience into the second of his two major prose works, *Eimi*. In 1932, he married Marion Morehouse, a model, actress, and photographer. It was his third marriage and it survived. She died in 1969. The three decades Cummings spent with Marion and the nearly four decades at Patchin Place deserve emphasis in a biographical sketch because they provide a perspective that brings some balance to the poet's reputation as a bohemian enfant terrible. Although he never lost the cutting edge of his capacity to shock, he lived a relatively settled life devoted to painting and writing poetry.

ANALYSIS

Since E. E. Cummings rarely used titles, all those poems without titles will be identified by reference to the Index of First Lines in *Complete Poems, 1913-1962*. An analysis of Cummings's poetry turns, for the most part, upon judgments about his innovative, highly idiosyncratic versification. Some of Cummings's critics have thought his techniques to be not only cheap and shallow tricks but also ultimately nonpoetic. There was, from the early stages of his career, general agreement about his potential as a lyric and satiric poet. As that career developed through his middle and late periods, negative criticism of his verse diminished as affirmation grew. Although there always will be dissenting voices, the consensus for some time has been that his innovative verse techniques and his lyric and satiric talents were successfully blended in the best of his work.

"R-P-O-P-H-E-S-S-A-G-R"

Cummings wrote both free verse and conventional verse, particularly in the form of quatrains and sonnets.

He also imposed on conventional verse the combination of typographical eccentricities and grammatical and syntactical permutations which constitute his distinctive hallmark. There is a considerable range between his most extreme free-verse poems, where the hallmark is superimposed, and his most conventional sonnets, where the hallmark is barely discernible. An example of the extreme is his "grasshopper" poem, "r-p-o-p-h-e-s-s-a-g-r," which is at the same time a masterpiece and a failure. The poem is a masterful blending of form and content, an achievement that might be described as pure technique becoming pure form. It fails as a poem, however, to move the reader or to matter very much except as a witty display of pyrotechnics. Its achievement, nevertheless, is a considerable one, and it serves as a useful model of one kind of poem for which Cummings is best known.

The poem "r-p-o-p-h-e-s-s-a-g-r" is structurally a free-verse poem in which Cummings employs many of his distinctive typographical devices. The word "grasshopper" occurs four times in the poem, its letters jumbled beyond recognition the first three times. The grasshopper's leap, capturing the essence of grasshoppers, brings its name into proper arrangement. Cummings also uses parentheses to break up words and to signal recombinations of letters and syllables resulting in conventional spelling, syntax, and meaning. At the literal and figurative center of the poem is the word "leaps," which links the first two versions of the word "grasshopper" to the final two, culminating in the resolution of the proper arrangement of letters. Cummings's diagonal typography for the word "leaps" is intended to render spatially, in the visual terms of a painter, the conceptual meaning of the word.

VISUAL EFFECTS

A poem of even less substance than "r-p-o-p-h-e-s-s-a-g-r," and therefore illustratively useful in the same way, is the "leaf-falling" poem "1(a." The four words of the poem, "a," "leaf," "falls," and "loneliness," are arranged along a vertical line with two or three letters or characters on each horizontal line, except for the final five of "iness." Thus, the poem begins with "1(a," with the rest of the poem directly below, two or three letters at a time, spaced out to suggest two triplets, set off by an opening, an intervening, and a closing single line. The use of the two parentheses, setting off "a leaf falls,"

actually helps in the reading of the poem. To the extent that the slender column of letters on the relatively vast whiteness of the page visually complements the theme of the poem, human loneliness engendered by the cyclical dying of the natural world in the fall of the year, Cummings has again succeeded in an effective union of form and content.

Other examples of this kind of verse are poems depicting a black, ragtime piano player ("ta"), a sunset ("stinging"), and a thunderstorm ("n(o)w/the"). The arrangement on the page of the portrait of the piano player is very much like that of "loneliness," as is the second half of the poem depicting a sunset by the sea. Cummings attempts in the thunderstorm poem to create visual effects to complement the conceptual meaning of the words "lightning" and "thunder." In one line, he states that the world "iS Slapped:with;liGhtninG"; thunder in the poems appears as "THuNdeR." These five poems represent some of Cummings's more effective uses of several of his most representative devices, particularly eccentric typography and spatial arrangement intended to create special visual effects. Often successful, these same devices at times fail completely, merely producing involved semantic puzzles hardly worth the effort necessary to solve them. More important, however, is the fact that the same features of versification exemplified by these poems of relatively little substance are to be found in his very best lyric and satiric poetry, the best of which stands between the highly eccentric versification of "r-p-o-p-h-e-s-s-a-g-r" and his relatively conventional uses of the sonnet form.

SONNETS

Cummings wrote many sonnets. A convenient sampling of his uses of the form is to be found in *Is 5*, which begins with five sonnets and closes with five. The first five are portraits or sketches of prostitutes and are among the few Cummings poems with titles—in this example, the respective names of each of the women. The subject matter of the final five sonnets of the collection, in sharp contrast to the portraits, is romantic love, and this set is more conventional than the portraits of the prostitutes. Cummings's best lyric poetry tends to be his more conventional verse: A comparative reading of the second and the tenth sonnets of *Is 5* will illustrate Cummings's mastery of conventional lyric forms.

Three observations can be made about the second sonnet of *Is 5*, the portrait of Mame ("Mame") and the tenth ("if I have made, my lady, intricate"). First, the former is a portrait of a prostitute, while the latter is addressed to "my lady." Second, Mame speaks in a Brooklyn dialect, such as "duh woild," "some noive," and "dat baby." What little quoted speech there is in "if I have made,my lady,intricate" is not dialect and would not be obtrusive in a Renaissance sonnet. Third, Mame's sonnet is relatively loose structurally, while my lady's is one of Cummings's most conventional. The loose structure of the former results largely from the dramatic presentation, particularly as it calls for the use of fragmented speech in dialect. Both sonnets are conventional syntactically, grammatically, and typographically. Formally and thematically, "if I have made,my lady,intricate" stands in dramatic contrast to "r-p-o-p-h-e-s-s-a-g-r." The sonnet is one of Cummings's better lyric poems, the best of which make use of the formal eccentricities of "r-p-o-p-h-e-s-s-a-g-r" in the poet's successful blending of traditional subject matter with his personally distinctive, modern verse forms.

LYRIC POETRY

Cummings's principal lyric subject matter is his celebration of romantic, sexual, and transcendental love and of the beauty, physical and spiritual, of lovers. A good example of a successful blend of his distinctive versification with a traditional lyric subject is "(ponder,darling,these busted statues." Formally, the poem might be thought of as standing near the middle of the range defined by the extremes of "r-p-o-p-h-e-s-s-a-g-r" and "if I have made, my lady, intricate." As such, it represents well the characteristics of Cummings's poetry. The blend of versification with a traditional subject is effective because of the appropriateness of the fragmented verse to the imagery of broken statuary and architectural ruins and of both to the poem's *carpe diem* theme.

The most obvious aspect of Cummings's distinctive verse is typographical, his sparse and erratic use of capitals and of parentheses. These particular details function in this poem of lyric substance to further understanding. Two sets of parentheses clearly delineate the three sections of the poem, the first and last being enclosed by them. The capitalization gives emphasis to the "Greediest Paws" of time and to the all-important "Horizontal"

business. In addition to the typography, two examples of Cummings's manipulation of syntax also contribute to understanding his style: verse paragraphs three and six. As with the typography, the unconventional syntax contributes to the unmistakable distinctiveness of Cummings's verse without in any way impeding the reader's comprehension and hence appreciation of the poem.

The poem "(ponder,darling,these busted statues" is the modern poet's address to the perennially coy mistress. As in Andrew Marvell's poem "To His Coy Mistress" (1650), the woman is asked to consider the mutability of all things and urged, since time passes irrevocably, to get on with meaningful "horizontal" business. Marvell's plea turns on his images of the grave and the desert of eternity. Cummings, the quintessential modern, stands with the woman among the architectural ruins of a past that must be not so much denied as ignored, or, at least, turned away from. Although it is a lesser poem than T. S. Eliot's *The Waste Land* (1922), it shares with that landmark of the modernist period the fragmented artifacts of the past. More important, Cummings, like Eliot, is addressing the fundamental question of their time: What does one do in the midst of such ruins? Cummings's answer, "make love," is direct, obvious, and highly ironic; it is not simply flippant and clever. The poet's urgent request to get on with the important horizontal business is one of the most traditional lyric responses to the overt awareness of mortality, one of man's principal talismans down through the centuries against the certainty of death.

The poems "somewhere i have never travelled,gladly beyond" and "you shall above all things be glad and young" provide good examples of Cummings's celebration of transcendental love. It should be noted that the categories, physical or sexual love and transcendental love, are not mutually exclusive. That is, nothing in "(ponder,darling,these busted statues" precludes the possibility that the lovers see something in each other deeper and more enduring than sex. Yet, it would be foolish to deny the sexual suggestiveness of the imagery of "somewhere i have never travelled,gladly beyond."

The poem "since feeling is first" is an explicit celebration of feeling, the wellspring of all lyricism. Examples of his affirmation of spontaneity, of nature, and of the natural and the childlike selves can be found in "when god lets my body be," "i thank You God for most this amazing," "in Just-," and "O sweet spontaneous." Cummings's intense tribute to his father, "my father moved through dooms of love," and his slight but moving poem for his mother, "if there are any heavens my mother will(all by herself)have," extend the range of lyric subject matter to include filial affection. The poem "anyone lived in a pretty how town" is Cummings's allegorical "everyman" which has a poignancy similar to that of Thornton Wilder's *Our Town* (1938).

These poems provide examples of Cummings's principal lyric subject matter. They also constitute a group useful for studying the formal variety found in some of his best poetry. Two of them, the poem on his father and "anyone lived in a pretty how town," are fairly conventional quatrains given a twist by Cummings's characteristic grammatical distortion: The parts of speech exchange roles. For example, the father moves "through griefs of joy" and sings "desire into begin." Everyman of "anyone lived in a pretty how town" "sang his didn't" and "danced his did." In general, the key to this special vocabulary, here and in other poems, is that the present, immediate, concrete, and spontaneous are being affirmed, while their opposites are being rejected. "Is" is superior to "was." The "dooms of feel" are to be celebrated; the "pomp of must and shall" scorned. In addition to these examples of Cummings's quatrains, this group also contains another of his fairly conventional sonnets, "i thank You God for most this amazing," and several free verse poems, including "in Just-," and "O sweet spontaneous." As a group, they illustrate and support the generalization stated earlier that Cummings makes the most effective use of his distinctive devices in his more substantive lyric poetry.

SATIRIC POETRY

Because satirists use lyricism to intensify their satirical thrusts, there is often no hard line between satiric and lyric poetry. The distinction for Cummings in particular is more a matter of emphasis than a clear-cut distinction. Because so much of his poetry is primarily satirical, however, it is profitable to consider several appropriate examples. It is also instructive to note that, as with his best lyric poetry, his best satiric pieces are those characterized by an effective blending of his distinctive devices with the resources of traditional verse. An excellent ex-

ample of such blending and of the use of lyric intensity for satiric purposes is "i sing of Olaf glad and big."

The poem looks and even sounds like free verse. It is, however, an intricately constructed set of interlocking quatrains and couplets in four-stress lines. The loosening of what sounds like very regular verse is effected by the spacing on the page and by the counterpoint of sentence or sense structure against the verse structure. That tension between verse and sense is intensified by the characteristic use of parentheses and syntactical inversions. As in "(ponder,darling,these busted statues," the parentheses are used conventionally for humorous asides, as when readers are told that colonel left the scene "hurriedly to shave," and for emphasis, as in the passages on Olaf's knees and Christ's mercy. The syntactical inversions effectively provide emphasis and hardly impede understanding. The hyphenating of the word "object-or" catches the genius of Cummings's style at its best. The poem is about a conscientious objector who becomes an "object" in the hands of his fellow soldiers.

The satire is directed not at the military or against war, but at the lockstep, group mentality which, although fostered particularly by the military, may be found in the highly organized structures of all institutions: corporate, religious, academic. For Cummings, affirmation of the bravery of the individual places heavy emphasis on "individual," and it is the group, crowd, or gang that is being indicated. The irony of the closing lines strongly suggests that the military is but the protective arm of the nation or culture locked into value systems symbolized by abstractions such as the nation's "blueeyed pride." Olaf, blond and blue-eyed, fits the abstraction and hence his culpability is compounded. He was "blonder," however (that is, nearer the ideal of bravery and of manhood), than most and willing to pay lip service to the ideal, while others lose themselves in the false security of the crowd.

Two other satires set in the context of war but directed at more fundamental targets are "my sweet old etcetera" and "plato told." The first satirizes, in a light vein, attitudes very close to those of the soldiers of "i sing of Olaf glad and big." Aunts, sister, mother, and father all think war is glorious, while the soldier, who describes them, lies in the muddy trenches, thereby refuting the grandiose notions of those safe and comfortable at home. The satire "plato told" comes closest to being an indictment of war, but its focus is really on the obtuseness of "him," on his failure to understand what everyone has been telling him, which is that war is hell. All three of these "war" poems satirize a failure to see reality.

"Poem: Or, Beauty Hurts Mr. Vinal," one of Cummings's few titled poems, is a harsh but clever indictment of modern advertising and, implicitly, of the culture from which it derives. Cummings piles up actual lines from advertisements for garters, gum, shirt collars, drawers, Kodaks, and laxatives juxtaposed with fragments of lines from "America the Beautiful" and fragmented allusions to Robert Browning in the sixth verse paragraph. The poem makes fun of the glibness and excessive claims of advertising but then takes a turn toward the end to focus on Cummings's primary satiric target: men and woman, "gelded" or "spaded," who have allowed themselves to be manipulated into anonymous units of the "market." Cummings makes the same point in one of his harshest sonnets, "a salesman is an it that stinks Excuse." Almost savage in tone, the poem once again links various seemingly incongruous activities in terms of the marketplace: the selling of "hate condoms education . . . democracy." The focus of Cummings's attack shifts from its ostensible targets—the military, advertising, and a salesman—to processes which rob people of their individuality and freedom of choice.

Cummings's innovative genius as a versifier, excessive in many of the lesser poems, is modified and restrained in his poems of substance, effecting in many of them happy unions of form and content. He is, as a result, a modernist poet of consequence.

OTHER MAJOR WORKS

PLAYS: *Him*, pb. 1927; *Tom: A Ballet*, pb. 1935; *Anthropos: The Future of Art*, pb. 1944; *Santa Claus: A Morality*, pb. 1946.

NONFICTION: *The Enormous Room*, 1922; *CIOPW*, 1931 (drawings); *Eimi*, 1933; *i: six nonlectures*, 1953; *Adventures in Value*, 1962 (photographs by Marion Morehouse).

TRANSLATION: *The Red Front*, 1933 (a selection of poems by Louis Aragon).

BIBLIOGRAPHY

Ahearn, Barry, ed. *Pound/Cummings: The Correspondence of Ezra Pound and E. E. Cummings*. Ann Arbor: University of Michigan Press, 1996. These interchanges cast light on both the poets and their times. Includes bibliographic references.

Dumas, Bethany K. *E. E. Cummings: A Remembrance of Miracles*. London: Vision Press, 1974. Presents a basic introduction, individual discussions of the poetry, prose, drama, and art, a biographical overview, and general theories. Emphasis is on helping the beginning reader get to know the man and his work. Includes a bibliographical note and indexes of first lines and subjects.

Friedman, Norman. *E. E. Cummings: The Art of His Poetry*. Baltimore: The Johns Hopkins University Press, 1960. Although dated in some respects, the book offers an easy, graduated approach to the poems that is particularly suited to the novice. Shows how Cummings's leading ideas generated his unique forms and devices. A good index helps draw related points and poems together.

Kennedy, Richard S. *E. E. Cummings Revisited*. New York: Twayne, 1994. Kennedy, using materials at the Cummings Collection of the Harvard Library, including previously unavailable materials, delivers an analysis of Cummings's oeuvre. Includes many illustrations, a few by Cummings himself.

Kidder, Rushworth M. *E. E. Cummings: An Introduction to the Poetry*. New York: Columbia University Press, 1979. Because of the separation in time between Cummings's life and the appearance of this volume, Kidder had gained some objectivity over earlier critics, enabling him to focus on enduring values in the poetry. His commentaries are fresh and insightful, often correcting existing misconceptions. Includes a bibliography and indexes.

Lane, Gary. *I Am: A Study of E. E. Cummings' Poems*. Lawrence: University Press of Kansas, 1976. A good reference for new readers. Reprints selected poems, appending detailed discussions designed to make the obscure and complicated devices transparent. The critical apparatus features complete notes, an index, and a bibliographical note.

Marks, Barry A. *E. E. Cummings*. New York: Twayne, 1964. Like all the volumes in this series, this book presents a chronological outline, a complete list of notes and references, an extensive bibliography, and an index. Unlike others, this introduction arranges a series of essays setting Cummings in his historical, social, cultural, and philosophical contexts. Hence, it is excellent on background.

Norman, Charles. *The Magic Maker: E. E. Cummings*. Rev. ed. Indianapolis: Bobbs-Merrill, 1972. First written while Cummings was still alive, this combination memoir and critical introduction grows out of a long and intimate relationship with the poet. The personal material bears a rich authenticity, full of telling anecdotes. The illustrations are unrivaled. A good index offers useful cross-references, but there are no notes.

Wegner, Robert E. *The Poetry and Prose of E. E. Cummings*. New York: Harcourt, Brace & World, 1965. More than the other sources, this book focuses on revealing the evolution of Cummings's style and the relationship between his life and work. It includes a chronology of publications rather than of his life. Includes footnotes and indexes of first lines and subjects, but no bibliography.

Lloyd N. Dendinger;
bibliography updated by the editors

J. V. CUNNINGHAM

Born: Cumberland, Maryland; August 23, 1911
Died: Waltham, Massachusetts; March 30, 1985

PRINCIPAL POETRY
The Helmsman, 1942
The Judge Is Fury, 1947
Doctor Drink, 1950
Trivial, Vulgar, and Exalted: Epigrams, 1957
The Exclusions of a Rhyme: Poems and Epigrams, 1960
To What Strangers, What Welcome: A Sequence of Short Poems, 1964

Some Salt: Poems and Epigrams . . . , 1967
The Collected Poems and Epigrams of J. V. Cunningham, 1971
Selected Poems, 1971
The Poems of J. V. Cunningham, 1997

OTHER LITERARY FORMS

J. V. Cunningham wrote scholarly and critical essays on Statius, Geoffrey Chaucer, William Shakespeare, and Wallace Stevens, as well as on a number of other poets and aspects of poetry. He edited a literary anthology, *The Renaissance in England* (1966), and wrote commentaries on his own poetry under the titles *The Quest of the Opal: A Commentary on "The Helmsman"* (1950) and *The Journal of John Cardan: Together with "The Quest of the Opal" and "The Problem of Form"* (1964). The volume into which his prose was collected is extremely valuable in the study of his poetry, not only for his penetrating essays on style and form but also for his scholarly discussions of literary modes and periods, which cast light on his own poetic practice.

ACHIEVEMENTS

During the early 1930's, when J. V. Cunningham was composing the first of the poems which he later considered worth printing, T. S. Eliot and Ezra Pound were exerting a powerful influence on modern poetry. In many respects a literary maverick, Cunningham objected particularly to the growing disregard of poetic meter and to Archibald MacLeish's dictum that "A poem should not mean/ But be." While pursuing degrees at Stanford University and beginning his career as an English instructor, Cunningham wrote uncompromisingly metrical poems which always meant something. Although he taught in several leading universities, he achieved prominence as scholar and poet only upon his appointment as chair of the English department at the young Brandeis University in Waltham, Massachusetts, in 1953; thereafter, he gained many honors: Guggenheim Fellowships in 1959 and 1967, a National Institute of Arts and Letters grant in 1965 and a grant from the National Institute for the Arts the following year, as well as designation as only the second University Professor at Brandeis in 1966. He was awarded an Academy of American Poets Fellowship in 1976.

His highly disciplined, concise, and intellectual poetry won acknowledgment from literary scholars such as Yvor Winters and Denis Donoghue, as well as from the makers of many poetry anthologies. In addition, Cunningham's teaching influenced a younger generation of poets, particularly Alan Shapiro.

BIOGRAPHY

Although born in Cumberland, Maryland, in 1911, James Vincent Cunningham's earliest recollections were of Billings, Montana, where the family settled when he was about four years old. After growing up in Montana and in Denver, Colorado, and briefly attending St. Mary's College in Kansas, he earned his A.B. and Ph.D. at Stanford University, where he also taught English.

From 1945, when he achieved his doctorate, until 1953, he taught at the Universities of Hawaii, Chicago, and Virginia, publishing two books of poetry and a book on Shakespearean tragedy during this period. Recognition followed at Brandeis University, where Cunningham taught from 1953 until his retirement in 1982.

Married and divorced twice earlier, Cunningham was married to Jessie MacGregor Campbell in 1950. Following his appointment to Brandeis, the Cunninghams settled in Sudbury, Massachusetts, between Waltham and Worcester, where she taught English at Clark University. He died on March 30, 1985, at the age of seventy-three.

ANALYSIS

J. V. Cunningham's small but distinguished corpus of poetry (he preferred to call it verse) challenges many modern assumptions. In an age dominated by freer forms, he devoted himself to meter, fixed stanzas, and—more often than not—rhyme. His poems are taut, plain, and philosophical, with the feeling tightly controlled. The proportion of general statement to sensory detail is high, as is that of abstract words to concrete and imagistic language. Although he eschewed the self as the focus of lyric, he had a highly proprietary attitude toward his poems, insisting that they belonged essentially to him rather than to his readers. He appeared quite content to reach a relatively select readership capable of appreciating the subtlety and precision of his work. In both theory and practice, he went his own way, often in contradistinction to, sometimes in defiance of, the norms of twentieth century lyric.

CLASSICISM IN THE COLLECTED POEMS AND EPIGRAMS OF J. V. CUNNINGHAM

As a scholar trained in the Greek and Latin classics and in English Renaissance poetry, he brought the predilections of his favorite literary periods to his own verse. His classicism emerges in a number of ways. Cunningham's favorite form, the epigram, was perfected in Latin by Martial in the first century C.E. and in English by Ben Jonson early in the seventeenth century. More than half the poems in *The Collected Poems and Epigrams of J. V. Cunningham* are termed epigrams, while a number of others have epigrammatic qualities. Although he called only one of his poems an ode, a number of others fall within the tradition of the Horatian ode. He frequently imitates—or rather seeks English equivalents for—Latin stanzas and meters. It is no accident that his favorite stanzas, like those of Horace in his odes, are quatrains, sometimes with the contours and movement of the Roman poet's alcaic meter, and couplets, which were Martial's and Ben Jonson's preferred way of rendering the terse and witty statements of epigram.

J. V. Cunningham (Courtesy of Brandeis University)

Another aspect of his classicism is his fondness for Latin titles such as "Agnosco Veteris Vestigia Flammae" (I recognize the traces of an old flame), "Timor Dei" (the fear of God), and "Lector Aere Perennior." The last of these illustrates his penchant for allusion, as it appropriates a famous Horatian phrase about poetry being a monument more lasting than bronze and applies it to the *lector*, the reader of the poetry. Wittily manipulating a Latin commonplace about the fame of poets, some basic concepts of medieval Scholasticism, and Pythagoras's theory of the transmigration of souls, Cunningham argues that the poet's immortality inheres not in the poet, who, except as a name, is forgotten, but in the reader—in each successive reader for whom the poem comes to life again. Adapting phrases from Horace is one of his favorite ploys. Horace wrote *odi profanum vulgus* (I hate the common crowd), Cunningham, "I like the trivial, vulgar, and exalted." He also appropriates the old but relatively rare Latinate word *haecceity*, meaning "thisness," to express Cunningham's own theory that the preoccupation with any particular "this" is evil.

Often, he takes advantage of Latin roots to extend meaning. One of his lines in "All Choice Is Error"—"Radical change, the root of human woe!"—reminds the reader that "radical" means root. His poem "Passion" requires for its full effect an awareness that *patior* (whose past participle, *passus*, provides the basis of the English word) means "suffer," that *patior* is a passive verb (he calls passion "love's passive form"), and that the medieval derivation *passio* was used not only in theological discourse, referring to Christ's suffering, but also in philosophical discourse, to indicate that which is passive or acted upon. Sometimes his employment of etymology is very sly, as in his phrase "mere conservative," where, clued by his awareness that "conservative" is an honorific to Cunningham, the reader benefits from knowing that *merus* means "pure," a fact now obscured by the English adjective's having changed from meaning "nothing less than" to "nothing more than."

Classical poets also manipulated syntax for emphasis in ways which are not always available to English poets, but Cunningham plays the sentence against the line variously, using enjambments in such poems as "Think" and "Monday Morning" to throw into striking relief words that might otherwise be obscured. He is fond of classical syntactical figures such as chiasmus. "So he may discover/ As Scholar truth, sincerity as lover" exhibits this reversal of word order in otherwise parallel phrases. It might be noted that Cunningham shares with many free-verse poets a liking for visually arresting enjambments and displacements; he differs primarily in adjusting them to the formal demands of meter.

What might be called Jonsonian neoclassicism favors poets such as Horace and Martial, who treat of their subjects in a cool and somewhat impersonal tone, carefully regulating—though not abjuring—feeling and striving for the general import of their subjects. Readers of Jonson's lyrics will recall his poem "On My First Son," which illustrates these traits well, though dealing with a heartrending experience, the death of a young son. Jonson generates not only a quiet but unmistakable sense of grief and resentment but also a corrective admonition against the moral dangers of selfishness and presumption in lamenting such a common occurrence too much. Cunningham's "Consolatio Nova" (new consolation), on the death of his publisher and champion, Alan Swallow, exhibits many of the same virtues. It generalizes, and no feeling overflows, but the careful reader sees that the loss is a specific and deeply felt one. A similarly quiet tone and controlled feeling mark "Obsequies for a Poetess."

A scholar himself, Jonson would have appreciated "To a Friend, on Her Examination for the Doctorate in English" and, except for the feminine pronoun and the latter-day degree, would have recognized in the title a perfectly appropriate theme for a poem, for in both classical and neoclassical Renaissance poetry, friendship rivaled love as a theme. "The Aged Lover Discourses in the Flat Style" is also Jonsonian from its title onward, Cunningham even adapting to his own sparer person some of Jonson's physical description in "My Picture Left in Scotland." The modern poet's fine "To My Wife," though more paradoxical than Jonson was as a rule, illustrates well the classical restraint in dealing with love. It is a poem of four quatrains in cross-rhymed tetrameter, the first two presenting images of landscape and the seasons, the last two modulating to quiet statement dominated by abstractions: terror, delight, regret, anger, love, time, grace.

Two more reputed classical virtues are simplicity and brevity. At first glance, Cunningham's poems do not seem unfailingly simple, for although the language itself is not notably difficult, the thought is often complex and usually highly compressed. Cunningham displays no urge to embellish or amplify, however, and his assessment of his own style as plain or "flat" is accurate. Brevity can test the reader's comprehension, and brevity is the very essence of Cunningham's poetic. Of the 175 original poems and epigrams in his collected verse, the longest is thirty-six lines, and many are much shorter. It is a small book for a man who wrote poetry for more than forty years. The classical model here is perhaps Vergil, traditionally thought to be happy with a daily output of an acceptable line or two. For Cunningham, the perfection of a lyric outshines any number of diamonds in the rough.

THE FOLLY OF PARTICULARITY

Although Cunningham's classically inspired challenge to modern poetry was thoroughgoing and persistent, he did modify it over his career. He disapproved vigorously of poetry that merely recounts experience or indulges in emotion, and his early poems in particular concentrate on interpreting experience and subduing emotion. An early poem, "All Choice Is Error," sets forth a conviction that because choice signifies not merely the preference of one thing for another but also the rejection of all other possibilities, choice must be seen as evil, even if it is necessary evil. Choices restrict life, and the habit of favoring particularities in verse—a habit of twentieth century poets, in Cunningham's view—is an especially lamentable habit. This poem develops the theme with reference to lovers' traditional fondness for carving their initials on such surfaces as tree trunks provide. Since there can be few people who have not reflected on the folly of thus publicizing a choice that all too soon may look silly or embarrassing, it is a clever motif to illustrate his point about the folly of particularity. The poem celebrates time and the elements, which smooth the lovers' initials. What remains is recognizable as love, but the specificity of the lovers is happily lost.

"Haecceity" carries this theme further. It is a more philosophical poem, based on the argument that the actualization of any possibility is the denial of all other possibilities. Cunningham knows that people must make choices and that morally it may be better to choose one thing over another, but, at the same time, choice is inherently evil because of the exclusions it necessitates. A consequence of this conviction that to restrict any general possibility to one manifestation constitutes evil is that any particular poem setting forth this idea is evil, a paradox that Cunningham does not hesitate to admit.

Since human beings have a fundamental urge to carry out choices, to achieve particularity, and since all choices are equally denials of the remaining possibilities, on what basis is choice to be made? Cunningham, struck by the arbitrary and even despairing nature of many human choices, reasoned that carefully considered judgments would assure the best, or least damaging, decisions. He came to doubt reason's capacity to best emotion, however, particularly since the latter is more likely to enlist the assistance of religion. (Cunningham was reared a Roman Catholic and gave up all religious beliefs in his maturity, but he realized that his early religious training continued to influence his imagination, and references to Catholic doctrine appear in some of his mature poems.) In his commentary *The Quest of the Opal*, Cunningham discusses the poems he wrote in his attempts to escape the consequences of his theory of the evil of particularity. Although his intellectual search bore little fruit, some interesting poems, including "Summer Idyll," "Autumn," and "The Wandering Scholar," resulted.

"THE HELMSMAN: AN ODE"

Meanwhile, Cunningham was discovering a more satisfying way of dealing with experience in "The Helmsman: An Ode." He had been much interested in Horace's ode 1.9, in which the poet describes Mount Soracte under its cap of snow and then modulates to his frequent theme of *carpe diem*, "seize the day," embodied in a celebration of young love. Cunningham hoped to imitate the way Horace's images delicately implied the theme rather than merely exemplifying it. "The Helmsman," a poem about "the voyage of the soul . . ./ Through age to wisdom," imitated Horace procedurally as well as formally. It builds on memories and disappointments along the way, asserting the need to strike out on one's own, ever alert lest he slip and drown like Vergil's Palinurus in the fifth book of the *Aeneid* (c. 29-19 B.C.E.). Wisdom "comes like the ripening gleam of wheat" to this voyager, "flashing like snakes underneath the haze." In the second half of the poem, the imagery imitates that of another Horatian ode, 1.7, in which Teucer, an ancient king of Troy, prepares festively for a dangerous voyage with his cohorts. Security is only an illusion: The wheat may not ripen, the voyage may come to naught. The voyager must acknowledge the possibility of defeat but not flag in his pursuit.

AUTOBIOGRAPHICAL THEMES

By his own admission, Cunningham's poetry was becoming more autobiographical, although hardly in the manner of, for example, Robert Lowell. The closing poem of the second group in *The Collected Poems and Epigrams of J. V. Cunningham* draws on recollections of the landscape of his childhood. "Montana Pastoral" is a good example of Cunningham's ability to revive old modes by unexpected departures from convention. Over the centuries, poets have rung many changes on pastoral, turning Theocritus's and Vergil's shepherds into other rural types, into pastors in the ecclesiastical sense (John Milton's "Lycidas") or even into denizens of Lewis Carroll's *Alice's Adventures in Wonderland* (1865), as William Empson has suggested in *Some Versions of Pastoral* (1935). Cunningham's speaker can find no evidence of the supposed pastoral virtues in the wild and bleak Montana landscape. More precisely, the poem is an antipastoral, gaining its effect by holding out in its title the perennially attractive promise of the simpler, more wholesome life but then detailing briskly and briefly the harshness of the land.

INNOVATIONS

Cunningham found other ways of being new. He experimented with meters, including syllabic ones freer than most free verse in all but line lengths. "Think," for example, uses a seven-syllable line with three variously placed stresses per line, while "Monday Morning" uses a nine-syllable line with four stresses per line. In his essay "How Shall a Poem Be Written?" Cunningham cites precedents for such types of syllabic lines, although chiefly ten-syllable ones, in Thomas Wyatt, John Donne, and Sir Philip Sidney. In the eighth poem of his *To What Strangers, What Welcome* sequence, he tries blank-verse tetrameter, extremely rare in English poetry.

TO WHAT STRANGERS, WHAT WELCOME

It is tempting to read this sequence autobiographically. The earlier of the fifteen short poems take a trav-

eler westward in the United States. Along the white lines of highways and barbed-wire fences, past tumbleweed and locoweed, the speaker wends his way. He stops in Las Vegas, takes in gaming and shows unenthusiastically, and finally passes through desert to the land of redwood trees and the Pacific surf. In the eleventh poem, the speaker turns back toward the East and, after more desert, prairie, and "stonewalled road," is found at the end relaxing in New England. The poems also allude to a love affair, although rather obscurely. While the nominal subject of the sequence is a transcontinental automobile trip, it may perhaps be read also as a telescopic account of Cunningham's career. Born in Maryland, he went west to Montana and Colorado with his family, received most of his higher education at Stanford University (not far from the redwoods and closer yet to the surf), and, after teaching mostly at points intermediate, gravitated to New England, specifically to Brandeis University in Massachusetts, where he received the swift academic preferment that had been denied him everywhere else and where he remained for the duration of his working life. The title of the sequence—an ironic twist on the western "welcome, stranger"— becomes more ironic if one reads into it a kind of career résumé, since by far the heartiest welcome Cunningham ever received was in that urban, New England university under Jewish auspices. It must be noted, however, that the sequence does not end triumphantly but in a series of questions about identity, as if "what welcome?" remains a query without an answer.

There is much more description and concrete detail than in Cunningham's earlier poetry. He seems more inclined to imply, rather than state, his theme. The "I" of the sequence is more like the first person in the work of his autobiographical or confessional contemporaries in verse, more often found in the midst of specific, yet offhand, experiences: "I drive Westward," "I write here," "I go moseying about." It is impossible to find, difficult to imagine, Cunningham "moseying" in his earlier poetry. The footloose sequence raises a series of questions about love, fulfillment, identity. While it does not appear to answer any of them, the tone is that of a modern man responding dryly and sarcastically to Walt Whitman, the ingenuous traveler of the open road, who reveled not only in the redwoods but even in their destruction by men determined to rival them in grandeur. Cunningham's road, with its boundaries of interminable white lines and barbed wire, speaks of a land whose greatness remains but whose lack of hospitality looms, and man no longer seems commensurate with it, save in degree of unfriendliness.

To What Strangers, What Welcome confirms what careful readers of Cunningham's verse had surely already recognized: that he was very much a man of his own time, a man whose poetic theory was in no danger of turning into a pale imitation of a Roman of the Empire or an Englishman of the age of Elizabeth I. Not only in subject matter but also in form, he seemed to be edging closer to the prevailing poetry of his time. His verse in the sequence is measured but flexible and untrammeled.

Despite his sometimes intransigent defiance of the poets in Whitman's train, Cunningham objected to *vers libre* far less than to the assumption, unfortunately still common among its advocates, the meter is passé and that free forms constitute the only defensible mode of poetry in the later twentieth century. Despite the strictness of so much of his practice, he conceded that much modern verse is also metrical, for it departs from, often returns to, and inevitably is measured against, meter as a norm. His attitude in this respect does not differ greatly from that of another strict metrist, Robert Frost, who also loved classical poetry, found the limitations of traditional forms an irresistible challenge, and even suspected free-verse poets of unacknowledged but nevertheless recurrent iambic tendencies.

EPIGRAMS

The epigrams, which are found at the end of his collection of original poetry, are more regular. They represent poems both early and late in his career and are the best exemplars of his fondness for wit, brevity, and a cool and often satirical tone. That they are also twentieth century poems is evident from the titles that some of them bear: "With a Detective Story," "History of Ideas," "For a College Yearbook," "New York: 5 March 1957," "Towards Tucson." In short, they are full of subjects, concepts, and attitudes unimaginable to Martial, Ben Jonson, or Walter Savage Landor. There are some for which Latin equivalents might have been composed two

thousand years ago, but only because they are about universal types and habits.

The epigrams are about love, drink, music, grief, wisdom, illusion, calculus, Freudianism, and many other things. They vary considerably in tone: reflective, cynical, sardonic, risqué, indecent, smug, earnest. They contain lapses in taste and judgment, but virtually all of them display an alert intelligence. Writing in an age not very interested in the epigram, Cunningham proves its durability and his right to be considered with the masters of this ancient form. A free-verse epigram would be a contradiction in terms; thus, to deny the legitimacy of Cunningham's art is to deny the possibility of the contemporary epigram.

POETRY IN TRANSLATION

The Collected Poems and Epigrams of J. V. Cunningham concludes with twenty-one translations of classical, medieval, and Renaissance Latin poems. Like the epigrams, these poems were written over many years. The most rollicking is his translation of "The Confession of Bishop Golias," attributed to the Archpoet of Cologne, a twelfth century figure. The finest, however, are of classical Latin poetry.

One might suppose that by the twentieth century, no one would be able to find a new way to render Catullus's famous couplet "Odi et amo," but Cunningham succeeded in finding a new equivalent for its final word, *excrucior.* This poem is about the lover who does not know why he both hates and loves his girl but feels it and is "tormented" or "tortured," as translators usually have it. Cunningham concludes with "I feel it and am torn." His choice, simpler and yet more graphic, is certainly justified, for the cross (*crux,* from which *excrucior* derives) tore the flesh of the crucified as the conflicting emotions tear Catullus's lover's psyche.

Cunningham also translated the Mount Soracte ode of Horace, whose procedure he found so instructive. Somewhat more formal and literal than other modern versions, his translation avoids the casual, even flippant, effect of those who bend over backward to avoid sounding archaic and bookish and, as a result, answers to the dignity of Horace's theme:

Tomorrow may no man divine.
This day that Fortune gives set down

> As profit, nor while young still
> Scorn the rewards of sweet dancing love,
>
> So long as from your flowering days
> Crabbed age delays.

Why Cunningham did not choose to translate more of Horace for publication is a nagging question; surely few writers have been as well qualified to do this poet justice.

In one of his most valuable critical essays, Cunningham discusses his translation of Statius's poem on sleep. By reviving a comparison first made in the late nineteenth century by the great Latin scholar J. W. Mackail between the Latin poem and William Wordsworth's sonnet "To Sleep," Cunningham establishes six points of contrast between the poetry of Horace, Vergil, Statius, and many modern poets, on the one hand, and William Wordsworth, along with many medieval and Tudor lyric poets, on the other. The first has to do with the relative complexity of the meter that was used by the earlier group, the second with the playing off of syntax against meter, which the medieval-Tudor group seldom did. The earlier group determined the length of the poem relatively freely, while the later group worked with a fixed idea of length. The earlier group did not match thought units to formal divisions, whereas the later group did. The paraphrasable meaning of the early group is implicit, of the later group explicit. Conceptually, the earlier group's poems exhibit continuity and degree, while the later group's are more likely to show discontinuity, identity, and contradiction. The reader must consult the essay "Classical and Medieval: Statius on Sleep" for clarification and exemplification of these differences.

What is important to see is that the group referred to above as the earlier includes not only Roman poets of antiquity but also much modern poetry. According to Cunningham, the tendency of the English lyric over the centuries has been from the medieval-Tudor practice to that best exemplified by Horace, Vergil, and Statius. Far from carrying on warfare with these modern poets, whom Cunningham does not name but who surely include T. S. Eliot, Wallace Stevens, and presumably even William Carlos Williams, together with their followers in contemporary poetry, Cunningham in effect finds these moderns to be classical in a number of important ways. In his own translation of Statius's poem, he employs the now unfashionable form of blank verse, but he has clearly attempted to achieve the six qualities which he has designated as at once classical and modern. The translation ends:

> If this long night some lover
> In his girl's arms should willingly repel thee,
> Thence come, sweet Sleep! Nor with all thy power
> Pour through my eyes—so may they ask, the many,
> More happy—: touch me with thy wand's last tip,
> Enough, or lightly pass with hovering step.

He has not declared a truce with modern poetry, and his diction will not impress many readers as typically modern, but in at least some respects, his verse and that of his contemporaries attain peaceful coexistence.

OTHER MAJOR WORKS

NONFICTION: *The Quest of the Opal: A Commentary on "The Helmsman,"* 1950; *Woe or Wonder: The Emotional Effect of Shakespearean Tragedy*, 1951; *Tradition and Poetic Structure: Essays in Literary History and Criticism*, 1960; *The Journal of John Cardan: Together with "The Quest of the Opal" and "The Problem of Form,"* 1964; *The Collected Essays of J. V. Cunningham*, 1976.

EDITED TEXTS: *The Problem of Style*, 1966; *The Renaissance in England*, 1966; *In Shakespeare's Day*, 1970.

BIBLIOGRAPHY

Cunningham, J. V. Interview by Timothy Steele. *The Iowa Review* 15 (Fall, 1985): 1-24. In this delightful and revealing look at Cunningham's life and ideas about poetry, the poet describes writing poetry as a "professional task," not a mystical act. He defends the practice of meter and abhors its decline in recent poetry.

Pinsky, Robert. "Two Examples of Poetic Discursiveness." *Chicago Review* 27 (Fall, 1975): 133-141. Pinsky sees Cunningham's "discursiveness" as a positive quality. It is "concise and accurate" and without the usual poetic devices of imagery and irony. He claims that this leads to poetry that has the power and authority found in Ben Jonson's poetry.

Rathmann, Andrew. "Review of *The Poems of J. V. Cunningham*." *Chicago Review* 43, no. 3 (Summer,

1997): 107-103. Rathmann gives a critical analysis of Cunningham's work and laments the fact that Cunningham is not more widely known despite the admiration of many contemporary poet-critics.

Shapiro, Alan. "'Far Lamps at Night': The Poetry of J. V. Cunningham," and "The Early Seventies and J. V. Cunningham." In *In Praise of the Impure: Poetry and the Ethical Imagination: Essays, 1980-1991.* Evanston, Ill.: TriQuarterly Books, 1993. Shapiro, a former student of Cunningham at Brandeis University, believes that Cunningham deserves to be more "highly esteemed." He analyzes a few poems and shows that Cunningham did not blindly follow traditions but set his poetry against them to create a fruitful intertextuality.

Stall, Lindon. "The Trivial, Vulgar, and Exalted: The Poems of J. V. Cunningham." *The Southern Review* 9 (Spring, 1973): 1044-1048. Stall claims that Cunningham's "intelligibility" is responsible for his lack of fame. Stall states that Cunningham has restored the epigram to seriousness and brought that ancient form a new power.

Stein, Robert A. "The Collected Poems and Epigrams of J. V. Cunningham." *Western Humanities Review* 27 (Fall, 1973): 23-25. An evenhanded review of Cunningham's poems. Stein states flatly that Cunningham has written some great poems. He also sees some liabilities, especially Cunningham's use of too many clever paradoxes.

Robert P. Ellis;
bibliography updated by the editors

CYNEWULF

Flourished: 775-825 (place of birth and death unknown)

PRINCIPAL POETRY
The Fates of the Apostles
Juliana
Elene
Christ II (Ascension)

OTHER LITERARY FORMS

Cynewulf's known literary works remain the four poems attributed to him in the Exeter Book and the Vercelli Book.

ACHIEVEMENTS

Since the discovery of his name in the nineteenth century, Cynewulf's reputation, like the size of his canon, has fluctuated widely. Certainly, a prolific poet who could count *The Dream of the Rood* among his works would deserve much respect, but the Cynewulf of the four signed poems has not fared so well. Scholars have always shown great interest in Cynewulf, primarily because of his runic signatures. Daniel Calder is probably right in suggesting that critical assessment of the poet has suffered "from the need to make him more important than he is." General histories and surveys of Old English poetry, for example, devote much space to this poet with a name, but have been essentially unimpressed by the poetry itself. Some have seen it as a diluted version of the earlier heroic style, a breakdown of technique, and the end of a great tradition. Commenting on *The Fates of the Apostles* in his history of medieval poetry, Derek Pearsall states that the poem "has the characteristic nerveless orthodoxy of treatment which prompts one to think of Cynewulf's poems in turn as the final product of a declining old age." Even the editors of Cynewulf have not been admiring. Rosemary Woolf, editor of *Juliana*, sees the poem as bringing "Old English poetry into a blind alley." What is not certain in these and numerous other such assessments of Cynewulf is the extent to which they reflect the quality of his poetry or the critic's preference for the heroic style of earlier English poetry. The modern distaste for the hagiographic subject matter and overt didacticism of these Christian poems may also account for Cynewulf's bad notices.

Later studies approaching Cynewulf's poems within the contexts of Christian exegesis, hagiography, and iconography, however, have signaled a general reevaluation of the poems. *Elene* and *Christ II* have been especially praised. Scholars have been impressed by the "sophisticated handling" of patristic motifs in *Christ II* and the "beauty of intellectual form" of *Elene*. Comparisons of Cynewulf's poems with religious pictorial art have been especially popular. *Juliana* has been compared to an icon, *Christ* to a triptych, and *Elene* to panels on a church wall. To judge these poems against Aristotelian and nineteenth century expectations of realism is as foolish as judging a Byzantine icon or a complex design in the *Book of Kells* against Renaissance expectations of linear perspective and verisimilitude in art.

As helpful as these new approaches to the structure and characters of Cynewulf's narratives are, the poems remain to be appreciated and analyzed as poetry. Clearly, poetry was very important to Cynewulf. His runic signatures may reflect his desire to elicit prayers, but they also imply that he believed the poems deserved reward. Whereas the earlier oral poets (the scops) probably saw their poetry as common property, Cynewulf's signatures and requests for prayers suggest "that he believed that he had a permanent claim on his work" (Barbara Raw, *The Art and Background of Old English Poetry*, 1978).

In *Christ II*, Cynewulf includes poetry and song among the gifts that Christ bestows on man. Thus, the composition of poetry itself is considered a pious act, the development of God-given talent, the manipulation of secular technique for religious purposes. Certainly, Cynewulf so manipulated Anglo-Saxon poetic technique. In his poetry, he borrows and adapts formulaic phrases, standard motifs, and established kennings (elaborate and traditional metaphors such as "swan-road" for "sea"). He continues the tradition of alliterative and accentual verse, dividing the poetic line into two half lines containing two stresses each. These half lines are joined by alliteration, the pattern of which varies from line to line but is generally controlled by the sound of the first stressed syllable in the second half line. The pattern of stressed and unstressed syllables also varies, allowing the poet a variety of rhythmic effects.

Cynewulf's poetry does differ in many respects from the earlier heroic poetry and even from the religious verse formerly attributed to Caedmon. On occasion, Cynewulf experiments with rhyme—something very unusual in Old English, as is also his use of runes. Some of the differences may be caused by Cynewulf's dependence on Latin texts, although detailed studies of his use of sources suggest that Cynewulf actually improved and clarified the syntax of his originals. His style has been described as "classic." Cynewulf's verse is also "looser," "lighter," and more varied rhythmically, developing a great number of secondary stresses. In contrast to the elevated tone of *Beowulf* (c. 1000), it is more conversational. Some consider this effect prosaic, the end of a poetic tradition, but more recently, Raw has explained the style as a deliberate attempt at informality, an effort to follow Augustine's advice to express Christian themes in a simple style. Cynewulf does vary his style according to his subject, from meditation to set descriptive passages and formal debates. In his introduction to *Anglo-Saxon Poetry* (1954), R. K. Gordon states that "Cynewulf is as deliberate and conscious an artist as Tennyson." Such an estimate may be overstated, but Cynewulf does deserve attention as a poet and not merely as a "monastic craftsman" with a name.

BIOGRAPHY

The discovery of Cynewulf's name has not meant the discovery of a biography for the poet. Working from a name deciphered from runes, scholars have made tortuous attempts to discover a Cynewulf in historical records who could be identified as the poet. Candidates have included Cenwulf, an abbot of Peterborough (died 1006), Cynewulf, a bishop of Lindisfarne (c. 780), and Cynewulf, a priest of Dunwich (c. 803). None of these identifications has been accepted, and scholars are left with what meager data can be deduced from the four poems. Based on the poetry's subject matter, dependence on Latin sources, and relationship to the liturgical calendar, scholars assume he was a literate poet, a cleric, and probably a monk. Based on dialect and linguistic analysis, Cynewulf is usually dated around the turn of the eighth and ninth centuries and placed within the broad area of the Anglian dialect, in northern and eastern England. Since the runes twice give the poet's name as "Cynewulf" and twice as "Cynwulf," suggesting a variation of spelling not known in texts from the north, scholars have further limited the dialect to Mercian. This conclusion is supported by the rhyming passages in *Elene* and *Christ II*, which are most effective when the Mercian, rather than the manuscript's West Saxon, dialect is followed.

The evidence nevertheless remains scanty. Elaborate arguments based on what the "I" persona says in the poems have suggested that Cynewulf was a wandering minstrel or that he led a riotous and sinful life until, through conversion, he became a religious poet. Such arguments misunderstand the traditions of the elegiac wanderer in Old English poetry and conventional Christian humility motifs. Like other attempts to deal with the unknown poet rather than with his known poetry, they are fruitless. As Daniel Calder concludes, after surveying what little is known,

> Barring the discovery of wholly new evidence, the pursuit of Cynewulf's identity and the spinning out of a biography remain idle tasks. He emerges from the anonymity of Anglo-Saxon poetry long enough to sign his name and then disappear again into that great obscurity he shares with all the other scops who left no trace.

ANALYSIS

Cynewulf's name is known to students of Old English poetry because, in the conclusions of the four poems which can with certainty be attributed to him, he "signed" his name in runic letters. The name, however, was not deciphered until 1840. Cynewulf did not write his name directly, but wove the runes into the concluding meditations of his poems, so that they can be read not only as letters spelling his name, but also as symbols representing words that form part of the poetry. This riddling device—with both personal and poetic purposes—is typical of Cynewulf's poetry, which often applies devices used in earlier heroic and secular poetry to his meditative religious verse.

CYNEWULF'S CANON

Cynewulf's four poems are extant in two of the four major manuscript collections of Old English poetry, both copied around the year 1000 in the West Saxon dialect. The Exeter Book, now in the Exeter Cathedral Library, contains *Christ II* and *Juliana*; the Vercelli Book, located in the northern Italian cathedral library of Vercelli, includes *The Fates of the Apostles* and *Elene*. Nineteenth century scholars, driven by the rare discovery of a poet's name from a period of general anonymity, attributed all the religious verse in these two manuscripts to Cynewulf. Just as Caedmon was considered to be the author of the poems dealing with Old Testament subjects extant in the Junius manuscript, so Cynewulf became the author of the saints' lives and

allegorical poetry of the Exeter and Vercelli manuscripts. Only *Beowulf*, found in the fourth major manuscript, escaped being attributed with confidence to Cynewulf.

This poetry does in some respects share stylistic and thematic features with the four poems of Cynewulf. The two *Guthlac* poems ("A" and "B") treat the life and death of the eighth century hermit Saint Guthlac. Like *Juliana*, Cynewulf's account of the martyrdom of Saint Juliana, these poems deal with a saint who was challenged and harassed by demons. Guthlac is a Mercian saint associated with Croyland Abbey in Lincolnshire, an area perhaps connected with Cynewulf. Furthermore, *Guthlac B*, based on the Latin *Vita Guthlaci* by Felix of Croyland, shares several stylistic devices with the "signed" poems. Since in the Exeter Book its conclusion is missing, it is possible that it may have closed with a passage containing Cynewulf's name.

Also stylistically related to Cynewulf's poetry is *The Dream of the Rood*. Found not only in the Vercelli Book but also in fragments inscribed in runes on the Ruthwell Cross (located in southwest Scotland), this dream vision shares certain descriptive passages with *Elene*. Whereas *Elene* describes Constantine's conversion and Saint Helena's discovery of the cross, *The Dream of the Rood* concentrates on Christ's crucifixion; nevertheless, both share a devotion to the glorious cross of victory. Now usually dated earlier than Cynewulf's poetry, *The Dream of the Rood* has been called one of the greatest religious lyrics in the English language. It certainly is the best of the "Cynewulfian group," those poems associated with, but not now attributed to, Cynewulf.

The other poems attributed by nineteenth century scholars to Cynewulf share fewer stylistic and thematic elements with the four signed poems. *Andreas*, a saint's legend based on the apocryphal Latin *Acts of Saints Andrew and Matthew*, was long tied to *The Fates of the Apostles*, a summary description of the deaths of Christ's disciples. Since *The Fates of the Apostles*—considered to be an epilogue to *Andreas*, which precedes it in the Vercelli Book—contained the runic signature, scholars reasoned that *Andreas* must also be by Cynewulf. Similarly, *Christ I (Advent)* and *Christ III (Last Judgment)* were attributed to Cynewulf before critical analysis subdivided *Christ* into three distinct poems.

Although the three may be thematically related and perhaps were even brought together by Cynewulf, only *Christ II* (lines 441-866) concludes with the runic signature. It is a meditation on, and explication of, the significance of Christ's Ascension. *Christ I*, a series of antiphons for use in Vespers during the week preceding Christmas, is, according to Claes Schaar, "fairly close to Cynewulf's poetry," whereas *Christ III*, a rather uneven picture of the Last Judgment and the terrors awaiting the sinful, is definitely not by Cynewulf. *The Phoenix*, an allegorical treatment of Christ's Resurrection; *Physiologus*, a series of allegorized interpretations of natural history; and *Wulf and Eadwacer*, once understood as a riddle containing Cynewulf's name, are today not associated with Cynewulf.

Nineteenth century understanding of the Cynewulf canon had a certain balance and symmetry which is attractive. If Caedmon dealt with the epic themes of the Old Testament, Cynewulf emphasized themes more exclusively Christian: allegories of salvation, events in the life of Christ, and the stories of the early martyrs. This poetry spanned Christian history from Palestine in the first century to England in the eighth; from Christ's birth (*Christ I*) to his death (*The Dream of the Rood*), Resurrection (*The Phoenix*), and Ascension (*Christ II*); from the foundation of the church by the first missionaries (*The Fates of the Apostles* and *Andreas*) to the suffering of the martyrs (*Juliana*), the official recognition of Christianity by the Empire (*Elene*), and the continuity of the tradition of the hermit saint in England (*Guthlac*). This broad survey of Christian history not unexpectedly concluded with a description of the Last Judgment (*Christ III*).

The analyses of S. K. Das and Schaar in the 1940's, however, have limited Cynewulf's canon to the four poems containing his name, leaving one to wonder whether even these rather varied and differing works would have survived the complex and thorough stylistic and linguistic analyses if they had not concluded with a runic signature. Resembling the effect of higher criticism of the Bible, Old English scholarship has reduced Cynewulf from being the author of a large and diverse body of verse to being the composer of 2,600 lines: *The Fates of the Apostles* (122 lines), *Juliana* (731 lines), *Elene* (1,321 lines), and *Christ II* (426 lines).

CYNEWULF'S FOUR POEMS

Cynewulf's four poems vary in length, subject, complexity, and style, yet they may be characterized as sharing similar source materials, purposes, and themes. All four are essentially didactic Christian poems, based on Latin prose originals, probably composed with the liturgical calendar in mind, and perhaps to be read as poetic meditations accompanying other monastic readings. The poems are didactic and specifically Christian in that their major purpose is to teach or celebrate significant events of salvation history. The four reflect a variety of Latin originals and specific types of monastic readings, meditative practice, and exegetical thought. In *The Fates of the Apostles*, Cynewulf notes that he borrowed from many holy books, and he clearly takes pride in his knowledge and use of the "authorities" throughout his work.

Thematically, Cynewulf's poems reflect an interest also typical of his time and of monastic literature, the cosmic conflict between the forces of good and evil. This conflict is portrayed in both human and supernatural terms, sometimes in brief summaries of Christian suffering, sometimes in long debates and complaints. To highlight this conflict, Cynewulf establishes polarities of good and evil. The devil and his cohorts are clearly opposed to Christ and his faithful. Emperors and the wealthy persecute martyrs and the poor, and the headstrong Jews oppose the reasonable Christians. Idols contrast with Christian worship; lust attacks virginity; the law cannot conquer grace.

Characters are either black or white, symbols of good or evil rather than individual. While imprisoned, Juliana is suddenly visited by a demon pretending to be an angel. Her suitor, who in the Latin sources is merely a pragmatic Roman official, is portrayed by Cynewulf as a champion of paganism. There must be no hesitation, no sense that characters may have a divided mind. When the actors in this cosmic drama do change, they do not develop characters but flip from one extreme to another, as if shifting masks. In *Elene*, Judas shifts from being a miracle-working Christian bishop. Paralleling the career of Saul in the New Testament, whose conversion from persecutor to persecuted is signaled by a change of his name to Paul, Judas's name is changed to Cyriacus. As in the New Testament, which lies behind Cynewulf's Latin sources, there definitely is no place for the lukewarm.

Cynewulf's poems draw on the recorded victories of the faithful in the past to teach Christians in the present to uphold their inheritance of truth. This didactic purpose is accomplished by two means: Cynewulf portrays past events as types or symbols which can be applied to contemporary Christians, and he inserts personal comments in the conclusion of his poems, confessing his own need to follow the examples of the past and to repent in the present. As in the past Christ gave power to the saints to withstand the forces of Satan, so in the continuing battle between good and evil, he gives power to overcome temptation. The monastic communities, which understood themselves to be the inheritors of the tradition begun by the martyrs, will likewise conquer evil. The cosmic battle, given personal application, is made urgent by the concluding meditations on the transitory nature of the world, on the Last Judgment, and on the joys of heaven. In the future, contemporary events will be judged according to their place in the battle lines, and those joining the forces of Christianity will be appropriately rewarded.

THE FATES OF THE APOSTLES

Basically a catalog listing the missionary activities and deaths of Christ's twelve apostles, *The Fates of the Apostles* is based on various Latin historical martyrologies, perhaps on a version of the *Breviarium Apostolorum* (The Breviary of the Apostles). Its brief accounts of the early Christian missionaries may have been intended for reading during November to celebrate the martyred saints. Of Cynewulf's four poems, *The Fates of the Apostles* is considered as "the least effective" and "inferior" by several critics. Such evaluations probably reflect modern contempt not only for the poem's subject but also for its form. Yet to the Anglo-Saxon Christian community, sharing strong missionary impulses, interested in converting pagans, and claiming to be both historically and universally established, the poem's subject is a proclamation of legitimacy. Its form, furthermore, would not seem odd in an age when Christian chronicles were often composed in poetry and the poet was caretaker of the community's memory. Such catalogs have an honorable parentage both in the Old and New Testaments and in classical literature—in the catalogs of Homer, for example.

More appreciative critics have sought through elaborate numerical and grammatical analysis to complicate the poem, to see it as more than a simple catalog, as mannered, mystical, and even ironic. Yet, what seems most obvious about *The Fates of the Apostles* is its simplicity of purpose and structure. It establishes in the clearest possible outline the conflict between good and evil: Christian heroes, courageously obeying Christ's command to go into all nations, preach to the heathen, and suffer martyrdom. These deeds are related to the poet, his world, and his heavenly goals through the poem's prologue and epilogue.

Mentioning each of the twelve apostles in turn, Cynewulf follows a simple pattern with appropriate variations: "We have heard how X taught the people in, or journeyed to, Y and died at the hands of Z." The specific acts are introduced by a personal comment on the poet's own weariness and similarly conclude with a personal request that those who hear the poem will pray to the apostles for him. Then follows the runic signature, which inverts the spelling of his name to read "FWULCYN." The runes are woven as a riddle into a meditation on the mutability of earthly joy and wealth. The poet then refers to himself as a wanderer—a motif of long standing in Christian thought, which rejects this world as a home—and concludes with a reminder of the true home of all Christians, Heaven.

JULIANA

Juliana is a classic saint's life. Based on a Latin prose life, perhaps Saint Bede's *Martyrology* (c. 700) or one of Saint Bede's sources, the poem narrates the various human and devilish tortures and temptations withstood by Saint Juliana, who died about 305-311 and whose martyrdom is celebrated in the Christian calendar on February 16. Like *The Fates of the Apostles*, *Juliana* has not fared well with critics. To Stanley Greenfield, for example, it is "the least impressive as poetry of the Cynewulf group" (*Critical History of Old English Literature*, 1965). In contrast to *The Fates of the Apostles* it is a lengthy and somewhat repetitious account (even though lacking approximately 130 lines) of the suffering not of numerous saints but of a single martyr.

The conflict between the opposing forces of good and evil is again drawn through stark contrasts. Juliana's suitor, Eleusius, is portrayed as possessing stores of treasure, representing earthly nobility and power. Repeatedly characterized by his wealth, he is the choice of

Juliana's father, who tells the virgin that Eleusius is better, nobler, and wealthier than she, thus deserving her love. In contrast, Juliana's heart is set on a different bridegroom, the noble ruler of Heaven, possessing eternal wealth and divine power. As in the traditional love triangle of romance—what Northrop Frye calls "the secular scripture"—the father is enraged by his daughter's intransigence and gives her over to her enemies. Here, however, the love triangle leads to supernatural conflict, as Juliana contrasts her Lord with Eleusius's devils. After forcing a long confession from a demon, "the enemy of the soul," and suffering numerous torments, Juliana is killed. Eleusius, driven mad by the ordeal of dealing with a martyr, is drowned, along with his companions.

The narrative concludes by describing the hellish destiny of Eleusius and his supporters, using the language of heroic poetry to deny the rewards traditionally given to the Germanic *comitatus* (the heroic band of warriors) by its chieftain. It is as if Cynewulf uses the heroic style to condemn an old heroism and to substitute a new Christian heroism, not based on violent deeds but on faithful suffering, for the destiny of Eleusius and the pagans is contrasted to the destiny of Juliana, whose martyred body is the occasion of joy in her native Nicomedia, and continuing glory for Christians. This continuity is then extended by Cynewulf to the present when he asks for aid from Saint Juliana in his own preparation for death. Weaving his name into a meditation on death—here using three groups of runes, "CYN," "EWU," "LF"—the poet again requests prayers from those who read his poem and asks that the ruler of Heaven stand by him at the final judgment.

ELENE

Also in the tradition of the saint's legend, *Elene* spins a more complicated narrative than does *Juliana*. Based on a version of the *Inventio Sanctae Crucis* similar to the *Acta Cyriaci*, it relates the discovery of the true cross by Saint Helena, the mother of Constantine. This event is celebrated in the liturgical calendar on May 3. *Elene* is generally considered to be Cynewulf's finest poem; its description of the glorious cross gleaming in the sky is often compared with the imagery of *The Dream of the Rood*. *Elene*'s popularity may also be the result of its development of several passages in the heroic style, including Elene's sea journey and Constantine's war

against the Huns. Using the vigorous language of battle poetry, Cynewulf here develops the motif of the beasts of battle: the raven, eagle, and wolf that traditionally frequent Old English poetic battles.

Nevertheless, *Elene*'s basic theme is Christian, and although it borrows epic devices, the poem's main subject is conversion. It describes three miraculous conversions related to the discovery of the cross: Constantine's conversion following his vision of the cross; Judas's conversion leading to the discovery of the cross; and the conversion of the Jews after the discovery of the nails used to crucify Christ. In relating these conversions, the poem may strike modern readers as inexplicable and even offensive. The suffering of the Christian martyr memorialized in *Juliana* becomes here the militancy of the Christian emperor. The cross becomes the banner of war, and the nails of the cross, hammered by Roman soldiers into the flesh of Christ, become amulets for the bridle of the Roman emperor, assuring that he will vanquish all. Similarly, in contrast to the protagonist of *Juliana*, Elene represents imperial power and can force her beliefs on others. Thus she has Judas cast into a cistern for seven days until he acknowledges the truth of Christianity. In Cynewulf's black-and-white view of salvation history, Elene is on the side of right, whereas the Jews, cursed for rejecting Christ, deserve humiliation and punishment.

An unsympathetic approach to *Elene*, however, misunderstands both the Christian background of the poem and its development of characters as types. The figure of Judas, particularly, needs careful attention. The poem introduces him after Elene asks to see the wisest among the Jews. Groups of three thousand, then one thousand, and finally five hundred wise men are rejected by Elene before Judas, "the one skilled in speeches," is found. The whole process resembles the Old Testament account of Abraham's bargaining with Jehovah over Sodom (Genesis 18:23-33), reducing the number of the righteous to Lot and his family. Judas shares features with Lot, for like him, he has ancient parentage and familial ties to the righteous, yet represents a doomed people. He knows the truth of Christianity from his father; furthermore, his brother was Stephen, the first Christian martyr. He refuses, however, to accept what he knows. Like his namesake, Judas Iscariot, the most despised

Jew in Christian history, he rejects Christ until driven to admit the truth by Elene. Then his role is reversed, a point emphasized by the demon who appears in the poem to complain of Christian interference in the designs of evil. This new Judas—like Christ, the new Adam—provides the way to salvation through the cross. By converting to Christianity and using his wisdom to discover the cross, Judas Cyriacus saves not only himself, but also the Jewish people, whom medieval Christians believed would ultimately be converted to Christianity.

Other characters in *Elene* are similarly given typological significance. Constantine is associated with Christ and Elene with *ecclesia*, the victorious Christian Church. The confrontation between Judas and Elene thus symbolizes a standard doctrinal topic of Christian apologetic and polemical literature: the confrontation between *synagoga* and *ecclasia*, the law of Judaism and the grace of Christ. The confrontation is settled by the elevation of the cross, the visible token of Christ's redemptive act and a disastrous defeat for the devil.

Like the missionary activities of the apostles and the martyrdom of the saints, however, this confrontation is only one of a series of battles in the larger war between good and evil. It remains for the individual to take sides in the war, to join forces with *ecclasia*, as Cynewulf emphasizes in his conclusion. In a passage developing internal rhymes, he relates his own conversion from sin to the cross. The poet takes the past event and gives it personal application, for his own conversion associates him with the three conversions of the narrative. Then, after weaving his name in runes into a meditation on the mutability of this world, Cynewulf describes doomsday and the respective rewards of the righteous and evil. This concluding radical perspective explains the militancy of the Christian emperor, the conversion of the Jews, and the poet's own dedication to the cross.

CHRIST II

Unlike Cynewulf's other poems, *Christ II* deals not with Christian saints but with a key event in the life of Christ, the Ascension. Rather than drawing from legendary sources, it closely parallels the last part of Pope Gregory's homily on the Ascension (homily 29), with some additions based on Saint Bede's *On the Lord's Ascension* (c. 700) and monastic readings for Ascension-

tide. Although Claes Schaar believed that in *Christ II* "the poet is some-what overwhelmed by the rhetoric of Gregory," others have praised Cynewulf's "masterful reworking" of the homily. Daniel Calder, comparing Cynewulf's treatment of Gregory to Gregory's treatment of the Bible, notes that the poet "takes liberties with Gregory's text" to arrive at the truth concerning the Ascension, sometimes expanding, other times rearranging, his Latin source.

The result is an imaginative exposition of the significance of the Ascension combining Christian allegory and exegesis with Germanic poetic techniques. The description of Christ's six leaps in his role as humankind's savior, from incarnation to Ascension, allegorically develops the exegesis of the Song of Solomon and establishes the Ascension as the final necessary step in the long process of man's salvation. Christ, "the famous Prince," leaves his band of retainers on earth (the disciples) and goes to join the band of angels in Heaven. The disciples, like the wanderers of Old English elegiac poetry, are overwhelmed by the loss of their leader, whereas the angels raise a song of joy and triumph. Yet, the apostles are not left helpless, for Christ bestows gifts on humankind, including not only the spiritual gifts of wisdom, poetry, and teaching, but also the physical gifts of victory in battle and seafaring.

Even the description of Christ's glorious Ascension, however, is understood in the context of the cosmic battle between good and evil. Christ is welcomed to Heaven by a song praising his harrowing of hell, his victory against the "ancient foes." In another passage experimenting with internal rhyme, Cynewulf establishes the significance of Christ's act, which makes possible man's choice between salvation and damnation. The passage, reflecting the poet's pronounced dualism, contrasts Heaven and hell, light and dark, majesty and doom, glory and torment.

Later, Cynewulf relates Christ's six redemptive leaps to man's need to leap by holy deeds to the rewards of Heaven. The Father of Heaven will help man overcome sin and will protect his faithful against the attacks of fiends in the cosmic battle. The importance of such reliance on Christ is underscored in the poem's conclusion, Cynewulf's elaborate treatment of doomsday. Introduced by his own confession of sin and fear of judgment, it includes the runic signature woven into the description of terror facing the worldly man before the almighty judge.

Thus, as in *The Fates of the Apostles*, *Juliana*, and *Elene*, Cynewulf in *Christ II* ties the events of Christian history, developed from his Latin sources, to his contemporary world through personal confession. The poems all teach a basic concept underlying the Christian liturgy and its understanding of sacred time: the close relationship between the past, present, and future. The victories of the past in the struggle between good and evil symbolized by the ministry of Christ and the lives of the saints must be repeated in the present by the individual Christian, for in the future all persons will face the judgment of God.

BIBLIOGRAPHY

Bjork, Robert E., ed. *The Cynewulf Reader.* New York: Routledge, 2001. A collection of essays that provide a comprehensive view of the Anglo-Saxon poet and his work.

Calder, Daniel G. *Cynewulf.* Boston: Twayne, 1981. This book-length critical analysis approaches its study by relating together all Cynewulf's poems. Augmented by a selected bibliography, these poems are studied for structural and thematic similarities to establish a base for in-depth examination.

Cook, Albert S., ed. *The Christ of Cynewulf.* Hamden, Conn.: Archon Books, 1964. While concentrating on the poem *Christ II*, Cook provides extensive information on the life of Cynewulf, including his theology. Supplemented by grammatical notes and a glossary, this book offers indispensable insight into this Old English poet.

Frese, Delores Warwick. "The Art of Cynewulf's Runic Signatures." In *Anglo-Saxon Poetry: Essays in Appreciation.* Notre Dame, Ind.: University of Notre Dame Press, 1975. Frese discusses how the runic signature of Cynewulf was intricately interwoven into the texts of his poetry, greatly affecting and shaping the vocabulary, imagery, and ideology.

Greenfield, Stanley B., and Daniel Calder. *A New Critical History of Old English Literature.* New York: New York University Press, 1986. Shows the importance of the writings of Cynewulf in the Old English tradition. Presents interesting background and information on Cynewulf's possible identity and analyzes his poetry as subtle Christian abstractions, reflective in their constructs.

Olsen, Alexandra Hennessey. *Speech, Song, and Poetic Craft: The Artistry of the Cynewulf Canon.* New York: Lang, 1984. Olsen stresses the fact that Cynewulf used poetic language to reinforce legends and used a conscious literary style to compose poems of high moral purpose. Augmented with an exhaustive bibliography that makes this work invaluable to the student of Old English poetry.

Schaar, Claes. *Critical Studies in the Cynewulf Group.* New York: Haskell, 1967. Complemented with an excellent bibliography, this volume critically examines not only Cynewulf's poetry but also other works from the same period. Includes analysis of subject, text, style, and manner, for an in-depth look at traditional writings and poetic personalities.

Wine, Joseph D. *Figurative Language in Cynewulf: Defining Aspects of a Poetic Style.* New York: P. Lang, 1993. A study of the use of Old English figures of speech in Cynewulf's poetry. Includes bibliography and index.

Richard Kenneth Emmerson;
bibliography updated by the editors

D

PHILIP DACEY

Born: St. Louis, Missouri; May 9, 1939

PRINCIPAL POETRY

The Beast with Two Backs, 1969
Fist, Sweet Giraffe, the Lion, Snake, and Owl, 1970
Four Nudes, 1971
How I Escaped from the Labyrinth and Other Poems, 1977
The Boy Under the Bed, 1979
The Condom Poems, 1979
Gerard Manley Hopkins Meets Walt Whitman in Heaven and Other Poems, 1982
Fives, 1984
The Man with Red Suspenders: Poems, 1986
The Condom Poems II, 1989
Night Shift at the Crucifix Factory: Poems, 1991
What's Empty Weighs the Most: Twenty-four Sonnets, 1997
The Deathbed Playboy: Poems, 1999

OTHER LITERARY FORMS

Philip Dacey has edited two anthologies, including the influential *Strong Measures: Contemporary American Poetry in Traditional Forms* of 1986, which he coedited with David Jauss. With Gerald M. Knoll he had earlier coedited *I Love You All Day: It Is That Simple* (1970). In his first years at Southwest State University, from 1971 to 1976, he edited the literary journal *Crazy Horse*. In addition to expressing his fascination with Walt Whitman in his own poetry, Dacey has explored the poet's life and character in a play in the first issue of *The Mickle Street Review*, published in 1979 by the Walt Whitman House Association.

ACHIEVEMENTS

Dacey's major career awards include a Woodrow Wilson Fellowship, in 1961; the New York YM-YWHA Discovery award, in 1974; two National Endowment for the Arts Fellowships, in 1975 and 1980; two Minnesota State Arts Board Fellowships, in 1975 and 1983; a Bush Foundation Fellowship, in 1977; the Loft-McKnight Fellowship, in 1984, awarded by The Loft; and a Fulbright lectureship in Yugoslavia, in 1988.

Dacey began winning awards for his poetry early in his career. Honors included the Yankee Poetry Prize in 1968, the Poet and Critic Prize in 1969, and the Borestone Mountain Poetry Award in 1974. He took first prize in the G. M. Hopkins Memorial Sonnet Competition in 1977, and the first prizes in poetry awarded by literary magazines *Prairie Schooner*, in 1977, and *Kansas Quarterly*, in 1980. Dacey won Pushcart Prizes in 1977 and 1982. Later awards include the Edwin Ford Piper Award, from the University of Iowa Press, in 1990; the Carolyn Kizer prize, awarded by *Poetry Northwest* in 1991; and the Flyway Literary Award for Poetry from Iowa State University, in 1997. He won the Peace Corps Writers Poetry Award in 2000 for *The Deathbed Playboy*.

Several of his works have been set to music. The poem "The Birthday" was set by David Sampson and performed at Carnegie-Mellon Institute in 1982. The long poem "The Musician" was set to music by Elizabeth Alexander for the American Master Chorale. It received its debut performance in 1994 with the Wisconsin Chamber Orchestra at the First Congregational Church of Madison, Wisconsin.

BIOGRAPHY

Philip Dacey spent his early years in Missouri and graduated from St. Louis University in 1961. He served in the U.S. Peace Corps as a volunteer high school teacher in eastern Nigeria from 1963 to 1965. He married Florence Chard in 1963. The marriage, which ended in 1986, produced two sons and one daughter. After his Peace Corps experience, Dacey served as an instructor at Miles College in Birmingham, Alabama, in 1966, and earned his M.A. in 1967 from Stanford University in California. He then returned to St. Louis to serve as an instructor in English at the University of Missouri until 1968. In 1970 he joined the faculty of the department of English at Southwest State University in Marshall, Minnesota, and served jointly as professor of English and coordinator of creative writing through 1990. He served as Distinguished Poet in Residence at

Wichita State University in 1985 and was awarded residencies by the Corporation of Yaddo and the Ragdale Foundation, also in the 1980's. Eventually he settled at Southwest State University, Marshall.

Dacey has long been active in arts organizations. He was founder and director of the Minnesota Writers' Festival, in 1978, and founder and director in 1986 and 1989 of the Marshall Festivals. He served as member of the arts review board for the Minnesota School and Resource Center for the Arts in 1988.

Dacey has given numerous readings from his own works, and in 1992 founded the performance trio Strong Measures with his sons, Emmett and Austin. In addition to readings in the United States, Dacey has given readings in Ireland, Yugoslavia, and Mexico.

ANALYSIS

While Philip Dacey initially nursed the ambition of becoming a novelist, he early realized that his talent was better adapted to considerably shorter forms. His poetry is often marked by a witty approach to those most personal of matters, loving and sex. Even so, some of the sensibility of the novelist can be detected in his preoccupation with historical figures, two of whom have become major characters in his poems. Many of his quasi-biographical yet imaginative poems have focused on Gerard Manley Hopkins and Walt Whitman. He has also turned his eye toward the painter Thomas Eakins.

In his poetry, Philip Dacey has consistently pursued an interest in poetic form, not only editing a volume of contemporary formal verse but also using traditional forms in his own work. This concern may parallel the difficulties he has faced in establishing his personal voice as a poet. Many of his works have suffered from an incomplete command of tone, especially noticeable when he takes a more humorous approach to his subjects.

His greatest accomplishments have tended to fall within two distinct areas. His early, somewhat haphazard pursuit of a poetry of sexuality and love has matured through the years into a more reflective approach to personal matters, as represented by such works as "North Broadway & Grand." His imaginative poems, employing such characters as Whitman and Hopkins, often seem to spring from the same font of inspiration as these more overtly personal poems.

Distinct from these are Dacey's works of a more purely imaginative nature, in which accidents of phraseology or the incongruities of contemporary life have inspired poems of a nearly absurdist nature. The accidents and incongruities serve as the building-blocks of a fabricated, artificial reality, as in the poems "The Shopping List" or "Four Men in a Car." These works immediately and unabashedly reveal themselves to the reader as artifice, and display Dacey's talent for witty and entertaining verse.

"THE SLEEP"

Dacey's 1977 Pushcart award-winning poem "The Sleep," a delicately balanced poem about the sexual act, approaches its subject through evocation rather than description: "The limbs begin to believe in their gravity./ The dark age of faith begins, a god below/ Draws down the body, he wants it/ And we are flattered." In the last of its three sections, the poem compares the point of sexual climax with a kind of departure. "Already we are forgetting/ Where we were/ And left from." Despite being a poem about so intense an experience, the language of the poem has a flattened and perhaps even melancholy feel to it. This may suit the poem's secondary subject, for it is also a poem offered in memory of poet Anne Sexton.

THE MAN WITH RED SUSPENDERS

The reflective and highly personal poem "North Broadway & Grand" opens the collection *The Man with Red Suspenders* as a kind of preface. Also a memorial, it is addressed to Dacey's brother Owen, who was "the Dancing Policeman of St. Louis," and to the memory of their late sister Joan. The poet immediately connects the strands of their separate lives in the opening lines: "O, when she died/ he was the traffic cop/ again." The poet describes Owen as being present, at least symbolically, at Joan's death:

> only this time he was there
> at the crossroads
>
> to lead her home,
> his sister, through
> the deepening dark,
> no light but that
>
> of his presence

The poem ends with what seems to be an official statement of Owen's abilities as traffic cop: He could direct moving traffic at the city's worst intersection, where even traffic-guidance machines had failed before him. The poet ascribes Owen's unusual success to a purely human element.

> Put Dacey in. And the human
> touch eased
> the knot, jam, block,
> and everyone got home
> safe, everyone.

"North Broadway & Grand" is a poem of reassurance, offering a vision of a loved one's death eased by the "human touch."

Numerous poems in *The Man with Red Suspenders* owe more to imagination than to experience, and often seem to play more upon shallow expectation than worldly wisdom. The poem "The Hitchhiker" speaks from the point of view of a figure apparently intent on being sheerly contrary: "If you are light,/ I am dark./ If you are clean/ I have grease/ on my knapsack." The short lines emphasize the brittle tension created by the intrusion of an unwanted presence in a private car. At the end of the poem, the discomfort prevails, for the hitchhiker switches places with the driver.

In the poem "Dialing a Wrong Number," Dacey creates a second-person figure, possibly a male, who has found himself talking with the wrong person on the telephone. Yet he had taken precautions against this: "You know you have dialed/ the right number./ You were careful." The person who answers is both the wrong person and the right one: "She says she gets nothing these days/ but wrong numbers/ and has come to need them." The unintended connection becomes, by the end of the poem, yet another hoped-for connection that may never get through again.

The poem "The Shopping List" takes a more decisive step toward imaginary circumstances. The first-person speaker of the poem is immersed in a dreamlike experience, in which he cannot make the items on his shopping list correspond to the items he takes off the shelf. The reader comes to presume the speaker is male, because of what he finds when he turns: "I U-turn into the next/ aisle and find women on display,/ parts and whole,/ frozen or fresh." When he makes this turn, not only the store but his shopping list, too, changes. "Now every item/ refers to women./ My mother is on the list/ and my sister." In plain, unadorned language, the poem moves the reader through a dreamlike shopping experience toward a vision of an empty soul full of yearning, lost among other lost souls: ". . . the store opens/ onto a vast plain./ People walk there,/ as if forever,/ shopping for nothing."

Other poems in the collection, such as "Someone," "He Restricts Himself to Reading One Poem a Day," and "Waiting for the Mail," take a similar approach in conjuring up an image or idea with some element of strangeness about it, and developing that image or idea in the manner of a narrative. All share a flatness of imagery and plainness of style, as if nonpoetic diction might lend a sense of reality to these episodes of unreality.

Perhaps appropriately, the sense of unreality is most pronounced in the title poem, "The Man with Red Suspenders," which is presented as a kind of improvisation on a theme suggested by a moment in a writing class. A teacher's comment, that "you can't write a story about a man with red suspenders," inspires the subsequent series of playful comments. It begins, "I am the man with red suspenders,/ alive in this poem./ For years I wandered from short story to short story,/ seeking admittance." The poem self-consciously embraces an artificial situation and remains at the level of simple artifice through to its end: "I am as pleased as Punch/ to be here."

THE DEATHBED PLAYBOY

The title poem, "The Deathbed Playboy," is a long narrative poem detailing the interaction between a son and father at the latter's deathbed. The father has requested a copy of *Playboy* magazine. The son supplies the copy and watches his father examining it, but he wonders if he had misheard his father. Whether correctly heard or not, the son comes to the conclusion that bringing the magazine was an appropriately life-giving and affirmative act at that near-death moment.

While the writing has a relaxed, unconstrained feel, the poem is written in iambic pentameter, with end-rhymes arranged in a quatrain pattern. The overall poem is not broken into quatrains, however, but into larger sections with varied numbers of lines. The end-rhymes, being often slant rhymes, are unobtrusive.

A second notable long poem in iambic pentameter, with slant-rhymed couplets, appears in this collection. "Harry Stafford: Whitman at Timber Creek" also presents a narrative of a young man caring for an older one. In this case the first-person narrator, Harry Stafford, is looking after "a famous poet, taken ill." In caring for and observing Whitman, who to a great degree oversees his own recovery through highly idiosyncratic rest and recreation, Harry Stafford plants within himself the seeds for what he will become when he, too, is older. Harry remembers Whitman's remarks to him and reflects that "my kind/ ways to him must somehow someday come round/ home to me, because everything came round." The maturity conveyed by this poem, and by "The Deathbed Playboy," stands in contrast to Dacey's earlier tendency to embrace the flip and coy, in both language and subject, in his poems.

The poem "North Broadway & Grand," from *The Man with Red Suspenders*, reappears in *The Deathbed Playboy* as the second part of a now longer poem, "Difficult Corners." The new first section, "Introduction to 'North Broadway & Grand,'" is a more pointedly narrative work, giving the background on "the traffic cop who dances as he works." It offers contrasts to the earlier work in its tone, imagery, and language.

The Deathbed Playboy also contains several of the poems of artifice typical of Dacey's work. Perhaps the most adroit is "Recorded Message," an improvisation on the theme of an answering-machine message reached by a caller at an unresponsive business. "Four Men in a Car" is a playful depiction of the situation stated in the title, colored by nursery-rhyme allusions. Other poems of this sort include "The Neighbors," which imagines Saddam Hussein and George Bush as the poet's suburban neighbors, and "Trousers," which presents a list of imaginative thoughts relating the idea of generosity to the article of clothing.

OTHER MAJOR WORKS

EDITED TEXTS: *I Love You All Day, It Is That Simple*, 1970 (with Gerald M. Knoll); *Strong Measures: Contemporary American Poetry in Traditional Forms*, 1986 (with David Jauss).

BIBLIOGRAPHY

Dacey, Philip. *Selections*. 1983. Kansas City, Mo.: New Letters on the Air, 1983. This twenty-nine-minute sound-cassette recording of a reading by Dacey, first broadcast on February 18, 1983, includes Dacey's own comments on the background of each poem.

Stitt, Peter. "The Necessary Poem." *The Ohio Review* 19, no. 2 (Spring/Summer, 1978): 101-112. Stitt's examination of Dacey's poetry is valuable for its discussion of tonal consistency. While appreciative of the poet's strengths, he takes an uncompromising look at Dacey's failures of voice.

Stuart, Dabney. "Sex and Violence." *Tar River Poetry* 26, no. 2 (Spring, 1987): 46-53. Stuart explores Dacey's concern with sexuality as a topic, especially in reference to the poems of *The Man with Red Suspenders*.

Wallace, Ronald. "An Air a Wound Sings." *The Chowder Review* 9 (1977): 93-94. Wallace's examination of Dacey's earlier work, couched in entirely positive terms, is useful for its assessment of Dacey's affirmative and celebratory approach.

Yesner, Seymour, ed. *Twenty-five Minnesota Poets*. 2d ed. Minneapolis, Minn.: Nodin Press, 1977. While not regional in his subject matter, Dacey nevertheless has become recognized as an important part of the Minnesota writing community. *Twenty-five Minnesota Poets* effectively places Dacey within a flourishing regional writing scene.

Mark Rich

ROBERT DANA

Born: Allston, Massachusetts; June 2, 1929

PRINCIPAL POETRY

My Glass Brother and Other Poems, 1957
The Dark Flag of Waking, 1964
Some Versions of Silence, 1967
The Power of the Visible, 1971
In a Fugitive Season: A Sequence of Poems, 1979
Starting Out for the Difficult World, 1987
What I Think I Know: New and Selected Poems, 1991
Yes, Everything: New Poems, 1994
Hello, Stranger: Beach Poems, 1996
Summer, 2000

OTHER LITERARY FORMS

Robert Dana is the editor of *Against the Grain: Interviews with Maverick American Publishers* (1986) and *A Community of Writers: Paul Engle and the Iowa Writers' Workshop* (1999).

ACHIEVEMENTS

Robert Dana's body of work was recognized with the 1984 Rainer Maria Rilke Prize, New York University's 1989 Delmore Schwartz Memorial Award, and the 1994 Carl Sandburg Medal for Poetry. Dana's landmark volume, *Starting Out for the Difficult World*, was short-listed for the 1988 Pulitzer Prize.

BIOGRAPHY

Robert Patrick Dana's Depression-era childhood was, by any measure, complicated, a trauma, he has said, "from which I never recovered." He never met his biological father, an Italian milliner who was already married with five children when he conducted a lengthy affair with Dana's Irish Catholic mother. Dana's mother simply picked the name Dana for her child. When he was seven, his mother, only forty, died of pneumonia. Abandoned by his father, he and an older half sister (who later would become a nun) were separated and sent to live with relatives; the troubled Dana ran away several times. Although an indifferent student, he recalled being entranced by the works of Edgar Allan Poe, "the right music for a morbid boy with a miserable past and a dark future." From 1946 to 1948, Dana served in the U.S. Navy as a radio operator in Guam. He returned to Massachusetts, briefly attending Holyoke Community College before buying a one-way ticket to Des Moines, Iowa, to attend Drake University, which he selected largely because a friend had received a postcard advertising it.

Dana thrived at the school. His faculty adviser, the poet E. L. Mayo, introduced him to the works of Robert Frost, T. S. Eliot, Ezra Pound, and W. H. Auden, none of whom Dana had read before. After completing his bachelor's degree in 1951, he tried teaching high school for a year before earning his master's degree in 1954 from the prestigious Writers' Workshop at the University of Iowa. For more than forty years, he taught English as Distinguished Poet-in-Residence at Cornell College in Mount Vernon, Iowa. He began publishing poetry in small presses in 1955, although he would not release his first major collection for more than a decade. He expressed his admiration for such presses in 1986 when he edited a collection of interviews he conducted with those who kept such presses active, *Against the Grain: Interviews with Maverick American Publishers*. Beginning in the mid-1970's, Dana traveled widely, accepting appointments as a visiting writer in residence at universities in the United States and abroad. After retiring in 1994, he remained in his adopted Iowa and continued to write verse.

ANALYSIS

A lapsed Catholic, Robert Dana offers a profound sense of a fallen, often brutal world compelled by chance rather than governed by any design. His approach is much like that of Robert Lowell, a teacher of his at Iowa. Although deeply impressed by the sheer force of the natural world, particularly the limitless edge of the ocean and the forbidding prairie of his adopted Midwest, Dana cannot sustain comfort in the unaffected love of such natural wonders. He is too aware of the insubstantiality of the natural world, how every part of it—and ultimately every person within it—must perish. His vision, then, is ultimately sobering, even tragic, despite touches of humor and the reassurance he has found in the experience of love with his second wife, Peg.

Dana studied Chinese philosophy and taught Asian literature. Not willing to dwell on the emotional calamities of his personal past or to anticipate the rewards of some dubious afterlife, he counsels, with Zen-like calm, the embrace of the moment. His poetry, particularly his later work, revels in the sheer delight of discovering the rich textures of the ordinary. For him, that is the poet's job: to cast the passing moment and the unobserved object into the noble shape and reassuring permanence of language. The poet's only magic, he said, "is with words . . . their sounds, their taste, their soft or their steel feel."

Although trained in formal poetics while at the Writers' Workshop at Iowa, Dana came to find natural expression in open verse. Its music, so apparently improvisational, often goes unheard by the impatient ear, but his verse manages syllables, stresses, and vowel and consonant sounds to create an engrossing aural event.

He once compared his verse lines to jazz: "I wanted to achieve in words what the jazz musician achieves in notes and time signatures."

SOME VERSIONS OF SILENCE

Dana's first major collection, published just two years shy of his fortieth birthday, divides into three strikingly different sections. In the first are traditional narrative poems in which Dana, like Robert Frost or Edwin Arlington Robinson, captures the anxieties, frustrations, and surprises of quotidian experience, the recollections of a poet locked in time, bound to the real. They are moments of generous inclusion for the reader, poems about resilient fall flowers, crowded supermarkets, signs along a highway, and the trying experience of love.

With disconcerting—and deliberate—abruptness, the second section forsakes such familiarity. These poems, like Ezra Pound's experiments in strict imagism, do not have the reassuring flow, music, or rhythms of free verse. These are spare, minimalist bits, cryptic occasions for meditation, like Zen koans that cannot be adequately explained or paraphrased. "What word./ One/ without syllable,/ without edge;/ more moving/ but more/ than moving." They are abstract reflections that eschew metaphor and image and refuse commentary on the events that occasioned them.

In the closing section Dana brings together these two impulses—the concrete and the abstract—to create quasi parables. Palpable objects are given a spiritual resonance. Under the poet's careful eye, caged birds, hawks in flight, a comb left in an empty room, autumn trees, lightning, and the descent of night can all be coaxed into suggestive symbols within slender lines that nevertheless sing. The closing poem, "The Stonecutter," tells of a craftsman fashioning from heavy stone the subtle curves of a woman. It is a fitting image of the isolated poet finding consolation in the exertion of craft itself as a strategy for discovering the spectacular in the unpromising.

THE POWER OF THE VISIBLE

The poems in this collection resist easy summary. They are Dana's most Eastern-influenced works, enigmatic, fragmentary verses with scant sense of plot, place, or character. These are cool, clean, precise, impersonal poems that speak, thematically, of the hunger for permanence amid flux, for stability amid the rush of inevitable movement. In "The Stone Garden" Dana offers a telling Zen allegory of the monumental efforts of a man to fashion a tidy garden; he then goes in to read the newspaper obituaries, a sobering reminder of the untidiness of the larger world. Love here is inaccessible, even a burden. Achingly close to a natural world that is frustratingly inscrutable, paralyzed within the vastness of time and space, many of the poems are slender presences, thin ribbons of words amid forbidding white spaces. Dana offers as solution the poem itself, the calming music of the lines. What transfixes the reader here is the language, particularly Dana's gift for unexpected coinages, striking figurative phrases, and unusual diction, that transmutes the ordinary into the delightful: "a boredom of summer storms"; "the sliding/ murder of the calendar"; skin that clings like "a jacket and gloves of ice"; a woman's face that is "a page of snow"; pink pigs that "blister the hillside." It is the poet as conjurer and alchemist (one selection concerns a dying Merlin) who provides the reader with what the poems so desperately seek: a place apart, albeit aesthetic, amid the chaos.

IN A FUGITIVE SEASON

The poems in Dana's third major volume mark the beginning of his reclamation of what he termed "the hard details of reality." These poems recall Dana's earlier sense of forbidding vastness but are vivid and concrete. The vastness is both natural (images include mountains, prairies, night skies, snowstorms, and the sun) and temporal (in a cycle of European poems, he visits Stonehenge and ruins of ancient civilizations). The contemporary world is a palpable presence, although harshly disappointing—Dana writes powerfully of the 1968 assassination of Senator Robert Kennedy, the anxieties of nuclear apocalypse, the political evil of the 1970's Watergate scandal. Love, specifically the heated connection of passion, is vividly re-created. Although such a world cannot offer meaning or logic, Dana refuses despair. As he counsels his cynical students:

> . . . this planet
> does its crazy slow turn under us
>
> And miles away
> even my midwestern burg
>
> twinkles
> through the blue drizzle.

Dana departs from his earlier solutions (withdrawal and meditation) and offers radically new strategies—engagement and observation, allowing the open eye to be stunned by the sheer sensual impact of the world, recalling the humane Imagism of William Carlos Williams, an influence Dana readily acknowledged. The poet, then, is to remind readers tempted to abandon wonder and to expect disappointment that the world around can shatter with its color, shade, and line. It is too much to expect meaning but enough to delight in the play of surfaces. The world is much like Dana's preferred syntactic strategy: fragments that come together to create a sense of wholeness.

> I see that I am what I always was
>
> that ordinary man on his front steps
> bewildered under the bright mess of the heavens
> by the fierce indecipherable language of its stars

STARTING OUT FOR THE DIFFICULT WORLD

The title might appear ironic, given that at its publication Dana was nearing sixty. The poetic argument here is decidedly different from earlier work, though, and represents a significant starting point for Dana. At long last ready to share in the intimacy of the reader-writer relationship, he violates the keen loneliness that had long haunted his poetry by bonding with the reader. Unlike previous collections, this one deploys direct address, manipulating a recognizable, consistent "I"—an orphan, brother, friend, husband, teacher—in a real place, a New Englander transplanted to the prairie. Dana reveals a generous eye and an aching heart as well as a deep fascination for the everyday—subzero mornings, a diving hawk, homemade bread, lightning storms, summer heat, gulls feeding on a beach, even cockroaches.

These poems, reassuringly concrete and accessibly written with the easy flow of conversational intimacy, boldly attest to a self that may not be significant but is nevertheless valuable. In the moving "At the Vietnam War Memorial, Washington, D.C.," Dana writes of locating a single name on the memorial wall and, determining to rescue that name's individuality from such a forbidding catalog, recalls a photograph taken shortly before the soldier's death. In a brutal world that oppresses with the implied inconsequentiality of the individual, Dana demands that "we shout our names, cut/ them, like these [names],/ into air/ deeper than any natural shadow." Within a flow of time that no one can ease, against the shapeless fears of the impending intrusion of mortality, Dana offers the generous notion that here and now must be enough, that love is worth the risk of its failure, and that every day the open eye can find consolation in the simplest objects.

YES, EVERYTHING

As if to confirm Dana's affirmation of the self in the real world, the poems collected in the 1994 *Yes, Everything* are about places—familiar and exotic, contemporary and ancient, domestic and foreign—that are very real: "This is short-grass/ prairie," he says in "Tanzania," "not a simile/ or a metaphor." Dana takes the reader to the Irish countryside; a campsite in Yellowstone National Park; a beach along the Indian Ocean; the Serengeti Plain in suffocating heat; a Helsinki railroad terminal, where he watches a couple furiously kiss; and a rain-spattered Paris sidewalk. Importantly, he includes the less exotic: a parking lot at a Florida Winn Dixie supermarket; a deserted Iowa golf course; and, in perhaps the collection's most affective moment, the slender "Genesis," Dana recalls being with his wife, quite naked and shivering "amid the stunned animals," in a field just outside their Iowa home, a place that, despite being literally in their back yard, Dana compares to Eden. Not simply lexical postcards, these poems speak to the relationship between the responding self and an unfamiliar world.

Dana's position as traveler/visitor/tourist and the experience of otherness implicit in travel allow him the opportunity to explore what has always fascinated him: the implications of loneliness and the cosmic self, rootless and homeless. In the volume's penultimate poem—whose title, "Here and Now," handily summarizes his larger philosophy—Dana unpacks a new hibachi and ponders the distant pain of his Massachusetts childhood ("I remember the gilded/ and pinched and downcast/ faces of Boston women") but affirms only the "pliers/ and screwdriver . . . I believe/ in this. Here. And now." The metaphor of travel thus allows Dana to suggest that the eye has every reason to be compelled by every glance it takes, that every place, even the familiar, has the capacity to stun.

Stylistically, the poems are opulently detailed and reassuringly concrete. Most of them are direct narratives with locales that are lovingly, sensually detailed, vivid with colors colliding in unexpected harmonies. Appropriately, the music here comes subtly in modulations of syllables and shifts in stresses that allow lines to fold gently into one another. It is a tonal effect best appreciated in reading the poems aloud. Particularly effective is "Rapture," a loving ode to a stretch of Carolina beach at night that captures the heaving surf in a complex medley of long vowels, rolling "ing" words, and soft consonants.

SUMMER

It is not altogether surprising that a poet so compelled by the urgency of now, so convinced that the material world has meaning beyond its obvious surfaces, would produce—at an age when most people are consumed by regrets, fears, or sentimental nostalgia— a volume of verse eloquently tuned to the power of the moment. Like the title, the poems are vibrant and urgent. The lines themselves flow, seldom stopped by end punctuation. "Why can't we," he asks in "Lines Written Between Dream & Sleep," "learn to sip the light/ as sweet bees do?" In "Awake," the poet recounts the quiet drama of a house stirring to life, each object speaking its own language of resurrection. These are not narratives but rather observations: a cold morning at his bird feeder, the first hard storm of winter, a twelve-tone wind chime, a clutch of robin's eggs, late morning coffee, a neighborhood sugared by an early morning snow, trees afire in autumn, a sleeping cat, a deep-dish pizza. They are moments snatched from the approach of mortality (in "Thyme," as he ponders a friend's cardiac scare, he is drying a bumper crop of thyme/time). Such is the treasure each is given every morning.

Dana's readers are cautioned not to be like his neighbors who "look at the sea and see only the sea." The volume closes with Dana strolling alone in a heavy beach fog, where he finds in the cloaking mist his voice suddenly stilled and useless. Dana does not panic. Rather he whistles: a sweet Chopin adagio and then "Stardust" and "On the Sunny Side of the Street," the irrepressible affirmation of, respectively, beauty, love, and hope in a forbidding environment that will not permit him either to look back from where he has come or see ahead to where he is going. Fogbound and making music: It is a fitting summary figure of the philosophy Dana has evolved over more than four decades of poetry.

OTHER MAJOR WORKS

EDITED TEXTS: *Against the Grain: Interviews with Maverick American Publishers*, 1986; *A Community of Writers: Paul Engle and the Iowa Writers' Workshop*, 1999.

BIBLIOGRAPHY

Brunner, Edward. "From Deep Space: The Poetry of Robert Dana." *Iowa Review* 22, no. 3 (1992): 115-134. Indispensable overview of Dana's verse that traces its evolution from early formalist verse and minimalist experiments. Particularly focused on Dana's strategy for violating the poet's profound isolation by offering art itself as mediating terrain. Close readings of several key Dana poems.

Holinger, Richard. "Transcendental Bouquet." *Iowa Review* 25, no. 3 (1995): 168-171. Review of *Yes, Everything* that explores Dana's Buddhist sense of the connectedness of everything and the beauty in the mundane. Places him within the Transcendentalist school of Emerson and Thoreau.

Jaeger, Lowell. "An Interview with Robert Dana." *Poets & Writers Magazine*, July/August, 1991, 13-21. Revealing discussion centering on Dana's sense of language and his place within twentieth century poetics. Engages in candid biographical information.

Joseph Dewey

SAMUEL DANIEL

Born: Taunton, England; 1562(?)
Died: Beckington, England; October, 1619

PRINCIPAL POETRY

Delia, 1592
The Complaynt of Rosamonde, 1592
The First Fowre Bookes of the Civile Warres Between the Two Houses of Lancaster and Yorke, 1595, enlarged in 1599 and 1601
Musophilus: Or, A Defence of Poesie, 1599, 1601, 1602, 1607, 1611, 1623
Poeticall Essayes, 1599

The Works of Samuel Daniel, 1601
Certaine Small Poems, 1605
Songs for the Lute, Viol and Voice, 1606

OTHER LITERARY FORMS

In 1594, for the third edition of *Delia*—which bore the title *Delia and Rosamond augmented*—Samuel Daniel included a play, *Cleopatra*, which was written in the "Senecan mode." Actually, the author entered the piece in the Stationers' Register as early as October 19, 1593, and dedicated it to his patron, Mary Herbert, Countess of Pembroke (1561-1621), the sister of Sir Philip Sidney. He stated that he wrote it at her request and as a companion to her own translation of the French playwright Robert Gainier's *Tragedy of Antonie* (1592). Six years later, Daniel began another play, three acts of a tragedy based on the story of Philotas, taken from Quintus Curtius, Justin, and Plutarch's *Life of Alexander*. Originally, he had intended the play to be acted at Bath during the Christmas season by certain gentlemen's sons; however, his printers urged him to complete other projects, and *The Tragedy of Philotas* was not completed and published until 1605. Daniel dedicated the work to Prince Henry, complaining that the public favor extended to him during the reign of Elizabeth had not been carried over to that of James I.

The Tragedy of Philotas caused Daniel some problems at Court, principally because suspicion arose that Philotas was actually a representation of the late earl of Essex. Such a conclusion meant that the author was trying to apologize for or to defend Essex's rebellion of 1601. Thus, the nobles summoned Daniel before them requesting him to explain his meaning; upon doing so, he was nevertheless reprimanded. In 1607, Daniel published a "corrected" edition of *The Tragedy of Philotas*, with an "apology" denying that his play warranted the aspersions that had been cast upon it. Finally, the poet published, in 1618, *The Collection of the Historie of England*, from the beginnings of English history to the end of Edward III's reign (1377).

ACHIEVEMENTS

Samuel Daniel's reputation has suffered the misfortune of history, the poet having lived and written during an age of literary giants. In a sense, he lies buried beneath the weight of Edmund Spenser, William Shakespeare, John Lyly, Sir Philip Sidney, Michael Drayton, Thomas Campion, and Ben Jonson. The existence of those personages was not itself sufficient to relegate Daniel to the second rank of poets; rather, the writer's own attitudes toward poetry and the state of the world contributed to his eventual position in the literary history of the later Elizabethan period. On the surface, Daniel appears as an intelligent and thoughtful poet, gifted with imagination and literary eloquence. No one has ever questioned his dedication to the craft of poetry, as he labored to write and then to polish his verse. He embraced all of the virtues associated with the best practitioners of his art: patience to correct and revise, and sensitivity to criticism. Those very virtues, however, restricted both his artistic and personal advancements. He was by nature reluctant to burst forth upon the world. Incessant labor and untiring revision became a refuge for his hesitancy and uncertainty, and he spent much time, both in and outside his poetry, reflecting upon and developing a variety of viewpoints.

Nevertheless, that hesitancy and uncertainty, as observed from a distance of almost three centuries, may well constitute the essence of Daniel's achievement as a poet. He never saw himself other than as a poet called upon to write poetry. With that purpose in mind, he sought perfection, although he fully recognized the impossibility of ever rising to that state. For example, he revised *The Complaynt of Rosamonde* five times and *Delia* on four occasions, while *Musophilus: Or, A Defence of Poesie* was altered substantially from its first appearance in 1599 through editions of 1601, 1602, 1607, 1611, and 1623—so often, in fact, that he almost ruined the piece. Still, the revisions reveal Daniel at work, striving to improve the verbal melodies of his lines, repairing what he thought were technical blemishes, purging the Elizabethan idiom from his language, seeking conciseness at almost any cost. Indeed, in discussing these revisions and alterations, a modern editor of Daniel's poetry has referred to the writer as "something of a neoclassicist born before his time," particularly in reference to his passion for accuracy.

Daniel may have been somewhat intimidated by his contemporaries, but he certainly could stand foremost among them in terms of his patriotism—the eagerness and sincerity with which he expressed his love for his country. Patriotism was a mark of the times; still, the careful reader of his poems will readily observe that he availed himself of every opportunity to support England. In his *The First Fowre Bookes of the Civile Warres Between the Two Houses of Lancaster and Yorke*, for example, he extols the virtues of the Talbots, dukes of Shrewsbury, and of Prince Henry at Agincourt with a passion equal to Shakespeare's history plays; he blames a French woman by the name of Margaret for the murder of Henry IV's youngest son, the duke of Humphrey; he cries out to Neptune as god of the sea and protector of his nation to shut out ungodly wiles, vile impieties, and all variety of corruption in order to keep England "meere English." Such expression, however, is not limited to patriotism for the sake of mere nationalism; indeed, Daniel recognized all aspects and varieties of patriotic virtue: the courage of the Welsh bowmen and the fortitude and religious conviction of Sir William Wallace, the principal champion of Scotland's independence. Kings are also given their due, as Daniel describes Edward I, a generous prince and Christian warrior who shed his blood for England's greatness. Richard Coeur de Lion (Richard I), on the other hand, and from a more objective point of view, is depicted as having found himself caught up in his campaigns against Philip II of France in an unjust and unprofitable war, deceiving both the world and himself.

Daniel's dedication to England can be related directly to his love of the past. In that respect, he stood equal to a select band among his contemporaries, principally Sidney and Spenser. He rose in anger at allusions by others to the vaunted infallibility of the Greeks and Romans. Such proclamations, he maintained, were but passions that clouded sound men's judgments and caused them to lose respect for the traditions of their own nations. Thus, as in *Musophilus*, Daniel sought out those times that, free from classical ornamentation and deformity, fashioned the wonderful architecture of England. Standing, regretfully, before Stonehenge, he sees it as a vague symbol of the nation's birth: "The misery of darke forgetfulnesse." Similarly, he looks back upon an early day to a peaceful and devout world, in which men of learning lived in a cloistered security. What happened to that cloister? It was a bubble of illusion, burst from

without by printing presses which spread controversy and by gunpowder which destroyed the ancient form and discipline of medieval warfare.

In the final analysis, however, Daniel must be seen as a poet of the Renaissance whose imagination grew out of Renaissance ideals of action—to pursue learning and to reconcile the ideal of action with that of culture. Such poetry, particularly in *Musophilus*, became prophecy in which Daniel looked to a new world that would continue to emphasize the civilization of times past. In that new world, the poet (perhaps Daniel himself) rises to considerable heights when he explicates the fine qualities of that former age. Like his contemporaries, Shakespeare and Spenser, Daniel represented the true Elizabethan poet because, as did all true Elizabethans, he tried very hard to transcend the boundaries of his age. "The Starres, that have most glorie," he wrote, "have no rest."

BIOGRAPHY

Although the exact date and place of Samuel Daniel's birth remain unknown, he was probably born near Taunton, in north Somerset, in late 1562 or early 1563, the son of John Daniel, a music master. A younger brother, John, became a musician of some reputation, having earned a bachelor's degree in music in 1604 from Christ Church College, Oxford, after which he published twenty songs titled *Songs for the Lute, Viol and Voice*—with words by his poet-brother. A third brother, also named John, engaged himself in the service of the Earl of Essex. He was later fined and imprisoned for having embezzled certain of Essex's letters to his wife and, in 1601, for conspiring with one Peter Bales to blackmail the countess.

Samuel Daniel entered Magdalen Hall, Oxford, in 1581, at the age of nineteen as a commoner. However, he did not remain quite long enough to earn a degree; after about three years, he found English poetry, history, and translation more to his liking than the stricter disciplines of logic and philosophy. Thus, in 1585 he published his first book, a translation of a tract on devices, or crests, titled *Imprese*, by Paolo Giovo, Bishop of Nocera. By 1586 he had obtained a position with Lord Stafford, Elizabeth's ambassador to France; in September of that year, he was found at Rye in the company of an Italian doctor, Julio Marino. If one is to trust the 1594 sonnet collection, *Delia* (numbers 47 and 48), Daniel had spent almost two years in Italy—either from 1584 to 1586, or at some period prior to 1589. Shortly after 1590, the poet became tutor to William Herbert, third earl of Pembroke, son of Sir Philip Sidney's sister, Mary, and the patron of Shakespeare. Thus, Daniel took up residence at Wilton, near Salisbury, the seat of the Pembrokes.

The real attraction for Daniel at Wilton was not his pupil, but the boy's mother, Mary Herbert, countess of Pembroke. A woman of excellent literary taste and of distinctive literary talent, she had married Henry Herbert in 1577 and became the most famous patroness of literature in her time, bestowing her favors and encouragement upon Spenser, Ben Jonson, Shakespeare, her brother Philip Sidney, and, of course, Daniel. Despite such support for his work, however, Daniel first appeared before the world without his consent or even foreknowledge. At the end of the 1591 edition of Sidney's *Astrophel and Stella*, the printer (or editor) attached twenty-seven of Daniel's sonnets; what really bothered him, however, was the fact that the pieces contained typographical errors which offended his sense of correctness. He countered by issuing, in February, 1592, his volume of *Delia*, with fifty sonnets dedicated to the countess of Pembroke. The volume was well received, with the result that Daniel published a new edition later the same year (with four new sonnets and *The Complaynt of Rosamonde*, a long narrative poem) and a third edition in 1594. In the latter collection, he replaced the prose dedication to the countess of Pembroke with a sonnet, added a number of sonnets and deleted others, enlarged *The Complaynt of Rosamonde* by twenty-three stanzas, and included his Senecan tragedy, *Cleopatra*.

Daniel's reputation grew and attracted Spenser's attention, the epic poet thinking highly of him and encouraging him to write tragedy. Daniel was not interested in such projects, however; instead, he produced a long historical poem, *The First Fowre Bookes of the Civile Warres Between the Two Houses of Lancaster and Yorke*; on the model of Lucan's ancient *Pharsalia*. For the next five years (1595-1599), Daniel published nothing new, principally because he was busily engaged at Skipton, Yorkshire, in tutoring Anne Clifford, daughter

of the countess of Cumberland, then eleven years of age. He enjoyed the relationship with the family but felt restricted by the work that kept him from writing poetry— especially the completion of his *Civile Warres*. Nevertheless, he managed to wrench himself free long enough to compose, in 1599, his poem *Musophilus* and a verse *Letter from Octavia to Marcus Antonius*. Two years later he published the first collected edition of his works, *Poeticall Essayes*. That was followed by a complete edition later in 1601, *The Works of Samuel Daniel*.

There are those who would maintain that, upon Spenser's death in 1599, Daniel succeeded him as poet laureate of England. However, before Ben Jonson received his patent and pension in February, 1616, the official position of poet laureate did not really exist. True, Spenser had received £50 a year from Queen Elizabeth, but that sum signified informal royal recognition rather than payment for a distinct position or office. Although Daniel occupied no formal position as a poet, he visited often at Court early in the reign of James I, where friends received him well. Further, Daniel had determined to be one of the first to congratulate James on the king's arrival in England; thus, he sent him *A Panegyricke Congratulatorie* while he traveled toward London. In 1602, the poet had dedicated a sonnet to "Her Sacred Majestie," Queen Anne. With his political fences fairly secure, he turned his attention to *The Tragedy of Philotas* (1605).

Daniel spent the better part of his later years reviewing his early poetry, preparing editions of his works, and writing second-rate entertainments for Court festivities: *The Vision of the Twelve Goddesses* (1604), *The Queenes Arcadia* (1605), *Tethys Festival: Or, The Queenes Wake* (1610), and *Hymens Triumph* (1615), the last piece to be published by Daniel during his lifetime. Such efforts yielded some reward, for he received the appointment of inspector of the children of the queen's revels, a post that he gave over to his brother John in 1619. In 1607, the poet served as a groom of the queen's privy chamber, which meant a stipend of £60 a year. He had moved out of London in 1603 and rented a farm in Wiltshire, near Devizes. There, in June, 1618, he wrote his last poem "To the Right Reverend Father in God, James Montague, Lord Bishop of Winchester," Dean of the Chapel and a member of the Privy Council, the purpose of which was to console the cleric during his sickness. Daniel himself died in October, 1619.

ANALYSIS

Perhaps the most sensible point at which to begin an analysis of Samuel Daniel's poetry is the commentary of his contemporaries. The poets of his day saw considerable quality in his work. Francis Meres, a rector, schoolmaster, and literary reviewer, believed that in the *Delia* sonnets, Daniel captured the matchless beauty of his titled subject, while the individual's passion rose at the reading of the distressed Rosamond's death. Meres also found the *Civile Warres* to be equal to Lucan's *Pharsalia*. The lyric poet and writer of romances Thomas Lodge gave him the highest praise for invention and choice of language, while Thomas Carew, one of Ben Jonson's principal disciples, labeled him the English Lucan. Daniel's rhyme caught the attention of the Scots pamphleteer and versifier William Drummond of Hawthornden, who believed it second to none, and a number of lesser poetic lights during the reigns of Elizabeth and James I heaped praise upon Daniel's sharp conceits, pure English, and choice of words. There were, of course, a like number of detractors, foremost among them being Ben Jonson, the dramatist John Marston, and Michael Drayton, who claimed that Daniel was only a historian in verse who should have written prose ather than poetry. Interestingly, the judgments of Daniel's contemporaries, both positive and unfavorable, were not too far off the mark.

Daniel's career as a poet must be viewed in two stages. In his early period, the poet committed himself to pageantry and the patriotism of Elizabethan England. He sought to glorify his nation, applying his imagination to its ideals and achievements. As he matured, however—as his experiences widened and his intellect developed and deepened—he learned how to control the complex combination of poetry and history. Further, he learned about the language of poetry. Once in command of the poet's art, of language, he began to understand the conflicts in which all Elizabethan poets engaged: confidence in and concern for the ability to write poetry; dedication to the notion of England, but doubt of the events of history; trust in beauty, but skepticism about surface materialism. Still, with all of these conflicts, Daniel

managed to succeed as a poet because, in the end, he appealed to custom and nature, both of which provided him "wings" to carry him "not out of his course, but as it were beyond his power to a faire happier flights."

DELIA

Daniel reached the height of his stature as a poet with the publication of his sonnet sequence, *Delia*, and its apparent companion piece, the long narrative poem *The Complaynt of Rosamonde*. Although the poet, by 1592, might have been expected to demonstrate some evidence of having been influenced by Sir Philip Sidney and his sister, the countess of Pembroke, *Delia*, in particular, differs significantly from *Astrophel and Stella*. The former contains little of the drama and personal tension found in Sidney's sequence, but it has considerably more melody and clear imagery. The majority of the sonnets follow the English (or Shakespearean) pattern, with three quatrains and a final couplet. Unlike those of Shakespeare, however, the poems lack any bursts of emotional surge or lift. Instead, Daniel clung to this pure diction, serene rhythms, and sparkling clarity that allowed his reader to see, without difficulty, such objects as a clear-eyed rector of a holy hill, a modest maid decked with the blush of honor, and the green paths of youth and love. True, the sonnets are supposed to reflect the passionate love adventures of the poet's youth; obviously, however, time, a series of careful revisions for later editions, and the quiet and placid nature of maturity created a unified series of sober, restrained, and mediated utterances. There are a number of interesting biographical and source problems surrounding *Delia*, particularly the identity of the lady of the title and accusations of plagiarism from several French sonneteers; these remain debates of a speculative nature and ought not to detract from the true poetic force of the complete sequence.

THE COMPLAYNT OF ROSAMONDE

The Complaynt of Rosamonde first appeared in 1592, bound with the authorized edition of *Delia*. Thus, scholars have quickly labeled it a companion to the sonnets, although it might be more accurately termed a transition. On one hand, its style and content relate it to *Delia*, but it also moves in the opposite direction, toward the serious, contemplative tone of later poems. In 106 seven-line stanzas, Daniel relates the story of Rosamond

Clifford, mistress of Henry II, but the poet does not forget entirely the Delia of his sonnets. The ghost of Rosamond, while pleading with the poet to attempt to relate her narrative, apologizes for intruding upon his own private griefs. However, the spirit strongly suggests that Delia's heart may be moved by evidence of poetic sympathy for one of her sex—namely, Rosamond. Before vanishing, the ghost appeals to Delia for a sigh to help her pass to a sweet Elysian rest. Thus, Daniel finds himself alone with his own sorrows concerning the errors of his youth. In another context, the despondent Rosamond reflects upon the cruelty of isolating beauty from the admiration of the world. She points to the beautiful women who come to town to display their loveliness—all except Delia, who has been left in a remote part of the country. *The Complaynt of Rosamonde* demonstrates the skill with which Daniel could construct a long narrative poem containing both story and moral, uncluttered with social, religious, or political complications. In *The Complaynt of Rosamonde*, he concentrated almost exclusively on the theme of personal tragedy and the contrast between exaltation and misery. Such concentration permitted him to develop a character, write a story reflecting universal melancholy, and place both in a context appropriate to and worthy of the term *complaint*.

CLEOPATRA

Daniel's *Cleopatra* is a carefully formed Senecan tragedy in alternate rhyme, justifiably dismissed as drama but not sufficiently appreciated for its poetry. The play, which focuses mainly on events subsequent to Anthony's death, was dwarfed by Shakespeare's *Antony and Cleopatra* (c. 1606-1607), which swept all rivals from the field. Nevertheless, Daniel's *Cleopatra* can be appreciated as literature. It contains an abundance of human feeling from which the reader may derive dramatic and poetic pleasure; further, its form and diction have been compared with that of Shakespeare's *Antony and Cleopatra* and John Dryden's *All for Love* (1677). Daniel concentrates his attention on Cleopatra to examine her at a moment of significant crisis, to view her from various perspectives. For example, he weaves into his verse-drama a number of seemingly peripheral scenes that function as comments on Cleopatra's resolve to die. Such scenes—Arius saving Philostratus from death,

Philostratus being ashamed of clinging to life so eagerly in time of national disaster—place the story of individual persons into the larger, more important context of politics and society. Certainly there is much to observe in the conflict between Cleopatra as queen and as mother. Daniel, however, does not lose sight of the "higher" moral issues: pride and riot out of control, government and citizens overcome by impiety and false security, and the entire society wallowing in what he terms "fat-fed pleasure."

CIVILE WARRES

Certainly, the historical and political issues in *Cleopatra* helped to establish Daniel's interest in those areas, and he never lost sight of his mission to give the world a memorable historical epic. Thus, almost exactly a year after entering *Cleopatra* in the Stationers' Register, the poet issued the initial version of his *Civile Warres*. After almost fifteen years of labor, beginning in 1594, Daniel managed to produce eight books amounting to about seven thousand ottava rima lines. The work began with Richard II in 1377 and was supposed to end with the marriage of Henry VII to Elizabeth of York in January, 1486, but the poet fell slightly short of the mark and arrived only at 1464 and the marriage of Edward IV and Lady Elizabeth Grey. Although it would be a disservice to Daniel's motives to term the project a mistake, it may well have been too ambitious an undertaking for one who was not a fully committed historian. Daniel set out to versify the truth, not to write a poem; he hoped that the result would serve all of his countrymen, a national epic that seemed right for the time. Unfortunately, his contemporaries viewed the *Civile Warres* as a verse chronicle, not as an epic poem. In fact, Ben Jonson complained that Daniel had written a poetic commentary on the civil wars, but had failed to include a single battle—a comment that was more figurative than factual.

Actually, the problems arising from the project were not entirely of Daniel's own making. He originally intended to establish himself as a legitimate epic poet and a loyal subject of Elizabeth by anchoring the *Civile Warres* to Tudor myth and history. Although the blood factions of the nation produced a bloody war, good eventually came from the evil. Elizabeth would serve as a symbol of peace following the civil strife, thus inspiring poets to record and comment upon the events. By 1609, however, prior to completing the final book of the *Civile Warres*, Daniel found himself without a subject: Elizabeth was dead. He had by that time, however, directed his attention to other forms of historical writing, especially prose, and he simply lost interest in the epic, as well as in the historical period he was attempting to versify.

MUSOPHILUS

History was not the only study to capture Daniel's interest and muse. His *Poeticall Essayes* of 1599 contain one of his most characteristic poems, *Musophilus*. It is certainly a very personal piece, yet it stands as a fine example of the verse dialogue. On the personal level, the poet contends that he must develop and defend his own art, not only for the benefit of those who are contemptuous of it but also to reestablish his faith in himself and in the career of letters to which he has dedicated himself. That personal level, then, dictates the structure of the poem. Philocosmus, the unlettered man of action, confronts Musophilus, the defender of culture and of all learning. Daniel maintained that the idea for the poem was his—from his own heart—but there are clear connections to Count Baldassare Castiglione's *Il Cortegiano* (translated into English in 1561). At any rate, Philocosmus (like the French) reflects the great heresy of knowing only the nobility of arms; he ignores and also abhors letters, and considers learned men rascals. Such thinking is of course countered with the idea of letters being profitable and necessary for life and culture. The mind, therefore, enters the contest against materialism and narrow utilitarianism in order to preserve reverence. Daniel seriously believed that religious innovation and reform would eventually alter all priorities—the good as well as the bad—thus eradicating the sacred traditions of religion. In other words, in defending poetry and learning, the lines of *Musophilus* clearly echo the poet's fear of the scientific spirit, of an arrogance wherein men strive to talk rather than to worship. The ideal for Daniel was for humility and modesty to accompany knowledge and learning.

OTHER MAJOR WORKS

PLAYS: *Cleopatra*, pb. 1594; *The Tragedy of Philotas*, pb. 1605.

NONFICTION: *The Defence of Ryme*, 1603; *The Collection of the Historie of England*, 1618.

MISCELLANEOUS: *The Works of Samuel Daniel*, 1601; *The Complete Works in Verse and Prose of Samuel Daniel*, 1885-1896, 1963 (5 volumes; Alexander B. Grosart, editor).

BIBLIOGRAPHY

Attreed, Lorraine. "England's Official Rose: Tudor Concepts of the Middle Ages." In *Hermeneutics and Medieval Culture*, edited by Patrick J. Gallacher and Helen Damico. Albany: State University of New York Press, 1989. Attreed places Daniel at the end of a tradition of Tudor apologists concerned with the legend of Tudor achievement and with the mythical connection to King Arthur, and she traces Daniel's growing discomfort with the simplistic tendencies of such historiography. Although not concerned exclusively with Daniel, this article provides important context for much of his historical writing in both verse and prose.

Bergeron, David M. "Women as Patrons of English Renaissance Drama." In *Patronage in the Renaissance*, edited by Guy Fitch Lytle and Stephen Orgel. Princeton, N.J.: Princeton University Press, 1981. Chronicling the importance of women as patrons of dramatic works, Bergeron shows the particular importance to Daniel of both Lucy Russell, the countess of Bedford, and Mary Herbert, the countess of Pembroke. The former arranged for Daniel to be commissioned to write *The Vision of the Twelve Goddesses*, and the latter made him part of her circle at Wilton. Both patrons were major influences on Daniel's career.

Daniel, Samuel. *Musophilus: Containing a General Defense of All Learning*. Edited by Raymond Himelick. West Lafayette, Ind.: Purdue University Press, 1965. After a brief biographical introduction, Himelick explains the main argument of Daniel's philosophical poem and examines its sources and analogues, the poet's revisions, and the style. This volume is a helpful commentary on a rather difficult and abstract work.

Harner, James L. *Samuel Daniel and Michael Drayton: A Reference Guide*. Boston: G. K. Hall, 1980. Harner collects all the major scholarly treatments of Daniel and Michael Drayton from 1684 through early 1979 and annotates each one briefly. The two poets are treated separately. General readers, as well as students, will find this book to be an indispensable guide to secondary materials, which are of uneven quality and often rather specialized.

Helgerson, Richard. "Barbarous Tongues: The Ideology of Poetic Form in Renaissance England." In *The Historical Renaissance: New Essays on Tudor and Stuart Literature and Culture*, edited by Richard Strier and Heather Dubrow. Chicago: University of Chicago Press, 1988. Tracing the sixteenth century argument for quantitative verse to a choice for the civilized tradition of Greece and Rome over the barbarous one of the Goths, Helgerson shows how Daniel answers that argument by repudiating the classical model and by celebrating the gothic origins of the English language and its poetry. Daniel's choice of rhyme is therefore patriotic as well as theoretical. Helgerson sees this choice in a consciously political context, coming as it does in 1603, the year of Queen Elizabeth's death.

Hiller, Geoffrey A., and Peter L. Groves, eds. *Daniel Samuel: Selected Poetry and "A Defense of Rhyme."* Asheville, N.C.: Pegasus Press, 1998. Annotated edition of Samuel Daniel's major poetry and selected prose which expands in scope and detail the Sprague 1930 edition. Spelling and punctuation have been modernized. Some selections are prefaced by a discussion of their literary characteristics, publication history, and thematic content.

Rees, Joan. *Samuel Daniel: A Critical and Biographical Study.* Liverpool: Liverpool University Press, 1964. Placing Daniel and his works in detailed biographical and historical context, Rees explains important influences on the poet and elucidates his main ideas. She is particularly informative on patronage and its effects on Daniel. Unlike many critics, Rees defends Daniel's play *Cleopatra*, but on the other hand, she thinks his masques show unease with the form and its symbolism. Contains four illustrations and a good, though not annotated, select bibliography.

Seronsy, Cecil. *Samuel Daniel.* New York: Twayne, 1967. This basic critical biography of Daniel is clearly and simply presented and is ideally suited for nonspecialists as well as students. Seronsy is particularly strong in showing the development of Daniel as a poet over the course of many years. The final chapter, "Poet and Thinker," offers an excellent introduction to Daniel's versification, characteristic imagery, and ideas. A carefully annotated short bibliography is included.

Samuel J. Rogal;
bibliography updated by the editors

GABRIELE D'ANNUNZIO

Born: Pescara, Italy; March 12, 1863
Died: Gardone, Italy; March 1, 1938

PRINCIPAL POETRY

Primo vere, 1879, 1880
Canto novo, 1882, 1896
Intermezzo di rime, 1884, 1896
Isaotta Gùttadauro ed altre poesie, 1886, 1890
San Pantaleone, 1886
Elegie romane, 1892
Poema paradisiaco—Odi navali, 1893
Laudi del cielo del mare della terra e degli eroi, 1899
Maia, 1903
Elettra, 1904
Alcyone, 1904 (English translation, 1977)
Merope, 1912
Canti della guerra latina, 1914-1918
Asterope, 1949
Le laudi, 1949 (expanded version of 1899 title, also includes *Maia*, *Elettra*, *Alcyone*, *Merope*, and *Asterope*)

OTHER LITERARY FORMS

In addition to poetry, Gabriele D'Annunzio's literary production encompasses many other genres: short stories, novels, autobiographical essays, political writings, and several plays, in Italian and in French.

The whole of D'Annunzio's production is available in three major editions: *Opera omnia* (1927-1936); *Tutte le opere* (1931-1937); and *Tutte le opere* (1930-1965), which also includes D'Annunzio's notes under the title *Taccuini*. Forty-one volumes of D'Annunzio's collected work were issued under the title *Opera complete* (1941-1943).

ACHIEVEMENTS

Gabriele D'Annunzio dominated the Italian literary scene from 1880 until the end of World War I. His literary work and his personal conduct challenged existing models with such an exuberant vitality that even the less positive aspects of his art and life have been influential, if only for the reaction they have provoked.

Extremely receptive to foreign influences, D'Annunzio, through a series of experiments with new forms and styles of composition, evolved an original poetic language. Replacing traditional grammatical links with paratactic constructions, he forged a style in which assonance, onomatopoeia, and alliteration prevail, achieving enthralling effects of pictorial and musical synesthesia.

Historically, D'Annunzio's most original achievement was to help break the highly academic literary tradition which had been dominant in Italy for centuries and to reintegrate Italian culture into the mainstream of European intellectual life. He was the first modern Italian writer. His literary work in its amplitude and variety served as an invaluable source of motifs, themes, and suggestions for the brilliant generation of poets who came to maturity in the 1920's. As Eugenio Montale has observed, an Italian poet who has learned nothing from D'Annunzio is truly impoverished.

BIOGRAPHY

Gabriele D'Annunzio was born in Pescara, a small port city in the Abruzzi region, on March 12, 1863, to a well-to-do family. He received a solid classical education at the Liceo Cicognini, in Prato, and when he was only sixteen years old, he published his first collection of verses, *Primo vere* (early spring).

In 1881, D'Annunzio moved to Rome, where he registered at the university in the department of Italian literature, but he never completed his university studies. He

Gabriele D'Annunzio (Library of Congress)

chose instead to pursue a writer's career, consolidating his fame as a young poetic genius in the literary and aristocratic circles of the capital. During that time, he contributed verses, short stories, and articles to several publications, while enjoying an intense social life punctuated by love affairs, intrigues, and scandals. His second collection of verses, *Canto novo* (new song), was both more accomplished and more personal than its predecessor.

D'Annunzio's Roman period, interrupted by adventurous cruises and occasional sojourns in the Abruzzi region, lasted until 1891. By that time, he had already gained national recognition, sealing his social and literary success with his marriage to Maria Hardouin, Duchess of Gallese, and with the publication of a novel. These were fruitful years for D'Annunzio, as witnessed by the production of numerous novels and collections of short stories. D'Annunzio led an extravagant and magnificent life, a life of debts and scandals, of new loves and adventures. At the same time, he maintained an unrelenting rhythm of work. Indeed, all of his activities were encompassed and absorbed by a total engagement in literature.

D'Annunzio also nourished political ambitions. In 1896, he published *Le vergini della rocce* (*The Maidens of the Rocks*, 1898), a novel whose antidemocratic message is emblematic of the writer's political choices. One year later, he entered the political arena and was elected as a representative to the Italian parliament. His activity there was unremarkable until 1900, when, during the controversy over the exceptional laws proposed by Luigi Pelloux's government, he theatrically shifted to the left wing, declaring: "I am going toward life." In the same year, he presented himself as a candidate in the Socialist list but was not elected; with this defeat, D'Annunzio closed his parliamentary experience.

In 1894, D'Annunzio had met Eleonora Duse, the great actress, who played a considerable part in his sentimental life and had a substantial influence on his literary activities. This union of love and art gave rise to a period of great literary achievements. At "La Capponcina," a villa in the hilly countryside of Florence, surrounded by horses, dogs, and works of art, D'Annunzio wrote another novel, a number of plays, and the first three volumes of *Le laudi*, which represent the highest expression of his poetic art. His relationship with Duse was interrupted in 1903 by new temptations. After a few years of extravagant expenses, D'Annunzio, driven by his taste for luxury and his passion for cars and planes, was insolvent. In 1909, "La Capponcina" was seized by the creditors, and one year later D'Annunzio left Italy for France, choosing what he pompously called a "a voluntary exile." There, he split his time between his residence in Arcachon and Paris, where he was soon introduced into the literary and social circles. To this period belong several works in Old French, the most prominent of which is *Le Martyre de Saint Sébastien*, a theatrical text with music by Claude Debussy, which was presented in Paris in 1911.

The French period came to a close at the outbreak of World War I. Faithful to the idea of traditional alliance between France and Italy, D'Annunzio returned to Italy to campaign in favor of Italy's intervention in the war against Germany. D'Annunzio's political speeches were a clamorous success, significantly contributing to the victory of the interventionist party.

As soon as Italy entered the war, D'Annunzio enlisted as a volunteer; he fought first on the front line and then participated in several actions on the sea and in the air. In January, 1916, as a result of a plane accident, he lost his right eye and had to spend three months immobilized and in darkness. During this period of forced inactivity, he painfully scribbled notes which were to become *Il notturno* (1921), a work in prose without a precise narrative line, in which he registered impressions and notations in a stream of consciousness in which past and present are intertwined.

The end of the war and the peace negotiations, quite unsatisfactory for Italy, found D'Annunzio in the role of the poet-prophet, the voice of the people demanding their rights. The polemics over the peace negotiations reached their height when it appeared that the city of Fiume would not be annexed to Italy. With his famous "Marci dei Ronchi," D'Annunzio, at the head of a group of volunteers, entered Fiume and established a temporary government. His action interrupted the diplomatic negotiations between Italy and Yugoslavia; the Italian government first ordered D'Annunzio to leave the city, and then sent the fleet to force him out.

Fiume was officially annexed to Italy in 1924. D'Annunzio's action may have had some weight in this decision, but its immediate result was a failure. Meanwhile, in Italy, D'Annunzio's prophetic role had been assumed by Benito Mussolini. D'Annunzio, disillusioned, retired to a large estate on Lake Garda which he renamed "Il Vittoriale." There, he spent the rest of his life, surrounded by a rich library and by the mass of disparate objects which he had collected with obsessive passion.

The relations between D'Annunzio and the Fascist government were respectfully cold. The poet, while subscribing to certain principles of Fascism, considered Benito Mussolini a poor imitator of his own style; Mussolini, for his part, chose to keep D'Annunzio at a proper distance while bestowing on him honors and subsidies.

When he was not traveling, D'Annunzio led a quiet life at "Il Vittoriale," devoting his time to editing his *Op-*

era omnia (1927-1936). In 1924, under the title *Le faville del maglio*, he gathered and published some of his previous writings; a second volume appeared in 1928. D'Annunzio's *Le cento e cento e cento pagine del libro segreto di Gabriele D'Annunzio tentato di morire* (1935) clearly referred to a strange accident in 1922 (he had fallen from a window) which could have been a suicide attempt. He died in 1938.

ANALYSIS

The "D'Annunzio phenomenon" has stirred a century-long argument between Gabriele D'Annunzio's admirers and detractors, and his reputation has endured alternating periods of favor and disfavor, often related to historical circumstances. Later, under the impetus of a revival both in Italy and abroad, his works were reevaluated in the light of new critical methods.

Considering the number of D'Annunzio's poetry collections, novels, plays, and memoirs, it would be unrealistic to expect a consistent artistic level throughout his oeuvre, but it should be recognized that, in its vastness and diversity, his work is an invaluable documentation of half a century of European intellectual life. In this perspective, it is difficult to isolate certain verse collections from the context of his entire production. The pattern of receptivity and experimentation that characterizes D'Annunzio's poetry can only be appreciated by following the arc of his poetic achievement from *Primo vere* to *Le laudi*, where the voice of the poet reaches the plenitude of his expressive means.

PRIMO VERE

In *Primo vere*, the choice of language, images, and versification is clearly inspired by Giosuè Carducci's model. A second edition of the work in 1880, enriched with fifty-nine new poems, offers greater insight. The delicate musicality of certain verses, the attention devoted to the description of landscapes as the privileged scenery for love encounters, anticipate the distinctive tone which D'Annunzio was to achieve in *Canto novo*. The driving inspiration of this collection is the poet's yearning for identification with nature. A pervasive pagan sensuality saturates the atmosphere as nature and man vibrate with the same impulses: A woman's breath has the perfume of the forest, and her haunches are like those of an antelope; lovers are entwined like "virgin trees interlacing their branches." The metaphors unify Earth, sea, and man in a vitalistic élan in which all forms merge.

CANTO NOVO

Canto novo establishes the alternation between two themes which constitutes a favorite pattern of D'Annunzio's dialectic: an unresolved conflict between the vitalistic impetus and a fin de siècle introspection and sadness. The tendency to magnify the elegiac and melancholic component in the poet's writings is evident in the prevalent interpretation of the collection's most celebrated poem, "O falce di luna calante" (oh, sickle of waning moon), which has often been read as an expression of weariness and consuming despair; as Barberi Squarotti has noted in *Invito alla lettura di D'Annunzio* (1982), this interpretation takes the poem out of its context in the collection, for the next poem is an invitation to another day of joyous life and love.

INTERMEZZO DI RIME

D'Annunzio's negative note decidedly does prevail, however, in *Intermezzo di rime*, which was later revised and published under the shorter title *Intermezzo*. This new collection presented a sharp change in versification, tone, and inspiration. Influenced by the French Parnassian school, D'Annunzio abandoned Carducci's versification for the traditional meters of sonnets and ballads. The volume also reveals a renewed taste for mythological reminiscence, while the polished elegance of the compositions suggests a new concern with aestheticism. Here, closed gardens substitute for natural landscapes, bucolic pagan eroticism gives way to a refined experimentation with morbid sensuality, and vitalism turns into sadistic cruelty. The entire collection is informed by a spirit of willful transgression. The protagonist, "l'Adolescente," dissipates his vital energies in enervating lust. His attempt to achieve full control of life through the exaltation of the senses results in failure, as the satisfaction of pure sensuality rapidly wears out in disgust.

Several other important themes make their first appearance in this collection: the promenade, a privileged moment for erotic emotions; woman, the luxurious female whose castrating power destroys man's energies; art, the fruit and carrier of corruption; the poet, the supreme artificer, the jeweler chiseling the hard, resistant metal of language. Other, less significant sections of *Intermezzo* reveal a taste for the macabre and the sadistic, quite in fashion at that time.

POEMA PARADISIACO

Following several collections of poems which refined the manner of *Intermezzo*, *Poema paradisiaco* (pb. as part of *Poema paradisiaco—Odi navali*) introduced a new style. Here, following the French Symbolists and influenced as well by Giovanni Pascoli's *Myricae* (1891; tamarisks), D'Annunzio proposes a new musicality studiously built on a rhythm of verses broken by enjambments and interrupted by exclamations, questions, and invocations, where rhymes are hidden and assonance prevails. Memory, contemplation, and melancholy govern this poem of gardens (from the Greek *paradeisos*, "of the garden"), where "gardens" signify the closed space of interiority and meditation away from intellectual and sensual turmoil.

Poema paradisiaco evokes the languid melancholy of things that are no more, of sentiments that could have been. The memory of a brief encounter rouses a longing for an opportunity forever lost. The poet recalls flowers that have not been gathered, loves that have not been lived, privileged moments that have not been enjoyed. In "La passeggiata," the poet prefers a sweet and melancholy relation with a woman to the ardor of love, concluding with a subtly ironic comment: "o voi dal dolce nome che io non chiamo!/ perchè voi non mi amate ed io non vi amo" ("You, with the sweet name I do not call!/ because you do not love me and I do not love you"). *Poema paradisiaco* remains one of the fundamental works of nineteenth century Italian poetry for its innovative language and rhythm and for its influence on the following generation of poets.

LE LAUDI

While all the preceding poetic works of D'Annunzio have provoked contrasting critical opinions, *Le laudi* has by general agreement been recognized as the poet's masterpiece. This vast work was to include seven books dedicated to the seven stars of the Pleiades, but only four books of the projected seven were published during D'Annunzio's lifetime: *Maia*, *Elettra*, *Alcyone*, and *Merope*. A fifth book, *Asterope*, published posthumously in 1949, includes the poems which D'Annunzio wrote during World War I.

Maia is mainly devoted to "Laus vitae," a long poem based on D'Annunzio's voyages in Greece in 1898 and 1899. In this poem, he celebrates the creative power of the classical world, comparing the vital drive of Greek civilization with the sterility of contemporary society. Hymns to Hermes, the creator, alternate with descriptions of modern cities where corruption and vice dominate, culminating with a vision of the "Great Demagogue," a mass leader who preaches the destruction of everything that is beautiful and noble. The populace is portrayed as an instinctively violent and somehow innocent animal, exploited by demagogues and sacrificed without pity. Destruction and suffering, the poet-prophet predicts, will be followed by the birth of a new society in which work and beauty will be equally respected and loved.

In these fiery images, D'Annunzio expresses his antidemocratic and aristocratic sentiments, inspired by Friedrich Nietzsche, but the complex system of the philosopher is narrowed down to serve a limited political program. The poem concludes with an invocation to Nature, the immortal Mother, who is the source of creation and renewal.

Elettra, named for the second star in the constellation, is divided roughly into two parts. In the first part, the celebratory and commemorative inspiration of many of the poems and their oratorical manner reveal D'Annunzio's ambition to create a new mythology, to become the epic bard of the new Italian nation. This effort is not always sustained by authentic inspiration, and in many poems rhetoric and artificiality prevail. The second part, "Le città del silenzio," is a celebration of the old Italian cities, silent and forgotten in the enclosure of their glorious past. Evocations of ancient events and descriptions of splendid monuments and palaces, dissolve into a subdued musicality tinted with melancholy.

In the third volume of the series, *Alcyone*, D'Annunzio reached his highest lyric expression. After the heroic tension of *Maia* and *Elettra* and their fervid affirmations and denunciations, *Alcyone* stands as a pause, a moment of total participation in the joyous blossoming of nature in its fullest season. The book opens with "La tregua," an invocation to "il magnanimo despota" (the generous despot), Nietzsche, the master of willpower. After a period of intense commitment to the fight against brutal ignorance, corruption, and vulgarity, the poet asks for a respite. He wants to be reinvigorated, forsaking public squabbles for the pure sources of life. The poem concludes with a celebration of pagan nature, the realm of fauns, nymphs, and satyrs.

In the following poems, a series of mythological passages translates the introductory hymn to nature into the apotheosis of poetry. In the poem "Il fanciullo," the divine flute player who modulates the most delicate murmurs of nature is the image of the youthful god of poetry: Here, poetry is the privileged activity where art and nature meet and merge. In "Lungo l'Affrico nella sera di giugno dopo la pioggia," a description of the fresh calm of nature in the twilight after a summer rain evolves into a meditation on the power of poetry. Nature offers itself like ductile clay to the poet, who shapes it into a durable work of art. In the following poem, "La sera fiesolana," this concept evolves into a conception of poetics which is central to an understanding of the collection. The landscape vibrates with a secret urge to express itself; hills and rivers, leaves and drops of rain, all of nature utters silent words that only the poet can hear. The voice of nature is the language of poetry itself. "La spica" and "Le opere e i giorni" carry the message even further, affirming that all forms of nature live only as a function of the poetic word, which, by naming them, calls them into existence.

After *Alcyone*, D'Annunzio was chiefly concerned with other literary genres. He seldom returned to poetry and then only for occasional lyric fragments. *Merope*, the fourth book of *Le laudi*, includes ten canzones composed on the occasion of the Italo-Turkish war. These poems do not add anything to D'Annunzio's reputation, the flamboyant rhetoric of the volume betrays its essentially political function.

With *Alcyone*, D'Annunzio's poetic inspiration achieved its fullest expression. The feeling of joyful participation in nature which informed his early verse reappeared in *Alcyone*, decanted, refined, and enriched by the variety of D'Annunzio's painstaking experiments with new forms and techniques and by his unrelenting meditation on poetry. Themes, motifs, and discoveries of the preceding collections merge in *Alcyone*. Mythology, no longer an artificial ornament, is integrated with nature, which speaks through myths and transfers to the

poet its creative force. In this world created by poetic language, everything harmonizes in a unique song celebrating the eternal beauty of life and nature in their multiform aspects.

D'Annunzio's art, based on classical culture yet renewed by the European avant-garde, represents the link between traditional and modern forms of poetry. Like all great writers, D'Annunzio created a personal poetic language to give life to his imaginative world; at the same time, his verse transcended personal concerns to serve as a testing ground for modern Italian poetry.

Other major works

LONG FICTION: *Il piacere*, 1889 (*The Child of Pleasure*, 1898); *Giovanni Episcopo*, 1892 (*Episcopo and Company*, 1896); *L'innocente*, 1892 (*The Intruder*, 1898); *Il trionfo della morte*, 1894 (*The Triumph of Death*, 1896); *Le vergini della rocce*, 1896 (*The Maidens of the Rocks*, 1898); *Il fuoco*, 1900 (*The Flame of Life*, 1900); *Forse che si forse che no*, 1910; *La Leda senza cigno*, 1916.

SHORT FICTION: *Terra vergine*, 1882, 1884; *Il libro della vergini*, 1884; *San Pantaleone*, 1886; *Le novelle della Pescara*, 1902 (*Tales from My Native Town*, 1920); *Le faville del maglio*, 1924, 1928 (2 volumes).

PLAYS: *Sogno di un mattino di primavera*, pr., pb. 1897 (*The Dream of a Spring Morning*, 1902); *Sogno di un tramonto d'autunno*, pb. 1898 (*The Dream of an Autumn Sunset*, 1904); *La città morta*, pb. 1898, pr. in French 1898, pr. in Italian 1901 (*The Dead City*, 1900); *La Gioconda*, pr., pb. 1899 (*Gioconda*, 1902); *La gloria*, pr., pb. 1899; *Francesca da Rimini*, pr. 1901 (verse play; English translation, 1902); *La figlia di Jorio*, pr., pb. 1904 (*The Daughter of Jorio*, 1907); *La fiaccola sotto il moggio*, pr., pb. 1905 (verse play); *Più che l'amore*, pr. 1906; *La nave*, pr., pb. 1908 (verse play); *Fedra*, pr., pb. 1909 (verse play); *Le Martyre de Saint Sébastien*, pr., pb. 1911 (music by Claude Debussy, choreography by Ida Rubinstein); *La Pisanelle: Ou, La Mort parfumée*, pr. in French 1913, pb. 1913 (music by Ildebrando Rizzetti and Pietro Mascagni); *Parisina*, pr., pb. 1913 (music by Mascagni); *La Chèvrefeuille*, pr. 1913 (*The Honeysuckle*, 1915).

SCREENPLAY: *Cabiria*, 1914.

NONFICTION: *L'armata d'Italia*, 1888; *L'allegoria dell'autunno*, 1895; *Contemplazione della morte*, 1912; *Vite di uomini illustri e di uomini oscuri*, 1913; *La musica di Wagner e la genesi del "Parsifal,"* 1914; *Per la più grande Italia*, 1915; *Il notturno*, 1921; *Il libro ascetico della giovane Itali*, 1926; *La penultima ventura*, 1919, 1931 (2 volumes); *Le cento e cento e cento pagine del libro segreto di Gabriele D'Annunzio tentato di morire*, 1935; *Teneo te, Africa*, 1936; *Solus ad solam*, 1939.

MISCELLANEOUS: *Opera omnia*, 1927-1936; *Tutte le opere*, 1930-1965; *Tutte le opere*, 1931-1937; *Opera complete*, 1941-1943 (41 volumes).

BIBLIOGRAPHY

Becker, Jared. *Nationalism and Culture: Gabriele D'Annunzio and Italy After the Risorgimento*. New York: P. Lang, 1994. Biography of D'Annunzio and history of Italy in the first half of the twentieth century. Includes bibliographical references and index.

Bonadeo, Alfredo. *D'Annunzio and the Great War*. Cranbury, N.J.: Associated University Presses, 1995. A biography of D'Annunzio as a narrative of his involvement in World War I. Includes bibliographic references and an index.

D'Annunzio, Gabriele. *Alcyone*. Edited by John Robert Woodhouse. Manchester, England: Manchester University Press, 1978. A collection of D'Annunzio's poetry in English with an informative introduction and annotations by the editor. Includes bibliography and index.

De Felice, Pampaloni, E. Paratore, and Mario Praz. *Gabriele D'Annunzio*. Bologna, Italy: M. Boni, 1978. A collection of biographical and critical essays on D'Annunzio published in Italian.

Gullace, Giovanni. *Gabriele D'Annunzio in France: A Study in Cultural Relations*. Syracuse, N.Y.: Syracuse University Press, 1966. Biographical and historical account of D'Annunzio's life.

Jullian, P. *D'Annunzio*. New York: Viking Press, 1973. An in-depth biography of D'Annunzio's career.

Rhodes, A. *The Poet as Superman: G. D'Annunzio*. New York: McDowell, Obolensky, 1960. Narrative biography of D'Annunzio's life in politics and literature.

Woodhouse, John Robert. *Gabriele D'Annunzio: Defiant Archangel*. New York: Clarendon Press, 1998. An authoritative biography, presenting D'Annunzio's relationships with the worlds of Italian culture, theater, and politics. Includes extensive bibliographic references.

Luisetta Elia Chomel;
bibliography updated by the editors

DANTE

Born: Florence, Italy; May or June, 1265
Died: Ravenna, Italy; September 13 or 14, 1321

PRINCIPAL POETRY

La vita nuova, c. 1292 (*Vita Nuova*, 1861; better known as *The New Life*)

La divina commedia, c. 1320 (3 volumes; *The Divine Comedy*, 1802)

OTHER LITERARY FORMS

Dante's prose works are not usually taken as major literary achievements in themselves, although they provide many useful sidelights and clarifications to a reader of *The Divine Comedy*. Dante titled the work *Commedia*. It was Giovanni Boccaccio, forty years after Dante's death, who called the work *La divina commedia*, the name by which it is commonly known. *Il convivio* (c. 1307; *The Banquet*, 1887) was probably written between 1304 and 1307. An unfinished work of some seventy thousand words in Italian prose, it is a commentary on three canzones or odes in which the poet proposes a theory of allegory for moral readings of his poetic compositions, so that it will be clear that virtue, not passion, is the topic. A digressive apologia, *The Banquet* is a mine of information about medieval literary culture. *De vulgari eloquentia* (c. 1306; English translation, 1890), a Latin prose work of nearly twelve thousand words, was probably composed in the period from 1304 to 1306. It is believed to be the first study ever written about vernacular language and poetic style and contains fascinating conjectures about the origin of language, Romance linguistics, verse forms, metrics, and poetic sounds. *De monarchia* (c. 1313; *On World Government*, 1957) is a Latin prose work of nearly eighteen thousand words, probably written in 1312 and 1313; it is a series of arguments for world rule unified under the Holy Roman Empire. Dante's explanations of his ideas about the separate but complementary functions of church and state are particularly valuable. Only a few of Dante's letters survive, but several of them contain seminal passages of Dantean thought.

Many of Dante's lyrics are probably lost forever, but if the eighty or so miscellaneous ones attributed to him are a fair sampling of his efforts, he put his finest in *The New Life*. Many of these smaller poems show only average craftsmanship and are interesting because they reveal a poet who actively participated in his society. Some of the sonnets are exchanges of opinions with friends; six are part of an invective, a contest both socially and intellectually (which was common then), between Dante and Forese Donati. There are love poems to various ladies, some of them real individuals, others clearly allegorical. The lyrics show a very human poet, playful and experimental, heated by anger and love, embittered by exile.

ACHIEVEMENTS

Dante is among the greatest and most influential figures in the long history of Western literature, and no brief summary can do justice to the scope of his achievements. Perhaps his most enduring legacy has been the astonishing supply of signs and symbols for describing and evaluating inner experience which succeeding generations of readers have found in *The Divine Comedy*. Dante was ultimately a mystic in his approach to God, but he wrote with systematic clarity about every spiritual event, stopping only at the point where language and reason had to be abandoned. Probably the most learned, articulate voice in the Christian West since Saint Augustine, Dante created a powerful mindscape able to reflect every movement of the soul. He did this without subjectivism and narcissism. Dante's vision is both a mirror of the self and a window onto the outside world, the cosmos, and the divine. His inward journey is recounted with great intensity and variety, but with no surprises, for that inner world is no more ambiguous or mysterious

than the outer world, and Dante did not confront either world in a metaphysical void. His vision is not a hallucinatory refuge, but a site where the interconnectedness of all things can be rationally presented and the consequent need for spiritual discipline and social duty can be argued.

Dante responded to two primary imaginative impulses. One drove him to put all of his experiences into an ordered relationship: eros, history, politics, faith. Behind these ideal forms and schematizations lies a genuine love of the created world in all its density. Dante insists that experience be known as actual *and* metaphorical, and that virtue be attained through historical processes. The other impulse moved him continually beyond each part of his creation, always ascending, so that each epiphany becomes a curtain to be drawn back to reveal a higher one. One reads Dante with an awareness of the elaborations of each part and the upward movement of the whole.

Dante was the most important voice in the vernacular love lyric before William Shakespeare. Dante's mastery of lyric form and meter was unparalleled, and he used the intellectually demanding conventions of *dolce stil nuovo* (sweet new style) with simplicity and ease. Had he taken Holy Orders, he could have given the world a pastoral voice worthy of John Donne or George Herbert. Dante's vocational decision was singular and uncompromising. He decided to be a citizen and a philosophical poet. The pains of citizenship fired the creator in him, so that he ultimately became the grandsire of Italian literature and indeed of much of Western literature written since his time. Dante excelled in the poetry of direct statement, in making thought melodic. He found ways to energize moral knowledge, so that it could both persuade and delight. He never wrote to be obscure or ambiguous, but it is important to remember that he was addressing keen, well-educated medieval minds. His mastery of narrative technique and symbolic detail encourages some readers to evaluate his art for its own sake, but Dante always wrote to make the reader look beyond his words to the vision that they served.

BIOGRAPHY

Dante Alighieri was a citizen, and his city was Florence. Medieval Italian cities were for the most part independent states, free of feudal allegiances, with power based not on land, but on harbors, commerce, and industry. The nobility within these cities had gradually yielded power to the new bourgeois interests, but the traditional lines of that struggle were still evident, the nobles seeking support from the emperor and the bourgeois and popular elements tending to oppose the empire and join with the pope.

Those in the imperial faction were called Ghibelines, and those in Papal, or at least the anti-imperial faction, were known as Guelphs. The faction one chose to support often had more to do with current and particular needs and where one's friends and enemies were than with hereditary considerations. Dante's Florence was Guelph, which was enough to make rival cities support the Ghibelline cause—not that the Florentine Guelphs were able to live peaceably for long among themselves. A feud between two branches of a family in Pistoia, who called themselves "Whites" and "Blacks," spread to the Florentine upper classes. The Whites attracted the older families and Papal supporters, while the Blacks tended to attract the newly rich commercial classes.

Little is known of Dante's youth in Florence. It is clear that he read widely among Provençal and contemporary Italian poets as well as classical Latin writers; his writing also reveals a practical knowledge of music and painting. He may have attended the University of Bologna. He fought in the Florentine army and seems to have enjoyed many friendships throughout his city. The most important event in his life occurred at a May Day festival when he was nine years old. There he first saw Beatrice Portinari, who was eight at the time. They did not see each other again until nine years later, but Dante's devout fascination with her image and its significance lasted throughout his life. When she died in 1290, Dante diverted his grief by plunging into the difficult politics of the city and the study of philosophy. Between 1296 and 1301, the government of Florence entrusted him with high responsibilities in politics, finances, and diplomacy. His election as one of the city's six priors in the summer of 1300 exemplifies the public trust he enjoyed, a trust he justified when he validated the banishment of his close friend, the poet Guido Cavalcanti.

The year 1300 brought a convergence of several crises, political, spiritual, and economic, in the poet's life. So far as Dante's personal misfortunes are concerned, there are few details in the historical records. The larger event involved Charles de Valois, whom Pope Boniface had invited into Italy to help with the reconquest of Sicily. Charles was permitted to enter Florence with all of his troops, after assurances that he would not take part in the struggle between the Whites and the Blacks. Almost immediately, Charles allowed the Blacks to have the upper hand, at which point they began severe reprisals against the Whites. Dante was in Rome at the time as part of a delegation sent to secure guarantees from the pope that the French forces would not interfere in Florentine politics. Dante was accused in absentia of barratry, extortion, impiety, and disloyalty, accusations which ulti-

Dante (Library of Congress)

mately carried with them the death sentence. Dante never returned to Florence. As an exile, he drew closer to the exiled Whites and Ghibellines, but neither negotiations nor armed conspiracy succeeded in restoring them to power in Florence. Dante became disenchanted and impatient with his fellow exiles, who resented him, and may even have blamed him for the military reversals they were suffering.

A restless Dante may have spent time in at least a half dozen Italian cities and perhaps Paris at one point. He was unable to right things between himself and Florence, so that he might return. When Henry VII was elected emperor, Dante envisioned an Italy unified under the empire, with an end to the destructive rivalry between church and state, but several key cities, aided by Florentine money, resisted Henry. When Dante angrily urged the Emperor to conquer Florence, he probably eliminated his last chance of entering the city alive. Florence excluded him from the general amnesty offered to the Whites, and then withstood the emperor's assault; Henry died shortly thereafter. In 1315, probably because it needed talented citizens to help against a rival army, Florence declared itself willing to have Dante return, but he proudly rejected the terms. He was in Verona shortly after that, at work on *The Divine Comedy* under the patronage of Can Grande della Scala and his family. He spent his last days in Ravenna at the court of Guido da Polenta. In 1321, da Polenta sent him on a diplomatic mission to Venice. On his return, Dante fell desperately ill and did not recover. He was buried in Verona wearing Franciscan dress.

ANALYSIS

THE NEW LIFE

Dante wrote *The New Life* to give an essential history of his own spirit, which was first aroused, then illuminated by his love for a woman. Here together are the narcissism and ecstasy of youth with the intricate design and perceptions of an older, uncompromising intelligence. The work consists of forty-two passages of prose commentary in which thirty-one poems are set at varying intervals. There are twenty-five sonnets, five canzones, and one ballad. The reader is not meant to abide the prose patiently until he reaches the next poem. Medieval poets believed that it should be possible to state in prose

the core idea of any poem they created. Furthermore, no poem existed for its own sake—that is, solely for an aesthetic purpose. The prose keeps the reader in touch with the invisible realities and spiritual implications which were far more important to Dante than personal expression or artistic technique. The poems of *The New Life* describe and deal with romantic and sexual passion. Within the close boundaries and strict internal laws of poetic form, they either exemplify the point Dante is making in prose, or give way to a prose examination of the meanings beneath their surfaces. The poetic voice contains the original turmoil; the prose voice carries the more complete understanding of later personal reflection. The reader is thus able to share in the warmth of the original feelings and the sequence of epiphanies about them.

The topic of *The New Life* is love-suffering, which the poet will complain about but never abandon, for love-suffering is a way of life—indeed, part of the credentials of a noble person. The nobles whom Dante addressed constituted an elite, intelligent group who shared a sensitivity about love and who communicated easily with one another about its subtle doctrines. Traditionally, the medieval love poet did not concentrate on the real presence of the lady so much as on his own feelings about her. The poet would cry out against the upheavals his passions were causing and voice his fear and resentment of her coldness and elevated distance. Despite it all, he would vow to continue his martyrdom. These conventions of refined love were distorted and exaggerated, but they proved fit equipment for capturing the values of romantic experience. They take the reader past appearances into mental and spiritual realities which a camera eye can never see. The new ideas about love, which began emerging less than a century before Dante was born, caused a revolution in the sensibilities of Western European culture. Dante mastered them, then added a revolution of his own. He transcended the devouring egotism of his predecessors by identifying his own erotic drive and the mental processes it stimulated with the Divine Love which beckons to every soul. The lady thus becomes not merely the outer boundary of the lover's consciousness but a mediating presence between self and Deity. No longer a mirror of the poet's feelings, she stands as a window onto the infinite beauty of the

Divine Presence and the way of salvation. *The New Life* records Dante's discovery of what he owed to several "God-bearing" ladies whom he encountered on his journey, Beatrice foremost among them.

The work begins with the intelligent and chastened voice of experience: Dante has learned to read the book of Nature, and he knows that the mystical significance of numbers can validate his spiritual discoveries. He has found a *vita nuova*, a new and miraculous life epitomized by the number nine, which the word *nuova* also signifies. Nine is the square of three, a number which, to the medieval imagination, represented perfection and the spiritual life. Dante explains how he first saw Beatrice when she was in her ninth year of life, and not again until nine years later, at the ninth hour of the day. Numbers are the clues to what Heaven has planned for him, so that when Dante writes this book of personal memory, made according to the laws of sequence and cause and effect, the reader is also aware of the perennial present of an unchanging ideal realm. For example, in section 3 of *The New Life*, Dante has a dream which is not only an erotic fantasy but also a prophecy. After he has seen Beatrice for the second time, the God of Love appears in a fiery cloud carrying Beatrice, who is asleep and flimsily clothed. Love wakens her and skillfully makes her eat of Dante's burning heart. Then the God begins to weep, folds his arms around her, and the two ascend heavenward. Dante notes that he had this dream at the first of the last nine hours of the night. Thus, the historical event of the lady's death, through the significance of numbers, reflects eternity.

The structure of Dante's book of memory suggests infinite harmony and reconciliation, particularly through the numbers three and nine. The thirty-one poems of *The New Life* fall into three groups, each group attached to one of the three canzones, or longer poems. At the center of the second or middle group is a canzone with four poems on either side of it. The first and third groups each have ten poems and one canzone; in the first group the poems precede the canzone, and in the second they follow it. Besides the obvious symmetry of the entire structure, there are nine poems in the middle group. If Dante had intended the first poem to be an introduction and the thirty-first to be an epilogue, the numbers nine and one would dominate the plan, although this is only a

reasonable conjecture. Of more significance is the merger of numerical sign and literary idea in the middle group: The canzone which is at the exact center of the work refers to Beatrice's possible death with imagery traditionally associated with the Crucifixion of Christ. Thus, the center of the poet's book of memory and the center of Christian history are connected, through the analogy drawn between Beatrice and Christ.

The cast of *The New Life* is small, and the narrative is almost without setting and background. There are really only two actors: the poet, and the feminine presence who provides all the imaginative milestones in his life. Some women are useful distractions to prying eyes, so that he can conceal his true love's identity. The death of one of them tunes his grief for the eventual death of Beatrice, as does the death of Folco Portinari, Beatrice's father. If one takes this little history of a pilgrim's soul as an analogy for God's created time, where events can be understood either to anticipate or to look back toward Christ's Passion, death, and Resurrection, one immediately appreciates the suggestiveness of the format. When Dante contemplates the possibility of Beatrice's death, it seems to him that the sun grows dark and violent earthquakes occur. The next dream presents Beatrice following her beautiful friend, Giovanna, just as Christ followed John the Baptist. Her death will be comparably momentous and fruitful for his own life and later ages. Not that these insights enabled the poet to bear the actual death of Beatrice; the sonnets and canzones which follow that event are almost all to which a lyric poet can aspire, fusing intellect and pathos so perfectly that readers are reminded how imperfectly united their own souls are; at the same time, they are uplifted by the unity Dante has found. For long moments, the reader can believe that the alleged incompatibility between poetry and philosophy is but a jealous rumor.

As Dante decorates his own love story with signs of what he would come to understand about it in retrospect, he also means to show the progress of his own mind as events teach and shape him. He remembers himself as a self-preoccupied courtly lover, more educated and intellectually demanding than the troubadour poets from whom he learned, but, like them, emaciated by love-suffering, anxious, easily embarrassed, inclined to enjoy nursing his wounds in private, and completely under the rule of his master, Love. When, out of concern for her good name, Beatrice refuses to recognize him, he takes to his bed like a punished child. Then he begins to realize the limitations of this infantile mode. That night in a dream, the god appears and tells Dante that not he, but Love, is at the center of things, equidistant from all points on the circumference. Until he can accept the possibilities of this subtler and more comprehensive definition, the paradoxically painful and pleasurable qualities of his subjective experience will continue to vex him. Then, some town women, gently ridiculing his emaciated condition, suggest logically what Love had put more mysteriously: Happiness can come from the words he uses to praise Beatrice, not the words which concentrate on his own condition. With this nobler theme, his new life begins.

The famous canzone from section 19 which begins "Donne ch'avete intelletto d'amore," or "Ladies who can reason out Love's ways," describes the source of the lady's nobleness and perfection, which make all in Heaven want her with them, so that Heaven itself can be more perfect. On Earth, her glance can banish an evil intention or transform it to a noble one, and the worthy will feel salvation from having looked at her, for God has granted that whoever has talked with her will not come to a bad end. Having shifted his attention to a site outside himself, and having identified Beatrice as an emissary of Divine Love (able like It to create something where nothing has existed), Dante now has a talismanic axiom that will help him meet all future experience—even Beatrice's death, for everything coming to him from her will lead heavenward.

After Beatrice's death, a disconsolate Dante is temporarily distracted by the earthly beauty and compassion of a lady who looks at him sympathetically, but a vision of Beatrice resolves his inner struggle between reason and sensuality, and from then on the image of Beatrice is all he contemplates. The last sonnet of *The New Life* tells how his sigh passed the world's outermost sphere, moved by a new intelligence to the radiance of Beatrice in Heaven. When the sigh tries to report what it saw, its words are too subtle for Dante's comprehension; he is certain only that he hears Beatrice's name again and again. The highest and most serene image of the poet's renewed life is, paradoxically, beyond words. In the final section, Dante tells of a miraculous vision which included sights so profound that he made the resolution to say no more about Beatrice until he could find a suitably elevated vehicle. He closes with the wish that the Lord will grant him a few more years, so that he can compose a work about her which will contain things never said about any woman.

A diary unlike any written before it, *The New Life* was the work of a poet ready for sublime tasks who chose to review the development of his spiritual vision and poetic powers as the first step in the direction of carrying out those tasks. A finished masterpiece in its own right, it also served as a prelude to the greatest sustained poetic achievement in the West since Homer.

THE DIVINE COMEDY

There probably never has been a piece of literary imagination as great in scope, as intricate in relationships among its parts, as fastidiously shaped to the smallest detail as Dante's *The Divine Comedy*. Besides the exacting challenge of maintaining poetic intensity for some fourteen thousand lines, there were the perils of dealing with interpretations of religious doctrine and Holy Writ in a fictional context. Even more perilous was the interpretation of Divine Justice, as it applied to specific historical incidents and individuals. Dante's genius and pious imagination flourished among these boundaries and obstacles. He used the appearances of the created world to describe the human heart in a theocentric universe. The three-part narrative pictures the soul deprived of God, in hope of God, and with God. Dante needed a design to mirror the unchanging realities beyond time and space, and he needed an action which would be an imitation of the soul's movements toward these realities. The symmetrical design of the entire work reflects divine perfection, as does its threefold narrative division and three-line stanzas. Each part, *Inferno*, *Purgatorio* (*Purgatory*), and *Paradiso* (*Paradise*), is divided into thirty-three cantos. With the introductory canto, these total one hundred, a number which also traditionally suggested divine unity and perfection.

The world of Dante's *The Divine Comedy* is vertical. The reader always moves downward or upward with the poet: the spiral descent into Hell, the climb up the purgatorial mountain, then up through the various planetary spheres, until the notions of movement up and down are no longer pertinent. The medieval model of the universe was similarly vertical, with Heaven above, Earth at the middle, and Hell below. Everything in God's creation was located at some point or other on a chain or ladder of being, which descended from His divine presence to the lowest form of inert matter. Each being was put at a particular step or degree on this scale, so that it could realize whatever purpose the Creator intended for it, but each thing or being was also understood in terms of what was above it and what was below it. The three realms of Dante's *The Divine Comedy* are vertically related, and each realm has its own vertical plan. The reader is continually urged to compare each spectacle with the one viewed previously and to ponder in retrospect its connection to the spectacle which follows it.

Writing a comedy was also imitating the world, at least as Dante used the term "comedy." In the medieval conception, comedy presented the happy resolution of a difficult situation. Thus, time and history could be seen as parts of a comic action, because Providence, working behind the superficial chaos of Fortune's wheel, would ultimately turn every earthly change to good. Human time and all of its pains began with the Fall of Adam, but that Fall looked forward to Christ's redemptive sacrifice. The sacrifice of Christ, who is often referred to as the "Second Adam," made it possible for the pattern of each life to be comic—that is, for man to conquer sin and win salvation. Dante's *The Divine Comedy* takes place at the end of Holy Week, during the most spiritually intense hours of the Christian year. For a time, darkness appears to triumph, as the God-Man is slain and buried, but out of seeming defeat comes a victorious descent into Hell and a resurrection which is the archetype of every spiritual rebirth which will come after it. When Dante descends into Hell on Good Friday and reaches Purgatory on Easter morning of the year 1300, the reader contemplates that holier comedy thirteen hundred years before.

The Divine Comedy offers more than structural symmetry and Christian values. It is also an imitation of the swarming variousness of the world of time and space: dreams, boasts, accusations, haunting beauties and catastrophes, wisdom, and reconciliation. The opening words hurry the reader into the narrator's dilemma and impasse, until, ninety-nine cantos later, the vision moves beyond human language and sensation. In his treatment of things invisible, Dante makes the reader touch with understanding almost every texture of earthly existence. To the medieval mind, the world was a book to be read, but a book could imitate the world by being an exhaustive compendium of information about geography, history, the nature of flight, even the spots on the moon. Dante's imagination is alert and curious, not satisfied with building a warehouse of facts. Dante further wishes the reader to visualize and experience the logistics of every step of the journey, feeling the heat, smelling the foulness, seeing different kinds of light and darkness, confronting the monstrosities, and struggling along the broken causeways.

The Divine Comedy is Dante's report of a journey he took into the anagogical realm of existence—that is, the afterlife—to witness the rewards and punishments which God's justice apportions to humankind on the basis of choices freely made in life. Dante himself said this much about his masterpiece. The reader learns while watching him learn, and because of that, even in the *Inferno*, moving toward the center of the earth, the place farthest from God, there is a sense of the intelligence and soul expanding. The journey around which the narrative is constructed is also about the movement of every individual life. It intended to provide equipment for living in a City of God on Earth until the grander city of Jerusalem can be attained.

Although the meticulous physical detail encourages the reader to imagine himself on a journey in time and space, he is moving in a mindscape, a spectacle of the sinful human heart. Nowhere in Hell is he shown an attitude or act of which every living soul is not capable. Dante's descent involves a lowering of self through the admission of fault and capacity for fault, and the realization that the difference between man's sin and Satan's sin is one of degree rather than kind. Self-accusation and contrition make cleansing and regeneration possible, so that the climb to salvation can begin. Dante makes himself fall so that he may rise a stronger man, but his is a controlled fall. The vision of Hell could lead to despair and insane fascination, but with a guide who has been there before, Dante can have this terrible knowledge and survive. Having a second individual on the journey is also a useful narrative strategy, because the guide can interact dramatically with Dante the pilgrim and provide a normative presence, so that Dante the poet need not stultify the narrative with endless digressions about what the pilgrim cannot see.

That Dante should choose Vergil, the greatest of all Latin poets, to accompany him is not surprising. In one way or another, Vergil's writings had nourished every medieval poet. In his epic, the *Aeneid* (29-19 B.C.E.), Vergil had described a hero's visit to the underworld, and in that sense had been there once himself. His medieval admirers believed him to be a saint, a moralist, a prophet, even a magician. He was also a pagan and, as Dante strictly reasoned, had not been saved, but he was thought to embody natural wisdom unaided by revelation, which would make him a fit companion for a trip into the region of the damned. Vergil was also a poet of the Empire. He used the story of the fall of Troy to celebrate the founding of Rome and all the achievements of the divinely favored nation which followed it. Vergil predicted an era of world order and prosperity under Roman imperial rule. Many Christians believed that he foresaw in one of his pastorals the coming of the Redeemer and the Christian era. In his essay *On World Government*, Dante had argued that the Empire and the Church were two discrete but complementary modes by which divine purposes could be realized in human history, one emphasizing reason, the other revelation. Vergil epitomizes both the grandeur and the limitations of that gift of natural reason. He travels with Dante as far as he—that is, reason—can, and then is replaced by Beatrice, who personifies the light of divine revelation denied to pagans.

PART I, INFERNO

The world of *The Divine Comedy* is so wide and various that a comprehensive introduction to it is not possible in a brief essay, but canto 1 of the *Inferno* is a useful place to begin observing how Dante's composition works. It is Maundy Thursday night, the day before Good Friday in the year 1300. The poet's first words are about personal time, the midpoint of life at which he awakened to discover himself in a dark wood, with no idea where the right road was. Because the very first line refers to a stage of life, the reader is not likely to imagine a search through a literal wood for an actual road. A few lines later, as Dante painfully recalls the harshness and recalcitrance of the forest, it becomes clear that he is talking about his own former willfulness. As horrid as this time of error was, says Dante, good came of it. This mixture of fear and optimism sets the tone perfectly for the *Inferno* and for the rest of *The Divine Comedy*. The opening lines involve the reader in the experiences of another being as though they were his own (which, in a sense, they are). Eschewing biographical or historical detail, Dante presents only the essential, the elementary: At a crossroads in life, another human realized that he had lost touch with an important part of himself.

The poet does not know exactly how he lost his way in that wood, but the torpor from which he suffered at the time was obviously spiritual. Struggling out of the wood, he is aware of a steep mountain, and as he looks up at the sun which lights the ways of men, he feels some comfort. Somehow, his awareness of his own poor spiritual state and the grace of a loving God have helped him through a dangerous maze, a place, he notes, from which no one has escaped, once entrapped there. Clearly, the forest is a form of spiritual death, or sin, but all the pilgrim has done so far is avoid the worst. To climb the mountain and achieve the spiritual perfection it implies, he will need to gain control of the complicated forces within himself.

A quick-stepping leopard first impedes his progress, but a look at the morning sun, as beautiful as it was during the first moments of Creation, restores Dante's hopes, which are again shattered when a lion, head held high, approaches menacingly. Most intimidating is a gaunt, ravenous wolf, which Dante says has conquered many men. The wolf begins to edge Dante back down the path into the dark forest. Dante does not say what each of these beasts symbolizes, but probably they represent types of sinful living. This notion exists because, to the medieval mind, beasts usually stood for the lower or unreasonable parts of the personal hierarchy. The leopard seems to have the flair and energy of youth, the lion the more powerful intellectual pride which can dominate later years, and the wolf the avarice for possessions which comfort advanced years. Any one of these sins could weigh down a traveler throughout life. Dante makes the point that inability to deal with the three brings despair and spiritual disaster. The light of the sun offers encouragement; grace is available, but it has to be used. As he stumbles downward, Dante sees a shadow. Although it seems unaccustomed to speaking, the shadow answers when Dante calls to it for help, just as the way out of the woods appeared when Dante admitted to himself that he was lost. The shadow is Vergil, who stands for the natural good sense that Dante had allowed to lie dormant.

Vergil does not want Dante to take on the she-wolf directly, for she has been the ruin of many. There is another way out of the wood, Vergil says. The person who confronts his own demons without a guide or a strategy is inviting failure. Dante first needs to use his reason to understand the nature of unforgiven sin and its punishment. Then he can visit the purgatorial realm, where the vestiges of forgiven sins are removed, and finally a worthier guide will show him the vision of ultimate reward. Vergil also cautions Dante against becoming preoccupied with the sins of his fellow countrymen. In time, says Vergil, a greyhound will come to chase the avaricious wolf from Italy. Whether this greyhound represents a great earthly prince or some divine apocalypse is not clear. The central point of this first canto is that, beginning with his own conscience, then using the legible signs in the book of the natural world and the revival of his own rational faculty, Dante is ready to journey toward whatever perfection he can hope to attain.

The above remarks are not an ambitious reading of obscure material. Dante saw clearly and wrote to be understood. He did, however, believe that it was natural and beneficial to require an audience to be alert to more than the literal in what he said. An extremely sophisticated tradition of biblical interpretation had prepared his audience to do that and to take pleasure in understanding more than surface meanings in a piece of writing. If the created world was a fair field of symbols, and if the revealed word could be read on several metaphorical levels, why not a story of the mind's journey to God? Thus, Dante wrote allegorical fiction, in which what is said is frequently intended to mean something else. The "literal" aspect of allegorical narrative is usually the least important, for it is the sense of the figurative and the symbolic which the author wants to exercise. The reader needs a fine set of interchangeable lenses in order to see the multiple levels.

Dante's Hell is in the center of the earth, which was thought to be the center of the created world, but in a theocentric universe, the earth was really on the outside looking in. The lowest point in Dante's Hell is therefore the farthest possible point from God; it is frozen, signifying the total absence of human or divine love. This Hell is fashioned from religious tradition and popular belief. Spectacular as some of the punishments are, the chief source of pain is indescribable: the eternal loss of the sight of God.

Although many modern readers reject the idea of eternal punishment, medieval Christian thinkers had concluded that an all-perfect Being had to embody justice as well as mercy. When an individual died, the reign of mercy ended and that of justice began. In this view, the damned have willfully rejected the power of grace, the teachings of the Church, and the Sacraments. If after this, God relented, He would be unjust. Justice also determines the nature of the punishments and the consequent degree of suffering. The punishment Dante imagines for each sin is a symbolic definition of the sin itself, which the sinner has to repeat for eternity. Only the living can learn from this infernal repetition. For all the uproar and movement in Hell, nothing changes. A medieval definition of change would be the movement of things toward the ideal form which God intended for them; not a single gesture in Hell does that.

Dante's Hell is an inverted hierarchy, with each level revealing a more serious sin below. Hell has nine circles, in addition to an outer vestibule. The upper five circles contain punishments for sins committed through misdirected or uncontrolled emotions; they reflect the perils of natural vitality and appetites, as the image of the leopard suggested. Next, behind the walls of the city of Dis, are crimes which require a stronger determination of the will to disrupt the plan of existence. The violence which appears here (circles six and seven) may be connected with the lion which threatened Dante earlier. The eighth circle is a long sheer drop below this and contains the violators of the various kinds of promise-keeping which make social life possible. The more complicated frauds of treason and betrayal in the ninth and lowest circle may be related to the ravenous wolf. Far more ingenious than the schematic layout of Hell is Dante's ability to keep a sense of spontaneity and discovery in what could have been merely a dutiful walk through a catalog of sin. Dante's skill at variation, which every medieval poet would have coveted, is perhaps the chief source of the poem's excellence. Even in *Purgatory*, where the treatment of each sin runs to a pattern, Dante somehow handles every section uniquely.

One of the sources of variety and sense of forward movement in the *Inferno* is the interaction between Dante and Vergil. Vergil chides, encourages, and revives his pupil as they travel through Hell. The pilgrim Dante becomes stronger and more sure of himself, less frightened by the nightmarish circus about him and more able to despise intelligently the evil he sees. At first, Dante does not believe himself to be fit for such a journey, but when Vergil tells him that Beatrice wills it, he immediately agrees to follow. Two cantos later, in Limbo, the greatest pagan poets are welcoming him to their company. Whenever he has need of Reason, Vergil is always there—even literally at one point—to lift and carry him out of danger. The danger and inhospitableness increase as the two proceed deeper. Everything they see is an inversion or distortion of Charity, the love of God and neighbor in which every Christian act is rooted. At the start, Charon, the underworld boatman, refuses to ferry Dante and Vergil across the river Acheron; in the ninth and lowest circle, Count Ugolino devours the head of the bishop whose betrayal caused the Count and his sons to be starved to death. The reader becomes increasingly aware of Dante's obsession with the two Florences: the City of God on Earth that he wanted it to become and the ungrateful zone of corruption it had been to him. In his darkest hour, Dante was nearer to Beatrice and all that she stood for than Florence would ever be to Jerusalem. Almost until the final instants of *Paradise*, Dante rails against the city that nourished and exiled him.

Somewhat like a gothic cathedral, *The Divine Comedy* is a huge structural support covered with crafted sections of varying size and content, each section somehow finding a place in the totality. A very limited sampling of sections might begin with Upper Hell, where the sins of the incontinent are punished. It may be surprising to find that lust is the first sin viewed here, which makes it the least serious offense in Hell. Medieval moralists tended to treat sexual love as a natural behavior in need of a supernatural perspective. This is quite different from treating sexuality as a taboo, as later ages would. Even so, the reader should consider the mixture of feelings within Dante—who began as a lyric poet in the tradition of erotic courtship—as he watches the souls of the lustful tossed on a roaring black wind, an image of the uncontrollable passion to which they surrendered their reasoning power. They are like flocks of starlings and cranes borne up and down forever, shrieking as they go. The scene conveys the restlessness of human passion and the crowded commonness of the sin itself. The world's most famous lovers are in those flocks: Dido, Helen, Paris, Tristram. Seeing them, Dante grows dizzy with sympathy.

Two of the lovers are still together, dovelike as they waft along hand in hand. They are Paolo and Francesca, who suffered and died for love at the hands of Francesca's husband. Francesca delivers a courtly lyric celebrating the power of love which brought her and Paolo together, a lyric which ends with the assurance that damnation awaits the one who murdered them. Deeply moved by the lovers' tragedy, Dante asks to know more. What he hears is not the spell of romance but a rather ordinary process of young lechery: leisure time, suggestive reading, and the knowing glances which precede coupling. Dante has to be true to the old conventions of love here, the ones he transformed in *The New Life*; he also has to maintain the clear-eyed antiromanticism of Christian morality. It is all too much for the pilgrim, who falls into a dead swoon, until he awakes to find himself in the third circle, with the Gluttonous.

Like the Lustful, the Gluttonous have allowed themselves to be controlled and distorted by a natural urge. The image Dante uses to describe the punishment here is startling in the manner of a metaphysical conceit. First, he describes a cold, heavy rain soaking a putrid earth. Cerberus, the three-headed watchdog of the Underworld, is there, each head gorging on the souls of the Gluttonous as they wallow in the mud. To distract the monstrous beast, Vergil throws filthy mud down its throats. Cold rain seems to have no connection with excessive eating, until one considers the motivation which is often behind that excess: self-centered loneliness with indiscriminate sieges of oral gratification. One Ciacco ("Fats"), a fellow Florentine, addresses Dante from the slime. He vents his own alienation and misery, then gives an acid survey of the rottenness which will continue to seep from their native city.

The metaphoric effect is equally powerful in canto 12, when Dante and Vergil enter the pathless wood of the suicides, where the souls have been turned to dead trees which bleed at the touch and are fed on by Harpies, who represent the guilt of self-destruction. Through this same wood run the souls of persons who in life madly spent all they owned. They are being chased and torn to pieces by hunting dogs. Dante's decision to put suicides here among souls who have been violent against themselves seems reasonable. That he should sense a comparable wish for death among those who are impatient to destroy their wealth shows a marvelous awareness of the darker corners of the human situation. Like the cold rain upon the Gluttonous, it is a superb reach of intelligence and intuition.

The last four cantos describe the ninth and lowest circle of Hell, which contains the perpetrators of the subtlest, most complicated frauds imaginable. First described are the giants of classical legend who tried to scale Heaven and challenge Jove, and the biblical Nimrod, who directed the attempt to build the Tower of Babel. At the bottom of Hell's pit is the frozen lake Cocytus. There, the traitors, who through intellect and will achieved the most drastic perversion of love, are frozen in unrepentant attitudes of hatred. These are the souls of those who betrayed kin, fatherland, guests, and, lowest of all, those who betrayed their lords. Fed ultimately by all the rivers of Hell, the ice itself may be blood-colored. Tears, a symbol of compassion, freeze instantly there. The famous agony of Count Ugolino of Pisa, who, with his children, starved to death in prison, mirrors perfectly these pitiless surroundings. Ugolino and the others are at Hell's bottom because they violated the promise-keeping which is the root of every social and spiritual relationship, for man becomes ethical on the basis of his fidelity to promises of loyalty, hospitality, and the like. The cannibalism which the traitor Ugolino enacts as he devours the skull of the person who betrayed him suggests the ultimate negation of social behavior, where humanity and bestiality are no longer distinguishable.

Satan, the angel once nearest to God, now occupies the lowest extremity of Hell, held in ice up to his chest. This is the summary image of the first third of *The Divine Comedy*. At the center of the heart of darkness is this living death, presided over by the first of God's creatures to defy Him. Satan has three faces here, red, yellow, and black, which probably refer to the races of humanity through which his first evil is continued. A parody of the Triune God, his face is the inversion of the spiritual number three. Two batlike wings flap under each face, making a freezing wind which keeps the lake frozen. There is no other movement observable here, unless one includes the tears from those three pairs of eyes, which drip in a bloody mixture from Satan's chins. The draft from his wings evidently freezes all tears but his own. If these tears and blood, which are appalling reminders of the sacramental water and blood which flowed from the side of the Redeemer on the first Good Friday, represent the misery which sin causes, they reveal no contrition whatsoever, for the wings are operated by a will which is still rebellious and an icy egotism which will never cease to oppose God. Even the blindly passionate wind which heaved Paolo and Francesca about would be a welcome alternative to those hopeless gusts.

Each of Satan's mouths chews on a famous traitor. Situated highest, the mouth of the red face tortures the most notorious traitor of all: Judas Iscariot. In the lower mouths are the two others who make up this Satanic Eucharist, Brutus and Cassius, who subverted God's plan for world empire under Rome by assassinating Julius Caesar. In Dante's conception, sacred and imperial history, although they are separate, are both founded on God's will, and therefore must stand responsible before His justice. In this sense, the things of God and the things of Caesar must ultimately converge. In the midst of these ironies is the supreme irony of Satan's powerlessness, which makes him, for all of his gigantic size, ridiculous. He and the giants are mastodons in a museum. Dante and Vergil climb down this hulk out of Hell and see the stars for the first time since early Friday morning.

When Vergil and Dante have climbed down past Satan's navel, they have reached the point farthest from God. What was below is now above them, and Satan appears upside down, a fitting final aspect of the Arch-Rebel. The pair are now in the earth's southern hemisphere, facing an island with a mountain called Purgatory, formed of the land which retreated to avoid Satan when he fell. The Earthly Paradise is on the top of that mountain. It was closed at the expulsion of Adam and Eve, but since Christ's death it has been open to souls purified in Purgatory. Actually, Scripture gives few specific details about Hell, and none at all about Purgatory.

In Purgatory, medieval Christians believed, the residual effects of sins admitted, confessed, and forgiven were removed before the soul entered Paradise. The soul permitted to enter Purgatory was saved and would surely see God someday. Furthermore, these souls could be helped by the prayers of people still on Earth and could enjoy communication with the suffering souls around them. This is quite different from the isolation and hopeless sense of loss in Hell.

PART II, PURGATORY

If the topic of the *Inferno* is the just punishment of sin, the topic of *Purgatory* is the discipline of perfection. It is a more serenely organized piece of writing, with a pace which is generally more constant. After the terraces of the ante-Purgatory, the mountain has seven cornices, each devoted to purging the stain of one of the deadly sins. Every cornice contains a penance, a meditation, a prayer, a guardian angel, and a benediction. The ascent from one area to another is often accompanied by a brief essay on some topic in natural or moral philosophy. The idea of an ante-Purgatory was probably Dante's own. In its two terraces are the souls of those who delayed repenting until the moment of their death. Having waited too long in life to do what was necessary to be saved, they must wait for some time before they can begin the ascent. In the first terrace, are the souls who, although excommunicated by the Church, delayed repentance until the last moments of life. In terrace two, are those who delayed similarly, although they always lived within the Church; included here are the souls of the indolent, the unshriven, and the preoccupied.

Saint Peter's Gate is the entrance to Purgatory proper. Three steps of Penance lead up to it: confession, contrition, and satisfaction. At the gate, an angelic custodian inscribes seven *P*'s, signifying the Seven Deadly Sins (*peccatum* is the Latin for sin), on the forehead of each soul. The letters will be erased one at a time as the soul passes from cornice to cornice. The Seven Deadly Sins were the most widely used description of human evil in the Middle Ages. Somehow or other, every transgression was thought to have come from one of those seven:

Lust, Gluttony, Avarice, Sloth, Wrath, Envy, and Pride. Each cornice has a penance appropriate to the stain left by one of those sins. The soul may be made to perform a penitential exercise which symbolically describes the effects of the sin committed, or as counterbalance it may have to perform actions which suggest the virtue directly opposed to the sin. Sometimes souls are assigned to do both.

The meditation in each cornice consists of a whip, or example of the opposing virtue, and a bridle, which is made up of horrid instances of the sin in question. These are followed by a prayer taken from the Psalms or hymns of the Church, then by a benediction (one of the Beatitudes), which is spoken by the angel of the cornice, who then erases a *P* from the soul's forehead. The soul then moves up the Pass of Pardon to the next cornice.

The boundary line for a Hell or Purgatory can be difficult for even a severely legalistic planner to draw. Those souls closest to the entrance of Hell had lost all hope of salvation, though by a narrow margin. In *Purgatory*, those closest to the boundary have avoided that loss by a similarly narrow margin. Dante's Hell begins with the neutrals, those who chose not to choose. They are a faceless mob condemned to chase a whirling standard forever. Next is the Limbo of the unbaptized and virtuous pagans. Dante could not imagine salvation for them, even though their poetry and ideas had nurtured him, but neither could he condemn them for light denied. Thus, the virtuous pagans appear in a dim but pastoral setting, and the poets among them admit Dante to their number. The first terrace of Purgatory also involves fine distinctions, but ones in which the poet is less personally involved. To be excommunicated was not a sin in itself, but a person who was separated from the Church by a sin which called for excommunication, and who put off repentance until the last minutes of life, was grasping salvation by its coattails. Appropriately, these excommunicates and the other late repentants in the second terrace are the only souls in Purgatory who have to undergo a punishment—that is, a wait. All of the others are cheerfully engaged in a healing process which will continue until they are ready for Paradise.

Ascending through the cornices of Purgatory is in one way like backing up the spiral road out of Hell. The lowest part of Hell, where the proudest act ever committed is being punished, corresponds to the first cornice, where the stains of pride are being removed. The cornice of Lust, the least of the Seven Deadly Sins, is nearest the top of the mountain, as Lust was farthest from the frozen lake at the bottom of Hell. The descent became increasingly difficult for Dante and Vergil as each circle delivered something more bleak or dangerous. The trek upward in Purgatory is a happy jettisoning of old heaviness, done in the midst of general enthusiasm and encouragement. Instead of Charon, who grudgingly ferried the two across Acheron, an angel of the Lord lightly takes a hundred singing souls across to the island where Mount Purgatory stands. Indeed, the change of mood exhilarates Dante so thoroughly that he all but loses his sense of mission as he listens to the singing of Casella, an old friend and musician.

There are subtle changes in Vergil's presence at this point. He is temporarily eclipsed in the early cantos by the appearance of the astringent Cato, who represents the discipline that will be needed for the lively chores ahead. Moreover, Vergil has not been here before, so although he is still a fount of good sense, he is seeing everything for the first time. He can only partly answer certain questions Dante asks, such as the one about the efficacy of human prayer. Dante will have to wait for Beatrice to explain such matters fully, and interpreters will come forth intermittently to talk about what Vergil cannot be expected to recognize.

Dante and Vergil emerge from Hell on Easter morning at dawn and reach the island shortly after that. They are in the second terrace of ante-Purgatory when the sun begins to set. Night-climbing is not permitted, so the two are led to a beautiful valley, where the souls of preoccupied rulers dwell. The cycle of day and night and the natural beauty of the valley indicate their presence still on Earth, in the middle state. The significance of not attempting a penitential climb in the dark is fairly clear, but as night falls, two angels descend to keep watch over the valley. They immediately chase off a serpent who has marauded there. Dante is brilliantly suggestive here. The sentry angels are dressed in green, which is a sign of both hope and penance, but that they should be there at all is puzzling. The point seems to be that, at least in ante-Purgatory, temptation is still a possibility. The fiery swords that the angels bear and the presence of the en-

emy serpent recall the Fall in Eden, and indeed the theme at the core of this journey is the return to that garden and man's state before he sinned.

The morning dream which Dante has in that valley is also charged with details which add significance to all that will happen. Having his own share of Old Adam's nature, he says, he nods off, and in the first light, the time of holy and prophetic dreams, he sees a golden eagle in midair, about to swoop toward its prey. He thinks of Zeus snatching the boy Ganymede up to Heaven, but then he conjectures that this eagle must always hunt here, so it need not have anything to do with him. Then the eagle comes for him like lightning, and takes him up to the circle of fire which surrounds the earth, where they burn together with a heat which wakens him and ends the dream. He finds that Saint Lucy has carried him to Saint Peter's Gate—the beginning of Purgatory proper.

This dream illuminates the rest of the story until the final line, although it is possible to interpret its simpler elements at once. Lucy is one of the three ladies (the other two are Beatrice and the Blessed Virgin) who decided to help Dante out of the dark wood earlier. Lucy personifies the beckoning power of Divine Light by literally transporting Dante to the start of this second phase of his journey. The golden eagle, a bird sacred to Jove and also an emblem of the empire, is doing a comparable thing. Here are two faces of the Godhead, one maternally encouraging, the other ravenously assertive, together making up a richly complicated insight which comes not from a Vergilian lecture or the remark of a dead soul, but from a dream, where the discourse is intuitive and mystical. The progress up the mountain will for the most part involve intellectual and ethical knowledge, but as it is happening the totality of Dante's being will be moving toward a Divine Love which is beyond language and rational understanding, and for which a burning heaven is the most appropriate metaphor. The movement up the cornices will be clear and steady, so uniform as to be tedious at times. It will require the light of day, but the total movement of the self with the Deity is perhaps best reflected in dream-light, because Dante is giving his readers not only an encyclopedia of morality but also an imitation of a psychological process.

The removal of the vestiges of sin will render the soul fitter and more able to see the Beatific Vision in its full glory. In Purgatory, all souls are headed homeward, and each step is easier and more satisfying. Innocence, man's state before sin, is the first destination, and from there a more glorious vision will begin, one which the most artful words can only partially describe.

Signs that Eden is near begin in the sixth cornice, with the Gluttonous. By this time, Publius Papinius Statius, a pagan Latin poet who became a Christian, has joined the party; Dante believes that Vergil's reason and literary art need the supplement of revelation so that everything that is about to happen can be fully appreciated. Vergil had pagan glimmerings of Eden and the prelapsarian state when he wrote of a virtuous Golden Age once enjoyed by humankind, but glimmerings are not enough. Before them in the path, they see a tall tree, watered from above by a cascade. The tree bears ambrosial fruit, but a voice forbids anyone to eat it. Examples of Temperance are then described, which are the goad or whip to counter the vice. The souls of the Gluttonous, all emaciated, suffer from being denied the sweet-smelling fruit, but, as one of them tells Dante, they come to the tree with the same desire that Christ brought to the Cross, for both sufferings bring redemption. They see another tree which also keeps its fruit from a gathering of gluttonous souls. A voice tells them to ignore the tree, which is the sort that fed Eve's greed. The connection between the sin of Gluttony and the eating of the forbidden fruit was a point commonly made from medieval pulpits. Particularly noteworthy here is the easy flow of allusions to the Fall of Man and to the suffering on the Cross which compensated for it. The classical story of Tantalus's punishment in the Underworld may have inspired Dante's description of the Gluttonous, but the tree of Eden and the tree of the Cross are clearly the central points of reference here.

PART III, PARADISE

When the three travelers finally reach the Earthly Paradise, they see not a garden but a forest, a sacred wood wherein dwells the primal innocence which seemed so far away in the dark wood of the *Inferno*, in canto 1. The sacred wood has a single inhabitant, Matilda, who is there to explain these environs and make straight the way of Beatrice, who appears in a spectacular allegorical event called the Procession of the Sacrament. Only eyes which have regained the first innocence are ready

for such a vision. Looking eastward, which is by tradition the holiest direction, Dante sees a brilliant light spread through the forest, and a procession led by seven candlesticks to a chanting of "Hosanna." Next come twenty-four elders, heads crowned with lilies, and after them four beasts surrounding the triumphal cart drawn by a griffin, whose birdlike features are gold, and elsewhere red and white. Three ladies, colored respectively, red, green, and white, dance in a circle by the right wheel; four in purple dance by the left wheel, led by one who has a third eye. Two old men come next, one dressed as a physician, the other carrying a sword. They are followed by four humbly dressed individuals, and then by a very old man, going in a visionary trance. These last seven all wear red flowers.

Medieval religious processions were usually staged to affirm a crucial matter of doctrine or devotion. The key notion in this masquelike procession is the unity of sacred revelation since the Fall of Man. The twenty-four elders refer to the books of the Old Testament, their lily crowns suggesting pure righteousness. The Benedictus they sing is a reminder that the Old Testament symbolically anticipates events in the New Testament. The four beasts are the beasts of the Apocalypse and the signs of the four Evangelists. The griffin, which is part eagle and part lion, traditionally refers to the two natures of Christ, its gold suggesting divinity, its red and white, humanity. White and red are also the colors respectively of the Old and New Testaments, and of the bread and wine in the Eucharist. The ladies by the right wheel are Faith (white), Hope (green), and Charity (red); by the left wheel are the four cardinal virtues: Prudence (with the third eye), Temperance, Fortitude, and Justice. Behind the cart are Luke, Paul, and the Epistles of Peter, James, John, and Jude. The old man is the Revelation of Saint John. The red flowers they all wear signify the New Testament.

Then Beatrice appears on the cart in a red dress and green cloak, her head crowned with olive leaves. At this moment, Dante realizes that Vergil, the man of natural wisdom, is no longer with him. Beatrice, who might as well be called Revelation here, tells Dante to look at the entire procession. All of it is she, Beatrice says. Beatrice's words are the fullest manifestation so far of the significance of one passionate event which occurred when the poet was nine years old. What the God-Man brought into history, she is. The Incarnation which the Old Testament faintly surmised, and which the New Testament celebrates, she is, with every holy virtue in attendance. The same can be said of the transsubstantiated Host on the altar.

After a rebuke from Beatrice for the wandering ways of his own life, which is perhaps his own rightful dose of the purgatorial suffering he has been content to watch, Dante faints with shame. When he revives, Matilda is drawing him across the stream of forgetfulness. With the memory of evil now gone, he can watch with original innocence as the procession heads toward the Tree of Knowledge, where human sin began. Many medieval writings connected the Tree of Knowledge with the tree on which Christ was crucified. Lore had it that the seeds of the fruit from the first tree were buried on the tongue of Adam and then grew to become the tree of the Cross. Christ was often referred to as the Second Adam, come to reverse the catastrophe caused by the first. Here, the Griffin (Christ) moves the cart with Beatrice (the Word and its Incarnation) past the site on which the temptation and Fall occurred and joins the shaft of the cart to a barren tree, which immediately blossoms. The Griffin then ascends, leaving Beatrice at the roots of the tree. She now represents the Church which Christ at his ascension left behind to care for the humankind He had redeemed.

The role of the Empire in God's plan is stressed here, too. An eagle slashes at the tree, just as Roman persecution maimed the Church. Then a gaunt fox appears, probably to represent the heresies of the Church's early history. After the fox has prowled about the cart, the eagle descends again, this time to feather the cart from its own breast. This no doubt represents the symbiotic relationship between church and state in the Holy Roman Empire. That liaison is followed by a dragon which damages the cart, causing it to change into the many-headed beast of the Apocalypse, on top of which is enthroned a whore consorting with giants. The imagery suggests the later corruption of the Church caused by its consorting with earthly powers. Thus, Dante sketches a symbolic history of the decay of the Church which Christ and Peter founded. The point is one he makes directly in many places: that in Christian history, Church and Empire need to maintain separate identities as they pursue God's plan. The atmosphere of these last cantos

has been gradually shifting toward Apocalypse, which Beatrice continues by prophesying revenge for what has been allowed to happen to Christendom, but the final canto returns to the theme of a purgatorial journey. Dante now drinks from Eunoe, the water of Good Remembrance, which renders him finally free from the tarnish of an earthly life and ready for a direct vision of the Godhead.

Readers who think of Dante as the poet of Hell often have read only the first third of his masterpiece. The joy which quickens every step of the *Purgatory* makes it an exhilarating sequel to the *Inferno*, but that joy is only a hint of what awaits Dante in the vision of Paradise. The *Inferno* and *Purgatory* are preparatory visions, the first stressing the reality of evil and its effects, the second showing that it is possible to remove every one of those effects. *Purgatory* and *Paradise* form the main part of the comedic structure, which leaves the unhappiness of the *Inferno* far behind.

Dante's *Paradise* is a description of Godhead, as much of it as his eyes could register, and as much as his memory could retain. Medieval literary audiences loved well-executed descriptions, and the *Inferno* and *Purgatory* contain some extraordinarily effective ones. Once the poet has left the substantive world, images on which to base descriptions are no longer obvious. Hell and Purgatory are constructed and described according to sinful human actions, which had been traditionally identified and discussed in concrete images. Social history abounds with vivid examples of depravity, but there has never been a great store of fictions or metaphors to describe the state of the soul enjoying Heavenly rewards. Moreover, the step-by-step journey into Hell and up the purgatorial mountain involves a sense of time and space which is inappropriate to the simultaneity of eternity. Thus, the metaphor of the journey does not quite fit a vision of Heaven, although to accommodate human communication and understanding, the vision had to be subdivided and presented in some sequence. Dante reminds his audience, however, that this is only a strategy to help them see.

Until one reaches the presence of God, the Being than Whom none is higher, one has to understand every phenomenon, even heavenly bliss, hierarchically. Every soul in Heaven is completely happy, but even heavenly bliss has its degrees. To describe Paradise, Dante looks outward from Earth to the concentric spheres of the planets and beyond them to the Empyrean, where the Divine Presence begins. Because, moving outward, each successive planet is closer to God, each one can be a gathering point for increasingly elevated forms of blessedness. With the rather technical exception of the souls on the Moon, the imagery Dante uses to describe the souls he meets is nonrepresentational, even approaching abstraction with voices, lights, and patterns. Dante was familiar with the tradition of the cosmic voyage, a literary form which went back to the Stoic philosophers, in which a guide takes a troubled individual to the outer spheres, to provide consolation by demonstrating the littleness of troubled Earth when compared to the grand harmony of all Creation. A powerful counterpoint develops in *Paradise* between accounts of the sordidness of contemporary Italian society and the charity and communion above. Part of the image of Paradise is thus accomplished through negative description, using earthly examples to emphasize what Heaven is not.

The *Inferno* does not start with a poetic invocation. Dante rushes directly into the troubled middle of things. *Purgatory* has an invocation to Calliope, the Muse of epic poetry. It is crucial but perfunctory, and it suits the hopeful premises of that work. The invocation to *Paradise* is a fitting start to a sublime task. It tells what a poet requires to describe his Creator. He starts with the notion that what he has seen is not possible to relate, because when the mind nears that which it has always wanted, memory weakens. Even so, he will sing about that part of it which has remained with him. He calls upon Apollo, a god traditionally associated with light, wisdom, and prophecy, to breathe into him and use him like a bellows to utter song worthy of what memory of Paradise he still has left. Dante's audience would have been comfortable with an invocation to a pagan deity, because they believed that many pagan myths were glimpses of Christian light which could be used to make poetry more articulate. As an inspiration to soul and art, Apollo resembles the Holy Spirit, but he also carries all the rich associations of the classical literary tradition.

If Apollo will be generous, Dante continues, he will approach the laurel tree to take those famous leaves, now so neglected by an unheroic and unpoetic age, to create poetry which will ignite better imaginations than his own. From that tree, then, may come light for all future ages. The highly prophetic *Paradise* deserves to be under the keeping of Apollo. The poet approaches the laurel tree sacred to Apollo as he gathers strength to take his pilgrim self from Eden and the last visible traces of earthly things. The tree of tantalizing punishment for the Gluttonous and the tree of the first sin are replaced here by a tree reflecting the highest moral calling of art. As the images of Eden and sin recede, the laurel tree and the tree of Redemption converge. Dante looks at Beatrice looking at the sun, which is both Apollo's planet and a traditional symbol for God. It is the same sun he saw that morning in the dark wood, but then he was looking through sinful eyes. The eagle, Dante's symbol for the Empire, was thought to be able to look directly into the sun; the suggestion here is that Beatrice, who stands for all revelation, and the eagle are one. It might seem curious that an image of imperial order should be presented at a moment of intimacy between self and Godhead, but Dante will make a similar point throughout *Paradise:* that religious mysticism and social history are different but not antithetical routes to God. The eagle which seized Dante in a dream and took him on high to burn was as much the call of empire as it was a private religious impulse.

Dante is not able to look directly at the sun for long. As he looks at Beatrice looking at eternity, he begins to hear the music coming from the harmonious motion of the heavenly spheres, a sound no mortal has heard since Adam sinned. Instantly, Dante realizes that he has left Earth with Beatrice. The vision which follows, the organization of which is only a metaphor for the ineffable, involves ten Heavens, each of the first seven associated with a planet—Moon, Mercury, Venus, Sun, Mars, Jupiter, Saturn—the eighth Heaven with the zodiac and fixed stars, the ninth the Crystalline Heaven of the *Primum Mobile*, or First Mover, through which motion was imparted to all the other spheres, and beyond that the Empyrean, or realm of God. In the first seven Heavens, the souls are located in the planet with which their earthly activities could be associated, although in actuality each of them is in the Empyrean with God. According to Dante, the first three Heavens are touched by the shadow of Earth. On the Moon, the planet nearest Earth, are those souls who through no fault of their own proved inconstant in vows they had made to God. They were not sinners, only less perfect in salvation. Next is the Heaven of Mercury, filled with souls who lived virtuous lives serving the social order, but who were motivated at least in part by worldly ambition. The sphere of Venus is for those who followed Eros in life but now are delighted to wheel with celestial movement.

In the Heaven of the Sun are spirits whose wisdom furthered the understanding of God on Earth. Mars houses those who gave their lives for the Christian faith, while Jupiter houses the souls of the Just. The second three Heavens (Sun, Mars, and Jupiter) celebrate the virtuous achievements of the active life, but the contemplatives abide above them, in the circle of Saturn. The theme of the eighth Heaven is the Church triumphant, with Christ and the saints in full radiance. The ninth and tenth Heavens, respectively the *Primum Mobile* and the Empyrean, are given to the various direct manifestations of God. They take up the last six cantos, which trail off as even Dante's imagination begins to fade before its task.

The mood of *Paradise* is perfect joy which has no end and which leaves not even a trace of unfulfilled desire. The spirits describe that joy by what they do and say. There is a hierarchy of blessedness here, but it exists without anyone feeling envy or deprivation. Just as the courtesy and charity of Purgatory take one above the hatred and cupidity of Hell, so the perfect happiness here lifts one even higher, particularly through the praises for its perfect Source. The points of Christian doctrine and philosophy which are explained to Dante as he moves from Heaven to Heaven with Beatrice are rarefied, some barely fixable in mind or language. To follow these thoughts, the reader must move with Dante past the recognizable specifics of time and place. This commentary can only sample that exquisite brightness. One might begin with the notion that the rewards of Heaven justify everything that man can know about God's plan. *Paradise* is a celebration and vindication of the Church and all of its traditions, and of the plan for justice on earth through empire. It is also an opportunity for a citizen poet and visionary to justify himself to the audience of the world.

The Heaven of the Sun provides a satisfying example of Dante's love for the true Faith and the ideal Church.

When he and Beatrice ascend to this Heaven, twelve lights carol around them, and one, Saint Thomas Aquinas, speaks. Aquinas belongs with the wisdom and illumination of the Sun. Mastering Aristotelian thought, he put its processes at the service of Christian theology. Among medieval Scholastic philosophers, he was supreme, and as a member of the Dominican Order (whose standard is a blazing sun), he studied and wrote to combat the heresies of unbelievers. Aquinas speaks not to praise a great university scholastic, however, but to praise Saint Francis of Assisi. Saint Francis was a street preacher, a disciple of the poor, whose spontaneous, instinctive love of God did not move through learned syllogisms. Aquinas tells a lively allegory about Saint Francis and the woman in his life, Lady Poverty. Poverty had been a neglected widow since her first spouse died on the Cross twelve centuries before. Indeed Poverty and Christ were so inseparable that during the Crucifixion she leapt on the Cross, like a wanton lover. Aquinas compares Francis's taking the vow of poverty to a wedding, an orgiastic celebration at which the guests (Saint Francis's followers) all hasten to follow this couple; as an Order, they will spread preaching and conversion throughout the world. This earthy description of Saint Francis's love for an ideal is no blasphemy: It is a charming reminder of how far the saint actually was from sensuality.

Then a Franciscan, Saint Bonaventura, praises the life work of Saint Dominic, founder of the order to which Aquinas belonged. Dominic, says Bonaventura, was the skillful gardener, sent to cull, trim, and order the plot of Faith and bring it new vitality. It is, like Aquinas's remarks about Francis, a graceful compliment, from lights which glow more brightly as they praise others. The ecstatic preacher and the systematizer of doctrine both work God's will and complement each other. At the same time, the reader cannot forget the diatribes of Aquinas and Bonaventura against the state of those orders.

Dante continually arranges his descriptions of Heaven to portray the idea of perfect happiness, although he relentlessly turns to bitter reminders of what human choice has rendered impossible on Earth. He never puts down the lash of satire for long. If *Paradise* is the happy conclusion of a comedy, it is also filled with astringent reminders that human history is a process of social and moral decay, much like the image of the Old Man of Crete in *Inferno* 14, which starts with a golden head and ends with rotting feet. At points Dante is apocalyptic about this decay, and he foretells destruction for his sinful age. He also implies that one day a strong figure will punish those selfish wrongdoers and usher in an age of justice.

Despite his outcries as an embittered satirist and doomsayer, Dante knows that both sacred and secular history are processes of God's justice, even when they seem to be operating at cross-purposes. In the Heaven of Mercury, Dante interviews Justinian, the Roman Emperor and codifier of law, who outlines the historic progress of the Empire. For Justinian, history is the flight of God's sacred eagle. He describes the earliest tribes in Italy, the Punic Wars, and the emperors. Justinian's most startling point is that the highest privilege of Roman justice was the punishment of Christ. The Crucifixion was a legal act, conducted by duly constituted Roman authority, with Pontius Pilate as the agent. It made the Redemption possible. At the same time, as Beatrice will later explain, the legality of the act under Roman law did not remove the need to avenge what had been done to Christ's person, so, somewhat paradoxically, the destruction of Jerusalem was also justified. The path of Divine Justice moved from ancient Rome to the Holy Roman Empire, thanks to Charlemagne, but that magnificent progress has fallen to puny, contemptible heirs, as the Guelphs and Ghibellines of Dante's time continually ruin that justice with their feuding.

Dante's view of the workings of Divine Justice comes with surprises, as when he puts in the Heaven of Jove one Rhipeus, whom Vergil in the *Aeneid* called the most just among the Trojans. Presumably, Rhipeus was a pagan. That he should be in Heaven and the author who wrote about him in Hell is an irony, but Dante means to emphasize the presence of an appetite for justice in the Trojan line even before it settled in Italy.

If the ways of Justice can seem mysterious, Dante had no doubt that they would someday set in balance all the wrongs he had suffered. In Hell, Dante's anger at old enemies sometimes made him spiteful and almost pruriently interested in their pain. He paid particular attention to the part of Hell where barratry, the crime of making personal profit out of public trust, is punished by immersion in a pit of boiling tar. The episode is personal, for Dante was convicted and sentenced to exile on charges of barratry. For all the thrashing about among devils and damned souls in the pit of barrators, not so much as a drop of tar touches the poet. That is his answer to the capricious charges against him.

By placing his fictional journey in 1300, several years before the beginning of the political turmoil in Florence which resulted in his exile, Dante was able to present himself as a pilgrim ignorant of what is to come. This allows the heavenly hosts to refer to his coming suffering as an unjust but transient ordeal. It is a powerful response to his oppressors, because it allows him to assert the righteousness of his own cause and the maliciousness of his enemies through voices which are not to be contradicted, because their foreknowledge comes from the Divine Presence. The highest and most justified reaction to his future sufferings will come when Dante sees how little they amount to in the eye of eternity.

Dante's self-justification in *Paradise* shows a legitimate holy pride in ancestry and a certainty about his own destiny, despite the disgrace which is brewing for him. In the Heaven of Mars, the souls of those who died for the Faith form a cross. One of them, Dante's great-great-grandfather Cacciaguida, reminds him of the simple and virtuous old stock from which he is descended, in a line extending back to ancient Roman times. Cacciaguida hails Dante as a solitary continuation of this earlier nobility, then names clearly what had been hinted about in Hell and Purgatory: exile, poverty, a life at tables and under roofs not his own. Cacciaguida instructs Dante not to temper so much as a word, but to be a gadfly to degenerate Florence as Justice works its way.

Paradise is always ascending toward the vision of God, at which paradoxically it will evaporate, because it is only a human artifact. Actually, Dante is given three manifestations of God's presence. In the *Primum Mobile*, he sees God symbolically as a point of light surrounded by nine rings, each ring representing an order of angels. These nine rings of angels are in pointed contrast to the geocentric world, where the most slowly moving sphere, that of the Moon, is closest to the corruptible center. Here, as Beatrice explains, the fastest and brightest angelic circle, that of the Seraphim, is closest to the point of light. The definition of God as an indivisible point of light may seem unusual, given the traditions of a transcendent, all-encompassing Divinity. Dante was familiar with a definition of God as a sphere whose center is everywhere and whose circumference is nowhere, a concept which neatly implies the traditional idea of God's absolute and indivisible simplicity and His absolute interminability and simultaneity. The image of the point of light and the concentric circles of angels is perhaps as close as the human intelligence can come through symbols to understanding God's essence.

The image of God which Dante is given when he enters the Empyrean is a product of faith and revelation; it is the closest Dante can come directly to God, and this is the image with which *The Divine Comedy* must end. The Empyrean contains the souls of the Blessed on ascending tiers of thrones arranged to form petals of a white rose, as they will appear on Judgment Day. With the rose, a symbol of Divine Love, Dante moves finally beyond time and space in a blinding brightness as a river of Divine Grace pours from an incalculable height. In the center of the rose is a circle of light, the glory of God. It is time now for the final vision, but Dante discovers that Beatrice has left him to take her place among the Blessed. She has sent the great mystic and contemplative Saint Bernard to be his final guide. Doctrine and revelation, which Beatrice represented, have advanced as far as they can. Only ecstasy can go beyond that.

Under Bernard's direction, Dante's journey ends where it was first conceived, for there are the Virgin, and Lucia, whom the Virgin had sent to Beatrice, who in turn summoned Vergil to aid Dante in the descent to Hell. Now Saint Bernard prays for Mary's intercession, so that they can look at God without the instruments of metaphor or symbol. It is, as Dante says, the end of all yearning, satisfying and rendering obsolete the last vestiges of desire in the soul. In one mystical moment, Dante sees all creation held together by love. Then he sees three circles, each one a different color, occupying one space. It is the Trinity. The first two circles (the Father and the Son) reflect on each other, and the third (the Holy Ghost) seems a flame coming equally from the first two. It is a vision beyond logic and intellect. In trying to encompass it, Dante falls, like Icarus, back to his everyday human self. Dante ends with the remark that,

whatever the limitations of his own understanding, Love was at the heart of what he saw, that same Love which moves the sun and the stars.

OTHER MAJOR WORKS

NONFICTION: *Epistolae*, c. 1300-1321 (English translation, 1902); *De vulgari eloquentia*, c. 1306 (English translation, 1890); *Il convivio*, c. 1307 (*The Banquet*, 1887); *De monarchia*, c. 1313 (English translation, 1890; also known as *Monarchy*, 1954; better known as *On World Government*, 1957); "Epistola X," c. 1316 (English translation, 1902); *Eclogae*, 1319 (*Eclogues*, 1902); *Quaestio de aqua et terra*, 1320 (English translation, 1902); *Translation of the Latin Works of Dante Alighieri*, 1904; *Literary Criticism of Dante Alighieri*, 1973.

BIBLIOGRAPHY

Fletcher, Jefferson Butler. *Dante*. Notre Dame, Ind.: University of Notre Dame Press, 1965. A short but helpful introduction to Dante's work. Does not focus on Dante's biographical details unless relevant to the literary discussion. Shows how the reader must appreciate Dante's work first for its poetic vitality, so as not to become lost in the intricacies of its philosophical, theological, and political details. However, Fletcher also points out that the power of Dante's poetry and the profundity of his thought work hand in hand.

Freccero, John. *Dante: A Collection of Critical Essays*. Englewood Cliffs, N.J.: Prentice-Hall, 1965. This work presents an introduction by the editor, followed by thirteen essays by various Dante scholars (such as Charles Williams and Charles Singleton) and writers (such as Luigi Pirandello and T. S. Eliot). The selections are somewhat focused in scope for the beginning reader, but some (notably those on medieval culture and Dante's philosophy) are more accessible.

Gallagher, Joseph, and John Freccero. *A Modern Reader's Guide to Dante's "The Divine Comedy."* Liguori, Miss.: Liguori, 2000. A canto-by-canto guide to *The Divine Comedy* that is especially helpful for beginning readers of the work. Provides insightful character analysis from a specifically Roman Catholic perspective, along with accessible explanations of Dante's many obscure references. Includes a helpful outline.

Hawkins, Peter S., and Rachel Jacoff, eds. *The Poets' Dante: Essays on Dante by Twentieth-Century Poets*. New York: Farrar, Straus & Giroux, 2001. A collection of twenty-eight essays by both contemporary modern poets (such as Robert Pinsky and Seamus Heaney) and poets such as T. S. Eliot and Ezra Pound, along with a brief introduction by the editors. Demonstrates Dante's ongoing influence on poetic thought.

Jacoff, Rachel, ed. *The Cambridge Companion to Dante*. New York: Cambridge University Press, 1995. An excellent guide to Dante's life, work, and thought. Especially useful for those readers of *The Divine Comedy* who want more information on specific allusions than most footnoted editions supply. Includes fifteen specially commissioned essays which provide both background information and critical commentary and a chronological outline of Dante's life.

Thomas A. Van;
bibliography updated by the editors

RUBÉN DARÍO

Félix Rubén García Sarmiento
Born: Metapa, Nicaragua; January 18, 1867
Died: León, Nicaragua; February 6, 1916

PRINCIPAL POETRY
Abrojos, 1887
Rimas, 1887
Azul, 1888
Prosas profanas, 1896 (*Prosas Profanas and Other Poems*, 1922)
Cantos de vida y esperanza, los cisnes, y otros poemas, 1905
Poema de otoño y otros poemas, 1910
Canto a la Argentina, oda a mitre, y otros poemas, 1914
Selected Poems of Rubén Darío, 1965 (Lysander Kemp, translator)

OTHER LITERARY FORMS

Rubén Darío's fame rests primarily on his poetry, but he wrote serious prose as well. *Azul* (azure), his first major publication, contained poems and short stories alike. Both the poetry and the prose portions were widely acclaimed, but Darío's mature work includes almost no fiction. He published several volumes of essays based on his experience as a foreign correspondent, a traveler, and a diplomat, and two such collections have gained international attention: *La caravana pasa* (1903; the caravan passes) was among the earliest chronicles of the experience of American artists in Paris, while *Tierras solares* (1904; the sunny lands) is a collection of affectionate and melancholy essays celebrating the countryside of southern Spain, which Darío considered the common ground of Spanish and Latin American history. Darío also published literary criticism, political commentary, an autobiography, and exegeses of his own works.

The most famous of Darío's critical works is *Historias de mis libros* (1914; stories of my books), a compilation of three explanatory pieces he wrote about his greatest works of poetry, *Azul*, *Prosas Profanas and Other Poems*, and *Cantos de vida y esperanza, los cisnes, y otros poemas*. In *Historias de mis libros* he responded to the most frequent criticism of his work, that he had abandoned the traditional themes of Latin America in pursuit of a European art. He branded the criticism "myopic" and answered that the literature of the New World needed no more stylized odes to nature or patriotic battle hymns.

ACHIEVEMENTS

Rubén Darío was a giant of Spanish-language literature and a pioneer of the literature of the American continents. One of the founders of the indigenous Latin American literary movement known as *Modernismo*, Darío introduced European influences—particularly from France—to the poetry of Latin America, but perhaps more important, he introduced the *Modernismo* of Latin America to Europe. His dramatic innovations in theme, language, meter, and rhyme influenced the poetry of both the New World and the Old.

The publication of *Azul* in 1888 was acclaimed by European as well as South American critics, and the book's title was adopted by the *Azure Review*, a Mexican journal that became a principal forum for South America's experimental *Modernista* poetry. When Darío was only twenty-one years old, the influential Madrid critic Juan Valera praised the Nicaraguan's "singular artistic and poetic talent" and the "pure Spanish form" of his writing. With the publication of later works, Darío's renown grew, and he was widely acknowledged as a spokesman for Latin American culture.

Darío was a colorful public figure, equally at home in Paris, Madrid, and Latin America. He traveled constantly and was acquainted with literary figures throughout Europe and Latin America. He exerted a profound cultural influence through his poetry, his literary criticism, and his journalism. At the height of his fame, he was Nicaragua's minister to Spain; an internationally celebrated lecturer, poet, and journalist; and an éminence grise among artists of Europe and the Americas. In a 1934 tribute, Chile's Pablo Neruda and Spain's Federico García Lorca pronounced Darío "the poet of America and Spain."

BIOGRAPHY

Rubén Darío's life was adventurous and Bohemian. He traveled constantly in Europe and the Americas, renowned for his literary achievements but dogged by debt, sickness, and alcoholism throughout his life.

Darío was born in 1867 to a poor, part-Indian family in rural Nicaragua. He published his first poem at the age of thirteen, and his early promise as a poet won for him scholarships which enabled him to gain an education.

In 1886, Darío left Nicaragua for Santiago, Chile. There, he suffered a life of severe poverty and wrote in obscurity until the publication of *Azul*. Through Darío's friend Pedro Balmaceda, the son of Chile's president, *Azul* came to the attention of Juan Valera, a Spanish critic attentive to South American literature. Valera published an encouraging review in Spain and Latin America in 1889, but although this brought Darío literary recognition, it did little to ease his poverty. In the same year, the poet returned to Central America, where his writing in literary journals and other periodicals won regional fame for him.

In 1892, Darío traveled to Europe as an assistant to a relative who was an official of the Nicaraguan government. He made his first visits to Madrid and to Paris, developing a lifelong love for the artistic communities of Europe. Upon his return to Central America, Darío called on Dr. Rafael Nuñez, a former president of Colombia, who was like Darío, a writer. Nuñez arranged for a consular appointment for Darío in Buenos Aires, Argentina. Darío remained in Buenos Aires from 1893 to 1898, writing for many Latin American newspapers and other periodicals, including *La nación*, Argentina's most influential newspaper. In the course of his Argentine stay, Darío's literary reputation continued to grow. *Prosas Profanas and Other Poems*, his second major volume, was published in 1896 and attracted critical attention in Spain and South America alike. Both the work's literary maturity and treatment of erotic themes ensured Darío's notoriety in the Spanish-speaking literary world.

In 1898, Darío returned to Europe as a foreign correspondent for *La nación*. In the course of the following ten years, he became a fixture of the literary life in Spain and France. He collaborated in establishing a number of fledgling literary journals, contributed to periodicals in Europe and Latin America, and produced important works of nonfiction as well as collections of poetry. Despite his commission from *La nación* and appointments to consular positions for Nicaragua in both Paris and Madrid, however, Darío's financial difficulties continued.

In 1907, Darío returned to Nicaragua to an enthusiastic public reception but stayed in his native country only briefly; he remained restless until his death, spending the last ten years of his life traveling throughout Central America and Europe, holding a variety of diplomatic and ceremonial posts, lecturing, and publishing poetry and essays in periodicals of both continents. In 1914, he published his last major work, *Canto a la Argentina, oda a mitre, y otros poemas*, commissioned by *La nación* on the occasion of Argentina's centenary of independence.

In 1915, Darío took his last trip home from Europe. His health was poor, and he died the following year in León, Nicaragua, at the age of forty-nine.

ANALYSIS

Rubén Darío is remembered as one of the first poetic voices of postcolonial Latin America, enormously influential as a founder of *Modernismo*. His work, however, underwent constant change, and no single school can claim him. He was acclaimed a Prometheus who brought modern trends of European art to newly independent Latin America; at the same time, he was an innovator in poetic form who exercised a major influence on the poetry of twentieth century Spain. In his later years, Darío retreated from the exotic imagery of *Modernismo* and returned to more traditional Latin American themes, including patriotism and religion.

The birth of *Modernismo* in Latin America coincided with South America's transition from colonialism to independence. The declining influence of Spanish culture made way for new literary sources. Latin American intellectuals had long recognized French culture as the navigational star for their society, which was throwing off the control of monarchies. Thus, in the late nineteenth century, with much of Latin America freed from the cultural sway of Spain, the influence of France was everywhere ascendant, particularly in the universities and in the world of the arts. Darío's work in particular and *Modernismo* in general derived primarily from the interplay between French and Spanish culture, with a rich diversity of other foreign influences.

At its heart, *Modernismo* was an assertion of artistic freedom—the manifesto of those whom Darío described as a "new generation of American writers [with] an immense thirst for progress and a lively enthusiasm." The *Modernistas* idealized art, seeking to range freely for symbolic images in the worlds of the fantastic, the mysterious, and the spiritual. Emphasizing the eclectic internationalism that characterized the movement, Darío spoke of a "close material and spiritual commerce with the different nations of the world. . . ."

Darío's work spanned thirty-five years. It consists of thousands of poems, most of them short and many of them in sonnet form. Darío's best-known works also include longer pieces, and his shorter works are sometimes grouped as suites of poems with common themes.

The most common subjects of Darío's poetry are the members of his international family of friends, his romantic loves, and the world of nature. In the tradition of French Parnassianism, he portrayed his subjects through dramatic ideals, using lavish symbolic imagery. Whatever the subject, Darío's portraits are rich in exotic imagery and symbolism. The world of his images is European as much as it is American. In places real and imagined, the reader finds unusual animals and woodland flora, and characters plucked from myth and history. Darío's poetry abounds in allusion, and he often arrays his poetic portraits of the most commonplace themes with the exotic trim of myth and history.

"A VÍCTOR HUGO"

Early evidence of Darío's debt to French art and literature appears in the 1884 poem "A Víctor Hugo" (to Victor Hugo), a paean directed not only to the French master but also to an enumerated multitude of figures who inspired the seventeen-year-old Darío: authors, scientists, and philosophers from Europe and the United States as well as figures from mythology and the Bible. The poem describes the explosion that Hugo touched off in the heart of the self-proclaimed "sad troubadour from the New World." Throughout the work, Darío blends his pious attention to the noise and movement of nature with the voices of myth and history. The influential Spanish critic Juan Valera acknowledged the obvious: The poetry of the young Darío was marked by an immersion in the images and ideas of centuries of Western civilization. Throughout his literary life, Darío wore his new religion proudly.

"A Víctor Hugo" explodes with pithy tributes to Darío's Olympus of heroes. Venus smiles. Apollo discourses with Erato, the Muse of love poetry, and with her sister Muses. Christ preaches and dies. Galileo utters his apocryphal words of defiance ("And still, I say, it moves"). Benjamin Franklin, Robert Fulton, and Ferdinand de Lesseps move the Earth with their inspired plans.

International recognition did not immediately follow the publication of "A Víctor Hugo," but the work heralded Darío's fame. In it, he affirmed his proud association with the artist. His profusion of references to the geniuses of Western civilization, too, reflected his captivation by European art and writing. Finally, his portrait of the world was of an extraordinary setting, a site of spectacular animation, anticipating explicitly *Modernista* works. While emotional and sincere, his descriptions were not so much true to life as true to an ideal.

At the close of "A Víctor Hugo," the New World's sad but well-read troubadour echoes a famous theme of Spain's first poet of the modern era, Gustavo Adolfo

Bécquer: the yearning to give voice to the transcendent and the frustration at the limits of language. Darío unconvincingly gasps: "Oh, but I am left breathless at my lyre/ And unable to continue my song." The breathless recollection of Hugo, France's "immortal genius" and "prophet," however, provides a reviving breeze: "Thoughts of your just fame/ Echo in my mind/ And ardor inflames my heart. . . ."

AZUL

The publication of *Azul* in 1888 marked the beginning of Darío's international recognition. An unusual combination of short stories and poetry, the collection revealed not only Darío's ebullience but also his sympathy with the Parnassian school, with its exotic symbolism, lavish portrayal of ideals through striking imagery, and departure from metric formalities.

The centerpiece of *Azul* is the suite of four poems that constitute "El año lírico" (the lyrical year), corresponding to the seasons and beginning with spring. The poems describe settings rich in exotic scenery and stirring with activity. "Primaveral" (spring) is by far the most dramatic. It portrays a vast forest alive with the awakening activity of nature. Darío's treatment of the arrival of spring, with suggestions of pagan and mythic ritual, reveals his fascination with a favorite theme of nineteenth and twentieth century European art and literature: the vision of untamed nature as the face of the savage world. The theme received its most celebrated treatment in Igor Stravinsky's ballet, *Le Sacre du printemps* (*The Rite of Spring*), which premiered in Paris in 1913. Darío's "Primaveral" begins with an invitation to the same celebration. The poem is composed of six stanzas of nearly uniform length, five of which end with the antiphonal cry: "Oh, my beloved, It is the sweet springtime!" The grand forest hosts the bathing nymphs, a stalking Pan, and the stirring Muses. Throughout the poem, colors flicker in the light. The locusts chirp to the sun, and all of nature highlights the beauty of a woman's face. "Primaveral" is not simply a seasonal celebration of love; the forest is the beautiful face of the world.

Azul also introduced influential formal innovations. The traditional Spanish sonnet of the nineteenth century consisted of rhymed lines with an even distribution of metric feet within the lines. Darío's sonnets generally abide by those conventions, but he experimented with longer lines and innovative patterns of rhyme. His sonnet "Caupolicán" (added to editions of *Azul* after 1890) is an early example. Each of its lines far exceeds the conventional eleven metric feet; in addition, Darío's rhyme scheme is unorthodox, and instead of the usual rhyming device of assonance, he employs sharp, syllabic rhymes. The first quatrain of the sonnet is representative:

> Es algo formidable que vio la vieja raza;
> robusto tronco de árbol al hombro de un campeón
> salvaje y aguerrido, cuya fornida maza
> blandiera el brazo de Hércules, o el brazo de Sansón.

> (They saw Something formidable, the now-gone ancient race:
> A robust tree trunk on the shoulder of the champion
> Savage and war-wise with the mighty mace
> Fit for the arm of Hercules or the arm of a Samson.)

Azul, if not the first *Modernista* work in Latin America, is a literary landmark and supremely representative of the movement. Its departure from formality and its thematic audacity reveal the literary freedom of what was then a new, and largely young, generation of artists in Latin America, apace of Europe's artistic evolution.

PROSAS PROFANAS AND OTHER POEMS

With his next major collection, Darío established his reputation as a mature poet and aroused controversy as well. Published in 1896, while Darío was living in Argentina, the work received considerable attention in Spain. Although it developed themes familiar to readers of *Azul*, it also included many poems exalting erotic love. The Spanish poet Pedro Salinas, a Darío partisan, describes the work as the "daydream of a cultured and erotic man."

In exploring sexual themes, Darío was both playful and frank, enhancing his reputation as a libertine and a rascal, and he provoked predictable outrage from some conservative critics. Others saw uncommon beauty and innovation in the work, and *Prosas Profanas and Other Poems* won acclaim, particularly among young readers in Europe.

One of the best-known poems in the collection *Prosas Profanas and Other Poems*, "Blasón" ("Blazon") is a panegyric to the swan (*Modernista* doctrine and French Parnassians). The work contributed to one of literary history's most colorful exchanges, a contest between Darío and his contemporary, the Mexican poet Enrique González Martínez, fought by symbolic proxies.

In "Blazon," Darío proudly adopts the swan as his blazon—his emblem. He sings of the swan's haunting unreality and decorative beauty in numerous poems, extolling its mythic and regal qualities—"Olympic is the swan, . . . Wings, short and pure . . . as the sun they seek." In time, the swan became closely associated both with Darío and with *Modernismo*, symbolizing the depiction of the exquisite, for which the *Modernistas* strived.

Some Latin American artists believed that Darío was guilty of excessive fidelity to the symbols, themes, and forms of European art. The growing "New World" movement did not entirely reject *Modernismo* but rather scolded what it perceived as its symbolic excesses and favored development of truly Latin American themes. In his later works, Darío himself showed just such an inclination, but at the height of his swan worship, he was a target of the New World movement.

González Martínez chose to attack the symbol of the swan in his famous repudiation of the elegant excesses of *Modernismo*, "Tuércele el cuello al cisne" ("Wring the Swan's Neck"), something of a New World credo. The 1911 work began, "Wring the neck of the deceitfully-plumed swan/ Who sings his white note to the blue of the fountain." Ironically, by the time "Wring the Swan's Neck" was published, Darío had turned to themes more conspicuously South American, including traditional Christian subjects and songs to the awakening continent.

CANTOS DE VIDA Y ESPERANZA, LOS CISNES, Y OTROS POEMAS

This growing South Americanism is obvious in the last of Darío's three great collections, *Cantos de vida y esperanza, los cisnes, y otros poemas*. Published when Darío was thirty-eight and in the depths of ill health and despondency, the work was widely acclaimed in Europe and South America and recognized as a new departure for the poet. Although it carries on themes associated with Darío's early works, it also includes a number of poems featuring traditional Christian imagery as well as several political poems—both uncommon in his previous collections.

"A Roosevelt" ("To Roosevelt"), the best known of the *Cantos de vida y esperanza, los cisnes, y otros poemas*, is sharply political. It voices a stern warning to the United States to forswear colonial designs on Latin America. The poem is a confident address to President Theodore Roosevelt, a celebrated big-game hunter, whose personification of the United States is clear.

"To Roosevelt" followed close on the heels of Spanish defeat in the Spanish-American War. Voicing as it did a solemn warning to the United States and a disarming affinity with Spain, the poem did much to enhance the reputation of Darío, then living in Europe, as a spokesman of Latin America. The poem boasts of the proud Spanish spirit and the strong literary traditions of Latin America—both ironic choices for Darío—as the sources of South America's potential resistance to the United States.

Darío enjoys a lasting place in Hispanic literature. His art reunited Spain and its former empire after the wars of independence. He infused Latin American literature with the cosmopolitanism of the European avant-garde, while his own achievement drew European critical attention to the literary activity of Latin America. He was, to many, the quintessential American artist: an earnest student of tradition and an eager captive of the future.

OTHER MAJOR WORKS

SHORT FICTION: *Cuentos completos de Rubén Darío*, 1950 (Ernesto Mejía Sánchez, editor).

NONFICTION: *La caravana pasa*, 1903; *Tierras solares*, 1904; *Historias de mis libros*, 1914.

MISCELLANEOUS: *Obras desconocidas de Rubén Darío*, 1934 (Raúl Silva Castro, editor); *Escritos inéditos de Rubén Darío*, 1938 (Erwin K. Mapes, editor); *Rubén Darío, Obras completas*, 1950-1953 (5 volumes).

BIBLIOGRAPHY

LoDato, Rosemary C. *Beyond the Glitter: The Language of Gems in Modernista Writers Rubén Darío, Ramón del Valle-Inclán, and José Asunción Silva*. Lewisburg, N.Y.: Bucknell University Press, 1999. A critical study of Latin American and Spansh modernist writers. Includes bibliographical references and index.

Mujica, Barbara. "Uncovering a Literary Treasury." *Americas* 44, no. 2 (1992): 53. A profile of the early modernist magazine *Revista de America* and its publishers, including Rubén Darío.

Solares-Larrave, Francisco. "A Harmony of Whims: Towards a Discourse of Identity in Darío's 'Palabras Liminasies.'" *Hispanic Review* 66, no. 4 (Autumn, 1998): 447-465. An examination of Rubén Darío's ability to manipulate words to evoke a "soul" and to create beauty.

Torres-Rioseco, Arturo. *The Epic of Latin American Literature.* Berkeley: University of California Press, 1964. History and criticism of Latin American literature. Includes commentary on Rubén Darío's poetry. Includes index.

Watland, Charles. *Poet Errant.* New York: Philosophical Library, 1965. A biography of Darío with bibliographic references.

David Nerkle;
bibliography updated by the editors

GEORGE DARLEY

Born: Dublin, Ireland; 1795
Died: London, England; November 23, 1846

PRINCIPAL POETRY

The Errors of Ecstasie: A Dramatic Poem, with Other Pieces, 1822
Nepenthe, 1835
Poems of the Late George Darley, 1890
The Complete Poetical Works of George Darley, 1908 (Ramsey Colles, editor)

OTHER LITERARY FORMS

George Darley might be called a literary hack. The profession of writer in the early nineteenth century was a precarious one, and Darley tried his hand at most of the popular literary forms of his time. Although his work was usually unsigned, in keeping with the tradition of anonymous reviewing and publishing at the time, Darley can be credited with lyrical dramas, or masques, in the Elizabethan style, and a large number of reviews of art exhibits and current plays.

Among Darley's major literary works were a series of "dramatic" poems, *Sylvia: Or, The May Queen, a Lyrical Drama* (1827); and two tragedies: *Thomas à Becket: A Dramatic Chronicle in Five Acts* (1840) and *Ethelstan: Or, The Battle of Brunaburh, a Dramatic Chronicle in Five Acts* (1841). The titles of Darley's dramatic pieces suggest that they were written to be publicly staged, but none ever made it to the theater. Finally, the letters of George Darley should be noted as a highly valuable commentary on the life of a professional writer at a critical phase in English literature. Darley's letters, even more than his various essays on literature and art, provide a useful series of insights into the events and problems of the time. In spite of Darley's shy disposition, he met many of the most famous poets and critics of his time, read widely in the literature of his day, and was a fair commentator on many pressing social issues.

It should be noted that Darley spent his last five years writing scientific textbooks for the use of students of secondary age. He may also have written a *Life of Virgil,* which is ascribed to him in the British Museum catalog.

ACHIEVEMENTS

George Darley never attained the recognition for his poetry and dramatic works that he earnestly sought throughout most of his adult life, although he pretended to be indifferent to the poetic fame that invariably eluded him and demanded that his friends be unsparing of his feelings in making their comments on his work. In truth, his poetry was seldom reviewed or even noticed by anyone outside the immediate circle of his friends. It is difficult to find references to his ideas or to his poetry in anything but the most exhaustive surveys of English Romanticism. Still, within the circle of Darley's friends, he was regarded as something of a poetic genius—the poet who would bring forth a new era of poetry. Charles Lamb, Thomas Beddoes, and John Clare were enthusiastic readers of his work and did their best to secure attention from the critical reviews. Even the proverbially churlish Thomas Carlyle remarked that Darley was one of the few poets of his day who really understood the spirit of Elizabethan tragedy, to the extent of being able to imitate it with any kind of success. Yet Darley never achieved more than a marginal place among the English poets of the early nineteenth century.

It was only some forty years after his death that readers took up Darley's poetry with interest. Part of this interest derived from the Celtic renaissance, but part also derived from Darley's ultimate claims to be read as a good minor poet.

BIOGRAPHY

George Darley was born in Dublin, Ireland, in 1795. He was the oldest of seven children of Arthur and Mary Darley. His parents were of the upper class, and for unknown reasons went to America for an extended visit when Darley was about three. The boy was reared by his grandfather, and he always referred to this period of his life as the "sunshine of the breast." At this time in his life Darley acquired an extreme stammer, so severe that even in his later years his closest friends could scarcely make out what he was saying. The stammer may have been important in determining his later career as a poet, and it partly accounts for one of the most common themes in the poetry: the isolation of the poet.

In 1815 Darley entered Trinity College, Dublin. He apparently made few friends there and, curiously, never mentioned the school in his later correspondence. The stammer interfered with his examinations, but he received his degree in 1820 and immediately left for London. Despite his speech defect and chronic shyness, Darley made friends with a number of writers who were emerging in the 1820's. His friends encouraged his work, and the letters he exchanged with such poets as Clare and Beddoes reveal their high regard for his work.

Darley spent almost ten years in London working at various literary and scientific projects, but late in 1830 he determined to go to France. He wrote occasional essays on art for the *Athenaeum* and (perhaps) another journal, titled *The Original*, but there are few records of his life in Paris or his tours to Italy. It is significant, however, that several members of the Darley family were, for a while, reunited. The older brothers toured Italy together, and later Germany. He had always been sickly and generally poor, but he was a good tourist, and the letters from this period are among his best.

Darley continued to review books on various subjects for the *Athenaeum*, earning a reputation for extreme severity. He adopted the role in his private life of a vivacious and often bitter critic; he died in November, 1846, having never revisited Ireland, which constituted the one subject that was above criticism.

ANALYSIS

George Darley's best poetry is the work of a man seeking escape from the world. The sorrows of his life, his poverty and his lack of recognition, are for the most part not present in his poetry. Many of his poems are about love, beautiful women, and the death of innocent women. This preoccupation suggests one of the more common Romantic motifs: the separation between a desirable realm of creativity and fertility and the sterile existence of the poet's life. In Darley's love poems there is a continuing search for perfection—the perfect woman, the perfect love. These poems show the influence of the Cavalier poet Thomas Carew, and it might be noted that one of Darley's most successful poems ("It Is Not Beauty I Demand") was published in the *London Magazine* with the name Carew appended to it. The fraud was not discovered until much later, after Francis Palgrave had included the poem in *The Golden Treasury*.

The women in Darley's poems are not the sentimental idols of so much nineteenth century love poetry, yet these lyrics are marred by Darley's frequent use of Elizabethan clichés: lips as red as roses, breasts as white as snow, hair as golden as the sun. In setting and theme as well, Darley's love poems are excessively conventional.

NATURE POEMS

In his nature poetry Darley was able to achieve a more authentic style and tone. His early years in the Irish countryside had given him an almost pantheistic appreciation of nature as the ultimate source of comfort; many of his nature poems border on a kind of religious veneration. It is nature that comforts man, not the Church; it is nature that speaks with an "unerring voice" and will, if attended to, provide man with the lessons in morality that he requires.

"A Country Sunday," one of Darley's finest nature poems, illustrates this idea of God-in-nature. The poem, given its reference to Sunday, is curiously barren of any directly religious references. It is the sun that gives joy and the wind that serves as the vehicle of prayer. Nature serves as the great link between man's sordid existence and heaven.

"IT IS NOT BEAUTY I DEMAND"

In several of the lyric poems the themes of nature and love are fused. "It Is Not Beauty I Demand"—Darley's one assuredly great poem—illustrates the blending of nature and love, though the intent of the poet is to raise human love to a level beyond anything that might be found in nature. Darley's method is to use many of the standard phrases about women's beauty ("a crystal brow"; "starry eyes"; "lips that seem on roses fed") in a series of ten rapidly moving quatrains, with eight beats to each line, and a simple rhyme scheme of *abab cdcd* through the whole of the poem. The quatrains move rapidly, in part because Darley uses the syntax and diction of one who is speaking directly to his reader.

In "It Is Not Beauty I Demand" the natural beauties of the perfect woman are rejected as mere ornaments, or "gauds." In the fourth stanza, Darley breaks from the Cavalier tradition of "all for love" and inserts a fairly traditional moral into the poem. Thus, the red lips are rejected because they lead to destruction, like the red coral "beneath the ocean stream" upon which the "adventurer" perishes. The same moral argument is continued in the following stanzas, in which the white cheeks of the woman are rejected because they incite "hot youths to fields of blood." Even the greatest symbol of female beauty—"Helen's breast"—is rejected because Helen's beauty provoked war and suffering.

Darley's ideal woman would be a companion, a comforter, one with "a tender heart" and "loyal mind." Despite Darley's obvious affinities in this poem with Thomas Carew and other Cavalier poets, the poem represents a rejection of the Cavalier ideals of going off to battle to prove one's love and honor; it also represents a challenge to the rich sensuality of much Romantic poetry. With its emphasis on the intellectual virtues of women and the pleasures of companionship (versus sex), "It Is Not Beauty I Demand" is an affirmation of the ideals of love and marriage associated with the Victorians.

VERSE DRAMAS VS. LYRICS

Mention must be made of Darley's two tragedies, which in spite of their obvious failure as stage plays rep-

resent his most sustained creative effort. Darley had always been an enthusiastic reader of William Shakespeare and other Elizabethan dramatists; one of the most striking themes in his dramatic reviews was the death of tragedy in his own time. He was especially sickened by the rise and popularity of domestic tragedy; he reviewed one of the most popular tragedies of his time (*Ion*) in an almost savage manner for its sentimentality. Darley was not able to reverse the tendencies of Victorian playwriting, but his two tragedies, *Thomas à Becket* and *Ethelstan*, whatever their shortcomings as plays (they can be characterized as dramatic verse), illustrate what he thought a tragedy ought to be. He invoked the Elizabethan ideal of a man in high place who is brought to his death through his own error and the malice of others. Darley, however, was not able to write dialogue, and his characters are much given to lengthy, histrionic speeches. In many instances, the speeches cover entire scenes. As far as the plays have merit, they serve to illustrate the Victorian preoccupation with the "great man." Darley's heroes and villains are indeed on the heroic scale, but they lack credibility and the blank verse is frequently bathetic.

By contrast, Darley's lyrics, his only lasting achievement, have a genuine but limited appeal. His speech impediment, aloofness, and chronic shyness seemed to have forced him into a career that would serve as a natural release to his emotions. In his poetry, Darley created a world of fantasy, of benevolent nature and beautiful maidens, an ordered universe that the poet never found in real life.

OTHER MAJOR WORKS

PLAYS: *Sylvia: Or, The May Queen, a Lyrical Drama*, pb. 1827; *Thomas à Becket: A Dramatic Chronicle in Five Acts*, pb. 1840; *Ethelstan: Or, The Battle of Brunaburh, a Dramatic Chronicle in Five Acts*, pb. 1841.

NONFICTION: *The Life and Letters of George Darley*, 1928 (Claude Abbott, editor of letters).

BIBLIOGRAPHY

Abbott, Claude Colleer, ed. *The Life and Letters of George Darley, Poet and Critic*. 1928. Reprint. Oxford, England: Clarendon Press, 1967. A rare biography of Darley, which presents him as a poet and critic of distinction. Includes a full analysis of Darley's lyric poetry and of his major work *Nepenthe*. Notes the weakness in the structure of his work and suggests that it should be read as a series of lyric episodes expressing the theme of spiritual adventure. Includes a complete bibliography of works by Darley.

Bloom, Harold. *The Visionary Company: A Reading of English Romantic Poetry*. 1961. Rev. and enlarged ed. Ithaca, N.Y.: Cornell University Press, 1971. This brief analysis is important because Bloom is one of the most influential of modern literary critics. He pays Darley a high compliment by including him in the "visionary company" of Romantic poets. Includes a reading of *Nepenthe*, which Bloom sees as a quest-romance in the tradition of Percy Bysshe Shelley's *Alastor* and John Keats's *Endymion*.

Brisman, Leslie. *Romantic Origins*. Ithaca, N.Y.: Cornell University Press, 1978. The most extensive treatment of Darley by a modern critic, although it makes difficult reading. Brisman argues that Darley's awareness of his rank as a minor poet provides him with a recurring theme: He deliberately cultivates a "myth of weakness." This is particularly noticeable in *Nepenthe*, a poem in which Darley transforms the romantic quest "into a search for images of poetic diminutiveness."

Heath-Stubbs, John F. *The Darkling Plain: A Study of the Later Fortunes of Romanticism in English Poetry from George Darley to W. B. Yeats*. London: Eyre & Spottiswoode, 1950. Perhaps the best brief overview of Darley's work, particularly *Nepenthe*. Heath-Stubbs links *Nepenthe* to works by Keats and Shelley, and also by William Blake. Argues that in its "continuous intensity of lyrical music and vivid imagery" *Nepenthe* is unlike any other poem of similar length in English.

Jack, Ian. *English Literature, 1815-1832*. Oxford, England: Clarendon Press, 1963. Brief assessment in which Jack argues that Darley was a better critic than he was poet. Of his poetry, Darley's lyrics are superior to his long poems, although his diction was often flawed. He may, however, have had an influence on Alfred, Lord Tennyson. One of Darley's weaknesses was that he did not have anything original to say.

John R. Griffin

SIR WILLIAM DAVENANT

Born: Oxford, England; February, 1606
Died: London, England; April 7, 1668

PRINCIPAL POETRY

Madagascar: With Other Poems, 1638
Gondibert, 1651 (unfinished)
The Seventh and Last Canto of the Third Book of Gondibert, 1685
The Shorter Poems and Songs from the Plays and Masques, 1972 (A. M. Gibbs, editor)

OTHER LITERARY FORMS

Although he produced a considerable body of lyric and epic poetry, the bulk of Sir William Davenant's literary work was designed for the stage. His early dramas, heavily indebted to William Shakespeare and Ben Jonson, included the tragedy *The Cruell Brother* (1627), the comedies *The Witts* (1634) and *News from Plimouth* (1635), and the pastoral romance *The Platonick Lovers* (1635). In the mid-1630's he began writing masques; the best and most elaborate of these, *Britannia Triumphans* (1638), was done in collaboration with Inigo Jones. *Salmacida Spolia* (1640), also with Jones, was the last masque in which Charles I performed. After the Civil War, Davenant produced a series of dramatic entertainments, comprising a mixture of set speeches, scenes, and musical interludes, designed to circumvent the Puritan prohibition of conventional drama. The first was *The First Days Entertainment at Rutland House* (1656). In more sophisticated pieces on heroic themes, *The Siege of Rhodes* (1656) and *The Cruelty of the Spaniards in Peru* (1658), Davenant collaborated with such composers as Henry Lawes and Matthew Locke to create the English opera. After the Restoration he devoted much of his time to rewriting William Shakespeare, and in 1667 produced in collaboration with John Dryden an immensely popular comic travesty of *The Tempest*.

ACHIEVEMENTS

Sir William Davenant's lyric poetry, although essentially derivative from John Donne, Ben Jonson, and the Cavalier mode, is both skillful and varied. Davenant's longest poem, the unfinished *Gondibert*, is competent but undistinguished in its artistry. Nevertheless, it is of major importance when considered in conjunction with *The Preface to Gondibert with An Answer by Mr. Hobbes*. *Gondibert* was one of the first neoclassical poems. Here Davenant advocates such neoclassical precepts as the importance of restraint in metaphor, image, and sentiment; the use of the balanced, closed line; and the importance of probability. His popularization of neoclassical decorum and his development of the opera and the heroic drama are Sir William Davenant's major achievements.

BIOGRAPHY

Sir William Davenant, or D'Avenant, as he styled himself in later years, lived a life which seems to cry out to be the subject of a historical novel. Born into the middle class, destined to be a tradesman, he rose to become one of the most honored poets and playwrights of his day, a general in the army of Charles I, a successful diplomat, and the friend and companion of some of the most glamorous men and women of his age.

John Davenant, a vintner, was mayor of Oxford in 1606, the year of his son William's birth. Shakespeare was supposedly a regular visitor at the Davenant tavern and was reputed to be the boy's actual father, a rumor that the young poet actively fostered. Intended for apprenticeship to a London merchant, Davenant, at his father's death in 1622, was instead preferred to the powerful duchess of Richmond as a page. At the duke of Richmond's death in 1624, Davenant took service with Fulke Greville, Lord Brooke, opening even further the doors of patronage and preferment. The elder poet was an early supporter of his talent and by 1627 Davenant was a working playwright with his first tragedy, *The Cruell Brother*, licensed for performance. New plays followed quickly, but in 1630 Davenant fell silent for several years, the victim, it is believed, of a nearly fatal case of syphilis, an illness which cost him his nose. By 1633, however, Davenant had returned to the stage, writing a number of successful plays, gaining a reputation as a poet, and in the later years of the decade, achieving great success as a writer of court masques. In 1638, he was named poet laureate.

Davenant served with distinction in the Bishop's Wars of 1640 and was later implicated in the First Army Plot against Parliament. When the Civil War broke out, he served under the duke of Newcastle as lieutenant-general of ordinance and later fought with the king's army, being knighted in 1642 at the siege of Gloucester. In the later years of the war, he specialized in procuring arms and ammunition, making several dangerous trips to the Continent. Eventually, upon the collapse of the Royalist cause, he fled to France and became one of Queen Henrietta-Maria's most trusted servants.

In France, Davenant began the collaboration with Thomas Hobbes which was to be instrumental in the development of neoclassical theory. In 1650, they published *The Preface to Gondibert with An Answer by Mr. Hobbes*. Meanwhile, Davenant was appointed governor of Maryland by the exiled Charles II, but his ship to the New World was captured by privateers commissioned by Parliament. He spent the next two years in prison. Although released in 1652, at John Milton's intervention according to one tradition, Davenant spent the next few years in poverty and was again arrested, for debt, in 1654.

In 1656 Davenant returned to writing for the stage and, in his attempt to circumvent Puritan restrictions, developed the rambling art form which was the direct ancestor of both modern opera and Dryden's heroic drama. His career for the next few years was a series of successes, although he has been accused of selling out to the Puritan government. After the Restoration his popularity continued, but he was never reinstated in his laureateship. Charles II frequently attended his plays and at the time of his death on April 7, 1668, Davenant was one of the two most successful theater managers in London.

ANALYSIS

Sir William Davenant began his career as a versatile, technically competent poet, adept at producing *à la mode* verse guaranteed to please his patrons. His shorter works, many of them clearly bearing the stamp of John Donne's or Ben Jonson's influence, cover the entire range of forms fashionable in Caroline England: odes, satires, panegyrics, songs, and occasional poems. His themes were essentially what one would expect from a man destined to become poet laureate: the heroism of Prince Rupert and the king, the importance of friendship and the good life, the nobility of any number of aristocrats, and the beauty of a variety of noble ladies, especially the queen. As a lyric poet, Davenant was a competent craftsman, one of the best of that "mob of gentlemen who wrote with ease" and who surrounded Charles I. In later years, however, he became a trailblazer and his heroic poem, *Gondibert*, taken in conjunction with its *The Preface to Gondibert*, is one of the most important poems of the middle years of the seventeenth century.

MADAGASCAR

Although many of his early verses had appeared in poetic miscellanies or editions of his or others' plays, the first collection of Davenant's poems to be printed was *Madagascar: With Other Poems* in 1638. It consisted of the long (446-line) title poem and forty-two shorter pieces, including poems addressed to the king and queen, to aristocrats such as the duchess of Buckingham and the earls of Portland and Rutland, and to friends such as Endymion Porter, Henry Jermyn, and Thomas Carew. Also present are satiric works, several poems commemorating deaths, including William Shakespeare's, Ben Jonson's, and a false rumor of Davenant's own, and a number of prologues, epilogues, and songs from plays. The volume opens with commendatory verses from Porter, John Suckling, Carew, and William Habington.

Like Michael Drayton's "To the Virginian Voyage" of 1606, Davenant's "Madagascar" is a patriotic poem designed to stir Englishmen to great deeds of exploration and conquest. Whereas Drayton's poem is occasional—although three voyages were undertaken to Virginia in the year the work appeared—Davenant's piece honors a nonevent, Prince Rupert's proposed but never attempted expedition to South Africa, a voyage which his uncle Charles I eventually forbade and which Rupert's mother compared to an adventure of Don Quixote.

As the poem opens, Davenant recounts his soul's dream journey south to the tropics, where he beholds Rupert, his "mighty Uncles Trident" in hand, disembarking on the island of Madagascar with an army. The natives immediately surrender, awed as much by Rupert's beauty as by his military prowess. Other Europeans, perhaps Spaniards, also invade, and each side chooses two champions to determine ownership of the island by single combat. The English champions, for

whom "The God-like *Sidney* was a Type," are Davenant's friends Porter and Jermyn. Their conflict is recounted in typically "high, immortall verse," charged with elaborate conceits. The English champions are victorious but the treacherous Spaniards renege on their vow to surrender, thus proving the justice of the English claim and providing Davenant with material for further elaborately depicted battle scenes. Eventually, Rupert is proclaimed "The first true Monarch of the *Golden Isle*" and Madagascar's great riches are described at length, its value to the English crown confirmed. Exhausted, the poet's soul returns to his body.

At bottom, the Madagascar proposal was not very well thought out and when it was submitted to the East India Company, that body responded with what Davenant's biographer, A. H. Nethercot, calls "diplomatic caution," essentially refusing to have anything to do with it. Virtually all of Charles I's advisers pointed out the impossibility of the project, and Archbishop Laud even went so far as to offer Rupert a bishopric to replace his supposed governorship. Thus, the historical background lends to the poem a faint air of the ridiculous. Perhaps realizing this, Davenant concluded it with a whimsical description of himself, twirling a chain of office, growing goutish, sitting on the island's judicial bench. The poem's intent, however, is clear. With an eye toward the main chance of preferment, the soon-to-be poet laureate was quite obviously cultivating Rupert, the rising young star of the Caroline court.

Many of the poems which Davenant addressed to individual courtiers and noblemen, such as the typically if somewhat simplemindedly Jonsonian "To the King on New-years day 1630," are occasional verse. This poem begins by praising Charles I as a ruler who teaches by example, and by offering him all the joy inherent in such standard Cavalier touchstones as "Youth . . . Wine, and Wealth." It continues by wishing the king and the nation, first, peace, but peace "not compass'd by/ Expensive Treaties but a Victorie," and, second, a successful Parliament, one consisting of "such who can obey./ . . . not rebell." These veiled references to recent and only partially successful treaties with France and Spain and to Charles's dissolving of Parliament in March of 1629 typify Davenant's method and belief with regard to politics. He was essentially a "yes-man," defending Charles

I's actions without reservation, or, if differing at all with the king's policy, arguing on the side of action, the side of victory without compromise.

Other poems in the volume include "Elizium, To the Duchess of Buckingham," which begins by describing one of those Arcadian utopias of friendship, love, and beauty so popular with Cavalier poets, and finishes by eulogizing the dead duke of Buckingham; "A Journey into Worcestershire," a mock travelogue of the sort popularly used to satirize the foibles and follies of country bumpkins, Puritans, and the author and his friends; "Jeffereidos," a satire recounting the kidnapping of Jeffery Hudson, the queen's dwarf; and a pastoral lament, "Written When Colonel Goring Was Believ'd to be Slaine," in which two swains, Porter and Jermyn, again bemoan Goring's supposed death, juxtaposing fairly standard pastoral and heroic references to Achilles, Hector, and Elizium with references to Christopher Columbus and Ferdinand Magellan, and a complex, Donne-like nautical conceit. References to ships, compasses, charts, and exploration appear over and over again in Davenant's work. Indeed the nautical world is his favorite source of metaphors.

WORKS AND POEMS ON SEVERAL OCCASIONS

Between 1660 and 1663 Davenant published three short panegyric poems, *To His Excellency the Lord General Monck* (1660), *Upon His Sacred Majestie's Return to His Dominions* (1660), and *To the King's Most Sacred Majesty* (1663). These are minor pieces, very much the sort of thing every other poet of the day was writing. They were republished in the 1673 *Works* along with *Poems on Several Occasions*, a volume of Davenant's short pieces that had been intended for separate publication in 1657 but that had never seen print. *Poems on Several Occasions* includes the long (624-line) *To the Earl of Orrey*, an elaborate panegyric written in the 1650's. Davenant praises Orrey, a noted statesman and soldier who was later to be instrumental in restoring Charles II to the throne, in an elaborate conceit in which the poet is an explorer sailing the marvelous coastline of the Earl's genius.

There are fifty shorter pieces in *Poems on Several Occasions*, some of them dating from the 1630's; most of them, like the *Madagascar* poems, are easily classifiable as occasional pieces, lyrics, and satires. Perhaps the finest verses in *Poems on Several Occasions* are the short lyrics. Davenant's "The Lark now leaves his watry Nest" is a lovely compliment, more Elizabethan than anything else, in which the standard metaphor of the lady's awakening being like the sun's rising is handled with uncommon grace. Another lyric, "Endimion Porter and Olivia," contemplates the fate of lovers after death and the danger of their being separated.

GONDIBERT

Davenant is remembered today primarily as the author of *Gondibert*. This heroic poem relates the maneuverings and martial engagements involved in establishing the successor to the aging Aribert, eighth century king of the Lombards. The king's heir is the beautiful Rhodalind, and the king wishes her to wed Duke Gondibert, a knight who equals her in excellence. Unfortunately, the immoral but otherwise extremely capable Prince Oswald also aspires to the princess's hand and will fight to gain it. Oswald's followers are all hardened veterans of many campaigns. Gondibert's, by contrast, are mere youths, brave, but inexperienced, and devout worshipers at the shrine of Love.

One day Oswald and his troops ambush Gondibert while he is returning from the hunt. Disdaining to take advantage of his superior numbers, the prince offers to meet the duke in single combat. Soon the several leaders of the two factions are similarly engaged and Davenant describes the battle in great detail and with considerable relish. Oswald and his men are noble foes, but because virtue and Gondibert must triumph, Oswald is killed. As was the case in the duel in "Madagascar," which clearly served as a thematic, though not a stylistic, rough sketch for the heroics of *Gondibert*, the defeated faction refuses to abide by its leader's promise and attacks the duke's small party. Gondibert, wounded, nonetheless defeats them, and, although they have already proved doubly treacherous, gallantly lets them depart.

The poem goes on to relate the hero's recovery from his wounds at the palace of Astragon, a scientist-philosopher modeled on Sir Francis Bacon or Sir William Gilbert. While civil war is brewing, Gondibert dallies with Astragon's daughter, Birtha, and falls in love with her shortly before discovering that he has been proclaimed fiancé to Rhodalind. Soon after, the work breaks off. Although he lived another seventeen years, Davenant never returned to it.

Gondibert's importance lies not so much in its innate excellence as in the theory behind it. In its own day it provoked both controversy and ridicule. The poem was praised by Thomas Hobbes, who had something of a stake in it, and by both Edmund Waller and Abraham Cowley; but the more common reaction was highly negative. Some, like John Denham, were reduced to obscenities.

THE PREFACE TO GONDIBERT

In the all-important *The Preface to Gondibert*, Davenant argues that Homer, despite his greatness, erred when he introduced the supernatural into poetry. It is acceptable, for example, for the poet to petition his Muse metaphorically, when it is clear that he is really speaking to what Davenant calls his "rationall Spirit," but it is not acceptable for the poet to treat the Muse as a person in her own right. Vergil is similarly at fault and, even more so, Torquato Tasso and Edmund Spenser, the great modern heroic poets, because they as Christians should know better. Davenant generally follows his own advice in *Gondibert*, grounding his characters' actions not in motivation provided by meddling deities, but in the desire for power, martial exercise, and love. He does, however, include an enchantress in the poem, and has the Duke give Birtha a magic emerald which will change color if he is unfaithful.

Davenant saw the heroic poem as, at least in part, a didactic tool and resolved to display characters who exemplified active Christian virtues, although his conflicting desire to promote the Cavalier virtue of martial prowess occasionally led him to extremes. To convey the moral message and to please the reader were for Davenant the first requirements of the heroic poem, and anything standing in the way was to be condemned. Thus, Spenser could be faulted for his archaic language, complex stanzas, and obscure allegories. Davenant's own language is lofty but contemporary, his stanza a simple four-line iambic pentameter, rhyming *abab*.

Davenant was attempting to define and put to use what is now thought of as the neoclassical poetic. Breaking with his own early use of the metaphysical manner, he emphasized decorum, arguing against extremes, whether of language, sentiment, metaphor, or wit, and insisting on the superiority of the familiar and the real. With Hobbes's aid Davenant set out to develop an active poetic which repudiated all use of the supernatural even in epic or heroic forms, and which insisted on a rationalist approach to human nature. The word "wit" had meant something very different to Donne from what it was to mean to Alexander Pope, and it was in Davenant's *The Preface to Gondibert* that many of the arguments were first expounded which were eventually to lead to that change.

OTHER MAJOR WORKS

PLAYS: *The Cruell Brother*, pr. 1627; *The Tragedy of Albovine, King of the Lombards*, pb. 1629; *The Just Italian*, pr. 1629; *The Siege: Or, The Collonell*, pr. 1629; *Love and Honour*, pr. 1634; *The Witts*, pr. 1634; *News from Plimouth*, pr. 1635; *The Temple of Love*, pr., pb. 1635 (masque); *The Platonick Lovers*, pr. 1635; *The Triumphs of the Prince d'Amour* pr., pb. 1636 (masque); *Britannia Triumphans*, pr., pb. 1638 (masque); *The Fair Favorite*, pr. 1638; *Luminalia: Or, The Festival of Light*, pr., pb. 1638; *The Unfortunate Lovers*, pr. 1638; *The Distresses*, pr. 1639 (also as *The Spanish Lovers)*; *Salmacida Spolia*, pr., pb. 1640 (masque); *The First Days Entertainment at Rutland House*, pr. 1656 (music by Henry Lawes); *The Siege of Rhodes, Part I*, pr., pb. 1656, *Part II*, pr. 1659, pb. 1663; *The Cruelty of the Spaniards in Peru*, pr., pb. 1658; *The History of Sir Francis Drake*, pr., pb. 1659; *Hamlet*, pr. 1661 (adaptation of William Shakespeare's play); *Twelfth Night*, pr. 1661 (adaptation of Shakespeare's play); *The Law Against Lovers*, pr. 1662; *Romeo and Juliet*, pr. 1662 (adaptation of Shakespeare's play); *Henry VIII*, pr. 1663 (adaptation of Shakespeare's play); *Macbeth*, pr. 1663 (adaptation of Shakespeare's play); *The Playhouse to Be Lett*, pr. 1663; *The Rivals*, pr. 1664; *The Tempest: Or, The Enchanted Island*, pr. 1667 (with John Dryden; adaptation of Shakespeare's play); *The Man's the Master*, pr. 1668.

NONFICTION: *The Preface to Gondibert with An Answer by Mr. Hobbes*, 1650 (with Thomas Hobbes).

MISCELLANEOUS: *Works*, 1673 (3 volumes), 1968 (reprint); *Dramatic Works*, 1872-1874 (5 volumes; James Madiment and W. H. Logan, editors); *The Shorter Poems, and Songs from the Plays and Masques*, 1972 (A. M. Gibbs, editor).

BIBLIOGRAPHY

Blaydes, Sophia B., and Philip Bordinat. *Sir William Davenant: An Annotated Bibliography, 1629-1985.* New York: Garland, 1986. Current as of publication, listing the most important studies.

Bold, Alan. *Longman Dictionary of Poets.* Harlow, England: Longman, 1985. The entry on Davenant postulates that he may have been William Shakespeare's godson. Cites "The Souldier Going to the Field" as his best-known poem and asserts that it is a "tender expression of regret on leaving love for war."

Bordinat, Philip, and Sophia B. Blaydes. *Sir William Davenant.* Boston: Twayne, 1981. Recommended as an introduction to Davenant. Mostly appreciative but acknowledges that his poetry is not "of the first rank." Nevertheless, acknowledges Davenant's competency and his influence on both his peers and antecedents. The chapter on Davenant's nondramatic poetry discusses *Madagascar* and *Gondibert.* Perceives the last poems to be richer and more varied than *Madagascar.*

Harbage, Alfred. *Sir William Davenant: Poet Venturer, 1606-1668.* New York: Octagon Books, 1971. A full-length, sympathetic study of Davenant, whom Hurbage calls the "most conspicuous of the Cavalier poets" and whose poetry was "sometimes inspired." Contains extensive coverage of his early life, his plays, and his poems, with a chapter devoted to *Gondibert.* A must for Davenant scholars.

Scheil, Katherine West. "Sir William Davenant's Use of Shakespeare in 'The Law Against Lovers' (1662)." *Philological Quarterly* 76, no. 4 (Fall, 1997): 369-386. An analysis of Davenant's adaptation of Shakespeare's drama. Scheil delivers an understanding of Davenant's aesthetic and political motives by illustrating the conditions of theatrical production in the early Restoration period.

Welsford, Enid. *The Court Masque: A Study in the Relationship Between Poetry and the Revels.* Reprint. New York: Russell & Russell, 1962. A perceptive and thorough study of the masque, useful for interpreting the work of Davenant.

Michael M. Levy;
bibliography updated by the editors

DONALD DAVIE

Born: Barnsley, England; July 17, 1922
Died: Exeter, Devon, England; September 18, 1995

PRINCIPAL POETRY

Brides of Reason, 1955
A Winter Talent and Other Poems, 1957
The Forests of Lithuania, 1959
A Sequence for Francis Parkman, 1961
New and Selected Poems, 1961
Events and Wisdoms: Poems, 1957-1963, 1964
Essex Poems, 1963-1967, 1969
Six Epistles to Eva Hesse, 1970
Collected Poems, 1950-1970, 1972
The Shires, 1974
In the Stopping Train and Other Poems, 1977
"Three for Water-Music" and "The Shires," 1981
The Battered Wife and Other Poems, 1982
Collected Poems, 1970-1983, 1983
Poems and Melodramas, 1996
Selected Poems, 1997

Donald Davie

OTHER LITERARY FORMS

Donald Davie was a highly respected man of many letters. In addition to his poetry, he published numerous works of literary theory and criticism, including important books on Ezra Pound and Thomas Hardy, and an abundance of material on various British, American, and European authors. He also wrote several cultural histories that discuss the impact of religious dissent on culture and literature and edited a number of anthologies of Augustan and Russian poetry; in addition, he published biographical essays and translated Russian poetry.

ACHIEVEMENTS

Donald Davie's high reputation in the United States is apparent in the many awards and other academic appointments he received. He was the recipient of three awards in 1973—a Guggenheim Fellowship, an honorary fellowship at St. Catharine's College in Cambridge, and a fellowship in the American Academy of Arts and Sciences. In 1978 he earned a doctorate in literature from the University of Southern California and was made an honorary fellow at Trinity College in Dublin, Ireland.

BIOGRAPHY

Donald Davie was born July 17, 1922, into a lower-middle-class Baptist family, the son of a shopkeeper and the grandson of domestic servants. He grew up amid the slag heaps of industrial West Riding. His mother frequently recited poetry, and, according to Davie, "Robin Hood . . . surely did more than any other single text to make me a compulsive reader for ever after." His father, a lively and emotionally expressive man, encouraged the young boy to take piano lessons. Even as a child, however, Davie rankled at the pretensions and philistinism of his more well-to-do neighbors.

In 1940, Davie began his studies of seventeenth century religious oratory and architecture at St. Catharine's College, Cambridge. He joined the Royal Navy in 1941, and between 1942 and 1943 was stationed in northern Russia, where he studied the poetry of Boris Pasternak, who was to become an important and lasting influence. He married Doreen John, from Plymouth, in 1945; they had three children. Davie returned to Cambridge in 1946 and studied under F. R. Leavis; he earned his B.A. in

1946, his M.A. in 1949, and his Ph.D. in 1951. Between 1950 and 1957, he taught at Trinity College, Dublin, where he met the writers and poets Joseph Hone, Austin Clarke, and Padraic Fallon. He spent 1957-1958 as visiting professor at the University of California, Santa Barbara, where he was introduced to Yvor Winters, Thom Gunn, and Hugh Kenner (whose teaching post he actually filled for the year); it was during this period that he joined the "Reactionary Generation" of poets.

In 1958, he returned to Cambridge as a lecturer in English at Gonville and Caius Colleges, worried about how the "sentimental Left occupied all the same positions." Commenting further on his isolation during this time, he said: "The politics of envy . . . [and] self-pity had sapped independence, self-help, and self-respect." In 1964, he cofounded and became professor at the University of Essex (he later became pro-vice-chancellor there). Then, only four years later, feeling utter disillusionment with a declining British society and the philistinism of even his fellow poets, and also feeling totally alienated from his university colleagues, he moved to the United States and joined the faculty of Stanford University, where he remained until 1978. In 1978, he became Andrew W. Mellon Professor of Humanities at Vanderbilt University. He retired from Vanderbilt in 1988 and returned full-time to the Devonshire village, where for many years he had spent his summers. "I take retirement seriously, in a way that puzzles others, including my wife. I mean that I seldom find reasons for leaving this village." His writing slowed during this period and he died in Exeter, Devon, on September 18, 1995.

ANALYSIS

In both his poetry and his critical commentary, Donald Davie advocated a poetry of formal structure and prose syntax, along with restrained metaphor and feeling. He urged repeatedly that art communicate rational statement and moral purpose in technically disciplined forms. His work, usually highly compressed, erudite, and formally elegant, is sometimes criticized for its lack of feeling and for tending toward the overly academic—in short, for the notable absence of the personal element. Davie, nevertheless, stood firm in his position that the poet is responsible primarily to the community in which he writes for purifying and thus correcting the spoken language: "The central act of poetry as of music, is the creation of syntax, of meaningful arrangement." The poet thus helps one understand one's feelings; he improves the very process of one's thinking, and hence one's subsequent actions. Ultimately, the poet helps correct the moral behavior of the community at large.

Davie's poetry, frequently labeled "neo-Augustan," is characterized by formal elegance, urbane wit, technical purity, and plain diction. A widely respected poet, Davie pursued a refined and austere art in order to counter the disorder of the modern world. Shortly after publishing his *Collected Poems, 1950-1970*, he described the spirit of mid-century as "on the side of all that was insane and suicidal, without order and without proportion, *against* civilization." To Davie, the artist's purification of the word might restore moderation, propriety, and control—the very values that inspire integrity and courage. The poet, in fact, improving the spoken language of his society, might actually inspire the creative, moral, and social betterment of civilization. Again and again, Davie explained that "the abandonment of syntax testifies to . . . a loss of confidence in the intelligible structure of the conscious mind, and the validity of its activity." The main activity of the mind is moral and social.

Davie gained recognition with the *New Lines* anthology and the "Movement" of the 1950's. His name was linked with John Wain, Kingsley Amis, Philip Larkin, Thom Gunn, Robert Conquest, D. J. Enright, Elizabeth Jennings, and John Holloway, along with the other reactionary poets who stood against the romantic excesses, "tawdry amoralism," and Imagism and Symbolism of the British poets of the 1940's, such as Dylan Thomas, T. S. Eliot, and Ezra Pound. The Movement argued for a return to conventional prose syntax and a more formal poetry that utilized the conservative metaphors of the eighteenth century Augustans. These poets, who shared a similar class background, as well as similar educational and professional goals, were, in addition, linked to various "Reactionary Generation" Americans such as Yvor Winters, Louise Bogan, the Fugitives, and even Hart Crane, and to those poets who were pursuing concrete poetry, such as H. D. and Pound. For Davie and the Movement, a decorous diction was to be selected ac-cording to subject or genre; so, too, structure was to be logical rather than musical.

BRIDES OF REASON

The first poem of Davie's first volume, *Brides of Reason*, introduces a theme that persisted throughout his career—English identity abroad: the would-be-exile-becomes-hero, the poet inhabiting and striving to unite two different national psyches. Now in Ireland, he describes his "Hands [as] acknowledging no allegiance./ Gloved for good against brutal chance" ("Demi-Exile. Howth"). He also wrote, again in neoclassical form, that his work is intended to appeal to the "logic" in his reader, so that "poets may astonish you/ With what is not, but should be, true,/ And shackle on a moral shape" ("Hypochondriac Logic"). The frequent obscurities and ambiguities of this volume reflect the influence of William Empson and F. R. Leavis, although more noteworthy is Davie's debt to the Augustans William Cowper, Oliver Goldsmith, Samuel Johnson, and Christopher Smart. "Homage to William Cowper," which proposes that "Most poets let the morbid fancy roam," goes on to insist that "Horror starts, like Charity, at home." Davie, admitting that he is "a pasticheur of late-Augustan styles," would work with rhetoric of the eighteenth century and attempt a rational structure through absolute clarity of premeditated logic ("Zip!"):

> I'd have the spark that leaps upon the gun
> By one short fuse, electrically clear;
> And all be done before you've well begun.
> (It is reverberations that you hear.)

"On Bertrand Russell's 'Portraits from Memory'" begins with a familiar Davie verse:

> Those Cambridge generations, Russell's, Keynes' . . .
> And mine? Oh mine was Wittgenstein's, no doubt:
> Sweet pastoral, too, when some-one else explains,
> Although my memories leave the eclogues out.

Davie's early poetry was frequently compared to Charles Tomlinson's because of their mutual equation of form and morality. Poise, control, and clarity of statement, both poets maintained, reflect moral imperatives and contribute toward the establishment of a society of common sense, human decency, and high moral principle. Nevertheless, with his admittedly high moral stance,

Davie began a long isolation from his more fashionable contemporaries—from the early Dylan Thomas to the confessional poetry of Theodore Roethke, Sylvia Plath, and Robert Lowell. Throughout his career, Davie remained aloof from even the great W. B. Yeats and T. S. Eliot, in whose vast mythmaking he sensed a distancing from the human condition. For Davie, the poet must speak directly to his reader and take on the role of "spokesman of a social [not mythic] tradition"; the poet is responsible for the rescue of culture from decline by "making poetry out of moral commonplace." Interestingly, although Davie's aims were not entirely unlike Yeats's and Eliot's—to inspire action and change in a philistine and unimaginative contemporary world—he would accomplish his ends not through imaginative participation in myth, but rather through conscious control of language, and thus thought, and, finally, action. Responding to Davie's example of proper diction and traditional meter and syntax, for example, one might feel inclined to affirm the proper values of a more stable and civilized past. In "Vying," Davie wrote:

> There I, the sexton, battle
> Earth that will overturn
> Headstones, and rifle tombs,
> And spill the tilted urn.

Over the years, Davie gradually moved toward shorter and brisker lines, as well as a less obscure poetry. There was also an increasing display of emotion and a greater revelation of self—a closer relationship between the speaker and his landscape, history, and metaphor. The specific and general became more closely integrated. His rejection of a poetry consumed with the "messy ego," nevertheless, remained absolute, like his insistence that language remain the starting point of moral betterment. He therefore continued to reject accepted modern usage: "the stumbling, the moving voices," "the Beat and post-Beat poets,/ The illiterate apostles" ("Pentecost"). What is wanting and necessary, instead, is a "neutral tone" ("Remembering the 'Thirties"), reasonableness, and common values.

"A Sequence for Francis Parkman" reveals Davie's fascination with the openness of North America with its empty and uncluttered spaces that lack the detritus of a long history of human failure. The continent functions not unlike a grand tabula rasa on which the poet can project his meditations. He wrote in "A Letter to Curtis Bradford":

> But I only guess,
> I guess at it out of my Englishness
> And envy you out of England. Man with man
> Is all our history; American,
> You met with spirits. Neither white nor red
> The melancholy, disinherited
> Spirit of mid-America, but this,
> The manifest copiousness, the bounties.

A Sequence for Francis Parkman, Davie's response following his first visit to North America during 1957-1958, contains brief profiles of Sieur de La Salle, the Comte de Frontenac, Louis Joseph de Montcalm, Pontiac, and Louis Antoine de Bouganville, as Davie adapted them from the historiographer Francis Parkman.

EVENTS AND WISDOMS

The volume *Events and Wisdoms*, while retaining Davie's witty, epigrammatic style, also introduces a more sensual imagery in its precise descriptions of nature. In "Low Lands," for example, Davie describes a river delta

> Like a snake it is, its serpentine iridescence
> Of slow light spilt and wheeling over calm
> Inundations, and a snake's still menace
> Hooding with bruised sky belfry and lonely farm.
> The grasses wave on meadows fat with foison.

Both *Events and Wisdoms* and *Essex Poems, 1963-1967* illustrate Davie's pastoral-elegiac mode ("I smell a smell of death," "July, 1964"). He focused on death and emptiness, moving away from the more self-conscious literary subject matter of the Movement poetry. In the well-known "Winter Landscapes," he wrote:

> Danger, danger of dying
> Gives life in its shadows such riches.
> Once I saw or I dreamed
> A sunless and urbanized fenland
> One Sunday, and swans flying
> Among electric cables."

The sense of exile both within and outside his native country was also pronounced in poems such as "Rodez" and "The North Sea." Davie once again projected a concrete geography upon which to elaborate his meditations on human history and personal conduct. There is even an immersion in the external world of human event and interaction. Like Pound, who exerted a complex influence upon him, Davie wandered through the traditions of history, reexamining and restating human values worthy of restoration. "Rodez" admits "Goodbye to the Middle Ages! Although some/ Think that I enter them, those centuries/ Of monkish superstition, here I leave them/ With their true garlands, and their honest masks." Davie also accepted Pound's regard for nonhuman nature in its purposive indifference and essential *quidditas*. The poems in this volume, many composed in his most direct and sparsest language, retain Davie's essential urbanity, what Eliot called "the perfection of a common language"—impersonal, distinguished, and well mannered—a language sometimes called by Davie's detractors uninspiredly chaste, versified prose, an academic and excessively moralistic statement removed from sense experience. Nevertheless, "The practise of an art," he insisted, "is to convert all terms/ into the terms of art" ("July, 1964").

SIX EPISTLES TO EVA HESSE

Six Epistles to Eva Hesse again reflects Pound's rich influence on Davie. Like Pound, Davie incorporated the influences of numerous older and foreign literary traditions; he remained, like Pound, the traveler through history—the connoisseur of historical value, time, place, and event. Yet Davie retained his rage against disorder and freewheeling individuality, along with a rejection of Pound's experimental dislocations of traditional syntax. *Six Epistles to Eva Hesse*, addressed to Pound's German translator, is, in fact, Davie's "Essay on Criticism." He asked rhetorically

> Is it time
> For self-congratulating rhyme
> To honour as established fact
> the value of the artefact?
> Stoutly to trumpet Art is all
> We have, or need, to disenthrall
> Any of us from the chains
> History loads us with?

Again utilizing the verse epistle form and experimenting with a mixture of didactic narrative, satire, and a fluid octosyllabic couplet structure, Davie contemplated the new and old:

> Confound it, history . . . we transcend it
> Not when we agree to bend it
> To this cat's cradle or that theme
> But when, I take it, we redeem
> This man or that one.

Thus Davie established a connection between the virtues of common sense, proportion, and compassion; linear and empirical history; and specific, fixed verse forms.

COLLECTED POEMS, 1950-1970

The highly praised *Collected Poems, 1950-1970* draws on Davie's experiences in both England and the United States. He applauded the "Atlantic" as a "pond" in "a garden." At the same time, he reiterated his "faith that there are still distinctively English—rather than Anglo-American or 'international'—ways of responding imaginatively to the terms of life found in the twentieth century." One is reminded of Davie's Baptist roots and the stern demand of his faith. "Dissentient Voice," with its clear reference to Dylan Thomas's "Fern Hill," reminds one of the severities of Davie's childhood: "When some were happy as the grass was green/ I was as happy as a glass was dark." "England" recalls the bitterness of expatriation: On his way back from the United States to Great Britain, Davie confessed:

> I dwell, intensely dwell
> on my flying shadow
> over the Canadian barrens,
> and come to nothing else
>
> . . . .
>
> Napoleon was right:
> A nation of purveyors.
> Now we purvey ourselves
> . . . [with] brutal manners, brutal
> simplifications as
> we drag it all down.

To be sure, many of Davie's poems focus on England, and many compare the Mediterranean and Northern worlds. *The Forests of Lithuania*, written earlier (1959), however, and based on Adam Mickiewicz's romantic epic *Pan Tadeusz* (1834; English translation, 1917), focuses on Lithuania during its 1811-1812 Russian occupation. In this experimental poem, Davie utilized novelistic techniques, explaining that his goal is to deal with "common human experiences in the way they are commonly perceived, as slowly and gradually evolving amid a wealth of familiar and particular images" in the effort to "win back some of this territory from the novelist." "The Forest," for example, builds upon a series of lush and classical descriptions, as the poet conveys the sensual, as well as visual and tactile, richness of the landscape:

> Currants wave their hop-crowned tresses,
> Quickbeams blush like shepherdesses,
> The hazel in a maenad's shape
> Crowned with her nuts as with the grape
> Twirls a green thyrsus, and below
> The striplings of the forest grow—

THE SHIRES

Davie's tour de force, told entirely about England, is the complex autobiographical *The Shires*. Consisting of forty poems, one for each county in England, it is arranged in alphabetical order from Bedfordshire to Yorkshire. *The Shires* consists primarily of reveries about English geography and history, and as Davie lamented the unfulfilled potential of entire communities, as well as of individuals, he revealed the influence of Thomas Hardy. Also, in a voice that ranges from the formal to the informal, Davie filled the landscapes with personal (sometimes obscure) allusions. He speaks of Monmouthshire, for example, as the location of England's "wedding" to Wales and his marriage to a Welsh woman. The volume treats major and minor events, the tragic and the trivial. At times, Davie is serious and bitter about the modern world; at other times, he is resigned, wry, and even witty. These are poems of dissent and praise, as they treat his own experience and contemporary and historical England. Their predominant subject, however, is human and social neglect, and the waste ultimately brought on by the indifference to precise language and thought.

In "Suffolk," Davie admitted: "My education gave me this bad habit/ Of reading history for a hidden plot/ And finding it; invariably the same one,/ Its fraudulent title always, 'Something Gone.'" The poems resound with historical and literary echoes and august figures such as Lord Nelson, Tom Paine, Robert Walpole, Sir Francis Drake, Jane Austen, William Wordsworth, A. E. Housman, W. H. Auden, and John Fowles. Compared with the past, the contemporary world is vulgar and uninspired: "We run through a maze of tunnels for our meat/ As rats might . . ./ Drake,/ This is the freedom that you sailed from shore/ To save us for?" ("Devonshire"). Once again, Davie blended the particular and the abstract. Each shire reveals its own lesson. "Essex," where Davie taught, speaks of how language—our means of experiencing order of the self and society—is corrupted: "Names and things named don't match/ Ever." "Cornwall" describes the decline of imagination and intelligence: We live, said the poet, with "black patches on both eyes." "Devonshire" treats the corruption of community, and in "Staffordshire," the unrealized potential of the past has blighted the future.

The "Dorset" sequence, of particular interest, is organized in the manner of Pound's *The Pisan Cantos* (1948), with reveries and shifts of perspective and multileveled allusions to scholarship, history, culture, and autobiography. In "Sussex," however, one truly hears the poet's elegiac sadness for the general vacancy and lovelessness that has blanketed all the shires and which extends into the future. He writes:

> The most poeticized
> Of English counties . . .
>
> "Brain-drain" one hears no more of,
> And that's no loss. There is
> Another emigration:
> Draining away of love.

Throughout, the modern world is characterized by empty ceremony, diminished political acumen, and imprecise language. Davie also portrayed a physically vast, industrialized, polluted, and drab landscape.

The extraordinary "Trevenen" is a verse biography and tragedy, composed in octosyllabic couplets. It tells the story of the late-eighteenth century Cornish naval officer who, after a heroic career, was driven mad by those he served. Trevenen lived in "an age much like our own;/ As lax, as vulgar, as confused;/ . . . / Where that which was and that which seemed/ Were priced the same, where men were duped/ And knew they were." Davie's portrayal of Trevenen's naïveté, heroism, and death are among his most moving lines. The octosyllabic line is truncated to three stresses in four or six syllables:

Aware man's born to err,
Inclined to bear and forebear.
Pretense to more is vain.
Chastened have they been.
Hope was the tempter, hope.
Ambition has its scope
(Vast: the world's esteem);
Hope is a sickly dream.

IN THE STOPPING TRAIN AND OTHER POEMS

In his poems after the mid-1970's, Davie moved toward a more open and personal statement, although his commitment to perfect language and syntax remained, he said, less for the purpose of strengthening social and moral law than as a means of coming to terms with his personal life, which, he also confessed, was "the man going mad inside me." The title piece of *In the Stopping Train and Other Poems*, for example, is clearly less obscure and more emotionally expansive than has been his custom; it portrays a divided sensibility, an "I" and a "him." Davie admitted that the poem "is an expression of a mood of profound depression and uncertainty about what it has meant for me personally, and for people close to me, that for so many years I have devoted myself to this curious activity we call poetry." The poet boards a slow train in a journey of personal and historical reverie that moves through time and engages him in the difficult struggle to understand himself and define poetry. He is bitter about his ignorance of the world around him—the smell of a flower—and corrupted by his obsession with language:

Jonquil is a sweet word.
Is it a flowering bush?

· · · · · · ·

he never needed to see,

· · · · · · ·

he never needs to use his
Nose, except for language.

Not unlike the confessional poets, from whom he has always separated himself, he indicts himself "With his false loves." Finally, he confesses, "The man going mad inside me" is rendered mad by history and must mount "a slow/ and stopping train through places/ whose names used to have virtue." Like *The Shires*, "In the Stopping Train" integrates the abstract and personal and accom-

plishes a tighter relationship between the human, social, and abstract. Its complex narrator is closely integrated into the vast experience of common humanity.

In "To Thom Gunn in Los Altos, California," Davie admits of the pleasures and fears of the poet-exile in search of meaning: "What am I doing, I who am scared of edges?" All the same, poetry remains an exulting experience—the means of social, and, ultimately, of spiritual transcendence, even though he knows that "Most poems, or the best/ Describe their own birth, and this/ Is what they are—a space/ Cleared to walk around in" ("Ars Poetica"). *Three for Water-Music*, which contains noticeably sensuous and colorful images, also reminds one of Eliot's *Four Quartets* (1943), with its complex philosophical subjects and difficult personal allusions set within carefully defined formal divisions. The poet contemplates specific geographies once again and specific historical dates, and from these, deals with the personal and abstract. There are "epiphanies all around us/ Always perhaps," he remarks, and his personal recollections and even mythic evocations merge within a broad variety of styles.

THE BATTERED WIFE AND OTHER POEMS

The Battered Wife and Other Poems focuses on Davie's early life in Ireland when he was "martyred" to words. The title poem is a straightforward but unusually moving narrative about unfulfilled love. "Screech-Owl" admits that "Nightingales sang to me/ Once, and I never knew." In "Artifex in Extremis," Davie writes, "Let him rehearse the gifts reserved for age/ Much as the poet Eliot did," and then proceeds to explore the consciousness of the dying poet. He measures his success "to confess" that "The work that would . . . speak for itself/ Has not, [and this awareness] comes hard." The poems have an unusual intimacy about them, and the reader can sense a lament for the time and passion that have passed and forever been lost.

As a critic, Davie's remarks shed an interesting perspective on his poetry and reinforced his continuing concerns. For example, in *Purity of Diction in English Verse* (1952), he reaffirmed that the

strength of statement is found most often in a chaste or pure diction, because it goes together with economy in metaphor; and such economy is a feature of such a diction. It is achieved by judgment and taste, and it preserves the tone of the centre, a sort of urbanity. It purifies the spoken tongue.

This sentiment continues through *The Poet in the Imaginary Museum: Essays of Two Decades* (1977), a collection of essays whose title refers to the artist's obligation to wander through history to absorb and utilize art in all its forms. Speaking of Pound, for example, Davie again reiterated the poet's responsibility to link poetics and politics: "One would almost say . . . that to dislocate syntax is to threaten the rule of law in the community."

OTHER MAJOR WORKS

NONFICTION: *Purity of Diction in English Verse*, 1952; *Articulate Energy: An Enquiry into the Syntax of English Poetry*, 1955; *The Language of Science and the Language of Literature, 1700-1740*, 1963; *Ezra Pound: Poet as Sculptor*, 1964; *Thomas Hardy and British Poetry*, 1972; *Pound*, 1975; *The Poet in the Imaginary Museum: Essays of Two Decades*, 1977 (Barry Alpert, editor); *A Gathered Church: The Literature of the English Dissenting Interest, 1700-1930*, 1978; *Trying to Explain*, 1979; *Kenneth Allott and the Thirties*, 1980; *English Hymnology in the Eighteenth Century: Papers Read at a Clark Library Seminar, 5 March 1977*, 1980; *Dissentient Voice: The Ward and Phillips Lectures for 1980 with Some Related Pieces*, 1982; *These the Companions: Reflections*, 1982; *Czesław Miłosz and the Insufficiency of Lyric*, 1986; *Under Briggflatts: A History of Poetry in Great Britain, 1960-1988*, 1989; *Slave Excursions*, 1990; *Old Masters: Essays and Reflections on English and American Literature*, 1992; *Essays in Dissent: Church, Chapel, and the Unitarian Conspiracy*, 1995; *With the Grain: Essays on Thomas Hardy and Modern British Poetry*, 1998; *Two Ways Out of Whitman*, 2000.

TRANSLATION: *The Poems of Doctor Zhivago*, by Boris Pasternak, 1965.

EDITED TEXTS: *The Late Augustans: Longer Poems of the Eighteenth Century*, 1958; *Pasternak: Modern Judgments*, 1969 (with Angela Livingstone); *Augustan Lyric*, 1974; *The New Oxford Book of Christian Verse*, 1981.

BIBLIOGRAPHY

Everett, Barbara. "Poetry and Christianity." *London Review of Books*, February 4-18, 1982, 5-7. Everett stresses the reticence of Davie's poetry. Davie avoids strong displays of emotion, enabling him to concentrate on stylistic effects. At his best, as in *Three for Water-Music*, his poetry is superlative. He strongly emphasizes the values of the English countryside and defends an ideal of Christian civilization that he regards as in decline. Many of his best effects are understated and tacit, although he often begins a poem with a sharp phrase.

Fowler, Alastair. *A History of English Literature*. Cambridge, Mass.: Harvard University Press, 1987. Fowler relates Davie to the other Movement poets such as Robert Conquest and Philip Larkin. Davie's poetry stresses local themes and avoids difficulty. The value of plain, strong syntax is rated very high by Davie, but less so, one gathers, by Fowler. Davie avoids foreign influences and adopts a no-nonsense attitude toward the problem of how poetry relates to the world. Fowler rates him below Larkin and appears to dislike the Movement poets.

Kermode, Frank. *An Appetite for Poetry*. Cambridge, Mass.: Harvard University Press, 1989. Kermode notes a paradoxical side to Davie's poetry. Davie adopts the view that the genuine tradition of English poetry is one stressing local values. Thomas Hardy exemplifies the correct manner of writing poetry, and T. S. Eliot is regarded as aberrant. Davie considers his own work part of a counterrevolution against the modernism of Ezra Pound and Eliot. Nevertheless, his poetry displays the influence of both of those poets. Kermode contends that Davie is more cosmopolitan than Philip Larkin.

Powell, Neil. "Donald Davie, Dissentient Voice." In *British Poetry Since 1970: A Critical Survey*, edited by Peter Jones et al. London: Persea Books, 1980. Powell notes that much of Davie's poetry is concerned with his English audience. His move to California indicates a disillusion with England, and *Essex Poems, 1963-1967* suffers from an undue display of anger toward his former country. In some instances, for example, in the sequence *In the Stopping Train*, Davie talks to himself. Often, the shifts between "I" and "he" are bewildering. At his best, Davie is forceful and clear.

Rosenthal, M. L., and Sally McGall. *The Modern Poetic Sequence.* New York: Oxford University Press, 1983. The authors discuss in an illuminating way Davie's display of emotion in his poetry. His mood is usually bleak and somber. Instead of adding lyrical meditations after his narrative, in the nineteenth century tradition, Davie emphasizes the subjective throughout his poems. A detailed discussion of "After the Accident," an account of an automobile crash that nearly killed Davie and his wife, elucidates these points.

Wright, Stuart T. *Donald Davie, a Checklist of His Writings, 1946-1988.* New York: Greenwood Press, 1991. A comprehensive bibliography of Davie's works.

Lois Gordon

SIR JOHN DAVIES

Born: Chisgrove, Tisbury, Wiltshire, England; April, 1569

Died: London, England; December 8, 1626

PRINCIPAL POETRY

Epigrammes and Elegies, 1590? (with Christopher Marlowe)

"The Epithalamion of the Muses," c. 1594

Orchestra: Or, A Poeme of Dauncing, 1596, 1622

Nosce Teipsum: This Oracle Expounded in Two Elegies, 1599

Hymnes of Astraea, 1599

A Contention Betwixt a Widdowe, and a Maide, pr. 1602

Yet Other Twelve Wonders of the World, wr. 1602 or 1603, pb. 1608 (also known as *The Twelve Wonders of the World)*

The Poems of Sir John Davies, 1975 (Robert Krueger, editor)

OTHER LITERARY FORMS

Throughout his literary career, Sir John Davies published various nonfiction prose works, including a history of Ireland and a political commentary.

ACHIEVEMENTS

Sir John Davies' reputation as a poet has shifted radically, depending on the taste of the reading public. His epigrams and occasional poems were very popular with his contemporaries; they survive in numerous manuscript copies. *Nosce Teipsum,* his long philosophical poem, went through five editions during his lifetime. Reprinted first by Nahum Tate in 1697, it went through several more editions and remained very popular in the eighteenth century. Alexander Pope paid Davies the compliment of imitating him, and Samuel Johnson praised his skill at arguing in verse. Samuel Taylor Coleridge, in *Biographia Literaria* (1817), adapts three stanzas from *Nosce Teipsum* to explain how the poetic imagination functions. In the modern era, Davies attracted the favorable attention of poets such as T. S. Eliot and Theodore Roethke but has fared less well in academic scholarship.

In his very influential work *The Elizabethan World Picture* (1943), E. M. W. Tillyard identified Davies as a principal intellectual spokesman for the Elizabethan "world picture" and described his verse as "typically Elizabethan." This approach to his poetry established Davies as a poet who should be read for his ideas, for the insights he offered regarding the Elizabethan mind. Davies' modern editor, Robert Krueger, takes precisely this position when he concludes his critical introduction to the standard edition with the following statement: "Davies will never again be read for profit or pleasure; his readers will always be students of the Elizabethan world" (*The Poems of Sir John Davies*).

While it would be foolhardy to conclude that Davies is an underestimated "poet's poet," the major works of a poet who continued to receive favorable commentary from other practicing poets should not be dismissed as mediocre. His place in political history is assured: He served as attorney general of Ireland under James I and assisted in planning the "Plantation of Ulster." His literary achievements are more difficult to assess: Popular in his own day as the author of *Nosce Teipsum,* his long philosophical poem, and of salacious, satirical epigrams, Davies is now mostly remembered for his *Orchestra.*

BIOGRAPHY

John Davies was born in 1569, just five years after William Shakespeare and two years before John Donne.

His life belongs as much to the Jacobean as to the Elizabethan period. He probably became interested in writing epigrams while he was attending Winchester School. This preparatory school produced a large number of important epigrammatists, including John Owen, Thomas Bastard, and John Hoskins, as well as Davies. After spending some time at Oxford, Davies attended New Inn, an Inn of Chancery associated with the Inns of Court, before entering the Middle Temple and formally beginning his study of the law. Located near the theaters, the Inns of Court, the four important law schools in London, attracted many young men with literary as well as legal interests. Sir Francis Bacon studied at Gray's Inn, John Donne at Lincoln's Inn, and Sir Walter Ralegh and John Marston at the Middle Temple.

In the fall of 1592, Davies visited the University of Leiden, arriving a week after William Fleetwood and Richard Martin, his fellow students at the Middle Temple. William Camden, one of the leading English antiquarians, wrote a letter introducing Davies to Paul Merula, a distinguished Dutch jurist. The trip may have been partially motivated by the need to improve Fleetwood's image with the Middle Temple Benchers. He and Richard Martin had been expelled on February 11, 1592, for their "misdemeanours and abuses to the Masters and Benchers." Davies was probably involved in the Candlemas disturbances, but he and Robert Jacob, a lifelong friend, were given the milder penalty of merely being excluded from commons.

By 1594 Davies had apparently been presented at court by Charles Blount, Lord Mountjoy, who, along with Sir Thomas Egerton, is described as Davies' patron in all of the manuscript sources for his biography. Queen Elizabeth had Davies sworn her servant-in-ordinary and encouraged him in his studies at the Middle Temple. He then served as part of the embassy to Scotland for the christening of Prince Henry at Stirling Castle on October 30, 1594.

On July 4, 1595, Davies was "called to the degree of the Utter Bar with the assent of all the Masters of the Bench." Since his admission to the Bar came after the minimum seven years of residence and since he was called with the permission of all the Masters of the Bench, not merely by a particular reader, he must have distinguished himself as a particularly brilliant student.

Much of his best poetry was written during this period. By 1595 he had probably written *Nosce Teipsum*, which he did not publish until 1599, and most of his epigrams. In 1596 he published the first printed version of *Orchestra*, an encomium of dancing, to which he attached a dedicatory sonnet to Richard Martin, addressing him as his dearest friend.

On February 9, 1598, Davies entered the Middle Temple Dining Hall while the Benchers were seated decorously at the table, preparing for the practice court and other exercises which followed dinner. Davies walked immediately to the table where Richard Martin was seated and broke a bastinado over his head. Before leaving, he drew his rapier and brandished it above his head. For this flagrant violation of legal decorum, he was expelled on February 10 "never to return." No entirely satisfactory explanation for this attack has been proposed.

In *John Marston of the Middle Temple* (1969), Philip Finkelpearl speculated that the attack was related to a satiric reference to Davies' descent from a tanner which was made during the Christmas revels at the Middle Temple. Richard Martin played the Prince d'Amour, the central figure in the festivities, but it was Matagonius, the prince's poet, who was responsible for the satire against Davies. The incident occurred on December 27, 1597, so long before Davies' attack on Martin that it is difficult to believe that the two events were closely related. Whatever the provocation, it must have seemed significant to Davies, so much so, that he was willing to risk his promising legal future for public revenge.

After his expulsion Davies may have spent some time at Oxford. By 1601 he was serving in the House of Commons as a representative from Corfe Castle, Dorset. During the debate over monopolies, a raging controversy in this parliament, he advocated that the House of Commons proceed to pass a bill canceling the monopolies or patents. The queen's loyal supporters vigorously recommended that the House humbly petition her to redress their grievances, since granting monopolies was part of her royal prerogative. Sir Robert Cecil singled Davies out for a special reprimand. Martin also served in the parliament of 1601 and also opposed monopolies; his active support of Davies' position suggests that the reconciliation between the two men may have been genuine. Davies' own outspoken demeanor is the more surprising because he had been readmitted to the Middle Temple only about a month before the debate.

After James came to the throne of England, Davies was appointed first solicitor general and then attorney general of Ireland. After receiving a knighthood in 1603, the first concrete evidence of his progress up the social ladder occurred in 1609 when he married Lady Eleanor Audeley, the daughter of George Touchet, Lord Audeley, later the earl of Castlehaven. By 1612, Davies had been created a sergeant-at-law, and by 1613 he was well enough off financially to be listed as one of the chief adventurers in a list of investors in the Virginia Company. In 1612 he published his major prose work, a history of Ireland titled *A Discoverie of the True Causes Why Ireland Was Never Entirely Subdued, nor Brought Under Obedience of the Crowne of England, Until the Beginning of His Majesties Happie Raigne.*

However socially advantageous Davies' marriage was, it cannot have been very pleasant. Lady Eleanor's brother, Mervyn Touchet, the second earl of Castlehaven, was criminally insane. He was sentenced to death for unnatural offenses after a notorious trial in the House of Lords; Charles I temporarily improved the moral image of the aristocracy by allowing the execution to take place. Lady Eleanor herself was a religious fanatic who believed that she was the prophet Daniel reincarnated. The truth was supposedly revealed to her in anagrams which she explicated in incoherent prophecies. By her own report, three years before the end, she foresaw Davies' death and donned her mourning garments from that moment: "when about three days before his sudden death, before all his servants and his friends at the table, gave him pass to take his long sleep, by him thus put off, 'I pray weep not while I am alive, and I will give you leave to laugh when I am dead'" (*The Lady Eleanor Her Appeal*, 1646). Lady Eleanor did not mourn, but she had little reason to laugh after Davies' death. She remarried Sir Archibald Douglas in three months, but he neglected and finally deserted her. He also burned her manuscripts, and she prophesied that he, like Davies, would suffer for it. According to her reports, while taking communion he was struck dumb so that he could only make sounds like a beast. He apparently left England.

These facts are significant for a critical analysis of the surviving biographical materials and manuscript verse of Davies. His daughter Lucy married Ferdinando Hastings and became the countess of Huntingdon. Since her uncle was criminally insane and her mother's self-righteous fanaticism verged on madness, she would naturally want to present her father as morally upright and be sure that he was remembered for his solemn philosophical poetry and weighty prose. If the "licentious" sonnets first printed in the Clare Howard edition of Davies' *Poems* (1941) had been left among Davies' papers instead of in the library at Trinity College, Dublin, it is unlikely that either Lucy or her son Theophilus would have printed them. In his biographical notes on Davies, which survive in manuscript in the Hastings Collection at the Henry E. Huntington Library, Theophilus describes each of Davies' political appointments in detail, alludes to royal favors, and devotes several paragraphs to a description of Lucy Davies' dowry: Sir John's poetry is never mentioned.

ANALYSIS

Sir John Davies' minor poetry falls into three general classes: dramatic entertainments written for court ceremonies or celebrations, occasional poems which he sent to prominent people, and satires commenting on a literary fashion or topical scandal. Of the entertainments which can be clearly attributed to Davies, the most important are "The Epithalamion of the Muses," presented at the wedding of Elizabeth Vere, daughter of Edward Vere, earl of Oxford, to William Stanley, earl of Derby, and preserved in the commonplace book of Leweston Fitzjames of the Middle Temple; *A Contention Betwixt a Widdowe, and a Maide* presented at the home of Sir Robert Cecil on December 6, 1602, in honor of Queen Elizabeth; and *Yet Other Twelve Wonders of the World*, twelve poems in rhymed couplets which were apparently inscribed on a dozen trenchers which Davies presented to the Lord Treasurer on New Year's Day in 1602 or 1603. John Maynard set *Yet Other Twelve Wonders of the World* to music in 1611.

Davies' occasional poems were addressed to influential people such as Henry Percy, Earl of Northumberland; Sir Thomas Egerton, Lord Chancellor of England; Sir Edward Coke, Attorney General; as well as King James and Queen Anne. His "Gulling Sonnets" belong to the third class of topical poetry. In these sonnets

Davies mocks the conventions of the Petrarchan sonnet sequences which were popular in the 1590's. These particular poems survived only in manuscript accompanied by a dedication to Sir Anthony Cooke. They must have been written between 1596, when Cooke was knighted, and 1604, when he died. An internal reference to *Zepheria* (1597), an anonymous sonnet sequence, suggests that they were completed by 1598. *Zepheria* was probably written by a young law student since it contains an awkward combination of learned legal terms and Petrarchan images.

In his nineteenth century Victorian edition of Davies' works, Alexander Grosart supplied a commentary on Davies which unfortunately has dominated twentieth century critical opinion of the poet's major works. *Orchestra*, a dialogue between Penelope and one of her wooers, is, according to Grosart, a *jeu d'esprit* which Davies tossed off in his youth. Grosart insisted that Davies' most valuable work was *Nosce Teipsum* and that the chief merit of this exhaustive compendium of knowledge about the soul and immortality was its originality. Responding to Grosart's claim, modern academic scholarship on Davies has largely consisted of arguments that Davies' ideas derive from Plato, Aristotle, Pierre de la Primaudaye, Philippe du Plessis-Mornay, and Michel de Montaigne.

Underlying the approach to Davies which Grosart initiated is the assumption that a sixteenth century writer would have aimed at or even particularly valued originality. Davies, however, belonged to an age which suspected novelty, valued intellectual tradition, and sought to imitate poetic models rather than to express personal feelings. Poets consciously modeled themselves on previous poets. Edmund Spenser, who hoped to win the title of the English Vergil, began by writing pastorals just as his Latin master had done.

T. S. Eliot, in what remains the best critical appreciation of Davies' works, calls attention to his metrical virtuosity, his clarity and purity of diction, and his independence of thought. In shifting the critical issue from originality to independence of thought, Eliot demonstrates historical as well as literary insight. While Davies' ideas on the soul and immortality are not original, one should not expect them to be. His synthesis of many diverse sources shows intellectual independence.

Each of Davies' major poems has to be assessed in relation to other works in that particular genre. He consciously works with certain established poetic conventions. His *Nosce Teipsum* should be examined in relation to other long philosophical poems, such as Lucretius's *De rerum natura* (c. 60 B.C.E.; *On the Nature of Things*), Aonio Paleario's *De immortalitate animae* (1536), Samuel Daniel's *Musophilus* (1599), and Fulke Greville's poetic treatises. *Orchestra* belongs to the genre of mythological wooing poems, which were later given the name *epyllia*, or minor epics. In writing *Orchestra*, Davies did not set out to write a poem about the Elizabethan worldview; he suggests that *Orchestra* relates a wooing episode that Homer forgot to include in the *Odyssey* (c. 800 B.C.E.) because he wants his readers to associate the poem with other amatory poems popular in England in the 1590's. Of these, two of the most popular were Christopher Marlowe's *Hero and Leander* (1598) and Shakespeare's *Venus and Adonis* (1593). *Orchestra*, however, lacks the sensuality of these two poems and seems to resemble the more philosophical efforts in the genre, such as Michael Drayton's *Endimion and Phoebe* (1595) and George Chapman's *Ovids Banquet of Sence* (1595). The *Hymnes of Astraea* belong to a genre treated with disdain by most modern scholars. They are acrostic lyrics intended as an Accession Day tribute to Queen Elizabeth. Like the many entertainments written to praise Elizabeth's beauty or her purity, they are intended as courtly compliments and should be approached as artful "trifles," excellent in their kind.

Finally, it is important to emphasize that Davies was a man of ideas. His poems are intended to delight, but also to teach and to inform. Critics who associate poetry with the expression of feelings or the description of scenery may find his verse less immediately accessible. He thrived on formal restraints; to appreciate his poetry requires a sensitivity to the technical difficulties of writing verse. It also requires that the reader accept verse in which, in T. S. Eliot's words, "thought is not exploited for the sake of feeling; it is pursued for its own sake."

EPIGRAMMES AND ELEGIES

Davies' *Epigrammes and Elegies* appeared without a date and with a title page reading "At Middleburgh." No satisfactory explanation has been offered for the posthumous combination of Christopher Marlowe's translation of Ovid's *Elegies* with Davies' *Epigrammes and Elegies*. It is unlikely that the first edition was a piracy because Epigrams 47 and 48, which balance 1 and 2 in the printed text, seem to have been written specifically for the printed edition; they are absent from all four of the most important manuscripts. Although some of the epigrams may have dated from his school days, the majority were probably written between 1594 and 1595.

The poems are obviously modeled on Martial's epigrams, but Davies supplies details of sixteenth century English life. In "Meditations of a Gull," he describes a young gentleman consumed by "melancholy," a young man uninterested in politics who wears a cloak and a "great black feather." He is clearly describing the *type* of young man who pretends to be an intellectual, rather than a specific caricature. Davies, in fact, claims that his epigrams tax under "a peculiar name,/ A generall vice, which merits publick blame." In June, 1599, the Bishop of London and the Archbishop of Canterbury ordered that "Davyes Epigrams and Marlowe's Elegyes" be burned. Since they seem less obscene than other works so condemned, it may be that one of the epigrams contained a libelous allusion unrecognizable today. Practice in this genre, which requires condensation and lucidity, assisted Davies in developing talents which he demonstrated more forcefully in *Nosce Teipsum* and *Orchestra*, but the *Epigrammes and Elegies* still have some interest because of the clever way in which they mirror life in sixteenth century London.

NOSCE TEIPSUM

Nosce Teipsum: This Oracle Expounded in Two Elegies was first printed in 1599, approximately one year after Davies was expelled from the Middle Temple. The poem has frequently been described as an attempt on Davies' part to "repair his fortunes with his pen," thus assuming that Davies wrote it to show that he repented his assault on Martin and that he had completed his reformation. The poem contains what could be interpreted as an autobiographical reference: Affliction is described as having taken the narrator by the ear to teach him a lesson. There is substantial evidence, however, that the poem was begun long before Davies attacked Martin and that it was revised over a period of several years.

The question of literary form has received little attention in discussions of *Nosce Teipsum*, but an understanding of the nature of the poem's form and structure is crucial. First, the argument, or organization of ideas, does not define the form. It is impossible to outline *Nosce Teipsum* thematically without reaching the conclusion that the poem is a loosely organized compendium of Elizabethan knowledge. The second elegy, for example, defines the soul in relation to the body, but then discusses the origin of the soul, the fall of man, and free will, before considering the way in which the powers of the soul are actually exercised in the body. The fall of man is discussed at the beginning of the first elegy and then examined again in stanzas 138-186 of the second elegy. Second, the poem is divided into two elegies of very different lengths, 45 stanzas in the first and 436 in the second. In the second elegy a description of the soul requires 273 stanzas with arguments for immortality requiring another 163 stanzas. Davies could have divided the second elegy into two separate sections; that he did not do so requires some consideration.

The relationship between the two elegies is suggested by the general title of the work, not by the separate titles of the two elegies: *Nosce Teipsum: This Oracle Expounded in Two Elegies*. The emphasis should be upon "oracle," not upon the broad tradition of self-knowledge. The first elegy, "Of Humane Knowledge," is a riddle which presents the dilemmas that individuals experience in attempting to acquire self-knowledge. Both biblical and classical illustrations are used because the riddle of self-knowledge puzzles Christians as well as pagans. The second elegy represents a solution to the riddle, and it is structured as a classical oration. Davies' structure reverses the procedure of the classical oracle in which a relatively clear question led to an enigmatic answer. Influenced by the Renaissance concept of the "oracle" as an obscure riddle, Davies intends the first elegy to represent the question put to the deity in the ancient oracles; it concludes with an enigmatic statement of man's nature. The second elegy presents a clear and straightforward answer to that enigmatic statement. The relationship between the two elegies explains why the form of *Nosce Teipsum* required a break between the two poems.

The second elegy uses the seven-part format of a classical oration, following the divisions of Thomas Wilson, the sixteenth century rhetorician, rather than the six sections recommended by Cicero. The "entrance" (stanzas 1-21) invokes divine light, showing the poet's need for divine assistance by summarizing the diversity of opinions about the soul (7-15). The "narration" (22-174) consists of two parts: a definition (22-100) and a history (101-174). The soul is defined as a spirit separate from the body; then, the history of how the soul and body were created is summarized. The "proposition" (175-189) answers the questions: why the soul is related to the body, in what manner it is related to the body, and how the soul exercises her powers in the body. The answers summarize the major themes of the "history," "definition," and "division." Davies uses the "division" (190-269) literally to divide the faculties of the soul and their functions; traditionally, the division explained the disposition of the material. The arguments for the immortality of the soul are presented as the "confirmation" (274-357); the refutation of arguments against the immortality of the soul follows in the "confutation" (358-420). In the "conclusion" (421-436) Davies links the two main subjects, the soul and immortality, and then admonishes his own soul to be humble. This admonition parallels the invocation to divine light presented in the entrance.

Brilliantly using the resources of rhetoric, Davies takes the reader from darkness and ambiguity in the first elegy to light and clarity as the answer to the riddle is discovered. The vision of man as a "*proud* and yet a *wretched* thing" at the end of the first elegy is corrected in the Acclamation which precedes the arguments for immortality in the second elegy:

> O! What a lively life, what heavenly poer,
> What spreading vertue, what a sparkling fire!
> How great, how plentifull, how rich a dower
> Dost Thou within this dying flesh inspire!

ORCHESTRA

Davies' most engaging poem, and probably his most interesting for the modern reader, is *Orchestra*, an encomium of dancing set within a Homeric frame. The poem is supposed to relate a dialogue between Penelope, Queen of Ithaca, and Antinous, one of the disorderly suitors who wants to marry Penelope. Antinous invites Penelope to dance, but she refuses, calling dancing "this new rage." He responds with a lengthy defense of dancing, its antiquity and order.

Davies successfully achieves an exuberant combination of fancy and learning by using the structure, imagery, and setting to suggest multiple levels of meaning. These levels overlap and reinforce one another, but they can be generally distinguished as philosophical, political, and aesthetic. On a philosophical level, the poem is an extended hyperbole which views the macrocosm and microcosm united in the universal dance of life. Davies, however, treats this traditional idea playfully as well as seriously. When he extends the central image of a dancing cosmos to include the description of the veins of the earth as dancing "saphire streames," and to include the personification of Echo, the "prattling" daughter of the air, as an imperfect dancer, the reader becomes keenly aware of the poet's artifice. One is amused by these unconventional extensions of the traditional metaphor, but one does not question its basic validity. The aesthetic effect that Davies achieves is to render the tone playful without undercutting the seriousness of the message.

Similarly, Davies interweaves the themes of love and beauty in ways which enrich the philosophical and aesthetic overtones of the poem. Love is described as the father of dancing and also functions as a major figure in the poem. Stanzas 28-76 are devoted to Antinous's description of Love's speeches and actions, and Love, disguised as a page, presents Antinous with the magic mirror which reflects an idealized view of Elizabeth and her court (stanzas 109-126). In stanzas 98-108 love also becomes the central issue in the dialogue between Penelope and Antinous. She attacks Love as "of every ill the hatefull Father vile" (stanza 98), supporting this charge with mythological examples (stanzas 99-100). She concludes with a rejection of both dancing and love in stanza 101: "Unhappy may they prove,/ That sitting free, will either daunce or love." Antinous replies by distinguishing mischievous Lust from that "true Love" who invented dancing, tuned the world's harmony, and linked men in "sweet societie." In stanzas 105-108, Antinous argues that Love dances in Penelope: Her beauty is "but a daunce where Love hath us'd/ His finer cunning, and more curious art." As E. M. W. Tillyard has suggested, these stanzas allude to the Platonic ladder in which the lover is first attracted to the physical beauty of his mistress and then to her spiritual beauty and virtue; he is led up the ladder to the point at which he values virtue for its own sake. In stanza 108, the imagined vision of Penelope's virtues dancing a round dance in her soul almost puts Antinous into a trance.

The philosophical and aesthetic levels are closely related. Not only is Penelope's beauty described as a dance in which Love has used his "more curious art," but Love's dance in Penelope is also developed by artistic illustrations: Love dances in her fingers when she weaves her web (stanza 106) or when she plays "any silver-sounding instrument" (stanza 107). This type of aesthetic statement is set forth quite overtly in the poem, but there are also two digressions from the central action which function aesthetically to symbolize the entire poem: (1) Antinous reports a long speech which the god Love delivered to disorderly men and women in order to persuade them to dance. This persuasion to dance, stanzas 29-60, is a rhetorical set piece; it is unrelated to the main action, Antinous's persuasion of Penelope to dance, and yet it mirrors it. Love's speech is a macrocosmic parallel to the microcosm in which Antinous is wooing Penelope. (2) Near the conclusion of the poem (stanzas 109-126), in the second digression, Antinous summons Love disguised as a page boy to bring a magic mirror which reflects a vision of Elizabeth's court in which the sovereign moon is surrounded by dancing stars. The heavenly bodies and the court, or body politic, are united in harmonious order. Each of the above digressions comments upon the poem and underlines Davies' political intentions.

Queen Elizabeth was in her sixties when *Orchestra* was written, but she was surrounded by suitors who wished to be named as her successor. The contemporary political situation offered a close parallel to the Homeric setting, but Davies could not afford to make the comparisons too explicit. He merely hints that his own Queen Elizabeth, like Queen Penelope, is reluctant to participate in the orderly movement of the universe by assuring for a transfer of power (stanzas 60, 57-58). In the first digression, Antinous parallels Love, the god, who is attempting to persuade the disorderly men and women to learn to dance; by implication, Penelope parallels them.

The mirror, like the rhetorical set piece, symbolizes in miniature the poem. Davies' *Orchestra*, like the mirror, has displayed the timeless and ideal forms of order in the macrocosm and the microcosm. It has shown the

past by describing Antinous's wooing of Penelope and hinted at the rejection of order in Penelope's refusal. The poem, like the mirror, also shows the present by describing the Queen surrounded by her courtiers as the moon surrounded by the stars, but there is no provision for the future. At the end of the poem, the reader does not know whether Queen Penelope will finally accept the invitation to dance and in so doing assure order throughout the macrocosm and microcosm. The invocation to Urania in stanza 127 is addressed to a "Prophetesse divine," not to the muse of heavenly love. This invocation, which follows the invocation in stanza 123 so closely, emphasizes that the poet cannot prophesy the future. He has shown the past, present, and the timeless ideal, but it is up to the Queen to provide for the future.

The epic trappings, in which the disorderly Antinous of the *Odyssey* becomes a spokesman for order, invite the reader to make parallels, but they are handled so playfully that *Orchestra* could, if need arose, masquerade as a simple wooing poem. The poem invites, but does not require a political interpretation. *Orchestra* is constructed so that it could pass as a *jeu d'esprit* or as a celebration of honor climaxing in a compliment to the Queen, but it was intended as Davies' "pithie exhortation" to Elizabeth to settle the succession so that an orderly transfer of power would be assured after her death.

Three versions of *Orchestra* have survived, and in each, Davies' handling of the conclusion reflects his views about the contemporary political situation. The only surviving manuscript of the poem (LF) is preserved in Leweston Fitzjames's commonplace book (Bodleian Library Add. MS. B. 97. fols. 258-38). LF contains only some stanzas of the first printed version: 1-108 plus 131. An entry in the Stationers' Register in 1594 suggests that LF preserves an early version composed in 1593-1594, a time when the publication of Father Robert Parsons's *Conference About the Next Succession to the Crown of England* had made the subject of the succession dangerous to discuss. The LF version omits the magic mirror sequence so that no celebration of order in the body politic is included in the poem.

The first printed version is titled *Orchestra: Or, A Poeme of Dauncing. Iudicially Prooving the True Observation of Time and Measure, in the Authenticall and Laudable Use of Dauncing.* This version consists of stanzas 1-131. Probably to render the political implications less explicit, Davies added stanzas 109-126, the mirror sequence, to the already complete manuscript version before he published the poem in 1596.

The final version of the poem appeared in 1622, nearly twenty years after the succession had been peacefully settled. The 1622 version substitutes a dedication to Prince Charles for the earlier one to Richard Martin, who had died a few years earlier. Stanzas 127-131, which contain veiled allusions to poets popular in the 1590's, are omitted. Following stanza 126 there is the curious note: "Here are wanting some stanzas describing Queen Elizabeth. Then follow these." Ironically, the five new stanzas (132-136) contain a description of Queen Elizabeth. The printer seems to have confused these stanzas in manuscript and not known where to insert them; to conceal his confusion he added a note suggesting that something had been left out and merely printed the stanzas at the end of the text. When the stanzas are reordered and inserted in the appropriate places, it is clear that in this version Davies did intend to suggest that Queen Penelope accepted the invitation to dance. The invocation to Urania is omitted, and the poem concludes with stanza 126. Davies, looking back nostalgically on the Elizabethan court of his youth, suggests that Elizabeth's reign was indeed England's Golden Age.

HYMNES OF ASTRAEA

Hymnes of Astraea, twenty-six acrostic lyrics, celebrates Queen Elizabeth as Astraea, the just virgin, who left the earth after the end of the Golden Age; these hymns suggest that the English Virgin Queen is an embodiment of Astraea, who has returned to usher in the golden age of England. The number twenty-six was associated with the astrological sign of the constellation Virgo, and Virgo, in turn, was associated with Astraea, the just virgin. In *Orchestra*, Davies indicated that "the fairest sight that ever shall be seene" would occur when "sixe and twenty hundreth yeeres are past" (stanza 121). This reference demonstrates his awareness of the Virgo-Astraea tradition and his desire to associate it with Elizabeth, who, by deciding the succession question, could bring a new golden age to England.

Hymnes of Astraea is an artful and brilliantly sustained tour de force. Each of the twenty-six acrostic lyr-

ics contains sixteen lines divided into stanzas of five, five, and six. In all twenty-six Davies follows a regular rhyme pattern of *aabab ccdcd* in the first two stanzas, with occasional variations from the dominant pattern of *eefggf* in the third stanzas. The meter is predominantly iambic tetrameter. *Hymnes of Astraea* was entered in the Stationers' Register on November 17, 1599, the Queen's Accession Day. Intended as an Accession Day tribute, the initial letters of the lines read downward spell the royal name: ELISABETHA REGINA.

OTHER MAJOR WORKS

NONFICTION: *A Discoverie of the True Causes Why Ireland Was Never Entirely Subdued, nor Brought Under Obedience of the Crowne of England, Until the Beginning of His Majesties Happie Raigne*, 1612; *Le Premer Report des Cases et Matters en Ley*, 1615; *A Perfect Abridgement of the Eleven Bookes of Reports of the Reverend and Learned Sir Edw. Cook*, 1651; *The Question Concerning Impositions, Tonnage, Poundage, Prizage, Customs*, 1656.

BIBLIOGRAPHY

Brink, Jean R. "Sir John Davies' *Orchestra:* Political Symbolism and Textual Revision." *Durham University Journal* 72 (1980): 195-201. Analyzes the way in which *Orchestra*, Davies' most important poem, comments both philosophically and politically upon the Elizabethan "worldview." The notes offer a useful summary of previous biographical and critical discussions of Davies.

Brooks-Davies, Douglas, ed. *Silver Poets of the Sixteenth Century*. Rutland, Vt.: Charles E. Tuttle, 1992. Examines work by Wyatt, Surrey, Ralegh, and Davies, including the long philosophical poems *Orchestra* and *Nosce Teipsum*.

Davies, John. *A Discovery of the True Causes Why Ireland Was Never Entirely Subdued [and] Brought Under Obedience of the Crown of England Until the Beginning of His Majesty's Happy Reign*. 1612. Edited by James P. Myers, Jr. Washington, D.C.: Catholic University of America Press, 1988. In this tract on Ireland, Sir John Davies, Attorney General of Ireland under James I, comments at length upon the Plantation of Ulster and many other facets of the

Jacobean settlement. Myers's edition is the first to be fully accessible to the modern reader. He has modernized the spelling, carefully glossed unfamiliar historical references, and explained legal terms.

_____. *The Poems of Sir John Davies*, edited by Robert Krueger. Oxford, England: Clarendon Press, 1975. The standard edition of Davies' poetry, but, as Krueger notes in the introduction, much of Davies' verse, especially his epigrams and occasional poetry, was still being recovered from manuscript at the time that this edition appeared.

Helgerson, Richard. *Self-Crowned Laureates: Spenser, Jonson, Milton, and the Literary System.* Berkeley: University of California Press, 1983. Although Helgerson offers only a brief discussion of Davies, his study of the social milieu in which English Renaissance poetry was composed is important. Helgerson distinguishes Davies, a gifted amateur, from both the professionals and the would-be laureate poets.

Klemp, P. J. *Fulke Greville and Sir John Davies: A Reference Guide.* Boston: G. K. Hall, 1985. Klemp presents a chronological bibliography of works by and about Sir John Davies from 1590 to 1985. Each entry in the bibliography has been annotated.

Pawlisch, Hans S. *Sir John Davies and the Conquest of Ireland: A Study in Legal Imperialism.* Cambridge, England: Cambridge University Press, 1985. Concentrates on Davies' legal and political career rather than his verse. Pawlisch argues that judge-made law offered the English monarchy a means of consolidating the Tudor conquest of Ireland.

Sanderson, James L. *Sir John Davies.* Boston: Twayne, 1975. Although the biography is out of date, this study of Davies is the only full-length discussion of his life and major poems. Sanderson comments on Davies' epigrams, *Orchestra, Nosce Teipsum*, and his religious and occasional verse.

Sneath, E. Hershey. *Philosophy in Poetry: A Study of Sir John Davies' Poem "Nosce Teipsum."* New York: Greenwood Press, 1969. A rare book-length focus on Davies's poem, addressed in terms of soul and body, materialism and sensationalism.

Jeanie R. Brink;
bibliography updated by the editors

PETER DAVISON

Born: New York, New York; June 27, 1928

PRINCIPAL POETRY

The Breaking of the Day and Other Poems, 1964
The City and the Island, 1966
Pretending to Be Asleep, 1970
Walking the Boundaries, 1974
A Voice in the Mountain, 1977
Barn Fever and Other Poems, 1981
Praying Wrong: New and Selected Poems, 1957-1984, 1984
The Great Ledge, 1989
The Poems of Peter Davison, 1957-1995, 1995
Breathing Room: New Poems, 2000

OTHER LITERARY FORMS

In addition to his life as a poet, Peter Davison has carved out a distinguished career as an editor, including his many years as poetry editor of *The Atlantic Monthly* and as a consulting editor at Houghton Mifflin. *Hello, Darkness* (1978), his posthumous edition of the collected poems of L. E. Sissman, won the National Book Critics Circle Award in Poetry in 1979.

Davison has also written two autobiographical works: *Half Remembered: A Personal History* (1973), which recounts the story of his life from birth until his early forties, and *The Fading Smile: Poets in Boston, from Robert Frost to Robert Lowell to Sylvia Plath, 1955-1960* (1994), which offers his personal perspective on a significant midcentury poetry renaissance. *One of the Dangerous Trades: Essays on the Work and Workings of Poetry* (1991) is a collection of essays on poetry and poets.

ACHIEVEMENTS

Peter Davison's poetic career was launched auspiciously after he won the Yale Series of Younger Poets Competition in 1964. From the very beginning, his work gave evidence that he is heir to what might be termed the New England tradition of self-examination, a process marked by a penchant for using the outer world as a metaphor for one's inner life. In this regard, he learned much from his early mentor, the American poet Robert Frost.

Davison also discovered his literary vocation during the 1950's and 1960's, when confessional poetry, a lyric mode of personal outpouring, was the vogue. His preference for formal regularities, however, distinguishes his work from that of other poets of the time, such as Sylvia Plath and Anne Sexton, because he has a tendency to use the artifice of the poem not to indulge in guilt and self-effacement and to risk drowning himself in his own feelings but to give shape to his emotions so that they can be clarified.

In the final analysis, Davison has succeeded in charting a conservative course, punctuated by flirtations with topical subjects and free verse. He won the Poetry Award of the National Institute of Arts and Letters in 1972, the James Michener Award of the Academy of American Poets in 1981, and the New England Book Award for Literary Excellence from the New England Booksellers Association in 1995.

BIOGRAPHY

Born in New York City to Edward and Natalie (Weiner) Davison, Peter Hubert Davison spent his formative years in Boulder, Colorado. His father, a poet and English expatriate, taught at the University of Colorado. Here his family hosted some of the most important poets and novelists of the day because of his father's management of a significant national writing conference each summer. Thus, Peter Davison grew up in a privileged intellectual environment.

After he graduated from Harvard University in 1949 with a bachelor's degree in history and literature, Davison spent a year as a Fulbright scholar at Saint John's College of Cambridge University in England. In 1951 he was drafted into the military, and he served for two years in the psychological warfare division of the United States Army. Following his discharge in 1953, Davison worked in New York City for two years as an editor at Harcourt, Brace and Company before moving to Boston in 1955 to join the staff of Harvard University Press and, in 1956, Atlantic Monthly Press.

Shortly after his move to New England, he also began to consider the possibility of writing poetry. Davison was influenced in this decision by a number of factors.

He was inspired by the example of the young poet Sylvia Plath, with whom he had a brief love affair, and by his acting success in verse plays produced by the Poets' Theatre in Cambridge. He also credits years of serious psychoanalysis with helping him not only come to grips with his own identity but also find himself as a writer.

By the end of the 1950's, the course of his subsequent life was set. His has been a life in letters, divided between poetry and publishing. Davison directed the Atlantic Monthly Press until 1979, when he became its senior editor. He left that position in 1985 to become a consulting editor at Houghton Mifflin, where he remained until 1998.

It is, however, his personal and not his professional life that his most informed his verse, especially his responses to family connections and places of residence. He married for the first time in 1959; that union produced two children, Edward Angus and Lesley Truslow Davison. His first wife, Jane Auchincloss Truslow, was a writer. After her death in 1981, Davison married architect Joan Edelman Goody in 1984, and from then on he

Peter Davison (© Jill Krementz)

divided each year between his country home in West Gloucester, about a mile from the ocean, and his city home in Boston, Massachusetts.

ANALYSIS

From the time he took up the pen, Peter Davison has characterized the act of writing poetry as an exercise in self-discovery. This assertion is validated by his very first volume, *The Breaking of the Day and Other Poems*, which set the stage for all his later work by establishing the poet's two principal approaches to charting the parameters of self-identity: the individual's relationship to other people (parents, lovers, friends, and mentors) and the individual's relationship to nature. Yet, for Davison, who understands with often somber irony that what he seeks is esentially unknowable, poetry is both a means and an end.

THE BREAKING OF THE DAY AND OTHER POEMS

The centerpiece of Davison's first volume, *The Breaking of the Day and Other Poems*, is probably the poem titled "Not Forgotten," a five-part elegy for the poet's mother, who died of cancer in 1959. This poem, one of many that Davison wrote in response to his some-times ambivalent relationship to his parents, was the earliest of his poems to attract considerable critical attention. It chronicles the poet's experience of loss, from a state of mute numbness to a faltering acceptance of his mother's death because of his abiding sense of her "hovering/ In a hundred places."

Similarly, the title poem of the volume, the seven-part "The Breaking of the Day," focuses on the parent-child relationship. In this case, the poet assumes the role of Jacob, a biblical patriarch of the book of Genesis, wrestling with his own personal angel until the crack of dawn. The struggle described in the poem is symbolic of Davison's own coming to grips with the double displacement that he felt because of his upbringing: the betrayal he felt because of his mother's suppression of her own heritage (only at the age of thirteen did he learn that he was half Jewish) and the inhibition he felt about his own writing goals because of his father's failure to live up to his early promise as a poet. In the end, there is no sign from God, his father's incarnation in the poem; there is only the continuing quest for identity, a journey

that the poet pursues from book to book for the next forty years. Davison learns only that he must "Put God in words," must find his own poetic voice.

PRETENDING TO BE ASLEEP

Perhaps as an outgrowth of his own experience with psychoanalysis, Davison devoted his third volume, *Pretending to Be Asleep* (1970), to the complexities of the psyche and his hope, as he explored his poetic vocation, to find some balance between ego and id, between a conscious response to external experience and the mysterious prompting of imaginative insight. "How are we to see what must be seen," the poet asks in a poem titled "The Losing Struggle," "before shaping our language to the sound of it?"

Achieving this equilibrium between awareness and what Davison calls "unawareness" is difficult at best. At times, as in "Old Photograph," another poem about summoning up memories of his dead mother, Davison registers a failure of the imagination: "How can I keep in touch/ When there is nothing to touch?" Yet, in other pieces, such as the fourteenth and final section of the title poem, "Pretending to Be Asleep," Davison marvels at finding poems on his desk ready for him to revise. "When did this happen?" he asks, amazed by the unconscious activity of his brain. Yet, once the id has done its work, the ego takes over. "I know my job," he avows. "Possession they say is nine points in the poem."

WALKING THE BOUNDARIES

With his fourth volume, *Walking the Boundaries*, Davison's focus shifts away from the desire to explore the boundaries of self as delineated by the relationships that one has with others, from the formative connections to one's parents and mentors to the adult interactions with friends and lovers. Instead, perhaps prompted by his purchase of a twelve-acre farm in Gloucester, Massachusetts, in the late 1960's, Davison turns to nature as a metaphor of the self.

The most resonant example of this new mode might be the four-part series titled "Walking the Boundaries." The first section "West, by the Road" speaks of autumn, a season when "Roots hunch and contract, their blood runs thin." The section "South, by the Wall" celebrates spring, when we will "breed till our brains burst/ with the bluebell music of flickers and grackles"; and "East, by the Cliff" registers a time when the "sleeping marsh" endures a "season of waiting for light." It is clear by the fourth section, "The Woodcock," that the seasons of the year have provided metaphors for the seasons of life.

"Body at least is bound within a landscape," the poet asserts, "an earth that holds us fastened to the seasons." This condition creates "boundaries we cannot cross" except through the exercise of song. Like the woodcock that creates "music that clambers skyward through the dark," the poet can strive beyond the limits imposed by prevailing conditions through the exercise of his creative imagination.

A VOICE IN THE MOUNTAIN

The next volume, *A Voice in the Mountain*, continues Davison's poetic use of nature and its rhythms as keys to unlocking the mysteries of the human experience. The poem "Cross Cut," for example, reveals that even though its "gangrened upper branches" seemed to indicate that it was "dying from the top," the stump of a recently hewn pear tree shows signs of life at the core. Even though the "cross-cut" tree had lived to twice the poet's age, there is a lesson for Davison to learn about his own persistent fertility.

In "Haskell's Mill," Davison imaginatively re-creates a now-lost, late seventeenth century grist mill that once used the tidal currents to turn a giant wheel to grind corn, and he conjures up the figure of the original miller, who "held the balance between sea and land,/ the sun and moon, the water and the stone." Contrasted to the uneasy present, when "nothing is produced and little earned," the mill represents a "primal world" and a way of life characterized by a harmony of human effort and natural force.

BARN FEVER AND OTHER POEMS

Although he continued to write of his relationship to others, especially his parents, his wife, and other poets, Davison's most heralded pieces in *Barn Fever and Other Poems* are the poems that use natural fact to illuminate personal experience. The seven-part "Wordless Winter," for example, compares the emotional paralysis he is experiencing as he bears witness to the death of his first wife, Jane, to the phenomenon of a winter drought in New England. "Snow has forgotten itself," the poet writes, just as his own heart is seized by a frozen aridity.

Nature is a subject that requires close observation and specificity of description. It is a challenge that Da-

vison faces with aplomb. In the title poem, "Barn Fever," for example, the poet describes his own barn, whose lower half of "Cape Ann stone" is two hundred years old. Inheriting such a barn that others have allowed slowly to decay, the poet puzzles over ways to "heal" it even though it has ceased to have any practical purpose since his farm is no longer meant for farming. As an "emblem of the past," a remnant of lives led closer to the land than most people's, the barn in this poem is a companion structure to the old mill in "Haskell's Mill." Both poems resonate with the nostalgia inherent in the country verses of Davison's early poetic mentor, Robert Frost.

BREATHING ROOM

Peter Davison is always experimenting with form. Most of the poems in *Breathing Room: New Poems*, for instance, are formatted in eight stanzas, seven tercets or triplets of lines followed by a concluding quatrain. As he explains in the preface to the book, Davison used this structure to create what he tentatively calls "audiographs," poems meant to be read aloud, to conform to the patterns of breathing.

In subject matter, these poems echo the concerns of earlier volumes; they attempt to define the self through one's engagement with other people and the natural world. As with his earlier work, the poems of relationships are generally not as satisfactory as the poems in which he plays the role of naturalist. In this book, he writes in "A Ballad" of the "immortal mismarriage" of poets Sylvia Plath and Ted Hughes, and he revisits in "My Father's Hundredth Birthday" his poet-parent's impressive declamatory talents. These people-centered poems contain no revelations for the committed reader of Davison's work.

Despite his insistence in "Getting over Robert Frost" that the most important lesson that he learned from the older poet was the "trick of not trusting a line// unless it flickered with/ my own odor," Davison's best poems remain those that can be labeled essentially Frost-inspired. They sing of regret in a rural setting.

The poem "Seaside Summer Quarry" offers a case in point. "Rapt" in the sights and sounds around him, the poet laments the futility of trying to fix upon the page the "stolen abstractions" inspired by how a "water lily shivers and/ shrugs its shadow over/ a green platter of leaf" or how "gold strands of sunlight thread/ through the hemlocks."

OTHER MAJOR WORKS

NONFICTION: *Half Remembered: A Personal History*, 1973, revised 1991; *One of the Dangerous Trades: Essays on the Work and Workings of Poetry*, 1991; *The Fading Smile: Poets in Boston, from Robert Frost to Robert Lowell to Sylvia Plath, 1955-1960*, 1994.

EDITED TEXTS: *Hello, Darkness: The Collected Poems of L. E. Sissman*, 1978; *The World of Farley Mowat: A Selection from His Works*, 1980; *The Book Encompassed: Studies in Twentieth-Century Bibliography*, 1992; *Night Music*, 1999.

BIBLIOGRAPHY

Contemporary Literary Criticism 28 (1984): 99-104. A significant sampling of book reviews from the beginning of Davison's career as a poet up to the publication of *Barn Fever and Other Poems*.

Hewitt, Geof. "Peter Davison." In *Contemporary Poets*. New York: St. James Press, 1996. A summary of the poet's life and work with commentary by Davison and some critical analysis.

Ratner, Rochelle. Review of *Breathing Room: New Poems*, by Peter Davison. *Library Journal* 125 (August, 2000): 109. A brief review of the collection *Breathing Room*. Ratner traces Davison's argument that poetry should be composed in keeping with the capacities of the human breath to an earlier contention by American poet and essayist Charles Olson in 1950. The reviewer favors Davison's nature-inspired poems because they are more precise in detail and more demanding.

Rotella, Guy. *Three Contemporary Poets of New England: William Meredith, Philip Booth, and Peter Davison*. Boston: Twayne, 1983. This is the most comprehensive treatment of the first half of Davison's poetic career. The author attempts to grapple with the themes and techniques of the poet's first six books in an effort to define Davison's place in the New England literary tradition. In this regard, Rotella contends that at the heart of Davison's creative achievement is his nature poetry.

Young, Vernon. "Raptures of Distress." *Parnassus* 3 (1975): 75-89. A laudatory piece on Davison's relationship to other poets who write of the somber realities of life's mutability.

S. Thomas Mack

CECIL DAY LEWIS

Born: Ballintubbert, Ireland; April 27, 1904
Died: Hadley Wood, England; May 22, 1972

PRINCIPAL POETRY
Beechen Vigil and Other Poems, 1925
Country Comets, 1928
Transitional Poem, 1929
From Feathers to Iron, 1931
The Magnetic Mountain, 1933
Collected Poems, 1929-1933, 1935
A Time to Dance and Other Poems, 1935
Overtures to Death and Other Poems, 1938
Poems in Wartime, 1940
Selected Poems, 1940
Word over All, 1943
Short Is the Time: Poems, 1936-1943, 1945
Poems, 1943-1947, 1948
Collected Poems, 1929-1936, 1948
Selected Poems, 1951
An Italian Visit, 1953
Collected Poems, 1954
The Newborn: D.M.B., 29th April 1957, 1957
Pegasus and Other Poems, 1957
The Gate and Other Poems, 1962
Requiem for the Living, 1964
A Marriage Song for Albert and Barbara, 1965
The Room and Other Poems, 1965
Selections from His Poetry, 1967 (Patric Dickinson, editor)
Selected Poems, 1967
The Abbey That Refused to Die: A Poem, 1967
The Whispering Roots, 1970
The Poems, 1925-1972, 1977 (Ian Parsons, editor)

Cecil Day Lewis (© Hulton-Deutsch Collection/Corbis)

OTHER LITERARY FORMS

Cecil Day Lewis's fiction can easily be placed into three categories, the first being the novels published prior to World War II: *The Friendly Tree* (1936), *Starting Point* (1937), and *Child of Misfortune* (1939). Then, under the pseudonym of Nicholas Blake, he became a significant contributor to the popular genre of detective fiction. Finally, there are two pieces of juvenile fiction. Day Lewis's output was, however, not confined to fiction and poetry. He also produced a large body of literary criticism, editorial projects, and translations.

ACHIEVEMENTS

Cecil Day Lewis was the most conscientious poet laureate in England's history—even surpassing Alfred, Lord Tennyson in his conception of the laureate's responsibilities. During his tenure, from 1968 until his death in 1972, a period in which he suffered from illness, Day Lewis produced a lengthy list of poems on national and topical themes, a majority of which stand on their own poetic merits, as opposed to personal and shallow tributes to specific royal personages. Indeed, during his period as the nation's laureate, Day Lewis underscored his own importance as a contributor to English poetry, as one who understood and accepted the tradi-

tion of English poetry and significantly enlarged upon it.

Day Lewis's poetic achievement was marked by a flexible attitude toward the political and social temper of his times. He never withdrew to some private shelter to ponder future poetical-political courses of action or to brood over loss or misfortune. On the contrary, he viewed poetry as being exceedingly public and the poet as being the property of that public. Thus, he tried to share himself and his work with as many people as possible through books of and about poetry for children, through lectures and radio broadcasts about poetry, and through societies and festivals for advancing the general state of the poetic art. Particularly in the later stages of his career when he served as laureate, Day Lewis spent almost as much time writing and talking *about* poetry as he did creating poems. His appointment, in 1951, as professor of poetry at Oxford allowed him, still further, to perform a distinct service to his art.

Finally, Day Lewis's achievement may be observed in the nature of his own work as a representation of what may conveniently be termed the poetry of the mid-twentieth century. The poetry of Cecil Day Lewis indeed represents the conflict within the modern poet of that period, a conflict between the old and the new. In *A Hope for Poetry* (1934), he elaborated upon that conflict as a confrontation between the idea of the poet forging ahead to shape a new society and a new society shaping artists in its own image.

Such poems as "The Conflict," "The Double Vision," "Marriage of Two," "The Misfit," and "The Neurotic" capture effectively the degrees of uncertainty that Day Lewis sensed about people of his place and time. He understood well the old injustices that prompted, in turn, men and women to perform new injustices against one another. For him, poetry served society by asking questions about those conflicts, by probing moral problems for answers to some very difficult questions. In the act of poetic questioning, he sought not only a personal answer but also one that would best serve the social good.

BIOGRAPHY

Cecil Day Lewis was born in 1904 at Ballintubbert, Queen's County, in Ireland, where his father, the Reverend F. C. Day-Lewis, served as a curate. His mother, Kathleen Blake Squires, claimed distant relationship to Oliver Goldsmith, while the poet himself once reported a connection between his grandmother and the family of William Butler Yeats. The original name of the paternal family had been, simply, Day; the family later acquired the Lewis and then carried both names in hyphenated form. However, the poet discarded the hyphen for the purpose of practicing what he termed, in his autobiographical *The Buried Day* (1960), "inverted snobbery."

In 1907, when Day Lewis was only three years of age, the family severed its Irish connection and moved to England; by age six, the youngster had achieved some competence as a writer of verse. His pursuit of formal learning took him first to Sherborne School (Dorsetshire), then to Wadham College, Oxford, where he developed a particular interest in Latin poetry. He published *Beechen Vigil and Other Poems* while still an undergraduate, and spent the years between his departure from Oxford and the onset of World War II writing poetry and teaching English in a number of public schools in England and Scotland: Summer Fields, Oxford (1927-1928); Larchfield, Helensburgh, on the Firth of Clyde (1928-1930)—where he was succeeded by W. H. Auden; and Cheltenham College, Gloucestershire (1930-1935). With the publication of *Collected Poems, 1929-1933* and *A Question of Proof* (1935, the first detective story by Nicholas Blake), Day Lewis abandoned pedagogy for full-time authorship, although he would return to teaching and lecturing on a far more sophisticated level after World War II.

During the war, the poet worked for the Ministry of Information, after which he received a number of prestigious academic appointments: Clark Lecturer, Cambridge (1946); Warton Lecturer, British Academy, London (1951); Professor of Poetry, Oxford (1951-1956); Byron Lecturer, University of Nottingham (1952); Chancellor Dunning Lecturer, Queen's University, Kingston, Ontario (1954); Sidgwick Lecturer, University of Cambridge (1956); Norton Professor of Poetry, Harvard (1964-1965); and Compton Lecturer, University of Hull

(1968). Day Lewis also served as director of the publishing house of Chatto and Windus, London, from 1954 until his death, as well as a member of the Arts Council of Great Britain from 1962 to 1967. His most significant appointment and honor came in 1968, when he succeeded John Masefield (who died on May 12, 1967) as poet laureate of England. Although the list of candidates was never published, speculation as to his competition focused upon such names as Richard Church, Robert Graves, Edmund Blunden, and W. H. Auden. The last named had, by then, however, become an American citizen, while the first three poets were all more than seventy years of age. As matters turned out, Day Lewis's tenure as laureate lasted only four years.

The poet's first marriage was to Constance Mary King in 1928; upon their divorce in 1951, he married Jill Balcon. His last residence was at Crooms Hill, outside London and west of Greenwich Park. After his death on May 22, 1972, Day Lewis's body was transferred for burial at Stinsford, Dorsetshire (one mile east of Dorchester), where he lies today, close to the remains of Thomas Hardy, whom he greatly admired.

ANALYSIS

During his Oxford years and the period of his preparatory school teaching, Cecil Day Lewis published his first volumes of poetry: *Beechen Vigil and Other Poems*, followed by *Country Comets*. Both constitute a high level of juvenile verse, the products of a student who had studied much about poets and poetry but who had learned little about life and had experienced even less. The two books demonstrate, however, that, prior to the age of twenty-five, Day Lewis had essentially mastered the craft of poetry. Further, the two volumes established that for him, a book of verse would emerge as a unified, thematic whole rather than merely as a collection of miscellaneous pieces.

The poet's earliest conflicts arose out of his inability to distinguish clearly the old values of his present and past worlds from the newly emerging ones of the present and the future. In two poems, for example, "Juvenilia" and "Sketches for a Portrait," the young man of privileged and comfortably secure economic class confronts a fundamental social problem: whether to continue to accept without question or challenge the comfortable conventions of his class, or to look beyond both the class and the comforts in an attempt to understand and then to identify with the problems of people who exist totally outside his sphere of experience and values. Day Lewis inserts into the poetic environment high garden walls that protect the young man's neatly manicured lawn from the grime of the outside, but, certainly, the day must come when the dirt will filter through the wall and smudge the laurel. Then what?

TRANSITIONAL POEM

The answers to that question did not come quickly or easily. Instead, in three separate volumes, Day Lewis portrayed the complexity of human experience as it unfolded in several stages. The first, titled *Transitional Poem*, represents a form of self-analysis wherein the poet initially rejected the romantic nature worship of the preceding century as no solution to what he perceived as the mind's "own forked speculation." At twenty-five, Day Lewis had little or no sympathy for those among his contemporaries who appeared as "intellectual Quixotes," propagandizing abstract values and superficial critical criteria. As a poet he sought, instead, to harness the chaos of a disordered world and beget a new age built upon the "crest of things," upon the commonplace "household stuff, stone walls, mountains and trees/ [that] Placard the day with certainties." Further, the word of the artist, of the twentieth century poet, cannot be allowed, like the Word of God, to stand remote and free from actuality. Instead, poetry must return to life: "Wrenching a stony song from a scant acre/ The Word still justifies its Maker."

FROM FEATHERS TO IRON

Two years later, in 1931, Day Lewis continued his spiritual self-analysis in *From Feathers to Iron*. The title of the piece came from an observation by John Keats: "We take but three steps from feathers to iron," in reference to the maturation process from a theoretical perception of life to an actual understanding of human existence. In this series of lyric poems, Day Lewis considered the theme of experience within the context of marriage and parenthood. Love, he maintained, cannot endure without the presence of children; two years seems the limit for the love of husband and wife to be "marooned on self-sufficiency," and thus new dimen-

sions must be added to the union. The poems in the volume concern fertility, the passion and the pain involved with the anguish of birth, and the hope that fatherhood may end what the poet terms the "indeterminate quarrel between a fevered head and a cold heart." The narrator of the volume occupies the long period of expectation with poems to both mother and child, while the final days seem to him "numb with crisis, cramped with waiting"; after man and wife have, together, explored the extremes of pain and fear, deliverance finally arrives and the multifaceted experience draws to a close. Day Lewis may well have been the first to attempt, in verse, a serious analysis of marriage as it relates to birth and parenthood, placing it squarely within the context of the modern world, in the midst of its complexities and technological by-products.

THE MAGNETIC MOUNTAIN

Careful readers may sense, in the final of the three works—*The Magnetic Mountain*—the influences of Gerard Manley Hopkins and W. H. Auden. Day Lewis divided the piece into four major sections, the beginning being especially reminiscent of Hopkins's "The Windhover." The poet invokes a "kestrel joy, O hoverer in wind," as he searches "beyond the railheads of reason" for a "magnetic mountain," for truth. He proposes to follow his friends—Auden and Rex Warner—along the political path toward truth, where, in the second section, he surveys some politically reactionary types: a clinging mother, a conventional schoolmaster, a priest, and a "domestic" man. Then, in the third section, Day Lewis exposes what he believes to be the real enemies of progress: the flattering spell of love, popular education and information, the "religion" of science, and false romantic ideals. The poem ends with a series of lyrics extolling a social effort governed by the duality of twentieth century man—as soarer ("windhover") and as an earthbound creature. Criticism of *The Magnetic Mountain* focuses upon the issue of influence; some critics maintain that it contains too much of Auden's political and social thought, not enough of Hopkins's language and rhythm, and even less of Day Lewis's own voice.

POLITICAL PHILOSOPHY

Although the emphasis in *Transitional Poem*, *From Feathers to Iron*, and *The Magnetic Mountain* may appear social and spiritual, the political implications of the three volumes should not be ignored. Scholars generally have been attentive to the political philosophy of the early, prewar poetry of Day Lewis, particularly in the light of the poet's interest, in company with a number of his intellectual and artistic contemporaries, in communism as the principal healing agent for an economically and politically sick world. Day Lewis's excursions along the highways of Marxist philosophy, however, do not provide an adequate background needed to evaluate his work of the 1930's. Certainly a knowledge of his communist sympathies helps to clarify certain attitudes and methods, particularly his bullying tone or even outright contempt toward middle-class men and women in pursuit of little else beyond their contented, individualistic careers. Nevertheless, standing steadily behind the signposts of political ideology can be seen the beauty and the momentum created by the language of poetry–*not* by the language of politics. Poetically, the pieces depend very little on their topical content, especially now, fifty years or so after the specific events have faded into the clouds of history. To his credit, Day Lewis remained a poet and held fast to the principles of his art—as did Auden and Stephen Spender, and as did George Orwell in his fiction. Although Day Lewis tried his hand at political pamphleteering, especially when his passions gained the upper hand, he could not function for very long in that capacity.

THE 1930'S

Once Day Lewis had turned away from politics, his poetry reaped considerable artistic profit from force and economy. During the 1930's, the young poet struggled to find some use for the dominant images of the modern world, especially for modern industry and transportation. Similarly, he appeared uncomfortable, sometimes overly aggressive, in his attempts to find a place for the serenities of nature amidst the noise and the movement generated by his political themes. After 1939, however, even with the coming of world conflict, Day Lewis seemed eager to turn toward nature, to write as a true child of the provinces, as one who delighted in plowed fields, elevated tracts of land, and cloud formations, in air and in landscape; as one who sought to inject a positive spirit into his poetry after so many years of despair, disillusionment, and political frustration. "For me there is no dismay," he announced in *Word over All*, seem-

ingly struck "Dumb as a rooted rock" by the tragedy of world events. Nevertheless, despite his unveiled Georgian mood, he could still communicate with a nation at war, declaring, in "The Assertion," that "Now is the time we assert/ To their face that men are love. . . ." Again, in "Lidice," he recognized the complexity and the composition of humanity, the good and the evil that existed everywhere and at all times, and he understood that "The pangs we felt from . . . atrocious hurt/ Promise a time when the killer shall see/ His sword is aimed at his own naked heart."

In *From Feathers to Iron* and *The Magnetic Mountain*, despite certain inclinations toward themes of social unrest, political upheaval, and general radicalism, Day Lewis rarely lost sight of the form and function of lyric poetry, of the beauty and the rhythm of poetic language. Both during and after the war, he intensified his mastery of and reliance upon the love song, especially those tender poems in which he attempted to trace the effect of love on the personality, as in "The Lighted House" and "The Album." With his change in thematic emphasis came, of course, certain regrets, particularly over having lost the wildness, the excitement, the rapture of youth. Thus, in "The Rebuke," the love song serves well as a means of asking some penetrating questions about "the sparks at random," the "spendthrift fire, the holy fire"; all that has passed without having left its proper, natural effect, and it is now too late to do anything about it. Day Lewis's lyric poetry is firmly in the tradition of Richard Lovelace, Andrew Marvell, and Alfred, Lord Tennyson; during his later years, he never really strayed far from those models.

AN ITALIAN VISIT

The most ambitious and impressive volume of Day Lewis's poetry appeared in 1953 under the title *An Italian Visit*. The book consists of a long work divided into seven parts: "Dialogue at the Airport," "Flight to Italy," "A Letter from Rome," "Bus to Florence," "Florence: Works of Art," "Elegy Before Death: At Settignano," and "The Homeward Prospect." In this work Day Lewis has changed his poetic mood from an austere evangelizing spirit to an acceptance of a lighter, more genial mode of existence. He describes those who flowered in the 1930's as "an odd lot," "sceptical yet susceptible,/ Dour though enthusiastic." The poem is an intellectual travel book, a voyage of discovery not only of scenes and cities but also of the latent faculties of the traveler's mind and heart. Day Lewis's traveler, however, is a composite of three people who, in turn, reflect three aspects of the poet's own personality: Tom's concern is for the present, and Dick looks to the past; Harry, on the other hand, focuses upon neither, but searches the future for the truth. Tom takes his pleasure in the immediate moment as he seeks to gratify the senses through "The real, royal, vulgar pageant—/ Time flying like confetti or twirled in rosettes." Dick, the scholar, thinker, artist, and lover of the perfect, evaluates the present through the supreme achievements of the past ("Reaching across generations to find the parent stock"), while Harry—a sociologist, rationalist, brooder upon the human condition, and seeker of reality under appearances—sees the world as a "provocative, charming/ Striptease universe."

At the conclusion of the holiday, each traveler returns to England after having experienced a different Italy: Tom returns "enriched," Dick "sobered," and Harry "lightened." Two sections of the poem, "Florence: Works of Art" and "Elegy Before Death: At Settignano," stand apart from the five. In the former, Day Lewis seems to have had a grand time practicing parodies of the styles of Thomas Hardy, William Butler Yeats, Robert Frost, W. H. Auden, and Dylan Thomas—all poets whom he enthusiastically endorsed and admired. The "Settignano" section is a stark contrast, a profoundly moving meditation on the subjects of love, time, and mortality. The ark of love embarks through a "pinprick of doubt into the dark," wherein "a whole life is drained off," while in "Rhadamanthine" moments lovers find "a chance to make our flux/ Stand and deliver its holy spark." Merely a quick glance at the first and second generation Romantic poets of the nineteenth century reveals how well Day Lewis has extended the conventions of meditative verse and has done so without any perverse effort at originality for its own sake. For him, the traditions still hold.

Perhaps the most appealing human quality of Day Lewis's poetry is his natural hesitancy and inconsistency. Throughout his literary career, marked by political, social, and philosophical sampling and experimentation, he never once embraced the banner of unwavering certainty—the standard of false intellectual pride. He was, indeed, a poet of several points of view who spoke—as in *An Italian Visit*—in and through several voices, a modest thinker and artist who needed to work within a poetic tradition.

LATER POETRY

In the postwar poems and beyond, Day Lewis seemed to find his tradition. He came to understand what may be termed his "Englishness," his need for skeptical inquiry into himself and his world. That tradition bred and nurtured such authors as Robert Burns, William Barnes, and Thomas Hardy. Day Lewis had learned, from Hopkins and especially from Hardy, that the poet did not have to obligate himself to the smart and the fashionable; he had learned that the poet's responsibility rested upon the freedom to create his own personal atmosphere of seriousness and charm. After he cast off the restrictive mantle of fashionable radicalism, after he endured the tragedy of world war, Day Lewis found his freedom, his tradition, and his own poetic voice.

OTHER MAJOR WORKS

LONG FICTION: *A Question of Proof*, 1935; *The Friendly Tree*, 1936; *Starting Point*, 1937; *Child of Misfortune*, 1939; *Malice in Wonderland*, 1940; *The Case of the Abominable Snowman*, 1941; *Minute for Murder*, 1947; *A Tangled Web*, 1956; *The Deadly Joker*, 1963; *The Private Wound*, 1968.

PLAY: *Noah and the Waters*, pb. 1936.

NONFICTION: *A Hope for Poetry*, 1934; *Revolution in Writing*, 1935; *The Poetic Image*, 1947; *The Colloquial Element in English Poetry*, 1947; *The Poet's Task*, 1951; *The Poet's Way of Knowledge*, 1957; *The Buried Day*, 1960; *The Lyric Impulse*, 1965; *A Need for Poetry?*, 1968.

TRANSLATIONS: *The Georgics of Virgil*, 1940; *The Graveyard by the Sea*, 1946 (of Paul Valéry); *The Aeneid of Virgil*, 1952; *The Eclogues of Virgil*, 1963.

BIBLIOGRAPHY

Daiches, David. *Poetry and the Modern World: A Study of Poetry in England Between 1900 and 1939*. Chicago: University of Chicago Press, 1940. Daiches devotes a full chapter to Day Lewis and the problems facing the poet: how to face the disintegrating civilization after World War I? What audience would a poet write for? Instead of turning to mysticism or religion as did William Butler Yeats and T. S. Eliot, Day Lewis seeks a singleness of personality in revolutionary hope and mature self-understanding. A major study of this important poet.

Day-Lewis, Sean. *Day-Lewis: An English Literary Life.* London: Weidenfeld & Nicolson, 1980. The first son of Cecil Day Lewis wrote this year-by-year biography of his father within a decade of his death. Family members and friends contributed material to an objective but intimate portrait of the poet. Both the poetry publications and the crime novels (Day Lewis used the pen name Nicholas Blake) are discussed. Two poems by W. H. Auden, a discography and American titles, twenty photographs, and an index complete this valuable book.

Gelpi, Albert. *Living in Time: The Poetry of C. Day Lewis.* New York: Oxford University Press, 1998. A full-length critical study of the works of C. Day Lewis, and a record of his poetry within the literary ferment of the twentieth century. Explores the three major periods of the poet's development, beginning with the emergence of Day Lewis in the 1930's as the most radical of the Oxford poets.

Riddel, Joseph N. *C. Day Lewis.* New York: Twayne, 1971. Riddel argues that Day Lewis should be known as more than a member of the "Auden group" of British poets of the 1930's. His poetry is considered chronologically with emphasis on the creative and radical period from 1929 to 1938. The problems of language, individual psychology, the "divided self," and the lyric impulse are enduring themes. An essential study supplemented by notes and a bibliography.

Smith, Elton Edward. *The Angry Young Men of the Thirties.* Carbondale: Southern Illinois University Press, 1975. In his first chapter, "C. Day-Lewis: the Iron Lyricist," Smith outlines the dilemma of British poets in the 1930's: a decade of worldwide economic collapse. He traces Day Lewis's attitudes on religion and public events through his more than five volumes of poetry, giving clear explications of many individual poems from the earliest period to the final poems.

Tolley, A. T. *The Poetry of the Thirties.* London: Gollancz, 1975. In chapter 6, "Poetry and Politics," Tolley discusses the political content of Day Lewis's poetry, his adherence to Marxism as a solution to the pressing contemporary problems, and the subsequent development away from the Party in "Overtures to Death." His concern for the Spanish Civil War conflict is apparent; the mood is somber and disaster seems imminent. Along with political events, the problem of a divided self continues to occupy the poet's thoughts.

Samuel J. Rogal;
bibliography updated by the editors

THOMAS DEKKER

Born: London, England; c. 1572
Died: London, England; August, 1632

PRINCIPAL POETRY

The Whole History of Fortunatus, 1599 (commonly known as *Old Fortunatus*, play and poetry)

The Shoemaker's Holiday: Or, The Gentle Craft, 1600 (based on Thomas Deloney's narrative *The Gentle Craft*, play and poetry)

The Wonderful Year, 1603 (prose and poetry)

The Honest Whore, Part I, 1604 (with Thomas Middleton, play and poetry)

The Honest Whore, Part II, c. 1605 (play and poetry)

The Double PP, 1606 (prose and poetry)

Lanthorn and Candlelight, 1608, 1609 (prose and poetry; revised as *O per se O*, 1612; *Villanies Discovered*, 1616, 1620; *English Villanies*, 1632, 1638, 1648)

Dekker, His Dream, 1620 (prose and poetry)

The Virgin Martyr, c. 1620 (with Philip Massinger, play and poetry)

The Witch of Edmonton, 1621 (with William Rowley and John Ford, play and poetry)

The Sun's Darling, 1624 (with John Ford, play and poetry)

OTHER LITERARY FORMS

Thomas Dekker was a prolific author. Although his canon is not easily fixed because of works presumed to be lost, disputed authorship, and revised editions, the sheer number of his publications is impressive. Dekker was primarily a dramatist. By himself he composed more than twenty plays, and he collaborated on as many as forty; more than half of these are not extant today. His plays come in all the genres that theater-hungry Elizabethans loved to devour: city comedies, history plays, classical romances, and domestic tragedies. Additionally, Dekker published about twenty-five prose tracts and pamphlets which catered to a variety of popular tastes: descriptions of London's lowlife, collections of humorous and scandalous stories, and jeremiads on the nation's sins and its impending punishment at the hands of an angry God. Dekker found time between writing for the theater and the printing press to compose complimentary verses on other poets' works and to twice prepare interludes, sketches, and songs for the pageants honoring the Lord Mayor of London.

The best edition of the plays, *The Dramatic Works of Thomas Dekker* (1953-1961), is edited by Fredson Bowers in four volumes. Those tracts dealing with the calamities befalling Stuart London are represented in *The Plague Pamphlets of Thomas Dekker* (1925; F. P. Wilson, editor). The bulk of Dekker's prose and verse is collected in the occasionally unreliable *The Non-Dramatic Works of Thomas Dekker* (1884-1886, 4 volumes; Alexander B. Grosart, editor). A more readable and more judicious sampling of the tales and sketches is found in *Thomas Dekker: Selected Prose Writings* (1968; E. D. Pendry, editor).

ACHIEVEMENTS

A writer such as Thomas Dekker, so prolific in output, necessarily produces a lot of chaff with his wheat. His plays often lack tightly knit plots and carefully proportioned form; his prose works, especially those satirizing the moral lapses of contemporaries, sometimes belabor the point. Two literary virtues, however, continue to endear Dekker to readers, virtues common to both plays and pamphlets, to both verse and prose.

First, Dekker is always a wordsmith of the highest rank. Although Ben Jonson complained of Dekker and his collaborators that "It's the bane and torment of our ears/ To hear the discords of those jangled rhymers," hardly any reader or critic since has shared the opinion. Since the seventeenth century, Dekker has been universally acknowledged as a gifted poet whose lyrical ability stands out in an age well-stocked with good lyric poets. Charles Lamb's famous pronouncement that Dekker had "poetry for everything" sums up the commonplace modern attitude. Not only Dekker's verse in the plays, however, but also his prose deserves to be called poetic. Dekker's language, whatever its form, is characterized by frequent sound effects, varied diction, and attention to rhythm. Thoroughly at home with Renaissance habits of decorative rhetoric, Dekker seemingly thought in poetry and thus wrote it naturally, effortlessly, and continually.

Second, Dekker's heart is always in the right place. His sympathetically drawn characters seem to come alive as he portrays the people, sights, and events of Elizabethan London. Dekker is often compared with Geoffrey Chaucer and William Shakespeare for his sense of the *comédie humaine*, for knowing the heights and depths of human experience and for still finding something to care about afterward. Dekker's keen observations of life underlie his sharp sense of society's incongruities.

BIOGRAPHY

Few specifics of Thomas Dekker's life are known. He was probably born in 1572, although this date is conjectural. He may have served as a tradesman's apprentice or a sailor before beginning (in 1595?) to write plays for companies of actors. By playwriting and pamphleteering he kept himself alive for the next thirty-seven years. The date of his marriage is uncertain, but it is known that his wife Mary died in 1616. Dekker lived his life almost completely in London, first in Cripplegate and later in Clerkenwell. He was imprisoned for debt on three occasions and once for recusancy. Presumably the Thomas Dekker who was buried in August, 1632, in Clerkenwell parish was Thomas Dekker, playwright and pamphleteer.

Although Dekker's personal life is mostly subject to conjecture, his professional career can be more closely followed. It revolves around three intertwining themes: the dramatic collaborations, the pamphlets, and a life-long struggle against poverty. No one knows how Dekker's career started, but by 1598, he was writing plays alone or jointly for Philip Henslowe. Henslowe owned and managed the Rose Theatre, where he commissioned writers to compose plays for his prime tenants, an acting company called the Lord Admiral's Men. In 1598 alone, Dekker had a hand in fifteen plays (all now lost) which Henslowe commissioned. The sheer quantity indicates how audiences must have clamored for new productions, and some of the titles indicate the taste of the age for popularizations of history (*The First Civil Wars in France*), reworkings of classical tales (*Hannibal and Hermes*), and current stories of eccentric persons or scandalous events (*Black Batman of the North*). All of the plays on which Dekker worked had catchy titles: *The Roaring Girl: Or, Moll Cutpurse* (pr. c. 1610), *The Honest Whore*, *The Witch of Edmonton*, and *Match Me in London* (pr. c. 1611-1612), to name a few.

As early as 1600, Dekker was writing for companies other than the Lord Admiral's Men. In the course of his career he would write for the leading acting companies of the time: the Children of St. Paul's, the Prince's Men, the Palsgrave's Men, and the Players of the Revels. More varied than his employers were his collaborators: As a young man Dekker worked with Michael Drayton, Ben Jonson, George Chapman, Henry Chettle, and even William Shakespeare. When he returned to the theater as an older man, the new young scriptwriters—a veritable "Who's Who" of Jacobean dramatists, including John Ford, Samuel Rowley, John Marston, Philip Massinger, and John Webster—worked with him.

Since his employers and collaborators changed so often, it is not surprising that at least once the intense dramatic rivalry characteristic of the age embroiled Dekker in controversy. In 1600, he was drafted into the brief but vitriolic "War of the Theatres," which had begun in the previous year when Marston satirized Jonson as a boorish and presumptuous poet. Jonson returned the compliment by poking fun at Marston in two plays and tried to anticipate a Marston-Dekker rejoinder with a third play, *Poetaster* (1601), which compares them to "screaming grasshoppers held by the wings." Marston and Dekker retaliated with *Satiromastix: Or, The Un-trussing of the Humourous Poet* (pr. 1601), an amalgam of tragic, comic, and tragicomic plots, portraying Jonson as a slow-witted and slow-working poet for hire.

In 1603, Dekker was forced to find another line of work when an outbreak of the plague closed the theaters. He produced a pamphlet, *The Wonderful Year*, which recounted the death of the queen, Elizabeth I, the accession of James I, and the coming of the disease that scourged humankind's folly. In the next six years, Dekker published more than a dozen pamphlets designed to capitalize on readers' interest in current events and the city's criminal subculture. In his pamphlets, as in his plays, Dekker provides a panorama of cutpurses, pimps, courtesans, apprentices, and similar types; he paints scenes of busy streets and records the sounds of loud voices, creaking carriages, and thumped pots. Dekker's purpose is not that of the local colorist who preserves such scenes simply because they typify a time and place. Rather, his interest is that of the moralist who sees the side of city life that the upper classes would like to ignore and that the academics shrug off as part of the necessary order of things.

Dekker himself knew this low world intimately—at least he never seems to have gotten into the higher. Unlike his fellow writers Jonson and Shakespeare or the actor Edward Alleyn, Dekker could not or did not take advantage of the aristocracy's interest in the theater to secure for himself consistent patronage and financial stability. Playwriting seems to have brought Dekker only a few pounds per play: Despite his prodigious outburst of fifteen collaborations in 1598, he was arrested for debt that year and the next. Fourteen years later, while both publishing pamphlets and writing plays, Dekker was again imprisoned for debt at the King's Bench, a prison notorious for its mismanagement. He remained in debtors' prison for six or seven years (1613-1619).

No wonder, then, that money is one of Dekker's favorite themes and gold one image to which he devotes loving attention. He neither worships the almighty guinea nor scorns sinful lucre. On the one hand, Dekker likes money: His best characters make shrewd but kindly use of the stuff; they work, and their labor supports them. He sometimes sees even confidence games as offshoots of a healthy capitalistic impulse. Old Fortunatus's claim, "Gold is the strength, the sinnewes of the world,/ The Health, the soule, the beautie most divine," may be misguided, but Dekker understands the impulse. He forgives prodigals easily. On the other hand, Dekker expects generosity from moneymakers. Even virtuous persons who do not use their wealth well come to bad ends; those who refuse to help the needy he assigns to the coldest regions of hell. According to E. D. Pendry in *Thomas Dekker: Selected Prose Writings*, the use of money is for Dekker an index of morality: Virtue flows from its proper use and vice from its improper.

The last decade of Dekker's life was a repetition of the previous three. He wrote for the theater, published pamphlets, and teetered on the edge of debt. Though his life was hard and his social rank was low, Dekker generally wrote as if his literary trade was, like the shoemaker's, a truly gentle craft.

ANALYSIS

Most of Thomas Dekker's best poetry is found in his plays; unfortunately, since most of his plays were collaborations, it is often difficult to assign particular poetic passages to Dekker, and perhaps even harder to assign the larger poetic designs to him. He is, however, generally credited with most of the poetry in *Old Fortunatus* and *The Honest Whore, Parts I* and *II*. He wrote the delightfully poetic *The Shoemaker's Holiday* almost unaided. Mother Sawyer's eloquent poetry in *The Witch of Edmonton* so closely resembles portions of his long pamphlet-poem, *Dekker, His Dream*, as to make it all but certainly his. Songs and verses occupy varying proportions of his journalistic works, from a few lines in *The Wonderful Year*, to several songs in *Lanthorn and Candlelight*, to most of *The Double PP*. In all his plays, verse comprises a significant part of the dialogue.

While the quality of thought and care in organization vary from work to work and almost from line to line in a given work, the quality of the sound rarely falters. According to George Price in *Thomas Dekker* (1969), one poem long attributed to Dekker, *Canaan's Calamitie* (1598), has been excluded from the canon largely because of the inferior music of its verse. Critics often attach words such as "sweet," "lovely," "gentle," and "compassionate" to Dekker's most popular passages, and the adjectives seem to cover both sound and theme

in works such as *Old Fortunatus* and *The Shoemaker's Holiday*.

OLD FORTUNATUS

An old-fashioned production in its own day, *Old Fortunatus* weaves a morality pageant in which the goddess Fortune and her attendants witness a power struggle between Virtue and Vice with a loose chronicle play about a man to whom Fortune grants a choice. Instead of health, strength, knowledge, and wisdom, old Fortunatus chooses riches. His wealth and native cunning enable him to steal knowledge (in the form of a magic hat). After Fortune claims the old man's life, his sons Ampedo and Andelocia, inheriting his magic purse and hat, make no better use of them than their father had done. Greedy Andelocia abducts a princess, plays assorted pranks at various courts, and ends up strangled by equally greedy courtiers; virtuous Ampedo wrings his hands, eventually burns the magic hat, and dies in the stocks, unmourned even by Virtue. Structurally, *Old Fortunatus* has the odd elegance of medieval drama. Fortune, Virtue, and Vice enter the human world five times, usually with song and emblematic show designed to judge men or to point out the choices open to them.

The play's allegorical pageantry demanded elaborate costuming and equally elaborate verse, ranging from songs in varied meters and tones to dialogues that are often more incantation than blank verse speech:

> *Kings:* Accursed Queen of chaunces, damned sorceresse.
> *The Rest:* Most pow'rfull Queen of chaunce, dread
>   soveraignesse.
> *Fortune:* . . . [*To the Kings*] curse on: your cries to me
>   are Musicke
> And fill the sacred rondure of mine eares
> With tunes more sweet than moving of the Spheres:
> Curse on.

Most of the chronicle play which is interwoven with the morality pageant employs blank verse liberally sprinkled with prose passages and rhymed couplets. Renaissance notions of decorum set forth rather clear-cut rules governing the use of prose and poetry. An iambic pentameter line was considered the best medium for tragedy and for kings' and nobles' speeches in comedy. Madmen, clowns, and letter-readers in tragedy and lowerclass characters in comedy can speak prose. Dekker refines these guidelines. He uses prose for musing aloud, for French and Irish dialects, for talking to servants, and for expressing disappointment or depression: The sons mourn their dead father and have their most violent quarrel in prose. Dekker keys form to mood much as a modern songwriter does when he inserts a spoken passage into the lyrics. Even Dekker's prose, however, is textured like poetry; except for the lack of iambic pentameter rhythm, prose passages are virtually indistinguishable from verse. Typical are the lilting rhythms of the following passage (one of the cruelest in the play): "I was about to cast my little little self into a great love trance for him, fearing his hart was flint, but since I see 'tis pure virgin wax, he shall melt his belly full."

Sound itself is the subject of much comment in the play. Dekker's natural gift for pleasing rhythms, his knack for combining the gentler consonant sounds with higher frequency vowels, and his ear for slightly varied repetitions all combine to make *Old Fortunatus* strikingly beautiful poetry.

The fame of *Old Fortunatus*, however, rests on more than its sound. Dekker's imagery deserves the praise it consistently gets. The Princess's heartless line is one of many that connect melting with the play's values—love, fire, gold, and the sun—in ways that suggest both the purification of dross through the melting process and the fate of rich Crassus. Other images connect the silver moon and stars with music, and both precious metals with an earth producing fruit-laden trees that men use wisely or unwisely. The allegorical figures with their emblematic actions and costumes would heighten the effectiveness of such imagery for a viewing audience, just as hearing the poetry greatly magnifies its impact over silent reading.

THE SHOEMAKER'S HOLIDAY

In *The Shoemaker's Holiday*, Dekker shows a more sophisticated use of poetry. As in *Old Fortunatus*, he shifts between poetry and prose, depending somewhat on the characters' social class but more on mood, so that in a given scene a character can slip from prose to poetry and back while those around him remain in their normal métier. In the earlier play, however, he made little attempt to connect certain characters with certain sounds or images. In *The Shoemaker's Holiday*, characters have their own peculiar music.

The play combines three plots. In the first, Rowland Lacy disguises himself as Hans, a Dutch shoemaker, in order to avoid being shipped off to war in France, far from his beloved Rose Otley. His uncle, the Earl of Lincoln, and her father, Sir Roger Otley, oppose the love match. In the second, the shoemaker Rafe leaves his young wife Jane to do his country's bidding; later, lamed and supposed dead, he returns to find Jane missing. He rediscovers her just in time to stop her marriage to the rich but shallow Hammon. In the third, master shoemaker Simon Eyre, the employer of Lacy, Rafe, and a crew of journeymen and apprentices, rises by common sense and enthusiastic shop management to become London's merriest Lord Mayor.

Two relatively minor characters illustrate Dekker's poetic sense. The Earl of Lincoln, despite his blank verse, speaks less poetically than most of the other characters, and Eyre's journeyman, Firke, despite his freer prose rhythms, speaks much of the best poetry. Lincoln's decasyllables in the opening scene, for example, summarize Lacy's situation with few rhetorical figures:

> 'Twas now almost a year since he requested
> To travel countries for experiences.
> I furnished him with coin, bills of exchange,
> Letters of credit, men to wait on him.

Lincoln's speech is not absolutely unpoetic. Its rhythm is varied, quickened by added syllables and made natural by inverted feet—but that is all. Lincoln has a prosaic mind; to him Lacy's love is mere nuisance, a mild threat to the family name. Dishonest about his own motives, he presumes that others are likewise motivated by self-interest. Thus, when he speaks, his words slip easily off the tongue, but rarely figure forth the imaginative connections between things that Dekker's other characters display.

By contrast, Firke's lines have more of poetry's verbal texture than does most modern free verse. Asked the whereabouts of the eloped Rose and Lacy, he answers in a pastiche of poetic allusions and a pun on the gold coin that Elizabethans called angels: "No point: shall I betray my brother? no, shall I prove *Judas* to Hans? no, shall I crie treason to my corporation? no, I shall be firkt and yerkt then, but give me your angell, your angell shall tel you." The passage shouts an emphatic dance rhythm, forcefully repeats the focal "no, shall I," employs assonance ("*Judas* to *Hans*"), alliteration ("betray my brother"), and rhyme ("treason to my corporation" and "firkt and yerkt"). It speeds along, then slows to a perfectly cadenced close. The speaker, a boisterous, rowdy, practical joker, is always ready to burst into song, or something so close as to be indistinguishable from song.

Dekker gives these minor characters distinctive poetic voices. To the major characters he gives individualizing linguistic habits. Bluff Simon Eyre's trick of repeating himself would be maddening in a less kindly fellow. He is the only character capable of speaking prose to the king. Hammon, suitor both to Rose and Jane, speaks courtly compliment in light, rhymed couplets in which vows about "life" and "wife" play too heavy a part. Though he enjoys the banter of stichomythic verse, his images are stuffily conventional. As wellborn characters, Lacy and Rose naturally speak blank verse. Lacy's voice, however, turns to a quick prose dialect when he is disguised as Hans; Rose occasionally startles by slipping out of her romantic preoccupations into a few lines of practical yet polished prose.

Perhaps the play's best poetry is that which Dekker gives to shoemaker Rafe and seamstress Jane. Surrounded by shopkeepers and unaccustomed to courtly compliment, these two must invent their own poetic images and rhythms. "I will not greeve you,/ With hopes to taste fruite, which will never fall," says Jane to Hammon. Hearing of Rafe's death, she dismisses her persistent suitor with lines remarkable for homespun grace. Rafe, in turn, gives the entire play its thematic unity in two passages which raise shoemaking from a craft to a communal act of love. As he leaves for France, Rafe gives Jane a parting gift: not the jewels and rings that rich men present their wives, but a pair of shoes "cut out by *Hodge*, Sticht by my fellow *Firke*, seam'd by my selfe,/ Made up and pinckt, with letters for thy name." The shoes are the epitome of the shoemaker's art, and they are individually Jane's. Dekker returns to the image at a pivotal point after Rafe comes home from the war. The shoes, now old and needing replacement, lead Rafe to reunion with the missing Jane. His homely poetry, the most original in a play full of original language, is more touching than preposterous:

> . . . this shoe I durst be sworne
> Once covered the instep of my *Jane:*
> This is her size, her breadth, thus trod my love,
> These true love knots I prickt, I hold my life,
> By this old shoe I shall find out my wife.

The simple language fits Rafe as well as the shoe fits Jane. In *The Shoemaker's Holiday*, craftsmen know their work as confidently as the master wordsmith Dekker knows his characters' individual voices.

Critics generally agree that the play is Dekker's poetic masterpiece. His other plays contain excellent poetry, nicely tuned to suit persona in sound, mood, and imagery, but none has the range and grace of *The Shoemaker's Holiday*. Of special interest to the student of Dekker's verse are two of the speeches in *The Honest Whore* plays. In *Part I*, Hippolito's furious diatribe against whoredom is a virtual monologue, rising in a hundred lines to a fine crescendo, which deserves careful metrical and figural analysis. Its counterpart in *Part II*, Bellafront's long argument against her former profession, deserves similar attention.

PAMPHLETS

Dekker's pamphlets continue the habit of mixing prose and verse; most of them contain some poetry, if only in the rhymed couplets signifying closure. As early as 1603, in *The Wonderful Year*, he was writing essentially dramatic poetry. In that pamphlet, he includes two poems supposed to be the prologue and a summary of the action of a play—the "play" of England's reaction to Elizabeth I's death. The poetic section ends with three short epigrams of a deliberately homespun sort. *Lanthorn and Candlelight* further reflects the dramatic in Dekker's poetry. In the opening chapter, poems are couched in cant, a special thieves' jargon. "To cant" means "to sing" but since "canters" are strange, they sing strangely: "Enough! With boozy cove maund nase,/ Tower the patring cove in the darkman case." Dekker includes both a "Canter's Dictionary" (largely plagiarized) and "Englished" translations. His habit of using dramatic voices in poetry finds a logical conclusion in such songs.

Poetry is sporadic in most of Dekker's pamphlets; in *The Double PP* and *Dekker, His Dream*, however, it dominates. The former alternates sections of prose and poetry in an exhibition of English nationalism as complete as Simon Eyre's. In an elaborate rhetorical figure, Dekker presents ten kinds of papists as ten chivalric shields attacked by ten well-armed classes of English Protestants. The generally shallow but occasionally penetrating stereotypes show the influence of the current fad for Overburian Characters.

DEKKER, HIS DREAM

Dekker, His Dream is a much better poem. Published shortly after his release from seven years in debtor's prison, the work is ostensibly autobiographical. Dekker claims to relate a dream he had after almost seven years of imprisonment in an enchanted cave. Using lines of rhymed iambic pentameter that vary with his subject in tone and tempo, Dekker describes the last day of the world, the final judgment, heaven and hell. Periodically he interrupts the narrative to justify his vision by quoting in prose from scripture or church authorities.

Structurally, *Dekker, His Dream* is among his best works, building slowly to a climactic conclusion in which Dekker turns out to be, as William Blake said of John Milton, "of the devil's party." The poem begins with covert reminders of what Dekker himself has recently suffered, then moves vividly through the tale of Earth's destruction. Calmly, it relates the majestic coming of Christ and the harmonious rewards given the good, then turns rather quickly to hell. (In fact, Christ and Heaven occupy eight of Dekker's fifty-two pages.) Like Dante, Dekker secures permission to walk among the damned; he finds a two-part hell. In the first, the cold region, he sees the "rich dogs" who refused to help the poor and sick. Tormented by whips, diseases, snakes, and salamanders, they react with "Yels, teeth-gnashing, chattering, shivering." Then he moves into the traditional fires to find the drunkards, gamblers, adulterers, and gluttons—"millions" of them, whipped and stung with their own longings and with the "worme of conscience." Among them is a young man cursing God and proclaiming loudly as the whips descend that he does not deserve eternal punishment. Dekker gives him a perfectly logical defense: He had only thirty years of life, fifteen of which were spent asleep, five more in childishness, and some at least in good deeds. Nature had given him little—drops of gall from her left breast instead of milk—and his sins were small. His lengthy defense contains some of Dekker's best images and rhythms; it is interrupted by a booming angelic voice which shouts about justice until the rest of the damned, angered, outshout it, waking the poet. Dekker, hands shaking from the experience, concludes that, reading the world, "I found Here worse Devils than are in Hell."

The dream vision has been largely misinterpreted, but close study of the quality of the imagery and the proportions of the whole indicate that Dekker was indeed leading his readers to question the justice shouted by the avenging angel. It is a subtly and effectively composed poem, deserving more attention than it has had.

OTHER MAJOR WORKS

PLAYS: *The Whole History of Fortunatus*, pr. 1599 (commonly known as *Old Fortunatus*, play and poetry); *The Shoemaker's Holiday: Or, The Gentle Craft*, pr., pb. 1600 (based on Thomas Deloney's narrative *The Gentle Craft*, play and poetry); *Patient Grissell*, pr. 1600 (with Henry Chettle and William Haughton); *Satiromastix: Or, The Untrussing of the Humourous Poet*, pr. 1601; *Sir Thomas Wyatt*, pr. 1602 (as *Lady Jane*), pb. 1607; *The Magnificent Entertainment Given to King James*, pr. 1603 (with Ben Jonson and Thomas Middleton); *The Honest Whore, Part I*, pr., pb. 1604 (with Middleton, play and poetry); *Westward Ho!*, pr. 1604 (with John Webster); *The Honest Whore, Part II*, pr. c. 1605 (play and poetry); *Northward Ho!*, pr. 1605 (with Webster); *The Whore of Babylon*, pr. c. 1606-1607; *The Roaring Girl: Or, Moll Cutpurse*, pr. c. 1610 (with Middleton); *If This Be Not a Good Play, the Devil Is In It*, pr. c. 1610-1612, pb. 1612 (as *If It Be Not Good, the Devil Is in It*); *Match Me in London*, pr. c. 1611-1612; *The Virgin Martyr*, pr. c. 1620 (with Philip Massinger, play and poetry); *The Witch of Edmonton*, pr. 1621 (with John Ford and William Rowley, play and poetry); *The Noble Soldier: Or, A Contract Broken, Justly Revenged*, pr. c. 1622-1631 (with John Day; thought to be the same as *The Spanish Fig*, 1602); *The Wonder of a Kingdom*, pr. c. 1623; *The Sun's Darling*, pr. 1624 (with Ford, play and poetry); *The Welsh Embassador: Or, A Comedy in Disguises*, pr. c. 1624 (revision of *The Noble Soldier*); *The Dramatic Works of Thomas Dekker*, pb. 1953-1961 (4 volumes; Fredson Bowers, editor).

NONFICTION: *The Seven Deadly Sins of London*, 1606; *News from Hell*, 1606; *The Bellman of London*, 1608; *A Work for Armourers*, 1609; *The Gull's Hornbook*, 1609; *Four Birds of Noah's Ark*, 1609; *Penny-Wise, Pound-Foolish*, 1631; *The Plague Pamphlets of Thomas Dekker*, 1925 (F. P. Wilson, editor).

MISCELLANEOUS: *The Wonderful Year*, 1603 (prose and poetry); *The Double PP*, 1606 (prose and poetry); *Lanthorn and Candlelight*, 1608, 1609 (prose and poetry; revised as *O per se O*, 1612; *Villanies Discovered*, 1616, 1620; *English Villanies*, 1632, 1638, 1648); *Dekker, His Dream*, 1620 (prose and poetry); *The Non-Dramatic Works of Thomas Dekker*, 1884-1886 (4 volumes; Alexander B. Grosart, editor); *Thomas Dekker: Selected Prose Writings*, 1968 (E. D. Pendry, editor).

BIBLIOGRAPHY

Berlin, Normand. "Thomas Dekker: A Partial Reappraisal." *Studies in English Literature* 6 (1966): 263-267. Although brief, this analysis of Dekker is important because it demonstrates that the playwright is a more complex person and writer than suggested by his most popular work, the cheerfully optimistic *The Shoemaker's Holiday*. Berlin sees Dekker as "essentially a stern moralist" who sometimes, when theatrical conditions demand, compromises his morality.

Brown, Arthur. "Citizen Comedy and Domestic Drama." *Jacobean Theatre* 1 (1960): 66-83. Brown compares Dekker with Thomas Heywood and Ben Jonson, two fellow dramatists, and concludes that Dekker's work is "the least complicated by adherence to literary, or even moral, theory." Brown also shows how Dekker's understanding of his craft and audience is apparent in the plays.

Champion, Larry S. *Thomas Dekker and the Tradition of English Drama*. New York: Peter Lang, 1985. This straightforward commentary deals primarily with the dramatic structure and tone of the plays, but also shows how Dekker often experiments with new approaches. Champion also discusses Dekker's links with his contemporaries.

Conover, James H. *Thomas Dekker: An Analysis of Dramatic Structure*. The Hague: Mouton, 1966. Conover traces the development of the plots of Dekker's major plays (including *The Shoemaker's Holiday*, *The Honest Whore*, *Old Fortunatus*, and *Satiromastix*) and concludes with a chapter on the structural traits he believes are peculiar to Dekker's works.

Dekker, Thomas. *The Shoemaker's Holiday*. Edited by Stanley Wells and Robert Smallwood. New York: St. Martin's Press, 1999. More than a reprint of the play, this edition provides a study of the text and the editors' historical introduction, including an examination of the play's relationship with contemporary life and drama and its place in Dekker's work, a stage history, analysis, and a reprint of source materials.

Hunt, Mary Leland. *Thomas Dekker: A Study*. 1911. Reprint. Reprint Services, 1992. The first book-length study of Dekker's life and work—prose as well as play. It remains useful not only for the critical summaries of the works but also for its chronological treatment of the poet's life. Of special interest are the comments about Dekker's friendships in the theater and his collaborators. Since M. T. Jones-Davis's two-volume, 1958 study, *Un Peintre de la vue londonienne, Thomas Dekker, circa 1572-1632*, is not in English, Hunt's book is a worthwhile substitute.

Krantz, Susan E. "Thomas Dekker's Political Commentary in *The Whore of Babylon*." *Studies in English Literature, 1500-1900* 35, no. 2 (Spring, 1995): 271. Dekker's *The Whore of Babylon* is one of the first texts to recast Elizabethan England nostalgically as a form of covert criticism of the Jacobean court. An examination of the Gunpowder Plot and its effect on the pro-Henrician and anti-Spanish themes of the play is offered.

Price, George R. *Thomas Dekker*. New York: Twayne, 1969. This brief but reliable study reviews Dekker's life, then proceeds to examine twelve plays (eight by Dekker alone and four collaborations) and some of his nondramatic works. The comments on the playwright's social and religious ideas are illuminating, and the bibliography includes plays that have sometimes been attributed to Dekker.

*Robert M. Otten and Elizabeth Spalding Otten;
bibliography updated by the editors*

Walter de la Mare

Born: Charlton, Kent, England; April 25, 1873
Died: Twickenham, Middlesex, England; June 22, 1956

PRINCIPAL POETRY

Songs of Childhood, 1902
Poems, 1906
The Listeners and Other Poems, 1912
A Child's Day: A Book of Rhymes, 1912
Peacock Pie: A Book of Rhymes, 1913
The Sunken Garden and Other Poems, 1917
Motley and Other Poems, 1918
Flora: A Book of Drawings, 1919
Poems 1901 to 1918, 1920
Story and Rhyme, 1921
The Veil and Other Poems, 1921
Down-Adown-Derry: A Book of Fairy Poems, 1922
Thus Her Tale, 1923
A Ballad of Christmas, 1924
Stuff and Nonsense and So On, 1927
Self to Self, 1928
The Snowdrop, 1929
News, 1930
Poems for Children, 1930
Lucy, 1931
Old Rhymes and New, 1932
The Fleeting and Other Poems, 1933
Poems, 1919 to 1934, 1935
This Year, Next Year, 1937
Memory and Other Poems, 1938
Haunted, 1939
Bells and Grass, 1941
Collected Poems, 1941
Collected Rhymes and Verses, 1944
The Burning-Glass and Other Poems, 1945
The Traveller, 1946
Rhymes and Verses: Collected Poems for Young People, 1947
Inward Companion, 1950
Winged Chariot, 1951
O Lovely England and Other Poems, 1953
The Complete Poems, 1969

Walter de la Mare (Library of Congress)

OTHER LITERARY FORMS

Walter de la Mare was a prolific author of fiction and nonfiction as well as poetry. His novels include modern adult fiction, such as *Memoirs of a Midget* (1921), and fiction for children, such as *The Three Mulla-Mulgars* (1910). His short stories fit into a variety of traditional genres; many are tales of the supernatural. The interests which manifest themselves in the poetry and fiction are more explicitly revealed in de la Mare's essays and his work as an editor. Not much given to analysis, as a critic he was primarily an appreciator and interpreter, much as he was as a poet. Of the anthologies he edited, *Behold, This Dreamer!* (1939) is perhaps the most revealing of the influences that de la Mare particularly valued in his work as a poet.

ACHIEVEMENTS

Walter de la Mare was one of the most popular poets of his time. Since his death his reputation has faded. His verse sometimes sounds too romantic for the sensibilities of a modern audience. Yet his children's verse remains in print, and the best of his adult poetry remains standard for inclusion in anthologies of twentieth century English poets. The present moderate eclipse of the popularity of his poetry is probably temporary, because his best verse has those iconoclastic qualities that make such poets as William Blake stand out from ordinary poets.

De la Mare's sensibility is deeply rooted in the Romanticism of the nineteenth century, and, like the works of Rudyard Kipling and George Bernard Shaw, his writings often seem reminiscent of the Victorian Age. Nevertheless, his subjects were from the twentieth century, and the resultant mixture of contemporary realism and Romantic style make him special among major poets. Of the various poetic modes represented in his works, the lyric was the one with which de la Mare had his greatest artistic success; he ranks among the best lyric poets in the English language, and he may be the best English lyric poet of his era. In his mastery of poetic form and metaphor, de la Mare compares favorably with the best the English language has to offer.

His blend of romance and realism, of the supernatural with the commonplace, inspired poets of his day. The term *delamarian* was coined sometime during de la Mare's middle years, and it is still used to identify works that employ techniques that are best represented by his work. The coinage of such a term is evidence of the esteem in which de la Mare was held by many of his contemporaries, and of the unique blend of form and ideas that makes him one of the twentieth century's best poets.

BIOGRAPHY

The first in-depth, full-length biography of Walter de la Mare was not published until 1993. He was, by the few published accounts of those who knew him, a quiet and unremarkable man. One can reasonably infer from the absence of autobiographical material from an otherwise prolific writer that he was a private man. He seems to have lived his adventures through his writing, and his primary interests seem to have been of the intellect and the spirit.

He was born in 1873 to James Edward de la Mare and Lucy Sophia Browning de la Mare, a Scot. He at-

tended St. Paul's Cathedral Choir School. While in school he founded and edited *The Choiristers' Journal,* a school magazine. In 1890, Walter de la Mare entered the employ of the Anglo-American Oil Company, where he served as bookkeeper until 1908. During these years he wrote essays, stories, and poetry, which appeared in various magazines, including *Black and White* and *The Sketch.* In 1902, *Songs of Childhood,* his first book—and one of his most lastingly popular—was published. There he used the pseudonym Walter Ramal. Then, after using it also for his novel *Henry Brocken* in 1904, he dropped it. He married Constance Elfrida Igpen in 1899, with whom he had two sons and two daughters. She died in 1943.

De la Mare's employment at the Anglo-American Oil Company ended in 1908, when he was granted a Civil List pension of one hundred pounds a year. Thus encouraged, he embarked on a life of letters during which he produced poetry, short stories, essays, and one play, and edited volumes of poetry and essays. These many works reveal something of de la Mare's intellect, if not of his character. They reveal a preoccupation with inspiration and dreams, an irritation with Freudians and psychologists in general (they were too simplistic in their analyses, he believed), a love of romance, and a love for the child in people. The works reveal a complex mind that, curiously, preferred appreciation to analysis and observation to explanation.

ANALYSIS

The poetry of Walter de la Mare falls superficially into two groups: poetry for children and poetry for adults. This obvious and misleading division is unfortunate, however, because many readers have come to think of de la Mare as principally an author for children. Much of his poetry is intended for an adult readership; that which is meant for children is complex enough in theme to satisfy demanding adult readers. Much misunderstanding of the nature of de la Mare's poetry comes from its childlike response to the world. De la Mare distinguishes between the typically childlike and adult imaginations. Children, he contends, view the world subjectively, making and remaking reality according to their egocentric desires. Adults are more analytical and tend to dissociate themselves from reality; they try to observe reality objectively. De la Mare prefers the childlike view, an inductive rather than deductive understanding of the world. Reality, he believes, is revealed through inspiration, an essentially subjective aspect of human imagination. The modern vogue of discussions of "higher planes of reality" would have had little meaning for de la Mare, but he would approve the notion that there is a reality beyond that which can be objectively observed. Time and nature are tyrants who rule humankind. Their effects can be observed, but they in themselves cannot. To understand the reality of time and nature, the poet uses his imaginative insight. In pursuit of such insight, de la Mare studied dreams; as a poet he strove to describe the world as if observing it while in a walking dream. He attempted to observe as he imagined a child might observe, and because childhood involves a continual discovery of both the physical reality and the spiritual reality of nature, de la Mare's poetry is alive with discovery, wonder, and—as discovery often brings—disappointment with the imperfections of the world.

De la Mare wrote more than a thousand poems over more than half a century. In any such body of work, written during a long lifetime, one can rightly expect to find much diversity in subject and tone. De la Mare's work is no exception. Although he was a lyric poet all his life, his work shifted from short poems to long ones, and his prosody increased in complexity. To read the body of de la Mare's poetry is to experience a mind of diverse and passionate interests, with some of those interests unifying the whole of the poet's verse. De la Mare was a careful craftsman whose verse rhythms can disturb and delight wherever the content of a poem dictates. He loved children and strove to experience the world like a child, inductively. He saw the world of everyday experience as only part of a greater universe; he believed in spirits and a supernatural world. He saw great value in nature, even if it could be indifferent to human suffering.

These beliefs and passions enliven de la Mare's work, forming a background that colors all of his poems. If his poetry may be said to deliver a particular message, it is one which is at once simple and complex in its implications, like his verse: People are partly spiritual and thus should never be indifferent to evil, should love in-

nocence, and should understand that each person is greater than he appears.

CHILDREN'S POETRY

De la Mare's interest in childlike inspiration led him to write poetry for children. His respect for childlike imagination is reflected in the absence of condescension in his children's verse. In fact, most of it resembles that which he wrote for adults, although his diction is at a level that children can understand. All the major concerns of de la Mare's intellectual life are expressed in his children's verse; in "The Old King" (1922), for example, he discusses death. The "old King of Cumberland" awakens in surprise and looks about his room for what had disturbed him, but all seems normal until he touches his chest "where now no surging restless beat/ Its long tale told." The King's heart has stopped and he is terrified. The whole of the poem is expressed in a manner which children can comprehend, and de la Mare makes three important points: that death is a fact, that there is a reality beyond death, and that death is dreamlike. He never means to frighten his young readers; rather, he means for them to understand. For example, in "Now, Dear Me!" (1912), he describes a fearsome ghost: "A-glowering with/ A chalk-white face/ Out of some dim/ And dismal place." The ghost turns out to be Elizabeth Ann, a child very much alive, done up to frighten her nurse. Children are invited to laugh at the very real fears that their imaginations can create.

A child is unlikely to miss the implied respect for his mind when he reads poetry that clearly states de la Mare's point of view on a subject of moral substance. "Hi!" (1930) is a lyric which presents a hunter's killing of an animal: "Nevermore to peep again, creep again, leap again,/ Eat or sleep or drink again, Oh, what fun!" De la Mare's dismay at the killing of wildlife is clear, as is his effort to speak of an important matter to his young readership. Wildlife plays an important role in his poetry. Bears and elephants and other animals are shown as friendly to children. When Elizabeth Ann takes a bath in "Little Birds Bathe" (1912), her tub is invaded by a "Seal and Walrus/ And Polar Bear." A host of other animals join them, from alligators to swans to pumas. Her bath sounds fun, and the poem is as cheerful a depiction of bathing and imagination as one could hope to read. In "Who Really?" (1930), bears and bees share a natural antagonism and similarity—they are both thieves. In "The Holly" (1930), the poet describes the natural beauty of the holly tree. Repeatedly, he depicts nature as other than frightening; it can be awesome, but a child's imagination can render it knowable.

DREAMS AND THE SUPERNATURAL

The supernatural and dreams are significant aspects of de la Mare's poetry for youngsters. His verse spans topics from Christianity to pagan mysticism. In "Eden" (1930), he discusses the fall of humanity from God's grace and its effect on all nature. When the sin of humanity leads to the Great Flood, trees and animals suffer the consequences. Thus, the banishment of Adam and Eve is bewailed by the nightingale.

The notion that the fates of Humanity and Nature are linked is unmistakable. Pagan mysticism in the forms of fairies and elves is common children's fare. Typical of de la Mare's respect for his young audience, he offers uncommon fairies. In "The Double" (1922), a fairy child joins a young dancer in a garden. The fairy is at once a reflection of the dancer and a part of the plants in the garden; it is at once substantial and incapable of leaving faintest marks of its footsteps. The poem is a sad evocation of childlike imagination; the fairy child disappears beyond recalling. Fairies and their kin are evocations of the natural world; they respond to people when people respond to nature. They are ephemeral, as much the products of imagination and dreams as of tradition and myth.

"The World of Dream" (1912) takes poetic tradition and uses it to portray a child's view of sleep. When dreaming, one often seems to be floating on air or water; death is often described similarly. De la Mare takes his sleeping child on a ride in a boat equipped with "elphin lanterns," a boat with "hundreds of passengers." The misty world of sleep sounds peaceful and much like death.

DEATH AND EVIL

The connecting of sleep and death is common in literature, yet death is not a customary topic intended for children. Although de la Mare writes for children, he spares them none of the topics that he deems important. Death is a part of nature; it is something that, as "Eden" shows, was brought into nature by humankind. Death is not inherently evil, although killing can

be. In de la Mare's poetry, dreams and death are often linked, and he commonly uses dreams to reveal a truer reality than is found in the nondreaming world. Thus, death itself is not meant to be evil or even exceptionally awful.

Even so, de la Mare did perceive evil in the world, and children are not spared its presence in his poetry. Evil is not trivialized for the sake of youthful readers. The poet shows children being punished for naughty behavior, as in "This Little Morsel of Morsels Here" (1912), but he does not lay the heavy burden of evil on the filching of gingery sweets: Bears can misbehave and so can children. Naughtiness is natural, although undesirable. True evil is profound. It can be personified as a "handsome hunting man" in "Hi!" or as the actions of a child slashing his toy sword through the grasses of a meadow in "The Massacre" (1906). The actions seem innocent, but the child imagines heads lopped off and "dead about my feet." Nature in the form of sunlight and air recoils in horror from the imaginary deeds that in a child foreshadow the potential evil of adulthood.

POETRY FOR ADULTS

Most of de la Mare's verse was directed at an adult audience. While his poetry for children reveals the bare forms of his poetic interests, it is primarily cheerful, concentrating on sympathetically helping children to use their imaginations; his adult poetry is more somber and even more mystical. The most famous of de la Mare's poems perhaps best exemplifies his characteristic blending of dreams, the supernatural, and the childlike imagination. "The Listeners" (1912) was once memorized by thousands of schoolchildren; it puzzled and enthralled de la Mare's contemporaries, and it is likely to survive the test of time, retaining its mystical and symbolic power.

"THE LISTENERS"

In "The Listeners," a Traveller knocks at the door of a house that is at once empty and filled with "a host of phantom listeners." The Traveller smites the door and is answered only by echoes in empty hallways. He repeatedly calls, "Is anybody there?" and listens for replies. Even though no one answers, the Traveller senses the presence of the listeners: "And he felt in his heart their strangeness,/ Their stillness answering his cry." The

Traveller strikes the door again and cries out, "Tell them I came, and no one answered,/ That I kept my word." The listeners who lurk in "the shadowiness of the still house" listen to him mount his horse and ride away. Throughout the poem, *silence* is as palpable as sound, and at its conclusion *silence* remains a part of the listeners' house. The poem exhibits the salient traits of most of de la Mare's poetry. Its tone, subject, and events all seem part of a dream, yet it is populated by mundane physical details: a horse dining on grass, the Traveller's "grey eyes," and a "dark stair." The poem's effect is mystification and strangeness; its appeal is emotional, rather than intellectual. The theme of *others* who are near-human beings but cannot be seen nor heard is important to an understanding of de la Mare's work. Humanity is surrounded by spirits and fairies in his poetry. The listeners might be spirits of the dead or of the supernatural world; they might be otherworldly memories of the presences of those who dwelt in the house. Their nature is ambiguous because human experience of the spiritual is usually ambiguous.

The Traveller himself offers another context besides the supernatural. He senses the listeners and speaks to them. His purpose is at once specific and general; he comes to fulfill a promise, but the circumstances under which the promise was made and the people to whom it was made are never presented, leaving ambiguity instead of specifics. The Traveller's purpose is general enough to represent general human purpose; the Traveller is symbolic of all people. The theme of life as a journey marks much of de la Mare's most evocative work, and the idea of humanity as an aggregate of individual travelers is an important part of de la Mare's poetic vision. The Traveller represents people, and the listeners, too, can be people. In a sense, all people are both travelers and listeners, and often communication between people can be vague and uncertain. Often people's purposes are as mysterious to others as is that of the Traveller. Often people's are as distant from the lives of others as the listeners are from the Traveller. Typical of much of de la Mare's poetry, "The Listeners" allows multiple readings.

"HAUNTED"

The eerie dream quality of "The Listeners" reflects de la Mare's understanding of the world. A theme that is found from his earliest to his latest poetry is that of reality as dream. The supernatural world can be more substantial than the world of common experience; dreams are at once reflective of how everyday reality compares with the more valid reality of the spirit and are connections between the natural and supernatural. Human beings are parts of both worlds because of their spiritual natures. In "Haunted" (1939), a persona—the poem's speaker—fears "Life, which ever in at window stares." His fear originates in the uncertainty of life: "You say, *This is*. The soul cries, *Only seems*." What the conscious mind perceives as real the spirit understands as insubstantial. The persona notes "And who, when sleeping, finds unreal his dreams?" Dreams can seem to be real, and thus earthly life can seem to be all there is to existence. Yet in each person is a soul, a part of the supernatural world, and the soul perceives the danger and the reality beyond ordinary physical sensation. In "Haunted," the dangers lie in "the Fiend with his goods," who can turn a seemingly mundane activity into a spiritual threat. Those who inhabit the supernatural world have their own purposes, and human beings can miss seeing those purposes.

"THE SLUM CHILD"

Even de la Mare's poetic depictions of contemporary life is imbued with his conception of humanity's mixed relationships with the commonplace and the otherworldly. "The Slum Child" (1933), for example, evokes with carefully selected detail the dreary, unnatural life of an urban child growing up in poverty. The poem features one of de la Mare's favorite topics, children, and one of the fundamental themes of his poetry, that nature is an important part of human experience. The youngster in "The Slum Child" suffers from lack of exposure to nature. The child lives in a world of stone, "lean-faced girls and boys," and beggary. De la Mare employs irony to convey the unnaturalness of the slum childhood, as when his speaker uses the word "harboured": "What evil, and filth, and poverty,/ In childhood harboured me." The best that can be said about childhood in a slum is that it is miserable.

A reader could interpret "The Slum Child" as simply a poem of social protest. De la Mare's love of children is well known, and his dismay at the abuse of children in the slum environment is clearly portrayed in the poem.

Such a reading, however, would have to ignore the poem's last four stanzas. The poem is spiritual and consistent with de la Mare's emphasis on emotional rather than intellectual impact on his readers. He notes that within the child, "Some hidden one made mock of groans,/ Found living bread in stones." The depiction of slum life elicits anger, sadness, and feelings of hopelessness; yet the child's life is not hopeless. The poem's speaker, as an adult, looks back at his own youthful face and "I search its restless eyes,/ And, from those woe-flecked depths, at me/ Looks back through all its misery/ A self beyond surmise." The soul exists beyond the body. Even in the horrible slum one can find hope in one's spirit, which exists in the cosmos as well as in the tiny microcosm of everyday life. Like most of de la Mare's best poetry, "The Slum Child" is complex; it expresses de la Mare's horror of the child's life, and it reveals the inherent hopefulness of his belief in the supernatural.

"The Traveller"

The notion of the relative unimportance of the physical in relation to the spiritual is another theme that unifies de la Mare's poetry, from his first publications to his last. In one of his best poems, "The Traveller," this theme is symbolically presented. The Traveller himself is Everyman, and his journey is the journey that all people must take through life. The Traveller begins his journey at Titicaca, in the land of the Incas, and travels into strange places with alien landscapes. Throughout, de la Mare creates marvelously beautiful images. In the beginning, the Traveller gazes at "a vast plateau, smooth as porphyry,/ Its huge curve gradual as a woman's breast." He rides his Arabian horse onto the plateau, the surface of which is "Branched veins of sanguine in a milk-pale stone," becoming "Like night-blue porcelain." His journey takes him over "A vitreous region, like a sea asleep,/ Crystalline, convex, tideless and congealed." Eventually, the Traveller reaches "an immeasurable well/ Of lustrous crystal motionless black/ Deeped on. As he gazed . . ./ It seemed to him a presence there gazed back."

In a poem that purports to represent symbolically the life not only of each human being but of each earthly creature as well, such particular descriptions as the foregoing can be mystifying. "The Traveller" is a mixture of the implicit and the explicit. The poem's protagonist explicitly sees animals following him on his journey; he explicitly ages; he explicitly contemplates the meaning of his life: "Could Earth itself a living creature be,/ And he its transitory parasite?" As Henry Charles Duffin points out in his *Walter de la Mare: A Study of His Poetry* (1949), the poem's Earth is alive; it is an eye, and the Traveller traverses its ball and iris to its pupil, the "well." Throughout his life, from youthful determination to middle-aged contemplation to aged despair, the Traveller is watched. "Even the little ant . . . conscious may be of occult puissance near"; even, the poem states, the smallest of creatures can feel the living presence of the Earth.

Some critics have emphasized the despair in the poem; the divine may be too remote from humanity and humanity too small to be noticed. Doris Ross McCrosson, in *Walter de la Mare* (1966), is a notable advocate of de la Mare's despair and uncertainty about the existence and possible nature of God. Others, such as Victoria Sackville-West in "Walter de la Mare and 'The Traveller,'" *Proceedings of the British Academy* (1953), find an affirmation of faith in the poem. Typical of much of de la Mare's introspective poetry, "The Traveller" depicts pain and frustration as parts of living; and, typical of the poetry, Earth, nature, and each human being have spiritual aspects that can defy evil.

Other major works

LONG FICTION: *Henry Brocken*, 1904; *The Return*, 1910; *The Three Mulla-Mulgars*, 1910 (reprinted as *The Three Royal Monkeys: Or, The Three Mulla-Mulgars*, 1935); *Memoirs of a Midget*, 1921; *At First Sight: A Novel*, 1928.

SHORT FICTION: *Story and Rhyme: A Selection*, 1921; *The Riddle and Other Stories*, 1923; *Ding Dong Bell*, 1924; *Broomsticks and Other Tales*, 1925; *Miss Jemima*, 1925; *Readings*, 1925-1926 (2 volumes); *The Connoisseur and Other Tales*, 1926; *Told Again: Traditional Tales*, 1927; *Old Joe*, 1927; *On the Edge*, 1930; *Seven Short Stories*, 1931; *The Lord Fish*, 1933; *The Nap and Other Stories*, 1936; *The Wind Blows Over*, 1936; *Animal Stories*, 1939; *The Picnic*, 1941; *The Best Stories of Walter de la Mare*, 1942; *The Old Lion and Other Stories*, 1942; *The*

Magic Jacket and Other Stories, 1943; *The Scarecrow and Other Stories*, 1945; *The Dutch Cheese and Other Stories*, 1946; *Collected Stories for Children*, 1947; *A Beginning and Other Stories*, 1955; *Ghost Stories*, 1956.

PLAY: *Crossings: A Fairy Play*, pr. 1919.

NONFICTION: *Rupert Brooke and the Intellectual Imagination*, 1919; *The Printing of Poetry*, 1931; *Lewis Carroll*, 1932; *Poetry in Prose*, 1936; *Pleasures and Speculations*, 1940; *Chardin, J.B.S. 1699-1779*, 1948; *Private View*, 1953.

EDITED TEXTS: *Come Hither*, 1923; *The Shakespeare Songs*, 1929; *Christina Rossetti's Poems*, 1930; *Desert Islands and Robinson Crusoe*, 1930; *Stories from the Bible*, 1930; *Early One Morning in the Spring*, 1935; *Animal Stories*, 1939; *Behold, This Dreamer!*, 1939; *Love*, 1943.

BIBLIOGRAPHY

Benntinck, Anne. *Romantic Imagery in the Works of Walter de la Mare*. Lewiston, N.Y.: Edwin Mellen Press, 2001. Devotes one chapter apiece to each of seven major Romantic themes or leitmotifs in de la Mare's poetry. Bibliography, index of works, general index.

Duffin, Henry Charles. *Walter de la Mare: A Study of His Poetry*. London: Sidgwick and Jackson, 1949. A friend and intimate of the poet, Duffin divides de la Mare's poems into two classes: the poetry of reality, which dominated his early life, and the poetry of truth, which was characteristic of his later years. The first type, Duffin's favorite, is dreamlike. It teaches that a spiritual world exists in addition to the flesh and blood world, which is by comparison unreal. The poetry of truth presents man as a despairing creature.

Fowler, Alastair. *A History of English Literature*. Cambridge, Mass.: Harvard University Press, 1987. Fowler considers de la Mare the strangest, most elusive poet of the early twentieth century. His interest in supernaturalism was no eccentricity, but it was the expression of a metaphysical puzzlement about the nature of reality. He was a genuine philosopher, comparable to John Donne and other Metaphysical poets. Primarily a connoisseur of darkness, he is absurdly undervalued by most critics.

McCrosson, Doris Ross. *Walter de la Mare*. New York: Twayne, 1966. This volume offers a good discussion of de la Mare's novels, as well as his poems. McCrosson notes that de la Mare's poetry for children presents childhood as containing evil rather than as being entirely blissful. De la Mare was not himself childish but was childlike, that is, intuitive in his perception. Death is a constant theme in the poems. De la Mare leaves open the question of whether human beings survive death, and he never affirms a belief in God. He displays a "bias toward the miniature," writing about small animals and scenes.

Perkins, David. "Craftsmen of the Beautiful and the Agreeable." In *A History of Modern Poetry*. Vol. 1. Cambridge, Mass.: Harvard University Press, 1976. Perkins emphasizes de la Mare's complicated relationship to the Romantics. Like them, he often wrote about the world as a dream. He was aware of the conventional nature of Romantic poetry and often the poems are about conventions. Unlike certain Romantics, he does not portray evil as sublime. He is a master at interrogative conversation and anticipates the modernist stress on the accents of daily speech.

Sisson, C. H. *English Poetry, 1900-1950*. Manchester, England: Carcanet Press, 1981. Sisson mentions that de la Mare was the last of the Romantics. His poetry combines Romantic themes with the more personal themes of twentieth century verse. It is characterized by purity of language and hushed, intimate accents, and it succeeds in capturing the intimate rhythms of speech. De la Mare was at his best in a limited range of subjects. His finest work pictures life on the edge of a dream.

Whistler, Theresa. *Imagination of the Heart: The Life of Walter de la Mare*. London: Duckworth, 1993. The first substantial (nearly five-hundred-page) biography. Bibliographical references, illustrations, index.

Kirk H. Beetz;
bibliography updated by the editors

TOI DERRICOTTE

Born: Detroit, Michigan; April 12, 1941

PRINCIPAL POETRY

The Empress of the Death House, 1978
Natural Birth, 1983, reissued 2000
Captivity, 1989
Tender, 1997

OTHER LITERARY FORMS

A 1997 memoir, *The Black Notebooks: An Interior Journey*, is Toi Derricotte's most popular nonfiction work. The book, expanded from twenty years of diaries, reveals how it feels to look white and be black in the United States. The work met appropriate controversy during a time when the nation, at the behest of then-president Bill Clinton, was trying to generate a dialogue on racial abuses past and present. Derricotte also cowrote with Madeline Tiger Bass *Creative Writing: A Manual for Teachers* (1985), published by the New Jersey State Council on the Arts. The Library of Congress's *The Poet and the Poem from the Library of Congress: Toi Derricotte* is an archival recording produced in October, 1998, by the Library of Congress's Magnetic Recording Laboratory in Washington, D.C. It is one of four video or audio presentations that profile Derricotte's life and work.

ACHIEVEMENTS

Toi Derricotte has forced the American poetry establishment to rethink its assumptions about African Americans and women. Her work evolved through the 1970's, during the rise in black feminist awareness and what some scholars call the second Renaissance in black writing, or the Black Arts movement. She first won recognition from the New School for Social Research with its 1973 Pen and Brush Award for an untitled poetry manuscript. She went to on to win recognition and fellowships from Academy of American Poets in both 1974 and 1978. The National Endowment for the Arts bestowed awards in 1985 and 1990. She won the nomination for the 1998 Pushcart Prize, a Folger Shakespeare Library Poetry Book Award, a Lucille Medwick Memorial Award from the Poetry Society of America, and a United Black Artists' Distinguished Pioneering of the Arts Award.

BIOGRAPHY

Born April 12, 1941, into a Detroit family separated from most of the city's African American community by class and lighter skin, Toinette Derricotte wrote as a way to find solace in an existence filled with alienation. "Tender," the title poem of her fourth major collection, opens, "The tenderest meat comes from the houses where you hear the least squealing." This insight says much about what it was like to be the daughter of Benjamin Sweeney Webster, a mortician, and Antonia Banquet Webster Cyrus, a systems analyst. The young girl quickly learned to hide her thoughts on the page.

Writing is a first passion, but after high school, the shy teen studied psychology at Wayne State University with visions of a doctorate. Plans changed in December, 1961, when she gave birth to son Anthony, and in July, 1962, Derricotte married artist Clarence Reese. The union lasted two years. In 1967, she married banker Bruce Derricotte. They separated in 1991.

Parenthood's realities led Derricotte to major in special education. She started teaching in 1964 with the Manpower Program. She finished a bachelor's degree in 1965. In 1966, Derricotte became a teacher for mentally and emotionally retarded students at Detroit's Farand School. In 1969, Derricotte left her hometown to teach remedial reading at Jefferson School in Teaneck, New Jersey. The job lasted a year.

She taught for money, but always wrote. In 1973, Derricotte began a four-year stint on the New York Quarterly staff. The following year she started a fifteen-year residency with the New Jersey State Council on the Arts Poet-in-the-Schools program. Those years set the direction of her life as author, mentor, and teacher.

The Empress of the Death House, her first collection, was published in 1978. The next year she founded a retreat to foster the development of African American poets in a culturally sensitive atmosphere. That involvement ended in 1982 but was reborn in 1996, when she collaborated with Cornelius Eady to create Cave Canem, a summer workshop in upstate New York.

In 1983, *Natural Birth* was published. Derricotte was graduated from New York University with a master's degree in creative writing the next year. The 1985 publication of *Creative Writing: A Manual for Teachers*, coauthored with Madeline Bass, followed.

In 1988, twenty-one years after she left home for New Jersey, Derricotte moved to Norfolk, Virginia, to teach at Old Dominion. The next year, *Captivity* was published. In 1990, she spent a year as Commonwealth Professor in the English department of George Mason University in Fairfax, Virginia. In 1991, she moved to the University of Pittsburgh.

Throughout her writing career, Derricotte immersed herself in classes, readings, and contributions to a various magazines and journals, such as *Pequod, Iowa Review, Ironwood, Northwest Review, Poetry Northwest, American Poetry Review, Bread Loaf Quarterly, Massachusetts Review, Ploughshares*, and *Feminist Studies*. Many of her poems and essays appear in anthologies, as well.

During 1992 and 1993, she served on faculties of summer workshops at Squaw Valley, the University of South Florida, and the College of Charleston. The decade ended with the publication of *Tender* (1997), the 1997 memoir *The Black Notebooks*, and, in 2000, a reissue of *Natural Birth*.

ANALYSIS

Toi Derricotte's candor has been compared with the simple clarity of Emily Dickinson and honest communication of Walt Whitman—but only by those unfamiliar with African American poetry. Derricotte's blunt eloquence is typical of poets in the period from the mid-1960's to the mid-1970's, known as the Black Arts movement, which some scholars have considered to be the counterpart of the Black Power movement. Derricotte's style and themes are more similar to those of Nikki Giovanni or Mari Evans than to those of nineteenth century white Americans.

Derricotte is unique in her confessional treatment of racial identity. "My skin causes certain problems continuously, problems that open the issue of racism over and over like a wound," she once wrote. That statement hangs over her photograph on the African American Literature Book Club Web site as tribute to the talent she displays in the ability to turn poignant racial episodes into instruments that sometimes strike readers' consciences with jackhammer force and, at others, soothe their souls.

"I'm not an Emily Dickinson scholar, but I have loved her for many, many years, for many reasons," she wrote in *Titanic Operas: A Poet's Corner of Responses to Dickinson's Legacy* (edited by Martha Nell Smith and Laura Elyn Lauth):

> One of the reasons is because of her great courage to look at things—the most terrifying, the most beautiful—without flinching.

"Her poems begin in ordinary experiences," Jon Woodson writes of Derricotte in *Contemporary Women Poets*, "but she dissects the routine definitions supplied by society as a way towards making discoveries about what unsuspected resources the self actually contains." That aptly describes what a reader will find in any of the author's poems.

The prizewinning writer treats womanhood and race as media through which she bares her torments and forces readers to look more closely than ever before at often evaded aspects of the human experience. She writes about being an African American woman in the late twentieth century, but the work is likely to resonate with readers in any culture and time who understand that life holds more questions than answers.

THE EMPRESS OF THE DEATH HOUSE

Derricotte's early works focused on death and birth. The theme is heavy in her first book, *The Empress of the Death House*, where "The Grandmother Poems" discuss her childhood experiences in her grandparents' Detroit funeral home. Her mother's stepfather owned the business. Although she was sickly, the woman used two thousand dollars of her own money to send Derricotte's father to mortuary school, so that he might join a more stable line of work.

The Empress of the Death House grapples with the plight of women who survive abuse in an effort to sort out her feelings about her grandmother and mother. The understanding was a step on the path to self-awareness and helped her to understand her personal reactions to motherhood. In *The American Book Review*, reviewer Joe Weixlmann, who wrote about *Natural Birth*, said *The Empress of the Death House* opens readers' eyes to the "indifference or contempt" with which the world treats African American women.

NATURAL BIRTH

Natural Birth, in both its 1983 and 2000 editions, is an extension of Derricotte's investigation into African American women. The collection candidly probes the birth process as an experience that hurts too much and humiliates. This poem is a "tour de force, at once a book-length experimental poem, an exploration of the extremes of human experience, and an examination of the social construction of identity," Woodson wrote of the 1983 Crossing Press version. Of the 2000 edition, Eileen Robinson wrote in *Black Issues Book Review:*

> Natural Birth is a triumph of one woman's spirit that will appeal to readers who are looking for depth, emotion, originality and truth. . . . Derricotte has completed a moving testament to teenage mothers, and mothers everywhere, who survive the miracle of birth. It is also a special gift to their children who grow stronger for understanding the very human fears and pains of the women who brought them here.

Natural Birth takes writings about death, birth, and transcendence to another level. Derricotte reaches for the truth that most unwed mothers might like to tell. She reaches inside the experience of childbirth for the thoughts that most mothers might want to share.

In *Contemporary Authors*, Derricotte is quoted as saying that her Catholic school education taught that confession made a person "whole" or "back into a state of grace." She concludes,

> As a black woman, I have been consistently confused about my 'sins,' unsure of which faults were in me and which faults were the results of others' projections. . . . truthtelling in my art is also a way to separate my 'self' from what I have been taught to believe about my 'self,' the degrading stereotypes about black women.

CAPTIVITY

Captivity shifted the focus from gender to race, sliding from portraits of general poverty to intricate sketches of urban students. The book places the U.S. slave experience at the root of many issues in today's black experience. The dehumanization and commercialization of African Americans' slave ancestors has been cited as a root cause of black poverty, fractured family structures, violence, and continued oppression. *Village Voice* reviewer Robyn Selman called the book "a personal exploration yielding truths that apply to all of us."

TENDER

Derricotte's fourth book of poetry, *Tender*, does a similar favor. The uncharacteristically short title poem appears to talk about meat and begins:

> The tenderest meat
> comes from the houses
> where you hear the least
>
> squealing.

It does not take much reflection to see the metaphor about pain-filled lives. In the collection's preface, Derricotte urges readers to use the poem as a hub in exploring, as she calls describes the book's structure, "a seven-spoked wheel." The poet continues to wrestle with the meanings of death, birth, and transcendence. She writes, "Violence is central to our lives, a constant and unavoidable reality."

Derricotte's enduring legacy might be that, as she herself observed of Emily Dickinson, she does not flinch, whether the subject is political or sexual, and that courage is especially well demonstrated in *Tender*. For example, in "Clitoris," she discusses oral sex and her emotional response to it graphically and with lush imagery.

Like many in her generation, Derricotte never let go of the optimism of the 1960's about a positive evolution U.S. attitude and treatment of women and blacks. At the same time, she does not hesitate to display bitter disappointment at where we are along the road. For example, in "After a Reading at a Black College," also from *Tender*, she looks forward with both hope and skepticism:

> Maybe one day we will have
> written about this color thing
> until we've solved it. Tonight
> when I read my poems about
> looking white, the audience strains
> forward with their whole colored
> bodies. . . .
> . . . . . .
> . . . though frightened,
> I don't stop the spirit.
> *Hold steady*, Harriet Tubman whispers,
> *Don't flop around.*

Once again, the best part of Derricotte's work is that, no matter how scathing, it is unapologetic. "People would like inspiring books that tell them what to do, something like *Five Steps Not to Be a Racist*," she told Don Lee in a 1996 interview in *Ploughshares*, the Emerson College literary journal. "That's just not the truth. The easy solutions don't really prepare one for the hard work that needs to be done." She goes on,

I feel the need to represent what's not spoken," she says. "I discover a pocket in myself that hasn't been articulated, then I have to find a form to carry that. Speaking the unspeakable is not that hard. The difficulty is in finding a way to make it perfect, to make it have light and beauty and truth inside it.

OTHER MAJOR WORKS

NONFICTION: *Creative Writing: A Manual for Teachers*, 1985 (with Madeline Bass); *The Black Notebooks: An Interior Journey*, 1997.

BIBLIOGRAPHY

Andrews, William, et al., eds. *The Oxford Companion to African American Literature*. New York: Oxford University Press, 1996. Contains a thorough, concise resume of the author's life.

Robinson, Caudell, M. "Where Poets Explore Their Pain While Others Beware the Dog." *American Visions* 14, no. 5 (October, 1999): 30. Profiles Derricotte's thoughts on writing and efforts to promote the art among African Americans through a summer workshop in upstate New York.

Powers, William F. "The Furious Muse: Black Poets Assess the State of Their Art." *The Washington Post*, October 1, 1994, p. H1. "For lots of reasons we have felt shut out of poetry that sits up there in the traditional canon," iconoclastic Derricotte says. The article reports on a Harrisburg, Virginia gathering of thirty African American poets and about 250 writers, critics and scholars to define qualities set black poetry apart from the American mainstream. The feature story offers insight into the author's personality.

Vincent F. A. Golphin

JAMES DICKEY

Born: Atlanta, Georgia; February 2, 1923
Died: Columbia, South Carolina; January 19, 1997

PRINCIPAL POETRY

Into the Stone and Other Poems, 1960
Drowning with Others, 1962
Helmets, 1964
Buckdancer's Choice, 1965
Poems, 1957-1967, 1967
The Eye-Beaters, Blood, Victory, Madness, Buckhead, and Mercy, 1970
The Zodiac, 1976
The Strength of Fields, 1979
Falling, May Day Sermon, and Other Poems, 1981
Puella, 1982
The Eagle's Mile, 1990
The Whole Motion: Collected Poems, 1945-1992, 1992

OTHER LITERARY FORMS

James Dickey was a novelist as well as a poet, having published *Deliverance* (1970) and *Alnilam* (1987). *The Suspect in Poetry* (1964) and *From Babel to Byzantium* (1968) are important collections of criticism on modern and contemporary poetry. *Self-Interviews* (1970), *Sorties* (1971), *Night Hurdling: Poems, Essays, Conversations, Commencements, and Afterwords* (1983), and *The Voiced Connections of James Dickey* (1989) are collections of essays, addresses, journal notes, and interviews. *Spinning the Crystal Ball* (1967) and *Metaphor as Pure Adventure* (1968) are influential pamphlets based on addresses Dickey delivered while serving as Consultant in Poetry to the Library of Congress. Dickey also wrote a number of essays and book reviews for popular periodicals and newspapers, as well as screenplays and music for several films, two children's books, and four coffee-table books (in collaboration with various graphic and photographic artists).

ACHIEVEMENTS

Though James Dickey's subject matter varies widely, the primary tension underlying most of his writing involves the relationship between romantic individualism and power. In Dickey's work this relationship is often played out through attempts to relate the self to the large rhythms of the universe, a process that Dickey depicts as a necessary, yet potentially destructive, catalyst in individuals' efforts to endow existence with consequence. This paradoxical vision often drew the ire of the critical establishment, but despite the controversy his writings generated, Dickey enjoyed an abundance of academic and popular acclaim for his work in a variety of genres. Among the awards he garnered are two fellowships from the *Sewanee Review*, the Vachel Lindsay Award, the Longview Foundation Prize, a Guggenheim Fellowship, the Bollingen Prize for *Helmets*, the National Book Award and the Melville Cane Award for *Buckdancer's Choice*, the French Prix Medicis for *Deliverance*, and *Poetry*'s Levinson Prize for *Puella*. Dickey was twice named Consultant in Poetry to the Library of Congress and was elected to the National Institute of Arts and Letters and the American Academy of Arts and Sciences. In 1977 President Jimmy Carter selected him to read at the inaugural concert gala, making Dickey and Robert Frost the only poets up to that time to read at an American presidential inauguration. In 1983, he was invited to read the poem "For a Time and Place" at the second inauguration of Richard Riley, governor of South Carolina.

Biography

Born to lawyer Eugene Dickey and Maibelle Swift Dickey in the Atlanta suburb of Buckhead, James Lafayette Dickey was a mediocre high school student who preferred the athletic field to the classroom. After becoming an acclaimed football player at North Fulton High School, Dickey went on to play wingback at Clemson College in 1941 before joining the Army Air Corps the following year. Dickey was assigned to the 418th Night Fighter Squadron because of his exceptional night vision. He flew more than one hundred combat missions in the South Pacific, for which he was awarded several medals, including the Distinguished Flying Cross. After World War II, Dickey enrolled at Vanderbilt University with the intention of pursuing a career as a writer. In 1949 he earned a B.A. in English magna cum laude; he stayed on at Vanderbilt to take an M.A. in English, writing a thesis titled "Symbol and Imagery in the Shorter Poems of Herman Melville." While at the university he also joined the track team and won the Tennessee State High Hurdles Championship. He published several poems in the campus literary magazine and one in *The Sewanee Review*; he also married Maxine Syerson, with whom he had two sons.

In 1951 Dickey began teaching at Rice University before being recalled by the Air Force to fight in the Korean War. Following his discharge, Dickey returned to teach at Rice briefly, before earning a fellowship from *The Sewanee Review*, which he used to travel and write in Europe. In 1956 he returned to teach at the University of Florida, but after disputes with the university administration over his teaching assignment and a sexually explicit poem he read to a group of faculty wives, he left Florida to become a copywriter and executive for an advertising firm in New York. A year later Dickey returned to Atlanta to work as senior writer and creative director for the local Coca-Cola bottler, later moving to other firms, where he engineered the Lay's potato chip and Delta Airlines accounts. During this period Dickey continued publishing poetry in little maga-

James Dickey (Washington Star Collection, D.C. Public Library)

zines, eventually winning several awards, including a Guggenheim Fellowship, which allowed him to quit advertising and spend 1961-1962 writing in Italy.

During the 1960's, Dickey's reputation underwent a meteoric rise, as he established himself as one of the major poets of his generation and won a series of major awards. After serving as poet-in-residence at several universities—including the University of Wisconsin, where he won the National Book Award and was the subject of a feature article in *Life* magazine—Dickey accepted the chair of Carolina Professor in English at the University of South Carolina, where he continued to teach. In 1976 Maxine Dickey died, and Dickey married Deborah Dodson, with whom he had a daughter in 1981. Dickey continued to live and write at a vigorous pace, producing two novels in the last ten years of his life. From 1989 to 1994 he served as a Yale Younger Poets contest judge. He died in Columbia, South Carolina, on January 19, 1997.

ANALYSIS

In his poetry and novels James Dickey often explored what extreme, and sometimes violent, situations reveal about the human condition. Dickey's poetry and fiction of the late 1950's to the 1970's are characterized by startlingly original images and a strong narrative thrust, through which he expressed, and assessed, the belief that volatile qualities are an inherent and necessary, yet potentially destructive, part of the human animal. In the late 1970's Dickey turned to a reflective, language-oriented approach, less immediately accessible and more self-conscious, but he continued to explore his previous themes. Though his themes remained fairly constant, it should be noted that stylistically Dickey was a relentless experimenter always looking to cover new ground in the terrain of poetic possibilities.

INTO THE STONE AND OTHER POEMS AND DROWNING WITH OTHERS

The poems of Dickey's first two collections, *Into the Stone and Other Poems* and *Drowning with Others*, are generally short, tightly structured, and highly rhythmic. While these poems are often anecdotal, they do not so much unfold in time as focus on a specific psychological experience. In essence, these poems are short dramatic parables, describing a moment in which the first-person narrator experiences an epiphany resulting in a more unified and aware self. Through the brief situation presented, Dickey attempted to make a visceral impact on the reader that would become a continuing part of that person's consciousness, intensifying and altering the way in which the person experienced the world by restoring, in Ralph Waldo Emerson's words, "an original relationship to the universe."

These qualities are apparent in "Sleeping Out at Easter," which suggests how Dickey handled the theme of communion with nature in his early work. The narrator's description of his "resurrection" on Easter morning resonates with Christian and pagan overtones, making the dramatic situation—a man waking at daybreak after sleeping out in his backyard—assume a mythic, mystic dimension: "My animal eyes become human/ As the Word rises out of darkness."

The steady, flowing, melodic quality of the anapestic meter enhances the feeling that the experience happens without encumbrance. In each of the first five stanzas, the last line repeats the stanza's first line. The concluding line of each stanza is italicized and used as a refrain, producing the hypnotic quality of an incantation, and the sixth and final stanza consists entirely of the italicized refrains. The result is a sense of continuity and unity, as the poem's lines echo themselves as effortlessly as the narrator accepts the dawn and his newfound self. Dickey captures an organic unity of theme and technique that arrests and annihilates time through the image of first light, creating a new world around the narrator as he grasps the "root," and "source," of all life and of his most elemental self; it is a moment of pure religious transcendence, involving a sense of immortality achieved through communion with the permanent essence of nature.

The poem is more than an account of its narrator, however, for Dickey clearly intended it to initiate change in the reader as well. He directly addressed the reader through the use of second person in the fourth and sixth stanzas (the other four stanzas are presented in first person). These stanzas are completely italicized, indicating a transcendent voice that reverberates through all things. Similarly, the light that accompanies the new day spreads everywhere, touching everything simultaneously, symbolizing the renewal and coming together of all things.

In the first stanza the man waking declares, "My sight is the same as the sun's," and in the fifth he describes his child, who, "mouth open, still sleeping,/ Hears the song in the egg of a bird./ The sun shall have told him that song." The transformation becomes complete in the poem's last three lines ("The sun shall have told you this song,/ For this is the grave of the king;/ For the king's grave turns you to light"): The reader ("you") is also included.

Aside from these two stanzas, Dickey primarily used first person in "Sleeping Out at Easter," as in most of his poems. When the narrator experiences transcendence he enters into a state of unity with nature ("My sight is the same as the sun's"), with the consciousness of the child, and with the reader. The narrator achieves this state without struggle; the tightly controlled, steady, almost monotonous metrics reflect the ease, godlike power, and control over experience that distinctly mark Dickey's first two books.

HELMETS

In *Helmets* Dickey continued to explore the themes of his earlier poetry; nevertheless, *Helmets* is a transitional volume in the Dickey canon. While there are still many short poems relying on radically subjective narrative images—poems that express control and metaphysical certainty—there also appear longer, more diffuse poems that suggest doubt and a reduced sense of control. While some of the poems in *Into the Stone and Other Poems* and *Drowning with Others* draw upon the everyday, the emphasis is (with one or two exceptions such as "A Screened in Porch in the Country") on achieving a "superhuman" transcendent state, and transcendence is always gained. Though there are still plenty of poems of this kind in *Helmets*, in some of the poems—"Cherry Log Road," "The Scarred Girl," "Chenille"—the epiphanies are more modest and more fully human. Other poems—"Springer Mountain" and "Kudzu"—represent a more purely comic vein than his previous work.

"Approaching Prayer," one of Dickey's finest poems, indicates the manner in which the visionary moment and the role of violence began to evolve in Dickey's later work. It begins with the lines "A moment tries to come in/ Through the windows, when one must go/ Beyond what there is in the room." Yet instead of being plunged right into a religious experience as in "Sleeping Out at Easter," the reader witnesses a struggle, as the narrator wanders around uncertain of what he is doing. He must "circle" and go "looking for things" before he can "produce a word" he is not even sure of.

Like an amateur shaman, the narrator begins to dress for a ritual ceremony he has never previously performed, as he accumulates objects that encompass a range of experience and retain contradictory associations. The things he gathers before attempting prayer are all associated with death—the head of a boar he killed, his dead father's sweater and gamecock spurs—but also hold positive value: The hog's head represents the narrator's "best and stillest moment"; the spurs and sweater contain the memory of his father. The spurs and the hog's head are also associated with violence, and the narrator declares that his "best" moment involved violence.

After putting on the objects, through the dead hog's glass eyes the narrator begins to discover another "best and stillest moment" by lining himself up with the stars in the night sky. A vision explodes before him, as "hunting" and being hunted become symbolic of the visionary moment: The narrator must experience the contrary roles. Hunting involves physical action requiring discipline and spontaneity; it also contains a deeply imaginative quality. In playing out their own parts, the predator and the prey each imaginatively enter the other's consciousness. The man must be able to think like the beast, and the beast must try to anticipate the man. When the narrator "draws the breath of life/ For the dead hog," he begins to experience the role of the prey. He is able to see himself through the eyes of the other, and a greater range of knowledge begins to open up before him.

When he views himself from the perspective of the hog, "stiller than trees or stones," the images of himself as hunter, prey, and praying freeze in his mind, shearing away time. As the narrator imagines himself goring a dog and feeling the hair on his (the hog's) back stand up, he also feels the hair that was on his head as a young man stand up. Through this thoroughly original moment, the past and the present, and the perspectives of predator and prey, merge.

As the narrator experiences killing and being killed at the same instant, the universe comes into balance, signaling his acceptance of life and death. This balance consists of stillness and motion—a universe where the "moon and the stars do not move" and where "frantic," violent action takes place. The arrow the narrator uses to kill the hog is characterized as a shaft of light—symbolic of unity and revelation—which connects the hunter and the hog. This culminates in a unity of vision that allows him to maintain his "stillest" moment until something he compares to a shaft of light from an exploding star (suggestive of the arrow that connected hunter and hog) shoots through him, letting him feel his own death. At this point he has participated in the complete gamut of life and death. He has seen his death as a "beast" (through the eyes of the hog) and as an "angel": He has felt the light of the cosmos flare through him. When his death becomes a reality for him, he realizes that the full cycle of life contains death and violence for himself as well as for the "other." Prayer here does not result in discovery of a god who holds out the promise of an immortal soul, but in a vision that holds many dimensions of experience. Only through experiencing the contraries can real prayer be achieved, because only through full knowledge of those contraries can life be fully comprehended.

SPLIT-LINE TECHNIQUE

The greater length and variety of metrical structure of "Approaching Prayer" demonstrate the increased poetical confidence and flexibility Dickey attained with *Helmets*. In subsequent collections, *Buckdancer's Choice; Falling, May Day Sermon, and Other Poems* (first released in *Poems, 1957-1967*); *The Eye-Beaters, Blood, Victory, Madness, Buckhead, and Mercy*, and *The Zodiac*, this trend continued through Dickey's development of the split-line technique, which aims at creating a type of poetic stream of consciousness.

Dickey did not describe the mental processes he depicted through the split line as orderly or logical but in terms suggesting revelation: "fits," "jumps," "shocks," "electric leaps," "word-bursts," "lightning-stamped." He saw "insight" as a matter of instinctual associations that intellectual reasoning disrupts. By breaking up his lines into "clusters of words," Dickey attempted to capture "the characteristics of thought when it associates rapidly, and in detail, in regard to a specific subject, an action, an event, a theme."

"MAY DAY SERMON TO THE WOMEN OF GILMER COUNTY, GEORGIA, BY A WOMAN PREACHER LEAVING THE BAPTIST CHURCH"

"May Day Sermon to the Women of Gilmer County, Georgia, By a Woman Preacher Leaving the Baptist Church" is a good example of Dickey's use of the split line. The woman preacher who narrates the poem speaks in long, sprawling sentences that form hyperbolic and melodramatic masses of language. She tells the story of a religious zealot who, after discovering that his daughter has been sleeping with her boyfriend, drags her naked into the barn, chains her, and whips her while reciting biblical passages. Frenzied and near mad, the woman preacher tells the story through a tidal wave of images from the rural South. Much of the imagery is mixed and contradictory, suggesting the confusion in her own mind and the paradoxical qualities of the relationship between Christian values, especially as embodied in Southern Fundamentalism, and natural sexual drives. Dickey saw the poem as a commentary on "the malevolent power God has under certain circumstances: that is, when He is controlled and 'interpreted' by people of malevolent tendencies."

Dickey expressed this theme by reversing traditional Christian symbols. He describes the female narrator and God in terms of a snake. The "Lord" referred to in the first line gives "men all the help they need/ To drag their daughters into barns," suggesting the brutal, sadistically sexual use of God by some in the Fundamentalist South. The psychosexual nature of the experience is indicated by the father's chaining the girl to the "centerpole," the opening of the barn door to show the "pole of light" that "comes comes," and the "unbending" snake. Sexual associations are also created through the narrator's use of snake imagery to describe God ("Jehovah . . . Down on His belly") and herself ("flickering from my mouth").

Sight, the imagination's ability to see the implications of events in order to find God, becomes the poem's central focus, as it takes on a deeply voyeuristic quality. First, the narrator asserts that the "Lord" watches the "abominations" the girl's father performs, but as the reader moves deeper into the passage it becomes increasingly clear that the vision is the narrator's. Instead of seeing the "abominations" she claims God witnesses, the narrator sees an orgiastic dance, as the animals "stomp" and the girl "prances": The narrator is imaginatively possessed by the scene, not simply relating it for the benefit of her audience.

As the girl is beaten, she fights against her father and "King James" by experiencing a vision of her lover, which is generated through her dance with the animals, giving her the power to transform the beating into a vision of God. Though a vision of the "torsoes of the prophets" begins to form, it quickly "dies out" as the naturalistic forces of "flesh and the Devil twist and turn/ Her body to love." Her God becomes a lover, "the dear heart/ Of life" located in the sexual urge. Like Christ on the cross refusing to recant, she refuses to deny the god she has just discovered, declaring "YOU CAN BEAT ME TO DEATH/ And I'll still be glad." Also like Christ, whose physical suffering on the cross resulted in a heightened state of spiritual awareness, the girl can "change all/ Things for good, by pain." The animals know "they shall be saved . . . as she screams of sin."

Rather than choking off her desires, the father's beating awakens her passion all the more intensely. Indeed, God, her lover, and her father are all conflated. The girl refers to "God-darling" as her "lover" and "angel-stud." Her cry "you're killing" after asking her God and lover to "put it in me" and to "give," like her use of the pronoun "YOU," can be seen as directed to God, the lover and the father. The beating assumes a sadistic sexual dimension for the woman preacher, whose "to hear her say again O again" is both part of her narrative to the congregation and a call for the beating and lovemaking to continue. Physical urges that, from a traditional point of view, are inspired by "flesh and the Devil" cannot be extinguished.

As God is pain and pleasure for the woman preacher, God is also death ("it is true/ That the kudzu advances, its copperheads drunk and tremendous"), birth ("young deer stand half/ In existence, munching cornshucks"), and, above all, sex. The woman preacher rants that the women of the congregation, like the girl, must every spring awaken to "this lovely other life-pain between the thighs." The girl has suffered her father's beating so that other women can "take/ The pain they were born for." This pain is not the sadistic torment the girl endures and transforms, but the pain that "rose through her body straight/ Up from the earth like a plant, like

the process that raised overhead/ The limbs of the un-injured willow." In other words, the woman preacher claims that women must discover God in the natural passionate ache of love and giving birth. This urge springs from the earth and is part of the continuing process of life, leaving the world "uninjured" and intact, unlike the pain the father inflicts with a willow branch torn from a tree.

Yet Dickey portrayed the father's beating as awakening the girl's—and the woman preacher's—sexual passion. Moreover, Dickey's woman preacher proceeds to present a male fantasy of women's perceptions and desires as she glorifies the phallus by demanding that the congregation "understand about men and sheaths." The images she uses to explain herself to the congregation are all of process, movement, "flowing," picturing existence as a constantly evolving cycle, in which male sexuality provides the impetus, "the very juice of resurrection." The poem concludes with the girl murdering her father by driving an icepick between his eyes, releasing all the animals on the farm, and roaring off with her lover on a motorcycle. The girl and her lover follow no man-made road or track but disappear on the "road of mist," which moves through and envelops all nature, and they can be heard returning each spring as a reminder of the primacy of the forces of the flesh. This mythic vision inspires the woman preacher to urge the congregation to leave "God's farm," find their lovers, and go to "Hell"—that is, experience the natural world of physical drives which she believes the Bible condemns.

Though "Sleeping Out at Easter," "Approaching Prayer," and "May Day Sermon" differ radically in style, like many of Dickey's poems they concern people's attempts to gain a greater intimacy with the vital forces of the natural world. Though these particular poems present this endeavor as an affirmative experience, in "The Fiend," the novel *Deliverance*, and other works Dickey portrays this process as menacingly destructive.

PUELLA

With *Puella* and *The Eagle's Mile*, Dickey continued to push the limits of his artistic achievements through even more intrepid experimentation. *Puella*, which is Latin for "young girl," consists of a series of relatively short poems written from the perspective of an adolescent emerging into womanhood. "Doorstep, Lightning,

Waif-Dreaming" typifies this collection through its emphasis on moments of revelatory manifestation and its use of audibly charged language. The poem begins with the line "Who can tell who was born of what?" and proceeds to capture the mystery of creation and self-creation by describing the young woman's thoughts as she watches a thunderstorm unfold from the doorstep of her home. Through acoustically resonant language— "vital, engendering blank/ The interim spraddling crack the crowning rollback/ Whited out *ex nihilo*"—Dickey described the "shifting blasts" of thunder and lightning that culminate in the young woman's realization of the vitality within her ("I come of a root-system of fire") as she beholds her powers of self-sufficiency. In its entirety *Puella* is a resounding celebration of natural processes, independence, and the strength and power of womanhood.

THE EAGLE'S MILE

With *The Eagle's Mile*, Dickey continued to foreground the sounds of poetic language while exploring the self's relationship to nature; however, instead of using narrative as does much of his previous work, these poems are deeply reflective meditations. "Daybreak" describes an individual's thoughts and sensations as he observes the forces of nature while standing on the beach. The narrator realizes that the auroral and tidal processes have no choice but to follow the laws that dictate their patterns, and finds that it is impossible not to think of the human condition while making such observations. While he considers that he has "nothing to say" to the waves, which show no signs of autonomy, he thinks that perhaps by staring into the shallows, which are "shucked of all wave-law," he can discover something about his relationship to the world. He imagines that by doing so he could see his own reflection and the reflection of the clouds and sky merging into one image, suggesting that some force, somewhere, must have conceived of and created a unified design that allows him and the world to exist.

"Daybreak" characterizes *The Eagle's Mile*, and much of Dickey's poetry, in its emphasis on the power of the psyche's imaginative capacities. Though in the past Dickey had shown that such idealism contains potential dangers, the rewards Dickey discovered reflect his belief in the human spirit's insatiable desire to extend itself beyond conventional boundaries, embracing a heightened state of emotional responsiveness and a capacity for glory.

OTHER MAJOR WORKS

PLAYS: *Deliverance*, pr. 1972 (screenplay), pb. 1981; *The Call of the Wild*, pr. 1976 (teleplay, based on the novel by Jack London).

LONG FICTION: *Deliverance*, 1970; *Alnilam*, 1987; *To the White Sea*, 1993.

NONFICTION: *The Suspect in Poetry*, 1964; *Spinning the Crystal Ball*, 1967; *From Babel to Byzantium*, 1968; *Metaphor as Pure Adventure*, 1968; *Self-Interviews*, 1970; *Sorties*, 1971; *The Voiced Connections of James Dickey*, 1989; *Striking In: The Early Notebooks of James Dickey*, 1996; *Crux: The Letters of James Dickey*, 1999.

MISCELLANEOUS: *Night Hurdling: Poems, Essays, Conversations, Commencements, and Afterwords*, 1983; *The James Dickey Reader*, 1999.

CHILDREN'S LITERATURE: *Tucky the Hunter*, 1978.

BIBLIOGRAPHY

Baughman, Ronald. *The Voiced Connections of James Dickey*. Columbia: University of South Carolina Press, 1990. This collection of interviews covers Dickey's career from the mid-1960's to the late 1980's. Baughman, who taught at the University of South Carolina with Dickey, has done a good job of selecting important and lively interviews that touch on practically every major component of Dickey's writing and career. The interviews are edited to avoid unnecessary repetition, and a useful chronology of Dickey's life and a helpful index are included.

Bowers, Neal. *James Dickey: The Poet as Pitchman*. Columbia: University of Missouri Press, 1985. This short study focuses on Dickey as a public figure who was not only a successful poet but also a successful promoter of his work and of poetry in general. Bowers's analysis of individual poems is sometimes thin, and his assessment of Dickey as "pitchman" for poetry is overly simplistic, but the study serves as a good introductory overview of Dickey as a media phenomenon.

Calhoun, Richard J., and Robert W. Hill. *James Dickey.* Boston: Twayne, 1983. The first book-length study of Dickey's work, this study covers his writing from the publication of *Into the Stone and Other Poems* to *Puella*. The authors attempt to analyze virtually everything Dickey wrote during a twenty-two-year period, so that at times the discussions are rather sketchy. Still, this book provides a solid introduction to Dickey, and the index provides easy access to treatment of individual works.

Hart, Henry. *James Dickey: The World As a Lie.* New York: Picador USA, 2000. A narrative biography that details the rise and self-destruction of a literary reputation. Little of Dickey's prose or verse is quoted for analysis, and the book relies on Dickey's interviews and the people around him who were held by the power of his personality.

Kirschten, Robert. *James Dickey and the Gentle Ecstasy of Earth: A Reading of the Poems.* Baton Rouge: Louisiana State University Press, 1988. This study uses R. S. Crane's concept of "multiple working hypotheses" to provide one of the best readings of Dickey's poems yet published. Kirschten employs four hypotheses—mysticism, neoplatonism, romanticism, and primitivism—to identify Dickey's characteristic techniques and thematic concerns. Kirschten's wide range of readings in Romantic poetry, anthropology, and mythology (from classical to American Indian) constitutes a rich context for many finely nuanced close readings. Whenever a poem is analyzed extensively, long sections of it are reprinted, so that the reader can follow the critic's insights.

_____, ed. *Critical Essays on James Dickey.* New York: Maxwell Macmillan International, 1994. A collection of essays including early reviews and selection of more modern scholarship. Authors of reprinted articles and reviews include Robert Bly, Paul Carroll, James Wright, and Wendell Berry. With bibliography and index.

Suarez, Ernest. "Emerson in Vietnam: Dickey, Bly, and the New Left." *Southern Literary Journal* (Spring, 1991): 100-112. Examining controversial elements—especially the use of violence—in Dickey's poems, and the adverse critical reaction to his work, this study demonstrates how the Vietnam War resulted in critics' valuing the didactic over the dialectical and the communal over the individual. Dickey's complex metaphysics collided with the politics of a historic particular, the war, generating a New Left critical agenda that could not accommodate the philosophical underpinnings of his poetry. The result was widespread misinterpretations of Dickey's work.

_____. "The Uncollected Dickey: Pound, New Criticism, and the Narrative Image." *American Poetry* 7 (Fall, 1990): 127-145. This article focuses on a vital phase of Dickey's poetic development that critics have been unaware of or have neglected. By examining Dickey's early uncollected poems and his correspondence with Ezra Pound, the article documents Dickey's struggle to move out from under modernism's domination and arrive at his mature poetic aesthetic, through the development of an image-centered poetry that accommodated his romantic sensibility and his affection for narrative forms.

Weigl, Bruce, and T. R. Hummer, eds. *The Imagination as Glory: The Poetry of James Dickey.* Urbana: University of Illinois Press, 1984. This collection of previously published essays represents the best articles on Dickey up to the early 1980's. Especially noteworthy is Joyce Carol Oates's essay "Out of the Stone and into the Flesh," which argues that Dickey is a relentlessly honest writer who explores human condition in a world of violence and chaos. This book also contains a checklist of secondary sources and two essays by Dickey based on addresses he delivered.

Ernest Suarez

EMILY DICKINSON

Born: Amherst, Massachusetts; December 10, 1830
Died: Amherst, Massachusetts; May 15, 1886

PRINCIPAL POETRY
Poems, 1890
Poems: Second Series, 1891

Poems: Third Series, 1896
The Single Hound, 1914
Further Poems, 1929
Unpublished Poems, 1936
Bolts of Melody, 1945
The Poems of Emily Dickinson, 1955
   (3 volumes; Thomas H. Johnson, editor)
The Complete Poems of Emily Dickinson, 1960
   (Thomas H. Johnson, editor)

OTHER LITERARY FORMS

In addition to her poetry, Emily Dickinson left behind voluminous correspondence. Because she was so rarely out of Amherst—and in her later life so rarely left her house—much of her contact with others took place through letters, many of which include poems. Like her poetry, the letters are witty, epigrammatic, and often enigmatic. They are available in *The Letters of Emily Dickinson* (1958, 3 volumes; Thomas H. Johnson and Theodora Ward, editors).

ACHIEVEMENTS

Reclusive throughout her life, Emily Dickinson garnered little recognition for her poetry during her lifetime, but her legacy to American literature in general and poetic form in particular is an achievement few have surmounted. As surely as William Faulkner and Ernest Hemingway, different as they were, brought American fiction into the twentieth century, so Walt Whitman and Emily Dickinson brought about a revolution in American poetry. By the mid-nineteenth century, American lyric poetry had matured to an evenly polished state. Edgar Allan Poe, Ralph Waldo Emerson, and Herman Melville were creating poetry of both power and precision, but American poetry was still hampered by certain limiting assumptions about the nature of literary language, about the value of regular rhythm, meter, and rhyme, and about imagery as ornamental rather than organic. Were the medium not to become sterile and conventionalized, poets had to expand the possibilities of the form.

Into this situation came Dickinson and Whitman, poets who—except in their commitment to writing a personalized poetry unlike anything the nineteenth century had thus far read—differ as widely as do Faulkner

and Hemingway. Whitman rid himself of the limitations of regular meter entirely. Identifying with the common man, Whitman attempted to make him a hero who could encompass the universe. He was a poet of the open road; Whitman journeyed along, accumulating experience and attempting to unite himself with the world around him. For him, life was dynamic and progressive. Dickinson, however, was the poet of exclusion, of the shut door. She accepted the limitations of rhyme and meter, and worked endless variations on one basic pattern, exploring the nuances that the framework would allow. No democrat, she constructed for herself a set of aristocratic images. No traveler, she stayed at home to examine small fragments of the world she knew. For Dickinson life was kinesthetic; she recorded the impressions of experience on her nerves and on her soul. Rather than being linear and progressive, it was circular: "My business is circumference," she wrote, and she often described the arcs and circles of experience. As carefully as Whitman defined himself by inclusion, Dickinson defined herself and her experience by exclu-

Emily Dickinson (Hulton Archive)

sion, by what she was not. Whitman was a poet of explanation; Dickinson, having rejected expansion, exploited suggestion.

Different as they were, however, they are America's greatest lyric poets. Although Dickinson was barely understood or appreciated in her own lifetime, she now seems a central figure—at once firmly in a tradition and, at the same time, a breaker of tradition, a revolutionary who freed American poetry for modern thought and technique.

BIOGRAPHY

"Renunciation is a piercing virtue," wrote Emily Dickinson, and her life can be seen as a series of renunciations. Born in 1830 of a prominent Amherst family, she rarely left the town, except for time spent in Boston and trips to Washington and Philadelphia. She attended the Amherst Academy and Mount Holyoke Female Seminary. Although she was witty and popular, she set herself apart from the other girls by her refusal to be converted to the conventional Christianity of the town. Her life was marked by a circle of close friends and of family: a stern and humorless father, a mother who suffered a long period of illness and whom Emily took care of; her sister Lavinia, who likewise never married and remained in the family home; and her brother Austin, who married Sue Gilbert Dickinson and whose forceful personality, like that of his wife, affected the family while Emily Dickinson lived, and whose affair with Mabel Todd, the editor of the poems, precipitated family squabbles that affected their publication.

Additionally, there was a series of men—for it almost seems that Dickinson took what she called her "preceptors" one at a time—who formed a sort of emotional resource for her. The first of these was Samuel Bowles, the editor of the neighboring Springfield, Massachusetts, *Republican*, which published some of her poetry. Charles Wadsworth was the minister of a Philadelphia church; a preacher famous for his eloquence, he preached one Sunday when Dickinson was in Philadelphia, and afterward they corresponded for several years. In 1862, however, he and his family moved from Philadelphia to the West Coast. Dickinson immediately sent four of her poems to Thomas Wentworth Higginson, at *The Atlantic Monthly*, for his advice, and they began a

long friendship; although Higginson was never convinced that Dickinson was a finished poet, he was a continuing mentor. Finally, late in life, Dickinson met Judge Otis Lord, and for a time it seemed as if they were to be married; this was her one explicitly romantic friendship, but the marriage never took place. There were also less intense friendships with women, particularly Mabel Todd, who, despite her important role in Dickinson's life, never actually met her, and with the writer Helen Hunt Jackson, one of the few to accept Dickinson's poetry as it was written.

The nature of the relationships with the "preceptors" and their effect on the poetry is a matter of much controversy. It is complicated by three famous and emotional "Master" letters which Dickinson wrote between 1858 and 1862 (the dates are partly conjectural). Who the master was, is uncertain. For Johnson, Dickinson's editor, the great influence was Wadsworth, and although their relationship was always geographically distant, it was he who was the great love, his moving to California the emotional crisis that occasioned the great flood-years of poetry—366 poems in 1862 alone, according to Johnson. For Richard B. Sewall, author of the standard biography, Bowles was the master.

Whatever the case, it is true that after 1862, Dickinson rarely left her house, except for a necessary visit to Boston where she was treated for eye trouble. She wore white dresses and with more and more frequency refused to see visitors, usually remaining upstairs, listening to the conversations and entering, if at all, by calling down the stairs or by sending in poems or other tokens of her participation. She became known as the "Myth of Amherst," and from this image is drawn the popular notion of the eccentric old maid that persists in the imagination of many of her readers today. Yet it is clear that whatever the limits of her actual experience, Dickinson lived life on the emotional level with great intensity. Her poetry is dense with vividly rendered emotions and observations, and she transformed the paucity of her outward life into the richness of her inner life.

Richard Wilbur has suggested that Dickinson suffered three great deprivations in her life: of a lover, of publication and fame, and of a God in whom she could believe. Although she often questioned a world in which such deprivations were necessary, she more frequently compensated, as Wilbur believes, by calling her "privation good, rendering it positive by renunciation." That she lived in a world of distances, solitude, and renunciation her biography makes clear; that she turned that absence into beauty is the testimony of her poetry.

ANALYSIS

During her lifetime, only seven of Emily Dickinson's poems were published, most of them edited to make them more conventional. After Dickinson's death, her sister Lavinia discovered about nine hundred poems, more than half of the nearly 1,775 poems that came to form the Dickinson canon. She took these to a family friend, Mrs. Mabel Loomis Todd, who, with Dickinson's friend Thomas Wentworth Higginson, published 115 of the poems in 1890. Together they published a second group of 166 in 1891, and Mrs. Todd alone edited a third series in 1896. Unfortunately, Mrs. Todd and Colonel Higginson continued the practice of revision that had begun with the first seven published poems, smoothing the rhymes and meter, revising the diction, and generally regularizing the poetry.

In 1914, Emily Dickinson's niece, Martha Dickinson Bianchi, published the first of several volumes of the poetry she was to edit. Although she was more scrupulous about preserving Dickinson's language and intent, several editorial problems persisted, and the body of Dickinson's poetry remained fragmented and often altered. In 1950, the Dickinson literary estate was given to Harvard University, and Thomas H. Johnson began his work of editing, arranging, and presenting the text. In 1955, he produced the variorum edition, 1,775 poems arranged in an attempt at chronological order, given such evidence as handwriting changes and incorporation of the poems in letters, and including all variations of the poems. In 1960, he chose one form of each poem as the final version and published the resulting collection as *The Complete Poems of Emily Dickinson.* Johnson's text and numbering system are accepted as the standard. His job was thorough, diligent, and imaginative. This is not to say, however, that his decisions about dates or choices among variants must be taken as final. Many scholars have other opinions, and since Dickinson herself apparently did not make final choices, there is no reason to accept every decision Johnson made.

Dickinson's poetry is at times sentimental, the extended metaphors occasionally too cute, the riddling tone sometimes too coy. Like any poet, that is, she has limitations; and because her poetry is so consistent throughout her life, those limitations may be more obvious than in a poet who changes more noticeably. They do not, however, diminish her stature. If she found her place in American literature only decades after her death, it is a place she will not forfeit. Her importance is, of course, partly historical: With Whitman she changed the shape and direction of American poetry, creating and fulfilling poetic potentials that make her a poet beyond her century. Her importance, however, is much greater than that. The intensity with which she converted emotional loss and intellectual questioning into art, the wit and energy of her work, mark the body of her poetry as among the finest America has yet produced.

THEMES AND FORM

One of Emily Dickinson's poems (#1129) begins, "Tell all the Truth but tell it slant," and the oblique and often enigmatic rendering of Truth is the dominant theme of Dickinson's poetry. Its motifs often recur: love, death, poetry, beauty, nature, immortality, the self. Such abstractions do not, however, indicate the broad and rich changes that Dickinson obliquely rings on the truths she tells. Dickinson's truth is, in the broadest sense, a religious truth.

Formally, her poetry plays endless variations on the Protestant hymn meters that she knew from her youthful experiences in church. Her reading in contemporary poetry was limited, and the form she knew best was the iambic of hymns: common meter (with its alternating tetrameter and trimeter lines), long meter (four lines of tetrameter), and short meter (four of trimeter) became the framework of her poetry. That static form, however, could not contain the energy of her work, and the rhythms and rhymes are varied, upset, and broken to accommodate the feeling of her lines. The predictable patterns of hymns were not for Dickinson, who delighted in off-rhyme, consonance, and, less frequently, eye-rhyme.

"I LIKE TO SEE IT LAP THE MILES"

Dickinson was a religious poet more than formally, but her thematic sense of religion lies not in her assurance, but in her continual questioning of God, in her attempt to define his nature and that of his world. Although she was always a poet of definition, straightforward definition was too direct for her: "The Riddle we can guess/ We speedily despise," she wrote. Her works often begin, "It was not" or "It was like," with the poem being an oblique attempt to define the "it." "I like to see it lap the Miles" (#585) is a typical Dickinson riddle poem. Like many, it begins with "it," a pronoun without an antecedent, so that the reader must join in the process of discovery and definition. The riddle is based on an extended metaphor; the answer to the riddle, a train, is compared to a horse; but in the poem both tenor (train) and vehicle (horse) are unstated. Meanwhile, what begins with an almost cloying tone, the train as an animal lapping and licking, moves through subtle gradations of attitude until the train stops at the end "docile and omnipotent." This juxtaposition of incongruous adjectives, like the coupling of unlikely adjective and noun, is another of Dickinson's favorite devices; just as the movement of the poem has been from the animal's (and train's) tame friendliness to its assertive power, so these adjectives crystallize the paradox.

"It sifts from Leaden Sieves"

"It sifts from Leaden Sieves" (#311), another riddle poem, also begins with an undefined "it," and again the movement of the poem and its description of the powerfully effacing strength of the snow, which is the subject of the poem and the answer to the riddle, is from apparently innocent beauty through detailed strength to a quietly understated dread. The emotional movement in the famous riddle poem "A Route of Evanescence" (#1463) is less striking, since the poet maintains the same awed appreciation of the hummingbird from beginning to end; but the source of that awe likewise moves from the bird's ephemeral beauty to its power.

"It was not Death, for I stood up"

Riddling becomes less straightforward, but no less central, in such a representative Dickinson poem as "It was not Death, for I stood up" (#510), in which many of her themes and techniques appear. The first third of the poem, two stanzas of the six, suggest what the "it" is not: death, night, frost, or fire. Each is presented in a couplet, but even in those pairs of lines, Dickinson manages to disconcert her reader. It is not death, for the persona is standing upright, the difference between life and death reduced to one of posture. Nor is it night, for the

bells are chiming noon—but Dickinson's image for that fact is also unnatural. The bells are mouths, their clappers tongues, which are "Put out"; personification here does not have the effect of making the bells more human, but of making them grotesque, breaking down as it does the barriers between such normally discrete worlds as the mechanical and the human, a distinction that Dickinson often dissolves. Moreover, the notion of the bells sticking out their tongues suggests their contemptuous attitude toward man. In stanza two, it is not frost because hot winds are crawling on the persona's flesh. The hackneyed phrase is reversed, so it is not coolness, but heat that makes flesh crawl, and not the flesh itself that crawls, but the winds upon it; nor is it fire, for the persona's marble feet "Could keep a Chancel, cool." Again, the persona is dehumanized, now grotesquely marble. While accomplishing this, Dickinson has also begun her inclusion of sense data, pervasive in the first part of the poem, so that the confrontation is not only intellectual and emotional but physical as well.

The second third of the poem changes the proportions. Although the experience is not actually any of the four things she has mentioned above, it is like them all; but now death, the first, is given seven lines, night three, frost only two, and fire is squeezed out altogether. It is like death because she has, after all, seen figures arranged like her own; now her life is "shaven,/ And fitted to a frame." It is like night when everything that "ticked"—again mechanical imagery for a natural phenomenon—has stopped, and like frosts, which in early autumn morns "Repeal the Beating Ground." Her vocabulary startles once more: The ground beats with life, but the frost can void it; "repeal" suggests the law, but nature's laws are here completely nullified.

Finally, in the last stanza, the metaphor shifts completely, and the experience is compared to something new: drowning at sea. It is "stopless" but "cool"; the agony that so often marks Dickinson's poetry may be appropriate to the persona, but nothing around her, neither people nor nature, seems to note it. Most important, there is neither chance nor means of rescue; there is no report of land. Any of these conditions would justify despair, but for the poet, this climatic experience is so chaotic that even despair is not justified, for there is no word of land to despair of reaching.

Thus, one sees many of Dickinson's typical devices at work: the tightly patterned form, based on an undefined subject, the riddle-like puzzle of defining that subject, the shifting of mood from apparent observation to horror, the grotesque images couched in emotionally distant language. All this delineates that experience, that confrontation—with God, with nature, with the self, with one's own mind—which is the center of Dickinson's best poetry. Whether her work looks inward or outward, the subject matter is a confrontation leading to awareness, and part of the terror is that for Dickinson there is never any mediating middle ground; she confronts herself in relation to an abyss beyond. There is no society, no community to make that experience palatable in any but the most grotesque sense of the word, the awful tasting of uncontrollable fear.

"I KNOW THAT HE EXISTS"

Dickinson often questions the nature of the universe; she senses that God is present only in one's awareness of his absence. She shares Robert Frost's notion that God has tricked man, but while for Frost, God's trick is in the nature of creation, for Dickinson it is equally in God's refusal to answer our riddles about that creation. She writes of the "eclipse" of God, and for Dickinson, it is God himself who has caused the obscurity. The customary movement in her explicitly religious poetry is from apparent affirmation to resounding doubt. Poem #338 begins with the line "I know that He exists." While Dickinson rarely uses periods even at the end of her poems, here the first line ends with one: a short and complete affirmation of God's existence, but an affirmation that remains unqualified for only that one line. God is not omnipresent, but exists "Somewhere—in Silence"; Dickinson then offers a justification for God's absence: His life is so fine that he has hidden it from humans who are unworthy. The second stanza offers two more justifications: He is playing with people, and one will be that much happier at the blissful surprise one has earned. Yet the play, in typical Dickinson fashion, is a "fond Ambush," and both the juxtaposition of incongruous words and the reader's understanding that only villains engage in ambush indicate how quickly and how brutally the tone of the poem is changing.

The last half begins with "But," and indeed 256 of Dickinson's poems, nearly fifteen percent, have a coordinate conjunction as the first word of the middle line: a hinge that links the deceptive movement of the first half with the oblique realization that takes place in the second. The lines of poem 338 then become heavily alliterative, slowing the reader with closely linked, plosive *p*'s before she begins the final question: "Should the glee—glaze—/ In Death's—stiff—stare." The quasi subjunctive, another consistent poetic stance in Dickinson, cannot mask the fact that there is no open possibility here, for death must come, the glee will glaze. Then the fun—it is God's fun of which she writes—will look too expensive, the jest will "Have crawled too far!" Although the last sentence is in the form of a question, the poem closes with an end mark stronger than the opening period, an exclamation point which leaves no doubt as to the tone the poem takes.

RELIGIOUS POEMS

This same movement appears in Dickinson's other overtly religious poems. Poem #501 ("This World is not Conclusion") likewise begins with a clear statement followed by a period and then moves rapidly toward doubt. Here God is a "Species" who "stands beyond." Men are shown as baffled by the riddle of the universe, grasping at any "twig of Evidence." Man asks "a Vane, the way," indicating the inconstancy of that on which man relies and punning on "in vain." Whatever answer man receives is only a narcotic, which "cannot still the Tooth/ That nibbles at the soul." Again, in "It's easy to invent a Life" (#724), God seems to be playing with man, and although the poem begins with man's birth as God's invention, it ends with death as God's simply "leaving out a Man." In poem #1601, "Of God we ask one favor," the favor requested is that he forgive man, but it is clear that humans do not know for what they ask forgiveness and, as in Frost's "Forgive, O Lord," it is clear that the greater crime is not man's but God's. In "I never lost as much but twice" (#49), an early but accomplished work, God is "Burglar! Banker—Father!" robbing the poet, making her poor.

One large group of Dickinson's poems, of which these are only a sample, suggests her sense of religious deprivation. Her transformation of the meter and rhythm of hymns into her own songs combines with the overt questioning of the ultimate meaning of her existence to make her work religious. As much, however, as Dickinson pretends to justify the ways of her "eclipsed" God to man, that justification never lasts. If God is Father, he is also Burglar. If God in his omnipotence finds it easy to invent a life, in his caprice he finds it just as easy to leave one out.

"I TASTE A LIQUOR NEVER BREWED" (#214)

Dickinson just as persistently questions nature, which was for her an equivocal manifestation of God's power and whims. Although there are occasional poems in which her experience of nature is exuberant ("I taste a liquor never brewed," for example, #214), in most of her work the experience is one of terror. A synecdochist rather than a Symbolist, she describes and confronts a part of nature, that scene representing the whole. For her nineteenth century opposite, Whitman, the world was one of possibilities, of romantic venturing forth to project oneself onto the world and form an organic relationship with it. For Dickinson, the human and the natural give way to the inorganic; nature is, if like a clock, not so in its perfect design and workings, but in its likeliness to wind down and stop.

"I STARTED EARLY—TOOK MY DOG"

"I started Early—Took my Dog" (#520) is characteristic in its treatment of nature, although uncharacteristic in the romantic venturing forth of the persona. For the first third of the poem, she seems to be in control: She starts early, takes her pet, and visits the sea. The sea is treated with conventional and rather pretty metaphor; it is a house with a basement full of mermaids. Even here, however, is a suggestion that something is amiss: The frigates extend "Hempen Hands"; the ropes that moor the ships are characteristically personified, but the substitution of "hempen" for the similar sounding and expected "helpin'" (the missing *g* itself a delusive familiarity) suggests that the hands will entwine, not aid, the poet. As so often in Dickinson, the natural world seems to be staring at her, as if she is the chief actor in an unfolding drama, and suddenly, with the coordinate conjunction "but," the action begins. The sea is personified as a man who would attack her. She flees. He pursues, reaching higher and higher on her clothes, until finally she achieves the solid ground, and the sea, like a docile and omnipotent train, unconcerned but "Mighty," bows and withdraws, his power there for another day.

"I DREADED THAT FIRST ROBIN, SO"

Whenever Dickinson looks at nature, the moment becomes a confrontation. Although she is superficially within the Puritan tradition of observing nature and reading its message, Dickinson differs not only in the chilling message that she reads, but also because nature refuses to remain passive; it is not simply an open book to be read—for books remain themselves—but active and aggressive; personification suggests its assertive malevolence. In #348 ("I dreaded that first Robin, so"), the initial part of the poem describes the poet's fear: Spring is horrible; it shouts, mangles, and pierces. What Dickinson finally manages is merely a peace with spring; she makes herself "Queen of Calvary," and in deference to that, nature salutes her and leaves her alone.

"A NARROW FELLOW IN THE GRASS"

The same accommodation with nature occurs in #986, "A narrow Fellow in the Grass," where the subject, a snake that she encounters, is first made to seem familiar and harmless. Then the poet suggests that she has made her peace with "Several of Nature's People," and she feels for them "a transport/ Of cordiality," although one expects a more ecstatic noun than cordiality after a sense of transport. Dickinson concludes with a potent description of her true feelings about the snake, "Zero at the Bone," a phrase which well reflects her emotion during most confrontations, internal or external.

"APPARENTLY WITH NO SURPRISE"

One of Dickinson's finest poems, #1624 ("Apparently with no surprise"), a poem from late in her career, unites her attitudes toward nature and God. Even as Frost does in "Design," Dickinson examines one destructive scene in nature and uses it to represent a larger pattern; with Frost, too, she sees two possibilities for both microcosm and macrocosm: accident or dark design. The first two lines of her short poem describe the "happy Flower." The personified flower is unsurprised by its sudden death: "The Frost beheads it at its play—/ In accidental power—/ The blonde Assassin passes on—." In common with many American writers, she reverses the conventional association of white with purity; here the killer, the frost, is blonde. While she suggests that the power may be accidental, in itself not a consoling thought, the two lines framing that assertion severely modify it, for beheading is rarely accidental; nor do assassins attain their power by chance.

Whichever the case, accident or design, there is finally little significant difference, for nothing in the world pays attention to what has happened. "The Sun proceeds unmoved," an unusual pun, since unmoved has the triple meaning of unconcerned, stationary, and without a prime mover; it measures off the time for a God who does approve.

SELF AND SOUL

Thus, when Dickinson turns her vision outward, she looks at essential reality translated, often appallingly, into human terms. The alternative vision for Dickinson is inward, at her own self, and despite the claims of her imperial language, what she sees there is just as chaotic and chilling as what she sees without. "The Soul selects her own Society," she writes (#303), and she makes that society a "divine Majority." "I'm Nobody," another Dickinson poem begins (#288); but in her poetry the explicit movement is from no one to someone, from the self as beggar to the self as monarch: empress or queen. Out of the deprivation of her small society, out of the renunciation of present pleasures, she makes a majority that fills her world with aristocratic presence. Yet, for all that affirmation, the poems that look directly inward suggest something more; her assurance is ambiguously modified, her boasting bravado is dissipated.

MADNESS AND REASON

Occasionally, Dickinson's poetry justifies her internal confusion in conventional terms. Poem #435, "Much Madness is divinest Sense," makes the familiar assertion that, although the common majority have enough power to label nonconformists as insane and dangerous, often what appears as madness is sense, "divinest Sense—/ To a discerning Eye." Usually, however, her poetry of the mind is more unsettling, her understanding more personal. "I Felt a Funeral, in my Brain" (#280) and "'Twas like a Maelstrom, with a notch" (#414), employing the drowning imagery of "It was not Death," are the most piercing of Dickinson's poems about the death of reason, the chaotic confrontation with the instability within. They also indicate the central ambiguity that these poems present, for the metaphor that Dickinson favors for the death of reason is literal, physical death: the tenor,

insanity; the vehicle, death. Yet one is never quite sure whether it might not be the other way around: the central subject death; the metaphoric vehicle, the death of reason. Through this uncertainty, these poems achieve a double-edged vitality, a shifting of idea and vehicle, foreground and background.

The awareness of one's tenuous grasp on his own reason seems clearest in "I felt a Funeral, in my Brain," for there the funeral is explicitly "in," although not necessarily "of," the speaker's brain. The metaphor is developed through a series of comparisons with the funeral rites, each introduced by "and," each arriving with increasing haste. At first the monotony of the mourners' tread almost causes sense to break through, but instead the mind reacts by going numb. Eventually the funeral metaphor gives way to that of a shipwreck—on the surface, an illogical shift, but given the movement of the poem, a continuation of the sense of confusion and abandonment. The last stanza returns to the dominant metaphor, presenting a rapid series of events, the first of which is "a Plank in Reason" breaking, plunging the persona—and the reader—back into the funeral imagery of a coffin dropping into a grave. The poem concludes with "And Finished knowing—then," an ambiguous finish suggesting both the end of her life and of her reasoning, thus fusing the two halves of the metaphor. These two readings of the last line do not exhaust its possibilities, for there is another way to read it: The speaker finished with "knowing" not as a gerund object, but as the participial modifier, so that even at the moment of her death, she dies knowing. Since for Dickinson awareness is the most chilling of experiences, it is an appropriately horrible alternative: not the end of knowing, but the end while knowing.

DEATH

Death is not merely metaphorical for Dickinson; it is the greatest subject of her work. Perhaps her finest lyrics are on this topic, which she surveyed with a style at once laconic and acute, a tone of quiet terror conveyed through understatement and indirection. Her power arises from the tension between her formal and tonal control and the emotional intensity of what she writes. She approaches death from two perspectives, adopts two stances: the persona as the grieving onlooker, attempting to continue with life; her own faith tested by the experience of watching another die; and the persona as the dying person.

In such poems as "How many times these low feet staggered" (#187), where the dead person has "soldered mouth," and "There's been a Death, in the Opposite House" (#389), where the windows of the house open like "a Pod," the description of death is mechanical, as if a machine has simply stopped. The reaction of the onlookers is first bewilderment, then the undertaking of necessary duties, and finally an awful silence in which they are alone with their realization of what has occurred.

"THE LAST NIGHT THAT SHE LIVED"

Poem #1100, "The last Night that She lived," best illustrates all of these attitudes. It oscillates between the quietly dying person—whose death is gentle, on a common night, who "mentioned—and forgot," who "struggled scarce—/ Consented"—and those, equally quiet but less capable of giving consent, who watch the death occur. First there is the conventional idea that they who watch see life differently: Death becomes a great light that italicizes events. Yet as the poem continues with the onlookers' random comings and goings and their feelings of guilt over continuing to live, there is little sense that their awareness is complete.

After the death, Dickinson provides one stanza, neatly summarizing the final understanding: "And We— We placed the Hair," the repeated pronoun, the little gasp for breath and hint of self-dramatization, fills part of the time with what must be done. Then there is nothing left to do or to be said: "And then an awful leisure was/ Belief to regulate." The strange linking of "awful" with "leisure," the disruption of syntax at the line break, and the notion that the best belief can do is regulate leisure, all suggest in two lines the confusion and disruption for those who remain alive.

"BECAUSE I COULD NOT STOP FOR DEATH"

By consensus the greatest of all Dickinson's poems, "Because I could not stop for Death" (#712) explores death from the second perspective, as do such poems as "I Heard a Fly buzz—when I died" (#465) and "I died for Beauty (#449), in which one who has died for beauty and one who has died for truth agree, with John Keats, that truth and beauty are the same—the poet adding the ironic commentary that their equality lies in the fact that the names of both are being covered up by moss.

"Because I could not stop for Death" unites love and death, for death comes to the persona in the form of a gentleman caller. Her reaction is neither haste to meet him, nor displeasure at his arrival. She has time to put away her "labor and . . . leisure"; he is civil. The only hint in the first two stanzas of what is really occurring is the presence of Immortality, and yet that presence, although not unnoticed, is as yet unfelt by the persona. The third stanza brings the customary metaphor of life as a journey and the convention of one's life passing before his eyes as he dies: from youth, through maturity, to sunset. Here, however, two of the images work against the surface calm: The children out for recess do not play, but strive; the grain is said to be gazing. "Grazing" might be the expected word, although even that would be somewhat out of place, but "gazing" both creates unfulfilled aural expectations and gives the sense of the persona as only one actor in a drama that many are watching.

Again, as is common in Dickinson, the poem is hinged by a coordinate conjunction in the exact middle. This time the conjunction is "Or," as the speaker realizes not that she is passing the sun, but that "He passed us." The metaphoric journey through life continues; it is now night, but the emotions have changed from the calm of control to fright. The speaker's "Zero at the Bone" is literal, for her clothing, frilly and light, while appropriate for a wedding, is not so for the funeral that is occurring. The final stop—for, like the first two stanzas, the last two are motionless—is before the grave, "a House that seemed/ A Swelling of the Ground." The swelling ground also suggests pregnancy, but this earth bears death, not life. The last stanza comments that even though the persona has been dead for centuries, all that time seems shorter than the one moment of realization of where her journey must ultimately end. Death, Dickinson's essential metaphor and subject, is seen in terms of a moment of confrontation. Absence thus becomes the major presence, confusion the major ordering principle.

OTHER MAJOR WORKS

NONFICTION: *Letters*, 1894 (2 volumes); *The Letters of Emily Dickinson*, 1958 (3 volumes; Thomas H. Johnson and Theodora Ward, editors).

BIBLIOGRAPHY

Boruch, Marianne. "Dickinson Descending." *The Georgia Review* 40 (1986): 863-877. Boruch, a gifted writer and poet, pays tribute to Dickinson in this lively, conversational discussion. She criticizes the parasitic "cottage industry" that feeds off speculative details of Dickinson's life and praises and explains Dickinson's heavy use of dashes. Includes a good explication of "I Heard A Fly Buzz" and notes to other criticism throughout. Contagious interests and excellent writing.

Carruth, Hayden. "Emily Dickinson's Unexpectedness." *Ironwood* 14 (1986): 51-57. This essay, one of seven in a special Dickinson issue, declares Dickinson's significance in Western literature and urges readers to read her as a poet, without constant reference to useless biographical information. Carruth explains four poems with great skill and sincerity, without overusing intellectual jargon.

Dickenson, Donna. *Emily Dickinson.* Oxford, England: Berg, 1985. A well-researched and accessible literary biography meant to fill the gap between the detailed scholarly criticism and the outdated popular image of Dickinson as the lovelorn recluse. The author does not try to make the poet's life explain her poetry, nor does she stretch the poetry to fit the life. The notes after each chapter indicate useful avenues for further study.

Eberwein, Jane Donahue. *An Emily Dickinson Encyclopedia.* Westport, Conn.: Greenwood Press, 1998. Edited by a founding board member of the Emily Dickinson International Society as well as a professor of English and a past committee member of the Modern Language Association's Division on American Literature to 1880. Covers a wide range of topics, from people important in Dickinson's life to her stylistic traits.

Ferlazzo, Paul, ed. *Critical Essays on Emily Dickinson.* Boston: G. K. Hall, 1984. This collection, edited and introduced by a leading Dickinson scholar, contains thirty-two essays that range in publication date from 1890 (Thomas Wentworth Higginson's "Preface to *Poems* by Emily Dickinson") to 1984. Includes a solid gathering of writings by well-known critics, Dickinson scholars, and both nineteenth century and contemporary fellow poets. A brief, comprehensive, and well-documented survey, with two essays written especially for the collection.

Grabher, Gudrun, Roland Hagenbüchle, and Cristanne Miller, ed. *The Emily Dickinson Handbook.* Amherst: University of Massachusetts Press, 1998. A collection of up-to-date essays covering Dickinson's poetry, poetics, and life. Useful reference with extensive bibliography.

Juhasz, Suzanne, ed. *Feminist Critics Read Emily Dickinson.* Bloomington: Indiana University Press, 1983. The title essay is a twenty-page introduction by the editor who explains how feminist criticism can correct some partial or "false" criticism that has always split Dickinson into "woman" and "poet"—elements that should go together. The feminist perspective is based on the assumption that gender informs the nature of art. Supplemented by a bibliography.

MacNeil, Helen. *Emily Dickinson.* New York: Pantheon Books, 1986. In this short critical biography intended for the general reader, as well as the student or specialist, the author reveals how strongly Dickinson distinguished between oral expression, which is restrained by convention, and written self-expression. Includes a bibliography, an index, and eight pages of plates.

Robinson, John. *Emily Dickinson: Looking to Canaan.* Winchester, Mass.: Faber & Faber, 1986. Accurate facts, deft insights, and a readable prose style make this volume of the Faber Student Guide series a useful introduction. Robinson reveals a Dickinson who sought to escape from history and time and whose work was satiric, yet defined by Protestant ethics.

Howard Faulkner;
bibliography updated by the editors

DIANE DI PRIMA

Born: Brooklyn, New York; August 6, 1934

PRINCIPAL POETRY

This Kind of Bird Flies Backward, 1958
Dinners and Nightmares, 1961, enlarged 1974, 1998
　(stories, poetry, prose)

The New Handbook of Heaven, 1963
Hotel Albert: Poems, 1968
Earthsong: Poems, 1957-1959, 1968
Revolutionary Letters, Etc., 1968
Freddie Poems, 1974
Selected Poems, 1956-1975, 1975
Loba, Parts I-VIII, 1978
Pieces of a Song: Selected Poems, 1990
Loba, 1998

OTHER LITERARY FORMS

With more than thirty-five published volumes of poetry, Diane di Prima is one of the most prolific contemporary American poets. While she is best known for her poetry, she has also written and produced a substantial number of plays. She is the author of two prose memoirs, the highly erotic novel-memoir *Memoirs of a Beatnik* (1969), which contributed significantly to making her the most widely known woman poet of the Beat generation, and *Recollections of My Life as a Woman: The New York Years, a Memoir* (2001), a remembrance of her growing feminist consciousness in the 1950's and 1960's. Di Prima has also translated poems from Latin and has written several treatises on Paracelsus, the famous sixteenth century alchemist and physician. She has expressed her opinions on poetics, politics, feminism, and the Beat generation in numerous interviews, many of them easily accessible on the World Wide Web.

ACHIEVEMENTS

Diane di Prima has received grants from the National Endowment for the Arts, in 1973 and 1979, and an honorary degree from St. Lawrence University in 1999. As a female member of the Beat generation, she has had to labor under the stereotype of "Beat chick," characterized by Jack Kerouac as girls "who say nothing and wear black." The last decades of the twentieth century brought a gradual revision of this stereotype and greater public recognition for her work. Although her poems have received little academic or critical attention, they have attracted a growing number of devoted readers.

George F. Butterick has argued that di Prima's greatest contribution to the poetry of her generation lies in her work as an organizer and editor/publisher, beginning with her collaboration in *The Floating Bear*, a monthly publication she published together with LeRoi Jones (Amiri Baraka) in 1961 and for which she served as editor until 1969. Also in the 1960's, she founded Poets Press, which published some thirty books of poetry and prose of such well-known figures as Herbert Huncke and Timothy Leary, as well as the anti-Vietnam War anthology *War Poems* (1968), edited by di Prima herself.

Even though di Prima has often been described as a minor constellation next to stars of the Beat generation like Jack Kerouac, Allen Ginsberg, William Burroughs, and Gregory Corso, her mature work since the 1970's deserves critical attention. She is an an important catalyst and chronicler of the bohemian counterculture of her generation.

BIOGRAPHY

Diane di Prima was born in Brooklyn, New York, to first-generation Italian immigrant parents. In interviews and in her autobiographical writings she emphasizes the strict, conservative upbringing to which a young girl of Italian ancestry was subjected during the 1930's, the years of the Great Depression. She credits her anarchist grandfather with sowing the seeds for her subsequent rebellion against this confinement by taking her to anarchist rallies and reading the works of Dante to her. At the age of fourteen she had already decided to become a poet. She enrolled at Swarthmore College in 1951, however, intending to major in theoretical physics. In 1953 she abandoned her academic career and moved to New York's lower East Side, beginning her bohemian life as a poet and activist. During this time she met Ezra Pound, who had been institutionalized at Saint Elizabeths, a mental hospital in Washington, D.C., where she visited him several times. Pound found encouraging words for her fledgling attempts at poetry, and the two corresponded for some time.

A decisive factor in di Prima's career was her introduction to the founding members of the Beat generation in 1957, a group with whom she remained closely connected for the next decade. Indeed, di Prima is considered the most important female writer of the Beat generation and features prominently in every anthology of that group. In 1958, LeRoi Jones (who later changed his name to Amiri Baraka) published her first collection of poetry, *This Kind of Bird Flies Backward*, the first in a list of more than forty works of poetry, prose, and drama.

During her years in Manhattan, she published and edited several poetry magazines and newsletters and helped found the New York Poets Theatre in 1961. She was married and divorced twice, eventually raising five children as a single mother—a life strongly reflected in her poetry. In 1965, she moved to upstate New York and participated in Timothy Leary's psychedelic community at Millbrook. At other times she traversed the continent in a Volkswagen bus, in the style of the male Beat writers and the Merry Pranksters, reading her poetry in churches, prisons, and schools.

In 1969 di Prima moved to the West Coast, a more hospitable place for female writers, and became involved with The Diggers, a radical political group of street actors. The move to the West Coast signals the beginning of a gradual move away from the radical social-political emphasis of the Beat writers and toward a more contemplative life, including the study of Zen Buddhism, alchemy, and Sanskrit.

In the 1980's she taught courses in the hermetic and esoteric traditions in poetry at the New College of California and at the Naropa Institute in Boulder, Colorado. She is the cofounder of the San Francisco Institute of Magical and Healing Arts, where she also teaches. Since the 1970's, she has worked on *Loba*, a long, visionary serial poem, published in expanded and revised form by Penguin in 1998.

The deaths of most of the male celebrities of the Beat generation led to a renewed interest in the women associated with this movement, resulting in a substantial number of autobiographies and memoirs, including di Prima's *Recollections of My Life as a Woman*, which candidly chronicles her involvement with the Beat movement in the 1950's and 1960's, as well as her growing self-confidence and autonomy as a woman poet determined to shed the groupie label of "Beat chick."

ANALYSIS

Diane di Prima's poetry falls into two clearly distinguished chronological and thematic categories. Her works from 1957 to 1975 are suffused with the idiom of

the Beat generation, the language of personal rebellion of the hipster. Di Prima considers her association with the poets of the Beat generation and the San Francisco Renaissance as seminal for her work, as she explained in an interview:

> Don't forget, however great your visioning and your inspiration, you need the techniques of the craft and there's nowhere, really to get them . . . they are passed on person to person and back then the male naturally passed them to the male. I think maybe I was one of the first women to break through that in having deep conversations with Charles Olson and Frank O'Hara.

Further evidence of this mentoring process can be seen in the fact that LeRoi Jones (Amiri Baraka) and his Totem Press published her first, slender collection, *This Kind of Bird Flies Backward*, and Lawrence Ferlinghetti wrote a brief "non-introduction by way of an introduction" for it. The volume is full of Beat terminology, such as "hip," "cool," and "crazy." While she saw herself, as most of the female Beat writers, inhibited by the "eternal, tiresome rule of Cool," she also acknowledges that Ginsberg taught her to have confidence in her own spontaneity, as well as emphasizing the importance of technical writing skills. The best view of this phase of di Prima's work can be found in her collection *Selected Poems, 1956-1975*, which extracts her favorite poems from *This Kind of Bird Flies Backward* to *Freddie Poems*.

The second part of her work covers the period after she permanently moved to Northern California in 1970. It is characterized by a less strident tone, a fading out of the Beat vocabulary, and a growing concern with spiritual and ecological matters, particularly her increasing involvement in Buddhism and her role as a woman and mother. Much of this changing perspective can be found in her collection *Pieces of a Song*; however, the long serial poem *Loba*, begun in 1971 and published in an expanded version in 1998, is considered by many commentators the most typical work of di Prima's mature creative period.

DINNERS AND NIGHTMARES

Di Prima's second collection of poems is dedicated to her "pads & the people who shared them with me." The first part consists of descriptions of meals she has shared with a variety of people in the bohemian milieu of New York, and there is good reason to believe that most of these sketches are in fact based on real people and events. The second part is a collection of poetic "nightmares," dark centerpieces to the more pleasant dinners of the first section. The nightmares deal with the squalid living conditions on the lower East Side, with thwarted or hopeless love affairs, or with standing in unemployment lines:

> Then I was standing in line unemployment green
>   institution green room
> green people slow shuffle. Then to the man ahead said
>   clerk-behind-desk,
> folding papers bored and sticking on seals
> Here are your twenty reasons for living sir.

Some of the "nightmares" are expressed in imagistic one-liners: "It hurts to be murdered" or "Get your cut throat off my knife."

The collection concludes with a section called "More or Less Love Poems," terse vignettes of love in the hipster pads, where "coolness" thinly disguises anguish and fear of loneliness:

> Yeah that was
> once in a lifetime
> baby
>
> you gotta be clean and
> with new shoes
> to love like I love you.
>
> I think it won't happen again.

Or even more pithily:

> You are not quite
> the air I breathe
> thank God.
>
> so go.

It is possible to see rebellion and defiance in these lines, an obstinate insistence on living life on her own terms, but while there is little self-pity (that would not have been "cool"), it is impossible to overlook the feeling of anguish and isolation.

EARTHSONG

This collection, which first appeared in 1968 and was enlarged for the 1974 version, was edited by di

Prima's then-husband Alan Marlowe and published by their Poets Press. In the introduction, Marlowe writes that "these poems contain the hard line of the fifties, and the smell of New York winters, cold and grey, as well as Miles Davis' jazz and the search for new forms." Di Prima reveals her extensive classical reading in a light-hearted Beat parody of Elizabethan poet/dramatist Christopher Marlowe's pastoral "The Passionate Shepherd to His Love" (1599), which she turns into "The Passionate Hipster to His Chick." The collection also includes probably her best-known and most frequently anthologized poem. Untitled in *Earthsong*, the poem appears in her *Selected Poems, 1956-1975* as "The Practice of Magical Evocation" and is a strident response to Gary Snyder's chauvinist 1958 poem "In Praise of Sick Women." In that poem, Snyder characterizes women as fertile and only confused by discipline. Di Prima's response is an unashamed acceptance of her femininity ("I am a woman and my poems/ are woman's: easy to say/ this"). She converts "fertile" into "ductile," emphasizing a woman's adaptability and strength in the face of male demands and expectations ("bring forth male children only"). Her final question, "what applause?" is rhetorical, indicating that women can expect no reward or even acknowledgment for their efforts. In her 2001 memoir *Recollections of My Life as a Woman*, di Prima sets the record straight when she writes:

> Disappointment or loss marked the men of that world. And silence; one simply didn't talk about it. Disappointment and silence marked the women too. But there the silence lay deeper. No tales were told about them. They did not turn from one career to another, "take up the law," but buried the work of their hearts in the basement, burned their poems and stories, lost the thread of their dreams.

LOBA

Di Prima began working on this long serial poem before 1973, when Part 1 of *Loba* first appeared in the Capra Chapbooks series. Expanded over the next decades, book 1 (parts 1-8) was published in 1978, and in 1998 Penguin published a full, though probably not final, version. The poem is characteristic of di Prima's post-Beat poetry: It is an attempt to emulate the mythical wanderings of the *Cantos* of her first mentor, Ezra Pound. The title is a reference to the figure of the she-wolf (the Spanish *loba*), the symbol of fierce maternal love in many cultures and particularly in Native American lore. *Loba* is a long journey of exploration of the feminine consciousness, beginning in primeval myths and archetypes.

Book 1 concentrates on matters of the flesh, while book 2 focuses on the soul. Di Prima has indicated that a yet-to-be-written book 3 would concern itself with the spirit. The work exhibits the poet's vast literary background, with allusions to Iseult, Persephone, and Lilith, all contained in a loosely joined series of philosophical, humorous, and lyrical poems. In one section di Prima invokes Ginsberg's "Howl" (1956) when she writes, "who walked across America behind gaunt violent yogis/ & died o-d'ing in methadone jail/ scarfing the evidence."

Loba is a difficult poem and should not be read with the intent of finding and recognizing all the references to literary characters and myths. The she-wolf is di Prima's fundamental female hero, whose mythical wanderings allow her to touch on all her favorite poetic subjects— politics, religion, eros, and ecology—and to display her great versatility in manipulating a wide variety of poetic forms and themes.

Di Prima's poetry has been criticized as uneven and sometimes obscure. There can be no doubt, however, that most of her poems, particularly of the early period, are accessible to the average reader and live up to the definition of poetry and the role of the poet she expressed in a 1978 interview:

> . . . the poet is the last person who is still speaking the truth when no one else dares to. . . . Pound once said, "Artists are the antennae of the race." . . . And we see very dramatically in our time how . . . the work of Allen [Ginsberg] and Kerouac in the '50's and so on has informed the '70's.

One can in good conscience add di Prima's name to that list.

OTHER MAJOR WORKS

LONG FICTION: *Memoirs of a Beatnik*, 1969, revised 1988; *The Calculus of Variation*, 1972.

PLAYS: *Paideuma*, pr. 1960; *The Discontent of a Russian Prince*, pr. 1961; *Murder Cake*, pr. 1963; *Like*, pr. 1964; *Poet's Vaudeville*, pr. 1964 (libretto); *Monuments*, pr. 1968; *The Discovery of America*, pr. 1972; *Whale Honey*, pr. 1975; *ZipCode: The Collected Plays of Diane di Prima*, pb. 1992.

NONFICTION: "Light / and Keats," in *Talking Poetics from Naropa Institute I*, 1978; "Paracelsus: An Appreciation," in *Alchemy: Pre-Egyptian Legacy, Millennial Promise*, 1979; *Recollections of My Life as a Woman: The New York Years, a Memoir*, 2001.

EDITED TEXT: *War Poems*, 1968.

BIBLIOGRAPHY

Blain, Virginia. "Diane di Prima." In *The Feminist Companion to Literature in English*. New Haven, Conn.: Yale University Press, 1990. The short essay discusses di Prima's work as a contribution to feminist literature.

Gibson, Sharon Slaton. *Diane di Prima: Beat, Hippie, and Feminist*. Master's thesis, University of Louisville. Ann Arbor, Mich.: University Microfilms International, 1984. A rare monograph-length work on di Prima. Includes bibliography.

Meltzer, David, ed. *San Francisco Beat: Talking with the Poets*. San Francisco, Calif.: City Lights, 2001. A volume of interviews with such Beats and associated poets as Gary Snyder and Philip Whalen, still working, in an effort to determine the true legacy of the Beats. Included are contributions by di Prima and Joanne Kyger.

Peabody, Richard, ed. *A Different Beat: Writing by Women of the Beat Generation*. In this anthology of writings by the women of the Beat generation, di Prima is set in context. Firsthand accounts of these women's experiences include those by Jan Kerouac, Joyce Johnson, Hettie Jones, di Prima, and others, who attest to the decidedly sexist times. An introduction provides an overview of the social and cultural background.

Reynolds, Persephone. *The Trickster as Facilitator: Contemporary American Women's Poetry*. Ph.D. thesis, Indiana University of Pennsylvania. Ann Arbor, Mich.: University Microfilms International, 1997. Includes a chapter on di Prima.

Waldman, Anne. "An Interview with Diane di Prima." In *The Beat Road*, edited by Arthur Knight and Kit Knight. [California, Pa.]: A. Knight, 1984. Waldman, herself a second-generation member of the Beat generation, talks with the poet about her early years in New York and about the specific problems of a woman writer of that period.

Franz G. Blaha

JOHN DONNE

Born: London, England; between January 24 and June 19, 1572
Died: London, England; March 31, 1631

PRINCIPAL POETRY

An Anatomy of the World: The First Anniversary, 1611
Of the Progress of the Soule: The Second Anniversary, 1612
Poems, by J. D.: With Elegies on the Authors Death, 1633, 1635, 1639, 1649, 1650, 1654, 1669

OTHER LITERARY FORMS

Although John Donne is known chiefly as a lyric poet, the posthumous volume *Poems, by J.D.*, which includes the lyrics, represents only a small part of his literary output. Donne was famous in his own age mainly as a preacher; in fact, he was probably the most popular preacher of an age when preaching held the same fascination for the general public that the cinema has today. Various sermons of Donne's were published during his lifetime, and several collections were published in the following decades. Without a commitment to Donne's religious values, few today would want to read through many of his sermons—grand as their style is. Donne must, however, be credited with the careful articulation of the parts of his sermons, which create a resounding unity of theme; and his control of prose rhythm and his ingenious imagery retain their power, even if modern readers are no longer disposed to see the majesty of God mirrored in such writing.

John Donne (Library of Congress)

Excerpts from Donne's sermons thus have a continuing vitality for general readers in a way that excerpts from the sermons of, for example, Lancelot Andrewes cannot. In the early seventeenth century, Andrewes had been the most popular preacher before Donne, and, as Bishop of Winchester, he held a more important position. He also had a greater reputation as a stylist, but for modern readers, Andrewes carries to an extreme the baroque fashion of "crumbling a text" (analyzing in minute detail). The sermons of Andrewes are now unreadable without special training in theology and classical languages. On the other hand, though also writing for an educated audience with a serious interest in divinity, Donne wears his scholarship more easily and can still be read by the general student without special preparation. His sermon to the Virginia Company is the first sermon in English to make a missionary appeal.

The single most famous of Donne's sermons was his last. *Death's Duell* (1632), preached before King Charles on February 25, 1631, is a profound meditation on mortality. Man's mortality is always a major theme with Donne, but here he reaches a new eloquence. Full of startling imagery, the sermon takes as its theme the paradox that life is death and death is life—although Christ's death delivers humankind from death. When this last sermon of Donne's was published, Henry King, Bishop of Chichester, remarked that "as he exceeded others at first so at last he exceeded himself."

A work of similar theme but published by Donne in his own lifetime is the *Devotions upon Emergent Occasions* (1624). Composed, as R. C. Bald has shown, with extreme rapidity during a serious illness and convalescence in 1623, this work is based on the structured meditational technique of St. Francis de Sales, involving the sensuous evocation of scenes, although, as Thomas F. Van Laan has suggested, the work is perhaps also influenced by the *Spiritual Exercises* (1548) of St. Ignatius Loyola. It is divided into twenty-three sections, each consisting of a meditation, an expostulation, and a prayer. The work is an artfully constructed whole of sustained emotional power, but the meditations have achieved a special fame with their vivid evocations of the theme that sickness brings man closer to God by putting him in touch with his frailty and mortality. Various meditations from the *Devotions upon Emergent Occasions* present famous pictures of the tolling of the death knell, of the body as a microcosm, and of the curious medical practices of the day, for example, the application of live pigeons to Donne's feet to try to draw the vapors of fever from his head. By this last practice, Donne discovers that he is his own executioner since the vapors are believed to be the consequence of his melancholy, and this is no more than the studiousness required of him by his calling as a preacher. While in past centuries most readers found the work's self-consciousness and introspection alienating, the contemporary sensibility finds these characteristics especially congenial. The three meditations on the tolling of the bells have, in particular, provided titles and catchphrases for popular writers.

A posthumously published early study of mortality by Donne is *Essayes in Divinity* (1651). The *Essayes in Divinity*, written in a knotty, baroque style, is a collection of curiously impersonal considerations of the Creation and of the deliverance of the Israelites from bondage in Egypt. The work shows none of the fire of the sermons and of the *Devotions upon Emergent Occa-*

sions. A very different sort of contemplation of mortality is provided in *Biathanatos* (1646). The casuistical reasoning perhaps shows evidence of Donne's Jesuit background. The same approach to logic and a similar iconoclasm are apparent in *Juvenilia: Or, Certaine Paradoxes and Problems* (1633; the first complete version was, however, not published until 1923).

The earliest of Donne's publications were two works of religious controversy of a more serious nature. These works also show Donne's Jesuit background, but in them, he is reacting against his upbringing and presenting a case for Anglican moderation in the face of Roman Catholic—and especially Jesuit—pretensions. *Pseudo-Martyr* (1610) was written at the explicit request of King James, according to Donne's first biographer, Izaak Walton. Here and throughout his subsequent career, Donne is a strongly committed Erastian, seeing the Church as properly subordinate in this world to secular authority.

The other of these early works of controversy, *Ignatius His Conclave* (1611), which appeared in Latin as well as English, is still amusing to modern readers who are unlikely to come to it with quite the strong partisan feeling of its original audience.

ACHIEVEMENTS

John Donne was a remarkably influential poet in his day. Despite the fact that it was only after his death that a substantial body of his poetry was published, the elegies and satires (and to a lesser extent the divine poems and the songs and sonnets) had already created a new poetic mode during Donne's lifetime as a result of circulating in manuscript. Thomas Carew, in a memorial elegy published in the first edition of Donne's poems, described him as ruling the "universal monarchy of wit." The poetry of the School of Donne was usually characterized in its own day by its "strong lines." This characterization seems to have meant that Donne and his followers were to be distinguished from the Sons of Ben, the poets influenced by Ben Jonson, chiefly by their experiments with rough meter and conversational syntax; Jonson, however, was also—somewhat confusingly—praised for strong lines. Donne's own characteristic metrics involve lines densely packed with syllables. He makes great use not only of syncope (dropping of an unstressed vowel within a word) and elision (dropping of an unstressed vowel at the juncture between words) but also of a device almost unique to Donne among English poets—synaloepha (speeding up of adjacent vowels at the juncture between words with no actual dropping). By hindsight Donne, Edward Lord Herbert of Cherbury, Henry King, George Herbert, John Cleveland, Richard Crashaw, Abraham Cowley, Henry Vaughan, Andrew Marvell, and others of the School of Donne share not only strong lines but also a common fund of imagery. Eschewing for the most part classical allusions, these poets turned to the imagery of everyday life and of the new learning in science and philosophy.

In the middle of the seventeenth century there occurred what T. S. Eliot has memorably described as a "dissociation of sensibility," after which it became increasingly difficult to see Donne's secular and religious values as part of a consistent whole. The beginnings of this attitude were already apparent in Donne's own day; in a letter, for example, he describes *Biathanatos* as the work not of Dr. Donne but of the youthful Jack Donne. Toward the end of the century, the change of perspective is complete when John Dryden describes Donne unsympathetically as one who "perplexes the Minds of the Fair Sex with nice Speculations of philosophy." The Restoration and the eighteenth century had lost Donne's sense of religious commitment and thus scrutinized a style in isolation from the content it intended to express. Donne's poetry was condemned as artificial, and his reputation disappeared almost overnight.

This was the situation when Samuel Johnson wrote the famous strictures on Donne in his "Life of Cowley." That these remarks occur in the *Life of Cowley* is perhaps a commentary on the fallen stature of the earlier poets: Donne did not himself merit individual treatment in *Lives of the Poets* (1779-1781). Conceding that to write like Donne "it was at least necessary to read and think," Johnson describes the wit of the School of Donne—accurately enough—as the "discovery of occult resemblances in things apparently unlike." While many readers of the earlier seventeenth century and of the twentieth century would consider the description high praise, for Johnson it was a condemnation. For him, the "most heterogeneous ideas are yoked by violence together." He popularized the term "Metaphysical poetry"

for this yoking; the term had, however, been used earlier, even in Donne's own day.

Donne's stature and influence today are equal to his great stature and wide influence in the seventeenth century, but the attitude represented by Johnson remained the norm for the centuries between. Donne's current prestige is based on values different from those that accounted for his prestige in his own day. The seventeenth century took its religion seriously but understood religion as part of the whole fabric of life. Donne's stature as a preacher was for this reason part of his prestige as a poet. In addition, the fact that he wrote love poetry and sometimes used graphic erotic imagery did not in his own day seem incongruous with his calling as a preacher.

The twentieth century did not, of course, recover the intense religiosity of the early seventeenth century, but what T. S. Eliot, Ezra Pound, and other poets of their circle had discovered in the 1920's was an aestheticism as intense as this religiosity. Their values naturally led them to praise lyric poetry in preference to epic and to prize intensity of emotion in literary work of all kinds. They disparaged the poetry of John Milton because it was an expression of ideas rather than of feeling and offered Donne as a model and a more appropriate great author for the period. The restoration of Donne's prestige was remarkably complete; but, paradoxically, precisely because the triumph of Donne was so complete, the denigration of Milton never quite occurred. The values that Eliot and others praised in Donne were looked for—and discovered—in Milton as well.

Although Donne was perhaps a more exciting figure during his mid-twentieth century "rediscovery" than he is today, because to appreciate him meant to throw over the eighteenth and nineteenth century allegiance to Milton as the great poet of the language, Donne's stature as a major figure is now assured. Contemporary scholarly opinion has, however, been moving inevitably toward seeing the divine poems as the capstone of his career. Scholarly opinion has, in fact, moved beyond Eliot's position and come to value literary works simply because they have religious content, since intensity of feeling will surely be found in a poetry of religious commitment. This is not a way of appreciating Donne and the Metaphysicals that would have been understood in the seventeenth century.

BIOGRAPHY

Born in St. Nicholas Olave Parish, London, sometime between January 24 and June 19, 1572, John Donne came from a Welsh paternal line (originally Dwn) with some claim to gentility. His father, however, was an ironmonger, although important enough to serve as warden of his professional guild. On his mother's side, Donne's connections were distinguished for both their intellectual attainments and their recusancy—that is, allegiance to the Church of Rome in the face of the Elizabethan Church Settlement. Donne's maternal grandfather was the epigrammatist and playwright John Heywood. A great-grandfather, John Rastell, was a minor playwright. Two of Donne's uncles were Jesuits who died in exile for their faith, as did his great-uncle Judge William Rastell; and another great-uncle, the monk Thomas Heywood, was executed, having been caught saying mass. Finally, a great-grandmother was the sister of Sir Thomas More, whose skull Donne inherited and very characteristically kept as a *memento mori*. Donne's brother, Henry, died in prison, where he had been sent for harboring a seminary priest; and Donne justifiably said in *Pseudo-Martyr* that no family had suffered more for the Roman Church.

His father died while Donne was still in infancy. His mother married twice more. The stepfather of Donne's youth was a prominent physician. At first educated at home by Roman Catholic tutors, in 1584, Donne and his younger brother, Henry, were admitted to Hart Hall, Oxford. While they were a precocious twelve and eleven at the time, they were entered in the register as even younger in order to circumvent the requirement that students of sixteen and over subscribe to the Oath of Supremacy. Donne spent probably three years at Oxford altogether.

Although records are lacking for the next period of Donne's life, one hypothesis is that he spent some of this time in travel abroad. With his brother, Donne eventually took up residence at the Inns of Court to prepare for a legal career. Unsettled in these career plans by the arrest and death of Henry, Donne began serious study of the relative claims of the Anglican and Roman Churches and finally abandoned the study of law entirely.

In 1596, he participated in the earl of Essex's military expedition to Cadiz. Donne's affability and his growing reputation as a poet—sustained by the private circulation of some of his elegies and lyrics—recommended him to a son of Sir Thomas Egerton who had also participated in the sack of Cadiz, and Egerton, who was Lord Keeper, was persuaded to appoint Donne as his secretary. In this position and also in Parliament, where he served briefly in 1601, he had many opportunities to meet people of note, and he improved his reputation as a poet by composing satires and occasional poems as well as additional lyrics.

In 1601, Donne was already in his late twenties, and, during Christmastide, he contracted a secret marriage with Anne More, the sixteen-year-old niece of Lady Egerton. Since the marriage was contrary to her father's wishes, Donne was imprisoned for his offense; he also permanently lost his position as Egerton's secretary, and the couple were forced to live for several years on the charity of friends and relations. A comment made at the time, sometimes attributed to Donne himself, was, "John Donne, Anne Donne, Undone."

Although his career hopes had been dashed by the impetuous marriage, his winning personality and poetic skill won for him new friends in high places. He traveled abroad with Sir Walter Chute in 1605; he became a member of the salon of Lucy, countess of Bedford; and he even attracted the attention of King James, who saw what a useful ornament Donne would be to the Church and urged him to take orders. Not completely resolved in his conscience to do so, Donne, for a considerable time, temporized. Yet, his activity during this period led him inevitably toward this step. A substantial body of Donne's religious verse was written during this period and sent to Magdalen Herbert, mother of George Herbert and Lord Herbert of Cherbury. Finally, he committed himself to seeking advancement within the Anglican Church with the publication of *Pseudo-Martyr*, a work of religious controversy on a problem strongly vexing the King—the refusal of Roman Catholics to subscribe to the Oath of Allegiance. Thereafter, the king refused to consider Donne for any post outside the Church. In 1610, Oxford University awarded an honorary master's degree to Donne, who had been prevented by his former religion from taking an undergraduate degree.

Having composed the *Anniversaries* under the patronage of Sir Robert Drury of Hawsted, he accompanied Sir Robert to Paris and then to Frankfort. After the return of the party to England in 1612, Donne and his family resided with Sir Robert. Although he continued to write occasional verse, Donne had definitely decided to take orders. Having prepared himself through further study, he was ordained early in 1615, and numerous avenues for advancement immediately became available to him. The king made him a royal chaplain. Cambridge awarded him the degree of doctor of divinity by royal command. Lincoln's Inn appointed him reader in divinity to the Society. In addition, he was able to turn down offers of fourteen country livings in his first year as a priest, while accepting two. The one blight on his early years as a priest was the death of his wife in 1617. In 1619, Donne took time out from his regular duties to serve as chaplain accompanying Lord Doncaster on an embassy to Germany.

Donne's fame as a preacher had been immediate, and it continued to grow each year. As Walton reports, even his friends were surprised by the continuous growth of his pulpit eloquence after such a striking beginning. Such genius received its proper setting in 1621, when Donne was appointed dean of St. Paul's Cathedral. The position was also a lucrative one, and the dean's residence was as large as an episcopal palace.

The winter of 1623-1624 was a particularly eventful time in Donne's life. Having contracted relapsing fever, he was on the verge of death, but with characteristic dedication—and also characteristic self-consciousness—he kept a meticulous record of his illness as an aid to devotion. The resulting work, *Devotions upon Emergent Occasions*, was published almost immediately. During the same period, Donne's daughter, Constance, married the aging Elizabethan actor Edward Alleyn, founder of Dulwich College. From circumstances surrounding the wedding, the publishing history of *Devotions upon Emergent Occasions* has been reconstructed. It now seems clear that Donne composed this highly structured work in just a few weeks while still physically incapacitated.

In 1624, he took on additional duties as vicar of St. Dunstan's-in-the-West. After the death of King James in the following year, Donne was chosen to preach the first sermon before the new king. This and other sermons were printed at the request of King Charles. Also printed was his memorial sermon for Lady Danvers, as Magdalen Herbert had become.

Even when Donne again became gravely ill in 1629, he would not stop preaching. Ever conscious of his mortality during these last months, he sat for a portrait wearing his shroud. When he delivered his last sermon on Ash Wednesday in 1631, it was the famous *Death's Duell*. Walton gives a vivid account of the writing and preaching of this sermon during Donne's last illness, and some of the sermon's special urgency is perhaps explained by the fact that the king's household called it Donne's own funeral sermon. Indeed, a few weeks later, on March 31, 1631, he died, having been preceded only a few months before by his aged mother.

ANALYSIS

The traditional dichotomy between Jack Donne and Dr. Donne, despite John Donne's own authority for it, is essentially false. In the seventeenth century context, the work of Donne constitutes a fundamental unity. Conventional wisdom may expect devotional poetry from a divine and feel a certain uneasiness when faced with love poetry, but such a view misses the point in two different ways. On one hand, Donne's love poetry is philosophical in its nature and characterized by a texture of religious imagery; and, on the other hand, his devotional poetry makes unexpected, bold use of erotic imagery. What Donne presents is two sides of a consistent vision of the world and of the mortality of man.

In the nineteenth century, when Donne's poetry did occasionally attract some attention from the discerning, it was not for the lyrics but for the satires. The satirical mode seemed the most congenial use that Donne had found for his paradoxical style. This had also been the attitude of the eighteenth century, which, however, valued metrical euphony too highly to accept even the satires. In fact, Alexander Pope tried to rescue Donne for the eighteenth century by the curious expedient of "translating" his satires into verse, that is, by regularizing them. In addition to replacing Donne's strong lines and surprising caesurae with regular meter, Pope, as Addison C. Bross has shown, puts ideas into climactic sequence, makes particulars follow generalizations, groups similar images together, and untangles syntax. In other words, he homogenizes the works.

While today Donne's lyrics are preferred to his satires, the satires are regarded as artistically effective in their original form, although this artistry is of a different order from that of the lyrics. Sherry Zivley has shown that the imagery of the satires works in a somewhat different way from that of the imagery of the lyrics, where diverse images simply succeed one another. With images accumulated from a similarly wide range of sources, the satires build a thematic center. N. J. C. Andreasen has gone even further, discerning in the body of the satires a thematic unity. Andreasen sees Donne as having created a single persona for the satires, one who consistently deplores the encroaching materialism of the seventeenth century.

"KIND PITY CHOKES MY SPLEEN"

Satire III on religion ("Kind pity chokes my spleen") is undoubtedly the most famous of the satires. Using related images to picture men as engaging in a kind of courtship of the truth, the poem provides a defense of moderation and of a common ground between the competing churches of the post-Reformation world. Although written in the period of Donne's transition from the Roman Catholic Church to the Anglican, the poem rejects both of these, along with the Lutheran and the Calvinist Churches, and calls on men to put their trust in God and not in those who unjustly claim authority from God for churches of their own devising.

In addition to the fully developed satires, Donne wrote a small number of very brief epigrams. These mere witticisms are often on classical subjects and therefore without the occasional focus that turns Ben Jonson's epigrams into genuine poetry. This is the only place where Donne makes any substantial use of classical allusion.

In his own day, Donne's most popular poems were probably his elegies. While in modern usage the term *elegy* is applied only to a memorial poem, Donne's elegies derive their form from a classical tradition that uses the term, as well, for poetry of love complaint written in couplets. Generally longer than the more famous songs and sonnets, the elegies are written on the model of Ovid's *Amores (Loves)*. Twenty or more such poems have been attributed to Donne, but several of these are demonstrably not his. On the basis of manuscript evidence, Dame Helen Gardner has suggested that Donne intended fourteen poems to stand as a thematically unified Book of Elegies and that "The Autumnal" (Elegy IX), which has a different manuscript history,

and "The Dream" (Elegy X), which is not in couplets, although authentic poems by Donne, do not form a part of it.

"THE AUTUMNAL"

Elegy IX, "The Autumnal," praises older women as more seasonable to the appetite because the uncontrollable fires of their youth have passed. There is a long tradition that this poem was specially written for Magdalen Herbert. If so, it is particularly daring since, although not a seduction poem, it is frankly erotic in its praise; inasmuch as Magdalen Herbert did take as her second husband a much younger man, however, it may be supposed that she would have appreciated the general recognition that sexual attractiveness and interest can endure and even ripen. On the other hand, the poem's praises are not without qualification. The persona admires autumnal beauty, but he can see nothing attractive in the truly aged, whom he rejects as death's heads from which the teeth have been scattered to various places— to the vexation of their souls since the teeth will have to be gathered together again for the resurrection of the body at the Last Judgment. Thus the poem shows Donne's typical combination of eroticism and contemplation of mortality in a mode of grotesque humor.

"TO HIS MISTRESS GOING TO BED"

In Elegy XIX, "To His Mistress Going to Bed," the persona enthusiastically directs his mistress in her undressing. Aroused, he uses his hands to full advantage to explore her body. In a famous passage, he compares his amazement to that of someone discovering a new land. He next directs her to bare her body to him as fully as she would to the midwife. This graphic request is followed by the poem's closing couplet, in which the persona points out that he is naked already to show his mistress the way and thus poignantly reveals that he is only hoping for such lasciviousness from her and not already having his wanton way. Even this poem uses religious imagery—most clearly and most daringly when it advocates a woman's baring of her body to her lover by analogy with the baring of the soul before God. In an influential explication, Clay Hunt suggests that Donne is, in fact, ridiculing the Neoplatonic school of love that could seriously advance such an analogy. If so, Donne is clearly having it both ways and making the analogy available for its own sake as well.

"THE CANONIZATION"

The songs and sonnets, as the other love poems are usually called, although no sonnets in the conventional sense are included, show an imaginative variety of verse forms. They are particularly famous for their dramatic, conversational opening lines. In addition, these poems are a great storehouse of the kind of verbal ambiguity that William Empson has shown the modern world how to admire.

In "The Canonization," the persona justifies his love affair in explicitly sacred terms by explaining that his relationship with his beloved makes the two of them saints of love. John A. Clair has shown how the structure of "The Canonization" follows the five stages of the process of canonization in the Roman Catholic Church during the Renaissance: proof of sanctity, recognition of heroic virtue, demonstration of miracles, examination of relics and writings, and declaration of worthiness of veneration. The poem is thus addressed to a devil's advocate who refuses to see the holiness of erotic love. It is this devil's advocate in love who is asked to hold his tongue, in the famous first line. "The Canonization" illustrates Donne's typical use of ambiguity as well as paradox, not as merely decorative wit, but to reveal deepest meanings. William H. Machett suggests that, for example, when the lovers in this poem become a "piece of chronicle," the word *piece* is a triple pun meaning masterpiece, fragment, and fortress. There is also a much more obvious meaning—piece of artillery—a meaning that interacts with the title to give a richer texture to the whole poem: The poem is not only about the making of saints of love; it is also about the warfare between this idea and conventional notions of sex and religion. Consequently, yet another meaning of *piece* comes into play, the sexual.

"THE FLEA"

"The Flea" is a seduction poem. Like many of the songs and sonnets, it takes the form of a logical argument making full use of the casuistries and indeed sophistries of the dialectic of Peter Ramus. In the first of the poem's three stanzas the persona asks the lady to contemplate a flea he has discerned upon her person. Since his blood and hers are mingled in the flea that has in succession bitten each of them, the mingling of the bloods that takes place during intercourse (as was then believed) has already occurred.

In the second stanza the persona cautions the lady not to kill the flea. By joining their bloods the flea has become the place of their joining in marriage, so for her to kill the flea would be to murder him and also to commit both suicide and sacrilege.

In the last stanza, the persona discovers that the lady has ignored his argument and killed the flea, but he is ready with another argument. When the lady triumphantly points out that they have survived this death of the flea, surely she is also showing how false her fears of sex are, since sex involves no greater loss of blood and no greater death. Implicit in these last lines is the traditional pun on "death," which was the popular term for sexual climax.

The pun and the poem as a whole illustrate Donne's characteristic mingling of the sacred and the profane. It should be noted that a love poem on the subject of the lady's fleas was not an original idea with Donne, but the usual treatment of the subject was as an erotic fantasy. Donne's originality is precisely in his use of the subject for dialectic and in the restraint he shows in ending the poem before the lady capitulates, in fact without indicating whether she does.

"THE ECSTASY"

"The Ecstasy," the longest of the songs and sonnets, has, for a lyric, attracted a remarkable range of divergent interpretations. The poem is about spiritual love and intermingling as the culmination of physical love, but some critics have seen the Neoplatonism, or spiritualizing of love, as quite serious, while others have insisted that it is merely a patently sophistical ploy of the persona to convince his mistress that, since they are one soul, the physical consummation of their love is harmless, appropriate, inevitable. If the critics who see "The Ecstasy" as a seduction poem are right, the conclusion is even more salacious than they have supposed, since it calls on the addressee to examine the lovers closely for the evidence of true love when they have given themselves over to their bodies—in other words, to watch them make love. In fact, the poem, like so many of Donne's, is quite content to be theological and erotic by turns—beginning with its very title, a term used of both religious experience and sexual experience. That the perfect soul brought into being by the union of the lovers should combine the flesh and spirit eternally is an understandable religious hope and also a good sexual fantasy. In this way, the poem illustrates Donne's philosophy of love. Although not all his poems use this theme, Donne has, in fact, a unique ability for his day to perceive love as experienced by equals.

"A VALEDICTION: FORBIDDING MOURNING"

Another famous poem of love between equals is "A Valediction: Forbidding Mourning." The poem rushes through a dazzling spectrum of imagery in just the way deplored by Samuel Johnson. In addition, in the *Life of Cowley* Johnson singles out the poem for his ultimate condemnation, saying that in the extended metaphor of the last three stanzas "it may be doubted whether absurdity or ingenuity has the better claim." During the present century, ingenuity has once again become respectable in poetry, and modern readers come with more sympathy than Johnson did to this famous extended metaphor, or conceit, comparing lovers who have to suffer a temporary separation to a pair of pencil compasses. Even the improbability of the image—which Johnson castigated as absurdity—has been given a context by modern scholarship. W. A. Murray, for example, has shown that the circle with a dot in the center, which is inscribed by the compasses reflecting the lovers who are separated yet joined, is, in fact, the alchemical symbol for gold, mentioned elsewhere in the poem and a traditional symbol of perfection. More ingeniously, John Freccero has seen Donne's compasses as inscribing not simply a circle but, as they close, a spiral. The spiral has some history of use in describing the motion of the planets. Since the spiral is also a conventional symbol of humanity, this spiral reading helps readers see in "A Valediction: Forbidding Mourning" Donne's characteristic balance of the celestial and the personal.

In fact, Donne's inclusiveness is even wider than it is usually assumed to be. He collapses not only physical and spiritual but also male and female. Donne has the unusual perspicacity to make the persona of "Break of Day" explicitly female, and although no critic has made the point before, there is nothing to prevent seeing a similar female persona in "A Valediction: Forbidding Mourning." Such a reading has the advantage of introducing some erotic puns in the compass conceit as the man (the fixed center in this reading) harkens after his beloved as she roams and then grows erect when she

returns to him. More important, such a reading makes further sense out of the image of a circle inscribed by compasses. The circle is a traditional symbol of woman, and woman's life is traditionally completed—or, as the poem puts it, made just—with a man at the center. Since the circle is a natural sexual image for woman, in this reading, the poem illustrates the practical sex as well as the theoretical sociology behind its imagery as the lover's firmness makes the woman's circle taut. An objection that might be made to this reading is that the poem's various references to parting show that it is the speaker who is going away. While a woman of the seventeenth century would be unlikely to do extensive traveling apart from her lover (or even in his company), a woman may have to part as well as a man, and lovers might well think of themselves as roaming the world when kept apart only by the daily round of pedestrian business. There is no more reason in the poem for believing that the absent one will literally roam than for believing that this absent one will literally run.

While Walton assigns this poem to the occasion of Donne's trip to France with Sir Robert Drury in 1611, the apocryphal nature of Walton's story is sufficiently indicated by the fact that it does not appear until the 1675 version of his *Life of Donne*. This dating would, at the least, make "A Valediction: Forbidding Mourning" extremely late for the songs and sonnets. Nevertheless, were the poem occasioned by Donne's preparation to travel to France in 1611, reading it as spoken by a woman would still be appropriate, since Donne prepared for this trip by sending his wife and children to stay with relatives on the Isle of Wight several months before he was himself able to embark. In addition, a general knowledge of how poets work suggests that a lyric inspired by a specific occasion is seldom in every particular a document congruent with the poet's actual experience. Perhaps the poem finally says that a woman can make a virtue of necessary separation as well as a man can.

"TWICKHAM GARDEN"

Among the songs and sonnets are a few poems that seem to have been written for patrons. Since Twickenham is the seat of the Earls of Bedford, "Twickham Garden" is assumed to have been written for Lucy, Countess of Bedford. According to the poem, the garden is a refuge like Eden, but the persona admits that with him the serpent has been let in. He wishes he were instead an aphrodisiac plant or fountain more properly at home in the place. In the last stanza, he seems to become such a fountain, but he is disappointed to discover that all the lovers who visit the garden are false. The poem ends—perhaps rather curiously for a patronage poem—with the obscure paradox that the only true woman is the one whose truth is killing.

"A Nocturnal upon St. Lucy's Day, Being the Shortest Day"

A similar depersonalization characterizes the riddling poem "A Nocturnal upon St. Lucy's Day, Being the Shortest Day." While the ironies of darkness and light and of the changing movement of time (*Lucy* means light, but her day provides less of it than any other) would have recommended the subject to Donne anyway, it must have been an additional stimulus that this astronomically significant day was the saint's day of one of his patronesses. Clarence H. Miller, seeing the poem as unique among the songs and sonnets in describing the union with the lady as exclusively sacred without any admixture of the profane, relates the poem to the liturgy for St. Lucy's Day. In the body of the poem, however, the persona sees himself as the epitaph for light, as every dead thing. Finally, he becomes St. Lucy's Day itself—for the purpose of providing lovers with a longer nighttime for lust. Despite a certain bitterness or at least coarseness of tone, the poem is usually seen as a lament for the countess's death (1627); the death of Donne's wife, however, has also been suggested, although Anne More has no special association with St. Lucy and his love for her could not have been exclusively spiritual. Richard E. Hughes has considered the occasion of the poem from a different point of view and usefully suggested that, though commemorating the countess of Bedford, the poem is not an improbably late lyric for the songs and sonnets but a lament from an earlier period for the loss of the countess's friendship. If the tone is considered in the least charitable light, the poem might even be read as an accusation of patronage withdrawn.

Verse letters

The familiar letter came into its own as a genre during the seventeenth century, and collections even began to be published. About two hundred of Donne's letters survive. This is a larger number than for any other figure of the English Renaissance except Sir Francis Bacon, and Bacon's correspondence includes many letters written in his official capacity. Since the familiar letter had only begun to surface as a genre, much of the impersonality and formality of earlier letter writing persist in Donne's correspondence. Donne's son was a rather casual editor, and in light of the sometimes general nature of Donne's letters, the date and intended recipient of many remain unknown. One curiosity of this period of epistolary transition is the verse letter. Almost forty of Donne's letters are written in verse. Some of these are true occasional poems datable from internal evidence, but many are of a more general, philosophical nature.

The most famous of the verse letters are "The Storm" and "The Calm," the first certainly and the second probably addressed to Christopher Brooke. Traditionally, shipwrecks and other dangers of the sea are used to illustrate the unpredictability of fortune in men's lives, but, as B. F. Nellist has shown, Donne does not follow this convention; instead, he teaches that frustration and despair are to be accepted as part of man's lot.

Epithalamia

While many of the verse letters seem to have been exchanged with friends as *jeux d'esprit*, some are attempts to influence patrons. A group of poems clearly written with an eye to patronage are the epithalamia. Among the weddings that Donne celebrated was that of Princess Elizabeth to Frederick V, elector of the palatinate and later briefly king of Bohemia. Donne also celebrated the wedding of the royal favorite Robert Carr, earl of Somerset, to Frances Howard, countess of Essex. Since the countess was shortly afterward convicted of murdering the essayist Sir Thomas Overbury for having stood in the way of her marriage, this epithalamion must later have been something of an embarrassment to Donne. An occasional poem for which no occasion is ascribed is the "Epithalamion Made at Lincoln's Inn." This is the most interesting of the epithalamia to contemporary taste. Its satiric tone, verbal crudities, and scoffing are a pleasant surprise in a genre usually characterized by reverence, even obsequiousness. The problem of what wedding could have been appropriately celebrated with such a poem has been resolved by David Novarr's suggestion that the "Epithalamion Made at Lincoln's Inn" was written for a mock wedding held as part of the law students' midsummer revels.

EPICEDES AND OBSEQUIES

Other poems written for patrons are those usually called the epicedes and obsequies. These are eulogies for the dead—elegies in a more modern sense of the term than the one Donne seems to have in mind. Donne was one among the many poets who expressed regret at the death of Prince Henry, the hope of the dynasty.

ANNIVERSARIES

Also in the general category of memorial verse are the two so-called *Anniversaries* (*An Anatomy of the World: The First Anniversary* and *Of the Progress of the Soule: The Second Anniversary*), but these two poems are so unlike traditional eulogies as to defy inclusion in the genre. In their search for moments of intense feeling, the Metaphysical poets, with their love of paradox, did not often try to write long poems. Most of the attempts they did make are unsatisfactory or at least puzzling in some fundamental way. The *Anniversaries* are, indeed, primary texts in the study of the difficulties of the long poem in the Metaphysical mode.

Ostensibly written as memorial poems to commemorate Elizabeth Drury, who died as a child of fourteen and whom Donne had never seen, these poems range over a broad canvas of history. "Shee," as the subject of the two poems is called, is eulogized in an extravagant fashion beyond anything in the obsequies. While O. B. Hardison has shown that these poems were not regarded as bizarre or fulsome when originally published, they were the first of Donne's works to lose favor with the passing of time. Indeed, of *An Anatomy of the World* Ben Jonson objected to Donne himself that "if it had been writ of the Virgin Marie it had been something." Donne's answer is reported to have been that he was describing not Elizabeth Drury specifically but the idea of woman; but this explanation has not been found wholly satisfactory. Many candidates have been suggested for Shee of the *Anniversaries*—from St. Lucy and Astraea (Goddess of Justice) to the Catholic Church and Christ as Divine *Logos*. Two critics have suggested Queen Elizabeth, but one finds her eulogized and the other sees her as satirized, indicting in a particularly striking way the problematic nature of these difficult, knotty poems.

Hardison and, later, Barbara Kiefer Lewalski, made the case for the poems as part of a tradition of epideictic poetry—poetry of praise. In this tradition, extravagant compliments are the norm rather than the exception, and all of Donne's individual extravagances have precedents. What such a reading leaves out of account is, on the one hand, the extraordinary density of the extravagant praise in Donne's *Anniversaries* and, on the other hand, the presence of satire, not only the possible satire of the heroine but also explicit satire in the exploration of the decay of nature that forms the subject of the poems. Marjorie Hope Nicholson sees the *Anniversaries* as companion poems, the first a lament for the body, the second a meditation on mortality. Louis L. Martz suggests, further, that the *Anniversaries* are structured meditations. Martz sees *An Anatomy of the World* as a mechanical application of Ignatian meditation and *Of the Progress of the Soule* as a more successful organic application. Meditation theory, however, fails to resolve all the interpretive difficulties. Northrop Frye's theory that the poems are Menippean satire, and Frank Manley's that they are wisdom literature, also leave unresolved difficulties.

Perhaps these interpretive difficulties are fundamentally beyond resolution. Rosalie L. Colie has usefully pointed out that, in the *Anniversaries*, Donne seems not to be trying to bring his disparate materials to a conventional resolution. The poems accept contradictions as part of the flux of life and should be seen within the Renaissance tradition of paradox. Donne is demonstrably a student of paradox in many of his other works. More specifically, Daniel B. Rowland has placed *An Anatomy of the World* in the Mannerist tradition because in it Donne succeeded in creating an unresolved tension. His purpose may be just to raise questions about the relative weight of praise and satire and about the identity of the heroine Shee. Mario Praz goes further—perhaps too far—when he sees all the work of Donne as Mannerist, as illustrative not of wit but of the dialectics of passion; Mannerism does, however, provide a useful description for what modern taste finds a strange combination of materials in the *Anniversaries*.

"INFINITATI SACRUM"

An even more difficult long poem is an unfinished one called "Infinitati Sacrum." This strange parable of original sin adapts Paracelsus's theory of the transmigration of souls to follow through the course of subsequent history the spirit of the apple plucked by Eve. W. A. Murray has seen in this poem the beginnings of a *Paradise Lost* (1667). While few other readers will want to go so far, most will agree with Murray and with George Williamson that "Infinitati Sacrum" is a preliminary use of the materials and themes treated in the *Anniversaries*.

Donne has been called a poet of religious doubt in contrast to Herbert, a poet of religious assurance; but Herbert has real doubts in the context of his assurance, and the bold demand for salvation in audacious, even shocking language characteristic of the holy sonnets suggests, on the contrary, that Donne writes from a deep-seated conviction of election.

HOLY SONNETS

Louis Martz, Helen Gardner, and others have shown the influence of Ignatian meditation in the holy sonnets. Dame Helen, in fact, by restoring the manuscript order, has been able to see in these poems a sequential meditative exercise. The sensuous language, however, suggests not so much the meditative technique of St. Ignatius Loyola as the technique of St. Francis de Sales. In addition, Don M. Ricks has argued cogently that the order of the poems in the Westmorland Manuscript may suggest an Elizabethan sonnet sequence and not a meditative exercise at all.

Holy Sonnet XIV (10 in Dame Helen's numbering), "Batter my heart, three-personed God," has been seen by Arthur L. Clements and others as hieroglyphically illustrating the Trinity in its three-part structure. This poem opens with the striking dramatic immediacy typical of Donne's best lyrics. Using both military and sexual imagery, Donne describes the frightening, ambivalent feelings called up by the thought of giving oneself over to God's power and overwhelming grace. The soul is a town ruled by a usurper whom God's viceroy, Reason, is inadequate to overthrow. The soul is also the beloved of God though betrothed to his enemy and longing for divorce. The resolution of this sonnet turns on a paradoxical sexual image as the persona says that his soul will never be chaste unless God ravishes him. A similar complex of imagery is used, though in a less startling fashion, in Holy Sonnet II (1), "As due by many titles I resign."

Holy Sonnet IX (5), "If poisonous minerals," begins audaciously by accusing God of unfairness in the consequences He has decreed for original sin. In the sestet the persona abruptly realizes that he is unworthy to dispute with God in this way and begs that his tears of guilt might form a river of forgetfulness inducing God to overlook his sins rather than actually forgiving them. While this poem does not turn on a sexual image, it does contrast the lot of fallen man unfavorably with that of lecherous goats, who have no decree of damnation hanging over them.

Holy Sonnet XVIII (2 in Dame Helen's separately numbered group from the Westmorland Manuscript), "Show me, dear Christ, Thy spouse so bright and clear," has some of the most shocking sexual imagery in all of religious literature. While the tradition of using erotic imagery to describe the soul's relationship with God has a long history, particularly in exegesis of the Song of Songs, that is helpful in understanding the other holy sonnets, the imagery here is of a different order. Like Satire III, the poem is a discussion of the competing claims of the various Christian churches, but it goes well beyond the courtship imagery of the satire when it praises the Anglican Church because, like a promiscuous woman, it makes itself available to all men.

A distinctly separate series of holy sonnets is "La Corona." Using paradoxes such as the fact that the Virgin is her Maker's maker, and including extensive allusions to the divine office, this sequence of seven poems on the life of Christ has been called by Martz a rosary of sonnets, not so much because of the devotional content as because of the interlaced structure: The last line of each poem is repeated as the first line of the next. While the ingenious patterning renders the sequence less personal than Donne's best religious poetry, within its exquisite compass it does make a beautiful statement of the mysteries of faith.

In "A Hymn to Christ, at the Author's Last Going into Germany," Donne exaggerates the dangers of a Channel crossing to confront his mortality. Then even in the face of death, the persona pictures Christ as a jealous lover to be castigated if He withdraws His love just because it is not reciprocated; yet the persona does call for a bill of divorcement from all his lesser loves. The poem ends with the thought that, just as dark churches (being free of distractions) are best for praying, death is the best refuge from stormy seas.

"Good Friday, 1613: Riding Westward" is a witty paradox built on Ramist dialectic. Forced to make a trip to the West on Good Friday, the persona feels his soul drawn to the East. Although the heavens are ordered for westward motion, he feels a contradiction even as he duplicates their motion because all of Christian iconology urges him to return to the East where life began—both human life in Eden and spiritual life with the Crucifixion. He reasons that through sin he has turned his back on the Cross—but only to receive the correction that his sins merit. He hopes such flagellation will so change his appearance that he will again become recognizable to God as made in His Own image. Then he will at last be able to turn and face God.

Another divine poem of witty paradox is "A Hymn to God the Father." Punning on *Son/sun* and on his own name, Donne demands that God swear to save him. Having done so, God will at last have Donne. Because of its frankness and its very personal use of puns, this poem is not really a hymn despite its title—although it has been included in hymnals.

The chapter headings of *Devotions upon Emergent Occasions* as laid out in the table of contents should also be included among the divine poems. Joan Webber has made the illuminating discovery that this table of contents is a Latin poem in dactylic hexameters. This is a particularly surprising element of artistry in a work composed in such a short time and under such difficult conditions. Thus even more self-conscious than had been supposed, *Devotions upon Emergent Occasions* can finally be seen as an explication of the Latin poem.

OTHER MAJOR WORKS

NONFICTION: *Pseudo-Martyr*, 1610; *Ignatius His Conclave*, 1611; *Devotions upon Emergent Occasions*, 1624; *Death's Duell*, 1632; *Juvenilia: Or, Certaine Paradoxes and Problems*, 1633, 1923; *Six Sermons on Several Occasions*, 1634; *LXXX Sermons*, 1640; *Biathanatos*, 1646; *Fifty Sermons*, 1649; *Essays in Divinity*, 1651; *Letters to Severall Persons of Honour*, 1651; *A Collection of Letters*, 1660; *XXVI Sermons*, 1660.

BIBLIOGRAPHY

Carey, John. *John Donne: Life, Mind, and Art.* Boston: Faber & Faber, 1981. Carey's exposition of the whole range of Donne's poetry is exact and detailed. Its arrangement is thematic rather than biographical, which produces some forceful new appraisals. Includes an index.

Docherty, Thomas. *John Donne Undone.* New York: Methuen, 1986. This poststructuralist reading of Donne seeks both a theoretical and a historical understanding of the poetry. He focuses particularly on the paradoxes, differences and irresolutions displayed. Contains an index.

Johnson, Jeffrey. *The Theology of John Donne.* New York: D. S. Brewer, 1999. A portrayal of the religious writings of John Donne as the result of a well-founded knowledge of Christian theology and Donne as a full-fledged religious thinker. Includes bibliographic references and an index.

Marotti, Arthur F., ed. *Critical Essays on John Donne.* New York: Maxwell Macmillan International, 1994. With newly commissioned and reprinted material the essays cover several critical stances to Donne's work. The introduction by the editor summarizes the history of Donne's inauguration as a modernist.

Sherwood, Terry. *Fulfilling the Circle: A Study of John Donne's Thought.* Toronto: University of Toronto Press, 1984. Attempts to trace Donne's understanding of the complex interrelationship of body and soul back from his later, more mature work. Theological and psychological perspectives are central. Includes an index.

Smith, A. J., ed. *John Donne: Essays in Celebration.* New York: Harper & Row, 1972. A collection of essays produced to mark the four hundredth anniversary of Donne's birth. Contains sixteen original essays by leading Donne scholars, and indexes.

Stein, Arnold. *John Donne's Lyrics.* Minneapolis: University of Minnesota Press, 1962. Stein deals not only with Donne in his time, or Donne in modern times, but also with the interplay of the two. Although he concentrates on Donne's songs, he demonstrates a full knowledge of Donne's works in seeking a re-reading. The book has stood the test of time better than some of its contemporaries. Supplemented by appendices and an index.

Winny, James. *A Preface to Donne.* 2d ed. New York: Longman, 1981. One of the Preface Books series, it is a useful background book touching on the religious, intellectual, and literary life of the time, with a short section of critical analysis. Includes a select bibliography and an index.

Edmund Miller;
bibliography updated by the editors

EDWARD DORN

Born: Villa Grove, Illinois; April 2, 1929
Died: Boulder, Colorado; December 10, 1999

PRINCIPAL POETRY

The Newly Fallen, 1961
Hands Up!, 1964
From Gloucester Out, 1964
Idaho Out, 1965
Geography, 1965
The North Atlantic Turbine, 1967
Our Word: Guerrilla Poems from Latin America, 1968 (translation with Gordon Brotherston of José Emilio Pacheco)
Gunslinger I, 1968
Gunslinger II, 1969
Gunslinger I and II, 1969
Twenty-four Love Songs, 1969
Trees Between Two Walls, 1969 (translation with Gordon Brotherston)
The Midwest Is That Space Between the Buffalo Statler and the Lawrence Eldridge, 1969
The Cosmology of Finding Your Spot, 1969
Songs, Set Two: A Short Count, 1970
Spectrum Breakdown: A Microbook, 1971
A Poem Called Alexander Hamilton, 1971
The Cycle, 1971

The Hamadryas Baboon at the Lincoln Park Zoo, 1972
Gunslinger Book III, 1972
Recollections of Gran Apachería, 1974
Semi-Hard, 1974 (with George Kinball)
Slinger, 1975 (includes *Gunslinger* books I-IV and *The Cycle*)
The Collected Poems, 1956-1974, 1975
Manchester Square, 1975 (with Jennifer Dunbar)
Selected Poems, 1976 (translation with Gordon Brotherston of César Vallejo)
Hello La Jolla, 1978
Selected Poems, 1978 (Donald Allen, editor)
Yellow Lola, 1981
Captain Jack's Chaps: Or, Houston, 1983
Abhorrences, 1984
High West Rendezvous, 1997

OTHER LITERARY FORMS

Edward Dorn wrote one novel, *The Rites of Passage: A Brief History* (1965, revised as *By the Sound* in 1971) and one book of short stories, *Some Business Recently Transacted in the White World* (1971). In addition, he published numerous books of essays and translations.

ACHIEVEMENTS

Edward Dorn's writing has been compared by critics to that of Walt Whitman for its joy in American themes, to that of Ernest Hemingway for its idiomatic speech, to that of Ezra Pound for its humor and erudition, and to that of Thomas Wolfe for its panoramic view. More accurate, however, are the criticisms claiming that his work defies paraphrasing and that his philosophy was likely to be different from that of his reader, who will emerge with a less inhibited and consequently more benevolent and tolerant view of the world. Dorn was called a "master of contemporary language," and *Gunslinger* has been called a "masterpiece of contemporary poetry."

Dorn taught at Idaho State University, at the University of Kansas, at Northeastern Illinois State University, at Kent State University, at the University of Essex (Colchester), at the University of California, Riverside and San Diego, and at Muir College. At the time of his death, he was an associate professor of English at the University of Colorado in Boulder and a director of the writing program. He was twice a Fulbright lecturer in American literature at Essex; he received National Endowment for the Arts grants in 1966 and 1968, a fellowship from the University of New Mexico in 1969, and the American Book Award in 1980. He was poet in residence at the University of Alaska and at the University of Michigan, Ann Arbor.

He read at the Folger Library, the Cambridge Poetry Festival, the University of Durham, England, King's College (the University of London), and Westfield College. He gave the Olson lectures at the State University of New York (SUNY) in 1981.

BIOGRAPHY

Edward Merton Dorn attended a one-room schoolhouse for most of his first eight grades. The poet he read most frequently was James Whitcomb Riley, whose writing appeared in the local newspapers because he was from the neighboring state of Indiana. Dorn attended the University of Illinois, Urbana, and Black Mountain College, where he was graduated in 1955. At

Edward Dorn (© Edward Dorn)

Black Mountain College, in a liberal, creative environment, Dorn was associated with the rector Charles Olson, the poets Robert Creeley, Robert Duncan, Joel Oppenheimer, John Weiners, and Paul Blackburn, as well as the painter Franz Kline, the composer John Cage, and many other stimulating people. He held such disparate jobs as those of a logger in Washington State and a reference librarian at New Mexico State University in Santa Fe. During the mid-1960's he was the editor of *Wild Dog* magazine.

In 1969 he married Jennifer Dunbar, and they had a son, Kidd, and a daughter, Maya. For the last two decades of his life, he led the University of Colorado's creative writing program. In his later years Dorn was much concerned, in his writing and teaching, with the culture and geography of the West, writing numerous essays on the subject that were eventually collected in *Way West: Stories, Essays, and Verse Accounts, 1963-1993* (1993). He died of pancreatic cancer on December 10, 1999, in Boulder, Colorado.

ANALYSIS

Typically called a Black Mountain poet, Edward Dorn commented that there is no Black Mountain "school" with a single style or ideology, but that instead Black Mountain College meant a "school" in the true sense of the word, a climate in which to acquire and satisfy a thirst for the "dazzle of learning" and an appreciation of its value.

Referring to the poetry of the much-revered Charles Olson, Dorn claimed that he was not sure what "breath-determined projective verse" is; he simply wrote in "clots" of words, and when a line begins to lose its energy, he began a new one. This intuitional line division leads to free verse, which utilizes some end-rhyme and, more often, internal rhyme. Dorn's long narrative poems (*Idaho Out* and *Gunslinger*) have the structure of an odyssey punctuated by stops and encounters.

DOMINANT THEMES

Dorn's major themes can be pinpointed by naming certain representative figures in his work. The eccentric entrepreneur and movie mogul Howard Hughes represents all that is wrong with today's world, from isolation to selfishness to unbounded competitiveness. Daniel Drew, the robber baron, is the prototype of earlier American acquisitiveness. Dick Tracy, the comic-strip detective, is a pop figure familiar to all. Parsifal is not only the ideal knight, symbolic of the unrecoverable past in the mistaken view of most Americans, but also a part of the mythology ever-present in Dorn's poetry. Composer John Philip Sousa, associated with a period of history that seems in retrospect more pleasing than the present, elicits both a love for music and an almost sentimental reminiscence about an Illinois childhood. There remains the geranium, the lovely scarlet bloom that flourishes in the West and represents in Dorn's poetry the feminine Indian principle, and the trees—the box elder of his youth and the piñon of his adult years.

THE WEST

Heeding the advice of Olson, his mentor at Black Mountain College, to "dig one thing or place" until he knew more about it than anyone else, Dorn chose the American West. That vast area became the locus and the vehicle for Dorn's major concerns: displaced persons and minorities, greedy entrepreneurs, ecology, the role of the poet, and, most important, survival. Believing that the United States government created its own first subdivisions with the passage of the Homestead Act, he noted that after a century of "planned greed," what remains are cowboys who live in ranch houses and pull plastic boats behind their highly horse-powered wagons. If a cowboy actually owns a horse, he does not ride it. Although Dorn generally loved this new world, he sometimes found it so evil that he thought it should not even have been discovered. Major villains are the realtors, who have converted SPACE to space by subdividing it, while the victims are the immigrants who came in "long black flea coats," Indians who now "play indian and scoff wieners and Seven Up," and the land itself.

"SOUSA"

While most ordinary citizens are relatively impotent in the face of money, acquisition, and imperialism, Dorn believed that the poet has the potential to alter perception and thought, to be, in Olson's phrase, "of the company of the gods." Art aids in man's survival. In the poem "Sousa," Dorn suggested that Sousa's music is an antidote to the present crash course on which the world is embarked, and even a means of figuratively irrigating the wasteland. In a Dylan Thomas-like phrase, he recalled "the only May Day of [his] mind," the octagonal bandstand, the girls' billowing summer dresses, and ladybugs—all associated with Sunday afternoon occasions. Pleading with "John" (Philip Sousa) to pick up his "phone," Dorn deplores the fact that the nation, which has lifted the "chalice of explosion," can no longer be amused by Sousa's martial music. Noting that Sousa's marches are benevolent—the kind in which no one is injured—the poet concludes the poem with a brief prayer that the friends he has loved and left will have "cut wood to warm them."

"THE RICK OF GREEN WOOD"

Wood is significant in Dorn's work, not only because it can literally warm bodies, but also because it is one of the natural objects to be lost in the despoliation of the West, and because Dorn himself worked as a logger. The box elder tree, associated with his youth in Illinois, and the piñon tree of the West and his adult life, appear frequently in the poems. "The Rick of Green Wood," which appears at the beginning of both *The Collected Poems, 1956-1974* and *Selected Poems*, serves to introduce not only the theme of wood and the comfort it will offer his family but also the poet himself: "My name is Dorn," he tells the woodcutter as the two converse in the November air. The friendly atmosphere is chilled by the warning that "the world is getting colder"—colder because of a lack of communication between its people and because of a depletion of its resources. Like Robert Frost's invitation to see the newborn calf and clear the pasture spring, and Emily Dickinson's "Letter to the World," Dorn's "The Rick of Green Wood" invites the reader to participate in the poet's world and to read on to learn more about the woodyard and the West beyond it.

ENGLAND

As Frost, Pound, and T. S. Eliot did before him, Dorn observed his homeland from England for a time; in all fairness, he admitted that America is "no more culpable" than England, and he finally decided that what happens in Minnesota was really more his business than what happens in England. Dorn took himself back home, but not before advising two jaded English poets who think that everything has already been said that they should make something up, "get laid" and describe that experience, or see what hope they can offer the world.

In the West once more, Dorn parodied the "Home on the Range," where Sacagawea wears a baseball cap and eats a Clark bar, and cowboys are good ole boys who ride in trucks with gun racks. Concerned as always with the fate of men living in the United States and on the North American continent, Dorn offered suggestions: Ignore the rigid patterns of society; the person who is different may be the one worth listening to.

LITERARY INFLUENCES

In his introduction to *The Lost America of Love: Rereading Robert Creeley, Edward Dorn, and Robert Duncan* (1981), Sherman Paul declares that his book concerns, much more than he had expected, the relationship of these poets to their "beloved predecessor," Walt Whitman. Dorn had affinities with the transcendentalists, with Henry David Thoreau (in spite of the fact that he refers to Thoreau as a "god damn sniveler") and his conception of the "different drummer," his attitude toward civil disobedience, and his love for land and nature; and with Ralph Waldo Emerson, who claimed to be "an endless seeker—with no past at my back." Dorn was closest, however, to Whitman. His poem "Wait by the Door Awhile, Death, There Are Others" recalls by its title and subject Whitman's "When Lilacs Last in the Dooryard Bloom'd" and contains several Whitmanesque references to his body, which Dorn said is younger than he is. Inviting himself to enter himself, Dorn confessed that he does so with great pleasure. One can almost smell Whitman's divine armpits. Some of Dorn's many "songs" could have been subtitled "Song of Myself"; in a burst of enthusiasm like that of the Transcendentalists, who thought man divine, Dorn announces that many of his gods have been men and women.

Other literary influences are numerous. Dorn's world was frequently like that of Lewis Carroll, where nothing is what it appears to be. "The New Union Dead in Alabama" recalls Allen Tate's "Ode to the Confederate Dead," but with a bitter difference: These men have died as a result of national hypocrisy, a gelding mentality, and a gelding culture. In "Home Again," the "green hand that rocks the cradle" is reminiscent of both Whitman and Dylan Thomas. The quotations and allusions in *The North Atlantic Turbine*, published in London, are reminiscent of Eliot. This is not to say that Dorn was not original. The opposite, rather, is true. He com-

bined old radio characters with Parsifal and Beowulf as adeptly and nimbly as Eliot did in *The Waste Land* (1922).

SATIRE: "WORLD BOX-SCORE CUP"

In spite of, or perhaps because of, all his literary kinships, Dorn was his own man. As Paul comments, "You don't mess with Dorn; he knows the score, and what is more . . . he has figured it out for himself." The score is, of course, lopsided, a fact satirically expressed in the poem "World Box-Score Cup," whose commentator, Stern Bill, broadcasts, from Yanqui-Go-Home Stadium, a game between the Haves (best fed, mostly English speaking) and the Havenots of the world. America, who can hardly be expected to be impartial, is the referee, and Al Capp is the captain of the Haves. Because the Havenots have no shirts, numbers are painted on their backs in whitewash; permanent paint is considered unnecessary, for obvious reasons. Players from the undeveloped squad have to be carried onto the field, an act distasteful to the developed players because of the smell of their nearly dead opponents. Stern Bill, who constantly uses the jargon of sportscasting, declares that this contest is one of the few places for people from both sides of the aluminum curtain to get together to work off their conflicting ideologies.

Stern Bill explains that the carcasses of undeveloped players will no longer be used in dog food because of the complaints of animal lovers that the meat was neither hygienic nor nutritional. At halftime he interviews Harry Carry (who has a Japanese accent) and John Malcom Fuggeridge, whose strangely dressed companion proves to be Truman Capote (also known as Trustworthy Kaput, a Southern degenerate). The last interviewees are Elizabeth Taylor's four dogs, who are accorded more dignity than are members of the Havenot team. As Dorn said, democracy has to be "cracked on the head" frequently to keep it in good condition. In this twentieth century "Modest Proposal," he is cracking at his caustic best. In an interview he once stated that one function of the poet is to stay "as removed as possible from permanent associations with power." Here he strikes out at the tendency of the United States to believe in its own invincibility and to interfere in other nations' affairs, at the same time condemning selfish greed in all nations—and all of this in sports jargon.

Dorn's satire was pointed, and he was not above using a few gimmicks. As the cover of *Hands Up!* is opened, two hands reach out to the reader, but as the book is closed, the hands suggest a nose-thumbing. In *Hello La Jolla*, Dorn apologized for the amount of "calculated" white space and invites the readers to fill it in. As he "roadtests" the language, he uses outrageous puns ("a mews," "pater"-"potter," "tiers of my country," "End-o-China," "Would you Bolivia it?," and "Vee-et," explained as the past tense of "eat"); archaic spelling ("sunne," "starre," "goe"); inversions (an Indian sings in his "daughter" tongue; a vacuum adores Nature; men go to the unemployment agency); and, in an age that has found such exact rhymes unfashionable, places "Trinity" with "infinity," "cuff" with "enough," and "cancer" with "dancer."

Gunslinger

His major opus, *Gunslinger*, years in the making, appeared one slim volume at a time but is available in a one-volume edition. Robert Duncan has called it an American *Canterbury Tales*, and indeed a crew of sophisticated Muppet-pilgrims could say, "To Taos we finally came." George Gugelberger has dubbed the work a space (-d out) epic, but under any name it entertains. The characters, who come out of Western motion pictures, comic books, and science fiction, include the Slinger himself, a "semidios" who drifts along the "selvedge of time" and who is a prototype of the Western strong man. A crack shot, he is headed toward Las Vegas in quest of Howard Hughes, who possesses the power once reserved for the gods. Robart (Rob-art), the foil for Gunslinger, is named for Howard Robard Hughes and is an evil, lawless, greedy entrepreneur.

"I" is the initiate, the likable dude who dies in Book II but is preserved for "past reference" when he is embalmed with five gallons of acid and finally revived as Parmenides' secretary. Gunslinger explains "I's" function as that of setting up the "bleechers" (*sic*) or booking the hall when the soul plays a date in another town. Lil, who is the Great Goddess, the female principle, and the prostitute with a heart of gold; Cool Everything, an acid freak; the Stoned Horse, Lévi-Strauss; and a "heliocentric" poet complete the list of pilgrims. The horse (horsepower) rides *inside* the stage and is, of course, a Pegasus. The travelers meet a Ph.D. named Doctor Flamboyant,

who confesses that he had to "take his degree," because the subject of his dissertation—last winter's icicles—could not be found.

Gunslinger, who observes that all the world is a cinema with Holy Writ as the script, visits a town called Truth or Consequence, whose residents ordered the truth and got the consequences. As the travelers get "inside the outskirts," the horse is horrified to learn that the green plots of the village contain the kind of grass that has to be *mowed*. When some local horses escape, their owner fires ten rounds so fast that the bullets stick together, his gun falls apart, and he becomes an Old Rugged Statue. The Stoned Horse, who sells the statue for twenty thousand pounds by starting a rumor that it is an Andy Warhol disguise, comments, "There's less to that village than meets the eye."

The townspeople crowd suspiciously around "I" because he looks strange. When they observe, "He has't got a pot. . .," "I" is saved by the magical appearance of a pot in his right hand. Slinger thanks the assembly for the "Kiwanis and Lions welcome," and Lil annotates (*sic*), "So this is Universe City," the name suggesting not only "university" but also the fact that people are much alike wherever one goes.

When the travelers "decoach" in Old Town and Cool Everything announces, "We're Here!" Slinger comments, "Sounds like an adverb disguised as a place." Amid puns on "head" and "para-dice," Cool Everything tells Lil his name, and she notes that if he does not stay away from tobacco, he might do just that. After a neat bit of internal rhyme: "'I is dead,' the poet said," Lil complains, "That aint grammatical, poet."

Gunslinger Book III

Gunslinger Book III introduces J. Edgar Whoever and the date February 31, along with the news that the horse had promised his mother not to join the Sierra Club. Slinger observes that everyone in this state (New Mexico) is fat because the citizens all think that "torque" is a relationship between tongue and fork. Their code is "Sllab," which must be spelled backwards to determine its true seriousness, and the first information it reveals is that Chester A. Arthur was America's first president, no matter what anyone says. The Slinger's quest is unsuccessful because his intended destination, Las Vegas, proves to be a "decoy" controlled by Big Money. The book ends at the Four Corners power plant, with "power" retaining a dual sense.

The speech of *Gunslinger* is that of hipsters, scientists, the media, bureaucracy, computers, comic books, Western slang, metaphysics, and pop culture. Dorn claimed he handles language like a material, keeping it in "instant repair." In *Gunslinger* he proved to be a virtuoso at juggling words, mining their ambiguous meanings, placing them in surprising positions, and finally using them "to make things cohere."

Why did Dorn choose the West as his Yoknapatawpha? The most obvious answer is that this is the area in which Americans were the last pioneers; the West is also the locale of America's principal myth—the same myth of the Wild West so effectively debunked by Stephen Crane and now treated more lovingly by Dorn. His poem "Vaquero" describes the last, delicate cowboy, his wrists embossed, his eyes as blue as the top of the sky, a wistful study in color by sometime painter Dorn. Another reason for his choice of the West is the admiration he held for the courtesy, humility, and hospitality of the Indians and Spanish-speaking people who live there; he also was attracted to the casual atmosphere of the West, a place as figuratively remote as possible from Wall Street, Detroit, and Pittsburgh.

THE POET'S ROLE

A summary of Dorn's concerns would have to include the tension between man and landscape brought on by greed. While man occasionally appreciates the beauties of landforms, as in *Gunslinger* ("Don't move . . . the sun rests deliberately on the rim of the sierra"), he has imposed a sameness on places by selling fast-food franchises, by constructing look-alike houses, by upsetting nature's balance, by allowing the careless rape of the land, by adopting a universal American dialect as standard, and by recognizing certain pop elements as part of national, not regional, culture. Space and place were at one time important, but thanks to man's avarice, they have lost much of their beauty as well as their identity.

To Dorn, a possible solution to this problem lies in the fact that language is a means of imposing order and discovering the natural order which man has disarrayed. The person who can best utilize language is, of course, the poet, who is equipped to communicate because of his facility with words. He can look objectively at what other men do with language as a means of justifying commerce and even war, at the same time demonstrating through his poetry what a marvelous weapon language can be—directly in the area of criticism, and indirectly by exuberant wordplay.

What, in Dorn's view, is the role of the poet? He wondered aloud about the familiar; he demonstrated the pleasure to be recovered from doubt; he rose above differences; he arbitrated because of his dexterity with words. He is, in short, a shaper.

OTHER MAJOR WORKS

LONG FICTION: *The Rites of Passage: A Brief History*, 1965 (revised as *By the Sound*, 1971, 1991).

SHORT FICTION: *Some Business Recently Transacted in the White World*, 1971.

NONFICTION: *What I See in the Maximus Poems*, 1960; *Prose I*, 1964 (with Michael Rumaker and Warren Tallman); *The Shoshoneans*, 1966 (with photographs by Leroy Lucas); *Book of Daniel Drew*, 1969; *Views and Interviews*, 1978, 1980 (Donald Allen, editor).

MISCELLANEOUS: *Way West: Stories, Essays, and Verse Accounts, 1963-1993*, 1993.

BIBLIOGRAPHY

Costello, James Thomas. "Edward Dorn: The Range of Poetry." *Dissertation Abstracts International* 44 (July, 1983): 167A. This work ambitiously examines Dorn's poetry as it relates to that of his post-World War II fellow writers and the influences on his works of the American West, contemporary politics, the Plains Indians, and even theoretical physics. Many of the major ideas in modern American writing are identified and explored. The range of Dorn's works cited spans *The Newly Fallen* to *Yellow Lola*.

Dorn, Edward. "An Interview with Edward Dorn." Interview by Tandy Sturgeon. *Contemporary Literature* 27 (Spring, 1986): 1-17. In this compelling interview, Dorn discusses the difficulty of characterizing and judging the effects of political poetry. Dorn also explains his scorn for the flaccid academic tradition in writing and expresses his desire to invigorate the genre. This extensive and well-conducted interview offers an extraordinary glimpse into the mind and art of Dorn.

Elmborg, James K. *A Pageant of Its Time: Edward Dorn's Slinger and the Sixties*. New York: P. Lang, 1998. This critical study explores the poet's depiction of life in the 1960's. The author argues that *Gunslinger* is best read as a reaction to the state of the nation in the 1960's. With bibliography and index.

Foster, Thomas. "Kick(ing) the Perpendiculars Outa Right Anglos: Edward Dorn's Multiculturalism." *Contemporary Literature* 38, no. 1 (Spring 1997): 78-105. Examines the book-length poem "Gunslinger."

Paul, Sherman. *The Lost America of Love*. Baton Rouge: Louisiana State University Press, 1981. A meditation on the poetry of Edward Dorn, Robert Creeley, and Robert Duncan, this book is a personal and intimate reflection on the power of these poets as experienced by the author. Paul explores Dorn's creative relationship to Walt Whitman, the effects of the Great Depression and World War II on his work, and the bedfellows of poetry and politics as they relate to Dorn's poetry.

Von Hallberg, Robert. *American Poetry and Culture, 1945-1980*. Cambridge, Mass.: Harvard University Press, 1985. The excellent chapter on Edward Dorn titled "This Marvellous Accidentalism" details the effects of Dorn's education, life experiences, and politics on his poetry. Dorn and his correspondence is frequently quoted, thereby giving authority to Von Hallberg's assertions. This is an accessible and well-blended account of the many influences at play in Dorn's poetry.

Wesling, Donald, ed. *Internal Resistances: The Poetry of Edward Dorn*. Berkeley: University of California Press, 1985. Wesling asserts that this collection of essays is the first book to address—as its sole concern—Dorn's poetic achievements. All phases of Dorn's poetry are represented in these lucid observations that illustrate Dorn as a self-reflexive, historical, ironic and, finally, post-postmodern poet. Dorn's opus, *Slinger*, is especially well studied in this book.

Sue L. Kimball;
bibliography updated by the editors

MARK DOTY

Born: Maryville, Tennessee; 1953

PRINCIPAL POETRY

Turtle, Swan: Poems, 1987
Bethlehem in Broad Daylight: Poems, 1991
My Alexandria: Poems, 1993
Atlantis: Poems, 1995
Sweet Machine: Poems, 1998
An Island Sheaf, 1998
"Turtle, Swan" and "Bethlehem in Broad Daylight": Two Volumes of Poetry, 2000
Source, 2001

OTHER LITERARY FORMS

Doty has written two memoirs; *Heaven's Coast: A Memoir* (1996) is a memoir of the illness and death from

Mark Doty (© Miriam Berkley)

acquired immunodeficiency syndrome (AIDS) of Doty's partner Wally Roberts. *Firebird: A Memoir* (1999) concerns Doty's early life and his discovery of his calling as a poet. *Still Life with Oysters and Lemon* (2001) is a meditation on the relationship between art and people's ability to see and understand the world around them. He has also contributed to anthologies such as Bill Moyers's *Fooling with Words: A Celebration of Poets and Their Craft* (1999).

ACHIEVEMENTS

Mark Doty has received numerous awards for his work. *My Alexandria* won the National Book Critics Circle Award (1994), the *Los Angeles Times* Book Award for Poetry (1993), and the T. S. Eliot Prize (1995) for the best book of poetry published in the United Kingdom. *Atlantis* won the Bingham Poetry Prize and the Lambda Literary Award. Doty has also received the Witter Bynner Poetry Prize from the American Academy of Arts and Letters and fellowships from several foundations including the Guggenheim Foundation. *Heaven's Coast* received the PEN/Martha Albrand Award for a first book of nonfiction.

BIOGRAPHY

As a child, Mark Doty moved often with his family (his father was a civilian employee of the Army Corps of Engineers). During his high school years in Tucson, Arizona, encouraged by poet Richard Shelton, Doty began to consider poetry seriously. He has said that he believes such mentoring is crucial to a beginning poet's development. Certainly Shelton and his household introduced Doty to an artistic world that was otherwise unavailable to him.

Doty received a B.A. from Drake University, in Des Moines, Iowa, where he also taught for a year. Duringthis time, uncertain how to deal with his sexual orientation, he was married for a short time. He also began to publish poetry, although he later repudiated his earliest volumes as being both immature and untrue to his own still-closeted identity. (He now considers his earliest book to be *Turtle, Swan*.) After he was divorced, he moved to Manhattan, where he fell in love with Wally Roberts, a window dresser for a department store. The two remained together for the rest of Rob-

erts's life. During this time Doty worked part time on an M.F.A. in creative writing from Goddard College in Montpelier, Vermont, where he and Roberts later lived for a time and renovated an old house. Later Doty taught at Goddard.

Turtle, Swan was published by Godine in 1987. Early reviews praised its quiet tone in presenting the gay experience in terms of the general human experience, which includes suffering. In 1989, Roberts was diagnosed with AIDS; the same year the couple discovered Provincetown, Massachusetts. Moved by the beauty of the place and reassured by the support of its gay community, they decided to settle there. Roberts died there in 1994. The experience was wrenching for Doty, who for a time was completely unable to write or even read. At last he found a release from grief in writing *Heaven's Coast*, the memoir in which he describes the experience of Roberts's illness.

In the latter half of the 1990's, Doty taught writing at various schools including the Iowa Writers' Workshop, the Columbia School of the Arts, and the University of Utah. When he began to teach one semester each year at the University of Houston, he and his partner, writer Paul Lisicky, started dividing their time between Texas and their two-hundred-year-old house in Provincetown.

ANALYSIS

Central to Mark Doty's work is his position as a gay poet; it informs all his poetic vision. Although he draws his subjects from a wide range of human experience, he views those subjects—as any writer must—through his own eyes. In Doty's case, those are eyes that have observed much beauty but also the painful experience of growing up gay in the 1950's and 1960's, the hatred expressed in American homophobia, and the grief of losing a lover to the ravages of AIDS. When a reviewer asked him about a "gay aesthetic," Doty noted that although gay people exist in as much variety as all human beings, a "sense of disjunction between surface and substance" is probably an essential part of gay life. A common theme in Doty's work examines the mutability of all things human; everything is ultimately scheduled to die, the poet says, but people must love anyway.

The relationship between surfaces and what lies beneath them is a recurrent motif in Doty's work both as he examines human experience and as he examines the external world. To discuss that relationship, he often uses the language of painting, a subject in which he is interested, as *Still Life with Oysters and Lemon* demonstrates. His diction draws frequently on the vocabulary of surface textures and colors.

A typical Doty poem is long, containing many short lines and short free verse stanzas, although he sometimes uses rhyme. His poems often incorporate a narrative element, but Doty's real goal usually lies in the meditation that accompanies the narrative, not in the event itself. Reading Doty's work, readers may feel they are accompanying the writer in the discovery of the meaning of the work as the poet leads them from the initial experience to its implications.

Doty has said that he is searching for ways to make his poetry political without relying on the language of the polemic or the harangue. He sees the possibility of making such poetry out of the materials of his own life, for he says that even when people tend their own gardens, they find that they have taken stances regarding social or political issues.

"Fog"

The poems of *My Alexandria* demonstrate this balance between the private and the political very powerfully as they address the AIDS epidemic and Wally Roberts's illness. In "Fog," Doty records the events that surrounded his and Roberts's being tested for the HIV virus. The poem's central metaphor is blood, like the color at the heart of the peony buds in the front garden or the blood Doty lost by a nick from the garden shears. As they wait the three weeks for the results, Doty sees blood everywhere, feels it welling up like a wine fountain. They pass time by consulting the Ouija board, and as they do, they find that all the spirits seem eager to speak "to someone who isn't dead yet." One of the spirits seems to say that "M. has immunity" (Doty was immune) and, enigmatically, that "W. has." Another spirit identifies God as being in the garden, and the speaker, Doty, concurs, perhaps because the garden is a place of so much dying as well as growth.

When they meet the public health care worker, they get the news. She gives Roberts "the word that begins with *P*"—positive, though Doty suggests that "planchette" (the marker for the Ouija board) or "peony" or any other word would be preferable. At last he asks what one of the Ouija spirits asked: "Kiss me,/ in front of the screen, please,/ the dead are watching." And he goes on: "They haven't had enough yet./ Every new bloom is falling apart." The fog of the title is the word the spirits use when "they can't speak clearly." Now, Doty says, it is the word he too must use for what he cannot say.

"The Wings"

The long poem "The Wings" uses an angel as its central metaphor. The poem begins at a country auction where a boy lies reading on the grass as he waits for his parents until he falls asleep The boy's parents waken him, and he leaves the magic world of dream and fiction to go back into "the world of things." As he slings his parents' purchase—a pair of snowshoes—across his back, he looks suddenly like "an angel/ to carry home the narrative of our storied,/ scattering things."

In the poem's next section, Doty recalls some of the things he and Roberts collected through the years. Once they picked apples in an abandoned orchard where the grasses were still flattened from where deer had been lying. Once they found a rabbit cage containing a pair of homemade painted pine rabbits—a find any collector would treasure. That day calls up memories of the German film *Der Himmel über Berlin* (1987; *Wings of Desire*, 1988), in which angels are willing to give up their immortality for the sake of human experience. Doty agrees with the angels—who wouldn't trade being an angel for such experiences? As he recalls the vivid scenes of that autumn day, he concludes "Don't let anybody tell you/ death's the price exacted/ for the ability to love. . . ."

The next section takes place as the AIDS quilt—the huge memorial quilt in which the hundreds of blocks are dedicated to people who died of AIDS—is being exhibited. Doty notes that many of the blocks are made of clothing of the dead; he concludes that these intimate blocks remind the viewer of "one essential, missing body." He goes on: "An empty pair of pants/ is mortality's severest evidence."

The poem's location moves into the autumn garden, a place in which errors can be corrected, plants can be lifted and reset in better places. The speaker says he is making an angel here, evidently using plantings to make an angelic shape. The image calls to his mind a dream in which he rescued a bird that loved him. When he took it from the closet and gave it water, "it began to beat the lush green music/ of its wings, and wrapped the brilliant risk/ of leaves all around my face."

Later, in Doty's class, his students puzzle over why the writer they are studying is so interested in mortality, and Doty says he longs to explain to them the image of the angel he has made, how it represents what is unthinkable between him and Roberts. It leans over his desk, over the bed where Roberts sleeps, just as the angels in the film watched their human charges. Doty names the angel *unharmed*. Its message seems to be that attachment to mortal beings is as futile as it is necessary to one's life as a human being: "You die by dying/ into what matters, which will kill you,/ but first it'll be enough."

ATLANTIS

The poems of Doty's next collection, *Atlantis*, form a testimony to the suffering AIDS causes both in those who have it and in the people who must watch them in their battle. The first poem of the collection, "Description," defends Doty's attention to the appearance of things: "What is description, after all,/ but encoded desire?"

"GROSSE FUGE"

The effects of AIDS are described in "Grosse Fuge." The title refers to the fugue, a form in classical music involving a series of variations on a motif. The poem uses this form as it recalls the autumn Robert Shore ("Bobby" in the poem) spent with Doty during Shore's last months with AIDS. The poem circles repeatedly through Bobby's incoherent but evocative pronouncements. At the same time, the speaker is studying the fugue form in order to appreciate Beethoven's "Grosse Fuge," the patterns and autumnal tone of which seem to match Shore's decline. The form, like the disease and even this poem, seems without resolution: What can I do but echo/ myself, vary and repeat?"

"ATLANTIS"

"Atlantis," the collection's long central poem, deals directly with Roberts's last days and with those of others who died of AIDS. The poem's six sections are linked by references to dreams. In the first, Doty recounts a dream in which his dog races into the road and is hit by a

car. In the second, Roberts tells a dream in which he sees a light at the end of a tunnel but says that he is not yet ready to join the beings streaming toward it. The third tells the dreams of others who have AIDS. The last three sections name other sorts of dreams. Section four introduces the dream city of Atlantis, apparently rising from the tidal marsh with an implied promise of life. The plumber's daughter in section five intends to cling to life for the sick loon she has found, just as Roberts stubbornly grasps this world, a commitment dramatized by his stroking the new dog that has joined the household in the last section, a sign of his doomed determination to live.

OTHER MAJOR WORKS

NONFICTION: *Heaven's Coast: A Memoir,* 1996; *Firebird: A Memoir,* 1999; *Still Life with Oysters and Lemon,* 2001.

BIBLIOGRAPHY

Bing, Jonathan. "Mark Doty: The Idea of Order on Cape Cod." *Publishers Weekly* 243 (April 15, 1996): 44-46. Doty discusses his working methods in reference to his recent prose work as well as to his poems.

Doty, Mark. Interview by Michael Glover. *New Statesman* 126 (May 30, 1997): 44-45. The interview contains some biographical detail about how Doty came to poetry. The poet also comments on the effect of Wally Roberts's death on his writing

Glover, Michael. Review of *Atlantis*. *New Statesman* 125 (July 26, 1996): 47. Glover calls Doty the best American poet since the death of Robert Lowell and gives some analysis to his imagery and diction.

Landau, Deborah. "'How to Live. What to Do.': The Poetics and Politics of AIDS." *American Literature* 68 (March, 1996): 193-226. Discusses the work of four poets as literary responses to the AIDS epidemic; examines Doty's work in detail.

Wonderlich, Mark. "About Mark Doty." *Ploughshares* 25 (Spring, 1999): 183-189. The profile contains some biographical information as well as brief discussions of *My Alexandria, Atlantis,* and *Sweet Machine.*

Ann D. Garbett

Rita Dove

Born: Akron, Ohio; August 28, 1952

PRINCIPAL POETRY

The Yellow House on the Corner, 1980
Museum, 1983
Thomas and Beulah, 1986
Grace Notes, 1989
Selected Poems, 1993
Mother Love, 1995
On the Bus with Rosa Parks, 1999

OTHER LITERARY FORMS

Rita Dove has published *Fifth Sunday* (1985), a collection of short stories; *Through the Ivory Gate* (1992), a novel; and *The Poet's World* (1995), a collection of essays. *The Darker Face of the Earth*, a verse drama, appeared in 1994.

ACHIEVEMENTS

Rita Dove's literary honors include grants and fellowships from the National Endowment for the Arts, the Academy of American Poets, the Guggenheim Foundation, and the General Electric Foundation. She spent 1988-1989 as a Senior Mellon Fellow at the National Humanities Center in North Carolina. In 1987 her collection *Thomas and Beulah* made her the first black woman since Gwendolyn Brooks to win the Pulitzer Prize. She has also been awarded the national Medal in the Humanities, the Heinz Award in the Arts and Humanities, and the Sara Lee Frontrunner Award. Dove served as poet laureate of the United States from 1993 to 1995. She was awarded the 1998 Levinson Prize from *Poetry* magazine and the 1999 John Frederick Nims Translation Award (together with Fred Viebahn).

BIOGRAPHY

Born in 1952 in Akron, Ohio, Rita Dove is the daughter of Ray and Elvira (Hord) Dove. She received a B.A. in 1973 from Miami University (Ohio) and then, on a Fulbright Fellowship, attended the University of Tübingen, Germany, to study modern European literature. She returned to the United States to earn an M.F.A.

at the highly regarded University of Iowa Writers' Workshop in 1977. She then held a number of teaching posts and traveled widely in Europe and the Middle East, later becoming a professor of English at the University of Virginia. During the summer of 1998, the Boston Symphony Orchestra performed her song cycle of a woman's life, *Seven for Luck*, with music by John Williams. Along with all her other activities, she writes a weekly column, "Poet's Choice," for *The Washington Post.* Dove married Fred Viebahn, a writer, and with him had a daughter, Aviva Chantal Tamu Dove-Viebahn.

ANALYSIS

In a period when much American poetry is condemned as being merely an exercise in solipsistic navel gazing, and when African American poetry more specifically seems to have lapsed into hibernation after the vigorous activity of the Black Arts movement, Rita Dove steps forth with a body of work that answers such criticism resoundingly. Hers is a poetry characterized by discipline and technical proficiency, surprising breadth of reference, a willingness to approach emotionally charged subjects with aesthetic objectivity, and a refusal to define herself only in terms of blackness. She combines a novelist's eye for action and gesture with the lyric poet's exalted sense of language. Rita Dove's distinguishing feature is her ability to turn a cold gaze on the larger world with which she has to interact as a social being— and as an African American woman. That gaze is filtered through an aesthetic sensibility that regards poetry as a redemptive force, a transformational power.

The startling scope of Dove's learning opens for her poetry a correspondingly vast range of topics and concerns, but the most persistent, and the one that most distinguishes her work from that of poets in the 1970's and 1980's, is history. She is constantly laboring to bring into focus the individual struggle in the ebb and flow of the historical tide. A second major concern is cultural collision, the responses of an outsider to a foreign culture, and she pursues this theme in a number of travel poems. Dove also plumbs the circumstances of her life as a way of confronting the puzzle of her own identity— as an African American, as a woman, as a daughter, as a parent—but she manages self-dramatization without self-aggrandizement.

Rita Dove (Fred Viebahn, courtesy of Pantheon Books)

Dove has been lauded for her technical acumen. While much contemporary poetry is best characterized by a certain casualness and laxity, she has created poetry in which no verse is "free." Each poem gives the impression of having been chiseled, honed, and polished. Her poems evolve into highly individual structures, rather than traditional forms, although it is possible to find an occasional sonnet neatly revised and partially hidden. More often she stresses rhythm and sound and uses interior rhyme, slant rhyme, and feminine rhyme to furnish her stanzas with a subtle organizing principle, what she calls the "sound cage" of a poem. Her idiom is predominantly colloquial, but she can adopt the stiffened, formal diction of the eighteenth and nineteenth centuries when evoking personas from those periods. In her mastery of the craft Dove reveals an attitude toward poetry itself—a deeply felt love and respect—that also influences the approach a reader must take to it. Her work makes demands upon the reader because of that love.

Dove's first two volumes, *The Yellow House on the Corner* and *Museum*, both provide a balance between the personal or individual and the social or cultural. Each is divided into sections that allow the author to address concerns that she wishes for now to remain separate. Yet it has also been noted that the titles of these two books signal a shift in Dove's emphasis from the homely and familiar, "the yellow house," to the more sophisticated and arcane "museum." This generalization should not, however, obscure the fact that the poet's interests in these books overlap considerably. *Museum* is the more consciously organized, with its sections pointedly titled and each dealing with a central topic—history and myth, art and artifact, autobiography and the personal past, life in the modern world.

Dove's next volume, *Thomas and Beulah*, represents her coming of age critically, a step into the position of a leading African American poet. It allows her to extend her continual dissertation on the single person striving in the midst of historical flux; at the same time she can pursue her abiding interest in her own family romance, the question of heritage. Following *Thomas and Beulah*, and still availing itself of a variety of themes, *Grace Notes* is by far the most intensely autobiographical of her works, becoming a study in limitation and poignant regret. How, she seems to ask here, does one grant to daily life that ornament or variation that magically transforms it? *On the Bus with Rosa Parks* examines the panoply of human endeavor, exploring the intersection of individual fates with the grand arc of history.

THE YELLOW HOUSE ON THE CORNER

Poems in *The Yellow House on the Corner* often depict the collision of wish with reality, of heart's desire with the dictates of the world. This collision is made tolerable by the working of the imagination, and the result is, for Dove, "magic," or the existence of an unexplainable occurrence. It is imagination and the art it produces that allow the speaker in "This Life" to see that "the possibilities/ are golden dresses in a nutshell." "Possibilities" have the power to transform this life into something distinct and charmed. Even the woman driven mad with grief over the loss of her son (or husband?) in "The Bird Frau" becomes a testament to possibility in her desire to "let everything go wild!" She becomes a bird-woman as a way of reuniting with her lost airman, who died in the war over France. While her condition may be perceived as pathetic, Dove refuses to indulge sentimentality, instead seeing her madness as a form of undying hope.

The refusal to indulge sentimentality is a mark of Dove's critical intelligence. It allows her to interpose an objectifying distance between herself and the subject. She knows the absolute value of perspective, so that while she can exult in the freedom that imagination makes possible, she recognizes that such liberty has its costs and dangers too. Two poems in particular reveal this desire and her wariness: "Geometry" and "Sightseeing." In the former, Dove parallels the study of points, lines, and planes in space with the work of the poet: "I prove a theorem and the house expands:/ the windows jerk free to hover near the ceiling,/ the ceiling floats away with a sigh." Barriers and boundaries disappear in the imagination's manipulation of them, but that manipulation has its methodology or aesthetic: "I *prove* a theorem. . . ."

In "Sightseeing" the speaker, a traveler in Europe after World War II, comes upon what would seem to be a poem waiting to happen. The inner courtyard of a village church has been left just as it was found by the villagers after an Allied bombing raid. It is filled with the shattered cherubim and seraphim that had previously decorated the inner terrace of the building: "What a consort of broken dolls!" Yet the speaker repudiates any temptation to view the sight as the villagers must—"A terrible sign. . . ." Instead she coolly ponders the rubble with the detached air of a detective: "Let's look/ at the facts." She "reads" the scene and the observers' attention to it as a cautionary lesson. The "children of angels" become "childish monsters." Since she distinguishes herself from the devout villagers, she can also see herself and her companion in the least flattering light: "two drunks" coming all the way across the town "to look at a bunch of smashed statues."

This ability to debunk and subvert expectations is a matter of artistic survival for Dove and a function of her calm intelligence. As an African American poet she is aware of the tradition of letters she steps into. Two other poems imply that this tradition can be problematic. In "Upon Meeting Don L. Lee, in a Dream" Dove encounters Lee (now known as Haki R. Madhubuti), a leading figure in the Black Arts movement, which attempted to generate a populist, specifically black aesthetic. The figure that emerges from Dove's poem, however, is unable to change except to self-destruct: "I can see caviar/ Imbedded like buckshot between his teeth." Her dreamportrait of Lee deflates not only his masculinity but his status as cultural icon as well. In "Nigger Song: An Odyssey" Dove seems to hark back further for a literary forebear and finds one in Gwendolyn Brooks, the first black woman to win the Pulitzer Prize. Although by 1967 Brooks would have come to embrace the black nationalism that Lee embodied, Dove's poem echoes the Brooks of an earlier time, the composer of "We Real Cool." In her evocation of "the nigger night" Dove captures the same vibrant energy that Brooks both celebrates and laments with the realization that the energy of urban African American youth is allowed no purposeful outlet and will turn upon itself. She writes: "Nothing can catch us./ Laughter spills like gin from glasses."

Some of the most compelling poems in Dove's first book are in a group of vignettes and portraits from the era of American slavery. These poems not only reveal her historical awareness but also allow her to engage the issue of race from a distance. Dove wants her poetry to produce anger, perhaps, but not to be produced only by anger. One example of this aesthetic distance from emotion might be "The Abduction," a brief foray in the voice of Solomon Northrup. Northrup is a free black lured to Washington, D.C., by "new friends" with the promise of good work, and then kidnapped and sold into bondage. Dove dwells on the duplicity of these men and Northrup's susceptibility to them. Yet no pronouncements are made. The poem ends with the end of freedom, but that ending has been foreshadowed by the tightly controlled structure of the poem itself, with each stanza shortening as the scope of the victim's world constricts to this one-line conclusion: "I woke and found myself alone, in darkness and in chains." The indignation and disgust that such an episode could call forth are left entirely to the reader.

MUSEUM

Dove's next volume, *Museum*, is itself, as the title suggests, a collection of historical and aesthetic artifacts. The shaping impulse of the book seems to be retrospective, a looking back to people and things that have been somehow suspended in time by legend, by historical circumstance, by all-too-human emotional wish. Dove intends to delve beneath the publicly known side of these stories—to excavate, in a sense, and uncover something forgotten but vital. The book is filled with both historical and mythical figures, all sharing the single trait of muted voice. Thus, "Nestor's Bathtub" begins: "As usual, legend got it all/ wrong." The private torment of a would-be martyr is made public in "Catherine of Alexandria." In "The Hill Has Something to Say" the poet speculates on the buried history of Europe, the cryptic messages that a culture sends across time. In one sense, the hill is a metaphor for this book, a repository of signs and images that speak only to that special archaeologist, the reader.

In the section titled "In the Bulrush" Dove finds worthy subjects in unlikely places and draws them from hiding. "Banneker" is another example of her flair for evoking the antebellum world of slavery, where even the free man is wrongly regarded because of his race. In the scientist Benjamin Banneker she finds sensitivity, eloquence, and intelligence, all transformed by prejudice into mere eccentricity. Banneker was the first black man to devise an almanac and served on Thomas Jefferson's commission to lay out the city of Washington, D.C., but the same qualities that lifted him to prominence made him suspect in the eyes of white society. Dove redeems this crabbed conception of the man in an alliterative final passage that focuses attention on his vision:

> Lowering his eyes to fields
> sweet with the rot of spring, he could see
> a government's domed city
> rising from the morass and spreading
> in a spiral of lights . . .

A third section of the book is devoted entirely to poems about the poet's father, and they represent her efforts to understand him. It is a very personal grouping, made to seem all the more so by the preceding sections in which there is little or nothing directly personal at all.

In the final section, "Primer for the Nuclear Age," Dove includes what is one of her most impressive performances. Although she has not shown herself to be a poet of rage, she is certainly not inured to the social and political injustice she observes. Her work is a way of channeling and controlling such anger; as she says in "Primer for the Nuclear Age": "if you've/ got a heart at all, someday/ it will kill you." "Parsley," the final poem

of *Museum*, summons up the rank insanity of Rafael Trujillo, dictator of the Dominican Republic, who, on October 2, 1957, ordered twenty thousand black Haitians killed because they could not pronounce the letter *r* in *perejil*, Spanish for parsley. The poem is divided into two sections; the first is a villanelle spoken by the Haitians; the second describes General Trujillo on the day of his decision. The second section echoes many of the lines from the Haitians' speech, drawing murderer and victim together, suggesting a disturbing complicity among all parties in this episode of unfettered power. Even though Dove certainly wants to draw attention to this event, the real subject here is the lyric poet's realm—that point at which language intersects with history and actually determines its course.

THOMAS AND BEULAH

Thomas and Beulah garnered the Pulitzer Prize, but it is more important for the stage it represents in Dove's poetic development. Her first two books reveal a lyric poet generally working within the bounds of her medium. The lyric poem denies time, process, change. It becomes a frozen moment, an emotion reenacted in the reading. In *Thomas and Beulah* she pushes at the limitations of the form by stringing together, "as beads on a necklace," a whole series of these lyric moments. As the poems begin to reflect upon one another, the effect is a dramatic unfolding in which the passing of time is represented, even though the sequence never establishes a conventional plot. To accomplish this end Dove creates a two-sided book: Thomas's side ("Mandolin," twenty-one poems) followed by Beulah's ("Canary in Bloom," twenty-one poems).

The narrative moves from Thomas's riverboat life and the crucial death of his friend Lem to his arrival in Akron and marriage, through the birth of children, jobs, illness, and death. Beulah's part of the book then begins, moving through her parents' stormy relationship, her courtship with Thomas, marriage, pregnancy, work, and death. These two lives transpire against the historical backdrop of the great migration, the Depression, World War II, and the March on Washington; however, these events are practically the only common elements in the two sides of the story. Thomas and Beulah seem to live separate lives. Their communication with each other is implicit in the survival of the marriage itself. Throughout, Dove handles the story through exacting use of imagery and character.

Thomas emerges as a haunted man, dogged by the death of his friend Lem, which occurs in the opening poem, "The Event." Thomas drunkenly challenges Lem to swim from the deck of the riverboat to an island in the Mississippi. Lem drowns in the attempt to reach what is probably a mirage, and Thomas is left with "a stinking circle of rags/ the half-shell mandolin." In "Courtship" he begins to woo Beulah, but the poem implies that the basis of their relationship will be the misinterpreted gesture and that Thomas's guilt has left him with a void. He casually takes a yellow silk scarf from around his neck and wraps it around her shoulders; "a gnat flies/ in his eye and she thinks/ he's crying." Thomas's gift, rather than a spontaneous transfer of warmth, is a sign of his security in his relative affluence. The show of vulnerability and emotional warmth is accidental. The lyric poet in Dove allows her to compress this range of possibility in the isolated gesture or image. Beulah's life is conveyed as a more interior affair, a process of attaining the wisdom to understand her world rather than to resist it openly. In "The Great Palace of Versailles" Beulah's reading becomes her secret escape from the nastiness of the whites for whom she works in Charlotte's Dress Shoppe. As she lies dying in the final poem, "The Oriental Ballerina," the contemplation of the tiny figurine seems a similar invitation to fantasy, but her sensibilities have always been attuned to seeing the world as it is, as it has to be, and the poem ends in a brief flurry of realistic details and an air of acceptance; there is "no cross, just the paper kiss/ of a kleenex above the stink of camphor,/ the walls exploding with shabby tutus. . . ."

GRACE NOTES

Grace Notes marks Dove's return to the purely lyric mode, but an autobiographical impulse dominates the work to an unprecedented degree. More than in any of her previous collections, the poet can be seen as actor in her own closet drama, whether as a young child learning a rather brutal lesson in the Southern black school of survival ("Crab-Boil") or as a mother groping for a way to reveal feminine mysteries to her own little girl ("After Reading *Mickey in the Night Kitchen* for the Third Time Before Bed"). The willingness to become more self-referential carries with it the danger of obscurity, the in-side joke that stays inside. Dove, however, seems to open herself to a kind of scrutiny and challenge that offer no hiding place, and that assay extends to her own poetic practice. In "Dedication," a poem in the manner of Czesław Miłosz, Dove seems to question the veracity of her own technical expertise: "What are music or books if not ways/ to trap us in rumors? The freedom of fine cages!"

In the wickedly ironic "Ars Poetica" she places herself on the literary chain of being with what might pass for self-deprecation. Her ambition is to make a small poem, like a ghost town, a minute speck on the "larger map of wills." "Then you can pencil me in as a hawk:/ a traveling x-marks-the-spot." Yet this hawk is not a songbird to be taken lightly. The very next poem in the book unleashes the bird of prey in Dove (a pun she surely intends); in the aptly titled "Arrow," she exposes the sexism and racism of an "eminent scholar" in all of its condescending glory. This focus on the autobiographical element is not to imply that the range of subjects in *Grace Notes* is not still wide-ranging and surprising. Echoes of her earlier books sound clearly; so does the wit that makes them always engaging: "Here's a riddle for Our Age: when the sky's the limit,/ how can you tell you've gone too far?"

MOTHER LOVE

In *Mother Love*, Dove survives her overused source material, the myth of Demeter and Persephone, by transforming it into something deeply personal. She allows herself to be inhabited by the myth, and Dove's Demeter consciousness reveals that every time a daughter walks out the door, the abduction by Hades begins again. Dove's persona adopts Persephone's stance in "Persephone in Hell"; here, Dove recalls, at twenty, enjoying the risks of visiting Paris. She felt her mother's worry but asserts, "I was doing what she didn't need to know," testing her ripeness against the world's (man's) treachery. Dove employs loose sonnet shapes in these poems, giving herself license in order to provide authentic contemporary voices. At once dramatic, narrative, and highly lyrical, these poems more than fulfill the expectations of those who anointed her at the outset of her career.

ON THE BUS WITH ROSA PARKS

On the Bus with Rosa Parks is a more miscellaneous collection, but with several cohesive groupings. The

"Cameos" sequence provides sharply etched vignettes of working-class life, a recurrent subject in Dove's writings. The closing sequence, from which the entire collection takes its name, explores the interface of public and private lives in contemporary African American history. As ever, Dove is a superb storyteller whose movie-like poems are energized by precise imagery and tonal perfection.

OTHER MAJOR WORKS

LONG FICTION: *Through the Ivory Gate*, 1992.
SHORT FICTION: *Fifth Sunday*, 1985.
PLAY: *The Darker Face of the Earth*, pb. 1994 (verse drama).
NONFICTION: *The Poet's World*, 1995.
EDITED TEXT: *The Best American Poetry*, 2001.

BIBLIOGRAPHY

Dove, Rita. "Coming Home." Interview by Steven Schneider. *The Iowa Review* 19 (Fall, 1989): 112-123. This interview is devoted almost entirely to a discussion of *Thomas and Beulah* and the process of its creation.

_____. Interview by Judith Kitchen and others. *Black American Literature Forum* 20 (Fall, 1986): 227-240. In this fine interview the bulk of attention is paid to Dove's *Museum*, especially the poem "Parsley," and to *Thomas and Beulah*. Dove is quite forthcoming in revealing certain writerly decisions and her method of working. She also discusses her short stories in *Fifth Sunday*.

Harrington, Walt. "A Narrow World Made Wide." *The Washington Post Magazine*, May 7, 1995, 13-19, 28-29. Harrington provides a close examination of Dove in the process of writing. Her ambitions, work habits, and revision strategies receive a clear, sympathetic, and nonacademic treatment.

McDowell, Robert. "The Assembling Vision of Rita Dove." *Callaloo: A Black South Journal of Arts and Letters* 9 (Winter, 1986): 61-70. This article provides an excellent overview of Dove's accomplishments in her first three books and places her in the larger context of American poetry. McDowell argues that Dove's distinction is her role as "an assembler," someone who pulls together the facts of this life and presents them in challenging ways.

Newson, Adele S. Review of *On the Bus with Rosa Parks. World Literature Today* 74, no. 1 (Winter, 2000): 165-166. Newson examines the collection section by section, suggesting that the book forms an overall story bonded by related imagery and linked through digressions. In it, we hear "the voice of a community's history and human response."

Pereira, Malin. "An Interview with Rita Dove." *Contemporary Literature* 40, no. 2 (Summer, 1999): 182-213. This wide-ranging interview includes Dove's comments on the writings of Breyten Breytenbach, the Black Arts movement, her own literary influences, and her experience living in the South.

Rampersad, Arnold. "The Poems of Rita Dove." *Callaloo: A Black South Journal of Arts and Letters* 9 (Winter, 1986): 52-60. In one of the best articles yet written on Dove, Rampersad places her in the context of African American poetry on the basis of her first two books of poetry (this article precedes *Thomas and Beulah*). He emphasizes particularly the tight control of emotion that is implicit in her poetic practice.

Shoptaw, John. Review of *Thomas and Beulah*, by Rita Dove. *Black American Literature Forum* 21 (Fall, 1987): 335-341. Although this is only a review of Dove's Pulitzer Prize-winning volume, it is still one of the best sources for isolating specific verbal tactics that Dove employs. It also addresses the problem of narrative and the difficult task Dove set for herself in telling the story as she did.

Nelson Hathcock,
updated by Philip K. Jason

MICHAEL DRAYTON

Born: Hartshill, England; 1563
Died: London, England; December 23, 1631

PRINCIPAL POETRY

The Harmonie of the Church, 1591
Idea, the Shepheard's Garland, 1593
Peirs Gaveston, 1593

Ideas Mirrour, 1594

Matilda, 1594

Endimion and Phoebe, 1595

The Tragicall Legend of Robert, Duke of Normandy,
    1596

Mortimeriados, 1596

Englands Heroicall Epistles, 1597

The Barrons Wars, 1603

The Owle, 1604

Poemes Lyrick and Pastorall, 1606

The Legend of Great Cromwell, 1607

Poly-Olbion, 1612-1622

Poems, 1619

The Battaile of Agincourt, 1627

The Muses Elizium, 1630

The Works of Michael Drayton, 1931-1941 (5 vol-
    umes; J. W. Hebel, Kathleen Tillotson, and B. H.
    Newdigate, editors)

OTHER LITERARY FORMS

Except for brief prefaces to his books and letters, four of which were published in the *Works* of his friend William Drummond of Hawthornden, Michael Drayton wrote exclusively in verse. Between about 1597 and 1602 he is reputed to have written or collaborated on twenty plays, all of which are lost except *The First Part of the True and Honorable Historie of the Life of Sir John Old-Castle the Good Lord Cobham* (pr. 1599). The titles indicate that these were chronicle history plays.

ACHIEVEMENTS

According to Francis Meres in 1598, Michael Drayton was "a man of virtuous disposition, honest conversation, and well-governed carriage; which is almost miraculous among good wits in these declining times." His early reputation was as a Spenserian, and as his life went on, friends perceived him as a conservative man increasingly out of sorts with the post-Elizabethan world. Though inevitably overshadowed by major contemporaries such as Edmund Spenser, his fellow-Warwickshirite William Shakespeare, John Donne, and Ben Jonson, he wrote well in virtually every popular literary genre of his day, and in his "heroical epistles" and Horatian odes introduced forms which, while not of major importance thereafter in English literature, he prac-

ticed with distinction. With reference to his longest work, Charles Lamb called Drayton "that panegyrist of my native earth; who has gone over her soul in his *Poly-Olbion* with the fidelity of a herald, and the painful love of a son." Drayton's odes in praise of English accomplishments, the "Ballad of Agincourt" and "To the Virginian Voyage," remain anthology favorites, as do several poems from *Idea*, one of the finest sonnet sequences in English.

As one of England's first professional poets, Drayton nearly always wrote competently and on occasion superbly, especially in his lyrics. In his best poems he blends an intense love of his native land with a classicism marked by clarity, decorum, careful attention to form, and—with respect to all passions except his patriotic fervor—calm detachment.

BIOGRAPHY

Most of the available biographical facts derive from Michael Drayton's own poems and dedications. He was born in northern Warwickshire in 1563 and seems to have been reared and well-educated in the household of Sir Henry Goodere at Polesworth, not far from his native village of Hartshill. To fulfill his lifelong desire to be a poet, he moved to London at least by 1591, although more likely in the later 1580's. Beyond reasonable doubt the "Idea" of his sonnets honors Sir Henry's daughter Anne. Drayton may have been in love with Anne; around 1595, however, she married a man of her own class, Sir Henry Rainsford. Of Drayton's ever marrying there is no record. In later years, the poet spent his summers at Clifford Hall, Gloucestershire, the Rainsfords' seat, and he is known to have been treated by Lady Rainsford's physician, Dr. John Hall, who was Shakespeare's son-in-law. Although he apparently lived the last forty years of his life in London, Drayton's fondness for rural England and his admiration for the values of the landed gentry were obviously genuine. He is credited with having been on familiar terms with nearly every important literary Englishman of his time. Dying near the end of 1631, he was buried in Westminster Abbey.

ANALYSIS

In an age when the writing of poetry was an avocation for actors, courtiers, clergymen, and landed gentlemen,

Michael Drayton devoted his life to poetry. In a verse epistle to a friend, Henry Reynolds, Drayton writes of how, at the age of ten, he beseeched his tutor to make him a poet. Being a man of the Renaissance, the teacher started him on eclogues, first those of "honest Mantuan," a currently popular Italian humanist, then the great Vergil himself, after which Drayton studied the English poets, beginning, of course, with Geoffrey Chaucer and working through to contemporaries such as William Shakespeare, Christopher Marlowe, Samuel Daniel, and Ben Jonson (Drayton having of course grown up in the meantime). Both the classics and the native poetical tradition continued to inspire him throughout his long career, and in his most characteristic work he adapts classical models to his own time, place, and language.

To a greater extent, perhaps, than any of his contemporaries, Drayton straddles the sixteenth and seventeenth centuries and raises the question of whether he was more Elizabethan or Jacobean. As he does not fall squarely into the usual categories of Spenserian, Jonsonian, or Metaphysical, his work challenges the usefulness—certainly the inclusiveness—of these categories of English Renaissance poetry. His career may be divided into three stages, the first and last of which are short but enormously energetic and productive, while the long middle stage demonstrates the characteristic development of his art while incidentally furnishing most of the poems for which he is best known today. In the first and, paradoxically, last stages he is most Elizabethan, or, to use a term popularized by C. S. Lewis in his *English Literature in the Sixteenth Century* (1954), most "golden."

EARLY PERIOD

His early period begins with the publication in 1591 of a drab religious exercise called *The Harmonie of the Church*, but between 1593 and 1595 he brought out three works which typify and enrich that most remarkable period in English letters: *Idea, the Shepheard's Garland; Ideas Mirrour*; and *Endimion and Phoebe*. The first of these demonstrates a young poet's preliminary pastoral, Vergil having worked from the shepherds' dale to epic heights—a program which the ambitious Spenser had already imitated and which many others, including John Milton, would imitate. The poems are eclogues, shepherds' dialogues on love, death, the de-

cline of the world, and poetry itself; they are meant to exercise a poet's versatility in song. Drayton's are not notable, except perhaps for their unusually frequent references to English topography; they do, however, demonstrate that the poet, at thirty, had long since learned his craft.

IDEAS MIRROUR

Ideas Mirrour is a sonnet sequence, not a classical form to be sure, but one associated with the great fourteenth century classicist, Petrarch. Since the posthumous publication of Sir Philip Sidney's *Astrophel and Stella* in 1591, poets had flooded England with sonnets featuring graceful tributes to beautiful ladies with stylized and often classical names such as Celia, Delia, and Diana, along with the laments of versifying suitors frustrated by the very aloofness that attracted them so fatally. Shakespeare's "Dark Lady," it might be noted, is in a number of respects the exception to the rule. *Ideas Mirrour*, fifty-one sonnets long, is conventionally melancholy, sometimes awkward, and regularly sensuous in the well-bred Elizabethan way.

ENDIMION AND PHOEBE

Endimion and Phoebe, in 516 pentameter couplets, is Drayton's contribution to the Ovidian love narrative, a genre that had already generated Shakespeare's *Venus and Adonis* (1593) and Marlowe's *Hero and Leander* (1598). Endimion is a shepherd lad who loves the fair goddess Phoebe at once passionately and chastely; she rewards him by wrapping him in a "fiery mantle" and lofting him to the empyrean, where he is shown a series of splendors both astronomical and divine. The poem is full of rich, smooth-flowing language—not so thoroughly a thing of beauty as John Keats's *Endymion* (1818) but a joy nevertheless.

MORTIMERIADOS

Myth, pastoral, and love lyrics provided only limited opportunities for another English obsession in the heady years following the defeat of the supposedly invincible Spanish Armada in 1588: the patriotism that rings forth in John of Gaunt's "Methinks I am a prophet new inspired" speech in Shakespeare's *Richard II* (1595-1596) and so many other poems of the 1590's. Thus, 1596 found Drayton issuing *Mortimeriados*, on the political struggles of the reign of Edward II. Drayton was again following the lead of other poets, this time Shakespeare and Daniel (who had published the first four books of his *Civil Wars* in 1595) more than Spenser and Marlowe. *Mortimeriados*, which can be considered the last of the poems of Drayton's early phase, is only one of a series, begun three years earlier in his *Peirs Gaveston* and continuing throughout most of his life, in which he delves into the history, topography, and presumed national virtues of England.

MIDDLE PERIOD

As the childless Queen Elizabeth grew old and crotchety, ambitious courtiers jockeyed for position, and as the problem of the succession loomed, England's mood changed. Spenser died in 1599, leaving *The Faerie Queene* unfinished and its shadowy heroine Gloriana unwed to Prince Arthur. Shakespeare turned increasingly to the writing of tragedy. Drayton's heart remained, as it always would remain, unabashedly Elizabethan. As his art matured, however, he welded his classicism and patriotism in poems of much greater originality.

ENGLANDS HEROICALL EPISTLES

Englands Heroicall Epistles marks a turning point. Of this work can be said what surely cannot be said of anything in Drayton's earlier poems: It is something new in English literature. His classical model, Ovid's *Heroides*, had been imitated as far back as Geoffrey Chaucer's *The Legend of Good Women* (1380-1386), but instead of retaining Ovid's subject matter—the plights of a group of legendary and historical women of the ancient world such as Dido, Medea, and Cleopatra—and forgoing Ovid's epistolary form, as had Chaucer, Drayton wrote his poem in the form of letters to and from such women as Eleanor Cobham, Rosamond Clifford, and Alice, Countess of Salisbury—that is, women involved in the political history of England, usually as royal wives or mistresses, although in the case of Lady Jane Grey, as the victim of political intrigue.

Drayton's changes are instructive. All the letters of the *Heroides* are purportedly those of the women, mostly complaints by women abandoned by their consorts, with Ovid avoiding monotony through the exercise of his considerable psychological insight. Drayton, who much preferred to build situations involving the interactions of characters, hit upon the idea of an exchange of letters between the man and the woman, with some-

times hers coming first, sometimes his. Notorious royal mistresses such as Rosamond Clifford and Jane Shore had spoken in verse before, but chiefly in the moralizing vein of that stodgy Elizabethan perennial, *A Mirror for Magistrates* (1599), in which the ghosts of people fallen from high place appear for the purpose of lugubriously advising and admonishing the reader. Thomas Churchyard ends his account of *Shore's Wife* (1563), for example: "A mirror make of my great overthrow;/ Defy this world and all his wanton ways;/ Beware by me that spent so ill her days." Drayton's Jane, on the other hand, concludes her letter to Edward IV: "thou art become my fate,/ And mak'st me love even in the midst of hate." He refuses to subordinate his lovers to an abstract moral, though, to be sure, he has selected them in the first place as manifestations of the national spirit.

THE BARRONS WARS

Drayton's professionalism drove him to protracted and extensive revisions, and many of the works of his middle period are reworkings of earlier poems. In *The Barrons Wars*, he turns the rhyme royal of *Mortimeriados* into ottava rima, explaining that although the former had "harmony," the latter possessed "majesty, perfection, and solidity." Drayton aspired to an epic, but he was no Vergil, and *The Barrons Wars*, though an improvement on *Mortimeriados*, was no *Aeneid* (c. 29-19 B.C.E.). In other cases, his critics find his "improvements" made in vain, as in his *Poemes Lyrick and Pastorall*, which surely made his contemporary readers wonder why, twenty-seven years after Spenser's *Shepheardes Calendar* (1579), Drayton insisted on reworking old eclogues. As for his modern readers, they generally prefer *Endimion and Phoebe* to the new version, *The Man in the Moon*.

ODES

The latter volume is nevertheless important for introducing another of Drayton's successful classical adaptations, his odes. A deservedly obscure poet named John Southern had made a few Pindaric odes in the 1580's, but Drayton is the first Englishman to imitate the Horatian type. After acknowledging in his preface both Pindar's triumphant and Anacreon's amorous odes, Drayton intimates a fondness for the "mixed" odes of Horace. Having written in both the Ovidian and the Vergilian manner, Drayton was now treading in the footsteps of a poet notable for understanding and working within his limitations. In contrast to the high-flying poets, Horace compares himself, in the second ode of his fourth book, to a bee gathering nectar on the banks of the Tiber. Eschewing the heroic and the passionate, he concentrates on such themes as moderation, hospitality, friendship, and the propriety of accepting one's fate. Although Drayton did not easily accept his fate as a leftover Elizabethan in the age of James I, he recognized in the Horatian ode the vehicle for a range of expression that had not found utterance in earlier English poetry. What he suggested in his odes, Ben Jonson and the neoclassicists of the new century would exploit more thoroughly.

For the ode to become a recognizable form in English, Drayton had to find an equivalent of Horace's favorite four-line Alcaic and Sapphic stanzas. He wisely avoided the English imitations of Latin quantitative verse which had so intrigued some of the Elizabethans but had defeated all of them except Thomas Campion in a handful of lyrics. Drayton favored a five- or six-line stanza with short lines and prominent rhymes. Coupled with his usual end-stopped lines, the rhymes not only create an effect entirely different from Horace's but also force Drayton into an unnatural syntax marked by ellipses, inversions, and the omission of transitions. English poets had tended to avoid short lines except in song lyrics, preferring the opposite risk of the hexameter line, which Alexander Pope would later compare to a "wounded snake," and the even longer fourteener. Whether Drayton thought of his odes as singable or not, he knew that short lines and obtrusive rhymes had been used most successfully for satiric and humorous purposes, as in Chaucer's "Tale of Sir Thopas" and John Skelton's *Phillip Sparrow* (c. 1508).

Except in a few instances, such as "The Sacrifice to Apollo," where he fell into a too self-consciously Horatian posture, Drayton avoided servility in the ode as he had in *Englands Heroicall Epistles* In the odes on Agincourt and the peak, in "To the New Year" and "To the Virginian Voyage," the reader senses an early seventeenth century Englishman responding directly to his milieu as Horace had responded to Rome in the first century B.C.E. The similarity between the two poets, less a formal or temperamental likeness than a kind of equiv-

alent spirit grounded in love for land and landscape, kept Drayton from sounding like an "ancient." He did not have to praise Horace's Bandusian fountain and Caecubian wine, for he had "Buxton's delicious baths" and good "strong ale" to celebrate. The whole "Ode Written on the Peak" is built on the proposition that England is as worthy of an ode as anything in ancient Rome. Drayton's classicism, then, takes the form of an Englishman singing his own island in a diction and rhythm assertively Anglo-Saxon. Before Drayton, Englishmen, uncomfortable with Horace's Epicureanism, had valued chiefly the Horace of the moral *Satires* (35, 30 B.C.E.) and *Epistles* (20-13 B.C.E.). Having learned from Drayton, the later Cavalier poets achieved (not without some loss of intellectual vigor) the gracefulness and urbanity that Drayton had not caught in their common master's odes.

POLY-OLBION

Drayton expressed the same patriotic convictions in a much more expansive way in his magnum opus, *Poly-Olbion*, on which he had been working for many years before its initial publication in 1612. His fondness for myth, the countryside, and antiquarian lore come together in this leisurely survey of England and Wales in which the favorite mode of travel is the river. The poem owes something to the researches of an early Tudor antiquarian, John Leland, and to Drayton's learned contemporary, William Camden. If his preoccupation with rivers needs a model, Spenser, whose *Colin Clouts Come Home Againe* (1595), *Prothalamion* (1596), and the now lost *Epithalamion* (1595) all feature rivers, probably is the man.

To assist the reader through his gigantic poem, Drayton employed the services of another learned man, John Selden, who wrote explanatory notes, and an engraver who furnished maps for each section of the poem. Not at all confident that the work would find a ready audience in what he called "this lunatic age," Drayton wrote an introduction excoriating those who would "rather read the fantasies of foreign invention than to see the rarities and history of their own country delivered by a true native muse." Ten years later, having "met with barbarous ignorance and base detraction" in the reception of the first edition, he nevertheless republished the poem with twelve additional sections.

Few readers today negotiate the full *Poly-Olbion*, but it is a pleasant, if sometimes prosaic, journey. Drayton probably did not visit all the localities described in the poem, and it is unlikely that the reader ignorant of his Warwickshire origin could guess it from this poem. It is an interesting section of the poem, however, detailing at length the Forest of Arden, which Shakespeare had used as the setting for much of *As You Like It* (1599-1600). There may be fools in Shakespeare's Arden, but Drayton's is populated by innumerable birds, beasts, hunters, and a happy hermit who has fled "the sottish purblind world." He also traces the several little rivers that flow into the Avon, which he follows past Stratford, though without mentioning Shakespeare. In this poem, Drayton is more interested in the past, and he tells the legend of Guy of Warwick, who is credited with defeating the Danish champion Colbrand and thus turning away the tenth century invasion. Like many historical poems written in late Tudor and early Stuart England, this one shows the transition from the earlier uncritical acceptance of myth and legend to a more skeptical attitude. The legends still have vitality, but the scholars of the seventeenth century—Selden, Francis Bacon, and the Earl of Clarendon—cast increasing doubt on their truthfulness and value.

IDEA

While at work on *Poly-Olbion*, Drayton was also overhauling his sonnets, now titled simply *Idea*. In this work his tireless revising paid off handsomely, for by 1619 he had added and rewritten forty-three new sonnets to go with twenty early ones, and the sequence had become a masterpiece. By this time John Donne, the first of the great Metaphysical poets, was writing love poems in other forms and reserving the sonnet for religious purposes, while Ben Jonson and his tribe scorned the sonnet and other nonclassical forms altogether. As a poet born in the decade before Donne and Jonson, Drayton had been enough of a working Elizabethan (and enough of a conservative) to prefer building on the accomplishments of that age. In this endeavor, however, he was alone; all the other Elizabethan poets of consequence—Sidney, Marlowe, Shakespeare, Sir Walter Raleigh, Daniel, all the people he might have wished to please, it must have seemed—were dead. Only Drayton worked on, increasingly testy and ill-humored in his prefaces but as devoted as ever to the perfection of poems of a kind now out of favor.

As far back as Sidney, English sonneteers had presented the lover as a sometimes comic figure. Despite certain resemblances to his creator, Sidney's Astrophel is a character at whom readers are sometimes encouraged to laugh. In *Idea*, Drayton's speaker even seems to laugh at himself. In the splendid Number 61, "Since there's no help, come let us kiss and part," the speaker, after asserting in a matter-of-fact tone and words chiefly of one syllable—the first thirty-three words, in fact, being monosyllables exclusively—that nothing but a complete break makes any sense, that he is willing to "shake hands" on it, reverts in the third quatrain to a sentimental deathbed scene of love personified, and closes with a couplet the irony of which the speaker surely recognizes: "Now if thou would'st, when all have given him over,/ From death to life, thou might'st him yet recover." The lover in these poems knows that love and passion are silly and that their stylized portrayal in language is sillier yet, but he also knows that to reject them outright is to reject life and the art that attempts to portray it. The perspective here is Horatian: a delicate balance, a golden mean, between involvement and detachment. The poet has mastered his form: He writes English sonnets which frequently retain the capacity of the Italian sonnet for a turning point just past the middle as well as a distinct closing couplet that sometimes brings another, unexpected turn.

Drayton's wit is on display in Number 21, about a "witless gallant" who has asked for and received from the speaker a sonnet to send to his own love. The speaker, however, has written it "as fast as e'er my pen could trot"—just the opposite of the correct, painstaking way. The third quatrain reports that the lady "doted on the dolt beyond all measure," the rueful couplet sadly concluding: "Yet by my troth, this fool his love obtains,/ And I lose you, for all my wit and pains." The reader understands that the "gallant's" success was a hollow one; Idea, whose name is Plato's word for that highest type of beauty and goodness, of which all ordinary earthly manifestations are but shadows, is worth the inevitable disappointments.

In Drayton's very Elizabethan sonnets, the reader comes upon many of the witty, argumentative ploys so characteristic of Donne and Jonson. For Drayton, such wit amounted to a perfecting of the now largely abandoned sonnet cycle in which he saw further possibilities for variety within unity, flexibility within firmness. He is not being Metaphysical or neoclassical, only bringing out the latent potential of the earlier poetry, while displaying in the process a wit, irony, and plainness of diction more characteristic of the new poetry that he was supposedly rejecting.

THE BATTAILE OF AGINCOURT AND ELEGIES UPON SUNDREY OCCASIONS

With the publication of the complete *Poly-Olbion*, Drayton's most elaborate tribute to the native land he had been praising so long, the poet, now entering his sixtieth year, might have been expected to taper off. Instead, he brought out two books composed primarily of previously unpublished poems. The first, named for a long historical poem, *The Battaile of Agincourt* (no improvement on his "ballad" and not to be confused with it), included another Horatian genre, the complimentary verse epistle, one of which was the letter to Henry Reynolds revealing his early desire to be a poet. He may not have been the first in the field, for Donne and Jonson were also writing them, but his *Elegies upon Sundrey Occasions*, as he called them, are more carefully adapted to the "occasions," suggesting that his primary aim was communication at once functional, artful, and expressive of genuine feeling. In this aim he came closer to the spirit of his Roman Master than did other poets of the time, whose style and tone tend to vary little with the occasion and the identity of the recipient.

SHEPHEARDS SIRENA

Two poems in *The Battaile of Agincourt* illustrate Drayton's final lyrical stage. *Shepheards Sirena* sings more purely than any of his earlier pastorals. Sirena dwells in the vicinity of the River Trent, here transmuted into a domestic Arcadia. While vestiges of the competitions and complaints of early English pastoral remain, the best part of the poem is its 170 liquid lines in praise of the lady—praise that never slides into the convolutions of Jacobean wit.

NIMPHIDIA

Nimphidia is quite different. It can be classified roughly as mock-heroic. Pigwiggen, in love with Queen Mab, entices her away from King Oberon and chal-

lenges the latter to a duel for the "dear lady's honor." Having secured seconds and gone through all necessary preliminaries, the champions hack briskly away at each other, though, when the contest threatens to get too bloody, Prosorpina administers the Lethe water that makes them forget their enmity entirely. At the end the King and Queen, as if nothing had happened, are sitting down to a good fairy meal. That the poem has a satirical purpose is indicated by Drayton's name-dropping: Sir Thopas, Pantagruel, and Don Quixote are all mentioned. The poem brims with parodies of heroic clichés. The emphasis, though, is on fun and fantasy in a delicate miniature world made of spiders' legs and butterflies' wings. Its eighty-eight tripping stanzas, rhyming *aaabcccb* (tetrameter except for the *b* lines, which are a syllable shorter with feminine rhymes), "carry the vein of Sir Thopas into the world of Oberon," as Oliver Elton puts it in *Michael Drayton: A Critical Study* (1966).

THE MUSES ELIZIUM

Drayton's final volume, issued thirty-nine years after his first and only one year before his death, includes three long "divine poems" on Noah, Moses, and David, but it is best remembered for its title poem, *The Muses Elizium*. Elizium, a "paradise on earth" whose name honors the queen who had now been dead twenty-seven years, can be seen as a nostalgic retreat from the realities of a nation now entered on the "Eleven Years' Tyranny" of Charles I. Made up of ten eclogues, or "nymphals," the work is, like *The Shepheards Sirena*, almost purely lyrical, full of flowery meadows and crystal springs, with occasional reminders of the prosaic real world.

One of these occurs in the tenth nymphal. Two nymphs discover a "monster" whom the shepherd Corbilus recognizes as an old satyr, refugee from "Felicia," which is the everyday world, now destroyed by "beastly men." After a suitable opportunity to lament the denuding of the forest by crass builders, the satyr is invited to "live in bliss" in Elizium until such time as the true Felicians reclaim the land. Thus, in his old age, Drayton metamorphoses his conservatism, love of the land, displeasure with the world of 1630, and perhaps—if readers take the satyr to represent the author—a disposition toward a bit of humor at his own expense, into a calm, dispassionate poem whose very preface is, for a change, sweet-tempered. In this last stage, Drayton has receded from the Stuart milieu to the extent of cultivating a pure, "irrelevant" art. The attitude is that of an old man, but one who has ceased to rage; the lyric freshness is that of a young poet not yet fully aware of the indifferent children of the earth whom Drayton has not forgotten.

With its delight in plain, shaggy, rural life, *The Muses Elizium* is likely to remind readers of classical pastoral more of Theocritus than of the more polished poet of the Roman Empire, Vergil. The style here is not of the Greek or Roman Golden Ages, but of the Elizabethan. Drayton had outlived his age, but this poem has outlived the seventeenth century strife in the midst of which it seemed so old-fashioned.

OTHER MAJOR WORK

PLAY: *The First Part of the True and Honorable Historie of the Life of Sir John Old-Castle the Good Lord Cobham*, pr. 1599.

BIBLIOGRAPHY

Brink, Jean R. *Michael Drayton Revisited*. Boston: Twayne, 1990. Offers an excellent introduction to Drayton's life and works. The first chapter substantially revises Drayton's biography. The other chapters deal chronologically with each of his major poems, and the concluding chapter discusses Drayton's impact on later writers. Supplemented by a chronology, notes, and a useful select bibliography.

Corbett, Margery, and Ronald Lightbown. *The Comely Frontispiece: The Emblematic Title-Page in England, 1550-1660*. London: Routledge & Kegan Paul, 1979. In this attractive collection of essays, the thirteenth chapter is devoted to the unusual frontispiece to Drayton's *Poly-Olbion*, his lengthy poetic description of the geography and history of Great Britain. An interpretation is offered of the engraving of Great Britain as a woman seated on an imperial throne. Beautifully illustrated.

Curran, John E. "The History Never Written: Bards, Druids, and the Problem of Antiquarianism in 'Poly Olbion.'" *Renaissance Quarterly* 51, no. 2 (Summer, 1998): 498-528. A study of the response of Drayton to the rise of antiquarianism as seen in his depictions of bards and druids in this poem.

Grundy, Joan. *The Spenserian Poets*. London: Edward Arnold, 1969. This older critical study argues that Drayton wrote in the tradition of Edmund Spenser. Grundy demonstrates that "cleare" had a complex meaning for Drayton, representing a heroic vision. Concentrates on *Poly-Olbion* and on Drayton's sonnets to his mistress Idea.

Hardin, Richard. *Michael Drayton and the Passing of Elizabethan England*. Lawrence: University Press of Kansas, 1973. This full-length study pays particular attention to Drayton's odes and to his historical poetry. Hardin argues that what distinguished Drayton from other Elizabethan poets was his consistent patriotism and his sincere devotion to England and English traditions.

Harner, James L. *Samuel Daniel and Michael Drayton: A Reference Guide*. Boston: G. K. Hall, 1980. Approximately one-half of this bibliography is devoted to books and articles written about Michael Drayton. The entries are arranged chronologically beginning with the seventeenth century and concluding with the twentieth. The annotations are reliable and extremely useful.

Hulse, Clark. *Metamorphic Verse: The Elizabethan Minor Epic*. Princeton, N.J.: Princeton University Press, 1981. This perceptive discussion of mythological narrative verse comments upon Edmund Spenser, William Shakespeare, and a number of other Elizabethan poets. Hulse includes a suggestive analysis of Drayton's verse complaints and poetic legends. Hulse's discussion emphasizes Drayton's *Peirs Gaveston* (1593), *Matilda* (1594), and *The Tragicall Legend of Robert, Duke of Normandy* (1596).

Norbrook, David. *Poetry and Politics in the English Renaissance*. London: Routledge & Kegan Paul, 1984. This extremely important study analyzes the intersection of politics and literature during the reigns of Elizabeth Tudor and James Stuart. Argues that poets such as Drayton who became disenchanted with the Stuart court deliberately adopted Spenserian themes and genres in order to criticize the present by idealizing the past. Comments upon Drayton's historical poetry, verse epistles, and late pastorals.

Robert P. Ellis;
bibliography updated by the editors

CARLOS DRUMMOND DE ANDRADE

Born: Itabira, Brazil; October 31, 1902
Died: Rio de Janeiro, Brazil; August 17, 1987

PRINCIPAL POETRY

Alguma poesia, 1930
Brejo das almas, 1934
Sentimento do mundo, 1940
Poesias, 1942
A rosa do povo, 1945
Poesia até agora, 1947
Claro enigma, 1951
Viola de bolso, 1952
Fazendeiro do ar, 1953
Cincoenta poemas escolhidos pelo autor, 1958
Poemas, 1959
Antologia poética, 1962
Lição de coisas, 1962
In the Middle of the Road, 1965
José e outros: Poesia, 1967
Boitempo, 1968
A falta que ama, 1968
Reunião: 10 livros de poesia, 1969
Menino antigo, 1973
As impurezas do branco, 1973
Esquecer para lembrar, 1979
A paixão medida, 1980
The Minus Sign: Selected Poems, 1980
Carmina Drummondiana, 1982 (with Silva Belkior)
Nova reunião: 19 livros de poesia, 1983
Corpo, 1984
Sessenta anos de poesia, 1985
Travelling in the Family, 1986
Amar se aprende amanda: Poesia de convívio e de humor, 1987
Poesia errante: Derrames líricos (e outros nem tanto, ou nada), 1988
Seleta em prosa e verso, 1971
O amor natural, 1992
A paixão medida: Poesia, 1993
José: Novos Poemas, 1993
Carlos Drummond de Andrade: Poesia, 1994

OTHER LITERARY FORMS

In addition to many books of poetry, Carlos Drummond de Andrade published three volumes of stories, nine collections of *crônicas* (journalistic "chronicles," or short prose pieces which may take the form of anecdotal narratives or commentary on current events or behavior), and numerous Portuguese translations of works of French literature. The language of many of his prose-narrative poems is closely related to that of his *crônicas*.

ACHIEVEMENTS

In a distinguished career spanning six decades, Carlos Drummond de Andrade produced a formidable body of poetry and prose. Appealing to connoisseurs of literature and the broader public alike, he became one of Brazil's most beloved modern writers. With a vast poetic repertory of considerable thematic and stylistic variety, Drummond is widely regarded as the leading Brazilian poet of the twentieth century; many consider him to be the most important lyrical voice in that nation's entire literary history. He rightly stands alongside the great Portuguese-language poets, the classic Luís de Camões and the modern Fernando Pessoa, as well as the major contemporary Latin American poets Pablo Neruda, César Vallejo, and Octavio Paz.

Brazilian *Modernismo* of the 1920's and 1930's sought to free poetry from the lingering constraints of Parnassian and Symbolist verse. Iconoclast writers combated conservative tradition, infusing poetry with New World awareness and revitalizing lyric through application of avant-garde techniques. Perhaps more than any other poet of *Modernismo*, Drummond was capable of crystallizing the aims of the movement to institute newness and give value to the national variety of the Portuguese language, while forging an intensely personal style with universal scope.

Drummond received numerous literary prizes in Brazil for individual works and overall contribution, including those of the PEN Club of Brazil and the Union of Brazilian Writers. He was twice nominated (in 1972 and 1978) for the Neustadt International Prize for Literature awarded by *World Literature Today*. In his modest way, Drummond refused many other prizes and declined to seek a chair in the Brazilian Academy of Letters. His work has had a tremendous and continuing impact on successive generations of Brazilian artists, influencing emerging lyric poets since the 1930's. On another front, more than seventy musical settings of his poems have been made. Composers inspired by Drummond include the renowned Heitor Villa-Lobos (who set Drummond's poems to music as early as 1926) and the popular vocalist Milton Nascimento. Academic studies of Drummond's work abound; hundreds of articles and dozens of book-length analyses of his poetry have appeared in Brazil.

Biography

Carlos Drummond de Andrade was born in a small town in the interior of Brazil, the ninth son of a rancher with strict traditional values. His rural origins and family life were to be constant sources of inspiration for his poetry. As a rebellious youth, he studied in Belo Horizonte, the capital city of the state, where the family moved in 1920. The young Drummond had already published several items when, in 1922, he became aware of the Modern Art Week in São Paulo, an event that officially launched *Modernismo* as a program of artistic renovation and nationalist spirit.

In 1924, two leaders of the movement from São Paulo, Oswald de Andrade and Mário de Andrade (no relation), took Swiss-French poet Blaise Cendrars on a tour of Brazil; Drummond met them in Belo Horizonte. The young poet from Minas corresponded with Mário de Andrade, one of Brazil's most influential men of culture, until the death of the latter. Still in his home state, Drummond was a cofounder, in 1925, of *A revista* (the review), a modernist organ which lasted through three issues. In the same year, Drummond received a degree in pharmacy, a profession which he never practiced. Instead, he began to earn his living in journalism. In 1928, Oswald de Andrade's radical literary journal *Revista de antropofagia* (review of anthropophagy) published a neoteric poem by Drummond which generated much controversy and some early notoriety for the author. His first two books of verse were published in 1930 and in 1934, the year Drummond moved to Rio de Janeiro, the political and cultural capital of the nation.

In Rio, the writer from Minas served as chief of staff for the minister of health and education and collaborated

on magazines and literary reviews. By 1942, he had been contracted by a major publishing house which would regularly publish cumulative editions of the poet's work, affording renewed exposure to poetry that had originally appeared in limited first editions of narrow circulation. Drummond lost his position in the ministry when the government fell in 1945. For a brief period, he was part of the editorial board of the tribune of the Communist Party. Later in that same year, he found work with the directorship of the National Artistic and Historical Patrimony, a bureaucratic position he held until his retirement in 1962.

During his years of public service, Drummond kept up a prolific pace as a journalist, narrator, and poet of diverse talents. In 1954, he obtained a permanent column in a major Rio daily to publish his *crônicas*; he maintained this activity until the early 1980's. Throughout these four decades, the author periodically joined the best of his journalistic prose pieces with other original writings for publication in volumes. Parallel to these endeavors, to which a significant part of his wide-ranging recognition and popularity can be attributed, Drummond's reputation as poet steadily grew. His work has been translated into Spanish, German, French, Swedish, Bulgarian, Czech, Russian, and English.

Analysis

In 1962, Carlos Drummond de Andrade edited an anthology of his own poetry. Rather than follow a standard chronological sequence or order selections according to the book in which they originally appeared, the author chose poems from each of his collections and organized them into nine representative thematic divisions. This self-characterization reflects, in very general terms, the main preoccupations of Drummond's poetry before and after the publication of the anthology. Each of what the poet calls his "points of departure" or "materials" corresponds to a titled subdivision: the individual ("Um eu todo retorcido," a totally twisted self); the homeland ("Uma província: Esta," a province: this one); the family ("A família que medei," the family I gave myself); friends ("Cantar de amigos," singing of friends); social impact ("Amar-amaro," better-bitter love); knowledge of love ("Uma, duas argolinhas," one, two jousts); lyric itself ("Poesia contemplada," contemplated poetry); playful exercises ("Na praça de conuites," in the square of invitations); and a vision, or attempt, of existence ("Tentativa de exploração e de interpretação do estar-no-mundo," efforts at exploration and interpretation of being-in-the-world).

These are, as the author himself noted, imprecise and overlapping sections. Indeed, any effort at classificatory or chronological categorization of Drummond's poetry, like that of any complex and prolific verse-maker, is subject to inconsistencies and inaccuracies. In addition to the wide thematic concerns enumerated above, several stylistic constants run through the whole of Drummond's work. Certain traits of form and content fade and reappear; other aspects merit consideration from a cumulative point of view. There is much transitional overlap between the broadly defined phases of his production. With these caveats in mind, the general lines of Drummond's poetic trajectory can be traced.

His earliest production, in the 1930's, following the antinormative paths of *Modernismo*, is direct, colloquial, and circumstantial. Sarcastic tones abound within a somewhat individualistic focus. Broader perspective is evident in the next stage, in the 1940's, as the poet explores the physical and human world around him. Existential questions are raised within the context of community; social and historical events move the poet, whose own anguish is a reflection of a generalized crisis of consciousness. A third phase, in the 1950's, incorporates personal and social concerns into an all-encompassing consideration of man and his environment from a philosophical standpoint. A certain formal rigidity accompanies this more contemplative and speculative poetry.

The development of Drummond's verse from the 1930's to the 1950's reveals, in broad strokes, a process of opening and expansion. This unfolding can be described with a tripartite metaphor of sight and attitude. The dominant voice of the early poetry is ironic yet timid; the poet *observes* but the lyric vision is uninvolved, hardly surpassing the limits of self. As the poet begins to confront the surrounding world, he *looks* more intently at the faces of reality. Existential meditations lead to a project of encounter; the struggles of others are seen and internalized. In his most mature stage, the poet not only observes and looks but also contemplates objects and subjects in an effort to see essences or the roots of contradictions. Having developed this broader vision, Drummond returns, in a cycle of books beginning in 1968, to examine his provincial origins. These latest works—in a reflection of the predominance of paradigms over temporal progression in Drummond's work—are permeated with the vigorous irony that characterized his earliest verse.

A thoroughly modern poet, Drummond can be inspired by and effectively use almost any source for his poetry. Much of his raw material is quotidian; the molding of everyday reality into poetic frameworks may be anecdotal or manifest utopian aspirations. One of his notable strengths is the ability to strike a balance between the light, vulgar, direct, or colloquial and the heavy, elevated, evocative, or contemplative. He is at home with the concrete and the abstract, finding the structures of language most adequate for a particular situation. His is a poetry of discovery, whether of a provincial past in its psychic and mythical dimensions or of the relationships and values that form modern society. Drummond's literary discoveries are not presented as truths or absolutes. His poetry is informed by a fundamental skepticism. Yet bouts with relativism and anguish do not result in nihilism or cynicism. His lyric universe is fundamentally secular; his speculative and metaphysical considerations of essences and human experience rarely involve concepts of god or divinity.

Throughout, there operates a dialectic of inner examination and outward projection, of introspection and denunciation of social problems. Expressions, of anguish and impotence unveil emblematic poetic selves threatened by technology and a hostile world. The poet seeks to apprehend the profound sense of unresolved differences and change for the individual, the family and affective relationships, society at large, his nation, and the community of humankind. When he bares himself and his personal psychic states, well-tuned devices filter or block the potential for self-indulgence or confessionalism. The revelation of oppressive senses of reality is related to a view of the human condition, to the crises of modern man and civilization. T. S. Eliot said that great poets writing about themselves are writing about their times. A clear sign of Drummond's greatness is his linkage of substances of private, public, and transcendent planes.

EXPRESSIVE MEANS

A particularly important aspect of Drummond's poetry is the explicit preoccupation with words and expressive means. At the outset, the poet expressed his disquiet through attacks on worn values and stale traditions. As his impulsive impressionism evolved, he undertook an ever-expanding search for nuances, key words, the secrets of language and its virtualities. Words themselves and the making of poetry are the themes of some of Drummond's most important poems. In such works, the necessity of expression may be played against incommunicability or the imperfections of language. There is no tendency or approach in his poetry without a corresponding questioning of linguistic instruments or the sense of poetry. The modernist period, in Western culture in general, has been characterized as the age of criticism. Drummond's poetry is marked by self-consciousness; he is a constant critic of his own art. After *Modernismo* had effectively dissolved as a movement in Brazil, only its most complete poet would be able to write: "And how boring it's become to be modern/ Now I will be eternal."

Drummond's prime linguistic concern is with meaning. In his poetry, conceptual dimensions are generally more important than visuality or sonorousness. Occurrence, idea, and conceit dominate over imagery or symbolism. He seeks to use words in unusual and provocative combinations. Drummond's verse, moreover, is not very musical, in the sense of melodious and harmonious formation of words. There is notable formal variety in the poet's repertory, which incorporates everything from minimalist epigrams to long prose poems, both lyrical and narrative. Much of the poetry seems direct or simple. In the fashion of an Ernest Hemingway character who can "know that it's complicated and write it simple," Drummond, in the realm of poetry, has an uncanny ability to sculpt seemingly spontaneous airs. The simplicity of the poet is deceptive or even duplicitous. While Drummond's customary approach is free verse, he has written in consecrated forms such as the sonnet. He has cultivated the ode, the ballad, and the elegy as well.

MODERNISMO: THE EARLY PHASE

Drummond's earliest work is written under the sign of *Modernismo* and demonstrates a combative frame of mind with respect to conservative notions of belles let-tres associated with Parnassian and Symbolist traditions, long surpassed in Europe but slow to die in South America. Following the Brazilian modernists who preceded him in the 1920's, Drummond sought, once and for all, to pierce the "sacred air" of poetry by abandoning the idea of "noble" thematics and insisting on a more colloquial approach. In 1930, *Modernismo* had already conquered some ground. Thus, Drummond's poetry could not constitute rebellion alone. He was presented with the challenges that liberation presents and had to forge an iconoclasm of the second degree. Drummond succeeded in delivering the *coup de grace* on propriety, academic language, and mandatory stylization of diction. Humor and irony, never perverse, permeate the early poems, several of which can be called, in the Brazilian fashion, "joke-poems."

"IN THE MIDDLE OF THE ROAD"

Two memorable selections from Drummond's first book, modestly titled *Alguma poesia* (some poetry), illustrate the poet's characteristically daring and provocative attitudes. In the ten lines of the poem "No meio do caminho" ("In the Middle of the Road"), the speaker simply announces, in a starkly unadorned and repetitive fashion, that he, with "fatigued retinas," will never forget that "there was a stone in the middle of the road." Readers wondered whether the poem was sheer mockery or designed to baffle. Conservative critics laughed at the author, some even suggesting that the poem demonstrated a state of schizophrenia or psychosis. The extent of the controversy enabled Drummond, many years later, to edit a book consisting solely of commentaries and critiques of the neoteric set of verses. On the positive side, the poem can be read as a drama of obsession with ideas or as an expression of a monotonous human condition. It can also represent confrontation with impediments of any kind, be they personal, related to self-fulfillment, or literary (that is, ingrained norms). "In the Middle of the Road" can further be considered as a premonition of the hermetic mode in which Drummond would operate in subsequent poetry.

"POEM OF SEVEN FACES"

Another symptomatic modernist work is the seemingly disjunct "Poema de sete faces" ("Poem of Seven Faces"). The opening lines—"When I was born, a crooked angel/ one of those who live in shadows/ said:

Go on, Carlos! be *gauche* in life."—embody senses of repudiation, marginality, and awkwardness that inform the poet's early work and never completely disappear. This is the first presentation of the "twisted self" that inhabits Drummond's poetic world. The penultimate group of verses of the heptagonal poem alludes to a neoclassical poem, well-known by Brazilian readers, to present aspects of a new poetics: "World world oh vast world/ If I were called Earl'd/ it would be a rhyme, it wouldn't be a solution." Here Drummond attacks the canons of rhyme and meter as external formalities that restrict expressive plenitude. This aggressive insistence on artistic freedom is again formulated with reference to rhyme in "Considera ção do poema" (consideration of the poem), in which the poet writes that he will not rhyme *sono* (slumber) with "the uncorresponding word" *outono* (autumn) but rather with "the word flesh/ or any other for all are good for me." Such statements should not be misconstrued, for Drummond has utilized delicately all manners of rhyme (verse-initial, verse-final, horizontal, vertical, diagonal, internal), especially in his middle years. The question is not rhyme per se but the adaptation of form to the exigencies of particular poetic situations. In the early years of modernist enthusiasm, free verse indeed dominates Drummond's output.

NATIONALISM

As for the nationalistic concerns of *Modernismo*, the young Drummond did present a series of poetic snapshots of Brazil, focused on his home state of Minas Gerais, but these poems were not strictly regionalist. Even the validation of national reality did not escape the ironic provocations of the young poet. In a poem titled "Também já fui brasileiro" (I have been Brazilian too), he writes: ". . . I learned that nationalism is a virtue/ But there comes a time when bars close/ and all virtues are denied." Unwillingness to be restricted by the imposition of new values can also be read between lines such as "A garden, hardly Brazilian . . . but so lovely." Drummond's all-encompassing irony is crystalline in a poem called "Hino naçional" (national anthem), which begins, in typical Brazilian modernist fashion "We must discover Brazil!" only to declare, toward the conclusion of this exercise in skepticism, "We must, we must forget Brazil!" This distancing effect is a good measure of the poet's independence and unyielding search for revelations beyond given and constituted frames of reference, above and below evident surfaces.

SOCIAL-HISTORICAL PHASE

The social phase of Drummond's poetry is identifiable not so much by formal development but rather by attitudinal and ideological shifts. The titles of his third and fourth collections, *Sentimento do mundo* (feeling of the world) and *A rosa do povo* (the people's rose, his most popular work), clearly indicate in what directions the poet moved. Personal and family preoccupations are linked to the surrounding world, as the poet explores the consequences of pragmatism, mechanization, and the reification of man. The disquiet of the ironic Self gives way to concerns with the Other and with more far-reaching societal problems. Within this orientation, one of Drummond's masterpieces is "Canto ao homem do povo Charlie Chaplin" ("Song to the Man of the People C. C."). Harry Levin has written that Chaplin was one of the greatest modernists for his brilliant renderings of the frustrations and incongruities of modern urban life. Drummond, master of Brazilian *Modernismo*, pays homage to that cinematographic genius and incorporates reverberations of his work into a long (226-line) Whitmanesque piece which speaks for the "abandoned, pariahs, failures, downtrodden." In general, Drummond's poetry of this period gives rise to an existential *raison d'être* that is determined via interaction and giving. Individuality is encompassed by new perspectives: ethics, solidarity with the oppressed and the international community. The symptomatic poem "Os ombros suportam o mundo" ("Shoulders Bear the World") establishes a vital perspective—"Just life without mystifications"—alongside "Mãos dadas" ("Hand in Hand"), which presents the poetic voice of commitment: "I am shackled to life and I see my companions/ They may be taciturn but they nourish great hopes/ It is among them that I consider the enormity of reality." The 1940's were marked by the ravages of world war, and events touched Drummond the poet. The effects of the war in Europe are reflected, for example, in his "Congresso internacional do medo" (international congress of fear). Anti-Fascist positions and Socialist sympathies are evident in such representative poems as "Carta a Stalingrado" (letter to Stalingrad) and "Con o russo em Berlin" (with the Russians in Berlin).

"RESIDUE" AND "SEARCH FOR POETRY"

In the midst of this social and historical commotion, Drummond wrote two of his most enduring poems, "Resíduo" ("Residue"), an instigating inventory of emotive and objective presences, and "Procura da poesia" ("Search for Poetry"), which voices an ideal poetics. Here the persona speaks against making poetry of events, feelings, memories, or thoughts. Instead, he advises one to "penetrate quietly the kingdom of words" and contemplate the "thousands of secret faces under the neutral face" of each word. This advice might seem to point out inner contradictions, for much of Drummond's poetry itself derives from the sources he seems to reject. Without discounting a touch of ironic self-commentary, a less literal reading would not hold occurrences, sentiment, recollection, and ideas to be, in themselves, ill-advised for poets. Indeed, unmediated experience will not yield poetry; the true search is for a linguistic craft capable of reformulating experience into viable art.

NEOCLASSICAL PHASE

Formal and thematic properties alike permit establishing a third phase in Drummond's poetic career, beginning in the 1950's and continuing into the next decade. The free-verse and colloquial emphases of his eminently modernist and *engagé* poetry give way to somewhat neoclassical methods. The poet rediscovers the sonnet (and other measured forms) and withdraws from events into a philosophical mode. Reflection on the self, the world, and words takes place at the level of abstract expression. Drummond's confrontation with issues of metaphysics and transcendence signify an interpretative poetry, which becomes somewhat hermetic. The book titles *Claro enigma* (clear enigma) and *Fazendeiro do ar* (farmer of the air) are suggestive of the evolution of the poet's endeavors, as are the names of specific poems such as "Ser" ("Being"), "Entre o ser e as coisas" ("Between Being and Things"). "Aspiração" ("Aspiration"), "Dissolução" ("Dissolution"), and "Contemplação no banco" ("Contemplation on a Bench"). In this more "pure" poetry, love (carnal and psychic) may constitute a means of sublimation. Consideration of family and of the past may evoke wonder about immortality or heredity as a cognitive category. What Drummond calls in the most representative poem of this period, "A máquina do mundo" ("The Machine of the World"), is not to be understood in terms of personal accommodation or social structure but as phenomenological totality with mythical and archetypal dimensions. The poet reports an awakening:

> the machine of the world half-opened
> for whom its breaking was avoiding
> and at the very thought of it moaning . . .
> the whole of a reality that transcends
> the outline of its own image drawn
> in the face of mystery, in abysms . . .

Such poetry of paradox and enigma is also present in *Poemas*, but narrative procedures and concrete referents are reminiscent at times of the more "realistic" poetry of earlier years. The title of the poem "Especulações emtornoda palavra homem" ("Speculations Around the Word Man") suggests its philosophical stance, but rather than affirmations the poem is made up entirely of questions. In this way, one is reminded of the celebrated poem "José," which portrayed disillusionment and the potential for resignation through a series of questions. "A um hotel em demolição" ("To a Hotel Under Demolition") is a long, digressive work which was inspired by an actual event and has prosaic moments. The wandering poem is anchored at the end of the metaphor of the hotel, as the speaker, who has "lived and unlived" in the "Great Hotel of the World without management," finds himself to be "a secret guest of himself." Here Drummond balances narrative and lyrical impulses, private and social dimensions, as well as observation and contemplation.

LIÇÃO DE COISAS

The two most important selections of *Lição de coisas* (lesson of things), which represents fully the author's mixed style, operate within strict binomial structures. Philosophical speculation is tempered in (by) "A bomba" (the bomb), an extended series of reactions to and statements about atomic explosive devices, the most humbling and frightening invention of modern technology. Each line begins with "the bomb," except the last, in which "man" appears with the hope that he "will destroy the bomb." The realism of this lyric contrasts, but ultimately links, with the experimental "Isso é aquilo" (this is that). This second work is measured and balanced, consisting of ten numbered sets of ten, two-item lines. The pairs of words or neologisms in each line are determined by free lexical, morphological, or semantic associations, for example, "The facile the fossil/ the missile the fissile. . . . the atom the atone . . . the chastity the castigate . . . " The final two lines have but one item—"the bombix/ the pytx"—and connect the playful linguistic exercise to the thematic of destruction. These two poems reflect how philosophical, humanitarian, and poetically inventive concerns can interpenetrate and synthesize in Drummond's poetry.

BOITEMPO

The publication of *Boitempo* (oxtime) begins a homonymous trilogy which incorporates hundreds of poems. This production constitutes a detailed return to historical roots and rural origins. The poet sets out to explore memories, incidents, and personages of his childhood and adolescence in Minas Gerais, much as he did in the 1930's. Inherent in this project is the potential for self-indulgence, cathartic sentimentalism, or autobiographical nostalgia. Yet Drummond undertakes this effort with all the perspective of his varied poetic activities—modernist struggles, committed verse, metaphysical divagations, metapoetics—and makes poetic distance of the chronological distance that separates him from his material. His moods are serene, and a generalized irony tempers the tenderness of memory. The poet is sufficiently detached to employ light, humorous tones in his review of a parochial (and paternalistic) past. There are certainly literarily self-conscious moments in the flow of Drummond's *Boitempo*. Passages which might appear to be dialogues with what was lived long ago are actually evocations of a literary oeuvre. There are returns to the birth of the "totally twisted self" as well as dramatizations of the genesis of nonconformity and rebelliousness. The poetry's comic character signifies a turning away from problematic relations as the center of poetic concern. Only about a tenth of the first set of the *Boitempo* poems are suggestive of Drummond's philosophical muses. The continuation of that mode is to be found in *A falta que ama* (loving lack) and in parts of the brief *A paixão medida* (measured passion).

LEGACY

The contributions of Carlos Drummond de Andrade to the modern art of poetry can be measured in re-gional, national, continental, and international terms. His regional role in *Modernismo* developed into Brazil's most powerful body of poetry. His reformulation of academic verse as idiomatic lyricism was unique in the diversity of tones, depth of psychological probing, and complexity of thought. With its linguistic flexibility, Drummond's poetry has the eminent capacity to represent metamorphoses, the mobility of sentiment, and the multiplicity of being. In his craft, he achieves a balance of emotion, intelligence, ethical senses, and irony. While Drummond's poetry has been a vehicle for expressions of social awareness, self-discovery, and transcendent inquiry, none of these is more fundamental than the poet's disquiet with the instrument of language itself. Drummond's truest vocation is not the profession of a literary creed or promulgation of any set of ideas but the very uncovering and shaping of words and verbal structures to reflect and explore multiple moods and attitudes.

OTHER MAJOR WORKS

SHORT FICTION: *Contos de aprendiz*, 1951; *70 historinhas*, 1978; *Contos plausíveis*, 1981; *O sorvete e outras histórias*, 1993; *As palavras que ninguém diz: Crônica*, 1997; *Histórias para o rei: Conto*, 1997.

NONFICTION: *Confissões de Minas*, 1944; *Passeios na ilha: Divagaçoes sôbre a vida literária e outras matérias*, 1952; *Fala, amendoeira*, 1957; *Cadeira de balanco*, 1966; *Versiprosa: Crônica da vida cotidiana e de algumas miragens*, 1967; *Caminhos de João Brandão*, 1970; *A bôlsa e a vida*, 1971; *O poder ultra jovem*, 1972; *Discurso de primavera e algumas sombras*, 1977; *Os dias lindos*, 1977; *Setenta historinhas: Antologia*, 1978; *Boca de luar*, 1984; *O observador no escritório*, 1985; *Tempo, vida, poesia: Confissões no rádio*, 1986; *Moça deitada na grama*, 1987; *O observador no escritório*, 1994; *Conversa de livraria, 1941 e 1948*, 2000.

TRANSLATION: *Fome*, 1963 (of Knut Hamsun).

CHILDREN'S LITERATURE: *Historia de dois amores*, 1985.

EDITED TEXTS: *Rio de Janeiro em prosa e verso*, 1965 (with Manuel Bandeira); *Minas Gerais*, 1967; *Uma pedra no meio do caminho: Biographia de um poema*, 1967.

MISCELLANEOUS: *Obra completa*, 1964; *De notícias e não notícias faz-se a crônica: Histórias, diálogos, divagaçoes*, 1974; *O avesso das coisas*, 1987 (aphorisms); *Discurso de primavera e algumas sombras*, 1994.

BIBLIOGRAPHY

Armstrong, Piers. *Third World Literary Fortunes: Brazilian Culture and Its International Reception*. Lewisburg, Pa.: Bucknell University Press, 1999. Contrasts Brazilian writers with their Spanish American counterparts, and compares Andrade's poetic persona to such "paradigmatic antiheroes" as T. S. Eliot and Franz Kafka.

Di Antonio, Robert Edward. "The Confessional Mode as a Liberating Force in the Poetics of Carlos Drummond de Andrade." *Quaderni ibero-americani* 8, nos. 61/62 (December/January, 1986/1987): 201-207. Considers Andrade an existentialist with a personal, often humorous vision of the absurdity of existence.

Lima, Luiz Costa. "Carlos Drummond de Andrade." *Latin American Writers*. Vol. 2. New York: Charles Scribner's Sons, 1989. This lengthy essay discusses Andrade's early work in the context of conflicting aspects of Brazilian *Modernismo*, his later work as evidence of "the corrosion principle," and his even later work as the "postcorrosion phase," in which memory is privileged over history.

Sternberg, Ricardo da Silveira Lobo. *The Unquiet Self: Self and Society in the Poetry of Carlos Drummond de Andrade*. Valencia, Spain: Albatros/Hispanófila, 1986. Analyzes Andrade's work as representing the inherent conflict in the relationship between self and other(s), and the tendency toward both withdrawal from and engagement with the world.

_____. "The World Within: Carlos Drummond de Andrade's *Alguma Poesia*." *Luso-Brazilian Review* 21, no. 2 (Winter, 1984): 57-69. Focusing on Andrade's "first phase," from 1930 to 1945, Sternberg examines *o choque social*, or social shock inherent in the conflicts between individual and society, self and others, in Andrade's poetry.

Charles A. Perrone;
bibliography updated by the editors

WILLIAM DRUMMOND OF HAWTHORNDEN

Born: Hawthornden, Scotland; December 13, 1585
Died: Hawthornden, Scotland; December 4, 1649

PRINCIPAL POETRY
Teares, on the Death of Moeliades, 1613
Poems, 1616
Forth Feasting, 1617
Flowres of Sion, 1623
The Entertainment, 1633
To the Exequies, 1638

OTHER LITERARY FORMS

William Drummond's only prose work published during his lifetime was *A Midnight's Trance* (1619), a meditation on death. In its revised form it was appended to *Flowres of Sion* as *A Cypresse Grove*. His *The History of Scotland from the Year 1423 Until the Year 1542*, his longest piece of prose, appeared posthumously in 1655. This volume also included a section of Drummond's letters, a reprinting of *A Cypresse Grove*, and "Memorials of State," a sample of the political pamphlets Drummond had written (but never published) in the two decades preceding his death. The 1711 edition of Drummond's works remains the most complete collection of the prose; in this edition *Irene*, *Skiamachia*, and other political pieces first appeared. Here, too, were first published notes on the famous conversations between Drummond and Ben Jonson.

In 1831, David Laing published *Extracts from the Hawthornden Manuscripts*, which includes "A Brief Account of the Hawthornden Manuscripts in the Possession of the Society of Antiquaries of Scotland, with Extracts, Containing Several Unpublished Letters with Poems of William Drummond of Hawthornden" (*Transactions of the Society of Antiquaries of Scotland*, Volume 5). In the second part of that volume, published in 1832, Laing presented the first complete edition of the *Notes by William Drummond, of Conversations with Ben Jonson*. Subsequent editions of Drummond's poetry have included manuscript material, but the prose remains uncollected.

ACHIEVEMENTS

By 1616 William Drummond was known as "the Scottish Petrarch." His first published poem went through three editions within a year, and the 1616 edition of the *Poems* quickly went into a second impression. John Milton read Drummond with approbation, and Milton's nephew, Edward Phillips, Drummond's first editor, in the preface to the 1656 edition of the poetry, called Drummond "a genius the most polite and verdant that ever the Scottish nation produced," adding "that neither Tasso, nor Guarini, nor any of the most neat and refined can challenge to themselves any advantage above him." For Charles Lamb, a century and a half later, "The sweetest names, and which carry a perfume in the mention, are, Kit Marlowe, Drayton, Drummond of Hawthornden, and Cowley."

What Alexander Pope observed of the last of these "sweet" poets, however—"Who now reads Cowley?"—is also applicable to Drummond. Though he was the first Scottish poet to produce a substantial body of poetry in English, and though much of that poetry demonstrates technical virtuosity, Drummond does not command many readers today. In large part this neglect has resulted from his theory of composition. Jonson warned him "that oft a man's modesty made a fool of his wit." Drummond's poetic modesty led him to translate and adapt the works of others instead of applying himself to invention. His poetry, therefore, while skillful, is rarely original, and, as Samuel Johnson stated, "No man ever became great by imitation." Drummond's skill with language and the details of prosody guarantee him a secure place among the second rank of Renaissance English poets, but his inability or refusal to go beyond such models as Sir Philip Sidney, Pierre de Ronsard, Petrarch, Battista Marino, and Baldassare Castiglione bars him from the first.

His history of the first five Jameses, like his poetry, is stylistically sound but derivative in content. Although much praised by Drummond's contemporaries and reprinted five times, it has not been reissued since 1711. David Laing commented more than a century ago in *Archaeoló gia Scotiá* (Volume 5) that the work is "only of subsidiary importance," and so it remains. *A Cypresse Grove* may have influenced Sir Thomas Browne's *Hydriotaphia: Urne-Buriall* (1658), but along with vir-tually all Drummond's other prose works it has fallen into neglect after enjoying a contemporary popularity. Yet for most students of early seventeenth century British literature, Drummond owes his reputation to a prose work, though it is one that he merely transcribed and that was never published in his lifetime. *Notes of Ben Jonson's Conversations with William Drummond of Hawthornden*, a record of Jonson's comments on himself and his contemporaries—and hence an invaluable primary source for literary historians—is the best known of Drummond's writings today. It is perhaps fitting that a man who shunned originality should owe his fame almost entirely to his transcription of the pronouncements of another.

BIOGRAPHY

The eldest son of John Drummond and Susannah Fowler, William Drummond was born on December 13, 1585, at Hawthornden, some seven miles southeast of Edinburgh. In 1590 Drummond's father was appointed gentleman-usher to King James VI; about this time, too, his uncle, William Fowler, became private secretary

William Drummond of Hawthornden (Hulton Archive)

to Queen Anne. Drummond thus grew up in a court dedicated to literary pursuits. James VI was a poet, and William Fowler translated Petrarch's *The Triumphs* (c. 1352-1374) and composed original verses as well. Such surroundings must have stimulated Drummond's own literary inclinations.

After taking a degree from the University of Edinburgh in July, 1605, Drummond set out for France to study law at Bourges. During the next four years, Drummond maintained a list of his readings: Of the numerous volumes he read, only one concerns jurisprudence—the *Institutes* (533) of Justinian. Other volumes deal in part with religion. Although Drummond was hardly a prejudiced sectarian, his poetry reflects a deep religiosity. Most of Drummond's reading at this time was, however, secular; during his years abroad he familiarized himself with the major works of the Renaissance, both English and Continental, which later served as the models for his own writings.

By the time he returned to Scotland in late 1608 he was intimately acquainted with the best of Spanish, French, Italian, and English literatures. These he not only read but also acquired: An inventory of his library in 1611 includes more than five hundred titles. This inventory suggests again that Drummond's interest in the law was less than overwhelming, for only twenty-four of those books deal with that field.

Fortunately for Drummond, he was not obliged to rely on the law for a living. On August 21, 1610, "about Noone," according to Drummond's "Memorials," his father died, leaving him laird of Hawthornden. Here Drummond remained for the rest of his life, reading and writing "farre from the madding Worldlings hoarse Discords" (Sonnet XLIII, Part I, *Poems*).

The death of Prince Henry in November, 1612, inspired Drummond's first published work, *Teares, on the Death of Moeliades*. Shortly afterward, perhaps as early as the next year, another volume appeared, consisting of a sonnet sequence in two parts. In the first section Drummond speaks conventionally of the pains of love, and in the second he mourns his mistress's death. Although both Dante and Petrarch had written of their dead mistresses, no one in English had yet done so. Drummond boasted that he was "The First in the Isle that did celebrate a mistress dead."

Life seems to have imitated art in this case. Drummond apparently had fallen in love with a Miss Cunningham in 1614 and had become engaged to her. Shortly before their marriage—but after the completion of most of the sonnets in *Poems*—Miss Cunningham died. Except for his abandonment of love poetry for religious verse, Drummond's writings do not reflect this personal tragedy, but he remained unmarried until 1632, and the woman he did marry—Elizabeth Logan—attracted him in part because she reminded him of his first love.

When the former James VI of Scotland, then James I of England, returned to his native land after a fourteen-year absence, Drummond welcomed him with the effusive encomium *Forth Feasting*, in which he imagines the river's rejoicing to receive her monarch. In general, the poem pleased the king, though his courtiers, and even James, questioned one line: "No Guard so sure as Love unto a Crowne" (line 246). The sentiment was hardly original with Drummond, going back to Aristotle's *Politics* (between 336 and 322 B.C.E.). The Stuarts, however, preferred to govern through fear. In his political pamphlets of the 1630's and 1640's Drummond would expand his view, recommending love and mercy to James's successor.

The following year Scotland received another visitor—the prince of poets, Ben Jonson. Jonson probably came to Scotland in search of literary material, but in late December, 1618, and early January of the next year he spent several weeks at Hawthornden conversing with Drummond. It is this visit that has kept Drummond's name alive, for Drummond kept careful notes of Jonson's observations. (The original manuscript apparently has not survived, but a transcription by the antiquary Sir Robert Sibbald [1641-1722] has preserved Jonson's remarks.) These observations contain much material about Jonson himself as well as about his contemporaries and so are invaluable to the student of the period, offering information not available elsewhere. They also suggest why Drummond and Jonson ceased corresponding within six months of the latter's return to England. Drummond's notes justify his comment that Jonson was "a great lover and praiser of himself, a contemner and Scorner of others."

Flowres of Sion, a collection of religious poetry, appeared in 1623; in 1630 Drummond published a revised edition of this work. In the interval between these editions, Drummond's thoughts turned for a time to earthly matters: He apparently sired three illegitimate children, and in 1627 he received a letter patent for sixteen military and naval inventions. There is no evidence that he ever went beyond theorizing about these weapons of destruction, but his very proposals suggest a concern with the Thirty Years' War raging on the Continent. The "madding Worldlings hoarse Discords" could penetrate even secluded Hawthornden. More consonant with the tenor of Drummond's temper, in 1626 he donated a large portion of his library—more than five hundred volumes—to his alma mater.

By 1633, when Charles I visited Edinburgh, Drummond was regarded as the unofficial poet laureate of Scotland. For the royal visit he wrote *The Entertainment*, a collection of poetry and prose. As in *Forth Feasting*, the praise is lavish. At the same time, just as *Forth Feasting* had advised James I on the proper way to rule, so *The Entertainment* cautions Charles to rule by love rather than by force and to avoid alienating his subjects through the imposition of new taxes or the creation of court favorites.

Unhappily for Charles I and England, Drummond's warnings went unheeded. Instead of attempting to win the love of Scotland, the king alienated the country by attempting to impose Episcopal rites on the Presbyterian kirk. In 1638, Scottish Presbyterians replied with the National League and Covenant to oppose liturgical alterations, and, after much negotiation, Charles yielded. *Irene*, a work never published during Drummond's lifetime though circulated in manuscript, urged both parties to abandon the quarrel. Drummond criticized the Covenanters for seeking to overthrow the natural order of society by rebelling against the king, but he also warned Charles not to pursue a harsh policy toward his subjects: "The drawing of your sword against them shall be the drawing of it against yourself; instead of triumphs, you shall obtain nothing but sad exequies and mournful funerals."

The struggle did, of course, continue. Though a Royalist, Drummond signed the Covenant in 1639 to escape being "mocked, hissed, plundered, banished hence," as he expressed his plight in one of his late poems. In another unpublished tract he nevertheless prophesied that

civil war would lead to "one who will name himself PROTECTOR of the Liberty of the Kingdom. He shall surcharge the people with greater miseries than ever before they did suffer . . . and in the end shall essay to make himself King." Drummond's Royalist sentiments surfaced again when the Parliamentary leader John Pym died; Drummond's poem on the occasion does not suggest regret:

> When Pime last night descended into Hell,
> Ere hee his coupes of Lethe did carouse,
> What place is this (said hee) I pray mee tell?
> To whom a Divell: This is the lower house.

In addition to composing political tracts urging moderation, Drummond was working on a history of Scotland during the reigns of the first five Jameses. He had begun his research at least as early as 1633, perhaps as an outgrowth of genealogical research he had undertaken for his kinsman John Drummond, second Earl of Perth. James I of Scotland, with whom *The History of Scotland from the Year 1423 Until the Year 1542* begins, was the son of Annabella Drummond and so related to the earl. This work, too, shows Drummond's desire for religious toleration and peace. Drummond also wrote "A Speech on Toleration" for one of the privy councilors of James V, urging the monarch to permit religious freedom. Yet Drummond sensed that his calls for moderation would go unheeded; immediately after this speech Drummond notes, "But the King followed not this opinione."

By the time of his death on December 4, 1649, Drummond had witnessed the fulfillment of his direst predictions. He was buried in the church at Lasswade. When he had been near death in 1620, he had written a sonnet to Sir William Alexander, a friend and fellow poet: "I conjure Thee . . ./ To grave this short Remembrance on my Grave./ Heere *Damon* lyes, whose Songes did some-time grace/ The murmuring Eske, may Roses shade the place." In October, 1893, a memorial with this inscription was at last erected over Drummond's grave.

ANALYSIS

In an undated letter to Dr. Arthur Johnston, court physician to Charles I and himself a poet, William Drummond expressed his theory of poetic composition. Conservative in his literary as in his political philosophy,

Drummond objected to the innovations of John Donne and his followers: "What is not like the ancients and conforme to those Rules which hath been agreed unto by all tymes, maye (indeed) be some thing like unto poesie, but it is no more Poesie than a Monster is a Man." Thus, Drummond valued imitation over invention. He would not seek to create new poetic forms or to develop original themes. For Drummond, as for Alexander Pope, the aim of poetry was to give fresh expression to old ideas. The result in Drummond's case is a body of work adapted from classical and Renaissance sources, elegantly phrased and carefully crafted but lacking the emotion and invention that elevate excellent versifying to the level of first-rate poetry.

TEARES, ON THE DEATH OF MOELIADES

Drummond's first published piece, *Teares, on the Death of Moeliades*, exemplifies the poet's habits of composition throughout his life and reveals his skill as a craftsman and his techniques of adaptation. According to L. E. Kastner in his 1913 edition of Drummond's poetry, the model for this elegy is one for Basilius in Sir Philip Sidney's *Arcadia* (1590, 1593, 1598). Kastner also points out various specific borrowings from Sidney's poem. Thus, Sidney writes, "O Hyacinth let AI be on thee still"; Drummond changes this line only slightly: "O Hyacinthes, for ay your AI keepe still" (line 127). Drummond's lines "Stay Skie thy turning Course, and now become/ A stately Arche, unto the Earth his Tombe" (lines 137-138) echo Sidney's "And well me-thinks becomes this vaulty sky/ A stately tomb to cover him deceased." Other lines are drawn from *Astrophel and Stella* (1591) and from Sonnet XVI of *Aurora* (1604) by Sir William Alexander. The poem is full of classical allusions, and the consolation, beginning with line 143, suggests Socrates' vision of heaven in Plato's *Phaedo* (probably one of the middle dialogues).

Despite all these borrowings, however, the poem is decidedly Drummond's rather than Sidney's or Alexander's. Drummond has transposed Sidney's lament into iambic pentameter couplets, a verse form which he handles effectively. Aware of the dangers of falling into sing-song monotony, Drummond repeatedly alters the position of the caesura; in the first three lines it occurs after the third, sixth, and fourth syllables respectively. He also alters the iamb. The poem begins with a spondee

("O Heavens!"), as do lines nine and nineteen; line twenty-three begins with a trochee. A potentially monotonous emphasis on the rhyme-words is overcome through frequent enjambment: "That (in a Palsey) quakes to finde so soone/ Her Lover set" (lines 33-34); "A Youth more brave, pale Troy with trembling Walles/ Did never see" (lines 61-62).

Another characteristic evident in this poem is Drummond's musicality. Some of his poetry is clearly intended to be sung, and he was a competent lutanist. Here the refrain—apparently original—repeats the liquid *l* and *r* and combines these with the long *e* and *o* sounds to infuse an appropriately watery sound (since the poet is addressing water spirits) as well as a gentle melancholy tone: "Moeliades sweet courtly Nymphes deplore,/ From Thuly to Hydapses pearlie Shore." (Less happily, this refrain reveals Drummond's fondness for inversion, which occasionally renders a line difficult to decipher.)

Even when he borrows, Drummond frequently improves a verse. He turns Sidney's "I never drank of Aganippe well;/ Nor never did in shade of Tempe sit" into "Chaste Maides which haunt fair Aganippe Well,/ And you in Tempes sacred Shade who dwell" (lines 97-98). The long *u* sounds here, coupled with "haunt," do indeed suggest the "doleful Plaints" that the poet is requesting of the nymphs. Again, Sidney's line about the hyacinths is not much altered, but Drummond does pun on the "AI" that the hyacinth supposedly spells. The sky is to serve as a tomb for both Basilius and Moeliades, but Drummond enriches his couplet by introducing the Copernican worldview of a turning rather than a stationary heaven. (Drummond's awareness of the New Science is evident again in *A Cypresse Grove*.)

Drummond's love of natural beauty is evident even as he asks for that beauty to be lessened in mourning: "Delicious *Meades*, whose checkred *Plaine* foorth brings,/ White, golden, azure Flowers, which once were Kings" (lines 121-122); "Queene of the Fields, whose Blush makes blushe the *Morne,*/ Sweet *Rose*" (lines 125-126); "In silver Robe the *Moone*, the *Sunne* in Gold" (line 160). The language is lush, suggesting Edmund Spenser and Sidney. At the same time, the description is general; here is no Romantic nature worship, no minute Wordsworthian observation.

The immortality that Drummond anticipates is decidedly Christian, but it is also Neoplatonic. In *Teares, on the Death of Moeliades* Drummond portrays heaven as the abode of perfection, where "other sumptuous Towres" excel "our poore Bowres" (lines 171-172), where songs are sweetest, where all is immutable; he describes God as the supreme exemplar of love and beauty, which those on earth can never truly experience. This Platonism, too, recurs throughout Drummond's poetry.

Teares, on the Death of Moeliades is a tissue of allusions, adaptations, and direct borrowings of phrases and ideas. Still, the poem as a whole is distinctly Drummond's in its techniques and themes. Hence, when Drummond turned from an elegy to a sonnet sequence, the poetry did not assume very different characteristics. One might be hard pressed to find the author of "The Extasie" in "Death Be Not Proud," but one would have no difficulty in recognizing the author of *Teares, on the Death of Moeliades* in *Poems*, despite their disparate subjects.

DEATH

Teares, on the Death of Moeliades is as characteristic of Drummond in its themes as in its technique. Drummond's last published poem, like his first, deals with death. He boasted of being the first to write a sonnet sequence in English on the death of a mistress, and the only prose piece he published during his lifetime is an extended meditation on death. The early seventeenth century was obsessed with this subject; yet even those who wrote most eloquently on the theme published on other subjects as well. Not so Drummond. Even his love poems are full of the imagery of graves, grief, and death. Clearly the subject was congenial to him.

Related to Drummond's love of death is a contempt for this world. This theme, too, is conventional, yet even before Drummond was imitating and adapting poetry, he wrote from France to Sir George Keith (February 12, 1607), "And truly considering all our actions, except those which regard the service and adoration of God Almighty, they are either to be lamented or laughed at." In his lament for the death of Prince Henry he presents the moral that he will repeat in numerous poems: "O fading Hopes! O short-while-lasting Joy!/ Of Earth-borne Man, which one Houre can destroy!" (lines 9-10). In his elegy on the death of Jane, Countess of Perth, he laments that

"fairest Thinges thus soonest have their End" (line 10). Even in *The Entertainment*, a splendid celebration of temporal power and magnificence, Drummond tells Charles I, "On gorgeous rayments, womanising toyes,/ The workes of wormes, and what a Moth destroyes,/ The Maze of fooles, thou shalt no treasure spend,/ Thy charge to immortality shall tend" (iv, 31-34).

POEMS

Like *Teares, on the Death of Moeliades*, Drummond's *Poems* are heavily indebted to Sidney. Where Sidney celebrates Stella, Drummond sings of Auristella. Kastner notes that Sonnet XXVII (the first part) is reminiscent of Sidney's Sonnet LXXIV in *Astrophel and Stella*, and Drummond's Sonnet V is reminiscent of Sidney's Sonnet XXX. The sequence also reveals Drummond's intimate knowledge of Italian, French, and Spanish models. The very form is of course traditional, though by 1616 the sonnet sequence was a dying, if not a dead, form. Drummond's use of this poetic model is yet another reflection of his desire to copy the best models instead of striking out on his own.

Drummond invariably ends each sonnet with a two-line summary in the manner of the English rather than the Italian form. Otherwise, however, he is flexible in both rhyme scheme and structure. Sonnet XXIV (the first part) has a rhyme scheme of *abab baba cdcd ee*. Two sonnets later, one finds *abba cddc effe gg*, and in the very next sonnet the pattern is different still—*abba abba cdcd ee*. Sonnet XXXI (the first part) consists of an octet and sestet in the Italian mode (though still with the concluding couplet); Sonnet XVI has three quatrains and a couplet in the English manner.

The lush language and musicality of *Teares, on the Death of Moeliades* are even more fully realized in *Poems*, aided by the use of feminine rhymes not present in the elegy. Song I (the first part) describes a luxuriant landscape. Often rich description appears in conjunction with an unusual word, as in Sonnet XVII (the first part), "The silver Flouds in pearlie Channells flow,/ The late-bare Woods greene Anadeams doe weare" (lines 3-4)—*anadeam* had entered the language only about ten years earlier. A bit later Drummond writes, "With Roses here *Shee* stellified the Ground" (Sonnet XXIII, the first part, line 7), and he writes of "Phoebus in his Chaire/ Ensaffroning Sea and Aire" (Song II, the first part, lines

39-40). This love of exotic diction leads him in at least two instances to new coinings; Drummond's is the only use of *deflourish'd* not rated by the *Oxford English Dictionary* ("Deflourish'd *Mead* where is your heavenly Hue?"—Sonnet XLV, the first part, line 9) and the same authority lists as the first use of *disgarland* his "Thy Lockes disgarland" (Song I, the second part, line 90). The descriptions, though rich, are nevertheless general; the landscape is merely a luxurious background for the human actions occurring there.

As in *Teares, on the Death of Moeliades*, Drummond repeatedly invokes mythology. In Song I (the first part) he invokes Phaeton, Elysian Fields, Venus, Mars, Adonis, and many other mythological figures. His use of mythology is usually conventional. In one instance, though, Drummond does cleverly invert the traditional story. Daphne and Syrinx were both turned into plants to preserve their chastity; Drummond imagines that he sees the process reversed as "three naked Nymphes" emerge from a myrtle (lines 84-86). This reversal of the traditional myths foreshadows a thematic reversal in the poem. Conventionally, the lover praises his mistress's chastity. When Drummond's mistress enters the "Fort of Chastitie," though, he bemoans his fate both asleep and waking.

Such playful invention is all too infrequent in the sonnets, the commonplace lamentations all too frequent. Drummond recognized the artificiality of such writing. In the first of "Galatea's Sonnets," a sequence of five poems that Drummond chose not to publish, a woman rejects Petrarchan conceits:

> I Thinke not love ore thee his wings hath spred,
> Or if that passion hath thy soule opprest,
> Its onlie for some Grecian Mistresse dead,
> Of such old sighs thou dost discharge thy brest.

Occasionally, Drummond can infuse sincerity into those old sighs, as when he regrets his failure to declare his love (Sonnet XXIII, the first part) or when he praises the green color of his mistress's eyes (Sonnet XVIII, the first part); neither of these pieces relies on a specific model. Here the emotions are not exaggerated, the incidents quotidian and hence credible. More often, unfortunately, he is willing to tear a passion to tatters. Sonnet XLVII (the first part) sounds like a parody from the rude

mechanical's *Pyramus and Thisbe* in William Shakespeare's *A Midsummer Night's Dream* (c. 1595-1596): "O Night, clear Night, O darke and gloomie Day!/ O wofull Waking! O Soule-pleasing Sleepe" (lines 1-2). Though this is the most egregious example, there are enough borrowings from Petrarch, Giambattista Marino, Pierre de Ronsard, and others to suggest that Drummond's inspiration for his sonnets was his library rather than Miss Cunningham.

The sonnet sequence ends with a vision corresponding to the dream in Song I of the first part. In that earlier song the poet meets his mistress for the first time; in this final song he becomes reconciled to her death. The poem apparently cost Drummond much effort, for among his manuscripts is a fragment of eight lines translated from Passerat, apparently a draft of this piece. Here one can trace the movement from literal translation to adaptation. The eight lines have been expanded to nineteen, the natural setting elaborated, and phrases repeated to heighten the melancholy musicality.

As the poem begins, Drummond's mistress appears to urge him to abandon his grief. Her arguments begin with stoical reflections: "Was shee not mortall borne? (line 45); "Why wouldst thou Here longer wish to bee?" (line 75). With line 93 the argument moves to Platonism, echoing the consolation in *Teares, on the Death of Moeliades*. Whereas *Teares, on the Death of Moeliads* ended with Platonic idealism, however, the song proceeds to a third stage (lines 181-240), explicitly Christian, exhorting the lover to think of heaven's joys rather than earth's sorrows.

A CYPRESSE GROVE AND FLOWRES OF SION

A Cypresse Grove, which Drummond appended to his next collection of poetry, *Flowres of Sion*, retraces these three stages. Indeed, the prose meditation on death is little more than an expansion of the song, with repetitions of phrases as well as ideas. To cite but one example, in the "Song" Drummond writes, "We bee not made for Earth, though here wee come,/ More than the *Embryon* for the Mothers Wombe" (lines 178-179). In *A Cypresse Grove* these lines become "For though hee be borne on the Earthe, hee is not borne for the Earth, more than the Embryon for the mothers wombe."

In fact, the entire volume of *Flowres of Sion* stems logically from the "song," elaborating on the Christian message that concludes that piece. In his edition of Drummond's writings, R. H. MacDonald notes that *Flowres of Sion* proceeds through the three stages of the religious meditation: Sonnets I-VI depict the poetry's memory of the evils of this world, Sonnet VII through Hymn III (which treat Christ's birth, life, and death) present an understanding of Christ's solution to those evils, and the rest of the poems adore God's love and meditate on the follies of this world.

The poetic techniques by now familiar to the reader of Drummond remain evident here: the love of exotic words (such as "Jubeling cries" in Hymn II, line 49; the *Oxford English Dictionary* notes only a single fifteenth century use of this word), borrowings from numerous sources, luxurious general description, virtuosity in the handling of the sonnet or couplet form. The themes, too, are familiar—the love of death, contempt for the things of this world, Christianity heavily tinged with Neoplatonism. This sonnet cycle mirrors Drummond's earlier one; both progress from despair to hope, from the pains of this world to the joys of the next. Here, however, the emphasis is on the latter rather than the former, so that, paradoxically, the sequence focusing on death is less depressing than the one supposedly treating love.

THE ENTERTAINMENT

In the last twenty-six years of his life Drummond published only two occasional pieces, *The Entertainment* in 1633 for King Charles's visit to Edinburgh, and, five years later, an elegy on the death of the son of his longtime friend and fellow poet, Sir William Alexander.

The first of these works combines prose and poetry in an elaborate tribute to the king. For the poetic sections, Drummond uses the heroic couplet almost exclusively, an apt choice to celebrate a grand event, and as usual he handles the verse form competently. Only one poem does not employ the couplet, instead containing three lines of six syllables followed by two lines of ten in each of the four verse paragraphs. This metrical pattern suggests the Italian *canzone*, the madrigal, and the dramatic chorus. The language is ornate, abounding in such epithets as "The Acidalian Queene" (Venus) and "Leucadian Sythe-bearing Sire" (Saturn). As these epithets suggest, Drummond again invokes mythological allusions, as Endymion, Saturn, Jove, Mars, Venus, and

Mercury address Charles. In choosing these particular deities, together with the Sun and Moon, Drummond implies that the entire universe rejoices at Charles's visit. Each of the gods ends his speech with a refrain: "Thus heavens decree, so have ordain'd the Fates," alternating with "Thus heavens ordaine, so doe decree the Fates." Drummond had effectively used this rhetorical device in *Teares, on the Death of Moeliades*; though the refrain here lacks the melody of the earlier one, the slight variation shows a concern for preventing monotony.

Although the excessive flattery is obligatory, it does not lack a hortatory edge. The king is urged to avoid excessive taxation and the raising up of favorites, to aid learning and the arts, and to rule through love rather than through fear. The political message thus anticipates such pamphlets as *Irene*.

A PASTORALL ELEGIE

The Entertainment is largely original, only occasionally hinting at other poets. *A Pastorall Elegie*, on the other hand, is virtually a translation of Baldassare Castiglione's "Alcon"; Drummond even refers to the dead Sir Antony Alexander as Alcon. The highly artificial pastoral form and the lack of originality suggest that Drummond was writing from a sense of obligation to his old friend; there is even less emotion here than in *Teares, on the Death of Moeliades*. The technique is as sound as ever, but only in one place does Drummond surpass his model. Ostensibly unaware of his friend's death, the poet imagines that "the populous City holds him, amongst Harmes/ Of some fierce *Cyclops*, Circe's stronger Charmes" (lines 183-184). These Homeric allusions, absent in Castiglione's poem, suggest that the youth in fact will not return but rather suffer the fate of Odysseus's companions. These references thus foreshadow the poet's discovery of the youth's fate.

During his lifetime Drummond suppressed almost as much poetry as he published. In general, he was a sound editor; few of the pieces published since his death add anything to his reputation. Occasionally, though, one of the posthumous poems demonstrates wit and imagination too often lacking in Drummond's published works. The quatrain on Pym's death quoted earlier is original and clever. The five sonnets of Galatea, supposedly written in response to verses such as those Drummond composed in the first part of *Poems*, wittily undercut the Petrarchan conventions by pointing out their artificiality and logical absurdity. "The Country Maid," though slightly bawdy, is mythopoeic. Drummond's decision not to publish poems such as these may have been less a judgment on their quality than an indication of the kind of literary reputation he wished to cultivate. Less concerned with originality and mythopoesis than with correctness, imitation, and technical virtuosity, Drummond published those works that embodied his poetic ideals. Working with established forms and themes, he was able to make these his own and to find a unique voice. His models rarely led him astray; he produced few bad poems, much competent verse, and a handful of memorable pieces such as the "Song" that closes the second part of the sonnet cycle of *Poems* or his sonnet to Sir William Alexander on his own illness. What Samuel Johnson said of another reclusive poet, Thomas Gray, may also be said of Drummond at his best: "Had [he] written often thus, it had been vain to blame, and useless to praise him."

OTHER MAJOR WORKS

NONFICTION: *A Midnight's Trance*, 1619 (as *A Cypresse Grove*, 1623); *The History of Scotland from the Year 1423 Until the Year 1542*, 1655; *Notes of Ben Jonson's Conversations with William Drummond of Hawthornden*, 1842.

MISCELLANEOUS: *The Works of William Drummond of Hawthornden*, 1711 (2 volumes).

BIBLIOGRAPHY

Cummings, Robert. "Drummond's Forth Feasting: A Panegyric for King James in Scotland." *The Seventeenth Century* 2, no. 1 (1987): 1-18. Cummings discusses Drummond's panegyric in relation to its tradition and the situation at the time. This article, though on a rather specialized subject, makes a useful addition to earlier critical approaches that stress the poet's sonnets and other short lyrics.

Fogle, French Rowe. *A Critical Study of William Drummond of Hawthornden*. New York: King's Crown Press of Columbia University, 1952. The most useful book on Drummond for the general reader, this critical account examines the poet's development with biographical background where necessary. One appendix lists Drummond's reading and a second describes and excerpts poems in the Hawthornden manuscript. Fogle does not deal with Drummond's prose works or conversations with Ben Jonson.

Masson, David. *Drummond of Hawthornden*. London: Macmillan, 1873. Masson's book, though out of date in many respects, is the fullest account of the events of Drummond's life. It is also one of the more readily available works on Drummond as it has been reproduced in a microform series (LEL) found in many colleges and some community libraries.

Rae, Thomas Ian. "The Political Attitudes of William Drummond of Hawthornden." In *The Scottish Traditions: Essays in Honour of Ronald Gordon Cant*, edited by G. W. S. Barrow. Edinburgh: Scottish Academic Press, 1974. Analyzes Drummond's political writings, with particular emphasis on "Irene: A Remonstrance for Concord, Amity and Love Amongst His Majesty's Subjects" (1638). Rae argues that Drummond based his political opinions on abstract (and largely obsolete) ideas of the order of the universe and of society. He illuminates a monarchist, conservative side of Drummond which, though less familiar than the poetic craftsman side, helps readers to understand the nostalgic nature of his personality.

Severance, Sibyl Lutz. "'Some Other Figure': The Vision of Change in *Flowres of Sion*, 1623." *Spenser Studies: A Renaissance Poetry Annual* 2 (1981): 217-228. Seeing the *Flowres of Sion* sequence as a whole rather than as a series of separate sonnets, Severance points out the importance of Drummond's idea of change (earthly mutability) versus permanence (eternity). The argument depends on a detailed numerological analysis of the sequence.

Spence, G. "The Theism of William Drummond." *Keats-Shelley Review* 14 (2000): 71-83. An examination of theological questions raised by Drummond's poetry.

Wallerstein, Ruth C. "The Style of Drummond of Hawthornden in Its Relation to His Translations." *PMLA* 48 (1933): 1090-1107. This detailed article examines the most important aspects of Drummond's poetic style against the background of his translations. Though somewhat technical for many readers, it remains the only thorough analysis of the poet's technique to be found in a major journal.

Joseph Rosenblum;
bibliography updated by the editors

JOHN DRYDEN

Born: Aldwinckle, England; August 19, 1631
Died: London, England; May 1, 1700

PRINCIPAL POETRY

Heroic Stanzas, 1659
Astraea Redux, 1660
"To My Lord Chancellor," 1662
Prologues and Epilogues, 1664-1700
Annus Mirabilis, 1667
Absalom and Achitophel, Part I, 1681
Absalom and Achitophel, Part II, 1682 (with Nahum Tate)
The Medall: A Satyre Against Sedition, 1682
Mac Flecknoe: Or, A Satyre upon the True-Blew-Protestant Poet, T. S., 1682
Religio Laici: Or, A Layman's Faith, 1682
Threnodia Augustalis, 1685
The Hind and the Panther, 1687
"A Song for St. Cecilia's Day," 1687
Britannia Rediviva, 1688
Eleonora, 1692
"To My Dear Friend Mr. Congreve," 1694
Alexander's Feast: Or, The Power of Music, an Ode in Honor of St. Cecilia's Day, 1697
"To My Honour'd Kinsman, John Driden," 1700

OTHER LITERARY FORMS

If one follows the practice of literary historians and assigns John Milton to an earlier age, then John Dryden stands as the greatest literary artist in England between 1660 and 1700, a period sometimes designated the Age of Dryden. In addition to his achievements in poetry, he excelled in drama, translation, and literary criticism. Dryden wrote or coauthored twenty-seven plays over a period of nearly thirty-five years; among them were successfully produced tragedies, heroic plays, tragicomedies, comedies of manner, and operas.

For every verse of original poetry that Dryden wrote, he translated two from another poet. Moreover, he translated two long volumes of prose from French originals—in 1684, Louis Maimbourg's *Histoire de la Ligue* and in 1688, Dominick Bouhours's *La Vie de Saint François Xavier*—and he had a hand in the translation of the version of Plutarch's *Lives* published by Jacob Tonson in 1683. The translations were usually well received, especially the editions of Juvenal and Persius (1693) and of Vergil (1697).

Dryden's literary criticism consists largely of prefaces and dedications published throughout his career and attached to other works, his only critical work published alone being *Of Dramatic Poesie: An Essay* (1668). As a critic, Dryden appears at his best when he evaluates an earlier poet or dramatist (Homer, Vergil, Ovid, Geoffrey Chaucer, William Shakespeare, Ben Johnson, John Fletcher), when he seeks to define a genre, or when he breaks new critical ground, providing, for example, definitions of "wit" or a theory of translation.

ACHIEVEMENTS

The original English poetry of John Dryden consists of approximately two hundred titles, or about twenty thousand verses. Slow to develop as a poet, he wrote his first significant poem in his twenty-eighth year, yet his poetic energy continued almost unabated until his death forty-one years later. His poetry reflects the diversity of talent which one finds throughout his literary career, and a wide range of didactic and lyric genre are represented. With *Mac Flecknoe* and *Absalom and Achitophel* Dryden raised English satire to a form of high art, surpassing his contemporaries John Oldham, Samuel Butler, and the earl of Rochester as they had surpassed their Elizabethan predecessors. He left his impression on the ode and the verse epistle, and his religious poem *Religio Laici* may be considered an early example of the verse essay. In the minor genre represented by prologues and epilogues, he stands alone in English literature, unexcelled in both variety and quality.

Of Dryden's poetic achievement Samuel Johnson wrote in his *Life of Dryden*: "What was said of Rome, adorned by Augustus, may be applied by an easy metaphor to English poetry embellished by Dryden. . . . [H]e found it brick and he left it marble." Johnson's praise applies primarily to Dryden's significant achievements in style and tone, for Dryden perfected the heroic couplet, the rhymed iambic pentameter form that was to remain the dominant meter of English verse for nearly a century. He demonstrated that a stanza form best suited to lucid and graceful aphoristic wit could be varied and supple enough to produce a range of tones. Building upon the achievements of his predecessors Edmund Waller and John Denham and drawing upon his own wide experience with the couplet in heroic plays, Dryden polished the form that became for him a natural mode of expression. His couplets are usually end-stopped and closed, achieving a complete grammatical unit by the end of the second line. He makes extensive use of colloquial diction to create a rational, almost conversational tone. The lines contain internal pauses that are carefully regulated, and the syntax usually follows that of idiomatic English. To keep tension in the verse, he relies primarily upon balance, antithesis, and other schemes of repetition.

Dryden brought to poetry of his age the energy and directness of expression that critics describe as the most masculine of styles. Accustomed to writing soliloquies and moral arguments in the speeches of heroic drama, he incorporated into his poetry extended passages of reasoning in verse that an age which valued reason found appealing. His inclination to choose for his poetry subjects of interest to contemporaries—science, aesthetics, religion, and politics—enhanced the popularity of his work.

Dryden is essentially a poet of urbanity, wit, and reason, perhaps seeking more to persuade readers than to move them. It has justly been pointed out that his poetry lacks emotional depth. He would rather arouse indignation and scorn over what he opposes than create admiration and appreciation for what he defends. The topical and occasional nature of his poetry suggest his preoccupation with issues of interest to his own day, which are of course less interesting to subsequent ages. His imagery and figures of speech are derived from classical literature, art, and society, not from nature. Even so, modern readers still find appealing those qualities that Dryden himself prized—grace and subtlety of style, rational tone, and vigorous and direct expression.

BIOGRAPHY

John Dryden was the eldest of fourteen children in a landed family of modest means whose sympathies were Puritan on both sides. Little is known of his youth in Northamptonshire, for Dryden, seldom hesitant about his opinions, was reticent about his personal life. At about age fifteen, he was enrolled in Westminster School, then under the headmastership of Dr. Richard Busby, a school notable for its production of poets and bishops. Having attained at Westminster a thorough grounding in Latin, he proceeded to Cambridge, taking the B.A. degree in 1654. After the death of his father brought him a modest inheritance in the form of rents from family land, he left the university and settled in London. Though little is known of his early years there, he served briefly in Cromwell's government in a minor

John Dryden (Library of Congress)

position and may have worked for the publisher Henry Herringman. He produced an elegy on the death of Cromwell, yet when Charles II ascended the throne, Dryden greeted the new ruler with a congratulatory poem, *Astraea Redux*. After the Restoration he turned his main interest to the drama, collaborating with Sir Robert Howard on one heroic play. He married Lady Elizabeth Howard, Sir Robert's sister, in 1663, a marriage which brought him a generous dowry and eventually three sons in whom he took pride.

Throughout his career Dryden was no stranger to controversy, whether literary, political, or religious; in fact, he seemed all too eager to seize an occasion to express his views on these subjects. In literature he challenged Sir Robert Howard's views on the drama, Thomas Rymer's on criticism, and Rochester's and Thomas Shadwell's on questions of literary merit and taste. After receiving encouragement from Charles II, he entered the political controversy over succession to the throne with *Absalom and Achitophel*. Later he explained his religious views by attacking Deists, Catholics, and Dissenters in *Religio Laici*; then he shifted his ground and defended Catholicism in *The Hind and the Panther*.

For a variety of reasons, certainly in some measure because of envy, Dryden was the most often assailed among major poets. In an age when almost everyone prized his own wit, Dryden attained eminence without obviously possessing more of that quality than many others. His willingness to plunge into controversy brought him a host of enemies, and his changes of opinions and beliefs—literary, religious, political—presented an even greater problem. Examining the changes one by one, a biographer or critic can provide a logical explanation for each. This task is perhaps most difficult in literary criticism, however, where Dryden will defend a position with enthusiasm only to abandon it later for another, which he advocates with equal enthusiasm. To his contemporaries, some of his changes coincided with interest, and, rightly or wrongly, he was frequently charged with timeserving.

In 1668, Dryden was appointed poet laureate, a position he held for twenty years, being deprived of it after the Glorious Revolution of 1688. During his term he received a two-hundred-pound annual stipend, which was later increased to three hundred when he became historiographer royal, but this was irregularly paid. His greatest efforts remained with the drama until his satire *Mac Flecknoe* and the beginning of the Popish plot in 1678, when he turned his energies to poetic satire.

When events surrounding the Plot posed a threat to the government of Charles II, Dryden wrote vigorously on behalf of the Tory cause, producing satires, translations, and then his religious poems. Initially he carried the field for the king, but after the fall of James II and the loss of his political cause, he also lost the laureateship and its accompanying pension.

During the final period of his life, 1688-1700, he made a brief return to the theater but devoted most of his considerable energy and talent to translation, achieving success with his patrons and public. Though he had taken unpopular political and religious positions, he experienced no decline in his literary talent; in his final decade he produced some of his best poems. Shortly before his death on May 1, 1700, he could look back upon his century and epitomize the era poetically in *The Secular Masque*. He represented the Stuart Era by Diana (James I), Mars (Charles I and the Civil Wars), and Venus (Charles II).

(to Diana)	All, all of a piece throughout; Thy Chase had a Beast in View;
(to Mars)	Thy Wars brought nothing about;
(to Venus)	Thy Lovers were all untrue; 'Tis well an Old Age is out, And time to begin a New.

ANALYSIS

To a greater degree than those of most other poets, John Dryden's poems are based upon real and not imaginary occasions or events, often of a public nature. His imaginative power lies not in creating original or dramatic situations but in endowing actual events with poetic and sometimes mythic significance. When one looks beyond the rich variety of his poetry, Dryden's art is likely to impress the reader most strongly for the following: his intricate craftsmanship and style, his sense of genre, and his reliance upon what he termed parallels, analogies used for both structuring and developing his poems. Craft and style are most readily revealed through analysis of selected passages from the poems, but some clarification of genre and the parallels may be useful at the outset.

Though Dryden possessed a keen sense of poetic genre, questions of classification in his poetry are not always easily resolved, for he writes in genres not well defined during his age. A poem may be assigned to one genre on the basis of its theme or purpose (an elegy, for example) and to another on the basis of form (such as an ode). Yet almost any poem by Dryden can be placed with assurance in one of the following genres: lyric forms, especially songs and odes; satires; ratiocinative poems; panegyrics praising public figures or celebrating public occasions; verse epistles, usually in praise of living persons; epigrams, epitaphs, and elegies commemorating the dead; and prologues and epilogues.

For his parallels, which often reveal his preoccupation with monarchy and hierarchy, Dryden goes to the Bible, classical antiquity, or history. They provide a mythic framework within which he develops rational positions or ideals, aided by a set of conventional metaphors such as the temple, the tree, or the theater. Dryden's use of parallels and conventional metaphors indicates his essentially conservative cast of mind, especially about human nature and political affairs.

POLARITIES AND OPPOSITES

The parallels also afford an opportunity for Dryden's favorite mode of thought—that of polarities or opposites. He delights in presenting contrasting viewpoints and then either defending one as an ideal or steering between them in a show of moderation. Normally such polarities or dichotomies contribute to a rational tone, enabling Dryden to ingratiate himself with the reader, as in his "Prologue to *Aureng-Zebe*" (1675). He contemplates retirement from the stage and contrasts his own plays with those of Shakespeare and his younger contemporaries such as William Wycherley:

> As with the greater Dead he dares not strive,
> He wou'd not match his Verse with those who live:
> Let him retire, betwix't two Ages cast,
> The first of this, and hindmost of the last.

The reader accepts the tone of humility, even though he realizes that it is not entirely ingenuous.

ANNUS MIRABILIS

Dryden's earliest poems are usually occasional pieces and panegyrics that reveal to some extent a debt to so-called Metaphysical poetry and to Abraham Cow-

ley, an influence he soon rejected for a style more regular and lucid. Yet as late as 1667, in *Annus Mirabilis*, a long poem on the London plague and fire and the Dutch war, Dryden still retained some tendency toward Metaphysical conceits. It is notable too that *Annus Mirabilis* employs the four-line heroic stanza from Sir William Davenant's poem *Gondibert* (1651), which Dryden had used earlier in the elegy on Cromwell. Perhaps a more reliable index to his poetic development during the 1660's is represented by the prologues and epilogues which he began publishing in 1664.

PROLOGUES AND EPILOGUES

During the Restoration, prologues and epilogues became normal complements to dramatic works. Over nearly four decades, Dryden wrote more than a hundred of them, not only for his own plays but for those of other dramatists as well. They employ straightforward, colloquial diction and syntax, and they are normally written in heroic couplets. In his early examples in this genre, Dryden follows established convention by having the poems appeal for the indulgence of the audience and a favorable reception of the play. Later he adapts the poems to varied subjects and purposes, some having little to do with drama. He writes prologues to introduce special performances at unaccustomed sites, such as Oxford, or to greet an eminent person in the audience (a duke or duchess, perhaps), or to mark some theater occasion, such as the opening of a new playhouse. In some of the poems he reflects upon the poor taste of the audience; in others he explains principles of literary criticism. He may take his audience into his confidence and impart his own personal plans. At times, as in the "Prologue to *The Duke of Guise*" (1684), he outlines his views on political questions, explaining how events chronicled in the play resemble those then current. In more than a few he titillates the audience with sexual humor, allusion, and innuendo. For all their variety, the poems evidence throughout some of Dryden's most characteristic poetic qualities—directness, clarity, colloquial tone, wit, and adaptability.

MAC FLECKNOE

Neither the occasion nor the time of Dryden's first satire, *Mac Flecknoe*, a mock-heroic attack on a rival playwright, Thomas Shadwell, is known with certainty. Dryden selects the demise of the poetaster Richard

Flecknoe (d. 1678) as the basis of his poem—a mock coronation, in which Flecknoe, dubbed the reigning prince of dullness, chooses Shadwell as his successor. This situation permits scintillating literary inversion; the kingdom of letters, Augustan Rome, and the seriousness of succession to the throne all provide contrasting analogy and allusion. The poem satirizes not only Shadwell but also bad taste in art. Establishing a polarity between true and false wit, Dryden creates by implication an aesthetic ideal.

In the first section of the poem, Flecknoe arrives at his decision regarding a successor. The poem then describes the festivities preceding Shadwell's coronation and the coronation itself, followed by the long oration and fall of Flecknoe. The opening lines invite the reader to assume that selecting a successor to the throne of dullness is serious business:

> All human things are subject to decay,
> And, when Fate summons, Monarchs must obey.
> This Flecknoe found, who, like Augustus, young
> Was call'd to Empire, and had govern'd long;
> In Prose and Verse, was own'd, without dispute
> Through all the Realms of *Nonsense*, absolute.

The sober aphorism in the opening lines, followed by comparison with Augustus, creates a tone of solemnity, to be overturned by the mockery of "Realms of *Nonsense*." As Flecknoe selects Shadwell, he catalogs a series of personal attributes praiseworthy in a dunce, usually deriving from the plays of Shadwell. Yet Dryden does not refrain from personal satire directed at Shadwell's size, perhaps because Shadwell himself had used his corpulent appearance as a basis for his resemblance to Ben Jonson:

> Besides his goodly Fabrick fills the eyes,
> And seems design'd for thoughtless Majesty:
> Thoughtless as Monarch Oakes that shade the plain,
> And, spread in solemn state, supinely reign.

Another satiric maneuver is to separate poets into two camps, with Shadwell relegated to the company of dullards. An example occurs when Flecknoe describes the site of the coronation:

> Great Fletcher never treads in Buskins here,
> Nor greater Jonson dare in Socks appear.
> But gentle Simkin just reception finds
> Amidst this Monument of vanish't Minds.

The polarity of artists includes such figures as Ben Jonson, John Fletcher, Sir Charles Sedley, and Sir George Etherege at one end; and John Ogleby, Thomas Heywood, John Shirley, Thomas Dekker, and Richard Flecknoe at the other.

As there is a difference between true and false writing, there is also a hierarchy of forms or genres. Flecknoe admonishes Shadwell to abandon the drama and turn to those poems developed through what Dryden's age considered false wit: pattern poems, anagrams, acrostics, and ballads—works appropriate to his dull wit. In *Mac Flecknoe* Dryden generally maintains a tone of exuberant good humor and mirth, seldom resorting to lampoon. The poem does, however, illustrate the problem of topicality, since many of its allusions are now obscure and others are altogether lost. Still, as Dryden explores the kingdoms of sense and nonsense, he clearly demonstrates his reliance upon parallels and polarities.

SATIRIC POEMS

Dryden's three later satiric poems–*Absalom and Achitophel, Part I*, *The Medal*, and *Absalom and Achitophel, Part II* (with Nahum Tate)—concern the struggle of the Whigs to alter the succession in England by excluding James, Duke of York, the King's brother, and giving the right of succession to James, Duke of Monmouth, the king's illegitimate son. This enterprise was ably led by the earl of Shaftesbury (Achitophel), though he could not prevail against the determined opposition of the king. Charles II (David) understood that permitting Parliament to change the established succession would alter the form of monarchy from a royal one, in which the king normally followed law and established tradition but could exercise extraordinary powers in times of crisis, to a constitutional monarchy in which the king's power became subject to parliamentary restrictions. Dryden's objective in the poem is to persuade readers to support the king in the conflict.

ABSALOM AND ACHITOPHEL

Thus in *Absalom and Achitophel*, Dryden (then poet laureate) employed his pen in the king's behalf—according to anecdote, at the king's own suggestion. He makes use of the biblical rebellion against David by his son Absalom, at the instigation of Achitophel (II Samuel 13-18), a parallel familiar to his audience. Dryden freely adds characters and alters the biblical parallel to make it apply to English political leaders and institutions, pointing out that while the biblical account ends with the death of Absalom, he hopes that a peaceful resolution with Monmouth remains possible.

The satire of *Absalom and Achitophel* differs somewhat from that of *Mac Flecknoe*. While Dryden believed satire to be a form of heroic or epic poetry, implying some narrative content, he had in *Mac Flecknoe* maintained a tone of ironic mockery and fine raillery throughout. *Absalom and Achitophel* represents a mixed or Varronian kind of satire, perhaps owing something to Juvenal as well as to Varro. The satiric elements are confined chiefly to the first section of the poem, where Dryden discredits the Whig opponents of the king. Instead of implying an ideal, as satire normally does, Dryden explains it directly in a passage that has come to be regarded as an essay on government (vv. 723-810). Finally, Dryden praises the supporters of the king individually and has the king appear in his own person at the poem's end, showing David (Charles II) facing his opponents with firmness and moderation.

In addition to the biblical parallel, Dryden makes effective use of characters, a technique that owes something to classical satirists but more to the character writers of the seventeenth century. A "character" in Dryden is a passage, sometimes satiric, sometimes serious, delineating a person and creating a unified impression. Though Dryden includes both satiric and complimentary characters, the satiric ones—Achitophel (Shaftesbury), Zimri (Buckingham), Shimei (Slingsby Bethel), and Corah (Titus Oates)—are the most memorable. In his character of Zimri (vv. 543-568), Dryden portrays the duke of Buckingham as foolishly inconsistent: "A man so various, that he seem'd to be/ Not one, but all Mankind's Epitome." In his perversity, Zimri is made to reflect a kind of frenetic energy:

> Stiff in opinions, always in the wrong;
> Was everything by starts, and nothing long;
> But in the course of one revolving Moon,
> Was Chymist, Fidler, States-Man, and Buffoon.

Such an indiscriminate course indicates that Zimri's judgment about human beings and political institutions cannot be trusted, as the character goes on to suggest.

The character becomes a major means of discrediting the king's chief opponents, yet it also permits Dryden to praise the king's loyal supporters.

RELIGIO LAICI

For his religious poem, *Religio Laici*, Dryden assigns no genre, giving as the subtitle "A Poem." In a lengthy preface he finds precedent for his work in the epistles of Horace. It is often called a ratiocinative poem, but it closely resembles the genre in English poetry designated "verse essay." It surveys a definite subject, presents a variety of positions, explores their bases, provides reasoned analysis, and gives the poet's personal positions. *Religio Laici* surveys religious movements in England during Dryden's day and rejects all except the established church, supporting the official view that the Church of England represents a *via media*—a middle way—avoiding the extremes of the Deists, Catholics, and Dissenters. Dryden upholds biblical authority against the Deists, citing reasons for belief in scriptural authority and arguing that the religious principles advocated by the Deists were first brought to man by revelation, not innate understanding, as Deists believed, for otherwise the Greeks and Romans would have discovered them. As the Deist relies too heavily on man's reason, the Catholic relies too heavily on tradition and the argument of infallibility, while the Protestant errs in the extreme in another direction, relying excessively on private interpretation of the Scriptures, an extreme which leads to disorder in society.

Dryden's conclusion indicates both his moderation and his intensely conservative outlook. Essential points of faith are few and plain. Since men believe more than is necessary, they should seek guidance from reliable ancient theologians on disputed points. If that does not provide adequate enlightenment, they can either leave the matter unsettled or restrain further speculation and inquiry in the interest of public peace and order.

"TO THE MEMORY OF MR. OLDHAM"

"To the Memory of Mr. Oldham" (1684), a poem that demonstrates the efficacy of heroic couplets for a serious theme, may be Dryden's finest elegy. John Oldham, a younger poet, had attained success with his satires against the Jesuits and had died young. Dryden pays tribute to a fellow satirist with whom he can identify. The opening lines establish the basic tone: "Farewell, too little, and too lately known,/ Whom I began to think and call my own." The classical simplicity of "farewell," the weight and seriousness of the long vowels and semivowels, and the balance within the lines ("too little and too lately" and "think and call") establish a serious, even tone which Dryden can vary, yet preserve. In a second part of the poem, he stresses the youth of Oldham and his early achievement, acknowledging its imperfection. The tone of unqualified praise has altered, but balance and tonal consistency remain. Dryden next demonstrates his exquisite sense of poetic sound when he turns to the defects of Oldham's poetry, choosing to downplay them: "But Satyr needs not those, and Wit will shine/ Through the harsh cadence of a rugged line." The cadence in the second line sounds harsher because it follows a perfectly balanced line. After further downplaying of the importance of a good ear in the insipid passage, "Maturing time/ But mellow what we write to the dull sweets of Rime," Dryden returns to the balanced and rational tone:

> Once more, hail and farewell; farewell thou young,
> But ah too short, Marcellus of our Tongue;
> Thy Brows with Ivy, and with Laurels bound;
> But Fate and gloomy Night encompass thee around.

Allusion to Marcellus enables Dryden to draw the parallel to Augustan Rome, where the nephew who might have succeeded Augustus dies young. Thus, the kingdom of civilized letters in Dryden's age resembles the finest earlier civilization. The balance within the verse ("Ivy and Laurels," "Fate and gloomy Night") ends the poem in a tone of serious, subdued expression of loss.

ODES

As one would expect, in the ode Dryden abandons the heroic couplet for a more complicated stanza and metrical pattern. His odes are occasional poems either upon the death of someone, as in "Threnodia Augustalis," on the death of Charles II, or "To the Pious Memory of the Accomplished Young Lady Mrs. Anne Killigrew," or commemoration of an occasion, as in his two odes for St. Cecilia's Day, written ten years apart (1687 and 1697), both commemorating the patron saint of music. They share a common theme, the power of music to influence man's emotions or passions. In the first "A Song for St. Cecilia's Day," Dryden employs the traditional association of instruments with particular human pas-

sions and develops his theme, "What Passion cannot Musick raise and quell," in a kind of linear fashion, the trumpet instilling courage and valor, the flute arousing love, the violin, jealousy, and the organ influencing devotion. Inclusion of the organ enables Dryden to allude to St. Cecilia, who is said to have invented that instrument. According to legend, while playing on her invention she drew an angel to earth, the harmony having caused him to mistake earth for heaven. In a concluding grand chorus, Dryden sees music, an element of the creation, as also befitting the end of creation:

> So, when the last and dreadful hour
> This crumbling Pageant shall devour,
> The Trumpet shall be heard on high,
> The Dead shall live, the Living die,
> And Musick shall untune the sky.

ALEXANDER'S FEAST

Alexander's Feast, the second St. Cecilia ode, is constructed according to a more ambitious plan, for Dryden imagines Alexander celebrating his victory over the Persian King Darius, listening to the music of Timotheus, which has sufficient power to move a hero of Alexander's greatness. The shifts are abrupt, as in the Pindaric ode, yet Dryden preserves the Horatian structure with a regular development of emotional response, as Timotheus causes the monarch to experience a sense of deification, a desire for pleasure, pity for the fallen Darius, and then love. No sooner has Alexander indulged his pleasure than Timotheus, in another strain, incites him to revenge, and the king seizes a torch to set the Persian city aflame. At the poem's end, Dryden compares Cecilia and Timotheus. In this ode Dryden achieves a remarkably complex, forceful, and energetic movement, and he lends dramatic strength to the familiar theme by creating a dramatic parallel that involves historical characters. While the ode attains a kind of Pindaric exuberance, Dryden nevertheless follows a regular, linear organization.

HORATIAN VERSE EPISTLES

One of Dryden's principal poetic forms is the Horatian verse epistle, a type of poetry he wrote over a period of nearly forty years. The genre permits a poet to address an individual, speaking in his own person, and revealing as much or as little about himself as he wishes.

Dryden's epistles are usually poems of praise, though wit may sometimes be the chief purpose. Two of his final epistles, "To My Dear Friend Mr. Congreve" and "To My Honour'd Kinsman, John Driden" (a poem addressed to his cousin who then served in Parliament), are among his most memorable. Dryden's reliance on kingdoms and monarchies comes to the fore in each—the state in the epistle to his kinsman and the kingdom of letters in the poem to the dramatist William Congreve.

A favorite device of Dryden's is to set up polarities between differing ages and make comparisons, as he does in his "Epigram on Milton": "Three Poets in three distant ages born/ Greece, Italy, and England did adorn." The contrasts constitute a witty means of expressing praise, an art which Dryden had mastered in both verse and prose—being as skilled in panegyric as he was in satire.

In "To My Dear Friend Mr Congreve," the colloquial tone of the opening line belies a more serious theme and purpose: "Well then; the promis'd hour is come at last;/ The present Age of Wit obscures the past." Speaking of the wits of his time, Dryden acknowledges that, owing to a deficiency of genius, they have not equaled the achievements of Shakespeare and Jonson, and thus, metaphorically, "The second Temple was not like the first." Having introduced his metaphor of the temple, Dryden exploits it by alluding to another age and comparing Congreve to the Roman architect Vitruvius. Dryden goes on to praise Congreve's specific abilities as a dramatist, comparing him with Jonson, Fletcher, George Etherege, Thomas Southerne, and Wycherley, and, in a further allusion to Rome, with Scipio, for achieving greatness in youth.

Becoming more personal, Dryden shifts the parallel to the kingdom of poetry and, specifically, to his own tenure as poet laureate:

> O that your Brows by Lawrel had sustain'd,
> Well had I been Depos'd, if You had reign'd!
> The Father had descended for the Son;
> For only You are lineal to the Throne.

It was a great irony in Dryden's life that the poet he had made successor to the throne of dullness in *Mac Flecknoe*, Thomas Shadwell, had succeeded instead to the laureateship. The poem concludes with Dryden speaking of his own departure from the stage and asking

the young Congreve to treat his memory kindly, a request which Congreve, to his credit, fulfilled by editing Dryden's plays and writing a personal testimony and memoir favorable to the older poet. The poem is vintage Dryden, displaying the polarities between ages, the temple metaphor, the Roman allusions, and, above all, the monarchical metaphor involving successions, coronations, and reigns.

OTHER MAJOR WORKS

PLAYS: *The Wild Gallant*, pr. 1663; *The Rival Ladies*, pr., pb. 1664; *The Indian Queen*, pr. 1664 (with Sir Robert Howard); *The Indian Emperor: Or, The Conquest of Mexico by the Spaniards*, pr. 1665; *Secret Love: Or, The Maiden Queen*, pr. 1667; *The Tempest: Or, The Enchanted Island*, pr. 1667 (adaptation of William Shakespeare's play; with Sir William Davenant); *An Evening's Love: Or, The Mock Astrologer*, pr. 1668 (adaptation of Thomas Corneille's *Le Feint Astrologue*); *Tyrannic Love: Or, The Royal Martyr*, pr. 1669; *The Conquest of Granada by the Spaniards, Part I*, pr. 1670; *The Conquest of Granada by the Spaniards, Part II*, pr. 1671; *The Assignation: Or, Love in a Nunnery*, pr. 1672; *Marriage á la Mode*, pr. 1672; *Amboyna: Or, The Cruelties of the Dutch to the English Merchants*, pr., pb. 1673; *Aureng-Zebe*, pr. 1675; *The State of Innocence, and Fall of Man*, pb. 1677 (libretto; adaptation of John Milton's *Paradise Lost*); *All for Love: Or, The World Well Lost*, pr. 1677; *Oedipus*, pr. 1678 (with Nathaniel Lee); *The Kind Keeper: Or, Mr. Limberham*, pr. 1678; *Troilus and Cressida: Or, Truth Found Too Late*, pr., pb. 1679; *The Spanish Friar: Or, The Double Discovery*, pr. 1680; *The Duke of Guise*, pr. 1682 (with Lee); *Albion and Albanius*, pr., pb. 1685 (libretto; music by Louis Grabu); *Don Sebastian*, pr. 1689; *Amphitryon: Or, The Two Socia's*, pr., pb. 1690; *King Arthur: Or, The British Worthy*, pr., pb. 1691 (libretto; music by Henry Purcell); *Cleomenes, the Spartan Hero*, pr., pb. 1692; *Love Triumphant: Or, Nature Will Prevail*, pr., pb. 1694; *The Secular Masque*, pr., pb. 1700 (masque); *Dramatick Works*, pb. 1717; *The Works of John Dryden*, pb. 1808 (18 volumes).

NONFICTION: *Of Dramatic Poesie: An Essay*, 1668; "A Defence of *An Essay of Dramatic Poesy*," 1668;

"Preface to *An Evening's Love: Or, The Mock Astrologer*," 1671; "Of Heroic Plays: An Essay," 1672; "The Author's Apology for Heroic Poetry and Poetic License," 1677; "Preface to *All for Love*," 1678; "The Grounds of Criticism in Tragedy," 1679; "Preface to *Sylvae*," 1685; *A Discourse Concerning the Original and Progress of Satire*, 1693; "Dedication of *Examen Poeticum*," 1693; "A Parallel of Poetry and Painting," 1695; "Dedication of the *Aeneis*," 1697; "Preface to *Fables Ancient and Modern*," 1700; "Heads of an Answer to Rymer," 1711.

TRANSLATIONS: *Ovid's Epistles*, 1680; *The History of the League*, 1684 (of Louis Maimbourg's *Histoire de la Ligue*); *The Life of St. Francis Xavier*, 1688 (of Dominique Bouhours's *La Vie de Saint François Xavier*); *The Satires of Juvenal and Persius*, 1693; *The Works of Vergil*, 1697.

BIBLIOGRAPHY

Bloom, Harold, ed. *John Dryden*. New York: Chelsea House, 1987. One of the Modern Critical Views series. Plays, prose, and poetry are discussed side by side in this collection of essays by leading Dryden scholars, focusing on Dryden's place in the Restoration ideologically and poetically. Contains a chronology, a bibliography, and an index.

Budick, Sanford. *Dryden and the Abyss of Light*. New Haven, Conn.: Yale University Press, 1970. A full study of Dryden's theological thinking, specifically as expressed in *Religio Laici* and *The Hind and the Panther*. Contains appendices and an index.

Gelber, Michael Werth. *The Just and the Lively: The Literary Criticism of John Dryden*. Manchester, England: Manchester University Press, 1999. Gelber provides a complete study of Dryden's criticism. Through a detailed reading of each of Dryden's essays, the book explains and illustrates the unity and the development of his thought.

Hammond, Paul, and David Hopkins, eds. *John Dryden: Tercentenary Essays*. New York: Oxford University Press, 2000. A collection of biographical and critical essays dealing with Dryden's life, work, and politics. Includes bibliographical references and index.

Miner, Earl. *Dryden's Poetry*. Bloomington: Indiana University Press, 1967. A combination of the scholarly and the critical, this authoritative study deals extensively with all the major long poems, the lyric poetry, and the fables. Both Dryden's ideas and his figures are extensively analyzed. Contains a bibliography and an index.

Roper, Alan. *Dryden's Poetic Kingdoms*. London: Routledge & Kegan Paul, 1965. Ten poems are studied in detail to demonstrate the close link between Dryden's royalist politics and his poetic practice. Includes an index.

Winn, James Anderson. *John Dryden and His World*. New Haven, Conn.: Yale University Press, 1987. A full biography that effectively replaces Charles Ward's. It ties Dryden's poetry and drama very closely to his life. Contains four appendices and an index.

Wykes, David. *A Preface to Dryden*. New York: Longman, 1977. One of the Preface Books series. Contains clear discussions of biography, beliefs, style, and a critical survey. Includes a short reference section and an index.

Zwicker, Steven N. *Politics and Language in Dryden's Poetry*. Princeton, N.J.: Princeton University Press, 1984. A scholarly work that traces, historically and analytically, Dryden's poetic strategies in dealing with his poetic views. Includes an index.

Stanley Archer;
bibliography updated by the editors

Du Fu

Tu Fu

Born: Gongxian, China; 712
Died: Hunan, China; 770

PRINCIPAL POETRY

Tu Fu: Selected Poems, 1962 (English translations; Zhi Feng, editor; Rewi Alley, translator)

OTHER LITERARY FORMS

Du Fu is known primarily for his poetry.

ACHIEVEMENTS

Born during the Tang Dynasty (618-907), the classical period in Chinese literary history, Du Fu was one of four poets whose greatness marked the era. Some fifty thousand poems from that period have survived, the large number resulting primarily from the talents of these four men. Wang Wei was basically a nature poet; Bo Juyi, a government official whose poetry often reflected official concerns; and Li Bo, probably the best known of all Chinese poets, a poet of the otherworldly or the sublime.

Du Fu sums up the work of all these poets' works with the wide range of topics and concerns that appear in his poems. Known variously as "poet-historian," "poet-sage," and "the Master," Du Fu may be China's greatest poet. His "Moonlit Night" is perhaps the most famous poem in Chinese literature. His more than fourteen hundred extant poems testify to his productivity; the range of topics in his poetry and the variety of verse that he employed constitute Du Fu's main contribution to Chinese literature.

One of Du Fu's major contributions to Chinese literature was his extensive occasional verse—poems inspired by a journey or by a mundane experience such as building a house. Many of Du Fu's occasional poems were addressed to friends or relatives at some special time in their lives. Distant relatives who held official positions and achieved distinction would receive a laudatory poem. These poems could also be addressed to special friends. Du Fu traveled much in his life, both by choice and involuntarily, relying on friends to shelter and support him, because, for the majority of his life, he was without an official governmental position and salary. His poems would therefore be addressed to these persons as expressions of gratitude and friendship on the occasion of his visit.

Poems about nature abounded during the Tang period, and Du Fu contributed extensively to this genre as well. In contrast to Li Bo, who followed the Daoist philosophy of withdrawal from the world, Du Fu was very much a poet of everyday life, both in his response to nature and the physical world and in his active engagement in the social and political life of his times. Indeed, it has been said that Du Fu's poetry provides a running history of the Chinese state during his era.

Finally, Du Fu was a master of poetic form; his verse forms were as varied as his content. During the Tang period, the *guti* (old forms) in Chinese poetry coexisted with the *lüshi* (new forms). The old, or "unregulated," forms placed no restrictions on the word tones used in the verse; they did not limit the number of lines in a poem; and they did not require verbal parallelism. The new forms, or "regulated verse," however, were much more demanding. They mandated certain tonal patterns, especially in rhyme words, a requirement which markedly affected word choice; they usually restricted the total number of lines in a poem; and they utilized verbal parallelism. Each of these two major categories of Chinese poetry was also divided into subcategories depending on the meter, which in Chinese poetry depends on the number of words in each line rather than on stressed and unstressed syllables, as in Western poetry. Du Fu adeptly used both old and new forms in his verse, justifying in this respect as in every other his reputation as "the Master."

BIOGRAPHY

Du Fu's life could best be described as one of frustration. Although his mother's family was related to the imperial clan, and both his father and grandfather held official positions in the government, much of Du Fu's life was spent in poverty. Unable to pass the examination for entrance into official service, Du Fu remained a "plain-robed" man, a man without official position and salary, more often than not. His poems from the mid-730's allude to "the hovel" in which he lived on the outskirts of the capital while the court members resided in the splendor of the palace. One of Du Fu's sons died from starvation in 755 because of the family's poverty, and the poet's sadness and anguish caused by his son's death is reflected in several of Du Fu's poems.

Du Fu was born in Gongxian, Henan Province, in 712. His natural mother died at an early age, and Du Fu's father remarried, eventually adding three brothers and a sister to the family. Du Fu was apparently a very precocious child. In his autobiography, he states unabashedly that at the age of seven he pondered "only high matters" and wrote verses about beautiful birds, while other children his age were dealing with puerile subjects such as dogs and cats. At an early age, Du Fu also mastered a great number of the characters which make up written Chinese. He was writing so extensively by the age of nine, he claims, that his output could easily have filled several large bags. Not much else is known about Du Fu's early years. As would be expected, he was schooled in literary matters in preparation for entrance into official service. A firsthand knowledge of the many facets of Chinese life and the geography of the country also became a part of Du Fu's education: He traveled for about three years before taking the official examination for public service. His poetry of this period reflects the experiences and sights he encountered while traversing the countryside.

In 735, at the age of twenty-three, Du Fu finally took the test to enter government service and failed. Apparently there was something in Du Fu's writing style, in the way he handled the Chinese characters, which did not suit the examiners. This setback in Du Fu's plans ushered in the first of several important phases in his life. Since the poet had failed the examination and was without a position, he resumed his travels. During these travel years, several significant changes occurred in his life. His father died in 740, which prompted a series of poems on the theme of life's impermanence. This event was followed by Du Fu's marriage to a woman from the Cui clan, a marriage which ultimately produced two sons and four daughters for the poet. Finally, and probably most important in terms of his literary work, Du Fu met Li Bo in 744.

Following the Daoist tradition, Li Bo, who was ten years Du Fu's senior, had become a "withdrawn" poet after his banishment from the court. As such, he represented a viewpoint opposite to that of Du Fu concerning a literate man's obligations to Chinese society at that time. Du Fu's poetry exhibits his grappling with these contending views. He was sometimes attracted to the simple lifestyle of Li Bo, but the Confucian ethic under which Du Fu had been reared persevered, and he returned to the capital in 746, eleven years after his first attempt, to repeat the test for an official position. He failed again; this time, according to the historians, one of the emperor's officials was afraid that new appointees to the bureaucracy would weaken the latter's power in the court, so he saw to it that *everyone* who took the examination failed. The frustration and humiliation resulting from this second failure to pass the examination, perhaps heightened by the fact that his younger brother had taken and passed the examination earlier, did not seem to deter Du Fu

from his goal of securing an official post. Although he was forced to move outside the capital with his family and to rely on support from friends and relatives to survive, Du Fu seemingly resolved to gain an official position through another route, this time by ingratiating himself with important people who could aid his quest.

Wei Ji was one such person. As an adviser to the emperor, he was in a position to help Du Fu when the occasion arose. Du Fu was also well acquainted with Prince Li Jin, a pleasure-loving, undisciplined figure who was an embarrassment to the court. The prince had a great appreciation for literature, however, and after Du Fu wrote several poems dealing with "The Eight Immortals of the Wine Cup," as the prince and his coterie were called, the prince took a special liking to the poet. Because of these friendships, Du Fu's name was heard around the court, and when he wrote the "Three Great Ceremonies" poems, their excellence and their laudatory treatment of the emperor engendered imperial recognition and favor. A third examination for an official position ensued as a result. Whether Du Fu passed or failed this one was of little consequence; finally, at the age of forty-four, he was given an official position by imperial decree. (Li Bo's position with the court had also been established by imperial decree, because he had refused to take the civil-service exam as a matter of principle.) Ironically, Du Fu refused the position. It apparently involved moving to a distant western district; because the position required him to be a part of the police administration, it would also have involved beating people for infractions of the law, something Du Fu was not inclined to do. The poet's refusal found some sympathy in the court, and he was appointed instead to the heir apparent's household. Thus, the years 755 and 756 stand as pivotal ones in Du Fu's life: He received his first official position in the government after many years of struggle, and, strangely enough, he gave up that position because he rapidly grew to dislike the servile aspects of the job. Amid all this, the An Lushan Rebellion began.

For the remainder of his life, Du Fu was one of the many who endured the misfortunes of this war. When the rebellion began in 756, the emperor was forced to flee the capital, as did Du Fu. The latter's poems from that period depict the many defeats of the imperial army. Once he had established his family in the relative safety of Fuzhou in the north, Du Fu set out to join the "Traveling Palace" of the displaced emperor, but he was captured by rebel forces and taken back to the capital, which they occupied. Held by the rebels for several months, he finally escaped and joined the Traveling Palace as a censor, an official responsible for reminding the emperor of matters which required his attention. During this period, Du Fu did not hear from his family for more than a year, and he wrote possibly the most famous poem in Chinese literature, a love poem to his wife and children entitled "Moonlit Night."

The capital was retaken the next year, 757, and Du Fu was reunited with his family. His "Journey North" describes the effects of the war on the Chinese people and countryside, and his homecoming to his family. With the government reestablished in the capital, Du Fu returned there with his family for official service. This period of service was also short-lived; he once again grew tired of the bureaucratic life and its constraints. Floods and the war had devastated the countryside around the capital, so Du Fu took his family west to flee the war and to find food. The war, however, also spread to the west, and as a result, Du Fu once again shifted his family, this time southward to Zhengdu, five hundred miles from the fighting.

The time he spent in the south has been labeled Du Fu's "thatched hut" period. This was something of a pastoral period in his life, during which he seemed to emulate Li Bo and the Daoist ethic to some degree. The war, however, persisted both in the countryside and in Du Fu's poems. The rebellion finally spread even to the south, and Du Fu was forced to leave his thatched hut in 765. He spent the remaining five years of his life in restless travel, cataloging in poetry his journeys and the events he witnessed. Du Fu, "the Master," died in 770, at the age of fifty-eight, as he traveled the Xiang River looking for a haven from the ill health and ill times which had beset him.

ANALYSIS

Du Fu's poetry deals with a multitude of concerns and events. His verses express the moments of self-doubt and frustration which plagued the poet, such as when he failed the civil-service examinations or when he became increasingly afflicted by physical ailments later in life, referring to himself in one verse as an "ema-

ciated horse." Du Fu's poems also deal with painting and the other arts, and they often employ allusions to outstanding figures in China's literary and political past to comment on contemporary conditions. It is, however, in his poems addressed to family and friends and in his nature poems that the substance and depth of his verse can be most clearly seen.

Among Du Fu's finest poems are those which express his love for friends and family. Poems addressed to friends constituted both a literary and a social convention in China during the Tang period. In literate society, men sought one another for friendship and intellectual companionship, and poems of the "address and answer" variety were often composed by the poet. Several examples occur in the poems which Du Fu wrote either to or about Li Bo, his fellow poet. After the two met in 744, they traveled together extensively, and a firm bond, both personal and scholarly, was established between them. In one poem commemorating the two poets' excursion to visit a fellow writer, Du Fu explained his feeling toward Li Bo: "I love my Lord as young brother loves elder brother/ . . . Hand in hand we daily walk together." In "A Winter Day," Du Fu writes that "Since early dawn I have thought only of you [Li Bo]," thoughts which may have been both pleasant and painful for Du Fu as he grappled with the question of whether he wanted to continue his quest for a governmental position or follow Li Bo's example and become a "withdrawn" poet. Du Fu also highly praised Li Bo's verses. In a later poem, "the Master" laments the fact that Li Bo has become unstable, but he also rejoices in the gift of Li Bo's talent: "My thoughts are only of love for his talent./ Brilliant are his thousand poems."

The concern and admiration which Du Fu felt and expressed poetically were not directed solely to other poets. Many of his poems of this type were addressed to longtime friends. "For Wei Ba, in Retirement" is one example which not only expresses Du Fu's friendship for Wei Ba but also describes the life stages the two have passed through together. The poet comments on how briefly their youth lasted, observing that "Though in those days you were not married/ Suddenly sons and daughters troop in." The two friends have not seen each other for twenty years, "both our heads have become grizzled," and Du Fu knows that the next day will separate them again. He is elated, however, by the "sense of acquaintance" his friend revives in him, and the poet captures that sense in his verse.

"MOONLIT NIGHT"

Du Fu was separated from his family several times, sometimes by the war, sometimes by economic conditions. His most famous poem, "Moonlit Night," expresses his deep concern for his wife as "In her chamber she alone looks out/ . . . In the sweet night her cloud-like tresses are damp/ In the clear moonlight her jade-like arms are cold." The poet wonders how long it will be before ". . . we two nestle against those unfilled curtains/ With the moon displaying the dried tear-stains of us both?" Essentially a love poem for the poet's wife, "Moonlit Night" was an unconventional work in its time. Wives in ancient China were seen primarily as pieces of reproductive machinery, with no intellectual capabilities. A poet might lavish great sentiment in verse on a male companion, but tender thoughts concerning a wife were rarely expressed in poetry.

"THE RIVER BY OUR VILLAGE"

In true classical fashion, Du Fu was also a nature poet. He could portray nature in an idyllic vein, as in "The River by Our Village," in which the poet describes how "Clear waters wind around our village/ With long summer days full of loveliness/ Fluttering in and out from the house beams the swallows play/ Waterfowl disport together as everlasting lovers." These lines reflect the contentment of Du Fu's pastoral or "Thatched Hut" period; he ends the poem by asking: "What more could I wish for?"

"THE WINDING RIVER"

While many of Du Fu's nature poems are distinguished by their vivid evocation of landscapes and wildlife for their own sake, he also treats nature symbolically. In "The Winding River," falling blossoms signify the changing of the seasons and cause the poet to ". . . grieve to see petals flying/ Away in the wind. . . ." This evidence of mutability engenders further reflection; as the poet watches "Butterflies going deeper and deeper/ In amongst the flowers, dragon-flies/ Skimming and flicking over the water," he is reminded that "Wind, light, and time ever revolve," that the only constant factor in life is change. In turn, the poet is led to reflect on the inconsequential and often futile nature of his and other men's ambitions: ". . . why should I be lured/ By transient rank and honours?" Nature instructs him ". . . to live/ Along with her" in a rich and full harmony rather than existing in the pale semblance of living which men have created for themselves.

Because of the range of his sympathy, Du Fu has been compared to William Shakespeare: Both were able to encompass in their works the whole teeming life of their times. Although Du Fu's declaration "In poetry I have exhausted human topics" may seem an overstatement, his many poems and their varied concerns seem almost to justify such a claim.

BIBLIOGRAPHY

Chou, Eva Shan. *Reconsidering Tu Fu: Literary Greatness and Cultural Context*. New York: Cambridge University Press, 1995. Criticism and interpretation of Du Fu by a well-known scholar of his works and time. Bibliographical references, index.

_____. "Tu Fu's 'General Ho' Poems: Social Obligation and Poetic Response." *Harvard Journal of Asiatic Studies* 60, no. 1 (June, 2000): 165-204. These two sets of poems from early in Du Fu's career follow the pattern of estate poems: an arrival poem, exit poem, and central poems describing the host and the estate. Chou discusses these works as a product of the "social, cultural, and economic forces of their time."

_____. "Tu Fu's Social Conscience: Compassion and Topicality in His Poetry." *Harvard Journal of Asiatic Studies* 51, no. 1 (June, 1991): 5-53. This essay presents Du Fu as a writer who frequently unites technical precision with a sense of seriousness and high moral purpose. Chou analyses Du Fu's choice of subjects, noting the moral stance that appears both in works about ordinary people and trivial details as well as works about politics, service to the state or rebellion. The article includes a detailed discussion of the types of poetic realism in his poetry.

_____. "Allusion and Periphrasis as Modes of Poetry in Tu Fu's 'Eight Laments.'" *Harvard Journal of Asiatic Studies* 45, no. 1 (June, 1985): 77-128. The article examines how narrative pace and lyricism are replaced by allusion and periphrasis in the "Laments." While the subject is technical, Chou provides detailed explanations and examples to allow the reader to understand the material in the article.

Davis, Arthur R. *Tu Fu*. New York: Twayne, 1971. Davis discusses Du Fu's use of and variance from the poetic forms of the High Tang period, as well as his role in Chinese literature, tracing his influence on other poets. The biographical details are interwoven with the discussion of the poetry which allows the reader to understand the development of major themes. A helpful annotated bibliography is also included.

Hawkes, David. *A Little Primer of Tu Fu*. Oxford: Clarendon Press, 1967. In this helpful introduction to Du Fu's poetry, Hawkes not only explains the subject matter of many of the most famous poems, he also provides historic background and context. Details about the construction, use of language, and techniques of Chinese poetry will give readers a clearer understanding of the genre. The author effectively combines the historical and literary perspective.

William. *Tu Fu: China's Greatest Poet*. Boston: Harvard University Press, 1952. Hung provides a detailed description of the poet's life based primarily on Du Fu's poetry, which has a strong autobiographical quality; the information is bolstered by the author's extensive research into the period. The book allows the reader to develop an understanding of the historical background and explore Du Fu's role in his society. The translations of the poems in this work are neither word-for-word nor poetic; instead the purpose is to provide the reader with a clear understanding of the meaning.

Kenneth A. Howe;
bibliography updated by Mary E. Mahony

NORMAN DUBIE

Born: Barre, Vermont; April 10, 1945

PRINCIPAL POETRY

The Horsehair Sofa, 1969
Alehouse Sonnets, 1971
The Prayers of the North American Martyrs, 1975
Popham of the New Song and Other Poems, 1975
In the Dead of the Night, 1975
The Illustrations, 1977
A Thousand Little Things and Other Poems, 1978
Odalisque in White: Two Poems, 1978
The City of the Olesha Fruit, 1979
The Everlastings, 1980
The Window in the Field, 1981
Selected and New Poems, 1983
The Springhouse, 1986
Groom Falconer, Poems by Norman Dubie, 1989
Radio Sky, 1991
The Clouds of Magellan, 1991
The Mercy Seat: Collected and New Poems, 1967-2000, 2001

OTHER LITERARY FORMS

Norman Dubie has contributed several critical pieces to such journals as *American Poetry Review*, *Poetry*, and *Iowa Review*, but he is known primarily for his poetry.

ACHIEVEMENTS

Norman Dubie is one of America's most important and innovative contemporary poets. Since the publication of his first volume of verse when he was twenty-three, Dubie has, on the average, published one book every two years, accumulating an impressive body of work. At a time when American poetry has been both praised and criticized for its preoccupation with intimate personal experience, Dubie has sought to see the world through the eyes of historical figures from many different times and places—painters, fellow writers, individuals of all sorts, whose distinctive perspective he adopts for the duration of a poem.

In 1976, Dubie won the Bess Hokin Award from *Poetry* and the Modern Poetry Association for "The Negress, Her Monologue of Dark Crepe." He has also been the recipient of creative writing fellowships from the National Endowment for the Arts and the Guggenheim Foundation. In honor of Dubie's literary achievements, the University of Iowa, where he received his M.F.A., houses the Norman Dubie Collection in its library.

BIOGRAPHY

Norman Evans Dubie, Jr., was born on April 10, 1945, in Barre, Vermont. His father, Norman Evans

Dubie, Sr., was a clergyman, and his mother, Doris, was a registered nurse. Dubie was educated in Vermont and received his undergraduate degree at Goddard College in Plainfield, being graduated from there in 1969. In 1968, while a student at Goddard, Dubie married the first of his wives, Francesca Stafford. This marriage would produce Dubie's only child, Hannah.

Leaving Vermont after his graduation, Dubie studied creative writing in the M.F.A. program of the Iowa Writers' Workshop at the University of Iowa. He received his degree in 1971 and began lecturing in the workshop afterward. From 1971 though 1972, Dubie was the poetry editor of *The Iowa Review*; from 1973 through 1974, he edited *Now*. During this period, his first marriage ended in divorce.

When Dubie left the University of Iowa, he became an assistant professor of English at Ohio University in Athens. He retained this position from 1974 through 1975; during this period, Dubie published three volumes of poetry: *The Prayers of the North American Martyrs*, *Popham of the New Song and Other Poems*, and *In the Dead of the Night*. Following the publication of these

Norman Dubie (© Chris Pickler)

collections, Dubie left Ohio University and accepted a position at Arizona State University.

Dubie was writer in residence at Arizona State from 1975 until 1976. He was a lecturer there from 1976 until 1983 and was then promoted to the rank of full professor of English. In 1976 he became the director of Arizona State's graduate writing program.

In 1975, Dubie was remarried, to Pamela Stewart, a poet and a teacher. Five years later, this marriage also ended in divorce. In 1981, Dubie remarried again, this time to Jeannine Savard, also a poet. They make their home in Tempe, Arizona. He frequently contributes to many magazines, including *The Paris Review*, *The New Yorker*, *The American Poetry Review*, *Antaeus*, *The Antioch Review*, *Field*, and *Poetry*.

ANALYSIS

In his introduction to Norman Dubie's *The Illustrations*, poet Richard Howard says that Dubie's poetry centers on "the experience which has the root of *peril* in it, the ripple of danger which enlivens the seemingly lovely surfaces, the 'ordinary' existence." That perilous quality is evident in nearly all Dubie's work; it is the very thing that guarantees its success. Still, "the ripple of danger" creates a difficult poetry, too, embracing experience in exciting, innovative ways. The ordinary becomes extraordinary. As Howard puts it, "Dubie identifies that experience, by reciting it, with his own life to a hallucinatory degree: We are not to know what is given and what is taken, what is 'real' and what 'made up.'"

The juxtaposition of "real" and "fiction" is particularly engaging in much of Dubie's early work. In *Alehouse Sonnets* and *The Illustrations*, Dubie wrote historically based poems in the form of dramatic monologues. Perhaps it is this for which Dubie is best known; not only do these monologues create a space in which the poet can move outside himself and the time in which he lives, but also they allow him the intellectual advantage of innovation as well as imagistic and allusive complexity. The result is an engaging, demanding verse. The reader must work to understand; he or she must either clarify the obscurity or be resigned to the "hallucinatory"; the reader must not relent in the attempt to discover the value of such complexity. These are imperatives; the reader has no choice.

Still, one reader will find Dubie's work elegant and beautiful; the next will find it distant and foreign, purposely ignoring accessibility. Both appraisals may be justified. Dubie's demands upon his poetry and upon his readers, however, set him apart from nearly all other contemporary poets. His is an original, fanciful voice, and often the distinction he makes between reality and fancy is fuzzy. This creates a sometimes lethargic, somnambulant effect, quite like walking along some foggy, hazed-over street under white lights, dreamy, disembodied, and more than a little disenchanted. The reader is much like the character in "Hazlitt Down from the Lecture Table" (*Alehouse Sonnets*) who ". . . just/ sat out the stupor in a corner."

This seems to be Dubie's exact intention, though. Dubie's imagination draws him—and the reader—away from the mundane, real world and intensifies that "stupor" by displacing him to a paradoxical, mundane, exotic world. The lives of Dubie's characters, their triumphs and their failures, are no more special than are those of his readers—and no worse. The difficulty, then, is the importance readers may attribute to the allusive figures or to the thick, ambiguous imagery. One assumes that the allusion *means* something essential or that knowledge of the allusion will clarify the poem. The reader may puzzle for an interminable time, trying to unravel an obscure image. Each of these, however, is a failed reading; such scrutiny may aid comprehension, but it will not guarantee tidy answers. The man who "sat out the stupor" knows and accepts this.

The importance of Dubie's contribution to the poetics of his time is evident. More than most of his contemporaries, Dubie has risked much to offer an unusual, resonant voice. Granted, his poems are difficult, evasive at times, incomprehensible at other times, yet his imagination addresses very real issues. That Dubie expects his reader to work is really no fault inherent in his poetry; already, too many other poets write easy, disposable verse. Dubie's poetry is not disposable. It will not let its readers let it loose.

ALEHOUSE SONNETS

While some of Dubie's critics find his work incomprehensible, still others accuse him of being too impersonal. This is especially so in Dubie's early writing. *Alehouse Sonnets*, for example, is characterized by a detached, unidentified persona. All one knows of the persona is his affinity to William Hazlitt, the nineteenth century English critic, whom he addresses throughout the book. One can imagine, after reading *Alehouse Sonnets*, a companionship made between men of two different centuries and, likely, two different lifestyles. Time and place cannot erase humankind's disappointments, however, for the characters in the poems share those experiences universally. In order to juxtapose the contraries of time and place, Dubie approaches his subjects and his characters with calculated distance. The poet hovers over the characters, sometimes coming in, intruding, but usually standing not far off, aloof and watchful.

To fault this as being impersonal is also a misreading of Dubie's work. As Lorrie Goldensohn has written of Dubie, "What mostly gets left out is the explicitly autobiographical self. The self, that darling of contemporary poetry, here has little to do; it appears to be just another dreamer, usually present as a disembodied voice rummaging around . . . interchangeable with others." Contemporary poetry is excessively burdened with poems of "self," and Dubie's poems offer a refreshing break from that tendency. The fanciful mind discovers commonality of experience, how the persona's life, Hazlitt's, the poet's, and the reader's are much the same. The verse does not need to be autobiographical, because Dubie is writing everyone's biography. The poem cannot be personal; as Dubie wrote in "Address to the Populous Winter Youths," "Nearness exasperates."

IN THE DEAD OF THE NIGHT AND ILLUSTRATIONS

In the several collections which immediately followed *Alehouse Sonnets*, Dubie continued to experiment with deliberate distancing. Rather than addressing only one allusive figure—Hazlitt, for example—Dubie would address numerous historical personages or speak through them. *In the Dead of the Night* and *The Illustrations* are most notably characterized by a profusion of allusions to artists. A quick listing of Dubie's titles present many: "The Suicide of Hedda Gabler," "Charles Baudelaire," "Seurat," "El Greco," "Sun and Moon Flowers: Paul Klee, 1879-1940," "The Czar's Last Christmas Letter: A Barn in the Urals," and "Horace." In particular, *The Illustrations* handles these monologues with mastery.

Quite literally, one can approach the poems of this volume as "illustrations." Dubie, himself, is the illustrator, the artist whose own perceptiveness becomes the voices of his characters. The illustrations are of any number of stories, and the reader involves himself in as many ways as his experience will allow. For,

> In a world that
>
> Belongs to a system of things
> Which presents a dark humus with everything
>
> Living

(an excerpt from "These Untitled Little Verses . . ." in *The Illustrations*), the reader discovers, as Dubie knows, vital connections.

SELECTED AND NEW POEMS

As his career has progressed, however, Dubie has discovered the limitations of his dramatic monologues. *Selected and New Poems*, while including a generous selection from earlier volumes, introduced a noticeable change in Dubie's manner. The emotional excessiveness of his earlier work was toned down, and many of the new poems eschewed the dramatic monologue for a more personal voice. David Wojahn, reviewing this book in *Western Humanities Review*, remarked that while the new poems "do not match the ambition of some of the earlier poems . . . they are often better crafted and more genuine." That Dubie's style changed is indicative of his desire to move ahead. It also puts Dubie into a certain degree of peril: His writing is turning inward, becoming personal, and—if more lyrical—more conventional.

THE SPRINGHOUSE

The Springhouse is a promising extension of the new material found in *Selected and New Poems*. What makes *The Springhouse* remarkable is Dubie's ability to move away from the style and subjects that brought him acclaim while still reveling in his mastery of rich verbal textures. The result is a collection of thirty highly intimate lyrics—poems of youth, religious belief, and love. The new note of intimacy in *The Springhouse* is unmistakable: Readers who found themselves fighting through the earlier dramatic monologues will find the poems of *The Springhouse* similarly dramatic but infinitely more delicate and accessible.

Consider, for example, "Hummingbirds," which suggests that the world is hostile to its fragile creatures:

> They have made a new statement
> About our world—a clerk in Memphis
> Has confessed to laying out feeders
> Filled with sulphuric acid. She says
>
> God asked for these deaths . . . like God
> They are insignificant, and have visited us
>
> Who are wretched.

The "new statement" is that human beings are wretched because they find hummingbirds and God insignificant; they are poorer because of it. This is hardly the Norman Dubie of the earlier collections, the one who distanced himself from his subjects and his readers, who disdained closeness. Similarly, "Old Night and Sleep," dedicated to Dubie's grandfather, moves the reader:

> A cold rain falls through empty nests, a cold rain
> Falls over the canvas
> Of some big beast with four stomachs
> Who eats beneath a white tree
> In which only a dozen dry pods are left . . .
>
> Some new sense of days being counted.

The poem is a lamentation, an emptiness of soul accounted for visually in sensuous imagery. Things are drizzly, vague, empty; loss of a loved one makes one feel this way, makes one aware of one's own temporal existence.

THE MERCY SEAT

With *The Mercy Seat*, Dubie rejoined the literary world after a ten-year publishing hiatus. The book is divided into two sections; the first chronicles his poems from 1967 to 1991, while the second half presents new poetry. Like past works, his language continues to be spare and often sorrowful but nonetheless rich and vigorous in its forms. Here Dubie continues his exploration of dramatic monologues with the recasting of the world's great tales, bringing forth lesser historic events and making them moments of redemptive, imaginative beauty. However, his foot is also placed firmly in the current era: By dedicating the book to the Dalai Lama, modern political realities and the true stakes of the world anchor his complexly balanced poems.

BIBLIOGRAPHY

Anderson, Jon. "On Norman Dubie's Poems." *The Iowa Review* 3 (Fall, 1973): 65-67. This article offers a reading of Dubie's work on two levels: the empathetic, which results from the poet's attempt at communication, and the aesthetic, which is the reader's personal judgment. Anderson's interpretation utilizes both sensibilities, although the latter is clearly favored in his examination of *Alehouse Sonnets*, "The Dugouts," and "Northwind Escarpment," among others.

Clark, Kevin. "Synchronous Isolations: 'Elegies for the Ocher Deer on the Walls at Lascaux' by Norman Dubie." *American Poetry* 5, no. 2 (Winter, 1988): 12-32. Clark draws upon the concepts of Carl Jung, Albert Einstein, and Søren Kierkegaard to illuminate Dubie's vision and technique in this important long poem. This is an exemplary study, its methodology applicable to much of Dubie's work.

Leavitt, Michele. "Dubie's 'Amen.'" *The Explicator* 56, no. 1 (Fall, 1997): 55-56. A close reading reveals Dubie's technique of multiple juxtapositions that create provocative but incomplete analogies. The poem insists that by evading responsibility for brutality, human beings inevitably come to share it.

Raab, Lawrence. "Illustrations and Illuminations: On Norman Dubie." *The American Poetry Review* 7 (July/August, 1978): 17-21. Raab examines the amalgamation of time periods and subjects in Dubie's poetry—from Greek mythology to Victorian England and Ovid to Nicholas I—and explores Dubie's methods of arguing and instructing his characters. Perhaps Raab's most valuable and insightful observation of Dubie's work concludes that his poetry is about the "little things," which, when seen clearly, appear large.

St. John, David. "A Generous Salvation: The Poetry of Norman Dubie." *The American Poetry Review* 13 (September/October, 1984): 17-21. St. John uses the collection of Dubie's poems, *Selected and New Poems*, as a jumping-off point for an examination of the poet's major themes, including a fascination with the living and dead, personal and historical realities, and the principle of "release." St. John assists the reader by publishing the full text of the poems discussed.

Slattery, William. "My Dubious Calculus." *Antioch Review* 52, no. 1 (Winter, 1994): 132-140. At once sarcastic and cautiously admiring, Slattery questions the value of perceived ambiguities and opacities in Dubie's style. Slattery discusses the structure of each volume in Dubie's "trilogy" (*Springhouse*, *Groom Falconer*, and *Radio Sky*), commenting on the lack of neat resolutions and the way in which Dubie's images suggest unforgettable stories about people in desperate situations.

Wojahn, David. "Recent Poetry." *Western Humanities Review* 38 (August, 1984): 269-273. Wojahn explores the transition of Dubie's style as it becomes more subdued and lyrical in his work, *Selected and New Poems*. Because this process was then incomplete, the value of Wojahn's article lies in its careful and evocative examination of Dubie's early style with its dramatic monologues, extreme situations, and idiosyncratic syntax.

Young, David. "Out Beyond Rhetoric." *Contemporary Poetry and Poetics* 30 (Spring, 1984): 83-102. The career and work of Dubie are carefully and thoroughly examined in this ambitious assessment of the poet's life, themes, and expression of his ideas, which can range from the difficult to the nearly incomprehensible. This important and insightful examination is worthy reading for the Dubie scholar and enthusiast alike.

Mark Sanders,
updated by Philip K. Jason and Sarah Hilbert

Jovan Dučić

Born: Trebinje, Yugoslavia; February 5, 1871
Died: Gary, Indiana; April 7, 1943

PRINCIPAL POETRY
Pjesme, 1901
Jadranski sonetti, 1906
Pesme, 1908
Plave legende, 1908 (*Blue Legends*, 1983)
Sabrana dela, 1929-1932 (5 volumes), 1969 (6 volumes)
Lirika, 1943
Izabrana dela, 1982

OTHER LITERARY FORMS

Although Jovan Dučić was preoccupied with poetry, he wrote in several other genres. His travelogues, *Gradovi i himere* (1932; cities and chimeras), contain his impressions gathered during journeys to Switzerland, France, Italy, Greece, Egypt, and other countries. More testimonies to his erudition than reports of his actual experiences, they deal with the history and cultural background of those places rather than with the present. *Gradovi i himere* is the best book of its kind in Serbian literature. A number of historical-cultural essays are collected in the book *Blago Cara Radovana* (1932; the treasure of Czar Radovan). They offer Dučić's views on happiness, love, women, friendship, youth, old age, poets, heroes, and prophets. Dučić also wrote numerous articles on Yugoslav writers, his predecessors as well as his contemporaries, in which he presented not only opinions on these writers but also glimpses of his own literary views and accomplishments. Toward the end of his life he wrote a book about a Serb who went to Russia and became an influential figure at the court of Peter the Great, *Grof Sava Vladislavič* (1942; Count Sava Vladislavič). It is an ambitious pseudohistorical study that reads more like a novel than history. Dučić also wrote numerous essays and articles about cultural, national, social, and political issues of the day.

ACHIEVEMENTS

Jovan Dučić appeared at a crucial point in the history of Serbian literature, at the turn of the century, when the epoch of Romantic and realist poetry was coming to a close and another, usually referred to as *Moderna*, was just beginning. By introducing new themes and sources of inspiration, Dučić was very instrumental in setting Serbian poetry on a new course. He was an aesthete, with a refined taste and an aristocratic spirit. In his poetry, he strove for formal excellence expressed through clarity, precision, elegance, musical quality, and picturesque images. His subject matter and unique style, reflecting the manner of French verse—Parnassian, Symbolist, *décadent*—brought a new spirit to Serbian verse. Unlike previous Serbian poets, who were either Romantically or realistically oriented, Dučić was attracted to esoteric, sophisticated, thought-provoking, and soul-searching themes, creating his own lonely world of imagination and reacting to it in a highly subjective manner. His poetry reveals a sensitive artist with a basically pessimistic outlook. He has sometimes been criticized for this, as well as for his inclination toward art for art's sake. His supreme craftsmanship, however, no one denies. Dučić represents one of the highest achievements in Serbian and in all south Slavic literatures, a fame that increases as time goes on.

BIOGRAPHY

Jovan Dučić was born into a prominent Serbian family in Trebinje, a picturesque little town in Herzegovina, at that time under Turkish occupation, in 1871. As a boy he moved to Mostar, a Herzegovinian cultural center, and later to Sarajevo. After he was graduated, he taught at schools in Bosnia and in Mostar, where he was frequently harassed by Austrian authorities for his nationalist activities. In Mostar, he participated in cultural activities, joined a literary circle, edited literary journals, and began to write poetry. Supported by the Serbian government, he studied liberal arts at the University of Geneva. During his study there and on frequent visits to Paris, he fell under the influence of French culture, particularly that represented by the *décadent* and Symbolist poets, which would have a decisive impact on his literary development. Upon his return to Serbia in 1907, he entered diplomatic service and served in that capacity for the rest of his life in various capitals of the world. At the same time, he published poetry and prose works and came to be recognized as one of the leading Serbian writers. He was in Lisbon during World War II and moved to the United States in 1941. Until his death less than two years later, Dučić actively supported the nationalist side of the guerrilla struggle against the Germans in his native country. His book *Lirika* (lyric poems) appeared the day he died. He is buried at the Serbian shrine in Libertyville, Illinois. At his request, his papers and library were sent to his native Trebinje.

ANALYSIS

Jovan Dučić wrote poetry during his entire mature life. His first poems followed in the footsteps of the leading Serbian poet, Vojislav Ilič, at the end of the nineteenth century. Ilič employed a mixture of Romanticism, realism, and neoclassicism, all of which appealed to the young Dučić, especially in view of his patriotic fervor. During his study in Switzerland and prolonged stays in France, Dučić moved away from national regionalism as a result of his falling under the influence of the Parnassians and, later, the Symbolists. Despite some striking similarities to French poets, however, he developed his own style, thus successfully transplanting foreign influences onto a soil uniquely his own. In the latter part of his poetic career, he was free from any foreign influence. Ironically, his own influence on Serbian poets was minimal despite attempts by many to emulate him.

There are three more or less distinct periods in his poetic development. The first (1886-1908) was the period of naïve beginnings, fervent patriotism, love of nature, pronounced musicality, and Romantic sentimentalism. The strong French influence later in this period manifested itself through accentuated pessimism, melancholy, affectation, and a strict attention to form. This development, as literary historian Milan Kašanin sees it, had not only aesthetic but also historical significance, for the French predilection for intellectualism and rationalism replaced in Dučić's poetry the emotion and folkloristic regionalism dominant in Serbian poetry up to that time. Changes in Dučić, in turn, paved the way for historical changes in Serbian poetry in the first decade of the twentieth century. Dučić carried these and other signs of French influence, notably that of Albert Samain, Henri de Régnier, Sully-Prudhomme, Charles Baudelaire, Théophile Gautier, and José Maria de Hérédia, into his second period (1908-1932), but during this period he was able to transform such influence into a synthesis of his earlier Romantic preoccupations and the French "linear" spirit and discipline. In this period, he turned inward, searching for lasting themes and grappling with such perennial problems as man's isolation, love, search for faith, and reconciliation with death. It was not until his third and last period (1932-1943) that he was able to give full expression to this synthesis. Refining it further, he wrote his most mature works, although they consisted more of prose than of poetry. His last poems, some of them undoubtedly his best, return to the simplicity of his earlier period, as if closing the circle.

Dučić wrote a great deal of poetry, but, always placing high demands on his craft, he later renounced much of it; in fact, he explicitly forbade the republication of his earliest poetry. As a consequence, his entire authorized poetic output consists of only one medium-sized volume. He was also versatile in his choice of subject matter and in his stylistic approaches. His poems can be grouped according to their overriding themes into patriotic-historical poems; poems focusing on nature; love poems; and predominantly meditative poems. Sometimes a poem is limited to one of these themes; more often, however, it combines two or more of them.

PATRIOTIC AND HISTORICAL POEMS

Dučić wrote poems on patriotic and historical themes, undoubtedly under the influence of folk poetry, the Serbian poets still writing in a Romantic vein, and the general patriotic enthusiasm of his countrymen. These early poems are rather bombastic, full of rhetoric, declamatory, though quite sincere. Later, he moved away from purely patriotic themes and turned to history. Only during the two world wars, especially during World War I, did he return to patriotic poetry, for obvious reasons. Inspired by the enormous suffering, valiant efforts, and glorious exploits of his people, he wrote several excellent poems, of which "Ave Serbia!" and "The Hymn of the Victors" are especially notable.

In somewhat intellectual fashion Dučić sings not of battles but of the suffering necessary for victory. Love for one's country he calls "a drop of poisonous milk," hinting at its opiumlike intoxication. Only that country is blessed "where children unearth a rusted sword" and "paths of greatness lead over fallen heroes." "Glory, that is the terrible sun of the martyrs," he exclaims in praise of the World War I victors. He would raise his voice once again during the second world cataclysm, this time more in anger and despair over the tragic fate of his people, whose end he did not live to see.

His historical poems are in a much lighter vein, devoid of the tragic aura of his patriotic poetry. In the cycle "Carski soneti" (the imperial sonnets) he returns to the glory of Serbian medieval empire, and in the cycle "Dubrovačke poeme" (the Dubrovnik poems) he extolls the virtues and the sunny ambience of the Ragusan Republic, which alone escaped several centuries of Turkish occupation. While the former cycle is unrestrained in its glorification of the pomp and strength of the old Serbian empire, the latter is amusing, humorous, at times irreverent, but above all lighthearted and warm. These poems are read today only out of curiosity and for amusement, although some of them show Dučić's craftsmanship at its best.

NATURE POEMS

Dučić's poems about nature are both varied and limited in scope. While it is true that he touches upon many phenomena and objects in nature, his approach tends to be somewhat one-sided. This one-sidedness can be seen in his choice of motifs, which are repeated time and again, although in endless variations. Among such often-repeated motifs are the sea, the sun, morning, evening, night, and natural objects that are usually isolated in their surroundings—no doubt reflecting the poet's own isolation and loneliness despite his appearance as a very happy and self-satisfied person. Even the titles of the cycles reveal the concentration on certain motifs: "Jutarnje pesme" (morning poems), "Večernje pesme" (evening poems), and "Sunčane pesme" (sun poems).

Dučić's nature poems are not descriptive per se; rather, description is used primarily to evoke an atmosphere or to underscore the poet's melancholy mood. In the poem "Sat" ("The Clock"), for example, the very first verse sets the desired tone: "A sick, murky day, the sky impenetrable." The tolling of the tower clock contributes to general hopelessness: "Last roses are slowly dying . . . poplars are shedding their last leaves." The entire scene is permeated with "a horrible foreboding and the panic of things." In his treatment of nature Dučić emulates the Parnassians and the Symbolists, but he also endeavors to "spiritualize" nature, as Pero Slijepčevič, a literary historian of Serbian literature, remarks, to present it as something outside and above the poet's perception of it. When a strong musicality is added to his regular versification, the impact of his poem, whether it is read or listened to, is powerful and lasting.

Other poems, such as those in "Sunčane pesme," are almost exactly the opposite: sunny, joyful, invigorating. Thus the poem "April" evokes a fairytale setting: The sky resembles a field covered with roses, the green hill is full of snails, and the sun's gold glitters in mud puddles. The titles of other poems in the Sun cycle—which translate as dawn, a forest, the sun, rain, a pine tree, the wind, and so on—suggest a symphonic picture of nature, as Miodrag Pavlović observes, a picture that nourishes one's imagination and captivates with its seemingly effortless simplicity.

Dučić is a poet of the Mediterranean *joie de vivre* and closeness to nature, his pessimistic posturing notwithstanding. This fact explains the abundance of sounds and acoustic impressions, with form and color following closely. As a native of a region close to the Adriatic Sea and having spent most of his life in cosmopolitan centers, he shows little interest in the inland territories of the Balkans and Europe, concentrating on landscapes at or near the sea, both in his poetry and in his travelogues, most of which depict places in the Mediterranean area.

Dučić goes to nature not so much to enjoy it as to meditate in it. Many of his poems depict silence as the most salutary state for the poet's musing about life and the meaning of existence. There he finds "loneliness, in eternal silence, pale, by the river" and "evening waters streaming in quiet sadness, and weeping willows rustling forgetfulness." It is hard to say whether such attitudes stem from affectation or from the need to give his mood adequate expression. Critics have often accused him of affectation and artificiality, but in doing so, they overlook his remarkable ability to create with a few masterful strokes a picture of a landscape capable of moving the reader. Despite certain mannerisms, clichés, and repetitiousness, Dučić's poems about nature are highly ingenious in approach and execution. They belong to the best of their kind in Serbian poetry.

LOVE POETRY

Dučić has been accused of even greater affectation and artificiality in his love poetry, probably because the woman in his poems is seldom a being made of flesh and blood but rather only a vision of an unknown woman, an eternal creature without specific abode or age. She does not exist nor did she ever exist, Dučić admits. Instead of endowing his emotions with a concrete substance, he creates a woman cult, placing her at the altar of an unrealizable dream. She is "the principle that builds and destroys, the God's spirit in every string and line . . . an inexhaustible well of pride and shame . . . an endless desert where the suns of despair rise and set" ("Poem to a Woman"). She is also a constant source of pain and unhappiness, mainly because she does not exist in her own right but only as the poet's chimera: "You have shone in the sun of my heart: for, everything we love, we have created ourselves." Seeing in woman a goddess, a cosmic principle, and destiny, it is not surprising that Dučič cannot find happiness and satisfaction in love. Even though he yearns for satisfaction, he is convinced beforehand of his failure. It is interesting that, as Slijepčevič remarks, Dučič never sings about the beginning or the duration of love but only about its end.

It is easy to see only affectation in attitudes such as these, but such an approach does not exhaust the complexity of Dučić's love poetry. The fact is that he did not always advocate such an ethereal relationship. In his earliest poems (later repudiated), as well as in his poems in prose, he does speak of lust, sensual excesses, and even devouring passion. In private life, he was known as an insatiable, often ruthless lover. As he matured as a poet, however, the ideal of a woman beyond reach—but also beyond corruption and decay—slowly took shape: "Remain unreachable, speechless, and distant—for, the dream of happiness means more than happiness" ("Poem to a Woman"). Yet, despite the withdrawal and lack of confidence, he refuses to dwell on the transience of love, counterposing love to death as one of the few forces that could overcome it. One cycle of his poems is entitled "Poems of Love and Death." By elevating woman to the level of deity, he establishes love as one of the three basic themes of high poetry: God, death, and love. Thus, Dučić's love poetry transcends the Romantic, realist, and Symbolist approach to love, all of which had, at one point or another, taken their turn in shaping his poetic profile. As in his nature poetry, he approaches love in a nontraditional, primarily intellectual way. Love is no longer a manifestation of only feelings but also of thought. In the process, Dučić has created some of the best love poems in Serbian literature, despite some admitted flaws.

POETRY OF MEDITATION

Many of Dučić's poems about nature and love show a distinct propensity for meditation, just as many of his purely meditative poems are related to nature and love. Dučić's meditative bent derives not only from his nature but also from his firm belief that only the meditative element and intellectualism could pull Serbian literature out of the confines of narrow regionalism. His time in France and Switzerland, as well as in other parts of the world, only confirmed that belief. In order to achieve that goal, he sometimes strained too hard. On the other hand, some of his meditative poems are genuine artistic achievements.

Dučić never developed his own philosophy, nor was he systematic in expressing his thoughts in his poems. There is no doubt, however, that he was fond of philosophizing and couching his thoughts on many subjects in poetic fashion. Even in his prose works, where his meditativeness is more pronounced, he often expresses his thoughts poetically. From the many poems which are either completely or partially suffused with meditation, several topics clearly emerge. In these works, Dučić frequently addresses God. Even though he sees him in all things, offering his hand "whenever my ship tilts," the poet cannot always suppress doubts about his whereabouts at the time "when a criminal sharpens his knife somewhere" ("Poems to God"). Most of Dučić's references to God are the result of the constant interplay of faith and doubt. Death, "the only thing we did not invent . . . more real than reality . . . the only truth and the only fairy tale, the sum of all symbols" ("Poems of Death"), is also often depicted by Dučić. In accord with his basically pessimistic attitude, he speaks of death as of an inevitable outcome that can be halted temporarily only by love. The experience of love, too, often gives Dučić an opportunity to reflect. Poetry itself is the subject of meditation, as in his famous "My Poetry," in which he pleads with his muse to be beautiful and proud only for him and to ignore the rest of the world as if it were hidden in a mysterious fog. This aptly illustrates his belief in *l'art pour l'art*, of which he was the leading proponent in Serbian literature.

Some critics maintain that the reflective poems are the weakest in Dučić's oeuvre. Others believe that this particular characteristic lends his poetry an aura of cosmopolitanism and sophistication that helped Serbian poetry overcome its century-long limitations, as Dučić believed it would. Moreover, far from being trite or superfluous, his meditativeness inspires the reader to do his own thinking.

BLUE LEGENDS

Dučić's poems in prose in *Blue Legends* stand out as a curiosity in Serbian poetry, because no other Serbian poet had written prose poems in such a sustained and dedicated fashion. They are also a further testimony to Dučić's versatility and poetic prowess. The thirty-seven poems in this collection cover the ground of his lyric poetry: One finds poems about nature, love, faith, gods, and human behavior in general. The most striking difference lies in the frequent depiction of the ancient world, of pagan and classical antiquity as well as of early Christianity. Dučić, who seldom concerned himself with the present, found in these escapes into the past a convenient idiom to give poetic expression to his thoughts and sentiments. His treatment of love here is much bolder and earthier and that of faith much less reverent than in his lyric poetry, and his conclusions about human nature seem to be more realistic. "The Sun" and "The Little Princess" are generally considered to be the best of these prose poems.

VERSIFICATION, STYLE, IMAGERY

Dučić's style has often been singled out as the most significant and accomplished aspect of his poetry, often at the expense of other qualities. He demanded of himself, as well as of other writers, rigorous attention to matters of style, considering himself to be a craftsman in a poetic workshop. He constantly revised his works, not hesitating to disown those he did not deem worthy. He remained a student of poetry even when others thought of him as a complete artist, and he had no patience with those who neglected style.

In matters of versification, Dučić shows a remarkable versatility. His most common form is a variation of the Alexandrine, which he used almost exclusively in his later periods (except in the last book published during his lifetime, *Lirika*). He started with hexameter, octameter, and decameter, and settled on the Alexandrine, although he used many variations of these and other meters. All his verses rhyme, but even here there is great variety from poem to poem, even within a single poem. Enjambment is not infrequent. Most of his poems consist of four to six quatrains. He wrote many sonnets; some of the cycles are composed entirely of them.

The texture of Dučić's verse is characterized above all by strong musicality, achieved through a skillful use of vowels, cadence, and resonance, and by avoiding harsh elements such as dissonant consonants, corrupted speech, and provincialisms. The inner rhythm is achieved by strict adherence to the rules of versification, especially those of meter, stress, and caesura, although he sometimes deviates if his highly sensitive ear tells him to do so. This is possible in Serbo-Croatian, where morphological and syntactic rules allow such variations.

The wealth of images and metaphors in Dučić's poetry has often been pointed out. The originality of such figures is undeniable: The armies of night are sailing, and the flags of darkness are waving; a horny moon has entangled itself in the branches of old chestnut trees; his poetry is quiet as marble, cold as a shadow; a sea willow resembles a nymph condemned to become a tree-rustling sadness. Dučić frequently employs personification: A row of black poplars marches through the wheatfield; water fountains are crying; the dawn looks into the window with the childlike eyes of a doe; a snake is taking off its shirt in the blackberry bush. Even with such a wealth of imagery and metaphor, Dučić's verse is always clear and fully expressed, never overloaded with meaning yet never devoid of it. The purity of his language, his striking and bold innovations, and his musical fluidity all contribute to a powerful total effect.

While it is true that many of these characteristics can be traced to the influence of the Parnassians and the Symbolists, it is also true that without his own immense talent Dučić could not have become what he was—a leading poet of his generation, a pathfinder and epochmaker in Serbian literature, and one of the important writers in world literature of the twentieth century. Only the fact that his skillfully composed poetry is extremely difficult to translate has limited his appeal and reputation in the rest of the world.

OTHER MAJOR WORKS
    LONG FICTION: *Grof Sava Vladislavić*, 1942.
    NONFICTION: *Blago Cara Radovana*, 1932; *Gradovi i himere*, 1932.

BIBLIOGRAPHY

Goy, Edward D. "The Poetry of Jovan Dučić." In *Gorski Vijenac: A Garland of Essays Offered to Professor Elizabeth Mary Hill*. Cambridge, England: The Modern Humanities Research Association, 1970. An expertly written essay by a noted British Slavicist. Goy discusses Dučić's poetry within the framework of European literature as well as his artistic virtuosity.

Mihailovich, Vasa D. "Jovan Dučić in America." *Serbian Studies* 4, no. 4 (1988): 55-69. An essay about Dučić's stay in America during 1941-1943, the last two years of his life. It covers his many activities among the Serbs of America. Even though he wrote relatively little poetry at this time, he penned political tracts in support of General Draža Mihailović. The essay chronicles those activities in detail.

Petrov, Aleksandar, ed. *Manje poznati Dučić—A Less Known Dučić*. Pittsburgh: American Srbobran, 1994. A valuable publication about lesser known writings of the poet, primarily his poems written during World War II. It contains the editor's informative essay about this period in the poet's life and translations of his last poems.

Popovi, Radovan. *Knjiga o Dučiću*. Belgrade: BIGZ, 1992. A very informative book about Dučić, who has been ostracized in his own country and declared a *persona non grata* because of his support of General Draža Mihailović. This is the first book to speak objectively about the poet's stance during World War II, after a long silence.

Puvačić, Dušan. "The Theme of Bosnia and Hercegovina in the Works of Jovan Dučić." *South Slav Journal* 15, nos. 1/2 (1992): 35-43. The author analyzes Dučić's attachment to his native region as expressed in his works. The political background is examined as well as his artistic excellence.

Vitanović, Slobodan. *Jovan Dučić u znaku Apolona i Dionisa*. Belgrade: Srpska akademija nauka i umetnosti, 1994. Vitanović discusses Dučić's thoughts and attitudes about love and the role of eros in his poems. He also discusses the poet's literary and aesthetic views and his place in the history of Serbian literature, as well as his thoughts about European culture and literature.

Vasa D. Mihailovich;
bibliography updated by Mihailovich

ALAN DUGAN

Born: Brooklyn, New York; February 12, 1923

PRINCIPAL POETRY

General Prothalamion in Populous Times, 1961
Poems, 1961
Poems Two, 1963
Poems Three, 1967
Collected Poems, 1969
Poems Four, 1974
Sequence, 1976
New and Collected Poems, 1961-1983, 1983 (includes *Poems Five*)
Poems Six, 1989
Ten Years of Poems: From Alan Dugan's Worshop at Castle Hill Center for the Arts, Truro, Massachusetts, 1987
More Poems: From Alan Dugan's Workshop at Castle Hill Center for the Arts, Truro, Massachusetts, 1994
Poems Seven: New and Complete Poetry, 2001

OTHER LITERARY FORMS

Alan Dugan's literary accomplishments have centered on the medium of poetry.

ACHIEVEMENTS

Alan Dugan had been publishing poems in literary magazines for a number of years—winning an award from *Poetry* as early as 1947—before his first book of poetry was published in 1961. That book, *Poems*, enjoyed one of the greatest critical successes of any first volume of poems in the twentieth century. Dudley Fitts awarded it the Yale Series of Younger Poets Award; it also won the National Book Award and the Pulitzer Prize. Poet Philip Booth called it "the most original first book that has appeared . . . in a sad long time."

Dugan published subsequent volumes of poetry, similar in style and range to his first volume, winning the Pulitzer Prize for Poetry again in 1967 for *Poems Three*. Dugan also won the Prix de Rome from the American Academy of Arts and Letters (1962-1962), a Guggenheim Fellowship (1963-1964). He was a Rockefeller Foundation fellow in 1966-1967 and won a Levinson poetry prize from *Poetry* magazine in 1967. In 1981, Dugan won the Shelley Memorial Award. In 2001, *Poems Seven* won the National Book Award for Poetry, awarded by the National Book Foundation.

BIOGRAPHY

Born in Brooklyn, Alan Dugan has spent most of his life in New York City. His stint in the Army Air

Alan Dugan in Truro, 1989. (Gillian Drake, courtesy of Provincetown Arts Press)

and two Pulitzer prizes, he received a Rome Fellowship from the American Academy of Arts and Letters in 1962-1963, a Guggenheim Fellowship in 1963-1964, and a Rockefeller Foundation Fellowship in 1967-1968. He was a member of the faculty at Sarah Lawrence College from 1967 through 1971, and he has been on the faculty of the Fine Arts Work Center in Provincetown, Massachusetts, since 1971. Dugan has given many poetry readings, and, after adjusting to his high voice and the purposely undramatic, cold presentation, audiences have found that his style of reading fits the poems.

ANALYSIS

Alan Dugan brought to his first remarkable volume, *Poems*, a completely developed style. That style was colloquial, spare, and tough, fitting the bleak vision of much of his poetry. Dugan has been characterized as a poet lacking in charm, and truly, there is no attempt to be charming, only intense and truthful. His mocking, ironic style fits the narrowness of his outlook, and both the achievement and the weakness of his poetry rest on it. Whether Dugan writes of war, love, or work (his key subjects), he confronts them with a similar ironic stance. His poetry is against sentimentality, even against transcendence, a kind of antipoetry.

Corps during World War II was of importance to him, and a number of his first published poems were portraits of servicemen. He attended Queens College and Olivet College, and received his B.A. degree from Mexico City College. He married Judith Shahn, the daughter of the painter Ben Shahn. After the war, he held a number of jobs in New York City, working in advertising and publishing and as a maker of models for a medical supply house. These jobs made him dissatisfied with the world of office work that he satirizes in his poetry.

The success of his first book of poems in 1961 led to his winning a series of awards that gave him more time for his poetry. Besides the National Book Award

Dugan's language makes it evident that he belongs to the colloquial tradition of American poetry. In a manner somewhat reminiscent of William Carlos Williams, Dugan reverses the expectations of the reader of love or nature poetry, turning sentiment into irony. Like Williams, and like contemporary poets such as James Wright and Philip Levine, Dugan sets his poetry in the city and expresses sympathy for, and identification with, the urban working class. Although Dugan's poems seldom rhyme, they often employ traditional meters and stanza as well as free verse. The emphasis on form—even, on a few occasions, the resort to pattern poems—often creates an interesting tension with his dominant plain style.

"How We Heard the Name"

"How We Heard the Name," the poem that Dudley Fitts, the judge of the Yale Series of Younger Poets, selected for its "strangeness" despite "the greyness of diction and versification," is typical of Dugan's work. In part, this poem depends for its meaning on a classical allusion, a surprisingly common technique in this tough-talking urban poet. At the center of the poem is the battle of Granicus, one of Alexander the Great's most famous victories, but Dugan has singled out a seemingly trivial historical oddity: Alexander wrote that he won the battle "with no help from the Lacedaemonians."

In Dugan's poem, the river brings down the debris and dead of the battle until it also brings down a soldier on a log. The speaker of the poem inquires about the source of this grim pollution, and the soldier sardonically tells him of the famous victory won by the Greeks "except/ the Lacedaemonians and/ myself." He explains that this is merely a joke "between me and a man/ named Alexander, whom/ all of you ba-bas/ will hear of as a god." The antiheroic stance, the directness of the language, the casualness of the mention of Alexander, and the comedy of "ba-bas" to characterize those who believe a mere man can be a god, make up a microcosm of Dugan's tone and style. This is a voice that has come to joke about Caesar, not to praise him, yet reserves its greatest contempt for the sheeplike followers of great leaders. No apologies are made for running away from the battle, and the reader is left with the feeling that it was the action of an intelligent man who, like the Lacedaemonians, knew when not to fight.

War poetry

Dugan often speaks sarcastically of war, whether it is one of Alexander's, the American Civil War, the two World Wars, or the Vietnam War—all of which make appearances in his poetry. In a "Fabrication of Ancestors," Dugan sums up his attitude toward all wars when he praises his ancestor, "shot in the ass," who did not help to win the war for the North but wore on his body a constant "proof/ of the war's obscenity." In the curious "Adultery," Dugan contrasts the insignificance of private immoralities with greater public evils— the world of "McNamara and his band" and "Johnson and his Napalm Boys," who wipe out the lives of entire cities in Vietnam. Dugan does not plan to be among "the ba-bas."

"Love Song: I and Thou"

Love is another dominant subject of Dugan's work, and he approaches it in much the same tone of fierceness and irony that informs his poems about war. In these poems he turns to the war between the sexes, its battles and betrayals. "Love Song: I and Thou" is one of Dugan's most skillful poems and is deservedly one of his most frequently anthologized. In a complicated brew, it mixes the techniques of allegory and allusion with Dugan's terse colloquial style. It illustrates the basic paradox of much of his verse: the dominant conversational, flat tone that all the reviewers have emphasized, merging with elaborate poetic devices—devices that only a few commentators have mentioned. The overriding figure is the comparison between a man's life and a house, a badly built house, in this case. The opening line of the poem declares how badly it is built: "Nothing is plumb, level, or square." It is a house with a corresponding life in considerable disarray, a house for which, on one level, the speaker insists on taking responsibility ("I planned it"), yet whose chaos, on some other level, must be blamed on a higher power ("God damned it"). The description of the house becomes a description of the ancient quarrel concerning the roles of free will and determinism in a person's life.

Also running throughout "Love Song: I and Thou" is a comparison-contrast between the speaker and Christ: "By Christ/ I am no carpenter." This reference concludes in the final lines about crucifixion in a passage that suddenly introduces the love song promised by the title. The title's "I and Thou" is a reference to the modern Jewish philosopher Martin Buber; *I-Thou* is the language he used to describe a true and vital love relationship between equals, as opposed to *I-It*. The ending of Dugan's poem, however, creates a highly ambiguous feeling. In what sounds like tender talk, "I need . . . a help, a love, a you, a wife," the speaker is asking for someone to nail his right hand to the cross. He cannot finish his crucifixion by himself; he needs a helpmate, a nailer. One critic finds the language very touching, but there seems to be a bitter joke at the heart of this complex poem.

"LETTER TO DONALD FALL"

Although Dugan sometimes praises the world of sexuality ("the red world of love"), his enthusiasms are almost always tempered by irony. In a "Letter to Donald Fall," he makes a list of "my other blessings after friendship/ unencumbered by communion." They include:

> a money making job, time off it, a wife
> I still love sometimes unapproachably
> hammering on picture frames, my own city . . .
> and my new false teeth. . . .

The words "sometimes unapproachably," which manage to go both forward and backward, suggest Dugan's attitude toward love. Even more typical is the comic introduction of his false teeth, which become a parallel to the approaching spring. The teeth seem to him to be "like Grails" and they talk to him, saying, "We are the resurrection/ and the life." Amidst some amusing images of spring coming to the city, Dugan comes as close as he can to satisfaction when he addresses his friend with the symbolic name in the final line of the poem: "Fall, it is not so bad at Dugan's Edge."

"COOLED HEELS LAMENT AGAINST FRIVOLITY, THE MASK OF DESPAIR"

The Muse, too, is tough in the poem with the amusing title, "Cooled Heels Lament Against Frivolity, the Mask of Despair"; she is a kind of distant boss, keeping the poet waiting in her office, as she swaps stories with the "star-salesmen of the soul." He seems to speak to her with slim hope of any positive response:

> Dugan's deathward darling; you
> in your unseeable beauty, oh
> fictitious, legal person, need
> be only formally concerned. . . .

If the fanciful Muse seems cold and indifferent, it is because there is not much to look forward to in one's encounters with the real world of bosses and work.

"ON A SEVEN-DAY DIARY"

That world of work is often portrayed in Dugan's poetry as a necessary but painful evil. "No man should work, but be" is the dream that cannot be fulfilled because "poverty is worse than work." "On a Seven-Day Diary" comically sums up Dugan's attitude with the insistent refrain, "Then I got up and went to work."

It is repeated five times for the five weekdays, but "Then it's Saturday, Saturday, Saturday!" The speaker excitedly proclaims that "Love must be the reason for the week!" as he lists the pleasures of the weekend. Yet he drinks so much on Saturday night that most of Sunday is lost, and—as one might expect from Dugan—the poem ends with "Then I got up and went to work."

"ON ZERO"

War, love, and work make a similarly dour pattern in Dugan's poetry—the grayness of Monday always returns. This is a poet whose longest published poem is entitled "On Zero," and whose attitude toward change might be summed up in the closing lines of "General Prothalamion in Populous Times": "the fall/ from summer's marching innocence/ to the last winter of general war." Reading a collection of Dugan's poems can be harrowing. His is a world where freedom is something to be feared, where to meet the morning is to confront "the daily accident," and where "sometimes you can't even lose"; yet Dugan often brings enough skill and humor to his work to overcome the darkness of the vision. What has been said of other writers who have been called cynical or misanthropic can be said of his work as well: The very energy of his language and the vitality of his wit belie his pessimism.

POEMS SIX

In a 1989 interview, Dugan himself complained about the slightness of the poems he wrote in the 1970's. In the same year, he published *Poems Six*, which attempts to get back to the more ambitious mode of his earlier volumes. Even for those accustomed to the bitterness of Dugan's work, however, the poems in this volume seem still bleaker in vision. The language of nausea and excrement often dominates Dugan's responses to the world's and his own difficulties.

In the opening poems of this volume, Dugan often confronts political subjects more directly than he had in the past. "Take on Armageddon" is addressed to Ronald Reagan. After talking about the final battle, the poem ends in a description of a world where there will be "no more insects, and no more you and your rotten God." In "Love and Money," Dugan describes a moment in Johnstown, Pennsylvania, when a steelworkers' strike and a convention of baton twirlers are taking place at the same time. The strikers "didn't touch the girls or the mills/ because they weren't theirs," but the speaker declares the mills do belong to the strikers since they built them and ran them. Their inability to recognize this, however, leads to the conclusion that "There is no left-wing politics in America left/ There is the International Baton Twirlers Association."

In *Poems Six*, Dugan continues to concentrate on his subjects of work, war, and love, and on occasions—as he did in his earlier volumes—to mix his tough-guy talk with allusions to classical literature and mythology. He tells his audience that as a child he used his statuette of Erato, Muse of lyric poetry, as an exercising dumbbell. He would "grab her by the neck and ankles when I got her alone/ and pump her up and down." Now the statue remains behind in silent rooms in Brooklyn as the traffic outside is leaving "for New York and the Wild West."

Possibly the most successful poem in *Poems Six* is the final one: "Night Scene Before Combat." The trucks moving in convoy outside his window in the middle of the night become a complicated symbol for the speaker, containing poetry, war, and death: "Did you know/ that metaphor means Truck/ in modern Greek? Truck. Carryall." He feels a battle within himself between staying with the woman he addresses and joining the convoy that rumbles by outside. The trucks, however, prevail, and the speaker turns to the woman "for one last time in sleep, love,/ before I put my uniform back on,/ check my piece, and say So long."

POEMS SEVEN

The year 2001 saw publication of the collection *Poems Seven*, a grand compendium four hundred pages in length and covering Dugan's entire forty-year career. Along with early war poems, three dozen new, previously uncollected, poems appear. The collection impressed the National Book Foundation sufficiently to garner for Dugan a nomination for the National Book Award for Poetry for 2001.

BIBLIOGRAPHY

Atlas, James. "Autobiography of the Present." *Poetry* 125 (February, 1975): 300-301. This review emphasizes Dugan's acute observations about commonplace moments in daily life. Atlas criticizes the later poems of Dugan for adopting a hectoring and polemical tone.

Boyers, Robert. "On Alan Dugan." In *Contemporary Poetry in America*, edited by Robert Boyers. New York: Schocken Books, 1974. A clear and thorough overview of Dugan's poetry. Despite his limitation in range, Dugan is praised as a moralist in difficult times. Boyers believes that the best poems make "a temporary truce with the miserableness of the world."

Dugan, Alan. "An Interview by J. C. Ellefson and Belle Waring." *American Poetry Review* 19 (May/June, 1990): 43-51. In this wide-ranging interview, Dugan talks about his childhood, his parents, his early jobs (including writing for *The New York Enquirer*, later to become *The National Enquirer*), and his attitude toward poetry. He expresses admiration for the poetry of Charles Bukowski and Philip Levine, contemporary urban American poets with whom he feels a kinship.

Howard, Richard. *Alone with America: Essays on the Art of Poetry in the United States Since 1950*. Enlarged ed. New York: Atheneum, 1980. In this complex and difficult-to-read book, Howard finds something like paranoia at the center of Dugan's work. He believes that the poetry displays an "honest and desperate resentment and hatred," a hatred sometimes directed at language itself.

Scharf, Michael. Review of *Poems Seven*. *Publishers Weekly* 248, no. 43 (October 22, 2001): 71. A review of the collection that garnered for Dugan his second nomination for a National Book Award.

Stepanchev, Stephen. *American Poetry Since 1945*. New York: Harper & Row, 1965. Stepanchev states that nothing is sacred to Dugan. He praises him highly for the colloquial directness and honesty of his work and discovers a kind of irony in the way his simple style confronts difficult and complicated subjects.

Michael Paul Novak;
bibliography updated by the editors

PAUL LAURENCE DUNBAR

Born: Dayton, Ohio; June 27, 1872
Died: Dayton, Ohio; February 9, 1906

PRINCIPAL POETRY
Oak and Ivy, 1893
Majors and Minors, 1895
Lyrics of Lowly Life, 1896
Lyrics of the Hearthside, 1899
Lyrics of Love and Laughter, 1903
Lyrics of Sunshine and Shadow, 1905
Complete Poems, 1913

OTHER LITERARY FORMS

Though Paul Laurence Dunbar is best known for his poetry, he was a fiction writer as well. His achievements in fiction include four volumes of short stories and four novels. Criticism of Dunbar's short fiction suggests that the stories contained in *Folks from Dixie* (1898) represent his best accomplishment in this literary form. His novels *The Uncalled* (1898) and *The Sport of the Gods* (1902) acquired more critical acclaim than his other two novels, *The Love of Landry* (1900) and *The Fanatics* (1901).

In addition to his work in these more traditional literary forms, Dunbar wrote an assortment of lyrics and libretti for a variety of theatrical productions. He also wrote essays for newspapers and attempted to establish a periodical of his own.

ACHIEVEMENTS

Paul Laurence Dunbar's literary career was brilliant, extending roughly across two decades. He can be credited with several first-time accomplishments: He was the first to use dialect poetry as a medium for the true interpretation of African American character and psychology, and he was the first African American writer to earn national prominence. In range of style and form, Dunbar remains the most versatile of African American writers.

BIOGRAPHY

Paul Laurence Dunbar was born to former slaves Joshua and Matilda J. Murphy Dunbar on June 27, 1872. He spent his early childhood in Dayton, Ohio, where he attended Central High School. Dunbar began to write at age sixteen and gained early patronage for his work, and he was introduced to the Western Association of Writers in 1892.

The next few years of his life found him in the presence of great black leaders. He met Frederick Douglass, Mary Church Terrell, and Ida B. Wells at the World's Columbian Exposition in Chicago in 1893. He met W. E. B. Du Bois in 1896 and Booker T. Washington in 1897. These encounters influenced Dunbar's literary tone and perspective significantly. He blended the creative perspective of Booker T. Washington with the social philosophy of Du Bois in order to present a valid scenario of African Americans after the Civil War.

Major James B. Pond, a Dunbar enthusiast, sponsored a trip to England for the writer which extended from February to August of 1897. Upon his return to the United States, Dunbar married Alice Moore and decided to earn his living as a writer. Between 1898 and 1903, Dunbar wrote essays for newspapers and periodicals, primarily addressing the issues of racial equality and social justice in America. He attempted to establish his own journalistic voice through a periodical which he named the *Dayton Tattler* in 1890. This effort failed.

During the latter years of his life, Dunbar wrote lyrics, including those for the school song for Tuskegee Institute. Dunbar died in Dayton, Ohio, on February 9, 1906.

ANALYSIS

The body of poetry produced by Paul Laurence Dunbar illustrates some of the best qualities found in lyrical verse. It is obvious that the poet concentrated on a creation of mood and that he was an innovator who experimented with form, meter, and rhyme. Equally apparent is the fact that Dunbar's creative style was influenced by the great British poetic innovators of the seventeenth and nineteenth centuries. Dunbar's commitment to speak to his people through his verse is reflected in his dialect poetry. Writing in all the major lyrical forms—idyll, hymn, sonnet, song, ballad, ode, and elegy—Dunbar established himself as one of the most versatile poets in American literature.

Paul Laurence Dunbar (Library of Congress)

The more than four hundred poems written by Dunbar are varied in style and effect. It is clear, however, that his dominant aim was to create an empathetic poetic mood resulting from combinations of elements such as meter, rhyme, diction, sentence structure, characterization, repetition, imagery, and symbolism. His most memorable poems display the influence of such masters as William Wordsworth; Robert Herrick; Alfred, Lord Tennyson; John Donne; Robert Browning; and John Keats.

Such an array of influences would ordinarily render one's genius suspect. There are common threads, however, which organically characterize the poetic expressions of Paul Laurence Dunbar. The undergirding strain in his poetry is his allegiance to lyrical qualities. He carries mood through sound patterns, he creates images which carry philosophical import, he shapes dramatic events in the pattern of movement in his syntactic forms, and he develops a rhythmic pattern which is quite effec-

tive in recitation. These lyrical qualities predominate in the best of Dunbar's poetry. Indeed, one might easily classify Dunbar's poetry in typical Romantic lyrical categories: The bulk of his poems can be classified as love lyrics, reflective lyrics, melancholic lyrics, or nature lyrics. Sometimes these moods overlap in a single poem. Consequently, an analysis of the features in Dunbar's poetry is necessarily complex, placing his lyrical qualities in the poetic traditions which shape them.

LOVE LYRICS: LYRICS OF THE HEARTHSIDE

Dunbar's lyricism is substantially displayed in his love poetry. In "A Bridal Measure," from *Lyrics of the Hearthside*, the poet's persona beckons maidens to the bridal throne. His invitation is spirited and triumphant yet controlled, reminiscent of the tradition in love poetry established by Ben Jonson. The tone, however, more closely approximates the *carpe diem* attitude of Robert Herrick.

> Come, essay a sprightly measure,
> Tuned to some light song of pleasure.
> Maidens, let your brows be crowned
> As we foot this merry round.

The rhyming couplets carry the mood and punctuate the invitation. The urgency of the moment is extended further in the direct address: "Phyllis, Phyllis, why be waiting?/ In the woods the birds are mating." The poem continues in this tone, while adopting a pastoral simplicity.

> When the year, itself renewing,
> All the world with flowers is strewing,
> Then through Youth's Arcadian land,
> Love and song go hand in hand.

The accentuation in the syntactic flow of these lines underlines the poet's intentions. Though the meter is irregular, with some iambs and some anapests, the force of the poet's exhortation remains apparent.

Dunbar frequently personifies abstractions. In "Love and Grief," also from *Lyrics of the Hearthside*, Dunbar espouses a morbid yet redemptive view of love. While the reflective scenario presented in this poem recalls Tennyson's meditations on death and loss, the poetic event echoes Wordsworth's faith in the indestructibility of joy. Utilizing the heroic couplet, Dunbar makes an opening pronouncement:

> Out of my heart, one treach'rous winter's day,
> I locked young Love and threw the key away.
> Grief, wandering widely, found the key,
> And hastened with it, straightway, back to me.

The drama of grief-stricken love is thus established. The poet carefully clarifies his position through an emphatic personification of Grief's behavior: "He unlocked the door/ and bade Love enter with him there and stay." Being a lyric poet of redemptive sensibility, Dunbar cannot conclude the poem on this note. The "table must turn," as it does for Wordsworth in such situations. Love then becomes bold and asks of Grief: "What right hast thou/ To part or parcel of this heart?" In order to justify the redemptive quality he presents, Dunbar attributes the human frailty of pride to Love, a failing which invites Grief. In so doing, the poet's philosophical intuitiveness emerges with a measure of moral decorum. Through the movement in the syntactic patterns, the intensity of the drama is heightened as the poem moves to resolution. Dunbar utilizes a variety of metrical patterns, the most significant of which is the spondee. This poetic foot of two accented syllables allows the poet to proclaim emphatically: "And Love, pride purged, was chastened all his life." Thus, the principal emotion in the poem is redeemed.

The brief, compact lyrical verse, as found in Browning, is among Dunbar's typical forms. "Love's Humility," in *Lyrics of the Hearthside*, is an example:

> As some rapt gazer on the lowly earth,
>   Looks up to radiant planets, ranging far,
> So I, whose soul doth know thy wondrous worth
>   Look longing up to thee as to a star.

This skillfully concentrated simile elevates love to celestial heights. The descriptive detail enhances the power of the feeling the poet captures and empowers the lyrical qualities of the poem with greater pathos.

LYRICS OF LOVE AND LAUGHTER

Dunbar's *Lyrics of Love and Laughter* is not the best of his collections, but it contains some remarkable dialect verse. "A Plea" provides an example of this aspect of his reputation. Speaking of the unsettling feelings experienced by one overcome with love, Dunbar exhorts a lover's love object to "treat him nice."

> I ain't don a t'ing to shame,
> Lovahs all ac's jes de same:
> Don't you know we ain't to blame?
>   Treat me nice!

Rendering a common experience in the African American idiom, Dunbar typifies the emotionally enraptured lover as one who has no control over his behavior:

> Whut a pusson gwine to do,
> W'en he come a-cou'tin' you
> All a-trimblin' thoo and thoo?
>   Please be nice.

The diction in this poem is not pure dialect. Only those portions which describe the emotions and behavior of the lover are stated in dialect, highlighting the primary emotions and enhancing the pathetic mood, which is apparently Dunbar's principal intent. Typical of Dunbar's love lyrics, "A Plea" is rooted in the experience of a particular culture yet remains universal in its themes. Through his use of diction, meter, and stanzaic form, Dunbar captures fundamental human emotions and renders them with intensity and lyrical compassion.

REFLECTIVE LYRICS: LYRICS OF LOWLY LIFE

Reflective lyrics form a large segment of Dunbar's poetry. Some of his best poems of this type are found in *Lyrics of Lowly Life*, including the long stanzaic poem "Ere Sleep Comes Down to Soothe the Weary Eyes." This poem utilizes one sensory impression as a focal point for the lyrical evolution in the style of Keats. The sleep motif provides an avenue through which the persona's imagination enters the realm of reflection.

Through sleep's dream the persona is able to "make the waking world a world of lies—/ of lies palpable, uncouth, forlorn." In this state of subconscious reflection, past pains are revisited as they "come thronging through the chambers of the brain." As the poem progresses, it becomes apparent that the repetitive echo of "ere sleep comes down to soothe the weary eyes" has some significance. This refrain begins and ends each stanza of the poem except the last. In addition to serving as a mood-setting device, this expression provides the channel of thought for the literary journey, which is compared with the "spirit's journeying." Dunbar's audience is thus constantly reminded of the source of his revelations.

Dunbar reveals his poetic thesis in the last stanza. He uses images from the subconscious state of life, sleep, to make a point about death. Prior to making this point, Dunbar takes the reader to the realm of reflective introspection: "So, trembling with the shock of sad surprise,/ The soul doth view its awful self alone." There is an introspective confrontation of the soul with itself, and it resolves:

> When sleep comes down to seal the weary eyes,
>
> . . . .
>
> Ah, then, no more we heed
> the sad world's cries,
> Or seek to probe th' eternal mystery,
> Or fret our souls at long-withheld replies.

The escape from pain and misery is death; there is no intermediary state which will eradicate that fact of life. Dunbar presents this notion with sympathy and sincerity. His metaphorical extensions, particularly those relative to the soul, are filled with compassion. The soul is torn with the world's deceit; it cries with "pangs of vague inexplicable pain." The spirit, an embodiment of the soul, forges ahead to seek truth as far as fancy will lead. Questioning begins then, and the inner sense confronts the inner being until truth emerges. Dunbar's presentation of the resolution is tender and gentle.

Dunbar wrote reflective lyrics in the vernacular as well. Espousing the philosophy of divine intention, Dunbar wrote "Accountability," a poem also found in *Lyrics of Lowly Life*. In this poem, the beliefs and attitudes of the persona are revealed in familiar language.

> Folks ain't got no right to
> censuah othah
> folks about dey habits;
>
> . . . .
>
> We is all constructed diff'ent,
> d'ain't no two of
> us de same;
>
> . . . .

> But we all fits into places dat
> no othah ones
> could fill.

Each stanza in this poem presents a thesis and develops that point. The illustrations from the natural world support a creationist viewpoint. The persona obviously accepts the notion that everything has a purpose. The Creator gave the animals their members shaped as they are for a reason and so, "Him dat giv' de squr'ls de bushtails made de bobtails fu' de rabbits." The variations in nature are by design: "Him dat built de gread big mountains hollered out de little valleys"; "Him dat made de streets an' driveways wasn't shamed to make de alley." The poet establishes these notions in three quatrains, concluding in the fourth quatrain: "When you come to think about it, how it's all planned out it's splendid./ Nuthin's done er evah happens, dout hit's somefin' dat's intended." The persona's position that divine intention rules the world is thereby sealed.

Introspection is a feature of Dunbar's reflective lyrics. In "The Lesson," the persona engages in character revelation, interacts with the audience toward establishment of appropriate resolution, and participates in the action of the poem. These qualities are reminiscent of Browning's dramatic monologues. As the principal speaker sits by a window in his cottage, reflecting, he reports:

> And I thought of myself so sad and lone,
> And my life's cold winter that knew no spring;
> Of my mind so weary and sick and wild,
> Of my heart too sad to sing.

The inner conflict facing the persona is revealed in these lines and the perspective of self-examination is established. The persona must confront his sadness and move toward resolution. The movement toward resolution presents the dramatic occasion in the poem: "A thought stole into my saddened heart,/ And I said, 'I can cheer some other soul/ By a carol's simple art.'" Reflective introspection typically leads to improved character, a fundamental tenet in the Victorian viewpoint. Sustained by his new conviction and outlook, the persona "sang a lay for a brother's ear/ In a strain to soothe his bleeding heart."

The lyrical quality of "The Lesson" is strengthened by the movement in the poet's syntactic patterns. Feelings of initial despair and resulting joy and hope are conveyed through the poet's syntax. The sequential conjoining of ideas as if in a rushing stream of thought is particularly effective. The latter sections of the poem are noteworthy in this regard. This pattern gives the action more force, thereby intensifying the feeling. Dunbar presents an emphatic idea—"and he smiled . . ."—and juxtaposes it to an exception—"Though mine was a feeble art." He presents a responsive result—"But at his smile I smiled in turn"—connected to a culminating effect—"And into my soul there came a ray." With this pronouncement, the drama comes full circle from inner conflict through conversion to changed philosophical outlook. Dunbar captures each moment with appropriate vigor.

MELANCHOLY: "YESTERDAY AND TO-MORROW"

The subjects of love and death are treated in Dunbar's lyrics of melancholy, the third major mood found in the poet's lyrical verse. "Yesterday and To-morrow," in *Lyrics of Sunshine and Shadow*, is an example of Dunbar's lyric of melancholy. The mood of this poem is in the tradition of the British Romantic poets, particularly that of Wordsworth. Dunbar treats the melancholy feelings in this poem with tenderness and simplicity. The persona expresses disappointment with the untimeliness of life's events and the uncertainties of love. This scenario intimates a bleak future.

"Yesterday and To-morrow" is developed in three compact quatrains. Each quatrain envelops a primary emotion. The first stanza unfolds yesterday's contentment in love. The lover remembers the tender and blessed emotion of closeness with his lover: "And its gentle yieldingness/ From my soul I blessed it." The second stanza is reminiscent of the metaphysical questionings and imagery of Donne: "Must our gold forever know/ Flames for the refining?" The lovers' emotions are compared with precious metal undergoing the fire of refinement: Their feelings of sadness are released in this cynical question.

In the third quatrain, Dunbar feeds the sad heart with more cynicism. Returning to the feelings of disappointment and uncertainty, the persona concludes: "Life was all a lyric song/ Set to tricksy meter." The persona escapes in cynicism, but the poem still ends on a hopeless note.

"COMMUNION"

"Communion," which is collected in *Lyrics of the Hearthside*, is another of Dunbar's melancholy lyrics and focuses the theme of love and death. The situation in the poem again evokes a cynical attitude, again reminiscent of Donne. The poem presents a struggle between life's memories and death. Life's memories are primarily of the existence of the love relationship, and death symbolizes its demise. This circumstance unfolds in a dramatic narrative in the style of Browning.

The first two stanzas of the poem introduce the situation and the mood begins to evolve in stanza three. The poet uses images from nature to create the somber mood. The "breeze of Death," for example, sweeps his lover's soul "Out into the unsounded deeps." On one hand, the Romantic theme of dominance of nature and man's helplessness in the face of it creeps through; on the other hand, faith in love as the superior experience resounds. The conflict between conquering Death, symbolized in nature, and Love creates tension in the poem. Consequently, though the breeze of Death has swept his bride away, the persona announces that "Wind nor sea may keep me from/ Soft communing with my bride." As these quatrains of iambic pentameter unfold, the poem becomes somewhat elegiac in tone.

The persona solemnly enters into reflective reminiscence in the fifth stanza and proclaims: "I shall rest my head on thee/ As I did long days of yore." Continuing in stanza 6, he announces: "I shall take thy hand in mine,/ And live o'er the olden days." Leading up to the grief-stricken pledge of eternal love, the melancholic feeling is intensified. The mourner details his impression as follows:

> Tho' the grave-door shut between,
> Still their love lights o'er me steal.
>
> I can see thee thro' my tears,
> As thro' rain we see the sun.

The comfort which comes from such memories brings a ray of light; the lover concludes:

> I shall see thee still and be
> Thy true lover evermore,
> And thy face shall be to me
> Dear and helpful as before.

The drama cannot end unless the persona interacts with his audience. The audience is therefore included in the philosophical conclusion: "Death may vaunt and Death may boast,/ But we laugh his pow'r to scorn." Dunbar illustrates an ability to overcome the causes of melancholy in his lyrics of this mood. He works with contrasting feelings, cynicism, and determinism to achieve this goal. His melancholic mood is therefore less gloomy than one might expect.

NATURE LYRICS: "IN SUMMER"

Since he was greatly influenced by the British Romantic writers, it is not surprising that Dunbar also wrote nature lyrics. "In Summer," from *Lyrics of the Hearthside*, and "The Old Apple-Tree," from *Lyrics of Lowly Life*, are representative of his nature lyrics. "In Summer" captures a mood of merriment which is stimulated by nature. The common man is used as a model of one who possesses the capacity to experience this natural joy. Summer is a bright, sunny time; it is also a time for ease, as presented in the second stanza. Introducing the character of the farmer boy in stanza 3, Dunbar presents a model embodiment of the ease and merriment of summer. Amid the blades of green grass and as the breezes cool his brow, the farmer boy sings as he plows. He sings "to the dewy morn" and "to the joys of life." This behavior leads to some moralizing, to which the last three stanzas of the poem are devoted. The poet's point is made through a contrast:

> O ye who toil in the town.
> And ye who moil in the mart,
> Hear the artless song, and your faith made strong
> Shall renew your joy of heart.

Dunbar admonishes the reader to examine the behavior of the farm boy. Elevation of the simple, rustic life is prevalent in the writings of early British Romantic poets and postbellum African American writers alike. The admonition to reflect on the rustic life, for example, is the same advice Wordsworth gives in "The Old Cumberland Beggar." Both groups of writers agree that there are lessons to be learned through an examination of the virtues of the rustic life. In this vein, Dunbar advises: "Oh, poor were the worth of the world/ If never a song were heard." He goes further by advising all to "taunt old Care with a merry air."

"THE OLD APPLE-TREE"

The emphasis on the rustic life is also pervasive in "The Old Apple-Tree." The primary lyrical quality of the poem is that the poetic message evolves from the poet's memory and imagination. Image creation is the medium through which Dunbar works here: His predominant image, dancing in flames of ruddy light, is an orchard "wrapped in autumn's purple haze."

Dunbar proceeds to create a nature scene which provides a setting for the immortalization of the apple tree. Memory takes the persona to the scene, but imagination re-creates events and feelings. The speaker in the poem admits that it probably appears ugly "When you look the tree all over/ Unadorned by memory's glow." The tree has become old and crooked, and it bears inferior fruit. Thus, without the nostalgic recall, the tree does not appear special at all.

Utilizing the imaginative frame, the speaker designs features of the simple rustic life, features which are typically British Romantic and peculiarly Wordsworthian. The "quiet, sweet seclusion" realized as one hides under the shelter of the tree and the idle dreaming in which one engages dangling in a swing from the tree are primary among these thoughts. Most memorable to the speaker is the solitary contentment he and his sweetheart found as they courted beneath the old apple tree.

> Now my gray old wife is Hallie,
> An I'm grayer still than she,
> But I'll not forget our courtin'
> 'Neath the old apple-tree.

The poet's ultimate purpose, to immortalize the apple tree, is fulfilled in the last stanza. The old apple tree will never lose its place in nature or its significance, for the speaker asks:

> But when death does come a-callin',
> This my last request shall be,—
> That they'll bury me an' Hallie
> 'Neath the old apple-tree.

The union of man and nature at the culmination of physical life approaches a notion expressed in Wordsworth's poetry. This tree has symbolized the ultimate in goodness and universal harmony; it symbolizes the peace, contentment, and joy in the speaker's life. Here Dunbar's indebtedness to the Romantic traditions that inform his entire oeuvre is most profoundly felt.

OTHER MAJOR WORKS

LONG FICTION: *The Uncalled*, 1898; *The Love of Landry*, 1900; *The Fanatics*, 1901; *The Sport of the Gods*, 1902.

SHORT FICTION: *Folks from Dixie*, 1898; *The Strength of Gideon and Other Stories*, 1900; *In Old Plantation Days*, 1903; *The Heart of Happy Hollow*, 1904.

BIBLIOGRAPHY

Alexander, Eleanor. *Lyrics of Sunshine and Shadow: The Tragic Courtship and Marriage of Paul Laurence Dunbar and Alice Ruth Moore*. Albany: New York University Press, 2001. Traces the tempestuous romance of America's most noted African American literary couple. Assistant professor of history Alexander draws on a love letters, diaries, journals, and autobiographies to tell the story of Dunbar and Moore's tumultuous affair, elopement, Dunbar's abuse of Moore, their passionate marriage, and the violence that ended it. An examination of a celebrated couple in the context of their times, fame, and cultural ideology.

Brawley, Benjamin, *Paul Laurence Dunbar: Poet of His People*. Port Washington, N.Y.: Kennikat Press, 1967. A dated but still useful early biographical and critical study of Dunbar, this book is a reprint of a 1936 edition. After placing Dunbar in his historical context, Brawley gives a chronological overview of Dunbar's life and career, with some general observations about individual poems. Includes some personal correspondence of the poet, as well as an appendix and a bibliography of primary and secondary material.

Gayle, Addison, Jr. *Oak and Ivy: A Biography of Paul Laurence Dunbar*. Garden City, N.Y.: Doubleday, 1971. This study of the life and work of Dunbar focuses particularly on the "mask" of the "Negro poet" that Dunbar assumed while desiring to be a much more serious, innovative poet. Contains excellent discussions of individual poems and short stories, a chronology of Dunbar's life, and a primary and secondary bibliography.

Gentry, Tony. *Paul Laurence Dunbar: Poet*. Los Angeles: Melrose Square, 1993. Covers Dunbar's personal life and his literary accomplishments, with excerpts from his works to exemplify his ideas. Heavily illustrated, providing a sense of his times. Well geared to the needs of younger and student audiences, as well as those new to Dunbar.

Hudson, Gossie Harold. *A Biography of Paul Laurence Dunbar*. Baltimore, Md.: Gateway Press, 1999. In-depth biography with biographical references.

Lawson, Victor. *Dunbar Critically Examined*. Washington, D.C.: Associated Publishers, 1941. Though somewhat dated, Lawson's book provides an excellent introduction to Dunbar's poetry and prose. Attempts to determine Dunbar's significance to American poetry and places him in his historical context, including the earlier and contemporary poetic traditions which influenced him, especially the works of Alfred, Lord Tennyson, and Edgar Allan Poe. Separates the literary and dialect poems for purposes of discussion. The bibliography is short and largely outdated.

Martin, Jay, ed. *A Singer in the Dawn: Reinterpretations of Paul Laurence Dunbar*. New York: Dodd, Mead, 1975. This collection of critical essays and personal reminiscences on Dunbar contains essays by Saunders Redding, Arna Bontemps, Darwin T. Turner, Dickson D. Bruce, Jr., and others. Four essays are devoted to Dunbar's poetic achievement, with especially important essays on myths about Dunbar's poetry and on Dunbar and the African American folk tradition. Also included are notes, a foreword by Jay Martin, and an afterword by Nikki Giovanni.

Okeke-Ezigbo, Emeka. "Paul Laurence Dunbar: Straightening the Record." *California Library Association Journal* 24 (1980/1981): 481-496. Arguing against the traditional myths concerning Dunbar the man and the poet, Okeke-Ezigbo demonstrates that Dunbar's dialect poetry reveals his condescending attitude toward African Americans. The comparisons between Dunbar and his mentor, James Whitcomb Riley, and literary predecessors such as Robert Burns, Geoffrey Chaucer, and James Russell Lowell help place Dunbar in a literary tradition.

Some references lead to sections of books which include short discussions of Dunbar.

Randall, Dudley. *The Black Poets*. New York: Bantam, 1971. According to Randall, "not only does this book present the full range of Black poetry, but it presents most poets in depths, and in some cases presents aspects of a poet neglected or overlooked before. . . . Turning away from White models and returning to their roots has freed Black poets to create a new poetry. This book records their progress." Dunbar is covered along with most other major plack poets.

Revell, Peter. *Paul Laurence Dunbar*. Boston: Twayne, 1979. An excellent introduction to the life and works of Dunbar, this study is organized according to the genres in which Dunbar wrote: "Poetry in Literary English," "Poetry in Dialect," "Black Theater," "The Short Stories," and "The Novels." Includes analyses of individual poems, both those in literary English and those in dialect, and an assessment of Dunbar as an important figure in African American literary history. Notes, references, and a selected annotated bibliography make this a considerable contribution to Dunbar scholarship.

Wagner, Jean. "Paul Laurence Dunbar." In *Black Poets of the United States from Paul Laurence Dunbar to Langston Hughes*, translated by Kenneth Douglas. Urbana: University of Illinois Press, 1973. After a lengthy introduction placing Dunbar in his historical context as an African American poet, Wagner devotes an entire chapter of this important work to Dunbar's poetry. Gives an excellent overview of Dunbar's career as a poet and some quite useful analyses of individual poems. Includes a short bibliography of secondary materials on Dunbar.

Patricia A. R. Williams;
bibliography updated by the editors

WILLIAM DUNBAR

Born: Lothian, Scotland; c. 1460
Died: Scotland(?); c. 1525

PRINCIPAL POETRY

"The Thrissill and the Rois," 1503
"The Dance of the Sevin Deidly Synnis," c. 1503-1508
"The Goldyn Targe," c. 1508
"Lament for the Makaris," c. 1508
"The Tretis of the Tua Mariit Wemen and the Wedo," c. 1508
The Poems of William Dunbar, 1884-1893 (John Small, editor)
The Poems of William Dunbar, 1892-1894 (Jakob Schipper, editor)
The Poems of William Dunbar, 1932 (W. MacKay Mackenzie, editor)
Poems, 1958 (James Kinsley, editor)
The Poems of William Dunbar, 1979 (James Kinsley, editor)
The Poems of William Dunbar, 1998 (Priscilla Bawcutt, editor)

OTHER LITERARY FORMS

There is no evidence that William Dunbar wrote in any genre other than short poetry.

ACHIEVEMENTS

William Dunbar has traditionally been grouped with Robert Henryson, Gavin Douglas, Sir David Lyndsay, and James I of Scotland, author of *The Kingis Quair* (1423-1424, *The King's Choir*), as a "Scottish Chaucerian," because he often used Geoffrey Chaucer's metrical forms and poetic conventions. He may also be considered a Chaucerian in the sense that he and his contemporaries, both in England and Scotland, acknowledged a large debt to Chaucer, the "flower of rhetoricians," who, they believed, raised the English language to a status equal to that of Latin and French, where it could be used for both philosophy and literature. Thus, the Chaucerians felt that one of their important duties was to consolidate this new status by practicing a highly ornate rhetoric, and Dunbar's rhetoric was as self-consciously artful as anyone's. At the same time, however, Dunbar was never a slavish imitator of the great English poet. Indeed, there are more than a few differences between them. Whereas Chaucer was an accomplished storyteller, Dunbar wrote mainly short lyrical poems. Whereas Chaucer was a sensitive creator of literary characters, Dunbar's interests lay elsewhere, and so his characters are never as fully developed. Finally, although Chaucer wrote warm human comedy, the tone of his work is quite different from that of Dunbar's raucous grotesqueries.

One of Dunbar's most noticeable poetic qualities is his professionalism, for he took his job as *makar*, the Scots term for "poet," very seriously. Like his fellow Scots poets, Dunbar had a highly developed sense of the different kinds of poetry that were possible, and thus he cultivated several different poetic forms and levels of language, each of which was chosen expressly to fit differing situations. He was much more a poetic virtuoso than were his contemporaries to the south, and in his small corpus one finds everything from the lowest scatological abuse to the most ornate high-minded panegyric. Furthermore, Dunbar had a gift for picking the correct meter, which he chose from a very extensive repertoire. Finally, Dunbar composed easily on at least three different levels of language: In his eldritch or bawdy poems, he used a very exaggerated Scots voice; in his moral poetry, he used a more normal speaking voice; and in his courtly or panegyric poems, he used a highly literate, aureate voice.

While his lyrical variety looks forward to the Renaissance, Dunbar is more often seen as coming at the end of the long medieval poetic tradition, for his work is usually rooted in traditional forms and themes. Moreover, though his poems may be called lyrical because of their short length and strong musical quality, they are not the products of personal emotion recollected in tranquillity. Dunbar was always a public poet; one never sees him in literary undress. Indeed, Dunbar's interests did not lie with presenting philosophical or moral concepts; still less was he interested in exploring his own emotional depths. He was interested, rather, in presenting traditional materials in highly finished packages. Following medieval thought on poetics, he considered himself primarily a rhetorician, and he wanted his poetry either to explode like colorful and noisy fireworks or to sit "enamelled," "gilded," and "refined," like a delicate piece of china, a precise and static work of art. In short, Dunbar was more concerned with language than with content, and for this reason his poetry has been called a poetry of surface effects. Commenting on Dunbar's unbounded vitality, C. S. Lewis once remarked: "If you like half-tones and nuances you will not enjoy Dunbar; he will deafen you."

BIOGRAPHY

How much one claims to know about the life of William Dunbar depends on how much one is willing to trust the claims to be found in his poems, for very little external evidence remains. From Dunbar's poetry, for example, John W. Baxter in his book *William Dunbar: A Biographical Study* (1952) surmises that the poet was descended from the noble house of Dunbar, the earls of which were both powerful and controversial figures in the history of Scotland. Descendants of a Northumbrian earl, Cospatrick, they more than once sided with the English in quarrels between the two countries. In 1402, for example, Henry Dunbar, earl of March, piqued over losses in a personal controversy with the earl of Douglas, aided King Henry IV of England at the Battle of Homildon Hill, thus earning his family the enmity of James I of Scotland, who stripped the clan of most of its lands. If Dunbar had noble blood, then he belonged to a family whose fortunes had fallen considerably.

However that may be, in many of his poems, Dunbar does speak distastefully of the lower classes and of social climbers. In "To the King" ("Schir, yit remember as befoir"), the poet calls himself a "gentill goishalk." This may be significant since the birds of prey were often associated with the nobility in medieval poetry, as, for example, in Chaucer's *Parlement of Foules* (1380). Furthermore, in the same poem Dunbar complains that while still a youth he was thought headed for a bishopric, but upon achieving maturity he stated, "A sempill vicar I can not be." In short, the tone of many of his poems seems to be that of a frustrated aristocrat.

Dunbar appears to have had a good education, and here again there is much speculation as to exactly where he received it. It was customary for Scottish students of the time to study on the Continent, especially at the University of Paris, but there is absolutely no evidence that Dunbar ever studied there. Again, though Dunbar wrote a poem on Oxford, it is doubtful that he ever attended that university. Rather, it is likely that he wrote his poem while visiting Oxford in 1501, when he helped to arrange James IV's marriage to Margaret Tudor, the daughter of Henry VII of England. On the other hand, records of St. Andrew's University in Scotland show that a William Dunbar, probably the poet, received a bachelor of arts degree there in 1477 and his licentiate in 1479.

Evidently not independently wealthy, Dunbar chose a vocation in the church and was ordained a priest later in life. The accounts of the lord high treasurer of Scotland show that he was given a sum of four pounds eighteen shillings in 1504 as a gift for his first Mass. Moreover, Dunbar spent most of his life waiting for a benefice—a grant of land and a parish from which he could make his living. One of Dunbar's poems, "How Dunbar Was Desired to be a Friar," has led some to speculate that the poet spent part of his early life as a traveling Franciscan novice. In the poem, a devil in the guise of St. Francis appears to Dunbar in a dream, exhorting him to take up the Franciscan habit. Dunbar, however, will have none of it, and he retorts that, if he must take a religious habit, he will take that of a bishop, for he has read in "holy legends" that more bishops than friars have become saints. Moreover—and this is the tantalizing part—he claims to have already worn the Franciscan habit all over England and France, to have preached openly, and also to have picked up "many a trick and wile" of the friars, who are "always ready to beguile men." Now, however, those days are long past, says the poet, and he is content to live a more honest life. Whether this poem is a reliable autobiographical document or merely an antifraternal jape cannot be determined.

That Dunbar moved in the aristocratic circles of the court of James IV can be determined. Beginning in 1500, Dunbar was awarded an annual pension of ten pounds per year from the king until he should receive a benefice worth at least forty pounds annually. In 1507, this amount was raised to twenty pounds per year, and in 1510, the poet was awarded a very substantial increase to eighty pounds annually. As a rough measure of what these sums were worth, Baxter reports that, when he was receiving a pension of ten pounds, Dunbar was on the same level as the king's steward and clerk of accounts. When he received a pension of twenty pounds, Dunbar

was raised above all other members of the royal household except the keeper of the king's silver vessels. His pension of eighty pounds raised the poet above even the principal of King's College, Hector Boece. Thus, despite Dunbar's frequent complaints to the contrary, he was well appreciated and rewarded by King James.

From these generous pensions and from his occasional court poetry such as "To Princess Margaret" and "The Ballade of Barnard Stewart Lord of Aubigny," one can infer that Dunbar held the position of unofficial poet laureate. Indeed, when the printing press was finally introduced into Scotland in 1507 by Walter Chepman and Andrew Myllar, Dunbar's poems were among the first writings to be printed.

Entries for Dunbar in the royal records cease in 1513. In June of that year, Henry VIII invaded France, and James IV, responding to calls for help from his old French allies, advanced southward with his armies into England. He met the English at Flodden on September 9, but, although his soldiers fought bravely, he was defeated. Most of the great houses of Scotland lost men in that battle, and the king himself was also killed. In its aftermath, Edinburgh fortified itself against an invasion, but Henry VIII decided not to follow up his victory: The new Scottish king, James V, was the son of Henry's own sister, Margaret, and he thus hoped for better relationships with Scotland. Nevertheless, the defeat was disastrous for the country, and it later led to continuous civil strife.

Dunbar was probably too old to have been among the troops at Flodden, but what became of him after that date is unknown. Did he perhaps finally find his long-awaited benefice, or was his pension simply cut off because of Scotland's financial difficulties? The question is further complicated by the fact that the Treasurer's records are often missing for the years between 1513 and 1529.

One poem, "Quhen the Gouvernour past in Fraunce," is often cited as proof that Dunbar continued to write after 1513, since it refers to the visit to Scotland, from 1515 to 1517, of John Stewart, Duke of Albany, for the purpose of restoring order to the kingdom. Although the poem is ascribed to Dunbar in an important manuscript, however, Dunbar's editor James Kinsley has deleted it from the poet's corpus, partly because "little else that is attributed to him is as clumsy and undistinguished as this." Since many scholars agree with Kinsley, one can safely say that Dunbar seems to have stopped writing about this time. In any case, in 1530 another Scottish poet, Sir David Lyndsay, noted, in his "Testament of the Papyngo," that Dunbar had died. If Lyndsay listed the poets in the order of their death, then Dunbar died before 1522, for that is when Gavin Douglas, the next poet mentioned, died.

ANALYSIS

Because William Dunbar wrote in his native Scots dialect, it is often difficult for modern English speakers to understand his poetry. Middle Scots, the language of the Scottish Lowlanders, was a development from the northern dialects of Middle English. Its rival, the Gaelic tongue spoken by the Highlanders, is a Celtic language related to Welsh, Irish, and Breton. Although his own Scots shows the influence of Gaelic, Dunbar often spoke scornfully of the Celtic tongue, as, for example, when he insulted Walter Kennedy, a Highlander, in "The Flyting of Dunbar and Kennedy."

Nevertheless, Scots did borrow many words from Gaelic, some of which, such as "canny," "dour," and "bairn," have been taken over into standard English. The Middle Scots dialect can be easily recognized by its diction, by certain grammatical forms, and also by certain peculiarities in spelling and pronunciation. For example, Scots used "qu" or "quh" in place of "wh" in such words as "quhat" (what), "quhilk" (which), and "quhen" (when). The dialect also retained the Old English "a" where it had been replaced by a more rounded vowel in the South: "stane" (stone) and "hale" (whole) are good examples. Also, the northern dialects preferred the plosive consonants "g" and "k" where the southerners adopted the softer "y" and "ch" sounds; thus one finds "kirk" for "church," "mikel" for "much," and "yaf" for "gave." These are only the most noteworthy of many dialectical peculiarities, but they will be of some help when one first encounters Dunbar's poetry.

Nowhere is Dunbar's ability with language more evident than in his "The Goldyn Targe." Although he draws heavily on medieval allegorical traditions, Dunbar here is less interested in the message of the love allegory than in the language with which it is conveyed. Furthermore,

this display of poetic virtuosity must have been appreciated in his own day, for "The Goldyn Targe" was one of the six poems of Dunbar printed by Chepman and Myllar in 1507, and it was later singled out by Lyndsay in his "Testament of the Papyngo" to prove that Dunbar "language had at large."

"THE GOLDYN TARGE"

"The Goldyn Targe" can be placed in the tradition of *Roman de la Rose* (*The Romance of the Rose*), a long narrative poem written some time in the thirteenth century by the poets Guillaume de Lorris and Jean de Meung. All the action of the French poem takes place in a dream; the characters are all personifications; and even the settings carry allegorical meanings: The idealized garden represents the life at court, and the rose-plot symbolizes the mind of a young lady. *The Romance of the Rose* was thus a psychological exposition of courtly love.

Although there is some disagreement as to whether courtly love was ever actually practiced or whether it was simply a literary convention, the idea sprang up in the eleventh century in the songs of the French troubadours. Chrétien de Troyes's Lancelot and Guinevere are perhaps the best known courtly lovers, though others such as Tristan and Iseult or Chaucer's Troilus and Criseyde could also be cited. The behavior of the lovers was highly codified in this system, with the woman holding the ascendancy. For his part, the man was to be humble, discreet, and courteous, complying with each whim of his mistress. How does one fall in love, and what are its results? Poems such as "The Goldyn Targe" attempted to explain the process through allegory.

Walking through an idealized garden on a fresh May morning, the narrator of "The Goldyn Targe" soon tires, falls asleep, and has a marvelous dream. He spies a beautiful ship laden with a hundred gods and goddesses from antiquity led by Nature and Venus. They are a merry group, dressed entirely in green, a color symbolic of youth, freshness, and vigor. When the Dreamer tries to get a better look at them, however, he is suddenly caught by Venus, who for no apparent reason orders her "troops" to attack him. The attacking platoons are made up of personified feminine qualities such as Beauty, Delight, and Fine Appearance.

The Dreamer is protected from this onslaught for a time by Reason, wielding his golden shield and successfully repelling all the missiles shot by the attackers. Reason is overcome, however, by Presence, who sneaks up and throws a blinding powder into the eyes of the warrior. Thus, Reason is defeated, and the Dreamer is soon enslaved by Venus. The effect of the victory is short-lived, however, for the goddesses and their partners depart as quickly as they came, leaving the Dreamer in a state of despair. A final trumpet blast from the ship wakens the Dreamer, who again finds himself back in the idealized countryside. The poem closes with a panegyric to Chaucer, John Gower, and John Lydgate, and with an envoy in which Dunbar sends his "lytill quair [book]" forth into the world, where it must be obedient to all.

The use of the panegyric and the envoy reinforce the fact that Dunbar was thoroughly grounded in medieval poetic conventions. Chaucer, for example, used much the same sort of envoy in his *Troilus and Criseyde* (c. 1382). Unlike Chaucer, however, Dunbar was not fundamentally interested in the story, his two-dimensional characters, or the obvious moral that the passions must be controlled by the higher faculty of reason, which, unfortunately, is not always invincible. The poem's greatness, then, necessarily lies in Dunbar's masterful use of language. His smooth iambic pentameter lines are grouped into nine-line stanzas, rhyming *aabaabbab*, the very difficult form which Chaucer first employed in *Anelida and Arcite* (c. 1380). Moreover, though Dunbar could use only two different rhymes per stanza, nowhere did that seem to pose any great difficulties for him.

The highly wrought surface of Dunbar's poem is very clearly seen in his descriptions of the garden. What is created here, in the words of Edmund Reiss (*William Dunbar*, 1979), is "a world combining heaven and earth, one showing nature in idealized, purified, and rarefied splendor." Take, for example, these lines from the second and third stanzas:

> *Anamalit* was the felde wyth all colouris
> The *perly* droppis schake in *silvir* schouris,
>
> . . . .
>
> The *purpur* hevyn, ourscailit in *silvir* sloppis,
>   [with silver trailing clouds scattered about]
> *Ourgilt* [gilded over] the treis, branchis, lef
>   and barkis. (emphasis added)

Here Dunbar uses aureate terms, together with the recurring images of various gems and precious metals, to create a visionary landscape, reminiscent of Paradise in the Middle English *Pearl* (c. 1350-1380). This is obviously not a personally experienced nature like that of the Romantic poets; Dunbar's nature is founded in the tradition of the *locus amoenus*, an idealized pastoral setting, the characteristics of which had already become standardized in late antiquity.

The word "aureate," signifying a highly wrought style and elevated diction, was coined by the English Chaucerian Lydgate, who borrowed many obscure terms from Latin for the sake of sonority and, hence, for dignifying his subject matter. Whereas Lydgate used his aureate terms basically for religious poetry, Dunbar went well beyond his predecessor and used aureate diction in other types of poems. The use of "artificial" words fit well into medieval poetic theory, and it was not until the nineteenth century, when William Wordsworth began to attack "poetic diction," that "aureate" came to have pejorative connotations.

"THE TRETIS OF THE TUA MARIIT WEMEN AND THE WEDO"

It is a steep descent from the elevated tone and subject matter of "The Goldyn Targe" to the rowdy burlesque of "The Tretis of the Tua Mariit Wemen and the Wedo," though the level of Dunbar's conscious artistry nowhere flags in the latter piece. The poem, written in 530 lines of alliterative verse, begins delicately in the courtly love tradition, but after the first forty lines the reader finds himself thrown into a crude display of female candor, where, in Kinsley's words, "Ideal beauty is exposed as the whited sepulchre of lust and greed."

Walking forth on a midsummer's night, the poet discovers a beautiful little garden, wherein are three courtly ladies, described in the typically idealized way: They all have beautiful blonde hair, white skin, fine features, rich clothing, and jeweled adornment. That they wear green mantles—reminiscent, perhaps, of the gods and goddesses of "The Goldyn Targe"—seems an innocent innovation at this point, but as soon as the poet notes that they "wauchtit" [quaffed] their wine, the reader suspects that something is amiss.

While the narrator discreetly hides, one of the three women, the Widow, sets the dialogue in motion with a *demande d'amour:* "Bewrie [reveal], said the wedo, ye woddit wemen ying,/ Quhat mirth ye fand in maryage sen ye war menis wyffis." She also wishes to know if they have had extramarital affairs; if, given the chance, they would choose another husband; and if they believe the marriage bond to be insoluble. These are hardly the questions one would expect from a "chaste widow," and what follows are hardly the timid responses expected from two modest young wives.

The first is married to an old man who, like Januarius in Chaucer's "The Merchant's Tale" (from *The Canterbury Tales*, 1387-1400), guards her jealously. The lusty young wife, however, reveals that her husband lacks the sexual vitality to satisfy fully her womanly desires, and she nonchalantly confesses that, if she were allowed, she would change husbands yearly, like the birds. For the time being her only satisfaction comes from the many gifts which her husband must give her before she consents to lovemaking.

Here, and in many other parts of this poem, Dunbar employs the style used in "The Flyting of Dunbar and Kennedy" to capture suitably the disgust of this young woman toward her spouse. In this style, a Gaelic poetic tradition, the poet piles up lists of epithets, uses various types of wordplay, and polishes the surface with obtrusive alliteration and rhyme. Generally employed when two poets publicly attacked each other, this style creates a tone that is a mixture of aggression, absurdity, and play. Dunbar's ingenuity and wit are shown when he incongruously transplants this harsh technique into the delicate context of courtly conversation.

The second wife is unhappy as well. Her young husband, though outwardly a ladies' man, is totally worn out from his earlier promiscuous behavior. Thus, she too, using suitably graphic metaphors, attacks her husband, reducing him from "rake" to "snivelling faker," and the three ladies laugh loudly, making "game amang the grene leiffis," and quaff more of the "sueit wyne." The two young wives, and the reader as well, are thus prepared for the presentation of the central character of the poem, the Widow, who is a literary cousin of Chaucer's Wife of Bath. Like Dame Alice, the Widow is both lecherous and proud of it. She is also outspoken, and she preaches the gospel of pleasure openly to her audience. Unlike Dame Alice, however, the Widow has no warmth or humanity; she is thoroughly calculating and vicious.

She begins her "sermon" with a mock invocation to God to send her "sentence," the medieval code word for an edifying moral. Religious parody was not uncommon in medieval literature, and, though Dunbar was a priest, he clearly was having fun here at the expense of the sacred rites. This parody, however, is slight compared to the poet's "The Dregy of Dunbar Maid to King James the Fowrth being in Strivilling," where he constructed a mock liturgical Office of the Dead to tease James out of his Lenten retreat.

This unholy preacher, the Widow, had been married twice: first to an old Januarius type, and then to a middle-aged merchant. She recounts all the cruel steps which she took to divest the merchant completely of both his goods and his masculinity. When he finally died, she felt no regrets at all, for then she could begin to play the field in church, at public gatherings, and on pilgrimages. She describes, for example, how her black widow's veil can be used to cover her face while she surveys the crowds of men "To se quhat berne [fellow] is best brand [muscled] or bredest in schulderis." Using the language of courtly love literature, the Widow confesses to being the common property of all her "servants" (lovers) and to being a nymphomaniac who "comforts" them all. As a good preacher, however, she cannot recount a tale without offering her moral as well: The secret of a happy life is guile. Her counsel to the young wives is neatly summed up in the following: "Be dragonis baith and dowis [doves] ay in double forme." Hence her "sentence" is as neatly packaged as proverbial wisdom, and the end of her tale is similarly furnished with religious terminology: "This is the legeand of my lif, thought Latyne it be nane." The reference here is to saints' lives, a very popular form of literature in her day, even among the laity.

Dunbar resumes the high style of courtly literature as the three women retire, having passed the night in drunken camaraderie. The coming of the new day is as pleasantly described as if the narrator had just witnessed the first tryst of Troilus and Criseyde, but he ends the poem with a final ironic question: "Quhilk wald ye waill [choose] to your wif gif ye suld wed one?"

The characters in "The Tretis of the Tua Mariit Wemen and the Wedo" are so outrageous that one wonders whether the poem could ever be considered serious antifeminist satire. Perhaps Dunbar's intention lay no further than to produce belly laughs from his audience, especially the women. The poem does, however, show Dunbar's skill in blending various medieval traditions: the tradition of the courtly love narrative, the tradition of the eavesdropping narrator, the antifeminist tradition, and the French tradition of *la chanson de la mal mariée* [the song of the unhappy wife].

ANGLO-SAXON ALLITERATION

Not only did Dunbar revive traditional themes, but he also revived, for one of the last times, a very ancient poetic device, the Anglo-Saxon alliterative line used by the poet of *Beowulf* and his contemporaries. This type of poetic line construction was based not on syllable count and not on metrical feet but on the principle of alliteration. The theory was fairly complex, but basically each verse was constructed from two half-lines, separated by a caesura, each having two, or perhaps three, stressed syllables. Ordinarily the first three stressed syllables per line were alliterated. Thus, Dunbar's "Bewŕie, said the wédo/ ye wóddit wémen ying," more than fulfills the requirements, actually adding an unnecessary fourth alliterated syllable. In practice, however, the alliterative line could vary widely in the total number of syllables and in the pattern of stressed alliterations. Moreover, rhyme was normally not used at all as a poetic device.

As Anglo-Saxon evolved into Middle English, chiefly owing to the effects of the Norman Invasion in 1066, alliterative poetry seemed to die out. The French tradition of decasyllabic rhyming verse came to be favored in England; Chaucer, for example, was highly influenced by just such Continental models. His character the Parson, however, does comment on the older verse form in the prologue to his sermon: "But trusteth well, I am a Southern man,/ I kan nat geeste [tell a tale] 'rum, ram, ruf,' by lettre." Nevertheless, there were those in the northwest of England, Chaucer's contemporaries, who could indeed "rum, ram, ruf," and thus English letters experienced an "alliterative revival" in such works as *Sir Gawain and the Green Knight* (c. fourteenth century) and *The Vision of William, Concerning Piers the Plowman* (1362-c. 1393). Dunbar's work, coming as it does roughly one hundred years after

these works, attests not only to a sort of poetic conservatism in Scotland, but also to Dunbar's poetic vigor, which enabled him to revive the old form so successfully.

"THE DANCE OF THE SEVIN DEIDLY SYNNIS"

Another traditional form which Dunbar used with imagination was the tail-rhymed stanza, commonly employed by long-winded medieval romancers and parodied by Chaucer in his "The Tale of Sir Thopas" (from *The Canterbury Tales*). The pattern called for four-beat rhyming couplets separated by three-beat lines in the following manner: *aabccb* (or, if a twelve-line stanza was desired, *aabccbddbeeb*). Dunbar's "The Dance of the Sevin Deidly Synnis," Part I of "Fasternes Evening in Hell," is composed of nine twelve-line stanzas with two additional six-line stanzas interspersed. They form another dream poem, like "The Goldyn Targe," but a strange one. The dream takes place on Fasternes Evening, the last day of the carnival before Lent. During this time the public celebrations included colorful pageants, filled with allegorical figures. Baxter notes that one must place the poem in just such a context, imagining the poet reacting to a group of revelers, costumed to represent sins, devils, fairies, and the like, dancing wildly under torchlight in the streets. Dunbar's poem captures them forever in their frenzy.

Indeed, Dunbar's portrait of the Seven Deadly Sins—Pride, Anger, Envy, Greed, Sloth, Lechery, and Gluttony—is probably the most lively of all the many such medieval portraits. In the poem, the Dreamer sees "Mahoun" (Satan) give orders for a dance in Hell, to which the personified vices immediately respond. The context explains why Dunbar's portraits are fairly realistic, and also why, perhaps, Dunbar took the opportunity to poke fun at his Highland foes. In the last stanza, Mahoun orders a Highland pageant to add some additional music to the festivities. Their Gaelic clatter, however, is too much even for Mahoun, who banishes them to the "depest pit of hell."

"LAMENT FOR THE MAKARIS"

An artistic cousin of the "The Dance of the Sevin Deidly Synnis" is perhaps the *danse macabre*, another medieval commonplace. In painting and in verse this motif shows the skeletons of people of all social classes dancing together as equals—in death. Dunbar takes up this theme in his poem "Lament for the Makaris," which Kinsley calls "one of the great elegiac expressions of a melancholy age." No longer the brazen poet of "The Tretis of the Tua Mariit Wemen and the Wedo" nor the frenetic poet of "The Dance of the Sevin Deidly Synnis," Dunbar here is saddened, pensive, and grave.

The poem is written in twenty-five stanzas of two tetrameter couplets each, a form which in Old French was called the *kyrielle*. The last line of each stanza is a Latin quotation from the Office of the Dead, "*Timor mortis conturbat me*" (The fear of death alarms me), a refrain that was often heard in an age of frequent war, great poverty, and the Black Plague. Lydgate, for example, used the same refrain in the poem entitled "*Timor Mortis Conturbat Me*," and it was probably Dunbar's model. Dunbar's poem, however, is much more compact and understated, and, as Gregory Kratzmann notes in *Anglo-Scottish Literary Relations, 1430-1550* (1980), these very qualities help give the poem the rhythm of a sober death dance.

The movement of the poem is from the universal to the particular. It begins with the sublunary principle that "Our plesance heir is all vane glory,/ This fals warld is bot transitory"; continues through a catalog of the various classes and professions, noting especially the deaths of his fellow poets; and concludes with the realization that his own death must be close at hand. By including the catalog of his fellow poets, Dunbar particularizes, and thus makes more poignant, this melancholy poetic form.

Dunbar's creativity, shown very well in "Lament for the Makaris," is manifest throughout his works; he seems always able to reinvest older poetic forms with new vigor. He is a poet of high energy, but not of inchoate effusions, for his power is always tightly controlled, each enameled word fitting carefully into a well-wrought framework. Variety is also a characteristic of Dunbar's work. His poetry always has a musical quality to it, for he was a master versifier with an extremely varied repertoire of patterns at his command. Even so, one might be forgiven for clinging to an image of Dunbar composing only his most energetic pieces, since, like his personified Deadly Sins, he seems always ready, in a literary sense, to "kast up gamountis [gambols] in the skyis."

BIBLIOGRAPHY

Bawcutt, Priscilla. *Dunbar the Makar.* New York: Oxford University Press, 1992. A comprehensive critical study of Dunbar's works. Includes a bibliography and an index.

_____. "William Dunbar and Gavin Douglas." In *The History of Scottish Literature: Origins to 1660 (Medieval and Renaissance)*. Vol. 1, edited by R. D. S. Jack and Cairns Craig. Aberdeen: Aberdeen University Press, 1988. Demonstrates the poet's debt to his Scottish predecessors. Notes the differences between Dunbar and Gavin Douglas, who were similar in terms of the lengths of their works, the subjects about which they wrote, and the total works they composed. Includes notes and works for further reading and lists primary and secondary sources.

Baxter, J. W. *William Dunbar: A Biographical Study.* Edinburgh, Scotland: Oliver & Boyd, 1952. Perhaps the seminal introductory volume of commentary on Dunbar, this work traces the poet's life and comments on his poems. Each of its sixteen chapters is highlighted by additional notes. This volume contains six appendices that range from Dunbar's textual sources to examinations of poems believed to be composed by Dunbar. Contains an extensive bibliography of primary and secondary sources and two indexes. The first index refers to individual poems in the volume; the second is a general index.

Davidoff, Judith M. "William Dunbar's Framing Fiction Poems." In *Beginning Well.* Cranbury, N.J.: Associated University Presses, 1988. In this interesting and novel chapter, Dunbar's parodies of traditional literary forms are discussed. Of particular importance is the demonstration of Dunbar's proficiency in handling traditional literary patterns in "The Goldyn Targe" and the observation that Dunbar comically turns old conventions to original uses.

Reiss, Edmund. "The Ironic Art of William Dunbar." In *Fifteenth Century Studies*, edited by Robert F. Yeager. Hamden, Conn.: Archon Books, 1984. While this study is brief, it offers insight concerning the eclectic nature of Dunbar's poems. These variations are introduced and distinguished in short order; the result is a precise compendium for further study.

The work's extensive notes provide a good starting point for anyone interested in Dunbar.

_____. *William Dunbar*. Boston: Twayne, 1979. One of Twayne's English Authors series. The six chapters in this important work are devoted to the various stages and writing styles in the literary career of Dunbar. The work traces his growth from court poet to Christian moralist and to writer of love poems and offers precise explication of many of his works. Contains a brief chronology of important dates and events in Dunbar's life, thorough notes and references, a short select bibliography that lists primary and secondary sources (including general studies, bibliographies, books, and articles), and a thorough index.

Scott, Tom. *Dunbar: A Critical Exposition of the Poems*. Edinburgh: Edinburgh University Press, 1966. Perhaps the definitive critical work on the poems of Dunbar. This study concentrates on the sociocultural milieu of Dunbar. Its primary importance is its value as a contextual approach to the works of Dunbar.

Waller, Gary. "Dunbar and Wyatt." In *Early Poetry of the Sixteenth Century*. London: Longman, 1986. This study remarks on the simplicity of the works of Dunbar and the impact which the English monarchy had on the Scottish court and its poets. It also gives a brief account of his life. This chapter is a small gem in a mine of information. Waller's work contains a concise chronology, a general bibliography, and notes on individual authors touched upon in the book.

Gregory M. Sadlek;
bibliography updated by the editors

ROBERT DUNCAN

Born: Oakland, California; January 7, 1919
Died: San Francisco, California; February 3, 1988

PRINCIPAL POETRY
Heavenly City, Earthly City, 1947
Poems, 1948-1949, 1950

Medieval Scenes, 1950 (reprinted as *Medieval Scenes 1950 and 1959*)
Fragments of a Disordered Devotion, 1952
Caesar's Gate: Poems, 1948-1950, 1956
Letters: Poems MCMLIII-MCMLVI, 1958
Selected Poems, 1959
The Opening of the Field, 1960
Writing, Writing: A Composition Book for Madison 1953, Stein Imitations, 1964
Roots and Branches, 1964
Passages 22-27 of the War, 1966
The Years as Catches: First Poems (1939-1946), 1966
Six Prose Pieces, 1966
A Book of Resemblances: Poems, 1950-1953, 1966
Epilogos, 1967
Names of People, 1968
Bending the Bow, 1968
The First Decade: Selected Poems, 1940-1950, 1969

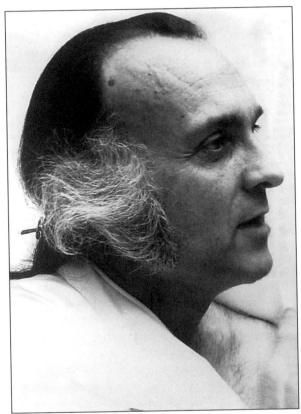

Robert Duncan (Matthew Foley, courtesy of New Directions Publishing)

Derivations: Selected Poems, 1950-1956, 1969
Achilles' Song, 1969
Play Time: Pseudo Stein, 1969
Poetic Disturbances, 1970
Tribunals: Passages 31-35, 1970
Ground Work, 1971
Poems from the Margins of Thom Gunn's "Moly," 1972
A Seventeenth Century Suite in Homage to the Metaphysical Genius in English Poetry, 1590/1690, 1973
An Ode and Arcadia, 1974 (with Jack Spicer)
Dante, 1974
The Venice Poem, 1975
Veil, Turbine, Cord, and Bird, 1979
The Five Songs, 1981
Ground Work: Before the War, 1984
A Paris Visit, 1985
Ground Work II: In the Dark, 1987

OTHER LITERARY FORMS

Besides the poetic oeuvre, Robert Duncan produced a limited but essential corpus of essays concerning both his own work and life, and the work of those other writers important to him. Although *The Truth and Life of Myth: An Essay in Essential Autobiography* (1968) was published separately, it also opens the volume of his collected essays, *Fictive Certainties* (1985), and constitutes a major touchstone for an understanding of Duncan's work. "Towards an Open Universe" and "Man's Fulfillment in Order and Strife," also gathered in the same collection, are essential statements on poetics and politics. "The H. D. Book," first conceived as a study of the poetry of H. D. (Hilda Doolittle), became an encyclopedic investigation of mythopoesis and modernism, eighteen sections of which appeared in magazines during the late 1960's and 1970's. Other titles include *The Sweetness and Greatness of Dante's "Divine Comedy"* (1965) and *As Testimony: The Poem and The Scene* (1964). Duncan is also the author of two plays, *Faust Foutu: An Entertainment in Four Parts* (1959) and *Medea at Kolchis: The Maidenhead* (1965). Duncan was a spell-binding reader of his own work as well as a truly phenomenal raconteur: A multitude of tapes preserved either in private hands or in university archives bear witness to this,

and future transcriptions of his talks and interviews will provide major additions to, and commentaries on, the oeuvre as it now stands.

ACHIEVEMENTS

Because of his erudition, his sense of poetic tradition, his mastery of a variety of poetic forms, and, most important, his profoundly metaphysical voice, Robert Duncan is a major contemporary poet. "Each age requires a new confession," Ralph Waldo Emerson declared, and Duncan presents his era with a voice it cannot afford to ignore. While Duncan called himself a derivative poet, revealing his penetrating readings of Dante, Walt Whitman, Ralph Waldo Emerson, William Shakespeare, William Blake, and others, at the same time he generated contemporary visions, Emersonian prospects of discovery and renewal. An impressive collection of more than thirty volumes of poetry, drama, and prose constitutes Duncan's literary achievement. His serious notion of the role of the poet is evident in his many statements about his work, including the prefaces to such works as *The Truth and Life of Myth* and "The H. D. Book." Duncan wrote in a wide range of voices, including a bardic, visionary persona of high seriousness and metaphysical concerns, but he never lost his wit and joy in language-play. Not only was he a masterful lyricist, capable of penetrating epiphanies such as "Roots and Branches," but also he excelled in longer closed forms such as the serial poem ("Apprehensions," "The Continent") and the symphonic form of *The Venice Poem*. Finally, Duncan did some of his finest work in the form that is America's most distinctive contribution to world poetry in the twentieth century: the long, open-ended poem that can accommodate an encyclopedia if need be. Duncan's ongoing open poems, "The Structure of Rime" and "Passages," are in the tradition of Ezra Pound's *Cantos* (beginning in 1925), William Carlos Williams's *Paterson* (1946-1958), Louis Zukofsky's *"A"* (1927-1978), and Charles Olson's *The Maximus Poems* (1960).

BIOGRAPHY

Robert Duncan was born Edward Howard Duncan in Oakland, California, on January 7, 1919, to Edward Howard and Marguerite Wesley Duncan. His mother died shortly after his birth, and his father was forced to put him up for adoption. His foster parents, "orthodox Theosophists," chose him on the basis of his astrological configuration. Duncan grew up as Robert Edward Symmes and published some two dozen poems under that name before resuming his original surname in 1942. The hermetic lore imparted by his family and the fables and nursery rhymes of his childhood constitute a major influence on his work.

He attended the University of California at Berkeley from 1936 to 1938, publishing his first poems in the school's literary magazine, *The Occident*, and joining a circle of friends that included Mary and Lilli Fabilli, Virginia Admiral, and Pauline Kael. For several years he lived in the East, associating with the circle of Anaïs Nin in New York City and with a group of poets in Woodstock which included Sanders Russell and Jack Johnson. Receiving a psychiatric discharge from the army in 1941, he continued publishing poems, and with Virginia Admiral edited *Ritual* (later *Experimental Review*). In 1944, he published his courageous essay, "The Homosexual in Society," in *Politics*.

Returning to Berkeley in 1946, he studied medieval and Renaissance culture and worked with Kenneth Rexroth, Jack Spicer, and Robin Blaser. In 1951 he began his continuing relationship with painter Jess Collins. Duncan directly addresses the significance of his homosexuality to his art: "Perhaps the sexual irregularity underlay and led to the poetic; neither as homosexual nor as poet could one take over the accepted paradigms and conventions of the Protestant ethic."

In 1952, he began publishing in *Origin* and then in the *Black Mountain Review*. In the mid-1950's he taught briefly at Black Mountain College, further developing his relationship with Charles Olson, whose important essay, "Projective Verse," had been published in 1950. Duncan remains the strongest link between the Black Mountain poets and the San Francisco Renaissance, although the name of such "schools" must be highly elastic to include such diverse poets as Olson, Robert Creeley, Ed Dorn, Allen Ginsberg, Lawrence Ferlinghetti, and Duncan.

The 1960's saw the publication of three major collections, the intense involvement with the poetry of H. D., and the writing of "The H. D. Book," as well as Duncan's strong commitment to antiwar politics, as evidenced in the "Passages" series of poems. By the early 1970's, his reputation had grown beyond the borders of the United States, and he often toured, giving poetry readings and publishing his works in Europe and elsewhere. In 1968, frustrated by his publishers' inability or unwillingness to print his work according to his own specifications, Duncan announced that he would let fifteen years elapse before publishing another major collection, although small, often private printings of work in progress would continue to appear throughout the 1970's and early 1980's. In 1983, he won the Shelley Memorial Award. In 1984, New Directions published *Ground Work: Before the War*, typeset under the poet's direct supervision. This volume was nominated for the National Book Critics Circle Award and won a National Poetry Award for Duncan. *Ground Work II: In the Dark* followed in 1987, only a few months before the poet's death in February, 1988.

ANALYSIS

Of the many metaphors that Robert Duncan applied to his poetry—and very few poets have been so perceptive and articulate about their own practice—those dealing with limits, boundaries, and margins are numerous and permit a coherent if partial survey of his complex work. Such references are frequent in his poetry and are rooted in his life and his way of seeing. Living in San Francisco, at the edge of the North American continent, Duncan was acutely sensitive to the centrifugal pressures of his culture. Having been an adopted child, his identity and very name were under question during his early years. As a homosexual, he felt distanced from "the accepted paradigms and conventions of the Protestant ethic." As a Theosophist, his way of thinking had been influenced by similarly unconventional assumptions. His very vision blurs distinctions and identities: He was cross-eyed, a way of seeing which he eloquently explored in such poems as "A Poem Slow Beginning" and "Crosses of Harmony and Disharmony," and which he relates to Alfred North Whitehead's "presentational immediacy."

Duncan referred to himself as "the artist of the margin," and the term is basic to an understanding of his vision and poetics. While the concept can be traced to a number of eclectic and overlapping influences, William James's *Principles of Psychology* (1890), with its theme of the fluidity of consciousness, provides an instructive point of departure. For James, with his great interest in the "penumbra" of experience, "life is at the transitions." As he says in "A World of Pure Experience," "Our fields of experience have no more definite boundaries than have our fields of view. Both are fringed forever by a *more* that continuously develops and that continuously supersedes them as life proceeds." For Duncan as for James, life is at the edge, at the point of relationship, surprise, novelty—at the transgression of boundaries. Conceiving the universe as a constant rhythm between order and disorder, both writers (with Whitehead and John Dewey) maintained that order develops. Rejecting the extreme poles of a world of mere flux without any stability and a static world without crisis, such a worldview embraces the moment of passage as that of most intense life. Appropriately, Duncan's major ongoing poem is entitled the "Passages Poems." Primary here too is John Keats's notion of "negative capability," an acceptance of "uncertainties, mysteries, doubts, without any irritable reaching after fact and reason." Indeed, Duncan defines Romanticism as "the intellectual adventure of not knowing."

Duncan was fully cognizant of the implications that such ideas have for his poetics, scoffing in *The Truth and Life of Myth* at the "sensory debunkers" who "would protect our boundaries, the very shape of what we are, by closing our minds to the truth." The poet's charge is to challenge the boundaries of convention, with direct impact on his poetry's form: "Back of each poet's concept of the poem is his concept of the meaning of form itself; and his concept of form in turn where it is serious at all arises from his concept of the nature of the universe." Duncan's poetry challenges the boundaries of conventional ideas and conventional forms. He speaks of his poetry as a collage, an especially appropriate form for a poetry which incessantly interrogates boundaries, edges, identities. "The great art of our time," he says in "The H. D. Book," "is the collagist's art, to bring all things into new complexes of meaning."

The theme appears early in his work, developing in the poems of the 1940's and 1950's. From the first decade, in "Heavenly City, Earthly City," the poet as

a "man in the solitude of his poetic form/ finds his self-consciousness defined/ by the boundaries of a non-committal sea." He apostrophizes the Pacific Ocean as an "Insistent questioner of our shores!" "A Congregation," similarly, sounds early poetic concerns of field, order, disorder, and fragmentation. In "The Festival," the fifth poem in *Medieval Scenes*, a strong early series, Duncan uses the motif of the dream to explore the unclear distinctions between wakefulness and sleep and, by extension, between ecstasy and madness, inspiration and inflated foolishness, the unicorn and the ass.

A pervasive concern with boundaries and limits is apparent in "The Venice Poem" (1948), Duncan's first indisputably major poem. In this work, based on Igor Stravinsky's *Symphony in Three Movements*, Duncan relates Berkeley to Venice and links his own lost love and self-questioning to the frustrations of Othello and Desdemona. The awareness of limits and edges crystallizes in a description of an image's coming into being: "She hesitates upon the verge of sound./ She waits upon a sounding impossibility,/ upon the edge of poetry." The final poem collected in *The First Decade*, "The Song of the Borderguard," announces by its very title Duncan's increasing awareness of transgressed boundaries: "The borderlines of sense in the morning light/ are naked as a line of poetry in a war."

The 1950's were productive years; poems written during that period include those published in *Derivations*; *Writing, Writing*; and *Letters*. While many of these poems are all too explicitly derivative, Duncan reprints them as testimony to his roots and his past. In his 1972 preface to *Caesar's Gate*, Duncan does not use Ezra Pound's term *periplum*, but his description of the writing conveys something of the sense of a poetry "fearfully and with many errors making its way . . . seeking to regain a map in the actual." The first poem collected in *Derivations*, "An Essay at War," opens with a description of the poem "constantly/ under reconstruction," as "a proposition in movement." The poem contrasts the foolish ad hoc "design" of war itself with the imperfect pattern or design of a poem true to a changing experience. The preface to *Letters* argues that a poet's process is one of revision and disorganization which takes place at the threshold. "I attempt the discontinuities of poetry," he announces, opening gaps which "introduce the peril of beauty." While cynics assume that such poetry must be inflated or impossible and while traditionalists abhor his assumption of a godlike role, Duncan answers both in deft lyrics such as "An Owl Is an Only Bird of Poetry," whose sure and witty inclusiveness articulates both design and disorder. Two poems near the end of *Letters*, "Changing Trains" and "The Language of Love," specifically employ the imagery of border-crossing and entering new territory, clear harbingers of Duncan's major phase.

While the early books are significant achievements, Duncan's reputation rests primarily on three major books of poetry published in the 1960's, *The Opening of the Field, Roots and Branches*, and *Bending the Bow*. Each is a unified whole rather than a collection of poems, and each manifests and extends Duncan's use of the theme of boundaries and margins.

THE OPENING OF THE FIELD

The terms of *The Opening of the Field* are proposed in the title, and the book's first and last poems reveal Duncan's awareness of beginnings and endings as they affect this book and much more. "Often I Am Permitted to Return to a Meadow" establishes the basic metaphor of the book, of poetry as an entry into a field of essences, "a scene made-up by the mind,/ that is not mine, but is a made place,/ that is mine." Granted entry into this field of poetic activity, the poet participates in the grand poem through his individual poems. Within this meadow, "the shadows that are forms fall," and in an act of faith ("as if"), the poet accepts it as a "given property of the mind/ that certain bounds hold against chaos." The poems seem to delineate boundaries or fields of order against chaos, but they *only* seem to do so because in the larger view Duncan has of poetry and the universe, chaos or disorder are parts of a larger order. The real boundary of this poem, then, is between a state of awareness and its absence. Delineating that boundary, or more fundamentally recognizing the difference, is the responsibility of the poet. In the "disturbance of words within words," the poet's poems are constructs, architectures, flowers which turn into "flames lit to the lady." The limits and definitions of physical reality must give way before the reality of the visionary imagination.

Duncan returns to these images—indeed he never leaves them—in the final poem of this book, "Food for Fire, Food for Thought," in which he self-consciously comments on the paradox of a last poem in an open poetics: "This is what I wanted for the last poem,/ a loosening of conventions and a return to open form." The attempt to define or limit is frustrating and necessarily progressive rather than definitive. The activity, however, is the poet's preoccupation: "We trace faces in the clouds: they drift apart,/ palaces of air—the sun dying down/ sets them on fire." Fire is the concluding image, again transformed into a flower, as an "unlikely heat/ at the edge of our belief bud[s] forth." In these two poems and those in between, Duncan explores the shifting borderlines between essence and form, childhood and adulthood, flame and flower. Even as Leonardo da Vinci did, he sees "figures that were stains upon a wall" as he operates "at the edge of our belief."

The Opening of the Field includes "A Poem Beginning with a Line by Pindar," perhaps Duncan's best-known poem. Beginning with a misreading of a line from the third Pythian Ode, the poem then proclaims his recognition of a "god-step at the margins of thought." The poem is a mosaic or collage of images playing between light and dark, Cupid-sensuality and Psyche-spirituality, East and West, past and present, and it cannot be summarized here. The fourth section begins, "O yes! Bless the footfall where/ step by step the boundary walker," echoing the footstep of the poem's opening, informs and clarifies the poet's memories and experiences. The poet, as a boundary walker, must be attuned to the elusive image or inspiration, even to a felicitous misreading of Pindar.

Other poems directly addressing the theme of boundaries include "After Reading *Barely and Widely*," a book by Louis Zukofsky, and the series "The Structure of Rime," in the second of which the poet interrogates the nature of poetry. "What is the Structure of Rime? I asked," and he is told, "*An absolute scale of resemblance and disresemblance establishes measures that are music in the actual world.*" Such a recognition of pervasive correspondences and rhymes inspires confidence in the face of difficulties and risks inherent in such poetry. In the eighth of the series, the poet is permitted to crawl through "interstices of Earth" in realizing the possible "from a nexus in the Impossible." The entire series, continuing in subsequent books and intersecting at times with other series, addresses major questions of poetry and reality.

ROOTS AND BRANCHES

Again, *Roots and Branches* enunciates in its title the basic metaphor of the book, "the ramifications below and above the trunk of vegetative life." The title lyric, one of Duncan's best, describes his delight in a monarch butterfly whose flight traces out an imaginary tree, "unseen roots and branches of sense/ I share in thought." The poet's epiphany, inspired by the correspondence between his spirit and the beauty of the common butterfly, denies yet another boundary respected by common sense, that between physical reality and a transcendent reality. Frank in its Romantic idealism, the poem evokes an Emersonian wonder at the harmony of physical and spiritual facts for a modern audience every bit as skeptical as Ralph Waldo Emerson's neighbors.

Roots and Branches closes with a more extended sequence of poems, the memorable series "The Continent," in which Duncan directly names and accepts his role as "the artist of the margin" who "works abundancies" and who recognizes that the scope of poetry "needs vast terms" because it is "out of earthly proportion to the page." On the literal level, Duncan calls for a long poem which will, like Whitman's, be creative and have "vista." Metaphorically and more significantly, he is calling for a poetry on the edge of consciousness, an expanding awareness of "marginal" realities, an openness to unusual or unconventional apprehensions. Unlike the coastal resident's awareness of the alien or the other, "The mid-Western mind differs in essentials." Without Buddhist temples or variant ways of seeing, midwesterners "stand with feet upon the ground/ against the/ run to the mythic sea, the fabulous." This is not praise for Antaeus.

The poem continues, describing a sparrow smashed upon a sidewalk. More than an allusion to William Carlos Williams's famous poem, the passage illuminates the difference between having a perspective in space and time and being "too close/ for shadow,/ the immediate!" The central image of the poem, the continent, itself examines horizons, especially those between shore and land and night and day. The closing sections link such imagery with Easter (evidently the time of the actual writing of the poem) and its denial of any clear distinction even between life and death.

Far from fragmenting our beliefs and dissociating our sensibilities, such a vision asserts the oneness of things: one time, one god, one promise flaring forth from "the margins of the page." In the apparent chaos of flux and change—"moving in rifts, churning, enjambing"—both continent and poem testify to a dynamic unity. Again, at the border, at the edge of meaning, like Christopher Columbus one finds not the abyss but new worlds.

"Apprehensions" is a poem closely related to "The Continent." The central theme is again that which "defines the borderlines of the meaning." The opening chord, "To open Night's eye that sleeps in what we know by day," announces the familiar concern with overcoming common sense and sensory limitations, and with the assertion of paradoxical oneness. Quotidian preoccupations obstruct our perspectives and limit our perceptions. In sharp contrast, the "Sage Architect" awakens "the proportions and scales of the soul's wonder" and lets light and shadow mix. The poem is a song to apprehension—both fearful and perceiving—of excavation of boundaries, resemblances, rhymes. The central apprehension is of concordances which overcome our limited sense of shifting time, place, and boundaries in favor of an overriding order.

BENDING THE BOW

Continuing his development, Duncan followed four years later with yet another major book, *Bending the Bow*. In his introduction, he discusses his poetry with his accustomed insight, beginning by criticizing the Vietnam War which, "as if to hold all China or the ancient sea at bay, breaks out at a boundary we name *ours*. It is a boundary beyond our understanding." Captured by a rigid form, by a fixed image of oneself, one is unable to adapt to new conditions and insights. In contrast, the pulse of the poet in moments of vision "beats before and beyond all proper bounds." The book's title establishes the contrasts of bow and lyre, war and music, Apollo and Hermes, whose tension generates this book's field. Duncan speaks of the poem not as a stream of consciousness but as an area of composition in which "the poet works with a sense of parts fitting in relation to a design that is larger than the poem" and which he knows "will never be completed."

The title lyric develops the bow and lyre analogy, articulating the central Heraclitean themes of design, connection, and unity in diversity: "At this extremity of this/ design/ there is a connexion working in both directions, as in/ the bow and the lyre." As Duncan explains in "Towards an Open Universe," the turn and return of prose and verses of poetry are phases of a dynamic unity, like the alternation of day and night or the systole and diastole of the heart. The focus of his poetry and poetics remains on the intensity of the point of transition.

While "The Structure of Rime" continues in this volume, a new series, the "Passages Poems," is also introduced, beginning with a telling epigraph: "For the even is bounded, but the uneven is without bounds and there is no way through or out of it." The first passage, "Tribal Memories," invokes "Her-Without-Bounds," and the importance of margins, borders, and boundaries continues. Describing "Passages Poems" in his introduction, Duncan states that "they belong to a series that extends in an area larger than my work in them. I enter the poem as I entered my own life, moving between an initiation and a terminus I cannot name. This is not a field of the irrational; but a field of ratios." Among the poem's many concerns are those ratios or correspondences, and some of the most provocative insights derive from the poetic theme of margins and transitions. "The Architecture, Passages 9" demands recesses so that "there is always something around the corner." In "Wine, Passages 12," the poet celebrates even as he is threatened by "the voice/ . . . the enormous/ sonority at the edge of the void." "In the Place of a Passage 22," the poet prays for passage in "the vast universe/ showing only its boundaries we imagine."

Like "The Structure of Rime," "Passages Poems" is an exciting achievement. Like most long poems, it resists the sort of cursory treatment that consideration of space dictates here, and the project may well be victimized by the "magnificent failure" syndrome so characteristic of criticism of American literature. Certainly it is ambitious, as Duncan acknowledges in "Where It Appears, Passage 4": "Statistically insignificant as a locus of creation/ I have in this my own/ intense/ area of self creation." Even here, the telling conditionals of "as if I

could cast a shadow / to surround / what is boundless" indicate Duncan's full, continuing, double-edged apprehension of his enterprise and its risks.

GROUND WORK: BEFORE THE WAR

Ground Work: Before the War, published fifteen years after *Bending the Bow*, carries on the concerns of the three major collections of the 1960's. If there had been fear of a possible waning of Duncan's powers, these were unjustified. The architectonics of this large volume are highly complex, though one can easily discern a moving back and forth between familiar modes: the large-scale "grand collage" manner of the ongoing "The Structure of Rime" and "Passages Poems," and sequences of smaller, more private and sentimental lyrics, such as the most delicately rhymed "Glimpse." Both kind of workings, however, involve Duncan's familiar subject matter: revelation, knowing, the "rimes" that the poet worries out of his sympathetic readings of the past masters ("A Seventeenth Century Suite" and "Dante Études"), as well as what George Butterick has called "protest against the violation of the natural order by systematic viciousness." The short lyrics seem a clear relief after the violent engagements with the political disasters of the time, as chronicled in the *Tribunals* section of "Passages Poems," and in what is Duncan's and, maybe, the age's best political poem: "Santa Cruz Propositions." The volume ends with "Circulations of the Song," a deeply moving love poem originating in the poet's reading of Jalal al-Din Rumi's work and celebrating the years spent with the painter Jess Collins, the "constant exchange" and the shared dance of the hearth-work: After the "Inferno" of the war poems, a kind of "Paradiso" has been achieved.

This delicate point of equilibrium, however, cannot last: It belongs to that specific book, that momentary configuration; the work, the oeuvre goes on, disrupting the gained *Paradiso*, as intimations of physical disease and death enter *Ground Work II*, the next and final volume of Duncan's late work, subtitled *In the Dark* and published just months before the poet's death. Even here, however, there is no weakening of Duncan's powers: The grand sweep of the late set of "Passages Poems" entitled "Regulators" is ample proof of the poet's unrelenting energy and vision. Duncan's long illness enters the preoccupations of the book—"my Death/ rearranged the date He has with me"—without ever being able to overcome that realm of the imagination from which the poet drew his breath and strength.

DUNCAN'S ART

It is another measure of Duncan's stature and complexity that all his work is of a piece and should be read entire. A single lyric, for example, can be read by itself, or as part of a longer series in many cases (several lyrics are parts of more than one series). It must also be seen as part of the book in which it appears, since Duncan has carefully ordered his collections, and as an integral part of Duncan's canon. Finally, as he says in his introduction to *The Years as Catches*, "Poems then are immediate presentations of the intention of the whole, the great poem of all poems, a unity." Appropriately, even the boundaries of his poems are fluid and dynamic.

In his pervasive border-crossing, Duncan brings his readers news of an other which is shut out by conventional boundaries. With his artful disclosures, his imaginative vision transcends false, self-imposed constrictions. His art ultimately dissolves the very restraints and boundaries he recognizes in the act of transgressing them, and it thus weds humans to nature and to other humans, a familiar but rarely realized ideal of art.

OTHER MAJOR WORKS

PLAYS: *Faust Foutu: An Entertainment in Four Parts*, pb. 1959; *Medea at Kolchis: The Maidenhead*, pb. 1965.

NONFICTION: *As Testimony: The Poem and the Scene*, 1964; *The Sweetness and Greatness of Dante's "Divine Comedy,"* 1965; *The Cat and the Blackbird*, 1967; *The Truth and Life of Myth: An Essay in Essential Autobiography*, 1968; *A Selection of Sixty-five Drawings from One Drawing-Book, 1952-1956*, 1970; *Fictive Certainties*, 1985.

BIBLIOGRAPHY

Altieri, Charles. *Enlarging the Temple: New Directions in American Poetry during the 1960's.* Lewisburg, Pa.: Bucknell University Press, 1979. If Altieri's self-defined critical categories of "postmodern" and "immanentist" seem open to debate, this is a groundbreaking book that offers insightful analyses of both the philosophical strictures and the post-Poundian poetics underlying the work of some of the major poets to emerge in the 1960's (chapter 4 deals more specifically with Duncan's work).

Bertholf, Robert J., and Ian W. Reid, eds. *Robert Duncan: Scales of the Marvelous.* New York: New Directions, 1979. The most wide-ranging collection of essays on Robert Duncan. Besides personal reminiscences (by Mary Tyler, Denise Levertov, and R. B. Kitaj), the book proposes essays by Robert Bertholf, Donald Byrd, Michael Davidson, Eric Mottram, Nathaniel Mackey, and others, arranged according to the chronology of Duncan's publications. Includes a selected checklist to Robert Duncan's published writings.

Davidson, Michael. *The San Francisco Renaissance: Poetics and Community at Mid-Century.* Cambridge, England: Cambridge University Press, 1989. Although only chapter 4 ("Cave of Resemblances, Cave of Rimes: Tradition and Repetition in Robert Duncan") of this study of poetics and community in the Bay Area is specifically centered on the poetics of Robert Duncan, the book as a whole is an invaluable guide to the social, political, and literary environment in which Duncan lived and worked.

Ellingham, Lewis. *Poet Be Like God: Jack Spicer and the San Francisco Renaissance.* Hanover, N.H.: University Press of New England, 1998. Criticism and biographic material about Spicer and the San Francisco Renaissance group that included Robert Duncan. With bibliographic references.

Everson, William. *The Last Letters.* Berkeley, Calif.: Oyez, 2000. A collection of correspondence between Everson and Duncan.

Faas, Ekbert. *Young Robert Duncan: Portrait of the Poet as Homosexual in Society.* Santa Barbara: Black Sparrow Press, 1983. A well-researched book about Duncan's early life, the complexity of being a foster child, the East Coast years so often neglected in Duncan studies, the early radical decision to assert his homosexual identity, and the effects this had on the development of Duncan as a writer.

Maps 6 (1974). A special magazine issue on Duncan's work that, besides several seminal letters from Duncan to Charles Olson and an excellent Duncan piece on his "The Structure of Rime," includes essays by Ronald Johnson, Ron Silliman, and Wendy MacIntyre.

Paul, Sherman. *The Lost America of Love: Rereading Robert Creeley, Edward Dorn, and Robert Duncan.* Baton Rouge: Louisiana State University Press, 1981. A sympathetic, if idiosyncratic, reading of the poetry of three of the major Black Mountain figures.

Sagetrieb 4 (Fall/Winter, 1985). A special Robert Duncan issue. This 350-page compilation, gathering an important three-hour interview with Robert Duncan as well as the Robert Duncan-William Everson correspondence, includes valuable essays on Duncan's late poetry by, among others, George Butterick, Michael André Bernstein, and Thomas Gardner, and is an essential tool for Duncan studies.

Mark A. Johnson;
bibliography updated by the editors

LAWRENCE DURRELL

Born: Julundur, India; February 27, 1912
Died: Sommières, France; November 7, 1990

PRINCIPAL POETRY

Quaint Fragment: Poems Written Between the Ages of Sixteen and Nineteen, 1931
Ten Poems, 1932
Bromo Bombastes, 1933
Transition: Poems, 1934
Proems: An Anthology of Poems, 1938 (with others)
A Private Country, 1943
Cities, Plains, and People, 1946
Six Poems from the Greek of Sekilianos and Seferis, 1946 (translation)
The King of Asine and Other Poems, 1948 (translation of George Seferis)
On Seeming to Presume, 1948
Deus Loci, 1950
Private Drafts, 1955
The Tree of Idleness and Other Poems, 1955

Selected Poems, 1956
Collected Poems, 1960
Penguin Modern Poets One, 1962 (with Elizabeth Jennings and R. S. Thomas)
Beccaficio Le Beofigue, 1963 (English; includes French translation by F. J. Temple)
Selected Poems, 1935-1963, 1964
The Ikons and Other Poems, 1966
The Red Limbo Lingo: A Poetry Notebook for 1968-1970, 1971
On the Suchness of the Old Boy, 1972
Vega and Other Poems, 1973
Collected Poems, 1931-1974, 1980

OTHER LITERARY FORMS

Lawrence Durrell wrote novels, plays, travel books, humorous sketches, and poetry. The differences in genre, however, cannot obscure his fundamental and single identity as a poet. He is best known for his novels, especially *The Alexandria Quartet* (1957-1960) and *The Avignon Quintet* (1974-1985). Any reader of these works will recognize the same hand at work in Durrell's poems. The beauty of language, the exotic settings, and the subtle treatment of the themes of love, death, and time are elements common to all Durrell's work. In addition, the novels are rife with interpolated poetry. The characters not only speak poetically, they also quote at length from Greek, Egyptian, French, and English poets. Some have questioned this plethora of verse as unrealistic; others insist that Durrell's use of language and interpolated poetry represents a more intense reality, not a fantasy.

Durrell's poetic drama has inevitably enjoyed less attention than his novels, but it provides an excellent showcase for his skill at characterization and his poetic gifts. Durrell himself considered several passages from *Sappho* (1950) good enough to include in his *Collected Poems*, and most readers would agree. A later play, *Acte* (1965), shows that his drama does not rely entirely on the author's magnificent English: It was first performed in German, three years before its publication.

Ultimately, Durrell was a word artist, a poet. All genres had for him their particular virtues, and he brought to them all a poetic impulse which no change in form could disrupt.

ACHIEVEMENTS

Lawrence Durrell's accomplishments in prose over-shadowed his work in verse. Most readers will turn to the *Collected Poems* only after having read *The Alexandria Quartet*, or perhaps one of the travel books. Durrell won no major awards for poetry, despite his consistent excellence from the 1940's on. His name rarely appears on the lists of major English poets of the twentieth century.

All this notwithstanding, Durrell's achievement as a poet is sound and his eventual recognition assured. His success in other genres left him well-off financially and under no pressure; he could write poetry as he pleased, with no fear of disappointing expectant readers and no burden of leadership. Precisely because Durrell made his formidable reputation as a novelist, he could approach his poetry as an alternative. This does not imply that he merely dabbled—on the contrary, every poem shows the mark of craft and diligence—but rather that the wealth of material afforded by his diverse experience and wide-ranging mind could find its expression in pure

Lawrence Durrell (© Rosemarie Clausen)

poetry. He was free to write only those poems that his good judgment told him to write.

Neither rigidly traditional nor wildly experimental, Durrell's poems represent the subtle innovations of a consummate and independent artist. In this respect, they are reminiscent of the work of Wallace Stevens. Like Stevens, Durrell balanced the demands of tradition and the modern psyche, creating poems which the eye and the mind can follow, but which the soul does not reject as obsolete. Some of them compare favorably with the best of the twentieth century and will someday be read for their own merits, not merely for their connection with the famous novels by the same author.

BIOGRAPHY

Born in India, Lawrence George Durrell led a wandering life that profoundly influenced all his work. His formal education was adequate but limited; ironically, he could never gain admission to Cambridge, which may have motivated his half-jesting claim that he became a writer "by sheer ineptitude." In any event, he managed to acquire an astonishing fund of knowledge, becoming competent as a painter, a jazz pianist, a race-car driver, a teacher, and a diplomat. In his turbulent career, he lived and worked in London, Paris, Cairo, Belgrade, Beirut, Athens, Cyprus, Argentina, and Provence. Naturally enough, he also became an accomplished linguist, particularly in Greek. Many of the places mentioned above are familiar to readers as settings of his novels or travel books; they are also prominent in his poems.

Durrell's personal life was no less an odyssey than his career. Married three times, he went through two divorces and became a widower in 1967. His friendships proved more lasting, in particular his evolving relationship with Henry Miller. Beginning as Miller's disciple and admirer, Durrell virtually turned the tables. Even so, the two remained close and mutually stimulating friends, as evidenced by *Lawrence Durrell and Henry Miller: A Private Correspondence* (1963).

After many years of working at odd jobs, teaching, and representing his country in various diplomatic posts, Durrell settled in Provence in 1957 and devoted his full time to writing. Always a rapid worker—he completed the monumental *The Alexandria Quartet* in less than a year of actual writing time—he published many novels, dramas, and collections of poetry from the 1960's to the 1980's. By the late 1970's his wanderlust seemed cured; he stirred only reluctantly. In his late seclusion, Durrell was perhaps like Prospero, from William Shakespeare's *The Tempest* (1611), a favorite character of his—he worked his magic and recalled his life at court. Both his poems and his prose reveal the fruits of an extraordinary life at many Mediterranean "courts." Durrell died in Sommières, France, in 1990.

ANALYSIS

Durrell's poetry has many rare qualities. His multi-faceted life gave him a breadth of vision and a balance of mind which, in combination with his natural gifts and hard work, enabled him to produce a body of poetry remarkable for its beauty, richness, and integrity. His poems afford a glimpse into the changeless world of the Mediterranean, and into the ever-changing lives of the people who live there. Yet the poems never become mere travelogues; part of Durrell's integrity lies in his adherence to the central purpose of poetry: to illuminate the human experience. He remains faithful to that goal throughout "the wooing and seduction of form."

Reading Lawrence Durrell's poetry for the first time, a discerning reader might be reminded of T. S. Eliot, echoed in Durrell's sparse but effective rhymes, his facility in finding the *mot juste*, and some of his astonishing single lines, and think of "The Love Song of J. Alfred Prufrock" (1915) and *The Waste Land* (1922). Reflecting further, the first-time reader would perceive that both Durrell and Eliot are philosophical poets, and that their work shows their common preoccupation with the Western tradition and certain of its key philosophical issues.

Truly discerning readers, however, will conclude that the resemblance ends there. For all his superficial likeness to Eliot, Durrell has a distinctive voice as a poet. The hypothetical discerning reader might well end up thinking of Durrell as a curious mixture of the qualities of Eliot, D. H. Lawrence, and Gerard Manley Hopkins, but even that remarkable formulation would not cover all the facts. Durrell is unique; he is the Anglo-Indian poet of the Mediterranean, craftsman, and thinker at once.

In an interview printed in the Autumn-Winter issue of *The Paris Review* for 1959-1960, Durrell reveals his guiding principle as a poet: "Poetry is form, and the wooing and seduction of form is the whole game." His poems *seem* rather traditional in their construction; a glance at the printed page reveals few typographical eccentricities. A careful reading, however, will turn up subtle variations in meter, line-length, and rhyme. Durrell worked hard and successfully at wooing and seducing form. He altered form almost imperceptibly, so that a sonnet by Durrell does not seem quite a sonnet. One re-counts lines and syllables and finally admits that the poem *is* a sonnet, but an odd one. Simply put, Durrell wrested the form away from tradition and made it his own. This victory makes possible—by no means inevitable—the success of the poem.

"A SOLILOQUY OF HAMLET" AND "STYLE"

An example of this phenomenon is the second of the fourteen poems in "A Soliloquy of Hamlet." The poet has already indicated that the fourteen poems are to be regarded as sonnets. The student of the form, however, will demur because of the lack of rhyme and the arrangement into couplets. On intensive reading, he will be compelled to concede that there *is* a six/eight structure, the usual arrangement of a sonnet *à rebours*—in short, that his beloved sonnet form has been seduced.

Durrell offers an intriguing, if somewhat deceptive, insight into his art in a poem entitled "Style." The poet strives for "Something like the sea;/ Unlabored momentum of water;/ But going somewhere. . . ." Subsequently, he wishes to write "the wind that slits/ Forests from end to end." Finally, he rejects sea and wind for a third alternative:

> But neither is yet
> Fine enough for the line I hunt.
> The dry long blade of the
> Sword-grass might suit me
> Better: an assassin of polish.

The choice is never really made, of course: Durrell can write in all these manners and many more. The poem serves more to convey a sense of his unending struggle for perfection, in his verse and in his prose, than to issue any artistic manifesto.

In this struggle for perfection, Durrell differed from other writers only in his relative success. Other differences are easier to define and more important to the understanding of his poetry. Here it helps to refer to his prose work. Any reader of the novels and travel books knows Durrell's powers of description, his subtlety in handling love relationships between his characters, and his flair for transforming the mundane into the magical. As a poet, he displays the same talents in a different medium.

THE IMPORTANCE OF PLACE

As mentioned above, Durrell was the Anglo-Indian poet of the Mediterranean. The phrase is perhaps a trifle awkward, but to omit any element would be to misrepresent the poet. As an Anglo-Indian, he enjoyed at once the benefits of an English education and a childhood in the East. He also suffered, virtually from birth, the plight of the exile, the man without a country. England was alien; English was not. Durrell's work depends on the English literary tradition, even though he could not bear the thought of living in Great Britain. He found a series of homes on the shores of the Mediterranean: Greece, Lebanon, Cyprus, Egypt, France. The Mediterranean is the sine qua non of his work; nowhere else could he have found such "cities, plains and people." Thus, every element in the description is vital, because Durrell's birthplace, education, and later environment together help to account for the unique nature of his poetry.

"THE ANECDOTES"

The importance of place in Durrell's poetry is nowhere more evident than in "The Anecdotes," a series of brief lyrics with subtitles such as "In Cairo," "At Rhodes," and "In Patmos." Durrell has an unsurpassed genius for evoking the peculiar atmosphere of locale, and he makes good use of the imagination-stirring names of Mediterranean cities. "The Anecdotes" concern people and emotions, but the geography helps the reader to understand both.

In the third poem, "At Rhodes," Durrell suggests the languorous beauty of Rhodes by way of a few deft images. The memory of the boats in the harbor, the antics of two Greek children, and the town, "thrown as on a screen of watered silk," becomes a compact poem: "twelve sad lines against the dark." The lines express

nostalgia for Rhodes through a few well-chosen emblems of the city, suggesting a lovely tranquillity which the poet now lacks. The personal association—Durrell missed Rhodes sorely during his tour of duty in Egypt—becomes a theme.

The sense of place in the poems generally does have an importance beyond mere exotic appeal. The countries, the cities, even the streets and cafés that Durrell mentions have associations with specific moods and memories. Sometimes the connection is obscure; more often, Durrell selects his images so skillfully that the reader shares the mood without quite knowing why. In the best examples, the poet achieves Eliot's ideal, the "objective correlative."

The fourteenth anecdote, "In Beirut," has the reader sighing with the melancholy of "after twenty years another meeting," though Durrell gives few details of the people involved or of their stories. Beirut takes on the withered nature of the old friends, "flesh murky as old horn,/ Hands dry now as seabiscuit." Even without specific background, the contrast between "breathless harbours north of Tenedos" in April and "in Tunis, winter coming on" is evident. Durrell's beloved Greece comes to represent life and youth; the cities of Asia and North Africa connote aging and death.

"MAREOTIS"

One of the best examples of Durrell's artistry in this regard is "Mareotis." The reader need not know beforehand that Mareotis is a salt marsh outside Alexandria; Durrell makes it clear enough, even as he draws the parallel between the atmosphere of the marsh and the climate of his soul. The wind of the place, "Not subtle, not confiding, touches once again,/ The melancholy elbow cheek and paper." The odd blend of discontent and self-knowledge matches the nature of the salt marsh. It misses the changes of spring, remaining the same, just as the poet does. Durrell has performed a sleight of hand, first alluding to a place, then subtly sketching its nature, and ultimately using the finished image to make his poetic point.

"CITIES, PLAINS AND PEOPLE"

It must be noted here that Durrell's reliance on images of place sometimes renders his poetry difficult to understand. Most readers know next to nothing of the world the poet inhabits, beyond a few clichés. In the novels, he overcomes this problem masterfully by means of long descriptions. In the poems, lacking this resource, he depends on a few striking images. This may account in part for the greater popularity of the fiction. To Durrell's credit, relatively few of his poems are seriously marred by his esoteric geography.

In "Cities, Plains and People," one of his major poems, Durrell approaches overwhelming questions in the course of a poetic autobiography. He begins under the shadow of the Himalayas, "in idleness," an innocent tyke to whom "Sex was small,/ Death was small. . . ." Both have become very large for the poet as he has grown, but the early years in British India stand as the time before the Fall. There in the mountains, only "nine marches" from inscrutable Lhasa, the boy grows up. He does not, however, go to Tibet:

> But he for whom steel and running water
> Were roads, went westward only
> To the prudish cliffs and the sad green home
> Of Pudding Island o'er the Victorian foam

The growing artist finds himself repelled and attracted by Europe; though he knows that "London/ Could only be a promise-giving kingdom," there are always "Dante and Homer/ To impress the lame and awkward newcomer." Impressed in both senses of the word, the Anglo-Indian struggles against the insidious examples of Saint Bede, Saint Augustine, and Saint Jerome, those deniers of the flesh, and mourns the dismal reality, "The potential passion hidden, Wordsworth/ In the desiccated bodies of postmistresses." The associations of place here serve to advance the story and to present the thought of the developing poet.

Durrell goes on to discover the escape hatch, the magic of Prospero's island. Here the literal and the fictive landscapes merge. William Shakespeare and the earthly Mediterranean both have a part in the choice, an eclectic mixture of the best of the British literary tradition and the best of the poet's several homes. The conflict is by no means resolved, but the two great forces have at least acknowledged each other. The Englishman born in India has found something worth having from Pudding Island.

The journey continues because the poet has found only a working arrangement, not an ultimate answer. He still has much to learn of those great matters which the child considered insignificant. He learns much of sex. It becomes "a lesser sort of speech, and the members doors." It is versatile, serving as a means of salvation both spiritual—"man might botch his way/ To God via Valéry, Gide or Rabelais"—the physical: "savage Chatterleys of the new romance/ Get carried off in sex, the ambulance." That Durrell can debunk in one stanza what he affirms so powerfully elsewhere implies not inconsistency but rather an appreciation of the complexity of the matter. The youth has lost his innocence and has also gone beyond a naïve faith in a simple solution. Sex may be an answer but not a simple answer.

Durrell goes on to probe beyond knowledge, "in the dark field of sensibility." As in the novels, he comes to no rigid conclusion. At the end of *The Alexandria Quartet*, Darley sits down to write; "Cities, Plains and People" ends with an analogous image:

> For Prospero remains the evergreen
> Cell by the margin of the sea and land,
> Who many cities, plains, and people saw
> Yet by his open door
> In sunlight fell asleep
> One summer with the Apple in his hand.

Between Durrell the poet and Durrell the novelist there lies only the difference in genre: The artist and the resolution are the same. Prospero remains, latent with magic—the magic to bring order and beauty to the chaotic world of cities, plains, and people. Darley on his island off the coast of Egypt and the poet somewhere in the Aegean represent Durrell/ Prospero, perhaps the key image of his work.

"Proffer the Loaves of Pain"

Durrell's repertoire is by no means limited to extended philosophical ruminations, nor his imagery to geographical references. He has estimable gifts as a lyric poet, which he demonstrates throughout his work. One particularly fine example, "Proffer the Loaves of Pain," shows Durrell's technical wizardry in the manipulation of rhyme. The four stanzas run the gamut of the seasons, echoing sadly: "they shall not meet." The first three stanzas feature half-rhymes: "quantum/ autumn," "saunter/ winter," and "roamer/summer." This tantalizing soundplay gives the true rhyme of the conclusion, "ring/

spring," a finality not inherent in the words of the stanza. The poem dodges and ducks until the last inexorable rhyme destroys the last hope—in spring, ironically enough.

The poem distinguishes itself in other ways as well. The economy of language requires close attention on the part of the reader, for the clues are subtle. For example, the poet employs the word "this" to modify the seasons in the first two stanzas. Summer and spring, however, serve as objects of the preposition "in." The specific negation of the first half of the poem becomes a chilling "nevermore" in the last two stanzas, by the simple device of a change in grammar.

"THE DEATH OF GENERAL UNCEBUNKE"

Durrell's melancholy wit and his fascination with the ever-lurking mystery of death come together in "The Death of General Uncebunke: A Biography in Little," which he labels "Not satire but an exercise in ironic compassion." The biography encompasses not only the general, a Victorian empire builder, but also the dowager Aunt Prudence. Despite the earlier gibes at "Pudding Island," the poet holds true to his word: The poem expresses no contempt for Uncebunke, even if the reader cannot stifle a chuckle or two at the man who "wrote a will in hexameters." Rather, Durrell transmutes the potentially absurd details of the old campaigner's life into symbols of his death. He rides horses, fords rivers, and crosses into Tartary, and the poet invests these adventures with a new and final significance.

Durrell's sentiment is noble and restrained, but his handling of language and form in the poem deserves even more attention. The fourteen "carols" begin in three fashions. Four start with the words "My uncle sleeps in the image of death"; five begin "My uncle has gone beyond astronomy"; the remainder open with references to Aunt Prudence. Thus, the poet achieves at once a compelling repetition and movement; the lines referring to the uncle maintain the elegiac tone, while the stanzas devoted to Prudence reinforce the sense of gradual decay.

A number of phonetic tricks bolster the ironic character of the poem and add to the reader's grasp of the characters. Of the uncle, for example, Durrell says: "he like a faultless liner, finer never took air." The sound play recalls Gerard Manley Hopkins, although the good

Jesuit would probably not have indulged in the irony. Aunt Prudence prays earnestly and ridiculously: "Thy will be done in Baden Baden./ In Ouchy, Lord, and in Vichy." By one of his own favorite ploys, here in a new guise, Durrell uses references of place to provoke a response.

Finally, Durrell tosses off one memorable line after another, each in itself worth an ode. Uncebunke in his dotage lives on a country estate, "devoted to the polo-pony, mesmerized by stamps." Aunt Prudence putters about, "feeding the parrot, pensive over a croquet-hoop." The horses in the stable "champ, stamp, yawn, paw in the straw." One suspects that Hopkins—or any other modern poet, for that matter—would have taken pride in such verses.

"BALLAD OF THE OEDIPUS COMPLEX"

To all his other virtues as a poet, Durrell adds a lively and whimsical sense of humor. Though the prevailing literary prejudices of the twentieth century keep most readers from appraising humorous verse at its full worth, no one who has suffered the slings and arrows of outrageous Freudians will read the "Ballad of the Oedipus Complex" unmoved. Besides poking fun at overworked psychological truisms, Durrell shows a fine English sense of fair play, plunging his own face into a custard pie:

> I tried to strangle it one day
> While sitting in the Lido
> But it got up and tickled me
> And now I'm all libido.

This ability to snicker at his own literary obsessions betokens a fine sensibility in Durrell, as well as a sense of humor so often lacking in his contemporaries.

OTHER MAJOR WORKS

LONG FICTION: *Pied Piper of Lovers*, 1935; *Panic Spring*, 1937 (as Charles Norden); *The Black Book*, 1938; *Cefalû*, 1947 (republished as *The Dark Labyrinth*, 1958); *Justine*, 1957; *Balthazar*, 1958; *Mountolive*, 1958; *Clea*, 1960; *The Alexandria Quartet*, 1962 (includes previous 4 novels); *Tunc*, 1968; *Nunquam*, 1970; *Monsieur: Or, the Prince of Darkness*, 1974; *Livia: Or, Buried Alive*, 1978; *Constance: Or, Solitary Practices*, 1981; *Sebastian: Or, Ruling Pas-*

sions, 1983; *Quinx: Or, The Ripper's Tale*, 1985; *The Avignon Quintet*, 1992 (includes previous 5 novels).

SHORT FICTION: *Esprit de Corps: Sketches from Diplomatic Life*, 1957; *Stiff Upper Lip: Life Among the Diplomats*, 1958; *Sauve Qui Peut*, 1966; *The Best of Antrobus*, 1974; *Antrobus Complete*, 1985.

PLAYS: *Sappho*, pr. 1950; *An Irish Faustus*, pb. 1963; *Acte*, pr. 1964.

NONFICTION: *Prospero's Cell*, 1945; *A Landmark Gone*, 1949; *A Key to Modern British Poetry*, 1952; *Reflections on a Marine Venus*, 1953; *The Curious History of Pope Joan*, 1954 (translation, revised as *Pope Joan: A Personal Biography*, 1960); *Bitter Lemons*, 1957; *Art and Outrage*, 1959; *Lawrence Durrell and Henry Miller: A Private Correspondence*, 1963 (George Wickes, editor); *Spirit of Place: Letters and Essays on Travel*, 1969 (Alan G. Thomas, editor); *The Big Supposer: Dialogues with Marc Alyn/Lawrence Durrell*, 1973; *Sicilian Carousel*, 1977; *The Greek Islands*, 1978; *Literary Lifelines: The Richard Aldington-Lawrence Durrell Correspondence*, 1981; *The Durrell-Miller Letters, 1935-1980*, 1988; *Caesar's Vast Ghost: A Portrait of Provence*, 1990.

CHILDREN'S LITERATURE: *White Eagles over Serbia*, 1957.

BIBLIOGRAPHY

Bengal, Michael H., ed. *On Miracle Ground: Essays on the Fiction of Lawrence Durrell*. Lewisburg, Pa.: Bucknell University Press, 1990. Limited to Durrell's major fiction, these essays reflect the variety of critical responses the novels elicited "from metafiction to close textual analysis to deconstruction to reader response theory." "Overture" by Durrell gives his own understanding of the forces that shaped him. Contains a useful bibliography of secondary sources.

Bowker, Gordon. *Through the Dark Labyrinth: A Biography of Lawrence Durrell*. New York: St. Martin's Press, 1997. Bowker reveals Durrell to be a complex man beset at times by incredibly painful circumstances that he was somehow able to transmute into his fiction.

Fraser, G. S. *Lawrence Durrell*. Essex, England: Longman Group, 1970. This monograph contains six essays on Durrell's career, poems, travel books, *The Black Book, The Alexandria Quartet*, and *Tunc* and *Nunquam*, which place individual works within the context of English writers contemporary to Durrell and within the context of their society and culture. Fraser provides excellent plot summaries of the prose and indicates the most significant elements of Durrell's poetry and drama.

Friedman, Alan Warren. *Lawrence Durrell and "The Alexandria Quartet": Art for Love's Sake*. Norman: University of Oklahoma Press, 1970. This pioneering study of Durrell's writing concentrates on *The Alexandria Quartet* as the culmination, at the time, of his writing. Durrell is placed as a leading experimental novelist in the traditions of the Impressionists and the stream-of-consciousness novelists. The bibliography, though out of date, is helpfully organized and contains primary and secondary sources.

Herbrechter, Stefan. *Lawrence Durrell: Postmodernism and the Ethics of Alterity*. Atlanta, Ga.: Rodopi, 1999. An investigation of the notions of alterity which underlie the work of Durrell and postmodernist theory. The introduction sketches the Levinasian ethics of alterity and reevaluates Durrell's fiction within the context of postmodernism.

Kersnowski, Frank, ed. *Into the Labyrinth: Essays Concerning the Art of Lawrence Durrell*. Rochester, N.Y.: University of Rochester Press, 1991. This collection of critical essays and biographical reminiscences contains essays on all forms of Durrell's writing and painting. The reproduction of art by Durrell and the chronology of his life provide information not readily available elsewhere.

Unterecker, John. *Lawrence Durrell*. New York: Columbia University Press, 1964. This brief, provocative study wisely delineates major interests in Durrell's writings and relates them to a sketch of the author's life. Most useful as a source of concerns and approaches for readers and critics to develop.

Vander Closter, Susan. *Joyce Cary and Lawrence Durrell: A Reference Guide*. Boston: G. K. Hall, 1985. This annotated bibliography of secondary material is essential to anyone writing about Durrell. Reviews, essays, and critical studies from 1937 to

1983 are listed chronologically. The index contains thematic listings, some of which refer to names of individual critics and to individual works by Durrell. The first half of the book concerns Joyce Cary and the second half concerns Durrell.

Weigel, John A. *Lawrence Durrell*. Rev. ed. Boston: Twayne, 1989. This revision of the 1965 study pro-vides a clear overview of Durrell's life and writing. The discussion of individual works is useful for students approaching Durrell for the first time. Although Durrell's poetry, drama, and criticism are discussed, the study focuses on the novels.

Philip Krummrich;
bibliography updated by the editors

E

CORNELIUS EADY

Born: Rochester, New York; January 7, 1954

PRINCIPAL POETRY

Kartunes, 1980
Victims of the Latest Dance Craze, 1985
BOOM BOOM BOOM, 1988 (limited edition chapbook)
The Gathering of My Name, 1991
You Don't Miss Your Water, 1995
The Autobiography of a Jukebox, 1996
Brutal Imagination, 2001

OTHER LITERARY FORMS

Given his willingness to experiment with bringing to the written word the rhythms of both jazz and blues and his belief in poetry as performed (that is, heard) art, Cornelius Eady, not surprisingly, has produced two experimental theater pieces, part of a projected trilogy for the New York City-based Music-Theater Group, both of which involved original scores written by jazz cellist and longtime friend Diedre L. Murray. The first production, in 1997, was a staged recitation based on *You Don't Miss Your Water* (1995), Eady's cycle of prose poems that recounts his father's death. In 1999 Eady provided the libretto for an experimental jazz opera based on the story of Murray's brother, a gifted man lost to a life of crime and heroin addiction. That production, *Running Man* (pr. 1999), won two Obie Awards and was shortlisted for both the New York Drama Critics Circle Award and the Pulitzer Prize. In 2001, *Brutal Imagination* was a finalist for the National Book Award in Poetry.

ACHIEVEMENTS

Cornelius Eady emerged within the first generation of African American poets to succeed the formidable work of the Black Arts movement of the mid-twentieth century. That literary movement, an extension of the era's Civil Rights movement, created new interest in black identity. Eady continued that exploration, using his own working-class upbringing and his position as a black poet in late twentieth century America. That compelling honesty, coupled with his experiments in the sheer music of language, has garnered Eady two nominations for the Pulitzer Prize; in addition to *Running Man*, *The Gathering of My Name* was nominated for the poetry prize. *Victims of the Latest Dance Craze* was given the Lamont Prize from the Academy of American Poets in 1985. A career academic, Eady has received fellowships from the Guggenheim Foundation (1993), the National Endowment for the Arts (1985), the Rockefeller Foundation (1993), and the Lila Wallace-*Reader's Digest* Foundation (1992-1993).

BIOGRAPHY

Born in Rochester, New York, Cornelius Eady began writing poems when he was only twelve. As chronicled in *You Don't Miss Your Water*, Eady's father posed a formidable emotional problem. High-school educated, the father, employed by the city water department, had difficulty accepting literature as a valid vocation. Consequently, Eady would struggle with feelings of estrangement until his father's death in 1993. After graduating from Empire State College and then earning his M.F.A. from Warren Wilson College, Eady held teaching appointments at Sweet Briar College, the College of William and Mary, Sarah Lawrence College, Tougaloo College, and City College of New York. While at the State University of New York at Stony Brook in the 1990's, he served as director of its famous poetry center. In 1999, Eady became distinguished writer in residence in the M.F.A. program at New York City's innovative New School. In 1996, along with poet Toi Derricotte, Eady founded the Cave Canem (literally, "Beware of the Dog"), a popular program of summer workshops for African American poets.

ANALYSIS

Cornelius Eady's poetry concerns the construction of identity, the dynamics of memory and reflection as part of the interrogation of the self, and the importance of recording that complex process. Like the blues, Eady's poetry centers on the struggle to define the isolated self within a chaotic world that harbors little possibility for redemption. Yet, like jazz, Eady's poetry also responds to a world that, given its essential unpredictability, can sustain authentic ecstasy. That texture, the self sustained between sadness and exuberance, is central to Eady's work. His poetry explores the roles he himself has played in the construction of his own identity. Not surprisingly, over the time Eady has been writing, this interrogation of the self has become more complex. Initially, Eady explored his role as urban poet; later, he examined more complex relational roles, that of husband, lover, teacher, and, supremely, son; he later began to confront his role as an African American, specifically the struggle to construct a viable black self amid the historical and social pressures of late twentieth century America.

The poetic line for such an investigation into the self is appropriately individual and resists conventional expectations of structure and sound. Rhythmic but not metric, Eady's line can appear deceptively simple, direct, even conversational. However, it is freedom within a tightly manipulated form. Like improvisational jazz, which can, at first hearing, seem easy and effortless, Eady's poetry is a complex aural event. His poems consciously manipulate sounds, unexpected syncopations and cadences, enjambment, irregular spacings and emphasis, line length, and sound repetition to create an air of improvisation that is nevertheless a carefully textured sonic weave.

KARTUNES

Kartunes is a portrait of the self as young poet, an exercise in testing the reach of the imagination and celebrating the role of a cocksure poet responding originally to the world. "I want to be fresh," he proclaims, "I want words/ to tumble off my lips/ rich enough/ to fertilize/ the ground." Giddy with imaginative possibilities, Eady improvises his narrative "I" into outlandish personas (the "cartoons" suggested by the title), many culled from pop culture: He is at turns an inept terrorist, a nerdy librarian, an unhappy woman forced into a witness protection program, a dying philanthropist anxious about the approaching afterlife, a man

Cornelius Eady (© Miriam Berkley)

contemplating torching his own house, the legendary Headless Horseman selecting the appropriate pumpkin to hurtle, Popeye's nemesis Bluto groomed for a date, even Adolf Hitler posing before a mirror and dreaming of greatness.

Given such wild fluctuations in the narrative center, the poetry is given over to irreverent exuberance. Despite often centering on alienated characters existing within a contemporary environment of absurdity and brutality, the poems resist surrendering to emotional heaviness. The poems, themselves innovative in structure and sound (witness the wordplay of the collection's title), offer as resolutions the sheer animation of the engaged imagination, the possibility of love, and the ability of the world to stun with its unchoreographed wonder. With the confident insouciance of a young man, Eady argues that nothing is nobler than "laughing/ when nothing/ is funny anymore."

VICTIMS OF THE LATEST DANCE CRAZE

The interest in defining the poet and that confident sense of play animates Eady's follow-up collection, thematically centered on the metaphor of the dance.

Here the world is in constant motion—the title poem, for example, details a pulsating urban neighborhood. Like William Carlos Williams (whose influence Eady has acknowledged), the poet responds to the seductive suasion of the world that too often goes unnoticed—to a cloud passing overhead, crows battling a strong wind, a waitress's purple nail polish, the leaden feel of November, the faint stirrings of April: "an entire world," he trumpets, "on the tip of my tongue." To respond to that world is to dance, a suggestive metaphor for the body's irresistible, spontaneous response to being alive, the electric moment of the "hands . . ./ Accidentally brush[ing] against the skirts of the world." Such animation, makes problematic the life of the poet so vital in *Kartunes*.

In the closing poem, "Dance at the Amherst County Public Library," the poet describes himself as a "dancing fool who couldn't stay away from words." He concedes his jealousy over those who live so effortlessly and of his own poor efforts to capture secondhand that rich experience within his poetry, his "small graffiti dance." Yet the poetic lines here boldly strive to match the urgent call to respond originally to the world, capturing the improvisational feel of jazz: irregular patterning of lines, multiple stops and starts, a delightful matching of sounds, and wildly unanticipated rhythms.

THE GATHERING OF MY NAME

In Eady's ambitious third major collection, the tone considerably darkens as jazz gives way to the slower pull of the blues. In the opening poem, "Gratitude," Eady audaciously proffers love to those who have not welcomed him nor his poetry and confesses his greatest weakness is his "inability/ to sustain rage." It is a familiar brashness, and, indeed, the second poem ("Grace") offers one of those unexpected moments when the world sparkles: the sight of the neighborhood reflected in the waxed hood of a black sedan.

Yet quickly the poems concede to a more disturbing world that crushes dreams and sours love. For the first time, Eady addresses race. Poems introduce figures such as the tormented blues singer Leadbelly or jazz great John Coltrane in the aftermath of the 1963 bombing of a Baptist church in Birmingham, Alabama. In others, a waitress in Virginia refuses to serve a black man, a passing motorist hurls racial epithets at a black man's white wife, a car breaks down in the "wrong" neighborhood. Like the blues, these are poems of pain and bad luck, the curse of awareness, the dilemma of disappointment, and the need to define the self in a harsh world. What is the poet to do? "Get it all out," Eady demands in "The Sheets of Sounds," the remarkable closing piece that is a tour de force of metrical audacity. Here, Eady captures in language the technical virtuosity and improvisational sound of Coltrane himself: "What do I have to lose,/ Actually,/ By coming right out/ And saying/ What I mean/ To say?" Honesty then compels the poet/jazz artist to let loose the spirit in all its outrage, to push art if only for a moment into uncompromising expression, the "loud humility" of a man giving himself the right to claim, as a refrain insists with typographical variations: "This is who I am."

YOU DON'T MISS YOUR WATER

Appropriately, then, in Eady's fourth collection readers feel (for the first time in his work) the nearness of the poet himself. Dropping his elaborate personas, Eady speaks forthrightly of his own life. The twenty-one prose poems are stark narratives without poetic frills and without clean chronological sequencing. The reader is given an unblinking record of a son's estrangement from a father in the face of mortality, the honest struggle to come to terms with the difficult wisdom of the blues lines, "You don't miss your water/ 'til your well runs dry." Eady refuses to sentimentalize the father (he is at turns miserly, stubborn, distant, even unfaithful) or himself (he cremates the body to save money), or even death (he records the indignities of hospital treatment and the impersonal efficiency of agencies that manage the paperwork). Titles recall traditional blues songs, and the mood is elegiac, sobering, eloquent: "This is how life, sharpened to a fine point, plunges into what we call hope."

If Eady's first three volumes speak of how the imagination takes hold of the world and shapes individual identity, here he acknowledges the depth of the inevitable experience of loss and how that experience is as well part of any construction of identity. In the volume's rich closing poem, "Paradiso," Eady decides that language itself, disparaged in his earlier work as secondhand graffiti, is the sole conjurer of the afterlife, that the "key to any heaven is language."

THE AUTOBIOGRAPHY OF A JUKEBOX

The Autobiography of a Jukebox is a kind of summary text. It is divided into four sections, each of which centers on themes drawn from earlier works: the heavy intrusion of loss; the ugly realities of racism; the glorious transcendence of art, specifically jazz, within this environment of oppression; and those small unexpected moments that trigger deep emotional responses and make such a world endurable. The volume begins where *You Don't Miss Your Water* ends: dealing with harsh loss—indeed, opening poems linger within recollections of Eady's father. With bluesy feel, other poems follow characters who discover the wounding of love, the certainty of bad luck, and the humiliations of poverty.

In the second section Eady confronts the angry indignation over the 1991 beating of citizen Rodney King by Los Angeles police, the federal trial in which the white officers were acquitted, and the riots that followed. It is Eady's first lengthy examination of the social dimension of the self and specifically how black identity must be defined within an oppressive white culture. To maintain dignity and to touch grace within such an environment Eady offers in the third section portraits of jazz artists (and pioneer rocker Chuck Berry), black musicians who forged from such oppression the stuff of their art: "What/ Hurts is beautiful, the bruise/ Of the lyric" However, it is not sufficient simply to relish such aesthetic artifacts.

In the closing section Eady quietly affirms what his first two volumes trumpeted: the imagination's ability to be stunned by the accidental encounter with something that triggers a minor epiphany in a flawed world that still permits awe—a woman with dreadlocks crossing a street, a tray of cornbread at a posh reception, the electric flow of an urban mall, the tangy smells of a bakery. Yet, hard on the death of Eady's father and the anger over the King beating, these slender moments of grace are suddenly significant in ways the earlier volumes could not suggest.

BRUTAL IMAGINATION

In *Brutal Imagination* Eady's career-long interest in defining the self takes on new maturity as he projects himself, within two unrelated poem cycles, out of the matrix of his own experience. In the first section Eady conjures the spirit, and voice, of the black kidnapper that mother Susan Smith invented as an alibi to cover the 1994 murder of her two infant sons. Eady uses that lie to investigate the white culture of anger, bigotry, and anxiety within which all black identity must be fashioned. In a biting middle section Eady suggests the dimensions of this dilemma by giving voice to the sorry racist stereotypes fashioned by a white imagination unwilling to grant blacks the dignity and complexity of legitimate selfhood: Uncle Tom, Uncle Ben, Aunt Jemima, Buckwheat, Stepin Fetchit. The faux-kidnapper—witty, articulate, probing, caring—dominates the cycle and, specifically, the symbiotic relationship between Smith and her invention, Eady suggesting how necessary the black stereotype is for whites. In the closing poem, "Birthing," which draws excerpts from Smith's actual confession, the conjured kidnapper extends compassion to the mother, imagining the actual killing and the desperate loneliness of Smith herself driven to do the unimaginable.

The second section contains pieces from the libretto of *Running Man*. Although offered without the haunting jazz score of the original production and without the dramatic interplay of performance, the pieces nevertheless succeed in a conjuring of a sort far different from Susan Smith's. A southern black family, devastated by the death of its only son, struggles to explain why such a promising young man succumbed to the very life of crime that made credible the vicious lie of Susan Smith. Within the interplay of their elegiac recollections, the poetic line tightly clipped for maximum effect, the young man himself is conjured and speaks of his own promise lost to the anger of limited social expectations within the white system and to the easy out of drug addiction and crime. He is the "running man" never sure where he was running from or to: "Where I come from/ A smart black boy/ Is like being a cat/ With a duck's bill." Chained to history—the cycle begins in an old slave cemetery—blacks, whatever their talent or aspirations, must withstand the larger predatory white culture that can leave them helpless, like "fish, scooped from a pond." It is a powerful assessment of black identity at the twentieth century's close.

OTHER MAJOR WORKS
PLAY: *Running Man*, pr. 1999 (libretto).
EDITED TEXTS: *Words for Breakfast*, 1998 (with Meg Kearney, Norma Fox Mazer, and Jacqueline

Woodson); *Vinyl Donuts*, 2000 (with Kearney, Mazer, and Woodson).

BIBLIOGRAPHY

Carroll, Rebecca. *Swing Low: Black Men Writing*. New York: Carol Southern Books, 1995. This book features interviews with sixteen authors along with excerpts from their work. Included are Eady, Charles Johnson, Yusef Komunyakaa, Ishmael Reed, and August Wilson.

Harper, Michael S., and Anthony Walton, eds. *Every Shut Eye Ain't Asleep: An Anthology of Poetry by African Americans Since 1945*. Boston: Little, Brown, 1994. Contains a selection of Eady's poetry with brief critical commentary within an anthology of Eady's generation of African American poets.

Hawkins, Shayla. "Cave Canem: A Haven for Black Poets." *Poets & Writers* 29, no. 2 (March/April, 2001): 48-53. Discusses the Cave Canem workshop and retreat founded by Eady and Toi Derricotte. Eady and Derricotte recognized the need for a "haven" for black writers.

Quashie, Kevin Everod. "Cornelius Eady." In *New Bones: Contemporary Black Writers in America*, edited by Joyce Lausch, Keith Miller, and Quashie. Saddle River, N.J.: Prentice-Hall, 2001. A helpful overview of Eady's career. The introduction assesses issues and themes of Eady's generation.

Young, Kevin, ed. *Giant Steps: The New Generation of African-American Writers*. New York: Perennial, 2000. A comprehensive introduction to Eady's generation.

Joseph Dewey

RICHARD EBERHART

Born: Austin, Minnesota; April 5, 1904

PRINCIPAL POETRY

A Bravery of Earth, 1930
Reading the Spirit, 1936
Song and Idea, 1940
A World-View, 1941
Poems, New and Selected, 1944
Burr Oaks, 1947
Brotherhood of Men, 1949
An Herb Basket, 1950
Selected Poems, 1951
Undercliff: Poems, 1946-1953, 1953
Great Praises, 1957
The Oak: A Poem, 1957
Collected Poems, 1930-1960, Including Fifty-one New Poems, 1960
The Quarry, 1964
Selected Poems, 1930-1965, 1965
Thirty-one Sonnets, 1967
Shifts of Being, 1968
Three Poems, 1968
Fields of Grace, 1972
Two Poems, 1975
Poems to Poets, 1976
Collected Poems: 1930-1976, 1976
Hour, Gnats: New Poems, 1977
Survivors, 1979
Four Poems, 1980
Ways of Light, 1980
New Hampshire: Nine Poems, 1980
Florida Poems, 1981
The Long Reach, 1984
Collected Poems, 1930-1986, 1986
Maine Poems, 1988
New and Selected Poems, 1930-1990, 1990

OTHER LITERARY FORMS

Of Poetry and Poets (1979) is a prose collection divided into three parts and an epilogue. The first section is a compilation of lectures and essays on the craft of poetry. The second is a critical section in which Richard Eberhart discusses the work of poets such as Wallace Stevens, Theodore Roethke, W. H. Auden, and Robert Frost. Five interviews and Eberhart's National Book Award acceptance speech round out the book.

Eberhart's verse plays also deserve mention. The first, "The Apparition," printed in *Poetry* (Chicago) in 1950, is a short play in which a salesman encounters a young girl who wanders into his room; she talks with him, enjoys a few drinks, and then disappears into the hallway. The second play, *The Visionary Farms*, was begun at Yaddo, the artists' colony near Saratoga Springs, New York, when the poet worked in a studio apartment next to William Carlos Williams. The play was produced in May, 1952, at the Poets' Theatre (of which he was cofounder) in Cambridge, Massachusetts. *The Visionary Farms*, which records the collapse of a family's fortune, is a satire on hucksterism. "Hurricane" Ransom misappropriates more than a million dollars from the protagonist, Fahnstock, and leaves him on the verge of financial ruin. On another level the play is a study of American enterprise and a protest against greed. Eberhart's verse dramas are largely considered to be experiments and, though they are interesting adjuncts of the poet's craft, they are not among his finer achievements.

ACHIEVEMENTS

Richard Eberhart fills one of the fifty chairs of the American Academy of Arts and Letters and has served as honorary president of the Poetry Society of America.

Among his other distinguished honors are the Bollingen Prize in 1962, the Pulitzer Prize in 1966 for *Selected Poems* (New Directions), the fellowship of the Academy of American Poets in 1969, and the National Book Award in 1977 for *Collected Poems*. He has served as consultant in poetry to the Library of Congress and as poet laureate of New Hampshire. In 1986 he won the Frost Medal. Philosophical and timeless matters of human life are explored throughout his work in unpretentious language and with gentle wit and humor. Eberhart's poetic career spans six decades, and the poet has served as a model of inspiration to such poets as Sydnea Lea, Dion Pincus, Richard Moore, Michael Benedikt, and Leo Connellan.

BIOGRAPHY

Richard Eberhart grew up on his family's estate, Burr Oaks, in Austin, Minnesota. His early life was almost idyllic. His father, Alpha LaRue Eberhart, the son of a Methodist minister, typified the American dream, having worked his way up from serving as a farm hand at the age of fourteen to owning a business at the age of twenty-one. Working for the Hormel company, where he trained as a salesman, he accumulated a fortune; by the time Richard Ghormley Eberhart was born, he had been able to buy Burr Oaks, an eighteen-room house on forty acres of land. Here the poet, his brother Dryden (b. 1902), and his sister Elizabeth (b. 1910) enjoyed financial security until the year following the poet's graduation from high school, when tragedy struck both his mother and his father.

In 1921, a trusted member of the Hormel enterprise was found to have embezzled more than a million dollars from the company. As a result, A. L. Eberhart lost his accumulated wealth. The more serious catastrophe, however, was the poet's mother's lung cancer, which caused excruciating pain from the fall of 1921 to her death on June 22, 1922. Richard Eberhart, who was then eighteen, stayed out of college a year to help take care of her. It was the most profound experience of the poet's life, and as such, provided an impetus for his poetry and for his exploration of the meaning of suffering, what is real and unreal, the mystery of creation, and the place of the imagination in art.

Eberhart was graduated from Dartmouth College in 1926. For a while he worked as a floor walker in a department store and as an advertising copywriter, and then shipped out as a deckhand on a tramp steamer going around the world. He jumped ship at Port Said, Egypt, and made his way to England. In 1927, he went to St. John's College, Cambridge University, where he took a second B.A. in 1929.

The following year, 1930-1931, he served as tutor to the son of King Prajadhipok of Siam. Upon his return to the United States, he became a graduate student at Harvard University but decided not to go on for his Ph.D. degree. He taught at St. Mark's School from 1933 to 1940; during this time, he was responsible for bringing W. H. Auden as a guest member of the faculty for a month.

Eberhart and his wife, Helen Elizabeth Butcher, were married on August 29, 1941. The couple would have two children: Richard Butcher Eberhart, called Dikkon, and Margaret Ghormley Eberhart, called Gretchen.

After Dikkon's birth, in 1942, the Eberharts moved to Florida, where the poet received a commission as lieutenant in the United States Naval Reserve and served as a theoretical gunnery instructor. He was later transferred to the Aerial Free Gunnery Training Unit in Dam Neck, Virginia, where he wrote "The Fury of Aerial Bombardment" in the summer of 1944.

The breakthrough in Eberhart's career came with his appointment to the faculty of Dartmouth in 1956. He also taught each spring term at the University of Florida in Gainesville in addition to serving as poet in residence at Dartmouth.

ANALYSIS

In his poems, Richard Eberhart returns again and again to the theme of death: death-in-life and life-in-death. His poems are, at once, a stay against oblivion and a bid for immortality. In his essay "Poetry as a Creative Principle," in *Of Poetry and Poets*, Eberhart claims that poetry is "a spell against death." As long as the essence of one's life exists in one's recorded work, there is immortality.

A Bravery of Earth, Eberhart's first published work, is a long philosophical and autobiographical narrative that establishes the dichotomy between the push toward life, harmony, and order and the corresponding horrors that are a constant pull toward the grave.

"THE GROUNDHOG"

"The Groundhog," perhaps Eberhart's most anthologized and acclaimed poem, is the epitome of the duality that characterizes his verse. The poem serves as a kind of memento mori that unites all living creatures in their temporality. Focusing on a dead groundhog, it develops the paradox of life-in-death. The poem additionally expresses the poet's belief that poetry is a gift of the gods—a mystical power that is relative, never absolute.

"The Groundhog" is one of four or five poems that Eberhart claims were given to him. In a 1982 interview printed in *Negative Capability*, he describes this mystical experience. These "given poems," Eberhart states, came from "far beyond or underneath the rational mind" and hence are unusually powerful. In such an experience, he speculates, one is "allied with world consciousness." Commenting specifically on "The Groundhog," he explains that the poem was composed in "twenty minutes of heightened awareness" after he saw a dead groundhog on a friend's farm.

The body was open and the belly was seething with maggots. So here was a small dead animal, as dead as could be, and yet he was full of life, an absolute paradox. . . . He seemed to have more life in him being eaten up by maggots than if he were running along in the fields with nature harmoniously in him.

The poem cites three encounters with a dead groundhog. The first takes place "in June, amid golden fields." Here, in "vigorous summer," the animal's form began its "senseless change." The sight of it without its senses makes the poet's own "senses waver dim/ Seeing nature ferocious in him." He pokes the animal with a stick and notes that it is alive with maggots.

In autumn the speaker returns to the place where he saw the dead groundhog. This time, "the sap [was] gone out of the groundhog,/ But the bony sodden hulk remained." The speaker's previous reaction of love and loathing, the revulsion that was the first response of the senses, is no longer present. "In intellectual chains, . . . mured up in the wall of wisdom," he brings intellect into play. He thinks about and applies reason to the experience of seeing the dead animal. In another summer, then, he takes to the fields again, "massive and burning, full of life," and chances upon the spot where the groundhog lies. "There was only a little hair left,/ And bones bleaching in the sunlight."

After three years, the poet returns again, but this time "there is no sign of the groundhog." It is "whirling summer" once more, and as the speaker's hand covers a "withered heart," he thinks of

China and of Greece,
Of Alexander in his tent;
Of Montaigne in his tower,
Of Saint Theresa in her wild lament.

Eberhart attributes the success of "The Groundhog" to the fact that he refused to delete these final lines. At a writer's discussion group in the Harvard area, where Eberhart joined other poets and read his work aloud, he was urged to end the poem with the description of the dead creature—before the mention of China and Greece, of the soldier, the philosopher, and the saint. Eberhart points out that the purposeful lives of these notable people distinguish them from a dead animal, the groundhog. Perhaps it can be said that an ordinary man would never have noticed the small rotting thing lying in the field had a poet not called attention to its demise. An animal leaves only bones that in time disappear. Yet the lives of great men and women endure throughout time and are recorded in their works. The final lines of Eberhart's poem celebrate human achievement, the life-in-death that is beyond decay.

"FOR A LAMB"

In juxtaposition to "The Groundhog," "For a Lamb," an earlier poem about a dead animal, anticipates and highlights the import of the later work. In a field near Cambridge, England, in 1928, the speaker sees a dead lamb among daisies. "But the guts were out for crows to eat." The speaker asks, "Where's the lamb?" and then answers, "Say he's in the wind somewhere,/ Say, there's a lamb in the daisies." Although there is the sense of death as a fusion with life, there is no person in the poem to give meaning to existence. The lamb lives only because someone, a poet with creative imagination, has marked its being in the world. When there is human significance, death-in-life is transformed into life-in-death.

Eberhart believes that poetry comes out of suffering, and it was his mother's death that brought this awareness. Before she died, he had stayed out of college a year to help take care of her. According to a 1983 essay published in *Negative Capability*, this was for Eberhart "the most profound experience of my life, one that begot my poetry, an experience of depth that was inexpressible." Fifty-five years later, in an essay entitled "The Real and the Unreal," the adult Eberhart ponders the meaning of this early suffering. From memory, he says, "as part of the mystery of creation, flow poetry and music, manifold works of the imagination." One of his poems asserts that it is "the willowy Day-Bed of past time/ that taught death in the substratum." These lines exemplify Eberhart's thoughts in "The Theory of Poetry" that the first experience of the death of a loved one teaches "the bitterness but the holy clarity of truth."

LIFE-IN-DEATH AND DEATH-IN-LIFE

The final stanza of the poem "1934," reprinted in *Collected Poems 1930-1986*, defines Eberhart's premise about poetry and "life-in-death."

> And I have eased reality and fiction
> Into a kind of intellectual fruition

> Strength in solitude, life in death,
> Compassion by suffering, love in strife,
> And ever and still the weight of mystery
> Arrows a way between my words and me.

As a philosophical poet, Eberhart explores life's dualities. In "How I Write Poetry," he states that "everything about poetry is relative rather than absolute." Commenting on "The Cancer Cells," a poem that brings to mind his mother's terminal illness, the poet writes that the cancer cells photographed in *Life* magazine aroused in him an awareness of the simultaneity of the lethal and the beautiful, another poignant reminder of death-in-life.

In "Meditation Two," Eberhart notes that since "the Garden of Eden/ When Eve offered man the fruit of the womb and of life," human beings have been locked in dualism, "so that from the opposites of good and evil, flesh and spirit,/ Damnation and redemption, he is never absent/ But truly is fixed in a vise of these opposites." Art is a "triumph of nature/ Before the worm takes over," and it is the poet's job to "sing the harmony of the instant of knowing/ When all things dual become a unity."

The duality of the person as human and as a kind of creator and god is evident in "New Hampshire, February." Eberhart says the poem was written in the late 1930's, before he was married. One cold winter evening, he was staying in Kensington, in a cabin heated only by a kitchen stove. Two wasps fell through the roof onto the stove. At first the insects were numb, but as they moved to the center of the stove, they became lively. The poet describes how he played God and shoved the creatures toward the heat, where they would become lively and buzz their wings; he would then push them away and watch them become gelid once more. The philosophical implications of this act in relation of persons to God led to the poem that concludes,

> The moral of this is plain.
> But I will shirk it.
> You will not like it. And
> God does not live to explain.

Humans' purposeful nature sets them apart from insects and animals, from wasps, spiders, gnats, seals, terns, cats, tree swallows, owls, field mice, groundhogs, and squirrels. Creatures obey "the orders of nature/ Without knowing them," but the poet who observes their blessed ignorance comments that "it is what man does not know of God/ Composes the visible poem of the world" ("On a Squirrel Crossing the Road in Autumn, in New England," *Collected Poems 1930-1986*).

HORRORS OF WAR

"The poetry of tragedy is never dead," Eberhart states in "Am I My Neighbor's Keeper?" "If it were not so," he says, "I would not dream/ On principles so deep they have no ending,/ Nor on the ambiguity of what things ever seem./ The truth is hid and shaped in veils of error." The question of death in war, of humankind's capacity for destruction and God's tolerance of evil, is addressed in a series of poems Eberhart wrote during World War II. "The Fury of Aerial Bombardment" seems to be the best known and most anthologized of the lot. This poem's speaker says, "You would think the fury of aerial bombardment/ Would rouse God to relent." Since the time of Cain, man has killed his brother. "Is God by definition indifferent, beyond us all?" the poet asks. The ruthlessness and senselessness of war are exposed in a lament over the death of two young men, Van Wettering and Averill, "Names on a list, whose faces I do not recall."

In "At the End of War," "God, awful and powerful beyond the sky's acre/ . . . looks down upon fighting men" and sees their bloody folly and their wickedness. The poet asks God to "forgive them, that all they do is fight/ In blindness and fury." The poem concludes with a further prayer: "And may he learn not to fight/ And never to kill, but love."

"Brotherhood of Men," an account of the death march of Bataan, similarly bewails the horrors of war. Its speaker tells what it was like to be a prisoner of war, "caught . . . on the Rock. At Corregidor/ Caged with the enemy." Here Eberhart is unsparing in graphic detail, telling of "bones softened by black malnutrition," of ulcerous legs and "heads swelled like cabbages before the soft death-rattle." He speaks of "days unendurable," when "madness was manifest, infernal the struggle."

> Urine was drunk by many, rampant was chaos,
> Came wild men at each other, held off attackers,
> Some slit the throats of the dead,

> Drank the blood outright, howled wailing,
> Slit the wrists of the living, others
> with knives, or with fangs ravenous,
> I saw them drinking the blood of victims.

Yet horrible as war is, the narrator finds redemption in the brotherhood of humankind. He has a profound conviction "that we were at our peak when in the depths." The tortured group of men who "lived close to life when cuffed by death,/ had visions of brotherhood when [they] were broken,/ learned compassion beyond the curse of passion."

LIFE'S BLESSINGS

Though Eberhart rails against the evil in human nature that leads to violence and war, he is able to transcend death and destruction to acknowledge simply that to be human is to be imperfect. The poem called "A Meditation" concludes with an exhortation to let one's awareness of evil and death purify and heighten one's enjoyment of life's blessings, "easing a little the burden of our suffering/ Before we blow like the wind away."

Eberhart states in "Learning from Nature" that he has been taught "acceptance of irrationality." He recognizes "the supreme authority of the imagination" because "life longs to a perfection it never achieves." In a poem whose title is an exit, "A Way Out," Eberhart notes the mocking nature of time: "but I would mock it,/ Throw hurricane force against its devil,/ Commanding it to stop." The poet acknowledges the Buddha and Jesus Christ, for they "give mankind examples of the way to go/ The ineffable, and the active means to know." The speaker wrestles with doubt and belief. His warfare is that of rationality, he says, and he "could not abrogate [his] reason East or West." In the end, however, "We can sense/ That old death will give way to new life/ As new mornings grow, Spring comes over the land."

"Love is the mystery in which to rejoice," Eberhart states in "Sphinx," and readers must not mistake his intense interest in and focus on death as indicating somberness or a lack of joy. "The Groundhog Revisiting" is a poem that celebrates life. The occasion is the wedding of the poet's daughter. A groundhog has come along and deflowered the garden; Eberhart wants to dissuade the groundhog from such destruction, not kill it, so he pours gasoline down its hole. "It's on with marriage, down with the groundhogs," he says, as he reflects on Gretchen as a child, when she could "turn six cart-wheels/ Outwitting my power to put on paper/ Pure agility and grace in action." The poet offers a kind of prayer. "Grace this company in some retrospect," he says. "We are here to celebrate love and belief,/ May time bless these believers, love give them grace."

It is because of humanity's impermanence that life is precious, and Eberhart recognizes this in "Three Kids," another poem inspired by his daughter, Gretchen. He fumbles for words to describe his feelings at seeing three frisky little goats frolicking around her in a bright meadow.

> If I lived a hundred years
> No ink of mine from a passionate hand
> Could communicate to you, dear reader,
> Essence of ecstasy, this ecstatic sight
> Of joy of life, limitless freedom,
> As the girl and the young kids leaped and played.

Eberhart's delight in such youthful exuberance is informed by his awareness of death. "Flux" serves up a litany of tragedy: "the gods of this world/ Have taken the daughter of my neighbor,/ Who died this day of encephalitis," a boy, "in his first hour on his motorbike,/ Met death in a head-on collision," and a sea farmer "was tripped in the wake of a cruiser./ He went down in the cold waters of the summer." Death is sudden and inexorable. "Life is stranger than any of us expected," the poet concludes; "there is a somber, imponderable fate" that will annihilate all.

DEATH AS PREEMINENT THEME

For Eberhart, is is necessary to acknowledge the horror of death in order to move beyond it, and poems that embrace the theme of death represent a sizable part of his canon.

"Orchard" pictures a family, the poet's own, sitting in an automobile among fruit trees, grieving in deep silence. They have learned of the mother's impending death. In the middle time of her life, when she is "most glorious" and most beautiful, she is "stalked/ By the stark shape of malignant disease,/ And her face was holy white like all desire." "All of life and all of death were

there" among the fruit trees in the evening, but the final line says that "the strong right of human love was there" as well.

In "Grave Piece," the speaker, presumably the poet himself, says, "Death, I try to get into you," and later repeats, "I must discover inexorable Death." He feels compelled to attempt the impossible, to make "poetry to break the marble word."

Although Eberhart believes that poetry is a gift of the gods, he recognizes that it requires a certain sacrifice: "Every poet is a sacrificial spirit." Yet the poet bears this burden gladly, "gay as a boy tossing his cap up," for even when he is called to write "of tragic things and heavy/ He lives in the senses' gaiety."

Eberhart believes that the ideal life would be lived "near the pitch that is madness." He explains that the crucial word is "near." To be mad or insane would be to fail to capitalize on one's potential, but to live *near* madness, without being mad, would afford heightened awareness that makes poetry. For Eberhart, poetry is the bid for immortality that ultimately defeats death. It is the only way to deal with the immutable fact of mortality.

CRITICAL COMMENTARY

Eberhart's poems seldom display a light touch; they are serious and philosophical, and critics sometimes claim that they are uneven. Two advocates offer strong counters to this claim. In *Negative Capability*'s Eberhart Symposium issue, Arthur Gregor asserts that "poetry is significant only if it articulates the great and time-less matters of human life, anything less than that falls short of its ancient obligation." He says that Eberhart's work reminds him "of the invisible realities" at a time when "trivia has replaced the great matters of poetry." In the same issue, Sydnea Lea says that "Dick's poems, like the man himself, are engaged with matters that matter."

Certainly an examination of Eberhart's work will show that "death-in-life" is a consistent and predominant theme. To celebrate life, according to Eberhart, it is necessary to probe its opposite—death. "It is not necessary to live long to sense the abysmal depths of despair," he writes as he catalogs some of the horrors: prolonged and problematical illness such as his mother's cancer, the pain of wrecked bodies in war, the deep eyes of those justly accused of crime, the awesome spectacle of mental imbalance. "It is impossible," Eberhart adds "to conceive of great poetry being written without a knowledge of suffering."

Eberhart stresses the fact that he is a meliorist who adjudicates between opposite ideas. "I don't accept anyone's idea as absolute, or I try not to," he says, and when one meets the poet, this aspect of his personality becomes immediately clear. "So what can one make of all of this?" is a typical Eberhart statement, and his poems set out to respond to that question—to determine what one is to make of the grand and knotty complexity that is life. Eberhart is a poet whose creativity is a spell against death. Words from "Hardening into Print" sum up his work:

> This glimpse is of an immaculate joy
> Heart suffers for, and wishes to keep.

OTHER MAJOR WORKS

PLAYS: *The Apparition*, pr. 1950; *The Visionary Farms*, pr. 1952; *Triptych*, pr. 1955; *The Mad Musician*, pr. 1962; *Devils and Angels*, pr. 1962; *Collected Verse Plays*, pr. 1962; *The Bride from Mantua*, pr. 1964; *Chocorua*, pr. 1981.

NONFICTION: *Poetry as a Creative Principle*, 1952; *Of Poetry and Poets*, 1979.

BIBLIOGRAPHY

Engel, Bernard F. *Richard Eberhart*. New York: Twayne, 1971. An introductory biography and critical study of selected works. Includes a bibliography of Eberhart's works.

Ginsberg, Allen. *To Eberhart from Ginsberg: A Letter About Howl, 1956, An Explanation by Allen Ginsberg of His Publication "Howl" and Richard Eberhart's "New York Times" Article "West Coast Rhythms."* Penmaen Press, 1976. Ginsberg's essay casts light on both Eberhart and their times.

Hoffman, Daniel G. *Hunting a Master Image: The Poetry of Richard Eberhart*. Special issue of *The Hollins Critic* 1, no. 4 (October, 1964). Devoted to Eberhart's poetics.

Lea, Sydney, Jay Parini, and M. Robin Barone, eds. *Richard Eberhart: A Celebration*. Hanover, N.H.: Kenyon Hill Publications, 1980. A collection of essays on Eberhart and his work.

Negative Capability 6 (Spring/Summer, 1986). This "Richard Eberhart Symposium Issue" contains letters to Eberhart, commentaries and critical articles on the poet's work, an interview, and poems, essays, and addresses by Eberhart. It is edited by Sue Brannan Walker and Jane Mayhall.

Roache, Joel. *Richard Eberhart*. New York: Oxford University Press, 1971. This book is a biography that covers the twists and turns of Eberhart's career from 1904 to 1961. Contains a selected bibliography.

Thorslev, Peter L., Jr. "The Poetry of Richard Eberhart." In *Poets in Progress*, edited by Edward Hungerford. Evanston, Ill.: Northwestern University Press, 1962. A critical appraisal of Eberhart's work, with an analysis of specific poems.

Van Dore, Wade. *Richard Eberhart: Poet of Life in Death*. Tampa, Fla.: American Studies Press, 1982. A small pamphlet that deals specifically with Eberhart's study of death.

Sue Walker;
bibliography updated by the editors

W. D. EHRHART

Born: Roaring Spring, Pennsylvania; September 30, 1948

PRINCIPAL POETRY

A Generation of Peace, 1975
Rootless, 1977
Empire, 1978
The Awkward Silence, 1980
The Samisdat Poems, 1980
To Those Who Have Gone Home Tired, 1984
The Outer Banks and Other Poems, 1984
Just for Laughs, 1990
The Distance We Travel, 1993
Beautiful Wreckage: New and Selected Poems, 1999

OTHER LITERARY FORMS

In addition to winning critical acclaim with his poetry, Ehrhart has distinguished himself in the fields of memoir and personal commentary. He has published four volumes on his Vietnam and post-Vietnam experiences as well as an investigative account and oral history of how the war affected the members of his boot camp platoon. He has published hundreds of personal essays and short opinion pieces on various topics in newspapers and magazines, many of which appear in his 1991 collection *In the Shadow of Vietnam: Essays, 1977-1991.*

Ehrhart has also made his mark as an editor and critic. He has edited two anthologies of Vietnam War poetry and has coedited an additional anthology of Vietnam War poetry and an anthology of Korean War literature.

ACHIEVEMENTS

While he has never enjoyed great commercial success, W. D. Ehrhart has been widely credited with establishing the American experience in Vietnam as a subject for poetry and, as Donald Ringnalda has written, is generally considered the "poet laureate of the [Vietnam] war." He has especially been in demand as a speaker and lecturer at academic conferences and universities. Heserved as a visiting professor of war and social consequences at the William Joiner Center, University of Massachusetts at Boston, in 1990; as writer in residence with the National Writers' Voice Project of the Young Men's Christian Association in Detroit, in 1996; and as a guest in residence at the University of Illinois at Champaign-Urbana, in 1998. In 2001, he held a research fellowship with the American Studies Department, University of Wales, Swansea, United Kingdom. He has received a grant from the Mary Rinehart Foundation (1980), fellowships in prose and in poetry from the Pennsylvania Council on the Arts (1981, 1988), the President's Medal from Veterans for Peace, and a Pew Fellowship in the Arts for Poetry (1993). He was also featured in episode 5, "America Takes Charge," of the Public Broadcasting Service's series *Vietnam: A Television History* and was invited to edit a special issue of the journal *War, Literature, and the Arts* (Fall/Winter, 1997).

BIOGRAPHY

William Daniel Ehrhart was born in Roaring Spring, Pennsylvania, but spent his formative years in Perkasie, Pennsylvania, where his father was a minister. The third of four sons, Ehrhart excelled in school, but the escalating conflict in Vietnam left him feeling honor-bound to postpone college in favor of military service. Reminding his parents that they had not reared him "to let somebody else's kids fight America's wars," he secured their reluctant permission to enlist in the Marine Corps at age seventeen, immediately following his high school graduation in June, 1966.

Ehrhart served in Vietnam with an infantry battalion from 1967 to 1968 and was wounded in the battle for Hue during the Tet Offensive of 1968. Discharged in 1969 with the rank of sergeant, he went on to Swarthmore College, where he became active in the antiwar movement and wrote his first published works before his graduation in 1973.

While still at Swarthmore, Ehrhart gained national recognition as a poet in *Winning Hearts and Minds* (1972), a collection of Vietnam War poetry dedicated to the cause of ending the United States' involvement. Eight of Ehrhart's early poems appeared in this collection.

After college, Ehrhart went to sea as a Merchant Marine and later tried both newspaper reporting and high school teaching along with earning an M.A. in creative writing at the University of Illinois at Chicago in 1978. He married in 1981, and in 1985 he made his home in Philadelphia, Pennsylvania. He earned the Ph.D. in 2000 from the University of Wales at Swansea, United Kingdom. Although he has occasionally taken short-term teaching assignments, he bills himself as an "independent scholar and teacher," earning his living primarily through his writing and his speaking engagements.

ANALYSIS

H. Bruce Franklin, in 1995, spoke for the critical consensus in praising W. D. Ehrhart for his "concision and avoidance of the mannerisms that have made 'poetry' seem like a coterie activity." Ehrhart's "distinctive flat voice speaking in a deceptively plain style," Franklin contends, gives his poetry a "visceral power" and forms the perfect stylistic complement to the "rare fusion of personal and historical vision" for which he has been widely praised. A constant theme throughout Ehrhart's poetry is the personal and collective disillusionment his generation suffered as a result of the U.S. intervention in Vietnam. Many of his poems are unabashedly polemical, and the great majority are written in free verse, Ehrhart's intention being to reach the widest possible audience. As Vince Gotera has pointed out, however, Ehrhart's apparent simplicity and earnestness belie a self-conscious artistry that involves a carefully considered selection and arrangement of language and even occasional forays into traditional poetic techniques and forms. Although he first came to prominence with his antiwar poetry, Ehrhart has not confined himself to that theme. His later poems, on a wide range of subjects, reveal a refreshing capacity for self-ironic reflection and an unabashed appreciation for the moments of grace, love, and contentment he continues to find in his own life.

Ehrhart's early collections are mostly out of print. Many of the poems that appeared in these collections, however, also appear in his 1999 collection *Beautiful Wreckage.*

A GENERATION OF PEACE

A Generation of Peace first established Ehrhart as a truth-teller par excellence and as an insightful interpreter of how the American cultural narrative failed the United States in Vietnam. His Vietnam experiences are crystallized in a series of seemingly simple and straightforward poetic vignettes illustrating the existential character of the war. The poem "Guerrilla War," for example, bespeaks his frustration at finding himself unable to distinguish between friend and foe. The poem concludes with the honest admission that "After a while,/ You quit trying."

The poem "Hunting" turns on the realization that, contrary to the American mythos that brought him to this point, Ehrhart has "never hunted anything in [his] whole life/except other men." Yet "such thoughts," he affirms, are quickly eclipsed by more immediate concerns, such as "chow, and sleep,/ and how much longer till I change my socks."

One of the most widely praised and culturally resonant poems to come out of this collection is "A Relative Thing," a title that Ehrhart intended as a play on the adage, "You can pick your friends but not your relatives."

The poem strikes a tone of bitter recrimination over the willful ignorance of the generation that sent its sons to fight in Vietnam and bears dramatic witness to the brutal realities behind much of the sanitizing rhetoric of the era. "We have been Democracy on Zippo raids,/ burning houses to the ground," the speaker complains, and made the "instruments/ of your pigeon-breasted fantasies."

"Making the Children Behave" likewise challenges the previous generation's vision of American rectitude and stands in opposition to a pervasive tendency among veteran-authors to focus on American trauma to the exclusion of the Vietnamese point of view. The poem culminates in an ironic epiphany occasioned by the speaker's earlier sense of cultural and even racial superiority. When the people in the villages through which he passed "tell stories to their children/ of the evil/ that awaits misbehavior," he wonders, "is it me they conjure?"

ROOTLESS, EMPIRE, AND THE SAMISDAT POEMS

The chapbooks *Rootless* and *Empire*, along with *The Samisdat Poems*, contain further reflections on the war's continuing effects on Ehrhart's life and the life of the country. The poem "Letter," for example, is addressed to the North Vietnamese soldier who almost killed Ehrhart in the battle for Hue during the Tet Offensive. The backdrop to the poem is the United States' 1976 centennial celebration, for which "we've found again our inspiration," the speaker wryly observes, "by recalling where we came from/ and forgetting where we've been." The poem ends with the speaker's fervent hope that Vietnam will "remember Ho Chi Minh/ was a poet" and not let their victory "come down/ to nothing."

These collections also contain reflections on perennial human themes, such as relationships, aging, and even the consolations to be found in nature. "After the Fire" is especially representative of Ehrhart's ability to celebrate the experience of love in poignant and even explicit imagery. "Turning Thirty," in fresh language, bespeaks the confusion of finding oneself suddenly older but not necessarily wiser.

TO THOSE WHO HAVE GONE HOME TIRED

A maturing of Ehrhart's vision as a public poet, one committed to addressing a growing political and popular amnesia over Vietnam, is evident in *To Those Who Have Gone Home Tired*. A restlessness and a self-ironic sense of frustration creep into many of the poems. The title poem is a far-ranging and bitter recrimination over the rapaciousness and brutality that Ehrhart sees as continuing to characterize post-Vietnam American life. "The Invasion of Grenada" likewise bespeaks his despair at popular and political appropriations of the Vietnam experience. Rejecting monuments and commemorative gestures, the speaker declares that he only wanted "a simple recognition" of the limits of U.S. power and an "understanding/that the world . . . is not ours." What he really wanted is "an end to monuments."

The collection also contains some of his finest and most moving poems on subjects other than war. "Gifts" and "Continuity" express Ehrhart's love for his wife, while "New Jersey Pine Barrens" and "The Outer Banks" recount idyllic retreats into the world of nature. Just under the surface, and often explicitly noted, is an anxious sense that the saving graces of love and nature are only transitory and never unalloyed for someone who has committed himself to the cause of truth-telling. From the world's standpoint, he realizes, he is too readily dismissed as a "farmer of dreams" ("The Farmer") and is even considered boorish for his persistent refusal to accommodate himself to the world as it is ("Sound Advice").

THE DISTANCE WE TRAVEL

Inspired by his own trip back to Vietnam, this collection is remarkable for illustrating Ehrhart's continuing capacity for reexamination and self-ironic reflection. His frustration now is directed at a culture that has appropriated the Vietnam experience for both political manipulation and popular entertainment ("For a Coming Extinction"). As the title poem and at least two others suggest, Ehrhart's former bitterness has been mitigated by the openness and friendliness he has found among the postwar Vietnamese. The result seems to have been a modicum of peace with his past, a resolution reinforced by two of his most revealing poems about his present joys, "Making Love in the Garden" and "Star Light, Star Bright."

MOSTLY NOTHING HAPPENS

One of Ehrhart's longest poems, running to 156 lines, *Mostly Nothing Happens* first appeared in two separate journals and was later reissued as a pamphlet. A frankly autobiographical and personal statement, the poem places Ehrhart's present life squarely within the ironic context of his past and explores America's still

unresolved legacy of racial tension. The backdrop is Ehrhart's refusal to give up on the American dream of brotherhood. He continues to live in an integrated inner city neighborhood in the hope that his child would not "reach the age of seventeen/ with no one in her life/ who isn't white." The realization that so many of the angry young African American men he must pass day after day have no inkling of his good intentions and even resent his presence leaves him feeling understandably anxious. This anxiety occasions a poignant reflection on the first African American friend Ehrhart ever made and how this man's gentle strength helped him get through Marine recruit training. His friend, however, later died in Vietnam—an ironic fate which Ehrhart seems to hold up as an example of how the war itself only helped to exacerbate the legacy of racial disharmony and distrust he now confronts. The result, he realizes, is a depressingly familiar feeling: "Every day I'm always on patrol."

BEAUTIFUL WRECKAGE

A retrospective as well as a collection of new poems, *Beautiful Wreckage* stands as a fine introduction to Ehrhart's poetry and themes. The title poem speaks to the issue of strictly factual accuracy versus authenticity in a larger literary sense.

The collection also contains some of his finest occasional poems reflecting on his life and on the manners and mores of contemporary American life. "Not for You" is a painfully honest statement of frustrated hopes and expectations. "Prayer for My Enemies" is an ironic statement of the hypocritical pretense that Ehrhart sees as endemic to organized religion. "Rehobeth, One Last Time" shows how our self-indulgent tendency toward serial monogamy has affected a friend's life. Other poems suggest that he has made peace with his parents and with his own past ("Visiting My Parents' Grave," "What Goes Around Comes Around"). "A Meditation on Family Geography and a Prayer for my Daughter" expresses his fervent wish that his daughter will grow up to find "a place in the world/ surrounded by people who care."

OTHER MAJOR WORKS

NONFICTION: *Vietnam-Perkasie: A Combat Marine Memoir*, 1983; *Going Back: An Ex-Marine Re-*

turns to Vietnam, 1987; *Passing Time: Memoir of a Vietnam Veteran Against the War*, 1989; *In the Shadow of Vietnam: Essays, 1977-1991*, 1991; *Busted: A Vietnam Veteran in Nixon's America*, 1995.

EDITED TEXTS: *Demilitarized Zones: Veterans After Vietnam*, 1976 (with Jan Barry); *Carrying the Darkness: American Indochina, The Poetry of the Vietnam War*, 1989; *Unaccustomed Mercy: Soldier-Poets of the Vietnam War*, 1989; *Retrieving Bones: Stories and Poems of the Korean War*, 1999 (with Philip K. Jason).

MISCELLANEOUS: *Ordinary Lives: Platoon 1005 and the Vietnam War*, 1999.

BIBLIOGRAPHY

Beidler, Philip D. *Re-writing America: Vietnam Authors in Their Generation*. Athens: University of Georgia Press, 1991. Argues that Ehrhart is best understood within the cultural context of his generation and sees his work as an attempt to reinscribe the values and ideals the country failed to live up to in Vietnam.

Gotera, Vince F. *Radical Visions: Poetry by Vietnam Veterans*. Athens: University of Georgia Press, 1994. Remains the best overall introduction to Ehrhart's themes and technique. Gotera establishes Ehrhart as a serious artist and acknowledges his influence as a critic and editor.

Ringnalda, Donald. *Fighting and Writing the Vietnam War*. Jackson: University Press of Mississippi, 1994. Argues that Ehrhart is one of a number of Vietnam-veteran writers whose disregard of literary convention reflects the unconventional nature of the war itself and forms a fitting strategy for challenging residual conventional wisdom.

Rottman, Larry, and Basil T. Paquet. *Winning Hearts and Minds: War Poems by Vietnam Veterans*. New York: McGraw-Hill, 1972. Ehrhart debuted in this anthology. One of his most striking Vietnam poems, "Hunting," first appeared here.

Smith, Lorrie. "Against a Coming Extinction: W. D. Ehrhart and the Evolving Canon of Vietnam Veteran's Poetry." *War, Literature, and the Arts* 8, no. 2 (1996): 1-30. A lucid and insightful survey of Ehrhart's career and of his influence within the field.

Tal, Kali. *Worlds of Hurt: Reading the Literatures of Trauma*. New York: Cambridge University Press, 1996. Places Ehrhart squarely within the "literature of trauma" school. Tal sees Ehrhart as bearing an intensely personal witness to his traumatic experience and as resisting any and all attempts at appropriating or generalizing upon his experience.

Edward F. Palm

JOSEPH VON EICHENDORFF

Born: Near Ratibor, Silesia; March 10, 1788
Died: Neisse, Silesia; November 26, 1857

PRINCIPAL POETRY

Gedichte, 1837 (*Happy Wanderer and Other Poems*, 1925)

Neue Gesamtausgabe der Werke und Schriften in vier Bänden, 1957-1958

OTHER LITERARY FORMS

Although Joseph von Eichendorff's reputation is based almost exclusively on the lyrical talents which both his poetry and novellas attest, his poems themselves compose but a small portion of his entire literary production. Epic poems such as "Robert Guiscard" and "Julian" are included among his more eloquent lyrical poems. His first prose work and the first of his two full-length novels, *Ahnung und Gegenwart* (1815; presentiment and the present), contains fifty poems which reinforce an already impressionistic, lyrical style. His second novel, *Dichter und ihre Gesellen* (1834; the word *Gesellen* is ambiguous: The title means both "poets and their companions" and "poets and their apprentices"), is more tightly constructed and reveals a writer somewhat less conditioned by his proclivities toward poetry. His nine novellas, highlighted by *Aus dem Leben eines Taugenichts* (1826; *Memoirs of a Good-for-Nothing*, 1866) and *Das Marmorbild* (1819; *The Marble Statue*, 1927), do not belie the lyricist and are strewn with some of Eichendorff's most appealing and musical verses. The strength of his narrative work lies not in plot but in allegorical content, landscape descriptions, dream content, and poetic language. Eichendorff's attempts at drama include *Krieg den Philistern* (published 1824; war on the Philistines), the comedy *Die Freier* (pb. 1833; the suitors), historical plays such as *Der letzte Held von Marienburg* (pb. 1830; the last hero of Marienburg), and a dramatic fairy tale. Among his translations are one-act religious dramas of Pedro Calderón de la Barca, some of the farces of Miguel de Cervantes, and Don Juan Manuel's *Conde Lucanor* (1335). Eichendorff is recognized also for his accomplishments as a critical historian of German literature and Romanticism, particularly in *Geschichte der poetischen Literatur Deutschlands* (1857; history of the poetic literature of Germany). He also wrote numerous treatises on history, politics, and religion.

ACHIEVEMENTS

Joseph von Eichendorff's reputation as a master craftsman among German lyrical poets is beyond dispute. No literary history fails to list him in the first rank of German Romantic poets, and such noted poetic successors as Heinrich Heine, Theodor Storm, and Hugo von Hofmannsthal enthusiastically acknowledged his major contributions to the genre. Well into the twentieth century, his work continued to be acclaimed by such literary connoisseurs as Thomas Mann and Werner Bergengruen. He has been called "the last knight of German Romanticism," and his works are said to represent both the climax and the crisis of German Romanticism. The popularity of many of his lyrics has transformed them into veritable folk songs. Four of Eichendorff's most memorable poems, "Das zerbrochene Ringlein" ("The Broken Ring"), "Der frohe Wandersmann" ("The Happy Wanderer"), "Mondnacht" ("Moonlit Night"), and "Sehnsucht" ("Yearning"), were set to music by Robert Schumann; others were used by Johannes Brahms, Hugo Wolf, Felix Mendelssohn-Bartholdy, Hans Pfitzner, and Othmar Schoeck. His novella *Das Schloss Dürande* (1837; the castle Dürande) was the basis for an opera by Schoeck. *Memoirs of a Good-for-Nothing* is one of the *most widely* read German novellas of the nineteenth century and is often regarded as the quintessential Romantic novella.

Somewhat less generally conceded, however, is Eichendorff's status as a religious poet and his function as a pedagogue and a critic of Romanticism. The didactic intent in his poetry is often overshadowed by the very obvious accoutrements of Romanticism with which it abounds. The simple musicality of Eichendorff's verses, the frequent repetition of rhymes and images, the limited scope of his themes, the recurrent expression of a simple but sincere piety, and particularly his *Taugenichts* character sometimes earn Eichendorff the label of a naïve, unsophisticated lyricist, albeit a pleasant and refreshingly healthy one. The immediate, conspicuous beauty of his rhythms and melodies may suffice for the superficial reader. A more persistent and careful reading of his verses, however, yields the insight that beyond the aesthetically pleasing exterior of his opus there is a very tenacious and vital religious faith communicated through a rather surprisingly rich range of variations on the Christian theme. Neither a monastic mystic nor a simplistic, uncritical "true believer," Eichendorff was a decidedly world-involved applier of his faith to life and vice versa. His poems testify to his deeply held conviction of the nec-

Joseph von Eichendorff (© Bettmann/Corbis)

essary interrelationship between his poetry and his religion, aim to convince the reader of the desirability of such a union, and caution against the dangers of a too subjectively oriented Romanticism which does not permit the freedom to choose and to serve a higher ideal.

Biography

Despite the depiction of incessant wanderings and frequent allusions to "die weite Welt" (the wide world) in the writings of Joseph Freiherr von Eichendorff, the poet himself actually had limited exposure to the world beyond the reaches of his native Upper Silesia in southeastern Germany. His journeys were primarily spiritual ones; even university days in Halle and Heidelberg, a student trip to Paris and Vienna, and eventual civil service posts in Breslau, Danzig, Berlin, and Königsberg did not take him to those distant, exotic, non-German-speaking lands, the *Welschland*, which his work often evokes. His birthplace, the Castle Lubowitz near Ratibor, remained at least the physical mecca to which he periodically returned until the deteriorating financial status of his aristocratic family forced the sale of all its properties in 1822.

By the age of ten, when Eichendorff first read the New Testament and was moved by the story of Christ's Passion, he had already been introduced through the Polish and German folk songs and fairy tales of his native region to the second guiding force of his life, the power of poetry. The poet's deep commitment to the Roman Catholic faith and his love for the music and beauty of words as well as his soon proven facility with them were to sustain him for his entire life, even when professional success as a governmental official was withheld from him and external pressures were overwhelming.

Eichendorff had ample discourse with gifted representatives of the Romantic movement, first in 1807, at the University of Heidelberg, where he heard the lectures of the philosopher Joseph von Görres and where he made the acquaintance of such leading literary figures as Clemens von Brentano, Achim von Arnim, and Adam Müller, and then years later, in Berlin, with Ludwig Tieck and E. T. A. Hoffmann, and in Vienna, with Friedrich von Schlegel. He was, however, to turn eventually from Romanticism and to take it to task figuratively in his poetry and literally in his expository writings. Any tendency to succumb completely to narcissistic Romantic musings on Eichendorff's part was confined to his year in Heidelberg. His conscious awareness of the Dionysian dangers of Romanticism is evident in the larger body of his poetry and is particularly clear in the narrative *Viel Lärmen um Nichts* (1833; much ado about nothing).

After completion of his civil service examinations in Vienna in 1812 and his participation in the Wars of Liberation against Napoleon in 1813 and 1815, Eichendorff married Aloysia von Larisch in 1815. They produced four children. The poet held various bureaucratic posts as governmental councillor in several North German cities until he took an early retirement in 1844 for reasons of ill health. From approximately 1816 to 1855, few details are available about Eichendorff's personal life except for the indirect information revealed in his writing; the diaries he had kept regularly from the age of twelve were not continued into that period. His apparently ineffectual career gained him no special recognition; the sole honor bestowed upon him was the Medal for Science and Art by King Maximilian II of Bavaria.

From the poet's retirement until his death thirteen years later at the home of his daughter Therese in Neisse, he resided for only brief periods of time in various East German cities and in Vienna. In the latter city, his acquaintances included the composer Robert Schumann and the writers Franz Grill-Parzer and Adalbert Stifter.

Although Eichendorff had a surprisingly wide circle of intellectual, artistic, and politically influential friends in the course of his life, he seems never to have been an overtly influential personal force among them or a dynamic contributor to their social gatherings but was noted rather for his pleasant, unassuming manner and the quiet grace and spirituality of his personality. After his retirement, he turned to the writing of theoretical treatises and translations from Spanish. It seems that the rigors of a profession to which the poet felt no true emotional commitment had to be balanced by the more pleasant practice of poetry; after the duties of that profession no longer had to be met, he could turn from the perspective of age and experience to objective evaluations of the cultural, historical, and literary developments which he had witnessed throughout his life.

ANALYSIS

Despite the fact that Joseph von Eichendorff is routinely classified among the German Romantic writers, his affiliation with them is primarily a superficial one. The idyllic nature descriptions, the wandering musicians and students, the nostalgic glance toward home and the glorious past, the veneration of the beloved, and an obvious acquaintance with the religious dogma of Catholicism play such a large role in his work that the temptation arises to accept such a generally accepted label without further question. Unlike many Romantics, however, Eichendorff demonstrated no utter abandonment to an introverted psyche but manifested instead a surrender to a specific, sharply focused ideal beyond the self and repeatedly warned against the perils of subjective self-indulgence. The wandering that is done so frequently in Eichendorff's work is not an aimless roaming, as it might at first appear, but a deliberately chosen pilgrimage to God. When Romanticism failed, in Eichendorff's eyes, to keep its promise to restore man's broken relationship with God, it ceased to have validity for the poet.

Eichendorff's poetry and his religious faith were one. Even a random reading of his verses should discourage any attempt to separate the two, despite the fact that his explicitly *geistliche Gedichte* (spiritual poems) do not make up the bulk of his poetic production and represent by no means his masterpieces. Eichendorff himself emphasized in his treatises on literature the importance not of Christian content in poetry but rather of religious orientation and a permeation of the poetry by religious attitudes. He felt that the talent of a poet should be placed in the service of God and that the Christian atmosphere thus created would permit the concealed but higher meaning of earthly life to manifest itself. When he maintained that all poetry is but the expression or the spiritual body of the inner history of a nation and that the inner history of a nation is its religion, he very clearly established the framework in which his poetry should be read.

Since poetry was not an escape from life for Eichendorff but an indispensable manifestation of the truth and beauty that he found inherent in his religious belief, he believed that the poet himself has a special calling. As he does among the Romantics, the poet enjoys a lofty position in Eichendorff's view, but instead of having the function of awakening nature in the Romantic sense for aesthetic purposes, Eichendorff's poet has the moral task of awakening man himself and of illuminating and promoting man's deepest desire and loftiest aim—that is, the search for and movement toward God. He is to caution against selfish, godless pursuits, encouraging human acceptance of heavenly love. The title of one of Eichendorff's most frequently quoted poems is often overlooked; if cognizance is made of the title "Wünschelrute" ("Divining Rod"), then it becomes clear that the *Zauberwort* (magic word) that is sought in order to set the world singing pertains to the living waters hidden underground which are mentioned in the Gospel of John. The sleeping world will awaken to the everlasting life promised by Christ, if the proper word is found—that is, if the truth of that promise of everlasting life can be articulated.

THE SEARCH FOR GOD

In his poem "An die Dichter" ("To the Poets"), Eichendorff paints a very graphic picture of the ethical responsibilities of the poet: As the "Heart of the World," wandering in the footsteps of the Lord, he is to save his fellowmen and set them free, for he has been given the power of the word that boldly names the darkness. To name the darkness is to tell the truth and to warn of the dark forces that threaten him who is caught unaware; the nature of that darkness Eichendorff discusses elsewhere. That the poet has an active role in the search for God is obvious in many poems, from the six sonnets produced early in his career, in which he speaks of various aspects of poetry and the poet, to much later ones, such as "Der Dichter" ("The Poet"), in which only the poet, in a mysterious fashion, is the recipient of the deepest beauties of life and the benefactor of the joy that God places in his heart. According to Eichendorff, the poet has special access through God to the truth and beauty of his religion, which he transforms into images and poetry which are reflections of that religion. One is reminded thereby of Friedrich Hölderlin's dictum: "That which endures is produced by poets." The poet's concern is religion within the larger context of human experience. For Eichendorff, poetry is a virtual spiritual personification and a governing spiritual principle of the life of humankind. The guidance of the poet is therefore essential for ordinary mortals; he is to use his divining rod to locate the living waters of his faith and to articulate them with his songs for the benefit of humankind.

EARTHLY INDULGENCE AND TEMPTATION

Eichendorff's frequently uttered admonition "Hüte dich, bleib wach und munter" (take care, stay awake and lively) is directed against two dangers, that of sensual and aesthetic excess, which he saw as the lure of Romanticism, and that of sterile, middle-class domesticity and the Philistine life. These two hazards are the substance of "Die zwei Gesellen" ("The Two Companions"). The first comrade succumbs to the snares of domestic bliss and is soon imprisoned by hearth and home; the second is seduced by the bewitching sirens of the deep, the enticements of abandoning oneself to eroticism and hedonistic self-indulgence. Interestingly, Eichendorff felt moved to treat the second danger at greater length; he apparently considered it the greater threat and articulated warnings against it more frequently in his poetry, most likely since it was this very indulgence which Romanticism tended to encourage. It is part of the poet's general protest against introversion of the personality. For the narrator of the poem, however, both extremes are distant from God, and he implores God that he be led to him.

Particularly during his student days in Heidelberg, where he was associated with the Romantic movement, Eichendorff concentrated on such poems as "Die Zauberin im Walde" ("The Sorceress in the Forest"), in which the demoniac power of a godless nature and physical beauty are the undoing of a naïve and undisciplined youth. The reader is introduced here to the evil charms of a sultry world where the fresh breezes of God's spirit can gain no entrance. In the poem "Zwielicht" ("Twilight"), the diminishing light of day permits a precarious state in which the usual clear contours are lost and distortions in human relationships are possible. Without the light, which for Eichendorff always means the light of the world, Christ, and consequently also his love, the world is in jeopardy and can be lost in darkness. That God provides the only refuge from earthly sorrows and temptations is clear

in "Das Gebet" ("The Prayer"). The pilgrim moving through life, encountering its pleasures and enchantments, experiences through them sorrow as well as joy and has as his only recourse prayer, which overcomes all the evil bewitchments of life when it victoriously reaches God.

POEMS OF MOVEMENT

Eichendorff's poems are poems of movement; when there are no wandering musicians, there are flowing streams, moving clouds, or rustling forests, and always there is at least the flow of song. The two possibilities for movement away from God against which the poet cautions have already been discussed. If one decides to follow either of these choices, he follows, according to Eichendorff, "earthly ponderousness"; if he chooses instead to move toward God, he is reacting to "intimations of Heaven" and he opens himself to God's light and love. Eichendorff speaks about the two influences operating on man as centrifugal and centripetal forces and sees human life as a constant battleground on which these opposing powers are raging. Centripetal force draws man away from himself and toward God as the true center; like the sun, which provides energy for physical life, the divine love of God reaches out to man and promotes spiritual growth. Man is free to accept that love and prosper or succumb to centrifugal forces and perish in the abyss of his own earthliness. The movement, then, that is always present in his work can usually be recognized as either of these choices and thus a descent into the darkness of the base individual self and spiritual death or an ascent upward toward the heavenly source of love and eternal salvation. When Eichendorff speaks of love, however, it need not be of divine love; its uplifting power may also be that of human love, which by itself has none of the redeeming features of divine love and which leads to an ever-diminishing world of the self if it is not touched by the light and love of God. Such ill-starred love is treated in poems such as "Verlorene Liebe" ("Lost Love") and particularly in the novella *The Marble Statue*.

"MOONLIT NIGHT"

One of Eichendorff's most famous and beautiful lyrics, "Mondnacht" ("Moonlit Night"), might at first glance appear to be solely a nature poem, even though it is listed among the religious poems in his collected works. Viewed within the framework of the poet's philosophy, the poem clearly appears to be an illustration of God's loving gesture toward his earthly creations. Somewhat in the Homeric manner of not directly describing physical traits of objects but rather depicting subjective reactions to them, Eichendorff here shows the effect of Heaven's kiss upon the Earth and nature's response to it. If one takes the sky or Heaven (the German word "Himmel" means both) as a representation of God, then one sees the spirit of God moving across the landscape; the rustling of the forests and the gently waving grain are manifestations of that movement. God's creation, the Earth, is visited by him and derives its beauty and holiness from that contact. The poem ends with the human reaction to such an association: The soul of the narrator moves through the quiet countryside in the presence of God's spirit as though it were already flying home.

That homeward journey is in ordinary Christian terms a return to heavenly origins. Eichendorff gives here an exceptionally effective poetic picture of heavenly love, the centripetal pull it exerts on God's creation, the beauty it produces in the physical world, and the spiritual reply to that love in the soul of man. It is likewise noteworthy that this occurs on a moonlit night; especially with Eichendorff, one must assume that the title of a poem is as important as the text itself and that the moonlight is a significant addition to the poem. Here the light of the moon serves the purpose of illuminating God's moving spirit; were the night not moon-bright, the shimmer of blossoms and the billowing of the grain would not be visible to any human observer. What initially appears to be a magnificently executed nature description is thus demonstrated as being a poetic statement of God's love, symbolized by the kiss of Heaven, reaching, like the moonlight, down to his creation, which in turn renders physical as well as spiritual evidence of the efficacy of that love.

RECURRING MESSAGES AND IMAGERY

Eichendorff is sometimes criticized for his repetitiousness and lack of originality, but such objections lose their force with the realization that the poet, in service to his well-defined worldview, is constantly and deliberately reiterating, rephrasing, rearranging, and recombining his relatively few basic concepts in the

manner of any dedicated teacher following the tradition of *repetitio est mater studiorum*. Eichendorff is not the aesthete who expresses himself in random variety, casting up beautiful images in a kind of verbal "light show" but rather the pedagogue who is "preaching with other means" the established religious convictions to which his ego and his poetic talents are subordinated and with which they are harmonized. He is a kind of religious philosopher who has achieved an exercise in the sublimation or apotheosis of his philosophy in and through his poetry as well as vice versa. He is used by his poetry and his philosophy as a "musician" of these two muses to create living word entities which embody and transfer to the reader the essence of his philosophy. His poems are thus written "through him" and tend to transcend his personal attributes and abilities as they take on a being and order of their own, culminating in an entity apart from and beyond the poet's own manipulation of words, themes, ideas, and forms.

Since Eichendorff himself spoke of the hieroglyphic language used in his poetry, it would be most profitable to take note of some of his most frequently used words and images. The confines of this essay unfortunately permit no thorough analysis of the function of such concepts as spring, gardens, *das Bild* (the image or picture), song, *der Quell* (source or fountain), water, forests, woman, and light which appear so regularly in Eichendorff's poetry. Such a study as well as an investigation of the changing contexts of these motifs would yield proof of the profundity of his often superficially read poems. Here, attention is drawn chiefly to the central concept of light. Even a quick survey of Eichendorff's poems indicates how frequently light, particularly morning light, is featured in his work. The morning is his favorite time of day and Aurora a favorite allegorical figure; the periodical which currently publishes articles on Eichendorff's works has appropriately chosen the name of the goddess of dawn for its title.

It may seem surprising that an ear-oriented poet such as Eichendorff emphasizes light so frequently in his work. Although Eichendorff's talent is that of a musician, his sensitivity is not limited to the auditory world; much of the joy he chooses to articulate is that which he experiences through a visual awareness of the beauty of nature. Instead of employing words to paint the detailed splendors of the visually perceptible physical world, however, Eichendorff was better able to sing praises of them. His frequent allusion to light is therefore both his acknowledgment of the spiritual source of the light which illuminates the wonder of God's creation and a kind of reduction and simplification of multitudinous visual phenomena to one comprehensive symbol. Eichendorff's light is always from above, and when it is not the daylight produced by the sun, it is the light of the moon or the stars, which mitigates and provides relief from the undifferentiated, ambivalent night. Light is for Eichendorff a verification of the Heavenly Father who provides it and of his love for his earthly creatures; it is, as in the poem "Jugendandacht" ("Youthful Devotion"), "des Himmels Kunden" (tidings from Heaven). In "Der himmlische Maler" ("The Heavenly Painter"), it is God and not the poet who is the painter: God's hand draws the contours of the landscape with the morning light, and as the light makes visible the colors of the countryside, his world is painted and shown in all its glory.

Because Eichendorff was so committed to the idea expressed by his contemporary Clemens von Brentano, that "In dem Lichte wohnt das Heil!" (in light there is salvation!), the arrival of light at dawn was an especially welcome occasion for him and the theme of a great many cheerful poems. For Eichendorff, the morning light clarifies the mysteries of the night and erases the worries, fears, and temptations that accompany the night. His morning poems are always expressions of a joyful new beginning; as in the biblical account of the Creation, light means the advent of new life. In Eichendorff's poems, the awakening of nature is heralded by the song of the birds; they seem to acknowledge the source of all light and life as they wing upward toward the heavens. Dawn often coincides with the start of the poet's frequently delineated journeys. Eichendorff was inclined also to write of the other daily transition between light and darkness, the twilight; the time of fading light exemplifies, in contrast to morning hope, an awareness of the bleakness of any diminution of God's light and love.

TECHNICAL AND STYLISTIC DEVICES

Neither in style nor in content does Eichendorff's poetry initially appear to be strikingly innovative; just as the poet's worldview has survived the test of time, so his poetic forms are well-practiced and time-honored. For the quintessential poet Eichendorff, however, perhaps more than for poets generally, the poem is itself the message; the "how" of its delivery is as important as the "what" of its content and serves as an additional aspect or reinforcement of the thought contained within it. Oskar Seidlin demonstrates in his study of "The Two Companions," for example, how intimately and intricately the structure, rhythm, and sounds of the poem are linked to the discourse.

Eichendorff is far more than a facile technician; the standard technical devices he uses are painstakingly chosen to complement the ideas in question, but the full subtleties of such an interrelationship of form and content are exposed only after thorough analysis. With justification, one can say that much of the poet's art conceals itself. Since Eichendorff is a master of *Liedform* (song form), in which the entire poem is one organic, melodic unit, his sense of style has been compared to that of Schumann. The cyclical structure the poet often employs involves not only a rephrasing of the initial message at the conclusion of the poem and therefore a full-cycle realization of the essential meaning, but also a counter-reflecting of individual parts internally, so that a wheels-within-wheels effect is created throughout the entire structure. Eichendorff's sonnets and ballads as well as his songs are best rendered orally, so that the sounds of nature he so frequently uses, the liquid rhythms, and the eloquent, poignant melodies, are clearly communicated.

The strength of Eichendorff's work rests therefore not upon superficial novelty but rather upon the quality of his expression and the integrity and skill with which he executed his mission as an artist. What is unique and extraordinary in Eichendorff's writing is the fervor of his belief in the interrelationship of his poetry and his faith and the consistency and emotive power with which he demonstrated that belief in practice. The journeys into "the wide world" which feature so prominently in his work become particularly inviting when it becomes clear that they are ultimately excursions of the soul into regions that promise spiritual nourishment.

OTHER MAJOR WORKS

LONG FICTION: *Ahnung und Gegenwart*, 1815; *Das Marmorbild*, 1819 (novella; *The Marble Statue*,

1927); *Aus dem Leben eines Taugenichts,* 1826 (novella; *Memoirs of a Good-for-Nothing,* 1866); *Viel Lärmen um Nichts,* 1833 (novella); *Dichter und ihre Gesellen,* 1834; *Eine Meerfahrt,* 1835; *Das Schloss Dürande,* 1837 (novella); *Die Entführung,* 1839; *Die Glücksritter,* 1841; *Das Incognito: Ein Puppenspiel,* 1841; *Libertas und ihre Freier,* 1849; *Julian,* 1853.

PLAYS: *Krieg den Philistern,* pb. 1824; *Ezelin von Romano,* pb. 1828; *Der letzte Held von Marienburg,* pb. 1830; *Die Freier,* pb. 1833; *Robert und Guiscard,* pb. 1855 (verse).

NONFICTION: *Zur Kunstliteratur,* 1835; *Die Wiederherstellung des Schlosses der deutschen Ordensritter zu Marienburg,* 1844; *Zur Geschichte der neueren romantischen Poesie in Deutschland,* 1846; *Über die ethische und religiöse Bedeutung der neueren romantischen Poesie in Deutschland,* 1847; *Brentano und seine Märchen,* 1847; *Die deutsche Salonpoesie der Frauen,* 1847; *Novellen von Ernst Ritter,* 1847; *Die neue Poesie Österreichs,* 1847; *Die geistliche Poesie in Deutschland,* 1847; *Die deutschen Volksschriftsteller,* 1848; *Zu den Gedichten von Lebrecht Dreves,* 1849; *Der deutsche Roman des achtzehnten Jahrhunderts in seinem Verhältnis zum Christentum,* 1851; *Zur Geschichte des Dramas,* 1854; *Erlebtes,* 1857; *Geschichte der poetischen Literatur Deutschlands,* 1857 (2 volumes).

MISCELLANEOUS: *Neue Gesamtausgabe der Werke und Schriften in vier Bänden,* 1957-1958.

BIBLIOGRAPHY

Goebel, Robert Owen. *Eichendorff's Scholarly Reception: A Survey.* Columbia, S.C.: Camden House, 1993. A critical study of Eichendorff's work and the German academic culture of his time. Includes bibliographical references and an index.

Lukács, Georg. *German Realists in the Nineteenth Century.* Translated by Jeremy Gaines and Paul Keast. Edited by Rodney Livingstone. Cambridge, Mass.: MIT Press, 1993. Seven essays on major nineteenth century figures in German literature, including Eichendorff, concerning the role of literature in history, society, and politics.

Purver, Judith. *Hindeutung auf das Höhere: A Structural Study of the Novels of Joseph von Eichendorff.* New York: P. Lang, 1989. In this comprehensive study of Eichendorff's novels in English Purver argues that the theological and didactic intentions in Eichendorff's work are vitally important.

Radner, Lawrence. *Eichendorff: The Spiritual Geometer.* Lafayette, Ind.: Purdue University Studies, 1970. A comprehensive critical interpretation of Eichendorff's works.

Schwarz, Egon. *Joseph von Eichendorff.* New York: Twayne, 1972. A short biography with a bibliography of Eichendorff's work.

Margaret T. Peischl;
bibliography updated by the editors

GUNNAR EKELÖF

Born: Stockholm, Sweden; September 15, 1907
Died: Sigtuna, Sweden; March 16, 1968

PRINCIPAL POETRY
Sent på jorden, 1932
Dedikation, 1934
Sorgen och stjärnan, 1936
Köp den blindes sång, 1938
Färjesång, 1941
Non serviam, 1945
Dikter I-III, 1949
Om hösten, 1951
Strountes, 1955
Dikter, 1932-1951, 1956
Opus incertum, 1959
En Mölna-elegi, 1960 (*A Mölna Elegy,* 1984; Muriel Rukeyser and Leif Sjöberg, translators)
En natt i Otočac, 1961
Sent på jorden med Appendix 1962, och En natt vid horisonten, 1962
Dikter, 1955-1962, 1965
Dīwān över fursten av Emgión, 1965
Sagan om Fatumeh, 1966
Vatten och sand, 1966

Vägvisare till underjorden, 1967 (*Guide to the Underworld*, 1980)

Selected Poems of Gunnar Ekelöf, 1967 (Rukeyser and Sjöberg, translators)

I Do Best at Night: Poems by Gunnar Ekelöf, 1968 (Robert Bly and Christina Paulston, translators)

Urval: Dikter, 1928-1968, 1968

Partitur, 1969

Selected Poems, 1971 (W. H. Auden and Sjöberg, translators)

Dikter, 1965-1968, 1976

Songs of Something Else: Selected Poems of Gunnar Ekelöf, 1982

OTHER LITERARY FORMS

In addition to fifteen original volumes of poetry published before his death in 1968, Gunnar Ekelöf wrote four books of essays: *Promenader* (1941; walks), *Utflykter* (1947; excursions), *Blandade kort* (1957; a mixed deck), and *Lägga patience* (1969; playing solitaire). He also published four books of translations, mostly poetry, from French, German, English, Latin, and Persian: *Fransk surrealism* (1933; French Surrealism), *Hundra år modern fransk dikt* (1934; one hundred years of modern French poetry), *Valfrändskaper* (1960; chosen kinships), and *Glödande gåtor* (1966; a translation of Nelly Sachs's *Glühende Rätsel*). Since his death, there have appeared two books containing letters, the poet's annotations to some of his own works, and various other materials drawn from Ekelöf's notebooks and manuscripts: *En självbiografi* (1971; an autobiography), selected, edited, and with an introduction by the poet's wife and literary executor, Ingrid Ekelöf, and *En röst* (1973; a voice).

ACHIEVEMENTS

Gunnar Ekelöf is widely recognized as the most original and influential Swedish poet of his generation. His reputation was well established in Scandinavia during his lifetime. Sweden honored him with many national literary prizes; the Danish Academy awarded him its Grand Prize for Poetry in 1964; and in 1966, the Scandinavian Council gave Ekelöf its prize for *Dīwān över fursten av Emgión* (1965; Diwan over the prince of Emgión). Although Ekelöf never completed his formal education, he was honored by academia. The University of Uppsala gave him an honorary degree in 1958, and in the same year, he was elected a member of the Swedish Academy. His contributions to Swedish literature were recognized: He expressed the voice of modernism and brought a new lyric tone to Swedish poetry. The concerns of Ekelöf's major poems are metaphysical and complex; to make them understood, Ekelöf continually tried to simplify poetic language. He pared away nonessentials—what he called "literary language"—until the tone of his poems became almost conversational. It is not, however, a casual voice that one encounters in the poems; it addresses the reader directly, intensely, passionately. Scandinavians recognize this voice as belonging to a major poet, and many scholars believe that if Ekelöf had written in a language such as English, he would be regarded as a key international figure in the development of contemporary poetry.

Gunnar Ekelöf (© Lütfi Özkök)

BIOGRAPHY

Bengt Gunnar Ekelöf was born in Stockholm, Sweden, on September 15, 1907. His father, Gerhard Ekelöf, was a wealthy stockbroker, and Ekelöf grew up in big, finely furnished houses. Ekelöf's childhood, however, was not a happy one, despite his comfortable surroundings. Gerhard Ekelöf had contracted syphilis, and his health was deteriorating when Ekelöf was a young boy. Before Ekelöf turned nine, his father died, and Ekelöf was sent away to boarding schools. When his mother, Valborg von Hedenberg, remarried several years later, Ekelöf felt rejected and homeless. Bengt Landgren and Reidar Ekner, the critics most familiar with Ekelöf's biography, point out that Ekelöf's relationship with his parents cultivated and reinforced his role as an "outsider." Ekelöf's failed love relationships—a 1932 marriage to Gunnel Bergström was dissolved after a few months, and an affair during 1933 and 1934 was broken off—reinforced Ekelöf's "outsider" perspective.

Ekelöf was particularly fascinated by two subjects as a student: music and Oriental mysticism. In 1926, he spent one semester at the London School of Oriental Studies, and in the next year he began studies in Persian at the University of Uppsala in Sweden. Ekelöf was often sick as a student, and he never earned a degree, but his studies inspired a lifelong interest in Oriental mysticism and led to his discovery of Ibn el-Arabi's poetry, which moved Ekelöf to write his first poems. The attraction of mysticism for Ekelöf, so compelling when he was young, did not wane as he matured. Strains of mysticism can be found throughout his oeuvre, particularly in the last three collections of original work published before his death: *Dīwān över fursten av Emgión*, *Sagan om Fatumeh* (the tale of Fatumeh), and *Guide to the Underworld*.

In the late 1920's, Ekelöf moved to Paris to study music. Soon, however, his attention shifted from music to the problems of poetic language, as he struggled through an emotional breakdown to write many of the poems which appeared in his first book, *Sent på jorden* (late hour on Earth). After the publication of this initial volume, Ekelöf published new volumes every three or four years, becoming a popular as well as a critically acclaimed poet.

In 1943, Ekelöf married Gunhild Flodquist. Their marriage was dissolved in 1950, and in 1951 Ekelöf married Ingrid Flodquist, who became his literary executor after his death. A daughter, Suzanne, was born to

them in 1952. As befitted a poet who sought to dissolve the boundaries of time and place, Ekelöf was a tireless traveler; in the last years of his life, he was increasingly drawn to the Middle East. His travels, particularly his 1965 trip to Istanbul, gave rise to the "eternal wanderers" of his later poetry. In 1968, he died of cancer of the throat. At Ekelöf's request, his ashes were placed in the ancient city of Sardis.

ANALYSIS

To discuss Gunnar Ekelöf's poetry is to discuss more than poetry: His books of poems also document evolving stages of Ekelöf's vision, the quest to resolve the great paradoxes of life and death and the boundaries of time. In his grappling with metaphysical questions, Ekelöf followed the path of the "contemporary mystic," in Eric Lindegren's words, and it is this quest which gives Ekelöf's poetry its distinctive character.

"EN OUTSIDERS VÄG"

In 1941, Ekelöf wrote an essay entitled "En outsiders väg" (an outsider's way), and readers have followed his lead in classifying Ekelöf's perspective as that of an "outsider." Certainly, the Byzantine and ancient Greek settings of his last books of poems are far removed from the life and landscape of his contemporary Sweden. One of the central themes in Ekelöf's poetry is the plight of the individual, both isolated and imprisoned within the conscious ego and subjective will of the "I" and "locked out" from all other people and things. The poet's first duty, Ekelöf has stated, is "to admit his unrelieved loneliness and meaninglessness in his wandering on the Earth." It is paradoxically this awareness, this outsider perspective, that allows the poet to create, for only then is the poet resigned enough to be uninhibited, to write truthfully—and thereby to be of some use to others. In typical Ekelöf fashion, total alienation and dejection are turned upside down to provide the starting point for genuine communication. Ekelöf never veers from his personal vision, his outsider's way, but at the same time he never loses his audience. His personal vision is expressed with such uncompromising honesty and conviction that his private questions and dilemmas assume universal significance. Thus, however cryptic and arcane his verse becomes, it is never merely art for art's sake: "It is not art one makes/ But it is oneself."

SENT PÅ JORDEN

By analyzing Ekelöf's volumes of poetry chronologically, one can trace the development of his vision from the desperation and anguish expressed in his early poems to the integration of the individual and the unity of time in a cosmic oneness expressed in the Byzantine triptych. Although *Sent på jorden*, Ekelöf's first volume of poetry, did not receive a great deal of attention when it was published, it has been of enormous consequence for the development of Swedish poetry: *Sent på jorden* ushered in lyric modernism. Ekelöf composed the volume in Paris, supposedly while listening to recordings of Igor Stravinsky:

> I placed one word beside another and finally with a great deal of effort managed to construct a whole sentence. . . . It was the hidden meaning that I was seeking—a kind of *Alchemie du verbe*. . . . [P]oetry is this very tensioned-filled relationship between the words, between the lines, between the meanings.

Like the Surrealists and the Dadaists, Ekelöf sought to exploit the associative and suggestive power of words, but he was not content with mere verbal fireworks; he stressed the arrangement of the whole as he carefully placed "one word beside another."

Ekelöf has called *Sent på jorden* a "suicide book," and many of the poems in the volume express an anguished desperation. The persona of the poems is "dying in [his] own convulsions" as he violently struggles for expression and meaning: "crush the alphabet between your teeth." The persona's identity is ready to shatter as "nerves screech silently in the dying light." Locked up in a room, completely isolated from the outside world and even from the objects of the room itself, the persona can only chant: "I don't want to die, I don't want to die and cannot live . . . it's late on earth." Death offers a solution to the persona's desperation, an annihilation of the self. Thus, death is a tempting liberator, able to free the persona from imprisonment in ego. In "Cosmic Sleepwalker," however, the persona, rather than seeking self-annihilation, dreams of communion with a cosmic mother. The choices for the persona, then, are spelled out in "Apotheosis," the final poem of the collection: "Give me poison to die or dreams to live." The fragmented isolation of the individual, prisoner of the "I," is

unbearable. In his first volume, then, Ekelöf defines one of his central themes. He also hints, however, at a resolution for the hysterical persona: a living cosmic oneness, where the individual is a part of a larger whole.

SURREALIST INFLUENCE

In 1934, the same year in which Ekelöf published *Dedikation*, he published a book of translations, *Hundra år modern fransk dikt*. The year before, in 1933, his translations of French Surrealist poems had been published in *Fransk surrealism*. Living in Paris in the late 1920's, Ekelöf was bound to feel the impulses of the various "isms" of the period, and many poems in his early volumes could be termed Surrealist. Ekelöf was attracted to the French Surrealists, particularly Robert Desnos, but ultimately found their methods contrived, artificial, and mechanical. On the title page of *Dedikation*, Ekelöf quotes a poet to whom he was more fundamentally drawn, Arthur Rimbaud: "I say: one must be a seer, one must make oneself a seer." In *Sent på jorden*, Ekelöf asked for "dreams to live," and Rimbaud offered a vision to synthesize life and dreams. Nevertheless, the "apotheosis" that Ekelöf sought in *Dedikation* failed; the glorified dream world of this volume later struck Ekelöf as false, and he rejected it. As Rabbe Enckell has pointed out, the romanticized images and prophetic voice in the volume seem an overcompensation for the desperate tone in *Sent på jorden*.

In *Sorgen och stjärnan* (sorrow and the star), the crucial problem remains the same: "One thing I've learned: reality kills! And something else: That no reality exists except this—that none exists!" In *Köp den blindes säng* (buy the blind one's song), the tone becomes calmer, though the perception is the same. The poet can, however, accept his condition, because it becomes a prerequisite for meaning. Ekelöf himself called *Köp den blindes säng* a transitional book; what he referred to as "the breakthrough" came with *Färjesång* (ferry song).

FÄRJESÅNG

The persona in *Färjesång* overcomes his desperation, assumes the role of the phoenix, and rises out of his ashes of anguish ready to "write it down." The tone is confident, at times assertive, and even lecturing: "In reality you are no one." The poet—who has experienced true vision—unmasks his readers and exposes the feeble self-deceptions they have invented to give significance and purpose to their lives. "Legal rights, human dignity, free will/ all of these are pictures painted with fear in reality's empty hall." Ekelöf asserts a new understanding of reality "beyond justice and injustice, beyond thesis and antithesis," a reality beyond individual personalities and perspectives. Exposing the meaninglessness of clichés and conventions of daily life, Ekelöf "surrenders" himself, "like the last rat on a sinking ship," in the hope of mystically uniting with all. The climax of the collection, the poem "Eufori" ("Euphoria"), clearly shows how Ekelöf's vision had evolved since the earlier volumes. The tone of the poem is calm. The persona is sitting in his garden, at peace with the natural world around him. The red evening glow, the moth, the candle, the aspen—all are pulsating with life, but in this transcendent moment, they pulsate with more than life: "All nature strong with love and death around you." The poet has a vision of the synthesis of life and death, of the individual consciousness and the awareness of all. In this poem, at least, the poet has an answer for himself and the reader: He can "sing of the only thing that reconciles/ the only practical, for all alike."

NON SERVIAM

The mood is much darker in *Non serviam*. In it the poet is estranged from the comforts of the welfare state: "Here, in the long, well-fed hours'/ overfurnished Sweden/ where everything is closed for draughts . . . it is cold to me." The ugly duckling, the odd one, "Svanen" ("The Swan"), surveys the "anemic blush over endless suburbs/ of identical houses." It is fall in this poem, the land laid waste with "worm-eaten cabbages and bare flowers." In a key poem of this collection, "Absentia animi," rotting mushrooms and tattered butterflies are omens of general oblivion. Echoing *Sent på jorden*, the poem repeats the refrain, "Meaningless. Unreal. Meaningless." The vision from *Färjesång* remains, however, although the intensity of the joyful tone is subdued:

> O deep down in me
> the eye of a black pearl reflects from its surface
> in happy half-consciousness
> the image of a cloud!
> Not a thing that exists
> It is something else
> It is in something existent
> but it does not exist

> It is something else
> O far far away
> in what is beyond is found
> something very near!

In "En Julinatt" ("A July Night"), a poem Ekelöf called central to the collection, the persona yearns for a prenatal state, suggesting "something else . . . beyond" as a state, or condition, of preconsciousness, before the intrusion of "I":

> Let me keep my world
> my prenatal world!
> Give me back my world!
> My world is a dark one
> but I will go home in the darkness
> through the grass, under the woods.

Despising the society and culture that produce "suburbs of identical houses," Ekelöf seems reconciled to the simple elements of nature. Like his predecessor, Edith Södergran, a Finno-Swedish poet he much admired, who declared that "the key to all secrets lies hidden in the raspberry patch," Ekelöf trusts nature's existence, concretely and as a revelation of "something else."

"A REALITY [DREAMED]"

In an essay published in 1941, Ekelöf wrote: "Kinship with the dead—or rather: the dead within one—is in many ways more alive than kinship with one's contemporaries, from whom one is separated by a thick layer of rhinoceros hide." The individual is alone—that is a central theme in Ekelöf's poetry—but teeming with life; the dead remain as integral parts of the individual's ego. In earlier volumes, Ekelöf had exposed the falsehoods of rational philosophies and denied their reality, but in "En verklighet [drömd]" ("A Reality [*dreamed*]"), from the collection *Om hösten* (in autumn), the poet's insight—somewhat akin to Ralph Waldo Emerson's "dream power"—enables him to construct a philosophy of life from his experience of nature. The persona overcomes all limitations, including time, space, and loneliness:

> every landscape, every shift in the landscape, contains
> all possible landscapes
> and this life contains all possible lives:
>
> . . . .
>
> the peopled worlds,
> and the life of the unseen, and the dead.

THE 1940'S AND 1950'S

Critics agree that Ekelöf's poetry of the 1940's assured him a place as one of Sweden's greatest lyric poets. The concerns of the poetry are abstract, metaphysical, speculative. Most of the key poems of this period are longer lyrics, varying in tone from the explosiveness of *Färjesång* to the romantic, elegiac tone of *Om hösten*. The poems of the 1950's move in a different direction. Ekelöf simplified his style in an attempt to write depersonalized poetry, and the poems of this decade are generally short, simple lyrics about familiar objects and situations, pruned of all literary baggage to achieve what Ekelöf called "poetry of the factual," or antipoetry. The collections published in the 1950's also reveal a joking, absurd side of Ekelöf's vision. In contrast to the speculative, metaphysical poems of earlier volumes, many of these poems focus on the body: sexuality, eroticism, obscenity. If Ekelöf's anti-poetry functions to balance the body-soul relationship by emphasizing feeling and existence here and now, as Pär Hellström's study of these volumes suggests, Ekelöf as seeker still permeates these collections. He continues as a solitary figure, affirming that "I do best alone at night," for then he can listen "to the talk of the eternal wanderers." Eternal wanderers, however, live an existence different from that of ordinary mortals, and many of these poems express a longing for death in the poet's desire to identify with and become a part of timeless existence. The poet's "self-reflecting waters" do not speak "of life but of Lethe's wave"; rebirth is to be found "in the swaddling cloth of death." This fascination with death, however, culminates in a turn toward life-giving uses of the past and tradition. Unable to exist in the isolation of his own ego, unable to accept the social alienation of his contemporary Sweden, Ekelöf turns to "ancient cities" to find his own "future." Thus, the publication of his next volume, *A Mölna Elegy*, marked a transition to the concerns that inform the trilogy which concluded his career.

A MÖLNA ELEGY

In his introductory notes to *A Mölna Elegy*, Ekelöf stated that the poem is concerned with "the relativity of the experience of time"; he hoped, he said, to capture a "traverse section of time, instead of a section lengthwise." In his attempt to analyze "the mood of a certain moment," Ekelöf revealed the complexity of consciousness. The life moment in *A Mölna Elegy* is a moment of mystical insight, with "time running wild" in the consciousness of the persona. The "I" comprises many personalities and undergoes many transformations as the present, past, and future are experienced as independent layers of consciousness. The life of the past—in the memory of the persona's relatives, for example—exists in the present, in the persona's consciousness, as well as in the lives of the dead. Any given moment, then, comprises images from a number of centuries and from various cultures and beliefs—from the past as well as the present. Demarcations of time and space are dissolved, borders between life and death eliminated. All existence is a unity: The reality "beyond" is all of it at once.

"I am of the opinion," Ekelöf once wrote, "that man carries humanity within himself, not only his father's and mother's inheritance but also his cousin's, his second cousins', and further, the animals', plants', and stones' inheritance." As Leif Sjöberg has so convincingly documented, the many "inheritances" which constitute the moment expressed in *A Mölna Elegy* are held together by the "I" of the poem—not only by means of his own observations, but also by means of dead relatives speaking through him, and through allusions to and quotations from dead poets. Ekelöf uses fragmentary allusions, many of them esoteric (such as authentic graffiti and inscriptions in Latin found on tombstones in Pompeii), and borrowings (for example, from Edith Södergran) to document a life and a piece of history. Ghosts, phantoms, spirits—the "dead ones"—still have a voice, and thus the past continues to live in the present, integral to the speaker's consciousness. People, things, and ideas can be fully comprehended only in the context of their connectedness to the past.

Ekelöf's 1965 trip to Istanbul, where he saw the Madonna icon of Vlachernes, inspired an outpouring of passionate lyrics. Poems came so quickly, Ekelöf wrote to a friend, that, "as far as I can understand, someone has written the poems with me as a medium. . . ." Within a few short months, Ekelöf composed the last three volumes he was to publish in his lifetime.

DĪWĀN ÖVER FURSTEN AV EMGIÓN

The Diwan trilogy ranges from the Byzantine Middle Ages to an unspecified epoch in the Oriental (that is,

Middle Eastern) world to classical antiquity and the Hellenic Age. In accepting the prize of the Scandinavian Council in 1966 for *Dīwān över fursten av Emgión*, Ekelöf stressed that these civilizations of the past can speak to modern times: "I have chosen Byzantium, long since lost, as a starting point from which I should be able to assail the present." His targets are "political decadence" and the "degradation" and "coldness" among persons he observes in modern life. These are familiar themes in Ekelöf's poetry, but they are given a particular intensity in the trilogy, an intensity derived from the controlled, pure passion they express.

In the Diwan trilogy, Ekelöf has been able to concretize "something beyond" into a female figure, lover-daughter-sister, and finally an all-embracing mother figure. His vision can therefore be expressed in passionate love lyrics, or in what Bengt Landgren has termed "erotic mysticism." The persona in *Dīwān över fursten av Emgión* is captured in battle, imprisoned, tortured, and finally blinded. Locked in darkness, his only means of "escape" and survival is his ability to dream and to remember. The Ekelöf persona recognizes both God and the Devil as "tyrants," as exponents of either/or, a world of duality he rejects. Love offers the persona an alternative to "the two locked in combat," a liberation from captivity in ego. The love for the mother figure allows a transition from life to death or the presence of death—or preconsciousness—in the present. The persona's dream power, or vision, enables him to "go home in the darkness" to that "prenatal world" Ekelöf called for in *Non serviam*. "Something else," something beyond, is now seen clearly as a "Mother to no man/ But who has breasts/ With milk for all."

SAGAN OM FATUMEH

The female persona in *Sagan om Fatumeh*, like the male persona in *Dīwān över fursten av Emgión*, suffers horribly. She is apparently deserted by the prince who has fathered her child. For a time she serves in a harem, but eventually she is thrown out on the street. As she becomes an old woman; she has to prostitute herself to survive. Yet her spirit is never crushed; her visions—the memories of her lover—sustain her. Fatumeh also sustains the prince, for she gives his "soul a shadow"; the love they feel for each other is

their realization of the unity of all things, of the soul's awareness of the eternal Mother. Only something that exists can cast a "shadow": The soul exists in its expression of love, as felt between two people, and as a vision of the encompassing love of an Earth Mother. In Fatumeh's final meeting with her beloved, the mystic identification is realized as the lovers are effaced in a cosmic union.

GUIDE TO THE UNDERWORLD

Early in his career, in a poem published in *Färjesång*, Ekelöf described his "underworld":

> Each person is a world, peopled
> by blind creatures in dim revolt
> against the I, the kin, who rules them.
> In each soul thousands of souls are imprisoned,
> in each world thousands of worlds are hidden
> and these blind and lower worlds
> are real and living, though not full-born,
> as truly as I am real . . .

In *Guide to the Underworld*, the last volume of poetry he published before he died, Ekelöf is able to free these "blind creatures" because the "guide" is free of the ego. He has discovered that, "alone in the quiet night," he can escape the limitations of his own identity and "hover" in his visions, "weightless," "empty," "floating." Life and death, past and present, history and dreams converge and dissolve into each other. In a key poem, "The Devil's Sermon," the persona unites with the Virgin, or Eternal She, in an act of love. Thus, the persona merges with the universe and is one with the infinite. Ekelöf finally resolves the great paradox—he embraces a reality that is life and death at once:

> I wanted both
>
> The part of the whole as well as the whole
> And that this choice would involve no contradiction.

OTHER MAJOR WORKS

NONFICTION: *Promenader*, 1941; *Utflykter*, 1947; *Blandade kort*, 1957; *Verklighetsflykt*, 1958; *Lägga patience*, 1969; *Ensjälvbiografi*, 1971; *En röst*, 1973.

TRANSLATIONS: *Fransk surrealism*, 1933; *Hundra år modern fransk dikt*, 1934; *Valfrändskaper*, 1960; *Glödande gåtor*, 1966 (of Nelly Sachs's poetry).

MISCELLANEOUS: *Skrifter*, 1991-1993 (8 volumes; collected works).

BIBLIOGRAPHY

Shideler, Ross. *Voices Under the Ground*. Berkeley: University of California Press, 1973. A critical study of Ekelöf's early poetry. Includes biobliographic references.

Sjöberg, Leif. *A Reader's Guide to Gunnar Ekelöf's "A Mölna Elegy."* New York: Twayne, 1973. A critical guide to *A Mölna Elegy*. Includes bibliographic references.

Thygesen, Erik. Introduction to *Modus Vivendi: Selected Prose*, by Gunnar Ekelöf. Norwich, England: Norvik Press, 1996. Thygesen's introduction and notes on each poem offer some biographical and historical background to Ekelöf's work.

Thygesen, Erik. *Gunnar Ekelöf's Open-Form Poem, A Mölna Elegy*. Stockholm, Sweden: Almqvist & Wiskell International, 1985. A critical study of *A Mölna Elegy*. Includes bibliographic references and an index.

C. L. Mossberg;
bibliography updated by the editors

T. S. ELIOT

Born: St. Louis, Missouri; September 26, 1888
Died: London, England; January 4, 1965

PRINCIPAL POETRY

Prufrock and Other Observations, 1917
Poems, 1919
Ara Vos Prec, 1920
The Waste Land, 1922
Poems, 1909-1925, 1925
Ash Wednesday, 1930
Triumphal March, 1931
Sweeney Agonistes, 1932
Words for Music, 1934
Collected Poems, 1909-1935, 1936
Old Possum's Book of Practical Cats, 1939

Four Quartets, 1943
The Cultivation of Christmas Trees, 1954
Collected Poems, 1909-1962, 1963
Poems Written in Early Youth, 1967
The Complete Poems and Plays, 1969

OTHER LITERARY FORMS

When he startled the poetic world with the publication of *Prufrock and Other Observations* in 1917, T. S. Eliot was already on his way to becoming a prolific, formidable, and renowned literary critic of extraordinary originality and depth. Between 1916 and 1920, for example, he contributed almost one hundred essays and reviews to several journals, some of which he helped to edit. While his most enduring and famous criticism (except for his superb work on Dante Alighieri) is contained in such essays as "Hamlet and His Problems" and "Tradition and the Individual Talent" (*The Sacred Wood*, 1920), he published thirty books and pamphlets and scores of essays, many of which remain uncollected. Chief among his other volumes of prose are *Homage to John Dryden* (1924), *Shakespeare and the Stoicism of Seneca* (1927), *For Lancelot Andrewes* (1928), the celebrated *Dante* (1929), *Selected Essays* (1932, 1950), *The Use of Poetry and the Use of Criticism* (1933), *After Strange Gods* (1934), *Essays Ancient and Modern* (1936), *Poetry and Drama* (1951), and *On Poetry and Poets* (1957). From its inception in 1922 until its last issue in 1939, Eliot was editor of *The Criterion* and an important contributor to that and other journals concerned with literary, cultural, political, and religious matters.

Eliot came to drama later than to poetry and criticism, though the seeds of drama are clearly in his early poetry, and the drama occupied much of his criticism. His dramatic writing ranges from religious pageant-plays in verse, *The Rock: A Pageant Play* (1934) and *Murder in the Cathedral* (1935), to quite diverse efforts such as *The Family Reunion* (1939), *The Cocktail Party* (1949), *The Confidential Clerk* (1953), and *The Elder Statesman* (1958). All his dramatic work has as one of its objects the restoration of poetic drama to the popular theater.

The record of Eliot's achievement is by no means complete. Many of his essays are available only in the journals in which they were published, and his notebooks have not been fully mined. *The Letters of T. S. Eliot: Volume I, 1898-1922*, edited by Valerie Eliot, his second wife, was published in 1988. The letters exemplify Eliot's characteristic civility, and they give glimpses of his occasional insecurities as a young American determined to succeed in England on England's terms. Eliot's thousand or so letters to Emily Hale have not been published; they are in the Princeton University Library and may be made public after January 1, 2020. Mrs. Valerie Eliot has edited and published *The Waste Land: A Facsimile and Transcript of the Original Drafts Including the Annotations of Ezra Pound* (1971) and Eliot's *Poems Written in Early Youth*. Several of Eliot's manuscripts are in the Berg Collection of the New York Public Library and in the Hayward Collection at King's College, Cambridge.

ACHIEVEMENTS

T. S. Eliot's achievements are such that he became the premier poet of his own generation and enlivened literary criticism by contributing such phrases as "objective correlative," "dissociation of sensibility," and "impersonal" poetry. He greatly helped to foster a resurgence of interest in Dante, in the Metaphysical poets of the seventeenth century, and in Elizabethan and Jacobean drama at a time when such a resurgence was needed. He also provided a strong critical and poetic voice that chided the Victorian and Edwardian poets while furnishing a new poetry that served as a practical criticism of theirs.

The one title he preferred, and the one by which he is best and justly remembered, is "poet." His poetry is not, on first acquaintance, easy; and it may not be so on second or third acquaintance. He is, as he said of his own favorite writer, Dante, "a poet to whom one grows up over a lifetime." His poetic originality, called into question in his early days by those who charged him with plagiarism, lies in the careful crafting and arrangement of lines and phrases, the introduction of literary, historical, and cultural allusions, and the elaboration of image and symbol in highly charged and often dramatic language that both describes and presents a personal emotion or experience and generalizes it. Eliot's careful husbanding of words, phrases, images, and symbols results in a recurrence of those elements and a

continuity of subject matter from his juvenilia through his first and second masterpieces ("The Love Song of J. Alfred Prufrock" and *The Waste Land*) to his last (*Four Quartets*). The themes of his greater poems, as of his lesser ones, involve indentity, sexuality, the nature of love, religious belief (or its absence), and the telling of a tale/writing of a poem in language adequate to the emotion or state that the telling/writing seeks to express.

It is a short step from the dramatic situations of Eliot's early and middle poetry, situations that owe something to the poetry of Robert Browning, more to John Donne and the Elizabethan and Jacobean dramatists, and most to the Symbolist poetry of Jules Laforgue. One of Eliot's chief aspirations and limited achievements countered the thrust of modern drama since Henrik Ibsen (the Nō drama of William Butler Yeats excepted): Eliot was dedicated to the revivification of verse drama

T. S. Eliot, Nobel laureate in literature for 1948. (© The Nobel Foundation)

in the twentieth century. He succeeded in doing this, to some extent, in *The Rock*, more so in *Murder in the Cathedral*, and less so in *The Family Reunion* and subsequent plays. Although his account of the martyrdom of Thomas à Becket clearly inspired Jean Anouilh's *Becket* (1959), Eliot's attempt to revive the poetic drama amounted to a false start, perhaps attributable in part to the highly poetic but *un*dramatic and static nature of his plays.

Eliot's achievements have led at least one critic to state that in the area of humane letters the larger part of the twentieth century may be called The Age of Eliot. Eliotatry aside, there is some merit in the remark. No stranger to prizes and awards, Eliot may have valued, and needed, the *Dial Award* of 1922 for *The Waste Land*. In the course of his long career he received doctoral degrees (*honoris causa*) from a score of British, European, and American universities; was Clark Lecturer at Trinity College, Cambridge (1926), and Charles Eliot Norton Professor of Poetry at Harvard University (1932-1933); and won the Hanseatic Goethe Prize (1954), the Dante Gold Medal (Florence, 1959), the Emerson-Thoreau Medal (American Academy of Arts and Sciences, 1959), and the U.S. Medal of Freedom (1964). In 1948 he achieved a dual distinction: Not only was he awarded the British Order of Merit, but he also won the Nobel Prize in Literature for, he surmised, "the entire corpus."

In another sense, Eliot's continuing achievement may be measured by the extent to which innumerable students, teachers, and researchers have surrendered to him. Each year several books or portions of books, as well as numerous essays, swell the number of works about him, his thought, and his writing; they stand as monuments to his still-unfolding mind and meaning. A legend in his own time, he remains one today.

BIOGRAPHY

To see Thomas Stearns Eliot's end in his beginning is to recall that Andrew Eliot (1627-1704) emigrated from East Coker, Somerset, to Beverly, Massachusetts, in a century that his twentieth century scion would explore and reexplore in poetry and criticism for most of his life. Eliot's grandfather, the Reverend William Greenleaf Eliot, forsook his native New England and went with

missionary zeal to the outpost of St. Louis, Missouri, in 1834. There he founded the (first) Unitarian church of the Messiah and later founded Washington University (originally, Eliot Seminary) where he became Chancellor (1870-1887). In the year after William Eliot's death, on September 25, 1888, Thomas Stearns Eliot, the seventh child of a second son, was born to Henry and Charlotte (Stearns) Eliot. As the Eliots did, the American Stearns family hailed from seventeenth century Massachusetts: Members of both families had done what they considered the right thing in the Salem witch trials, Andrew Eliot as a juror, a Stearns as a judge. Eliot's schooling at Smith Academy was punctuated by summers in New England, chiefly at Gloucester and Rockport, Massachusetts (on Cape Ann), not far from the Dry Salvages. After a year at Milton Academy, Eliot matriculated at Harvard College, where he received a B.A. degree (1909) and pursued graduate studies (1910-1914), completing but not defending a doctoral dissertation on the philosophy of F. H. Bradley (published, 1964).

During the years 1910 to 1917, Eliot visited Paris and Germany (1910-1911) and studied at the Sorbonne; back in Cambridge (1911-1914), he studied philosophy (with Bertrand Russell), Sanskrit, Pali, along with other subjects, and received a fellowship stipend to study at Marburg, Germany, in 1914—an award which he promptly transferred to Merton College, Oxford, at the onset of World War I. On September 22, 1914, Eliot met Ezra Pound; it was an event that marked the forging of a spiritual bond that endured for the rest of Eliot's life. Since much has been made of Pound's influence on Eliot's poetry, especially *The Waste Land*, it may be useful to recall Pound's statement that Eliot had "trained himself *and* modernized himself *on his own*." It was largely through Pound's influence, however, that the poems of *Prufrock and Other Observations* were first published in American and English periodicals.

Eliot's marriage to Vivien Haigh-Wood, on June 26, 1915, was followed by brief periods of teaching (High Wycombe Grammar School, Highgate School) and lecturing (Oxford University Extension Lectures, 1915-1917). In March, 1917, Eliot secured a post in the Colonial and Foreign Department of Lloyd's Bank, London, where he worked continuously, except for three months' leave for reasons of health in the autumn of 1921, until he joined the publishing firm of Faber and Gwynn (later, Faber and Faber) in 1925. His marriage lasted until Vivien's death in 1947, although she and Eliot were officially separated (by letter) in 1933, and thereafter, according to written accounts, they met again only once, and briefly (at one of Eliot's lectures). Several critics have seen the extremely unhappy marriage as fundamental to some of his poems.

Eliot's literary activity between 1916 and 1922 was prodigious: It was the time of his numerous essays and reviews for *The Egoist, The Dial*, the *Athanaeum*, the *Times Literary Supplement*, and many other journals, of *Prufrock and Other Observations, Ara Vos Prec, Poems*, and his masterpiece, *The Waste Land*. That work would catapult him to a prominence attained by no other poet of the twentieth century. In 1922 he assumed the editorship of *The Criterion*. In 1927 Eliot experienced a sea-change: First, he became a communicant in the Church of England (June 29); then he became a British subject (November). In 1928 a statement in *For Lancelot Andrewes* characterized his newly adopted perspectives: "The general point of view may be described as classicist in literature, royalist in politics, and Anglo-Catholic in religion." The formulation is one that should be approached with caution. Although accurate in some respects and misleading in others, it does help to explain the many turnings in the road from "The Hollow Men" (1925) through the Ariel poems to *Ash Wednesday*.

Before returning from his post as Norton Professor of Poetry at Harvard (1932-1933), Eliot obtained a legal separation from his wife (to whom he had dedicated *Ash Wednesday*) and lectured at the University of Virginia on Christian apologetics, a subject of increasing interest for him. His poetry of the 1930's centered on verse drama and on such disparate efforts as "Five Finger Exercises," "Triumphal March," and *Old Possum's Book of Practical Cats*, but the poetic highlights of the decade are *Ash Wednesday, Murder in the Cathedral*, and his best poem of those years, "Burnt Norton."

The first of the poems later to comprise *Four Quartets*, "Burnt Norton" was followed by "East Coker" (1940), "The Dry Salvages" (1941), and his own *Paradiso*, "Little Gidding" (1942). In the years follow-

ing the publication of *Four Quartets*, Eliot wrote little poetry, but he kept on writing verse drama and began to enjoy generous recognition of his work; notably, he received the Nobel Prize in Literature in 1948, a year after the death of Vivien. His marriage to Valerie Fletcher (January 10, 1957) marked another of the many turning points of his life—this time a turn for the better in a happy marriage. Eliot truly became, in the 1940's, 1950's, and 1960's, the elder statesman of letters. His position in the history of modern poetry became unassailable.

Eliot died on January 4, 1965, survived by his wife, Valerie. His ashes were interred in the parish church at East Coker, Somerset, the church of his English ancestors, and a memorial was placed in the Poets' Corner, Westminister Abbey.

ANALYSIS

One useful approach to T. S. Eliot's poetry is to examine voices and fragments as they announce and illustrate themes. In the concluding section of *The Waste Land*, one of Eliot's speakers provides a key to that poem, to Eliot's poetry generally, and to the theory and practice of poetic composition that marked his career as a writer: "These fragments I have shored against my ruins." These fragments consist mainly of highly allusive phrases and quotations, of intricately wrought verbal symbols, of lines of direct simplicity and complex opacity, of passages of sheer beauty and crabbed commonality fixed in formulated phrases, arranged and rearranged until, in the best of the poetry, one finds the complete consort dancing together. Upon first coming to Eliot's poetry, especially to "The Love Song of J. Alfred Prufrock" or *The Waste Land*, the reader's usual (and perfectly acceptable) reaction is one of bewilderment, excitement, and, at best, an appreciation of the poetic statements that does not necessarily involve an understanding of precisely what is said, the conditions under which it is said, the full nature of the speaker, or his or her aims, intentions, or situation.

The fragments owe much to Eliot's youthful experience in St. Louis, summers on the New England coast, his Harvard education, his visits to Paris and Munich, and the Oxford and London years. Furthermore, they stem from his lifelong immersion in Dante and the Bible and from his omnivorous reading. He was particulary drawn to French Symbolist poetry (especially Laforgue), the Elizabethan and Jacobean playwrights, especially John Webster, Cyril Tourneur, Christopher Marlowe, William Shakespeare, and Donne and the other Metaphysical poets. To come to Eliot's poetry with such a literary background is to see the phrases of other writers whom Eliot admired take on new and sometimes surprising meanings. To read Eliot's work without such a background may mean that the reader will miss both the larger and the particular allusions, but still the reader may grasp possible meanings of individual poems. The unwary reader may be carried along on the surface of the poem or find himself in sympathy with an expressed emotion without clearly knowing what is at issue. All readers should have recourse to those works to which Eliot seems to allude so that they may proceed the more intelligently with the poem at hand. The fragments that Eliot quotes or alludes to are the necessary baggage of the intelligent reader, *impedimenta* that include much of the Western European tradition and elements from Middle and Far Eastern culture.

In many respects, Eliot the poet became not unlike Joseph Conrad's Mr. Kurtz or, indeed, Marlow: He became "A Voice," an "invisible poet" (Hugh Kenner's phrase) who speaks. The voice or voices in the poems are usually those that repeat formulas embedded in literary, cultural, and religious traditions—uncertain voices that often betray their speakers' lack of self-knowledge or clear identity; they may be voices (especially in the Ariel poems) whose certitudes are affirmed only as they speak them (word becomes act) and which may be truly chimerical. The voices speaking the fragments, even the unified voice of *Four Quartets*, are the voices of humanity (though often a special order of humanity) seeking, as they turn over the fragments and seek the sense of sounds, to understand, explain, and identify themselves in terms of the past, present, and future. The voices, desiderative, expectant, seek in the expression of a word or words to communicate themselves to other communicants (the reader) and to educate those communicants in the mystery of a common life, the implications of action or inaction, the generalizable elements of a particular experience or emotion.

Long before his Paris year (1910-1911), Eliot had read Arthur Symons's *The Symbolist Movement in Literature* (1899) and had come under the sway of French Symbolist poetry. He had published some undergraduate poetry (phrases of which he used in later poems) and had begun two major poems, "Portrait of a Lady" and "The Love Song of J. Alfred Prufrock." He completed the latter at Munich (1911) but it remained in manuscript until Ezra Pound persuaded Harriet Monroe to publish it in *Poetry* (1915); it then formed the nucleus for Eliot's first volume of poetry, *Prufrock and Other Observations*, in which he may justly be said to have inaugurated modern poetry in English. It is with "The Love Song of J. Alfred Prufrock," the first masterpiece of an apprentice, that a just appreciation of Eliot's oeuvre should begin.

"THE LOVE SONG OF J. ALFRED PRUFROCK"

Like "Portrait of a Lady" and most of his poetry prior to *Four Quartets*, "The Love Song of J. Alfred Prufrock" is a dramatic, if static, monologue. It is heavily influenced by Jules Laforgue's poetic technique in that it presents an interior landscape of atomized consciousness. The male narrator (the voice) worries about the possibility of an erotic encounter as he worries and puzzles over his own identity, his too conscious sense of self, his meaning and place in a surreal and menacing universe of his own devising, and his observations (objective and subjective genitive, as James Joyce phrased it) while he confides to a reader (who is called upon to become part of Prufrock's divided self) the fragmented perceptions of himself and his situation. Prufrock does not, however, arrive at any conclusions about the encounter or about his own identity and meaning.

The epigraph (Dante, *Inferno*, XXVII) provides a key to the incongruous "love song" of an impossible lover and sets the reader squarely in Hell listening to a reluctant speaker (who cannot say what he means) who will confide in the auditor/reader as Guido did in the character Dante, "without fear or infamy," without fear that the secret will be revealed on earth (will become the subject of "observations"), particularly in the hearing of the perplexing women who "come and go" in the troublesome room or of the desirable but distant and somewhat fearsome recumbent woman. It is possible to exclude the "reader" as the addressee of this poem and to read it as an interior dialogue between "self" and "soul": Such a reading would heighten to a clinical level the disorder of identity that is sensed in Prufrock's divided self.

The voice that addresses the reader in scraps of experience remembered and fearfully anticipated and in fragments of historical- and self-consciousness does so in response to a question, presumably posed by the reader in a Dantesque role. As Hugh Kenner aptly points out, the reader enters a "zone of consciousness" in the poem, not a verifiable or constant "realistic" setting. Prufrock is not a "real" character who tells a logical or temporally sequential story. Indeed, the reader participates in the unfolding narrative by hearing and deciding what is part of the world of recognizable experience and what is intrinsic to a fragmented, disjointed, disordered, diseased consciousness that speaks familiarly ("you and I") of a shared boredom of social rounds and obligations, of the terror of rejection, and (the greater Prufrockian terror) of acceptance and surrender in sexual contact—all of which contribute to a sense of cognitive and emotional paralysis for which Prufrock finds a disordered "objective correlative" in the "sky/ Like a patient etherised upon a table."

The literary fragments in the poem include the central situational analogue in the *Inferno*, the Polonian self-caricature, and grotesque visions of St. John the Baptist and Lazarus returned from the dead. None of the characters in the fragments belong to the realm of the living and all represent an inability "to say just what I mean."

"GERONTION"

"Gerontion" (1919) carries on the pattern of monologue that Eliot established in "The Love Song of J. Alfred Prufrock" and "Portrait of a Lady." Here Eliot presents another voice speaking, besides words of his own devising, words from the Bible, William Shakespeare, Cyril Torneur, Thomas Middleton, Ben Jonson, and George Chapman. He intended "Gerontion" to be a prolegomenon to *The Waste Land*, and as such it is more than adequate: It deals with concerns and embodies themes common to the longer poem: themes such as aridity, the inadequacies of the common experience of sexuality and love, history's "contrived corridors," the

function of memory, the Christian economy of salvation, and the attempts of consciousness to order disparate experiences and make them comprehensible. Structurally, both works are collages that use allusive language to make human history manageable; technically, they both employ a stream of consciousness tentatively centered in the centrifugal thoughts of a "dry brain in a dry season."

Gerontion and the foreign figures who flit through the Inferno and Purgatorio of his memory are figures of desolation who have reaped the whirlwind of their own personal histories and of history generally. The characters, from Mr. Silvero to Mrs. Cammel, represent some of the dry thoughts that Gerontion houses. They typify one major difficulty that the poem presents: the tension between the past, the past remembered in the present, and the present—the past dominating the present and vitiating it as memory mixes with desire in a futile nostalgia that prevents the narrator from acting (reaching conclusion). This temporal tension is at the poem's core and is resolved only in the poem's emphasis on the act of remembering. Once again, as in "The Love Song of J. Alfred Prufrock" and *The Waste Land*, the self-conscious voices utter personal and historical fragments that illuminate consciousness speaking. The point of remembering these fragments is to identify a fundamental problem of meaning that attaches to peripheral love (of art, for example) and to *love* (possibly of the poem's addressee), its meaning in personal and general historical context, and the relationship of those meanings to the meaning of the death for which Gerontion waits and the possibility of another kind of life hereafter.

THE WASTE LAND

The transition from "Gerontion" to *The Waste Land*, in which Gerontion is transformed into Tiresias, is a movement from considerable opacity to relative clarity, though the later poem is indeed perplexing. In 1953, Eliot wrote that he did not look forward with pleasure either to literary oblivion or to a time when his works would be read only by a few graduate students in "Middle Anglo-American, 42B." Together with "The Love Song of J. Alfred Prufrock" and *Four Quarters*, *The Waste Land* ensures that neither of those ends is probable. Eliot stunned all, and outraged some, of the literary world in 1922 with the publication (in *The Criterion* and

The Dial) of *The Waste Land*, a work that has engendered more commentaries, interpretations, and discussions than any other poem of the twentieth century. Structurally, the work is a series of five poems that constitute one poem; parts of it were written and rewritten over the course of at least seven years, with editorial help for the final version from Ezra Pound. When he published it in book form, Eliot added more than fifty notes to the poem, some of which are not helpful and some of which emphasize the importance of vegetation ceremonies and direct the reader to Sir James Frazer's *The Golden Bough* (1890-1915) and to Jessie L. Weston's work on the Grail legend, *From Ritual to Romance* (1920).

The wealth of literary fragments, clues, and allusions to other works, the inclusion of foreign words and phrases and of arcane material, may produce some bafflement and has inspired numerous exegetical tracts. It is of primary importance not to treat the poem as a highly sophisticated double-cross; instead, one should, before beginning a search for sources and analogues, surrender to it as an emotional, intellectual, puzzling, and disquieting poem. It is only in allowing for the experience of communicable and precisely incommunicable emotion that the poem can work as a poem rather than as an occasion for the exercise of literary archaeology.

Eliot wrote (note to 1.218), "Tiresias, although a mere spectator and not indeed a 'character,' is yet the most important personage in the poem, uniting all the rest . . . What Tiresias *sees*, in fact, is the substance of the poem." One may, on Eliot's authority, read the poem as an account of Tiresias's observations as he guides the reader through his own memory to various locations in *The Waste Land* as seen or remembered on a journey that is both in and out of time. Thus, many elements fall into place as Tiresias subsumes all the characters or speakers in a multilayered, cyclical ritual of death and rebirth. Alternatively, one may read the poem as a series of fragmented monologues, in the manner of "The Love Song of J. Alfred Prufrock," so that Tiresias's becomes only one among many voices. So to read it is to find Eliot's note somewhat misleading.

Assuming that this is a Symbolist poem, perhaps *the* Symbolist poem of the twentieth century, the historical and cultural dimensions that many critics have so ably attributed to it (as being a poem about the disillusionment of a particular generation, about the 1920's, about London, and so on) recede. So, too, do the ubiquitous anthropological considerations of barren land, infertility, initiation rites, and the death of gods. Both sets of data may, then, be treated as "objective correlatives" for emotions that the poet seeks to express. What remain as underlying themes are sexual disorder (basic to the Grail and to vegetation myths), the lack of and need for religious belief (accented negatively by the presence of Madam Sosostris and positively in "The Fire Sermon" and "What the Thunder Said"), and the process of poetic composition (fragments "shored against my ruins"). These may be seen as elaborations in *The Waste Land* of themes present in "Portrait of a Lady," "The Love Song of J. Alfred Prufrock," "The Hippopotamus" (1917), and "Gerontion"; they are themes that also relate directly to Eliot's lessons from Dante's *La vita nuova* (c. 1292; *The New Life*) and *La divina commedia* (c. 1320; *The Divine Comedy*).

The diverse interpretations of what the poem is about have obvious implications for how one values the fragments of which it is composed and, to return to the question of voice, how one identifies the speaker and the burden of his speech. If, for example, one assumes that the blind, androgynous Tiresias speaks in many voices and does so with foreknowledge of all, one may conclude that the work stands as a monument to the disillusionment not of one generation but of many. One may also find that the slight progress of the Fisher King from the dull canal behind the gashouse (III) to the shore (V) has slight significance and that the question about setting his lands in order is, like shoring fragments against ruins, all that can be done before capitulating to the inevitable continuation of a condition in which the land will remain waste. Tiresias has, after all, foreseen this, too. If one assumes a multiplicity of voices, however, beginning with Marie, the Hyacinth Girl (or, in the epigraph, with the Sibyl's complaint and the voice speaking of it), and ending with the Fisher King, the Thunder, and a new voice (or many voices) speaking in the poem's last lines, one has a quite different experience of the poem. In the second reading one treats the work as a series of soliloquies or monologues all mixing memory with quite different desires, all commenting on various meanings (or lack of meaning) or love, and all concerned with hope or its opposite, hope negated in self-irony, hope centered on the release from individual prisons, hope tempered by trepidations attendant upon the "awful daring of a moment's surrender," and, possibly, hope that the Fisher King has finally thrown off accidia by asking himself the one needful question.

In either reading, how one treats the speaker and the meaning of the fragments raises other questions that drive one back into the poem, and each new reading raises new questions. There is no doubt that sexual disorder is a dominant theme, that the disorder concerns the dissociation of appetitive action from the intellectual and emotional aspects that would make the action human and not merely a reflex action, and that the symptoms of disorder are common to such characters as the typist, Mr. Eugenides, Mrs. Porter, Elizabeth I, Tiresias, Philomel, and the Fisher King. Add to this the abiding sense of death and its meaning, and the spiritual teachings of Buddhism and the mystery religions (Christianity among them), and new complexities emerge, as do new questions that only the Thunder can answer.

The poem's last verse paragraph displays little overt coherence once the Fisher King asks his question, but it does nevertheless offer a direct key to understanding the poem. That the Fisher King has traversed the arid plains, has put them behind him and now may have some power to set his kingdom in order, provides a sense of closure. In the next line (1. 427), London Bridge, crossed by so many who had been undone by death in the unreal City (Part I), is falling down: This action will end the procession of dead commuters; in the nursery rhyme there is no adequate means to rebuild the bridge permanently. The next line is from Dante, who is a source for many of the attitudes, emotions, and possibly the situational contexts of many of the poem's speakers: Here Arnaut Daniel, suffering in Purgatory for sins of lust, leaps back into the refining fire of his own accord; this may be seen as a gloss on the "Fire Sermon" and as a cure for the various forms of lust in the entire poem. There follow lines from "Pervigilium Veneris," a reference to Philomela (echoes of Parts II and III) and from Gérard de Nerval's "El Desdichado." This last may have metapoetical im-

plications for the authorial Eliot and may also recall another quest for rightful inheritance—in Sir Walter Scott's novel *Ivanhoe* (1819). In "These fragments I have shored against my ruins" (1. 430), "these fragments" are the preceding 429 lines, the immediately preceding seven lines, the fragmented speeches, the fragments of poetic and religious traditions, and the fragments of verses composed over many years to form the poem itself. The reference to Thomas Kyd's *The Spanish Tragedy* (c. 1585, 1. 431), in which Hieronymo proposes to "fit" a play using fragments of poetry in several languages (tongues) could, as Bernard Bergonzi indicates, comment directly on *The Waste Land* itself. The penultimate line repeats the Thunder's statements, giving them more point; and the final line is translated by Eliot as equivalent to "The Peace which passeth understanding."

What do these keys unlock? Surely they suggest what a reader should know of European and Eastern literary, cultural, and religious traditions in order to grasp some of the poem's meanings. They may also serve to help the reader see, to paraphrase Eliot, the end in the beginning and the beginning in the end. Having come to the end of the poem, one must be prepared to read it anew from the beginning. Bernard Bergonzi, following C. K. Stead's analysis of the pattern and meaning of *Four Quartets*, provides an invaluable guide to the significance of each of the poem's five sections. "The Burial of the Dead" concerns movement in time (seasons, change, reluctant birth); "A Game of Chess" reveals patent dissatisfaction with worldly experience; "The Fire Sermon" leads through purgation in the world and a divesting of the soul of love for created things; "Death by Water" is a brief lyric containing a warning and an invocation; "What the Thunder Said" deals with the issues of spiritual health and artistic wholeness. To read the work as a poem about the artist's concern for artistic wholeness allied to spiritual health offers extraordinary and suggestive possibilities for revaluing it and the poetry that preceded it.

"THE HOLLOW MEN"

"The Hollow Men" has often been read as a poem written at the nadir of the poet's emotional life, a depressing and depressed poem. This may be a correct reading; it may also be, however much it is favored by scores of writers who seek autobiographical confessions in Eliot's poetry, wide of the mark. The poem seems, indeed, to have been composed from fragments discarded from earlier drafts of *The Waste Land*. Again, voice and fragment should guide the wary reader. The epigraph, from Joseph Conrad's *Heart of Darkness* (1902), should put the reader on guard: The speech is that of an African worker reporting the death of Mr. Kurtz to Conrad's narrator-once-removed, Marlow, whose account is passed on to the reader by one who heard him tell the tale. The reader is, like the hollow men, at several removes from anything like experience at first hand; and several emotional layers separate Conrad's reader from Kurtz: Eliot adds another emotional layer of separation but strikes a responsive note of limited sympathy in his readers who have read Conrad. This is only one small reflection of the ways in which *Heart of Darkness* stands in relation to this poem and, by extension, to *The Waste Land* and its "preface," "Gerontion."

This poem, like earlier poems and the later *Ash Wednesday*, is obsessed with death. One of Dante's dead, a "hollow man" (*Inferno*, III) who lived, without blame and without praise, a life of accidia, addresses the reader in self-explanation and communal confession. Two other major sources inform the poem and quicken the sense of death: the history of the Gunpowder Plot and the Elizabethan dramatic account of assassination found in Shakespeare's *Julius Caesar* (c. 1599-1600, in which the phrase "hollow men" occurs). The reader is clearly in the presence of the dead, just as Dante's Pilgrim listened to the hollow men, who were neither for Jehovah nor against him, in the Hell of their own making. Like the addressee of *Heart of Darkness* the reader hears, perhaps seated in a club chair, a story of Marlow telling a tale prompted by his observation that his present location (seated on a yawl on the Thames) was once one of the dark places of the earth (and may still be so). In each case, the reader/addressee is told a story of darkness, a story of the Shadow, a story of failure and, ultimately, of inconsequence, a story told to pass the time.

ASH WEDNESDAY

In *Ash Wednesday*, so named for the first day of Lent, a day for the turnings of Christian metanoia, Dante's mysticism and its correlative tension between flesh and spirit are elaborated. The situation of which the voice speaks, a conversion that is not without difficulty and contention, is told not in logical, sequential narrative but in a disciplined Symbolist dream. Here, for example, the Lady subsumes many ladies (the rejected one of blesséd face, Beatrice, Theologia, Ecclesia) and Eliot's earlier expressions of dehumanization (such as the classic "ragged claws" of "The Love Song of J. Alfred Prufrock") now become expressions of Christian humility. Unquestionably influenced by Eliot's own turning to the Anglican church in 1928, this poem, together with the Ariel poems, represents poetic pilgrimages of hope that do not necessarily find resolution of the tensions between flesh and spirit but which indicate possibilities for subliminal resolution in transcendence.

FOUR QUARTETS

The assured masterpiece of his poetic maturity, *Four Quartets* is more immediately accessible than Eliot's early and middle work. The poems which comprise it, like his earlier poetry, grew incrementally from "Burnt Norton," which sprang from lines discarded from *Murder in the Cathedral*, to "Little Gidding," with "East Coker" and "The Dry Salvages" intervening. Unlike his earlier poetry, the poems of *Four Quartets* lack a dramatic character who speaks; instead, they are in the lyric tradition of direct poetic speech in which the speaker has a constant voice that may well be the poet's own. Unfortunately, the speaker sometimes assumes the hortatory voice of the preacher. This shift in poetic style, away from masks and personae, is a new element in Eliot's verse.

Each of the poems adopts a musical and frequently iterative pattern, as if the reader is meant to hear the instrumental conversations endemic to musical quartets. In reading these poems, one is frequently reminded of Walter Pater's dictum that "all art continually aspires to the condition of music." The poems are set pieces in the eighteenth century tradition of verse inspired by a visit to a specific place. Taken together, they constitute some of Eliot's most beautiful (and, in places, most banal) poetry, as the lyricist adopts a consistent poetic voice that muses on the process of cognition and composition.

The essential structure of these poems, filled as they are with local references dear to Eliot, follows the five-part structure of *The Waste Land*. C. K. Stead admirably analyzes the fivefold structure of each of the sections of *Four Quartets* as follows: (1) the movement of time, in which brief moments of eternity are caught; (2) worldly experience, leading only to dissatisfaction; (3) purgation in the world, divesting the soul of love of created things; (4) a lyric prayer for, or affirmation of the need of, intercession; and (5) the problems of attaining artistic wholeness which become analogues for, and merge into, the problems of achieving spiritual health.

The poems of *Four Quartets* in some way negate, by their affirmations, the fragmented, disparate, and "unreal" elements in Eliot's earliest poems, but, on the whole, they present a synthesis of Eliot's poetic conerns and his varied statements about the problems and business of being a poet. They stand not at the end of his artistic career but at the summit of his career as a poet whose later work, in both bulk and intensity, is minimal. *Four Quartets* constitutes a compendium of the themes that Eliot pursued from his earliest days as a poet, but with the decided difference that sex has become part of love, belief has been ratified, and the world has become flesh again. The fire and the rose are one.

OTHER MAJOR WORKS

PLAYS: *Sweeney Agonistes*, pb. 1932 (fragment); *The Rock: A Pageant Play*, pr., pb. 1934; *Murder in the Cathedral*, pr., pb. 1935; *The Family Reunion*, pr., pb. 1939; *The Cocktail Party*, pr. 1949; *The Confidential Clerk*, pr. 1953; *The Elder Statesman*, pr. 1958; *Collected Plays*, pb. 1962.

NONFICTION: *Ezra Pound: His Metric and Poetry*, 1917; *The Sacred Wood*, 1920; *Homage to John Dryden*, 1924; *Shakespeare and the Stoicism of Seneca*, 1927; *For Lancelot Andrewes*, 1928; *Dante*, 1929; *Thoughts After Lambeth*, 1931; *Charles Whibley: A Memoir*, 1931; *John Dryden: The Poet, the Dramatist, the Critic*, 1932; *Selected Essays*, 1932, new ed. 1950; *The Use of Poetry and the Use of Criticism*, 1933; *After Strange Gods*, 1934; *Elizabethan Essays*, 1934; *Essays Ancient and Modern*, 1936; *The Idea of a Christian Society*, 1939; *The Music of Poetry*, 1942; *The Classics and the Man of Letters*, 1942; *Notes To-*ward the Definition of Culture*, 1948; *Poetry and Drama*, 1951; *The Three Voices of Poetry*, 1953; *Religious Drama: Medieval and Modern*, 1954; *The Literature of Politics*, 1955; *The Frontiers of Criticism*, 1956; *On Poetry and Poets*, 1957; *Knowledge and Experience in the Philosophy of F. H. Bradley*, 1964; *To Criticize the Critic*, 1965; *The Letters of T. S. Eliot: Volume I, 1898-1922*, 1988.

BIBLIOGRAPHY

Ackroyd, Peter. *T. S. Eliot: A Life*. New York: Simon & Schuster, 1984. The first comprehensive biography based on Eliot's published and unpublished writing, as well as on extensive interviews with his friends and associates. Ackroyd has been praised in several reviews for his handling of both Eliot's life and work, especially the poet's disastrous first marriage and *The Waste Land*.

Donoghue, Denis. *Words Alone: The Poet, T. S. Eliot*. New Haven, Conn.: Yale University Press, 2000. A wide-ranging critical examination in the form of an intellectual memoir, and an illuminating account of Donoghue's engagement with the works of Eliot. Includes bibliographical references and index.

Eliot, Valerie, ed. *The Letters of T. S. Eliot, 1898-1922*. Vol. 1. New York: Harcourt Brace Jovanovich, 1988. Includes all the poet's significant extant correspondence up to the age of thirty-four. An important addition to the biographical and critical literature on Eliot, none of which had access to this complete collection of letters. His correspondence contains drafts of poems and reveals both his extremely correct and whimsical sides.

Gordon, Lyndall. *Eliot's Early Years*. New York: Oxford University Press, 1977. Reviewed by Richard Ellmann and other important critics as the most through treatment of Eliot's early career, Gordon's study is a superb meld of biography and criticism, drawing upon unpublished diaries, letters, and poems by the poet's mother. Should be read in conjunction with Peter Ackroyd's equally important biography.

_____. *Eliot's New Life*. New York: Farrar, Straus & Giroux, 1988. A continuation of Gordon's biography of the early years, concentrating on the religious phase of the poet's life, his separation from his first wife, his friendships with two other women, and his marriage to Valerie Fletcher in 1957. Gordon is equally sound on Eliot's later poetry, especially on the development of *Four Quartets*.

_____. *T. S. Eliot: An Imperfect Life*. New York: Norton, 1999. In this exhaustive biography Gordon builds on the efforts from her first two books covering Eliot's early years. She assiduously tracked down Eliot's correspondence and manuscripts to address the issue of Eliot's anti-Semitism and misogyny. Gordon reinforces her thesis that Eliot's poetic output should be interpreted as a coherent spiritual biography.

Litz, A. Walton, ed. *Eliot in His Time: Essays on the Occasion of the Fiftieth Anniversary of "The Waste Land."* Princeton, N.J.: Princeton University Press, 1973. Eight essays by eminent poets and scholars on the development, the achievement, and the impact of Eliot's great poem. Each essay assesses Eliot's place in literary history and examines not only his published poetry but also the facsimile publication of Eliot's manuscripts of *The Waste Land*.

Matthews, T. S. *The Great Tom: Notes Toward a Definition of T. S. Eliot*. New York: Harper & Row, 1974. Coming from a religious and upper-middle-class background similar to Eliot's, Matthews sensitively probes Eliot's conversion to the Anglican faith. While not one of Eliot's close friends, Matthews did meet the poet on several occasions, and his biography, while superseded by Peter Ackroyd's and Lyndall Gordon's biographies, nevertheless supplies keen insights into the poet and his work.

Schuchard, Ronald. *Eliot's Dark Angel: Intersections of Life and Art*. New York: Oxford University Press, 1999. A critical study demonstrating how Eliot's personal voice works through the sordid, the bawdy, the blasphemous, and the horrific to create a unique moral world. Schuchard works against conventional attitudes toward Eliot's intellectual and spiritual development by showing how early and consistently his classical and religious sensibility manifests itself in his poetry and criticism.

John J. Conlon;
bibliography updated by the editors

PAUL ÉLUARD

Eugène Grindel
Born: Saint-Denis, France; December 14, 1895
Died: Charenton-le-Pont, France; November 18, 1952

PRINCIPAL POETRY

Le Devoir et l'inquiétude, 1917
Poèmes pour la paix, 1918
Les Animaux et leurs hommes, les hommes et leurs animaux, 1920
Les Nécessités de la vie et les conséquences des rêves, 1921
Mourir de ne pas mourir, 1924
Capitale de la douleur, 1926 (*Capital of Pain*, 1973)
L'Amour la poésie, 1929
À toute épreuve, 1930
La Vie immédiate, 1932
La Rose publique, 1934

Paul Éluard

Faciles, 1935

Les Yeux fertiles, 1936

Thorns of Thunder: Selected Poems, 1936

Les Mains libres, 1937

Donner à voir, 1939

Médieuses, 1939

Le Livre ouvert I, 1938-1940, 1940

Choix de poèmes, 1914-1941, 1941

Le Livre ouvert II, 1939-1941, 1942

Poésie et vérité, 1942 (*Poetry and Truth, 1942*, 1944)

Au rendez-vous allemand, 1944

Dignes de vivre, 1944

En avril 1944: Paris respirait encore!, 1945

Le Dur Désir de durer, 1946

Poésie ininterrompue, 1946

Corps mémorable, 1947

Le Livre ouvert, 1938-1944, 1947

Marc Chagall, 1947

Poèmes politiques, 1948

Premiers Poèmes (1913-1921), 1948

Une Leçon de morale, 1949

Le Phénix, 1951

Poèmes, 1951

Tout dire, 1951

Poèmes pour tous, 1952

Les Derniers Poèmes d'amour de Paul Éluard, 1963
  (*Last Love Poems of Paul Éluard*, 1980)

OTHER LITERARY FORMS

Paul Éluard wrote many critical essays explaining the theories of the Surrealist movement, in which he played so large a part, and delineating his personal aesthetic theories as well. These critical works include the various Surrealist manifestos (many coauthored with André Breton), *Avenir de la poésie* (1937), *Poésie involuntaire et poésie intentionelle* (1942), *À Pablo Picasso* (1944), *Picasso à Antibes* (1948), *Jacques Villon ou l'art glorieux* (1948), *La Poésie du passé* (1951), *Anthologie des écrits sur l'art* (1952), and *Les Sentiers et routes de la poésie* (1952). Since the Surrealists were little interested in the limitations of genre, much of Éluard's poetic work falls into the category of the prose poem. His complete works are published in *Œuvres complètes* (1968). Some of his letters are published in *Lettres à Joe Bousquet* (1973).

ACHIEVEMENTS

Paul Éluard was, with André Breton and Louis Aragon, a cofounder of Surrealism, one of the principal artistic movements of the twentieth century. Earlier, he had also been instrumental in the Dada movement. As one of the primary theoreticians of Surrealism, Éluard helped to outline its aesthetic concepts in a number of manifestos and illustrated its techniques in his huge output of poetry. He published more than seventy volumes of poetry in his lifetime, many of which reveal his ability to set aside Surrealist theories in favor of poetic effect. As a result, many critics have called him the most original of the Surrealist poets and the truest poet of the group. His love poetry in particular is singled out for praise. Eluard's *Capital of Pain*, *La Rose publique*, and *Les Yeux fertiles* are widely regarded as among the finest products of Surrealism in French poetry.

BIOGRAPHY

Paul Éluard was born Eugène Grindel on December 14, 1895, in Saint-Denis, a suburb of Paris. His background was strictly working-class—his father was a bookkeeper and his mother (from whom he took the name Éluard) a seamstress—and most of his early years were spent in the vicinity of factories in Saint-Denis and Aulnay-sous-Bois. Éluard was a good student at the École Communale, but later, when the Grindels moved to Paris and the boy was enrolled at the École Supérieure Colbert, his scholastic performance declined. His education was cut short by illness, and he was placed in a sanatorium in Davos, Switzerland, when he was sixteen. He returned to Paris two years later and almost immediately entered the army; his experiences in the trenches of World War I crystallized his growing awareness of the suffering of humanity. Suffering from gangrene of the bronchi as a result of poison gas, Éluard spent more time in a sanatorium, reading much poetry, especially the works of Arthur Rimbaud, Lautréamont, and Charles Vildrac. He also read Percy Bysshe Shelley, Novalis, and Heraclitus, and he developed a special feeling for Walt Whitman, whose *Leaves of Grass* (1855) he read many times.

In 1917, Éluard published his first book of poetry, *Le Devoir et l'inquiétude*. The following year, his *Poèmes pour la paix* was published, and he met Jean Paulhan, "impresario of poets," who advanced his career. He also met André Breton, Louis Aragon, Tristan Tzara, Philippe Soupault, and Giorgio de Chirico—the writers and artists who would eventually become, with Éluard, the leading figures of the Surrealist movement. Surrealism, however, was preceded by Dada; Éluard, Breton, Aragon, Francis Picabia, Soupault, Marguerite Buffet, and others, according to Tzara, all took part in the public "debut" of Dada in January, 1920, at a matinee organized by *Littérature*, a Dadaist review. The spectacle caused an enormous uproar, and a week later, Éluard joined Breton, Soupault, and others in a public debate at the Université Populaire. Éluard began to publish a review called *Proverbe*, to which all the Dadaists contributed. Wrote Tzara, "It was chiefly a matter of contradicting logic and language."

As Dada moved toward the more rigorous Surrealism, Éluard's name appeared on various manifestos. His poetry changed as a result of his allegiance to Dada and Surrealism; under the influence of the Surrealists' enthusiasm for "automatic writing," his language became freer. He also developed friendships with some of the most influential artists of the time, including Pablo Picasso, Max Ernst, Salvador Dalí, and Joan Miró.

In 1917, Éluard married Gala (Elena Dimitievna Diakanova), whom he had met in Switzerland in 1912, and though they had a daughter, Cécile, in 1918, the marriage disintegrated when Gala turned her affections toward Dalí. Brokenhearted, Éluard disappeared without explanation in March, 1924. Rumors circulated that he had died. In fact, he had sailed on the first available ship out of Marseilles, beginning a mysterious seven-month voyage around the world. He was seen in Rome, Vienna, Prague, London, and Spain, and he visited such distant locales as Australia, New Zealand, the Antilles, Panama, Malaysia, Java, Sumatra, Ceylon, Indochina, and India.

On his return, Éluard once again enthusiastically threw himself into the Surrealist movement, becoming editor and director of the movement's reviews, *La Révolution surréaliste* and *La Surréalisme au service de la révolution*. Following Surrealist theories, he experimented in his poetry with verbal techniques, the free expression of the mind, and the relation between dream and reality. These inquiries led to *L'Immaculée*

Conception (1930), which he wrote with André Breton. That same year, he made a final break with Gala, having met Maria Benz (affectionately called Nusch), who was the subject of numerous works by Picasso. The publication of *Capital of Pain* had established Éluard as an important poet, and with *La Rose publique* and *Les Yeux fertiles* he became the leading poet of Surrealism.

Éluard's world trip and his memories of proletarian life and of the war had made him sensitive to the political trends of the 1930's. These feelings came to the fore at the outbreak of the Spanish Civil War. The fascist armies in Spain seemed to Éluard the forerunners of a total destruction of the modern concept of freedom. In response, his poetry became more politically oriented. He wrote in *L'Évidence poétique* (1936) that "the time has come when poets have a right and a duty to maintain that they are profoundly involved in the lives of other men, in communal life." He became exasperated with the detachment of his Surrealist colleagues and separated from the group.

In 1939, Éluard once again found himself in the French army, and after the disastrous defeat, he courageously worked for the Resistance in Paris and Lozère, helping to found the weekly newspaper *Lettres françaises*. He was constantly in danger of arrest, and he and Nusch, whom he had married in 1934, where forced to move every month to avoid the Gestapo. He joined the outlawed Communist Party in 1942 (he had been affiliated with it for nearly fifteen years). He used the pseudonyms Jean du Hault and Maurice Hervent, and the *maquis* circulated his poems underground. One poem, "Liberté," published in 1942 in the Nazi-denounced collection *Poetry and Truth, 1942*, has been called one of the "consecrated texts of the Resistance." For a brief period, he was forced to hide in an asylum at Saint-Alban. He was deeply affected by the suffering of the inmates and the experience could be seen in his subsequent writings.

After the war, Éluard's life was shattered by the sudden death of Nusch. He sought a solution to his sorrow in his poetry and in extending his love to embrace all humankind. During this period, he was very active in the Communist Party, traveling to Italy, Yugoslavia, Greece, Poland, Switzerland, and the Soviet Union, which awarded him the International Peace Prize. In Mexico, attending the Congress of the World Council on Peace, he met Dominique Lemor, and his love for her did much to restore his moral vision. He married her in 1951, but a heart attack in September, 1952, weakened him, and he died of a stroke that November in his apartment overlooking the Bois de Vincennes, outside Paris.

ANALYSIS

Paul Éluard is regarded by many critics as Surrealism's greatest poet. Dubbed the "Nurse of the Stars" by Philippe Soupault, he was central to the movement from the beginning. Breton once answered the question "What is Surrealism?" by saying, "It is a splinter of the sparkling glass of Paul Éluard." It is therefore ironic that when Éluard's work is praised, its "non-Surrealistic" elements are generally singled out as having made his work better than that of the poets around him. Critics point out his permanent and universal themes, present even before the birth of Surrealism. He continually explores the themes of love, human suffering, and the struggle of the masses against hunger, slavery, and deprivation. His avoidance of shock and violence, employed programmatically by many of the Surrealists, is also pointed out as evidence of his internal distance from the movement in which he played such a central role. Finally, unlike many of his fellow Surrealists, who regarded the world of dreams as a higher reality, sufficient unto itself, Éluard used dreams to interpret his experience: In his poetry, the dreamworld helps make the "real" world more comprehensible.

Nevertheless, Éluard's poetry can be understood only in the context of Surrealism. His works strongly reflect the Surrealist rejection of nineteenth century values, which had led not to the paradise promised by progressives of that century but to the abject horror of World War I. It was necessary, therefore, to reject the worldview that brought about the enslavement of the human imagination. The enemy was not only order but also the *belief* in order. Religion and science are both inherently limiting, the Surrealists argued, and fail to take account of the most fundamental element of existence: disorder.

When Éluard found a mystical revelation in six consecutive lines beginning with the letter *p* in Tzara's

Grains et issues (1935), he was expressing the Surrealist faith in a truth beyond the surface of things, a truth that could be explored only through absolute freedom. Naturally, this freedom must exist in the political sphere as well, that Éluard, like a number of Surrealists, embraced an idealistic vision of communism is not surprising, given the context of the times. Communism preached the destruction of religion and of the bourgeoisie, and it was an avowed enemy of the fascism taking hold all over Europe in the 1920's and 1930's.

Above all, however, the Surrealists turned inward; love, a privileged theme in their works, is treated as a means of altering consciousness, analogous in its effects to hallucinogenic drugs. Love becomes, paradoxically, both a way of escaping the world and the profoundest way of knowing it. Éluard adamantly holds that all real knowledge comes from love, and his finest poems express a longing for transcendence through sexual love.

"PREMIÈRE DU MONDE" AND "A WOMAN IN LOVE"

In Éluard's works, woman, as the object of love, is a mirror for which men reach; seeing themselves reflected there, they discover "surreality." Woman, in Éluard's poetry, is simultaneously a particular woman (Gala, Nusch, Dominique) and a universal woman, timeless, embodying womanhood and all women. She is a vision of light, and images of brightness, transcendence, and purity are associated with her. The poet, on the other hand, suffers in darkness, isolation, limitation, and impurity. He addresses her: "You who abolish forgetfulness, ignorance, and hope/ You who suppress absence and give me birth . . . / You are pure, you are even purer than I." In "Première du monde," his woman is the first woman in the world. She is simultaneously held captive by the Earth and possessed by spirit. The light hides itself in her. She is a complex of wheels; she is grass in which one becomes lost; she resembles the stars; she takes upon herself a maze of fire. In another poem, he writes, "I love you for your wisdom that is not mine . . . / For this immortal heart which I do not possess." In other poems, he relates the image of the mirror to the image of woman so that her eyes become mirrors and she plays a mirrorlike role. Woman is mirror is poetry is woman: Each reflects the other;

each *is* the other. One sees this most strikingly in "L'Amoureuse" ("A Woman in Love," from *Mourir de ne pas mourir*), when the lover becomes one with the beloved: "She has the shape of my hands/ She has the color of my eyes/ She is swallowed in my shadow/ Like a stone against the sky."

SURREALIST INFLUENCES

Éluard's poetic vision of woman is representative of the constant shifting between opposites that characterizes his work. He moves between light and dark, despair and hope, mystery and knowledge. This subtle play between opposites is very much characteristic of Surrealism in general, but Éluard handles it with simple, direct language. Like many great writers dealing with enormously complex and difficult conceptions, Éluard simplifies his language, choosing ordinary words and rearranging them in extraordinary ways. One of his early short poems, "Enfermé, seul" (from *Les Nécessités de la vie et les conséquences des rêves*), illustrates his passionate simplicity: "Complete song/ The table to see, the chair to sit/ And the air to breathe./ To rest,/ Inevitable Idea,/ Complete song."

When Éluard is at his best, this plain language becomes exquisite, as in lines such as: "Dawn fallen like a shower"; "We were tired/ Of living in the ruins of sleep"; "The prism breathes with us"; "The fountain running and sweet and nude." Unlike traditional metaphors, which are based on logical resemblances between things, Éluard's metaphors come out of dreams, revealing the power of the mind to find meaning in "illogical" juxtapositions. The line "She is standing on my eyelids" from "A Woman in Love," for example, could be a literal transcription of a dream: Thus, the poet achieves expression of the previously inexpressible. Like Dalí's famous melting clocks, Éluard's images broaden the vision of the reader. This quality makes Éluard's poetry easy to grasp and yet extraordinarily difficult, immediately meaningful yet provoking endless reflection.

OTHER MAJOR WORKS

NONFICTION: *L'Immaculée Conception*, 1930 (with André Breton; *The Immaculate Conception*, 1990); *L'Évidence poétique*, 1936; *Avenir de la poésie*, 1937; *Poésie involuntaire et poésie intentionelle*, 1942; *À*

Pablo Picasso, 1944; *Jacques Villon ou l'art glorieux*, 1948; *Picasso à Antibes*, 1948; *La Poésie du passé*, 1951; *Anthologie des écrits sur l'art*, 1952; *Les Sentiers et routes de la poésie*, 1952; *Lettres à Joe Bousquet*, 1973; *Letters to Gala*, 1989.

MISCELLANEOUS: *Œuvres complètes*, 1968.

BIBLIOGRAPHY

Fontville, Agnès. *Le Mot vide et l'expression lexicale du vide dans l'œuvre de Paul Eluard*. Villeneuve d'Ascq, France: Presses Universitaires du Septentrion, 1998. Minutely examines the distribution of the word *vide* (empty) and its parasynomyms *désert* (desert) and *mur* (wall) to demonstrate how these manifestations of absence and obstacle function not as particular representations but rather signify the closing-in and importance of the gaze, which point back to the poetic act itself. In French.

Gaitet, Pascal. "Eluard's Reactions, Poetic and Political to World War Two." *Literature and History* 2, no. 1 (1991): 24-43. Examines Éluard's shift from the destabilizing, anti-bourgeois doctrines espoused by the Surrealists toward a more conventional use of symbolism, reinforcing traditional values, and a unifying rhetoric during the Resistance era. Gaitet depicts Éluard's poetic output during this era as embracing a more utilitarian, propagandist function, much in keeping with the Communist Party, which he rejoined in 1942.

Strauss, Jonathan. "Paul Éluard and the Origins of Visual Subjectivity." *Mosaic* 33, no. 2 (2000): 25-46. Offers close readings of passages taken from *Capital of Pain* to demonstrate Éluard's agile usage of the visual and his redefinition of subjectivity in terms of impossible images that can only be expressed through language. This tying of the sensuous to the abstract becomes the cornerstone of Éluard's attempt to create a new theory of subjectivity.

Tsatsakou, Athanasia. *La Grèce comme espace-temps chez Paul Éluard*. Paris: L'Harmattan, 2000. Utilizing Mikhail Bakhtin's concept of the chronotope to determine spatial-temporal correlations in literature, Tsatsakou focuses on Greece as a recurring element in Éluard's poetry, focusing especially on his *Grèce ma rose de raison*, to show that Greece functions as a chronotope of presence which can be broken down in multiple nuances, such as ideal space, stage of human activity, an emerging eternity, and the eternal present. In French.

Vanoyeke, Violane. *Paul Éluard: Le Poète de la liberté.* Paris: Julliard, 1995. Well-researched biography that clearly traces Éluard's public and private life and places him at the heart of the French literary and artistic community of the 1920's through the post-World War II era. In French.

Watts, Philip. *Allegories of the Purge: How Literature Responded to the Postwar Trials of Writers and Intellectuals in France.* Stanford, Calif.: Stanford University Press, 1998. Chapter 4 examines Éluard's poetic output during the Occupation and the period of purge trials in France directly following the end of World War II to show that Éluard's shift from the linguistic and image play of his earlier writings to a strictly metered verse can be seen as a political act calling for the purge of collaborationist writers.

J. Madison Davis;
bibliography updated by David Harrison Horton

ODYSSEUS ELYTIS

Odysseus Alepoudhelis

Born: Iraklion (also known as Heraklion), Crete; November 2, 1911
Died: Athens, Greece; March 18, 1996

PRINCIPAL POETRY

Prosanatolizmi, 1939
Ilios o protos, mazi me tis parallayies pano se mian ahtidha, 1943
Azma iroiko ke penthimo yia ton hameno anthipolohagho tis Alvanias, 1945 (*Heroic and Elegiac Song for the Lost Second Lieutenant of the Albanian Campaign,* 1965)
To axion esti, 1959 (*The Axion Esti,* 1974)
Exi ke mia tipsis yia ton ourano, 1960 (*Six and One Remorses for the Sky,* 1974)

O ilios o iliatoras, 1971 (*The Sovereign Sun,* 1974)
To fotodhendro ke i dhekati tetarti omorfia, 1971
To monogramma, 1971 (*The Monogram,* 1974)
The Sovereign Sun: Selected Poems, 1974 (includes *Six and One Remorses for the Sky, The Monogram, The Sovereign Sun,* and various selections from his other collections)
Maria Nefeli, 1978 (*Maria Nephele,* 1981)
Ekloyi, 1935-1977, 1979
Odysseus Elytis: Selected Poems, 1981
What I Love: Selected Poems of Odysseus Elytis, 1986
Ek tou plision, 1998
The Collected Poems of Odysseus Elytis; 1997

OTHER LITERARY FORMS

Principally a poet, Odysseus Elytis, in the eminently pictorial, imagistic, "architectural" nature of his verse, revealed his other, parallel propensity. Had he received any formal artistic education, he might have been a distinguished painter as well. As early as 1935, he produced a number of Surrealist collages; in 1966, he painted some thirty-odd gouaches, all but four of which he destroyed; and in the years from 1967 to 1974, the period of the dictatorship of the "colonels," he produced about forty remarkable collages, nineteen of which are reproduced in Ilías Petropoulous's book *Elytis, Moralis, Tsarouhis* (1974). Elytis's longstanding interest in the arts and his friendship with some of the most prominent modern artists in Greece and France have qualified him as an acute art critic as well.

Elytis translated poets as varied as Le Comte de Lautreamont, Arthur Rimbaud, Pierre-Jean Jouve, Paul Eluard, Giuseppe Ungaretti, Federico García Lorca, and Vladimir Mayakovsky. Elytis's prose works include essays and monographs on sympathetic writers and painters. His most important work in prose, an invaluable companion to his poetry, is *Anihta hartia* (1974; open book), a work of widely ranging, often aphoristic reflections, in which Elytis spoke extensively about his poetics and his development as a poet.

ACHIEVEMENTS

Odysseus Elytis's constantly renewed originality, his wise optimism, and his glorification of the Greek world in its physical and spiritual beauty have gradually won for him wide popularity and recognition as well as several distinctions, honors, and prizes—most notably the Nobel Prize for Literature in 1979. In 1960 he also won the National Poetry Prize and the National Book Award, both for *To axion esti*. He won the Order of the Phoenix in 1965. He was honored with several honorary doctorate degrees from institutions such as the University of Thessaloniki (1975), University of Paris (1980), and University of London (1981). In 1989 he was commander in the French Legion of Honor.

BIOGRAPHY

The offspring of a family originating on the island of Lesbos (or Mitilini), in the eastern Aegean, Odysseus Elytis was born Odysseus Alepoudhelis in Heraklion, Crete, the sixth and last child of Panyiotis Alepoudhelis, a successful soap manufacturer, and Maria Vranas, of Byzantine extraction. In 1914, the family settled permanently in Athens, where Elytis went to high school, but summers spent in Lesbos, Crete, and other Aegean islands provided him with what was to be his poetic world in terms of imagery, symbols, language, and cultural identity.

Elytis's early literary interests were given an outlet and direction through his chance discovery of the poetry of Paul Éluard in 1929. From 1930 to 1935, Elytis attended the law school of the University of Athens but never was graduated. His meeting with the orthodox Surrealist poet Andreas Embiriíkos (1901-1975) in 1935 decidedly enhanced his own Surrealist inclinations. That same year, Elytis published his first poems in the periodical *Nea Ghramata*, recently founded by the poet and critic Andréas Karandonis (1910-1982); under Karandonis's editorship, *Nea Ghramata* soon became the rallying center of the new poetry and prose in Greece. Elytis's first collection of poems, *Prosanatolizmi* (orientations), appeared in December, 1939.

Fascist Italy attacked Greece from Albania in 1940, and in 1940-1941 Elytis served as a second lieutenant on the Albanian front, where he almost perished in a military hospital from typhoid. During the Nazi occupation of Greece, his second book of poetry, *Ilios o protos,*

mazi me tis parallayies pano se mian ahtidha (sun the first together with variations on a sunbeam), was published, followed, soon after the liberation, by *Heroic and Elegiac Song for the Lost Second Lieutenant of the Albanian Campaign*. In 1945-1946, Elytis served as director of programming and broadcasting for the National Broadcasting System in Athens. From 1948 to 1952, Elytis lived in Paris, where he studied literature at the Sorbonne, and traveled in England, Switzerland, Italy, and Spain. During this period he associated with Andre Breton, Paul Eluard, Tristan Tzara, Pierre Jean Jouve, Henri Michaux, Giuseppe Ungaretti, Henri Matisse, Pablo Picasso, Alberto Giacometti, and Giorgio de Chirico. In 1950, Elytis was elected as a member of the International Union of Art Critics, and in 1953, after his return to Greece, he was elected to the Poetry Committee of the Group of Twelve, which annually awarded prizes for poetry. Elytis served once again as director of programming and broadcasting of the National Broadcasting System in Athens until 1954. From 1955 to 1956, he was on the governing board of the avant-garde Karolos Koun Art Theater, and from 1956 to 1958 he was president of the governing board of the Greek Ballet.

The publication of his two epoch-making books of verse, *The Axion Esti* and *Six and One Remorses for the Sky*, broke Elytis's poetic silence and won for him the National Prize for Poetry in 1960. A selection from *The Axion Esti*, set to music by the composer Mikis Theodhorakis in 1964, brought the poet wide popularity.

In 1961, Elytis visited the United States for three months at the invitation of the State Department, and in 1962 he visited the Soviet Union on the invitation of its government. From 1965 to 1968, he was a member of the administrative board of the Greek National Theater.

In 1967, the government of Greece was toppled by a military coup. For the next seven years, the colonels (as the ruling junta was known) ruthlessly suppressed opposition to their regime, exercising severe censorship and otherwise curtailing civil rights. From 1969 to 1971, Elytis lived in France, primarily in Paris. Following his return to Greece, he published seven poetry books, including *The Monogram, The Sovereign Sun*, and *To fotodhendro ke i dhekati tetarti omorfia* (the light tree and the fourteenth beauty), as well as the prose work

Odysseus Elytis, Nobel laureate in literature for 1979.
(© The Nobel Foundation)

Anihta hartia. Elytis was awarded the Nobel Prize for Literature in 1979, and in 1980 he received an honorary doctorate from the Sorbonne. He died in Athens, Greece, on March 18, 1996.

ANALYSIS

The suicide of the Greek poet Kostas Karyotakis in 1928 may be said to have marked the end of an era in Greek poetry, which had long abided in Parnassianism, *poesie maudite*, Symbolism, and *poésie pure.* A spirit of discomfort, decadence, and despair prevailed, intensified by the military defeat suffered by Greece in Asia Minor in 1922. The year 1935 has generally been considered to mark the beginning of a great change in modern Greek poetry—a renaissance in which Odysseus Elytis, along with George Seferis and others, was most instrumental. Rejecting a tired traditionalism, these modernists invigorated Greek poetry by the adoption and creative assimilation of Western trends. The renaissance which they initiated is still flourishing; indeed, twentieth century Greek poetry is as rich as that of any nation in its time.

Adopting Surrealism as a liberating force with his extraordinary lyrical gifts, Elytis brought to Greek poetry a spirit of eternal youthfulness, beauty, purity, sanity, and erotic vigor. His inspiration sprung from nature, particularly from the Aegean archipelago, as well as from the Greek world throughout the centuries. At the same time, however, Elytis's mature vision was shaped by his experiences in World War II, which enriched and deepened his brilliant, careless, pictorial lyricism with historical awareness—an awareness of suffering as an essential and unavoidable part of life, which it is the poet's duty to recognize and transcend. A moderated Platonic idealism, earthly in its roots, characterized most of Elytis's work.

Elytis's early poetry broke new ground in Greek verse. Its youthful, optimistic freshness; its genuine, powerful lyricism; the graceful richness of its imagery drawn from nature; and its free Surrealistic associations—all conspired to liberate Greek poetry from its Symbolist melancholy and despair. In Surrealism, Elytis found a force of sanity and purity, of liberating newness, but he quickly abandoned the automatism of Surrealist orthodoxy, choosing instead to subject the effusions of his unconscious to formal demands. Inspired by the Apollonian clarity of the Greek sunlight, yet without excluding its mystical, its Dionysian essence, he thus accomplished an imaginative, creative assimilation, an acclimatization of the positive elements in Surrealism to the Greek world, its reality and spirit.

The physical elements of the Aegean archipelago, its landscapes and seascapes, provided Elytis with the material for a radiant, sun-drenched poetic realm, a setting in which adolescent youths learn of Eros as the all-mastering, all-penetrating, all-revealing, all-uniting procreative and inspiring force. Elytis identified man with nature in terms of analogies existing between them: Nature is anthropomorphized in a joyful exchange that no deep sorrow dares to tint.

Throughout his long career, with its constant experimentation, inventive metamorphoses, renovations, and striking changes, Elytis remained faithful to certain fundamental beliefs concerning the objectives of his art:

> The lesson remains the same: it is sufficient to express that which we love, and this alone, with the fewest means at our disposal, yet in the most direct manner, that of poetry.

PROSANATOLIZMI AND ILIOS O PROTOS, MAZI ME TIS PARALLAYIES PANO SE MIAN AHTIDHA

Elytis's first book, *Prosanatolizmi*, experimental in manner and form, features free rhythmical verse, gently sensual, mostly of imagery set in motion. Although there is in this collection no deepening into thought and emotion, there are some poems of exquisite beauty and power, including "Anniversary," "Ode to Santorini," "Marina of the Rocks," "The Mad Pomegranate Tree," and others that won instant acclaim and lasting popularity, earning Elytis the title of "the poet of the Aegean."

In Elytis's second book, *Ilios o protos, mazi me tis parallayies pano se mian ahtidha*, the idealized "countryside of open heart," the paradise of carefree and unaging youth, the world of an eternal present which ignores the past and hopes in the future, is more consciously mastered and revealed. This early collection demonstrated the poet's conscientious craftsmanship, his sensitivity to the Greek language in all of its expressive power, its visual and musical richness and beauty. A more thoughtful tone is apparent here as well.

THE AXION ESTI

The experience of the war, reflected in the long poem *Heroic and Elegiac Song for the Lost Second Lieutenant of the Albanian Campaign*, permanently altered Elytis's vision. Fourteen years passed between the publication of this wartime elegy and the appearance of Elytis's next book, *The Axion Esti* (its title meaning "worthy it is," appears in the liturgy of the Greek Orthodox Church as well as in several Byzantine hymns).

The Axion Esti may be viewed as the worldly equivalent of a Greek Orthodox mass, with its three parts corresponding to Christ's life, His Passion, and His Resurrection. The poem is not a Christian epic in the strict sense of the term; it is, however, much indebted to Byzantine hymnology. Its middle section consists of three types of poetic units corresponding to liturgical ones.

Eighteen "psalms" alternate, in strictly mathematical, symmetrical order, with twelve "odes" and six "readings." The readings are objective, powerfully realistic prose accounts of representative scenes and episodes of the 1940's, while the psalms, in free verse, are lyrical and thoughtful reactions, and the odes are songlike in their various intricately metrical stanzas. On the whole, the poem is a tour de force in the technical variety of its forms and modes, in the richness of its language and imagery, and in its superbly conscious craftsmanship; it was on this poem in particular that the Swedish Academy bestowed its highest praise in awarding the Nobel Prize to Elytis. In this epic in lyric form, the poet of the impulsive unconscious presented a poetry that is described by Andreas Karandonis as "highly programmed, totally directed to a final goal, and measured in its every detail as if with a compass." Thematically, this epic may be said to have its first conception in Elytis's heroic elegy on the Albanian campaign, for it returns in part to the suffering and the heroism which he witnessed in the war, yet in its epic grandeur and technical variety, *The Axion Esti* widens to embrace the physical and spiritual identity of the Greek nation and the Hellenic world.

Of the three major sections of this poem, the first, "Genesis," is an imagistic and lyrical account of how light, the Aegean sunlight, defined the physical, ethical, spiritual, and psychological characteristics of the Greek world. Parallel to the growth of Greek culture and the Greek nation is the poet's own growth, for in him a personified sun, the divine creator, has its axis. This identification of the poet with the giver of life establishes the rhythm of the poem, which shifts constantly from the individual to the archetypal, from the microcosm to the macrocosm. The small world of Greece is identical with the "great world," as the "now" is with the "ever."

Following this account of the past, "The Passion"—the centerpiece of the poem, the longest, most stylistically varied, and most significant of the three sections—turns to the present, to the war decade (1940-1949), during which the "created world" is submitted to a major test of suffering. The third and last section, "Gloria," is highly lyrical and prophetic, earthy yet "meteoric," physical yet metaphysical. The disturbed and challenged world is waiting to be restored to its inherent beauty and worth as a "regained paradise," enriched by the lessons learned through hardship.

Speaking of the insistent "search for paradise" in his work, Elytis has remarked: "When I say 'paradise,' I do not conceive of it in the Christian sense. It is another world which is incorporated into our own, and it is our own fault that we are unable to grasp it." Almost always connected with Elytis's notion of paradise are the "girls" ever present in his poetry, embodiments of beauty and inspirers of Eros, both physical and transcendental. Elytis's informing vision was described as a "solar metaphysics," the metaphysics of Greek sunlight. As Elytis remarked: "Europeans and Westerners always find mystery in obscurity, in the night, while we Greeks find it in light, which is for us an absolute. . . . *Limpidity* is probably the one element which dominates my poetry at present," where "behind a given thing something different can be seen."

TO FOTODHENDRO KE I DHEKATI TETARTI OMORFIA

Elytis's solar metaphysics found seminal expression in the collection entitled *To fotodhendro ke i dhekati tetarti omorfia*. These poems depict "the full miniature of a solar system, with the same tranquillity and the same air of eternity, the same perpetual motion in its separate constituent parts." The senses reach their "sanctity," becoming organs of poetic metaphysics and extensions of the spirit. In suggestive dreams, Elytis's "girls" became angelic phantoms, not earthly any more but inhabitants of a paradise which grows melancholy and mysterious. The "light tree" mentioned in the title, which Elytis once saw magically growing in the backyard of his childhood home, is symbolic of the light of life, of revelation and inspiration, of love and communion with the universe; when in his old age he returns in search of it, the tree is gone. In a series of nostalgic, intimate, imaginative recollections of his childhood and youth, he tried to recapture and decipher the meaning of his experience. These poems are apparently progressive stages in the day or week of his whole life, starting from a Palm Sunday morning, progressing to the sunset, then passing into night and the astral metaphysics of his old age. There, with mystical and occult insinuations, all opposites meet and are reconciled.

MARIA NEPHELE

A work that was later regarded to be the summa of Elytis's later writings, *Maria Nephele* was initially received by a curious yet hesitant public. As one critic noted, "some academicians and critics of the older generations still [wanted] to cling to the concept of the 'sun-drinking' Elytis . . . the monumental *Axion Esti*, so they [approached it] with cautious hesitation as an experimental and not-so-attractive creation of rather ephemeral value."

The issue lay with its radically different presentation. Whereas his earlier poems dealt with the almost timeless expression of the Greek reality that were not directly derived from actual events, *Maria Nephele* was based on a young woman he actually met. Moreover, unlike the women from his earlier work, the woman in Elytis's poem had changed to reflect the troubled times in which she lived, becoming a new manifestation of the eternal female. Maria stands opposed to the more traditional women figures of his early poems by serving as an attractive, liberated, restless, and even blasé representative of today's young woman. American youth radicalism hit its apex in the late 1960's, but it took another decade for its force to be felt in Greece. In *Maria Nephele* the tensions produced from the radicalism interact with some more newly developed Greek cultural realities: increased cosmopolitanism (with its positive and negative aspects), technological advances, and concern with material possessions.

As one critic wrote, the urban Maria Nephele "is the offspring, not the sibling, of the women of Elytis's youth. Her setting is the polluted city, not the open country and its islands of purity and fresh air."

The poem consists of the juxtaposed conversations of Maria Nephele, who represents the ideals of today's emerging woman, and Antifonitis, or the Responder, who stands for more traditional views. Maria forces the Responder to confront issues which he would rather ignore. Both characters are sophisticated and complex urbanites who express themselves in a wide range of styles, moods, idioms, and stanzaic forms.

OTHER MAJOR WORKS

NONFICTION: *O zoghrafos Theofilos*, 1973; *Anihta hartia*, 1974; *I mayia tou Papadhiamandi*, 1976;

Anafora ston Andrea Embiríko, 1978; *Ta dimosia ke ta idiotika*, 1990; *En lefko*, 1992; *Open Papers*, 1995.

TRANSLATION: *Dhefteri ghrafi*, 1976 (of Arthur Rimbaud and others).

BIBLIOGRAPHY

Books Abroad (Fall, 1975). Special Elytis issue.

Bosnakis, Panayiotis. "*Ek tou plision.*" *World Literature Today* 74, no. 1 (Winter, 2000): 211-212. A critical analysis of Elytis's posthumously published *Ek tou plision.* (from close)

Friar, Kimon. *Modern Greek Poetry: From Cavafis to Elytis*. New York: Simon and Schuster, 1973. Informative introduction, an essay on translation, and annotations to the poetry by the editor. Includes bibliography.

Glasgow, Eric. "Odysseus Elytis: In Memory of a Modern Greek Poet." *Contemporary Review* 270, no. 1572 (January, 1997): 33-34. A brief biographical article.

Ivask, Ivar, ed. *Odysseus Elytis: Analogies of Light*. Norman: University of Oklahoma Press, 1981. A collection of critical essays on Elytis's work.

Andonis Decavalles,
updated by Sarah Hilbert

RALPH WALDO EMERSON

Born: Boston, Massachusetts; May 25, 1803
Died: Concord, Massachusetts; April 27, 1882

PRINCIPAL POETRY

Poems, 1847
May-Day and Other Pieces, 1867
Selected Poems, 1876

OTHER LITERARY FORMS

Ralph Waldo Emerson's *The Journals of Ralph Waldo Emerson* (1909-1914), written over a period of fifty-five years (1820-1875), were ultimately the source of everything else he wrote. These have been edited in ten volumes by Edward W. Emerson and Waldo Emerson Forbes. From this set a fine one-volume collection has been edited by Bliss Perry, *The Heart of Emerson's Journals* (1926). Ralph L. Rusk has also edited *The Letters of Ralph Waldo Emerson* in six volumes (1939). Emerson was a noted lecturer in his day, although many of his addresses and speeches were not collected until after his death. These appear in three posthumous volumes—*Lectures and Biographical Sketches* (1884), *Miscellanies* (1884), and *Natural History of Intellect* (1893)—which were published as part of the Centenary Edition (1903-1904). A volume of Emerson's *Uncollected Writings: Essays, Addresses, Poems, Reviews, and Letters* was published in 1912. A sixteen-volume edition of journals and miscellaneous papers was published between 1960 and 1982.

ACHIEVEMENTS

Although Ralph Waldo Emerson's poetry was but a small part of his overall literary output, he thought of himself as very much a poet—even in his essays and lectures. He began writing poetry early in childhood and at the age of nine composed some verses on the Sabbath. At Harvard he was elected class poet and was asked to write the annual Phi Beta Kappa poem in 1834. This interest in poetry continued throughout his long career.

During his lifetime he published two small volumes of poetry, *Poems* and *May-Day and Other Pieces*, which were later collected in one volume for the Centenary Edition of his works. Altogether, the Centenary volume contains some 170 poems, of which perhaps only several dozen are noteworthy.

Although Emerson produced a comparatively small amount of poetry and an even smaller number of first-rate poems, he stands as a major influence on the subsequent course of American poetry. As scholar, critic, and poet, Emerson was the first to define the distinctive qualities of American verse. His broad and exalted concept of the poet—as prophet, oracle, visionary, and seer—was shaped by his Romantic idealism. "I am more of a poet than anything else," he once wrote, although as much of his poetry is found in his journals and essays as in the poems themselves. In *The American Scholar* (1837) he called for a distinctive American poetry, and in his essay "The Poet" he provided the theoretical framework for American poetics. Scornful of imitation, he demanded freshness and originality from his

Ralph Waldo Emerson (Library of Congress)

democratic culture would embrace the facts of ordinary experience rather than celebrate epic themes. It would be a poetry of enumeration rather than elevation, of fact rather than eloquence; indeed, the democratic poet would have to struggle for eloquence, for poetry of the commonplace can easily become flat or prosaic. Even Emerson's own best verse often seems uneven, with memorable lines interspersed with mediocre ones.

Part of the problem with Emerson's poetry arose from his methods of composition. Writing poetry was not for him a smooth, continuous act of composition. Nor did he have a set formula for composition, as Edgar Allan Poe advocated in "The Philosophy of Composition"; instead, he trusted inspiration to allow the form of the poem to be determined by its subject matter. This "organic" theory of composition shapes many of Emerson's best poems, including "The Snow-Storm," "Hamatreya," "Days," and "Ode." These poems avoid a fixed metrical or stanzaic structure and allow the sense of the line to dictate its poetic form. Emerson clearly composed by the line rather than by the stanza or paragraph, in both his poetry and prose, and this self-contained quality often gives his work a gnomic or orphic tone.

Although some of his poems appear to be fragmentary, they are not unfinished. They lack smoothness or polish because Emerson was not a lyrical but a visionary, oracular poet. He valued poetry as a philosophy or attitude toward life rather than simply as a formal linguistic structure or an artistic form. "The poet is the sayer, the namer, and represents beauty," he observed in "The Poet." With Percy Bysshe Shelley he believed that the poet was the visionary who would make men whole and teach them to see anew. "Poets are thus liberating gods," Emerson concluded, because "they are free, and they make free." Poetry is simply the most concentrated expression of the poetic vision, which all men are capable of sharing.

Thus Emerson's poems seek to accomplish what the essays announce. His poems attempt to reestablish the primal relationship between man and nature that he sought as a substitute for revelation. Emerson prized the poet as an innovator, a namer, and a language-maker who could interpret the oracles of nature. In its derivation from nature, all language, he felt, was fossil poetry.

verse, even though he did not always achieve in practice what he sought in theory. Rejecting the derivative verse of the "Hartford Wits" and the sentimental versifiers of his day, he sought an original style and flavor for an American poetry close to the native grain. The form of his poetry was, as F. I. Carpenter argues (*Emerson Handbook*, 1953), the logical result of his insistence upon self-reliance, while its content was shaped by his Romantic idealism. Thus his cumulative influence on American poetry is greater than his verse alone might imply.

Expression mattered more than form in poetry, according to Emerson. If he was not the completely inspirational poet called for in his essays, that may have been more a matter of temperament than of any flaw in his sense of the kind of poetry that a democratic culture would produce. In fact, his comments often closely parallel those of Alexis de Tocqueville on the nature of poetry in America. Both men agreed that the poetry of a

"Always the seer is a sayer," he announced in his Harvard Divinity School address, and through the vision of the poet "we come to look at the world with new eyes."

Of the defects in Emerson's poetry, the chief is perhaps that Emerson's muse sees rather than sings. Because his lines are orphic and self-contained, they sometimes seem flat and discontinuous. Individual lines stand out in otherwise undistinguished poems. Nor do his lines always scan or flow smoothly, since Emerson was virtually tone-deaf. In "The Poet" he rejects fixed poetic form in favor of a freer, more open verse. For Emerson, democratic poetry would be composed with variable line and meter, with form subordinated to expression. The poet in a democracy is thus a "representative man," chanting the poetry of the common, the ordinary, and the low. Although Emerson pointed the way, it took Walt Whitman to master this new style of American poetry with his first edition of *Leaves of Grass* (1855), which Emerson promptly recognized and praised for its originality. Whitman thus became the poet whom Emerson had called for in "The American Scholar"; American poetry had come of age.

BIOGRAPHY

Born in Boston on May 25, 1803, Ralph Waldo Emerson was the second of five sons in the family of William and Ruth Emerson. His father was a noted Unitarian minister of old New England stock whose sudden death in 1811 left the family to struggle in genteel poverty. Although left without means, Emerson's mother and his aunt, Mary Moody Emerson, were energetic and resourceful women who managed to survive by taking in boarders, accepting the charity of relatives, and teaching their boys the New England values of thrift, hard work, and mutual assistance within the family. Frail as a child, Emerson attended Boston Latin School and Harvard, where he was graduated without distinction in 1821. Since their mother was determined that her children would receive a decent education, each of her sons taught after graduation to help the others through school. Thus Emerson taught for several years at his brother's private school for women before he decided to enter divinity school. His family's high thinking and plain living taught young Emerson self-reliance and a deep respect for books and learning.

With his father and step-grandfather, the Reverend Ezra Ripley of Concord, as models, Emerson returned to Harvard to prepare for the ministry. After two years of intermittent study at the Divinity School, Emerson was licensed to preach in the Unitarian Church. He was forced to postpone further studies, however, and travel south during the winter of 1826 because of poor health. The next two years saw him preaching occasionally and serving as a substitute pastor. One such call brought him to Concord, New Hampshire, where he met his future wife, Ellen Louisa Tucker. After his ordination in March, 1829, Emerson married Ellen Tucker and accepted a call as minister of the Second Church, Boston, where his father had also served. The position and salary were good, and Emerson was prepared to settle into a respectable career as a Boston Unitarian clergyman. Unfortunately his wife was frail, and within a year and a half she died of tuberculosis. Grief-stricken, Emerson found it difficult to continue with his duties as pastor and resigned from the pulpit six months after his wife's death. Private doubts had assailed him, and he found he could no longer administer the Lord's Supper in good conscience. His congregation would not allow him to dispense with the rite, so his resignation was reluctantly accepted.

With a small settlement from his wife's legacy he sailed for Europe in December, 1832, to regain his health and try to find a new vocation. During his winter in Italy he admired the art treasures in Florence and Rome. There he met the American sculptor Horatio Greenough and the English writer Walter Savage Landor. The following spring, Emerson continued his tour through Switzerland and into France. Paris charmed him with its splendid museums and gardens and he admired the natural history exhibits at the Jardin des Plantes. Crossing to England by August, he met Samuel Taylor Coleridge in London, then traveled north to visit Thomas Carlyle in Craigenputtock and William Wordsworth at Rydal Mount. His meeting with Carlyle resulted in a lifelong friendship.

After returning to Boston in 1833, Emerson gradually settled into a new routine of study, lecturing, and writing, filling an occasional pulpit on Sundays, and assembling ideas in his journals for his essay on "Nature." Lydia Jackson, a young woman from Plymouth, New

Hampshire, heard Emerson preach in Boston and became infatuated with him. The young widower returned her admiration, although he frankly confessed that he felt none of the deep affection he had cherished for his first wife. During their engagement he renamed her "Lidian" in their correspondence because he disliked the name Lydia. She accepted the change without demur. Within a year they were married and settled in a house on the Boston Post Road near the Old Manse of Grandfather Ripley. Emerson was now thirty-two and about to begin his life's work.

The next decade marked Emerson's intellectual maturity. *Nature* was completed and published as a small volume in 12836. In its elaborate series of correspondences between man and nature, Emerson established the foundations of his idealistic philosophy. "Why should not we also enjoy an original relation to the universe?" he asked. Man could seek revelations firsthand from nature, rather than having them handed down through tradition. A year later Emerson gave his "The American Scholar" address before the Harvard Phi Beta Kappa Society, an event that Oliver Wendell Holmes later called "our intellectual Declaration of Independence." In his address, Emerson called for a distinctively American style of letters, free from European influences. Invited in 1838 to speak before the graduating class of Harvard Divinity School, Emerson affirmed in his address that the true measure of religion resided within the individual, not in institutional or historical Christianity. If everyone had equal access to the Divine Spirit, then inner experience was all that was needed to validate religious truth. For this daring pronouncement he was attacked by Harvard President Andrews Norton and others for espousing "the latest form of infidelity." In a sense each of these important essays was an extension of Emerson's basic doctrine of self-reliance, applied to philosophy, culture, and religion.

His self-reliance served him equally well in personal life, even as family losses haunted him, almost as if to test his hard-won equanimity and sense of purpose. Besides losing his first wife, Ellen Tucker, Emerson saw two of his brothers die and a third become so feeble-minded that he had to be institutionalized. Worst of all, his first-born and beloved son Waldo died in 1841 of scarlet fever at the age of six. Emerson's melioristic phi-

losophy saw him through these losses, although in his journals he later chided himself for not feeling his son's death more deeply. Despite the hurt he felt, his New England reserve would not allow him to yield easily to grief or despair. Nor would he dwell in darkness while there was still light to be found.

During these years, Emerson found Concord a congenial home. He established a warm and stimulating circle of friends there and enjoyed the intellectual company of Nathaniel Hawthorne, Henry David Thoreau, and Bronson Alcott. As his fame as a lecturer and writer grew, he attracted a wider set of admirers, including Margaret Fuller, who often visited to share enthusiasms and transcendental conversations. Emerson even edited *The Dial* for a short time in 1842, but for the most part he remained aloof from, although sympathetic to, the transcendentalist movement that he had so largely inspired. His manner at times was even offhand. When asked for a definition of transcendentalism, he simply replied, "Idealism in 1842." When George Ripley invited him to join the Brook Farm Community in 1840, Emerson politely declined. Reform, he believed, had to begin with the individual. Thoreau later rebuked him for not taking a firmer stand on the fugitive slave issue, but Emerson was by nature apolitical and skeptical of partisan causes. His serenity was too hard-won to be sacrificed, no matter how worthy the cause.

So instead he continued to lecture and write, and his essays touched an entire generation of American writers. Thoreau, Whitman, and Emily Dickinson responded enthusiastically to the appeal of Emerson's thought, while even Hawthorne and Herman Melville, although rejecting it, still felt compelled to acknowledge his intellectual presence. Lecture tours took him repeatedly to the Midwest and to England and Scotland for a second time in 1847-1848. Harvard finally awarded him an honorary degree in 1866 and elected him overseer the following year. His alma mater also invited him to deliver a series of lectures on his philosophy in 1869-1870. When Emerson's home in Concord burned in 1877, friends sent him on a third visit to Europe and Egypt, accompanied by his daughter Ellen, while the house and study were rebuilt with funds from admirers. He spent his last few years in Concord quietly and died in the spring of 1882. Of his life it can be said that perhaps more than any of his contemporaries he embodied the qualities of the American spirit—its frankness, idealism, optimism, and self-confidence. For the American writer of his age, all things were possible. If, finally, he was as much prophet as poet, that may be due to the power of his vision as well as to its lyrical intensity, a power that suffused his prose and was concentrated in his poems.

ANALYSIS

Ralph Waldo Emerson's poetic achievement is greater than the range of his individual poems might suggest. While perhaps only a handful of his poems attain undisputed greatness, others are rich in implication despite their occasional lapses, saved by a memorable line or phrase. As a cultural critic and poetic innovator, moreover, Emerson has had an immense influence through his essays and poetry in suggesting an appropriate style and method for subsequent American poets. He tried to become the poet he called for in *The American Scholar*, and to a degree his poems reflect those democratic precepts. Determined to find distinctively American art forms, he began with expression—not form—and evolved the forms of his poems through their expression. Inspired by the "organic aesthetic" of the American sculptor Horatio Greenough, whose studio in Rome he visited in 1833, Emerson abandoned traditional poetic structure for a loose iambic meter and a variable (though often octosyllabic) line. Instead of following a rigid external form, the poem would take its form from its particular content and expression. This was the freedom Emerson sought for a "democratic" poetry.

Emerson's best poetry is thus marked by two qualities: organic form and a vernacular style; his less successful pieces, such as "The Sphinx," are too often cryptic and diffuse. These strengths and weaknesses both derive from his attempt to unite philosophical ideas and lyricism within a symbolic form in which the image would evoke its deeper meaning. "I am born a poet," he wrote to his fiancé, Lydia Jackson, "of a low class without doubt, yet a poet. That is my vocation. My singing, to be sure, is very 'husky,' and is for the most part in prose. Still I am a poet in the sense of a perceiver and dear lover of the harmonies that are in the soul and in matter, and specially of the correspondence between

these and those." Correspondence, then, is what Emerson sought in his poetry, based on his theory of language as intermediary between man and nature.

In his essay "The Poet," Emerson announced that "it is not metres, but metre-making argument that makes a poem." His representative American poet would be a namer and enumerator, not a rhymer or versifier. The poet would take his inspiration from the coarse vigor of American vernacular speech and in turn reinvigorate poetic language by tracing root metaphors back to their origins in ordinary experience. He would avoid stilted or artificial poetic diction in favor of ordinary speech. This meant sacrificing sound to sense, however, since Emerson's "metre-making arguments" were more often gnomic than lyrical. As a result, his poems are as spare as their native landscape. They are muted and understated rather than rhapsodic, and—with the exception of his Orientalism—tempered and homey in their subject matter, since Emerson was more of an innovator in style than in substance. Emerson's "Merlin" provides perhaps the best definition of what he sought in his poetry:

> Thy trivial harp will never please
> Or fill my craving ear;
> Its chords should ring as blows the breeze,
> Free, peremptory, clear.

"DAYS," "THE PROBLEM," AND "THE SNOW-STORM"

Emerson's poems fall into several distinct categories, the most obvious being his nature poems; his philosophical or meditative poems, which often echo the essays; his autobiographical verse; and his occasional pieces. Sometimes these categories may overlap, but the "organic" aesthetic and colloquial tone mark them as distinctly Emersonian. Two of his most frequently anthologized pieces, "Days" and "The Snow-Storm," will serve to illustrate his poetic style.

"Days" has been called the most perfect of Emerson's poems, and while there is a satisfying completeness about the poem, it resolves less than might appear at first reading. The poem deals with what was for Emerson the continuing problem of vocation or calling. How could he justify his apparent idleness in a work-oriented culture? "Days" thus contains something of a self-rebuke, cast in terms of an Oriental procession of

Days, personified as daughters of Time, who pass through the poet's garden bringing various gifts, the riches of life, which the poet too hastily rejects in favor of a "few herbs and apples," emblematic of the contemplative life. The Day scorns his choice, presumably because he has squandered his time in contemplation rather than having measured his ambition against worthier goals. The Oriental imagery employed here transforms a commonplace theme into a memorable poem, although the poet never responds to the implied criticism of his life; nor does he identify the "morning wishes" that have been abandoned for the more sedate and domestic "herbs and apples," although these images do suggest meanings beyond themselves.

A thematically related poem is "The Problem," in which Emerson tries to justify his reasons for leaving the ministry, which he respects and admires but cannot serve. Perhaps because he was more poet than priest, Emerson preferred the direct inspiration of the artist to the inherited truths of religion, or it may have been that, as a romantic, he found more inspiration in nature than in Scripture. The third stanza of "The Problem" contains one of the clearest articulations of Emerson's "organic" aesthetic, of form emerging from expression, in the image of the artist who "builded better than he knew." The temples of nature "art might obey, but not surpass."

This organic theory of art reached its fullest expression in "The Snow-Storm," which still offers the best example in Emerson's poetry of form following function, and human artistry imitating that of nature. Here the poem merges with what it describes. The first stanza announces the arrival of the storm and the second stanza evokes the "frolic architecture" of the snow and the human architectural forms that it anticipates. Nature freely creates and man imitates through art. Wind and snow form myriad natural forms that man can only "mimic in slow structures" of stone. As the wind-sculpted snowdrifts create beauty from the materials at hand, the poem rounds upon itself in the poet's implicit admiration of nature's work.

CYCLE OF LIFE METAPHOR

One of the most intriguing of Emerson's poems is "Hamatraya," which contains an attack on Yankee landgreed and acquisitiveness, cast as a Hindu meditation on the impermanence of all corporeal things. In "Hama-traya" the crass materialism of his countrymen evokes Emerson's serenely idealistic response. No one finally owns the land, he asserts, and to pretend so is to be deceived. The land will outlive successive masters, all of whom boast of owning it. In the enduring cycle of things, they are all finally returned to the earth they claimed to possess. Emerson uses dramatic form and the lyrical "Earth-Song" as an effective counterpoint to the blunt materialism of the first two stanzas. His theme of all things returning unto themselves finds its appropriate metaphor in the organic (and Hindu) cycle of life. Hindu cosmology and natural ecology complement each other in Emerson's critique of the pretensions of private landownership.

Another of Emerson's Oriental poems, his popular "Brahma," is notable for its blend of Eastern and Western thought. Here Emerson assumes the perspective of God or Brahma in presenting his theme of the divine relativity and continuity of life. Just as Krishna, "the Red Slayer," and his victim are merged in the unity of Brahma, so all other opposites are reconciled in the ultimate unity of the universe. This paradoxical logic appealed to Emerson as a way of presenting his monistic philosophy in poetic terms. The poem owes much to Emerson's study of the Bhagavad Gita and other Oriental scriptures, the first stanza of "Brahma" being in fact a close parallel to the Hindu text. The smooth regularity of Emerson's ballad stanzas also helps to offset the exotic quality of the Hindu allusions and the novelty of the poem's theme.

"URIEL" AND "EACH AND ALL"

Religious myth is also present in the poem "Uriel," which Robert Frost called "the greatest Western poem yet." Even if Frost's praise is overstated, this is still one of Emerson's most profound and complex poems. Again it deals with the reconciliation of opposites, this time in the proposed relativity of good and evil. Borrowing the theme of the primal revolt against God by the rebellious archangels, Emerson uses the figure of the angel Uriel as the prototype of the advanced thinker misunderstood or rejected by others. Uriel represents the artist as the rebel or prophet bearing unwelcome words, roles that Emerson no doubt identified with himself and the hostile reception given his *Divinity School Address* in 1838 by the Harvard theological faculty. Uriel's words, "Line in nature is not found;/ Unit and universe are round; In vain produced, all rays return;/ Evil will bless, and ice will burn," speak with particular force to the modern age, in which discoveries in theoretical physics and astronomy seem to have confirmed Emerson's intuitions about the relativity of matter and energy and the nature of the physical universe.

Emerson's monistic philosophy also appears in "Each and All," in which the poem suggests that beauty cannot be divorced from its context or setting without losing part of its original appeal. The peasant, sparrow, seashell, and maid must each be appreciated in the proper aesthetic context, as part of a greater unity. Beauty cannot be possessed, Emerson argues, without destroying it. The theme of "Each and All" perhaps echoes section III on Beauty of his essay *Nature*, in which Emerson observes that "the standard of beauty is the entire circuit of natural forms—the totality of nature. . . . Nothing is quite beautiful alone; nothing but is beautiful in the whole. A single object is only so far beautiful as it suggests this universal grace." The poem "Each and All" gives a more concentrated and lyrical expression to this apprehension of aesthetic unity. The poetic images lend grace and specificity to the philosophical concept of the beauty inherent in unity.

"GIVE ALL TO LOVE" AND "THRENODY"

Emerson's fondness for paradoxical logic and the union of apparent opposites appears in yet another poem, "Give All to Love," which initially appears to falter upon the contradiction between yielding to love and retaining one's individuality. The first three stanzas counsel a wholehearted surrender to the impulse of love, while the fourth stanza cautions the lover to remain "free as an Arab." The final two stanzas resolve this dilemma by affirming that the lovers may cherish joys apart without compromising their love for each other, since the purest love is that which is free from jealousy or possessiveness. Emerson reconciles the demands of love and those of self-reliance by idealizing the love relationship. Some commentators have even suggested that Emerson envisions a Neo-platonic ladder or hierarchy of love, from the Physical, to the Romantic, to the Ideal or Platonic—a relationship which in fact Emerson described in another poem titled "Initial, Daemonic, and Celestial Love"—but the theme of "Give All to Love" seems to

be simply to love fully without surrendering one's ego or identity. The last two lines of the poem, "When half-gods go,/ The Gods arrive," are often quoted out of context because of their aphoristic quality.

A poem that has led some readers to charge Emerson with coldheartedness or lack of feeling is "Threnody," his lament for the loss of his beloved son Waldo, who died of scarlet fever at the age of six. Waldo, the first-born child of his second marriage, died suddenly in January, 1842. Emerson was devastated by grief, yet he seems in the poem to berate himself for his inability to sustain his grief. In his journals Emerson freely expressed his bitterness and grief and he gradually transcribed these feelings into the moving pastoral elegy for his son. "Threnody," literally a death-song or lamentation, contains a mixture of commonplace and idealized pastoral images that demonstrate Emerson's ability to work within classical conventions and to ameliorate his grief through his doctrine of compensation. Some of the most moving lines in the poem describe the speaker's recollection of the child's "daily haunts" and unused toys, although these realistic details are later muted by the pathetic fallacy of external nature joining the poet in mourning the loss of his son.

NATURE POEMS

Emerson's muse most often turned to nature for inspiration, so it is no accident that his nature poems contain some of his best work. "The Rhodora" is an early poem in which Emerson's attention to sharp and precise details of his New England landscape stands out against his otherwise generalized and formal poetic style. The first eight lines of the poem, in which Emerson describes finding the rhodora, a northern azalea-like flower, blooming in the woods early in May of the New England spring, before other plants have put out their foliage, seem incomparably the best. Unfortunately the second half of the poem shifts from specific nature imagery to a generalized homily on the beauty of the rhodora, cast in formal poetic diction. Here Emerson's impulse to draw moralistic lessons from nature reminds us of another famous early nineteenth century American poem, William Cullen Bryant's "To a Waterfowl." This division within "The Rhodora" illustrates some of Emerson's difficulties in breaking away from the outmoded style and conventions of eighteenth century English landscape poetry to find an appropriate vernacular style for American nature poetry. Here the subject matter is distinctly American, but the style—the poem's manner of seeing and feeling—is still partially derivative.

"THE HUMBLE BEE" AND "WOODNOTES"

"The Humble Bee" is a more interesting poem in some respects, in that Emerson uses a form adequate to his expression—a tight octosyllabic line and rhymed couplets—to evoke through both sound and sense the meandering flight of the bumble bee. As the poem unfolds, the bee gradually becomes a figure for the poet intoxicated by nature. Some of the poem's conceits may seem quaint to modern taste, but "The Humble Bee" is innovative in its use of terse expression and symbolic form. Its style anticipates the elliptical language and abbreviated form of Emily Dickinson's poetry.

"Woodnotes" is a long and somewhat prosy two-part narrative poem that appears to be extracted from Emerson's journals. Part I introduces the transcendental nature lover ("A Forest Seer") in terms perhaps reminiscent of Thoreau, and Part II describes the reciprocal harmony between man and nature, in which each is fully realized through the other. The vagueness of Part II perhaps illustrates Emerson's difficulty in capturing transcendental rapture in specific poetic language.

OCCASIONAL POEMS

"Ode" ("Inscribed to W. H. Channing") and "Concord Hymn" are both occasional poems that otherwise differ markedly in style and technique. "Concord Hymn" is a traditional patriotic poem in four ballad stanzas that Emerson composed to be sung at the placing of a stone obelisk on July 4, 1837, to commemorate the Battle of Concord, fought on April 19, 1775, on land later belonging to Reverend Ezra Ripley. The lines of the first stanza, now so well known that they are part of our national folklore, demonstrate that Emerson could easily master traditional verse forms when he chose to do so. The images of the "bridge" and the "flood" in the first stanza ripen imperceptibly into metaphor in the poem's implied theme that the Battle of Concord provided the impetus for the American Revolutionary War.

Emerson's "Ode" is a much more unconventional piece, written in terse, variable lines, usually of two or three stresses, and touching upon the dominant social and political issues of the day—the Mexican War, the Fugitive Slave Law of 1850, the threat of secession in the South, and radical abolitionism in the North. This open form was perhaps best suited to Emerson's oracular style that aimed to leave a few memorable lines with the reader. His angry muse berates Daniel Webster for having compromised his principles by voting for the Fugitive Slave Law, and it denounces those materialistic interests, in both the North and the South, that would profit from wage or bond slavery. Emerson's lines "Things are in the saddle,/ And ride mankind" aptly express his misgivings about the drift of American affairs that seemed to be leading toward a civil war. His taut lines seem to chant their warning like a Greek chorus, foreseeing the inevitable but being helpless to intervene. By the 1850's Emerson had become an increasingly outspoken opponent of the Fugitive Slave Law, and on occasion risked his personal safety in speaking before hostile crowds.

LEGACY

Despite his commitment to a new American poetry based upon common diction and ordinary speech, Emerson's poetry never quite fulfilled the promise of his call, in *The American Scholar* and "The Poet," for a new poetics. Emerson wanted to do for American poetry what William Wordsworth had accomplished for English lyrical poetry, to free it from the constraints of an artificial and dead tradition of sensibility and feeling. Yet he was not as consistent or as thoroughgoing a poetic innovator as the Wordsworth of the "Preface" to the second edition of *Lyrical Ballads* (1800), who both announced and carried out his proposed revision of the existing neoclassical poetic diction, nor did he apply his theory to his poetic composition as skillfully as Wordsworth did. Emerson could envision a new poetics but he could not sustain in his poetry a genuine American vernacular tradition. That had to wait for Whitman and Dickinson. Perhaps Emerson was too much the philosopher ever to realize fully the poetic innovations that the sought, but even with their flaws his poems retain a freshness and vitality lacking in contemporaries such as Henry Wadsworth Longfellow and James Russell Lowell, who were probably more accomplished versifiers. Emerson's greatness resides in the originality of his vision of a future American poetry, free and distinct from European models. It can be found in the grace of his essays and the insights of his journals, and it appears in those select poems in which he was able to match vision and purpose, innovation and accomplishment. His "Saadi" was no less a poet for the restraint of his harp.

OTHER MAJOR WORKS

NONFICTION: *Nature*, 1836; *An Oration Delivered Before the Phi Beta Kappa Society, Cambridge*, 1837 (better known as *The American Scholar*); *An Address Delivered Before the Senior Class in Divinity College, Cambridge . . .* , 1838 (better known as *Divinity School Address*); *Essays: First Series*, 1841; *Orations, Lectures and Addresses*, 1844; *Essays: Second Series*, 1844; *Addresses and Lectures*, 1849; *Representative Men: Seven Lectures*, 1850; *English Traits*, 1856; *The Conduct of Life*, 1860; *Representative of Life*, 1860; *Society and Solitude*, 1870; *Works and Days*, 1870; *Letters and Social Aims*, 1875; *Lectures and Biographical Sketches*, 1884; *Miscellanies*, 1884; *Natural History of Intellect*, 1893; *The Journals of Ralph Waldo Emerson*, 1909-1914 (10 volumes; E. W. Emerson and W. E. Forbes, editors); *The Letters of Ralph Waldo Emerson*, 1939 (6 volumes; Ralph L. Rusk, editor); *The Journals and Miscellaneous Notebooks*, 1960-1982 (16 volumes).

EDITED TEXT: *Parnassus*, 1874.

MISCELLANEOUS: *Uncollected Writings: Essays, Addresses, Poems, Reviews, and Letters*, 1912.

BIBLIOGRAPHY

Bloom, Harold. "Emerson: The Self-Reliance of American Romanticism." In *Figures of Capable Imagination*. New York: Seabury Press, 1976. Bloom's innovative discussion focuses upon the parable of literary influence as it relates to Emerson's creative output. In Bloom's view, the Emersonian dialectic pits imaginative autonomy against necessity.

Burkholder, Robert E., and Joel Myerson, eds. *Critical Essays on Ralph Waldo Emerson*. Boston: G. K. Hall, 1983. Burkholder and Myerson avoid the "standard" critical works on Emerson. Instead, they select a wide range of pivotal essays and reviews, as well as more obscure works that help to define how Emerson's public received his writings. Contains a bibliography and references.

Myerson, Joel, ed. *A Historical Guide to Ralph Waldo Emerson*. New York: Oxford University Press, 2000. A collection of essays that provide an extended biographical study of Emerson. Later chapters study his concept of individualism, nature and natural science, religion, antislavery, and women's rights.

Neufelt, Leonard. *The House of Emerson*. Lincoln: University of Nebraska Press, 1982. Discusses the nature of Emerson's literary work and its underlying assumptions, using the writer's life as a reference point. Examines how Emerson's ideology, his "house," shaped his writing. Contains a bibliography.

Porte, Joel, and Saundra Morris, eds. *The Cambridge Companion to Ralph Waldo Emerson*. New York: Cambridge University Press, 1999. Provides a critical introduction to Emerson's work through interpretations of his writing and analysis of his influence and cultural significance. Includes a comprehensive chronology and bibliography.

Thurin, Erik Ingvar. *Emerson as Priest and Pan: A Study in the Metaphysics of Sex*. Lawrence: University Press of Kansas, 1981. Discusses Emerson's views on love and sex as illustrated in his writing. Thurin points out the many types of love that Emerson believed human beings are capable of experiencing. The author also addresses how Emerson's work reconciles the ideas of love and sex. Autobiographical information and the intellectual history of the period augment Thurin's analysis. Includes a bibliography.

Waggoner, Hyatt Howe. *Emerson as Poet*. Princeton, N.J.: Princeton University Press, 1974. Waggoner offers an insightful survey of past criticism on Emerson. Discusses how to read Emerson's poetry and what values can be derived from the verses. Examines the naturalism of Emerson's style, the reasons for some of his poetic failures, and the relationship of his poetry to his prose. Ends with an assessment of the relative value of Emerson's poetry. Contains a bibliography.

Yanella, Donald. *Ralph Waldo Emerson*. Boston: Twayne, 1982. In this brief but penetrating work, Yanella offers an introduction to the works of Emerson for the nonspecialist in the field of nineteenth century literature. Concentrates on Emerson's poetry and essays. Considers Emerson's philosophical and religious views, traces his influences, and assesses his impact on the development of nineteenth century American literature. Includes a chronology of Emerson's works.

Andrew J. Angyal;
bibliography updated by the editors

WILLIAM EMPSON

Born: Yokefleet, England; September 27, 1906
Died: London, England; April 15, 1984

PRINCIPAL POETRY
Poems, 1935
The Gathering Storm, 1940
Collected Poems, 1949, 1955
The Complete Poems, 2000

OTHER LITERARY FORMS

William Empson, better known for his criticism than for his poetry, is both famous and notorious for his doctrine of poetic ambiguity. Empson has argued that all good poetry is characterized by ambiguity, by uncertainties and tensions that are sometimes planned, sometimes fortuitous, frequently demanding variant interpretations. As a Cambridge undergraduate, Empson worked with I. A. Richards, whose pioneering "scientific" approach to literature, *Principles of Literary Criticism* (1924), inspired his protégé to judge poetry by its success in exploiting linguistic and semantic possibilities, rather than by concentrating on its affective powers. Indeed, Empson sees "tension" or unresolved conflict as the formative principle of poetry.

Growing out of his work at Cambridge with Richards, as well as his familiarity with *A Survey of Modernist Poetry* by Robert Graves and Laura Riding (1922), Empson's *Seven Types of Ambiguity* (1930) is a systematic and elaborate argument for close textual analysis of the semantic indeterminacy which is inherent in language. This remarkable study, which has remained Empson's most influential and celebrated work, demon-

strates how various shifting and equivocal denotative and connotative meanings both illuminate and complicate the experience of a poem. Empson conceded, however, that there is a good deal to be said for avoiding ambiguity. Observing that unequivocal, straightforward, prosaic, expository expression certainly leads "to results more direct, more communicable," he warns poets never to be ambiguous "without proper occasion," especially never to exploit plurisignification merely for decorative effect.

Such a brilliant critical work as *Seven Types of Ambiguity* appears even more impressive when one considers that it was an effort by an undergraduate not yet twenty-four years old. Accused of pedantry for his doctrinaire insistence on "scientific" classifications, Empson appears to have anticipated this response, for he explains first that ambiguity in his "extended sense" means whatever he wants it to mean. For the less flexible reader, however, he defines ambiguity as that which "gives room for alternative reactions to the same piece of language." He feels that such categories as his are justified because they provide a "useful set of distinctions" for the critical reader of poetry by both heightening his consciousness of nuance and involving him actively in the process of careful exegesis to determine what the poem means. One may be convinced by Empson's argument for such painstaking *explication du texte,* or may heatedly oppose it, but one cannot ignore it.

Thus Empson takes his place, along with T. S. Eliot and his mentor Richards, as an English exponent of what would come to be known as the "New Criticism," that formal and objective position which limits itself to the autonomous context of the work itself, rejecting any historical or biographical concern with either the poem or its creator. Though more open-minded in practice, especially in the glosses and notes which he appended to his own poetry, Empson still stressed the "disassociation of sensibility." He thus aligned himself with the New Critics in opposition to the Romantics and his contemporary neo-Romantics.

Five years after the appearance of *Seven Types of Ambiguity,* Empson continued to extend his concept of essential linguistic complexity, publishing *Some Versions of Pastoral* (1935), a somewhat misleading title for a more mature development of his critical method of

William Empson in 1946. (Hulton Archive)

creative artist's particular brand of linguistic complexity, the publication of this ambitious and learned work seemed to coincide with Empson's ceasing to write poetry, provoking speculation that he had found the satisfaction in criticism that he was unable to achieve in his verse. Ten years later, in 1961, another major work of criticism appeared, *Milton's God*, and a revision followed in 1965. Nothing innovative or brilliantly perceptive is evident here. His best later criticism continued to appear in the form of individual journal essays. Posthumous collections of his critical essays include *Essays on Shakespeare* (1986) and *Argufying: Essays on Literature and Culture* (1987).

As an undergraduate at Cambridge, Empson not only formulated his theory of poetic ambiguity but also edited and contributed to several literary publications, writing poetry and reviews of books, films, and theater productions. He even wrote a play, *Three Stories* (1927), now lost, in which he acted in a campus production. His lively talents have also been demonstrated in recordings of his poems. It is on *Seven Types of Ambiguity*, however, that Empson's critical reputation rests. Its intellectual gusto, engaging wit, jauntiness of tone, and provocative thesis all reflect the brilliant Cambridge undergraduate who would subsequently influence contemporary poetry and its appreciation to a remarkable degree.

ACHIEVEMENTS

To many, William Empson will always be the author of one book and recognized as the legendary "ambiguity man"; indeed, his poetry is often completely overlooked when he is identified only as "a British literary critic." Yet he wrote far more than the four critical volumes which established and expanded his analytical theory of linguistic complexity.

After publishing early poems in Cambridge undergraduate magazines, in 1935 he collected what he had written into his first slim annotated volume, *Poems*, all but ten of which were from his Cambridge days. Among the young poets breaking new ground in England in the 1930's, Empson would prove less successful than his contemporaries, for his style revealed that his work was so "difficult," so eccentrically brilliant, that general acclaim beyond academic circles was improbable. Cer-

verbal analysis. In this series of difficult yet controlled essays (entitled *English Pastoral Poetry* when it was published in America in 1938), Empson illustrates his theories with entire works rather than with excerpts, approaching a sophisticated Gestaltic position. Seeing the pastoral as the artificial cult of simplicity ("the process of putting the complex into the simple"), rather than as a conventional genre of poems about rustic life, he demonstrates a sociological bias in choosing his examples, claiming that he is trying to demonstrate how "the social ideas" resulting from such a literary inversion "have been used in English literature."

Empson's third major critical work is *The Structure of Complex Words* (1951), another collection of essays in which he moves away from the traditional aesthetic values of literature, seeing instead expressions of cultural and societal interest—no doubt a reaction to shifts in attitudes around him. Though still concerned with a tainly Empson himself knew that his verses would not suit popular taste.

In 1940, after returning to England from teaching positions in the Far East, Empson published his second collection of twenty-one poems, the ostensibly topical *The Gathering Storm*, including only ten poems which were previously unpublished. In his view, the work "is all about politics, saying we're going to have this second world war and we mustn't get too frightened about it," when in fact all the poems do not reflect the threatening world crisis then provoking contemporary public anxiety. Demonstrating a static clarity not evident in the first volume of verse, the new poems revealed not so much the elegance of a clever and precocious undergraduate as a less-concentrated profundity growing out of personal pain and conviction, and the volume drew public attention. Winston Churchill, in fact, appropriated the title for a volume of his history of World War II.

In the 1950's Empson found himself the somewhat surprised paragon of what was then seen by some as the goal of poetic expression, a curious and ironic position for one who had given up writing poetry almost a decade earlier. Those who now venerated him, calling themselves collectively "The Movement," were part of a loosely organized highbrow English reactionary group opposing both the apocalyptic, extreme neo-Romantic work best exemplified by the spectacularly sensual Dylan Thomas and that of the Symbolist tradition and of the so-called Imagists. Members of The Movement were attracted by Empson's urbane wit and control, his penchant not for emotional excess but for "argufying in poetry." In an illuminating article appearing in 1963, Empson declares that without recognizing the fact, he must have had "strong feelings" about John Donne for a long time, not for his being Metaphysical but because of his "argufying," a desirable and dynamic process that Empson saw as both mental and muscular and also as a revolt against Symbolism.

John Wain, one of the best-known members of The Movement, seeing Empson as the heir to Eliot, called attention to Empson's poetic work, which exemplified this rhetorical stance, in his 1950 essay "Ambiguous Gifts," which would have a profound formative impact in fashionable academic circles. Empson's functional and concrete imagery, especially that suggesting scientific ideas,

as Wain saw it, is most effective when it forms a series of intellectually ingenious conceits, much in the manner employed by the Metaphysical poet John Donne, and in this characteristic Empson's work found its greatest strength. In deprecating current "romantic scribblers" and their adverse influence on literary taste, Wain wondered if Empson could be appreciated by the general public, his cerebral gifts being beyond their scope. Nevertheless, just as the shrine is not liable for the acts of the pilgrims, Empson could not be held responsible for his vocal and encomiastic disciples who, incidentally, soon generally repudiated him and moved elsewhere for stylistic inspiration.

Perhaps as a result of interest in Empson stirred up by enthusiastic Movement members forced to use the 1949 American edition of the *Collected Poems*, an English edition appeared in 1955, but by that time much of the fervid excitement for his work had died down. This volume brought together all but a few of those poems that Empson chose to publish, including the three poems he wrote during World War II. Again he provided extensive notes at the end and even included an explanatory "Note on Notes." He has published no new poems since this volume appeared. In fact, his poems total only sixty-three.

BIOGRAPHY

A Yorkshireman of the landed gentry by birth, William Empson spent his early childhood at Yokefleet, a remote village, separated from his four older brothers and sisters by four years. He began his education at Folkestone Preparatory School, then entered Winchester College as a scholar in 1920, where he was an active debater. He went up in 1925 to Magdalene College, Cambridge, on a mathematics scholarship. After passing several levels of degree examinations in mathematics, he shifted his interest to literature and read under the tutelage of the renowned professor I. A. Richards. Before taking his degree with highest honors in English in 1929, Empson was caught up in the interdisciplinary intellectual fervor then at high pitch in Cambridge and made a name for himself in this heady atmosphere. Excitement grew from individual involvement in widely diverse disciplines, and C. P. Snow, the physicist who would later explore the status of the "two cultures," was then actively involved in the Cambridge life, where at that time the gap between literature and science was slight.

Obviously there was much for Empson to ponder and discuss after both Gertrude Stein and T. S. Eliot lectured at Cambridge in 1926, the latter on the Metaphysical poets, a universally recognized influence on Empson's poetry. In 1927 the undergraduate's first poem was published, and those that followed in his *annus mirabilis* of 1928 reflected the "difficult" mode of the early Andrew Marvell and John Donne as well as that of Eliot. Empson, then, owed much of his success as an undergraduate not only to his natural intellectual gifts but also to the stimulating and congenial atmosphere of Cambridge in the late 1920's.

After the publication in 1930 of his undergraduate thesis as *Seven Types of Ambiguity*, Empson accepted a teaching position from 1931 to 1934 as professor of english literature at Buneika Daigaku University in Tokyo, having been recommended for the post by his tutor Richards. In 1937, after a return to England, he accepted another position in the Orient; by this time he had published his first collection of poetry and his second volume of criticism. His new teaching assignment was on the English faculty of the Peking National University, but those were the uneasy years of the Sino-Japanese War, and for two years Empson followed academic refugees on the Great March across China in retreat from the invading Japanese forces, teaching from memory, constantly in peril, yet still writing poetry. Forced to return to London on "indefinite wartime leave" during the years of World War II, he served as a writer of propaganda and as Chinese broadcaster for the British Broadcasting Corporation from 1941 to 1946 and published his second collection of poems, many of them the result of his Far East experiences.

During this period in his native country he married and assumed responsibility for a family. In 1947 he took his wife and two sons to Peking where he returned to his teaching post, again, however, facing unsettling conditions in China, now under the regime of Mao Zedong. By 1953 he felt the need to settle his family in England and accepted a post as professor of english literature at Sheffield University, where he remained until his retirement in 1971. His involvement with advocates of the "New Criticism" brought him to America on several occasions during his active teaching career, for he always enjoyed traveling. He lived in active retirement in the London suburb of Hampstead until his death on April 15, 1984.

ANALYSIS

William Empson, assessing the inherent relationship between theory and performance, observed in *Seven Types of Ambiguity* that "the methods I have been describing are very useful to critics, but certainly they leave a poet in a difficult position." In his own case, the dilemma is compounded, as even the inexperienced reader naturally seeks to find in Empson's poetic works exemplification of his personal critical doctrine. Without question, Empson's ideas about ambiguity and the tensions generated by contradictions in poetry point directly to the core of what might be a meaning of his "specialized kind" of poetry.

One way to approach Empson's canon might be to note varying degrees of complexity, exemplification of possible multiple meanings discoverable in the poetry. Indeed, his puzzling knotted lines and verses ("my clotted kind of poetry," as Empson himself describes it) prompted the poet to furnish annotative notes with his published collections, admitting, however, that "the better poems tend to require fewer notes." Such finely wrought poetic works reflect Empson's recognition that he "grew up in the height of the vogue for the seventeenth century poet Donne," and that when he started as a poet, he "thought it would be very nice to write beautiful things like the poet Donne," recalling that he began composition by "trying to think of an interesting puzzle."

This familiarity with the Metaphysical poets would seem to illuminate Empson's work—sophisticated, scientific analyses of intensely personal and impassioned emotional states; fantastic, audacious, extremely extended conceits; intellectual, witty, and often unconventional diction—all exploited to unite feeling with thought, to attempt communication of restless, unreasonable expectation beyond reasonable limits. Such taut, controlled technique generally reflects a profound sense of life's difficulties and contradictions, what Empson described as a "conflict which is raging in the mind of the writer but hasn't been solved."

Empson's idea of poetry as the expression of an unresolved conflict ("Verse likes despair," he observes in "Success"), opposing forces seeking some form of equilibrium, is reflected throughout his characteristically argumentative work. One of his most quoted beliefs is that "life involves maintaining oneself between contradictions that can't be solved by analysis." Here his affinity with the American poet and New Critic John Crowe Ransom comes sharply into focus; a line in Ransom's "The Equilibrists" (1927), "Leave me now, and never let us meet" describes the equally unresolved torture of the unfulfilled lovers also seeking a tentative balance in Empson's "Aubade" (1937): "It seemed the best thing to be up and go."

Empson's attempt to reconcile opposing forces may have led to his fascination with Buddhism. Such a philosophical acceptance of human suffering as a way of apprehending reality so appealed to Empson that he put together "The Faces of Buddha," a collection of articles written in Japan and China; the manuscript, however, is regrettably lost. In "Missing Dates" (1937), the despairing refrain of the poem laments that despite man's efforts "the waste remains, the waste remains and kills." Whether the ambiguous key word here denotes emptiness, exhaustion, loss, or prodigality, its reality is fatal; nirvana is unattainable. Furthermore, in his published collections of poetry, Empson chose for an epigraph Buddha's "Fire Sermon," recognizing, as did Eliot, that modern man shares a universal dilemma.

EARLY POEMS

An awareness of contradictions, of ideas and emotions held in tension, characterizes Empson's work from the beginning. An early poem which appeared in an undergraduate Cambridge literary journal, "Value Is in Activity," is a recondite, sardonic statement of the ultimate futility of man's attempt to determine his fate, revealing the poet's sense of the relationship between the macroscopic and individual instance. Here man is a "juggler" endlessly tossing rotting apples, exhibited in a "circus" that is the world. Because of his unceasing activity, he cannot eat the Edenic fruit, which is, in any case, worthless, both maggot-filled and sterile ("Dwarf seeds unnavelled" by a blighting frost). Yet man cannot be idle, though knowing full well the ultimate waste of his frenetic activities and the futility of his situation. Thus

Empson challenges us to question what gives value to our actions; he does not, however, rationalize or philosophize.

Bafflement is also in the conclusion of "Plenum and Vacuum," its title suggesting antithetical states of existence. In a particularly characteristic "clotted style," the three stanzas have seven compound hyphenated words, which abound in ambiguities, and utilize typically Empsonian scientific imagery that reflects the teeming world of Cambridge. Yet any exegetic effort ultimately rests on acceptance of the axiom in stanza three that "Matter includes what must matter enclose," describing both the ontological statement and the poem itself.

Another important undergraduate poem is "High Dive," in which the subject again recognizes "value in activity," knows that he must "dive" into life ("the enclosed bathing-pool") rather than spend his time in neurotic contemplation, must join those who "tear him down" into a society both "menacing" and "assuring." Empson ominously and admonishingly cites the disastrous dives or falls of Lucifer and Jezebel, however, and the poem ends in desperate recognition that the pool's water is ultimately a vortex that will destroy the diver.

In "To an Old Lady," a tribute to his mother, Empson uses the classic Metaphysical image of the compass to praise her style and confidence; she is not to be pitied, for she is "certain of her pole," not "wasted" as some might presume. Empson concludes the poem with an astronomical conceit pointing up the paradox of proximity and distance between a mother and her son: "Strange that she too should be inaccessible./ Who shares my son."

One of the most beautiful and Donne-like of Empson's university poems is "Camping Out"; fellow-poet Richard Eberhart called it "a brain-tickler which exercised many hours of drawing-room discussion in Cambridge, and withheld its ultimate ambiguous secret for years." Here as the man is watching a desired young woman go about her usual activities (the poem opens with "And now she cleans her teeth into the lake"), he realizes that only in his imagination can any amorous consummation occur.

RHYME AND METER

At this point it should be noted that despite his startling exploitation of a number of devices of Metaphysical poetry, in many ways Empson's poetics are quite conservative. Criticizing *vers libre*, he declares in his poetic creed, "I am in favor of rhyme and metre"; and he particularly favors terza rima, a three-line stanza, usually in iambic pentameter, rhyming *aba*, *bcb*, *cdc*, and so on. An outstanding example of such an interlocked rhyme scheme is "Arachne," one of Empson's most critically acclaimed early poems. Here the ubiquitous muddling young man, as Empson put it, "being afraid of girl, as usual," walks "Twixt devil and deep sea," in precarious existential tension that illustrates Buddha's extremes, "between void and void," balancing like a spider on a filmy cobweb that "is at a breath destroyed." Like Andrew Marvell's lover arguing with his coy mistress, however, the man warns the reluctant threatening female of the reciprocal dangers of imbalance, that "Male spiders must not be too early slain."

"This Last Pain"

"This Last Pain" is invariably included in selections of Empson's best poetry. The speaker appears to be working out a means to survive, a rational acceptance of limitations both as a person and as a poet. Here Empson's total opposition to Victorian certitude and sophistry is set down without equivocation. If Robert Browning optimistically observed that "There's many a crown for who can reach," the characteristically pessimistic yet courageous Empson counters such a sanguine challenge with his belief that the damned "know the bliss with which they were not crowned." Browning proclaimed that "A man's reach should exceed his grasp,/ Or what's a heaven for?" but Empson doggedly holds that only on earth "Is all, of heaven or hell."

Even though man might pry into the possible bliss of the soul, "may know her happiness by eye to hole," yet he is eternally denied its enjoyment. As Empson stated in his notes to "This Last Pain," "the idea of the poem is that human nature can conceive divine states which it cannot attain." Knowing this, both man and poet must nevertheless preserve the ontological fiction of "those large dreams by which men long live well," feigning belief and imagining that which "could not possibly be true,/ And learn a style from a despair." In the final analysis, as Empson developed earlier in "Value Is in Activity" and "High Dive," activity is better than passivity, and even self-deception and pretense are preferable to

nothing, imagination being among the gods' "ambiguous gifts."

"Bacchus"

In the laconically entitled "Note on Local Flora," Empson first alludes to Bacchus, that "laughing god" that would be the focus of his personal favorite and most ambitious and complex poem, "Bacchus," a work begun in Japan in 1933 and not finished until 1939 in China. Published in various fragments and first appearing in completed form in 1946, the poem assumes that the reader is familiar with the mythological details of the god's birth. Bacchus is the son of Zeus and Semele, who had asked that the supreme deity appear to her in all his glory. This was a foolish request, for as the god of lightning his presence was fatal, and she was consumed by fire and turned to ashes, an ambiguous emblem of the price one pays for fulfilling knowledge. Zeus, however, snatched their unborn child from the charred remains and carried it in his body until birth. Thus Bacchus, in the earlier brief poem, would "ripen only" as a result of fire, analogous to the cones of an exotic tree in Kew Gardens—"So Semele desired her deity" just as the tree craves fire. In the later poem, Empson characterizes the young god as "born of a startling answer" to the request of the rash Semele, who ultimately is apotheosized and borne away "robed in fire," for "The god had lit up her despair."

Notes to "Bacchus" fill almost six pages, and Empson informs the reader that "a mythological chemical operation to distil drink is going on for the first four verses." Here, by means of chemical analogy, the poet reiterates his belief that one must find existence between contradictions and explains that he chose the metaphor of drink (and Bacchus, the god of wine, as his image) because of its power to make one "most outgoing and unself-critical," and therefore better able to maintain the precarious fictions essential to emotional equilibrium and survival. This is a familiar Empson theme (he elsewhere observes that "It is not human to feel safely placed"), but here it is developed in complexity, surprising at a time when the poet was ostensibly committed to simplifying his knotted, recondite verse. In the conclusion of "Bacchus," Empson also reaffirms his admiration for those who cope, for those who maintain optimistic fictions in the face of overpowering deterministic forces.

"AUBADE"

Empson's "Aubade" is curiously conversational, unusually self-revealing, yet evasive in its details. Obviously about his Japanese experience in the 1930's, it is his only original poem of his years there. When asked its subject, Empson responded enigmatically that it was "about a sexual situation." Far less "clotted" than his previous verse, the poem describes an intensely personal relationship between "two aliens" parted by both the forces of nature ("Hours before dawn we were woken by the quake") and the darkening political situation, from which the European flees homeward, only to encounter "the same war on a stronger toe." As he sadly concludes, "It seemed the best thing to be up and go"; yet he is powerfully and angrily drawn to the opposite course of action. The poem, then, is another evocation of Empson's recognition of the tension inherent in contradiction and ambiguity, a poetic antithesis.

THE GATHERING STORM

Continuing to reflect a change in both style and subject, Empson's collection *The Gathering Storm* included among its twenty-one poems several that reflect the rising political tensions of the preceding decade: "Reflection from Rochester," with its overt reference to "race of armament"; "Courage Means Running," also in terza rima stanzas, restating Empson's belief that "To take fear as the measure/ May be a measure of self-respect"; and the chatty "Autumn on Nan-Yueh," Empson's longest and least difficult poem, a description of his peripatetic adventures in China in 1937. Uncongenial critics saw this calmer despair in his later work as evidence of a loss of nerve, of "rot set in," of hollowness, or as smoothly surfaced mannerist verse, without substance or depth of experience. Such opinions, however, may reflect more the critical taste of the times than the quality of Empson's verse.

These later Empson poems appear to have been written with a real audience in mind, not that of the previously idealized intellectual university milieu. They are more centripetal in effect, infused with a deeper warmth, and reflect a moral awareness missing in his earlier, flashier work. The informing intelligence now seems to suggest the acceptance of the limits of the rational mind ("this deep blankness"), and the recognition that destructive personal chaos cannot be ordered by logical

process ("talk would . . . go so far aslant"). Instead, a static heroism emerges; a more practical stance in facing life's crises is offered.

Among these poems is "Missing Dates," a villanelle, a complex and challenging nineteen-line French verse form aimed at the appearance of spontaneous simplicity. "Missing Dates" is often anthologized and recognized for its intense and sustained pessimistic mood, the refrain being "Slowly the poison the whole blood fills./ The waste remains, the waste remains and kills." As a poet sensing his atrophying powers, seeing himself "not to have fire," Empson echoes the blight and despair of *The Waste Land* (1922), a sterile land of ambiguous "partial fires," a failed situation when *carpe diem* should have been the prevailing philosophy.

In "Success," as Empson draws toward his concluding poetic efforts (he felt "how right I was to stop writing"), he asserts that by his marriage "I have mislaid the torment and the fear," and his wife "should be praised for taking them away." If "verse likes despair," and he no longer suffers, then in his new state "Lose is Find." He recognizes that as an artist "I feed on flatness" and may have sacrificed by his new happiness his poetic voice: "All loss haunts us."

A final brief poem, "Let it go," almost casual in tone, is one of only three which he wrote during World War II. In two tercets, rhyming *abc*, *abc*, Empson recalls his pervasive concern with "blankness," whether emptiness, disinterest, barrenness, lack of success, or whatever denotative or connotative meaning the word might suggest. In "Ignorance of Death" he admitted that "I feel very blank upon this topic," adding, however, that death "is one [topic] that most people should be prepared to be blank upon." In "Aubade" he "slept, and blank as that I would yet lie." Empson's comment that "Let it go" is "about stopping writing poetry" is not surprising. Each of the three lines in the second stanza is end-stopped; the effect is valedictory. Thus Empson appears to offer here an alternative to continuing his dialectic of despair: a self-protective posture of blankness in the face of a personal and global "madhouse and the whole thing there."

Empson's memorable lines can be eminently savored, as Eberhart noted, "out of context with their grammatical relation to previous or succeeding lines." Total understanding is both undesirable and impossible in poetry so freighted with ambiguous contradictions. Eliot observed that "True poetry can communicate before it is understood"; in Empson's case, poetry often communicates meaning *without* comprehension.

William Empson's efforts to fuse thinking and feeling urge the reader to accept life for what it is, to maintain sustaining "fictions," and in some way to "build an edifice of form/ For house where phantoms may keep warm" ("This Last Pain"). His forms—his poems as well as his critical essays—explore dialectically the possibilities of making limited connections, both personal and linguistic, and demonstrate by metaphysical means that reconciliation of antinomies in human existence is ultimately futile and that resolution is possible only in art, in the poems themselves.

OTHER MAJOR WORKS

PLAY: *Three Stories*, pr. 1927.

NONFICTION: *Seven Types of Ambiguity*, 1930, revised 1947; *Some Versions of Pastoral*, 1935 (also known as *English Pastoral Poetry*); *The Structure of Complex Words*, 1951; *Milton's God*, 1961, revised 1965; *Using Biography*, 1984; *Essays on Shakespeare*, 1986; *Argufying: Essays on Literature and Culture*, 1987; *Faustus and the Censor: The English Faust-Book and Marlowe's Doctor Faustus*, 1987; *Essays on Renaissance Literature*, 1993-1994 (2 volumes); *The Strengths of Shakespeare's Shrew: Essays, Memoirs, and Reviews*, 1996.

EDITED TEXT: *Coleridge's Verse: A Selection*, 1972 (with David Pirie).

BIBLIOGRAPHY

Constable, John, ed. *Critical Essays on William Empson*. Brookfield, Vt.: Ashgate, 1993. A collection of reviews, articles, and excerpts on the work of the poet/critic. Includes bibliographic references.

Fry, Paul H. *William Empson: Prophet Against Sacrifice*. New York: Routledge, 1991. Provides an account of this versatile critic's career, and discredits the appropriation of his name by the conflicting parties of deconstruction and politicized cultural criticism. Includes a bibliography and index.

Gardner, Philip, and Averil Gardner. *The God Approached: A Commentary on the Poems of William Empson*. London: Chatto & Windus, 1978. A fairly thick book (226 pages) among the few devoted to Empson's poetry. Includes a brief bibliography.

Gill, Roma, ed. *William Empson: The Man and His Work*. Boston: Routledge & Kegan Paul, 1974. This Empson celebration features contributions by such luminaries as W. H. Auden and I. A. Richards. Some of the pieces specifically take up Empson's poetry. A hefty bibliography is provided.

Haffenden, John, ed. *The Complete Poems of William Empson*. Gainesville: University Press of Florida, 2001. Not merely a collection of all the poetry, including some discovered after Empson's death, this four-hundred-page book draws on unpublished papers, interviews, readings, and broadcasts to add copious appendices along with a detailed introduction by editor Haffenden. Also includes Empson's own notes, which complement the poems, and an iterview with Christopher Ricks.

Norris, Christopher. *William Empson and the Philosophy of Literary Criticism*. London: Athlone Press, 1978. Empson was known more for his literary criticism than he was for his poetry. Norris describes how Empson developed and applied his doctrine of poetic ambiguity. Contains bibliographical references and an index.

Sale, Roger. *Modern Heroism: Essays on D. H. Lawrence, William Empson, and J. R. R. Tolkien*. Berkeley: University of California Press, 1973. Sale analyzes these three twentieth century writers in terms of the way they utilized the theme of courage. Technological changes in the twentieth century shifted the meaning of heroism in literature, and these writers have helped shape a new definition. For advanced students.

Willis, John H. *William Empson*. New York: Columbia University Press, 1969. A brief (45-page) review of the poetry and criticism. Calls attention to Empson's debt to T. S. Eliot and the Metaphysical poets, and to his use of images and analogies from mathematics and science. Provides brief explications of many of Empson's significant poems. Contains a bibliography.

Maryhelen Cleverly Harmon;
bibliography updated by the editors